JIMMY SWAGGART
BIBLE COMMENTARY

- Genesis (639 pages) (11-201)
- Exodus (639 pages) (11-202)
- Leviticus (435 pages) (11-203)
- Numbers
  Deuteronomy (493 pages) (11-204)
- Joshua
  Judges
  Ruth (329 pages) (11-205)
- I Samuel
  II Samuel (528 pages) (11-206)
- I Kings
  II Kings (560 pages) (11-207)
- I Chronicles
  II Chronicles (528 pages) (11-226)
- Ezra
  Nehemiah
  Esther (288 pages) (11-208)
- Job (320 pages) (11-225)
- Psalms (688 pages) (11-216)
- Proverbs (320 pages) (11-227)
- Ecclesiastes
  Song Of Solomon (11-228)
- Isaiah (688 pages) (11-220)
- Jeremiah
  Lamentations (688 pages) (11-070)
- Ezekiel (508 pages) (11-223)
- Daniel (403 pages) (11-224)
- Hosea
  Joel
  Amos (496 pages) (11-229)
- Obadiah
  Jonah
  Micah
  Nahum
  Habakkuk
  Zephaniah *(will be ready Spring 2014)* (11-230)
- Matthew (880 pages) (11-073)
- Mark (606 pages) (11-074)
- Luke (626 pages) (11-075)
- John (532 pages) (11-076)
- Acts (697 pages) (11-077)
- Romans (536 pages) (11-078)

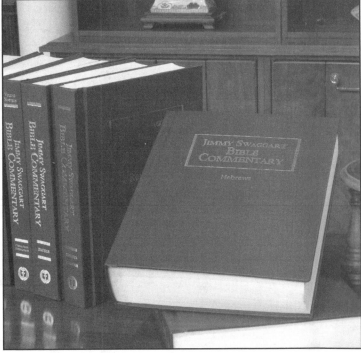

- I Corinthians (632 pages) (11-079)
- II Corinthians (589 pages) (11-080)
- Galatians (478 pages) (11-081)
- Ephesians (550 pages) (11-082)
- Philippians (476 pages) (11-083)
- Colossians (374 pages) (11-084)
- I Thessalonians
  II Thessalonians (498 pages) (11-085)
- I Timothy
  II Timothy
  Titus
  Philemon (687 pages) (11-086)
- Hebrews (831 pages) (11-087)
- James
  I Peter
  II Peter (730 pages) (11-088)
- I John
  II John
  III John
  Jude (377 pages) (11-089)
- Revelation (602 pages) (11-090)

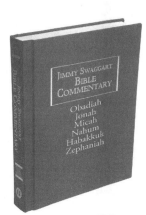

OBADIAH
JONAH
MICAH
NAHUM
HABAKKUK
ZEPHANIAH

For prices and information please call: 1-800-288-8350
Baton Rouge residents please call: (225) 768-7000
Website: www.jsm.org • E-mail: info@jsm.org

JIMMY SWAGGART BIBLE COMMENTARY

Romans

Jimmy Swaggart Bible Commentary

Romans

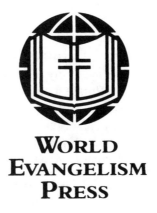

WORLD EVANGELISM PRESS

ISBN 978-1-934655-09-2

11-078 • COPYRIGHT © 1998 Jimmy Swaggart Ministries®
P.O. Box 262550 • Baton Rouge, Louisiana 70826-2550
Website: www.jsm.org • E-mail: info@jsm.org
(225) 768-8300

13 14 15 16 17 18 19 20 21 22 23 24 25 26 27 28 29 / CK / 22 21 20 19 18 17 16 15 14 13 12 11 10 9 8 7 6

TABLE OF CONTENTS

INTRODUCTION

A PRIVILEGE OF UNPARALLELED PROPORTIONS

I have looked forward with great anticipation in making the attempt concerning the writing of this Commentary on Romans. However, my reasons for strongly desiring to do so, have absolutely nothing to do with my ability, which I consider to be extremely limited. My desire is rather centered in my love for the Word of God, and more specifically, for this great Epistle.

Perhaps my love for this Book, is wrapped up in the great victories, and I speak of victories from a personal basis, which the Lord has given me concerning that which the Holy Spirit gave to Paul respecting this Epistle. Of necessity that would carry great meaning for me, as it would for anyone.

So, my love for this work I suppose more than all is ensconced in that of which has meant so much to me on a personal basis, which is of such magnitude, that I really have very little way to properly express myself.

THE FIRST EPISTLE

Someone has referred to the Book of Romans as the Magna Carta of Salvation, which it no doubt is.

It is only proper and fitting that the Epistle which explains Salvation, and in its totality, as well as all of Satan's efforts to dilute this Message, be placed first after the Book of Acts. It alone sets the Standard, as it alone can set the Standard, thereby supplying the Foundation for all which follows.

One Expositor made the statement that the Book of Romans is the viewpoint of Paul respecting the great Plan of Salvation; however, I beg to disagree.

These are not Paul's viewpoints, or those of any other man, but rather the Truth of Salvation as outlined by the Holy Spirit, and given to Paul in order that it may be given to the world. There is no other Plan of Salvation, no other Way of Salvation, at least given by God, which God will recognize. Anything, and I mean anything, which differs from the Salvation Plan offered in the Book of Romans, irrespective of its intellectual content, is persuasive philosophy, or its appealing allurement, is purely and simply, a lie. I realize that is blunt, but I mean for it to be that way, and would use a statement more blunt, were such available. There is nothing in the world worse than a false way of Salvation!

PAUL, THE WRITER

Paul was the writer, in effect the instrument. However, the Author of the Book of Romans, as well as the entirety of the Bible, is the Holy Spirit. Consequently, setting aside the translation, as all translations must be set aside, respecting perfection, because it is impossible for such to be inerrant due to the fact that such originates with man, however, the original Text *is* inerrant, i.e., error free, and, thereby perfect.

Paul was given the New Covenant, which in effect, made him the Moses of the New Testament. As a result, this Great and Glorious Covenant, containing better Promises to which the First Covenant pointed, and guaranteed by Jesus Christ, is found altogether in Paul's writings. No, that does not mean the Word written by Peter, James, Jude or John the Beloved, is any less the Word of God, or that their writings do not contribute to that given to Paul by the Holy Spirit, for they definitely do! Perhaps one could say that this given by the Holy Spirit to the other writers mentioned, deals in many ways with the practicality of the New Covenant, even as Paul dealt with such himself.

As well, neither are these statements meant to project the idea that Paul, and for instance Peter, differed in any way, for such would be grossly incorrect. As stated, the same Holy Spirit Who inspired that of which Paul wrote, as well, inspired Peter and all the other writers for that matter. There is no contradiction and neither are there differences of direction.

Some have attempted to put Paul and Peter in two different categories, in other words, somewhat contradicting each other. In view of that of which we speak concerning the Word of God, such thinking is not just unscriptural, but *grossly* unscriptural. While Paul alone was definitely given the New Covenant, even as Moses was given the Old Covenant, all else given are meant by the Holy Spirit to complement those Covenants, whether in the Old Testament or the New. Consequently, to sectionalize the two Apostles is grossly wrong!

THE ORIGIN OF THE BOOK OF ROMANS

Of course this great Epistle originated with God, but was penned by Paul probably in the Spring of A.D. 58. As well, it is conclusive, I think, that it was written from Corinth.

The purpose of the Holy Spirit in giving this great Epistle was, and to which we have already alluded, to provide, as it is said, the ABC's of Christian education. Until its lessons are learned, the Believer is ignorant of True Christian Principles. As stated, it is the very foundation of Church Teaching, and if we are wrong in understanding here, we shall be wrong elsewhere.

The great Theme of this Book is the Revelation of God's Wrath against sin, and the Righteousness through Faith as the grounds of Justification.

Romans makes the whole world guilty before God and in need of Salvation through Jesus Christ. As such, it also gives the whole world the opportunity of Salvation through Christ.

DOCTRINE

The Epistle to the Romans pure and simple is Doctrine. Paul makes that clear at the very outset, calling it *"The Gospel of God"* (Rom. 1:1).

He then emphatically states that this great Gospel is actually the *"Promise"* of the Old Testament (Rom. 1:2).

He then states unequivocally, that all of this, *"The Gospel,"* which is the *"Promise,"* is all wrapped up in *"Jesus Christ our Lord"* (Rom. 1:3).

So, in effect one can say that Doctrine must not be divorced from Jesus Christ, and, in effect, Doctrine is Jesus and Jesus is Doctrine. The Scripture says, *"He taught them many things by Parables, and said unto them in His Doctrine"* (Mk. 4:2).

The Scripture also says, *"And they were astonished at His Doctrine: for He taught them as One that had authority, and not as the Scribes"* (Mk. 1:22).

Doctrine becomes contentious only when it is devoid of Christ. That is the reason we must preach Jesus. If we properly preach Jesus, we will at the same time, properly preach Doctrine.

ROMANS AND GENTILES

Even though greatly dealing with the Jewish position, as is necessary, Romans is mainly addressed to Gentiles, and for the obvious reasons. Consequently, it could probably be called, and without doing violence to the Text, *"The Epistle of Paul the Apostle to the Gentiles."* In effect, and which was the intention of the Lord all along, Salvation is opened up to the entirety of the world and on the same basis, and without the Law, except the One to Whom the Law pointed, The Lord Jesus Christ (Gen. 12:3). As a result, it speaks to both Jew and Gentile, in effect, making all and everyone, both one and the same. The problem of sin is the problem of all, and the solution of Salvation is the solution of all, even as Jesus is the Saviour of all.

STYLE

For those of you who have one or more of our Commentaries, hopefully, our style is apparent.

We attempt to make these Commentaries a little more than the name implies. For instance, in many cases, and especially these of the New Testament, they are at least in part, a Word Study, a Bible Dictionary, a Bible Encyclopedia, along with the Commentary. As such, you will find, I think, that we address the great Subjects of the Bible, in a much more involved and extended manner than most Commentaries. Consequently, you will see in this Commentary, or one of the others, extended treatment respecting the great Foundations of the Faith, such as *"Justification by Faith," "Sanctification," "The Baptism with the Holy Spirit and the evidence thereof," "Grace,"* etc., to name just a few. We believe this helps the Bible Student to have a far greater understanding of these great Subjects, which is the intended purpose, and is so very valuable to the Child of God, which should be obvious.

As well, sprinkled throughout the Chapters of all our Commentaries, at least where we feel it would be complementary, we have included personal experiences, which we feel the Holy Spirit would have us do. The Holy Spirit through Paul plainly said, *"The husbandman that laboureth must be first partaker of the fruits"* (II Tim. 2:6). If one is to notice, Paul did this at times concerning his own experiences.

Actually that is what the Bible is all about! It is not philosophy, but rather the Word of God which is designed to Save the Soul and to change one's life. In fact, if it does not do that, it is not the Gospel, or else we have not allowed it a proper place in our lives.

SUBJECT MATTER

The Subject of the Epistle to the Romans is that God declares righteous the guilty sinner who believes upon the Atoning Saviour, whether that sinner be a degraded heathen, a cultured Greek, or a Hebrew moralist.

The Doctrine of this Epistle answers the ancient question (Job 9:2), *"How can a man be just with God?"* — by stating that the Gospel reveals a Righteousness from God (Rom. 1:17) even for those who merit the Wrath of God (Rom. 1:18).

The Doctrine of this Epistle also distinguishes between *"sin"* and *"sins,"* i.e., man's sinful nature (Chpts. 5-8) and the works of that nature (Chpts. 1-5); and it reveals in relation to that nature and its works, the sufficiency of God's activities in Justification and Sanctification.

Actually, the distinction between *"sin"* and *"sins,"* i.e., between the corrupt tree and its evil fruit, provides the key to the whole teaching of this Epistle.

JESUS CHRIST

Christ as the Believer's Justification and Sanctification releases him from the doom of sins and from the dominion of sin. Justification has to do with the Believer's *"Standing"* and Sanctification with the Believer's *"State."* These should not be confounded.

It is the entry of the new nature in Regeneration which originates the never-ceasing conflict between the *"flesh"* and the *"spirit"* (Williams).

RIGHTEOUSNESS

Paul dealt with the efforts of the Jew to establish his own Righteousness by imagined strict conformity to Law. But the Apostle well knew the vanity of this pretention; how it was a delusion, put man in a false position before God, and lowered the true ideal of Divine Righteousness.

He himself had once been *"Touching the Righteousness which is in the Law, blameless"* (Phil. 3:6), but he was painfully conscious how, when he would have done good, evil was present with him. The Jew might trust to Sacrifices to expiate his own shortcomings, but Paul knew, and Scripture itself confirmed, how impossible it was for the blood of bulls and goats to be in themselves of avail in the spiritual sphere of things.

On that memorable journey to Damascus the spark fell, and the illumination came. Jesus from Heaven,

Whose Voice at length penetrated Paul's soul, now rose clearly before his eye of Faith as the King of Righteousness, foretold of old, Who was to bring the Righteousness of God to man.

To complete our view of what Jesus has given us regarding Righteousness, we must further note that the full manifestation of God's Righteousness is regarded by Him as still future: the Gospel is but the dawning of the full day: *"the earnest expectation of the creature"* still *"waiteth for the manifestation of the sons of God"* (Rom. 8:19); *"even we ourselves groan within ourselves, waiting for the adoption, to wit, the Redemption of our body"* (Rom. 8:23); it is not till *"the end"* that *"all things shall be subdued unto Him, . . . that God may be All in All"* (I Cor. 15:28).

But meanwhile Believers are regarded as already partaking of the Righteousness of God, revealed and brought home to them in Christ; Faith, aspiration, and earnest endeavor (which are all man is capable of now) being accepted in Christ for Righteousness.

LAW

Paul, in this great Epistle, also deals with the fundamental thought of *"Law."* Even though he speaks primarily of the Law of Moses given at Mt. Sinai, he also uses the word in a wider sense, so as to denote general requirement of obedience to a moral code, appealing to the conscience.

In this, the Holy Spirit teaches us through him, how that the Law given through Moses, Holy and Divine as it was meant to be, at the same time, proved so inoperative for conversion of the heart, but rather intensified the guilt of sin, with no power to deliver from it.

Consequently, he tells us what the Office and Purpose of the Law really was and hence, of Law generally, as expressing the principle of obedience, under threat of punishment, to moral behests. He found that all that Law in itself could do was to restrain from overt transgressions such persons as would not be restrained without it.

GRACE

Paul ever views the Gospel as being the True Fulfillment of the Old Testament and all of the Prophetic yearnings, which can be spelled out in one word, and that word is *"Grace."* What Law could not do and in fact, was never intended to do, can and is done through and by the Grace of God.

So, he shows us, at least the Holy Spirit through him shows us, that what the Law could not do, in that it was weak through the flesh, could in fact, be brought about by the Grace of God, which is the Free Gift of Jesus Christ, received by the sinner upon Faith.

I think by now the Reader should grasp and understand that this Study of Romans is going to be very profitable. If you will earnestly study with us as we go through this great Epistle, I think when you finally conclude, you will be stronger in the Lord than when you began. That is our goal, *"Christian Growth."*

AND FINALLY . . .

Without Frances taking upon herself almost all the duties of the Administration of this Ministry, which employs approximately 200 people, I could not even think of devoting the time and attention to work of this sort; consequently, her efforts in Administration are not only of tremendous blessing to the Work of God in that capacity, but as well, if there is blessing in our efforts respecting this Commentary and, in fact, all of our Commentaries, then I owe a great part of it to her.

I can say the same regarding Donnie. Along with traveling all over the world in Revival Crusades, Donnie also serves as one of the Associate Pastors of Family Worship Center in Baton Rouge. As well, he attends to many things as it regards the Church and the Ministry, relieving me of that responsibility.

And then there are the people who perform the tedious work of making a Book out of these efforts. I speak of Donna Simpson, Sharon Whitelaw, and Barbara Eversburg. I have listed these three according to their seniority at the Ministry, but yet, each one provides a service that is indispensable.

Irrespective of who did what, if in fact your knowledge of the Lord and nearness to Him are enhanced by our labor in this Commentary, then all the efforts have been worthwhile. Otherwise, it is of no consequence.

Perhaps it would be best to rest this Introduction on the following:

"Jesus! Jesus! Jesus! Sing aloud the Name;
"Till it softly, slowly, sets all hearts aflame."

"Jesus! Name of Cleansing, washing all our stains;
"Jesus! Name of Healing, balm for all our pains."

"Jesus! Be our joy note, in this veil of tears;
"Till we reach the homeland, and the eternal years."

THE
BOOK OF ROMANS

◼

(1) "PAUL, A SERVANT OF JESUS CHRIST, CALLED TO BE AN APOSTLE, SEPARATED UNTO THE GOSPEL OF GOD,"

The phrase, *"Paul, a servant of Jesus Christ,"* in effect, has Paul labeling himself as a *"bondslave"* of Christ. This refers to one who is the entire property of another (Mat. 20:27; I Cor. 6:19-20; II Cor. 4:5).

As well, if it matters, Paul is the only one of the Bible Writers who discarded his Jewish name (Saul) for his Gentile name.

Actually, his Gentile name gains the ascendancy on his first Missionary Journey as he deals with the Roman Officer on Cyprus, and thereafter marks him out as the Apostle to the Gentiles, which was his Calling (Acts, Chpt. 13).

The word *"servant"* or *"doulos"* in the Greek Text, actually denotes, as stated, a slave, even in the most abject and servile of meanings.

The word designated one who was born as a slave, one who was bound to his master in cords so strong that only death could break them, one who served his master to the disregard of his own interests, one whose will was swallowed up in the will of his master.

Paul was born a slave of sin at his physical birth, and a bondslave of his Lord through Regeneration. The cords that bound him to his old master Satan, were rent asunder in his identification with Christ in the latter's death. The cords that bind him to his new Master will never be broken since the new Master will never die again, and is Paul's New Life, and ours as well, I might quickly add.

Paul's will, at one time swallowed up in the will of Satan, now is swallowed up in the sweet Will of God. In this he calls himself *"A bondslave of Christ Jesus."*

Actually, there were certain individuals in the Roman Empire designated *"Slaves of the Emperor."* This was a position of honor. One finds a reflection of this in Paul's act of designating himself as a slave of the King of kings. If one is to notice, he even puts this ahead of his Apostleship (Wuest).

The phrase, *"Called to be an Apostle,"* actually says in the Greek *"A called Apostle."*

The word *"called"* in the Greek is *"kletos"* and means *"called to an Office and Divinely selected and appointed to fill it"* (I Cor. 1:1; Gal. 1:15). In other words, his calling came from the very Highest Source, the Lord Himself.

In fact, the three statements of verse 1, emphasize the Apostle's independency of the Twelve at Jerusalem, or anyone else for that matter. He was chosen by the Holy Spirit. He was not their servant, neither was he chosen by them to be an Apostle, nor ordained by them to preach the Gospel.

However, in no way is the Salutation meant to impugn the Twelve, or anyone else for that matter, but is simply meant to state that God is the One Who does the calling, and as it held true for Paul, it holds true for all others as well.

Paul wished to emphasize, for the sake of his authority and the authority which his position would give the letter he was writing, that he was already in possession of the Office of the Apostle, and exercising the authority it conferred upon him. The word *"Apostle"* means *"sent on a commission."* The noun was used of an envoy, namely, one sent on a commission to represent another person, the person sent being given credentials and the responsibility of carrying out the orders of the one sending him. Actually, our word *"Ambassador"* adequately translates it. Paul thought of himself as an *"Ambassador of the King of kings"* (Wuest).

The idea and tenor of Acts and the Epistles regarding all those called by God, always denote the Call as independent of human instrumentation; consequently, the Called one must answer first of all to God. In fact, the only thing the Called one owes to his brother and sister in Christ, and this would hold true for all Believers, is to *"Love one another"* (Rom. 13:8).

Of course, and as should be overly obvious, if one truly loves another, one would never do anything to hurt or to harm that person in any fashion.

The phrase, *"Separated unto the Gospel of God,"* in essence means that Paul was separated by God from all mankind for his Apostleship. In other words, what Paul was called to do, no one else could do, at least as it would be done by Paul. In a sense, that is true respecting all who are called by God.

The word *"Gospel"* simply means *"Good News,"* but such as would be expected from God, God-like Good News.

It is *"Good News"* that man who is lost, does not have to remain lost, thereby, living forever in eternal darkness, but can be Saved from all sin by simple Faith in what Jesus did at Calvary and the Resurrection. It is truly *"Good News"* that upon Faith in Christ the enmity between God and man is removed, simply because the sin question has been cleared up. It is *"Good News"* that fellowship can now be restored between God and man, which within itself, is a Blessing unparalleled. It is *"Good News"* that this cleansed temple can now be filled with the Holy Spirit, Who leads us and guides us into all Truth. It is *"Good News"* that the Spirit-filled Believer has power over the powers of darkness, and as such can continue the Works of Christ. It is *"Good News"* that Believers upon Faith in Jesus Christ now have Eternal Life, thereby, passing from death to Life. It is *"Good News"* that one day the Trump of God will sound, and all Believers, whether dead or alive, will have part in the First Resurrection of Life, over which the second death will have no power.

Actually, the *"Good News"* is unending, and it is all found in Christ and what He did at Calvary, the Resurrection, and the Exaltation.

WHO IS PAUL?

From Paul's birth until his appearance in Jerusalem as a persecutor of Christians there is little information concerning his life. Although of the Tribe of Benjamin and a zealous Pharisee (Acts 23:6; Rom. 11:1; Phil. 3:5), he was born in Tarsus a Roman citizen (Acts 16:37; 21:39; 22:25).

Jerome cites a tradition that Paul's forbears were from Galilee. It is not certain whether they migrated to Tarsus for commercial reasons or were settled there as colonists by a Syrian ruler. That they were citizens suggests that they had resided there for some time.

THE EARLY YEARS

Sir William Ramsay and others have shown that Tarsus truly was *"No mean City."* It was a center of learning, and Scholars generally have assumed that Paul became acquainted with various Greek philosophies and religious cults during his youth there.

However, others place Paul in Jerusalem as a very small child, beginning his education at the feet of Rabban Gamaliel as a young man, possibly even at 12 years of age, now a *"Son of the Law."*

We do know that Paul was given official authority to direct the persecution of Christians and as a member of a Synagogue or Sanhedrin Elementary Council (not the great Sanhedrin) did cast his vote against Christians (Acts 26:10).

In the light of Paul's education and early prominence we may presume that his family was of some means and of prominent status; his nephew's access to the Jerusalem Leaders accords with this impression (Acts 23:16, 20).

HIS CONVERSION

While there is no evidence that Paul was acquainted with Jesus during His earthly Ministry, his experience of the martyrdom of Stephen (Acts 8:1), plus the conduct of other Christians he persecuted (Acts 26:10-11) must have made an impact upon him. The Glorified Jesus' question in Acts 26:14 implies as much. The result of Paul's encounter with the risen Christ gives ample assurance that it was an experience of a healthy mind; and it can be adequately interpreted, as indeed Luke does interpret it, only as a miraculous act, which transformed Christ's greatest enemy into His Apostle.

(2) "(WHICH HE HAD PROMISED AFORE BY HIS PROPHETS IN THE HOLY SCRIPTURES,)"

The phrase, *"Which He had promised afore by His Prophets,"* proclaimed these Prophets belonging exclusively to God, exactly as Paul belonged to God, and all others who are called for that matter.

Even though all Saints belong to God, as should be obvious, the emphasis by the Holy Spirit regarding the separation unto God of those who are called for Ministry, and in whatever capacity, is of a greater degree. This is brought out extensively so, due to the fact that Satan seeks to usurp the authority of such a Call, and most of the time does so by using religion in some form. Actually, this conflict has raged from the very beginning, even with Cain killing his brother Abel. As well, the Prophets who were killed down through the centuries, as mentioned by Jesus, were killed without exception by the Religious Hierarchy of Israel (Mat. 23:37). Also, those who fought Paul the greatest respecting his Message, in effect attempting to silence his voice, and using any means to do so, even murder, again was the Religious Hierarchy of Israel.

The Dark Ages witnessed the most horrifying persecution that possibly the world has ever known. Untold thousands were murdered by the torture racks or burned alive, by Roman Catholic authorities, because they would not give allegiance to the Pope. In other words, the Catholic Church demanded this allegiance under the penalty of death, and nothing was to be taught or preached unless it was sanctioned by that Church.

Really it has not changed presently. Through Denominational Hierarchy, this spirit of control is very much alive, and rears its head in many and varied ways. If it is not Denominations, oftentimes it is certain people in the local Church who threaten to withhold their giving, or to take other measures,

NOTES

if the preaching and teaching are not to their satisfaction. The Preacher who submits to such, and irrespective as to its direction, ceases to be a Preacher of the Gospel, and, in fact, becomes a hireling.

Nothing must stand between the preacher and God. The direct line must be kept ever open. It is our business to hear what He says, and then to deliver what He has said unsullied, uncompromised, and unchanged. Naturally, all Preachers desire for their Message to be accepted, and for Godly results to be forthcoming. Nevertheless, as important as that is, and it is very important, the most important thing is that we deliver the Message which God has given. It must never be trimmed in order to appeal to the public in any fashion.

The phrase, *"In the Holy Scriptures,"* speaks in this case of the Old Testament. They are called *"Holy"* because they are given by the Holy Spirit, even though they were penned by man.

Consequently, the Word of God, both the Old and New Testaments, is to serve as the criteria and foundation of all that we do. Nothing must ever usurp authority over the Bible. If something is demanded that is not Scriptural, it must be ignored and refused.

The Old Testament in its entirety, pointed to Christ, while the New Testament reveals Christ.

By Paul's statement in this verse, with one stroke he cuts away all objections to his message from the Jews who said he was introducing something new and opposed to the Mosaic economy. Consequently, Paul's Old Testament training is manifest, with him probably being the greatest Old Testament Scholar in the world of his day.

Naturally, in beginning the more precise description of the New Revelation, he refers to its connection with ancient Prophecy. As well, the term *"Prophets"* as used here does not limit the writers to those we know as the Major and Minor Prophets, but includes writers such as Moses and David, who were not normally thought of as Prophets, but actually were, with them also speaking the *"Good News"* (Wuest).

(3) "CONCERNING HIS SON JESUS CHRIST OUR LORD, WHICH WAS MADE

OF THE SEED OF DAVID ACCORDING TO THE FLESH;"

The phrase, *"Concerning His Son Jesus Christ our Lord,"* speaks of Jesus being the Central and Core Message of the Old Testament.

Actually, this phrase speaks of the Deity of Christ, while the latter phrase of this verse speaks of His Humanity. Jesus Christ is God! He became Man in order to redeem the human family!

The phrase, *"Which was made,"* signifies entrance into a new condition. It actually means *"to become,"* and in this case, assuming a human body, putting Himself under human limitations. Of course it speaks of the Incarnation, God becoming Man.

THE MEANING OF THE WORD *"INCARNATION"*

The word *"Incarnate"* or *"Incarnation"* is not found in the Bible. However, Paul said in I Timothy 3:16, *"He was manifested in the flesh,"* which adequately describes the English word *"Incarnation."* It simply refers to God taking on a human body of flesh.

The Bible sees physical flesh as a theologically significant symbol — a symbol, namely, of the created and dependent sort of life which men and even animals share for that matter, a sort of life which is derived from God and which, unlike God's Own Life, requires a physical organism to sustain it in its characteristic activity. Hence, *"flesh"* is a generic term for men, or animals, or men and animals together, viewed as creatures of God, whose life on Earth last only for the comparatively short period during which God supplies the breath of life in their nostrils. Consequently, *"flesh"* in this Biblically-developed sense, is thus not something that a man has, but something that he is. It marks his creaturely weakness and frailty (Isa. 40:6), and in this respect it stands in contrast to *"Spirit,"* the eternal and unflagging energy that is of God, and is God (Isa. 31:3; 40:6-31). That is the reason the Lord said of Israel, *"For He remembered that they were but flesh; a wind that passeth away, and cometh not again"* (Ps. 78:39).

JESUS AS MAN AND, THEREFORE, FLESH

To say, therefore, that Jesus Christ came

NOTES

and died *"in the flesh"* is to say that He came and died in the state and under the conditions of created physical life: in other words, that He Who died was Man.

But the New Testament also affirms that He Who died was eternally God, and continues to be God. The formula which enshrines the Incarnation, therefore, is that in some sense God, without ceasing to be God, was made Man. This is what John asserts in the prologue of his Gospel: *"The Word* (God's agent in creation), *Who in the beginning, before the creation, not only was with God, but Himself was God"* (Jn. 1:1-3). This same God, John declares *"Was made flesh, and dwelt among us"* (Jn. 1:14).

THE ORIGIN OF THE BELIEF REGARDING THE INCARNATION OF CHRIST

While the Jews in Jesus' day were definitely expecting the Messiah, they were not expecting Him to be the Son of God. Son of David, yes! Son of God, no!

They were expecting some type of superhuman, charismatic individual, with the military strategy of David and the wisdom of Solomon. As such, He would lead them as a Nation to glory, power, and supremacy once again.

Actually, the Jews were the only monotheistic people in the world, meaning they were the only ones who worshiped One God, with all the other Nations of the world worshiping many gods, etc. Of course, this which the Prophets gave to them was correct. There is only One God (Deut. 6:4).

Consequently, when Jesus came referring to God as His Father, even His Own Unique Personal Father, it was something the Jews did not understand. This type of terminology meant that Jesus was God as well!

What they did not understand, but in fact should have, is that Elohim is not one person, or one in number, but one in Unity. Elohim is not a divided Deity, but Three Persons in *"One God,"* or One Deity. The word *"Elohim"* does not say there are Three, but merely that Deity is in the Plural. (Elohim is a uni-plural noun meaning *"Gods."*)

The Hebrew word for *"Lord"* in Deuteronomy 6:4 and used several thousand other times in the Old Testament, means *"The*

Self-existent, Eternal and Immutable One, or Unity." As stated, it does not tell us how many persons are in the *"One (Unified) Lord,"* but the Scriptures mention Three Persons Who are called *"Lord"* and Who are *"Self-existent"* and *"Eternal"* and, therefore, all of Them can be called *"Jehovah."*

As stated, the Jews should have known this, and then they would not have been upset by the statements made by Jesus. So, the Jews would not accept that there is One God, manifested in Three Persons, *"God the Father, God the Son, and God the Holy Spirit."*

Neither would they accept God becoming flesh, even though Isaiah plainly predicted it (Isa. 7:14), with the Lord predicting it first of all in the Garden of Eden after the Fall of man (Gen. 3:15).

Also, they should have known and understood this concerning the Promise of God to Abraham, on which was built the warp and woof of Judaism (Gen. 12:1-3).

WHY DID THE JEWS NOT BELIEVE IN THE INCARNATION?

First of all, the Incarnation appears to mean that the Divine Maker became One of His Own Creatures, which is a prima facie contradiction in theological terms.

As well, they simply no longer believed the Word, having twisted and turned it to suit their own purposes. Paul said of them, *"For unto us was the Gospel preached, as well as unto them: but the Word preached did not profit them, not being mixed with Faith in them that heard it"* (Heb. 4:2).

To understand how the Creator could become One of His Creatures is not easy, and probably in the strict sense of the word, impossible. Consequently, once again Faith comes into view, which must be evidenced in order to accept what God did for the human family. Israel did not evidence that Faith and, in fact, would not do so!

So, how do we explain the beautiful but yet strange statement given by John, referring to God becoming flesh and dwelling among us?

In fact, how did the Early Church accept and understand this Miracle of Miracles, and yet of total necessity, if man was to be Redeemed, must be believed personally by man,

if man is to be Saved?

THE EARLY CHURCH

That which the Early Church believed concerning the Incarnation of Christ, God becoming Man, had absolutely nothing to do with, and had no roots in, Jewish speculations about a pre-existent superhuman Messiah, or to the myths about redeemer-gods which were characteristic of Hellenistic (Greek) mystery-religions and Gnostic cults.

So, those who proposed such things, and some did, made no headway, simply because the claims of the Early Church regarding the Incarnation of Christ were so different than the speculations, that no actual similarities existed.

First of all, the study of the four Gospels, and especially the Gospel of John, proclaims the Words of Jesus as making constant claims to Deity. As well, a total acceptance of these claims was fundamental to the Faith and Worship of the Early Church, even as pictured in the first Chapters of Acts (Jn. 1:51; 2:19; 3:13-18; 4:10, 14, 26; 5:19-47; 6:29, 35-40, 47-51, 53-63; 7:37-38, etc.).

In fact, the impact of Jesus' Own Life, Ministry, Death and Resurrection, convinced His Disciples of His Personal Deity even before He ascended. To be frank, the Early Church had no question whatsoever about the Deity of Christ, and not only because of the things we have said, but as well, because of the Person, Office, and Ministry of the Holy Spirit.

THE HOLY SPIRIT AND CHRIST

Error comes into the Church, and great error at that, because of the lack of Holy Spirit Presence. He is either rejected altogether, as in most old-line Denominational circles, or ignored, as He is in many Pentecostal and Charismatic circles, etc. His absence always spells error, and He is absent primarily because man usurps authority over Christ Who is the Head of the Church, grabbing the headship for himself. When this happens, the Holy Spirit always pulls aside. Jesus plainly said concerning the Holy Spirit, *"Howbeit when He, the Spirit of Truth, is come, He will guide you into all Truth: for He shall not speak of Himself; but whatsoever He shall hear, that shall He speak: and*

He will shew you things to come.

"He shall glorify Me: for He shall receive of Mine, and shall shew it unto you" (Jn. 16:13-14).

The Early Church was full of the Holy Spirit, so they did not question the great fundamentals of the Faith, as men later began to do, and which continues unto this hour.

They knew that Jesus was Lord; consequently, they proclaimed Him as the One Who accepts Repentance and gives Remission of Sins (Acts 5:31).

If one is to notice, the New Testament writers had no questions whatsoever about the mode of the Incarnation, or questions about the Incarnate State. Actually, their interest in the Person of Christ was not physical, philosophical or speculative, but rather Spiritual and Evangelical. In other words, they believed He was God as well as Man, even though they did not understand it all, and, in fact, no one has ever understood it all. To be frank, if one could understand everything about this subject of God becoming Man, he would have to be God to do so. Due to the fact that such is not the case, Faith is demanded, as should be obvious.

However, that is not to say that the proof of His Deity is not absolutely abundant, for it is. Even if one cannot prove the Virgin Birth, which of course is impossible for anyone to prove, with it as well taken by Faith, the Miracles which Jesus performed were so absolutely extraordinary, that they within themselves were proof enough. Jesus said, *"If I do not the Works of My Father, believe Me not.*

"But if I do, though ye believe not Me, believe the Works: that ye may know, and believe, that the Father is in Me, and I in Him" (Jn. 10:37-38).

As well, the Statements Jesus made concerning Himself and His Deity, which are mostly recorded in John, are so absolutely astounding, that it would not be possible for Him to be anything other than what He claimed, and actually is. In the entirety of history no one even came close to making such claims. As well, the claims were so correct, so right, so obvious, and so fulfilling of Old Testament Scriptures, that even though one would not believe them, even as the

Jewish Leadership, there was no way they could claim that His Statements were silly, unbelievable, or foolish, etc.

The point is this, unless Jesus knew exactly what He was talking about, and was actually What and Who He said He was, there is no way such things could be said. If one will take the time to read the host of Scriptures given from John, concerning what He said, and study those statements even to a small degree, one will see exactly what I am speaking about (Jn. 1:51; 2:19; 3:11-21; 4:10,14,26; 5:19-47; 6:35-40, 44-51, 53-58, 62-64; 7:17-19, 37-38; 8:12-19, 23-58; 9:5; 10:1-18, 25-32, 36-38; 11:25-26; 12:44-50; 14:1-21, 23-31; 15:1-27; 16:1-16, 19-28, 32-33; 17:1-26; 18:37; 20:17).

THE NEW TESTAMENT WRITERS
THE MYSTERY OF HIS PERSON

As stated, these men in penning the Words of the New Testament, which were inspired by the Holy Spirit, never spoke of Christ as a metaphysical problem (how God became Man, other than relating the account of the Virgin Birth, and what little Paul said in Philippians 2:6-8), but as a Divine Saviour. All they say about His Person is prompted by their desire to glorify Him through exhibiting His Work and vindicating His centrality in the Redemptive Purpose of God.

Actually, they never attempt to dissect the mystery of His Person; it is enough for them to proclaim the Incarnation as a fact, one of the sequence of Mighty Works whereby God has wrought Salvation for sinners. In fact, the only sense in which the New Testament writers ever attempt to explain the Incarnation is by showing how it fits into God's over-all Plan for redeeming mankind (Jn. 1:18; Rom. 8:3; Phil. 2:6-11; Col. 1:13-22; Heb. Chpts. 1-2; 4:14; 5:10; 7:1; 10:18; I Jn. 1:1-2:2).

THE VIRGIN BIRTH

The writers of the New Testament nowhere reflect on the Virgin Birth of Jesus as witnessing to the conjunction of Deity and Manhood in His Person, except merely to state the fact.

This silence need not mean that any of the New Testament writers were ignorant of the

Virgin Birth, as some have supposed. It is sufficiently explained by the fact that New Testament interest in Jesus centers upon His relation to the Saving Purposes of God. Proof of this is given by the way in which the Virgin Birth story is itself told by Matthew and Luke, the two Evangelists who recount it. Each lays all his stress, not on the unique constitution of the Person thus miraculously born, but on the fact that by this Miraculous Birth God began to fulfill His long-foretold intention of visiting and redeeming His people (Mat. 1:21; Lk. 1:31, 68-75; 2:10, 29-32).

THE DEITY AND MANHOOD OF JESUS

The Apostolic writers clearly see that both the Deity and the Manhood of Jesus are fundamental to His Saving Work. That Jesus is God the Son, they are to regard His disclosure of the Father's Mind and Heart as perfect and final (Jn. 1:18; 14:7-10; Heb. 1:1), and His Death as the Supreme Evidence of God's Love for sinners and His Will to bless Believers (Jn. 3:16; Rom. 5:5-10; 8:32; I Jn. 4:8-10).

They realize that it is Jesus' Divine Sonship that guarantees the endless duration, sinless perfection, and limitless efficacy, of His High-Priestly Service (Heb. 7:3, 16, 24-28).

They are aware that it was in virtue of His Deity that He was able to defeat and dispossess the Devil, the *"strong man armed"* who kept sinners in a state of helpless bondage (Mk. 3:27; Lk. 10:17; Jn. 12:31; 16:11; Heb. 2:14; Rev. 20:1). Equally, they see that it was necessary, and absolutely so, for God to *"become flesh"* for only so could He take His place as the *"Second Man"* or *"Second Adam"* through Whom God deals with the race (Rom. 5:15-19; I Cor. 15:21, 47); only then could He mediate between God and men (I Tim. 2:5); and only so could He die for sins, for only unglorified flesh can die.

HERESY

We should, therefore, expect the New Testament to treat any denial that Jesus Christ was both truly Divine and truly Human as a damning heresy, destructive of the Gospel; and so it does.

In fact, during the time of the Early Church, a man named Cerinthus did deny

the reality of Christ's *"flesh"* (I Jn. 4:2) and, hence, of His Physical Death (Blood), (I Jn. 5:6). John denounces this in his first two Epistles as a deadly error inspired by the spirit of Antichrist, a lying denial of both the Father and the Son (I Jn. 2:22-25; 4:1-6; 5:5-12; II Jn. vss. 7, 9).

Actually, it is suggested that the emphasis in John's Gospel, among other things, on the reality of Jesus' experience of human frailty (His weariness, Jn. 4:6; thirst, 4:7; 19:28; tears, 11:33) is intended to cut at the root of this error and, therefore, heresy.

THE NATURE OF THE INCARNATION

When the Word (God) *"became flesh"* His Deity was not abandoned, reduced, or contracted, nor did He cease to exercise the Divine functions which had been His before. It is He, we are told, Who sustains the creation in ordered existence, and Who gives and upholds all life (Jn. 1:4; Col. 1:17; Heb. 1:3), and these functions were certainly not laid aside during His time on Earth.

While it is true, that when He came into the world He *"emptied Himself"* of outward glory (Jn. 17:5; Phil. 2:7), and in that sense He *"became poor"* (II Cor. 8:9), but this does not at all imply a curtailing of His Divine Powers, even though He did not use those Powers in preaching, living, or performing Healings and Miracles, as that was done by the Power of the Holy Spirit (Lk. 4:18-19).

However, let me again state, that the New Testament stresses that the Son's Deity was not reduced through the Incarnation. In the Man Christ Jesus says Paul, *"Dwelleth all the fulness of the Godhead Bodily"* (Col. 1:19; 2:9).

The Incarnation of the Son of God, then, was not a diminishing of Deity, but an acquiring of manhood. It was not that God the Son came to indwell a human being, as the Spirit was later to do, it was rather that the Son in Person began to live a fully human life.

He did not simply clothe Himself in a human body, taking the place of its soul, as some have maintained; He took to Himself a human soul as well as a human body, i.e., He entered into the experience of human physical life. His Manhood, in other words, was complete; He became *"The Man Christ Jesus"* (Gal. 4:4; I Tim. 2:5; Heb. 2:14, 17).

As well, His Manhood is permanent. Though now exalted He *"Continueth to be God and Man in two distinct Natures, and One Person, for ever"* (Heb. 7:24).

WHAT DID THE INCARNATE STATE OF THE SON OF GOD REPRESENT? FIRST, A STATE OF EXAMPLE

To understand, at least somewhat, the Incarnate State of Christ, other than the all-important purpose of dying on Calvary and being Resurrected in order to redeem man, one must understand that this State was also a State of *example*. In other words, in the Incarnate State as Man, Jesus set the pattern for all Believers to follow.

As the prime example, Believers are to follow accordingly, hence Jesus beginning His Earthly Ministry in this respect by saying to His prospective Disciples, *"Follow Me"* (Mat. 4:19). In fact, that Command extends to all Believers and which Satan ever attempts to circumvent by inserting demands made by other men, and especially religious men.

THE INCARNATE STATE WAS ONE OF DEPENDENCE AND OBEDIENCE

Actually, the Incarnation of Christ in no way changed the relationship between the Son and the Father. They continued in unbroken fellowship, the Son saying and doing what the Father gave Him to say and do, and not going beyond the Father's known Will at any single moment.

An example is given in the first temptation (Mat. 4:2). As well, He confessed ignorance of the time of His own return (Mk. 13:32). To be sure, this was not a pretense as some claim, nor evidence of His having laid aside His Divine Knowledge for the purpose of the Incarnation, but simply as showing that it was not the Father's Will for Him to have this knowledge in His Mind at that particular time. As the Son, He did not wish or seek to know more than the Father wished Him to know.

THE STATE OF THE INCARNATION WAS ONE OF SINLESSNESS AND IMPECCABILITY

In fact, the Incarnation did not change

NOTES

the Nature and Character of the Son, but it did make His nature and character subject to the flesh. However, that His whole Life was sinless is several times asserted (Mat. 3:14-17; Jn. 8:46; II Cor. 5:21; Heb. 4:15; I Pet. 2:22; I Jn. 2:1). As well, that He was exempt from the original sin of Adam is evident from the fact that He was not bound to die for sins of His Own (Heb. 7:26), and, hence, could die vicariously and representatively, the Righteous taking the place of the unrighteous (Rom. 5:16; II Cor. 5:21; Gal. 3:13; I Pet. 3:18).

Deviation from the Father's Will was totally unthinkable for Him in the Incarnate State. However, the teaching that it was impossible for Him to sin, or to deviate from that Will, does not hold true with the very fact of the Incarnation, or its purpose.

While it is certainly true that as God He could not sin or deviate from that Will, at the same time the very fact of Him becoming Man, was not only to furnish a Perfect Sacrifice for the Redemption of the human family, in that God cannot die, but as well, to serve as the Second Adam, in order that Satan may have the same access to Him as he did the First Adam. For Him to be the Representative Man, as He certainly was, this part of His Purpose was just as important as His being the Perfect Sacrifice, for they both flow together.

I say these things, because many claim that it was not possible for Jesus to sin in the Incarnate State, for the simple reason that He at the same time continued to be God, and God cannot sin.

While it is certainly true that Jesus in the incarnation never ceased to be God, and it is also true that God cannot sin, nevertheless, the very purpose of God becoming Man, was for Jesus to be the Representative Man, as well as the Perfect Sacrifice. He could not be such, unless the possibility of sinning and falling was always there.

For instance, and as stated, He grew weary (Jn. 4:6), and we know that God cannot grow weary, at least as humans think of such. As well, He did thirst (Jn. 4:7), and we know that God does not get thirsty. Also, He shed tears (Jn. 11:33), and we know that God does not weep. As well, God does not get hungry, does not lack in knowledge concerning anything, or a host of other things that one could name, which in fact were a part of the Manhood of Christ.

If He had not faced the onslaughts of Satan, even as we face, He could not have been the Representative Man, which of necessity, must include temptation and the possibility of failure. So the answer is: while never ceasing to possess Deity, He did lay aside the expression of Deity (Phil. 2:5-8).

THE INCARNATE STATE WAS ONE OF TEMPTATION AND MORAL CONFLICT

The Incarnation was a true entry into the conditions of man's moral life. As God, He could not be tempted, but as Man, He definitely could be and was. In fact, what type of temptations did He face?

He was not tempted, as some think, to commit adultery, to steal, to lie, etc., but rather to step outside of the Revealed Will of God. Actually, this was the Genesis of His temptations, as recorded respecting His tryst with Satan in the wilderness (Mat. 4:1-11; Lk. 4:1-13). As well, this is the Genesis of every single temptation engineered by Satan against man.

The Evil One tempted Jesus to take the Power that God had given Him, and to use it for purposes other than the Revealed Will of God, such as gratifying His Own desires, etc. Hence, he told Him, to turn the stones to bread, etc. So Satan does the same with us.

He knows, and the Believer should know, that there is a Revealed Will of God for all people and for everything. Such is found in the Word of God, which makes it absolutely imperative that one know the Bible. Satan attempts to get the Believer to step outside of that Will, in order to gratify his own purposes and desires, which are not of God.

Consequently, stepping outside of that Will amounts to self-will. This was the sum total of Satan's subtle approach to Christ, and he uses the same tactics on Believers presently.

This means that sin committed by Christians, and in whatever capacity, is actually the *result* of self-will and not the Will of God. Such is temptation and such is sin.

One writer contends that it was not possible for Jesus to sin, but was necessary for

Him to fight temptation in order to overcome it. His statement contradicts itself. How could one fight and overcome something, if it was not possible for him to yield to that thing?

He went on to say, *"What His Deity ensured was not that He would not be tempted to stray from His Father's Will, nor that He would be exempt from the strain and distress that repeated insidious temptations create in the soul, but that, when tempted, He would fight and win."*

As stated, he contradicts himself. How can one win what one cannot lose? Satan was no fool! To tempt God was not possible; however, to tempt the human Jesus was definitely possible, even though Jesus never ceased to be God. As previously said, *"On becoming Man, God laid aside His expression of Deity, while never losing its possession."* If it were not possible for Jesus to sin or to fall, Satan would not have wasted his time, and, as repeatedly stated, Jesus could not have been the Representative Man.

Consequently, in view of Him facing Satan with the same Power that Redeemed man has (the Holy Spirit), with the possibility of failure, but yet overcoming him completely, and never failing, He is able to extend effective sympathy and help to tempted and distraught Christians (Heb. 2:18; 4:14; 5:2, 7).

(Bibliography: J. Denney, *"Jesus and the Gospel"*; L. Berkhof, *"Systematic Theology"*; G. C. Berkouwer, *"The Person of Christ."*)

The phrase, *"Of the Seed of David according to the flesh,"* is used in the context of the ancestry of David. That is, the Son of God, so far as His human ancestry is concerned, comes from the line of David. Consequently, He comprised within His Person two natures, that of Deity and that of humanity.

Why was the lineage of David necessary?

DAVID

David, as most know, was the youngest son of Jesse, of the Tribe of Judah, and the second King of Israel. (It was God's Will that he be the first King, as Saul was an aberration, i.e., a work of the flesh and not the Spirit. However, this aberration did not circumvent the Plan of God, as such never circumvents the Greater Plan of God.)

In Scripture the name *"David"* is his alone, typifying the unique place he has as ancestor, forerunner, and foreshadower of the Lord Jesus Christ — *"Great David's Greater Son."*

There are 58 New Testament references to David, including the oft-repeated title given to Jesus — *"Son of David."* Paul states, even as we are studying here, that Jesus is *"descended from David according to the flesh."* Jesus Himself is recorded by John as saying, *"I am the Root and the Offspring of David"* (Rev. 22:16). In fact, the name of David is the first human name in the New Testament (Mat. 1:1), and the last name in that Wondrous Work (Rev. 22:16).

FAMILY BACKGROUND OF DAVID

David was the great-grandson of Ruth and Boaz, presenting the cursed Moabitess as coming to Faith, and, thereby, having the distinct honor and privilege of being in the lineage of Christ. David was the youngest of eight brothers (I Sam. 17:12) and was brought up to be a Shepherd. As such, the type fits the great Anti-type, the Lord Jesus Christ, Who, as well, is *"The Good Shepherd"* (Jn. 10:11).

As well, David suffered from the ill-will and jealousy of his brothers, exactly as did Jesus (Jn. 7:5).

Also, David's birthplace was Bethlehem, as was the birthplace of His Divine Seed, The Lord Jesus Christ (Lk. 2:4-7).

THE ANOINTING OF DAVID BY SAMUEL

Whenever the Lord said to Samuel, *"Fill thine horn with oil, and go, . . . for I have provided Me a King . . ."* He was speaking of far more than David, but, as well, the Son of David, Jesus Christ (I Sam. 16:1).

There was an awesome Revelation of Divine Purpose in the Providence by which David, who was to replace Saul in the favor and Plan of God, is selected.

In a sense, Saul was a type of the coming Antichrist, who Israel will claim as the Chosen One, in other words, her Messiah. However, they will soon find that this man is a work of the flesh, exactly as Saul of long ago was such. And even as Israel rejected David at first, they also rejected Jesus at first. However, as they ultimately accepted him, they

NOTES

ultimately will accept Christ (Zech. 13:1, 6; Rev. Chpt. 19).

Likewise, as David was Anointed with oil, typifying the Holy Spirit, the Greater Son was Anointed with the Holy Spirit, as no one has ever been Anointed (Lk. 4:18-19).

As David ultimately became King at Jerusalem, likewise, Jesus will reign supremely from Jerusalem in the coming Kingdom Age.

THE PURPOSE AND NECESSITY OF THE DAVIDIC LINEAGE

In Genesis 3:15 the Lord made a prediction to Satan, that the Evil One would ultimately be destroyed, and that Righteousness would prevail. He used terminology which was strange, and probably was not understandable by Satan at the time. He said, *"And I will put enmity between thee and the woman, and between thy seed and her Seed; It shall bruise thy head, and thou shalt bruise His Heel."*

In other words, the Lord was telling Satan, *"You have used the woman to bring about your evil which has resulted in the Fall, and I will use a Woman to bring Righteousness into the world."* Of course, the *"Seed"* of which the Lord was speaking, was Jesus, Who would ultimately be born of the Virgin Mary. But at the time it probably did not make much sense to Satan, because, in effect, the woman has no seed, that being the prerogative altogether of the male gender.

Due to the manner in which God had made man and woman and the manner in which they would bring offspring into the world, Satan knew that avenue was destroyed forever. In other words, Satan could spoil the first Adam and due to the fact that he was the representative man, all after him would be destroyed as well, due to his seed being poisoned. He was correct in that, but he did not figure on the Lord sending a Second Adam, which would be the Seed of the Woman.

WHY DID IT TAKE SO LONG?

From the time the Lord made this prediction to Satan, it was about 4,000 years before Jesus was born. In the meantime, the world was in a horrible state. We may think situations are bad presently; however, due to what Jesus did at Calvary and the Resurrection and taking into account His Exaltation, with the Holy Spirit now being able to come into the hearts and lives of Born-Again Believers, the world has been made infinitely better. So why did it take so long for the Lord to do this thing?

In fact, Adam and Eve were very well aware of this Promise by the Lord. So much so in fact, that when Cain was born, their first child incidentally, Eve said, *"I have gotten a man from the Lord"* (Gen. 4:1).

By using the title or appellative *"Lord,"* Eve was referring to the Covenant in which the Redeemer would come into the world through the Woman. She thought this was the fulfillment of that Covenant. (The Name or Title *"Lord"* represents the most sacred Hebrew Name for God, as their Covenant God.) However, Cain was not the Promised Seed, but, in fact, a murderer.

After a period of time, Adam and Eve had another child, *"And* (she) *called his name Seth."*

She then said, *"For God, hath appointed me another seed instead of Abel, whom Cain slew"* (Gen. 4:25).

By her using the Title *"God,"* instead of *"Lord,"* this tells us that she had now lost Faith in the Covenant due to her disappointment concerning Cain.

Unto the time of Noah, about 1600 years after the Fall, concerning man, the Bible says, *"And that every imagination of the thoughts of his heart was only evil continually"* (Gen. 6:5). Consequently, the situation during this time was so awful, that God had to perform major surgery on the Earth, in effect taking out the entirety of the human family with the exception of Noah and his family, or else the entirety of everything would have been forever lost.

So, the reason that the Lord did not send His Son at that time, is because the world was so evil that precious few would have accepted Him. In fact, the Bible only records two people as Saved up to the time of Noah; Abel and Enoch (Gen. 4:4; 5:21-24).

THE AWFULNESS OF SIN

Considering that God could speak worlds into existence (Gen. Chpt. 1), yet could not

NOTES

speak Redemption into existence, but instead had to send His Son to die on Calvary in order that man might be Saved, tells us just how awful that sin really is. In fact, it is impossible for a human being to even begin to comprehend how terrible this scourge is.

Once again we emphasize, that if God by the Power of His Word could literally speak creation into existence, but yet could not do so with Redemption, especially considering that He is Omnipotent (all-powerful), Omniscient (all-knowing), and Omnipresent (everywhere), then we begin to get the idea as to exactly how awful this thing really is, at least as far as a poor human being can grasp such.

That is what makes the Church so absolutely foolish in accepting Humanistic Psychology as a panacea or solution for the sinful aberrations of man. If the Lord could not speak Redemption into existence, how in the world does the Church think that Psychologists can talk these problems out of humanity? One must understand, that Psychologists have no wonder drugs, no antibiotics, no certain types of medicine that can be given to one concerning these terrible problems which beset humanity. As well, when they speak of Psychological Therapy, they are not speaking of some antibiotic or body of learning that will help someone in this capacity. They are merely speaking of talking to a person and having the person talk to them.

Again I emphasize, that if one can talk these problems out of a person, Jesus Christ wasted His Time in coming down here to this mortal coil and dying on Calvary. How absolutely ludicrous can one be?

No! Humanistic Psychology has no answers whatsoever concerning the problem of mankind. That problem is sin, and can only be handled by the Lord Jesus Christ and what He did at Calvary and the Resurrection. Faith in Him, and Faith in Him Alone, is the only, and I emphasize, the *only* solution! (Jn. 3:16; Rom. 10:9-10, 13).

In fact, if one wants to know what man really is, one only has to read Romans Chapter 3. And when one understands, that this description given by the Holy Spirit through Paul, in fact, describes the entirety of mankind without Christ, and with no exceptions, we learn just how bad the situation really is.

No! The *"Seed of the Woman"* is the only answer, and that Seed is Jesus Christ and not just Jesus Christ as a man, but rather the Crucified, Risen, and Exalted Lord.

ISRAEL

For God to bring this *"Seed of the Woman"* into the world, a special people would have to be prepared for the entrance of the Second Adam (I Cor. 15:22, 45). This Last or Second Adam, would win or purchase back what the first Adam lost. That Last Adam, of course, was Jesus (Isa. Chpt. 53).

To prepare these special people, the Lord would choose a man by the name of Abraham (Gen. 12:1-3). From his loins and through Sarah his wife, the Seed of these people would be brought into the world, in effect, God creating a special people for the task of bringing the *"Seed of the Woman"* into the world. They were to be holy, and, in fact, were the only people on Earth who had any knowledge of the One True God.

Even with these special people prepared by the Lord, due to their many failures and rebellion against God, the situation became very precarious at times, as becomes overly obvious when one studies their history. As we have stated, all during this time, the world was not ready to receive the Redeemer and Israel was not ready to receive her Messiah, Who, in fact, was that Redeemer.

Approximately one thousand years after Abraham, and with the Nation of Israel becoming strong and powerful, the Lord told David that it was through his personal seed, that the Redeemer, *"The Seed of the Woman"* would come into the world (II Sam. Chpt. 7). Only now, even after a thousand years of preparation, was it possible to select this man of the Israelites, who would serve as the lineage. Spiritually, Israel simply was not ready before now, and to be frank, was barely ready at this moment.

In fact, the Lord had told Abraham that He would provide a Redeemer, actually continuing what He had said in the Garden after the Fall. Hence, Abraham referred to the Lord at that time as *"Jehovah-Jireh,"* which actually means, *"The Lord will provide."*

Provide what?

Provide a Redeemer for fallen humanity.

About 200 years after Abraham, the Lord spoke through Jacob, concerning the various Tribes of Israel, which had now become strong, that it would be through the Tribe of Judah that *"Shiloh"* or the *"Seed of the Woman,"* would come (Gen. 49:10). (Shiloh is an epithet of the Messiah.)

And now the Lord tells David that his family in the Tribe of Judah, will, in fact, be the promised lineage.

About 300 years after David, with his seed continuing to occupy the Throne of Israel (Judah), the Lord spoke through the Prophet Isaiah that through this family of David, in the Tribe of Judah, and the Nation of Israel, that *"A Virgin shall conceive, and bear a Son, and shall call His Name Immanuel,"* meaning *"God with us"* (Isa. 7:14). So now, Israel knows exactly how this *"Seed of the Woman"* will come into the world.

However, if one is to notice, this *"Seed"* could not come into the world through just any woman of the family of David, but she would have to be a Virgin, one who has never known man. The reason being, if Jesus had been conceived by the normal manner of procreation, He would have been born in sin exactly as all others before Him, consequently, unable to be the Perfect Sacrifice.

To be frank, this is the reason that Satan did not really understand as to how the Lord would do this thing, considering that not only was Adam and Eve destroyed, but the seed of Adam was destroyed as well, because the original fountain (Adam) was polluted. Satan did not realize that the Lord would bypass the normal manner of procreation, having a Virgin to conceive, thereby eliminating the poisoned seed of Adam. In fact, the Lord could do this and not destroy the type, because the original Adam was not born of normal procreation, but was, in fact, created or made by God. Therefore, the Last Adam, the Lord Jesus Christ, could be brought in the same way, even as He was, without the type of the first Adam being abrogated. In other words, the Last Adam must come in the same manner, in a sense, as the first Adam, that is, if He was to be the Representative Man for fallen humanity.

However, even now, at the time of Isaiah,

Israel was not ready for the Redeemer to be brought into the world. It would take approximately another 750 years, with conditions barely being ready even at that time which, of necessity, included not only Israel, but the entirety of the world of that day. Nevertheless, from the time this great prediction was given to David by the Lord concerning his family being the Sacred lineage, all of Israel knew that the Messiah would be *"The Son of David,"* hence, Paul using the term *"Of the seed of David."*

ACCORDING TO THE FLESH

The words, *"According to the flesh,"* concerned the lineage of David, and referred to the fact that the Last Adam had to be *"flesh"* exactly as the first Adam. In this manner alone could God Redeem humanity. As the first Adam was of *"flesh"* and was created and formed by God to be the representative man for all mankind, likewise, God would have to send another Representative Man into the world in the same manner. It would literally be God becoming Man, Who was Christ.

In this manner, man fell, and in this manner, man must be Redeemed.

This tells us that God had invested much in the original Adam and I speak of supremacy and dominion (Gen. 1:28; Ps. 8). This means that the Adam was not some animal-crawling primate, as perverted education likes to claim, but rather, a man of such magnitude and proportion, that his wisdom and power were literally beyond our comprehension. In fact, except in Jesus Christ, it is impossible to look at man presently and comprehend the original creation. It simply cannot be done in this manner. Even Redeemed man still suffers the effects of the Fall, which will not be totally erased until the coming Resurrection of Life (I Cor. 15:51-57).

As well, and considering, even as we have said, that all of humanity theoretically was in Adam's loins, Satan by destroying him, destroyed the entirety of humanity. So the Lord sent a Second or Last Adam, with the word *"Last"* simply referring to the fact, that another one will never be needed. Jesus would pay it all, Redeeming humanity from the clutches of the Evil One. As well, He would do so *"according to the flesh,"* in effect, being

the perfect, sinless Sacrifice, as He was, in the offering up of His Own Body on the Tree (I Pet. 2:24).

(4) "AND DECLARED TO BE THE SON OF GOD WITH POWER, ACCORDING TO THE SPIRIT OF HOLINESS, BY THE RESURRECTION FROM THE DEAD:"

The phrase, *"And declared to be the Son of God with power,"* in effect, the Son of God, so far as His human ancestry is concerned, came from the line of David.

This individual, comprising within His Person two natures, that of Deity and that of humanity, is *"Declared to be the Son or God."* *"Declared"* in the Greek Text is *"horizo,"* and means *"to mark out the boundaries or limits"* of anything, *"to appoint, decree, determine."*

Thayer says, *"For although Christ was the Son of God before His Resurrection, yet He was openly appointed such among men by this transcendent and crowning event."*

Vincent says, *"As respecting Christ's earthly descent, He was born like other men, at least as far as the womb of Mary was concerned. However, as respecting His Divine Essence, He was 'declared'"* (Wuest).

The Formula *"According to the flesh"* (vs. 3) and *"According to the Spirit"* (vs. 4) define His human and Divine Natures (Williams).

The use of the words *"With Power"* regarding Jesus and more specifically, *"The Son of God,"* has reference to several things.

First of all, His Ministry was *"With Power"* and, in fact, such Power as the world had never seen before. The sick of every description were healed, with not one single failure. Actually it was not possible for there to be a failure of healing or miracles. The dead were raised, even Lazarus who had been in the tomb for some four days. In fact, even though the Religious Leadership of Israel hated Him, they in no way denied the veracity of His Miracles and Healings. They accused Him of doing these things by the powers of Satan, but in no way did they try to claim that the Healings and Miracles were fakes. The evidence was so overwhelming otherwise, that they would have made no headway whatsoever with that claim, had it even been suggested.

As well, He had been raised from the dead,

which was the greatest representation of Power of all. And, in fact, now *"All Power is given unto Him"* (Mat. 28:18).

The phrase, *"According to the Spirit of Holiness,"* presents another Name for the Holy Spirit, Who, in fact, superintended the entirety of the Ministry of Christ (Lk. 4:18-19), and raised Him from the dead (Rom. 8:11).

As well, this *"Power"* operated *"According to the Spirit of Holiness,"* in contrast with *"According to the flesh."*

Some have claimed that the *"Spirit of Holiness"* referred to here, is not the Holy Spirit, but, rather, the Spirit of Christ. While Christ certainly did have a *"spirit,"* exactly as all other men, still, all the things He did were by and through the Power of the Holy Spirit (Lk. 4:18-19).

The phrase, *"By the Resurrection from the dead,"* in essence means, that the Jews crucified Jesus because He claimed to be the Son of God. God Resurrected Him because He *was* the Son of God. The Resurrection manifested and demonstrated what He was, and wrought a real transformation in His Mode of Being, namely, a Glorified State. In effect, the Resurrection only declared Him to be what He truly was (Wuest).

Concerning His Resurrection *"From the dead,"* the Greek Text does not have *"ek nekron"* as it generally does, which means *"out from among the dead,"* but only *"nekron,"* which means *"of the dead."* Consequently, the phrase refers to the Resurrection of all the dead in other places in the New Testament, and *here*, to their Resurrection as included and involved in the Resurrection of our Lord (Vincent). It is Christ's Resurrection which demonstrates His Deity after assuming humanity, but His Resurrection viewed together with the Resurrection of all the Righteous, the Resurrection of the latter being made possible by the former (Wuest).

In other words, Jesus was not only raised from the dead in order to ratify what was done at Calvary, but, as well, to ensure the coming Resurrection of all the Sainted Dead, of which He was the *"Firstfruits"* (I Cor. 15:20, 23).

(5) "BY WHOM WE HAVE RECEIVED GRACE AND APOSTLESHIP, FOR OBEDIENCE TO THE FAITH AMONG ALL NATIONS, FOR HIS NAME:"

NOTES

The phrase, *"By Whom we have received Grace and Apostleship,"* presents Paul speaking here solely of himself; however, the same principle would apply to all who are called by God.

"Grace" was the Apostle Paul's great theme and his, so to say, trademark (II Thess. 3:17-18).

The idea is, that this *"Apostleship"* did not come about through any good works on his part, or any merit whatsoever, but solely and completely by the *"Grace of God."*

Actually, this is the basis on which God gives all things to all men. In its most simplistic form, grace means *"unmerited favor."* In other words, man is not worthy of these great Gifts of God and, in fact, cannot do anything within himself that will make him worthy. Consequently, the only thing that is required to receive from God what man must have, which is Righteousness, or anything for that matter, is simple Faith in Who Christ is and What Christ has done for sinners at Calvary and the Resurrection (Eph. 2:8-9).

The phrase, *"For obedience to the Faith among all Nations, for His Name,"* proclaims the principle of Faith as opposed to works.

Trying to earn something from the Lord on the principle of works, constitutes disobedience, simply because such cannot be done. Man simply has no works that God will accept, at least in this vein.

Having *"Faith"* in what Christ did at Calvary and the Resurrection, constitutes obedience, and pleases God (Heb. 11:6).

As well, this principle of Salvation by Faith is the same *"Among all Nations,"* and one might quickly add, *"Among all races."* There is One Salvation for all, whether Jew or Gentile. All of this is *"For His Name,"* simply because it is Jesus, Who is the Saviour, Who has made all of this possible.

(6) "AMONG WHOM ARE YE ALSO THE CALLED OF JESUS CHRIST:"

Paul now places these Romans and all other Believers as well, as *"Also the Called,"* even as He was Called. However, that does not mean that the Calling of these Romans, as well as all other Believers, was identical to that of Paul. And yet, there is a little bit of every Calling in all Callings. The reason should be obvious!

First of all, all are Called by the same One, the Lord Jesus Christ. Also, even though Callings differ, all are of God and, therefore, of necessity, tend toward the carrying out of the Plan of God.

To say such in a little different way, as Paul was called to take the Gospel to the Gentiles, every Believer was to do the same in whatever way the Lord made such possible; however, few, if any, would have the same responsibility as Paul regarding this task. All that is truly of God must flow in the same general direction, and will do so if the Holy Spirit has His Way.

There is no such thing as one Calling of God opposing another Calling which is of the Lord. Such does not and, in fact, cannot exist. So, this means that those who fought or hindered Paul in the carrying out of this Calling, plus anyone else who is truly Called of God, are not doing the Work of God, but rather that of the Devil.

(7) "TO ALL THAT BE IN ROME, BELOVED OF GOD, CALLED TO BE SAINTS: GRACE TO YOU AND PEACE FROM GOD OUR FATHER, AND THE LORD JESUS CHRIST."

The phrase, *"To all that be in Rome,"* refers to the Church which was in Rome, and not the entirety of the population. The salutation refers as well to any and all Believers and for all time.

The phrase, *"Beloved of God,"* actually says in the Greek Text, *"God's loved-ones."* The word *"Love"* is *"Agape,"* and means *"The Love that was shown at Calvary."*

The phrase, *"Called to be Saints,"* presents the two words *"To be"* as improperly supplied by the translators. Consequently, the meaning can be changed somewhat to the future tense, when it is meant to be in the present tense. In other words, the idea as given here by the Holy Spirit, is not that Christians will finally work themselves into Sainthood, but that they are *"Saints"* the very moment they make Christ their Saviour.

In fact, a Saint is one who was once a sinner, but who in answer to his Faith in the Lord Jesus has been set apart by the Holy Spirit for God, set apart from sin to Holiness, from Satan to God, out of the dominion of the first Adam, into the dominion of

the Last Adam, to live a set-apart life of separation (Wuest).

The idea is that of separation *from* to separation *to*, from that which is unholy to that which is holy. Actually, the word *"Saint"* is God's designation of a Believer, and for every single Believer at that, and awarded them the very moment they accept Christ.

The world, and especially those in Western Countries, have been influenced by the Catholic Church respecting Sainthood. The Catholic Church has made up its own rules respecting this place and position, awarding it only to those who have died, and who fit their description. But of course, this is *"sainthood"* which God will not accept, because it is man-made sainthood and not that which is ordered by the Lord. In other words, it is sainthood by merit, which is opposed to everything the Gospel teaches.

God awards Sainthood instantly upon Conversion, and not on any merit whatsoever, but upon one's simple Faith in the Lord Jesus Christ. Consequently, the Righteousness afforded the Believer, and given instantly upon Faith, is the only Righteousness (freely imputed) which God will recognize, because it is that bought and paid for by the Shed Blood of the Lord Jesus Christ. As a result, He can legally declare the person a *"Saint."* The legal words for this are *"Sanctification and Justification."*

As the sinner cries to God for Salvation, which in itself is an act of Faith, the person is instantly Sanctified, which actually means *"made clean."* Justification immediately follows, in which the person is *"declared clean"* by God (I Cor. 6:11).

The phrase, *"Grace to you and Peace from God our Father, and the Lord Jesus Christ,"* tells us several things:

1. This statement by Paul implies the Deity of Christ no less than any dogmatic statement could do. It is impossible to associate with the Godhead, as Paul is doing here, one who is merely a human being, and not God. So, the Son is God, even as the Father is God!

2. Grace is spoken of strongly here, because these Romans and, in fact, all sinners, were Saved by the Grace of God. Meaning that no one has earned this great Salvation,

but upon Faith it is freely given to any sinner.

As well, as one continues to look to Christ for all things, more and more Grace is supplied which, in effect, translates into more and more power (II Cor. 12:9).

Conversely, when the Believer begins to look to himself instead of Christ, Grace is withdrawn, which means that Power is also withdrawn, and the Believer is now about to fall into sin, no matter how hard he fights against that monster. Grace and, therefore, Power continue, only so long as the Believer continues to look to Christ.

3. Peace with God is instantly given and continues, as long as the Believer continues to trust Christ for all things. The moment the Believer begins to trust in his own works, thereby looking to his own merit, at that moment Grace and Power are not only withdrawn, but *"Peace"* as well! Then the Believer enters into a troubled state, which tells us, that our Peace with God is anchored totally in Jesus, and our Faith in Him.

4. As well, the *"Grace"* and *"Peace"* mentioned here, proceed from both the Father and the Son. They can be obtained no other way.

As well, it is not possible to have the *"Peace"* of God, without first partaking of the *"Grace of God."* They go hand in hand, but *"Peace"* is always predicated on *"Grace,"* which is always predicated on *"Faith."*

5. The appellative or title *"Lord Jesus Christ"* is the Resurrection Name of Jesus. He is Lord, i.e., *"God,"* Jesus, i.e., *"Saviour,"* Christ, i.e., *"Messiah."*

(8) "FIRST, I THANK MY GOD THROUGH JESUS CHRIST FOR YOU ALL, THAT YOUR FAITH IS SPOKEN OF THROUGHOUT THE WHOLE WORLD."

The phrase, *"First, I thank my God through Jesus Christ for you all,"* proclaims the Apostle, as was his custom, beginning with a compliment, and an expression of thankfulness for the good he knew to be in his readers. Consequently, this proclaims to them that his intentions are good and honorable, which will hopefully, predispose them more favorably toward that which the Holy Spirit wants him to say.

He begins this salutation by using the word *"First,"* but which is not followed by second

NOTES

or third, etc. He is meaning by the use of the word *"First,"* that the most important thing to God is those who have made Christ their Saviour. As it is most important to the Lord, as well, it should be the most important thing to us also.

The phrase, *"That your Faith is spoken of throughout the whole world,"* speaks of the Roman Empire. Paul is using a part for the whole, actually a euphuism, which in this case means the Church throughout the Roman Empire. In fact, the far greater majority of the people in this Empire had no knowledge whatsoever of the Faith possessed by the Believers in Rome.

However, the Holy Spirit has Paul to use this term for the simple reason, I believe, that as far as God is concerned, His Church, and wherever it truly is, is the *"Whole world."* In other words, God noticed and acted toward the might and power of the Roman Empire, only as it impacted the True Church. To be frank, it has not changed presently:

That which interests the world is of little interest or consequence with God, His concern resting mostly in how situations in the world affect His Body, i.e., Church. In fact, that has always been His interest, and His interest Alone!

It is interesting that their *"Faith"* is the Crown Jewel of their Walk with God.

Why?

1. Faith is the Foundation on which all stands. Whatever its position, whether weak or strong, so is everything else respecting the Believer.

Simple Faith in God means to trust Him and to have reliance on Him. That comes in three directions: A. We trust Him for Salvation; B. We trust Him for Leading and Guidance by the Holy Spirit in all we do; and, C. We trust Him to meet our needs and to protect us.

2. Rome was where persecution would break out at the beginning against Christians by demon-possessed Nero.

Some years before, the Roman Senate had voted that *"Caesar"* be invested as well with Deity, in other words, looked at as *"God."* Thankfully, most Roman Caesars ignored this, all too well recognizing their human frailties. However, when Nero came to power, almost immediately he began demanding that the appellative *"Lord"* or *"Augustus"* (which meant *"Lord"*) be applied to him.

Later on, he began to enforce this Law, demanding he be referred to as *"Lord"* by all.

In fact, this was basically the criteria for execution regarding Christians in the Roman arenas, whether in Rome or elsewhere. Instead of proclaiming Jesus as *"Lord,"* the Believer would be ordered to proclaim that *"Caesar is Lord,"* and if not, they would die. Consequently, untold thousands went to their death in the Roman Arenas, torn to pieces by wild beasts, or burned to death at the stake, simply because they would not say *"Caesar is Lord."* As stated, Rome became the beginning and center of such persecution. Consequently, one's *"Faith"* now took on a brand-new meaning. In fact, extreme persecution always does two things:

1. It rids the land of false Prophets, as would be obvious. No one wants to claim something that might get them killed, when in reality they do not have that which they claim.

2. As well, extreme persecution always tests one's *"Faith"* whether it is real or imagined.

(9) "FOR GOD IS MY WITNESS, WHOM I SERVE WITH MY SPIRIT IN THE GOSPEL OF HIS SON, THAT WITHOUT CEASING I MAKE MENTION OF YOU ALWAYS IN MY PRAYERS;"

The phrase, *"For God is my witness,"* places Paul's claim at the very highest level. It means, *"One who avers or can aver what he himself has seen or heard or knows by the highest of means."* So, he is saying that the Lord Who hears him saying these words, knows it is true.

The word *"witness"* is *"martus"* in the Greek Text, and means, at least concerning the Lord, *"One who testifies to what he knows concerning the Lord Jesus, even though that Testimony may cost him his life."*

THE SPIRIT AND SOUL OF MAN

The phrase, *"Whom I serve with my spirit,"* refers to Paul's human spirit, that part of man which gives him God-consciousness and enables him, when regenerated, to worship and serve God.

What is meant here, is that Paul's service to the Lord is not mere ceremonial function, which characterizes most of the religious world and, in fact, is no service or worship at all, at least as far as God is concerned. Sadly, most people who engage in religious ceremony are not even Saved; therefore, it is not even possible for them to serve or worship God, for man can only serve and worship the Lord from a regenerated spirit, which comes about at Salvation, and is a Work of the Holy Spirit. Actually, it makes up the born-again experience.

The spirit of man is the intellect, will, mind, conscience, and other invisible faculties, whether born again or not, that makes him a free moral agent and a rational being. Both the soul and the spirit of man are immortal.

However, they are so closely related that it is hard to distinguish the finest details of difference between them, but there is a difference. This is clear from I Thessalonians 5:23; Hebrews 4:12.

In general we can say that the spirit of man is that which knows (I Cor. 2:11), and the soul is that which feels (Job 14:22). Both make the inner man, which leaves the body at death (James 2:26).

THAT WHICH IS SAVED

As well, there is no such thing as the spirit of man being Saved, with the soul and body not Saved, as some teach. Also, there is no such thing as the spirit and soul being Saved, without the body being Saved, as others teach. As well, there is no such thing as the body sinning and the soul and spirit not sinning, or the body and soul sinning and the spirit not sinning, as some teach also.

When a person comes to Christ, they are Saved; spirit, soul, and body. As well, when the Believer sins, every part of him sins; spirit, soul, and body (I Thess. 5:23).

While it is true that the spirit and soul leave the body at death, whether the person is Saved or not, that is done only because the body has not yet been Glorified, at least as far as the Believer is concerned. That will take place at the Resurrection of Life (I Thess. 4:16-17).

The phrase, *"In the Gospel of His Son,"*

proclaims his sphere of service. Paul labored diligently to proclaim the Gospel of Jesus Christ, which should be the labors of every Believer.

The phrase, *"That without ceasing I make mention of you always in my prayers,"* tells us much about Paul:

PRAYER

1. I think it is obvious that the man had a strong prayer life. In fact, it is impossible for anyone to be drawn close to the Lord, or to establish a relationship with Him, without a strong prayer life. Actually, Prayer and the Study of the Word of God are the two absolute requirements in this capacity. And yet, sadly and regrettably, most who call themselves Christians hardly pray at all, and then only in the case of emergencies, etc.

Due to this neglect, if one was able to materially see the spirit of most Christians, they would see a weak, thin, emaciated spirit, with hardly the strength to walk, if even that.

2. Paul knew that God answered prayer, or he would not have wasted his time otherwise. To be frank, the very reason most Christians do not pray, I suspect, is because they really do not believe that God hears and answers prayer. If they did, they would seek His Face far more often.

3. As well, Paul was close enough to the Lord, that he knew the Mind of God; therefore, he did not make foolish requests of the Lord, in other words, using God's Word against God. This simply means that God will not allow His Word, and irrespective of the content of the Promises (Mk. 11:24), to be used against Him, thereby bringing things to pass which are not His Will. The great Promises of God are always predicated on His Will, and not our wills.

4. Paul had enough burden for souls, that he sought the Face of the Lord earnestly for the Romans, even though he had never seen them. For the most part, and maybe altogether, none of these people were his converts. But yet, they were a part of the Body of Christ and, as such, he sought the Lord earnestly for them. What a lesson for us!

5. Also, he sought the Lord for these people *"Without ceasing,"* meaning that he had not prayed for them sometime in the past, but that they were always included in his supplication before the Lord.

What an honor to have been mentioned to the Lord by Paul the Apostle!

(10) "MAKING REQUEST, IF BY ANY MEANS NOW AT LENGTH I MIGHT HAVE A PROSPEROUS JOURNEY BY THE WILL OF GOD TO COME UNTO YOU."

A HOLY DESIRE

The phrase, *"Making request,"* has to do with seeking the Lord about a certain thing, in this case, the privilege of ministering to the Church at Rome.

Why was Paul so desirous of this, especially considering that he had not planted this particular Church?

First of all I think the Holy Spirit placed this desire in his heart, which occasioned this constant petition. In the Lord's dealings with His Children, I personally think that most of the time He places a desire in one's heart for certain things, even long before one has ascertained its total direction or exactly what the Lord wants. This desire, as with Paul, is meant to generate prayer, which then occasions things being set in motion.

Everything the Believer does, at least for God, is first begun in the spirit world. In other words, it begins with God and not man. Any plans berthed by man, and no matter how Godly the man may be, and no matter how well motivated, can never come out to a victorious, helpful conclusion. All such efforts are doomed to failure even before they begin. Everything, and I mean everything, must begin with God.

The Lord has given Believers the privilege of helping Him carry out His vast Plan respecting all of humanity and for all time. It is not that He needs man, for He does not, in that He is Self-sufficient in all things. He does such simply for our benefit and welfare, and not for His.

RESPONSIBILITY OF BELIEVERS

And yet, He has given His Body (the Church) such a vast part in this great Work, that the Work simply will not be done, if Believers fall down in this task. In other words, if David does not obey the Lord, earnestly seeking His Face, the giant will not be killed, and

NOTES

Israel will suffer a devastating defeat. If Joshua does not obey God respecting everything He was told to do regarding the crossing of the Jordan and the taking of Jericho, the City will not be taken, and Israel would have spent more time in the wilderness.

It is the same presently with modern Believers. God calls men and women to do certain things, and if they fall down in this effort, and irrespective of the reason, whatever they are delegated to do by the Holy Spirit, and irrespective of its effect on the world, it simply will not be done, with great loss being the result.

The idea, that if a Believer who is truly called of God to do a certain thing, in fact fails in its doing, that God will easily pick up someone else to carry out the task, is simply untrue. The Bible is replete with such examples.

For instance, those in Israel who were assigned special tasks by the Lord, but failed in that task, caused Israel to be destroyed by the Babylonian Monarch, despite the prophesying of Jeremiah. The terrible destruction of Jerusalem and the Temple, with Judah going into captivity, was not the Plan of God. It came about because of the failure of certain individuals to carry out what the Lord had called them to do, whatever that was, and despite the fact that these were God's Chosen People, the end result was destruction.

THE CALLING

It is the same in the modern Church! I am positive that the Reader knows and understands that God is constantly delegating certain things to be done by certain people in the Church, even on a worldwide basis. Whoever fails in their assigned task, simply means that which God planned, at least with that person, will not get done. And if enough fail, the Church and the world suffer very serious consequences.

So, when the Lord appoints someone a certain task, first, He *never* lifts that Call (Rom. 11:29), and, second, that particular Calling, failed or not, is never given to another. That is the reason, as should be obvious, that the Call of God on a person's life, and irrespective as to what it is, must never be taken lightly and, as well, must never be

NOTES

given over to other men or women for guidance and direction, but rather the Called one always looking to the Lord.

As I think should be obvious to all, as the carrying out of such a task is so very, very important, likewise, the response of other Believers toward that which God has delegated one to do, is extremely important as well! The sad fact is, the Church oftentimes seeks to hinder that which God has called someone to do, which is a travesty of travesties. Again, another example is Paul.

While there were some few in the Early Church who sought to help Paul anyway they could, respecting the great Call of God upon his life concerning World Evangelism, still, there were many others in the Church of that day, who did the very opposite, attempting to hinder him greatly (II Cor. 2:12-13, 17; 7:5; 11:12-15; Gal. 1:7; 2:12-14).

I think we should consider carefully how it must anger the Lord, for those who claim His Name, to purposely oppose that which He is doing. Not long after Paul, this problem of men in the Church opposing that which is the Plan of God became more and more acute, until the world ultimately was ushered into the Dark Ages. During this approximate one thousand years, the Work of God suffered greatly, with precious few people during that time being Saved, at least regarding the overall population, and all because of men who were supposed to be following the Lord, thereby doing what He desired, but instead greatly opposing that which God was doing, which destroyed the Church.

So that of which we speak, the Call of God and the carrying out of that Call, is the single most important thing on the face of the earth.

The phrase, *"If by any means now at length I might have a prosperous journey,"* proclaims this prayer being answered greatly in the spiritual sense regarding Paul's trip to Rome, but not so much in the physical and material sense. We are given a description of that journey in Acts Chapters 20-28. As well, this gives us further insight into that done by the Lord.

All things carried out victoriously in the spiritual sense, will always be contested greatly by Satan, using any and every means at his disposal. Consequently, there may be hardships, difficulties, and persecutions, which can take their toll physically and financially, as well as other ways. So, the situation is not to be judged in the natural, but in the spiritual! Paul's trip was very prosperous spiritually speaking, but not so otherwise.

The phrase, *"By the Will of God to come unto you,"* proclaims that Paul was ever seeking the Leading and Direction of the Holy Spirit, and would settle for nothing else.

Everything that comes into the heart of a Believer is not necessarily of God. Sometimes it may look like the Lord, sound like the Lord, and give every appearance of being of the Lord, but in reality be something else altogether. The Believer is to *"Try the spirits whether they are of God: because many false Prophets are gone out into the world"* (I Jn. 4:1).

As well, everything, and I mean everything, must come under the searching light of the Word of God, which the Holy Spirit always does. If it does not match up with the Scriptures, it must be abandoned out of hand and construed as not the Will of God.

At this stage in Paul's life, even though the desire to go to Rome was in his heart, he was not exactly certain if it was the Will of God or not. Consequently, he would continue seeking the Lord about this matter, and shortly as we know, the Lord's Will would be made known and graphically so (Acts 23:11).

(11) "FOR I LONG TO SEE YOU, THAT I MAY IMPART UNTO YOU SOME SPIRITUAL GIFT, TO THE END YE MAY BE ESTABLISHED;"

The phrase, *"For I long to see you, that I may impart unto you some Spiritual Gift,"* does not mean as some think, that Paul could impart one or more of the nine Gifts of the Spirit to Believers (I Cor. 12:8-10). Concerning that, Paul himself wrote, *"But all these worketh that one and the selfsame Spirit* (the Holy Spirit), *dividing to every man* (every Believer) *severally as He* (the Holy Spirit) *will"* (I Cor. 12:11). So, the impartation of these Gifts are according to the Will of God and not man.

However, at the same time Believers are told to *"Covet earnestly the best Gifts"* (I Cor. 12:31). As well, we are told to *"Desire*

Spiritual Gifts" (I Cor. 14:1).

Consequently, it is perfectly proper for Believers to seek the Lord for Gifts of the Spirit and, as well, to ask the Lord for the *"Best Gifts,"* i.e., the Gift or Gifts which the Holy Spirit wants us to have. As well, it is perfectly proper to ask a Minister to lay hands on us in order that this prayer may be answered.

So, under this context Paul was speaking of imparting unto these Romans *"Some Spiritual Gift."*

Also, the *"Spiritual Gift"* which Paul speaks here of, concerns the teaching of the Word of God regarding any of its great Subjects. As Paul would open up the Word to these Romans, as he constantly did to all others who were privileged to sit under his Ministry, great Truths would be given to them, which were *"Spiritual Gifts,"* but yet, having little to do with the nine Gifts of the Spirit per se. Actually, this impartation of various Truths is probably what he had in mind, even though the other was definitely a focus as well.

The phrase, *"To the end ye may be established,"* lends credence to the statement we have just made regarding Paul opening up the Truths of the Word of God to these people, rather than one or more of the nine Gifts of the Spirit, even though these may have been included as stated.

The word *"established"* in the Greek Text, is *"steridzo,"* and means *"to strengthen or to fix."*

One must understand that Believers in those days had two major problems that most Believers presently do not have, which of course were a hindrance:

1. Bibles, which then consisted of the Old Testament, were not easy to come by. The various Books had to be laboriously copied by hand, and, consequently, were expensive.

2. As well, the Lord was only then giving the New Covenant to Paul, with only some of his Epistles now written. Copies of these, although easier to obtain, still, were not as easy as presently purchasing a New Testament or an entire Bible for that matter.

Even though a visit from any of the Apostles would have been greatly beneficial, still, a visit from Paul would have been the greatest of all I think, especially considering that he was the one to whom the New Covenant was given, consequently, understanding it better than anyone else.

(12) "THAT IS, THAT I MAY BE COMFORTED TOGETHER WITH YOU BY THE MUTUAL FAITH BOTH OF YOU AND ME."

The phrase, *"That is, that I may be comforted together with you,"* carries the idea that Paul, by the previous statement, was not talking down to these people. In other words, he did not want them to think by his statement, that he was implying spiritual weakness or instability on their part. That was not the idea at all. What a beautiful lesson for all of us to learn.

This is but another sign of the humility of this Apostle. Paul, in effect, was the Moses of the New Testament. As Moses had been given the Old Covenant (Genesis through Deuteronomy), Paul had been given the New Covenant (Romans through Hebrews). But yet, he considers the feelings of these people, and above even that, does not even remotely consider himself to be anything great at all, irrespective of the great Revelations given unto him by the Lord (II Cor. 12:1-12).

The phrase, *"By the mutual Faith both of you and me,"* carries the idea of a mutual strengthening, brought about by his Ministry among them, and their Love shown to him.

The word *"comforted"* in the previous phrase generally carries with it the idea of consolation, but is not used by Paul in that sense here. The Greek word he actually used was *"sumparakaleo,"* and means *"to strengthen with others."* As stated, it was a mutual strengthening.

While his *"Faith"* was stronger than theirs as would be obvious, still, the *"Faith"* which they possessed, was from God and His Word, exactly as that of Paul. Consequently, this *"Mutual Faith"* as contained by both, would be a blessing to each other.

As he strengthened them from the Word of God, their Faith would strengthen him in the sense that he knew they had been pulled out of the quagmire of sin which characterized Rome, one of the most licentious cities in the world. These Miracles of Grace, for that is what they were, carried a special Blessing, especially to someone such as Paul.

(13) "NOW I WOULD NOT HAVE YOU IGNORANT, BRETHREN, THAT OFTENTIMES I PURPOSED TO COME UNTO YOU, (BUT WAS LET HITHERTO,) THAT I MIGHT HAVE SOME FRUIT AMONG YOU ALSO, EVEN AS AMONG OTHER GENTILES."

The phrase, *"Now I would not have you ignorant, Brethren,"* is not at all meant to talk down to these people, for this seems to be somewhat of a cliche used by Paul quite often, actually some six times in his writings (Rom. 1:13; 11:25; I Cor. 10:1; 12:1; II Cor. 1:8; I Thess. 4:13).

The phrase, *"That oftentimes I purposed to come unto you, (but was let hitherto,)"* simply means that several times Paul thought he would be able to go to Rome, but something always hindered him and, in this case, it would have meant that he was busy with the Work of God in other places. The word *"let"* as it is here used, means *"hindered."*

The phrase, *"That I might have some fruit among you also, even as among other Gentiles,"* tells us that this Church was predominantly Gentile, as should be obvious.

The *"fruit"* spoken of here, refers to the Salvation of souls and, as well, the spiritual growth of those in the Church in Rome, who of course, were already Saved.

Considering that Paul was the Apostle to the Gentiles, and especially called for this purpose, and having already been the first agent in carrying the Gospel into Europe (Acts 16:9-10), and having established it there in important centers of population, he ever kept in view an eventual visit to the Imperial City itself, in the hope, no doubt, of its thence permeating the whole Western World.

If one follows the Missionary Journeys of Paul as they are outlined in the Book of Acts, one will find that as he was zealous for every single soul, be they rich or poor, likewise, he attempted to build Churches in some of the great cities of the Empire, such as Ephesus, Corinth, Thessalonica, etc. Of course, he was sent by the Lord to these places, the plan being that a great central Church would be built in a great metropolitan area, with it then evangelizing everything within a particular radius.

(14) "I AM DEBTOR BOTH TO THE

GREEKS, AND TO THE BARBARIANS; BOTH TO THE WISE, AND TO THE UN- WISE."

The phrase, *"I am debtor,"* refers to that which is actually incumbent upon every single Believer. The Lord in His Mercy and Grace had brought the Gospel to Paul, and due to that act of Mercy, Paul felt, and rightly so, that the only way he could properly show his gratitude to the Lord for this great kind- ness shown to him, was to take the Message, at least as far as was possible, to every person in the world. Any Believer who does not feel the same way, and act accordingly, I would have to surmise that they little know or un- derstand this great Salvation afforded them, or else they are not really Saved at all!

In this Passage, the Holy Spirit plainly tells us that this must be the feeling of all Believers. Inasmuch as someone brought us the Gospel, we in turn, now that we know Christ as our own Personal Saviour, must try to take this Message to all others also.

WORLD EVANGELISM

At this particular time it is possible by Television to reach unheard of numbers of people with the Gospel, which was not pos- sible even a few decades ago. Especially con- sidering that God has called me for this particular task, even as He called Paul for his Ministry and scores of others, this is some- thing I see before my eyes day and night. I see the lost and hear their cries. I sense their bondage, even as they are unable to extricate themselves from their dilemma, at least by their own power and strength. The sadness is, no other human being can effect their release as well.

At the same time, I know that Jesus Christ is the Answer to every single problem, every single bondage, every single sin. And I might quickly add, that He is not just one answer, but in fact, the only Answer. In other words, I am not on Television because I have seen a need and have responded to that need; rather, I am especially called of God for this very purpose. That is the reason we see so many people brought to Christ. I am called for this task.

At the same time, this is the reason the Evil One fights with such a tenacity to try to

stop this Message which the Lord has given unto me. However, irrespective of the oppo- sition and even persecution, I must continue on to do the very best I can, to take this Gospel to the world. I have no choice, nei- ther do I seek or desire a choice. As Paul said, *"I am debtor . . . ."*

The phrase, *"Both to the Greeks, and to the Barbarians; both to the wise, and to the unwise,"* presents, as is obvious, all people, irrespective as to their nationality or social standing.

Paul was not being rude when he used the word *"Barbarians,"* for that was the com- mon usage referring to those who did not speak the Greek language.

FOR ALL!

Paul is stating in this Passage, that the Gospel of Jesus Christ is for everyone on the face of the Earth, and that means everyone. Consequently, there is no such thing as a West- ern Gospel, etc. As well, there is no such thing as Christianity being the *"white man's religion,"* etc. All of that are lies of Satan!

When the Lord sent His Son down to this world, He sent Him to the entirety of the world. Actually, John 3:16 says, *"For God so loved the world . . . ."*

Also, the idea that Christianity is for the whites and Islam is for the blacks, is again, a total fabrication.

When Jesus died on Calvary, He died for all of humanity, irrespective of race, color, nationality, social standing, or the lack thereof. The Barbarian is just as important as the Greek and the unwise as the wise.

In this statement, and the inclusion of all, Paul does not neglect the poor and un- learned, and neither does he neglect the civi- lized and cultivated community. Speaking of going to Rome, he seems to have before him the prospect of his address reaching the educated and intelligent classes of society in the Imperial City.

And the Epistle, as it goes on, is in accor- dance with such an aim. For its arguments are addressed, not merely to Believers in the Old Testament, but also generally to philo- sophical thinkers.

The state of the world is reviewed, human consciousness is analyzed, deep problems which had long exercised the minds of Philosophers are touched on, and the Gospel is, in fact, commended to the world as God's Answer to man's needs (Barmby).

While the Gospel is the only Hope for the poor and the downtrodden, and simply because the Lord is the only One Who truly cares for them; however, one is to never think that the Gospel is only for the poor and uneducated, because nothing could be further from the Truth. Actually, the Gospel of Jesus Christ stimulates the intellectual prowess of man as nothing else. It alone addresses the great questions of life, and it alone holds the answers. As someone has truly said, irrespective of the education that one may have, no man can truly call himself educated, unless he has a working knowledge of the Bible. The sadness is, it is really not possible for one to have such knowledge, unless one knows the Author of the Book. No matter how hard he tries, *"the natural man,"* irrespective of his education, *"Receiveth not the things of the Spirit of God: for they are foolishness unto him: neither can he know them, because they are spiritually discerned"* (I Cor. 2:14).

(15) "SO, AS MUCH AS IN ME IS, I AM READY TO PREACH THE GOSPEL TO YOU THAT ARE AT ROME ALSO."

"So, as much as in me is," speaks of the Glory of God in his soul, and, as well, the burden for a lost world. It was something which consumed him day and night and which constituted his very being, whether the intellect or his passions, and above all, his spirit. In other words, that was all that was within him and ever how much it was, there was room for nothing else.

Paul's desire to Preach the Gospel, to win the lost, to tell others about Jesus, was literally his world. His time was not divided between Christ and golf courses, hobbies, or other pursuits.

Burnout does not spring from a lack of leisure time, or a burden too heavy to bear, as some claim, but rather from a lack of relationship with Christ. A proper Prayer Life, along with the Word, will ensure a proper Relationship with the Lord, which handles these problems readily.

The phrase, *"I am ready to preach the*

Gospel to you that are at Rome also," refers to several things:

1. Rome, as the center of the world at that time, was very significant concerning the Kingdom of God. The Church there would have great influence not only on the City itself, but as well, over the entirety of the Roman Empire. Actually, even though it took several centuries, the far superior morality of Christianity ultimately won out over the political and military power of Rome. Unfortunately by this time, the Church was well into apostasy; consequently, it could take little advantage of the tremendous price paid in the past to bring this opportunity about.

2. When Paul spoke of Preaching the Gospel, he was primarily speaking of preaching the *"Cross of Jesus Christ."* He said, *"For Christ sent me not to Baptize, but to Preach the Gospel: not with wisdom of words, lest the Cross of Christ should be made of none effect"* (I Cor. 1:17).

He knew the reaction of the Intelligentsia in Rome, as well as elsewhere, would be a smirk at such a Message, if they would bother to even give it that much attention; however, he also knew that some would accept Christ, as some always did. In Truth, this is the great danger for the Church and, in fact, has always been.

Men do not enjoy being ridiculed, and the preaching of the Cross brings ridicule. Most Preachers do not preach the Cross. Consequently, and irrespective of the depth, thrust, wisdom, knowledge, or power of their Message otherwise, nothing, and I mean nothing, without the preaching of the Cross, will be done for the Lord Jesus Christ. In other words, no souls will be Saved, no lives miraculously changed, no bondages broken, no sick bodies healed, no Believers will be Baptized with the Holy Spirit.

Even though there are peripheral Doctrines of great significance, as should be obvious; however, everything must point toward the Central Core of the Cross, with every spoke leading to that hub.

(16) "FOR I AM NOT ASHAMED OF THE GOSPEL OF CHRIST: FOR IT IS THE POWER OF GOD UNTO SALVATION TO EVERY ONE THAT BELIEVETH; TO THE JEW FIRST, AND ALSO TO THE GREEK."

The phrase, *"For I am not ashamed of the Gospel of Christ,"* is said in reference to the Cross.

Of all people, Paul was fully aware that the pride of Greek Philosophy would despise the Message of the Cross, referring to it as *"foolishness"* (I Cor. 1:18).

In fact, such a Message would be totally strange to them and out of accord with their intellectual speculations, even as it continues to be presently. But Paul also knew that in the Message of the Cross was the one view that could meet human needs and, as such, would commend itself to some hungry hearts and thirsty souls, even some of those who called themselves *"thinkers."* The Reader needs to understand exactly what the Cross meant in that day. Even though the reproach of this Message still hangs heavy at the present hour, still, nearly 2,000 years of its Miracles of Redemption have softened the blow somewhat.

Crucifixion was the most used form of execution in the Roman world of Paul's day. However, it was reserved only for those who were not Roman citizens. Its form of death was so ignominious and terrible, that no Roman citizen was ever subjected to its torture and humiliation, with some few exceptions. If execution were demanded in their case, they were quickly dispatched with the sword. Thus, tradition, which says that Peter, like Jesus, was crucified, but Paul was beheaded because he was a Roman citizen, is in line with ancient practice.

In fact, it was a common thing on the outskirts of any Town or City of any size in the Roman Empire to see the horror of crucifixions in process. These horrifying scenes were always enacted by the side of a major road or thoroughfare in order that all could observe the might of Roman power and, consequently, be fearful of offending that power. Contemporary writers describe it as a most painful form of death.

WHY DID JESUS HAVE TO DIE ON A CROSS?

In fact, had Jesus died any other way, by stoning, the thrusting through with a spear, etc., it would not have sufficed for that which God intended. The Cross, as ugly

and humiliating as it was, was an absolute necessity, that is, if Jesus was to serve as the appropriate Sin-Offering and, thereby, Redeem humanity.

In the Mosaic Law, those who committed the most heinous crimes, at times, were crucified (Deut. 21:22-23). The word *"Tree"* as it is used in this Passage, symbolizes the Cross, because all crosses were made of wood.

Even though Jesus committed no crimes nor sin of any nature, the entirety of the human family was guilty of such horrid malefaction. I speak of original sin that came into the human family with the Fall in the Garden of Eden. Romans Chapter 3 describes the results of that Fall, at least as it affects man. Respecting that, God had decreed, and of necessity, that *"The wages of sin is death"* (Rom. 6:23). So the sentence was passed upon the entirety of the human family.

Due to man being dead to all spiritual things, at least in his unsaved state, he cannot know or understand how bad that sin really is. As stated at the beginning of this Chapter, it is the destruction of everything that is good. In fact, it is so powerful and so terrible, that even though God could speak Creation into existence (Gen. Chpt. 1), He could not speak Redemption into existence. That Great Work could only be brought about with God taking upon Himself human flesh, and then serving as a Sin-Offering at Calvary, thereby paying the terrible sin debt.

THE CURSE OF THE LAW

The Law of Moses gave man a pattern for living, telling him what was right and what was wrong. It dealt with man's responsibility toward God and his responsibility toward his fellowman. In fact, it was the only Law of God in the world at that time, therefore, the only fair and just law.

While the Law of Moses did carry Blessing (Obedience) with it (Deut. 28:1-14), it did not have any Salvation and as far as the spiritual was concerned, it only carried a Curse (Deut. 28:15-68).

The Curse of the Law was death, but in effect, spiritual death, which meant separation from God, and if continued, an eternal separation from God.

At Calvary Jesus did for man what man

could not do for himself. If man had died on the Cross, it would have served no purpose, because it would have been a Sacrifice which God could not accept, because it was polluted with original sin. Therefore, One had to die Who had no sin, which Sacrifice Alone God would accept. Jesus Christ was that Man, in effect, God manifest in the flesh (Isa. 7:14).

When Jesus died on Calvary, He *"Redeemed us from the Curse of the Law, being made a Curse for us"* (Gal. 3:13-14). So, it was imperative that Jesus die on a Cross, which He did, thereby suffering the penalty in our place. As should be obvious, He did none of this for Himself, but all for man, and unredeemed man at that! Consequently, for anyone to be Saved, all they have to do is believe in what He did on the Cross, and at that moment, the Lord removes the Curse of sin from the sinner, simply because Jesus took that Curse upon Himself, and then imparts to the sinner Eternal Life. That is the reason the Cross is so important (Jn. 3:16; Rom. 10:9-10, 13; Rev. 22:17).

THE NEW TESTAMENT WRITERS

The interest of Paul and the other Apostles respecting the Epistles of the New Testament which they wrote, was neither archaeological nor historical, but rather Christological. In other words, they were concerned with the Eternal and Spiritual significance of what happened once for all in the Death of Jesus Christ, the Son of God, on the Cross. Consequently, the word *"Cross"* was used as a summary description of the Gospel of Salvation, that Jesus Christ *"Died for our sins,"* so the *"Preaching of the Gospel"* is *"The Word of the Cross," "The Preaching of Christ Crucified"* (I Cor. 1:17).

Therefore, the Apostle glories *"In the Cross of our Lord Jesus Christ,"* and speaks of suffering persecution *"For the Cross of Christ."* Clearly the word *"Cross"* stands here for the whole glad announcement of our Redemption through the Atoning Death of Jesus Christ.

THE WORD OF RECONCILIATION

"The Word of the Cross" is also *"The Word of Reconciliation"* (II Cor. 5:19). This theme

NOTES

emerges clearly in the Epistles, especially in Ephesians and Colossians. It is *"Through the Cross"* that God has reconciled Jews and Gentiles, abolishing the middle wall of partition, the Law of Commandments (Eph. 2:14-16).

It is *"By the Blood of His Cross"* that God has made Peace in reconciling *"All things to Himself"* (Col. 1:20).

This Reconciliation is at once personal and spiritual. It comes because Christ has set aside the bond which stood against us with its legal demands, *"Nailing it to the Cross"* (Col. 2:14).

A SYMBOL OF SHAME AND HUMILIATION

The Cross, in the New Testament, is a symbol of shame and humiliation, as well as of God's Wisdom and Glory revealed through it. Rome used it not only as an instrument of torture and execution, but also as a shameful pillory reserved for the worst and lowest. To the Jews, as stated, it was a sign of being accursed (Deut. 21:23; Gal. 3:13).

This was the Death Jesus died, and for which the Religious Leadership clamored. He *"Endured the Cross, despising the shame"* (Heb. 12:2). The lowest rung in the ladder of our Lord's humiliation is that He endured *"Even Death on a Cross"* (Phil. 2:8). For this reason it was a *"stumblingblock"* to the Jews (I Cor. 1:23; Gal. 5:11).

The shameful spectacle of a victim carrying a patibulum was so familiar to His hearers that Jesus three times spoke of the road of Discipleship as that of Cross-bearing (Mat. 10:38; Mk. 8:34; Lk. 14:27).

UNION WITH CHRIST

Further, the Cross is the symbol of our union with Christ, not simply in virtue of our following His Example, but in virtue of what He has done for us and in us.

In His Substitutionary Death for us on the Cross, we died *"In Him"* (II Cor. 5:14), and as well, *"Our old man* (the sinner) *is crucified with Him,"* that by His indwelling Spirit we might *"walk in newness of Life"* (Rom. 6:4; Gal. 2:20; 5:24; 6:14), abiding *"In Him."*

(Bibliography: M. Hengel, *"Crucifixion"*; J. H. Charlesworth, *"Exposition"*; W. Barclay,

"Crucified and Crowned.")

The phrase, *"For it is the Power of God unto Salvation,"* presents Paul choosing the Greek word *"dunamis* (power)," to describe the effectual working of the Good News of Salvation.

Dunamis is power, natural ability, inherent power residing in a thing by virtue of it nature, or, power which a person or thing exerts or puts forth. In other words, the Gospel is the inherent, Omnipotent Power of God operating in the Salvation of a lost soul that accepts it. It results in Salvation to the one who believes. *"The Gospel is the Power of God."*

Vincent says that the Gospel is *"Not merely a powerful means in God's Hands, but in itself a Divine Energy."* It is the Good News of Salvation energized by the Holy Spirit.

Our word *"dynamite"* is the transliteration of this Greek word, and very well describes it.

One Greek Scholar said that even though *"dynamite"* is the correct translation, still, it is not its true meaning. He went on to say that the Gospel does not refer to an explosive powder, as does dynamite, but rather a sweet and loving Message of Mercy and Grace which the Holy Spirit in Sovereign Grace makes operative in the heart of the sinner who comes to Christ.

While the latter is certainly correct, he is overlooking the fact that as it is definitely Mercy and Grace to the believing sinner, it is also an explosive powder or power to Satan and the world of spiritual darkness.

While the words *"dynamite of God"* would not be a correct description, even as our brother has stated, respecting the Grace of God, it definitely is an apt description concerning the world of darkness, which must be defeated and, in fact, was defeated on Calvary's Cross. In fact, Satan and all his minions were so defeated at Calvary, that they will never again know supremacy over the human family, at least those who will believe God, and ultimately will be banished forever. Only raw, naked, forceful, Omnipotent power could do such a thing!

The phrase, *"To every one that Believeth,"* proclaims the requirement on the sinner's part.

Believe what?

The sinner must believe the Truth.

The Truth is, the sinner is lost, unable to save himself. He must believe that. As well, he must believe that God loved this world enough to give His Only Begotten Son to pay the price for dying humanity.

He must also believe that Jesus did pay that price by His Death on Calvary's Cross. As well, the sinner must believe that Jesus rose from the dead on the third day, thereby victorious over sin and death. If he believes that, making Jesus' Work his own, he is instantly Saved (Jn. 3:16; Rom. 10:9-10, 13; Eph. 2:8-9).

This of which we have said is far more than mere mental affirmation. In fact, merely believing this as an historical fact, will effect Salvation for no one. The sinner must take it unto himself, thereby believing that all of this was done for him, which it was (I Tim. 1:15).

The phrase, *"To the Jew first, and also to the Greek,"* simply means that all are included, as the designation *"Greek"* stands for all Gentiles, irrespective of race, color or nationality.

However, having said that, the Gospel, in fact, was offered to the Jews first, even as it should have been. It was to the Jews to whom Jesus first came, and rightly so, even though His Coming in the aggregate, was for the entirety of the world.

Why the Jews first?

These ancient people were raised up by God from the loins of Abraham and the womb of Sarah. They were raised up by the Lord, sustained by the Lord, and for a special purpose. They were to serve as the womb of the Messiah, and to give the world the Word of God, which they did. In this context, and because it was right, they were offered the Kingdom first of all (Mat. 3:1-2; 4:17). The Plan of God was, that Israel would accept the Kingdom, for which they had actually been groomed, and then share it with the Gentile world. However, as a body politic or Nation, it was rejected. As a result, the few Jews who did accept it, then gave it to the Gentiles, even as Paul is now saying.

Nevertheless, even though Israel rejected their Messiah and the Kingdom, they will soon be restored and will then receive the Kingdom. This will take place at the Second

Coming (Zech. Chpts. 12-14; Rev. Chpt. 19).

Paul said concerning Israel, *"I say then, have they stumbled that they should fall* (remain fallen)*? God forbid: but rather through their fall* (temporary fall) *Salvation is come unto the Gentiles* (which the Jews would not have given otherwise), *for to provoke them to jealousy"* (Rom. 11:11).

He then said, *"That blindness in part has happened to Israel, until the fullness of the Gentiles be come in* (which this time will be finished at the Second Coming).

"And so all Israel (at that time) *shall be Saved"* (Rom. 11:25-26).

(17) "FOR THEREIN IS THE RIGHTEOUSNESS OF GOD REVEALED FROM FAITH TO FAITH: AS IT IS WRITTEN, THE JUST SHALL LIVE BY FAITH."

The phrase, *"For therein is the Righteousness of God revealed,"* has to do with the *"Gospel of Christ"* which is centered up in the Cross.

WHAT IS RIGHTEOUSNESS?

The word *"Righteousness"* is a key word in Romans, and demands a careful and detailed treatment.

In the Greek Text there is a single family of words which expresses the concept. *"Dikaiosyne"* means *"Righteousness," "Uprightness."*

"Dikaios" means *"Just," "Upright," "Righteous."*

The verb *"dikaioo"* means *"To pronounce or to treat a person as Righteous,"* or *"to acquit," "to vindicate."*

In the Judaism of Jesus' Day, Righteousness was viewed as behavioral conformity to written or oral Law. There was no stress on, and little awareness of, the relationship with God that generates the Righteousness that the Law reveals. No wonder Jesus called His listeners to a Righteousness that exceeds the righteousness of the Scribes and Pharisees of His Day (Mat. 5:20).

The Righteousness which God recognizes, or Righteousness in a Biblical sense, is not determined by man nor by any external consideration, but by God, and that by Divine Fiat. Actually, Righteousness as it is looked at and defined by the world, is the total opposite of the Righteousness defined by God.

Righteousness in the Biblical sense is a condition of rightness, the Standard of which is God, which is estimated according to the *Divine Standard*, which shows itself in behavior conformable to God, and has to do above all things with its relation to God, and with the walk before Him. It is, and it is called, a *"Righteousness of God"* (Rom. 3:21) — Righteousness as it belongs to God and is of value before Him, God-like Righteousness; with this Righteousness, thus defined, the Gospel comes into the world of nations, which had been wont to measure by a different standard.

(Righteousness in the profane mind is merely a social virtue, only with a certain religious background of some type.)

THE RIGHTEOUSNESS OF GOD

Righteousness, which is of God, and that alone which He recognizes, always understands that God is the Goal and Standard of Integrity, and not that devised by man. Actually, this is one of the great underlying thoughts of Scripture to which Paul proclaims in this and other instances, with peculiar acuteness and clearness, which distinguishes him in apprehending its clear meaning.

Vincent says, *"The Righteousness revealed in the Gospel is described as a Righteousness of God. However, this does not merely mean Righteousness as an Attribute of God, but Righteousness as bestowed on man by God."*

It is obvious that God is Righteous, and by contrast, that man is unrighteous and cannot change that fact within himself. Consequently, the only way man can be Righteous, is for God to *freely give* man His Righteousness, which He does upon man exhibiting Faith in Him. When this happens, the sinner immediately becomes Righteous and Justified, with his state due entirely to God.

The Righteousness which becomes his is that which God declares to be Righteousness and ascribes to him. Righteousness thus expresses the relation of being right into which God puts the man who believes.

RIGHTEOUSNESS MADE POSSIBLE BY JESUS CHRIST

The Righteousness which the Gospel offers the sinner is God's Own Righteousness, which in effect, is afforded by Jesus Christ, which will cause the Believer to stand in right relation to God forever.

The sinner's guilt is taken away, borne by another on the Cross, and a positive Righteousness, Jesus Christ, is given him in Grace. The Tabernacle of old is an excellent example.

The white linen curtains which surrounded the Tabernacle symbolized three things: A. The Righteousness which God is; B. The Righteousness He demands of any person who would be in right relation to Him; and, C. The Righteousness which He bestows in answer to Faith.

The linen curtains kept the sinner out of God's Presence, but the door or gate afforded entrance to the sinner to the Holy of Holies through the Blood Sacrifice.

The same linen curtains that originally kept the sinner out of God's Presence, now keep him in. The Righteousness of God that will damn a sinner for all eternity who rejects it, Saves and keeps Saved for all eternity, the sinner who accepts it.

For a long time, Martin Luther saw only the condemning Righteousness of God, and he hated it. But when he came to see that the Righteousness that condemns when rejected, also Saves when accepted, the Light of the Gospel broke into his darkened soul.

REVEALED RIGHTEOUSNESS

This is what Paul is talking about when he says that this *"Righteousness is revealed."* The word *"revealed"* in the Greek Text is *"apokalupto,"* and means *"to uncover what has been hidden."*

In fact, if the sinner sees God at all, it is in this Eternal Righteousness of God which smites all sin and sinners. Hence, they have little desire to have anything to do with Him. But when the Gospel is preached to them, if they exhibit any Faith whatsoever, they are instantly made to know as it is revealed to them, that this *"Righteousness"* which they have formerly detested, can now be given to them, and in fact will be given upon Faith (Wuest).

The Gospel reveals a Righteousness from God on the principle of Faith as opposed to merit, and this Righteousness is to be received by Faith.

The phrase, *"From Faith to Faith,"* has a double meaning:

"From Faith" represents Justification by Faith as opposed to works.

"To Faith" refers to Justification accepted by Faith.

So, *"From Faith"* relates to God as the Provider, and *"To Faith"* relates to man as the receiver. The one offers Life on the Faith Principle; the other accepts the Gift on the same Principle (Williams).

The phrase, *"As it is written, the Just shall live by Faith,"* proclaims Paul showing that Righteousness by Faith is no new idea, but found in the Prophets (Hab. 2:4).

The idea is, that all Faith is one. This means that Paul is not guilty of forcing the words given by Habakkuk into the present purpose.

The Greek Text actually says, *"Moreover the Just out of Faith* (by his Faith) *shall live."* That is, the Source of the sinner's new life in Christ Jesus is Faith, the appropriating medium by means of which he receives Righteousness and Life. Actually, this was the spark that lit the Reformation (Wuest).

(18) "FOR THE WRATH OF GOD IS REVEALED FROM HEAVEN AGAINST ALL UNGODLINESS AND UNRIGHTEOUSNESS OF MEN, WHO HOLD THE TRUTH IN UNRIGHTEOUSNESS."

The phrase, *"For the Wrath of God is revealed from Heaven against all ungodliness and unrighteousness of men,"* tells us several things:

1. As the Righteousness of God is revealed to those who have Faith in Christ, likewise, *"The Wrath of God"* is revealed against those who reject that Righteousness.

2. The *"Wrath"* or anger of God is here revealed, along with the purpose of the Revelation.

It is absolutely imperative that God hate evil, because if He did not do so, He could not love good. If there is to be one (to love good) of necessity, there must be two (to also hate evil). In other words, God must do both or neither.

The Greek word for *"Wrath"* is *"Orge."* It is used of Jesus when, after healing the man with the withered hand, He observed the hardness of heart of the Pharisees, and looked upon them with anger (Mk. 3:5). *"Orge"* is an anger *"Which Righteous men not merely may, but as they are Righteous, must feel; nor can there be a surer and sadder token of an utterly prostrate moral condition than the not being able to be angry with sin — and sinners."*

Vincent describes *"Orge"* as God's personal emotion with regard to sin. It represents God's abhorrence and hatred of sin.

3. These Passages tell us that inasmuch as God has revealed His Righteousness from Heaven to sinful men, if that Light is rejected, as it mostly is, the Wrath of God automatically follows. In fact, Paul said, *"And the times of this ignorance* (the world before Jesus came) *God winked at; but now Commandeth all men every where to repent"* (Acts 17:30).

This tells us that the Judgment of God is even more severe now than it was in Old Testament times, which is the opposite of what most people believe. However, it should not be difficult to understand.

To where little Light of the Gospel was given, the Lord did not step in until there was absolutely no other choice. I speak of the flood, the destruction of Sodom and Gomorrah, the proposed extermination of certain Tribes, the threat and ultimate destruction of Nineveh, plus others. As should be obvious, there was some Light before Christ, but it was ensconced almost altogether in Israel, who at times hindered its illumination.

Since Jesus came and died on Calvary, thereby paying the sin debt, and rose from the dead, the Holy Spirit now has much more access to the world and to men in general, thereby, providing much greater opportunity for acceptance of the Lord. In other words, considering the proliferation of the Gospel, ignorance is no longer an excuse.

I think the record will show, that inclement weather, wars, famines, disease, and pestilence is the judgment of God against *"ungodliness and unrighteousness of men."*

A man asked me once if I believed that AIDS was a judgment from God?

My answer is an unequivocal *"Yes!"*

I realize that many would say, and rightly so, that all sickness and disease originate with Satan. However, even though that is correct, the Lord is still in control of everything.

In other words, Satan can only do what the Lord allows him to do (Job Chpt. 1). To not understand that, is to deny the Omnipotence, Omniscience, and Omnipresence of God!

The phrase, *"Who hold the Truth in unrighteousness,"* does not represent here the Gospel, but the fact of a Supreme Being with Divine Attributes to Whom worship and obedience are due.

This *"Truth"* being seen by all men through their observation of the created Universe, thus demands a Creator to answer for its existence.

The human race, possessing this Truth which is overly obvious, yet holds it down in the sense of refusing to acknowledge its moral implications, continues on in its sin, despite the proliferation of *"Light."*

The primary thrust of this particular Passage deals with evolution, which without a doubt has to be the biggest farce ever perpetrated upon gullible humanity. The promoters of this drivel, and drivel it is, claim to be scientific, which has no place for Faith, etc. The Truth is, it takes much more Faith to believe in evolution than it does the Biblical account of Creation.

The purveyors of this lie claim that all the evidence is available, with the exception of the *"missing link."* The Truth is, the whole chain is missing.

It is amazing that educators will teach this fabrication, especially considering that there is not one single specimen of evolution in the world. The simple fact is, were the teaching of evolution correct, there would be hundreds of millions of beings who are half ape and half man, or any such combinations. The answer that it takes billions of years to produce such, is no answer at all.

Once again, the simple fact is, if through these millions or billions of years evolution has produced the human family from apes, if we now have the finished product, or even a stage toward the finished product, there would also be other stages in between. Of necessity, that is a must, that is if there is any truth to evolution!

However, in this of which the Holy Spirit says through Paul, the *"Holding of the Truth in unrighteousness,"* not only applies to evolution, but as well to psychology. It too is an insult to God.

As evolution denies the Creator, psychology denies the Saviour. It claims it holds the answer for the sin and aberrations of humanity. In other words, man can save or rehabilitate himself.

As I have stated many times, and will continue to do so, if man is able to do that, then Jesus wasted His time coming down to this sinful world. He should have read a few of the books written by modern Psychologists and saved Himself the trouble.

No! As evolution is a lie pure and simple, psychology (psychoanalysis) falls into the same category.

It is ironical that two of the standards of atheistic Communism are *"evolution and psychology."*

And yet the modern Church, even the Pentecostal variety, has accepted and bought into this lie pretty much totally.

(19) "BECAUSE THAT WHICH MAY BE KNOWN OF GOD IS MANIFEST IN THEM; FOR GOD HATH SHEWED IT UNTO THEM."

The phrase, *"Because that which may be known of God is manifest in them,"* simply means it can be known if so desired. It speaks of the universal objective knowledge of God as the Creator, which is, more or less, in all men.

The phrase, *"For God hath shewed it unto them,"* means that in Creation is His Signature.

As we have stated, the Gospel reveals a Righteousness from God on the principle of Faith, as opposed to merit. Those who reject this Righteousness are justly exposed to the Wrath of God not only because they are without Righteousness, but because they are wholly unrighteous and corrupt and desire to remain that way. As well, all humanity is declared here to be sunken in this corruption.

The heathen world then as now, debased the gift of reason, degraded God to *"a creeping thing,"* and conduct being determined by creed, they gave themselves to vile affections.

Twenty-four of these are particularized, to which we will address ourselves momentarily, all of them together proving fallen human nature to be sunken into an appalling abyss

NOTES

of moral putridity.

This true picture of sinful man is fiercely denied by modern thinkers, as energized by the evil author of ancient and modern thought.

The Greeks and Romans who were the Disciples of Philosophy, condemned the heathen. One of the greatest of the Greek Philosophers was Socrates, and one of the most celebrated of the Romans was the Emperor Marcus Aurelius. But these cultured Nations disobeyed, degraded, and corrupted the wisdom which they had, for while applauding virtue they practiced vice, and taught that man being impotent to do what was right was not to be condemned if he practiced what was wrong.

To the Hebrew people was granted by Divine Election the most precious of all gifts — Revelation. Since man is a creature it was reasonable that his Creator should have made a Revelation of Himself to him. But just as the Rationalists and the Philosophers degraded the Light given to them, so Israel corrupted the Law, and became proud and self-righteous.

Thus, all men are by voluntary action subject to the Wrath of God; and the Holy Spirit places this terrible Truth in the forefront of the Gospel in order that the Doctrine of Justification by Faith might be based upon the fact of universal guilt and condemnation, and so open wide the door of boundless Salvation.

For the Gospel can only be truly preached, or embraced, as being the Good News of Life and Pardon to all who are lost beyond recovery and know it.

So the first Foundation Doctrine of the Gospel which the Apostle preached (vs. 15) announced the Wrath of God (vs. 18). This dogma angers self-righteous man (Williams).

(20) "FOR THE INVISIBLE THINGS OF HIM FROM THE CREATION OF THE WORLD ARE CLEARLY SEEN, BEING UNDERSTOOD BY THE THINGS THAT ARE MADE, EVEN HIS ETERNAL POWER AND GODHEAD; SO THAT THEY ARE WITHOUT EXCUSE:"

The phrase, *"For the invisible things of Him from the Creation of the world are clearly seen,"* proclaims this verse explaining verse 19. All invisible things are made obvious by the things which are *"clearly seen,"* which speak of God's Creation (Deut. 29:29). What a paradox, invisible things which are visible. This state of things has been true and has existed since the creation of the Universe. The Eternal Power and Godhead of the Creator which have always existed, are now understood by the things that have been made, namely, the material creation.

CAUSE AND EFFECT

Man, reasoning upon the basis of the law of cause and effect, which law requires an adequate cause for every effect, is forced to the conclusion that such a tremendous effect as the Universe, demands a Being of Eternal Power and of Divine Attributes. That Being must be God Who should be worshiped.

In fact, God purposely made man in such a way, that man is ever dependent upon Him for continued sustenance and life (spiritual life). As Creator and Redeemer, God demands worship.

Why?

It is not that He needs such, for one glimpse into Revelation, Chapters 4 and 5, portrays the fact that the worship God now receives from His Created Hosts, and in fact has always received, makes pale any other type of worship, including that of man.

The reason for the demand of worship on the part of God, is that God may reveal Himself to man. In other words, the worship of God is for our benefit.

EVOLUTION?

The phrase, *"Being understood by the things that are made,"* proclaims even as we have stated, that such a Creation, demands a Creator. That all of this could have come into being by blind chance, defies all logic, all understanding of true science, and in fact does not make sense at all. Once again as we have stated, to believe in evolution requires far greater Faith than to believe in the Biblical account of Creation.

A perfect example has to do with everything in the world other than the original Creation. I speak of all that man has done, such as buildings, roads, machines, etc. None of this just happened, it was created by men.

If evolution were a proper science, its logic

NOTES

would carry forth respecting everything else as well. Some would hold that logic does not hold true respecting man-made things, because they are not alive as the original Creation. However, I remind the Bible Student that it is no more illogical for machines to evolve on their own, than for living things. The reason is simple!

As machines on their own and without man's help, tend to wear out, and ultimately be reduced to a far lower form, such as scrap metal, etc., likewise, living things do not at all improve without proper help and care. In fact, they all tend to degenerate. In other words, if the pear tree is left entirely alone and allowed to proceed according to its own growth, without man's cultivation, etc., the luscious fruit now enjoyed, will degenerate into only a mere semblance of what it now is. This within itself disproves evolution. For if evolution were true, living things would need no cultivation or improvement whatsoever, but would generate on their own, which simply does not happen in any case. The answer to this is obvious.

God gave man dominion over all of His Creation, which meant that he could seek to improve the species, even as he has, but he could not push one species into another (Gen. 1:28).

CLONING

In the last few months, at least as I dictate these notes, the whole world has watched with fascination as particular types of animals have been cloned which opens the door for the cloning of man, etc. Debates have raged about this and rightly so, claiming that in doing this, at least with human beings, that men are *"playing God."*

While there is some truth to that latter statement, still, if such a thing ever is done, the cloning of human beings, they will find that it is not the same as the animals. Other than the physical body, men have a soul and spirit which are totally different than the animals, in that it is in essence the Breath of God (Gen. 2:7). So, even though human beings can no doubt be cloned in the physical sense, it is impossible to clone their souls and spirits. Consequently, considering that the soul and the spirit is that which really make man what he is, in other words, the fountain of either good or evil, with the physical body only serving as a house for the inner man (II Cor. 4:16; Eph. 3:16), the results will not be with human beings as the Scientists presently think.

SALVATION

The phrase, *"Even His Eternal Power and Godhead,"* takes man even further than the mere Revelation that a Creation demands a Creator. Paul is here declaring how much of God may be known from the Revelation of Himself which He has made in nature, from those vestiges of Himself which men may everywhere trace in the world around them. In other words, the wonder and splendor of the Creation tell us of the Eternal Power of God, in a sense, just how awesome that Power actually is.

And yet, man must not confuse the recognition of God as Creator, which the Creation proclaims all around us, with that of Salvation. On a personal basis, at least as it regards Salvation, God can only be known by the Revelation of Himself in His Son, the Lord Jesus Christ.

In fact, Paul did not use the word *"Godhead"* in Romans 1:20 as it is normally used. Normally it is translated *"theotes"* which Paul used in Colossians 2:9, which declares that in Jesus there dwells all the fullness of absolute Godhead. In other words, His Godhead was not mere rays of Divine Glory which gilded Him, lighting up His Person for a season and with a splendor not His Own, but rather, that He was, and is, absolute and perfect God.

However, in Romans 1:20, Paul used the Greek word *"theiotes"* which is slightly different than *"theotes."*

The latter word is more vague, more abstract, which is meant to portray God only as Creator and not Saviour.

From God's Works of Creation, men cannot know Him as Saviour, which can only be known through the Revelation of His Eternal Word, The Lord Jesus Christ (Trench).

THE CREATED UNIVERSE

Thus, through the Light of the Created Universe, unsaved man recognizes the fact (or should do so) that there is a Supreme

NOTES

Being Who created it, Who has Eternal Power and Divine Attributes, a Being to Whom worship and obedience are due. This is the Truth which unsaved man is repressing. Herein lies the just condemnation of the entire race, since it has not lived up to the Light which it has.

The phrase, *"So that they are without excuse,"* means that man is without defense.

It is not that he does not know the Truth, but that he will not admit to the Truth, which is obvious all around him.

In fact, Paul's appeal in this Chapter is not so much from the basis of the Old Testament, but rather by facts which are obvious to all.

He is offering the world, in a sense, a philosophy of human history to account for the present perplexing state of things — his purpose being to show universal guilt on the part of man. But his position here is quite consistent with what he says elsewhere of Adam's original transgression, as it would have to be, respecting its Inspiration by the Holy Spirit.

His whole argument in this Chapter involves the Doctrine of the Fall of man, who is conceived to have been originally endowed with Divine Instincts, and to have forfeited his prerogative through sin, and this is the essential meaning of the picture given us in Genesis Chapter 3 of the original transgression.

Actually, the entire drift of the Chapter is against the view of the condemnation of mankind being due simply to the sin of Adam being imputed to the race. While that certainly plays a heavy part, Paul also stresses the fact, that succeeding mankind is not innocent, as is obvious, and is thereby, represented as guilty, in that all have sinned against Light which they might have followed.

UNFAIR?

Some would claim, that God is unfair in condemning men who have been placed in their present position by the fault or act of another, namely Adam.

In reply to this argument, it may be said that Scripture nowhere says that men are finally condemned for Adam's transgression as such. On the contrary, the Gospel reveals to us the Atonement, preordained from the first by the offering of animal Sacrifices, for the avoidance of such final condemnation.

So, man was given a way out even from the very beginning, but for the most part has ignored or rejected that Way, Who has always been Christ, which makes the transgression of all who followed Adam as far-reaching as was the original transgression. So man is lost not only because of original sin, but even more so because of his rejection of God's Solution for that sin (Jn. 3:16). Once again, as Paul said, man is *"Without excuse."*

THE BIBLICAL DOCTRINE OF CREATION

This must not be confused or identified with any scientific theory of origins. The purpose of Biblical Doctrine, in contrast to that of scientific investigation, is not so much to inform man as to how God created things, at least in the total sense, but that, in fact, He did create them. In other words, the purpose of Biblical Doctrine in this respect is ethical and spiritual. Reference to the Doctrine of Creation is widespread in both the Old Testament and the New Testament, and is not confined to the opening Chapters of Genesis. The following references may be noted: (Neh. 9:6; Ps. 33:6, 9; 90:2; 102:25; Isa. 40:26, 28; 42:5; 45:18; Jer. 10:12-16; Amos 4:13; Jn. 1:1; Acts 17:24; Rom. 1:20, 25; 11:36; Col. 1:16; Heb. 1:2; 11:3; Rev. 4:11; 10:6).

BY FAITH

A necessary starting-point for any consideration of the Doctrine of Creation is Hebrews 11:3, *"By Faith we understand that the worlds* (plural) *were created by the Word of God."* This means that the Biblical Doctrine of Creation is based on Divine Revelation and understood only from the standpoint of Faith. It is this that sharply distinguishes the Biblical approach from the Scientific, but yet does not at all contradict true science.

In effect, the Work of Creation, no less than the Mystery of Redemption, is hidden from man and can be perceived only by Faith. (And yet as we have said, it takes far more Faith to believe in evolution than it does the Biblical account of Creation.)

THE TRINITY

The Work of Creation is variously attributed to all Three Persons of the Trinity: To the *Father*, as in Genesis 1:1; Psalm 33:6; Isaiah 44:24; 45:12; to the *Son*, as in John 1:3, 10; Colossians 1:16; to the *Holy Spirit*, as in Genesis 1:2; Job 26:13.

This is not to be taken to mean that different parts of Creation are attributed to different Persons within the Trinity, but rather that the whole is the Work of the Triune God. It might be better explained in the following fashion:

In construction there is normally the Owner, the Architect, and the Builder. Perhaps the same account, at least in part, can be used respecting Creation.

God the Father, God the Son, and God the Holy Spirit are the Owners of all things. However, in the manner in which the Trinity is now understood, due to the Revelation of Jesus Christ in the Gospels, we know that God the Father is the Head of all things (I Cor. 15:24). As such the *Father* is the Head of all Creation.

According to John 1:3, *Jesus Christ* served and serves as the Architect of all Creation. In Genesis 1:2, the *Holy Spirit* obviously serves as the actual Builder.

PREEXISTENT MATERIALS?

The words in Hebrews 11:3, *"What is seen was made out of things which do not appear"* taken with Genesis 1:1, *"In the beginning God created the Heaven and the Earth,"* indicate that the worlds were not made out of any preexistent material, but out of nothing by the Divine Word, in the sense that prior to the Divine creative fiat there was no other kind of existence.

To be sure, this has important theological implications. Among other things it precludes the idea that matter is eternal, which is basically taught in evolution. (Genesis 1:1 indicates that matter had a beginning.)

As well, Genesis 1:1 destroys the theory that there was any other type of Creation in the Universe(s) in which another kind of existence or power stands over against God and outside His control.

Likewise Genesis 1:1 indicates that God is

distinct from His Creation, and it (Creation) is not, as pantheism maintains, a part of God. In other words, when men worship the Sun, the Moon, the Stars, or any part of the Earth, etc., they are not, in fact, worshiping God, as many claim.

(Pantheism is the belief that God and Creation are one and the same, or in a worship of many gods.)

However, Creation as described in Hebrews 11:3 does not apply to man. In fact, man was not created out of nothing, but rather out of the dust of the ground (Gen. 2:7), and that includes the beasts of the field and the fowls of the air (Gen. 2:19).

This has been called secondary creation, a creative activity making use of already created materials, and stands alongside primary Creation as part of the Biblical Testimony.

GOD IS INDEPENDENT
OF HIS CREATION

Statements such as Ephesians 4:6, *"One God and Father of all, Who is above all, and through all, and in you all,"* indicate that God stands in a relationship of independence to His Created Order. In that He is *"above all"* and *"over all"* (Rom. 9:5), states that He is independent of His Creation, Self-existent and Self-sufficient. Thus, Creation must be understood as a free act of God determined only by His Sovereign Will, and in no way a necessary act. In other words, He did not *need* to create the Universe(s) (Acts 17:25). He chose to do so.

It is necessary to make this distinction, for only thus can He be God the Lord, the unconditioned, uncaused, unformed, unmade, eternal One, Who is above all and over all.

On the other hand, in that He is *"Through all, and in all,"* He is involved in His Creation, though distinct from it. In other words, the Creation is entirely dependent on His Power for its continued existence. *"In Him all things hold together"* (Col. 1:17) and *"In Him we live and move and have our being"* (Acts 17:28).

The words, *"By Thy Will they existed and were created"* (Rev. 4:11), *"Created through Him, and for Him"* (Col. 1:16), indicate the purpose and goal of Creation.

God created the world *"For the manifes-*

tation of the Glory of His Eternal Power, Wisdom and Goodness." Creation, in other words, is intended to display the Glory of God; to be, as Calvin says, *"The theatre of His Glory."*

Sadly, that *"theatre"* has been sullied because of the Fall, but will one day soon be cleansed and perfected, and once again will shine forth with all its resplendent glory.

THE GENESIS ACCOUNT
OF CREATION

The basic Genesis Account of Creation is Genesis 1:1-2:4. It is a lofty, dignified statement devoid of those coarser elements that are to be found in non-Biblical Creation stories.

Genesis Chapter 1 makes a series of assertions about how the visible world came into being. Its form is that of a simple eye-witness account and no attempt is made to introduce side glances of a kind which would be appreciated by modern Scientific knowledge. Even granting the fact of Revelation, a simple Creation Story would describe the origin of only those elements in the world around that which were visible to the naked eye. In other words, it does not go into any detail whatsoever as to how it was done, but the fact that it was done, and that God did it.

The explanation is not given for the obvious reasons. Even though Hebrews 11:3 gives us a little more light on the subject, still, even that Passage does not tell us exactly how the Lord did these things, other than by His Word which was sent out by Faith. The reason is obvious:

To try to explain Faith apart from God is literally impossible. In other words, to totally explain how God did these things, He would have to explain Himself in totality, which is beyond the capabilities of man to understand. Even though philosophy students will not accept this explanation, still, Paul said, *"O the depth of the riches both of the Wisdom and Knowledge of God! How unsearchable are His Judgments, and His Ways past finding out!*

"For who hath known the Mind of the Lord? Or Who hath been His Counsellor?" (Rom. 11:33-34).

As stated, one cannot understand Faith apart from God, and even then, other than

God, we really cannot tell how it works.

In fact, the secular world uses Faith constantly, but it is the Faith of logic. In other words, if certain things are done, logic demands that certain things follow. That is the type of Faith man has without God.

However, the type of Faith which comes from God, does not in any way operate on the basis of logic, or at least logic as we understand it.

Human logic says that if a man is blind, there is no way he can be made to see, without whatever is causing the blindness to be corrected. That has to be done by surgery or some such way, that is if possible at all. However, Faith with God, which operates through His Spoken Word, says in the Words of Jesus concerning blind Bartimaeus, *"Thy Faith hath made thee whole,"* and the Scripture says, *"Immediately he received his sight"* (Mk. 10:46-52).

Pure and simple, that is not logical, but yet it happened!

So, other than the fact of its happening, which is based on the Foundation of the Word of God, man has no other explanation, and in fact, cannot understand its ramifications.

THE FACT OF INSPIRATION

When the Lord gave the Genesis Account of Creation to Moses, to which we have alluded, He did not tell Moses how it was done, but only that it was done, with the finished product as the proof, and that He did it. While He did give Him the time factor involved, the language portrays that this was not the original Creation of the Earth, but rather a refurbishing or a bringing back to a habitable state.

Because of the simplicity of the Genesis Account, and the strange phenomenon of a serpent being used as a tool or instrument of Satan, many have discounted it as mere fable. However, they only do such because they do not know God and they have no knowledge whatsoever of the spirit world. While Satan used the serpent as an instrument at that time, the Lord later used a mule to speak to Balaam, the wayward Prophet (Num. 22:28).

(There is evidence that the serpent before the Fall, was the most beautiful of all reptiles

or animals, and even had a capability of limited speech. Adam and Eve were not surprised at all at his speaking to them, which insinuates that this was not the first time that this reptile had spoken. As well, there is evidence that the serpent had some type of willpower respecting choice, over and above instinct. Otherwise the Lord would not have placed a curse upon it, even as He did.) (Gen. 3:14).

So, the account given by Moses, was not the mere telling of a story by the great Lawgiver, but was related exactly as God gave such to him. In other words, even down to the structure of every sentence. It was inspired by the Holy Spirit to guarantee against error in any shape, form, or fashion.

THINGS CREATED

Using this account in Genesis exactly as the Lord gave it to Moses, and to all of humanity for that matter, we learn that the first item is the bringing of *"Light"* back to its former state of service. Consequently, this is one of the simplest of all human observations, that day and night occur in regular sequence, and that Light is an indispensable necessity for all life and growth.

"Who caused this to be so?", in a sense, asks the Holy Spirit. The answer is, God did (Gen. 1:3-5).

A second simple observation is that not merely are there waters below, which form the Seas and the underground Springs, but there are waters above which provide the source of rain. Between the two is the Firmament (something beaten out, or something in between). Who caused this to be? God did (Gen. 1:6-8). Again, it is a matter of common experience that Seas and landmasses are distributed in specific areas of the Earth's surface (Gen. 1:9-10). That too is God's doing.

Then, the Earth has produced vegetation of many kinds (Gen. 1:11-13). That too is God's Handiwork. There are no subtleties of botanical distinction. Actually, there are only three broad groupings of vegetation listed: A. Grass which grows close to the Earth; B. Herbs, which yield seed after its kind; and, C. Trees, which yield fruit whose seed is in itself.

Even as at the beginning, that classification of three groupings continue to cover the vegetable, plant, and tree world.

The next observation is that heavenly bodies are set in the Firmament, Sun, Moon, and Stars (Gen. 1:14-19). It was God Who placed them there to mark off times and seasons.

Turning to the spheres in which Living Creatures are to be found, Moses observes that the waters brought forth *"The moving creature that hath life"* (Gen. 1:20), *"swarms of living creatures"* and great whales and all that moves in the Seas (Gen. 1:21).

There is no attempt to make fine distinctions between the various species of Sea animals in the zoological sense. It suffices to say that God made the animals of the Sea, both small and great.

(However, we do know that Adam gave names to all the living creation, at least *"To every beast of the field, and every fowl of the air."* And at those names which described them in totality and remain unto this day, very well may have been zoological distinctions.)

Along with the Sea animals, we know that God also made the birds that fly in the Firmament (Gen. 1:20-22), along with all the living creatures of the land (Gen. 1:24-25).

Finally, God made man, which was on the sixth day along with all the animals, etc., in His Own Image and Likeness, a phrase that is immediately defined as having dominion over the denizens of Earth, Sea and Firmament (Gen. 1:26-28).

Actually, God created man composite, male and female (Gen. 1:27).

THE CHRONOLOGY OF EVENTS

Close examination of this Chapter will reveal a schematic presentation in which the creative acts are compressed into a pattern of six days, there being nine creative acts introduced by the words *"And God said."* (Some have insisted that the ninth act of the Lord was not creative; however, that is not correct in that the Lord made certain of the plant life edible, and did so by His Spoken Word. In fact, it seems that man before the Fall was intended to be vegetarians, but after the Fall certain types of animals were allowed to be eaten.) (Gen. 9:3; I Cor. 6:13; I Tim. 4:3-5)

Some seem confused by the Lord bringing

"Light" into existence on day one, and then seeming to do the same thing again on day four. However, such is not the case at all!

On day one the Light was brought into being, with the word *"Let"* telling us from the Hebrew that it was Light which had already existed from the Sun, also previously created by the Lord (Gen. 1:1), but with the barriers now removed in order that its Light may cover the Earth.

Day four was merely a regulation of the Light which had already been given. Such clears up the mystery, which in fact, is not such a mystery at all.

THE DIVINE CREATIVE WORD

The emphasis in Genesis Chapter 1 is on what God said. It is the Divine Creative Word that brings order out of chaos, Light out of darkness, Life out of death. More weight should be given to the word *"Said"* than to the words *"Create"* or *"Make,"* for Creation is asserted to be the produce of God's Personal Will.

Actually there were a number of words used which together stress the Divine activity. But the essential activity springs from the Word of God, i.e., *"God said."*

THE MEANING OF THE WORD *"DAY!"*

The word *"Day"* seems to occasion difficulties with some, at least as it is proclaimed in Genesis Chapter 1 and referring to the Lord doing all of this in six literal 24-hour days.

In fact, in the Bible this word has several meanings. In its simplest form it means a Day of 24 hours. But it is also used of a time of Divine Judgment, *"Day of the Lord"* (Isa. 2:12), an indefinite period of time *"Day of Temptation,"* (Ps. 95:8), a long period of (say) 1,000 years (Ps. 90:4). On that basis, some have insisted that six literal 24-hour days are not the meaning respecting the Creation.

Such thinking is incorrect. In fact, the Lord actually means six literal 24-hour days in Genesis Chapter 1.

The word *"Day"* is used 2,182 times in Scripture, and always speaks of twenty-four hour days, unless otherwise specified. The specification refers to terms such as *"the Day of the Lord,"* or *"the Day of God,"* etc. Consequently, this is speaking of an indeterminate period of time.

However, there is no such qualification concerning the "days" of Genesis, Chapter 1. In fact, the Holy Spirit qualifies those particular days as beginning with "evening" and "morning," which refers to ordinary twenty-four hour days.

Actually if one is to notice, the description of these 24-hour days begins with the *"evening"* and closes with the *"morning,"* which is backwards from our present reckoning.

Our days are reckoned now as beginning with the morning (12 a.m.) whereas then, the Lord began the new day with the going down of the Sun, or *"evening."* As well, this is the way the Jews reckoned the day during the time of Jesus. For instance, instead of the Sabbath beginning at 12 o'clock midnight on Saturday morning, it rather began at approximately 6 p.m., or at the going down of the Sun on what we now refer to as Friday.

People do not desire to believe that God did this in six literal days, simply because they want to limit God. They refuse to admit that He is Almighty and, therefore, capable of doing anything. In fact, that has been man's problem from the very beginning, limiting God, or denying His existence!

THE SEVENTH DAY

In the Genesis account of Creation, many great truths are given to us, with the following, I think, one of the greatest of all. Moses wrote:

"Thus the Heavens and the Earth were finished, and all the host of them.

"And on the Seventh Day, God ended His Work which He had made; and He rested on the Seventh Day from all His Work which He had made.

"And God blessed the Seventh Day, and sanctified it: because that in it He had rested from all His Work which God created and made" (Gen. 2:1-3).

While the sanctifying of the Seventh Day here no doubt had something to do with the Sabbath, as it regards the Law of Moses, still if we limit it to that, we're missing the point altogether.

All too often when studying the Word of God, we fail to see what the Holy Spirit is

NOTES

actually saying, with our attention many times being drawn to the particular work involved.

THE NUMBERS *"SIX"* AND *"SEVEN"*

Animal life and man were created on the sixth day. Throughout the Bible, we find that the number of man is *"six,"* which refers to the fact that man, although made in the Image of God, is not, in fact, God. So, the number *"six"* proclaims the fact that man falls short of being on the same par with his Creator, although man is made in His Image.

God's number is *"seven,"* which relates to perfection, totality, and universality.

THE SANCTIFICATION OF A DAY

As it regards the Seventh Day, we find that God *"blessed the Seventh Day, and sanctified it"* (Gen. 2:3). This means the following:

1. That it was thereby declared to be the special object of the Divine favor.

2. That it was thenceforth to be a day or epoch of blessing for God's creation.

3. That it was to be invested with a permanence which did not belong to the other six days, every one of which passed away and gave place to a successor.

The sanctifying of this day means that God declared it holy, i.e., He set it apart for holy purposes.

REST

The Scripture says that God *"rested on the Seventh Day from all His Work which He had made"* (Gen. 2:2).

To be sure, He didn't rest because He was tired, for such is impossible. He rested because the Work was finished. And in this scenario, we find the greater Truth being proposed here, far greater than the Seventh Day being a special day, etc.

The *"rest"* enjoined here by the Lord presents a type of Redemption rest, which follows the Atonement, at least for those who accept Christ.

While the keeping of the Sabbath (the Seventh Day) was a symbol of the Old Covenant, likewise, serving Christ presently, which means that we enter into *"His Rest,"* serves the same purpose, i.e., *"constitutes Sabbath keeping."*

Paul said: *"Let us therefore fear, lest, a promise being left us of entering into His Rest, any of you should seem to come short of it.*

"For unto us was the Gospel preached, as well as unto them: but the Word preached did not profit them, not being mixed with faith in them who heard it.

"For we which have believed do enter into rest, as He said, As I have sworn in My Wrath, if they shall enter into My Rest: although the works were finished from the foundation of the world.

"For He spoke in a certain place of the Seventh Day on this wise, And God did rest the Seventh Day from all His Works.

"And in this place again, If they shall enter into My Rest.

"Seeing therefore it remains that some must enter therein, and they to whom it was first preached entered not in because of unbelief:

"Again, He limited a certain day, saying in David, Today after so long a time; as it is said, Today if you will hear His voice, harden not your hearts.

"For if Joshua had given them rest, then would he not afterward have spoken of another day.

"There remains therefore a rest to the people of God.

"For he who is entered into His Rest, he also has ceased from his own works, as God did from His.

"Let us labor therefore to enter into that rest, lest any man fall after the same example of unbelief" (Heb. 4:1-11).

Because it is so important, let us say it again:

REST IN CHRIST

The Sabbath Day of the Old Covenant and keeping that Sabbath Day involved a day of *"rest,"* and not necessarily a day of worship. It was meant to symbolize the *"rest"* which would be brought about in Christ, even as Paul so graphically brought out.

When Jesus came, thereby fulfilling the Law in totality, which included the Sabbath Day, we find that keeping such a day is not brought over into the New Covenant. Why? It is not brought over into the New Covenant, simply

because it was satisfied in Christ. It represented Christ and the *"rest"* we would find in accepting Him as Lord and Saviour; therefore, to continue to keep such a day, as was kept under the Old Covenant, in effect denies Christ. As stated, when one now accepts Christ, thereby serving Him, one is, at the same time, keeping the Sabbath, which was a Type of Christ and the *"rest"* that we find in serving Him.

The Sabbath Day always pointed to Christ, always pertained to Christ, and always symbolized Christ; with the Coming of Christ, Who satisfied all the demands of the Law, the symbol is no longer needed.

THE CROSS: ENTERING INTO HIS REST

The *"rest"* which Paul so graphically illustrated in the Fourth Chapter of Hebrews has always reposed in Christ. However, it took the Cross, which satisfied the terrible sin debt, which man could not pay, for that *"rest"* to be given to us. Of this *"rest,"* Christ is the Source, while the Cross is the Means.

When the Lord sanctified the Seventh Day, this also had reference to the fact that what Jesus did at the Cross, Who is the True Sabbath, makes it possible for the Believer to live a sanctified life. Many Christians understand somewhat the part the Cross plays in Salvation, but understand almost nothing regarding Sanctification. But it is impossible for the Believer to live a sanctified life unless he understands the Cross as it regards the great work of Sanctification.

SANCTIFICATION

The word *"Sanctification"* simply means *"to be set apart exclusively unto the Lord."* Sanctification is a place and position to which the Holy Spirit strives to bring each and every Believer, but to which the Believer cannot attain of his own ability and strength, which can be done only by the Holy Spirit. In other words, the Believer cannot sanctify himself, irrespective as to his zeal, his consecration, or his holy desires. This which God requires of every Believer is totally outside the pale of one's personal strength and ability. It simply cannot be done in that fashion. As stated, this work can only be done by the Holy Spirit.

HOW THE HOLY SPIRIT WORKS

First of all, the Holy Spirit works exclusively within the realm of the Finished Work of Christ. This means that He works entirely within the parameters which are defined by the Cross (Rom. 8:2, 11). That's what Jesus was talking about when He told His Disciples just hours before His Crucifixion, *"And I will pray the Father, and He shall give you another Comforter, that He may abide with you forever;*

"Even the Spirit of Truth; Whom the world cannot receive, because it sees Him not, neither knows Him: but you know Him; for He dwells with you, and shall be in you" (Jn. 14:16-17).

Before the Cross, the Holy Spirit dwelt with Believers; but, since the Cross, where the sin debt was paid, the Holy Spirit can now *"be in you"* (I Cor. 3:16).

WHAT DOES THE HOLY SPIRIT REQUIRE OF US?

The Holy Spirit requires, and stringently so, that our Faith be anchored solely in the Cross of Christ, because the price was paid at the Cross. When our Faith is properly placed, in other words, that the Cross is ever the object of our Faith, the Holy Spirit will then work mightily within our lives (Rom. 6:3-5; 8:1).

One cannot sanctify oneself by works, although good works definitely will be the result of proper Sanctification. One can only bring about Sanctification by exhibiting proper Faith in Christ and what Christ did at the Cross, not allowing our Faith to be moved elsewhere. The greatest problem with the Believer is that he doesn't know, most of the time, what the object of his faith ought to be. Without exception, it must be Christ and the Cross, hence Paul saying, *"We preach Christ crucified"* (I Cor. 1:23).

The work at the Cross was a legal work. This means that what Jesus did at the Cross gives the Holy Spirit the legal right to do what He does, as it regards the Sanctification process within our hearts and lives. As stated, all that is required of us is faith, but it must be faith in the correct object; that correct object, without exception, always is

"the Cross of Christ."

OBJECT OF FAITH

Not understanding the Cross as it regards Sanctification, the object of faith for most Christians is something else entirely, which the Holy Spirit can never honor. For instance, millions make the object of their faith the confession of certain Scriptures, and the reciting of them over and over again, thinking that this somehow will move God to action. While the memorization of Scriptures is very good (and should be done by every Believer), still, the act of doing such will not bring about victory whatsoever in the heart and life of the Believer. The reason is simple:

When the Believer's object of faith is in such, it means it's not in Christ and the Cross, which means the Holy Spirit will not honor such. He honors Christ and the Christ Alone! This must never be forgotten.

In fact, this original Creation, which was not the Creation or Work of Genesis Chapter 1, could very well account for the existence of dinosaurs, etc., which it no doubt does, and which the Genesis Chapter 1 account does not give. It stands to reason that if these huge animals had been a part of the Creation before Noah's flood, that the Bible would have mentioned them. However, they are not mentioned, because they were not in existence at that particular time, having been destroyed in the first flood of Genesis 1:2.

Some Scientists have attempted to pull certain scientific phenomena into the last approximate 6,000 years. I speak of the Poles changing from the East/West axis, to their present North/South position. This is indicated by the remains of huge Mastodons found beneath the ice in extreme North/South positions, with green grass in their mouths, showing they died instantly, and that these areas were once tropical. Such could only mean a shifting of the Poles.

As well, a close friend of Albert Einstein, both of whom were Jewish, attempting to explain some of the Miracles in the Old Testament, and especially the Crossing of the Red Sea by Moses and the Children of Israel, suggested that before Moses, the possibility existed that the Sun rose in the West instead of the East as it now does. And at this great

Miracle of the Crossing, there was a shifting of the Earth on its axis.

According to the Word of God, I think these phenomena such as the changing of the Poles and other such like events actually took place, but before the first flood of Genesis 1:2. In fact, this answers many questions!

(Incidentally, the term *"prehistoric"* is often used, but in fact is incorrect. Its manner of usage refers to evolution, and goes back in that theory past recorded history. However, the Bible gives the history of man all the way back to creation as is recorded in Genesis Chapter 1. Consequently, as far as man is concerned, there is no such thing as a prehistoric time.)

(21) "BECAUSE THAT, WHEN THEY KNEW GOD, THEY GLORIFIED HIM NOT AS GOD, NEITHER WERE THANKFUL; BUT BECAME VAIN IN THEIR IMAGINATIONS, AND THEIR FOOLISH HEART WAS DARKENED."

The phrase, *"Because that, when they knew God, they glorified Him not as God,"* refers to an abundant knowledge of God as Creator, which was available to all, even overwhelming evidence. Nevertheless, they closed their eyes to this obvious knowledge, and refused to honor Him as God. If men do not understand God in the realm of Creation, they will not understand Him in anything else.

The phrase, *"Neither were thankful,"* means that they did not, and in fact would not, honor God as Creator in the giving of all good things on the Earth. Refusing to glorify Him as God, or even recognize Him as God, resulted in a lack of gratitude for His Gifts such as food, clothing, shelter, and even the Gift of Life itself.

Bengel says, *"They did neither; in their religion, they deposed God from His place as Creator, — in their lives, they were ungrateful by the abuse of His Gifts."*

Denney said, *"Nature shows us that God is to be glorified and thanked, i.e., nature reveals Him to be great and good."*

The phrase, *"But became vain in their imaginations,"* presents the only direction that fallen man can go, considering that he has rejected God. *"Vain"* in the Greek Text is *"mataioo,"* and means, *"devoid of force, truth, success, result."* It refers to an unsuccessful

attempt to do something or be something. It refers to that which does not measure up to that which it should be.

Solomon said, *"Vanity of vanities, all is vanity."* That is, *"Futility of futilities, all is futile."* All that man tried and tries was and is futile, therefore, unsuccessful in giving him complete satisfaction. Consequently, the results are wreckage and destruction.

(Incidentally, the word *"vain"* as it is now used, means *"proud."* However, the Greek word as it is used here, means lack of success and even destruction, and not pride, even though man is guilty of that sin as well.)

The phrase, *"And their foolish heart was darkened,"* speaks of the rejection of Light, which means that what they thought was Light was not, which left them with nothing but darkness. Ever let it be understood, that there is only One True Light, and that is Jesus (Jn. 8:12).

While Jesus did say of Believers, *"Ye are the Light of the world,"* He was referring to reflection and not Source. In other words, Believers are only a reflection of the Light which comes from the Source, The Lord Jesus Christ (Mat. 5:14).

(22) "PROFESSING THEMSELVES TO BE WISE, THEY BECAME FOOLS."

This statement by the Holy Spirit through the Apostle lays waste all so-called wisdom which is not of God. If men do not recognize God as the first cause of all things, they cannot be right thereafter. It is the same as mathematical equations. If the original numbers are figured wrong, irrespective of conclusions reached thereafter, all will be wrong, as is obvious.

THE MYTHS OF FOOLS

Concerning Creation, because that is where man began to go wrong, at least after the Fall, there are a number of stories linked with the supremacy ascribed to various ancient cities and the deity(s) conceived to have first dwelt there.

The City of Nippur, located about 60 miles southeast of Babylon, was thought to have been inhabited only by gods prior to the Creation of mankind.

Sumer, another City, says that Enki, the god of the deep and of wisdom, chose their

City and then set about founding neighboring territories, including the paradise Dilmun. He first, as they say, appointed the rivers, marshes and fishes, and then the Sea and the rain.

Another myth tells of the paradise Dilmun in which the mother-goddess Ninhursag produces offspring without pain or travail, though Enki, after eating plants, is cursed and falls sick until cured by a specially created goddess Ninti, whose name means *"The lady of the rib"* or *"The lady who makes live,"* both reflecting the name of Eve.

Marduk was one of the gods of Babylon, who, it is claimed, created the Firmament of Heaven and Earth. He then set in order the Stars, Sun and Moon, and lastly, to free the gods from menial tasks, with the help of another god called *"Ea"* created mankind from the clay mingled with the blood of *"Kingu,"* the rebel god who had led the forces of another god called *"Tiamat."*

We have only named a few from Babylonia, with Egypt basically falling into the same direction, along with ancient Greece.

To the Greeks in general the gods they worshiped were not responsible for the creation of the world, they said, but rather were beings created, or begotten, by vaguely conceived deities or forces which they replaced.

It is claimed in many of these tales, that Earth was impregnated by Heaven, then becoming the mother of all. Rather than Creation, there is an automatic development, they say, mainly by procreation, from undefined beginnings. Actually, there are many variations in detail, and the Philosophers rationalized them in various ways.

For instance, the Epicureans attribute it all to chance, nations of atoms, and the pantheistic stoics conceived of a *"logos,"* or impersonal world-principle.

Once again, *"Professing themselves to be wise, they became fools."*

Regrettably, the modern theory of evolution is no better than the worship of these silly claims of the past, and due to the great enlightenment resulting from Biblical Christianity, is probably put in a much worse category by the Lord.

In fact, many of these myths of old concerning Creation, have some remote resemblance to the actual Creation Story given in

NOTES

Genesis Chapter 1. So, as the Moslem Koran borrowed liberally from the Bible, so did these ancient tales!

(23) "AND CHANGED THE GLORY OF THE UNCORRUPTIBLE GOD INTO AN IMAGE MADE LIKE TO CORRUPTIBLE MAN, AND TO BIRDS, AND FOURFOOTED BEASTS, AND CREEPING THINGS."

The phrase, *"And changed the Glory of the uncorruptible God,"* presents the sin of the ages, and points not only to the heathen of old, but even much of modern Christendom.

Mankind is regarded as having lost a truer perception of God once possessed, idolatry being a sign of culpable degradation of the human race — not, as some would have us now believe, a stage in man's emergence from brutality, as taught by evolution.

Scripture ever represents the human race as having fallen and become degraded; not as having risen gradually to any intelligent conceptions of God at all. And it may well be asked whether modern Anthropological Science has really discovered anything to discredit the Scriptural view of the original condition and capacity of man? The answer is a resounding *"No!"*

Looking at Christendom, any time a Preacher, or anyone for that matter, adds to, or takes away from the Word of God, rather instituting their own interpretation, they are actually *"changing the glory of the uncorruptible God"* whether they realize it or not.

Worshiping Mary by the Catholics is a case in point. In fact, the denial of the Book of Acts' account of the Holy Spirit as relevant to the modern Church, is also a *"Changing of the Glory."* Actually, anything which pertains to God, and yet is man-devised, falls into the same category.

The phrase, *"Into an image made like to corruptible man, and to birds, and fourfooted beasts, and creeping things,"* proclaims, as is obvious, the degeneration from God down to snakes. Consequently, man is not getting better, but rather worse! In Truth, the only thing that has kept this world on a halfway even keel is the Advent of the Holy Spirit on the Day of Pentecost, Who has occupied the hearts of millions since that time, which has had the *only* positive effect other than the Giving of the Law some 1600 years before Christ, and the Life, Death, and Resurrection of Christ, which made it possible for the Holy Spirit to come.

That is one of the reasons that the Antichrist will not have too much difficulty in the world after the Rapture of the True Church. With all the *"Salt"* and *"Light"* gone, evil will reign supreme.

(24) "WHEREFORE GOD ALSO GAVE THEM UP TO UNCLEANNESS THROUGH THE LUSTS OF THEIR OWN HEARTS, TO DISHONOUR THEIR OWN BODIES BETWEEN THEMSELVES:"

The phrase, *"Wherefore God also gave them up to uncleanness through the lusts of their own hearts,"* presents mankind not merely drifting toward depravity, but actually in a sense being shoved by God in that direction.

Since men chose to give up God and worship the creature, God could do nothing but give men into the control of the sinful things they preferred. In other words, God would not violate man's will and force him to do something he did not want to do. When men persisted in following their totally depraved natures, God allowed them free reign. The natural result was immorality of the vilest kind (Wuest).

Alford says of God's act of delivering mankind over into the control of utter human depravity, *"Not merely permissive, but judicially, God delivered them over. As sin begets sin, and darkness of mind, deeper darkness, Grace gives place to judgment, and the Divine Wrath hardens men, and hurries them on to more fearful degrees of depravity."* God delivered man to uncleanness.

The word *"lusts"* is *"epithumia"* in the Greek Text, and means, *"a passionate craving, longing, desire,"* and in this sense, an inordinately sinful one.

Alford again says, *"Not by or through the lusts; the lusts of their heart were the field of action, the department of their being in which the dishonor took place."* In other words, this was what their hearts wanted.

The phrase, *"To dishonour their own bodies between themselves,"* carries with it more than the mere profligacy in the satisfaction of natural lust, but rather bestiality, which refers to impurity in the physical, and not

only in the social and religious sense. In other words, man is grossly immoral.

It speaks of adultery, fornication, pedophilia (sex with children), bestiality (sex with animals), lesbianism and homosexuality.

(25) "WHO CHANGED THE TRUTH OF GOD INTO A LIE, AND WORSHIPPED AND SERVED THE CREATURE MORE THAN THE CREATOR, WHO IS BLESSED FOR EVER. AMEN."

The phrase, *"Who changed the Truth of God into a lie,"* refers back to verse 23, which speaks of spiritual and sexual uncleanness.

In the realm of idolatry, this refers to anything that is placed before Christ.

Most people presently are not inclined to make idols out of pieces of wood as they did many centuries ago; however, if we allow anything to come between Christ and us, whether we realize it or not, such becomes an idol. That's why John the Beloved said, *"Little children, keep yourselves from idols"* (I Jn. 5:21).

However, this condition of men's hearts in purposely refusing the Truth of God, led to the Lord using no restraining force over man whatsoever, allowing him without restraint to push headlong into this lie of darkness, which in effect is the same as God giving man a push. Considering man's already depraved condition, the slide even further downward was terrible, to say the least!

As we see here, the words, *"God also gave them up,"* as given in verse 24, is a restraining force exercised by God even on unregenerate mankind, unless refused, which it was and continues to be.

As well, there is a far greater restraining force on Believers as should be obvious (Job 1:10; Ps. 91; Rom. 8:28).

However, this restraining force even on Believers can be removed as well through disobedience and rebellion.

The phrase, *"And worshipped and served the creature more than the Creator,"* presents that of which Paul spoke in his Message to the Athenians (Acts 17:29-30).

For man to worship and serve the creature, means that he is doing such to something he has made with his hands, and is, therefore, less than him.

Regarding the *"creature,"* even if man

worships himself or other men and women, which most of the world does, still, what good does such do him?

The phrase, *"Who is blessed for ever,"* should have been translated, *"bless-ed,"* because it refers to God.

The word *"blessed"* refers to one receiving a Blessing, in which as should be obvious, God needs nothing.

The word *"bless-ed,"* in effect, two syllables, refers to the One doing the Blessing, in this case, the Lord.

The idea is, all True Blessings come exclusively from the Lord, with idols or anything else for that matter, able to produce none at all.

The word *"Amen"* means that this is anchored in the Word of God, and as such, will not change.

WOMEN AND HOMOSEXUALITY

(26) "FOR THIS CAUSE GOD GAVE THEM UP UNTO VILE AFFECTIONS: FOR EVEN THEIR WOMEN DID CHANGE THE NATURAL USE INTO THAT WHICH IS AGAINST NATURE:"

The phrase, *"For this cause God gave them up unto vile affections,"* presents once again the people purposely and with forethought rejecting God, desiring instead a way of gross evil, with the Lord removing His restraints and, therefore, giving them unimpeded access to their desires. It must be remembered that the way down picks up speed as it goes, therefore, making it more and more difficult to stop or turn around, even though desire to do so may ultimately come about.

I speak of the untold millions who are hooked on alcohol, drugs, immorality, gambling, or any vice one may name. It begins oftentimes as a lark, but as the acceleration downward increases, it becomes more and more difficult to stop, actually impossible without the help of God.

DISHONOR

The word *"vile"* in the Greek Text is *"atimia,"* and means *"dishonor, ignominy and disgrace."*

The first word in this meaning is *"dishonor,"* and looking at the meaning of its opposite *"honor,"* means to evaluate the worth of a person and to treat him with the consideration, respect, and love due his character and position.

To dishonor a person is to either put an incorrect appraisal upon his worth and treat him accordingly, or, having properly evaluated his character, to refuse to treat him with the respect and deference which are his due.

Paul is using this in the sense of the world putting an incorrect estimate upon the sacredness, dignity, and purity of the physical body which was made by God, and in effect, in God's Image, and thus using it in a way which dishonors it.

In that this was what the world wanted, they were given over to a *"condition,"* and not merely to an evil desire (Wuest). It is one thing for an individual to do something which is very evil, but something else altogether for that person to *become* what they do, which is always where sin leads one. As stated, the problem can only be rectified by the Saving Grace of the Lord Jesus Christ.

The phrase, *"For even their women did change the natural use into that which is against nature,"* in short speaks of lesbianism — unnatural sexual relations between women (homosexuality). Several things are here said:

1. The word *"women"* as used here is not the word used as in John 4:9, which simply speaks of designation, but rather the Greek word *"thelus"* which means *"a female."* In other words, the Holy Spirit through Paul is pointing to the gender, and meaning that it is to stay that way.

2. That women tried to *"change"* the *purpose* of their gender, is the reason that Paul used the Greek word for *"female."* They were not trying so much to change the gender, but rather its purpose respecting the sexual sense.

Consequently, they were changing what God had designed, and doing so in a rebellious, base, ignominious way. They went from a far higher use down to a far lower use.

Even though this is one of the worst, or possibly the very worst example, still, this is the great sin of man, changing God's Ways for man's ways, and in every capacity.

3. The *"natural use"* presents that intended by God, in this sense the way sexually, that

women were originally created.

The word *"natural"* in the Greek is *"phusis,"* and means *"the nature of things, the force, laws, order of nature, as opposed to that which is monstrous, abnormal, perverse."*

4. That which is *"against nature"* respects that which is against nature's laws, or God's Laws, which are one and the same.

MEN AND HOMOSEXUALITY

(27) "AND LIKEWISE ALSO THE MEN, LEAVING THE NATURAL USE OF THE WOMAN, BURNED IN THEIR LUST ONE TOWARD ANOTHER; MEN WITH MEN WORKING THAT WHICH IS UNSEEMLY, AND RECEIVING IN THEMSELVES THAT RECOMPENCE OF THEIR ERROR WHICH WAS MEET."

The phrase, *"And likewise also the men,"* presents the word *"men"* used in the same fashion as the word *"women"* in the previous verse.

The Holy Spirit through Paul is not pointing out the mere designation of man, but rather the male as distinguished from a female. These terms are used because only the distinction of sex is contemplated (Vincent).

The phrase, *"Leaving the natural use of the woman,"* speaks of the sex act which is to be performed between the man and his wife. This natural way formed and made by God, is set aside, in favor of that which is far, far lower.

Let it ever be understood, that man can never improve upon that which God has done. He cannot add to it, or take away from it, at least with any positive results. He always drops down to a lower level, which is the problem with the world, and always has been since the Fall.

The Holy Spirit through the Apostle is using this example of lesbianism and homosexuality, because it portrays in the most glaring way, the obvious truth of these statements. In other words, this example portrays in the worst way the folly of changing God's designed direction, and designed, I mighty quickly add, for our good and not harm. Actually, this is one of Satan's greatest ploys, even as he tempted Adam and Eve in the Garden. He tried to make them think that God was withholding some good things

NOTES

from them, exactly as men think today. However, let it ever be known, that all good things are found in the Ways of God, and not outside those Ways. Satan has no good ways, only bondage. While he is able to offer some pleasure and can titillate the flesh somewhat, without exception, his efforts will lead to destruction. In other words, the Marlboro man dies of cancer.

The phrase, *"Burned in their lust one toward another,"* refers to that which is terrible in its intensity.

The word *"burned"* in the Greek is *"ekkaio,"* and means *"to burn out,"* and can be explained as *"the rage of lust."* Robertson defines it as, *"to enflame with lust."*

In other words, this type of lust satiates or consumes the entirety of the individual. It is an all-out endeavor to satisfy their totally-depraved natures. Once again, we are speaking here of homosexuality.

The phrase, *"Men with men working that which is unseemly,"* specifies its direction.

PEDOPHILES

The word *"working"* in the Greek is *"katergazomai,"* which means *"to perform, accomplish, achieve, to do that from which something results, to carry to its ultimate conclusion."* It is a *"lust"* which will not be satisfied until it obtains its desired results.

Many would ask as to how a man could take advantage of a little boy, sexually molesting him, when the man knows in his heart the child will be greatly affected mentally and emotionally?

The answer is obvious, it is the *"lust"* which drives the person and will not quit until it is momentarily satisfied. As well, each act takes the man lower and lower in its depravity.

At this stage, it is not why the man does such a thing, but that he has reached the point to where he has no choice in the matter. That is the reason that many pedophiles openly state, if given the opportunity they will do such again. They are right! Within themselves it is not possible for the situation to be changed.

At this stage and even long before, the favorite word used, and even by the Church is, *"They need professional help!"* Of course they are speaking of psychological counseling, etc.

However, I must remind the Reader, that there is no *"professional help"* for something of this nature, or any sin for that matter, be it great or small. The only Answer is Jesus Christ. As I have said, and will continue to say it over and over again, if, in fact, man has the answer for these problems in the realm of psychoanalysis, or in any other way, Jesus Christ made an unnecessary trip down to this sin-benighted world to die at Calvary, thereby paying a terrible price to redeem humanity. Once again I remind the Reader, that man's problem is sin, not environment, association, education, even though these things certainly may have some effect. And once again I say, that man's Solution is Jesus Christ, and Christ Alone! Also I again remind the Reader, that Jesus needs no help in this capacity, for in effect, He has already effected the cure, which is His Shed Blood coupled with His Power. For the Church to look elsewhere, to do otherwise, to think otherwise, is not just sin, but actually, rank, raw, ignominious blasphemy.

ALTERNATE LIFESTYLE?

The word *"unseemly"* in the Greek is *"aschemosune,"* and means *"want or form, disfigurement, deformed, one's nakedness, shame."*

It does not matter that modern man may attempt to label homosexuality as merely an *"alternate lifestyle,"* insinuating that there is nothing wrong with this direction, the Truth is the opposite, and irrespective of what type of erroneous laws that Congress may make, or the Supreme Court may judge. Man's law in no way changes God's Laws, i.e., that which God has deemed will happen! The awful results will always come about, irrespective of how much seal of approval that man may attempt to apply to this issue, or any other issue pertaining to Life and Godliness.

The phrase, *"And receiving in themselves that recompence of their error which was meet,"* refers to the penalty which is attached to wrongdoing, and if persisted, will always be brought about.

"Recompence" in the Greek is *"antimisthian,"* and means *"a reward given in compensation, requital, recompense."*

The word here refers to that natural result of their sin which pays them back for what they have done. The evil consequences are necessary as ordained by Divine Law. When one violates the laws of nature (God), one must pay the price.

The word *"error"* in the Greek is *"plane,"* and means *"a wandering, roving, or wrong action."* It carries the idea of an individual leaving the natural instincts created by God and forcing those instincts into perversion. The *"wandering, roving, wrong action"* steadily gets worse and worse, with the *"error"* becoming more and more pronounced.

An excellent example is the many homosexuals and lesbians who have had their physical, emotional and even mental appearances changed, and for the worse. In other words, their homosexuality shows in their mannerisms, which again are unnatural and repulsive.

THE SIN OF HOMOSEXUALITY

The Bible has much to say about this sin, as it does all sin.

Historically, according to the Bible, homosexual behavior was linked with idolatrous cult prostitution (I Ki. 14:24; 15:12; 22:46). However, the stern warning against this practice is included in Levitical Law, and upheld under the New Covenant as well, even respecting these Passages in Romans which we are now studying (Lev. 18:22; 20:13).

In this Chapter, to which we have already alluded, Paul greatly condemns homosexual acts, lesbian as well as male, putting them in the same breath in a sense as idolatry. However, his theological canvas is broader than the expression of the homosexual act regarding idolatry, but is rather held up as the terrible exchange fallen man has made in departing from his Creator's intention. Seen from this angle, every homosexual act is unnatural, not so much because it cuts across the individual's natural sexual orientation, or even infringes Old Testament Law, which it definitely does, but rather because it flies in the face of God's Creation Plan for human sexual expression.

OTHER WARNINGS

Paul makes two more references to

homosexual practice in other Epistles. Both occur in lists of banned activities and strike the same condemnatory note. In I Corinthians 6:9, practicing homosexuals are included among the unrighteous who will *not* inherit the Kingdom of God; however, Paul then adds a redemptive note, saying, *"And such were some of you"* (I Cor. 6:11). In other words, the Lord Saved these once practicing homosexuals, cleansing them of their sin, and made them new creatures in Christ Jesus.

The idea is, as should be obvious, that the Lord does not save in sin, but from sin.

A Newsman asked me once if God would save homosexuals? My answer to him was very clear and concise: *"Yes, God will save homosexuals, or anyone who comes to Him for that matter. Actually, that is the very reason Jesus came and died on Calvary."*

"However," I quickly added, *"but that means they will have to give up their sin of homosexuality, just as the drunkard gives up his drink, etc."*

In I Timothy 1:10, Paul again speaks of the sin of homosexuality, and by inference declares the lost condition of those who practice this sin, as well as other sins.

It has been suggested that the meaning of *"arsenikoites"* in I Corinthians 6:9 and I Timothy 1:10 may be restricted to that of *"male prostitute."* However, Greek linguistic evidence to support this view is lacking.

It is beyond reasonable doubt that Paul intended to condemn homosexual conduct in any capacity, but not homosexual people. As Creator, Law-Giver, and King, the Lord's condemnation of such behavior is absolutely plain, but yet He loves the sinner.

Following are some questions respecting homosexuality with hopefully some answers which will be helpful:

ARE HOMOSEXUALS BORN THAT WAY?

In a word, *"No!"*

While it is true that the seed of original sin carries with it every type of deviation, aberration, perversion, and wrongdoing, the Homosexual cannot claim to have been born that way anymore than the drunkard, gambler, killer, etc. However, I think it correct

to say that the gene pool which constitutes the character and personality makeup of every individual, is more predisposed toward some aberrations in certain persons than others. However, in the spiritual sense, the perverted or abnormal number of genes in any particular direction, is *not* the cause of these situations, but rather the *results*. The genes are that way because of man's fallen condition in a spiritual sense. So, even if Scientists one day can find a way to control the genes, the problem will still not be solved, because that which feeds the genes, which is the soul and the spirit of man, cannot be changed by medical or psychological procedures, but only by the Power of God. It is called the New Birth, and is referred to in the Word of God as *"Regeneration."* The actual Passage says, *"Not by works of Righteousness which we have done, but according to His Mercy He Saved us, by the washing of Regeneration, and renewing of the Holy Spirit"* (Titus 3:5).

The word *"Regeneration"* in the Greek Text is *"Paliggenesia,"* and means *"once more or again,"* in other words, *"regened."*

Him and Him Alone, the Lord Jesus Christ can change the person, i.e., *"Regene the individual, hence, Regeneration."*

Again we state, that even though there are greater propensities toward certain proclivities in some than in others, and because they were born that way, does not mean the thing is set in concrete, but only that there is a little lean in that direction. In fact, the Lord does not condemn the sinner for what he is, but rather for refusing to accept God's Way out of the situation, which is the Salvation afforded by Christ at Calvary. That goes for every sinner, homosexuals included!

WILL GOD SAVE HOMOSEXUALS?

Actually, this is a question we have already answered.

Yes, the Lord will save homosexuals, or anyone who comes to Him, irrespective as to who or what they may be. That is the very reason Jesus came to this world, *"To save sinners"* (I Cor. 6:9-12).

However, the Homosexual upon coming to Christ, must abandon the former lifestyle immediately, and that goes for the drunk, gambler, or anyone.

When a person comes to Christ, he leaves something (the old lifestyle), and comes to something, and more particularly to someone, The Lord Jesus Christ. As such, we take upon ourselves and by His Help, His Lifestyle.

WILL PSYCHOLOGICAL COUNSELING HELP THE HOMOSEXUAL?

No! Biblical Counseling will help but not Psychological Counseling.

Biblical Counseling will simply direct the person to Jesus in order that one may be Saved. Once this happens, the Power of the Risen Christ through the Person and Ministry of the Holy Spirit, takes up abode within the heart and life of the Redeemed sinner. As such, the former Homosexual, and any Believer for that matter, now has a Power within him greater than the power of Satan (Gal. 2:20; I Jn. 4:4).

In fact, psychology holds no help at all for the Homosexual, or anyone else for that matter, only harm. It is harm because it attempts to make the person believe a lie, and it keeps them from their only Source of help, The Lord Jesus Christ.

First of all, psychological counseling, for the most part, attempts to make the Homosexual *"feel good about himself,"* in other words, to accept his orientation, as it is called. If the Truth be known, many psychologists claim that the guilt felt by the Homosexual (or anyone), is the real problem, and is present because of certain myths called the Bible, etc.

While it is true that the *"Law"* of the Bible, does point out man's terrible sins, still if the Bible did not exist, the guilt of man's fallen condition would remain. That guilt can only be removed by Jesus Christ. (The Bible does not originate guilt — sin being the fault — it only defines it.)

ARE ALL HOMOSEXUALS INSTANTLY DELIVERED AT THE MOMENT OF SALVATION?

In fact, yes! Actually, it can be no other way, if Salvation is to be Salvation (II Cor. 5:17-18). However, whereas this terrible bondage, as with other problems such as temper, alcohol, nicotine, etc., are at times broken

NOTES

immediately, with some it does not come quite so quickly. In other words, at times it is a struggle.

However, the Lord does not throw us over if we fail or slip back, but in fact instantly forgives us as we ask for such (I Jn. 1:9). Consequently, the new Believer must continue to believe God, pressing forward toward victory. (Please read carefully the Commentary of Romans Chapters 6, 7 and 8, regarding this very subject.)

WILL HOMOSEXUALITY CAUSE ONE TO BE ETERNALLY LOST?

Yes, that is if the person does not repent and, thereby, forsake that lifestyle. Of course, the same can be said for alcoholism, drug addiction, or religion for that matter (Gal. 5:19-21).

The age-old problem of mankind is the desire to live in sin and have Salvation at the same time. However, those who would attempt such a thing, have not truly been Born Again.

When the person truly turns to Christ, making Him the Lord of one's life, affections change totally and completely. Actually, the Scripture is rather implicit about this, saying, *"Old things are passed away; behold, all things are become new"* (II Cor. 5:17). In other words, the new Believer does not want the old sinful lifestyle any longer, even though he may at times sense its pull. He is now a *"New creature in Christ Jesus."*

WHAT ABOUT THE LAWS OF CERTAIN STATES WHICH LEGALIZE HOMOSEXUAL MARRIAGES, OR THE COURTS ALLOWING HOMOSEXUAL COUPLES TO ADOPT CHILDREN, ETC.?

First of all, the Courts legalizing something, does not legitimize it in the Eyes of God. The Word of God does not change irrespective of what others may do. That is the reason it is referred to as Objective Truth, which means it is the same Standard forever and for everyone.

The recognition of homosexual marriages by the Courts is an abomination in the sight of God.

As well, the allowing of homosexual couples to adopt children, is again, an abomination. Putting a child in such an abnormal environment, can do nothing but have an adverse effect on that child, which will affect it negatively for the rest of its life.

Regrettably, this is also the case in most straight homes, for the simple reason that most do not know Jesus. Only Jesus can make a marriage, and He definitely will not do so with such an unscriptural, perverted lifestyle of homosexuality, irrespective of claims to the contrary.

However, if a home does have Jesus Christ, it has the only Solution for its problems and the only Guarantee for success.

HOW SHOULD CHRISTIANS REACT TOWARD HOMOSEXUALS?

To which we have alluded elsewhere in our comments on this subject, the Lord loves the Homosexual just as much as he does anyone else. When He died on Calvary, He died for these people just as well as He died for you and me. In fact, His Atonement is no different for them than for us.

Likewise, Christians must show kindness and the God kind of Love toward homosexuals, as they do for others. That means, at least as far as is possible, to treat them as human beings and that means with respect and dignity. However, the Believer must never leave the impression that such a lifestyle is condoned, while at the same time not leveling condemnation on the person. No one has ever brought people to Christ with a club, but millions have been brought to the Saviour because they felt somebody cared for them.

At the same time I do not think it is possible that a Christian could be close friends with a homosexual, or anyone outside of Christ for that matter! The Believer and the unbeliever have absolutely nothing in common, at least on which to build and sustain a friendship. One serves Christ, while the other serves himself (or herself).

(28) "AND EVEN AS THEY DID NOT LIKE TO RETAIN GOD IN THEIR KNOWLEDGE, GOD GAVE THEM OVER TO A REPROBATE MIND, TO DO THOSE THINGS WHICH ARE NOT CONVENIENT;"

The phrase, *"And even as they did not like to retain God in their knowledge,"* carries the

NOTES

idea of the human race putting God to the test for the purpose of approving or disapproving Him.

They wanted a God to their liking, and finding that He did not meet those specifications, the world refused to approve Him as the God to be worshiped, or have Him in its knowledge.

The *"knowledge"* spoken here, in the Greek is *"epignosis,"* and means *"full and precise knowledge."* In other words, their knowledge of God, due to their rebellion against Him and, therefore, going into deep sin, was only a dim memory, and that perverted!

If one wants to know what is wrong with the modern School System in America, despite the fact of hundreds of billions of dollars being thrown at this ever-worsening situation, it is because Educators *"did not like to retain God in their knowledge."* So, and speaking of the Public School System, we have Godless schools, which means that the schools are filled with Satan. We have Godless education, which means that what knowledge the students do have is largely warped and twisted, ill preparing them for life. We have Godless direction, consequently we have erroneous ways.

The phrase, *"God gave them over to a reprobate mind,"* presents the third time such a statement is used (vss. 24, 26). Once again, humanity wanted that which was licentious and evil and the Lord took away the restraining forces, allowing them to have what they desired.

The words *"Reprobate mind"* in the Greek Text is *"adokimon noun."* It carries the idea of the human race putting God on trial, and because it rejected Him after trial, God gives it a *"trialess"* mind, in other words, one incapable of discharging the functions of a mind with respect to the things of Salvation (Wuest).

As they did not think it fit to keep God in their knowledge, God gave them over to a mind which has no way to comprehend God. In other words, Light rejected is Light withdrawn. The one thing answers to the other.

Virtually, they pronounced the True God disapproved, and would have none of Him, and He in turn gave them up to a disapproved mind, a mind which is no mind and cannot discharge the functions of one, a mind in which the Divine distinctions of right and wrong are confused and lost, so that God's condemnation cannot but fall on it at last.

This speaks of people who are completely perverted, and as the Canaanites of old, who did their abominations unto their gods, then the last deep of evil has been reached.

The phrase, *"To do those things which are not convenient,"* concerns wrong direction which will affect the person in every capacity, and in a very negative way.

The Greek word for *"convenient"* is *"katheko,"* and means *"It is becoming, it is fitting."* So, the human race does things which are not fitting.

It is like an old abandoned building, the home of bats, spiders and snakes, not a very pleasant place to be (Robertson).

(29-31) "BEING FILLED WITH ALL UN-RIGHTEOUSNESS, FORNICATION, WICK-EDNESS, COVETOUSNESS, MALICIOUS-NESS; FULL OF ENVY, MURDER, DEBATE, DECEIT, MALIGNITY; WHISPERERS,

"BACKBITERS, HATERS OF GOD, DE-SPITEFUL, PROUD, BOASTERS, INVEN-TORS OF EVIL THINGS, DISOBEDIENT TO PARENTS,

"WITHOUT UNDERSTANDING, COV-ENANT BREAKERS, WITHOUT NATURAL AFFECTION, IMPLACABLE, UNMERCIFUL:"

The phrase, *"Being filled with all,"* literally means to *"fill up,"* and with this which is listed, presenting the cause and the reason for the problems in this Nation and anywhere in the world for that matter.

These who had disapproved of holding God in their knowledge were completely filled as a consequence with the 21 sins mentioned in verses 29-32, with the result that they remained in a full condition of putridity (Wuest).

The following presents the meaning of these words:

1. Unrighteousness: The Greek is *"adikia,"* which means *"unjust, injustice, what is not comfortable with justice, what ought not to be, that which is wrong."* It is that which is 180 degrees opposite of the Righteousness of God. In fact, when men reject the Righteousness of God, there is an automatic unrighteousness which comes to

them. Despite education, environment, or man's efforts in any capacity to ameliorate the situation, the unrighteousness remains, and will do so and even deepen, unless Jesus Christ is allowed into the situation.

2. Fornication: The Greek is *"porneia,"* which means *"unlawful sex sins of single and married people."* Some people have the erroneous idea that adultery pertains to those who are married, with fornication pertaining to those who are unmarried. That is incorrect.

Fornication pertains to anyone and it includes sex outside of marriage, homosexuality, lesbianism, bestiality, pedophilia, etc.

3. Wickedness: The Greek is *"athesmos,"* which means *"lawless, unprincipled, not in conformity to acceptable custom."* For instance, the homosexuals of Sodom and Gomorrah are called *"athesmoi"* in II Peter 2:7.

4. Covetousness: The Greek is *"pleonekthes,"* which means *"avaricious."*

5. Maliciousness: The Greek is *"kakias,"* which means *"not only doing evil, but being evil."*

6. Envy: The Greek is *"zelou,"* which means *"a jealousy which makes war upon the good it sees in another."*

7. Murder: The Greek is *"phoneus,"* which means *"one who commits homicide."*

8. Debate: The Greek is *"eridos,"* which means *"strife, contention, wrangling."*

9. Deceit: The Greek is *"apatao,"* which means *"to deceive or seduce into error."*

10. Malignity: The Greek is *"kakoetheia,"* which means *"taking everything with an evil connotation and giving a malicious interpretation to the actions of others, a nature which is evil and makes one suspect evil in others."*

11. Whisperers: The Greek is *"psithuristeas,"* which means *"a secret slanderer, an accuser, a backbiter."*

12. Backbiters: The Greek is *"katalalia,"* which means *"evil speaking, railing, defamation, accusation."*

13. Haters of God: The Greek is *"echthra,"* which means *"enmity, hatred, hostility, defamation, active malice."*

14. Despiteful: The Greek is *"enubrizo,"* which means *"to use reproachfully, to treat with despite."*

15. Proud: The Greek is *"alazoneia,"* which means *"ostentatious, boasting about

what one is not or does not possess, some-one going about with empty and boastful professions of cures and other feats."

16. Boasters: The Greek is *"alazon,"* which means *"vaunting in those things one does not possess."*

17. Inventors of evil things: The Greek is *"epheuretes,"* and means *"to invent, to find, to devise."*

18. Disobedient to parents: The Greek is *"anupotaktos,"* which means *"disobedient to authority, disorderly."*

19. Without understanding: The Greek is *"agnoeo,"* which means *"not to recognize or know, to be ignorant, unacquainted with."*

20. Covenant-breakers: The Greek is *"ausunthetos,"* which means *"a breaker of a covenant or agreement, faithless, treacherous."*

21. Without natural affection: The Greek is *"astorgos,"* which means *"without family love, hostile to benevolence, odious, hateful."*

22. Implacable: The Greek is *"aspondos,"* which means *"the absolutely irresponsible person who, being at war, refuses to lay aside his enmity or to listen to terms of reconciliation."*

23. Unmerciful: The Greek is *"aneleemon,"* which means *"without mercy, not compassionate."*

(32) "WHO KNOWING THE JUDGMENT OF GOD, THAT THEY WHICH COMMIT SUCH THINGS ARE WORTHY OF DEATH, NOT ONLY DO THE SAME, BUT HAVE PLEASURE IN THEM THAT DO THEM."

The phrase, *"Who knowing the Judgment of God,"* means that they traveled this path with eyes wide open. In other words, they thumbed their nose at the *"Judgment of God,"* in essence saying, *"Do your worst, and it will not stop us."*

And people wonder why there is a Hell!

The phrase, *"That they which commit such things are worthy of death,"* means that they knew what God had said about such sins, but went into them despite that knowledge, in effect, daring God to kill them, etc. It should be understood that Divine Judgment is implied.

Paul constantly denotes in a general and comprehensive sense, the penal consequence of unatoned sin due to the Divine Laws.

The idea is, that the wages of sin is death

and, as such, the guarantee is that ultimately the sentence will be carried out.

The phrase, *"Not only do the same, but have pleasure in them that do them,"* proclaims the evidence of the *"Reprobate mind."*

It is not simply that such things are done occasionally under temptation, but that they are in the habits of people's lives. And still more: such habits are not only participated in by those who have knowledge enough to perceive their guilt, but even condoned and approved.

In other words, there was no general protest or indignation in society against the prevalent abominations.

So, and as stated, if one wants to know the reason for the problems of this world, which fall out to a gross increase in crime, man's inhumanity to man, etc., he need look no further than Chapter 1 of Romans.

"When I survey the wondrous Cross on which the Prince of Glory died,
"My richest gain I count but loss, and pour contempt on all my pride."

"Forbid it, Lord, that I should boast, save in the death of Christ my God;
"All the vain things that charm me most, I sacrifice them to His Blood."

"See, from His Head, His Hands, His Feet, sorrow and love flow mingled down,
"Did e'er such love and sorrow meet, or thorns compose so rich a crown?"

"Were the whole realm of nature mine, that were a present far too small;
"Love so amazing, so Divine, demands my soul, my life, my all."

CHAPTER 2

(1) "THEREFORE THOU ART INEXCUSABLE, O MAN, WHOSOEVER THOU ART THAT JUDGEST: FOR WHEREIN THOU JUDGEST ANOTHER, THOU CONDEMNEST THYSELF; FOR THOU THAT JUDGEST DOEST THE SAME THINGS."

The phrase, *"Therefore thou art inexcusable, O man, whosoever thou art that judgest,"* presents this segment or Chapter as directed basically to the Jew.

They held themselves high and lofty, consequently pronouncing all Gentiles to be born in sin and under condemnation. In other words, they were the people who judged others. However, they forgot that the same principle on which the Gentiles were condemned, namely, that he does evil despite the fact of available knowledge to the contrary (Rom. 1:32), condemned the Jew also. In fact, his very impeachment toward the Pagans is his own condemnation. Actually, the sin of the Jews was far worse, because they had far greater Light, and despite their claims to the contrary, were sinning greatly against that Light.

The word *"inexcusable"* in the Greek is *"anapologetos,"* and means *"without an apology or defense."* The word *"apology"* as it is used here is different than the normal sense of asking one's forgiveness, or trying to prove a point, but is rather used in the sense of denying guilt. In other words, the Jew is unable to offer an apology or defense from the charge of failing to live up to the Light he has (Wuest).

The word *"judgest"* is *"krino"* in the Greek, and means *"to separate, to determine, to pronounce judgment."* It refers to censorious criticism and judgment. It refers to a derogatory *appraisal* of another's character, the forming of a *judgment* of his character (Wuest).

The idea is, that the Jew placed himself on a very high spiritual pedestal, with the rest of the world far beneath him. In other words, they considered themselves to be vastly superior in a spiritual sense, separating themselves from all of mankind in a holier-than-thou, self-righteous attitude. In fact, this spirit had become so bad by the time of Christ, that the Pharisees, who incidentally hated Christ, had even segmented themselves away from the rest of Israel in the same segmented, self-righteous position. This attitude of judging others, had pushed them into the place and position of secondary separation, even as it always does. This means they separated themselves from certain ones, and even from those who were friendly to those they despised. As stated, it is called secondary separation. The person

or people in his or their own eyes become more and more spiritual, looking down on others. Luke spoke of the Pharisees, saying, *"And He spake this Parable unto certain which trusted in themselves, that they were righteous, and despised others:"* (Lk. 18:9).

Jesus then gave the Parable of the Pharisee and the Publican, claiming that the criminal who admitted his sin and begged forgiveness from the Lord, went away Justified, while the Pharisee, who bragged about his spirituality, experienced no Justification at all, and in fact died lost.

Please let the Reader understand, that these Words of warning concerning the judging of others, as given by the Holy Spirit to the Apostle, were intended not only for the Jews, but all others as well, even us presently. In fact, Paul's warnings tell us several things:

1. The judging of the spirituality of others from a standpoint of supposed personal righteousness is terribly wrong.

2. There is no excuse for anyone who calls himself a Believer to do such a thing. When they do such, and in fact this problem is rampant, their sin is inexcusable.

3. The basis of their righteousness, even as we shall see, is not the finished Work of Christ, but rather their own opinion of themselves. Even though they talk a lot about the Lord, as the Jews of old, in fact, they do not know the Lord, and are actually far beneath, at least in a spiritual sense, the very one who they are criticizing and judging. (I am not speaking of judging Biblical Doctrine, which all must do, using the Scriptures as the yardstick, but rather the person himself or herself.)

As well, the word *"whosoever"* tells us that all fall into this category. Paul is not speaking to Jews only!

The phrase, *"For wherein thou judgest another, thou condemnest thyself,"* in effect says that God judges one who judges another, in the same manner in which he himself has judged, hence, *"Condemning himself"* (Mat. 7:1-2).

The phrase, *"For thou that judgest doest the same things,"* in effect says much more than appears on the surface.

The Jew looked down, way down, on the Gentiles, calling them *"dogs,"* etc. They were the people of God, while these Gentiles were idol-worshiping Pagans. In effect, everything Paul said in the First Chapter, which actually concerned the Gentiles, would have been applauded by the Jews, even Paul's strident enemies among this group. The Gentiles had refused the obvious, respecting God as Creator, etc. However, what the Jew did not see or understand was, as the Gentiles had purposely rejected the Light given them concerning God as Creator, Israel had rejected the Light given to them concerning Christ as Redeemer. In fact, Israel had far more Light than the Gentiles ever had, but rejected it all, even to the point of killing their Messiah, of which there could have been no worse sin. So they were even more guilty than the ones they were accusing.

Why didn't they see that?

They did not see it because of their self-righteousness. Self-righteousness by its very nature blinds men to what they really are. How could anyone have needed to repent, especially considering how religious they were, or so they thought? The idea was preposterous, hence, the Pharisees as a whole totally rejected the Ministry of John the Baptist and especially that of Christ.

The moral of this phrase as well, is that those who place themselves in the position of judging others, at least in this capacity, are in fact, guilty of the same sin, and even worse. However, *"Judges"* of such nature, can little see their own faults, or else they make excuses and allowances for themselves, while critically pointing out others.

The Reader must understand, that the Book of Romans, that is if it is understood correctly, lays waste much of that which refers to itself as *"Church!"* In its portrayal of the True Plan of Salvation, it hits broadside all the glosses of religious man. It cuts straight to the core, and in doing so, it angers many people. To be frank, the great controversy always has been over the issue of works and Grace. It may go under other labels, or be identified in some other measure, or be ignored, but *that* is the controversy.

When the modern Church will not accept True Repentance, which is God's Way, but insists upon adding other things, this automatically tells us exactly where the

NOTES

Church is relative to these great Foundational Doctrines of the Word of God.

Consequently, the Holy Spirit through Paul is not only pointing out the self-righteousness of the Jews, but as well is proving the position that all mankind is guilty before God. That is the idea of this summary.

So far this has been shown with regard to the mass of the heathen world, its general moral corruption, prevalent and condoned, having been pointed out finally as a glaring proof; the main point of the argument having been to trace this state of things to man's own fault, in that he had refused to retain and act on a Knowledge of God originally imparted to him through nature and through conscience. From such refusal had ensued idolatry.

Thence, as a judicial consequence, profligacy and the general prevalence of abominable practices.

At last, in many at least, the *"reprobate mind,"* threw aside all moral restraint, not only committing such terrible sins, but as well approving of them.

Thus, it is sufficiently proved that the heathen world, regarded as a whole, is under sin, and liable to the Wrath of God (Barmby).

THE WHOLE WORLD

But the required proof that the whole of mankind is guilty is not yet complete. It might be said that there are many still who disapprove of all this wickedness, and sit in judgment on it, and who are, therefore, not themselves implicated in the guilt.

To such persons the Apostle now turns, his purpose being to show that their judging others does not exempt themselves, unless they can show that they are themselves sinless. All, he argues, are tainted with sin, and, therefore, implicated in the guilt of the human race, while the very fact of their judging others condemns them all the more.

IT INCLUDES ALL . . .

It is usually said by Commentators that, the sin of the heathen world having been established in the First Chapter of Romans, the Second Chapter has reference exclusively to the Jews. But that is not so.

The expressions as used by Paul, evidently

include all who judge others, both Jew and Gentile.

However, Paul nowhere suggests that there is no difference between man and man with regard to moral worth before God. In this very Chapter he forcibly declares the moral excellence of some, without the Law as well as with the Law.

What he does straightly state, is that morality, as commendable as it is, does *not* imply Salvation.

Paul is stating, and unequivocally so, that Salvation is on another basis alone, that of Faith and not of works.

As well, he is stating that irrespective of the superior morality of some, that none whatever are so exempt from sin as to be in a position to judge others; and it is the judging of others that he especially attacks here, as increasing, rather than exempting from, condemnation.

THE SIN OF PRESUMPTION

Judging always involves in itself the sin of presumption, unless those that judge are sinless, which none are!

(Presumption is the ground, reason, or evidence lending probability to a belief. It is the inference as to the existence or truth of a fact not certainly known that is drawn from the known or proved existence of some other fact. In other words, it is a rush to judgment on something other than proof.)

(2) "BUT WE ARE SURE THAT THE JUDGMENT OF GOD IS ACCORDING TO TRUTH AGAINST THEM WHICH COMMIT SUCH THINGS."

The phrase, *"But we are sure that the Judgment of God is according to Truth,"* proclaims that which is never of presumption.

TRUE AND TRUTH

God being Omniscient (All-knowing), is qualified to judge, because He knows all things, even down to the motives of the heart. Consequently, His Judgment is always based on Truth, and in fact is Truth.

Actually, that which is *"True"* and that which is *"Truth"* are two different things altogether. All type of things are *"True,"* but that doesn't at all mean they are *"Truth."*

The Courts of man can come to judgment

only on the basis of that which is *"True,"* even if they get that close. That is the reason the Courts are so much found wanting. Actually, they have very little knowledge as to what *"Truth"* really is, in effect, with it actually being banned from the Courtroom, i.e., the Ten Commandments, or any part of the Bible for that matter. Such are not allowed in any type of Government Building, at least as regarding a Standard of Righteousness. This is done under the guise of the separation of Church and State. While such separation is right and commendable and even Scriptural, the actual Truth is, that it is more so a separation of God and State, which is the ruin of any Nation.

AN EXAMPLE

Some time back observing a Television program featuring a symposium of legal experts, addressing themselves to these very problems, something happened which further proves my point.

Someone ventured the question, *"But aren't we seeking Truth in the Courtroom?"*

The answer was revealing. One of the Judges answered that question by saying, *"There are two kinds of Truth, a Truth for the Prosecutor and a Truth for the Defense."*

Sitting there looking at this thing, my mouth fell open, at the absolute absurdity of such an answer. How in the world can there be two kinds of Truth?

SUBJECTIVE TRUTH AND OBJECTIVE TRUTH

Of course this man was operating on the premise of Subjective Truth. In other words, what may be Truth to you is not Truth to me, which means that Truth is relative, and, therefore, changes according to circumstances. In reality, such Truth is no Truth at all.

The type of *"Truth"* which Paul mentions here concerning God, is always Objective Truth, which, as well, is the Truth of the Word of God. It is *"Truth"* which never changes, because in real life terms, Truth cannot change, because if it does, it is really not Truth.

Sadder still, the man who gave this answer was Anthony Scalia, one of the sitting

Justices of the Supreme Court of the United States, the highest Court in the land.

The phrase, *"Against them which commit such things,"* proclaims a perfect Judgment, because it comes from Truth, and, consequently, cannot be denied.

Even though it is a negative, Truth must always be *"against"* the foul deed, but as well against the person who commits the deed, and will not repent.

(3) "AND THINKEST THOU THIS, O MAN, THAT JUDGEST THEM WHICH DO SUCH THINGS, AND DOEST THE SAME, THAT THOU SHALT ESCAPE THE JUDGMENT OF GOD?"

The beginning of the question, *"And thinkest thou this, O man, that judgest them which do such things, and doest the same . . . ?",* presents that which is very specific, and is meant to be. The *"thou"* is emphatic, *"you the Jew."*

Paul wants there to be no doubt whatsoever, as to what he is saying, and to whom it is directed.

However, let not the Church think that it is excused here, or anyone else for that matter. The Jew is singled out, because their argument was then the most predominant in the world. However, in the eyes of the Holy Spirit, they merely serve as an example for all.

The completion of the question, *"That thou shalt escape the Judgment of God?",* once again presents the *"thou"* as emphatic.

The Jew certainly thought, in many cases, that the privilege of his birth would of itself ensure his entrance into the Kingdom (Mat. 3:8-9): this was his practical conviction, whatever might be his proper creed.

Yet the emphatic *"Thou"* indicates that of all men the Jew, so distinguished by Special Revelation, should *least* have fallen into such an error. He is *"The servant who knew his Lord's Will,"* and whose judgment will be most rigorous if it is neglected, as will all who reject Light (Wuest).

THE MAN AND HIS MESSAGE

One can well imagine the anger in the hearts of many Jews, at least those who would bother to read this Epistle, regarding the Apostle's blunt statements respecting the lost

condition of the House of Israel. I speak of the Jews who were not followers of Christ, and, in fact, had rejected Christ. This is the reason they desired to kill Paul, and sought every means to do so.

Of course, the Apostle was writing exactly what the Holy Spirit told him to write; however, let it ever be said that such terminology used presently, would not be greeted by most in the modern Church with enthusiasm or approval. Paul would have been grievously labeled as a divider of men and a destroyer of unity. In fact, he was called those things, plus much worse!

Modern Preaching too much deals only with the safe issues, and not at all with that which will bring controversy. For instance, the self-righteousness of the modern Church is seldom mentioned, because it would upset some who indeed, fall into this category. I speak of so-called Religious Leaders! Catholicism is not to be mentioned either, despite the fact that this hellish Doctrine is taking untold millions to Hell. Catholics kick in quite heavily of their finances to particular Television Networks which call themselves *"Christian"*; consequently, those who Minister over those Networks are not allowed to deal with any of these pernicious Doctrines of works which are embraced by Catholicism, as well as many Protestants!

I suppose the Preachers on these Networks, take the position that at least they can preach some Truth, and better that than nothing at all. However, Paul said, *"I have not shunned to declare unto you all the Counsel of God"* (Acts 20:27).

THE JUDGMENT OF GOD

Men do not like to be told that they are going to face the *"Judgment of God,"* and that all of their good works and avid religion are not going to save them. They love to be told pleasing things, and made to feel comfortable in their error. Sadly, there are many Preachers who are ready and willing to oblige them.

However, I remind the Reader, that failure to preach all the Truth will in no way exempt those who are dying lost. In fact, those who would have been Saved had the Truth been presented to them, even as unsavory as it may have been, will in fact be lost forever. However, the blood of these lost souls will be required at the hands of the Preachers who *for whatever reason* would not preach all the Truth (Ezek. 3:17-21).

In fact, if a Preacher for any reason, refuses to preach all of the Truth, and irrespective of extenuating circumstances, I personally do believe that whatever Truth he does preach, will have little effect. The Holy Spirit is the One Who drives the Truth home to the sinner. As such, I do not believe He will allow the man of God, that is if he is truly a man of God, to pick and choose as to what he desires to deliver. Those who do that, are Teachers or Preachers with itching ears (II Tim. 4:3).

Paul said *"Preach the Word,"* and he did not mean part of the Word! (II Tim. 4:1-2).

Men are facing the *"Judgment of God,"* and I mean all men. The only thing that will stop this Judgment is the Whole Truth of the Word of God, and not a half-truth, etc. That is about like the Bailiff asking the prospective witness to put his hand on the Bible, and swear to tell some of the Truth, or what part he deemed nonoffensive!

(4) "OR DESPISEST THOU THE RICHES OF HIS GOODNESS AND FORBEARANCE AND LONGSUFFERING; NOT KNOWING THAT THE GOODNESS OF GOD LEADETH THEE TO REPENTANCE?"

The beginning of the question, *"Or despisest thou the riches of His Goodness and Forbearance and Longsuffering . . . ?"*, presents the Jew holding these things being graciously offered by God in contempt!

The idea is, that Judgment not coming immediately, causes some to think it is not coming at all, or else that they are right in their direction. Men love to justify themselves, and look for any opportunity to do so.

The idea is, that God is rich in *"Goodness"* which in this case means kindness. As well, He is rich in *"Forbearance"* which speaks of *"a holding back."* It implies something temporary which may pass away under new conditions. The idea is of a sinful, rebellious condition passing away due to Repentance. As well, He is rich in *"Longsuffering"* which speaks of *"patience and slowness in avenging wrongs."*

The word *"despiseth"* means *"to look down one's nose at a thing,"* in this case, the *"Goodness, Forbearance, and Longsuffering"* of God.

The conclusion of the question, *"Not knowing that the Goodness of God leadeth thee to Repentance?"*, means that this Grace of God is *intended* to lead the guilty party to Repentance. But Israel was looking down her nose at this Grace.

It is thought that Paul wrote the Book of Romans about 10 or 12 years before Jerusalem was totally destroyed by the Romans.

In fact, even though the Religious Leadership of Israel had crucified Christ not too much short of some 30 years before, they had suffered little or no ill effect regarding Judgment from God, or so it seemed. Jerusalem was prosperous at this time, with things going well. In A.D. 64 the long rebuilding of the Temple-Courts, which had begun in 19 B.C., was concluded. The 18,000 workmen thrown out of employment appeared to have been given *"unemployed work"* in *"paving the City with white stone."*

In A.D. 66 the long-smoldering discontent of the Jews against the Romans burst forth into open rebellion under the criminal incompetence of the present Roman Governor, Gessius Florus.

At that time, Palaces and Public Buildings were fired by the angered multitude, and after but two days' siege, the Fortress Antonia itself was captured by the Jews, set on fire and its garrison slain. (The Antonia was the Roman fortress situated on the edge of the Temple enclosure.)

FURTHER DEFEAT OF THE ROMANS

Cestius Gallus, hastening from Syria, was soon engaged in a siege of Jerusalem. The third wall was captured and some of the suburbs burned. But, when about to renew the attack upon the second wall, Gallus appears to have been seized with panic, and his partial withdrawal developed into an inglorious retreat in which he was pursued by the Jews down the pass to the Beth-horons as far as Antipatris.

SUPPOSED VICTORY

Defeating the Romans at this stage, caused the Leaders of Israel at this time to think they were about to gain their independence from the Roman yoke, and thereby gain their place once again of prominence and prestige. As such, they more than likely praised God for His helping them, when in reality He was not helping them at all. Actually, this victory cost the Jews dearly in the long run, as it led to the campaign of Vespasian and the eventual crushing of all their national hopes.

Vespasian commenced the conquest in the North, and advanced by slow and certain steps. Being recalled to Rome as Emperor in the midst of the war, the work of besieging and capturing the City itself fell to his son Titus.

None of the many calamities which had previously happened to the City are to be compared with this terrible siege. In none had the City been so magnificent, its fortifications so powerful, its population so crowded. In fact, it was Passover time, but, in addition to the crowds assembled for this event, vast numbers had hurried there, flying from the advancing Roman Army.

The loss of life was enormous, well over one million people, with the rest taken as slaves, and sold on the slave markets all over the world of that day.

THE SIEGE

The Siege commenced in the early part of A.D. 70, even though the war had begun some two years earlier with Vespasian taking Galilee. The Siege of Jerusalem lasted a total of 134 days.

Certain elements in Jerusalem desired to make peace with Titus, but were repulsed. Consequently, the constant demands for surrender by Titus were ignored. As a result, the miseries of the Siege and the destruction of life and property were at least as much the work of the Jews themselves as of their conquerors.

When the City finally fell, it was totally and completely destroyed. The Temple, exactly as Jesus had predicted, was torn down block by block, with even a harrow pulled by Oxen over the Temple site. In other words, nothing was left.

AFTER

For 60 years after its capture silence reigned over Jerusalem. We know that the

NOTES

site continued to be garrisoned, but it was not to any extent rebuilt. In A.D. 130 it was visited by the Roman Emperor Hadrian, who found but few buildings standing. Two years later (A.D. 132-135) occurred the last great rebellion of the Jews in their last uprising. It was put down with little difficulty.

With the suppression of this last effort for freedom, the remaining traces of Judaism were stamped out, and it is even said, as stated, that the very site of the Temple was plowed up by T. Annius Rufus. An Altar of Jupiter was placed upon the Temple-site, and the Jews at that time were excluded from Jerusalem on pain of death.

In A.D. 138 Hadrian rebuilt the City, giving it the name *"Aelia Capitolina."*

The Goodness of God in continuing to extend Mercy to the Jews, even after they had murdered His Son and their Messiah, was ridiculed and held in contempt. Consequently, it ultimately came to an end, with everything destroyed. They left God no alternative or choice, even as most of the world.

How Merciful is our God, how Gracious and Longsuffering. But yet, most mistake such for what it actually is, a plea for Repentance.

(5) "BUT AFTER THY HARDNESS AND IMPENITENT HEART TREASUREST UP UNTO THYSELF WRATH AGAINST THE DAY OF WRATH AND REVELATION OF THE RIGHTEOUS JUDGMENT OF GOD;"

The phrase, *"But after thy hardness and impenitent heart,"* speaks of a hardness toward God, with a refusal to repent. As is obvious, Paul is continuing to speak of the Jew, but actually these statements apply to anyone and for all time.

To understand the situation a little better, it was not so much that Israel needed to repent and refused to do so, but rather that they did not even admit that there was any need for Repentance. Actually, they were so spiritually blind and deaf from continued rebellion against God, that they could no longer properly evaluate anything which was spiritual. That is the trouble with rebellion which instigates wrong direction, it carries with it a frightful baggage.

"Impenitent" in the Greek is *"ametanoetos,"* and means *"unrepentant."* However, the idea of the word presents a

haughty, self-righteous, stubborn attitude, which refuses to believe or see.

To properly understand this situation, one has to compare Chapter 1 which is addressed to the world, with Chapter 2 which is primarily addressed to God's Chosen People, Israel. There is a difference!

ISRAEL EVEN WORSE . . .

Even though the condition of the world is frightful as would be obvious, the condition of Israel is even worse. As we have previously stated, the world was given some Light respecting Creation, but Israel was given great Revelation, consequently, held far more responsible. The consequence of their rebellion was a far harder heart even than those of the Gentiles. It is the same in the Church presently, and in fact, always has been.

The hardest hearted people in the world toward God, are not necessarily found in the dens of iniquity, etc., but rather sitting in Church!

To prove this point, Israel was totally destroyed in A.D. 70 as a direct result of what we are saying, while the world did not suffer such a fate, although certainly experiencing judgment of many sorts.

The phrase, *"Treasurest up unto thyself wrath against the Day of Wrath and Revelation of the Righteous Judgment of God,"* presents a frightful perspective.

The word *"treasurest"* in the Greek is *"thesauridzo."* It means *"to increase or store up"* (Mat. 6:19-20; II Cor. 12:14; II Pet. 3:7).

Sin is never overlooked by God. The Scripture plainly says, *"For the Wrath of God is revealed from Heaven against all ungodliness and unrighteousness of men, who hold the truth in unrighteousness"* (Rom. 1:18). This means every person has a choice. It is either the Wrath of God or Jesus Christ.

Paul is referring here to the Great White Throne Judgment which will take place at the Second Resurrection of Damnation, which will immediately follow the Thousand-Year Reign of Christ on Earth (Rev. Chpt. 20).

It is the Day of Judgment, the final display of Eternal Righteousness, when the *"forbearance"* will be forever over. It speaks not only of Israel, but the entirety of mankind and for all time. The persistently impenitent will

answer here (II Thess. 1:9).

It may be observed again here that it is against whom these indignant denunciations are hurled, and on the very ground of his, thus, setting himself up to judge while being himself guilty. Of him it is implied, not only that he shares the guilt of mankind, but also that he especially will not escape the Final Judgment.

Of others who, conscious of their own failings, seek sincerely after good, this is not said, however liable to condemnation on their own mere merits they may be. Indeed, the contrary is emphatically asserted in the verses that follow; nay, even Eternal Life is assured to such, whoever they may be, and under whatever dispensation, though it does not fall within the scope of the argument to explain in this place why or how.

It is important for us to see this clearly for an understanding of the drift of the Chapter, and of Paul's whole Doctrine with respect to human sin and its consequences (Barmby).

GRACE AND MERCY

In the core of the Text, we find that the denunciation hurled at the impenitent heart thundering with the Wrath of God, at the same time promises Mercy and Grace to the repentant one. This is the core and center of the Gospel. However, the implied Promise of Mercy and Grace, only make the Judgment more severe for those who refuse such Mercy and Grace.

It must ever be understood, that unlike man, the *"Judgment of God"* is always *"Righteous."* This means that no one will be able to look God in the Face and claim unfairness or ill-treatment. The idea is that the Mercy and Grace of God have been spurned over and over again, with the coming Judgment totally justified.

These two Chapters answer to us, at least in part, as to the disposition of the heathen who have never heard a Gospel Message. Some would claim that it is not fair for God to condemn them, especially considering that they have had little or no opportunity whatsoever. The answer is as follows:

1. The Creation itself is enough to alert all to the fact of the Creator, hence, God (Rom. 1:19-20).

2. Knowing from Creation there is a God, Paul said, *"That they should seek the Lord, if haply they might feel after Him, and find Him, though He be not far from every one of us"* (Acts 17:27).

It is here plainly said, that if man truly seeks after God, he will *"find Him."*

3. David wrote, *"The Eyes of the Lord are upon the Righteous, and His Ears are open unto their cry"* (Ps. 34:15).

As well, this Passage means that the Eyes of the Lord are also upon those, although not Righteous, but seek to be so. Jesus said, *"Come unto Me, all* (Righteous and unrighteous) *ye that labour and are heavy laden, and I will give you rest"* (Mat. 11:28-30).

In these who seek after the Lord, even as recorded above, the Lord answers by somehow getting the Gospel to them. But yet, if the Gospel is preached in any locality, far more will come to Christ as should be obvious, than if left to their own discretion. That is the reason that Jesus commanded that *"This Gospel of the Kingdom . . . be preached in all the world for a witness unto all Nations . . ."* (Mat. 24:14).

As well, those who have had the opportunity to hear the Gospel, as the Jews of old, if refused, will bring upon themselves a much more severe Judgment than those who have had little opportunity (Lk. 12:47-48).

(6) "WHO WILL RENDER TO EVERY MAN ACCORDING TO HIS DEEDS:"

This short verse gives us insight into several things:

1. First of all, it shoots down the idea of a sinning Salvation. Recognizing that no Believer is perfect, and that all of us have flaws because we still retain the sin nature, still, the Believer nowhere in the Word of God is given a license to sin. The *"sin a little bit every day"* religion is not found in the Bible.

2. The *"Deeds"* mentioned here, refer to those which have not been forgiven. In other words, God stands ready to forgive, wash, and cleanse any and every sinful act, if the Believer will only ask Him to do so (I Jn. 1:9); however, if forgiveness is not sought, the *"deed"* and its penalty stand. Of course, such could only come about because of rebellion and a hardened heart, especially considering

NOTES

that forgiveness is so easy to obtain.

3. God being God, and, therefore, Omnipotent, Omniscient, and Omnipresent, can and will make a Righteous Judgment, of that one can be sure.

4. *"Every man"* means that none are exempt. In fact, this is stated in this manner, because Paul is speaking here of the Jews, God's Chosen People. As such, they felt they were above the Judgment of God, but are told here that such is not so. Let all others understand accordingly!

5. Also, the *"Deeds"* mentioned here, refer both to good and bad. God notes all, and all will be addressed, of that all can be sure.

6. In no way is this speaking of a *"works"* Salvation as some might claim. The idea is that Salvation which is received only by Faith, and in fact, maintained by Faith, still, in no way sets aside the significance of good deeds, or the responsibility incurred respecting bad deeds. For that, all Believers will give account.

Likewise, just because a person is not a Believer, and in fact may not even believe there is a God, such conduct or thought in no way absolves one of responsibility respecting each and every action. They will give account.

7. Last of all, this points to personal responsibility. In other words, it is *"his deeds,"* meaning that responsibility or blame for one's personal actions cannot be shifted to others. Actually, this is one of the requirements for Repentance. The person must take responsibility before God, owning up to the sin, and not attempt to lay blame on others for one's personal wrongdoing. While there may be contributing factors by others, still, wrongdoing must be laid solely at the step of the perpetrator. Adam blamed Eve, and Eve blamed the Serpent, but such had no bearing on God and His Judgment.

(7) "TO THEM WHO BY PATIENT CONTINUANCE IN WELL DOING SEEK FOR GLORY AND HONOUR AND IMMORTALITY, ETERNAL LIFE:"

The phrase, *"To them who by patient continuance in well doing,"* now portrays those who are not trusting in place or position for their Salvation, but rather in Jesus Christ.

The statement points to the Jews who thought they were safe and secure simply because God had originally chosen them respecting great and mighty things. It was true, that they were the only people in the world who had a true knowledge of the Lord. But still, these things were Blessings extended through Mercy and Grace, and not because of personal worthiness. However, they had come to believe that they *were* personally worthy, and as such crucified their Lord.

The same problem is a danger to all Believers, and especially to Religious Denominations which the Lord has blessed. Somehow the Blessing once experienced and now enjoyed, tends to make one think that one has personally contributed something toward such, at least if one is not very careful.

The idea is, that one set one's mind, heart, soul, and strength on serving God, and continuing to do so, even though it may seem as if such is not being rewarded.

Jesus mentioned this when He said, *"Who then is a faithful and wise servant, whom his Lord hath made ruler over His household, to give them meat in due season?*

"Blessed is that servant, whom his Lord when He cometh shall find so doing."

He then addressed the one who evidently had begun in well-doing, but had ceased, saying to him, *"But and if that evil servant shall say in his heart, My Lord delayeth His Coming;*

"And shall begin to smite his fellow servants, and to eat and drink with the drunken;

"The Lord of that servant . . .

". . . shall cut him asunder, and appoint him his portion with the hypocrites: there shall be weeping and gnashing of teeth" (Mat. 24:45-51).

The phrase, *"Seek for glory and honour and immortality, Eternal Life,"* once again by using the word *"seek,"* abolishes place and position.

These things listed, are given on conditions of seeking them and by *"continuance in well-doing."*

To be sure, acts of obedience do not merit such Blessings, nor can they, because such are always provided by Grace; however, the seeking of such demonstrates that the seeker understands the worth of such Blessings and presents to God a proof of conformity to His

Will (Phil. 2:12; James 1:21-27).

Most of the world is seeking for glory, but it is the glory of man. As well, many seek for honor, but again it is honor bestowed by man. However, this speaks of *"Glory and Honour"* as given by God. Such always accompanies Salvation, and guarantees *"Immortality, Eternal Life."*

There could be nothing greater, as should be overly obvious!

(8) "BUT UNTO THEM THAT ARE CONTENTIOUS, AND DO NOT OBEY THE TRUTH, BUT OBEY UNRIGHTEOUSNESS, INDIGNATION AND WRATH,"

The phrase, *"But unto them that are contentious,"* carries the idea of contending with God.

Living for God is totally different than anything else one may imagine regarding the system of the world. One does not bargain with God, does not question God, and does not disobey.

The idea is not that of a Dictator, even as such would symbolize a worldly system, but rather that of the Creator.

First of all, every person must understand that God has our welfare at heart. He wants to do us good. He desires to give us good things. As well, He Alone knows the Way, which due to the Fall of man in the Garden of Eden, such Way has been obscured.

The idea is, that we do not know the Way, and must look to God constantly for Leading and Guidance. Also, we must understand that we are fallen creatures, and as such, are not worthy of even the least of God's Blessings. That is the reason the Lord said, *"To this man will I look, even to him that is poor* (understands that within ourselves we are spiritually and morally bankrupt) *and of a contrite spirit, and trembleth at My Word"* (Isa. 66:2).

To be frank, contention with God is the problem of the world. They may not look at it in that respect, but that is what it is. They do not want to obey Him, they do not want to follow Him, therefore, they either attempt to deny that He exists, or else attempt to ignore Him, or else make up their own religion, claiming that they are truly serving Him, when in reality it is of their own making! That is contention!

The phrase, *"And do not obey the Truth,"* proclaims the problem in a nutshell.

A SUBSTITUTION OF TRUTH

The Truth is the Word of God. It alone sets the Standard. It alone gives the right direction, because it is the Word of God.

Just last night, a man attempted to tell me that the Book of Mormon was the Word of God as well!

Pure and simple, no, it is not! It as the Koran is the work of man, and, therefore, of Satan. Those words may seem hard, but there is no other way in which they can be said. Man's problem has ever been that he has attempted to substitute something else for the Truth. That was Israel's problem, it is the problem of the world, and it is our problem if we are not very, very careful.

WHAT IS TRUTH?

First of all, and as we have said many times, Truth cannot adequately be explained as a philosophy, which is actually a pursuit of wisdom, or a search for a general understanding of values and reality by investigative means. However, one's viewpoint of wisdom or reality, at least according to their understanding changes constantly, according to outside influences. Therefore, such cannot be Truth, for Truth does not change, and in fact, cannot change, for if it does, it is not Truth! Truth is not an idea, it is a Person, and that Person is the Lord Jesus Christ, Who changes not (Mal. 3:6).

Actually, the Bible speaks of four things from which Truth springs:

1. Jesus is Truth (Jn. 14:6).
2. The Bible is Truth (Jn. 17:17).
3. The Holy Spirit is Truth (I Jn. 5:6).
4. The Anointing of the Holy Spirit is Truth (I Jn. 2:27).

The Holy Spirit Who is Truth, will not anoint anything which is not Truth, as should be obvious.

One must understand that the four listed here do not merely contain Truth, but are Truth. There is a vast difference in containing Truth, as all True Believers do, than being the Source of Truth, of which these four are.

It was not necessary to list the Father as

NOTES

being Truth, for Jesus is in the Father and the Father is in Jesus (Jn. 14:11). Actually, the same could be said of the Holy Spirit and not do violence to Scripture; however, the office work of Each will not allow such. For instance, Jesus came to reveal the Father to the world (Jn. 14:8-9). He did not come to reveal the Holy Spirit, inasmuch as the Holy Spirit came to help Him reveal the Father (Lk. 4:18-19). In fact, after His exaltation, Jesus sent back the Holy Spirit to more perfectly reveal the Son to the world as the True Revelation of the Father (Jn. 16:13-15).

SUBJECTIVE TRUTH

This is so-called Truth which changes with one's experience, which in reality is no Truth at all.

This aspect of Truth, at least as spoken here, is never primary in Scripture, unless in the question of Pilate before Jesus, when he posed the question, *"What is Truth?"* (Jn. 18:38).

He had so far missed the profound ethical sense in which Jesus used the word — everyone that is of the Truth heareth My Voice — that Jesus did not at all answer him, nor, indeed, does Pilate seem to have expected any reply to what was probably only the contempt of a skeptical attitude (Jn. 18:37).

Respecting that which is referred to as Subjective Truth, there is in the whole of Scripture a subjective idea, the product of Revelation or Inspiration in some form of working, that constitutes an ideal to be realized objectively. In this sense, Truth in its subjective form is correct, *but only as it corresponds with the Word of God.*

The Kingdom of God for example, is the formative idea of Scripture Teaching. In a definite sense the Kingdom exists now; however, it is still yet to be created. Respecting that which is to come, one could refer to such as subjective; however, Bible Students know that such is definite, because God's Word cannot fail, and, therefore, can look at it as objective.

It must be kept in mind, therefore, that only vaguely and indirectly does Truth have abstract meaning to the Biblical writers. The Holy Spirit through them was always direct and, therefore, concrete — in other words, not subjective, but rather objective.

LOGICAL TRUTH

This type of so-called Truth, once again which is no Truth at all, deals with logic. In other words, a series of events which lead to a predictable conclusion.

Truth in this sense involves the correspondence of concepts with facts. While this meaning of Truth is involved in Scripture, it is not the primary meaning anywhere save in a practical spiritual application, as in Ephesians 4:21; I John 2:4, 21.

While logic is not completely thrown out respecting the Bible, it definitely does not serve as a foundational principle. The reason is obvious:

God works from the principle of Faith which is not logical, at least according to the definition of the world, and in fact, defies all logic.

Actually, this is the reason that much of the Church world does not believe in Miracles. Miracles do not follow logic, and cannot be explained logically. So in many cases they are denied! The Truth is, that most who claim to follow Christ, do not at all actually know Him. In other words, they have never really been born again, so they cannot function from a realm of Faith, with logic being their only recourse, as such is the recourse of the world.

MORAL AND OBJECTIVE TRUTH

This is the Truth which changes not and is, therefore, the Truth of the Bible.

As someone has said, *"Taken in its full meaning of correspondence of idea with fact, of expression with thought and with intention, of concrete reality with ideal type, this is the characteristic sense of the meaning of the word 'Truth' in the Scriptures."* The aim of the Holy Spirit through the Word of God is to relate man to God in accordance with Truth. The idea is that man can know God and His Order as it is given in the Word of God. In achievement man is to make true in his own experience the idea of God that is given to him in the Word.

Truth is thus to be apprehended and thus to be produced in the life of the Believer.

NOTES

Actually, the characteristic teaching of Biblical Christianity is that the will to produce Truth, to do the Will of God, is the required attitude for apprehending the Truth.

In spotlighting this, Jesus said, *"If any man will do His Will, he shall know of the Doctrine, whether it be of God, or whether I speak of myself"* (Jn. 7:17). This accords with the entire teaching of the Bible.

Ephesians 1:18 suggests the importance of right attitude for learning Truth, while Ephesians 4:18 shows the effect of a wrong attitude in ignorance of vital Truth.

THE BIBLE IS THE STANDARD

Philosophy has continuously tried to find tests for Truth, and so has wrought out many theories, etc.

While this is done outside the Bible, the tendencies have been toward skepticism, which permeates much thinking. There is, therefore, a conclusion in religion (that which is not of the Lord) and morals (that which is not of the Bible) a tendency to obscure the distinction between what is and what ought to be. As a result, we find before us Subjective Truth, which in reality, is no Truth at all, at least if it is not based squarely on the Bible.

In the Bible the known Will of God is final for man as a Standard of Truth, not as arbitrary, but as expressive of God's Nature. In other words, the Will of God is not Truth simply because it is the Will of God, but rather because it *is* Truth. To say it another way, something is not necessarily right simply because God does it, but He does it because it *is* right.

God's Nature is all-comprehensive of fact and goodness, and so is, all and in all, the Source, Support, and Objective of all concrete being. The Will of God thus reveals, persuades to, and achieves the ideals and ends of complete existence. Consequently, the term *"Truth" is equivalent to the revealed Will of God.*

TRUTH IN MAN

Truth in man is in response to Truth in God, and is to be acquired on the basis of a Gift from God. This Gift comes by the way of Salvation as one accepts Christ, which then, and only then, opens up the Way of the Lord to the new Believer. The Holy Spirit then takes the Word of God and begins to make it real in the heart and life of the Believer, both in a spiritual and practical sense.

Highest Truth in correspondence to ideal is possible only by the working of *"The God of Truth"* in the spirit of man. Man's freedom to realize his being is dependent upon his receptive attitude toward the Son of God. Hence, Jesus saying, *"Come unto Me, all ye that labour and are heavy laden, and I will give you rest.*

"Take My yoke upon you, and learn of Me . . ." (Mat. 11:28-30).

Truth is reality in relation to the vital interests of the soul. It is primarily something to be *realized* and *done*, hence, coming to Jesus, rather than something to be learned or known. In other words, one learns about Jesus by coming to Him in the realm of Salvation, rather than by trying to study Him as one would study another man.

In the largest aspect Truth is God's Nature finding expression in His Creation, in Revelation, in Jesus Christ in Whom *"Grace and Truth came"* (Jn. 1:17).

It is impossible to find, understand or know Truth without first accepting and knowing Jesus Christ in the realm of Salvation, which then opens up the Word of God by the Holy Spirit. Otherwise, Truth is a blank, which reason the so-called great thinkers of this age, or any age, never seem to find. To do it without Jesus is impossible.

Truth is Personalized in Jesus Christ. He truly expresses God, presents the true ideal of man, in Himself summarizes the harmony of existence and becomes the Agent for unifying the disordered world. Hence, He *is* the Truth (Jn. 14:6), as well as its true expression (Jn. 1:1).

Similarly, the Holy Spirit is the Spirit of Truth because His function is to guide into all Truth, which He does relentlessly.

GOD AS TRUTH

God's Truth is especially noteworthy as a guaranty of merciful consideration of men. This is an extremely important element in the theology of the Old Testament, as it points to the Redeemer Who is to come, and

NOTES

in the New Testament, as it reveals the Redeemer Who has come.

However, the Redeemer rejected, corresponds as well with the Truth of God as an assurance to men of Righteous Judgment in condemnation of sin and sinners (I Sam. 15:29; Ps. 96:13; Rom. 2:2-8).

In general, the Truth of God stands for the consistency of His Nature and guarantees His full response in all the relations of the universe of which He is the Maker, Preserver, and End.

As related to God in origin and obligation, man is bound morally to see and respond to all the demands of his relations to God and to the order in which he lives under God.

Truth is not merely in utterance, nor is it only response to a specific command or word, but lies in the response of the will and life to the essential obligations of one's being (Ps. 15:2; 119:30; Prov. 12:19; 23:23; Isa. 59:4, 14-15; Jer. 7:28; 9:3; Hos. 4:1; Rom. 1:18, 25; Eph. 4:15; II Thess. 2:10-12).

THE FOUNDATION OF ALL TRUTH

Jesus Christ as the Truth of God becomes the Standard and Test for Truth in the spiritual obligations of men. As well, Jesus and the Word will always agree, because in Truth, Jesus is the Living Word (Jn. 1:1).

Whenever Jesus ceases to be the focal point in all things, one can rest assured that such religion is not of God, but rather man devised.

For instance, just a few nights ago, a man attempted to tell me that Mormonism was God's Way, with the Mormon Church His Church. In essence, he was saying that one had to belong to the Mormon Church to be Saved, which in effect, makes the Church the Saviour, which in effect, makes the whole thing a lie. In fact, the Catholic Church says the same thing. Regrettably, even some Protestant Churches have that idea, whether spelled out as succinctly or not.

Jesus Alone is the Saviour, and does not need the help of any Church, or religion. That is the reason True Christianity is not a religion but rather a relationship, and more particularly, a relationship with a Man, The Man, Christ Jesus (Jn. 3:16).

This is what makes the basic teaching of

the modern *"Promise Keepers"* so wrong. It teaches a man-devised unity, which ignores False Doctrine, claiming that we are to all love one another and accept one another.

I must remind the perpetrators of this thought, that True Love does not really lie to people and make them feel they are Saved when they really aren't. In other words, sending so-called converts back to Churches which do not teach the Word of God, is tantamount to consigning that person to spiritual death. No, it is never Love, at least as the Bible describes Love, to tell man a lie, and especially a lie of such horrifying consequences as this.

Jesus Christ is the Standard, but if we divorce Jesus from the Word of God, in effect, we have *"another Jesus,"* who Paul describes, and which most of the modern Church world presently has (II Cor. 11:4).

(Some of the material on Truth was derived from the teaching of William Owen Carver.)

The phrase, *"But obey unrighteousness, indignation and wrath,"* portrays the opposite of verse 7, contrasting the two — good and evil.

We observe here how the expressions as given by the Holy Spirit are heaped up, significant of the Divine indignation against high-handed sin, unrepented and unatoned for, of which the Apostle, in very virtue of his view of the Eternal, had an awful sense.

"Unrighteousness" in the Greek Text is *"adikia,"* and means *"legal injustice and wrongfulness of character, life and acts."*

"Indignation" in the Greek is *"thumos,"* and means *"fierceness."*

"Wrath" is *"orge,"* and means *"violent passion."*

Consequently, we have in this one statement by Paul the results of man's fallen condition.

Outside of God man simply cannot do right. That is the reason force of Law is required, whether for individuals or Nations.

The United States is the policeman of the world at this time, whether we like it or not. That responsibility is thrust upon us for the simple reason, that the United States probably has more Christians per capita than any other Nation in the world, or else is near the

NOTES

top of that list. Whether it is confessed or not, Bible Christianity sets the only right and sensible Standard for Life and Godliness (II Pet. 1:3-4). If one thinks not, let one study Islam, the major adversary of Bible Christianity, and the difference and reasons will become quickly obvious.

Sadly and regrettably, concerning the Fall of man, mankind continues to address his terrible problem, for the most part, outside of God. The trouble is, man is so deceived by his lost condition, that he doesn't really realize his actual state. Being spiritually blind, deaf, and lost, he has no way to properly evaluate his condition, continuing to think that the problem is minor, and can be corrected with a slight adjustment. As sad as it is, it is understandable that the world would be in that plight, but not so understandable respecting the Church. It too falls into lockstep with the world, recommending everything but Jesus, Who Alone can rectify this terrible situation.

(9) "TRIBULATION AND ANGUISH, UPON EVERY SOUL OF MAN THAT DOETH EVIL, OF THE JEW FIRST, AND ALSO OF THE GENTILE;"

The phrase, *"Tribulation and anguish, upon every soul of man that doeth evil,"* presents the natural results of the unnatural act of sin. When one gets to the bottom line, *"evil"* is the cause of all the problems in the world, and more specifically, the evil that man commits. In other words, he brings it upon himself.

This is the Scriptural logic of God which man denies, but which is guaranteed in its conclusion. If men follow the Lord, God's logic demands Blessing. Otherwise, it demands *"tribulation and anguish."*

Deuteronomy Chapter 28 in the Old Testament gives a perfect example of both — Blessings and Curses. Actually, one of the very purposes of the Law was to spell out what God meant by Righteousness and unrighteousness. In that 28th Chapter of Deuteronomy He lists the rewards of both. To be sure, that part of the Law did not die with its fulfillment by Christ, but holds true unto this hour, and will ever continue to do so. The reasons are obvious, it cannot do otherwise, for the simple fact that the Goodness of God will never change, and the results of sin cannot change as well.

Also, and that there be no mistake, this is binding on *"every soul of man."* None are exempt!

The phrase, *"Of the Jew first, and also of the Gentile,"* is said in this way for the obvious reasons.

First of all, the Jews had come to believe that they were exempt from the same type of judgment heaped upon the Gentiles, due to the fact that they were the people of the Book, in effect, God's Chosen. However, the Holy Spirit through the Apostle makes it abundantly clear, that these results whether of Righteousness or of unrighteousness, cannot vary, due to the very nature of what they are. In other words, poison does not discriminate, and as Paul will say in a moment, neither does God.

By Paul placing the Jew first, he is saying that the Truth is actually the opposite of what the Jew thinks. They were the first to be given the Righteousness of God in respect to the Prophets and the Law of Moses. Consequently, they will be the first to taste of the Wrath of God as well, which they were.

THE JUDAISM OF JESUS' DAY

The Judaism of the First Century was no longer that supernaturally revealed system in which the Israelite was taught to look ahead in Faith to a coming Sacrifice which God would offer for his sins, this Sacrifice being typified by the Tabernacle Offerings and Priesthood. It was merely an ethical cult, preaching a Salvation-by-works Message. Consequently, it little, truly, knew God anymore. In fact, that was the world of Paul before his Conversion, hence, his terrible persecution against the followers of Christ. Regrettably, much of the modern Church falls into the same category as the Judaism of old.

THE MODERN CHURCH

Three sins characterize the modern Church even as Israel or Judea of the First Century.

1. The first sin is *"control."* As the Religious Leadership of Jesus' day had taken the control away from God, exerting that prerogative for themselves, so has the modern Church. The Headship of Christ has been abrogated in favor of man. Actually, that is the reason the Sanhedrin hated Jesus so much, they simply could not control Him. Consequently, they would destroy Him, even as the modern Church seeks to destroy all that it cannot control, and for the simple reason, as the Sanhedrin of old, what it cannot control it sees as a threat.

2. *"Self-righteousness"* is the second great sin. It was acute during the time of Christ and is acute presently. The modern Pentecostal Denominations are a case in point.

When the Holy Spirit began to fall at the turn of the century, fulfilling that of the Prophet Joel, which he had spoken in the Second Chapter of his Book, concerning the Latter Rain, etc., the old-line Religious Denominations fought it severely, and primarily because of self-righteousness. Strangely enough, the situation has now come full circle, with those who were once opposed now doing the opposing. Once again it is self-righteousness.

3. The third sin is a *"denial of the Word of God."* Of course they deny their denial. Nevertheless, when one sets aside the Word of God in favor of their own rules and regulations, which in fact oppose the Word of God, no other conclusion can be reached. In Jesus' day, Israel had done the very same thing. Jesus plainly said, *"Thus have ye made the Commandment of God of none effect by your tradition."*

He then said, *"But in vain they do worship Me, teaching for Doctrines the commandments of men"* (Mat. 15:6-9).

Men very easily become lifted up within themselves, and religious men most of all. Israel was boasting so much of God, but in reality had very little of God. Most of the modern Church does the same, and with the same results.

(10) "BUT GLORY, HONOUR, AND PEACE, TO EVERY MAN THAT WORKETH GOOD, TO THE JEW FIRST, AND ALSO TO THE GENTILE:"

The phrase, *"But glory, honour, and peace, to every man that worketh good,"* once again, and even as we have said, presents God's logic, which proclaims if certain things are done, certain things will follow.

"Glory" in the Greek is *"doxa,"* and means

"dignity and praise," referring to the fact, that the Lord literally praises those who follow Him.

"Honour" in the Greek is *"time,"* and means *"esteem,"* referring to the fact that this is God's True Self-esteem, which is actually brought about by hiding self in Christ, making Him All in All. Consequently, the modern self-esteem teaching is error and actually devilish (James 3:14-15).

"Peace" in the Greek is *"eirene,"* and means *"prosperity, quietness, rest, to set at one again,"* referring to the enmity of God against man being removed, because of Salvation.

Once again, and irrespective of the individual whether Jew or Gentile, bad sinner or so-called good sinner, the results will be the same.

The phrase, *"To the Jew first, and also to the Gentile,"* is given again to show the place of prominence respecting the Jew, but which they forfeited.

However, it also brings out in a striking way the clear Doctrine of the New Testament that the Jews had no monopoly of Divine favor with respect to final Salvation. Whatever advantages certain races of mankind seem undoubtedly to have above others in this world (and that this has been, and is so, with other races as well as the Jews is obvious), all men are described as standing on an exactly equal footing at the bar of eternal equity (Barmby).

(11) "FOR THERE IS NO RESPECT OF PERSONS WITH GOD."

In the Greek *"Respect of persons"* is *"prosopolempsia,"* and means literally *"an accepter of a face."* Literally translated, the verse reads, *"For there is not a receiving of face in the Presence of God."* That is, God does not receive or accept anybody's face.

One who has respect of persons, which is the opposite of God, is one who has respect to the outward circumstances of men and not to their intrinsic merits, and so prefers, as the more worthy, one who is rich, highborn, or powerful, and has little or no respect for one who is destitute of such gifts.

Paul is primarily saying that though the Jew has had great advantages, he shall be justly judged for his use of them, not treated as a favorite of Heaven. Even though there

were great advantages, as well there was great responsibility, as it always is with God (Wuest).

(12) "FOR AS MANY AS HAVE SINNED WITHOUT LAW SHALL ALSO PERISH WITHOUT LAW: AND AS MANY AS HAVE SINNED IN THE LAW SHALL BE JUDGED BY THE LAW;"

The phrase, *"For as many as have sinned without Law shall also perish without Law,"* tells us two things:

1. First of all, God will not hold the Gentile world accountable to the Law of Moses, for this is the Law of which He speaks, as He will hold responsible the Jews.

2. However, all Gentiles during the time of the Old Testament, will answer for their sins, and be eternally lost, except for those few who accepted God's Covenant, which a few did. In fact, merely having the Law of Moses, as important as that was, and as beneficial as it was in many ways, did not within itself guarantee Salvation.

In other words, while the Lord will not hold the Gentiles accountable to the Law of Moses in Old Testament times, in no way means that He will not hold them accountable for their sin. The fact of sin is not abrogated in any case respecting ignorance.

The phrase, *"And as many as have sinned in the Law shall be judged by the Law,"* in effect places the Jew in a more responsible and even fearful situation. In fact, the Jews will be judged for their sins and as well, the added Light of the Law of Moses.

It is ironical, the Jews had come to the place that they thought that merely having the Law guaranteed Salvation, while the Gentiles thought that ignorance of the Law exonerated them. Neither was true!

(13) "(FOR NOT THE HEARERS OF THE LAW ARE JUST BEFORE GOD, BUT THE DOERS OF THE LAW SHALL BE JUSTIFIED."

The phrase, *"For not the hearers of the Law are just before God,"* verifies my statement that the mere having of the Law, or even hearing the Law, saves no one. It is the same with the Gospel, having and hearing it affords no Salvation within itself.

As well, the word *"hearers"* refers to constant hearers who were educated in the Law of Moses. The Truth presented here is, that no degree of familiarity with the Law or with the Gospel avails if it is not obeyed.

By the Law of Moses was the *knowledge* of sin and consequent guilt, but not the power of avoiding sin.

The phrase, *"But the doers of the Law shall be justified,"* is used by Paul in this manner to merely make a point, and not to aver in any manner that the keeping of the Law actually justified, which it didn't. In other words, the Jew was shot down on both counts.

First of all, merely having the Law did not save, and as well all attempts at keeping it, even as they should have done, did not save. As we have previously stated, there was Blessing in attempting to keep the Law, but there was no Salvation (Deut. Chpt. 28).

Considering how much that Paul refers to the Old Testament (and which Jesus did for that matter), it is extremely hurtful that many Christians little know or understand the Old Testament. They incorrectly reason that it is a Covenant which applied only to the Jews, and inasmuch as Jesus has now come, the Old Covenant is of no more consequence. Nothing could be further from the Truth.

While Jesus definitely has come, and definitely has fulfilled the requirements of the Law, even down to the taking of its curse, still, if the Believer does not have a working knowledge of the Old Testament, which is actually the Foundation of the New, then it is frankly impossible for him to understand the New Testament. That is the reason that many Preachers come up with weird Doctrines, they simply don't know the Old Testament. Actually, every single Word of Instruction in the New Testament, is already found somewhere in the Old.

(14) "FOR WHEN THE GENTILES, WHICH HAVE NOT THE LAW, DO BY NATURE THE THINGS CONTAINED IN THE LAW, THESE, HAVING NOT THE LAW, ARE A LAW UNTO THEMSELVES:"

The phrase, *"For when the Gentiles, which have not the Law,"* refers to Old Testament times, and that Gentiles did not have the Law of Moses.

THE LAW OF MOSES

The Law of Moses was an instrument which went into exact detail as to how that man should conduct himself toward God and his fellowman. Absolutely nothing was left out, even down to the most minute detail, so that everyone would know and understand. Being the only Law of God in the world, it was the only Law which was fair and equal for all, and, consequently, provided a standard of living for the Jews which was the envy of the world of that day.

As well, within the myriad of instructions pertaining to the Law, were the Sacrifices, which in fact, were instructions within themselves. They were meant to portray the coming Redeemer, in effect serving as a substitute until His arrival.

The Sacrifices instructed man that he was a sinner, and in no way could save himself. As well, it taught him that he needed Blood Atonement which was symbolized by the shedding of blood from the innocent victim, which pertained to Lambs, Goats, Bullocks, and Rams. The fires on the Brazen Altar spoke of the Judgment of God on sin, with the animal itself symbolizing the coming Christ, Who would give His Own Life as a Sin Offering, in order to pay the terrible price demanded by sin, which is death (Rom. 6:23).

The Gentiles had none of this, and were, therefore, ignorant regarding the specifics.

THE GENTILES

The phrase, *"Do by nature the things contained in the Law,"* refers to several things:

1. While the Gentiles did not have the Law of Moses, still, their conscience told them some semblance of right and wrong.

2. This means that no man is absolutely without the knowledge of God's Will, though he have little truthful information.

3. While this inbred instinct or knowledge does not translate into Salvation, still, it does once again show, even as Paul has already said, that man is *"without excuse"* (Rom. 1:20).

The phrase, *"These, having not the Law, are a Law unto themselves,"* proclaims that their judgment will center around that which they do know. Once again, this has nothing to do with Salvation.

THE JUDGMENT

In the Judgment which is to come (Rev.

20:11-15), the Judgment in effect will be twofold:

1. All without Christ and for all time, are immediately judged as lost. Actually, only the lost will appear at the Great White Throne Judgment.

2. The amount of punishment prescribed, which is the second part of the Judgment, will depend on many things. Actually, the idea even as Paul opens up this scenario, is that the Jews who refuse to walk in the great Light which was given them, will be punished far more severely in eternal Hell, than the Gentiles who had very little Light (Lk. 12:47-48).

The same holds true pertaining to the Gospel. To use a phrase, *"Hell will burn extremely hot for those who have heard the Gospel of Jesus Christ over and over, or else had the opportunity to hear, but little heeded, by comparison with those who have had little opportunity at all."*

The sinful condition is somewhat like a disease. Whether it is fair or unfair, the person still has the disease. As such, those who obtained it unfairly will suffer the same results of dying prematurely, even as the one who contracted such by his own misconduct. The results are the same in both cases, as would be obvious. The fact of sin follows the same course.

CONDEMNATION

As we have previously stated, God does not really condemn men for their sinful condition, knowing they were born into such, actually a condition over which they had no control. However, that in no way alters the fact of their lost condition. What God does condemn, and He does so strongly, is man's failure to take advantage of the Atonement provided by the Lord at great price. In essence, that is why men die without God and go to Hell (Jn. 16:8-11).

Due to Adam, man cannot help what he is, namely a sinner, and which he is a victim through no fault of his own; however, he is woefully responsible for failing to accept the Redemption freely given by the Lord Jesus Christ.

That is at least one of the reasons, and actually I think the great reason, that the

Lord insists upon all having the opportunity to hear the Gospel. That is also the reason the Great Commission of taking the Gospel to the world was the last Message given by Jesus Christ (Mk. 16:15). Man must have the opportunity to hear, whether he accepts or rejects. If he has the opportunity to hear even once, he will not then be able to point a finger of accusation at God at the Great White Throne Judgment.

Even though such condition will not save him, even though legitimate, it *will* cause the Church to look very bad, considering that it is our responsibility to tell this story to all of mankind, and without fail.

WORLD EVANGELISM

That is why I have a consuming burden to personally take the Gospel to the world. Not only am I called to do this, and as directly as one could ever be, I know how important all of this is, at least as much as a poor human being can know.

I firmly believe that when Christians stand before Christ to give account for this great Salvation afforded unto us, I think very high on the list will be our participation individually in the realm of World Evangelism. Did we do what we could do? Did we pray as much as we could have for the lost of the world, and did we give of our means as much as we could to help carry out this task?

I am afraid the answer to those questions is going to be one of shame for many, if not most!

(15) "WHICH SHEW THE WORK OF THE LAW WRITTEN IN THEIR HEARTS, THEIR CONSCIENCE ALSO BEARING WITNESS, AND THEIR THOUGHTS THE MEAN WHILE ACCUSING OR ELSE EXCUSING ONE ANOTHER;)"

The phrase, *"Which shew the work of the Law written in their hearts,"* means that no one, even if they have never heard of the Name of Jesus, is absent of all Light.

The idea is, that the Fall in the Garden of Eden did not erase totally and completely every vestige of the Image of God in man. This does not mean that he has any inbred spirituality in his fallen state, but that the knowledge of right and wrong, although greatly jaded and weakened, still remains to some small degree. Actually, the laws which men attempted to formulate before the Law of Moses was given, are proof of that fact. Even though these laws were greatly unequal, thereby strongly leaning toward certain favored segments of society, still, they were attempts to address murder, stealing, lying, etc. The reason is simple, such instinct of right and wrong is written in the heart.

The phrase, *"Their conscience also bearing witness,"* presents that which is obvious in all, but yet not a very reliable guide, and because it is easily seared or jaded.

WHAT IS THE CONSCIENCE?

All of us know the inner nagging that drags our thoughts to that which is right and wrong. If one does something wrong, one is smitten in one's conscience, making one feel badly about the act, that is, if the conscience is not jaded or seared as said.

However, it being there at all, proclaims the veracity of that which Paul addresses.

THE GREEK WORD FOR CONSCIENCE

Conscience is a Greek concept, with a few of its aspects expressed by that complex Old Testament term *"heart."*

For the average inhabitant of the New Testament world, the idea of conscience was familiar — and distasteful, and because it always signified wrongdoing, that is if it signified anything at all.

The Greek word for *"conscience"* is *"syneidesis."* Originally the word signified a look back into one's past, an evaluation of remembered events in relationship to good and evil.

To the Greeks, as reflected in their literature, conscience was usually a *"bad conscience,"* one that relentlessly plagued its owner by accusations about past failures.

The Bible shows how God deals with our bad consciences, and this revelation adds much to our understanding of human moral nature.

THE PAGAN CONSCIENCE

Paul argues that those with Old Testament Law and those without it are equally without Righteousness, even as we are now studying; he writes that Pagans *"show that*

the requirements of the Law are written on their hearts, their consciences also bearing witness, and their thoughts now accusing, are defending them." What Paul describes is the moral faculty that God has designed into human nature.

Even those without specific knowledge of God's Standards realize intuitively that moral issues exist, and they go on to establish standards in moral areas. But being sinners, they fall short of the goodness that is expressed in their standards, hence, the problems in America at present, as well as the entirety of the world. In fact, if man leaves God out of the picture, he doesn't even come up to his own standards, much less those which are of God.

Consequently, aware of guilt in this matter, they attempt to quiet an accusing conscience by blaming others and/or by excusing their own actions due to extreme circumstances, etc.

The unbeliever, even the Pagan has a conscience. Its existence stands as a witness to man's moral nature.

THE INFORMED CONSCIENCE

Paul graphically points out that the Jew took comfort in knowing God's Will, being *"instructed by the Law"* (Rom. 2:18). Consequently, the Jews not only shared humanity's moral sense, but they also had unique access to true moral content, namely the Law.

In the Law, the Jews had a Revelation from God of His Own Standards of right and wrong. Thus, moral faculty was wedded with accurate knowledge of moral content.

But Paul goes on to argue that just as the Pagans act against their uninformed conscience, the Jews have acted against their informed conscience. All humans break the moral code in which they themselves believe. Consequently, Gentiles and Jews are all sinners.

Conscience serves as a witness to the rightness of moral standards. But conscience also serves as a witness against those who violate those standards. Yet, conscience has never succeeded in producing a truly moral person, simply because, as the Law, it can only point out the evil, not give power to bring about Righteousness.

THE INADEQUACY OF CONSCIENCE

Scripture suggests a number of reasons why conscience is inadequate as a moral guide, although a witness:

1. Conscience exists as a faculty of moral evaluation. There is no guarantee that one's personal evaluation, however, is correct. What a person's conscience says is right may not agree with what God says is right.

2. Even a Believer's conscience may be weak. Such can be linked to one that has not yet attained a mature understanding of Christian Faith. In Paul's day, those with weak consciences were troubled about matters such as eating meat and determining which days should be considered special (Rom. 14:1-6). By focusing on inconsequentials, such Believers began to judge or to look down on those who disagree with them (Rom. 14:9-10). Thus, a weak conscience may trap a person into serious sins.

3. A person's conscience can be *"defiled."* Someone with a weak conscience is particularly susceptible to acting against what he or she believes is right, and thus, this person is made to feel guilty (I Cor. 8:7). Continual violation of conscience can corrupt a conscience and bring a constant state of defilement (Titus 1:15).

It should be clear from these observations that Scripture does not regard conscience as an infallible guide anymore than as a motivator of good behavior.

THE CLEANSED CONSCIENCE

The Book of Hebrews shows us another aspect of conscience. The writer looks back at the Old Testament Sacrificial system, with its repeated Sacrifices for sins, noting that they were *"not able to clear the conscience of the worshipper"* (Heb. 9:9).

The endless Sacrifices were in fact a *"constant reminder of sins"* (Heb. 10:3), and, as well, a constant testimony to the worshiper that his past was with him and that he stood guilty before God. All of an individual's acts of sin were stored up in his conscience, shouting out his guilt and draining away any confidence in the possibility of a different future.

GUILT

Actually, guilt does this to us. It saps our strength and makes us unwilling to evidence Faith. It robs us of the hope that our future will be different from our past.

Hebrews presents this argument to show a contrast. What the Old Testament Sacrifices could not do, the Blood of Jesus accomplishes. That Blood, offered to God, does *"cleanse our conscience from acts that lead to death, so that we may serve the Living God"* (Heb. 9:14). Through Christ we are cleansed *"once for all"* (Heb. 10:2, 10, 14).

With our sins forgiven and ourselves cleansed, we have the assurance that God Himself no longer remembers our lawless acts (Heb. 10:17).

Cleansing is both objective, accomplished by Jesus' Sacrifice, and subjective, experienced increasingly as we appropriate what Jesus has done for us. There will be times when our conscience will still drag our glance back to the past and shout out accusations. Then we must remember that our sins are forgiven (and the past gone). We must forget them (and it) and look ahead to how we can serve the Living God.

As we continue to have confidence in God's Word and to act on the Promise of a fresh future, our confidence will be rewarded. As we do the Will of God, we will receive the fulfillment of that Promise (Heb. 10:35-36). Our consciences will be cleansed, never to nag us again. And we will be freed to look only ahead, enthusiastic about our opportunities to serve the Lord.

THE CLEAR CONSCIENCE

God's forgiveness cleanses the conscience. A clear conscience is something else. It is the testimony of our conscience that we have chosen and have done what is right. Paul writes, *"I strive always to keep my conscience clear before God and man"* (Acts 24:16).

The Christian maintains a clear conscience by living in harmony with the Truths unveiled in God's Word (II Cor. 1:12; I Tim. 1:5, 19; 3:9; II Tim. 1:3; I Pet. 3:16, 21).

We of course want to keep our conscience clear. But we also need to remember that God, not the conscience, is our Judge. *"My conscience is clear,"* Paul writes, *"but that does not make me innocent. It is the Lord Who judges me"* (I Cor. 4:4-5). Thus, we see again the inadequacy of conscience. With all its other deficiencies, it is not even capable of penetrating to inner Truth about our own guilt or innocence.

RESPONSIBILITY TO THE CONSCIENCES OF OTHERS

Scripture is the objective criteria by which we evaluate not only our actions but also the content of our conscience.

As we have seen, some Believers have weak consciences. They have not matured to distinguish clearly between what is truly good and what is evil, nor to discern what is morally indifferent.

This is particularly a problem in matters of person conviction. In matters about which God has spoken, Believers should have no trouble seeing what is right. But there are many things about which God has no definite word, and Believers have different beliefs and convictions on those things.

Such issues are considered in Romans Chapter 14. In each case discussed, Believers are told to remember that Jesus Alone is Lord. No one has the right to take Christ's place by judging or by imposing his or her own standards on others (Rom. 14:1-10).

Thus, each person must act in accordance with his or her own conscience and be careful not to make the attempt to influence others to act against their convictions (Rom. 14:13-16). We are to make every effort to *"do what leads to peace and to mutual edification"* (Rom. 14:19).

How are we to do this? Paul says, *"Whatever you believe about these things keep between yourself and God"* (Rom. 14:22), warning us not to fall into foolish debates about secondary issues.

AND FINALLY . . .

Conscience provides evidence of humanity's moral nature. But conscience is not an adequate guide to moral behavior. The conscience cannot move us to do right, and all too often its judgments are faulty.

Moreover, conscience reminds us constantly of past failures and of guilt. It robs

NOTES

us of confidence and hope for a better future. But God has acted in Christ to provide a forgiveness that cleanses our conscience, releasing us from bondage to our past. With God's forgiveness, that past is wiped away, and you and I can go on to live in obedience to God.

Believers want to maintain a clear conscience. This is accomplished by doing what we believe to be God's Will, and what is obvious in His Word. Our understanding of God's Will grows, and our consciences become stronger as we mature in our Faith.

Within the Christian community, conscience can become a problem. This happens with some insisting that their personal convictions are the standard that should govern the believing community. God's Word on this issue is clear.

We are to recognize the inadequacy of conscience and acknowledge the Lordship of Jesus. Where there is no clear Word from God, each individual must be free to respond as he or she believes Jesus desires.

Rather than make such matters issues in the Christian community, *"Whatever you believe about these things,"* as stated, *"keep between yourself and God"* and build unity through Love for one another and by mutual commitment to Jesus.

(The statement on conscience was derived from the teaching of Lawrence O. Richards.)

The phrase, *"And their thoughts the mean while accusing or else excusing one another,"* as is here obvious, does not prove a reliable guide, but at least claims the existence of a conscience, which pertains more or less, to the right way.

(16) "IN THE DAY WHEN GOD SHALL JUDGE THE SECRETS OF MEN BY JESUS CHRIST ACCORDING TO MY GOSPEL."

The phrase, *"In the day when God shall judge the secrets of men by Jesus Christ,"* lays to rest any idea that Judgment will be on any other basis. In other words, even though conscience will be a witness, as possibly will be many other things, still, Jesus Alone is the criteria. The whole world, and for all time, must answer to Jesus Christ.

I realize that many will claim that before He was born into the world, that men could not be responsible to someone Who did not exist!

First of all, Jesus is God, and even though He had not previously existed as a man, as God He has always existed. As such, the entirety of the human race is answerable to Him and for all time.

Admittedly, His Coming into the world in the Incarnation, made it much easier to receive and accept Him, but, still, He was typified in the Sacrifices even from the beginning (Gen. 4:3-5).

As well, whether men believe that Jesus is the Son of God or not, has no effect or bearing on them one day answering to Him at the Judgment. He is God's Son, and the One Who paid the price for man's Redemption, and, consequently, to Him man will answer!

In that day, no one will be able to attempt to shift the blame to others, or to extenuating circumstances, etc. God knows every single secret of every heart, and will judge accordingly. In other words, the judging will be perfect and beyond question.

The phrase, *"According to my Gospel,"* speaks of the New Covenant which was given to Paul, in effect making him the Moses of the New Testament. That *"Gospel"* spans Romans through the Book of Hebrews, a total of some 14 Epistles.

(This does not mean the other Epistles written by Peter, John, James and Jude are not a part of the Gospel, for they are in every respect. However, they complement what Paul has already said, rather than add other material.)

WHAT IS THE GOSPEL?

In the New Testament, *"The Gospel"* is the sum total of Saving Truth about Jesus as it is communicated to lost humanity. The Gospel is called the Good News about Jesus (Mk. 1:1) and the *"Gospel of God"* (Rom. 1:1; 15:16; II Cor. 11:7; I Thess. 2:8-9; I Tim. 1:11), of *"Christ"* (I Cor. 9:12; II Cor. 2:12; 10:14; Gal. 1:7; I Thess. 3:2; II Thess. 1:8), and of our *"Salvation"* (Eph. 1:13).

JESUS

Through Jesus, the Good News comes. His Shed Blood on Calvary's Cross allows God to forgive sinners of all their sins. In Jesus the invitation is given to accept that forgiveness as a free gift and so to come into personal

relationship with God.

When distorted by a denial of Who Jesus is, or by rejection of the Truth that everything that God works in us is of Grace, appropriated by Faith, and guaranteed by the Holy Spirit, that Gospel is *"a different Gospel — which is no Gospel at all"* (Gal. 1:6-7).

THE GOSPEL AND THE KINGDOM

While in the Epistles the word *"Gospel"* is clearly focused on the Saving Work of God in Jesus, it is important to note that at times in the Gospels (Matthew - John) a different Message of Good News is in view.

This is the Good News that God's Kingdom is at hand, and because Jesus was Personally and Physically present on Earth at that time. Regrettably, the offer of the Kingdom was refused by Israel at that time, which subjected the world to continued war, strife, pillage, sickness, etc. However, that will be rectified at the Second Coming, when Israel will finally accept the Kingdom, but only because they have accepted the King, The Lord Jesus Christ as their Messiah and Saviour. The Kingdom will then be established throughout the entirety of the Earth, and called *"The Kingdom Age."*

Consequently, it is important when reading the Gospels (Matthew - John) to note that when the phrase *"of the Kingdom"* is added to *"Gospel,"* a somewhat different Message is in view than that intended by the Epistles.

THE GOSPEL — THE WORD OF GOD

Inasmuch as all of humanity will be judged by, and according to, what Jesus Christ has done in His Great Work of Redemption, and that the particulars are given to us in Paul's Epistles, we should learn all we can about this which is so very, very important.

First of all, to the many who entered into the Old Covenant with the Lord, as would be obvious before the First Covenant was given, their Salvation was what one might call *"on credit."* In other words, even though Jesus had not yet come, they were credited Salvation by the means of simple Faith. In fact, it is the same presently, with one exception. Jesus has now come, fulfilling all the predictions of the Prophets, and, consequently, making Salvation a Finished Work.

THE VERACITY OF OUR MODERN BIBLES

When I say *"modern Bibles,"* I am primarily speaking of the King James Version. Although there are many Versions, it is my opinion that most of them are more interpretations than anything else, which tends to favor particular Doctrines, etc.

After some investigation, it is my thinking that the King James is closer to the original Texts, with one or two others possibly holding similar credibility.

The New Testament was originally written in Greek. This was the unified language of the Roman Empire in the First Century, actually a language of international exchange. Where a person knew more than one language during that time, it was usually the case that he knew Greek as his second language, which almost all did.

This is one of the factors that caused the tremendous and rapid spread of Christianity in the Roman World. The language was one, which presented a greater understanding.

For 1500 years, until the age of printing, the Manuscripts of the New Testament were copied by hand. During this time mistakes crept in, as would be obvious. But through the labors of Textual critics, these mistakes have been eliminated, with the result that in the best Texts of the Greek New Testament in use today, Scholars tell us that 999 words out of every 1000 are the same as those in the original Manuscripts. As well, they say that the 1000th word over which there is some dispute, is of so minor a consequence that it effects no historical fact nor Doctrine.

These Textual critics have a vast amount of material with which to work, some 4,000 Greek Manuscripts, some 8,000 copies of the Latin Vulgate, and some 2,000 copies of the New Testament in other languages, some 14,000 available sources from which to reconstruct a correct Text.

Furthermore, these Greek Manuscripts go back to the Third Century in an unbroken succession, and with the writings of the Apostolic and Church Fathers, which are Commentaries on the Greek New Testament, and which quote the entire Greek Text with the

NOTES

exception of the first 11 verses of John Chapter 8, form a direct link with the original Manuscripts of the New Testament.

Tertullian, an early Church Father, tells us that the original Manuscripts were still in existence in A.D. 200. Thus, the record of the Greek New Testament is correct, and in its every word, is the Inspired Word of God.

So, we presently have the New Covenant just as it was given to Paul, at least as far as is possible for such to be translated from the original language to another. Actually that applies to the entirety of the Bible both Old and New Testaments. Even the enemies of the Lord admit to the purity of the Text.

THE REASON FOR THESE CLAIMS

Professor John A. Scott says in his book, *Luke: Greek Physician and Historian, "there is one great advantage which the New Testament can claim over all the writings of classical Greece, and that is the age and excellent condition of its Manuscripts."*

Homer lived about a thousand years before Christ, yet the oldest Manuscripts concerning his work are hardly older than the Tenth Century of the Christian era, meaning that the oldest Manuscript copy of that particular work is about 2,000 years from the original writing. In other words, the copy of the copies of the copies, etc., is that far removed, presenting more opportunity for error.

Again, most of the poetry of Pindar, who died about 500 years before Christ, has been lost, but the oldest Manuscript of his poetry which has survived was written very near the year A.D. 1150. In other words, there is an interval of about 1600 years between Pindar and the date of his oldest Manuscript, once again, leaving room for much error.

Another example is, Demosthenes who died about 300 years before Christ, with the oldest Manuscript of his work being about a thousand years after Christ. These selected are the ones of which we have especially old and reliable Manuscripts, and despite the great gaps of which we have spoken between the original and the existing copy, scholarship grants their accuracy.

With the New Testament we are in completely another world, for we have two Manuscripts (copies) which were certainly written before A.D. 340, perhaps as early as A.D. 325. This means there is far less room for error, as would be obvious.

Actually, the final Book of the New Testament, which is the Book of Revelation written by the Apostle John, was probably written in about A.D. 100. Hence, we have Manuscripts of the New Testament which are removed from the compilation of that Book by little more than two centuries, while in the case of the greatest writers of Greek poetry and philosophy, the average interval is more than eight times as great, or some 16 centuries.

THE WORD OF GOD

Well meaning Christians often say that we must take the Gospels on Faith, meaning that we really cannot be sure of the accuracy of the Text. While Faith definitely plays a part in any and all things pertaining to the Gospel, still, we *can* be sure of the Text, even as we *should* be sure of the Text. In other words, it is not guess work.

Just last night in our Prayer Meeting, I warned our people that they should understand the Word of God in the realm of its every word, and not merely the general thought. In other words, the Holy Spirit certainly did inspire the thoughts, but even far greater than that, He inspired every single Word. Consequently, each and every Word of the Bible is of great significance. Jesus said, *"It is written, man shall not live by bread alone, but by every word that proceedeth out of the Mouth of God"* (Mat. 4:4).

He also said, *"For verily I say unto you, till Heaven and Earth pass, one jot or one tittle shall in no wise pass from the Law, till all be fulfilled"* (Mat. 5:18).

"Jot" is the smallest letter and *"Tittle"* the smallest ornament placed upon certain Hebrew letters.

So from these statements coming from the Lord Himself, we surely should realize how important the Word of God really is, and that means not only the thought itself, but down to every single Word, even to the slightest little mark above one of those Words, of which Jesus was speaking, which gives a certain meaning to that particular Hebrew Word, etc. That is the reason that

Believers should be very careful concerning the translations they use for their personal study regarding the Bible.

(17) "BEHOLD, THOU ART CALLED A JEW, AND RESTEST IN THE LAW, AND MAKEST THY BOAST OF GOD,"

The phrase, *"Behold, thou art called a Jew,"* presents Paul summoning the Jew exclusively to the Bar of Judgment, whose claims to exemption from the general condemnation have come to the front in the preceding verses of this Chapter.

Actually there were three titles applied to these people, Hebrew, Jew, and Israelite, which should be distinguished.

The first distinguishes a Hebrew-speaking Jew from a Greek-speaking one. The second distinguishes a Jew from a Gentile, and denotes nationality. The third (Israelite) is the most august title of all, speaking of the fact that the Jew is a member of the theocracy, and thus an heir of the Promises (Trench).

The point of Paul's argument is that the Jews were notoriously at that time no better than other Nations in moral conduct — nay, their national character was such as to bring their very religion into disrepute among the heathen, thus, their whole ground for national exemption from judgment was taken away.

In fact, even as we have stated, even long before Jesus, Israel had long since ceased to look ahead in Faith to a coming Sacrifice, typified in the Tabernacle Offerings and Priesthood. It was now merely an ethical cult, preaching a Salvation-by-works Message, hence, their Crucifixion of Christ. Despite their bold religious claims, they had long since left the Ways of God.

The phrase, *"And restest in the Law,"* presents a picture of a blind and mechanical reliance on the Mosaic Law, which could not save, and had never been meant to save. In fact, Jesus had invited them to *"rest"* on Him, but to no avail (Mat. 11:28-30).

Untold millions at this present hour are resting upon particular *"Churches"* and are in fact, in the same condition as Israel of old. The Law could not save and neither can the Church. Sadly, this means that most every single Catholic in the world is lost. (Yes, some Catholics definitely are Saved; however, once they are truly born again, they will have to leave out of that grossly unscriptural Doctrine, which they will truly want to do.)

The phrase, *"And makest thy boast of God,"* proclaims them glorying in who they were, and what God had originally done for them. In effect, the Jew gloried, as against the heathen, in his knowledge and worship of the One True God. If there was anyone who understood this, Paul did.

He had once boasted accordingly, and had lived in that same self-righteous, pretentious attitude *"which trusted in themselves that they were righteous, and despised others"* (Lk. 18:9).

There are none so blind as those who will not see, and there are none who have such sight as those who were once blind, but who miraculously were delivered by the Lord, even as Paul.

(18) "AND KNOWEST HIS WILL, AND APPROVEST THE THINGS THAT ARE MORE EXCELLENT, BEING INSTRUCTED OUT OF THE LAW;"

The phrase, *"And knowest His Will,"* has reference to the fact that Israel had the literal Word of God, which the other Nations of the world did not have, which meant there was no excuse in them not knowing His Will. The Bible is the revealed Will of God. That is the reason the Believer should make the study of it a daily habit. It should mold one's life.

Regrettably, some, even as the Jews of old, seek to make the Word of God fit their interpretation, instead of making their interpretation fit the Word of God. The criteria is and ever shall be, *"What does the Bible say?"*

The phrase, *"And approvest the things that are more excellent,"* means to put to the test for the purpose of finding that the person or thing tested, meets the specifications laid down. In other words, they had proved the Word over and over, until there was absolutely no shadow of doubt as to its veracity, and in every capacity. They proved the Word of God as being *"more excellent"* than the philosophical speculations of man.

The phrase, *"Being instructed out of the Law,"* in essence means that they were instructed by the very Mouth of God.

(19) "AND ART CONFIDENT THAT THOU THYSELF ART A GUIDE OF THE

BLIND, A LIGHT OF THEM WHICH ARE IN DARKNESS,"

The phrase, *"And art confident that thou thyself art a guide of the blind,"* concerns the idea that the Jews were actually meant by God to be the guides of the Gentiles, for Salvation is of the Jews, as Jesus said (Jn. 4:22) . . . , but this intention of God about the Jews had resulted in a conceited arrogance on their part (Robertson).

The phrase, *"A light of them which are in darkness,"* presents God's intentions, but which they abrogated, and presents the responsibility of the Church as well (Mat. 5:13-14).

In fact, the only True Light on the Earth during the time of the Law, a period of about 1500 years, was Israel. However, that light dimmed extremely low, so low in fact that the Lord was forced to extinguish what little illumination it actually did have (II Chron. 36:15-21). The Lord took the scepter of power away from the Sons of David, for whom it was originally intended, giving that power to the Gentiles, where it has remained ever since (Lk. 21:24). Up to now that has been a time of approximately 2600 years; however, the *"times of the Gentiles"* will end at the Second Coming of the Lord, when Israel will then accept Jesus as her Messiah and Saviour, with the power once again returning to the Throne of David, where it will remain forever.

(20) "AN INSTRUCTOR OF THE FOOLISH, A TEACHER OF BABES, WHICH HAST THE FORM OF KNOWLEDGE AND OF THE TRUTH IN THE LAW."

The phrase, *"An instructor of the foolish,"* presents that which they actually were.

The heathen world, which included all except the Jews, was foolish in their worship of their gods of human invention, etc. Even the Greeks who excelled in philosophy, still, had no idea whatsoever of the true things of life. In Greek philosophy, as it is with all philosophy, the great questions of life were left unanswered. Who is man? Where did he come from? Where is he going? More particularly, what is man?

The Greeks had no answers, lumbering from one hypothesis to the other, even as their modern counterparts. These answers were found only in the Word of God as it was given to the Jews.

It is the same presently, the Church is to be the instructor of those who do not know God, consequently holding no answers!

The phrase, *"A teacher of babes,"* presents the Holy Spirit, at least as far as true knowledge and wisdom are concerned, looking at the great Greek philosophers as no more than infants. Actually, the word *"babes"* in the Greek is *"nepios,"* and means *"an infant or simple-minded person."*

To be frank, and irrespective of the amount of education, and irrespective of the plaudits of the world, without God and His Word, the celebrated are called *"simple-minded"* by the Lord.

The phrase, *"Which hast the form of knowledge and of the Truth in the Law,"* has been debated by Scholars.

The word *"form"* in the Greek is *"morphosis,"* and means *"the mere form or rough sketch,"* but can also mean, *"the form befitting the thing or truly expressing the fact."*

I personally think the latter is in view, when one takes into consideration all the things said by Paul. In other words, the Jews had the Knowledge of the Lord, and knew the Truth of the Law.

While it is true that they corrupted this Knowledge and Truth, still, that did not mean ignorance, but rather the very opposite. In other words, this made their sin even worse.

Actually the word *"knowledge"* in the Greek is *"gnosis,"* and means *"experiential knowledge,"* not a mere passing acquaintance. The Jews had tested and proven the Word of God, even as Paul had said, and knew it to live up to its Promises. In other words, the Word of God was 12 inches to the foot, 36 inches to the yard, and 5,280 feet to the mile.

THE LAW OF MOSES

The Law of Moses, was not simply a kind of ideal, civil code, or Law for Israel. It was far more than that.

Moses was moved by God to express Israel's relationship to Jehovah in the form of a Covenant, by which a Great King (in this case, God, the King of kings) bound to Himself a vassal-people (here, Israel).

For Israel, the basic stipulations of their Covenant were the Ten Commandments, in

effect the Moral Law as the expression of God's Will; and the detailed Covenant-obligations took the form of *"civil"* Statue rooted in the Moral Law of the Ten Commandments (Ex. Chpts. 21-23; Deut. 12:26). Of course, there were a myriad of other Laws and stipulations tied to the central core of the Ten Commandments.

Israel's life in every way was to be marked by Righteousness and Holiness as issuing from obedience to the Covenant, or, in other words, fulfilling the Law. Attainment, however, waited upon further Divine provision, which Israel never seemed to learn (Gal. 3:23).

TOTAL LAW

Because Israel's Covenant was not merely a treaty of political obligations but regulated their daily life before God, its Ordinances served also as a basis of *"civil"* Law for the people. In other words, the Law of Moses dealt with every facet of life in Israel, be it political, economical, social, domestical, mental, and above all spiritual.

However, the number or quantity of *"civil"* Laws in the Pentateuch is in no way excessive or exceptional when compared with other Nations of the world. In fact, it was much less detailed, even though it touched every area of life. Actually, as far as volume is concerned, if that really matters, the Law of Moses as given by God, was only about half the size of the Hammurabi Code, or the Middle Assyrian Laws, which were in vogue at that particular time.

(21) "THOU THEREFORE WHICH TEACHEST ANOTHER, TEACHEST THOU NOT THYSELF? THOU THAT PREACHEST A MAN SHOULD NOT STEAL, DOST THOU STEAL?"

The question, *"Thou therefore which teachest another, teachest thou not thyself?"*, proclaims the great problem of Israel. In other words, despite their claims, and the great Light given unto them, they little allowed the Law to guide them as it was intended. They desired in fact, to be the teacher of others, holding themselves as superior, but little allowed that which they taught to be learned of themselves. The idea is, if the Word of God does not have its intended effect in the life of the

Teacher, and all Believers fall into that category in one way or the other, the Teacher can little Teach.

The idea is not perfection, because none have ever remotely reached that status, with the exception of Christ, Who was Perfect in every respect; however, a consecration to the highest ideals of the Word of God is demanded, with latitude given the Holy Spirit that He may ultimately bring the Believer into the Image of Christ. That ever must be the intended goal.

The question, *"Thou that preachest a man should not steal, dost thou steal?"*, is meant to delve far deeper into the Jewish heart than appears on the surface. The idea is this:

WHAT THE LAW WAS MEANT TO DO

The Law of Moses was meant to do several things, one of those things being the definition of sin. In other words, the Law was intended to specify what sin was, and its type. As well, as all Law, it was demanded by God that it be kept, with a penalty attached for a lack of obedience. The penalty was called the *"Curse of the Law"* (Deut. 28:15-68; Gal. 3:13). The Curse was severe, and the penalty, in its worst form, was death (Rom. 6:23).

However, even though God demanded the Law to be kept and perfectly, even with a severe penalty attached, He gave no power for man to keep the Law, even though He knew that man could not do it within himself.

On the surface that would seem cruel, but actually it was the Mercy of God instead of the opposite.

The intention was that man would see his hopeless position and throw himself on the Mercy and Grace of God, which was provided in the Sacrifices. However, Israel turned the whole thing into a matter of pride — prideful that she had the Law which placed her above all other Nations, and prideful that she attempted to keep the Law, at least in a convoluted way. In other words, she trumpeted loudly the Laws she kept, and conveniently ignored or covered up those she constantly broke. So, if God had given Israel the power to keep the Law, it would have only exacerbated the ever-present problem of pride which already is the bane of humanity,

NOTES

even the Jews.

SELF-RIGHTEOUSNESS

However, Israel little threw herself on the Mercy and Grace of God, but rather did the opposite, which automatically made them powerless to resist sin, which they readily committed. In their great religious effort which built itself around the keeping of the Law, but which they really did not do, they developed an elaborate system of hypocrisy, which always occurs in such cases, which fastened to them in the form of self-righteousness, which Paul is addressing here.

Refusing to seek the Lord for strength in these areas, they were helpless in the face of the weakness of the flesh, which they actually tried to overcome by the flesh, which is impossible.

So, when Paul asked these questions, in effect he is addressing their real problem — a problem incidentally, which he faced himself even after he came to Christ. Since he is now Saved and Baptized with the Holy Spirit, surely, he thinks, he will have no more problem with the flesh. However, the 7th Chapter of Romans bears out that the problem did continue, with Paul earnestly seeking the Lord for the answer, which was given to him, with him relating it in Romans Chapter 6. Paul gave the solution in the 6th Chapter, and then told us in the 7th Chapter as to how he was brought to this place. Of course, the great 8th Chapter tells how the Holy Spirit makes Christ's great victory at Calvary and the Resurrection real in the Believer's life, which is the only source of victory.

(Some think that Paul's experience in Romans Chapter 7 was before his Conversion. However, such is not the case, as Commentary on that Chapter I think will show.)

Consequently, Paul addressing Israel in this fashion, is not only from the position of Biblical Knowledge, which he certainly had, but as well from experience.

One could probably say that Israel's experience was not necessarily that of a willful hypocrisy, at least as we think of such, but rather a misinterpretation of the Law, which breeds self-righteousness. Then it is somewhat like a person who commits a crime he really does not intend to commit, and then perfects an elaborate scheme of hypocrisy to cover up. Quite possibly that is an understatement, but in overly simplistic form, that seems to have been their experience.

To which we have already alluded, instead of asking the Lord for Mercy, they continued to enlarge their religious scheme, making the matter ever worse, which resulted in them crucifying their own Messiah.

(22) "THOU THAT SAYEST A MAN SHOULD NOT COMMIT ADULTERY, DOST THOU COMMIT ADULTERY? THOU THAT ABHORREST IDOLS, DOST THOU COMMIT SACRILEGE?"

The question, *"Thou that sayest a man should not commit adultery, dost thou commit adultery?"*, presents Paul choosing the most awful of sins.

The question, *"Thou that abhorrest idols, dost thou commit sacrilege?"*, places Israel in the same state as the Gentile world which knew not God. The only difference was, that Israel claimed to know the True God, Who, in fact, could pull an individual above these vices, whereas the heathen world while applauding virtue practiced vice, and taught that man being impotent to do what was right was not to be condemned if he practiced what was wrong. So Israel pointed a finger at the Gentile world, and in a very negative way, while committing the same sins, but I think not fully understanding why.

An individual or an entire people such as Israel, can trap themselves into an ever-widening dilemma, while trying with all their strength to do otherwise. In this I do not for a moment mean to lessen Israel's terrible guilt, nor do I mean to make excuses, but I do hope to show what I think may have been the cause of their great problem. In fact, every Believer faces this problem in one way or the other. Admittedly, it is much more severe in some than in others and for the obvious reasons. The difference is this:

When Paul faced this great dilemma of trying to overcome the flesh with the flesh, and failing, as fail he must, he cried, *"O wretched man that I am! Who shall deliver me from the body of this death?"* (Rom. 7:24).

Israel would not admit to such, but kept maintaining that she had great Righteousness and Holiness, when in reality, she was

NOTES

spiritually bankrupt.

Jesus Christ was the Answer for Paul, exactly as He was the Answer for Israel. But they would not accept Him, and, therefore, were condemned to remain in their sin and, therefore, to die in their sin.

(23) "THOU THAT MAKEST THY BOAST OF THE LAW, THROUGH BREAKING THE LAW DISHONOUREST THOU GOD?"

The beginning of the question, *"Thou that makest thy boast of the Law . . . ?"*, carries two directions.

First of all, they boasted that they had the Law, and secondly, they boasted that they kept the Law, when in effect they did not keep the Law, because they really could not keep the Law. Only Jesus could, and did in fact, keep the Law of Moses.

The Religious Leadership of Israel lied about the situation, instead of seeking Mercy and Grace from God. It is very hard for a man to admit he is wrong, and it is harder still for one who serves God to admit such, and even harder still for those who serve in the capacity of leadership to do such. The situation spins its own trap.

In Israel's mind they were trying to impress the world, but were actually doing the very opposite. Pride imagines if it admits that it is helpless, throwing itself on the Grace of God, it will be destroyed. Actually, the opposite is the Truth, but it is very difficult for religious man to see that.

The completion of the question, *"Through breaking the Law dishonourest thou God?"*, is posed by Paul to the Jews, in order that they may see what is actually happening.

By their very elaborate religious scheme of ethics, which in fact were no ethics at all, and by piling more and more rules and regulations on one another, they imagined that the world applauded them for their great religiosity. Whenever they suspected this was not the case, they only drew themselves up more tightly in their religious superiority, berating the ignorant Pagans who did not know any better.

Paul is telling them, that their scheme has not fooled anyone, and in fact, they have dishonored God by their actions, and as well they are hated by the Pagan world instead of respected. Of course it was a Message they did not want to hear and, therefore, would not hear! This is what Paul meant in Acts 28:27, when he said, *"For the heart of this people is waxed gross, and their ears are dull of hearing, and their eyes have they closed; lest they should see with their eyes, and hear with their ears, and understand with their heart, and should be converted, and I should heal them."*

(24) "FOR THE NAME OF GOD IS BLASPHEMED AMONG THE GENTILES THROUGH YOU, AS IT IS WRITTEN."

The phrase, *"For the Name of God is blasphemed among the Gentiles through you,"* refers to the Jews, who, of all people, should have known better, but who had become so corrupted, especially their leadership, that the Word of God was actually being blasphemed. In fact, the office of the High Priest presented itself now as a commodity to be bought and sold, which it was.

The robbery of Temples as practiced by the Jews is inferred from Acts 19:37.

The Greek Scholar, Trench, remarks upon the mournfully numerous group of Greek words which expresses the different aspects of sin as used in these Passages by Paul.

They are *"hamartia,"* the missing of a mark; *"parabasis,"* the overpassing of a line; *"parakoe,"* the disobedience to a voice; *"paraptoma,"* a falling when one should have stood; *"agnoema,"* ignorance of what one should know; *"hethema,"* a diminishing of what should be rendered in full measure; *"anomia,"* or *"paranomia,"* non-observance of Law; *"plemmeleia,"* discord.

The phrase, *"As it is written,"* refers to Ezekiel 36:20, 23, as well as other similar Passages in the Old Testament.

THE PERFECT RIGHTEOUSNESS OF JESUS

As one reads these Words as given by the Holy Spirit through Paul, one begins to see and understand the terrible spiritual condition of Israel at the time of Christ. Until He came, their religious scheme of hypocrisy, which had been whetted and formed over the centuries, was little exposed. However, the perfect Righteousness of His Ministry and the perfect Holiness of His Person, was a constant rebuke to who they were and what they were doing.

In their misinterpretation of the Law, which began almost with its giving to Moses on Mt. Sinai, barring Repentance which was the only cure, they were left with only one recourse. That recourse was hypocrisy which led, as it always does, to a terrible self-righteousness. Over and over again Jesus referred to them as hypocrites (Mat. Chpt. 23), and I speak primarily of the leadership; however, it was not the type of hypocrisy which normally wears two faces. Of course, that was readily obvious as well, but their hypocrisy was of much worse conclusion.

The entirety of their system, to which low level Judaism had sunk, was that of hypocrisy, which is the only way it could go. Trying to make the Law into a Saviour which it wasn't, left them vulnerable to the powers of darkness of which Satan took full advantage.

HYPOCRISY

Whenever men leave the tried and true, and I might say proven Word of God, this course of ancient Israel is the only direction left open to them. Please allow me to mention regrettably so, some of the major Pentecostal Denominations of this present hour.

Inasmuch as most of them have instituted an unscriptural form of Church Government, which has little resemblance to the Book of Acts and the Epistles, which must serve as our Standard, that is if we desire to follow the Bible, the result as always is hypocrisy.

For instance, if these Denominations had been in existence at the time of Christ, Peter would not have been able to have preached the Inaugural Message on the Day of Pentecost, nor would the tremendous Miracles recorded in Acts Chapter 5 have taken place. As well, Paul would have little undertaken his Missionary Journeys, nor would he have written any of his Epistles, for the simple reason that he was not handpicked by the Jerusalem Church. Actually, he would have been labeled as a *"maverick,"* or a *"lone ranger,"* etc.

Regarding Peter, he would have had to have dropped out of Ministry for approximately two years, or some such period of time and Paul would not have been accepted for the simple reason that he could not be

SWAGGART BIBLE

controlled. Actually, they would have looked at Paul as a much greater threat than Peter because of his insistence on hearing directly from the Lord and then obeying what he had heard irrespective of what men thought (Gal. 1:1).

Going back to Peter, if his problem of denial had been little known, they would have taken little or no position at all. However, if it was public, which it was, they would have instituted all types of unscriptural demands. That is what I mean by the double standard. The Biblical Way does not change whether something is public or not. The remedy is the Precious Shed Blood of the Lord Jesus Christ, and not some man-instituted unscriptural form of penance, which is constantly changed to suit the occasion. Consequently, the whole thing breeds hypocrisy.

I realize that most laity reading this would show little concern, because they feel this is among Preachers and does not involve them. However, nothing could be further from the Truth.

Anything that is unscriptural, sooner or later affects everyone.

(25) "FOR CIRCUMCISION VERILY PROFITETH, IF THOU KEEP THE LAW: BUT IF THOU BE A BREAKER OF THE LAW, THY CIRCUMCISION IS MADE UNCIRCUMCISION."

The phrase, *"For Circumcision verily profiteth, if thou keep the Law,"* presents Paul zeroing in on the age-old problem of Israel, as well as the modern Church.

The remainder of this Chapter is devoted to a clear and final exposition of the principle involved throughout all the previous verses, that Jewish privileges were of no profit in themselves, especially without their meaning and purpose being understood and acted on.

The thought now passes exclusively to Circumcision, as being the original token of the Covenant, and the Jew's Rite of initiation into his whole privileged position (Gen. Chpt. 17).

When the Jew had come to be the peculiar designation of the children of the Covenant, persons were said to become Jews by Circumcision. It may be here observed as well, that the known fact of other races practicing Circumcision, is not the same thing

NOTES

as the Scriptural view of its being a peculiarly Jewish rite. For to the Jew alone it had a peculiar significance of spirituality far beyond the physical (Barmby).

The phrase, *"But if thou be a breaker of the Law, thy Circumcision is made uncircumcision,"* proclaims the fact that religious rites, no matter how much God-given, contain no properties of Salvation. As Paul will say in the last verse of this Chapter, it is the condition of the *"spiritual heart"* which really matters, and not some prescribed ceremony.

The same applies presently to the Church, in that millions think that their joining a Church, or being Baptized in Water, or partaking of the Lord's Supper, affords them some type of Salvation. It is the age-old act of being religious, which tends to make people think they are something which they aren't. How easy it is for man to be fooled by religion, and for the simple reason he desires to be fooled.

Men ever seek religious ceremony which will allow them to continue on in their sin. In Truth, this pertains to the far greater majority of the Church public. Most aren't truly Saved, have never been born again, have no personal relationship with Christ, do not know Him at all as Saviour, much less Baptizer with the Holy Spirit, have no interest in the Bible, and have experienced no change within their lives. They have a *"form of Godliness, but deny the power thereof."* Paul said, *"From such turn away"* (II Tim. 3:5).

The idea of Paul's statement is, that the Circumcision of the Covenant as practiced by the Jews, was looked at by God as no Covenant at all, because it was all based on an entirely wrong premise. The same can be said for modern rites or symbolisms. Most Water Baptisms are not looked upon at all by God as a True Baptism, but merely someone getting wet. The same can be said for the Lord's Supper, which serves as no symbol whatsoever of His Shed Blood or Broken Body, but merely the imbibing of grape juice and a cracker.

(26) "THEREFORE IF THE UNCIRCUMCISION KEEP THE RIGHTEOUSNESS OF THE LAW, SHALL NOT HIS UNCIRCUMCISION BE COUNTED FOR CIRCUMCISION?"

The beginning of the question, *"Therefore if the uncircumcision keep the Righteousness of the Law . . . ?"*, presents Paul taking Salvation to its rightful position, a changing of the heart, of which the Jews generally had lost sight.

Holding firmly to their Rite of Circumcision, they looked at all Gentiles as *"uncircumcised dogs."* The idea is, at least as the Apostle makes the case here, that irrespective as to how much Gentiles had accepted Christ, with their lives miraculously and gloriously changed, the Jews still counted them as nothing, that is, if they did not become a Proselyte Jew as well, entering into all the Ceremonies and Rites, etc.

To be frank, many modern Churches conduct themselves exactly as the Jews of old, considering God's Way of Salvation as insignificant, unless it is joined by the keeping of their prescribed rules, etc. In other words, one has to ask the Lord to forgive them as well as do a thousand Hail Marys, or some other such foolishness. The Truth is, Repentance before God in these circles is given less and less credence, with the keeping of their unscriptural rules more and more prominent. Again I emphasize, it is the same as the Jews of old.

Also, it should be noted that there is a *"Righteousness"* in the Law, which should be obvious, considering that it was given by God. However, this is the very thing that caused Israel's downfall, and is the same presently with many.

Israel tried to attain that Righteousness by their own supposed merit or religious Ceremony, completely misunderstanding the intent of the Law. In fact, there was no way they could keep the Law at least within themselves, no matter how hard they tried. Consequently, the *"Righteousness"* which they sought, but in the wrong way, was denied them.

In Truth, Jesus fully kept the Law, and in every respect, and thereby obtained its Righteousness, which in fact, He did not need inasmuch as He already had such. However, all that He did was not for Himself anyway, but for sinners.

In other words, upon simple Faith in Him and what He did at Calvary and the Resurrection, the believing sinner is granted the

NOTES

Righteousness of the Law, and judged by God because of his Faith, as a Law-keeper, instead of a Lawbreaker as he had been. It is a beautiful thing, but misunderstood and unseen by most.

In fact, the moment an individual attempts to earn this Righteousness in any manner, he automatically nullifies and makes void for himself, any Righteousness which is of God, which is the only kind God will accept. Consequently, whenever modern Religious Denominations demand something other than the Shed Blood of Jesus as an Atonement for sin, they are nullifying the Grace of God, and whoever submits to such demands as well, is nullifying his plea to God for forgiveness. This is exactly what Paul said in Galatians 5:4, *"Christ is become of no effect unto you, whosoever of you are justified* (attempt to be justified) *by the Law* (or any man-devised rule)*; ye are fallen from Grace."*

To receive God's great benefits, we must without exception, go God's Way, which is His Word. If men deviate from such in the slightest, especially in this manner, exactly as Paul said, *"Christ is become of no effect unto you."*

The conclusion of the question, *"Shall not his uncircumcision be counted for Circumcision?"*, proclaims in a nutshell, that one's trust in Jesus satisfies the demands of the Law, and without all the Rites and Rituals, and, thereby, secures the *"Righteousness of the Law."* In other words, what the Circumcision symbolized is now a reality, because it is a *"heart"* experience.

(27) "AND SHALL NOT UNCIRCUMCISION WHICH IS BY NATURE, IF IT FULFIL THE LAW, JUDGE THEE, WHO BY THE LETTER AND CIRCUMCISION DOST TRANSGRESS THE LAW?"

The beginning of the question, *"And shall not uncircumcision which is by nature, if it fulfil the Law, judge thee . . . ?"*, proclaims the obvious results of the changed life upon Faith in Christ, as the proof of what Paul is saying.

The term *"By nature"* simply means that Circumcision is a physical act within itself, and as such, cannot have any bearing or influence upon one's heart before God.

So, the Apostle is saying that the Jew

should take stock of his situation, admitting to himself, even as the facts bear out, that all the things he was doing, Circumcision, Sabbath keeping, keeping the Feast Days, Offering Sacrifices, etc., in fact, wrought no moral change in his life whatsoever, despite all his claims! Conversely, those who accepted Christ into their hearts, even though not engaging in any of these Rituals at all, enjoyed lives which were gloriously changed, and which within themselves were a judge of Israel. It did not mean that the Believers served as judges, but that the fact of their changed lives did.

It is the same with modern Church members, if all of their religiosity does not change their lives, they really have nothing in their souls, and are in fact the same as the Jews of old.

The conclusion of the question, *"Who by the letter and Circumcision dost transgress the Law?"*, speaks of the Jews, who despite trying to keep the letter of the Law and engaging in all of its Rituals, continued to transgress the Law. In other words, and to use an old expression, *"The proof of the pudding is in the eating."* A Gospel which does not change people's lives, is no Gospel at all.

For instance, Mormonism places great credence on the family, which within itself is right. However, the State of Utah, which headquarters Mormonism, and which makes up the majority of the population of the State I think, suffers a worse divorce rate than most other States in the Union.

Why?

Mormonism is a false religion, projecting a false way of Salvation, which in effect places Mormonism itself with all of its rituals along with the Mormon Church per se, as the Saviour. While Jesus is spoken about, in fact, it is *"another Jesus"* of which they speak (II Cor. 11:4).

A false religion has no positive affect on troubled marriages, or anything else for that matter; consequently, despite all the show of religion in those circles, no lives are truly changed, because only the Power of God can effect such, which comes only through the born-again experience as one truly makes Christ one's Saviour, which is done by Faith (Jn. 3:16; Rom. 10:9-10, 13; Eph. 2:8-9).

NOTES

(28) "FOR HE IS NOT A JEW, WHICH IS ONE OUTWARDLY; NEITHER IS THAT CIRCUMCISION, WHICH IS OUTWARD IN THE FLESH:"

The phrase, *"For he is not a Jew, which is one outwardly,"* completely destroys national Salvation. In other words, the Jew had come to believe that he was right with God, simply because he was a child of Abraham (Mat. 3:9). All the outward trappings of religion, despite their involvement and abundance, serve no spiritual purpose whatsoever, at least in a positive sense.

Such is the Catholic Church and most Protestants for that matter. With sorrow one observes all the rituals of the Catholic Church which are demanded of its followers, but bring no Salvation. It is all an outward show of religion!

How many Christians are such outwardly only?

The phrase, *"Neither is that Circumcision, which is outward in the flesh,"* has the simple meaning, that if this is all it is, an outward show, it is not that which God intends, and, in fact, is no true Circumcision at all!

(29) "BUT HE IS A JEW, WHICH IS ONE INWARDLY; AND CIRCUMCISION IS THAT OF THE HEART, IN THE SPIRIT, AND NOT IN THE LETTER; WHOSE PRAISE IS NOT OF MEN, BUT OF GOD."

The phrase, *"But he is a Jew, which is one inwardly,"* actually has two very important meanings:

1. As is obvious, and with which Paul has been dealing, it is only the work carried out by Christ inwardly, which constitutes Salvation. Outward trappings of religious ceremony have absolutely nothing to do with the inward experience, which should be obvious. The New Birth alone changes one's life.

2. This tells us that man's problem is not outward, i.e., environment, association, education, or religious ceremony. This means that humanistic psychology which can only deal with the outward, can have no positive effect.

SIN

If a person has cancer, rubbing some type of salve over the surface of this disease, will affect it not at all. To remove the cancer, surgery in some manner must be performed, in order to dig out the roots. If the roots are not killed, even though the outward may be momentarily affected in a positive way, the problem will quickly arise again.

Man's root problem is sin, and it has its source in man himself. That source is deep in his vitals, actually in his spirit and soul, which of course, affects his body and mind as well.

Inasmuch as the problem is spiritual, the medical profession cannot alleviate the situation, and neither can the Sociologist. As well, the Psychologist deals with symptoms, which manifest themselves outwardly, but that is the best he can do. The root remains, and consequently will continue to grow. So, there is no help for man's dilemma from these sources, which of all people, the Church ought to know. But yet, the Church has become one giant referral system, referring the *"hard cases"* to the Psychologists, under the guise that they need *"professional help."*

In the first place, there is no help from that source for this problem, and adding the word *"professional"* to the lie, only seeks to make a big lie bigger.

JESUS

Jesus Christ Alone (I said, Alone), can deal with this problem and save man from sin. Even then, it was so bad that He could not do so by a simple fiat (decree), or by His Virgin Birth, or sinless life, or Miracles, etc., but only through His vicarious Death on Calvary's Cross. Only then was the sin grip broken and Satan totally defeated. Only then could the person be totally and completely changed by the Power of God.

The phrase, *"And Circumcision is that of the heart, in the spirit,"* refers to the *"heart"* of the individual being changed, which is the seat of his passions, his will, his feelings, emotion and determination. It is done in his spirit, which is where the real problem is, and carried out by the Holy Spirit, which is a work of Regeneration. This great thing is obtained solely and totally by Faith, which the sinner exhibits toward Christ. He may not understand much about what the Lord has actually done for mankind, but he understands enough to know that Jesus is the

NOTES

only Answer (Eph. 2:8-9).

The phrase, *"And not in the letter,"* refers to the rules and regulations of the Law of Moses, which could not save, and was never intended by God to save. But Israel reduced the great gift of Judaism down to the far lower level of a mere *"ethic."* As such, it became a system of trying to effect Salvation by being ethical, even as does much of the world presently. The sadness is, they were not ethical and neither did they have Salvation.

As an example I refer to the several men, heads of the giant tobacco companies in America, who stood before a Congressional Investigative Committee in Washington, when asked if they believed that nicotine was not addictive, responded by all raising their hands.

One must understand that all of these men were well educated, considered to be pillars of society in the community, were wealthy, and yet, so much for ethics. For the dollar bill, each would lie before the entirety of the Nation, because it is impossible that they did not know that nicotine was addictive.

While ethics do have their place of course, they cannot change a person, and neither do most live up to them very much. However, ethics are man-devised, and because as such, never really address the real problem. They are all surface, because that is all they can be.

For instance, one is reminded of the Greek Philosopher Socrates, whose ethics were so exalted that he said that he never did anything in his life which his reason told him was wrong. Knowing totally depraved nature as we do, one simply cannot accept this statement at its full face value (Wuest).

The phrase, *"Whose praise is not of men, but of God,"* lets us in on a big secret.

Men will readily praise outward show, but seldom that which is inward. Only God will praise the inward, so man has a choice.

When a person says that he is going to trust Christ solely, one would think that the Church would readily applaud such. However, for the most part, nothing could be further from the Truth.

Why?

It is either Scriptural and Spiritual ignorance, or else the person has come to the place that he simply does not believe God any longer. I suspect the latter is the case, at least among Preachers.

When it comes to the Pentecostal and Charismatic varieties, one would think that surely these know the Ways of God. In fact, most of them do. So that means they are sinning against Light, which is the worst sin of all.

However, if the whole world says *"no"* and God says *"yes,"* guess which decision is going to win out!

> *"Guide me, O Thou great Jehovah, Pilgrim through this barren land;*
> *"I am weak, but Thou art mighty; hold me with Thy powerful Hand;*
> *"Bread of Heaven, Bread of Heaven,*
> *"Feed me till I want no more, feed me till I want no more."*

> *"Open now the Crystal Fountain, whence the Healing Stream doth flow;*
> *"Let the fire and clouded pillar, lead me all my journey through;*
> *"Strong Deliverer, Strong Deliverer,*
> *"Be Thou still my Strength and Shield, Be Thou still my Strength and Shield."*

> *"When I tread the verge of Jordan, bid my anxious fears subside;*
> *"Death of Death, and Hell's destruction, land me safe on Mercy shore;*
> *"Songs of Praises, Songs of Praises,*
> *"I will ever give to Thee, I will ever give to Thee."*

CHAPTER 3

(1) "WHAT ADVANTAGE THEN HATH THE JEW? OR WHAT PROFIT IS THERE OF CIRCUMCISION?"

The question, *"What advantage then hath the Jew?"*, proclaims the Apostle asking such, after he has shown that the mere possession of the Law does not exempt the Jew from Judgment, but that God requires its fulfillment.

He has shown that Circumcision in the flesh, sealed though it be of the Covenant and Pledge of its Promises, is only of value if it represents inward heart Circumcision; he

has, it may be argued, reduced the Jew to a position of entire equality with the Gentile. But the consciousness of the Jewish people must protest against such a conclusion.

"Salvation is of the Jews," is the Word of Christ Himself, and the Apostle is obliged to meet this instinctive protest of the ancient people of God.

The advantage of the Jew is admitted. However, if God's Character as Righteous Judge of the world be maintained — as it must be — these admissions do not exempt the Jew from that liability to Judgment which has just been demonstrated (Denney).

Considering Paul's question, if being a Jew, if Circumcision itself, which in effect was a sign of the entirety of the Covenant of Law, gives one no advantage over the Gentile, what was the use of the Old Covenant at all? It is thus shown to have been illusory; and God's Own Truth and Faithfulness are impugned, if He is supposed to have given, as conveying advantages, what really conveyed none.

The answer is obvious, God's Great Gift to these people, was not illusory; it did convey great advantages in the way of privilege and opportunity; this advantage first, not to mention others, that *"The Oracles of God"* (vs. 2) were entrusted to the Jew, even as we shall see in Paul's answer.

If some (more or fewer, it matters not) have failed to realize these advantages, it has been their fault, not God's. It is man's unfaithfulness, not His, that has been the cause of the failure.

The question, *"Or what profit is there of Circumcision?"*, embodies, as stated, as a symbolism the entirety of the Law.

As we have said repeatedly, Israel was far and away the greater of all people on Earth, and for the simple reason that they had the Word of God, while the rest of the world stumbled in spiritual darkness. As also stated, that they were not faithful to that which God gave them, was not the fault of God or His Word, but rather their fault.

I suppose one would have to wonder, if the Church has done much better?

The first 20 verses of this Chapter declare that all mankind whether enlightened by Reason, Philosophy, or Revelation, are, without distinction, equally guilty before God; and the conclusion is stated that no one is Righteous.

This conclusion is rejected and denied by much of modern Theology and many prominent Religious Teachers are not afraid to contradict the Holy Spirit and to charge Him with saying what is not true. These Teachers point to particular individuals of high education and of what they refer to as noble character, and they say that to class such men with those described in Romans 1:29-32 and 3:10-18 is an outrage. But God reads the heart, and all who claim to be wiser than He proclaim their own folly.

As an example, one piece of ground may be full of flowers, and the next piece full of weeds because left to nature. But the ground in both cases is similar, and equally in the power of a principle of evil hidden in the soil which originates thorns and brambles. So is it in human society. No man is Righteous as to his nature. All are unrighteous, and, therefore, subject to the Wrath of God, whether man wants to admit such or not.

Man's greatest need consequently is a Righteousness in which God can discover no flaw. That is the Righteousness which the Gospel offers; and it offers it on the Principle of Faith in an Atoning Saviour (Williams).

(2) "MUCH EVERY WAY: CHIEFLY, BECAUSE THAT UNTO THEM WERE COMMITTED THE ORACLES OF GOD."

The phrase, *"Much every way,"* proclaims the tremendous advantages, but none of which could save their souls, other than simple Faith. However, these advantages and of every description, made them so far superior to the other Nations of the world, that there simply was no contest. In fact, the Jews even halfway attempted to follow the Lord, God blessed them to such an extent that it literally defied description. During these times, they were the head of all Nations (Deut. 28:13). This leadership was not taken from them until about 600 years before Christ, with it remaining in the hands of the Gentiles from then until now, and will do so unto the Second Coming of the Lord.

Concerning economic blessings, during Solomon's time, the Nation was rich beyond belief. In fact, much of the wealth of the world of that day, flowed into its coffers, and that without war or even the threat of such.

NOTES

Truly their advantages were exactly as Paul said, *"Much every way."*

The phrase, *"Chiefly, because that unto them were committed the Oracles of God,"* presents the Holy Spirit's title for the Old Testament. He here declares its authority, and states that its Utterances were the Utterances of God. Many who profess to be Christian Ministers boldly deny this, and declare the Sacred Book to be the Oracles of man, but to their detriment I might quickly add! (Williams).

In effect, the Greatest Glory of Israel is affirmed here to be the possession of the Bible. Those who stand upon religious ceremonies esteem its greatest Glory to have been the Temple and the Priesthood. But Inspiration points to the Scriptures and to nothing else.

The Church now has both the Old and New Testaments, with the same said now as well. The Bible is far and away the Greatest Glory of the Church. It must serve as the Criteria for all things, the Standard for all Righteousness, the Course for all Doctrine, the Final Authority for all disputes. In fact, if it is not followed minutely, it will always lead to great trouble.

This is actually Satan's greatest effort against the Church. He tries to pull it away from the Word of God. The great question is and always has been, *"Is it Scriptural?"*

When man stands before God, he will not be judged according to what his Church taught, or Preachers for that matter. He will not be judged according to tradition, or education, or social position, etc. He will be judged strictly from, and according to, the Word of God.

In fact, millions will be consigned to Eternal Hell, while all the time pointing to their particular Church, but to no avail. Many will attempt to say that the Priest or Preacher told them certain things which they believed, but which were wrong. They will attempt to shift the responsibility, but again to no avail! While the Priests and Preachers will definitely answer, no one will be able to shift blame or liability at the Great White Throne Judgment. Each person must stand or fall on his own actions. Again, the Word of God will be the Standard.

That is the reason I strongly plead with people to know and understand what the Bible says about all things. Tragically and sadly, most have little knowledge as to what it really says, only what their Church teaches. In the Catholic Church the Bible for all practical purposes is an unread Book. Regrettably, in many Protestant Churches the situation is identical. I marvel as I see Preachers advocate certain things which are blatantly unscriptural, and Preachers I might quickly add, who should know better. However, they do not seem to know, or else they do know, and are purposely charting their own course in order to find favor with certain people. However, as Paul said in verse 4, *"Let God be true, but every man a liar."*

(3) "FOR WHAT IF SOME DID NOT BELIEVE? SHALL THEIR UNBELIEF MAKE THE FAITH OF GOD WITHOUT EFFECT?"

The question, *"For what if some did not believe?"*, proclaims the unbelief which rejected the Bible, but by no means nullified its Truthfulness or the Faithfulness of its Divine Author. On the contrary unbelief only proved man to be a liar.

The question, *"Shall their unbelief make the Faith of God without effect?"*, proclaims far more than meets the eye:

1. The unbelief of Israel in no way affected the Great Plan that God has provided for humanity, which is built on the premise of Faith.

2. The Great Plan of God is not affected at all, irrespective of what man does throughout the entirety of the world. God's Plan stands, as God's Plan must stand and ever shall stand.

3. Any person who exhibits Faith toward God in the prescribed manner of His Son, Jesus Christ, will without fail reap the results which God promises. The actions of Israel nullified this not at all, nor the Church for that matter. A billion people can reject the Plan of God, but if the billion and first person accepts God's Promises at face value, he will receive all the results and without fail.

What a mighty God we serve!

(4) "GOD FORBID: YEA, LET GOD BE TRUE, BUT EVERY MAN A LIAR; AS IT IS WRITTEN, THAT THOU MIGHTEST BE JUSTIFIED IN THY SAYINGS, AND

NOTES

MIGHTEST OVERCOME WHEN THOU ART JUDGED."

The phrase, *"God forbid,"* proclaims Paul's answer to the questions of verse 3.

The phrase, *"Yea, let God be true, but every man a liar,"* shows us that the problem is always of man, but never of God.

The truth is: God has never failed to keep His Word, irrespective as to what it was. If any person will obey the Lord, they will find that God always does what He says that He will do.

Paul evidently took this statement from Psalm 116:11, *"Every man a liar,"* even though the general thrust of that Psalm does not bear upon the present argument. The Apostle takes this phrase from it as expressing well what he wants to say, that though all men were false (in the sense expressed and implied by the previous verse), yet God's Truth stands (Barmby).

The phrase, *"As it is written, That thou mightest be justified in Thy Sayings, and mightest overcome when Thou art judged,"* is quoted from Psalm 51:4.

In quoting this verse, which is David's Repentance after his sin in the matter of Uriah, Paul in essence is saying, that, sin having been committed, man alone is guilty, and that God's Truth and Righteousness can never be impugned.

Some have attempted to imply that man's sin, instead of impugning the Righteousness of God, rather enhances it, as it makes it shine all the more. To follow that logic, it is claimed that God allowed David and even Israel to fall into even deeper sin with the view of establishing God's Righteousness all the more.

However, that teaching somewhat springs from the erroneous understanding of the Doctrine of Predestination, or else, an improper understanding of Grace. Paul answered that readily when he asked the question, *"Shall we continue in sin, that Grace may abound?"*

He then said, *"God forbid,"* using the same expression as he did respecting the Faith of God (Rom. 6:1-2).

God does not need anything, much less sin and more particularly, greater sin, to exhibit His Righteousness. God is not dependent on anyone or anything, and if He was, He certainly would not be dependent on sin.

(5) "BUT IF OUR UNRIGHTEOUSNESS COMMEND THE RIGHTEOUSNESS OF GOD, WHAT SHALL WE SAY? IS GOD UNRIGHTEOUS WHO TAKETH VENGEANCE? (I SPEAK AS A MAN)"

The question, *"But if our unrighteousness commend the Righteousness of God, what shall we say?"*, is meant to elicit the following answer:

While it may be true that the unrighteousness of man in no way negatively affects the Righteousness of God, but rather exhibits it, still, in no way does this mean that God places an approval upon sin of any nature.

Even if it is true that man's *"lie"* causes God's *"Truth"* to shine more beautifully, this in no way excuses the lie. The Judgment of God will ultimately come upon the lie and the liar, unless there is Repentance.

The question, *"Is God unrighteous who taketh vengeance? (I speak as a man)"* is meant to be answered *"No!"*

Just because the Righteousness of God shines brighter the more that the unrighteousness of man is portrayed, in no way means that God will forego vengeance upon sin.

His phrase, *"I speak as a man,"* is meant apologetically, in that only a foolish man would ask such a question. Paul asks it because he knows that some people will ask such a thing, so he answers it in advance. God is never unrighteous, and even the idea that He might be so, is silly to say the least!

Man is ever attempting to condemn God in order to justify his own sin. Consequently, Paul addresses the subject.

(6) "GOD FORBID: FOR THEN HOW SHALL GOD JUDGE THE WORLD?"

The phrase, *"God forbid,"* once again serves as Paul's answer to the preposterous question of the previous verse.

The question, *"For then how shall God judge the world?"*, presents the claims of man, if in fact carried to a conclusion, as setting aside the coming Great White Throne Judgment (Rev. 20:11-15). The fact that this Judgment cannot be avoided, means that the hypothesis of man is foolish indeed.

(7) "FOR IF THE TRUTH OF GOD HATH MORE ABOUNDED THROUGH MY LIE UNTO HIS GLORY; WHY YET AM I ALSO JUDGED AS A SINNER?"

The beginning of the question, *"For if the Truth of God hath more abounded through my lie unto His Glory . . . ?"*, is meant to be answered in the negative, for such a thing cannot be done.

The question, *"Why yet am I also judged as a sinner?"*, is meant to portray the foolishness of such a line of thinking, for if true, it would mean that sin glorifies God, which is preposterous. Were that so, God could in no way be Righteous for judging sinners. They should rather be rewarded!

(8) "AND NOT RATHER, (AS WE BE SLANDEROUSLY REPORTED, AND AS SOME AFFIRM THAT WE SAY,) LET US DO EVIL, THAT GOOD MAY COME? WHOSE DAMNATION IS JUST."

The phrase, *"And not rather, (as we be slanderously reported, and as some affirm that we say,)"* presents the reason that Paul is addressing this subject. Because of Paul's strong Teaching on Grace, his detractors, of which there seemed to be many, were slandering him by claiming that he was teaching several particular Doctrines which were grossly unscriptural. Those doctrines were:

Lie number one: Sin doesn't matter that much because Grace covers it all.

Lie number two: The Believer should not concern himself with trying to overcome sin because Grace is sufficient.

Lie number three: The more that one sins, the more that Grace abounds; consequently, the more the Believer sins, the more Glory he brings to God.

Lie number four: It doesn't really matter what one does, because it is covered by Grace.

One of Satan's favorite tactics in combatting True Biblical Doctrines, is to do exactly what he did here with Paul. The Truth is subtly twisted in order that it means something else entirely, and always extremely negative, at least toward that which is right. Regrettably, there seems to be altogether too many Believers who enjoy hearing such, and believing it for that matter! As well, Paul's situation was doubly difficult.

GRACE

The great Covenant of Grace, even as it was given to the Apostle, has now come into full flower, even as the Lord always intended.

However, it seemed far more radical than it really was, for the simple reason that the Jewish Salvation by works was so prominent. In fact, God had always dealt with the human race by Grace, for the simple reason that this was the only manner in which man could be reached, at least after his Fall in the Garden of Eden.

Due to the fact that Jesus had not yet come and removed the terrible sin debt against man, Grace was somewhat in shadow during Old Testament times. But since Calvary and the Resurrection and the Exaltation, that which God had planned all along could now be brought into full fruition, and in fact was. Irrespective, there were many Jewish Believers in Christ in Jerusalem, who were as well, attempting to hold on to the old Jewish Law, which they now tried to attach to Bible Christianity. Naturally, Paul hit this effort hard, which no doubt angered these people greatly (Gal. 1:6-10). So some of them are now resorting to any measures, even lying, to hinder the Apostle.

The question, *"Let us do evil, that good may come?"*, sums up what these detractors were accusing Paul of teaching.

The phrase, *"Whose damnation is just,"* proclaims the Apostle as saying that those who report such slander are liable to a just damnation.

They were holding themselves aloof from his Teaching concerning Grace, claiming that some people were committing the very worst of sins, sins for which they should be damned, but Paul was teaching them, they said, that such did not matter, because Grace covered it all, and besides that, they could feel free to continue committing these sins.

Satan's greatest efforts have always come from inside the Church. From there he wreaks his greatest destruction. As someone has well said, *"We have met the enemy, and he is us!"*

(9) "WHAT THEN? ARE WE BETTER THAN THEY? NO, IN NO WISE: FOR WE HAVE BEFORE PROVED BOTH JEWS AND GENTILES, THAT THEY ARE ALL UNDER SIN;"

The question, *"What then?"*, presents as we shall see, one of the reasons the Judaizers hated Paul so much.

Now the Reader must keep in mind, that the Judaizers were followers of Christ as well. Many, if not most, were members of the Church in Jerusalem. Not only did they not want to give up the old Law of Moses, which Paul had strongly proclaimed was fulfilled by Jesus, but as well, it angered them greatly that the Apostle placed them on the same level with Gentiles, and to be held even more responsible because of the great Light given to Jews through the centuries.

Giving up the Law in favor of Grace was bad enough, but to be placed on the same level as Gentiles was adding insult to injury. This was the core problem of many of the Jewish Believers.

As we said in Commentary on the Book of Acts, if James had given the same ruling for Jews as he did for Gentiles, which is recorded in Acts Chapter 15, this problem may have been solved completely, or at least greatly weakened. He certainly followed the leading of the Holy Spirit when he set the Gentile Believers free from the shackles of the Law. However, it was only proper that all followers of Christ, Jews included, be placed in the same category. This situation caused Paul great difficulties, and was a great hindrance to that which the Holy Spirit was doing.

As the Reader should understand, this did not mean that the Law of Moses was bad, because it wasn't. It was the Law of God and during its time, was the greatest thing that ever happened to Israel and the world. However, it was always intended to merely serve a purpose and when that purpose was completed, which it was in Christ, it was to be set aside. Jesus fulfilled it in totality, and even satisfied its Curse, taking it upon Himself on the Cross of Calvary. Consequently, it was binding no more upon Believers, because it had been satisfied in Him.

The question, *"Are we better than they?"*, is answered immediately by Paul, *"No, in no wise:"*

This, even as we have stated, is what greatly angered many of these Judaizers. So, the same self-righteous spirit which caused the Sanhedrin to crucify Christ, inculcates itself, at least to a degree, even in these Jewish followers of the Lord. To be told by Paul that they were no better than Gentiles, was like a slap in the face. Their pride simply could not allow themselves to admit such. Consequently, they struck out against the man who bravely told them the Truth. Such is human nature when it is not controlled by Christ.

Considering what the Jewish Leaders had done to Christ, it would seem that the Judaizers would have known and understood the spirit which prompted that, was also prompting them! However, pride is a powerful factor. As well, we must understand that these people were Spirit-filled Believers, but not at all Spirit-led, as should be obvious. Being Baptized with the Holy Spirit in no way guarantees correct Doctrine. Such comes about only as the Believer fully allows the Holy Spirit to have His Way, thereby leading into all Truth (Jn. 16:13). Regrettably, many Spirit-filled Believers allow more self-will to be prevalent than God's Will, which greatly hinders the Holy Spirit in all that He attempts to do. However, as should be overly obvious, all of this wrong direction is not the fault of the Spirit, but of the individual.

It is my belief, that at some point these people lost their way with God, unless they allowed the Holy Spirit to pull them in the right direction. Paul said as much in Galatians 5:4.

The phrase, *"For we have before proved both Jews and Gentiles, that they are all under sin,"* points to the supposed claim of the Jews for superiority, which is refuted.

The connection of thought is plain. The conclusion of Chapter 2 had left the Jews on the same footing with the Gentiles before God in respect of sinfulness. But then objections had been raised on the ground of the acknowledged privileges of the chosen people; and such objections had been met.

The Apostle now sums up the results:

What, then, is the state of the case? Have we any advantage to allege? No, not at all in the sense intended; the previous argument stands; and he proceeds to confine his position from the Testimony of the Old Testament itself (Barmby).

ALL THE WORLD GUILTY

In Chapter 1 of Romans, Paul deals with the state of the Gentile world. Obviously, it's

NOTES

not a very pleasant picture. He places the Gentile world into idol worship and sexual perversion, with the Scripture saying that God has *"given them over to a reprobate mind"* (Rom. 1:28). However, in Chapters 2 and 3, he deals with the Jewish question. He concludes by saying, *"For all have sinned* (both Jews and Gentiles), *and come short of the Glory of God;*

"Being justified freely by His Grace through the Redemption that is in Christ Jesus" (Rom. 3:23-24).

So, Chapters 1 through 3 proclaim the entirety of the human race being bound by sin, with the only solution being Jesus Christ, and, more particularly, *"Jesus Christ and Him Crucified."* Paul said:

"Whom God has set forth to be a propitiation (Atonement) *through Faith in His Blood* (all of this is made possible by the Cross), *to declare His Righteousness for the remission of sins that are past* (refers to all who trusted Christ before He actually came, which covers the entirety of the time from the Garden of Eden to the moment Jesus died on the Cross), *through the forbearance* (tolerance) *of God* (meaning that God tolerated the situation before Calvary, knowing the debt would be fully paid at that time, which it was!)" (Rom. 3:25).

(10) "AS IT IS WRITTEN, THERE IS NONE RIGHTEOUS, NO, NOT ONE:"

The phrase, *"As it is written,"* proclaims Paul going to the Old Testament as the Foundation for his Doctrine.

The way he uses the phrase, denotes the fact that the Old Testament is the Word of God, and that it is error free, simply because it is of God. As well, the statement not only proclaims the veracity of the Word, but as well portrays the fact that all other so-called sacred books, which claim to be the Word of God, in fact are not. This holds true at present exactly as it did then.

That which Paul proclaims to have been previously written, spans verses 10 through 18. Actually, what he says is not quoted from a particular Passage, but from several Old Testament Books on the same subject.

Verses 10-12 are from Psalms 14:2-3; 52:2-4; Eccl. 7:20. Verses 13-18 are from Psalms 5:9-10; 10:7; 36:1-2; 140:3; Isa. 59:7-8.

The phrase, *"There is none Righteous, no, not one,"* addresses the complaints of the Jews, and clenches the argument by the Scriptures which the Jews could not deny.

The type of *"Righteousness"* of which Paul speaks here, is the Righteousness of God. It is not referring to man's contrived righteousness in any manner.

WHAT IS THE RIGHTEOUSNESS OF GOD?

First of all, the Righteousness of God, which is the only kind He will accept, and which He demands of all men, is *"perfection."* More perfectly, it is *"moral perfection."* As well, it is His definition of morality, and not man's. To be more particular, this *"moral perfection"* which portrays *"God's Righteousness,"* is ensconced in Jesus Christ, God's Only Son. So, one could say without fear of contradiction, that Jesus is the perfect definition of the *"Righteousness of God."*

Within one's self, it is impossible for Righteousness to spring forth, at least the type God demands. The reason is simple. The wellspring is poisoned, but it is not poisoned from something outward, but rather from something inward.

Man refuses to admit that, thinking that his problem is external, hence the changing of environment or association, or the betterment of education, which he thinks will solve the problem. However, such is impossible!

If a well is poisoned, one can change the atmosphere around the well, build a beautiful house over the well, or make a beautiful garden around the well, but the water out of the well is still poisoned with nothing changed.

Also, if the water is poisoned by something for which man has no cure, he can treat the water after it comes from the well in any manner he so desires, but the poisoned water will be unaffected. The former speaks of man's social programs, while the latter speaks of humanistic psychology, which really treats only symptoms, because that's all it can treat.

The Truth is, the source of the well is poisoned, and until that is corrected, there is nothing that can be done to alleviate the situation of the poisoned water. All efforts are futile. In effect, there is no remedy, even

as there is no earthly remedy for sin. Man's source is Satan because of the Fall. Consequently, man must be born again, which alone addresses itself to the source, and which alone can change the poisoned water. In other words, the problem is spiritual, not psychological, not social, not economic, not philosophical, not educational. Inasmuch as it is spiritual, Jesus Christ Alone can deal with the situation, and because He Alone knows the problem and has paid the price for man's Redemption.

When Paul spoke of there being none Righteous, he was speaking of those outside of Christ. All Believers are Righteous, but it is not Righteousness of their own making or choosing, for such as we have explained, is not possible within themselves. That which True Believers have, is the Righteousness of God, which is given freely by the Lord Jesus Christ, upon one's Faith in Him. That is the reason that the Lord said of Abraham, *"And he believed in the Lord; and He counted it to him for Righteousness"* (Gen. 15:6).

(11) "THERE IS NONE THAT UNDERSTANDETH, THERE IS NONE THAT SEEKETH AFTER GOD."

The phrase, *"There is none that understandeth,"* refers to man on his own, having no way to understand God. That means the most brilliant Scholar, if not a Believer, has no more understanding of God, than a six year-old child. To be frank, the child probably has greater understanding, because its mind is uncluttered by many false things as opposed to the Scholar.

So, God cannot be learned or understood by education or scientific investigation. Every conclusion arrived at concerning God by unregenerate man, is so off the wall as to defy description. Whenever the Holy Spirit through Paul said there was *no* understanding, He meant exactly that.

Consequently, the only way for man to know anything about God, at least that which is Biblically correct, is for God to reveal Himself to man, which He did in the Person of His Son, Jesus Christ. As well as coming to redeem man from sinful bondage, Jesus also came to reveal the Father. So, when one sees Jesus one has seen the way and manner in which the Father is and works. It is a beautiful presentation to say the least!

However, that Revelation on its own is not enough to bring man to God. While it is true that Jesus is the *"Way"* and the *"Door"* (Jn. 14:6; 10:7), still, the understanding of man remains so skewed that the Holy Spirit must convict him of sin before he can be Saved. This is brought about as the Word of God is ministered in one way or the other (Jn. 16:7-11). Only after he is born again, can man fully begin to understand God, at least as He is revealed to us, and as well, the Word of God.

The phrase, *"There is none that seeketh after God,"* tells us that man left on his own, will not seek God, and, in fact, cannot seek God.

Many times, all of us have used the phrase *"He found the Lord!"* However, while that may be true in the broad sense, in the strict sense of the word, we didn't find the Lord, He found us. The story of the Gospel is Jesus seeking lost sinners. This is beautifully portrayed in the story of the lost sheep and the seeking Saviour (Mat. 18:11-13). Once again, this speaks of the unsaved, as is obvious.

Sinful man only seeks after God when the Holy Spirit moves upon Him, revealing to him his wicked and lost condition, with the ultimate results of Hell. Only then will some men seek after God.

(12) "THEY ARE ALL GONE OUT OF THE WAY, THEY ARE TOGETHER BECOME UNPROFITABLE; THERE IS NONE THAT DOETH GOOD, NO, NOT ONE."

The phrase, *"They are all gone out of the way,"* speaks of the lost condition of all men, and without exception. The *"Way"* spoken here, is God's Way. All other ways or directions are false, destructive, and simply will not work in any capacity.

The phrase, *"They are together become unprofitable,"* refers to the terrible loss in every capacity respecting wayward man. Looking at the situation clearly and honestly, the word *"unprofitable"* is the right word. The Holy Spirit is speaking of all things, but the greater thrust is toward the spiritual. Man left to himself, is altogether unprofitable in a spiritual sense. In Truth, unredeemed man is dead to all things spiritual. That is the reason that within himself, he cannot know God or serve God.

NOTES

The phrase, *"There is none that doeth good, no, not one,"* presents a sober indictment to say the least!

The word *"good"* in the Greek is *"chrestotes,"* and means *"moral goodness, integrity, and kindness."*

The idea comes from the word *"unprofitable,"* which, in the Greek, is *"achreios."* The actual meaning is: *"of no worth, useless."*

Considering what few things that unredeemed man does which seem to be *"good,"* the Truth is, his motivation for doing such is wrong, for the simple reason that it is truly impossible for this poisoned fountain to produce good water of any nature. It simply cannot be done.

A case in point is the life and death of the Catholic Nun, Mother Teresa.

Regarding her soul's Salvation, I cannot conclusively say. However, if she was Saved, it was not because of being a good Catholic, or doing good works.

Doing my best to make a Righteous judgment, if the things she said are any indication, and I will not go into detail, I must come to the conclusion that she did not know Jesus Christ as her own Personal Saviour (Jn. 3:16; Rom. 10:9-10, 13; Eph. 2:8-9).

If in fact she did not know Jesus as her Saviour, then all of these good deeds are not labeled by the Lord as *"good,"* simply because the motivation was wrong.

I have used her as an example for the obvious reasons. However, the entirety of the world falls into this category in one way or the other. Totally left on his own, man is incapable of doing good, and that means all men and for all time. As we have repeatedly said, a bitter fountain cannot bring forth sweet water. So that shoots down every idea of man attempting to solve his own problems. He simply cannot do such.

(13) "THEIR THROAT IS AN OPEN SEPULCHRE; WITH THEIR TONGUES THEY HAVE USED DECEIT; THE POISON OF ASPS IS UNDER THEIR LIPS:"

The phrase, *"Their throat is an open sepulchre,"* begins that which man does. The previous three verses tell what he is. He does what he does because of who and what he is.

The idea is, of an open grave, even with the casket open, and the rotting remains sending forth a putrid stench.

In essence it is saying, that man has no capability of producing life, only death. Everything he touches he pollutes, and everything he addresses he kills. *"The wages of sin is death,"* so death is all that man can produce (Rom. 6:23).

The phrase, *"With their tongues they have used deceit,"* speaks of guile, deception, hypocrisy, and smoothness, with the intent of entrapment.

The phrase, *"The poison of asps is under their lips,"* speaks of the Egyptian Cobra, a deadly serpent. Its poison is contained in a bag under the lips.

This is one of the reasons that the world is filled with lawyers. Man cannot be trusted in anything he says, so everything has to be documented several times over and by many witnesses.

(14) "WHOSE MOUTH IS FULL OF CURSING AND BITTERNESS:"

If one is to notice, the Holy Spirit strikingly portrays man's speech as being that of the most vile. Even though it certainly includes profanity and vulgarity, still, the idea is of far greater significance than that. Dealing with this very subject, Jesus said, *"O generation of vipers, how can ye, being evil, speak good things? For out of the abundance of the heart the mouth speaketh"* (Mat. 12:34). So it speaks more so of the deceit of the heart which guides the direction of the mouth.

The word *"Cursing"* in the Greek is *"ara,"* and means *"to place a curse on someone,"* by wishing them evil or hurt.

"Bitterness" in the Greek is *"pikria,"* and means *"bitter and reproachful language."* It has reference to railing out against people with gossip, innuendo, slander, etc.

(15) "THEIR FEET ARE SWIFT TO SHED BLOOD:"

The world is filled with murder, killing and violence. It has always been this way, but is worse now, at least in America, than it has been in my lifetime. In view of the fact that the world is racing toward Judgment, this problem, plus all other manner of evil, is going to get worse and worse. There are three basic symptoms of this, at least in this country: the Movies, Television, and a departure from the Bible. The first two are

caused by the third, with the spiritual problem always being the paramount cause.

This generation is called the MTV (Music, Television) generation. In other words, was and is raised on the fanfare as promoted by that particular Entertainment Channel. It promotes Homosexuality, Lesbianism, Acid Rock Music, Fornication and Adultery, Pornography, living together without the benefit of marriage, while at the same time denigrating the Bible, and actually every value taught in the Word of God.

The Movies have done, and are doing the same thing, but on a bigger screen. However, kids are tremendously influenced by these particular things. The people who appear as the stars serve as the role models, and the more evil, the better.

I saw a news clip the other day which said that there is more smoking in the Movies by the actors than ever before. They went on to elaborate as to how damaging this is respecting the efforts to keep kids from starting to smoke. One Movie, with one or more of the stars in that Movie setting the example by smoking, will start more kids down that path than anyone could ever think or believe. The warnings are forgotten when they see their star *"light up."*

As stated, regrettably the situation is not going to get better, but rather worse.

(16) "DESTRUCTION AND MISERY ARE IN THEIR WAYS:"

Destruction and misery are brought about by sin, and I speak of sin in the hearts of men. Modern Psychology claims that there is no such thing as sin; however, such an absurd conclusion in no way lessens the terrible impact of its wake of death.

I have travelled all over the world, and the problem is easy to identify. All the destruction and misery can be laid at the feet of sinful man. These are man's ways, and not God's *"Ways."* So, man has a choice, his ways or God's!

One would think that man's ways would not be too appetizing, but, regrettably, Satan is so adept at deception and blindness, that most of the world opts for the ways of man.

(17) "AND THE WAY OF PEACE HAVE THEY NOT KNOWN:"

For the approximate 33 1/2 years that Jesus

was in this world, for the first time in its history, it knew Peace. At His Birth the Scripture says that the *"Heavenly Host began Praising God,"* saying, *"Glory to God in the highest, and on Earth peace, good will toward men"* (Lk. 2:13-14).

It is said that for the first time in the history of the Roman Empire, the great war gates of Janus in Rome during this time were closed. Not a single Roman Army was on the march, and it stayed that way for the span of the Life of Jesus. The Prince of Peace was here, and there was Peace. Without Him there is no Peace, and in fact, there cannot be any Peace.

Regrettably, Israel rejected Him and the Kingdom, with war almost immediately commencing upon His Ascension. Such has remained the order of events from then until now, and will continue until His Second Coming. Then, and then alone, will the world know Peace.

Considering what man is and what man does, there is no way that man can have Peace, at least without Christ, irrespective of the United Nations, or whatever else is attempted in this vein.

(18) "THERE IS NO FEAR OF GOD BEFORE THEIR EYES."

In the heart of the True Believer, there is an apprehension somewhat of the Living God, as there should be. According to Luther, the natural man cannot fear God, at least as he should; according to Rudolph Otto, he is *"Quite unable even to shudder or feel horror in the real sense of the word."*

HOLY FEAR

Holy fear, on the other hand, is God-given, enabling men to reverence God's Authority, obey His Commandments and hate and shun all form of evil (Gen. 22:12; Jer. 32:40; Heb. 5:7). Moreover, the *"Fear of God is the beginning* (or principle) *of wisdom"* (Ps. 111:10); the secret of uprightness (Prov. 8:13); a feature of the people in whom God delights (Ps. 147:11); and the *"whole duty of man"* (Eccl. 12:13). It is also one of the Divine qualifications of the Messiah (Isa. 11:2-3).

In the Old Testament, largely because of the Law's legal sanctions, true spirituality is often regarded as synonymous with the Fear

of God (Ps. 34:11; Jer. 2:19), and even in New Testament times the term *"walking in the Fear of the Lord"* (Acts 9:31) was used in connection with the early Christians.

In the New Testament generally, however, emphasis is laid on God as loving and forgiving, the One Who through Christ gives to men the spirit of Sonship (Rom. 8:15), and enables them boldly to face up to life (II Tim. 1:6-7) and death (Heb. 2:15) without Fear.

Nevertheless, a Reverent Fear remains; for the awesomeness of God has not changed, and there is a Day of Judgment to be met by all, whether the Judgment Seat of Christ for Believers, or the Great White Throne Judgment for unbelievers (II Cor. 5:10; Rev. 20:11-15).

Godly Fear stimulates the Believer to seek Holiness (II Cor. 7:1), and is reflected in his attitude towards his fellow-Christians (Eph. 5:21).

NO FEAR OF GOD

The reason there is no Fear of God in the hearts of unbelievers is because, as we have previously stated, unbelieving man does not really know God. Unless he has been raised in a Christian home, or been influenced by Christianity in some way, unbelievers for the most part are not even sure if there is a God. In their minds, whether there is one or not, they do not respect His Authority, or even recognize that He has any authority. To obey His Commandments is a joke, because in their thinking, the Bible is basically a book of fables.

The only time they evidence any Fear toward God, or whatever type of name they would ascribe to Him, that is if they admit His existence at all, is during a time of personal or national tragedy. Someone has said that there are no atheists in the foxholes. However, once the danger is past, the fear quickly passes as well.

(19) "NOW WE KNOW THAT WHAT THINGS SOEVER THE LAW SAITH, IT SAITH TO THEM WHO ARE UNDER THE LAW: THAT EVERY MOUTH MAY BE STOPPED, AND ALL THE WORLD MAY BECOME GUILTY BEFORE GOD."

The phrase, *"Now we know that what things soever the Law saith, it saith to them who are under the Law,"* is meant first of all to inform the Jews that verses 10-18 apply to them as well as the Gentiles.

As we have previously stated, this must have been extremely galling to the Jews for Paul to say such a thing; however, the Holy Spirit wanted it said in such a way that there would be absolutely no mistake as to its meaning, and so it was.

By contrast, just because Paul specifies the Law, which the Gentiles did not have, one is not to draw the conclusion that his statement applied to Jews only and not Gentiles. In other words, and as he had already stated in Chapter 1, the Gentile world definitely could not claim ignorance due to the fact of not having the Law as the Jews did. *All* were equally guilty before God.

The phrase, *"That every mouth may be stopped,"* means exactly what it says. As stated, the Gentiles were claiming ignorance, while the Jews were claiming exemption from Judgment. This which the Holy Spirit gave Paul stops the mouths of all. Once again we go back to Paul's statement, *"Let God be True, but every man a liar"* (Rom. 3:4).

The phrase, *"And all the world may become guilty before God,"* very simply and clearly states the situation exactly as it is. Irrespective of who they are, where they are, what they are, or why they are, every human being on the face of the Earth who has ever been born, with the exception of Jesus Christ, is *"guilty before God."*

Now as we have stated in Commentary on Chapter 1, the fact of sin, which is graphically outlined here, and shown to be far, far worse than anyone could ever think or believe, is not really the cause of the coming Day of Judgment (Rev. 20:11-15). The real reason is the rejection by man of the great Redemption afforded by God's Only Son, and made available to all.

(20) "THEREFORE BY THE DEEDS OF THE LAW THERE SHALL NO FLESH BE JUSTIFIED IN HIS SIGHT: FOR BY THE LAW IS THE KNOWLEDGE OF SIN."

The phrase, *"Therefore by the deeds of the Law there shall no flesh be justified in His Sight,"* should read, *"by works of the Law,"* i.e., by personal religious efforts and ceremonies to obtain moral perfection, which simply cannot be done.

The structure of the sentence in the Greek includes the Mosaic Law, but goes much further, including Law in a deeper and more general sense as written both in the Ten Commandments and in the hearts of the Gentiles, and, consequently, embracing the moral deeds of both Gentiles and Jews.

So, let not the Reader think that the Holy Spirit through the Apostle is speaking only of the Law of Moses, but that He also is referring to every single man-devised effort that has ever existed, hoping to assuage guilt and bring about Righteousness. Irrespective of what it is, and even as religious as it may be, it is not something that God will accept.

It makes no difference if it's a billion dollar Church built by the Mormons, or ten Hail Marys, or reliance on being a third generation Baptist, Pentecostal, Holiness, etc., all are out and out totally.

In these Texts, the Mosaic Law may indeed be regarded as the primary reference, but only as representing a universal legislation which must of necessity include all the efforts of man to justify himself.

The phrase, *"For by the Law is the knowledge of sin,"* now swings back to the Law of Moses exclusively, and states its purpose.

The Law in itself was only meant to define sin and, consequently, make it sinful, but it in no way emancipated from it, nor was it designed to do so! However, man consciously or unconsciously keeps trying to earn Salvation by keeping rules, doing things, being religious, carrying out good deeds, ad infinitum.

Please believe this Evangelist, the problem did not die with Judaism, but continues to be the greatest hindrance to Salvation in the world today, and in fact, ever has been. As stated, it began with Adam and Eve in the Garden immediately after their Fall, when *"they sewed fig leaves together, and made themselves aprons"* (Gen. 3:7). However, the Lord *"made coats of skins, and clothed them,"* which was meant to portray the coming Redemption, which would be afforded by a sinless Victim, the Lord Jesus Christ (Gen. 3:21).

Regrettably, the proposed solution of the *"fig leaf"* did not end with the first couple, but in one form or the other, almost always religious, continues unto this hour.

The terrible declaration of verse 20 that not one member of the human family, however good and beautiful morally, at least they think, can procure by meritorious efforts a Righteousness that God will accept, and the added statement that the Law of Moses was given not to enable man to furnish himself with this needed Righteousness, but to make him conscious that he was a sinner, and therefore unrighteous — this terrible pronouncement destroys all hope of Salvation by works (Williams).

(21) "BUT NOW THE RIGHTEOUSNESS OF GOD WITHOUT THE LAW IS MANIFESTED, BEING WITNESSED BY THE LAW AND THE PROPHETS;"

The phrase, *"But now the Righteousness of God without the Law is manifested,"* should read, *"apart from Law,"* i.e., from works of merit.

The word *"Righteousness"* is the result of Justification by Faith. It is the act or process by which a man is brought into a right state as related to God.

In simple nontechnical language it refers to the Act of God removing the guilt and penalty of sin from the sinner who places his Faith in the Lord Jesus as Saviour. It also refers to the bestowal of a positive Righteousness, found only in Jesus Christ, in Whom the Believer stands a Righteous person before God's Law for time and eternity. All of this is made possible by and based upon the satisfaction (propitiation) which Jesus Christ offered on the Cross as a complete payment of the penalty imposed by the Law because of human infractions of that Law, thus satisfying His Justice, maintaining His Government, and making possible the bestowal of Mercy upon the basis of justice satisfied.

This is a legal standing, and does not within itself change nor affect the character of the person, which later is changed by the Work of the Holy Spirit in Progressive Sanctification (Wuest).

While there was a Righteousness in the Law, it was a Righteousness to which man within his own abilities could not attain. The Law of Moses required perfect obedience of which man was not capable.

NOTES

Consequently, God manifested His Righteousness in Christ in a different way, and on a different principle, from that of Law. As we have stated, the principle of Law is to enjoin and forbid, and to require complete obedience.

However, this manifestation of God's Righteousness in and through His Son Jesus Christ, though *"apart from Law,"* is not in any way in opposition to the Teaching of the Law and the Prophets, being, in fact, anticipated by them (Barmby).

The phrase, *"Being witnessed by the Law and the Prophets,"* proclaims as stated, the Testimony of the Law to the Divine Principle of Justification by Faith and is found in Genesis 15:6; the Testimony of the Prophets is that of Habakkuk 2:4.

(The term *"The Law"* in the New Testament frequently means the Old Testament, consisting of the Law, the Prophets, and the Psalms, Lk. 24:44; the Testimony of the Psalms to Justification by Faith is that of Ps. 32:1-2.)

In fact, the entirety of the Old Testament points exclusively to Christ, which includes all of the accoutrements of the Tabernacle, etc. Everything pointed to what Christ would do, regarding His Mediatorial, Atoning, and Intercessory Work.

(22) "EVEN THE RIGHTEOUSNESS OF GOD WHICH IS BY FAITH OF JESUS CHRIST UNTO ALL AND UPON ALL THEM THAT BELIEVE: FOR THERE IS NO DIFFERENCE:"

The phrase, *"Even the Righteousness of God which is by Faith of Jesus Christ,"* concerns Imputed Righteousness, and tells how it is obtained.

First of all we are talking about the *"Righteousness of God,"* which is as stated, *"perfection,"* but a standard which is far and beyond anything that man may label as *"perfect."* As well, it speaks of *"moral perfection,"* which again is a perfect morality, far and away beyond anything man could grasp or understand. That is *"God's Righteousness."*

There is only one way for this *"Righteousness"* to be obtained. It is through and by the Lord Jesus Christ. As the Apostle has repeatedly stated, no amount of good works, or privileged position, even as the Jews, can attain to this which God demands.

So if Jesus Alone can impart this Righteousness, how is it obtained from Him?

BY FAITH

It is obtained *"by Faith,"* and what does that mean?

It simply means that the sinner believes that Jesus is the Son of God, and that He became Man in order to become the Perfect Sacrifice which God would accept. The sinner must believe that Jesus died on Calvary, and in doing so, offered up Himself as an Atonement for the sin of man. In the offering up of Himself, man's terrible sin debt was instantly paid, with Satan holding no more claims over the head of man.

The sinner must also believe that Jesus rose from the dead on the third day, which guarantees the Resurrection of every Saint of God who has ever lived on that coming Glad Day.

The believing of this of which we have stated, is what it means to have Faith in Christ Jesus. The moment the sinner does that, he is instantly Saved (Jn. 3:16; Rom. 10:9-10, 13; Eph. 2:8-9; Rev. 22:17).

This is the reason that it is impossible to be Saved without trusting and believing in Jesus Christ. He is the One Who paid the price for man's Redemption; consequently, He is the One in Whom we must believe.

TO BELIEVE

The phrase, *"Unto all and upon all them that believe,"* states two things:

1. The way given here is *"unto all,"* meaning that all are on the same level, be they rich, poor, great, small, educated, uneducated, or whatever race, nationality, or creed. It is one Saviour and thereby one Salvation for all of humanity.

2. It is given to them only who *"believe."* By the word *"believe"* we are speaking of far more than mere mental affirmation, but rather an acceptance unto oneself of what Jesus did at Calvary nearly 2,000 years ago.

To be frank, millions believe in a historical Jesus, with many even believing that He died on Calvary, and with some even believing that He rose from the dead, but they are not Saved. They merely witness to the fact, which within itself brings about nothing.

The believing is that He did it for you, and without what he did, one cannot be Saved. We are to believe that He took our place and suffered the penalty, which was rightly ours.

To be sure, I dare not complicate the issue, considering that this great Plan of Salvation as afforded by God is so simple that even a child can understand, believe, and receive. I know, because He Saved me when I was eight years old!

If reading this at this moment, you feel that you are not Saved, in other words, that you have never really, fully accepted Christ as your own Personal Saviour, now is the time that this great and wonderful thing be done.

If you will simply read the following words, and believe them with all your heart, Salvation will instantly be yours.

Please read them slowly, and if you so desire, read them out loud.

"Dear Heavenly Father, I come to you in the Name of Your Son and my Saviour The Lord Jesus Christ. I am sorry for my sin and my rebellion against You. Please forgive me and cleanse me with the Precious Blood shed by Your Only Son, The Lord Jesus Christ.

"With my mouth I confess Him as Lord, and in my heart I believe that God has raised Him from the dead.

"At this moment, I accept Jesus as my Saviour and as my Lord. I believe that He has washed away every sin and stain. I believe now that I am Saved.

"Lord I thank You for hearing me, and above all I thank You for saving me. I will do my best to live for You, and I will be careful to confess Your Name as my Lord and Saviour. Amen."

The phrase, *"For there is no difference,"* simply means that Salvation, as we have stated, is for all, and comes on the same basis which is by Faith, whether the person is a Jew or Gentile.

Isn't it wonderful that the same requirements apply to all! Isn't it wonderful that any and all may come! Isn't it wonderful that He has never turned one away, who sincerely came to Him!

(23) "FOR ALL HAVE SINNED, AND COME SHORT OF THE GLORY OF GOD;"

The phrase, *"For all have sinned,"* presents

all men being placed in the same category, that of sinners.

The word "sinned" in the Greek is "hamartano," and means, "to miss the mark," thus, "to fail in obeying the Law."

In essence it means, that God the Creator has set the Standard for Righteousness, and man has failed to meet that Standard. To make it even worse, *all* men and without exception, have failed to meet that Standard, with one exception, and that is the Lord Jesus Christ. Also, it is not a matter of having failed to keep the Law one time or even a few times, but constantly. God has ever laid out the Standard, which ever abides, and man is ever failing to come up to the Standard, and in fact, no matter how hard he tries, cannot come up to the Standard, at least within himself.

Consequently, all having sinned, and all continuing to sin at least in some fashion, and no one possessing any merit, the Principle of Justification by Faith is universal in its application. In other words, all are lost and all, therefore, can be Saved.

SIN, THE CAUSE

The Old and New Testaments explain that the tragedy and suffering that mark human experience are the results of sin. The Biblical concept of sin, which is the only True Concept there is, has been clouded in modern culture. But the experience of each individual, like the history of every society provides overwhelming Testimony to the existence and the impact of what Scripture calls "sin."

IN THE OLD TESTAMENT

The principle Hebrew word in the Old Testament for sin is "hata," and means, as stated, "to miss the mark" (Judg. 20:16; Prov. 19:2).

In the Old Testament this word group, which is used some 580 times, typically speaks of missing the Standard that God sets for man. While in much of the Old Testament, "sin" involves a failure to obey the Mosaic Law, we see the concept of sin used prior to the giving of the Law. Genesis 13:13 identifies the men of Sodom as great sinners. Joseph was repelled when his master's wife tried to seduce him; he refused to "sin against God" (Gen. 39:9).

Reuben resisted when his brothers wanted "to sin against the boy," that is, to kill the young Joseph (Gen. 42:22). In each of these cases there is what may be called a sin against nature. That is, God has expressed His Character and Standards in the design of human nature, so that certain actions are perceived as violations of right, even though no Law had been given (Rom. 2:14-15).

Thus, the structure of human nature and the Revelation of Divine expectations both provide valid Standards for humanity. Violation of these Standards by falling short of performing what is expected, is sin.

There are many other Old Testament words in the vocabulary of sin. All of them imply the existence of a Divine Standard, which is the only Standard that matters. Most portray human actions in some relationship to that Standard.

"Hata" indicates missing the mark, "pesa" ("rebellion," "transgression") indicates a revolt against the Standard, and "awon" ("iniquity," "guilt") is a deviation from, or a twisting of, the Standard.

THE LANGUAGE OF REDEMPTION

In Scripture, the language of sin is also the language of Redemption. An example of this is the Hebrew word "hatt't." This word means both "Sin" and "Sin Offering." It speaks of both the fact of failure and the wonderful reality of a forgiveness provided by God through the Sin-Offering that removes guilt.

In the Old Testament, the "Sin-Offering" was an Animal Sacrifice, which incidentally could not really take away sin, but only cover it from the Righteous Eyes of God, and, therefore, pointed toward the One Sin-Offering Who was to come, and in fact did come, The Lord Jesus Christ.

God confronts us in Scripture, calling us to acknowledge our sin. But God also comforts us in Scripture, promising Restoration and reassuring us of His Love in the forgiveness and cleansing of sin, if men will only believe Him (Mat. 1:21; I Jn. 1:9).

THE EXAMPLE OF DAVID

The Hebrew language is not shaped to deal with philosophical issues. It rather focuses on concrete realities. Yet the Old Testament is filled with hints of the perspective on sin developed fully only in the New Testament.

The first verses of Psalm 51, David's prayer of confession of his sin with Bathsheba, draw together the Old Testament's view of sin in a fascinating way.

"Have Mercy on me, O God, according to Thy Lovingkindness; according to Your great Compassion blot out my transgressions (Hebrew 'pasa').

"Wash away all my iniquity ('awon') and cleanse me from my sin ('hatta't').

"For I know my transgressions ('pasa'), and my sin ('hatta't') are always before me.

"Against You, You Only, have I sinned ('hata') and done this evil ('ra') in Your Sight, so that You are proved right when You speak and justified when You judge.

"Surely I was sinful ('awon') at birth, sinful ('het') from the time my mother conceived me.

"Surely you desire Truth in the inner parts; You teach me wisdom in the inmost place.

"Cleanse ('hata') me with Hyssop, and I will be clean; wash me, and I will be whiter than snow.

"Let me hear joy and gladness; let the bones you have crushed rejoice.

"Hide Your Face from my sins ('het') and blot out all my iniquity ('awon').

"Create in me a pure heart, O God, and renew a steadfast spirit within me.

"Do not cast me from Your Presence or take Your Holy Spirit from me.

"Restore to me the joy of Your Salvation and grant me a willing spirit, to sustain me.

"Then I will teach transgressors ('pasa') Your Ways, and sinners ('hatta') will turn back to You.

"Save me from bloodguilt ('dam'), O God, The God Who saves me, and my tongue will sing of Your Righteousness."

GOD'S LOVE AND MERCY

Looking at the development of the Psalm, we note that David identifies his sin by all three major Old Testament terms. In sinning with Bathsheba he rebelled against God's Standards, fell short of them, and deviated from the path they marked out. Thus, God's Mercy and Love were the only

basis for David's appeal to God for cleansing from sin.

Whereas he could not find the type of Love and Mercy in the Law needed for cleansing from sin, David went all the way back to the deliverance of the Children of Israel from Egyptian bondage. He appealed to the Love and Mercy which applied the Blood to the doorposts of all the homes of the Children of Israel, which gave them protection and safe passage (Ex. 12:13).

That is the reason he said in the 51st Psalm, *"Purge me with Hyssop, and I shall be clean"* (51:7). On those houses in Egypt, the blood of the slain lamb was applied to the doorposts with *"Hyssop"* (Ex. 12:22-23).

(Hyssop is a small bushy plant, which grew between the cracks of stones and such like. It was used in several Jewish rituals [Lev. 14:4-6, 49-52; Num. 19:6, 18; I Ki. 4:33; Ps. 51:7; Jn. 19:29; Heb. 9:19].)

Consequently, the Precious Shed Blood of Jesus Christ (in type) which delivered the Children of Israel, and irrespective as to who they were and what they had done, also delivered David, as it will deliver anyone who places their Faith and Confidence in Him.

SIN ACKNOWLEDGED

David acknowledged his sin, rebellion and failure, as such always has to be done by any sinner, before Repentance can be enjoined. Only when sin is acknowledged as such can human beings begin to deal with the misery sin causes. Even more, David confesses to God, *"Against You, You Only have I sinned,"* which is actually the case altogether of sin — it is against God.

This does not mean his sin did not harm Bathsheba or her husband, for it did, and greatly so, as would be obvious. Rather, it is an admission that God is the One Who establishes the Standard of right and wrong. A relativistic morality that measures sin only by harm done to others must always fall short of the Biblical position.

Other people belong to God, and He has established His Standards for their protection as well as for our own. So sin is against God, and because it is against God, the Lord is *"proved right"* and *"justified"* when He acts in Judgment.

THE CONSTANT COMING SHORT

Psalms 51:5 has a hint of the Doctrine developed by Paul which we are now studying in the first three Chapters of Romans.

From the time of his conception, David had fallen short of the Divine Standard, and from birth he had deviated from God's Norm, as have all. However, original sin is not the result of rebellion, at least this of which we speak, because in that stage there is no conscious act of sin implied. As stated, we are speaking now of original sin, with which every baby has as a result of the Fall of Adam and Eve in the Garden of Eden.

These seeds of sin take root deep within our personalities, so deeply in fact, that there is no way that one can be separated from this dread malady, except through the New Birth.

TRUTH IN THE INWARD PARTS

In the inner person, the core of the human personality, God desires Truth. The reference to cleansing with Hyssop is a reference to Blood Sacrifice; as we have stated, the plant was used to sprinkle the Cleansing Blood of the Old Testament Sacrifices.

In view of his own moral and spiritual bankruptcy, David then called on God to act — in effect to hide His Face from (not look at, not respond in judgment to) David's sins (51:9). God was asked to do a creative work within David's heart and empower him by His Spirit.

After God answered these pleas, David would be able to move transgressors to follow the path he himself had taken — turning back to God, to rely, not on human righteousness, but on the Righteousness of God (51:11-14).

Thus, the Old Testament sees sin as involving a person's conscience, responsible choice measured against a known Divine Standard. But sin is more basic than that; the individual's propensity to react against the Divine Norm can be traced back to human nature itself.

Helpless people can only recognize their need and appeal to God for forgiveness, inner cleansing, and spiritual power. Those who do not see themselves in this capacity — helpless — do not seek God for that which only He can give.

NOTES

THE NEW TESTAMENT

Like the Old Testament, the New Testament is filled with words related to the concept of sin: fault, guilt, injustice, offense, transgression, unrighteousness, and wickedness, to name a few. And of course there are scores of specific sins mentioned, such as murder, theft, lying, adultery, idolatry, etc.

There are, however, two major word groups in the Greek language that sum up the concept of sin. One word *"adikia,"* means *"wrongdoing," "unrighteousness," "injustice."* Its focus is on the concept of sin as conscious human action that causes visible harm to other persons in violation of the Divine Standard.

As well, sin is also seen in the New Testament as rebellion and as conscious deviation from known right.

"Sin" is used in a descriptive sense in the Gospels, and there it is almost always associated with forgiveness. The Epistles, especially those of Paul, penetrate beyond observation of human behavior to explore its cause. Paul takes the concept of sin hinted at in Psalm 51:5 and implied in the Old Testament Doctrine of the New Covenant, and develops the portrait of a humanity distorted and twisted by the brutal power of sin (Rom. Chpt. 1).

Consequently, sin is not only missing God's mark; it is an inner reality, a warp in human nature, and a malignant power that holds each individual in an unbreakable grip.

THE HUMAN RESPONSE TO DIVINE STANDARDS

The Old Testament views sin in terms of the human response to Divine Standards. People fall short, deviate, and rebel against the norms that God has established. Such actions result in guilt, but a remedy is implied in the very Hebrew terms themselves. Thus, *"sin"* and *"Sin Offering,"* like *"trespass"* and *"Trespass Offering,"* are from the same roots. God calls on human beings to acknowledge their sin, and in that Call God invites the Believer to look to Him for forgiveness.

SIN IS MORE THAN A DEVIATION

In the New Testament, sin is still viewed as deviation from Divinely-established Norms. But sin is more, much more, than that. It is deeply rooted in the nature of the fallen race, a reality that holds human beings in slavery to hostile spiritual powers and to baser passions and desires. Because of the corruption of human nature by sin, no person can achieve the Standard of Righteousness God must require, and no one, apart from Redemption, can please the Lord.

JESUS THE ONLY ANSWER FOR SIN

Jesus' entry into the world to deal with sin must be understood on multiple levels. Jesus does forgive sins, and His Death on Calvary was a Sacrifice that satisfied the demands of Heavenly Justice that sin be punished. But Jesus also is the Source of a New Life that renews the individual from within.

Through Jesus we are provided with the capacity not to sin. But even this is not the full provision. By surrender to God and reliance on the Holy Spirit Whom Jesus has sent, the influence of the sin nature in the Believer can be dampened, and the Christian can live according to God's Will. Jesus saves *from* sin not in sin.

The Promise of Resurrection's full release from every taint of sin is tasted here, and at each moment the possibility of living without sin's corrupting impact does exist.

In I John we even have that Promise extended. God will not guarantee us sinlessness now. But the reality and the power of His Life within is a major motivation not to keep on sinning, which now is repugnant and repulsive to the Believer in Christ (Richards).

The phrase, *"And come short of the Glory of God,"* carries the idea in the Greek Text to *"right now come short."* In other words, the Believer not only came short of the Glory of God before his Conversion, but even continues to do so at present.

By that we do not mean that the Believer has a sinning Salvation, or that one must sin a little bit every day, as some claim, for as stated, Jesus does not save us in sin but rather, from sin. And yet, no Believer is perfect, and in fact, sinless perfection is not taught in the Word of God, at least in the here and now. The idea is, that no True Believer can practice sin (I Jn. 3:9).

SANCTIFICATION

When we speak of the Believer's walk before

NOTES

God, we are really referring to Sanctification. While there is only one Sanctification, still, it works in our lives in two distinct ways:

1. There is the *"Standing"* of Sanctification which comes to every sinner at the moment of their Conversion. This is the part that makes us clean and is a necessary work in the heart and life of the sinner as should be obvious (I Cor. 6:11).

This position never changes or varies, and is actually looked at by God as *"perfect."* This is because God has reckoned us accordingly due to the great Price paid by His Son and our Saviour, The Lord Jesus Christ, and our Faith in Him.

Jesus lived a perfect life on this Earth, keeping the Law in every respect, and as a consequence, having the Righteousness of the Law. All of this was done for sinners, and upon Faith in Him, His Perfection (perfect walk) is freely granted unto the Believer. In that manner, the Believer becomes a Lawkeeper instead of a Lawbreaker. But once again, it is all through Christ.

It is a perfect Life, a perfect Walk, a perfect Salvation, but all in Christ. As stated, that *"Standing"* in Christ doesn't vary and never changes from its position of *"perfection."*

2. Our *"State"* of Sanctification, however, is something else altogether. In fact, it does vary and is up and down constantly (I Thess. 5:23). Consequently, the Holy Spirit in His tireless efforts, seeks to bring our *"State"* up to our *"Standing."*

This is where the struggle between the flesh and the spirit comes in, which is a never-ceasing activity with the Child of God. To be frank, one's victory in Christ is actually just as simple as one's Salvation. However, the *"Promise"* of the Land is one thing, while the *"Possession"* is something else altogether. In fact, Jesus has totally possessed this land of victory for us, even as Romans Chapter 6 bears out, but it is very difficult for us at times to fully realize and understand all the implications of this. We find ourselves trying to fight battles all over again, which Jesus has already fought and won. As I have said many times, if the Believer is fighting and winning, after a while he will fight and lose.

To be frank, there is only one fight that the Believer should engage, and that is the *"good fight of Faith"* (I Tim. 6:12). If we attempt to fight any other fight, we will ultimately lose.

Perhaps the greatest problem in each and every Believer's life, is the folly, through ignorance or otherwise, of attempting to do all over again what Jesus has already done, which in the first place, is impossible!

The key to all of this is the Holy Spirit, even as Romans Chapter 8 brings out. But yet, when God takes our account, He doesn't look at our *"State"* of Sanctification, but always at our *"Standing."* Thank God, that Standing never changes, and because it is in Jesus.

ENTIRE SANCTIFICATION

The Teaching of Entire Sanctification is quite prominent in some Church circles. The Doctrine is correct if understood properly. However, in most cases it is misunderstood.

The idea is, at least as it is taught in some circles, that a person is first Saved, and then Sanctified, and then Baptized with the Holy Spirit (the Holiness people leave off the Baptism with the Holy Spirit).

They teach that one is Sanctified at some point in time, after being Saved. It is called Entire Sanctification, with one then becoming sinless, in other words, sinless perfection. Pure and simple, this is error, of which of course, the Bible does not teach.

The Bible teaches two Works of Grace: A. Salvation (Jn. 3:16); and, B. The Baptism with the Holy Spirit (Acts 1:4; 2:4).

THE SIMULTANEOUS THREE-STEP PROCESS

The Apostle Paul said, *"And such were some of you: but you are washed, but you are sanctified, but you are justified in the Name of the Lord Jesus, and by the Spirit of our God"* (I Cor. 6:11).

The first step in this process, as is obvious, is *"washing."* This is done automatically, by the Precious Blood of Christ, that is, when the believing sinner evidences Faith in Christ.

The next step is *"Sanctification."* The word simply means *"to be made clean."* In fact, this is done simultaneously with the *"washing."* Once again, it comes about as

NOTES

the believing sinner expresses Faith in Christ.

The third step, also carried out simultaneously, is *"Justification,"* which means *"to declare one not guilty."* Consequently, it's easy to see that one must be *"made clean,"* which is Sanctification, before one can be *"declared clean,"* which is Justification.

Washing and Sanctification are the practical Works of the Holy Spirit, while Justification is the legal Work of the Holy Spirit, all done at Conversion (I Cor. 6:11).

So as one can see, a second Work of Grace called *"Entire Sanctification"* would not make much sense, considering that this Work was carried out at Conversion. People come up with weird Doctrines when they do not properly follow the Word of God.

ABOUT PERFECTION

The Biblical idea of Perfection is of a state of ideal wholeness or completion, in which any disabilities, shortcomings, or defects that may have existed before have been eliminated or left behind.

Perfection is a relative term, meaning simply the attainment of a due end, or the enjoyment of an ideal state. What that end and state is varies in different cases. The Bible speaks of Perfection in three distinct connections.

THE PERFECTION OF GOD

Scripture speaks of God (Mat. 5:48), His *"Work"* (Deut. 32:4), His *"Way"* (II Sam. 22:31; Ps. 18:30), and His *"Law"* (Ps. 19:7; James 1:25) as perfect.

In each context some feature of His Manifested Moral Glory is in view, and the thought is that what God says and does is wholly free from faults and worthy of all praise. In Matthew 5:48, Christ holds up the ideal conduct of the Heavenly Father (particularly, in the context, of His Kindness to those who oppose Him) as a pattern which His Children must imitate.

THE PERFECTION OF CHRIST

The writer to the Hebrews speaks of the Incarnate Son of God as having been made *"perfect through sufferings"* (Heb. 2:10). The reference here is not to any personal probation of Jesus as Man, but to His being fitted by His experience of the power of temptation and the costliness of obedience for the High Priestly Ministry to which God had called Him (Heb. 5:7-10; 7:28).

As High Priest, having *"offered for all time a single Sacrifice for sins"* (Heb. 10:12), He became *"The Source of Eternal Salvation to all who obey Him"* (Heb. 5:9), securing for them by His Intercession constant access to God (Heb. 7:25; 10:19) and giving them the constant sympathy and help that they need in their constant temptations (Heb. 4:14).

It was His Own firsthand experience of temptation that fitted Him to fulfill this latter Ministry (Heb. 2:17; 5:2, 7).

THE PERFECTION OF MAN

This is spoken of with reference: A. To God's Covenant Relationship with man; and, B. To His Work of Grace in man.

The Bible speaks of man's Perfection in the Covenant with God. This is the Perfection which the Old Testament demands of God's people (Gen. 17:1; Deut. 18:13) and ascribes in certain ways to individual Saints (Noah, Gen. 6:9; Asa, I Ki. 15:14; Job, Job 1:1); loyal, sincere, wholehearted obedience to the known Will of their Gracious God. It is Faith at work, maintaining a right relationship with God by reverent worship and service.

This Perfection is essentially a matter of the heart (I Ki. 8:61; II Ki. 20:3; I Chron. 29:9); outward conformity to God's Commands is not enough if the heart is not perfect before God (II Chron. 25:2).

Perfection is regularly linked with uprightness, as its natural outward expression (Job 1:1, 8; 2:3; Ps. 37:37; Prov. 2:21).

GOD'S COVENANT RELATIONSHIP WITH MAN

The Bible also speaks of God's perfecting of His Covenant Relation with man. This is the perfecting of men through Christ with which the writer to the Hebrews deals. *"The perfecting of men refers to their Covenant condition . . . to per-fect . . . is to put the people into the True Covenant Relation of worshipers of the Lord, to bring them into His full fellowship."*

God did this by replacing the Old Covenant,

Priesthood, Tabernacle and Sacrifices with something better. The *"Old Covenant"* in Hebrews means the Mosaic system for establishing living fellowship between God and His people; but, says the writer, it could never *"per-fect"* them in this relationship, for it could not give full assurance of the remission of all sins, for Jesus had not yet come and died on Calvary (Heb. 7:11, 18; 9:9; 10:1-4).

Under the New Covenant, however, on the ground of Christ's Single Sacrifice of Himself, Believers receive God's assurance that He will remember their sins no more (Heb. 10:11-18). Thus, they are *"per-fected forever."* This Perfection of fellowship with God is something that Old Testament Saints did not know on Earth (Heb. 11:40) — though, through Christ, they enjoy it now, in the Heavenly Jerusalem (Heb. 12:23).

GOD, GRACE, AND MAN

The Bible speaks of God's perfecting of His people in the Image of Christ. God means those who through Faith enjoy fellowship with Him, to grow from spiritual infancy to a maturity (perfection as it applies to maturity) in which they will lack nothing of the full stature of Christ, in Whose Likeness they are being renewed (Col. 3:10).

They are to grow till they are, in this sense, complete (Gal. 3:14; Eph. 4:13; Col. 4:12; Heb. 5:14; 6:1; I Pet. 2:2). This thought has both a corporate and an individual aspect: the Church corporately is to become a *"perfect man"* (Gal. 3:28; Eph. 2:15; 4:13), and the individual Christian will *"be perfect"* (Phil. 3:12).

In either case the conception is Christological and Eschatological. This means, that the realm of perfection is *"in Christ"* (Col. 1:28), and perfection of fellowship with Christ, and likeness to Christ, is a Divine Gift that will not be enjoyed till the day of His Coming, the Church's completing, and the Christian's Resurrection (Eph. 4:12-16; Phil. 3:10-14; Col. 3:4; I Jn. 3:2).

Meanwhile, however, mature and vigorous Christians may be said to have attained a relative perfection in the realms of spiritual insight (Phil. 3:15), tempered Christian Character (James 1:4) and confident love towards God and men (I Jn. 4:12, 17).

PERFECTION?

The Bible nowhere relates the idea of Perfection directly to Law, nor equates it directly with sinlessness. While absolute sinlessness is a goal which Christians must seek (Mat. 5:48; Rom. 6:19; II Cor. 7:1), still, it is a place which they do not yet find (James 3:2; I Jn. 1:8-2:2). No doubt when the Christian is perfected in Glory he will be sinless, but to equate the Biblical idea of Perfection with sinlessness and then to argue that, because the Bible refers to some men as perfect, therefore, sinlessness on Earth must be a practical possibility, would be to darken counsel.

Actually, when the Bible speaks of Perfection relative to particular individuals, it is speaking of a certain aspect of their lives and not sinless perfection. Job is a perfect example (Job 1:8).

The word *"perfect"* here speaks of his efforts to please the Lord, which he tried to do, evidently, with all his strength. However, when he finally saw the Lord, Who always must be the Standard and Example, he said of himself, *"Behold, I am vile"* (Job 40:4).

The present Perfection, which, according to Scripture, a Christian may attain is a matter, not of sinlessness, for as Paul said, we are constantly coming short of the Glory of God, but of strong Faith, joyful patience, and overflowing Love.

(Bibliography: Arndt; Trench, *"New Testament Synonyms"*; B. B. Warfield, *"Perfectionism"*; and, R. N. Flew, *"The Idea of Perfection in Christian Theology."*)

(24) "BEING JUSTIFIED FREELY BY HIS GRACE THROUGH THE REDEMPTION THAT IS IN CHRIST JESUS:"

"Being Justified freely by His Grace," contains four powerful words relative to Salvation:

1. Justified: This speaks of Justification by Faith, which means that one is Justified in the Eyes of God, meaning that he is declared by God *"not guilty."* This phrase tells us how this is done.

2. Freely: The Greek word is *"dorean,"* and means *"gratis, gratuitously, without just cause."*

The idea is, that God exacts or requires no price of any nature from the sinner respecting this great Gift of Salvation. It is

absolutely free of charge. Actually, any payment presented by the sinner not only is not accepted, but nullifies that which God freely gives. So, the attempt for one to justify oneself by his own good works, is serious indeed!

3. Grace: The Greek is *"charis,"* and *"signifies a favor done out of the spontaneous generosity of the heart without any expectation of return."* As well, the age-old explanation of *"unmerited favor"* is unequalled. However, there is an extension to this which is little carried in the definition.

Of course, when the Greeks exhibited Grace, this favor of whatever nature was always done to one's friend, never to an enemy. But when *"Grace"* comes into the New Testament, it takes an infinite leap forward, for the favor God did at Calvary was for those who hated Him. It was a favor done out of the spontaneous generosity of God's Heart of Love with no expectation of return. There are no strings attached to Grace, as there can be no strings attached to Grace. It is given gratuitously, or it is not Grace.

Of course, Grace in the form of Salvation is so adjusted that the one who receives it, turns from sin to serve the Living God and live a Holy Life, for Grace includes not only the bestowal of a Righteousness, but the inward transformation consisting of the power of indwelling sin broken and the Divine Nature implanted, which liberates the Believer from the compelling power of sin and makes him hate sin, love Holiness, and gives him the power to obey the Word of God (Wuest).

4. Redemption: This Grace shown the believing sinner is made possible, Paul says, through the Redemption which is in Christ Jesus. *"Redemption"* in the Greek is *"apolutroscos,"* which means *"to redeem by paying the price."*

Actually, there are three Greek words which beautifully explain the word *"Redeem,"* adding more light to the subject:

1. *"Agorazo"*: This means *"to buy in the slave market"* (I Cor. 6:20, 7:23; II Pet. 2:1). Christ bought us in the slave market of sin by His Own Blood.

The sinner most of the time, does not think of himself as a slave to sin and Satan, but that's exactly what he is.

So the sinner has a choice, he can serve Satan as a slave, or serve Jesus as a bondslave, but he cannot serve both. However, I will remind the sinner that the Yoke of Christ is *"easy"* (Mat. 11:28-30), while that of Satan becomes increasingly harder.

2. *"Exagorazo"*: This means *"to buy out of the slave market"* (Gal. 3:13; 4:5). The extension of that is, that the Believer is never to be put up for sale in any slave market again. One can only shout *"Hallelujah!"*

3. *"Lutroo"*: This means *"to set free by paying a price"* (Tit. 2:14; I Pet. 1:18); the Believer is set free from sin and free to live a life pleasing to God in the Power of the Holy Spirit. As well, there is an extension to this also.

The *"price"* paid by Jesus was of such magnitude, that no one in the ceaseless ages of Eternity future, be they Satan, demon, spirit, Angel, or man, will ever be able to say, that the price paid was insufficient. When Jesus said *"It is finished,"* in effect, God said, *"It is enough!"*

The Redemption Price, the Precious Blood of Jesus, makes it possible for a Righteous God to justify a believing sinner on the basis of Justice satisfied.

The phrase, *"That is in Christ Jesus,"* tells us plainly that all Salvation is in Christ. There is no other, as there needs to be no other!

(25) "WHOM GOD HATH SET FORTH TO BE A PROPITIATION THROUGH FAITH IN HIS BLOOD, TO DECLARE HIS RIGHTEOUSNESS FOR THE REMISSION OF SINS THAT ARE PAST, THROUGH THE FORBEARANCE OF GOD;"

The phrase, *"Whom God has set forth to be a propitiation,"* refers to the atoning process, which was carried out at the Cross of Calvary, which satisfied the Righteousness of a Thrice-Holy God.

SET FORTH . . .

The words *"set forth"* in the Greek are *"protithemi,"* and means *"to set forth to be looked at, exposed to public view."*

This means that all that God did in order to bring Salvation to mankind through His Son Jesus Christ, was done completely in the open, with nothing kept secret, all in full

view. This spoke of His Birth, at least for those who cared to investigate. As well, His Life was lived in full view of all, given no special treatment by God, if anything, as a Peasant He was treated roughly and crudely.

As well, His Ministry was before the masses and constantly. His Healings were done in full view of all, with Miracles performed before friends and enemies alike.

His trial was at night only because the Jewish Sanhedrin was fearful of conducting it during daylight hours. Even though it was somewhat secretive, such was not on the part of Christ, but because of the wickedness of the Religious Leaders of Israel.

Above all, His Death on Calvary was a spectacle literally *"set forth"* in all of its shame and humiliation before any and all.

As well, He publicized His coming Resurrection over and over, even telling His enemies, *"Destroy this Temple,"* no doubt at this time, pointing to His Body, *"and in three days I will raise it up."* So, if there were no great crowds at His Resurrection, it was not due to any secrecy on His part, but rather because of unbelief, because it, the greatest happening in human history to date, was completely *"set forth"* as all else pertaining to Him.

His appearances after the Resurrection were many and varied, with His Ascension observed by possibly some 500 people. Once again, if so desired, no doubt there could have been thousands there that particular day when He went back to the Father. The only reason for their absence, at least for the most part, was unbelief.

From that moment until now, His Salvation has been heralded to the entirety of the world, *"set forth"* as nothing else in human history. Despite the fact, that it has not been preached enough, and in fact, could never be preached enough, still, the Message of His *"Redemption"* is the most heralded Message that man has ever known, seen, heard, witnessed, or experienced. Exactly as God said, it has been *"set forth,"* and, if men go to Hell, it will be because of their own rebellion and volition, not because of ignorance (Jn. 3:16; Rom. 1:20).

As Paul said to Governor Festus and King Agrippa, *"This thing was not done in a corner"* (Acts 26:26).

PROPITIATION

"Propitiation" in the Greek is *"hilasterion"* and means, *"an Atonement or reconciliation."*

This word in its classical form was used as the act of appeasing the Greek gods by a Sacrifice of rendering them favorable toward the worshiper. In other words, the Sacrifice was offered to buy off the anger of the god and buy his love. Such a use is not brought over into the New Testament, for our God does not need to be appeased nor is His Love for sale.

"Propitiation" refers to the act of getting rid of sin which has come between God and man.

In its strict form it referred to the Golden Cover on the Ark of the Covenant, called the *"Mercy Seat"* (Lev. 16:14). In the Ark, below this Cover, were the Tablets of Stone upon which were written the Ten Commandments which Israel had violated. Before the Ark stood the High Priest representing the people. When the Sacrificial Blood was sprinkled on this Cover, it ceased to be a place of Judgment and became a place of Mercy. The Blood comes between the violated Law and the violators, the people.

Before the Blood was applied, the Cherubim at either end of the Ark, were looking down on the Mercy Seat, in effect seeing the Broken Law, the Stone Tablets in the Ark. However, when the Blood was applied, its presence shielded the Broken Law, which is what happened when Jesus died on Calvary. His Precious Shed Blood, covers all sin, and actually washes it away. Consequently, the Blood of Jesus satisfied the just requirements of God's Holy Law which mankind broke. It paid the penalty for man, and thus removed that which had separated between a Holy God and sinful man, sin, its guilt and penalty. Thus, our Blessed Lord is Both the Mercy Seat and the Sacrifice which transform the former from a Judgment Seat to One where Mercy is offered a sinner on the basis of Justice satisfied (Wuest).

JESUS

The phrase, *"Through Faith in His Blood,"* sets forth Jesus as the Satisfaction for our sins. However, Paul is careful to explain that the benefits of that Sacrifice were only available

to one when he placed his Faith in the efficacy of that Blood which was shed.

It is not enough to have Faith in a historical Jesus or even in His Virgin Birth. Faith in His Perfect Sinless Life is required, but still, those things within themselves, as wonderful and important as they may be, effect no Salvation.

Sin is a dirty, evil, rotten, hellish business. Regrettably, its penalty could not be paid, nor Heaven's Justice satisfied, until Blood was shed. However, it could not be just any blood. It had to be the Blood of a Perfect, Sinless, Flawless Sacrifice, which is the reason that God became Man, and was born of the Virgin Mary. Had He been born by the normal way of procreation, He would have been born a sinner just like any other man, therefore, unfit as a Sacrifice.

Due to the fact that He was Virgin Born, He escaped that penalty, and was, therefore, unsullied, untainted. As well, Satan did everything that Hell could do to make Him fall during His years of Life and Ministry, but without success. As God, Satan had no chance respecting such an effort. But as Man, Jesus was vulnerable and subject to temptation, and had to be, if He was to be The Representative Man, which He was.

THE ERROR OF THE *"JESUS DIED SPIRITUALLY"* DOCTRINE

So when He died, He was the Perfect Sin-Offering, which completely refutes the error of what some call the *"Jesus Died Spiritually"* Doctrine.

This error teaches that Jesus actually became a sinner on the Cross, died and went to Hell like all other sinners, and was born again in Hell, etc. However, there is nothing in Scripture which even remotely validates such speculation.

First of all, had He actually become a sinner, that would have meant that He was polluted, and, therefore, unfit to serve as the Perfect Sin-Offering, which He had to do, in order that Heaven's Justice be satisfied.

As well, He went to Hell, but it was not in the burning side of the pit, but rather to Paradise (Lk. Chpt. 16; Eph. 4:8-10). As well, Jesus went to Paradise, not in order to be born again, but rather, to lead all those captive souls, which consisted of all the Old Testament Saints, to Heaven. The price had been paid, and Satan now had no more hold on them. They were free to go, and go they did.

The *"Jesus Died Spiritually"* Doctrine, comes about because of a misunderstanding of II Corinthians 5:21, *"For He hath made Him to be sin for us, Who knew no sin; that we might be made the Righteousness of God in Him."*

The word *"sin"* is used twice in this Scripture, with both coming from the Greek word *"hamartia."* However, even though it is the same Greek word, there are two different meanings.

SIN-OFFERING

The first word *"sin,"* means *"one who is treated as if he is a sinner, but is not."* In other words, He was the *"Sin-Offering."* Actually, in the Hebrew that very word means *"Sin-Offering."*

The second time *"sin"* is used in II Corinthians 5:21, it means *"missing the mark."*

So, this Scripture could be translated, *"For He* (God) *hath made Him* (Jesus) *to be sin* (a Sin-Offering) *for us, Who* (Jesus) *knew no sin* (never missed the mark)."

Or, *"For He* (God) *has treated Him* (Jesus) *as if He were a sinner, making a Sin-Offering of Him, Who had never missed the mark even one time."*

Those who teach the *"Jesus Died Spiritually"* Doctrine, misinterpret the first word *"sin"* in II Corinthians 5:21, thinking it means He became an actual sinner on the Cross. Consequently, were that so, He would need to be born again, hence Jesus going to the burning side of Hell like any other sinner, etc. However, none of that happened, because Jesus was not a sinner, even though He took the penalty for our sin, which is what He came to do. As we have already stated, had He literally become a sinner on the Cross as they claim, He would have been unfit to serve as the Sacrifice which had to be spotless, clean, without flaw, and without blemish. Thank God He was without sin and, consequently, without flaw, and, therefore, could serve as the Sin-Offering, which He did, paying the horrible debt demanded by Heavenly Justice.

NOTES

SALVATION

Most, if not all of this Teaching comes from the *"Word"* people, who too often times, don't really know the Word as they should. In fact, this error of the *"Jesus Died Spiritually"* Doctrine is far more serious than one realizes, striking at the Atonement, which is the single most important aspect of Salvation by Faith. To misunderstand what Jesus actually did at Calvary, is to misunderstand the very core of what Salvation is all about. Thankfully, the Lord overlooks much ignorance in all of us, rather accepting the motives of our hearts, than some of the erroneous directions we take. How grateful we are for that!

The phrase, *"To declare His Righteousness for the remission of sins that are past,"* presents to us a tremendous amount of information respecting the great Plan of Salvation. It is as follows:

FAITH AND RIGHTEOUSNESS

1. God set forth the Lord Jesus as the One Who would be the Satisfaction for our sins, but Paul is careful to explain that the benefits of that Sacrifice are only available to one when he places his Faith in the efficacy of that Blood which was shed.

2. It is *"His Righteousness"* to which God looks, and counts it sufficient for all people, for all sins, for all time. It is the only Righteousness which God will accept, which actually presents the bone of contention between God and the entirety of the human family. Man continues to put on display his own righteousness, which God will never accept.

In Truth, the moment any other type of supposed righteousness is presented, God not only refuses to accept such, but as well, withdraws the Righteousness of Christ, leaving the sinner with nothing.

3. God set forth our Lord in the First Century *"to declare His Righteousness for the remission of sins that are past,"* referring to all those who trusted Christ before He actually came. This covers the entirety of the time from the Garden of Eden to the moment Jesus died on Calvary's Cross.

Before He came, men were Saved by looking forward to Calvary, as they are Saved now by looking backward to Calvary. Calvary is ever the focal point.

During the time before He came, the Sacrifices of clean animals were used as a substitute in His place, even though their blood could not take away sin, only cover it. Consequently, the sin debt, in a sense, still hung over all pre-Calvary Believers, and was not actually removed until Jesus died on Calvary, paying the full price.

4. The word *"remission"* actually has two meanings in the Greek Text, with two distinct Greek words:

A. The first is *"aphesis,"* and means literally *"to put off"* or *"put away"* and is used in such places as Matthew 26:28; Ephesians 1:7; Colossians 1:14; Hebrews 9:22.

B. The second Greek word is *"paresis,"* and is the word used in this 25th verse. It means *"passing over, or letting pass."* The idea in this case is, that all the sins of all pre-Calvary Believers were passed over, with the future intent of remitting them entirely when Jesus came and paid the price. In other words, sins were not then removed at the time of Faith, but merely covered by the Blood of the Sacrifices, serving as a substitute until Jesus came.

God's Justification of a sinner is an action of His Grace based upon, and because of, the Redemption that is in Christ Jesus. It is only because of Christ's Atoning Sacrifice that God not only pardons but justifies sinners.

The phrase, *"Through the forbearance of God,"* refers to all sins committed by the people of God prior to, and up to, the One Great Sacrifice of Calvary. All these were put aside by God in His forbearance and then judged there; and all sins committed since Calvary were equally judged there. Thus, Calvary stands at the center of human history.

"Forbearance" in the Greek Text is *"anoche"* and means, *"tolerance."* In other words, God tolerated the situation before Calvary, knowing the debt would be fully paid at that time. Once again and as stated, everything focused on Calvary then, and everything focuses on Calvary now. As eagerly as some looked forward to that day, ugly and horrible though it might be, as eagerly and wondrously we should look back to that moment presently.

"Years I spent in vanity and pride,
"Caring not my Lord was crucified,
"Knowing not it was for me He died,
"At Calvary."

(26) "TO DECLARE, I SAY, AT THIS TIME HIS RIGHTEOUSNESS: THAT HE MIGHT BE JUST, AND THE JUSTIFIER OF HIM WHICH BELIEVETH IN JESUS."

The phrase, *"To declare, I say, at this time His Righteousness,"* refers to God's Righteousness which at all times must be satisfied.

The idea all along has always been the Righteousness of God.

THE RIGHTEOUSNESS OF GOD

Scripture often speaks of God as Righteous, which means that everything He does is right, and not just because He does it, but because it *is* right. As well, it is His Standard of *"Rightness,"* with which the world has quarreled since the Fall.

Just the other day I heard a Jewish Journalist say, *"God gave the Jews the Ten Commandments, which is the Standard for 'Rightness' and the world has never forgiven them since."*

He is the *"Righteous God"* (Ps. 4:1; 7:9; Isa. 45:21). His acts are *"always Righteous"* (Judg. 5:11; Ps. 71:24; Jer. 12:1) because all He does is in harmony with His Character. As He is the Moral Judge of the Universe, the very Character of God is the ultimate Standard of Righteousness, as it must be.

God's Righteousness finds expression in the Decrees and Laws that He gave to govern His people. Moses expressed this when he asked the generation of Israelites about to enter the Promised Land: *"What other Nation is so great as to have such Righteous Decrees and Laws as this Body of Laws I am setting before you today?"* (Deut. 4:8; Ps. 119:7, 62, 75, 106, 138, 160, 164, 172).

THE PORTRAYAL OF GOD

The Old Testament has two special ways of portraying God as acting righteously:

1. *"He will judge the world in Righteousness"* (Ps. 9:8; 96:13; 98:9). As Moral Judge God hates wickedness (Ps. 45:7). His Acts of Judgment thus are expressions of His intrinsic Righteousness.

2. We find in the Old Testament the realization that our Righteous God is also a Saviour (Isa. 45:21). The Psalmist cries, *"Deliver me in Your Righteousness"* (Ps. 31:1; 119:40).

God's Saving Acts are viewed as being in total harmony with His Righteousness, something that deeply concerned Paul as he developed his argument in Romans.

GOD'S RIGHTEOUSNESS IN SALVATION

Even though God had to drive Adam and Eve out of the Garden of Eden after their Fall, the wonder of it is that He went with them, and in essence promised to bring them back, at least respecting the human family.

(His driving them out was an act of Mercy, in that if they had eaten of the Tree of Life and lived forever, they would have done so in horrible sin which could only worsen, and would have made a Hell of unimagined proportions. Imagine Hitler living forever.)

So, at the very outset we find God setting everything in motion to save the human race. He will save them not merely because He has promised to save them, which He in fact did do (Gen. 3:15), but because He must save them. The must is moral.

To those who show themselves unworthy, with unworthiness defined as rejecting God's Salvation, God must punish them. The morality of God demands such. But if a Remnant, even a small Remnant show themselves faithful (accepting His Salvation), God must show His favor toward them.

Moral worth is not conceived of as something that is to be paid for by external rewards, but if God is moral He must not treat the Righteous and the unrighteous alike. That's what this is all about.

This conception of what God must do as an obligated Creator and Saviour influences profoundly the entire course of human history.

THE RIGHTEOUSNESS OF GOD
PORTRAYED IN JESUS

These various lines of Moral Laws come, of course, to their crown in the New Testament, in the Life and Death of Christ as set before us in the Gospels and interpreted by the Apostles.

Jesus stated certain moral axioms so clearly

NOTES

that the world will never escape their power. He said some things once and for all, and He did some things once and for all; that is to say, in His Life and Death He set on High the Righteousness of God at once as moral obligation and self-sacrificing Love (Jn. 3:16) and with such effectiveness that the world *has not* escaped and *cannot* escape this Righteous influence (Jn. 12:32).

Moreover, the course of Apostolic and subsequent history has shown that Christ put a winning and compelling power into the idea of Righteousness that it would otherwise have lacked, at least in the realm of understanding its power (Rom. 8:31-32).

THE RIGHTEOUSNESS OF GOD
IN THE BELIEVER

Understanding God as Creator and Saviour, at least as far as we creatures can understand Him, portrays the purpose of His Great Salvation, as the impartation of the Righteousness of God in the inner life of the Believer, which portrays itself in outward conduct. This is the Idea and Work of the Holy Spirit. God's Righteousness has been made our Righteousness, through the Lord Jesus Christ.

All of this comes through Faith in Christ, and is a Work of the Holy Spirit in the life of the Believer, and will not end until He *"presents us faultless before the Presence of His Glory with exceeding joy"* (Jude vs. 24).

The phrase, *"That He might be just, and the Justifier of him which believeth in Jesus,"* presents the great question. How can God be just, in effect maintaining His Justness, while at the same time being the Justifier of sinners?

He did it through His Son, The Lord Jesus Christ.

He judged Christ as a sinner on the Cross, even though He was not a sinner. He did this by making Him serve as a Sin-Offering, taking the penalty of sin, which only a sinner deserved, and not Him. That's what was meant when it said that He was *"stricken, smitten of God, and afflicted"* (Isa. 53:4).

He took the blows we should have taken and suffered the penalty of the Curse which we should have suffered. Consequently, the Righteousness of God was satisfied.

Now, God could freely be the *"Justifier"* of sinners and not impugn His Righteousness. The only requirement of the sinner is that he have Faith in what God demanded and what Christ freely did.

THE CROSS

Let it ever be understood, that Jesus did all of this freely and from one motivation, which was Love. There was nothing in Heaven's Laws that said such a thing had to be. It was done by God because He loved us (Jn. 3:16), and for no other purpose.

The Cross not only exonerated God from the charge that He passed by sin before the Crucifixion, but also demonstrated that when He declared a believing sinner Righteous, He at the same time was able to maintain His Righteousness.

It was a just as well as a merciful act for God to save a sinner, for Mercy was bestowed upon the basis of Justice satisfied, which it was in Christ Jesus.

The demands of the Broken Law were satisfied. Sin was paid for, not condoned. Thus, the believing sinner is Saved not only by the Mercy of God, but by the Righteousness of God, for his Salvation rests upon the fact that his sins are paid for and justice has been maintained. Thus, God is just and at the same time the One Who justifies the believing sinner (Wuest).

Please allow us to say it again, *"Believing in Jesus"* is the key. As well, it is the only key. So, when Peter said, *"Neither is there Salvation in any other: for there is none other name under Heaven given among men, whereby we must be Saved,"* he was not overstating the case at all (Acts 4:12).

(27) "WHERE IS BOASTING THEN? IT IS EXCLUDED. BY WHAT LAW? OF WORKS? NAY: BUT BY THE LAW OF FAITH."

The question, *"Where is boasting then?"*, refers primarily to the Jews boasting of who they were, as a result of the Law of God given to them.

Paul has shown that the Law did not save, and in fact, could not save. He has also shown, that according to the Light given, Israel had not even lived up to the standard of the Gentiles, which was despicable to say the least.

Also, Paul has proven that Salvation is totally in and of God, through Jesus Christ, with man playing no part in it at all. As a result, what did Israel have to boast about, or anyone for that matter?

The phrase, *"It is excluded,"* not only means that God will not accept such boasting, but that it actually serves as keeping one from Salvation, hence the majority of the Jews since Christ, dying eternally lost.

Not one single human being has anything at all to boast about, respecting Rightness with God. Every single person is deserving of Hell, and with no means or ways to save ourselves. We were and are helpless!

Therefore, everything we have respecting Salvation, has come totally and completely as a Free Gift from God, brought about by God, and carried through in His Son, The Lord Jesus Christ. And one might quickly add, at a fearsome, frightful price! We must never forget that.

The question, *"By what Law? Of works?"*, in a sense tells us, where and how the boasting originated. When one considers that not one single Jew ever fully kept the Law of Moses, where did the boasting come in?

THE LAW

As we have said in past Commentary, the very fact of having the Law, should have humbled Israel; however, it had the opposite effect. They grew very proud and haughty thinking somehow that God giving such to them was because they were morally superior in some way, etc.

By them failing to see and understand what the Law was all about, at least the majority of them, they created an ethical system out of the Law, which completely abrogated its true purpose.

(Its true purpose was to define sin and to show man his spiritual weakness and inability to do that which God commanded.)

The system they created out of the Law, as stated, was a system of ethics, which in the very doing of such sounded good, and made them feel as if they were holy, or at least superior to all other Nations. In this perversion of the Law, they developed a terrible self-righteousness, which such always will do, and that is the real cause.

Self-righteousness always produces a *"boasting"* or *"glorying!"*

(One must not overlook the fact, that there was always a small Remnant in Israel, even during its darkest times, which loved God, did their very best to obey Him, and who truly saw Him and His Word for what it was, and did not attempt to subvert it. They are the ones who were Saved.)

The phrase, *"Nay: but by the Law of Faith,"* proclaims to all and sundry, the manner in which Salvation is obtained from God, and anything else for that matter.

WHAT DOES PAUL MEAN BY USING THE TERM *"LAW OF FAITH?"*

In the way that human beings understand Law, it can be defined as *"a rule laid down for the guidance of an intelligent being, by an intelligent being having power over him."* This could be classified as *"Laws set by God to His human creatures, and Laws set by men to men."*

It could be said that there are three ideas respecting Law. The first is *"Command"* which refers to the expression of a particular desire. The second is *"Duty or Obligation"* signifying that one is bound or obliged by the Command to pursue a certain course of conduct. The third is *"Sanction,"* which indicates the evil likely to be incurred by disobedience.

To sum it up, as Law is used in the New Testament, it carries with it *"Command,"* *"Duty,"* and *"Sanction."*

This *"Law of Faith"* as Paul uses it, sets forth the Great Redemption of Jesus Christ, with the Apostle showing that it provides what the Law of Moses had failed to provide, a Righteousness which can satisfy the requirements of the Law.

And yet, it is a Righteousness that is indeed *"apart from the Law,"* apart from all men's attempts to keep the Law, but is nevertheless in deepest harmony with the principles of the Law, and has been witnessed *"by the Law and the Prophets."*

Actually, Faith–Righteousness never undermines the Law, but rather through the Law of Faith, which is a much higher Law of God, the Law of Moses, at least the moral part, is established in the heart of the Believer.

NOTES

This higher *"Law of Faith,"* which is exactly what Paul says it is, a Law, but yet is the total opposite of the Law of Moses.

The Law of Moses placed the responsibility on the person, while the *"Law of Faith"* places the responsibility on God. Consequently, it cannot fail. All the Believer has to do to receive the benefits of all that Jesus did, is to exercise the *"Law of Faith,"* which simply means to *believe* what the Lord has done. It is no more than that and no less than that (Jn. 3:16). Unfortunately, many Preachers make Faith difficult to understand and especially difficult, even impossible to receive. That is totally wrong.

If one reads and studies the Word of God, which is the Way Faith comes, and believes what the Word says, that person has Faith, actually the *"Law of Faith"* (Rom. 10:17).

By the *"Law of Moses"* man did it all, or attempted to do so, while with the *"Law of Faith"* God does it all, and in fact, has already done it all.

And finally, if the person, whether sinner or Believer will simply believe God, at least for what He has promised, the *"Law of Faith"* is guaranteed of fulfillment. It has never failed, because it cannot fail. As stated, it is a *"Law."*

(28) "THEREFORE WE CONCLUDE THAT A MAN IS JUSTIFIED BY FAITH WITHOUT THE DEEDS OF THE LAW."

The phrase, *"Therefore we conclude that a man is Justified by Faith,"* brings to an end the dialogue between Paul and the Jew.

Paul has proven from Verse 9, and especially from Chapters 2 and 3, that the Jews are in the same condition as the Romans, as it regards the need for a Redeemer; however, this didn't sit well at all with the Jews. They felt that inasmuch as they were (had been) God's chosen people, i.e., the people to whom the Word of God had been given, the people of the Prophets, and, above all, the people of the Law, that this merited them some type of special favor from God. The idea that they were no better than Gentiles, as stated, did not sit well, at all!

Surely, this counts for something, but yet Paul throws it all out as having no worth in the sense of special favor with God. While those things definitely had been a blessing to them, still, their having these things did not rule out their need for a Redeemer, for all of those things could not save from sin.

The phrase, *"Without the deeds of the Law,"* means that keeping these Commandments, or attempting to keep them, affords no Salvation whatsoever. This is the same as trusting in the Church to save, Water Baptism, the Lord's Supper, or performing good deeds, etc.

To be sure, the questions as posed by the Jews of so long ago, continue to be asked by the Gentiles even to this very moment.

Was not the Law meant to be kept?

Is the Law of Moses of no significance whatsoever?

Most certainly the Law of Moses as given by God was meant to be kept, as all Laws are meant to be kept. And yes, the keeping or not keeping of the Law was of great importance. As previously stated, the Lord even promised Great Blessings for those who tried to keep it (Deut. Chpt. 28).

Paul's argument is not that the Law of Moses was insignificant. In fact, it was of extreme importance. However, it was not meant to save one's soul and in fact, could not save the soul.

WORKS

The Jews tried to make it something which it wasn't, just as many today attempt to make the Church something it isn't. The Church per se cannot save as the Law could not save. Being Baptized in Water and taking the Lord's Supper cannot save, even as attempting to keep the Commandments of the Law could not save, although extremely important.

Men seem bent on devising their own way of Salvation, irrespective of the Word of the Lord. It is not a difficult thing to simply have Faith in Christ, which is demanded, and the only thing demanded. And yet, the Jews of old would not accept Him, and neither will most of the world presently.

Why?

The terrible deceptive powers which resulted in the Fall of man in the Garden of Eden, continue with him unto this hour. He was deceived then, and he continues to walk in deception unto now. He believed a

lie then, and finds it far easier to believe a lie now. He disobeyed God then, and finds it much easier to disobey God now. He obeyed Satan then, and finds it far easier to obey Satan now. In other words, one could say that man contracted a disease called *"sin,"* then, and with all of its attendant problems, continues to have that disease unto this moment (Isa. 1:4-6).

The only Remedy is Jesus and more particularly, Jesus and Him Crucified, but due to the incumbent of this disease called *"sin,"* he finds it very difficult through unbelief to simply accept Christ (I Cor. 1:18; 2:2).

(29) "IS HE THE GOD OF THE JEWS ONLY? IS HE NOT ALSO OF THE GENTILES? YES, OF THE GENTILES ALSO:"

The question, *"Is He the God of the Jews only?"*, hits at the very heart of Jewish thinking, because they did feel that Jehovah was God of the Jews only. They placed all Gentiles, which included the rest of the world, outside the scope of Salvation.

To be sure, they believed that a Gentile could be Saved but only if he became a Jew, thereby undergoing all types of Rituals and Ceremonies, most of them devised of themselves and not God. Jesus addressed this by saying, *"Woe unto you, Scribes and Pharisees, hypocrites! For ye compass sea and land to make one proselyte* (convert to Judaism), *and when he is made, ye make him twofold more the child of Hell than yourselves"* (Mat. 23:15).

The question, *"Is He not also of the Gentiles?"*, refers to God's Plan which included the Gentiles as well. From Genesis 12:3, we learn that God intended for the Gentiles to be brought into Salvation all along. In fact, one of the very purposes of the Jews was to evangelize the Gentile world. However, in their self-righteousness, they shut the rest of the world out, and in doing so, condemned themselves as well.

If one is to notice, when the Church is on fire for God, obeying Him, doing His Will, the greatest thrust always will be the Evangelism of the lost all over the world. However, when the Church begins to lose its way, it becomes inward, using all its resources to perpetuate itself, in effect, taking such out of the Hands of God.

When it does this, it doesn't seem to realize that instead of perpetuation, the very opposite effect is brought to bear. In other words, if a husband and wife does not have children, their line ceases with them. It is the same with the Church, the only way it can perpetuate itself, is to win the lost.

The phrase, *"Yes, of the Gentiles also,"* means that such was on God's Terms of Faith, instead of the Jewish terms of Law.

The Church as well, has a habit of falling into lockstep with Israel of old, by presenting something other than Faith in Christ. With the Catholic Church it is the Church itself, which also holds true with some Protestant Churches. Also, with many Protestant Churches, the Ordinances of the Church are presented instead of Christ, with Jesus only used as window dressing, or in some auxiliary mix.

(30) "SEEING IT IS ONE GOD, WHICH SHALL JUSTIFY THE CIRCUMCISION BY FAITH, AND UNCIRCUMCISION THROUGH FAITH."

The phrase, *"Seeing it is One God, which shall Justify the Circumcision by Faith,"* places the Jew on the same level as the Gentile. So the Jew had two problems: A. They did not accept Jesus as the Fulfillment of the Prophecies as Messiah and Saviour; and, B. They did not accept Salvation by Faith. In essence Paul is saying that it is *"One God"* for *"one world."*

While the Jews accepted the Doctrine of *"One God"* which actually was their Foundation, in comparison to the many gods of the heathen, they could not accept, and, in fact, would not accept the idea, that there was one Salvation for all. They considered this a gross comedown for them, not realizing it was the very opposite. However, it was self-righteousness which promoted this erroneous direction.

The phrase, *"And uncircumcision through Faith,"* puts the Gentile on the same level respecting the need for Salvation, and the manner of Salvation.

The conclusion is that God declares the Believer, whether Jew or Gentile, to be a Righteous person apart from and independently of personal moral merit; and this principle of Grace not only embraces all men whether

NOTES

Jew or Gentile, but establishes the moral teaching of the Old Testament as well, even as we shall see.

WHAT THE HOLY SPIRIT SAYS

Thus, in the short Passage of verses 19-28, in which the Holy Spirit declares through the Apostle the rudiments of the Gospel, we find that God declares Righteous the Believer in Jesus. Verse 19 declares all men guilty; verse 20 that it is impossible by religious effort or moral culture or by Priestly Ceremonies to obtain a Righteousness that God will accept; verse 21 reveals a Divine Righteousness independent of human effort; verse 22 assures such Righteousness to all who plead the Person and the Atoning Sacrifice of Christ, and assures it so effectually that all such persons become the Righteous of God through Faith in Christ (II Cor. 5:21).

Romans Chapter 3 verse 25 sets forth the Righteous Foundation upon which the Doctrine of Justification is set up, i.e., the Atonement.

Justification, therefore, is not a religious emotion felt by the repentant sinner, nor an experience and degree of sanctity reached by him, but it is the action of God declaring him to be a Righteous person, in other words, a legal act.

It is of the utmost importance to learn that Justification is the action of a Judge, in this case the God of all the ages, declaring an accused person to be Righteous according to Law, but by Faith and, therefore, blameless. For such a person there is no condemnation.

The expression, *"The Righteousness of God,"* in its personal sense, may be defined as God's activity in harmony with all that He has committed Himself to in Revelation. For example, He has committed Himself to eternally judge the unbeliever and to eternally save the Believer. His so acting is His Righteousness.

"A Righteousness from God" is the Righteousness of God reckoned to the Believer (Williams).

(31) "DO WE THEN MAKE VOID THE LAW THROUGH FAITH? GOD FORBID: YEA, WE ESTABLISH THE LAW."

The question, *"Do we then make void the*

Law through Faith?", Paul now answers in bold relief.

The kernel of his statement concerning Law and Faith, is not that Faith is a brand-new entity, not taking into consideration the Law at all, which is what many claimed that Paul was doing, but rather its very opposite.

A TYPE OF CHRIST

The phrase, *"God forbid: yea, we establish the Law,"* proclaims in effect that Christ is the Subject of the Law in all of its Rites and Ceremonies (Lk. 24:44; Col. 2:14-17; Heb. Chpts. 8-10).

Paul shows that the *"Just demands of the Law"* are fulfilled in Believers, and Believers only. The claim which the Apostle makes here, and established in these two Passages, is the same as that in our Lord's Words: *"I came not to destroy* (the Law and the Prophets), *but to fulfil"* (Mat. 5:17). In other words, Christ was and is the End of the Law, meaning its intended destination.

As we have said over and over, everything about the Law was a Type of Christ. The Brazen Altar symbolized Jesus on Calvary, and the Judgment of God coming upon Him for our sins. The Brazen Laver, pictured Jesus as the Word, as the Table of Shewbread pictured Him as the Bread of Life, etc. In fact, every function, every direction, every Command and every Ritual of the Law of Moses, were meant to serve as a Type of Christ, and, consequently, to point to Christ.

Law means the declaration of Righteousness, and requirement of conformity to it on the part of man. That is established throughout all the Old Testament, and reinforced by Paul in the necessity of Atonement for man's defect of sin. Consequently, when Christ is given His rightful due, the Law is placed on its true base.

In this proper position, it is shown not to justify, which it couldn't, but to convince of sin, i.e., define sin, point out sin, and so lead one to Christ.

In pursuing this thought, the Apostle, in the next Chapter, shows that in the Old Testament itself it is *"Faith,"* and not *"Law,"* which is regarded as justifying; as in the first place and notably, in the case of Abraham (Gen. 15:6).

NOTES

In Chapter 7 he treats the subject of the operation of the Law in the human soul and so brings out all the more clearly its true meaning and purpose (Barmby).

As should be obvious, when Christ came, Who was intended to be the End or Fulfillment of the Law, the Ceremonial part of the Law of necessity was set aside. Why should one want the symbol when the reality is present?

THE MORAL LAW

However, and as we will see, the Moral Part of the Law is incumbent upon Believers under the New Covenant, just as it was under the Old Covenant. However, there is a vast difference:

While the Moral Part of the Law loomed large above Israel, and I speak of the Ten Commandments, no strength was given from God to enable their obedience. However, under the New Covenant, Christ becomes our Strength, and actually lives this Moral Life through us (Gal. 2:20).

However, having said that, many Believers tend to take the living of the Moral Law out of the Hands of Christ, into their hands. In other words, all Believers at one time or the other, whether through ignorance or for whatever reason, have attempted to add to the Finished Work of Christ, by attempting to gain victory through works or Law. Such is not to be, and, in fact, such cannot be.

The same Faith in Christ, even as we shall see in Chapters 6-8, which brought us into Salvation, is meant to keep us in Salvation. That's the reason that Jesus plainly and clearly said, *"Come unto Me, all ye that labour and are heavy laden, and I will give you rest"* (Mat. 11:28).

In other words, Salvation in Christ, and Victory in Christ, are not *"labour,"* i.e., *"works,"* but rather *"rest,"* i.e., *"resting in Jesus."* To do otherwise frustrates the Grace of God, meaning that the very thing we are seeking through our works, victory over the flesh, we forfeit.

As the songwriter said, and as it ever must be, *"Nothing in my hands I bring, simply to the Cross I cling."*

"O soul, are you weary and troubled?
No light the darkness you see?

"There's light for a look at the Saviour, and life more abundant and free!"

"Through death into life everlasting He passed, and we follow Him there;
"Over sin no more hath dominion, for more than conquerors we dare!"

"His Word shall not fail you — He promised; believe Him, and all will be well:
"Then go to a world that is dying, His Perfect Salvation to tell!"

"Turn your eyes upon Jesus, look full in His wonderful Face;
"And the things of Earth will grow strangely dim in the Light of His Glory and Grace."

CHAPTER 4

(1) "WHAT SHALL WE SAY THEN THAT ABRAHAM OUR FATHER, AS PERTAINING TO THE FLESH, HATH FOUND?"

The beginning of the question, *"What shall we say then . . . ?"*, presents Paul as having stated his case, that the Old Testament teaches that God justifies the sinner on the Faith Principle as opposed to the Merit Principle.

The Holy Spirit now brings forward Abraham (vss. 1-5) and David (vss. 6-8) as illustrating this Truth. Both these men were *"ungodly"* by nature (vs. 5), and both had a Divine Righteousness reckoned to them, not because of any meritorious actions that they performed, but because they believed God and made Him their Salvation.

Abraham and David were progenitors of the Promised Messiah, and, as such, they held a unique place in the Faith and veneration of the Jewish people. If, therefore, they had no personal righteousness, and were sinners by nature, i.e., *"ungodly,"* it was evident that all members of the Commonwealth of Israel were in a similar moral condition before God; and if these eminent men were Justified by Faith, apart from works, then all men must be similarly Justified (Williams).

The phrase, *"That Abraham our father,"* presents a great part of the Plan of God regarding Salvation by Faith, and, as well, the coming Incarnation of Christ, which was an absolute necessity respecting the Salvation of mankind.

As Paul stated in Romans 3:25, God in effect, regarding the Salvation of all sinners before Christ, gave a promissory note, which was ratified by the blood of bulls and goats, that the great sin debt would ultimately be paid and by no less than His Only Son, The Lord Jesus Christ. Consequently, the idea is as the Holy Spirit speaks through the Apostle, that if one with the stature of Abraham, who was given such a momentous role in the Great Plan of God, could not merit Salvation, how does anyone else think that such is possible, especially considering that Abraham was the spiritual father of all Believers.

In fact, Abraham was *not* chosen because of any merit on his own, for he was a Gentile, *"a Syrian ready to perish"* (Deut. 26:5) and an idolater (Josh. 24:2-3). Grace chose him and promised a Redeemer through him (Gen. 15:6); because he believed what God said to him, his Faith was reckoned to him for Righteousness, and God Justified him, i.e., declared him to be a Righteous man.

The conclusion of the question, *"As pertaining to the flesh, hath found?"*, now is proclaimed by Paul as earning nothing from God by merit. Consequently, Paul will now prove Salvation by Faith from the Old Testament, and that this had always been God's Plan. In other words, Paul was not projecting something new, and that being the case, did not leave the Jews with no Spiritual or Scriptural recourse, at least apart from Faith.

WHAT IS THE FLESH?

First of all, the Biblical view differs in very significant ways from the ideas associated with the use of the word *"flesh"* in our society.

Even though it is used many ways in the Bible, such as referring to one's *"kindred"* (relatives), *"physical body"* (Gen. 40:19; Num. 19:7; I Ki. 21:27; II Ki. 9:36), *"self"* (Ps. 16:9-10), *"all living creatures"* (Gen. 6:12, 19; Ps. 145:21), and *"intimate interpersonal and family relationships"* (Gen. 2:23-24; 29:14), the greater use of the word *"flesh,"* especially as used by Paul, is to signify the frailty and weakness of man and as well, a twisted, perverted, fallen, human nature.

THE MANNER IN WHICH THE HOLY SPIRIT USES THIS WORD THROUGH PAUL

The most significant uses of the word *"flesh"* throughout the entirety of the Bible are found in Paul's Epistles.

According to Paul, human nature is not just frail and weak; human nature is also twisted and tangled. Human perspectives, human understanding, and human efforts are actually hostile to the perspective, understanding, and Plan of God. Consequently, the *"flesh"* denotes moral inadequacy and rebellion toward God.

Ancient Philosophers and popular modern Psychology contrast the flesh with the spiritual part in human nature. The New Testament, however, makes no such comparison.

Instead, the New Testament uses *"flesh"* to denote human nature apart from God. The contrasts drawn are between human powers, perspectives, and abilities and the powers, perspectives, and abilities of God, most importantly His Ability to enable people to do His Will.

The whole of human nature, not merely a *"part"* of human beings, is in view when Scripture uses *"flesh"* in a moral or theological sense to make statements about human nature.

The flesh speaks of human beings in isolation from God. Essentially, when human beings are cut off from the Lord, they are morally inadequate to rectify the situation (Rom. 6:19; 7:7-11, 15-20; 8:3). To live according to the flesh (in the realm of one's own abilities and strength) is completely different from living according to God's Spirit (Rom. 8:4-13; Gal. 5:16-26).

Apart from God, humanity is characterized by a complex web of thoughts, desires, values, and actions that are in opposition to God's intended pattern for us, which all denote the flesh.

ROMANS

Greater than any other of Paul's writings, and in the entirety of the Bible for that matter, Romans Chapter 7 gives us an idea

NOTES

of the frailty of the flesh, perhaps as no other Passages.

(Some mistake Romans Chapter 7, or at least part of it, as pertaining to Paul before his Conversion; however, that is incorrect. The entire Chapter pertains to the Apostle after coming to Christ, but attempting to gain victory over the flesh by the flesh — through one's own efforts. We know this from Romans 7:15 and other similar Passages in that Chapter. There he stated how he hated sin, which is the attitude and feelings of a Believer. In fact, while unbelievers may hate the result of their sin, none hate the sin, actually enjoying it.)

The Law of God is spiritual, meaning that it is all of Him, and available to all Believers; however, Paul, as Chapter 7 proclaims, was attempting to overcome through his own efforts, and, was consequently, trapped by sin. He then realized that *"nothing good"* lived in him, that is, in his *"flesh"* (in his sinful nature).

Trapped by his moral frailty, even as we all are, Paul found he could not live the Righteous life, revealed in God's Law, at least within his own strength. Seeking God earnestly about this matter, he was given the great Plan of Victory for the Believer, which he outlined in Romans Chapters 6 and 8, with 7 in the middle proclaiming his inadequacy.

(Please see Commentary on those three Chapters.)

GALATIANS

In Galatians 5:16-26, the word *"flesh"* could be translated *"sinful nature"* and would probably give the Reader a greater understanding.

Here Paul describes the flesh as energized and motivated by desires that find expression in a number of actions, ranging from sexual immorality to jealousy and even fits of rage. In contrast, Believers are called on to *"live by the Spirit."* God Himself is the Source of transformed desires that can motivate a New Life.

What's more, He is also the Source of Power for such a Life. When we keep in step with the Spirit rather than the flesh, God will fill us and our actions with Love, Joy, Peace, and other aspects of the Fruit of the Spirit.

I CORINTHIANS

In I Corinthians 3:1-4, the word *"carnal"* is used four times. In the Greek it is *"sarkikos,"* and means *"fleshly,"* or doing certain things which are wrong, because of yielding to the sin nature.

These verses describe the behavior of some of the Christians at Corinth. Their bickering and factions show that despite their relationship with Jesus, they were acting like *"mere men."* Their outlook was human, rather than being shaped by God's Perspective on the issues they found so important.

We Christians do have the potential to live beyond the possibilities of our human nature, but only through the Lord. However, such an enabled life is not guaranteed even though one is Saved and Baptized with the Holy Spirit, even as Paul found out in Romans Chapter 7. We must make daily choices, beyond our initial choice of Trusting and Loving Jesus, that affect our experience of the Christian Life.

To break out of the fleshly (carnal) pattern these Corinthians had to return to God's Word and search out God's Perspective, which refers to the manner in which something is viewed.

THE RELEASE FROM THE LIMITATIONS OF OUR HUMAN NATURE

Romans Chapter 8, as the Holy Spirit gave it to Paul, explains God's remedy for the limitations and sins of the flesh. That remedy is not found in the Law of Moses. In fact, Law was unable to lift us to Righteousness, even though it did contain Righteousness, because it was *"weakened by our sinful nature,"* in other words, man under the Law of Moses had only his own strength to enable him to keep that Law, which was woefully insufficient. In fact, God at that time had not given His Holy Spirit in this respect, and in fact could not do so, until Jesus came and paid the price for man's sins, lifting that terrible debt (Jn. 7:37-39). However, once Jesus came and paid this price, it was now possible for God through Christ to provide the Holy Spirit to Believers. Now Believers have the possibility of being controlled by the Spirit, not by the flesh.

It is the Spirit of God Whose Life-giving Power raised Jesus from the dead, and it is the Spirit Who can bring us Life and Power despite our mortality.

If the Spirit of God could raise Jesus from the dead, even though He was in a mortal body, with Satan trying to hold Him accordingly, then the Spirit of God can help us maintain our Victory as purchased by Jesus at Calvary and the Resurrection. Respecting this, when He was raised from the dead, in essence, we were raised with Him, signifying that what was done in Him spiritually, was done in us likewise, at least if we believe (Rom. 6:3-5).

If we choose to rely on the Spirit, and we must remember that it is a choice and not automatic, and if we commit ourselves to His Control, we will experience a Resurrection kind of Life — now. The limits imposed by our fleshly human nature will no longer contain us, and we will be free from the mastery of the flesh, consequently walking after the Spirit (Rom. 8:1).

THE BIBLICAL VIEW

In both Testaments, *"flesh"* even as we have stated, is a complex word with many meanings. However, its most significant meanings pertain to the statements made about human nature, of which is our subject.

The Old Testament emphasizes the frailty of human beings. Because of our weakness, we must look to God for everything good, not relying on ourselves at all. He Alone is the Source of our help. To recognize His Power brings us release from fear of other persons, who are ultimately as powerless as we are.

The New Testament emphasizes humanity's moral inadequacy. When we are isolated from God, we are energized by evil desires and guided by perceptions that distort God's Will and His Nature. The word *"flesh"* reminds us that we are caught in the grip of sin.

Even a desire for Righteousness cannot enable us to actually become Righteous. That can only be done by walking after the Spirit, understanding what Jesus did for us at Calvary and the Resurrection.

God deals with our flesh in a surprising way. He does not free us now from the sinful nature. Instead, He provides a Source of Power that will release us from the domination of the flesh. He has done it in this way, in order that we may constantly rely upon Him.

In a way, this is similar to the Law of Moses, which no one could keep, at least within themselves, but with one great difference. The New Covenant provides us with the Holy Spirit Who Alone can give us what is needed to maintain our Victory over the flesh. Jesus has paid for sins generated by our flesh, whether sins of our past or those yet in our future, that is, if we properly trust Him. However, and as stated, He has also provided us with His Holy Spirit.

The Spirit lives within us, and He is the Source of new desires and a new perspective. Even more, the Spiritual Power unleashed in the Resurrection is made available to us in the Spirit.

Hallelujah!

The bonds of our mortality and all that mortality implies can be shattered if we live according to the Spirit, with our desires and motives shaped by Him, with His Power enabling us to do what is truly good (Richards).

So, as regarding the *"flesh,"* or our own ability and strength, Abraham found absolutely nothing, at least that which is of God. As well, his results in the area of the flesh, are the results of all others — failure.

(2) "FOR IF ABRAHAM WERE JUSTIFIED BY WORKS, HE HATH WHEREOF TO GLORY; BUT NOT BEFORE GOD."

The phrase, *"For if Abraham were justified by works,"* presents a moot point, for it was something which could not be; however, Paul uses the statement in this manner to make a point.

The idea refers to *"a source of works."* In speaking of the relation of works to Justification, Paul never uses the Greek word *"dia,"* which means *"by means of"* or *"through."* Instead, he uses the Greek word *"ek,"* which means *"out of."* It refers to works being regarded by the Jew as the *"meritorious source of Salvation,"* which of course, and even as Paul solidly proclaims, God will not accept (Vincent).

The idea is, that Paul was not speaking of

"works" as a result of one's Salvation, which should follow every Believer, but rather, trying to make *"works"* the source or cause of one's Salvation, which cannot be.

The phrase, *"He hath whereof to glory,"* in essence means *"to boast."*

When people try to make works the source of Salvation, the flesh is glorified, but if Faith in God is the Source, then God is Glorified.

This was Israel's problem. They were very boastful in their self-righteousness, due to the fact of their trusting in their works instead of the Lord. Admittedly, He was spoken of constantly, but the Truth was, they had long since ceased to look at Him as He actually was, or to themselves as they actually were. To His Standard of Righteousness they could not even begin to hope to attain, but yet, thought they had and then some. Being told by Paul that this was not the case, and, furthermore, that spiritually speaking they were in no better shape than the Gentiles, in no way endeared the Apostle to his fellow countrymen.

The phrase, *"But not before God,"* gives us that alone which really matters.

The Modern Church glories in itself and others, which is a glory that God will not recognize. His Eyes alone are the Eyes that matter. His Approval alone, is the Approval that matters. If we please all men and not God, it is of no consequence at all. And as well, if we please God and displease all men, we haven't hurt ourselves at all. To be frank, if one pleases God, which means to go God's Way instead of man's way, just about all men will be displeased. The Christian can glory in man or God, but not both! And that's where the Church runs aground. In fact, this is probably the Christian's greatest problem. The Christian is often prone to trust men instead of God. If so, this stifles much of the work of the Holy Spirit within one's heart and life. To be sure, it affects every avenue of our life and living.

(3) "FOR WHAT SAITH THE SCRIPTURE? ABRAHAM BELIEVED GOD, AND IT WAS COUNTED UNTO HIM FOR RIGHTEOUSNESS."

The question, *"For what saith the Scripture?",* proclaims it and its proper interpretation as the foundation for all things which pertain to Life and Godliness. Inasmuch as we are here discussing Salvation, that means there is nothing in the world more important.

Furthermore, considering that Paul resorted to the Word of God which the Jews claimed to believe, and that above all he referred to Abraham in whom they gloried as their spiritual father, and he showed that the head of the race himself was Justified not by works, but by Faith, they were left with no ground whatsoever on which to stand.

The phrase, *"Abraham believed God, and it was counted unto him for Righteousness,"* presents the very heart of the Gospel. It is as follows:

THE MANNER OF SALVATION HAS ALWAYS BEEN THE SAME

First of all, Salvation was given to Abraham long before the Law, or even Circumcision. Remember, it is impossible to have it both ways. Placing oneself in the thinking of the Jews of old, if Circumcision and the Law of Moses were required in order to be Saved, as many claimed, then Abraham was not Saved, which is a direct contradiction of the Word of God. Men have always been Saved in exactly the same identical way, by looking to Christ, and more importantly, the Crucified, Risen Christ. This is the very reason that the Sacrifice of certain animals before Christ was demanded. They were to serve as a Symbol of the Coming One. As well, there was no reason for the Jews not to understand this, as it was clear.

BELIEVE GOD

The only requirement of Abraham, even as it has always been the only requirement, is that he *"believe God." "Believe"* in the Greek Text is *"pistikos,"* and means simply to *"trust a person or thing, in this case Christ."* More particularly it refers to *"having reliance upon Christ for Salvation."* It has respect as well to the *"Truthfulness of God."*

FAITH

The word *"It"* must be defined here, at least as it here refers to Faith.

The Believer must *not* look at the word *"Faith"* as a *"work"* or *"merit,"* for such

nullifies its very purpose. In other words, it was not the *"act of believing"* which was reckoned to Abraham as a Righteous act, or on that account of which Perfect Righteousness was laid to his charge, but that the fact of his trusting God to perform His Promise introduced him into the Blessing promised. What happened here, and which is very, very important, is that Abraham's Faith was the act of placing himself in such an attitude of trust in, and acceptance of, God's Blessings that made it possible for God to bestow Righteousness upon him. It could be described as the outstretched hand of a drowning man that makes it possible for the lifeguard to save him.

There is nothing meritorious in the act of a drowning man in stretching out his hand in order to be Saved. It is the efficient medium through which he is Saved. Thus, the Act of Faith on the sinner's part is not of merit but only the efficient medium through which God is able to save him.

Consequently, the *"It"* as defined here, and which is the single most important thing there is respecting one's Salvation, is the outstretched hand of Faith of a sinner reaching out for Salvation, which God grasps in His Own to lift him out of the mire of sin and place him upon the Rock, Christ Jesus (Alford — Wuest).

THE DANGER — FAITH BECOMING WORKS

As well, one cannot help but briefly mention the fact, that much, if not most, of today's Teaching on Faith falls into the attitude of *"works"* which automatically nullifies the principle of True Faith. The Believer must ever understand, that nothing is ever received from God on the merit or principle of *"works."* The very moment *"works"* are presented, at least as a means of receiving, God's Gift, and in whatever capacity, is instantly withdrawn. It should be ever understandable as to why.

We are plainly told that Salvation and all its peripheral Blessings, which actually include every single thing received by the sinner or Believer, is predicated on the principle of *"Gift."* In other words, *"For by Grace are ye Saved through Faith; and that not of yourselves: it is the Gift of God:*

"Not of works, lest any man should boast" (Eph. 2:8-9).

Therefore, it becomes very clear, that the moment one offers *"works"* to God as payment in any form, or turns Faith or any Attribute of God into *"works,"* all are immediately nullified. Once again I emphasize, that most modern Faith Teaching falls into this category, and, consequently, nullifies itself.

TO ONE'S ACCOUNT

The Holy Spirit here uses the word *"counted,"* which in the Greek is *"logizomai"* and means, *"to put down to one's account."* Thus, God put to Abraham's account (and every other believing sinner), actually placed on deposit for him, or credited to him, Righteousness.

However, the actual payment at that time (before Christ) had not been made; consequently, the actual bestowal of Righteousness had not been consummated. So, Abraham possessed Righteousness in the same manner as a person would possess a sum of money placed in his account in a bank as a loan. In God's Mind it was a legal, as well as a spiritual act. I suppose one could say, that Abraham, plus all Believers before Christ, were Saved on credit. When Jesus came, He paid off the loan leaving nothing owing. However, let it never be thought that those Saved in this time period were less Saved than those after Christ. In the Mind of God they were just as Saved as if Jesus had already come and paid the price.

In the Mind and Word of God it had already been done, therefore, Faith could legally claim the benefits without doing violence to the Justice of God.

Since the Resurrection, Old Testament Saints share with New Testament Believers the possession of Christ as the Righteousness in which they stand, guiltless and Righteous for time and for eternity (Wuest).

RIGHTEOUSNESS

The *"Righteousness"* mentioned here, is the Righteousness of God which is *"Moral Perfection."* As well, and as previously stated, it is God's definition of *"Moral Perfection,"* and not man's. It is so much higher than anything to which man could ever hope to

aspire, that the only way it can be received is by *"Faith."*

PERSONAL

As well, this is a Personal Salvation, therefore, *"accounted unto him,"* i.e., *"Abraham."*

Each person must evidence his own Faith in order to receive his own Salvation. It is not possible for one to evidence Faith for another when it comes to receiving anything from God. While one's Faith definitely can help, aid and abet another, there must at the same time, be a spark of Faith in the heart of the one who would receive the *"Gift."* In other words, he must *"stretch out his hand"* toward God in some sense of the word.

THE CORE OF SALVATION

This one Passage (Rom. 4:3), taken by Paul from Genesis 15:6, is the pivot point of the entirety of the Bible, at least regarding God's Great Plan of Salvation. If this is misunderstood, considering how important it actually is, then everything else is misunderstood as well!

As we have previously stated, Paul's argument as used by the Holy Spirit would be peculiarly telling as addressed to the Jews, who made such a point of their descent from Abraham, as the root of all their position of privilege (Ps. 105:6; Isa. 51:2; Mat. 3:9; Lk. 3:8; Jn. 8:39).

(4) "NOW TO HIM THAT WORKETH IS THE REWARD NOT RECKONED OF GRACE, BUT OF DEBT."

The phrase, *"Now to him that worketh,"* presents Paul turning the argument around, in other words explaining the same thing in another way, in order that there be no misunderstanding whatsoever as to what the Holy Spirit is saying.

The word *"worketh"* in the Greek is *"katergazomai,"* and means *"to do that from which something results."* In other words, the workman works in order to earn wages. Paul continues to speak of Salvation from God.

If one is going to attempt to earn one's Salvation by working for it, there are some things one must understand:

First of all, the debt owed by man to God is so absolutely astronomical, that it is literally impossible for the sinner to calculate or even understand the amount. So, the efforts to *"earn"* Salvation are shot down before one even begins.

At one point in His Ministry, Jesus referred to the extreme difficulty of a rich man being Saved, and for the reason that they tend to trust in their own ability and wealth. Due to the fact that the Jews believed, and extensively so at the time of Christ, that riches were the very epitome of the Blessings of God, and a sign of Salvation, Jesus' Disciples instantly asked, *"Who then can be Saved?"*

Jesus answered them by saying, *"With men this* (Salvation) *is impossible; but with God all things are possible"* (Mat. 19:23-26).

THE ATTEMPT TO EARN SALVATION

The Reader may think that this problem of attempting to earn one's Salvation is practiced by few. However, it is the single greatest problem in the world today, and, in fact, always has been.

All the Religions of the world fall into this category. Religion, as it is used Biblically, refers to man attempting to reach God, or some type of spiritual goal, and by devising his own means and in whatever capacity. (True Bible Christianity is God reaching down to man with His means, which is the very opposite.)

Christianity is not a Religion, but a relationship, and more particularly, a relationship with a Man, The Man, Christ Jesus. But yet, even in Christianity, I think one can say without any fear of exaggeration, that most in some way or the other attempt to earn their Salvation, which automatically nullifies the Grace of God. Consequently, that person is lost.

I had a Mormon say to me just the other day words to this effect: *"The Mormon Church is God's Church; consequently, to be Saved, one has to belong to the Mormon Church."*

What he is promoting is a Gospel of works pure and simple, and, consequently, is totally rejected by God. However, let not the Reader think that Mormonism, which is totally a fabrication of man, is that much different from many in the so-called mainstream of Christianity. In fact, Catholicism, which actually is a Religion is totally of works. Sadder still, many who claim to

NOTES

be Fundamental in belief, which means to adhere strictly to the Bible, fall into the same category.

PENANCE

For instance, a Lawyer Friend of mine was speaking with the Leader of a major Pentecostal Denomination. Actually, several of these Leaders were discussing a particular situation pertaining to the Work of God, etc.

The Leader of highest rank made a particular statement in which he was obviously speaking of someone doing *"penance,"* of which he felt should be done.

My Friend later said to me, *"I wonder if he knew what he was saying?"*

Penance is not taught in the Word of God, and, in fact, is the very opposite of everything which pertains to God's Grace and Plan of Salvation. One cannot have it both ways. One is either solely trusting God, or their own works, etc.

Now the question must be asked, *"Did in fact, this Pentecostal Leader know and understand what he was saying?"*

In fact I know the man, and actually know him quite well. Were you to ask him this question, he would give you the correct Biblical answer. So, he would deny any form of a *"works"* Salvation, or penance, etc., as having any sway with the Lord whatsoever. However, here is the irony:

Much of the system which they constantly practice, is a works, penance type of thing, which they do not even attempt to coincide with the Word of God. They claim these measures, which they change from time to time are Scriptural, but they never offer any type of Scriptural proof, at least that I've ever seen. As well, I know that some of their most renowned Pastors have in fact, demanded Scriptural proof for such positions, but none has ever been forthcoming, because it does not exist.

So, I think all of us would be truly surprised if we actually examined ourselves, even as the Holy Spirit demanded through Paul, in order to prove *"whether ye be in the Faith"* (II Cor. 13:5).

PAYMENT

The phrase, *"Is the reward not reckoned*

of Grace, but of debt," places this situation of works in its rightful posture.

The word, *"reward"* as used here by Paul in the Greek is *"misthos,"* and means *"dues paid for work, wages."* So, if we are attempting to earn our Salvation in this manner, we in fact are offering to God our works, demanding that He pay us, and that the payment should be in the realm of Salvation.

To use a type of analogy, it would be about the same as someone owing a billion dollars at the bank, with no money to pay or no way to pay. They would then pick up some litter on the lawn of the bank, and then ask for payment, with the expectation being that the account would be settled regarding their massive debt. Of course such a thing is ludicrous, but even that does not properly illustrate the disparity of the situation respecting the sinner's true condition.

However, the idea as presented by Paul is not necessarily to portray this disparity, but rather the absolute impossibility of such a direction. He who embarks upon the course of attempting to earn his Salvation, has embarked upon an impossible quest.

Why does one desire to attempt to do so anyway, especially considering that Jesus has paid it all!

The idea as expressed here by Paul, especially considering his use of the word *"debt,"* is that God owes us something, because of some certain things we are supposed to have done for Him.

First of all, one must ever realize, that God does not need anything at all from us. There is absolutely nothing we can do for Him which He needs, or even wants for that matter, at least in these particulars. So, that shoots down any type of service we may perform, supposing it earns us some type of merit, etc. And yet, many Believers function on that basis.

They ask the Lord to bless them, or to heal them, or to do some certain thing, on the basis that they have earned it by doing certain good things, etc. The Lord never responds to such, because as stated, He doesn't need anything that we may have.

On the other hand, everything we truly need as human beings, can be obtained only from the Lord. Inasmuch as we have

NOTES

nothing He needs or even wants, it has to be on the basis of a free Gift, for it cannot be offered or received in any other manner.

(5) "BUT TO HIM THAT WORKETH NOT, BUT BELIEVETH ON HIM THAT JUSTIFIETH THE UNGODLY, HIS FAITH IS COUNTED FOR RIGHTEOUSNESS."

The phrase, *"But to him that worketh not,"* refers to the sinner not at all depending on any supposed good works he may have performed, but rather on the Mercy and Grace of God.

The Doctrine of verse 5 stumbles and offends the carnal religious mind. It declares that whoever does no works but believes upon a God Who declares sinful men Righteous, to such a Believer God reckons his Faith for Righteousness, that he from that moment is Justified, and, consequently, stands in a Righteousness before God in which a flaw can never be found (Williams).

UNGODLY!

The phrase, *"But believeth on Him that justifieth the ungodly,"* seems to be a contradiction of terms, and especially to the self-righteous.

How can the ungodly be declared Godly?

That is the great question before humanity, and one which he attempts to answer in different ways:

1. Most will not admit to being ungodly, but which denial not at all changes their situation. It is not what man says anyway that counts, but what God says, and the Holy Spirit through the Apostle has declared the entirety of mankind and for all time, as ungodly (Rom. 3:10, 23).

2. Others attempt to evade the issue by embracing another religion which does not recognize God, as if their doing such will exclude them from the Judgment.

3. Others attempt to make up their own Salvation in one way or the other, whether by good works, excessive religion, or any number of things. However, none of these things address the problem, because none of these things can address the problem.

The only answer for humanity is *"believing on Him,"* i.e., The Lord Jesus Christ. And as we have said many times, this is far more than a mere mental assent that Jesus actually lived and was a good Man, etc.

BELIEVING ON HIM

"Believing on Him" refers to accepting Him as one's Saviour, and more particularly what He did at Calvary's Cross and the Resurrection. This alone Redeems lost humanity.

As well, Jesus is not One Redeemer among several, but the Only Redeemer, because He Alone is the Son of God, and paid the price for fallen man. That means that Mohammed is out, Joseph Smith is out, the Pope is out, Buddha is out, Confucius is out, plus any other proposed Saviour, whether human or philosophical.

In *"believing on Him,"* even though the sinner little understands such at the beginning, the idea is, that God loaded on Jesus all of our ungodliness, with Him suffering its penalty which we by rights should have suffered, which is death, and then because of our simple Faith in Him, He loads on us the Godliness of Christ. In that manner alone can the sinner be Justified, and in that manner alone can God be Just, or rather maintain Justice, in carrying out the act of Justification, which in essence means that one is *"declared not guilty."* It is without doubt, the most beautiful and wonderful display of Love that humanity has ever known, and that humanity will ever know.

FAITH

The phrase, *"His Faith is counted for Righteousness,"* presents Faith in Christ, and the only commodity which God recognizes, on which basis He will then impute Righteousness to the believing sinner.

To say it in another way, in the realm of the moral and spiritual, if a sinner does not perform good works in an effort to earn Salvation, but instead puts his Trust in the God Who justifies the ungodly person, that Act of Faith is put down to his account as the efficient medium through which God bestows a Righteous Standing upon that person.

Going back to Abraham, who Paul uses as an example, the Apostle completely rules out salvation by works. In fact, he is at pains to make certain that the Reader understands that Abraham, who is the father of us all, didn't gain justification by works, but rather

by Faith, and by Faith exclusively.

So, this forever lays to rest the idea that Salvation can be obtained by works or merit.

Setting the Church aside for a moment, the world has a terrible time accepting Salvation by Grace. Mother Teresa is a perfect case in point. The world lauded her before she died and when she died, held up these *"good works"* as proof of her being a *"Saint,"* etc. But of course, with God these things counted not at all, at least as far as Salvation was concerned.

In fact, most of the world operates on the basis of what I refer to as a *"brownie point system."* In other words, they weigh their so-called good deeds up beside their bad deeds, and always the good deeds come up higher, which in their minds constitute Salvation, or some type of favor, etc.

Regrettably, many in the modern Church fall into the same category. It is very difficult for most Church people to understand, that through Faith in Christ, one can be totally unrighteous one moment and totally Righteous the next. Even the Church, at least to a great degree, believes in some form of penance, or *"works Salvation."* However, let all know and understand, that the only thing that *"counts for Righteousness"* in the Eyes of God, Whose Eyes Alone matter, is *"Faith in Christ."*

(6) "EVEN AS DAVID ALSO DESCRIBETH THE BLESSEDNESS OF THE MAN, UNTO WHOM GOD IMPUTETH RIGHTEOUSNESS WITHOUT WORKS,"

The phrase, *"Even as David also describeth the Blessedness of the man,"* presents Paul using the Sweet Singer of Israel as the second example of Faith without works.

To make the point as to how much the modern Church is still into *"works,"* and at the same time denies *"Faith,"* if the scenario of David was transferred by God to this present time, there is no way the majority of the Church would accept David as an example for anything. Considering the terrible sin with Bathsheba and her husband Uriah, David would have been blacklisted forthwith. But the Holy Spirit accepted him and even presents him as an example of Righteousness.

Abraham is used as an example of one Saved before the Law of Moses was given, and David as an example after the Law was given. However, they were both Justified the same identical way, which was by Faith alone, and without the Law and works (Ps. 32:1-2). So, in these two men we actually have a complete compendium of what it means to have Faith in God. It is as follows:

1. Both are used as examples, even as we have said, of being Justified by Faith without works.

2. David as well, serves as a glaring example of a Believer who has sinned grievously, and who finds no Mercy whatsoever in the Law, for it demands death. However, on the same basis of Faith David received forgiveness and cleansing from this terrible sin, in the same manner in which he had originally received Salvation. It is all on the same premise — the premise of Faith in Christ (I Jn. 1:9).

No wonder David used the word *"Blessedness"* to describe such a man. In the Greek *"Blessedness"* is *"makarismos,"* and means *"a declaration of Blessedness."* In classical Greek it means *"prosperous,"* and in the New Testament, it is used in the sense of *"spiritually prosperous."*

Of course it is clear, that David is speaking of one who totally puts his trust in the Lord.

Once again, placing David in this modern setting, most so-called Church Leaders, would have demanded that he step down from being King of Israel for a period of two years, or some such time. As well, he would have been given a regimen of certain other things he must do, all which have no Scriptural or Spiritual bearing whatsoever, and are actually a form of penance, i.e., *"works."* Consequently, those who demand such a thing are nullifying the Grace of God, and those who submit to such a thing are likewise, nullifying the Grace of God.

It is impossible to have the situation both ways. Either we trust Christ fully, or we trust Him not at all.

Sin is a horrible, debilitating, destructive, wicked aberration that hurts all it touches as should be obvious. In fact, it is so bad, that the only thing which can cleanse and wash the terrible stain is the Precious Shed Blood of Jesus Christ. Faith and Trust in that alone, cleanses the stain, takes away the guilt, and restores spiritual prosperity. Truly,

NOTES

all who trust Christ completely and Christ Alone, are *"blessed."*

The phrase, *"Unto whom God imputeth Righteousness without works,"* seals the case. It means that God freely gives Righteousness to sinners who trust Him, and does so without any merit or *"works"* on the part of the sinner. In fact, and as we have stated, a presentation of *"works"* of any nature, automatically stops the presentation of Righteousness given by God.

IMPUTATION

At this stage we should look at the Doctrine of *"Imputation."*

The Greek word for *"impute"* is *"logizomai,"* and means *"to put on one's account, to credit him with, to put on deposit."* In other words, *"Imputation"* is the Lord granting Salvation to a Believing sinner, and doing so freely, after that sinner has expressed Faith in Christ and what Christ has done at the Cross. It simply means that Salvation is a free gift, which God freely imputes upon Faith (Rom. 3:24-31; 4:1-25).

In the case of Redemption, God credits to one's account His marvelous Salvation, and on the basis of the sinner having Faith in Christ. In fact, and as we keep saying, it is on this basis alone that He will impute Righteousness.

THE CROSS AND THE IMPUTATION OF RIGHTEOUSNESS

There is no way that man can earn Righteousness, irrespective as to what he might do. And yet, God demands Righteousness of all people.

But man is loath to admit that he cannot make himself righteous.

When Mother Theresa died, she was held up by the Catholic Church, and as well, by many in the Protestant Church, as stated, as the epitome of Righteousness. It was all credited to her because of her good works.

But despite what the Catholic Church said, or the Protestant Church, for that matter, was this lady righteous because of her good works?

No! Good works cannot bring about Righteousness, although, true Righteousness will always bring about good works.

Despite all the good works, there is little or no evidence at all that the dear lady just mentioned actually knew the Lord. She was depending exclusively, as far as can be determined, on her good works. In fact, the entirety of the Catholic Church functions in that capacity, and regrettably, most of the Protestant Churches follow suit in one way or the other.

RELATIVE RIGHTEOUSNESS AND WORKS RIGHTEOUSNESS

Our Lord gave a perfect example to us regarding self-righteousness, in one of His parables.

He spoke of two men who went to the Temple to pray, *"The one a Pharisee, and the other a publican."* Jesus said:

"The Pharisee stood and prayed thus with himself, God, I thank You that I am not as other men are, extortioners, unjust, adulterers, or even as this publican.

"I fast twice in the week, I give tithes of all that I possess.

"And the publican, standing afar off, would not lift up so much as his eyes unto Heaven, but smote upon his breast, saying, God be merciful to me a sinner.

"I tell you, this man went down to his house justified rather than the other: for every one who exalts himself shall be abased; and he who humbles himself shall be exalted" (Lk. 18:10-14).

Jesus addressed *"relative righteousness"* first. The Pharisee compared himself to other men, and that's what we mean by relative righteousness. To be sure, the Lord has no interest in such comparisons.

While we may think that we can always find someone who has done worse than we have, this, to be blunt, cuts no ice with God.

The Lord then addressed *"works righteousness."* The Pharisee also spoke of how much money he gave to the Work of the Lord, and how he fasted twice a week, etc. The Lord would not accept that either.

He then told of the publican, who in the eyes of the Pharisee, and all of Israel for that matter, was no more than a common criminal, who did not lift up himself at all, but merely cried, *"God, be merciful to me a sinner."*

NOTES

Our Lord said that this man was saved, and the Pharisee was lost, and despite his good works, etc.

If we look at this example closely, we will find that in the realm of *"relative righteousness,"* and *"works righteousness,"* which translates into *"self-righteousness,"* that it covers far too much of modern Christianity. That is sad but true!

THE CROSS AND RIGHTEOUSNESS

The only Righteousness that God will accept is the Righteousness that comes from Christ. It is made possible to us through what Jesus did at the Cross. To obtain this Righteousness, all we have to do is simply place our Faith and trust in Christ, and what He did for us at the Cross, and the Righteousness of God will immediately be imputed unto us.

There is a Righteousness in the Law, but for this Righteousness to be obtained, the Law must be kept perfectly, which is beyond man. But yet, Jesus did keep the Law, kept it perfectly, thereby gaining its Righteousness.

Please understand that He didn't need this for Himself, inasmuch as He had always been Righteous, was Righteous, and would ever be Righteous. But as the *"Last Adam"* (I Cor. 15:45), He had to do for us what we could not do for ourselves. In other words, He had to keep the Law perfectly, which He did, thereby gaining its Righteousness. But there remained the problem of unrighteousness being dealt with, in other words the broken Law. He had to pay the penalty of the broken Law, actually, *"being made a curse for us"* (Gal. 3:13).

Bearing the sin penalty on the Cross, thereby paying to God the terrible sin debt owed to Him by sinful man, this made it possible for God to justify man upon believing Faith, and thereby impute to him a perfect Righteousness (Rom. 5:9; II Cor. 5:21).

The Righteousness demanded by God can only be obtained by and through Jesus Christ, and more particularly, what He did for us at the Cross. We obtain it simply by exhibiting Faith in Christ, and His Finished Work (Gal. 5:6). Upon believing Faith, not only is a perfect Righteousness imputed to us, but it is given to us totally and completely. In other words, the Lord does not give it to us by degrees, but rather in totality at the moment of Faith. But let the Reader understand that when we say *"Faith,"* we are always speaking, and without exception, of Christ, and what Christ did at the Cross. On that basis alone, Righteousness, a perfect Righteousness, the Righteousness of Christ, is imputed to us (II Cor. 5:21).

(7) "SAYING, BLESSED ARE THEY WHOSE INIQUITIES ARE FORGIVEN, AND WHOSE SINS ARE COVERED."

The phrase, *"Saying, Blessed are they whose iniquities are forgiven,"* proclaims the spiritual prosperity of such a one, and which can only be obtained by throwing oneself on the Mercy and Grace of God, trusting fully in what He did for humanity at Calvary and the Resurrection.

David supports this Testimony in Psalm 32 by speaking of the happiness of the man to whom Righteousness is reckoned apart from works. The man is described as *"ungodly,"* in Psalms 32:5, for he has iniquities which need forgiveness and sins which require Atonement. Such a man has no Righteousness of his own.

David sings of what God was in Grace to such a man, and not of what the man was to God. His happiness was that God did not impute to him the sins he had committed, but covered and forgave them.

His Blessedness was not based upon any personal Righteousness which he had in himself before God, but it was based upon the activity of God in providing him with a Divine Righteousness, which being of God, and from God, was infinitely acceptable to God. David describes God as the Justifier, and man as the passive Believer (Williams).

The phrase, *"And whose sins are covered,"* implies Atonement and Justification. Atonement can mean *"at one ment"* as some claim, but also means expiation of guilt by a Blood-Sacrifice which covers it.

If one is to notice, the word *"covered"* is used and in the Greek is *"epikalupto,"* and means *"to conceal."*

David used that term because in Old Testament times, the blood of bulls and goats could not take away sin, only cover it. However, when Jesus died on Calvary, He did not merely cover our sins, but actually *"took them away"* (Jn. 1:29).

(8) "BLESSED IS THE MAN TO WHOM THE LORD WILL NOT IMPUTE SIN."

From verses 6 and 8 we learn that the Lord can either *"impute"* Righteousness or sin.

In other words, He freely imputes Righteousness to those who approach Him from the position of Faith instead of works. However, if sinners approach Him from the standpoint of works, that He will not accept, and, thereby, imputes them *"sin."* That means their sin is not forgiven, and, in fact, cannot be forgiven, unless Faith in Christ is offered.

Inasmuch as the Holy Spirit uses David as an example here, it can be observed that these verses represent and suggest the general tenor of the Book of Psalms, in which human righteousness is never asserted as constituting a claim to reward. *"My trust is in Thy Mercy,"* is, on the contrary, the ever-recurring theme (Barmby).

(9) "COMETH THIS BLESSEDNESS THEN UPON THE CIRCUMCISION ONLY, OR UPON THE UNCIRCUMCISION ALSO? FOR WE SAY THAT FAITH WAS RECKONED TO ABRAHAM FOR RIGHTEOUSNESS."

The question, *"Cometh this Blessedness then upon the Circumcision only, or upon the uncircumcision also?"*, is posed to the Jews, who taught that Gentiles must become Jews (Proselytes) in order to be Saved.

Paul has used two examples, Abraham who lived before the Law of Moses was given, and David who lived under the Law. He showed that both of them obtained Righteousness apart from Law, and, in fact, could not obtain such by Law. Righteousness was and is obtainable only by Faith in Christ.

The phrase, *"For we say that Faith was reckoned to Abraham for Righteousness,"* presents Faith alone as the ingredient. Actually, *"Righteousness"* was granted freely to Abraham upon his Faith in God some 14 years before the Rite of Circumcision was enjoined as a token of the Covenant (Gen. 15:6; 17:1-14).

Once again we go back to the principle that Salvation has always been given only on the premise of Faith in Christ. The giving of the Law of Moses did not change that, nor did the institution of the Church effect any change. The reason is simple:

Jesus is the One Who paid the price for man's Redemption, not the Law of Moses, or the Church for that matter. The Sacrifices before His Coming pointed to Him, and the Cross now points back to Him. Thus, is Jesus the Central Figure for all time, and, more particularly, the Crucified, Risen, Exalted Jesus.

(10) "HOW WAS IT THEN RECKONED? WHEN HE WAS IN CIRCUMCISION, OR IN UNCIRCUMCISION? NOT IN CIRCUMCISION, BUT IN UNCIRCUMCISION."

The question, *"How was it then reckoned?"*, is in at least one sense of the word, the greatest question of all time.

If one does not understand as to how Justification or Righteousness are reckoned, it is almost certain he will be led astray. The word *"reckoned"* in the Greek is *"logizomai,"* and means *"to take an inventory, to count, or conclude."* The idea is, that God will only accept His Computations, and not man's.

The question, *"When he was in Circumcision, or in uncircumcision?"*, is obvious as to its answer.

The phrase, *"Not in Circumcision, but in uncircumcision,"* proclaims the argument of verses 9-12 as that Abraham was declared by God to be a Righteous man while he was yet uncircumcised, i.e., outside of the Covenant within which Israel afterwards stood in its unique relation to God.

Actually, had the Promise of heirship of the world been based on the principle of Law, i.e., of merit, that would have set Abraham aside, for the inheritance was given him by Promise, and, therefore, on the principle of Faith.

Faith does not fulfill a Promise made to it, but believes it; and such Faith was reckoned to Abraham for Righteousness. This principle consequently opened wide the door of Grace to all men (Williams).

(11) "AND HE RECEIVED THE SIGN OF CIRCUMCISION, A SEAL OF THE RIGHTEOUSNESS OF THE FAITH WHICH HE HAD YET BEING UNCIRCUMCISED: THAT HE MIGHT BE THE FATHER OF ALL THEM THAT BELIEVE, THOUGH THEY BE NOT CIRCUMCISED; THAT RIGHTEOUSNESS MIGHT BE IMPUTED UNTO THEM ALSO:"

NOTES

The phrase, *"And he received the sign of Circumcision,"* presents such taking place about 14 years after he had been made Righteous by Faith in Christ. So, as should be obvious, this *"sign of Circumcision"* played no part in that Justification.

The phrase, *"A seal of the Righteousness of the Faith which he had yet being uncircumcised,"* plainly states that his Righteousness was by Faith, and was received long before Circumcision.

These things are portrayed so graphically, because man has a tremendous tendency to look toward the *"Sign"* instead of *"Faith."* Regrettably, he much easier puts his trust in a Ceremony or Ritual than he does Christ. Of course, he attempts to make it work, by claiming that the Sign, Ceremony, or Ritual are in effect, the acceptance of Christ by Faith. However, it isn't, and, in fact, cannot be. If a Sign or Ceremony is attached to Faith, it ceases to be Faith, and becomes works. That is the reason untold millions are lost. They have equated joining the Church, or being Baptized in Water, or taking the Lord's Supper, or doing other such things, with Faith. As stated, it isn't!

In fact, Circumcision was meant to imply a *"Seal of Righteousness,"* meaning that Abraham and all who followed in his train, would receive Righteousness solely by Faith and not by works. However, the Jews turned it around, making Circumcision the Salvation instead of it merely being the Seal or Symbol. As we have repeatedly stated, millions continue to do the same thing with Church Ordinances, etc.

The phrase, *"That he might be the father of all them that believe, though they be not Circumcised,"* places the ground or foundation of Salvation squarely on Faith instead of works.

In other words, the Lord was saying that being Circumcised or uncircumcised had nothing to do with Faith, and, consequently, nothing to do with Salvation. It was merely a *"Seal"* of what the Lord was going to do. Of course, when Jesus came, the *"Seal"* was no longer needed, as should be obvious.

The phrase, *"That Righteousness might be imputed unto them also,"* proclaims the insistence by the Holy Spirit that Righteousness be given to all who believe, whether they be Jew or Gentile.

In other words, the word *"also"* tells us that God raised up the Jews from the loins of Abraham that the Gospel may be given to the entirety of the world. However, Israel turned inward, refused to accept God's Plan of Salvation, but in effect, instituted her own, thereby excluding all others, except for those who became Proselyte Jews.

As well, the Church has to be very careful that it does not fall into the same trap. It is sad, but the more that a Religious Denomination leaves the Word of God, instituting their own particular rules and regulations which have little or no bearing on the Word of God, they become more and more wrapped up in their own religious affiliation, actually projecting the idea that association with them guarantees Salvation, or at least an elitist Christianity. The Truth then becomes the opposite.

(12) "AND THE FATHER OF CIRCUMCISION TO THEM WHO ARE NOT OF THE CIRCUMCISION ONLY, BUT WHO ALSO WALK IN THE STEPS OF THAT FAITH OF OUR FATHER ABRAHAM, WHICH HE HAD BEING YET UNCIRCUMCISED."

The phrase, *"And the father of Circumcision to them who are not of the Circumcision only,"* presents Abraham as being the father of all Believers, whether Circumcised (Jews) or not (Gentiles), providing they seek for Justification by Faith only.

Abraham is the father of us all, in that the Lord gave him the rudiments of Justification by Faith (Vs. 11). So, this means that Abraham, at least in a sense, was the father of both the Gentiles and the Jews, at least as far as Faith is concerned.

The Jews boasted greatly of Abraham, but the Apostle shows them that both Jews and Gentiles come under the same umbrella, at least by Faith.

The phrase, *"But who also walk in the steps of that Faith of our father Abraham,"* refers simply to him believing God, and God accounting his Faith to him for Righteousness (Gen. 15:6).

The phrase, *"Which he had being yet uncircumcised,"* clenches the argument, and opens up Salvation to all who come by Faith in

Christ, irrespective as to whom they may be.

(13) "FOR THE PROMISE, THAT HE SHOULD BE THE HEIR OF THE WORLD, WAS NOT TO ABRAHAM, OR TO HIS SEED, THROUGH THE LAW, BUT THROUGH THE RIGHTEOUSNESS OF FAITH."

The phrase, *"For the Promise, that he should be the heir of the world, was not to Abraham, or to his seed, through the Law,"* actually means in virtue of obedience to the Law. As the Reader knows, it is speaking of the Law of Moses.

Also, the Reader may tend to discount this great lesson given by the Holy Spirit through Paul, as being of little consequence presently, considering that we are no longer under Law but Grace. However, the Reader must be assured that the Holy Spirit had a great purpose in all of this, and that it is of extreme significance to each and all at this present time. At least some of the reasons are as follows:

1. First of all, while the Law of Moses is addressed here, it is used only as a symbol, actually referring to any Law or method one may use in order to effect Salvation. The Law of Moses served as an excellent symbol, because it was the Law of God. The idea is, that if the Law of God could not bring Salvation, how in the world does one think that man's puny and pitiful laws would be any better? In fact, the Law of Moses was never meant to save, only meant to portray and define sin.

2. The efforts of men to earn their own Salvation apart from God's Plan of Redemption, is a worldwide problem. As well, the problem is not isolated, but actually affecting almost all of humanity. Consequently, this of what Paul is Teaching affects all of humanity, and for all time.

3. In all of this, Faith in Christ is held up as the only Way of Salvation, which applies to all, and again, for all time.

The phrase, *"But through the Righteousness of Faith,"* refers to the Righteousness of God, which alone can be obtained by Faith in God. This speaks of the virtue of Faith in the Divine Promise.

The contrast here is between Law-keeping versus Promise-Believing.

The idea is, and as has been already

explained, that Law simply declares what is right, and requires conformity to it, but does not provide any Power to obey, or Atonement for not obeying, which man desperately needs. Hence, in itself, it worketh not Righteousness, but wrath, which is all that any Law can do.

(14) "FOR IF THEY WHICH ARE OF THE LAW BE HEIRS, FAITH IS MADE VOID, AND THE PROMISE MADE OF NONE EFFECT:"

The phrase, *"For if they which are of the Law be heirs, Faith is made void,"* in essence proclaims, that Abraham's Faith was of no consequence, which would as well, include all who lived before the giving of the Law, that is if Law-keeping affords Salvation.

This reminds me of some Churches or particular Doctrines which claim certain things other than Faith as a foundation or premise for Salvation. By declaring such, whatever it may be, the instigators are actually claiming that no one was Saved before their particular Doctrine became known, etc. In other words, the Faith of all others is *"void."*

Let's use the Catholic Church as an example. They claim that one must be faithful to the Catholic Church and keep its Ordinances in order to be Saved. The Mormons plus several others, proclaim similar foolishness. So, what about all those who lived before the Catholic Church or the Mormons, etc.?

Another example is the United Pentecostals who claim that one must speak in Tongues and be Baptized in Water to be Saved, and, as well, be Baptized according to a certain Baptismal formula. Of course, if that Doctrine is fully believed, that means that all those who lived before the Day of Pentecost were not Saved, even though they trusted Christ. As well, it also means that none are Saved now except those who are a part of that particular Church.

Once again, all of these Beliefs and Doctrines, plus many we have not named, make void the Faith of untold millions, which means they are not of God, that is if such is true.

The phrase, *"And the Promise made of none effect,"* pertains to the Great Promise of God Which, or rather Who in reality, is Jesus Christ. He Alone is the actual *"Promise."*

NOTES

This was the *"Promise"* given in Genesis 3:15, and that given to Abraham (Gen. 12:1-3; 15:6; 17:1-14, 19; 21:12; 22:13-14).

This is why it is so everlastingly bad, even evil and wicked, for anything to be added to the Finished Work of Christ. To do so, abrogates the *"Promise"* and makes it of *"none effect."* In other words, and as repeatedly said, if any Law or works, are added, everything is nullified, i.e., *"made void."*

(15) "BECAUSE THE LAW WORKETH WRATH: FOR WHERE NO LAW IS, THERE IS NO TRANSGRESSION."

The phrase, *"Because the Law worketh wrath,"* proclaims that which Law must do, because it's all it can do. All Law has a penalty, i.e., *"wrath"* or else, it is not Law.

In other words, if a person attempts to earn their Salvation by thinking they are keeping some type of Law, they are doomed to failure, and besides that, must suffer its penalty. Considering that there has never been an exception to this rule, I think one would be very foolish to think that he or she would be an exception.

The phrase, *"For where no Law is, there is no transgression,"* is actually saying, *"The more that one attempts to keep some type of Law, the more transgressions there will be."* The reason is simple, the very purpose of Law is to point out and define transgressions.

So what are we saying?

Even though Paul is not extending this subject at this particular time, as he will in Romans Chapters 6-8, the idea is, that if one attempts to overcome sin by a certain regimen or the keeping of certain rules, not only will he not overcome, but the sin will become even worse, no matter how hard he tries otherwise. That should be a sober thought.

For example, this means that the facing of problems in our lives can only be handled by Christ living through us and in us, and not by the Believer attempting to keep some types of Laws, etc.

For instance, millions have thought that by reading so many Scriptures a day, or praying so much each day, that such would bring victory. While these things are definitely important, and do bless greatly in other ways, they do not, however, effect the results which one seeks. As stated, that can only come through Christ. As Israel of old, it is very easy to make a *"Law"* even out of the Bible or prayer, fasting, etc. While these things definitely should be done, we must keep them in their rightful place, and not make of them that which were never intended.

Now I trust that one can see just how important this which Paul gives actually is! The last thing the Believer wants to do, is to embroil himself in something which increases transgressions, which is the very opposite of that which he desires.

The whole idea is, that the Law which God originally gave, called the *"Law of Moses"* was faced and kept totally by the Lord Jesus Christ in His Earthly Walk. No one else ever succeeded in doing such, even though God commanded such be done.

Upon Faith in Christ, the Lord freely imputes to the Believer the *standing* and *position* of *"Law-keeper,"* which is what God demands, but which the Believer on his own could never do.

Consequently, my life now as a Believer is not made up of my faithfulness to laws, rules, and regulations, which can only breed more transgressions, but rather to Christ Who has done all of these wonderful things, and in fact, did them for me. Simple Faith in Him, grants me all the victories He has won.

This is the reason it is so improper for Churches to institute all types of rules and regulations, etc. The only requirement to belong to any Church, should be a confession of one's simple Faith in their Lord and Saviour, Jesus Christ. Anything else, can only breed hypocrisy, transgressions, and defeat.

(16) "THEREFORE IT IS OF FAITH, THAT IT MIGHT BE BY GRACE; TO THE END THE PROMISE MIGHT BE SURE TO ALL THE SEED; NOT TO THAT ONLY WHICH IS OF THE LAW, BUT TO THAT ALSO WHICH IS OF THE FAITH OF ABRAHAM; WHO IS THE FATHER OF US ALL,"

The phrase, *"Therefore it is of Faith,"* means that the effect of the Law is condemnation, even as we already have stated, while the action of Grace is Justification.

Paul argues that the Law did not give Salvation, because in fact, it could not give Salvation; consequently, inasmuch as the

NOTES

Law could only condemn, the Inheritance, i.e., *"The Promise,"* must be of Faith and Faith alone!

These are the terms laid down by none other than God as to how the Inheritance, Eternal Life, is dispensed by God and appropriated by the sinner. He is to exercise Faith (exercise a simple trust in the Lord Jesus Christ) rather than perform works (joining a Church or becoming religious, thinking that such brings Salvation).

This does not mean that joining a Church is wrong, or a host of other good things one may name, but rather that they must not be done for the wrong reason.

The phrase, *"That it might be by Grace,"* means that God's Gift is just that, a Gift, which is given to the sinner upon simple Faith in Christ. The act is referred to as *"Grace,"* because it means *"unmerited favor."* God favors the sinner through no merit on the part of the sinner, but simply because the sinner has Faith in Christ. This is God's Way, and, actually, the only Way in which this Great Plan can function and operate.

As we have attempted to say several times, God does not so much condemn a person for what they are, as much as for what they refuse to become, i.e., *"Righteousness,"* which He will freely provide upon the sinner simply saying and meaning it, *"I believe."*

If the sinner earns Salvation by his works (which he cannot), Salvation would not be by Grace, would not be an unmerited gift given out of the spontaneous generosity of the Heart of God. But since Faith is the supplicant's hand outstretched for Salvation, the latter can be a Gift given in Pure Grace. And this is so construed also that Salvation is available to both Jew and Gentile on the same basis.

In fact, the Law of Moses was only given to the Jew, and if Salvation would have been given on the basis of works, only the Jew could be Saved, for the Gentile was never given the Law. However, Salvation is imparted on Faith alone and never by Law.

The phrase, *"To the end the Promise might be sure to all the seed,"* refers to the whole of humanity and for all time. This is what God was speaking of when He said to Abraham, *"And in thee shall all families of the Earth be blessed"* (Gen. 12:3).

The *"Sure Promise"* carries the idea, as is obvious, that God's Plan of Salvation by Faith, in order that it might be by Grace, will not change.

The phrase, *"Not to that only which is of the Law, but to that also which is of the Faith of Abraham,"* speaks to both Jews and Gentiles, and that they all must come the same way. But more so, as we have stated, even though the Jews were greatly favored by God in that they were given the Law of Moses, still, that favor had nothing to do with Salvation; consequently, regarding Salvation, everyone begins on a level playing field, but which the Jews would not accept.

They found it difficult, even impossible to believe, that a group of people so favored by God, surely would be looked at in a different light than Gentiles. In one sense of the word, they were!

When Jesus came, He came to the Jews first, offering them the Kingdom, which was a Blessing of such magnitude that it defies description (Mat. 3:2; Jn. 4:22). However, it was refused and forfeited, for the simple reason that they refused to humble themselves to accept Him as Saviour (Mat. 3:5-12).

The phrase, *"Who is the father of us all,"* proclaims the Patriarch being used as an example of Faith (Gen. 15:6).

ABRAHAM AS THE FATHER OF US ALL

In the New Testament we are astonished at the wealth and variety of comments respecting Abraham. As in the Old Testament, his position of ancestor lends him much of his significance, not only as ancestor of Israel (Acts 13:26), but specifically as ancestor, now of the Levitical Priesthood (Heb. 7:5), now of the Messiah (Mat. 1:1), now, by the peculiarly Christian Doctrine of the unity of Believers in Christ (Gal. 3:16-29).

All that he received through Divine Election, by the Covenant made with him, is inherited by his seed and passes under the collective names of the Promise (Rom. 4:13), the Blessing (Gal. 3:14), Mercy (Lk. 1:54), the Oath (Lk. 1:73), the Covenant (Acts 3:25). The way in which Abraham responded to this peculiar Goodness of God makes him the type of the Christian Believer.

NOTES

ABRAHAM AND HIS FAITH

It is his Faith in the Divine Promise, which, just because it was for him peculiarly unsupported by any evidence of the senses, becomes the type of the Faith that leads to Justification (Rom. 4:3), and, therefore, in this sense again he is the *"father"* of Christians, as Believers (Rom. 4:11). For that Promise to Abraham was, after all, a *"preaching beforehand"* of the Christian Gospel, in that it embraced *"all the families of the Earth"* (Gal. 3:8).

The obedience that Faith wrought in him is especially praised by the author of Hebrews (Heb. 11:8-17).

In accordance with this high estimate of the Patriarch's piety, we read of his eternal felicity as well, not only in the current conceptions of the Jews, but also in the express assertion of our Lord (Mat. 8:11; Lk. 13:28).

However, whatever may be said of him, the light that shines brightest in his life, and that which gives him great credence with God, was and is, his Faith. That alone shines like a beacon and refuses to be extinguished. On that, and that alone, he is given the title *"Father of us all."*

This tells us as well, that simple Faith in God, even with Abraham as our example, possesses an eternal quality which will never dim. Its consequences are eternal, and meant to be that way.

For a Christian to simply say *"I believe God,"* presents the greatest music to the Ears of God, that could ever be. God honors Faith. As well, He honors it in such a way, that it is made the foundation of all things (Heb. 11:6).

(17) "(AS IT IS WRITTEN, I HAVE MADE THEE A FATHER OF MANY NATIONS,) BEFORE HIM WHOM HE BELIEVED, EVEN GOD, WHO QUICKENETH THE DEAD, AND CALLETH THOSE THINGS WHICH BE NOT AS THOUGH THEY WERE."

The phrase, *"As it is written, I have made thee a father of many Nations,"* is taken from Genesis 17:4-5. To be sure, it was fulfilled even before New Testament times.

At the present time, all of the Arab Nations in the world have their origin in Abraham, through his son Ishmael. The

Jews, through his son Isaac (Gen. 17:19-21). In essence, the age-old conflict between the Jews and the Arabs stems from the two sons, Ishmael and Isaac. The Moslems claim through the Koran that Ishmael is the Promised Seed, while the Bible declares Isaac to be such, and which history bears out, I might quickly add (Gen. 17:19).

THE PROMISED SEED

The history of the Jews includes the Prophets who were given the Word of God, which includes the Old Testament. Islam which did not begin until some 600 years after Christ, boasts no Prophets, with the exception of Mohammed, who was a false Prophet.

(Ishmael was a work of the flesh, which has caused so many problems from then until now, and which portrays to us how that ones who are Faith-filled, such as Abraham and Sarah, can also give birth to that which is not of God, but rather of the flesh, and which will happen if one steps out of Faith into feelings.)

The phrase, *"Before Him Whom he believed,"* refers to Abraham believing God, but believing for what?

Of course we know that the Holy Spirit through the Apostle is referring to Abraham believing God for the Promised Seed, who would be Isaac. However, Isaac represented far more than a mere addition to the family. It was through him and his lineage that the Redeemer would come, which made this the single most important thing in the history of man.

For God to redeem man, he would have to become Man, in order that He may serve as a Sin-Offering, which Alone would satisfy the terrible sin debt. Of course, the Creator becoming a Creature, is beyond understanding.

Naturally, all of humanity goes back to Adam and Eve as the original parents, but due to the flood, all go back as well to the family of Noah. This means that all five races sprang from the three sons of Noah, Ham, Japeth, and Shem. However, according to the Prophecy as given by Noah, the lineage of Shem would bring forth the Promised Redeemer (Gen. 3:15; 9:26). Abraham was born in the lineage of Shem some 400 years after that Patriarch, approximately nine

NOTES

times removed (Gen., Chpt. 11).

THE JEWS

Through the loins of Abraham and the womb of his wife Sarah, the Lord would bring forth a very special people who would serve in essence, as the womb of the Messiah, and as well, give the world the Word of God. From the time of Abraham to the Birth of Jesus, would be approximately 2,000 years.

So, Abraham's believing God, even as the Scripture portrays here, was of far greater magnitude than meets the eye, literally involving every human being on the face of the Earth who would ever be born, even from the time of Adam and Eve. In that sense, and as stated, he is the *"Father of us all."*

The phrase, *"Even God, Who quickeneth the dead,"* has respect to the Miracle-working Power of Jehovah. It pertains to the coming Resurrection, but more particularly it pointed to the Lord quickening Abraham, in order that he could have children, even at his advanced age. Actually the Scripture says of him, *"Therefore sprang there even of one, and him as good as dead, so many as the stars of the sky in multitude, and as the sand which is by the sea shore innumerable"* (Heb. 11:12). The same was true of Sarah!

The phrase, *"And calleth those things which be not as though they were,"* presents a description of the use of Faith, as well as its power.

FAITH IN GOD

If it is in the Plan of God, Faith can address the situation as if it has already come to pass, even though it is yet future.

As an example, the Lord spoke to my heart in 1985 (I believe it was) respecting the Gospel going to every Village, Town, and City throughout the entirety of the Soviet Union. Of course at that time, such was impossible, due to that vast area being a Soviet Police State. However, God said it, and I believed it.

About three years later we began to translate Television Programming from English into Russian on the premise of what the Lord had spoken to my heart. In the natural there was no way such a thing could come to pass, and I speak of airing our Telecast over that vast area.

However, to the shocked amazement and surprise of the State Department in Washington, and the balance of the world for that matter, the wall began to come down in the latter part of 1989.

There was not a single political pundit in the world to my knowledge, who dreamed that such a thing would happen. But happen it did, and it was something of course of which the Lord knew would happen. Therefore, He told us to get ready, and on that premise, the premise of Faith alone, we began to translate programming, believing God that shortly this door would open, which it did.

We began televising first in the client State of Latvia. However, in a short time we were airing the Telecast over T.V. One out of Moscow, the number one Television Network in what had formerly been the Soviet Union. This Network had formerly been the Government Propaganda Channel, and was of course the most powerful in Russia, actually covering all 15 Republics. For nearly two years we televised the Gospel over that Network, covering one-sixth of the world's land surface, and nearly 300,000,000 people. Exactly as the Spirit of God had spoken to my heart, the Gospel went into every single Village, Town, and City, as predicted. Believing God, we were able to call those things which were not as though they were, and the Lord brought to pass that which He had said.

As well, I would be remiss if I did not credit Jim Woolsey with the Faith given to him by the Lord in order that this door be opened. He spearheaded and sparked that effort that brought untold thousands to a Saving Knowledge of Jesus Christ.

Due to this vast area being cut off from most of the world for some 70 years, without a doubt this was and is one of the greatest happenings of the Holy Spirit in this century. We give the Lord all the Praise and Glory, as He Alone is worthy of all Praise and Glory.

FAITH AS IT IS USED HERE

We learn from Romans 4:17 and Hebrews 11:3, that God works and functions, that is if we are allowed to use such terminology, from the realm of Faith. Consequently, it

would not be improper to refer to Him as *"The God of Faith."* In other words, everything that He has done, has been from the premise of Faith. Exactly as Paul wrote, He *"Calleth those things which be not as though they were."* Therefore, when the Believer functions in the capacity and principle of Bible Faith, he has locked into the same Force and Power used by God to create all things. As we have already stated, this is why Abraham was held up as such an example. He trusted God, even though appearances said otherwise.

For instance, Abraham had few fellow Believers to encourage him. In fact, other than Melchizedek, King of Salem (Jerusalem), there is no evidence that there was a single other Believer on the face of the Earth other than Abraham, Sarah, his servant Eliezer, and his nephew Lot (Gen. 14:18; 15:2; 19:1). So, the Church of that day was small. As well, Abraham did not have the privilege of the Holy Spirit residing in him, as we now do under the New Covenant. Nevertheless, despite these hindrances, plus many we have not named, Abraham believed God.

The ingredient of Faith is to be judged not only according to that which it can create, but as well to the circumstances in which it must function.

FAITH AND THE BELIEVER

Probably Faith could be described better by saying that it is reliance upon God Who is known to be trustworthy. Such reliance enables the Believer to treat the future as present and the invisible as seen. This relates to Hebrews 11:1, and translates into Power.

Actually, I think one could say that the Supreme Message of the Lord Jesus was *"reliance,"* and that means reliance on God. He passed that Message on to His Apostles. Through their lips and pens *"Faith,"* in that sense, became the supreme watchword of Christianity.

THE CENTRAL PLACE OF FAITH IN CHRISTIANITY

As being, in its true idea, a reliance as simple as possible upon the Word, Power, and Love, of Another, it is precisely that, which, on man's side, adjusts him to the living and merciful presence and action of a trusted God.

In the nature of Faith, it is the one possible receptive attitude, in which a person brings nothing to the Throne of God except his Faith, and leaves with everything. Thus, *"Faith"* is our side of union with Christ. And thus, it is our means of possessing all His Benefits, Pardon, Purification, Justification, Life, Peace, and Glory.

FAITHFULNESS AS THE ACTION OF FAITH

Faithfulness is a quality or attribute applied in the Scripture to both God and man. As we apply such to God, Faithfulness is one of the characteristics of God's ethical Nature. It denotes the firmness or constancy of God in His relations with men, especially with His people. It is, accordingly, one aspect of God's Truth and of His unchangeableness.

God is True not only because He is really God in contrast to all that is not God, and because He realizes the idea of Godhead, but also because He is *constant* or *faithful* in keeping His Promises, and, therefore, is worthy of Trust. God, likewise, is unchangeable in His ethical Nature.

This unchangeableness the Scripture often connects with God's Goodness and Mercy, and also with His constancy in reference to His Covenant Promises, and this is what the Bible means by the Faithfulness of God.

THE FAITHFULNESS OF GOD TO HIS COVENANT PROMISES

God's Faithfulness to His Covenants is frequently emphasized by Paul. He argues in Romans, Chapter 3 that the unbelief of the Jews cannot make void God's Faithfulness. Both Jew and Gentile, the Apostle said, are on the same footing regarding Justification. Nevertheless the Jews had one great advantage in that they were the people to whom the Revelation of God's Gracious Promises had been committed.

These Promises will certainly be fulfilled, notwithstanding the fact that some of the Jews were unfaithful, because the fulfillment of these Promises depends not on human conduct but on the Faithfulness of God, which cannot be made void by human faithlessness

and unbelief.

And to the supposition that man's faithlessness could make of none effect God's Faithfulness, Paul replies, *"Let God be true* (faithful) *and every man a liar* (unfaithful)*"* (Rom. 3:4). By this, Paul means that in the fulfillment of God's Promises, despite the fact that men are faithless, the Faithfulness of God will be abundantly vindicated, even though thereby every man should be proven untrue and faithless. And not only so, but human faithlessness will give an opportunity for a manifestation of the Faithfulness of God, abounding to His Glory (Rom. 3:7).

God's Faithfulness here is His unchangeable constancy and fidelity to His Covenant Promises; and it is this fidelity to His Promises, or the fact that God's Gracious Gifts and Election are without any change of mind on His part, which gave to Paul the assurance that all Israel should finally be Saved (Rom. 11:25-29).

FAITHFULNESS, THE NATURE OF GOD

Moreover this Covenant Faithfulness of God is grounded in His Very Nature, so that Paul's hope of Eternal Life rests on the fact that *"God, Who cannot lie, promised it before the world began"* (Titus 1:2); and the certainty that God will *"abide faithful"* notwithstanding human faithlessness rests on the fact that *"God cannot deny Himself"* (II Tim. 2:13).

It is because God is faithful that His Promises in Christ are *"yea"* and *"Amen"* (II Cor. 1:18-20). This attribute of God, moreover, is the basis of Paul's confident assurance that God will preserve the Christian in temptation (I Cor. 10:13); and establish him and preserve him from evil (II Thess. 3:3).

And since God is faithful and His Gracious Promises trustworthy, this characteristic attaches to the *"faithful sayings"* in the Pastoral Epistles which sum up the Gospel, making them worthy of trust and acceptance (I Tim. 1:15; 4:9; Titus 3:8).

A SURE TRUST AND HOPE

This Faithfulness of God in the sense of fidelity to His Promises is set forth as the object of sure trust and hope by the writer of the Epistle to the Hebrews.

It was the basis of Sarah's Faith that she would bear a child when she was past age (Heb. 11:11); and it is because God is faithful to His Promise in Christ that we can draw nigh to Him with full assurance of Faith, holding fast without wavering the profession of hope (Heb. 10:23).

GOD'S FAITHFULNESS IN THE FORGIVENESS OF SIN

John also ascribes this attribute to God. Since one of the most precious of God's Promises through Christ is the pardon of sin through the *"Blood of Jesus Christ,"* John says that God's Faithfulness, as well as His Righteousness, is manifested in the forgiveness of sin (I Jn. 1:9).

Even as I dictate these words I greatly sense the Presence of God. How many times has the Evil One told us that God has lost patience with us, and that it was no use importuning Him again concerning this terrible problem of sin. However, every single Believer who has ever lived, and who has approached God asking for forgiveness, irrespective of the number of times involved, not a single one has ever been turned away. His Faithfulness shines in this attribute to such an extent, that it is literally impossible for the Believer to fully and properly express himself regarding one's thankfulness to God for this Faithfulness.

Think of it! He has never turned a deaf ear to a sinner seeking Salvation, nor to a Believer seeking forgiveness. The song says:

"The record is clear today, He has washed my sins away.
"The old account was settled long ago."

Thank God for I John 1:9, *"If we confess our sins, He is faithful and just to forgive us our sins, and to cleanse us from all unrighteousness."*

THE FAITHFULNESS OF GOD IN PERSECUTION AND SUFFERING

God's Faithfulness in this respect is viewed from a slightly different viewpoint by Peter when he tells his readers that those who suffer as Christians and in accordance with God's Will should *"Commit their soul's in well-doing unto a Faithful Creator"* (I Pet. 4:19).

The quality of Faithfulness, which in the Scripture is more frequently ascribed to God in His relation to man as Gracious Saviour, and as the ground of hope in His Gracious Promises, is applied here by Peter to God in His relation to man as his Creator, and is made the ground of comfort under persecution and suffering.

By Peter using the words *"Faithful Creator"* he makes it emphatic that this is a characteristic of God as Creator, and the position of the words in this sentence throws great emphasis on this attribute of God as the basis of comfort under suffering. It is as if Peter would say to suffering Christians, *"You suffer not by chance but in accordance with God's Will; He, the Almighty Creator, made you, and since your suffering is in accordance with His Will, you ought to trust yourselves to Him Who as your Creator is faithful."*

It is, of course, Christians who are to derive this comfort, but the Faithfulness of God is extended here to cover all His relations to His people, and to pledge all His attributes in their behalf.

FAITHFULNESS AND THE LORD JESUS CHRIST

This attribute of Faithfulness is also ascribed to Christ in the New Testament. Where Jesus is called a Faithful High Priest, the idea expressed is His fidelity to His obligations to God and to His Saving Work (Heb. 2:17; 3:2:6). But when in the Book of Revelation Jesus Christ is called the *"Faithful Witness"* or absolutely the *"Faithful and True,"* it is clear that the quality of Faithfulness, in the most absolute sense in which it is characteristic of God in contrast with human changeableness, is also ascribed to Christ (Rev. 1:5; 3:14; 19:11).

This is especially clear in the last-named Passage. The Heavens themselves open to disclose the Glorified Christ, and He appears not only as a Victorious Warrior Whose Name is Faithful and True, but also as the One in Whom these attributes have their highest realization, and of Whom they are so characteristic as to become the Name of the Exalted Lord. This clearly implies the Deity of Jesus Christ.

THREE THINGS CONCERNING GOD'S FAITHFULNESS

1. This Characteristic of God is usually connected with His Gracious Promises of Salvation, and is one of those attributes which make God the firm and secure Object of all our trust and confidence.

As is the case with all Scriptural Teaching concerning God, it is the spiritual value of His Faithfulness which is made prominent.

2. The so-called moral attributes, of which Faithfulness is one, are essential in order to constitute God the Object of worship, along with attributes such as Omnipotence, Omnipresence, and Unchangeableness. Take away either class of attributes from God, and He ceases to be God, the Object of worship, veneration, and trust.

3. God is Faithful in such an absolute sense as to contrast Him with men who are faithful only in a relative sense, leaves us with no comparison at all. Compared to the Faithfulness of God, even the best of men appear as changeable and faithless.

No wonder He spoke of Himself through Baalim so long ago, and said, *"God is not a man, that He should lie; neither the son of man, that He should repent: hath He said, and shall He not do it? Or hath He spoken, and shall He not make it good?"* (Num. 23:19).

(18) "WHO AGAINST HOPE BELIEVED IN HOPE, THAT HE MIGHT BECOME THE FATHER OF MANY NATIONS, ACCORDING TO THAT WHICH WAS SPOKEN, SO SHALL THY SEED BE."

The phrase, *"Who against hope believed in hope,"* presents a description of Abraham's Faith.

The word *"hope"* in the Greek is *"elpis,"* and means, *"to anticipate, usually with pleasure."*

The idea is, that Abraham's Faith was contrary to hope, at least as far as nature could give hope, but rested on hope that God could do what nature could not do.

"Against" in the Greek is *"para,"* and means *"beyond."* In other words, Abraham's situation was beyond hope. Yet he based his expectation upon hope. His situation was beyond human hope, but despite that he rested it upon hope in God, which is

NOTES

something else altogether.

BIBLICAL HOPE

Biblical Hope is inseparable from Faith in God. Because of what God has done in the past, particularly in preparing for the Coming of Christ, and because of what God has done and is now doing through Christ, the Christian dares to expect future blessings which are at present invisible (II Cor. 1:10).

The majority of secular thinkers in the ancient world did not regard hope as a virtue, but merely as a temporary illusion; and Paul was giving an accurate description of Pagans when he said they had no hope (Eph. 2:12; I Thess. 4:13), the fundamental reason for this being that they were *"without God."*

However, the Believer in Christ alone has hope for the future. The reason being, that the Goodness of God for the Believer is never exhausted. As good as the present may be, the best is yet to come. His hope is increased as he reflects on the activities of God in the Scriptures (Rom. 12:12; 15:4). Christ in him is the Hope of future Glory (Col. 1:27).

THE ANCHOR OF THE SOUL

The Believer's final Salvation rests on such Hope (Rom. 8:24); and this Hope of Salvation is a *"Helmet,"* an essential part of the Believer's defensive armor in the struggle against evil (I Thess. 5:8).

Hope, to be sure, is not a kite at the mercy of the changing winds, but *"a sure and stedfast anchor of the soul,"* penetrating deep into the invisible eternal world (Heb. 6:19).

Because of his Faith the Christian has an assurance that the things he hopes for are real (Heb. 11:1); and his Hope never disappoints him (Rom. 5:5).

HOPE AND THE TEACHING OF JESUS

Actually, there are no explicit references to Hope in the Teaching of Jesus, because He is the very essence of Hope. He taught His Disciples not to be anxious about the future, because that future is in the Hands of a Loving Father. He also leads them to expect that after His Resurrection renewed spiritual power will be available for them, enabling them to do even greater works than He did, to overcome sin and death, and to look forward to sharing His Own Eternal Glory.

Consequently, even though He never directly mentioned the Word, the undergirding strength of His Teaching proclaimed it grandly and gloriously.

The Resurrection of Jesus revitalized their Hope, simply because Jesus is the Hope of all humanity. Consequently, when He taught of Himself, He was Teaching of Hope. In fact, and as we have stated, His Resurrection was far and away the mightiest Act of God wrought in history, and the greatest display of Hope that ever was.

Before it *"panic, and despair flee away."* Christian Faith is essentially Faith in God Who raised Jesus from the dead (I Pet. 1:21). This God, towards Whom the Christian directs his Faith, is called *"The God of Hope,"* Who can fill the Believer with joy and peace, and enable him to abound in Hope (Rom. 15:13).

Because of the Resurrection, the Christian is Saved from the miserable condition of having his Hope in Christ limited to this world only (I Cor. 15:19). Christ Jesus is his Hope for time and eternity (I Tim. 1:1). His call to be Christ's Disciple carries with it the Hope of finally sharing His Glory (Eph. 1:18). His Hope is laid up for him in Heaven (Col. 1:5) and will be realized when his Lord is revealed (I Pet. 1:13).

FAITH, HOPE, AND LOVE

The existence of this Hope makes it impossible for the Christian to be satisfied with transient joys (Heb. 13:14); it also acts as a stimulus to purity of life (I Jn. 3:2-3) and enables him to suffer cheerfully if necessary.

It is noticeable how often Hope is associated in the New Testament with *"patience"* or *"steadfastness."* This virtue, to be sure, is vastly different from Stoic endurance, precisely because it is bound up with a Hope unknown to the Stoic (Rom. 5:3-5; I Thess. 1:3).

In the light of what has been said, it is not surprising that Hope should so often be mentioned as a part of Faith. The heros of Faith in Hebrews Chapter 11 are also beacons of Hope. What is perhaps more remarkable is the frequent association of Hope with Love as well as with Faith. This threefold combination of Faith, Hope, and Love is

found in I Corinthians 13:13; Galatians 5:5-6; I Thessalonians 1:3; 5:8; Hebrews 6:10-12; I Peter 1:21-22.

By its connection with Love, Christian Hope is freed from all selfishness. The Christian does not hope for blessings for himself which he does not desire others to share. When he loves his fellowmen, he hopes that they will be the recipients of the good things that he knows God longs to give them.

Paul gave evidence of his Hope just as much as his Love and his Faith when he returned the runaway slave Onesimus to his master Philemon. Faith, Hope, and Love are thus inseparable. Hope cannot exist apart from Faith, and Love cannot be exercised without Hope. These three are the things that abide (I Cor. 13:13) and together they comprise the Christian way of life in Christ.

The phrase, *"That he might become the father of many Nations,"* presents that which was brought about by Faith, as verse 17 presents that which was promised by Faith. Even though the Promise was made by the Lord, Abraham had to activate his Faith in order that the Promise be realized, which it was.

But yet when the Patriarch died, in reality there were no Nations except in the Mind of God and the Faith of Abraham. Nevertheless, that Promise was fulfilled in totality, literally speaking, pointing to Israel and the Arab Nations. However, in a spiritual sense, every Nation in the world will ultimately fall into this category, as all ultimately will be brought unto Christ.

The phrase, *"According to that which was spoken, so shall they seed be,"* is taken from Genesis 15:5.

At that time, the Lord asked Abraham if he could count the stars, which then covered the heavens like a canopy, promising him that his seed would be accordingly.

The idea was, that Abraham was having difficulty believing the Lord for one son, especially considering the barrenness of Sarah, along with the age of them both; however, the Lord in effect tells him, that not only will he have the one, but millions as well!

Such has been fulfilled in Christ and continues to be fulfilled in Christ, exactly as the Lord said. Such is Faith!

Considering this great Faith mentioned

here, one must understand that it was all in the spiritual sense, and of tremendous consequences. In other words, the Patriarch was believing God for spiritual things, even though Isaac was physical.

It is sad when one considers that many in the modern Faith Movement, which in reality is mostly *"another Faith,"* have attempted to change the Faith of Abraham to temporal blessings. The *"Blessing of Abraham"* is referred to as financial blessings only, as I heard one so-called Faith Teacher say. Such thinking borders on blasphemy.

While the Lord certainly does bless His people in every way, including material things, etc., His Mission for us, however, is of far greater magnitude than that. Our lives in Christ are to have eternal consequences, and not merely the price of the suit of clothes we may wear.

Picking up on what the Lord said to Abraham, what will our seed be? Abraham's *"Seed"* ultimately was Christ (Gal. 3:16), as Jesus is to be the Ultimate Conclusion of all Faith (Heb. 12:2).

(19) "AND BEING NOT WEAK IN FAITH, HE CONSIDERED NOT HIS OWN BODY NOW DEAD, WHEN HE WAS ABOUT AN HUNDRED YEARS OLD, NEITHER YET THE DEADNESS OF SARAH'S WOMB:"

The phrase, *"And being not weak in Faith,"* refers as is later said, to *"Strong Faith."* However, Abraham did not come to this place of *"Strong Faith"* easily or quickly.

The Patriarch had to get past *"Fear"* and even the *"Hagar"* situation, in order to come to this place of Faith (Gen. 15:1; 16:1-4). And then there was the situation with Abimelech, to whom Abraham again lied respecting Sarah (Gen. Chpt. 20). An old sin is an easy sin. However, the idea is, that in all these difficulties, Abraham never stopped believing.

The Faith Walk is not an uneventful walk, but rather the very opposite. To be frank, this is the walk which Satan contests the most, and for the obvious reasons.

I heard someone say many years ago, that every single attack against the Child of God by Satan, and irrespective of its nature, is but for one purpose, and that is to weaken and ultimately destroy one's Faith in God.

NOTES

Taking a lesson from Abraham, none of us are perfect, but if we will not quit, God will not quit. Actually, that is the story of Faith.

To be frank, the Faith Walk has its problems the same as any other effort; however, the difference is, when doubt and unbelief fall flat on their faces, they stay there. However, Faith gets up, brushes itself off, and then starts again toward the designated goal.

The phrase, *"He considered not his own body now dead, when he was about an hundred years old,"* presents the obstacles of Faith, but which did not deter the Patriarch.

The word *"considered"* in the Greek is *"katanoeo,"* and means *"to consider attentively, to fix one's eyes or mind upon."*

There are two schools of thought respecting this phrase. Some Greek Scholars translate the phrase as Abraham not paying any attention to his physical deformities, which is implied in the English Text.

Others claim that it actually means, and which is probably the case, that Abraham considered very attentively his physical condition, which was hopeless, staring these obstacles right in the face, but refused to consider them.

Nowhere in the Word of God and especially as it deals with Faith, are we told to deny the obstacles or difficulties. The idea rather is, that we fully acknowledge them, but refuse to allow them to stop us. Abraham could not deny that he was a hundred years old, and that so far as procreative functions were concerned, his body had died (ceased to function) and was as a result in a condition in which it would stay dead, at least in this capacity (never function again). The door was absolutely and forever closed so far as having offspring was concerned.

The phrase, *"Neither yet the deadness of Sarah's womb,"* placed her in the same situation as her husband.

Why was it necessary that Abraham and Sarah be brought to this place, actually a place of impossibility, at least as far as natural ability is concerned, before the miracle child could be born?

The answer to that question is the answer to us all, and the answer to the Work of God on Earth.

The hope of the flesh had to die in every

respect, and that means that Abraham and Sarah had to be brought to a place to where it was absolutely impossible in every conceivable capacity, for this great Promise of God to be brought about through their own ability, or the ability of others. The work that was to be done, which constituted this child being born, had to be totally and completely of the Spirit and none of the flesh. Consequently, the Patriarch and his wife had to literally come to the end of themselves before the great Promise of God could take effect. The Spirit of God, Who Alone can bring about these things, cannot do so, and, in fact, will not do so, as long as there is a vestige of the flesh remaining. The Work must be all of God and none of man.

As an example, the work of the flesh which Abraham and Sarah did bring into the world respecting Hagar and Ishmael, has proved to be a source of contention from that moment until now, as are all works of the flesh (Gen. 21:9-12). It is one thing for the world to bring forth a work of the flesh, which is actually all they can do, but something else altogether, for a champion of Faith to do such. As such it will always contend with that which is born of the Spirit, which seems to never stop. So, the Believer must be very careful, that only that which is of the Spirit be brought forth, which always and without exception is the Mind and Will of God.

Consequently, not only should the great lesson of Faith as given by Abraham be a Teacher for us all, but as well, we should learn from his mistakes.

(20) "HE STAGGERED NOT AT THE PROMISE OF GOD THROUGH UNBELIEF; BUT WAS STRONG IN FAITH, GIVING GLORY TO GOD;"

The phrase, *"He staggered not at the Promise of God through unbelief,"* presents a tremendous statement. He did not allow the obstacles or difficulties and even failures at times, to deter him from the intended conclusion.

The word *"staggered"* in the Greek is *"diakrino,"* and means *"to judge between two,"* thus, *"to vacillate between two opinions or decisions."* The idea is, that Abraham did not vacillate between belief and unbelief with respect to his difficulty and the ability

of God to meet it. He did not waver (Wuest).

Vincent says the word implies a mental struggle. In other words, he did not allow his mind to dwell on difficulties, thereby, weakening his Faith. He was not divided in his mind by unbelief.

The phrase, *"But was strong in Faith, giving Glory to God,"* tells us what God did for him.

The words, *"Was strong"* in the Greek is *"endunamao,"* and means *"to make strong, endue with strength."* In other words, he was strengthened or endued with strength. This strength is qualified by the words *"in Faith,"* which means *"with respect to Faith."* The idea is this:

His Faith was strengthened in God and by God to meet his impossible difficulty with a Miracle. The thought here is not that Abraham's Faith was strengthened so that his physical powers again became equal to bringing children into the world. The idea is, that Isaac was the result of a biological Miracle performed by God in answer to Abraham's Faith, which meant that the Glory would go to God and not otherwise (Wuest).

What we are seeing here is a Law of God, called the *"Law of Faith"* (Rom. 3:27).

The contention is the more that one exercises Faith in God, the more Faith is granted unto that person. By contrast, to those who evidence unbelief, they sink deeper and deeper into more unbelief.

(21) "AND BEING FULLY PERSUADED THAT, WHAT HE HAD PROMISED, HE WAS ABLE ALSO TO PERFORM."

The phrase, *"And being fully persuaded,"* speaks of a guarantee of no turning back. The word *"persuaded"* in the Greek is *"plerophoreo,"* and means *"completely assured or totally convinced."*

The Patriarch looked at the physical obstacles which confronted he and Sarah, but judged them as nothing in comparison to the Power of God. He firmly believed in the ability of God to fulfill His Promise, and no difficulty shook him.

His Faith rested upon a God of Creation and of Resurrection; and these facts are recorded, not as mere history, but as illustrations for all time of God's method of Justification by Faith.

The phrase, *"That, what He had promised, He was able also to perform,"* presents the idea that no matter how impossible the situation may seem to be in the natural, Abraham knew that God was able to do what He said He would do. And so He did!

As well, when one reads this 21st verse, one should well understand that it applies not only to the Promise made to Abraham and Sarah of old, but as well, it covers the entirety of the span of the Word of God, all the way from the Book of Genesis through the Book of Revelation. What He has Promised, He will perform!

(22) "AND THEREFORE IT WAS IMPUTED TO HIM FOR RIGHTEOUSNESS."

How is it that the Promise of the child could translate into Salvation?

This child had to do with the lineage which made up the Incarnation of Christ, Who came to Redeem the world from sin, and did so by dying on Calvary's Cross, and being raised from the dead. So, in essence, Abraham's Faith was of a far greater magnitude than the mere answer to a prayer, as wonderful and miraculous as that would have been. It pertained to the great Salvation Plan and for all of humanity, and for all time. Abraham knew and understood this.

(23) "NOW IT WAS NOT WRITTEN FOR HIS SAKE ALONE, THAT IT WAS IMPUTED TO HIM;"

The phrase, *"Now it was not written for his sake alone,"* in effect has two meanings:

1. His struggle of Faith was meant to serve as an example to all others, especially as it portrayed the Plan of Salvation.

2. His struggle was not only for himself, but in a sense for all who would follow him. In essence, His Victory became my Victory, and I would trust that my Victory could become the Victory of others, as it should be with all of us.

The phrase, *"That it was imputed to him,"* served as the manner in which the sinner comes to Christ, and is fully Justified by the Power and Grace of God.

So as not to confuse us, all of this simply means that *"Abraham believed God, and it was counted unto him* (accredited to him) *for Righteousness* (the type of Righteousness which God would recognize)" (Gen. 15:6).

(24) "BUT FOR US ALSO, TO WHOM IT SHALL BE IMPUTED, IF WE BELIEVE ON HIM THAT RAISED UP JESUS OUR LORD FROM THE DEAD;"

The phrase, *"But for us also, to whom it shall be imputed,"* tells us that we can have that which Abraham had, and in fact, is meant to have what he had. That is the idea of all things presented here.

What a wonder, what an honor, what a privilege, to be included *"also!"*

The phrase, *"If we believe on Him that raised up Jesus our Lord from the dead,"* proclaims the condition for Salvation.

The bringing forth of Isaac was a Miracle, considering that the bodies of Abraham and Sarah were dead, at least as far as procreation was concerned. Consequently, for the Lord to bring this about, the birth of Isaac, He had to use Resurrection Power. Hence, the Holy Spirit through the Apostle likens this Miracle of Isaac to the Resurrection of Christ.

(25) "WHO WAS DELIVERED FOR OUR OFFENCES, AND WAS RAISED AGAIN FOR OUR JUSTIFICATION."

The phrase, *"Who was delivered for our offences,"* had to do with Jesus dying on the Cross for our sins. He had none of His Own.

(In type, Isaac suffered the same thing as he was offered up, or at least would have been, had not the hand of Abraham been stopped at the last moment. At any rate, the type was served.)

The phrase, *"And was raised again for our Justification,"* pertains to the Resurrection of Christ, which effected our Justification. In other words, if Christ had not risen from the dead, the price paid in His Death would have been to no avail.

(Isaac not being literally killed, but yet in the Mind of God having been so, and having served as a Type of His Coming Son, now coming back down the mountain in the company of his Father, pictures the Resurrection of Christ. Actually, all were typified by God's Revelation of Himself to Abraham and Isaac as *"Jehovah-Jireh,"* which means *"The Lord will provide."* It speaks of providing a Redeemer, Who would be The Lord Jesus Christ) (Gen. Chpt. 22).

In order to be Saved, all sinners must exercise Faith in God Who judged sin in Christ, and then raised Him from the dead. In thus believing God, Faith embraces the whole extent of His Redemptive Work.

By believing in such a God the Believer accepts the Testimony of Scripture that He delivered up His Beloved Son for the expiation of the Believer's offenses, and raised Him from out of the death-world in order to the justifying of the Believer's person.

The activity of God in Grace, through Righteousness, is here declared in abolishing sins, in declaring innocent the sinner, and in vindicating His Righteousness, which is what Justification by Faith actually means.

Abraham's Faith, being marvelous, cannot have been of, and from himself, but must have been a Divine Gift in Grace (Eph. 2:8), and, therefore, not in itself a justifying work.

The conclusion of the argument is that God declares the guilty Righteous on the principle of Faith as opposed to works; and that He never Saved men on any other principle.

The Doctrine of Justification by Works generates religious pride — that of Justification by Faith produces contrition and humility, which was evidenced in Abraham, the Father of us all.

In the matter of Justification, Faith and Works are opposite and irreconcilable — as opposed as Grace and Debt. Since God declares ungodly men Righteous, works cannot in any sense furnish a ground for Justification, and hence, the first step towards Salvation on the part of a sinner is to humble himself and accept the Divine Pronouncement that he is *"ungodly"* exactly as the Scripture says (Rom. 4:5).

Then the second and concluding step is to repose Faith in Him Who Justifies the ungodly. Nothing gives more Glory to God than simply believing Him.

Justification is not a change in character but a declaration by God as to the Believer's standing before Him. It is objective (changes not).

Sanctification affects one's character and is subjective (has to do with our experience).

"My Faith looks up to Thee, Thou Lamb of Calvary,
"Saviour Divine! Now hear me while I pray,

"Take all my guilt away, Oh let me from this day be wholly Thine."

"May Thy rich Grace impart strength to my fainting heart,
"My zeal inspire; as Thou hast died for me,
"Oh may my love to Thee, pure, warm, and changeless be,
"A living fire."

"When life's dark maze I tread, and griefs around me spread,
"Be Thou my Guide; bid darkness turn to day;
"Wipe sorrow's tears away, nor let me ever stray from Thee aside."

CHAPTER 5

(1) "THEREFORE BEING JUSTIFIED BY FAITH, WE HAVE PEACE WITH GOD THROUGH OUR LORD JESUS CHRIST:"

The phrase, *"Therefore being Justified by Faith,"* presents Paul stating a fact.

In coming to this place Paul has clearly come to several conclusions. In Romans 1:18-3:20 he proves man's need for the Righteousness of God. In Romans 3:21-30 he shows how such Righteousness comes, and how it is appropriated. In Romans 3:31-4:25 he shows by the example of Abraham, and the Testimony of David, that Righteousness appropriated by Faith does not upset, but rather establishes the Spiritual Order revealed in the Old Testament.

In Romans Chapter 5, to which we will now address, the Apostle now enlarges on the happiness and security of the Justified, and especially on their assurance of God's Love and of future Blessedness (Wuest).

WHAT THEN IS JUSTIFICATION?

It is the action of a Judge declaring a prisoner innocent. The accused says nothing and does nothing. The Judge is the sole actor — he justifies the man, i.e., he declares him Righteous (Williams).

This Beautiful Work comes about as one expresses simple Faith in Christ and what He did at Calvary and the Resurrection.

Paul by using the word *"therefore,"* points to a conclusion. In verses 1 through 8 of Romans Chapter 4, he tells us that we are not Justified by *"works."* In verses 9 through 12 of that same Chapter, he adds *"Ordinances,"* and then *"Law obedience"* in verses 13-25. These three things never give Peace to the soul. Faith does! (Wuest).

The phrase, *"We have Peace with God through our Lord Jesus Christ,"* points to Justifying Peace, in other words a legal standing with God, which does not, and in fact, cannot change. There are two types of Peace incumbent upon the Believer. They are as follows:

TWO KINDS OF PEACE

1. Justifying Peace: This is Peace *with* God, and as stated, a legal standing — that which we are now studying.

There is an enmity between God and unredeemed man. It is because of unconfessed and unrepentant sin, and more particularly, because of the sinner's refusal to accept God's Plan of Redemption, the Blood Atonement of Jesus Christ (Rom. 8:7; Eph. 2:14-15). *"Enmity"* means *"mutual hatred or ill will."* The sinner does not want to have anything to do with God (Rom. 1:21-23), and *"God is angry with the wicked every day"* (Ps. 7:11). In other words, and because of sin, there is a war going on between God and unredeemed man. However, God feels this enmity far more than the sinner, simply because it is God Who has been wronged and offended and not man. So, as a result of this war, there is no *"Peace"* between God and the sinner.

Actually, this very thing (lack of Peace with God), is the cause of all guilt and no doubt contributes toward all manner of stress, mental disorder, as well as sickness and disease. As one doctor said, *"I can remove the diseased physical organs, but actually that is only treating the symptoms, with the root cause being something else."*

When the sinner hears the Word of God and is convicted by the Holy Spirit, he is made to feel his wrong against God. Consequently, this is where Repentance comes in (Acts 20:21).

Upon Faith by the sinner, all sin is washed away by the Blood of Jesus, with the enmity

NOTES

instantly removed. The New Believer now has Justifying Peace, which is a result of Justification. That is what is meant by the phrase, *"Making Peace with God."* This type of Peace is abiding and never changes, and is what Paul is speaking about here.

2. Sanctifying Peace: This is the Peace *of* God in the heart. While the first has to do with Justification, the second has to do with Sanctification (Rom. 8:6; 14:19; 15:13; Gal. 1:3).

The first, as stated, is the result of a legal standing, the second, the result of the Work of the Holy Spirit. The first is static, never fluctuates, the second changes almost from hour to hour. The first, every Christian has, the second, every Christian may have.

AN EXAMPLE OF JUSTIFYING PEACE AND SANCTIFYING PEACE

When Israel was told by Moses to apply the Blood to the doorpost, this represented *"Justifying Peace"* (Ex. Chpt. 12).

One can well imagine that many Israelites that fateful night went to bed and slept well. That is *"Sanctifying Peace."*

However, one can also imagine that many did not sleep well that night. While they had *"Justifying Peace,"* they did not have *"Sanctifying Peace."* This was a lack of trust on their part, which robbed them of this Peace. And yet, their *"Justifying Peace"* was not disturbed in the least, because the Blood was on the doorpost. As well, those who slept well were no less secure than those who paced the floor, or vice versa.

Sanctifying Peace has to do with our trust in the Lord and is, as stated, up and down.

The more we grow in the Lord, however, the more we learn to trust Him, all which has to do with Sanctification, and our Sanctifying Peace.

Incidentally, *"The Lord Jesus Christ"* is the Resurrection Name of the Saviour, which guarantees our Justification (Rom. 4:25).

The Greek word for *"Peace"* is *"eirene,"* and means *"to bind together that which has been separated."* In other words, and getting back to Justifying Peace, our Lord made Peace through the Blood of the Cross (Col. 1:20) in the sense that through His Atonement He binds together again, those who by reason of their standing in the First Adam had been separated from God and who now through Faith in Christ are bound again to God in their new standing in the Last Adam, The Lord Jesus Christ. This is Justification. That is, a Justified sinner has Peace facing God.

He stands in the Presence of God, guiltless and uncondemned and Righteous in a Righteousness which God accepts, in the Lord Jesus (Wuest).

(2) "BY WHOM ALSO WE HAVE ACCESS BY FAITH INTO THIS GRACE WHEREIN WE STAND, AND REJOICE IN HOPE OF THE GLORY OF GOD."

The phrase, *"By Whom also we have access by Faith,"* speaks of access to the Throne of God and at any time.

Jesus said, *"At that day ye shall ask in My Name: and I say not unto you, that I will pray the Father for you"* (Jn. 16:26).

This Statement as made by Christ, would have probably been better translated, *"When you come before the Throne of God in prayer to make a petition in My Name, please know that you have instant and constant access to the Father even as I. The Father grants you this because He loves you, because you have loved Me and have believed that I came out from God."*

Once the sinner comes to Christ, he is then made a New Creature, and as well, a part of the Family of God. Consequently, there are many privileges, with *"access"* to the Throne being among that number.

This speaks of prayer and more particularly of Intercession, which is instant access, which can be had on the spur of the moment, and at any place and time.

"Access" in the Greek is *"prosagogue,"* and refers to *"a landing stage."* The total idea of the word pertains to access into, and rest in, a haven or harbor.

This of which Jesus did at Calvary and the Resurrection provides so much more for the Believer than most any of us even dare to think. Before Calvary, and due to the sin debt not yet having been paid, even the strongest of Believers at that time, did not have the privileges in Christ which are now available to even the least Child of God. Concerning this, Jesus lauded John the Baptist

by saying of him, *"Among them that are born of women there hath not risen a greater."*

But then He said, *"Notwithstanding he that is least in the Kingdom of Heaven is greater than he"* (Mat. 11:11).

John the Baptist closed out the Old Covenant, actually the last Prophet of that era. Jesus ushered in the New Covenant, with all of its greater privileges and blessings, solely because of the great price He had paid and the victories He won. So, anyone in this New Covenant is greater as far as privileges are concerned, than anyone in the Old Covenant.

THE SINS OF THE BELIEVER

The phrase, *"Into this Grace wherein we stand,"* refers to the fact that the Believer is set before the Throne of God in a Righteousness that is spotless, a life that is endless, and in a dignity that is glorious.

All of the sins of the Believer are canceled by God in the Death of Christ; God has consequently no sins to impute to him. That matter has been eternally settled by Christ's sufficing Atonement, and His Resurrection attests the fact. There is, therefore, no longer any question as to the Believer's sins between him and God. That question — the sin question — was the looming, all-encompassing and disturbing factor in relation to God, and Christ removed it according to the requirements of Divine Righteousness.

He bore infinitely all the Wrath of God due to sin and its fruit and satisfied and vindicated all the claims of the Throne of God against man as a sinner.

Consequently, this Great Salvation is, therefore, founded upon Eternal Righteousness, and is the result of the Divine activity operating in Grace.

As stated, Peace is the result of Justification and is, consequently, distinct from it. Faith enjoys this Peace, and glories not only in Salvation and all that it embraces, but in its Divine Author God Himself (Williams).

Grace here is seen as a haven or harbor.

The French have a word for this entrance or access. They call it *"entree."* It refers to one being brought before a Potentate by a friend, who has properly attired him, in order to present him into the presence of the King.

That is exactly what Jesus does for a believing sinner. He clothes him with Himself as His Righteousness, cleanses him in His Own Precious Blood, and brings him into the full favor (Grace) of God the Father. As stated, this is *"entree."*

The phrase, *"And rejoice in Hope of the Glory of God,"* portrays three things:

REJOICING

1. If the Believer even halfway understands the tremendous privileges and favor afforded him, as a result of his standing in Christ, such will bring a perpetual rejoicing. Man is a spiritual being, as well as physical and mental. As such, only God can truly satisfy the hunger and thirst of the soul. When He is given His rightful place in the Believer's heart and life, as Peter said, it is truly *"Joy unspeakable and full of Glory"* (I Pet. 1:8).

2. The *"hope"* here presented, does *not* mean that hope is that wherein we glory, but that, being in a state of hope, we glory (Barmby).

The idea is, that the future is guaranteed respecting these great things that God will do, but we do not know exactly when it will happen. This is our state of hope.

3. The *"Glory of God"* is that which is coming.

Even though we are given much evidence in the Word of God concerning that which is to come, still, it is so far beyond what we now see or know, that one is little able to properly evaluate such coming Glory. Consequently, Paul said, *"For now we see through a glass, darkly"* (I Cor. 13:12). The hope here is that of ultimately participating in the Glory of Heaven.

(3) "AND NOT ONLY SO, BUT WE GLORY IN TRIBULATIONS ALSO: KNOWING THAT TRIBULATION WORKETH PATIENCE;"

The phrase, *"And not only so, but we glory in tribulations also,"* does not simply mean *"when we are in tribulations,"* but also *"because we are,"* the tribulations being the ground of the glorying. To be sure this requires Supernatural Grace supplied by the Holy Spirit.

It is not that Paul was exulting, or that we are to exult because of the tribulations themselves, but because of their beneficial

effect upon the Christian Life. This the Saint must learn to do. He must look at these trials and difficulties as assets that develop his Christian Character.

"Tribulations" in the Greek is *"thlipsis,"* and means *"a pressing, pressing together, pressure, oppression, affliction, distress, straits."* In the Greek Text it is preceded by the definite article (the tribulations), marking these out as things naturally expected in a Christian's life (Wuest).

We are to perceive how they serve for our probation now: they test our endurance; and proved endurance increases hope.

The idea is that tribulations test, and endurance under them proves, the genuineness of Faith (Barmby).

TRIBULATION AND THE MODERN GOSPEL

Much of the so-called modern Faith Teaching denies any and all tribulations for the Believer, claiming that such are basically brought about because of a lack of Faith or proper confession, etc. Of course, such Teaching defies not only the peripheral aspects of the Gospel, but actually, its very core. Not a one of these Teachers, at least of those of whom I am aware, would even think of quoting the statement of Paul concerning the *"glorying in tribulations."* Or else they would define *"tribulations"* in an improper manner.

The tribulations came to Paul and come to all True Believers, not because of a lack of Faith, but because of Great Faith. Actually, I think the Scripture plainly teaches *"the greater the Faith, the greater the tribulations."* Job is an excellent example whom we will mention momentarily.

THE PATTERN AND THE NORM

The tribulations of the Christian are the pattern and norm for the experience of the Christian Community. Thus, tribulations are inevitable and to be anticipated (Mat. 13:21; Jn. 16:33; Acts 14:22; Rom. 8:35; 12:12; I Thess. 3:3; II Thess. 1:4; Rev. 1:9).

The tribulations of Israel under the Old Covenant finds its counterpart in the tribulations of the Church under the New (Heb. 11:37; 12:1). Thus, tribulations are particularly the lot of the Apostles who exemplify in a special manner the path of Suffering Discipleship (Acts 20:23; II Cor. 1:4; 4:8, 17; 6:4; Eph. 3:13).

A PARTICIPATION IN THE SUFFERINGS OF CHRIST

The tribulations of the people of Christ are in some sense a participation in the Sufferings of Christ (II Cor. 1:5; 4:10; Phil. 3:10; Col. 1:24; I Pet. 4:13).

Underlying the New Testament Teaching here may be the notion of the so-called *"afflictions of the Messiah,"* a tally of suffering to be endured by the Righteous before the consummation of the Redemptive Purpose of God.

TRIBULATIONS AND THE LIKENESS OF CHRIST

The tribulations of the people of Christ are instrumental in promoting their moral transformation into the Likeness of Christ (Rom. 5:3; II Cor. 3:18; 4:8-12, 16).

In particular the experience of tribulations promotes the upbuilding of the Christian Community through enabling the comforting of others in similar experiences (II Cor. 1:4; 4:10; Col. 1:24; I Thess. 1:6).

TRIBULATIONS AND THE COMING GLORY

The tribulations of the people of God are Eschatological, meaning that they point to the last age, the Kingdom of the End Time.

As such, they are a witness to the inbreaking and presence of the Kingdom (Mat. 24:9-14; Rev. 1:9; 7:14). In other words, tribulations tell us that a better time is coming, when there will not be such to endure.

A certain intensification of these tribulations will prelude the return of Christ and the consummation of the Kingdom (Mat. 24:21; Mk. 13:24; II Thess. 1:5-6; II Tim. 3:1).

Actually, this speaks of the Coming Great Tribulation, before which the Church will be raptured (I Thess. 4:16-17; 5:9). That tribulation, the greatest of all, will pertain to many things, but most of all the humbling of Israel, in order that she finally come back to God and the acceptance of her Messiah and Saviour, The Lord Jesus Christ (Jer. 30:7; Mat. 24:21).

NOTES

The phrase, *"Knowing that tribulation worketh patience,"* points to the characteristic of a man who is unswerved from his deliberate purpose and his loyalty to Faith and piety by even the greatest trials and sufferings.

"Worketh" in the Greek is *"katergazomai,"* and means *"to accomplish, achieve, to do that from which something results."* So, the *"tribulation"* is to generate or *"produce patience."*

"Patience" in the Greek is *"hupomone,"* and means *"steadfastness, constancy, endurance."*

It also has reference to *"remaining under,"* thus, to remain under trials in a God-honoring way so as to learn the lesson they are sent to teach, rather than an attempt to get out from under them in an effort to be relieved of their pressure.

So we can see from all of this, how that the Holy Spirit is directing and orchestrating all events, some which seem to be hurtful to the flesh, but all which are invigorating to the spirit.

(4) "AND PATIENCE, EXPERIENCE; AND EXPERIENCE, HOPE:"

The phrase, *"And Patience, Experience,"* points to an end result.

"Experience" in the Greek is *"dokimen,"* and means *"the result of trial, approvedness"* (Phil. 2:22). It is a *"tried integrity, a state of mind which has stood the test."* This is done for the purpose of approving, and finding that the person tested meets the specifications, in order for approval to be put upon him. Its results are a spiritual state which has shown itself proof under trial.

The spiritual metal of the Believer must be tested exactly as any product is tested respecting its veracity. The idea is *not* that God is to see what the test brings forth, for He already knows. The test is carried out for the benefit of the Believer. It shows us where we are, and we generally find that we are much weaker than we thought.

The problem of self-reliance rears its ugly head in the Believer just as it does in the unbeliever. Unfortunately, this ever-present problem cannot be rooted out by the laying on of hands, or by the manifestation of any of the Gifts of the Spirit.

In the natural, these things are somewhat

similar to a computer program which says that an instrument or piece of equipment should function in a certain way. Irrespective, the equipment still must be put to the test before it can be released to the public.

Spiritually we know what Salvation does. The instructions are given to us in the Word of God. However, it is only when we are put to the test that we actually know how well that we have allowed these great qualities to function within our lives. Finding out our weaknesses, which tests will always bring out, keeps the Believer humble and on his knees.

The phrase, *"And experience, hope,"* presents the natural product of an approved experience. The experience of what God can do, or rather of what He does, for the Justified amid the tribulations of this life, animates into new vigor the hope with which the Life of Faith begins (Denney).

A disapproved experience generates no hope whatsoever, as would be obvious. However, when one is put to the test, and there finding that the Grace of God is sufficient for all things, such causes *"hope"* to spring forth.

Job illustrates the discipline of verses 3 and 4. He exercised patience and so had the experience, or proof, that the issue of the Divine action is that God is full of pity and of tender mercy (James 5:11), so that he could boast of the tribulations which had disciplined him, and rejoice in the hope that made him not ashamed (Williams).

(5) "AND HOPE MAKETH NOT ASHAMED; BECAUSE THE LOVE OF GOD IS SHED ABROAD IN OUR HEARTS BY THE HOLY SPIRIT WHICH IS GIVEN UNTO US."

The phrase, *"And hope maketh not ashamed,"* in effect tells us that this is not a false hope. It will not shame us in the end, as being baseless and without fulfillment. As we have previously said, the type of *"hope"* mentioned here is guaranteed of fulfillment, with the only question being as to the fullness of time.

To the contrary, the type of hope which characterizes the world is the exact opposite. To be frank, the world never fulfills its promises, simply because it has no ways or means to do so. The system of the world is of Satan, and he is a liar and the father of

it. Consequently, all he can do is lie, because there is no truth in him (Jn. 8:44). Therefore, there is no hope in anything Satan does.

The phrase, *"Because the Love of God is shed abroad in our hearts,"* proclaims that all these Christian experiences and hopes rest upon an assurance of the Love of God. It is obvious from verse 5 and the whole connection, that the Love of God to us is meant, and not our Love to Him. It is the evidence of God's Love to us which the Apostle proceeds to set forth (Denney).

THE *"AGAPAO"* KIND OF LOVE

This *"Love"* tells us that everything God allows to come upon us, is for our good and not our hurt, irrespective as to the difficulties of the moment.

This *"Love"* of which Paul speaks is *"Agapao"* and speaks of a Love which is awakened by a sense of value in an object which causes one to prize it. It springs from an apprehension of the preciousness of an object. It is a Love of esteem and approbation. The quality of this Love is determined by the character of the one who loves, in this case the Lord Himself, and that of the object loved.

Consequently, God's Love for a sinful and lost race springs from His Heart in response to the high value He places upon each human soul. Every sinner is exceedingly precious in His Sight.

THE *"PHILEO"* KIND OF LOVE

The Greek word *"Phileo"* is another word for Love, a Love which is the response of the human spirit to what appeals to it as pleasurable. Such type of Love will not do here, for there is nothing in a lost sinner that the Heart of God can find pleasure in, but on the contrary, everything that His Holiness rebels against.

However, even though there is nothing in the sinner which is pleasurable to God, but rather the very opposite, still, each sinner is most precious to God. First of all, because he bears the Image of His Creator even though that Image be marred by sin, and second, because through Redemption that sinner can be conformed into the very Image of God's Dear Son.

This preciousness of each member of the human race to the Heart of God is the constituent element of the Love that gave His Son to die on the Cross. The decree of the preciousness is measured by the Infinite Sacrifice which God made.

The Love in John 3:16 for instance, is a Love whose essence is that of self-sacrifice for the benefit of the one loved, this Love based upon an evaluation of the preciousness of the one loved.

THE *"EROS"* KIND OF LOVE

The Greek word *"eros"* speaks of a type of Love which can only be described as self-serving. This type of Love is extended to individuals providing they are of some worth or value. In other words, the person is loved because he or she is rich, famous, or of some supposed worth or value. The idea is, when the worth or value is no longer there, the person is no longer desired.

The Holy Spirit thought so little of this type of Love, that it is not once mentioned in the New Testament. One can well understand why! It is the very opposite of *"Agape"* Love.

Regrettably, this type of love characterizes the world and even sad to say, much of the Church. If the person makes the system look good, the world showers accolades on the individual. However, when that ceases to be the case, the person is discarded like a broken piece of furniture.

Regrettably, many Churches fall into the same category. If the person is wealthy or famous or of some supposed value, he is a welcomed member. However, if that ceases to be the case, in too many Churches the individual is no longer wanted or desired. Consequently, far too often, the very ones who need what True Christianity provides, are left out in the cold, for the simple reason that they do not make the Church look good.

I hope the Reader can see how utterly ungodly such an attitude and spirit are, as stated, the very opposite of the True Love of God. These Preachers in Churches must realize, that when God Saved them, that is if they are Saved, there was absolutely nothing in them of any worth or value to the Lord. He loved them simply for their sake alone and

NOTES

nothing else. In turn, we must evidence the same type of Love toward others, even those who are the most unlovable.

The Word, *"is shed abroad,"* in the Greek Text is *"ekcheo,"* and means *"to pour out, or has poured in, and keeps pouring in."*

Inasmuch as the Love of God keeps pouring into our hearts, likewise, it is meant to pour out of our hearts onto others. If it doesn't, the implication is that the flow will cease from God to us. As it was *"shed abroad"* to us, it is meant by us to be *"shed abroad"* to others.

As well, this Love must never be diluted, lest it mean something else altogether. It must remain the same type of Love given to us by God, the God Kind of Love.

A DEMONSTRATION OF THE LOVE OF GOD

Jesus Christ is the greatest Personification of the Love of God. As someone has said, He is Love Incarnate and Personified (I Jn. 3:16), in fact, is God's Self-Revelation.

Jesus is not recorded in Matthew, Mark or Luke, as using the word *"Agapao"* to express God's Love for men. Rather He revealed it by His countless Acts of Compassionate Healing (Mk. 1:41; Lk. 7:13), His Teaching about God's acceptance of the sinner (Lk. 15:11; 18:10), His grief-stricken attitude to human disobedience (Mat. 23:37; Lk. 19:41), and by being Himself a Friend of sinners and outcasts (Lk. 7:34).

In other words, He did not talk so much about it, but rather revealed it, which is the exact opposite of many of us Christians.

This Saving activity is declared in John to be a demonstration of the Love of God, imparting an eternal reality of Life to men (Jn. 3:16; I Jn. 4:9). The whole drama of Redemption, centering as it does on the Death of Christ, is Divine Love in action (Rom. 5:8; II Cor. 5:14; Gal. 2:20).

MAN'S LOVE FOR GOD

Man's natural state is to be God's enemy (Rom. 5:10; Col. 1:21), and to hate Him (Lk. 19:14; Jn. 15:18), this enmity being seen for what it is in the Crucifixion.

In other words, if one wants to know what man thinks of God, one only has to look at the Crucifixion, and the enmity becomes crystal clear.

However, the manner in which this hatred of man toward God is changed, is always brought about by the Love of God. In other words, God loves man into accepting Him as Saviour, etc. Even acts of Judgment are in reality the Love of God, even though unregenerate man thinks the opposite.

In applying pressure, and using whatever capacity to do so, such is meant to bring man to his spiritual senses, which it often does. To be sure, that is God's Love in action, even though it may be painful for the moment.

A PERSONAL EXAMPLE OF JUDGMENT WHICH WAS LOVE

When my parents heard the Gospel of Jesus Christ for the first time, I was only five years old. Sadly, even as so many others, they rebelled against the pleas of the Holy Spirit, refusing to accept the Lord as their Saviour. They even thought they could pull up stakes in our hometown and go to a distant city and things would be different.

They did not realize that they were under Conviction by the Holy Spirit, and wherever they went, or whatever they did, this Conviction would remain. It did exactly that.

It is freeze-framed in my mind the morning we left our home in Louisiana and the Church I might quickly add, where my parents had first heard the Gospel. My Mother and Dad were going to South Texas where my Dad hoped to go into business, etc. The year was 1940.

Things did not go well in Texas, for the simple reason that my Mother and Dad were running from God. It is a trek which one cannot hope to win.

Very shortly after arriving in that beautiful area, my Baby Brother who was only a few months old, contracted pneumonia. This was before the days of the wonder drugs; however, inasmuch as the Hand of God was in all of this, I don't think the drugs would have mattered anyway.

Once again I remember it distinctly. We were living in a small Tourist Court. I had been to the hospital with my Dad much of the day where my Baby Brother had been taken. My Mother as well had come down with pneumonia and was herself hospitalized.

Some time that night, my Dad and I came back to the Tourist Court and went to bed. At about daylight there was a knock at the door.

I awakened along with my Dad, that is if he had ever been asleep. I remember distinctly him raising up in the bed and asking as to who was at the door?

The voice of my Uncle came through the door, with Dad instantly arising, opening the door for him to come in.

My Uncle just stood there for a few moments saying nothing, with my Dad looking at his face. Once again this moment is freeze-framed in my mind. My Dad looked at my Uncle and said to him, *"It's Donnie, isn't it?"* That was my Brother's name.

My Uncle dropped his head and his voice broke as he said, *"He died about an hour ago."*

I do not remember what my Dad said or did at that time, as that is lost from my memory. However, I distinctly remember the funeral which took place, I suppose, the next day.

The casket was tiny, inasmuch as my Baby Brother was only a few months old. But I'll never forget seeing him that last time.

When I was a kid, my hair was so blonde, that it was almost white. By contrast, my Brother's hair was jet black and in ringlet curls all over his head.

THE FUNERAL

The only ones at the funeral were the Morticians and an Assembly of God Pastor, with the short service being conducted at the graveside.

Inasmuch as we had just arrived in this part of the world, I have no idea as to how this Pastor knew my parents. My Mother was not there because she was too sick to come.

I remember the Pastor and the Mortician helping my Dad out of the car and walking with him to the graveside. Being only five years old, I really did not understand the terrible reality of death and what it meant. But this I do remember:

After the short service, they opened the casket the last time, and my Dad looked at my Baby Brother laying in the casket. He said, *"I promise you, I will meet you in Heaven."*

A few days later, when my Mother was able to travel, my parents came back to our home in Louisiana, to the Church which they had left, and a short time later made Jesus the Saviour and Lord of their lives.

Even though the death of my Baby Brother was of great sorrow, still, it was the Hand of God bringing my parents to their senses, in order that they would say yes to Him, which they did. As stated, even though it was hurtful for the time, that which was done was the Love of God, and must always be understood as such, and should be obvious to all!

The phrase, *"By the Holy Spirit which is given unto us,"* plainly proclaims, that this great attribute of God shed abroad in our hearts, is altogether a Work of the Holy Spirit. In fact, every single thing received by man from God, and in any capacity, is always through and by the Person, Office, Agency, Work, and Ministry of the Holy Spirit.

I realize that many Greek Scholars claim that the mention of the Holy Spirit in this fashion has nothing to do with the Acts 2:4 experience, but is rather the act of Regeneration carried out by the Spirit in the heart and life of the believing sinner. In fact, that is true up to a point, but not altogether.

While it is true that the Holy Spirit definitely comes into the Believer's heart and life at Conversion, still, it is not true that this is the entirety of His Work.

Actually, if the Believer does not go on and be Baptized with the Holy Spirit according to Acts 2:4, while the Holy Spirit certainly is in his heart and life, one could say without fear of exaggeration, that in this mode He (the Holy Spirit) is pretty much helpless. It is only when the Believer is Baptized with the Holy Spirit, which is always accompanied by the speaking with other Tongues (Acts Chpts. 2, 10, 19), that He is then given the latitude to properly do His Office Work in the heart and life of the Believer. The Book of Acts graphically portrays this.

(Regrettably, there are many who actually have been Baptized with the Holy Spirit, even most one probably could say, but still have not allowed Him the latitude and control He must have in order to do His complete Work. However, this is not the fault of

NOTES

the Spirit but of the person.)

(6) "FOR WHEN WE WERE YET WITHOUT STRENGTH, IN DUE TIME CHRIST DIED FOR THE UNGODLY."

The phrase, *"For when we were yet without strength,"* pertains to an extremely negative scenario respecting the unbeliever.

First of all, this Passage proclaims, in effect, the doctrine of *"Total Depravity."* The sinner does not know God, does not understand God, and does not understand anything about God. In fact, the Apostle also states that the sinner is *"dead in trespasses and sins"* (Eph. 2:1). The sinner, in fact, is constantly at war with God, whether he realizes it or not.

In this state, the sinner is helpless, unable to reach God, actually little believing in God, if at all! As well, he is so blinded spiritually that he has no idea as to how despicable his true state actually is. Whatever that state is, at least in his mind, he feels he has the necessary resources to correct it, whether with education, money, ability, or even brute force.

"Without strength" in the Greek is *"asthenes,"* and means *"feeble, impotent, sick, weak,"* and refers to such in the spiritual sense.

All of this means that God had to reach man, for man had no way to reach God. Absolutely void of any true spirituality, it is impossible for him to recognize or understand his true state. Consequently, the only way this spiritual death can be awakened is for the Word of God to be ministered unto the sinner, with the Holy Spirit energizing that Word, which seizes upon the heart of the person, placing him under conviction. For the first time, he then begins to realize his undone spiritual state. That is the reason the Preaching of the Gospel is so very, very important (Mk. 16:15).

The phrase, *"In due time Christ died for the ungodly,"* declares the nature of God's Love.

Man can sacrifice himself when he thinks he has an adequate motive, as is evidenced in war, but the unique character of God's Love is displayed in the fact that Christ died for men when there was no motive to move Him to do so, but every reason to the contrary; for man is morally impotent, and actively ungodly, sinful, and hostile.

It was God's Own Heart that prompted Him to pity and redeem lost men. He could not possibly have found in us any adequate reason or moral worthfulness to justify His action; and this is clear from the declaration as to man's impotency, ungodliness, sinfulness, and hostility.

No non-Christian would lay down his life for a Nero or a Hitler. Consequently, the extraordinary Character of God's Love is seen in that Christ died for the temporal and eternal welfare of men who hated Him.

In the entirety of this Scripture, the context clearly indicates that *"Substitution"* is meant. Thus, our Lord died instead of us, taking our penalty on behalf of us, in that His Death was in our interest.

IN DUE TIME

The words *"due time"* in the Greek is *"kairos,"* and means *"a strategic time, a time determined by a set of circumstances which make that particular point of time part of the efficient working of an action or set of actions."*

In fact, considering that the Promise of the Coming Redeemer was given immediately after the Fall of man in the Garden of Eden (Gen. 3:15), why was Jesus some 4,000 years in coming?

We learn from the words *"due time"* that there was a specific time, in effect ordered by events, in which this great Plan of Redemption could be carried out.

Among other things, this terrible delay or length of time before the First Advent of Christ, tells us how actually awful and terrible that sin really is. Even though God could speak worlds into existence, He could not simply decree Redemption, but, in fact, had to carry out a certain order of events before this great thing could be done.

This is what makes it so absolutely unreasonable and even pitiful, for the Church to think that humanistic wisdom such as Psychology would have any bearing whatsoever on this dread malady called sin. If it took the Death of Christ on the Cross, along with His Resurrection, to satisfy the claims of Heavenly Justice, and to break the grip of sin, how does poor mortal man, who is fallen himself, think that he can effect any type of

NOTES

cure, healing, or deliverance?

THE FIRST ADVENT OF CHRIST

For the First Advent of Christ, certain things had to be in place. Jesus not only had the task of redeeming mankind, but as well, had to take back His Title and Position as King of kings, which had been usurped by Satan, at least on Earth. Satan as the *"god of this world"* had become such by the default of Adam and Eve. As the First Adam had lost his way, the Second Adam would have to establish that *"Way"* again. Jesus would do this as a Man which was of necessity, and not as God.

A particular people would have to be raised up through whom the Redeemer would come, which was Israel. A particular Throne would have to be established in order for Kingship to be regained. That Throne was the Throne of David. As well, that Throne Lineage must play out until the Romans ruled the world, at least of that day. This was necessary for several reasons.

It had been prophesied by Daniel that the rule of the Romans would be the *"due time"* (Dan. 7:7; 9:24-26). This was necessary for several reasons:

As we have already stated, the Salvation of man was and is far more complex than meets the eye, and even that is a gross understatement. Man has to somehow come to an end of himself, before he will finally admit his need for God. Even as this is true on an individual basis, it is also true respecting the entirety of mankind.

Consequently, man had to exhaust his mental resources respecting his philosophical quests, which ripened under the Greeks with their philosophy, but which did not, and, in fact, could not, satisfy the thirst of the human heart. It took some 4,000 years for all of this to be brought about.

Rome now ruled with its universal language and universal power. This was the time prophesied by Daniel. As degraded and evil as it was, the world was now ready, it was *"due time."*

(7) "FOR SCARCELY FOR A RIGHTEOUS MAN WILL ONE DIE: YET PERADVENTURE FOR A GOOD MAN SOME WOULD EVEN DARE TO DIE."

The phrase, *"For scarcely for a Righteous man will one die,"* has Paul using the word *"Righteous"* not in the usual New Testament sense, but in its normal meaning, i.e., a type of human goodness, at least as the world describes such.

Paul is saying that a few might die for such a man.

The phrase, *"Yet peradventure for a good man some would even dare to die,"* puts the situation on a slightly higher plain.

In other words, once every several centuries a man may arise, who would attempt to do right things for the betterment of others, and would be labeled by the world as *"good."* Down through the centuries some have died for such a man, but such is rare.

Even though Paul is not actually addressing such at this time, it might be proper at this juncture to call attention to the untold millions who have willingly laid down their lives for the Lord Jesus Christ.

During the time of the Early Church, Rome made the floors of her sporting arenas slippery with blood, blood one might quickly add, shed by untold thousands of Christians, who laid down their lives for Christ. It was demanded of them that they simply say, *"Caesar is Lord,"* and to do so would instantly grant them pardon. However, as simple as this was, the takers were few, with untold numbers instead saying *"Jesus is Lord."* That they paid with their lives, history is replete.

The same could be said for the Dark Ages, when Roman Catholicism attempted to further their perverted version of the Kingdom of God by torture and the sword. Only God knows the uncounted numbers who paid the full price for their allegiance to the Lord Jesus Christ. Their number known only to God, will one day stand in splendor in the Portals of Glory, having died for His Cause.

It must be quickly asked, does anyone seriously think that these untold millions would have willingly laid down their lives even as they did, for an imposter? I think it should go without saying, that these millions did not, and in fact, would not have died for such a man. They died for their Redeemer, even though Man, but yet God.

(8) "BUT GOD COMMENDETH HIS LOVE TOWARD US, IN THAT, WHILE WE WERE YET SINNERS, CHRIST DIED FOR US."

The phrase, *"But God commendeth His Love toward us,"* pertains to the fact that Christ's dying for the ungodly is a proof of Love immeasurably beyond what is common among men. To say it another way, it is that the Love of God towards ungodly men was displayed in the Death of Christ.

Commendeth in the Greek is *"sunistemi,"* and means *"to put together by combining or comparing, hence to show, prove, establish, exhibit."* Denney says, *"How greatly is this utmost Love of man surpassed by the Love of God."*

Another Expositor called attention to the fact that the word *"commendeth"* is in the present tense, meaning that God continuously establishes His Love in that the Death of Christ remains as its most striking manifestation (Vincent).

So, Calvary ever remains at the forefront of God's Thoughts toward man, even grossly wicked, ungodly, sinful man. Whatever it is that men think of God, they only have to look to Calvary to know Who and What God really is, and more particularly, Who and What He is toward them. There is no way that His Love could be better, or more visibly displayed, than by that single act of so long ago.

The phrase, *"While we were yet sinners, Christ died for us,"* points to the fact that Jesus died for those who are at enmity with Him and who bitterly hate Him.

Going back to the previous phrase, the pronoun *"His"* before *"Love,"* carries the weight of *"His Own,"* in other words, not in contrast with human Love, but rather a type of Love so set apart from man's understanding of such, that there is no comparison.

When we look at this Divine Love displayed in the Atonement, we have to ask ourselves as to how this is consistent with the Divine Wrath against sin. The same Love that gave such respecting Calvary, is equally opposed to sin. However, the ideas are not irreconcilable.

The answer is, that God not only portrayed such great Love by the act of Calvary, but at the same time displayed His Righteous Anger and Wrath against sin. So, it is a twofold display.

God will not, should not, in fact cannot, in any capacity, not even in the slightest, overlook even the smallest manifestation of sin, much less the gross evil of man's fallen condition. The answer is that His Wrath which of necessity must be exhibited against sin, was poured out upon the Person of His Son, The Lord Jesus Christ, even though He had never sinned. He became the voluntary Sin-Offering agreeing to take the punishment of the Wrath of God which was necessary of display, that is if God is to retain His Righteousness, which He must do. In fact, that is the story of Isaiah Chapter 53.

The Prophet said, *"Surely He hath borne our griefs, and carried our sorrows: yet we did esteem Him stricken, smitten of God, and afflicted."*

It went on to say, *"But He was wounded for our transgressions, He was bruised for our iniquities: the chastisement of our peace was upon Him; and with His Stripes we are Healed."*

As well, this did not pertain to only a part of the human race, with the Prophet further adding, *"All we like sheep have gone astray; we have turned every one to his own way; and the Lord hath laid on Him the iniquity of us all"* (Isa. 53:4-6).

(9) "MUCH MORE THEN, BEING NOW JUSTIFIED BY HIS BLOOD, WE SHALL BE SAVED FROM WRATH THROUGH HIM."

The phrase, *"Much more then,"* carries the idea that if Christ died for us while we were yet sinners, and He most definitely did, which means that we had no merit whatsoever, this should make us realize how much He will actually do for us, now that we are redeemed, in effect, a Child of God, adopted, in fact, into the family (Rom. 8:31-34; Heb. 7:25).

Many Believers have the problem of self-condemnation which is so graphically outlined in Romans Chapter 8. Struggling at times with sin in the flesh, Satan takes advantage of us, by claiming that God's Patience is about expended with us, due to our many failures.

To be sure, in no way is this meant to condone sin, failure, or wrongdoing of any nature, but rather to express God's Love to the Believer, that if He loved us so much while we were yet sinners, even that He would

die for us, even while we were in that terrible state, how much more does He love us now that we are His, and in no way will He ever lose patience with us and thereby cast us over, as Satan the liar suggests.

While the Believer must never become complacent toward failure or weakness, at the same time he must understand that as long as he places his trust in Christ, God will never level condemnation at him. So, if in fact there is condemnation, it is from the Evil One, and not God.

In other words, the one pointing an accusing finger at the Believer is the Devil and not the Lord. So, the Believer must understand that, and refuse to accept Satan's condemnation, resting firmly in Christ, with the assurance that God always forgives and cleanses the supplicant Believer (I Jn. 1:9), and guarantees ultimate victory.

Hallelujah!

The phrase, *"Being now Justified by His Blood,"* tells us several wonderful things, so wonderful in fact, that it is almost beyond contemplation.

First of all, we are *"Now Justified."* That means, that the Believer is just as fully Justified now, as he will be when he at long last stands before God in Glorified Form.

It also means, that the new Convert, in fact, the one who gave his heart and life to Jesus just a few minutes ago, is as Justified now as the greatest Saint of God who has ever lived, or will ever live. As far as Justification is concerned, it is a total, complete, absolute, Finished Work, in the life of the Believer, even immediately upon Conversion. While it is true that all the results of this Work are not yet done, and in fact will not be done until the Resurrection of Life, still, the *"fact"* of this Work is done and completed.

It is this way because of the Finished Work of Christ. When the sinner believes Him, accepting what He did at Calvary and the Resurrection, the Work is then done and in totality. Were the Work dependent upon us, to be sure it would in no way be a Finished Work, but it is not dependent on us, but rather Christ. So, in Him it is done, finished, complete, absolute, total, and as well, everlasting.

*"Sinners Jesus will receive; sound this
Word of Grace to all,*
*"Who the heavenly pathway lead, all
who linger, all who fall."*

*"Come, and He will give you rest; Trust
Him, for His Word is plain;*
*"He will take the sinfulest; Christ
receiveth sinful men."*

*"Now my heart condemns me not; pure
before the Law I stand;*
*"He Who cleansed me from all spot,
satisfied its last demand."*

*"Christ receiveth sinful men, even me
with all my sin;*
*"Purged from every spot and stain,
Heaven with Him I enter in."*

RIGHTEOUSNESS

As the Reader surely by now knows, Justification is a legal Work carried out by God in the believing sinner's heart and life. In other words, upon Faith in Christ, God declares the sinner to be clean, perfect, pure, without spot, without blemish, and as a consequence, everlastingly Righteous. But once again, He declares that believing sinner in this fashion only after Christ. In other words, the pure, spotless, absolute Righteousness of Christ, is freely given to the believing sinner, with him taking upon himself that spotless Righteousness, while at the same time shedding the evil and the iniquity of his wickedness and sin.

This is all done *"by His Blood,"* meaning, that Jesus poured out His pure, untainted, unstained Life's Blood at Calvary's Cross, which paid the price for man's Redemption, satisfying Heaven's just demands.

HEAVEN'S DEMANDS

So, what Jesus did at Calvary was far more to satisfy Heaven's demands, than anything it had to do with Satan or sin.

The way it affected Satan and sin, was that Satan now had no more claim on the believing sinner, once Heaven's demands were satisfied. Before then, he could point an accusing finger at all of mankind and claim them as captives, simply because they were stained and polluted by hellish sin,

NOTES

which Satan knew that God in no way could accept. As the sin is automatically condemned by God, and even as it must be, the sinner containing the sin, is at the same time condemned. It is the same as a person having a contagious disease. Of necessity, the person must be quarantined, not because the person is hated, but because of his condition. It is the same way with sinners.

God did not and does not hate sinners, even as verse 8 so loudly proclaims. In fact, He loves sinners. But due to the fact, that sinners carry a disease called *"sin,"* they must be quarantined in a place called Hell, unless they accept the Atonement provided by God's Own Son in the shedding of His Precious Blood.

The phrase, *"We shall be Saved from wrath through Him,"* proclaims in stark clarity, that the Wrath of God is turned away from the sinner, once Faith is enjoined by the sinner toward Christ.

As stated, God had to cleanse man from this deadly malady called sin, or else the whole of humanity would be lost.

In the Greek Text the phrase actually says, *"We shall be Saved from the wrath through Him."* This points out a particular wrath, which is the Lake of Fire, the manifestation of God's Wrath against sin.

This is the reason that we have pointed several times to the fact, that God does not so much condemn sinners simply because they are sinners, but rather because they refuse to accept His Atonement for sin.

Consequently, in this one verse we are guaranteed present peace and future safety. *"Now Justified"* assures the one and, *"We shall be Saved"* makes absolute the other.

These are based, not upon the pious emotion or personal moral merit of a religious man, but upon Christ's Person and Atoning Sacrifice. This Divine Foundation is displayed in the words *"His Blood,"* and *"Through Him."* Notice also the expression, *"Christ died"* in verse 8, set over against man's fourfold demerit — morally impotent (vs. 6), ungodly (vs. 6), sinful (vs. 8), and hostile (vs. 10).

Modern Theology denies Christ's Atonement and God's Wrath. Both these Foundation Truths of the Gospel are here declared to be fundamental. Those who believe there is no wrath to fear, naturally seek no Saviour, and so cut themselves off from the Salvation that is in Christ Alone.

Christ's obedience unto Death (Phil. 2:8) — and that His Death was a Sin-Offering (I Cor. 15:3) — is the Central Truth of the Gospel. The effort to rid humanity of this Foundation Truth, or to minimize it, or to substitute the Incarnation for it, is one of the saddest features of what is proudly termed *"Modern Thought."*

The expiatory Sacrifice of Christ is the one and only eternal ground on which God can act in declaring ungodly men Righteous.

Galatians 3:21 and many similar Divine Declarations, reveal the hopelessness of standing before God in a Righteousness which He will accept upon any other principle than that of Faith in a Crucified Sin-Bearer.

CHRIST THE LAW-KEEPER

Christ's perfect obedience to the Law of God formed His Own Righteousness and gave virtue to His Sacrifice — for a Sacrifice for sin must have neither spot nor blemish. But it was not the spotlessness of the Lamb which made the Atonement, but its out-poured Blood, i.e., its surrendered life, for the Blood is the Life. The Judgment pronounced upon sin being death, that claim could only be vindicated and discharged by the suffering of death. Christ suffered that penalty, and, in consequence, saves the Believer from it.

FAITH BRINGS MAN CHRIST'S PERFECTION

If Christ's Perfect Obedience and Perfect Life alone would redeem man, then there was no need for Jesus to die. However, His Incarnation, His Virgin Birth, His spotless Life, His Healings and Miracles, could not redeem man, for such, as important as they were, did not pay the price, for such could not pay the price.

But the Scripture declares that He died for sinners, so that it is His Death that provides a spotless Righteousness for sinners who believe in Him; and it was His obedience in life which gave the power to His Suffering in Death (Williams).

ROMANS, THE ABC'S OF THE GOSPEL

An intelligent grasp of this Teaching is necessary to a Knowledge of the Gospel, i.e., the principle on which God can declare guilty men Righteous.

All of this which Paul proclaims, sets out Christ's Work for the believing sinner.

However, it is not necessary at all for the sinner to understand all the rudiments of what is explained here, for if so, no sinner would be Saved, because no sinner understands anything of the Gospel, much less all that Christ did for the sinner.

So, all that is necessary for the sinner to be Saved, is for him to simply believe that Jesus is the Son of God, and that He died for sinners. Believing that, instantly transforms the sinner with all his unrighteousness, into a Believer, cloaked in the Righteousness of God. That is the reason John 3:16 is so important. The sinner only has to believe.

However, having said that, it is imperative for the sinner once he has become a Believer, to learn and understand the great rudiments of the Gospel, here laid out by the Holy Spirit through Paul. He should take it upon himself to learn and understand, in which the Holy Spirit will grandly help him do, all that Jesus has done for us. To fail in that, is to fail in victory.

WHY DID GOD DEMAND THE BLOOD OF JESUS AS PAYMENT OR ATONEMENT FOR SIN?

We have learned very graphically and succinctly as to how Jesus shed His Life's Blood for the sin of man, and of the necessity that it should be done, but why was this the price demanded by God?

When reading the Bible, we find that *"Blood"* which is *"dam"* in Hebrew and *"haima"* in Greek, is theologically significant in both Testaments. In both, this word is linked with life and death. In both, Blood introduces us to the depths of God's Love for us and to His unique Forgiveness.

THE OLD TESTAMENT

The word *"dam"* in the Old Testament

occurs about 360 times. It is found most often in the Pentateuch and in Ezekiel. *"Blood"* is used generally in one of two ways.

Often it indicates violence (the shedding of Blood in war or murder), the usual outcome being death.

In other instances it is associated with the shedding of Blood done in making a Sacrifice to the Lord. Three Old Testament Passages show the respect for life that God demanded from human beings, and they show the significance of Blood.

GENESIS

At the very outset of time the Lord said, *"Whoever sheds the Blood of man, by man shall his Blood be shed"* (Gen. 9:6). In context, the Blood of every living creature must be accounted for, because that fluid is *"lifeblood."* To shed the Blood is to take the life; and although all life is precious, the life of human beings, made in God's Image, is uniquely precious (Gen. 9:4-6).

In fact, this is the reason for the demand for Capital Punishment for Capital Crimes. It is not to deter crime, but to show how precious that life really is, respecting the Image of God. Consequently, when a person takes the life of another in cold blood, he is showing disdain for the Image of God, and the Word of God declares that the murderer must forfeit his own life.

LEVITICUS

"The life of a creature is in the Blood, and I have given it to you to make Atonement for yourselves on the Altar" (Lev. 17:11).

In Old Testament Sacrifices the Blood of the Sacrificial animal was drained, then sprinkled on the Altar or ground, and the lifeless body was burned. The Blood represented life; Blood sustains mortal life and may be offered to God in place of the sinner's life, which it was in Christ Jesus with His Death on the Cross.

DEUTERONOMY

"Be sure you do not eat the Blood, because the Blood is the life, and you must not eat the life with the meat" (Deut. 12:23).

Blood is neither to be drunk nor eaten with meat (Gen. 9:4). Blood is sacred fluid:

once taken from an animal, its sole use was the Sacrifice through which the Old Testament Saint was assured of the forgiveness of his sins, and because it pointed to the One Who was coming, namely, The Lord Jesus Christ.

In fact, the Holy Spirit reinforced this Command even under the New Covenant in the statement given by James at the Great Council in Jerusalem, recorded in Acts Chapter 15.

He said, and pertaining to New Covenant Believers, *"That ye abstain from meats offered to idols, and from Blood, and from things strangled, and from fornication"* (Acts 15:29).

This shows us how much this all-important Truth was inculcated into the very spirit of Israel. They full well knew and understood the meaning of the offering of the animal Sacrifices, and what the shedding of their Blood actually meant. As solemn and somber as this ceremony was, they knew beyond the shadow of a doubt as to what it represented. Understanding perfectly the Promise given by God in the Garden of Eden concerning the Coming Redeemer (Gen. 3:15), they well understood that the Sacrifices were only a substitute until the Reality came, Who would be Christ.

Above that, the Prophets reinforced this over and over again, and especially the Prophet Isaiah in the giving of his great 53rd Chapter. This left absolutely no doubt as to that which the Redeemer would do.

So they knew and understood perfectly well the preciousness of the Blood, and why it was precious. Consequently, this is what made it so awful, their Crucifixion of Christ. Their denying and crucifying their Redeemer, and in fact the Redeemer of the world, was the most horrendous act in human history. There is no way that one could adequately describe the horror of what they did, and the suffering they have enjoined because of this one act.

While it was necessary that Christ die on the Cross, at least if man was to be Redeemed, still, it was not at all ordained that Israel, God's Chosen People, would do this horrible thing. God being God, could have effected the Crucifixion in many and varied ways, without His Own People carrying out this dastardly act. His Death was absolutely necessary, even as we are explaining here, but that Israel did this thing, was totally and completely of their own doing, and despite the pleas of Christ otherwise.

THE NEW TESTAMENT

The word *"Blood"* or in the Greek *"haima,"* occurs 99 times in the New Testament. Often it refers to human bloodshed, representing violence and death, even as in the Old.

Five times the New Testament speaks of *"flesh and blood"* to indicate human limitations and weakness. Blood is used in Revelation to express the terrors of those days of Judgment and is found 14 times in references to Old Testament Sacrifices.

Thirty-eight times the word is used in reference to the Blood of Christ.

THE BLOOD OF OUR LORD AND SAVIOUR JESUS CHRIST

When the Blood of Christ is mentioned, it is always in reference either to the institution of the New Covenant or to Jesus' Death as a Sacrifice of Atonement.

Covenant plays a central role in the theology of the Old Testament. A Covenant is an agreement or contract. The Old Testament Covenants entered into by God took on the character of an Oath or Promise, for in them God bound Himself to do certain things for His People. He also told individuals how they could experience the benefits promised.

There were a number of ways to make a Covenant in Old Testament times, but the most binding was a Covenant instituted and sealed by Blood (Gen. 15:8-21).

In the Old Testament, God promised that one day He would make a New Covenant with His People. Under the New Covenant, God promised to provide forgiveness and a new heart (inner transformation, Jer. 31:33-34).

The Death of Jesus (more specifically, the Blood that He shed on Calvary) instituted this New Covenant. Christ's Blood sets the seal of God's Promise on His Offer of Forgiveness through Faith in the Son (Heb. 9:15-28).

THE LORD'S SUPPER

We meet the New Covenant again in the Cup of Communion (Mat. 26:28; Mk. 14:24; Lk. 22:20; I Cor. 11:25-27). We are told to drink, recognizing the Blood of Jesus, as a sign of our *"participation in the Blood of Christ"* (I Cor. 10:16).

This language reflects Jesus' discourse on the Bread of Life, where He urged His hearers to *"drink"* His Blood (Jn. 6:53-56).

This metaphor, which was so startling to His audience, calls for appropriating by Faith the Sacrifice by which Jesus instituted the New Covenant, while Communion affirms our Faith in that Sacrifice.

Consequently, and as should be obvious, Jesus was not meaning that people literally drink His Blood, nor does the Grape Juice turn into His literal Blood in the Communion, as claimed by Catholics and others. As stated, Christ was using a metaphor in both cases.

THE SACRIFICE OF CHRIST

Most references to the Blood of Christ are linked directly with Calvary and recall the Old Testament link between Blood and Sacrifice. Thus, Romans 3:25 calls Christ's Blood the *"Blood of Atonement."* Jesus offered Himself up as a Sacrifice for our sins.

The emphasis in many New Testament references is laid on the benefits won for us by Jesus' Blood. It is by the Blood of Christ that we are Justified, which we are here studying (Rom. 5:9).

Through the Blood of Christ we have Redemption (Eph. 1:7; Heb. 9:12) and have been delivered from our old, empty way of life (I Pet. 1:19). Jesus' Blood has brought us near to God in the most intimate of relationships (Eph. 2:3) and has made Peace for us by bringing us into harmony with our Lord (Col. 1:20).

Likewise, the Blood of Christ has been effective in doing away with sin (Heb. 9:24-26). This involves forgiveness (Eph. 1:7), continual cleansing (I Jn. 1:7), and freedom from sin's binding power so that we can actively serve God with a cleansed conscience (Heb. 9:14; Rev. 1:5).

Against the background of the Old Testament, we understand the meaning of the

Sacrifice of Jesus on Calvary. However, it is through the Teaching of the New Testament that we grasp the wonderful benefits purchased for us by the Shed Blood of our Lord.

The wages of sin was and is death. Consequently, when man fell, he was poisoned totally and completely, spirit, soul and body. This meant that his life flow of Blood was contaminated, now containing death instead of Life.

To assuage this, or to nullify its binding result of death, a Perfect Life had to be offered up. However, there was no Perfect Life, in that all in Adam were judged as fallen creatures, unable to provide a Sacrifice.

Consequently, God became Man, the Second Adam, and in doing so was born of the Virgin Mary. Therefore, He was not tainted as all of humanity otherwise was. He would pour out His Perfect, unpolluted, untainted, unstained, Precious Blood as an Offering for sin, which Heaven would accept.

In fact, Perfect Shed Blood was the only thing that could be accepted, and because the Life was in the Blood (Richards).

(10) "FOR IF, WHEN WE WERE ENEMIES, WE WERE RECONCILED TO GOD BY THE DEATH OF HIS SON, MUCH MORE, BEING RECONCILED, WE SHALL BE SAVED BY HIS LIFE."

The phrase, *"For if, when we were enemies, we were reconciled to God by the Death of His Son,"* speaks of man being reconciled to God, and not God being reconciled to man, which is unscriptural.

God hasn't needed to be reconciled to man, at least in the sense in which we think, especially considering that He loves sinners, so much in fact, that He gave His Only Begotten Son in order to save sinners. God reconciles men to Himself by changing their hearts and converting them from sin by the manifestation of His Love in Christ.

This Reconciliation is spoken of as effected once for all, for all mankind in the Atonement, independently of, and previously to, the Conversion of sinners (Barmby).

Once again, this leads back to the statement of Paul, that *"While we were yet sinners, Christ died for us."* In fact, this Reconciliation is available to all mankind, and can be appropriated by Faith to any sinner.

As we have already stated, the word *"enemies"* applies only to man. In other words, man is the enemy of God, and not God the enemy of man. Now, the Truth is, man thinks of God as an enemy, and because the Righteousness of God is always opposed to the sin of man. While it is certainly true that He is opposed to sin, He in no stretch of the imagination, could be said to be opposed to the sinner.

Any parent is opposed to drugs or alcohol, or any other vice which may tend to destroy the life of their child, at least if the parent is halfway sensible. So, because God is unalterably opposed to sin, even as He should be, in no way makes Him an enemy.

REBELLION

Man is in a state of rebellion against God, and not God against man. This rebellion has persisted since the Fall, and takes upon itself the personality of the reason for the Fall. At that time, Adam and Eve, the representative parents of us all in a sense, stepped outside of the Revealed Will of God. They did it purposely, knowingly, and in direct violation of what God had said. Satan made them believe that God was withholding something good from them, by demanding that they not eat of the Tree of the Knowledge of Good and Evil. So, man carries that same thought with him presently, and in fact, always has. If he believes at all there is a God, he imagines God as interfering with him, in effect, not allowing him to have his full latitude. He has been deceived into thinking that for which his soul and spirit craves, can be fulfilled in the world. In other words, he believes the lie of Satan.

That is the reason that nothing can change man's attitude and spirit, with the exception of the proclamation of what Jesus did for man on Calvary's Cross, with the Holy Spirit bringing to bear His Work of Conviction on the human heart.

"Reconcile" in the Greek is *"katalasso,"* and means *"to change, exchange, to reconcile those at variance."* It means primarily to exchange, and hence to change the relation of hostile parties into a relation of Peace; to reconcile (Vincent). This involves four things:

RECONCILIATION

1. It begins with a Movement of God toward man with a view to break down man's hostility, to commend God's Love and Holiness to him, and to convince him of the enormity and the consequence of sin.

It is God Who initiates this Movement in the Person and Work of Jesus Christ, and He does it through the Office and Ministry of the Holy Spirit (Jn. Chpt. 16; Rom. 5:6, 8; II Cor. 5:18-19; Eph. 1:6; I Jn. 4:19).

2. For the Reconciliation to be complete, as should be obvious, a corresponding movement on man's part toward God must be effected. This speaks of man yielding to the Appeal of Christ's Self-Sacrificing Love, laying aside his enmity, renouncing his sin, and turning to God in Faith and Obedience.

3. As a result of man hearing the Gospel, and accepting the Gospel, a consequent change of character results in man. This is brought about by the forgiving and cleansing of all sin, which brings about a thorough revolution in all his dispositions and principles.

4. This change on man's part, effects a change of relation on God's Part as well, that being removed (sin) which rendered Him hostile to man, so that God can now receive him into fellowship and let loose upon him all His Fatherly Love and Grace (I Jn. 1:3, 7). Consequently, there is a complete reconciliation (Wuest).

The phrase, *"Much more, being reconciled, we shall be Saved by His Life,"* speaks of the Resurrection of Christ, whereas the previous phrase spoke of the Crucifixion of Christ. Whereas the first had to do with one's Salvation, the latter has to do with one's victorious walk in this life before God and man. This is found in Romans 6:4.

SANCTIFICATION

Paul was writing about Justification in the first phrase, he is here writing about our Sanctification.

Even though Sanctification is a Finished Work of Christ received by the sinner at Conversion, which means to be made clean, pure and to be set apart exclusively for the Lord, which must be done before the sinner can be Justified, which actually all happens at

NOTES

once, (I Cor. 6:11), still, there is also a Progressive Sanctification which begins with the Believer by the Holy Spirit at the moment of Conversion.

So as not to confuse the Reader, one must think of Sanctification as pertaining to two different works.

1. First of all, the new Believer has a *"Standing"* in Christ which never changes, and is made possible by the work of Sanctification, which is freely imputed and given as stated, at the moment of Conversion. That *"Standing"* never varies, because it is anchored in Christ and based upon His Perfect Righteousness.

2. However, the *"State"* of our Sanctification as we begin to live for God, is something else altogether. Whereas the *"Standing"* never varies, the *"State"* is constantly going up and down, pretty much according to our knowledge of the Word of God, and our Faith, or the lack of such, in appropriating what Christ has done for us in our own hearts and lives. This is what Paul is talking about here.

In our life lived for God, Satan constantly attempts to foster upon us sins of the flesh, in which he will greatly succeed if we do not know our rightful place in Christ, which pertains to the Resurrection. In other words, when Jesus came out of the Tomb, He came out different than when He went in, now with a Glorified Body. He is victorious over all sin and every power of Satan. Consequently, we must understand, even as we will study more succinctly in Romans Chapter 6, that all of this was done for us, in other words, we were in Christ when He died, in Him when He was placed in the Tomb (buried), and in Him when He was raised from the dead. Consequently, we are to allow Him to live the Resurrected Life in us, which gives us victory over all of the flesh and every attempt by Satan (Gal. 2:20-21). This is all done by Faith, and is carried out by the Power of the Holy Spirit, even as Paul outlines in Romans Chapter 8.

Once again, even as verse 9 says, if God Saved us when we were enemies, even upon the premise of our simple Faith in Christ in what He did at Calvary, how *"much more"* will He give us victory in the flesh after we have become His Child.

I say these things because at times the struggle can be severe, with the Believer wondering if victory is possible. However, it is possible, and in fact it is *not* something which is to be done, but actually has *already* been done in Christ. It is a matter of appropriating Faith, and understanding what Jesus really did for us, which we hope to open up more fully in Commentary on the next Chapter.

Incidentally, the words *"Saved by His Life,"* here do not speak of His Perfect Example respecting the some 33 1/2 years in which He lived above all sin, which within itself could save no one, but rather the pouring out of His Life's Blood at Calvary. While it is true that He wants us to have His Perfect Walk, still, the fact of that example cannot grant such to us in any capacity. The example only becomes real when we appropriate unto ourselves, incidentally by Faith and by the Power of the Holy Spirit, all that He did for us in His Death, Resurrection, and even His Exaltation.

The world has ever attempted to emulate the Life of Christ, while ignoring what He did at Calvary and the Resurrection, but such cannot be done. This is not a matter of mere ethics, but actually of Life and Death — the Life of Christ imparted to the sinner who is dead in trespasses and sins. All of that is anchored squarely in Calvary.

(11) "AND NOT ONLY SO, BUT WE ALSO JOY IN GOD THROUGH OUR LORD JESUS CHRIST, BY WHOM WE HAVE NOW RECEIVED THE ATONEMENT."

The phrase, *"And not only so, but we also joy in God through our Lord Jesus Christ,"* tells us several things:

1. Considering that all sin has now been removed by our Faith in Christ, and we have been reconciled unto God, this should be the occasion of constant joy expressed at what the Lord has done for us. In fact, the Believer is to *"glory* (boast) *in the Cross of our Lord Jesus Christ,"* which has made all of this possible (Gal. 6:14). However, our trust in Christ is no false confidence, and provides the only true *"Joy"* that a human being can actually have.

2. All of this is *"Through our Lord Jesus Christ,"* which incidentally, is His Resurrection Name. We truly owe it all to Jesus.

NOTES

The phrase, *"By Whom we have now received the Atonement,"* takes us even further.

3. We have Salvation *"now,"* even though we do not yet have all the results of Salvation, with the final results coming about at the Resurrection of all Believers, which is made possible by the Resurrection of Christ. At that time, every Saint will be *"Glorified"* which will then complete the Salvation process.

4. The word *"Atonement"* here should have been translated *"Reconciliation,"* because that is what it actually means.

However, the word *"Atonement"* not only means *"to cover,"* but it also means *"the making of two estranged parties at one,"* hence, *"Reconciliation."*

THE JOY OF THE LORD

A number of words in both Testaments express the Joy that human beings experience. Joy is found in the good things of this life and in expectation of God's Work in the future.

Tracing the concept of Joy through the Bible helps us realize that our happiness, like our hope, is founded on realities that are unaffected by conditions in this world, which can be claimed only by followers of Christ.

THE OLD TESTAMENT

A number of different Hebrew words are translated *"Joy."* Some of the key terms are: A. *"Gil,"* which is Joy at God's Works or Attributes; B. *"Ranan,"* jubilant shouts expressed at times of Sacrifice and over God's Saving Works; C. *"Sus,"* glad enthusiasm provoked by God and His Word; and, D. *"Samah,"* a glad or joyful disposition.

Often in the Old Testament, Joy is not so much a private emotion as it is the enthusiastic response of a feasting company or worshiping community to God's tangible and intangible Blessings. This Joy is an expressed Joy: it is expressed in glad shouts, in praise, in laughter, and in enthusiastic commitment to God's Ways.

RELATIONSHIP WITH GOD AS THE SOURCE OF A BELIEVER'S JOY

There is no doubt that the Old Testament portrays Joy, like every other aspect of life on

Earth, as dependent on God's Goodness. Although there is a direct Joy that comes from a personal relationship with the Lord (Ps. 16:11), all other Joy is from Him as well.

Obedience to God led to rich harvests and to Joy expressed in celebration of the Feast of Tabernacles. *"The Lord your God will bless you in all your harvest and in all the work of your hands, and your Joy will be complete"* (Deut. 16:15).

The memory of God's Saving Acts was a constant source of Joy as well. We sense the Joy of Praise in David's Psalm recorded in I Chronicles Chapter 16: *"Sing to the Lord, all the Earth; proclaim His Salvation day after day.*

"Declare His Glory among the Nations, His Marvelous Deeds among all peoples.

"For great is the Lord and most worthy of Praise; He is to be feared above all gods.

"For all the gods of the Nations are idols, but the Lord made the heavens.

"Splendor and Majesty are before Him; Strength and Joy in His Dwelling Place.

"Ascribe to the Lord, O families of Nations, ascribe to the Lord Glory and Strength,

"Ascribe to the Lord the Glory due to His Name.

"Bring an Offering and come before Him; worship the Lord in the splendor of His Holiness.

"Tremble before Him, all the Earth! The world is firmly established; it cannot be moved.

"Let the heavens rejoice, let the Earth be glad; let them say among the Nations, 'The Lord reigns!'" (I Chron. 16:23-31).

THE OBEDIENT BELIEVER

The Believer's relationship with God is a source of Joy in another way. The obedient Believer finds God's Word to be a Source of Joy (Ps. 19:8; 119:14); likewise, the Trusting Believer rejoices in God's Promises (Ps. 119:162). It is in commitment to God that the Believer finds an inner and hidden spring of Joy bubbling up within the heart.

In the Old Testament as well as the New Testament, a person's relationship with God is characterized by Hope and by Faith. Often one's situation is difficult or even dangerous. In times of trouble the Believer finds Joy in the expectation that God will act to deliver.

NOTES

Psalm 33 expresses this theme beautifully:
"No King is saved by the size of his army; no warrior escapes by his great strength.

"A horse is a vain hope for deliverance; despite all its great strength it cannot save.

"But the Eyes of the Lord are on those who fear Him, on those whose Hope is in His unfailing Love,

"To deliver them from death and keep them alive in famine.

"We wait in Hope for the Lord; He is our Help and our Shield.

"In Him our hearts rejoice, for we trust in His Holy Name.

"May Your unfailing Love rest upon us, O Lord, even as we put our Hope in You" (Ps. 33:16-22).

THE NEW TESTAMENT

There are three different Greek word groups in the New Testament that express the idea of Joy:

1. *"Agalliao"* is a loud, public expression of Joy in worship. It focuses attention on God and His past and future work for the Believer.

2. *"Euphraino"* emphasizes a community Joy, expressed by Believers in times of Revival and Movings of the Holy Spirit. It does not describe the feelings of the individual as much as the atmosphere of shared enjoyment.

3. *"Chairo"* is the word for Joy that is used most often in the New Testament. It has reference to both the subjective state of Joy (one's experience) and the things that bring Joy (that which is objective, and pertains to what is unchanging relative to the Word of God).

Each of these words is used in the Septuagint to translate several of the Old Testament terms for Joy as well. Consequently, the New Testament retains the basic Old Testament outlook on Joy.

THE BELIEVER'S JOY

Every human being is hungry for Joy. The New Testament provides a number of insights into how those who know Jesus can experience Joy through Faith.

Intimate relationship with Jesus is a Source of Joy. Two Teachings of Christ, reported by John, describe this relationship:
"If you obey My Commands, you will

remain in My Love, just as I have obeyed My Father's Commands and remain in His Love.

"I have told you this so that My Joy may be in you and that your Joy may be complete" (Jn. 15:10-11).

"Until now you have not asked for anything in My Name. Ask and you will receive, and your Joy will be complete" (Jn. 16:24).

The Believer's Joy is produced within, by the Holy Spirit (Lk. 10:21; Rom. 14:17; Gal. 5:22; I Thess. 1:6). The Joy of the Pagan is found in God's material blessings (Acts 14:17), but the Christian's Joy is unique in that it is an outcome of Salvation (Acts 8:8; 16:34) found through Trust in God (Rom. 15:13).

JOY AND PERSECUTION

The New Testament often links Joy with persecution. Jesus spoke in prayer of the antagonism of the world to Him and to His followers and asked that His followers might have *"the full measure"* of His Joy within them (Jn. 17:13).

The reaction of the early Missionaries to persecution was a glowing, inner Joy that seemed to deny circumstances (Acts 13:52; II Cor. 7:4; James 1:2). In his first Epistle, Peter describes the Believer's Joy despite suffering:

"In this (Salvation) *you greatly rejoice, though now for a little while you may have had to suffer grief in all kinds of trials.*

"These have come so that your Faith — of greater worth than gold, which perishes even though refined by fire — may be proved genuine and may result in Praise, Glory and Honour when Jesus Christ is revealed.

"Though you have not seen Him, you love Him; even though you do not see Him now, you believe in Him and are filled with an inexpressible and Glorious Joy,

"For you are receiving the goal of your Faith, the Salvation of your souls" (I Pet. 1:6-9).

This Saving Work of God within us provides an inexpressible Joy, whatever our circumstances.

Joy is most often linked in the New Testament with God's Work in fellow Believers whom we Love and whom we serve. This thought is behind the Joy spoken of in a number of Passages (Rom. 16:19; II Cor.

NOTES

1:24; 7:7; Phil. 1:4, 25-26; 2:2, 29; 4:1; I Thess. 2:19-20; 3:9; II Tim. 1:4; Phile. vs. 7; Heb. 13:17; I Jn. 1:4; II Jn. vss. 4, 12; III Jn. vss. 3-4).

THE ESSENCE OF BIBLICAL JOY

A sense of Joy pervades the Bible. The Old Testament looks most closely at the Joy of the believing community gathered to worship and praise God, which is carried over into the New Testament as well.

Joy is an emotion that is evoked by remembering God and His Work and by the confident expectation that God will act to deliver when troubles come.

One's relationship with God, maintained by obedient response to His Word, is a Source of Joy. Joy is surely associated with an abundance of the good things of this life. But Joy is essentially a spiritual experience in Christ.

PERSONAL RELATIONSHIP WITH CHRIST

The New Testament suggests that Pagans find Joy in God's material blessings. But, again, True Joy is essentially a spiritual experience, as stated in Christ. It is found in a saving relationship with God and in maintaining fellowship with Him.

Love, expressed in prayer and obedience, is the key to the Christian's full experience of Joy. The New Testament sees Joy as something that is independent of circumstances, which is very important. The Believer's Joy is found in the inner Work of the Holy Spirit, Who, despite trials or suffering, is bringing us Salvation.

Thus, Joy, like Peace, is rooted in Trust in the Lord. As for externals, the greatest Source of Joy for the Christian is found in serving other Believers and in seeing God work in their lives (Richards).

Inasmuch as the word *"Atonement"* is used here by the translators, and which in effect describes *"Reconciliation,"* and is that to which Paul is here addressing himself, perhaps a more fuller treatment of this word would be appropriate at this time.

ATONEMENT

How can a sinful human being approach God? How do we deal with the sins and the failures that alienate us from Him?

God's solution to this basic problem is pictured in the Atoning Sacrifices of the Old Testament. Although Sacrifices picture what became a reality in the Death of Jesus on Calvary. Consequently, a more proper understanding of this word opens up the greater reality of what the Lord has done for sinners in the realm of Salvation.

THE OLD TESTAMENT

The Hebrew words universally translated *"Atonement"* in modern English versions are *"kippur"* and *"kapar."*

The root (kapar) and its related words are used about 150 times in the Old Testament and are intimately linked in the Bible with Forgiveness of Sin and with Reconciliation to God. It is often said that the idea expressed is one found in a possibly related Arabic root that means *"to cover or conceal."*

Atonement would then denote a covering that conceals a person's sin and makes it possible for him to approach God.

However, there is some controversy concerning this particular definition.

Other Hebrew Scholars claim that the word *"Atonement"* actually means *"At-one-ment,"* the making of two estranged parties at one.

I personally think that both meanings have their place and, consequently, can be read into the Text and the Word *"Atonement."*

What is certain is the role that Atonement played in the Plan of God respecting Israel — a role one might quickly add, given to Atonement by God to carry a vital Message about our Faith.

THE ATONEMENT AND OBJECTS

In the Old Testament, Atonement was made to purify objects ritually and set them aside for God's Service (the Tabernacle Altar) (Ex. 29:36-37).

Atonement was also associated with ordaining persons for God's Service (Priests) (Ex. 29:35-36). But the primary connection of Atonement was with sin, guilt, and forgiveness.

UNINTENTIONAL SINS

Leviticus Chapter 4 deals with unintentional sins that were committed by Priests

(Lev. 4:3-12), the whole community (Lev. 4:13-21), the Leaders (Lev. 4:22-26), and the humblest members of the Faith Community (Lev. 4:27-35).

In each case the formula is repeated: the one who sins unintentionally, *"he is guilty."* The guilty sinner then brings an animal to the Priests, who offer it in Sacrifice. *"In this way he* (the Priest) *will make Atonement for the man's sin, and he will be forgiven"* (Lev. 4:26).

RESTORATION

Leviticus Chapter 14 makes it clear that this Sacrificial prescription was to be followed for both ritual and moral uncleanness and that the Atoning Sacrifice restored the guilty party or unclean object to harmonious relationship with God and the believing community.

Whatever the root meaning of *"kapar,"* it is clear that Atonement involves a Sacrifice that in some significant and just way deals with guilt so that God extends forgiveness, reconciling the person or group to Himself.

THE ATONEMENT AND SACRIFICE

In the Old Testament, Atonement for sin is consistently linked with the Sacrifice of a living animal (a clean animal). Even references to *"Atonement money"* make a link with Sacrifice, for Israel was told to *"use it for the service of the tent of meeting"* (Ex. 30:16).

Leviticus 17:11 teaches that the death of a Sacrificial animal was required for Atonement. The Israelites were told not to eat Blood, *"for,"* God told them, *"the life of a creature is in the Blood, and I have given it to you to make Atonement for yourselves on the Altar; it is the Blood that makes Atonement for one's life."*

The images in the Old Testament Worship System, then, are quite plain. As soon as God introduced Law (Ex. Chpts. 19-24), the reality of sin as Law-breaking was established. Persons who broke the Law of Moses became guilty before God (Rom. 7:7-13).

It thus became necessary for God to deal with guilt, for implicit in the Old Testament notion of sin is not only guilt as personal responsibility for one's actions but also the conviction that God must act to punish sin.

At Sinai, God acted immediately to deal

with this problem. He gave Moses plans for the Tabernacle (Ex. Chpts. 25-26). Worship there involved Sacrifices that would be offered in Atonement (Ex. Chpts. 27, 30). The Priesthood was established to make the Sacrifices (Ex. Chpts. 28-29).

With the establishment of the Tabernacle, the Sacrificial System, and the Priesthood, Atonement could be made after a person sinned, and the guilty individual could thus be restored to right relationship with God.

Old Testament Atonement called for the life of an animal. The guilty party laid his hand on the head of the animal, identifying himself with it (Lev. 4:4, 15, 24, 29). Then the animal was slain, symbolically taking the sinner's place. The imagery tells us that sin merits death but that God will accept another life in place of that of the sinner.

THE GREAT DAY OF ATONEMENT

Members of Israel's community could come to the Tabernacle to seek forgiveness when they discovered they were guilty of some unintentional sin. But what could be done about intentional sins?

Leviticus Chapter 16 gives instructions for a Special Sacrifice to be offered just once a year, on the 10th day of the 7th month, Tishri.

On that day, a male representative of each family in Israel was to assemble at the Tabernacle. Wives and children could accompany if so desired. On this particular day, all of Israel was to *"fast"* and do no work, actually, the only *"fast day"* required by the Law of Moses in the space of a year.

The High Priest, following carefully the prescribed steps, brought the Blood of the Sacrifice into the inner room (Holy of Holies) of the Tabernacle and there sprinkled the blood on the Cover (Mercy Seat) of the Ark of the Covenant.

The Sacrificial Animal was a *"Sin-Offering for the people"* (Lev. 16:15) and is specifically said to have been *"because of the uncleanness and rebellion of the Israelites, whatever their sins have been"* (Lev. 16:16, 21). That annual Sacrifice, made before the Lord, was an *"Atonement . . . to be made once a year for all the sins of the Israelites"* (Lev. 16:34).

Following it, Israel was told, *"You will be*

clean from all your sins" (Lev. 16:30).

The Old Testament Sacrificial System made provision, then, for Atonement of both unintentional and willful sins. It assured Israel that God could and would forgive sins when His people came to Him in the way He prescribed.

ATONEMENT IN THE NEW TESTAMENT

In the New Testament *"Atonement"* translates the Greek words *"hilasterion"* (Rom. 3:25; Heb. 9:5), *"hilaskomai"* (Heb. 2:17), and *"hilasmos"* (I Jn. 2:2; 4:10). One Translation has it *"Mercy Seat"* in Hebrews 9:5 and *"Propitiation"* in the other Passages.

In Greek culture, the word group denoting *"Propitiation"* carried with it the idea of acting in some way to avert the terrible, destructive powers of the gods and, if possible, to win the gods over to act favorably.

The Greek Translation of the Old Testament (the Septuagint) chose this word group when translating *"kippur."* Thus, the *"Atonement"* reflects the Old Testament, and the *"Propitiation"* reflects the Greek emphasis. So, all of these words reflect the word *"Atonement."*

When we look into the New Testament Passages themselves, we learn much about how the Coming of Jesus filled the Old Testament Sacrifices with special meaning.

THE ATONEMENT AND FAITH

In Romans 3:25, Paul raises a question: How can God justly have left past sins unpunished? The implication of this question is that Sacrificial Animals surely could *not* have fairly satisfied the Justice of God. People and animals are of different orders and value.

Yet from the beginning, God was willing to accept a person's Faith in the place of Righteousness, and, admittedly, this seems unfair.

Paul's answer is that we can understand the fairness of it now that Jesus has been presented as *"A Sacrifice of Atonement."* It is on the basis of the Atonement Jesus accomplished that God is shown to have been just and fair in forgiving those who have Faith.

THE INCARNATION AND THE ATONEMENT

Hebrews 2:17 argues that Jesus must have

become a True Human Being to serve both as the High Priest Who offered the Atoning Sacrifice to God and as the Sacrifice Itself. Hebrews Chapter 9 develops this theme.

The Ark, with its Golden Cover (Mercy Seat) on which Atoning Blood was spilled (Heb. 9:5), was *"an illustration for the present time"* (Heb. 9:9). All the Sacrifices offered there were *"not able to clear the conscience of the worshiper"* (Heb. 9:9).

In fact, those repeated Sacrifices only reminded Israel that they were sinners who constantly needed forgiveness. But these Sacrifices have now been superseded by the Single Sacrifice of Jesus Christ Himself. This Sacrifice does make the Believer holy and takes away all sins (Heb. 9:23-10:14).

JESUS AS THE ATONING SACRIFICE FOR OUR SINS

John explores the meaning of Jesus' Atonement for you and me as we live in this world as Believers and, at times, fall into sin (I Jn. 1:8-9). When we come to God and confess our sins, He forgives and cleanses us, for Jesus, *"The Atoning Sacrifice for our sins"* (I Jn. 2:2), speaks up in our defense (I Jn. 2:1).

The Love that God has for us is fully and decisively seen in the fact that God *"sent His Son as an Atoning Sacrifice for our sins"* (I Jn. 4:10).

Each of the elements found in the Old Testament Doctrine of Atonement is present in the New Testament. Here too are guilty human beings who have sinned and deserve punishment. Here too is a Sacrifice, provided by God. Here too is forgiveness for sins, won by identifying by Faith with the Atoning Sacrifice.

The wonder of the New Testament Revelation is that at last we see the Glory of God's Eternal Plan. He has Himself in Christ chosen to become the Sacrifice through which humanity can be released from the grip of sin and death.

JESUS' DEATH AS ATONEMENT

The history of theology has seen several theories advanced to explain how the Death of Jesus wins Forgiveness. One early theory noted that Jesus' Death frees the Believer from the dominion of Satan (Col. 2:15).

Therefore, some assume that Jesus died to pay a ransom to Satan. But this completely overlooks the need for forgiveness.

In the 12th Century, a *"moral influence"* theory was promulgated. According to this theory, the Life and Death of Jesus demonstrated God's Love so dramatically that human beings, who mistrusted God, were relieved. They learned in Jesus that God was never angry with them, and it is this discovery that moves human beings to Love God and to turn from their sins. But this theory as well, completely overlooks the fact of guilt and the need for forgiveness.

Anselm of Canterbury clearly stated the Orthodox Theory in the 11th Century: he taught that Jesus' Death was Substitutionary. God's Justice demanded that sin's debt be paid. God's Love sent Jesus to pay this debt for us.

The whole Bible speaks to these Truths. The Teaching of the New Testament corresponds, as reality does to shadow, with the practices of the Old Testament.

By Faith the sinner, guilty and deserving punishment, identifies with the One Who died as a Sacrifice in place of the sinner. That Sacrifice which is ordained by God, is accepted by God, and the sinner is pronounced forgiven. Actually, it is the Doctrine of Substitution and Identification.

The Symbolism as well as the direct Teaching of the New Testament shows that Jesus did take our place on the Cross and died there as our Substitute. United now with Jesus by Faith, we are considered both to have died with Him and now to be raised to New Life with Him, and one could even say, *"In Him"* (Rom. 6:1-10).

SUBSTITUTION AND IDENTIFICATION

The Old Testament shows us that Atonement calls for a Sacrifice: a life given for our life. The guilty must come in God's prescribed Way, trusting God to accept the Substitute (Jesus) that He Himself has ordained, and trusting Him to extend the Promised Forgiveness.

The New Testament shows us that the Sacrificial Practices ordained in the Old Testament were instructive: they foreshadowed the Death of Jesus on Calvary and prepared us to understand the meaning of that Death.

Jesus died as the Lamb of God, as our Substitute, and it is on the basis of His Shed Blood that God offers full and free Forgiveness to all who accept Him by Faith.

As stated, He Alone is our Substitute, ordained by God and acceptable by God, and we in our identification with Him, having Faith in Him, receive the benefit of His Sacrifice, which frees us from all sin and removes the guilt. It is called *"Justification by Faith."* However, in our Identification with Him, even though it pertains to all He is and all He has done, more particularly, it points to Calvary and the Resurrection. It is in that Atoning Work that we must be careful to identify with Him, for it was in that alone in which we were Redeemed.

(Most of the thoughts on Atonement were derived from Lawrence O. Richards.)

(12) "WHEREFORE, AS BY ONE MAN SIN ENTERED INTO THE WORLD, AND DEATH BY SIN; AND SO DEATH PASSED UPON ALL MEN, FOR THAT ALL HAVE SINNED:"

The phrase, *"Wherefore, as by one man sin entered into the world,"* narrates the facts as to the entrance of sin and death by one man Adam. As well, this argument includes the introduction of Life and Sanctification by the Second Man, the Lord from Heaven.

These two great Federal Heads of their respective sons are here contrasted; and the old nature and the new nature exhibited in opposition.

The argument of verses 12 and 18 is that the one disobedience of the first man (Adam) assured death for all men, and the one obedience of the Second Man (Christ Jesus) secured Life for all men.

That is, all the sons of the first Adam by reason of their relationship to him and because they possess his sinful nature, stand in death, and all the sons of the Second Adam in virtue of their relationship to Him, and because they possess His Spirit, stand in Life (Williams).

"World" in the Greek is *"kosmos,"* and means *"the human race."* It is the same word used in John 3:16 of the world of sinners.

Sin originated with the Angel Lucifer, who in rebelling against God contracted a sinful

NOTES

nature. Adam in his disobedience was the channel through which sin entered the human race. Through sin, death entered the race, physical and spiritual.

The literal Greek which follows is, *"And thus into all men death came throughout."* That is, when death entered the race, it went throughout the race, affecting everyone.

The reason why death affects all, Paul says, is that all sinned. Here Adam is looked upon as the federal head of the race, and that when he sinned all of humanity sinned in him. It is Adam's initial sin that constituted him a sinner in which all human beings participated, and which brings death upon all. In other words, we are sinners, not necessarily because we have committed acts of sin, but because Adam sinned (Wuest).

THE MANNER OF CREATION

Every evidence is that when God created the Angels, He created them all at the same time. Consequently, even though Angels have different ranks, as far as age is concerned they are all the same. Consequently, there have never been any baby Angels.

So, when the Angel Lucifer sinned (Isa. 14:12-15; Ezek. 28:11-19), his sin affected only himself. Even though a third of the Angels threw in their lot with him, such was by their own volition, which made their sin even worse (Rev. 12:4).

As to whether the Lord made any attempt to redeem these fallen Angels, the Scripture is silent.

HUMAN BEINGS AND PROCREATION

After bringing the world back to a habitable state (Gen. Chpt. 1), God then set about to create the human family (Gen. 1:26-27). However, He did this totally different than His Creation of Angels, in that He only made a pair of human beings (male and female), and gave them the power of procreation, i.e., to bring offspring into the world.

Whereas this was a tremendous honor and privilege bestowed upon humanity, still, it also imposed a great risk. The risk being that the seed of Adam carried with it the potential not only of great Blessing and Life, but also of death. Whatever he did, be it positive or negative, would affect the entirety of the coming human race, and irrespective as to how many there would be. Whatever he was, the offspring would be.

In his original Creation before the Fall, Adam was destined to bring sons and daughters of God into the world, which as stated, was an honor of unprecedented proportions, even that far above the Angels (Lk. 3:38). In fact, every indication is, that before the Fall Adam outranked the Angels (Ps. 8).

Due to the fact that Adam was originally created in the Image of God (Gen. 1:27), He also had the power to create even as God, and which has passed down to his offspring. There is no record in the Word of God that Angels have the power to create anything, even though they are powerful creatures within themselves.

Observing man in his fallen state, it is not easy to grasp the fact that he was originally created higher than the Angels, but the evidence is that he was, and will be again. David wrote, *"What is man, that thou art mindful of him? And the son of man, that thou visitest him?*

"For Thou hast made him a little lower than the Angels (God), *and hast crowned him with Glory and Honour.*

"Thou madest him to have dominion over the Works of Thy Hands; Thou hast put all things under his feet" (Ps. 8:4-6).

The word *"Angels"* in Psalm 8:5 should have been translated *"God,"* because David used the Hebrew word *"Elohim,"* which means *"God,"* and is so translated some 239 times elsewhere in the Old Testament.

However, when Adam fell from his lofty spiritual position given to him by God, he no longer had the ability or power to bring sons and daughters of God into the world, but now only sons and daughters *"in His Own Likeness, after His Image"* (Gen. 5:3). That speaks of the fallen state and original sin. In other words, every baby born thereafter, which has now numbered billions, was born with the awful poison of death.

THE DEGREE OF THE FALL

Adam fell from total God consciousness, which is bliss and security unparalleled in human thinking, down to the far, far lower level of total self-consciousness. In other

words, man lost all consciousness of God.

It is very difficult for man, even Redeemed man, to understand exactly how far that man has fallen, due to the fact that it is impossible to relate to something of which there is no example.

And yet, there has been one example, and I speak of the Lord Jesus Christ. In Him, the Second Adam, we observe total God-consciousness, but at the same time the perfidy of the fallen race which murdered Him. In Him we see what man was before the Fall, and the total depravity of man in murdering, in cold blood one might quickly add, the only Good Person Who has ever lived.

THE EFFECT ON MAN

Due to the Fall, man is a perverted creature. In revolting against the purpose of his being, which is to live and act entirely to the glory of his Sovereign and Beneficent Creator and to fulfill His Will, he ceases to be truly man.

His true manhood consists in conformity to the Image of God in which he was created. This Image of God is manifested in man's original capacity for communion with His Creator; in his enjoyment exclusively of what is good; in his rationality which makes it possible for him alone of all creatures to hear and respond to the Word of God; in his knowledge of the Truth and in the freedom which that knowledge ensures; and in Government, as the head of God's Creation, in obedience to the mandate to have dominion over every living thing and to subdue the Earth.

THE IMAGE OF GOD

Yet, rebel as he will against the Image of God with which he has been stamped, man cannot erase it, because it is part of his very constitution as man.

It is evident, for example, in his pursuit of scientific knowledge, in his harnessing of the forces of nature, and in his development of culture, art and civilization. But at the same time the efforts of fallen man are cursed with frustration.

This frustration is itself a proof of the perversity of the human heart. Thus, history shows that the very discoveries and advances which have promised most good to mankind have through misuse brought great evils in their train. The man who does not Love God does not Love his fellowmen. He is driven by selfish motives. The image of Satan, the great hater of God and man, is superimposed upon him. The result of the Fall is that man now knows good and evil.

TRUTH

The Spiritual and Ethical effects of the Fall are nowhere more graphically described than by Paul in Romans 1:18. All men, however ungodly and unrighteous they may be, know the Truth about God and themselves; but they wickedly suppress this Truth. It is, however, an inescapable Truth, for the fact of the *"Eternal Power and Godhead"* of the Creator is both manifested within them, by their very constitution as God's Creatures made in His Image, and also manifested all around them in the whole created order of the Universe which bears eloquent Testimony to its origin as God's Handiwork (Ps. 19:1).

DARKNESS RATHER THAN LIGHT

Basically, therefore, man's state is not one of ignorance but of knowledge. His condemnation is that he loves darkness rather than Light. His refusal to glorify God as God and his ingratitude lead him into intellectual vanity and futility.

Arrogantly professing himself to be wise, he in fact becomes a fool (Rom. 1:21). Having wilfully cut himself adrift from the Creator in Whom Alone the meaning of his existence is to be found, he must seek that meaning elsewhere, for his creaturely finitude makes it impossible for him to cease from being a spiritual creature. And his search becomes ever more foolish and degrading.

It carries him into the gross irrationality of superstition and idolatry, into vileness and unnatural vice, and into all those evils, social and international, which give rise to the hatreds and miseries that disfigure our world.

The Fall has, in brief, overthrown the true dignity of man (Rom. 1:23).

THE BIBLICAL DOCTRINE

It will be seen that the Scriptural Doctrine of the Fall altogether contradicts the

NOTES

popular modern view of man as a being who, by a slow evolutionary development, has succeeded in rising from the primeval fear and groping ignorance of an humble origin to proud heights of religious sensitivity and insight. However, the Bible does not portray man as risen, but as fallen, and in the most desperate of situations.

It is only against this background that God's Saving Action in Christ takes on its proper significance. Through the grateful appropriation by Faith of Christ's Atoning Work, what was forfeited by the Fall is restored to man: his true and intended dignity is recovered, the purpose of life recaptured, the Image of God restored, and the way into the paradise of intimate communion with God reopened.

Even though modern thought denies such, the New Testament proclaims the Fall as a definite event in human history — an event, moreover, of such critical consequences for the whole human race that it stands side by side with and explains the other great crucial event of history, namely the Coming of Christ to save the world (Rom. 5:12; I Cor. 15:21). Consequently, mankind, together with the rest of the created order, awaits a third and conclusive event of history, namely the Second Advent of Christ at the end of this age, when the effects of the Fall will be finally abolished, unbelievers eternally judged, and the renewed creation, the new heavens and new earth wherein Righteousness dwells, be established in accordance with Almighty God's immutable purposes (Acts 3:20; Rom. 8:19; II Pet. 3:13; Rev. Chpts. 21-22).

Thus, by God's Grace all that was lost in Adam, and much more than that, is restored in Christ.

(Bibliography: N. P. Williams, *"The Ideas of the Fall and of Original Sin"*; J. G. Machen, *"The Christian View of Man"*; J. Murray, *"The Imputation of Adam's Sin."*)

The phrase, *"And death by sin,"* speaks first of all of spiritual death, and by consequence, physical death.

When one reads these phrases, he is reading the cause of all of the suffering, sorrow, heartache, war, sickness and man's inhumanity to man, which characterizes the world and has done so since the Fall.

The phrase, *"And so death passed upon all men, for that all have sinned,"* consists of a two-pronged thrust.

The first prong consists of original sin. Inasmuch as the wages of sin is death, the dread malady of spiritual and physical death passes to every baby that is born. The well is poisoned, and it can only produce death.

Inasmuch as man is born in sin, this means he has a depraved nature, and, consequently, cannot live above sin, at least within himself.

Man keeps denying the fact of original sin and the depraved nature, claiming that proper education, environment, association, or even scientific research, can alleviate the situation. However the terrible sin problem remains, even as it must remain, at least as it responds to man's efforts.

The 20th Century is supposed to have been the most enlightened century of all the ages. To be sure, it has spawned the greatest scientific achievements in the annals of human history. And yet, the early 1940's witnessed the most horrifying spectacle of human history in the slaughter of some 6,000,000 Jews by Hitler's henchmen.

The 1920's on up through the 1970's witnessed as well, the deaths of untold millions more at the hands of Russian and Chinese Communism. Each decade in this century in fact, has brought a fresh horror whether in Africa or Europe, etc. So much for modern enlightenment!

Even though the Old Testament graphically outlines the horrors of sin, holding forth the Atonement as the only answer, the New Testament while agreeing with the Old, at the same time holds out an astounding difference. All the old terms and concepts of the Old Testament are brought over into the New, but deepened and strangely transformed.

The one factor which makes this great difference is the Work of Jesus Christ. He provides something which the Saints of the Old Testament yearned for but could never find: real and certain victory over sin.

The Doctrine of sin in the New Testament is dominated by the assurance that Christ has come to conquer this monster. Thus, whatever is said to emphasize sin's deadliness and seriousness serves to magnify the greatness of the Salvation from sin which Christ has obtained.

NOTES

As we should expect, each of the New Testament writers has a characteristic way of speaking about sin. However, Paul is by all counts the most profound. But there is no essential disharmony amid the variety. Above all, they are all dominated by the assurance of Christ's effective answer to sin.

As the first prong dealt with the fact of sin, i.e., *"original sin,"* the second prong deals with the nature of sin, which stems from the depraved nature, and guarantees that man will sin. So, man is shot down in two ways. He is a sinner by birth and a sinner by choice.

(13) "(FOR UNTIL THE LAW SIN WAS IN THE WORLD: BUT SIN IS NOT IMPUTED WHEN THERE IS NO LAW."

The phrase, *"For until the Law sin was in the world,"* pictures Paul now proceeding to explain what he has said about all having sinned.

First of all, he is speaking of the Law of Moses, which is obvious. This Law properly exposed sin and defined it, which of course, Law is supposed to do.

From the time of Adam unto Moses was a period of about 2400 years. During this time there was no Law given by God regarding sin. In other words, due to the lack of Law sin was not exposed and defined. Nevertheless, the absence of the Law did not mean that sin was absent. In fact, it was in the world just as much as ever, so bad in fact, that the Lord was forced to drown the entirety of mankind during the flood, with the exception of one family, that of Noah. In other words, sin had become so absolutely awful that the Lord had to perform major surgery on the Earth, or else the entirety of the creation would be lost, which it almost was anyway.

The phrase, *"But sin is not imputed when there is no Law,"* simply means that those living between Adam and Moses had no sins charged to their account by reason of the non-existence of the Written Law. However, that in no way meant they were not sinners, and as well would reap the result of their sin. It just meant that God did not reckon to their account each individual sin (Rev. 20:12).

(14) "NEVERTHELESS DEATH REIGNED FROM ADAM TO MOSES, EVEN OVER THEM THAT HAD NOT SINNED AFTER THE SIMILITUDE OF ADAM'S TRANSGRESSION, WHO IS THE FIGURE OF HIM THAT WAS TO COME."

The phrase, *"Nevertheless death reigned from Adam to Moses,"* proclaims the fact that even though individual sins were not reckoned to the account of each person, and because the Law had not yet been given, still, each person ultimately died, which proved the fact of their sin. Logic leads us to conclude that their death came by reason of Adam's sin and that they sinned in him, their Federal Head.

The phrase, *"Even over them that had not sinned after the similitude of Adam's transgression,"* has reference to the fact that death did not come to these people by personal sin, as it did in the case of Adam. Irrespective, they were just as guilty even though thy did not commit the same transgression he did. In fact, their guilt was in his *"transgression,"* as is the guilt of all!

The subject is sin and its reproductive energy. One command was given to Adam. He disobeyed it. Many commands were given to Moses. They were all disobeyed. So the trespass abounded, i.e., the principle of evil which caused one trespass in Adam caused countless trespasses under Law, and so manifested sin's abounding fertility.

A fact of science illustrates the matter. A germ when acted on by a certain temperature produces one deadly microbe, but on the temperature being raised, it produces millions.

Such was the moral effect that followed the introduction of Law. The nature of the principle of evil (termed *"sin"*) and its venomous energy, were made apparent to man's consciousness and to history (Williams).

The phrase, *"Who is the figure of Him that was to come,"* actually speaks of Christ.

It is used in a Doctrinal sense of a type, a person or thing prefiguring a future (Messianic) person or thing; in this sense Adam is called a Type of Jesus Christ, each of the two having exercised a preeminent influence upon the human race (the former destructive, the latter, saving) (Thayer).

This is added so as to bring around the thought to the main subject of the Chapter, the Reconciliation of all mankind through Christ, to which the Scriptural account of the condemnation of all mankind through Adam is given here. Adam is used as an analogy.

"Who" refers to Adam, who has just been for the first time named; *"He that was to come"* is Christ Who is called, in I Corinthians 15:45, *"The Last Adam."*

As stated, Adam was a Type of Christ in that both represented entire humanity; one as the representative and author of the fallen, the other of restored, humanity — the transgression of the one and the obedience of the other alike affecting all (vss. 18-19).

However, there is a vast difference between the two cases; and this is pointed out in verses 15, 16, and 17, which follow (Barmby).

(15) "BUT NOT AS THE OFFENCE, SO ALSO IS THE FREE GIFT. FOR IF THROUGH THE OFFENCE OF ONE MANY BE DEAD, MUCH MORE THE GRACE OF GOD, AND THE GIFT BY GRACE, WHICH IS BY ONE MAN, JESUS CHRIST, HATH ABOUNDED UNTO MANY."

The phrase, *"But not as the offence, so also is the free gift,"* would have probably been better translated, *"As the offence, much more the free gift."* Paul is here drawing an analogy, by drawing a contrast.

In other words he is saying, that Adam's offense touched the entirety of the world and for all time, at least until Jesus rectified all things, but as well, so did the Grace of God in His Free Gift of Salvation. However, the idea is this:

The Grace of God was not merely on the same level as the *"offence,"* but of a much greater proportion. That's what he means by the phrase, *"But not as the offence."*

"Offense" in the Greek is *"paraptoma,"* and means *"a falling alongside, a deviation from the right path."* Adam's original sin was the violation of the known Will of God.

"Free Gift" is *"Charisma,"* and means *"A Gift of Grace, a favor which one receives without merit of his own,"* referring here to the Gift of Eternal Life in Christ Jesus.

The one transgression or *"offence"* of Adam resulted in the physical and spiritual death of all. However, as the Fall of Adam caused great evil, the far greater Work of the Far Greater Christ shall much more cause far greater results of good (Vincent). And yet, there is even a greater thrust in this statement:

The Character of God is such from a Christian point of view, that the comparison gives a much more certain basis of belief, in what is gained through the Second Adam, than in the certainties of sin and death through the first Adam (Schaff and Riddle). In other words, much was lost in the Fall, but that will be gained back and even much more.

The phrase, *"For if through the offence of one many be dead,"* speaks of all who have died without God. Starting at the beginning and counting all the generations, this number would be in the billions. It speaks of spiritual death which is separation from God, which is the most horrible thing that could ever happen to anyone. (In effect it speaks of the whole of humanity.)

SPIRITUAL DEATH

Spiritual Death is a Divine Penalty, and was brought about, as is obvious here, because of Adam's transgression. Romans 6:23 regards death as *"the wages of sin,"* i.e., as the due reward for sin. In addressing this, Paul spoke of certain sinners who knew God's Decree, but violated it anyway, with him adding that those who do such things deserve to die (Rom. 1:32).

It is this thought of God's Decree that underlies John's reference to the *"mortal sin"* (I Jn. 5:16). In essence this speaks of blaspheming the Holy Spirit, of which we will not now go into its many nuances. However, John's statement, plus many others in the Bible present to us a very important Truth. It enables us to see the full horror of spiritual death (being without God forever).

At the same time, these dire warnings give us hope. Men are *not* caught up in a web woven by blind fate, so that, once having sinned, nothing can ever be done about it. God is over the whole process, and if He has decreed that death is the penalty of sin, which He has, He has also determined to given Eternal Life to sinful men, that is if they will only take advantage of the Atonement provided by Christ at Calvary.

NOTES

THE SECOND DEATH

Sometimes the New Testament emphasizes the serious consequences of sin by referring to *"the second death"* (Jude vs. 12; Rev. 2:11). This expression signifies eternal perdition.

It is to be understood along with Passages wherein our Lord spoke of *"eternal fire prepared for the Devil and his Angels"* (Mat. 25:41), *"eternal punishment"* (set in contrast to *"Eternal Life"*) (Mat. 25:46), and the like.

The final state of impenitent man is variously described as death, punishment, being lost, etc. As stated, it is a state to be regarded with horror.

GOD, LOVE, AND DAMNATION

Many years ago I preached a Message entitled, *"Can A Loving God Condemn A Soul To Eternal Hell, Burn Him There Forever And Forever, And Justify Himself In Doing So?"*

It is quite a question!

Sometimes the objection is made that Eternal Hell (spiritual death) is inconsistent with the view of God as a Loving God. However, such overlooks the fact that spiritual death is a *state* (in other words, all who are without God are spiritually dead at this very moment), as well as an *event* (the ultimate eternal conclusion being the Lake of Fire).

When we have grasped the Truth that death is a state, we see the impossibility of the impenitent (those who refuse to repent) being Saved. Salvation for such is a contradiction in terms. For Salvation a man must pass from death into Life, which can only be done by the born-again experience, and is brought about only through Jesus Christ (Jn. 5:24).

No! Considering what God has done to save lost humanity in the giving of His Only Son, Jesus Christ, to serve as a Sacrifice of death that men may be Saved, God is not only just in condemning to Eternal Hell those who refuse such Salvation, but contrary to modern thinking, He would be unjust in not doing so.

The phrase, *"Much more the Grace of God,"* proclaims the inexhaustible power of this attribute.

If one man's trespass had such far-reaching

effects, much more must the Grace of God have no less far-reaching effects. In effect, God's Grace must be more powerful than man's trespass, which it is! As well, it is not just somewhat more, but *"much more."*

THE FREE GIFT

The phrase, *"And the Gift by Grace,"* presents Jesus as that *"Gift."*

The one trespass of the one original transgressor did indeed render all mankind liable to condemnation; but the Free Gift in Christ annulled the effect, not only of that one trespass, but also of all subsequent trespasses of mankind; an immense debt, accumulating through the ages of human history, in addition to the original debt, was by that one free grant obliterated.

However, we are not to gather from these statements that the Holy Spirit through Paul is speaking of a Universal Salvation to the extent that due to what Christ did, all are Saved. The Truth is, all can be Saved, but the Truth also is that all are not Saved, and in fact, most will not be Saved, with only a *"few"* actually accepting Eternal Life, at least considering the whole of mankind (Mat. 7:13-14).

Irrespective, the fault is not God's but man's. The Lord has made Salvation available to all, and while it is true that some have more opportunity than others, still, if anyone wants to come, they can (Rev. 22:17).

The phrase, *"Which is by One Man, Jesus Christ, hath abounded unto many,"* signifies that this *"One Man"* The Lord Jesus Christ, nullified the offense of the *"One Man"* Adam.

In fact, the original trespass introduced a temporary reign of death, while the Free Gift of Righteousness introduced Life, in which the partakers of the Gift themselves — triumphant over death, will live and reign forever in Christ.

As stated, this *"Gift of Grace"* has *"abounded unto many,"* but in effect, it could abound unto all, that is, if they will only believe.

(16) "AND NOT AS IT WAS BY ONE THAT SINNED, SO IS THE GIFT: FOR THE JUDGMENT WAS BY ONE TO CONDEMNATION, BUT THE FREE GIFT IS OF MANY OFFENCES UNTO JUSTIFICATION."

The phrase, *"And not as it was by one that sinned, so is the Gift,"* presents the same thing as the first phrase of the last verse. Paul is once again drawing a contrast. One man Adam, brought the transgression, while One Man Christ, brought Eternal Life. However, there the similarity ends.

The contrast of Eternal Life as given by Christ up beside the offense of Adam, quickly becomes obvious.

Adam's one transgression affected all, even though all the billions had not yet been born and as a result, could not have committed any sin. However, they were judged as sinners, and, in fact, must be judged as sinners, because all were in Adam.

By comparison, the *"Free Gift"* of Salvation as purchased by Christ at Calvary, was not for the unborn, but for those who actually were sinners, in effect having committed many trespasses. Irrespective, simple Faith in Christ, would wash clean all sin, in effect cleansing from all unrighteousness.

The phrase, *"For the Judgment was by one to condemnation,"* respected Adam failing God, and then incurring the Judgment of God which was an absolute necessity. Perfect Righteousness must condemn all sin in the flesh, for there is no alternative as should be obvious. Consequently, the *"condemnation"* came upon all, because theoretically, all were in Adam's loins.

The phrase, *"But the Free Gift is of many offences unto Justification,"* verifies what we have said about the Eternal Life offered by Christ to believing sinners. As stated, this *"Free Gift"* cleanses from *"many offences,"* in effect, *"all offences."*

As well, this *"Free Gift"* not only addresses itself to all offenses, but as well effects a Legal Work which God can justly recognize, and declare the sinner *"not guilty."* He can do such because of the sinner's Faith in Christ, Who took the penalty for all of these offenses, thereby, wiping the slate clean, at least for all who will believe. Once again, this is *"Justification by Faith,"* which is the bedrock of Paul's argument respecting the New Covenant.

(17) "FOR IF BY ONE MAN'S OFFENCE DEATH REIGNED BY ONE; MUCH MORE THEY WHICH RECEIVE ABUNDANCE OF

GRACE AND OF THE GIFT OF RIGH-
TEOUSNESS SHALL REIGN IN LIFE BY
ONE, JESUS CHRIST.)"

The phrase, *"For if by one man's offence
death reigned by one,"* refers to Adam's failure, with the result being *"death."* Consequently, *"death reigns"* over all of mankind.

Reign in the Greek is *"basileuo,"* and
means *"to rule from a foundation of power."*
As a result, man who is God's choicest creation, is little able to utilize his ability and
energy, with death overtaking him even on
short notice.

In fact, man was not originally created
to die. Even though he was of flesh, even
as the Resurrected Body will be of flesh, still,
it was flesh that was incorruptible and immortal. Corruption and mortality came after
the Fall.

The phrase, *"Much more they which receive abundance of Grace,"* proclaims unlimited, unmerited favor. It is not just
"Grace," but *"Abundance of Grace!"* All of
this comes upon one exhibiting simple Faith
in Christ. The idea is, that the *"Grace"* is
more, *"much more"* than the debilitating
effects of sin.

The phrase, *"And of the Gift of Righteousness,"* once again proclaims *"Righteousness,"*
in effect, God's Righteousness, which speaks
of the essence of perfect morality. As stated,
it is a Free Gift, and in fact must be a *"Free
Gift,"* if it is to be by Grace.

The phrase, *"Shall reign in life by One,
Jesus Christ,"* proclaims the Believer as
"reigning," even as death had reigned, but
from a position of much greater power than
that of death. All is in *"Jesus Christ."*

In this verse, Death and Life are here contrasted; but while it says *"death reigned"* over
man it does not say that life reigns over the
Believer, for that would invest life with tyranny, but it says that the Believer reigns in
life, and thus the environment of freedom
and liberty is preserved. This life is legally
secured by the Life and Death of Christ.

If in fact Life reigned over humanity, it
would be the same as Adam and Eve eating
of the Tree of Life after the Fall, and thereby
living forever on Earth in that fallen state.
They would have continued to fall deeper
and deeper into depravity without physical

NOTES

death bringing this hell to a halt. The results would have been unthinkable, which is
the reason God drove them out of the Garden (Gen. 3:22-24).

Christ's one Righteous act of obedience was
His obedience unto Death (Phil. 2:8); but this
was the climax for His whole Mission on Earth,
which was one great act of obedience.

"The many," therefore, who are born of
Adam, and consequently possess his sinful
nature, are hopelessly lost, for they cannot
undo the fact of their birth, and the many
who are born of the Second Adam, and, consequently, possess His Nature, are absolutely
Saved, as much and even more, as those of
Adam are absolutely lost. However, this Salvation is afforded only to those who are *"in"*
Christ Jesus.

VICTORY OVER DEATH

An interesting feature of New Testament
Teaching on Death is that the emphasis is
on Life. If we look up a concordance we find
that in most places where the word *"dead"* is
used, it is of Resurrection from the dead or
the like. The Scripture faces death, as it
faces all reality. But its interest is in Life,
and death is treated more or less incidentally as that from which men are Saved.

Christ took upon Him our nature (the
Incarnation) *"That through death He might
destroy him that had the power of death,
that is, the Devil"* (Heb. 2:14).

CHRIST CAME TO PUT
AN END TO DEATH

The Devil's power is always regarded as subject to God's overruling (Job 2:6; Lk. 12:5).
He is no absolute disposer of death. Nevertheless death, the negation of Life, is his
proper sphere.

Christ came to put an end to death. It
was through death, as the Passage in Hebrews indicates, that He defeated Satan. It
was through death that He put away our sin.
*"The death He died, He died to sin once for
all"* (Rom. 6:10).

Apart from Christ, death is the supreme
enemy, the symbol of our alienation from
God, the ultimate horror. But Christ has
used death to deliver men from death. In
other words, He died that men may live.

It is significant that the New Testament can speak of Believers as *"sleeping rather than as dying"* (I Thess. 4:14).

Jesus bore the full horror of death. Therefore, for those who are *"in Christ"* death has been transformed so that it is no more than sleep.

THE RESURRECTION

The extent of the victory over death that Christ won is indicated by His Resurrection. *"Christ being raised from* (the) *death will never die again; death no longer has dominion over Him"* (Rom. 6:9).

The Resurrection is the great Triumphal Event, and the whole of the New Testament note of victory originates here. Christ is *"The Author of Life"* (Acts 3:15), *"Lord both of the dead and of the living"* (Rom. 14:9), *"The Word of Life"* (I Jn. 1:1).

His Victory over death is complete. And His Victory is made available to His People. Death's destruction is certain (I Cor. 15:26, 54; Rev. 21:4). The Second Death has no power over the Believer (Rev. 2:11; 20:6).

In keeping with this the New Testament understands Eternal Life not as the immortality of the soul, but in terms of the Resurrection of the body. Nothing could more graphically illustrate the finality and the completeness of death's defeat.

A GLORIOUS PRESENT AND
A GLORIOUS FUTURE

Not only is there a glorious future for the Believer, there is also a glorious present. The Believer has already passed out of death and into Life (Jn. 5:24; I Jn. 3:14). He is *"free from the Law of sin and death"* (Rom. 8:2).

Death cannot separate him from God (Rom. 8:38). Jesus said, *"If anyone keeps My Word, he will never see death"* (Jn. 8:51). Such words do not deny the reality of biological death. Rather they point us to the Truth that the death of Jesus means that the Believer has passed altogether out of the state which is death.

He is brought into a new state, which is aptly characterized as life. He will in due course pass through the gateway we call death. But the sting has been drawn. The death of Jesus means victory over death for

His followers.

(Bibliography: *"The Shape of Death,"* K. Rahner; *"On the Theology of Death,"* Leon Morris.)

(18) "THEREFORE AS BY THE OFFENCE OF ONE JUDGMENT CAME UPON ALL MEN TO CONDEMNATION; EVEN SO BY THE RIGHTEOUSNESS OF ONE THE FREE GIFT CAME UPON ALL MEN UNTO JUSTIFICATION OF LIFE."

The phrase, *"Therefore as by the offence of one Judgment came upon all men to condemnation,"* proclaims Paul saying the same thing that he has said several times and for purpose.

When the Holy Spirit repeats something of this nature and especially in as many ways as Paul has repeated it, among other things, He is proclaiming the significance of the event and that we should understand what is being said. As should be obvious, for man to know the reason for his present dilemma is necessary. If he does not know the dilemma and what caused such, at the same time, he will not as well know and understand the solution.

Once again, Paul states the cause of the terrible Judgment which has come upon all men — even a Judgment of Condemnation. It came by the Fall of the Federal Head, Adam.

The phrase, *"Even so by the Righteousness of One the Free Gift came upon all men unto Justification of Life,"* now proclaims the glorious solution.

Man had no Righteousness, and in fact, could not obtain any Righteousness, that is, the type which God would accept. Therefore, the *"Righteousness"* which is of *"One,"* i.e., *"Jesus Christ,"* is freely given to all who will simply believe. It is called *"Justification of Life."*

This means that sinners are made Righteous by simply believing Christ, and are thereby, declared as *"Justified,"* which means *"not guilty."* Sin had brought death, but Justification brings *"Life."*

(19) "FOR AS BY ONE MAN'S DISOBEDIENCE MANY WERE MADE SINNERS, SO BY THE OBEDIENCE OF ONE SHALL MANY BE MADE RIGHTEOUS."

The phrase, *"For as by one man's disobedience many were made sinners,"* actually refers to all, which are *"many."*

"Disobedience" in the Greek is *"parakoe,"* and means *"to mishear, or to disobey — neglect to hear."* This is one of the nine words for sin in the New Testament.

It describes the nature of Adam's first act of sin, the one act that plunged the entire race into sin with its accompanying degradation and misery.

Disobedience in a more fuller sense, is *"a failing to hear"* or *"a hearing amiss,"* the notion of active disobedience which follows on this inattentive or careless hearing, being superinduced upon the word; or, it may be, the sin being regarded as already committed in the *failing to listen when God is speaking.* It need hardly be observed how continually in the Old Testament, disobedience *is* described as a refusing to hear (Jer. 11:10, 35:17); and it appears literally as such in Acts 7:57 (Trench).

The phrase, *"So by the obedience of One shall many be made Righteous,"* pertains to the obedience of Christ as opposed to the disobedience of Adam.

Though the Doctrine of the Atonement, in all its depth, is beyond our comprehension, yet it is important for us to observe the various aspects in which it is presented to us in Scripture. Here the idea suggested is that of Christ, as the Representative of humanity, satisfying Divine Righteousness by perfect obedience to the Divine Will, and thus offering to God for man what man had lost the power of offering. To do this, Jesus had to *"become obedient unto death, even the death of the Cross"* (Phil. 2:8) (Barmby).

"Obedience" in the Greek is *"hupokoe,"* and means *"to hear,"* literally *"to hear under."* The idea is that of a willing listening to authority. Thayer defines it; *"obedience, compliance, submission."*

By the one act of Adam in disobeying God, the human race was constituted sinful, and this by the Judicial Act of God. Likewise, by the One Act of Obedience of the Lord Jesus, all who believe are constituted Righteous, and this by the Judicial Act of God.

The word *"made"* as it refers to *"Righteous"* in the Greek is *"poieo,"* and *"refers to a mechanical operation such as that of making a spear out of wood and iron."* It refers

NOTES

to the act of changing a certain material object so as to fit it for a certain purpose (Wuest).

This is the reason that Salvation is far more than mere philosophy, in fact, the sinner must be made new, in effect a *"New Creature"* (II Cor. 5:17).

This completely shoots down the psychological approach of *"rehabilitation,"* which word is not even found in the Bible. Rehabilitation, as stated, stems from humanistic psychology, which claims *"to restore to a former capacity,"* or *"to restore to a condition of health or useful and constructive activity."*

The thought is good, but the actual results are zero.

First of all, how can anyone be rehabilitated who has never been habilitated?

Psychology starts from the erroneous premise that all men are good, and if they go bad, it is because of external forces, etc. So, they attempt to expose these external forces, whatever they may be, isolate them, bringing the individual around these things hopefully, to a position of health, etc.

The Bible teaches the very opposite, in that man is inherently bad (Rom. Chpts. 1, 3). Consequently, bad is all he can do, or worse! Understanding that, there is nothing to which man can be rehabilitated.

So, the Holy Spirit through Christ starts out on an entirely different premise, with the object in view of making a completely *"New Creature"* out of the sinner. In other words, He has to *"make"* Righteousness for that sinner, which He will do, and will freely impute such to him upon simple Faith in Christ (Jn. 3:16).

Surely, it should be overly obvious as to the simplicity of the Gospel as given here by Paul, that no one need misunderstand. In view of that, how can Preachers who call themselves Saved and even Spirit-filled, fall for the lie of Psychology, which is so obviously contradictory of the Gospel?

The work that man desperately needs, which is to be made a New Person in Christ, and can only be done in Christ, is not in the power of man to bring about. In fact, it is literally impossible. Common spiritual sense tells one, that if such were possible, Jesus would not have had to have come to this sinful world, especially paying the terrible price He paid for the Redemption of humanity. That should go without saying! And yet, almost the entirety of the Church, even the Pentecostal varieties whose very claim once was the Power of God, have bought into this lie. As I have asked, *"Why?"*

I think the Truth is, that these Preachers, whomever they may be, simply do not believe God anymore. They may claim to do so, but their actions speak otherwise!

(20) "MOREOVER THE LAW ENTERED, THAT THE OFFENCE MIGHT ABOUND. BUT WHERE SIN ABOUNDED, GRACE DID MUCH MORE ABOUND:"

The phrase, *"Moreover the Law entered, that the offence might abound,"* has reference to the Law of Moses.

As it has already been stated, sin was active and real before the Law, but because there was no Law, it was not imputed as offenses by the perpetrators. Nevertheless, they were still sinners and died lost.

However, when the Law of Moses was given, which was about 2400 years after Adam, its very purpose was to expose sin and define it. When it did this, offenses abounded, as would be obvious. Denney says, *"The offense is multiplied because the Law encountering the flesh, evokes its natural antagonism to God* (antagonism of the flesh to God), *and so stimulates it into disobedience. As the offense multiplied, and for several reasons, the need of Redemption, and the sense of that need were intensified."* Vincent explains, *"Not primarily of the greater consciousness and acknowledgment, but the increase of actual transgressions."*

Why did Law cause sin to abound?

First of all, Law always has that effect, even the Law of God. That is not to be misunderstood as to think that the Law of God was unholy or unrighteous. Actually, it was the very opposite! The things that God demanded of Israel, were right and proper and what man ought to do everywhere.

As we have stated previously, even though the Law had many peripheral commands and statutes, still, the central core always was the Ten Commandments. Everything as spokes on a wheel led to that hub. However, as simple as the Ten Commandments were, Israel still could not obey them, at least in her

NOTES

own power, and neither can man presently. He is totally lacking in capability of doing such, no matter how hard he tries. This is because of the depraved nature of man, due to the Fall, which Paul is addressing here.

In setting out to keep these Laws, man always failed. Actually, the harder he tried, the more he failed! The reason points to *"The Law of Sin and Death"* in his flesh (Rom. 8:2).

As well, the very presence of Law created a desire to do the very opposite of what the Law demanded. That again is *"The Law of Sin and Death."*

It should be quickly added, that the very moment the modern Christian or Church institutes Law of any nature, it will have the same effect upon the Believer as the old Law of Moses. The efforts to keep such, instead of bringing about Holiness and Righteousness as some think, do the very opposite, increases failure. The reason is obvious. That is what it is designed to do. And yet I think that every single Christian at one time or the other, has attempted to bring about Righteousness by means of some type of Law, whether originated of himself, or his Church. Such may sound good to the religious mind, but it will bode ill every time.

Actually, the design of the Law was that Israel would see that it was impossible of obedience, and then would throw themselves on the Mercy and Grace of God through the Sacrifices. However, the majority in Israel did the very opposite, actually making a Law out of trying to keep the Law, and, thereby, instituting a religion of ethics, which in reality, was no Salvation at all.

The phrase, *"But where sin abounded, Grace did much more abound,"* sums up the entirety of this scenario as delineated by Paul. Even though sin was rampant from the very beginning (after the Fall), and then abounded to mountainous proportions after the Law was given, still, Grace abounded even more, *"much more."*

Paul actually said, *"Where sin increased, Grace superabounded, and then some on top of that."* However, just because Grace abounded, did not and does not mean that one is free to sin. Paul addresses this in the next Chapter.

NOTES

The idea is, that irrespective as to how bad sin is in the life of an unbeliever, irrespective of its depths, its depravity, its death or its horror, there is always enough of the Grace of God to cleanse the sinner of all sin, in effect, setting the captive free. Regarding the Believer, Grace never gives a license to sin, but rather liberty to live a Holy Life, for Grace has power.

(21) "THAT AS SIN HATH REIGNED UNTO DEATH, EVEN SO MIGHT GRACE REIGN THROUGH RIGHTEOUSNESS UNTO ETERNAL LIFE BY JESUS CHRIST OUR LORD."

The phrase, *"That as sin hath reigned unto death,"* actually refers to reigning as a *"King."*

Here sin is personified, and refers to a nature, the totally depraved nature of the unsaved person. That reigns as an absolute monarch in his being. *"Unto death"* actually means *"in the sphere of death."* It is not a very pretty picture!

The phrase, *"Even so might Grace reign through Righteousness unto Eternal Life by Jesus Christ our Lord,"* presents what Jesus has done in order to save men from this death of sin.

Sin reigns unto death, Grace reigns unto Life — but it reigns *"through Righteousness,"* i.e., because of God's Righteous Judgment of sin at Calvary executed in the Person of His Son Jesus Christ (Williams).

"To God be the Glory, great things He
  hath done,
"So loved He the world that He gave
  us His Son,
"Who yielded His Life an Atonement
  for sin,
"And opened the lifegate that all may
  go in."

"Oh Perfect Redemption, the purchase
  of Blood,
"To every Believer the Promise of God;
"The vilest offender who truly believes,
"That moment from Jesus a pardon
  receives."

"Great things He hath taught us, great
  things He hath done,
"And great our rejoicing thro' Jesus the
  Son;

"But purer, and higher, and greater
  will be,
"Our wonder, our transport, when Jesus
  we see."

"Praise the Lord, Praise the Lord, let
  the Earth hear His Voice!
"Praise the Lord, Praise the Lord, let
  the people rejoice!
"Oh come to the Father thro' Jesus the
  Son,
"And give Him the Glory; great things
  He hath done."

CHAPTER 6

(1) "WHAT SHALL WE SAY THEN? SHALL WE CONTINUE IN SIN, THAT GRACE MAY ABOUND?"

The question, *"What shall we say then?"*, is meant to direct attention to the 20th verse of the previous Chapter.

To be sure, Paul is not asking these questions because he doesn't know the answer, but rather because of erroneous interpretations by others placed upon the great Doctrine of Grace as preached by Paul.

The Doctrines of Grace — especially that which declares Justification to be by Faith apart from works — excites the enmity of the natural heart, and this enmity expresses itself today, as it has from the first, by the outcry of verse 1.

Here human reasoning conflicts with Divine Teaching. The latter declares that man is absolutely ruined by sin and wholly unable to restore himself to God's Favor; the former teaches that man is not wholly ruined, that he can by self-culture merit God's Favor and secure his own happiness. Actually, such is modern Psychology.

The question, *"Shall we continue in sin, that Grace may abound?"*, was asked by someone, or else made as a statement by Legalists who did not understand Grace, or else understood it, but did not believe in Grace.

This person was either claiming that he could sin all he wanted to, and Grace would cover it, or else he was claiming that Paul was teaching something that gave people a license to sin. No doubt these erroneous interpretations, willful or otherwise, were coming from all directions.

To be sure, there were not too many in the Church of that day, especially those in Jerusalem, who were very much in sympathy with Paul's Message of Grace, in any case. They wanted to continue in the Law of Moses and just simply add Jesus to that Law. So, and as stated, a Justification which was altogether by Faith and totally apart from works, did not set well. From this source most of the complaints arose.

It is highly unlikely, that new converts would have developed this reasoning. The very nature of the complaints rests with those who claimed spiritual maturity.

SIN

The first thing we must settle regards the word *"sin."* Does it refer here to acts of sin committed by the Believer, or to the depraved nature (sin nature) still in him?

Inasmuch as the definite article appears before the word *"sin"* in the Greek Text, in other words *"the sin,"* this means we are referring here to the sin nature, actually to sin reigning as a king (Rom. 5:21).

Every time the word *"sin"* is used in this Chapter as a noun, if the Reader will substitute the words *"sinful nature"* or *"sin nature"* in its place, interpretation will be much easier (Wuest).

Someone has said that Romans Chapter 6 presents the machinery or mechanics of the Holy Spirit in telling the Believer how to have victory over sin. That which Jesus Christ did at Calvary and the Resurrection is beautifully outlined respecting the Believer's position in Christ. That position is not one of attempting to gain the victory, but rather maintaining what Jesus has already done for us.

THE HOLY SPIRIT

In Romans Chapter 8 we have the dynamics of the Holy Spirit as the Source of Power which enables the Believer to appropriate to himself these great things Christ has done.

In Romans Chapter 7 we find the self-dependence problem rearing its ugly head which prevents the Holy Spirit from giving

the Believer victory over the sinful nature, which stops the Fruit of the Spirit from being developed.

In this 6th Chapter we are presently studying Paul is *not* talking about what *kind* of life the Believer should live, but by *what* method or *how* he should live that life (Wuest).

As Romans Chapter 8 graphically portrays, and which we will hopefully learn more about when we arrive at Commentary on that most important work of Paul's, we must understand the absolute necessity of the Holy Spirit in all of this. Actually, it is not possible for anyone to properly understand the Word of God, without the aid, leading and guidance of the Spirit of God; however, when it involves great and salient Truths such as we are studying here, and especially considering their complication, it is absolutely imperative that the Holy Spirit have complete control of our lives in order that He may perform His Office Work as He desires, without interference and hindrance. Unfortunately, that is not quite as simple as it sounds.

The last question in verse 1 could be asked in this fashion, *"Shall we continue in the sinful nature?"* *"Continue"* in the Greek is *"meno,"* and means *"to remain, abide."*

Considering the word *"continue,"* this question could be asked as well, *"Shall we as Believers, continue habitually to sustain the same relationship to the sin nature that we sustained before we were Saved?"* Of course, the answer is *"No!"* And yet many Believers are continuing to be ruled by this evil impulse; however, there is victory outlined in this great 6th Chapter.

The above fundamental question asked by Paul is not so much with regard to particular acts of sin, but with respect to the Believer's relationship to the sin nature. This is after all basic acts of sin in one's life, being the result of the degree of one's yieldedness, to the sin nature.

Some of the following material on the *"sin nature"* is taken from the teaching of the Greek Scholar, Kenneth Wuest. However, even though I greatly respect his work, we do have differences, mostly in the realm of the Baptism with the Holy Spirit. Consequently, my thrust respecting direction would be a little different than his. Nevertheless, I in no way question his motives, and feel that his contribution to the Work of God has been of tremendous magnitude. I have borrowed heavily from him, definitely believing that his treatment of this all-important subject is of tremendous benefit.

WHAT IS THE SIN NATURE?

The sin or evil nature is actually the Adamic nature which imprisoned man at the Fall. It has poisoned the entirety of the human race and for all time. It is the nature which encourages sin and which against, man is powerless.

At Calvary Jesus broke the hold of this deadly yoke. However, He did allow it to remain, but powerless. Its remaining is a disciplinary measure. If the Believer correctly follows Christ, there is no problem; however, if we yield to temptation and sin, and then try to overcome in the flesh, the sin nature comes alive with serious consequences.

So, in this Chapter we will study this all-important subject of sin in the life of the Christian, why it is there, and the victory afforded by Christ — the only victory there is incidentally.

THE BELIEVER AND THE ISOLATION OF THE SIN NATURE

Every individual has evil impulses. Heredity, environment, education, training, circumstances, all play a part in one's behavior. The average individual does not allow too many of these evil impulses to run rampant through his experience. But there are some impulses over which he has no control. He has fought them with all the willpower he could muster, but with little or no success.

In the pages of the Bible, we find the way of deliverance. It is found in one of the most profound, metaphysical Passages in all the Bible. Paul, the Hellenistic Jew, probably trained in the University of Tarsus, the foremost Greek School of Learning of the time, and in the Rabbinical School of Theology at Jerusalem, is the writer, but the Holy Spirit is the Author.

One must read carefully, to follow him through the intricate mazes of the inner workings of man's personality. Are you,

gentle Reader, longing for victory over certain evil impulses? Then read Paul in the following pages.

THE MANNER IN WHICH GOD ATTACKS SIN IN THE HUMAN RACE

1. He *Justifies* the believing sinner, that is, He removes the guilt and penalty of the person's sin, and bestows a Positive Righteousness, even Jesus Christ Himself, in Whom the Believer stands Guiltless and Righteous before God's Law for time and eternity.

2. He *Sanctifies* the person in that He breaks the power of the indwelling sinful nature and imparts His Divine Nature, thus freeing the individual from the power of sin and enabling him to live a life pleasing to God, doing this at the moment the sinner puts his Faith in the Lord Jesus as Saviour.

Actually, this act is followed by a process (a continued process of Sanctification) which goes on during the Believer's life as he yields himself to the Ministry of the Holy Spirit, Who eliminates sin from his life and produces a life in which the Christian virtues are present.

3. He will *Glorify* the Believer in that He will transform his physical body at the time when the Lord Jesus comes back to take out His Church. This will make the body immortal, perfect, and free from any indwelling sin. However, it is concerning the second of these phases, the Sanctifying process, to which we now wish to speak.

THE CHRISTIAN AND THE EVIL NATURE

When the medical profession speaks of a disease germ that has not yet been isolated, it means that germ has never been identified and thus isolated from those germs which are known. Since that germ has never been identified, medicine has not been able to discover a remedy for it. Once the germ has been isolated, a remedy can usually be found. It is so in the case of the Believer.

The Christian who has never isolated the evil nature — that is, who has not discovered the Truth of Romans Chapter 6 where God through the Apostle Paul describes the inner change which occurs at the moment he is Saved, and also the Christian's adjustment to this inner change, does not have consistent victory over it. But when in the Christian's thinking, this matter is cleared up and this nature isolated, he has the remedy which will enable him to gain consistent victory over sin in his life.

THE IDENTITY OF THE EVIL NATURE

The Scriptures are very clear as to the identity of the sin nature which indwells an individual as he is born into the world. It is the result of Adam's Fall, and is incumbent upon every human being.

One only has to glance at such portions as the following, in order to appraise the character of this sinful nature: *"And God saw that the wickedness of man was great in the Earth, and that every imagination of the thoughts of his heart was only evil continually"* (Gen. 6:5):

". . . there is none Righteous, no, not one:

"There is none that understandeth, there is none that seeketh after God.

"They are all gone out of the way, they are together become unprofitable; there is none that doeth good, no, not one.

"Their throat is an open sepulchre; with their tongues they have used deceit; the poison of asps is under their lips:

"Whose mouth is full of cursing and bitterness:

"Their feet are swift to shed blood:

"Destruction and misery are in their Ways:

"And the way of peace have they not known:

"There is no fear of God before their eyes" (Rom. 3:10-18):

"Now the works of the flesh are manifest, which are these; Adultery, fornication, uncleanness, lasciviousness,

"Idolatry, witchcraft, hatred, variance, emulations, wrath, strife, sedition, heresies,

"Envying, murders, drunkenness, revellings . . ." (Gal. 5:19-21).

The Bible has thus isolated the germ called sin; identifying it as the fallen nature received from Adam. This nature remains in the individual even after God has Saved him, as we learn from I John 1:8, *"If we say that we have no sin* (sin nature), *we deceive ourselves, and the Truth is not in us."*

God, in Salvation breaks the power of this sinful nature over the Believer, but leaves it in him as a disciplinary measure. When the Believer refuses its behests, saying a complete *"Yes"* to Jesus Christ, he glorifies God, defeats Satan, and grows in spiritual strength and stature.

If the Believer expects to gain consistent victory over this nature, he must know two things: A. What God has done in his inner being with regard to that nature; and, B. What adjustments it is necessary for him to make in relation to it. These two things Paul takes up in Chapter 6, which we are now studying.

TWO QUESTIONS

Paul's presentation consists of two questions and their answers. The two questions are as follows, and to which we have already briefly addressed: *"What therefore shall we say? Shall we who profess to be Christians, continue to sustain habitually the same relationship to the evil nature which we sustained before we were Saved, in order that God's Grace might abound, thus forgiving our sins?"* (Rom. 6:1):

"What then? Shall we commit occasional acts of sin because we are not under the uncompromising rule of Law, but under the lenient Sceptre of Grace?" (Rom. 6:14).

The above questions are a paraphrase of what Paul said.

Neither of these questions ever occurred to Paul, for he knew Grace. They were asked him by some person who had listened to the great Apostle preach on Grace, a person who did not understand the implication of God's Grace, but who lived under Law. Or else, and as we have stated, they were posed by some of the Judaizers, who were not in agreement with Paul concerning the great Gospel of Grace, in other words the New Covenant.

Paul answers the first question in verses 2-14, by showing that it is a spiritual impossibility for the Believer to sustain the same relationship habitually to the evil nature which he sustained before he was Saved. He answers the second question by showing that the Believer has changed masters, before Salvation, having Satan as his master, and since Grace has wrought an inward change, now having Jesus as his Master.

UNDERSTANDING ROMANS CHAPTER 6

The key to understanding this great Chapter is the definite article (a rule of the Greek language) which precedes the word *"sin"* of verse 1 in the Greek Text. In effect it says *"the sin."*

A rule of Greek syntax refers the sin mentioned in this verse back to the sin mentioned in Romans 5:21. In that verse, sin is looked upon as reigning as a king, and it is clear that the reference there is to the sinful nature, not to acts of sin, as we already have explained in previous Commentary. Thus, the sinful nature is spoken of in verse 1 and throughout this 6th Chapter where that word occurs.

When Paul says, *"What shall we say then?"*, he refers back to his statement in Romans 5:20, *"Where sin abounded, Grace did much more abound."*

In view of that statement by Paul, perhaps some questioner asked Paul the following: *"Paul, do you mean to say that God is willing to forgive sin as fast as a man commits it? If that is the case, shall we who profess to be Christians, continue to sustain the same relationship to the evil nature which we did before we were Saved, thus allowing acts of sin to enter our experience, thus allowing God to forgive those sins and display His Grace?"*

The question thus simmers down to the relationship of the sinful nature to the Christian.

(2) "GOD FORBID. HOW SHALL WE, THAT ARE DEAD TO SIN, LIVE ANY LONGER THEREIN?"

The two words, *"God forbid,"* presents Paul's answer to the question. *"Away with the thought, let not such a thing occur."* His first reaction is an emotional one, with his second answer being a rational one.

The question, *"How shall we, that are dead to sin, live any longer therein?"*, portrays in a nutshell the hardcore principle of what the Believer *now is* in Christ. Please allow me to emphasize it again, that Paul is speaking of a spiritual quality which the Believer has at the moment of Salvation, which is that

he is now *"dead to sin."* However, the Christian must remember that death is not extinction but separation.

When Paul asked as to how it is possible for the Believer to continue to live in sin, he is not asking a question for information, but is rather presenting a rhetorical question designed to declare the impossibility of the thing. He is actually saying that it is an impossibility for a Christian to habitually sustain the same relationship to the evil nature that he sustained before God Saved him.

If a person subscribes to the *"sin a little bit every day"* religion, claiming that the Believer sins just as much as the unbeliever, etc., that is a sure sign that this person has really never been born again. Actually, the new nature is the prime characteristic of the Child of God. However, at the same time, the evil nature or sin nature also remains in the Believer, which is the cause for Paul's treatment of this subject.

THE CHRISTIAN AND SIN

The Christian has died to sin in the sense that God in supernatural Grace, while leaving the sinful nature in the Believer, has separated him from it. There has been a definite cleavage, a disengagement of the person from the effects of the evil nature, even though it is still present in the Believer. However, this evil nature or sin nature is a dethroned monarch. Before Salvation, it was the master of the individual. Since Salvation, the Believer is its master.

When the Believer begins to see this Truth, he has isolated this nature, identified it in its proper character, and has within his grasp the remedy for it. However, many Believers have little or no knowledge whatsoever of this particular subject, which leaves them at a serious disadvantage.

WHY DOES THE LORD LEAVE THE SINFUL NATURE IN THE BELIEVER AFTER CONVERSION?

It is for our discipline. However, before I go into that a little more fully, let me address myself to some erroneous teaching which seems to be prevalent in some circles.

One particular teaching is *"sinless perfection."*

NOTES

This stems from an erroneous understanding of Sanctification. Such teaching claims that a person comes to Jesus at Conversion, and then some time later, hopefully soon, the individual is then Sanctified. At that time, at least according to this teaching, the person has reached sinless perfection. Actually, this Doctrine came out of the old Holiness teaching, and is carried over into some Pentecostal circles.

AN EXAMPLE

Years ago a friend of mine, actually one of the greatest Bible Scholars I have ever personally known, and who is now with the Lord, was discussing this issue with some of the Leaders in a major Pentecostal Denomination. They were teaching *"sinless perfection,"* and he, although a member of that particular Denomination, was rebutting this error.

First of all, they should have had more forethought than to argue with this man, considering his vast Scriptural knowledge.

To make the story brief, in a few minutes time my friend proved his point from the Bible to such an extent, that his opponent, who was incidentally *"perfect,"* lost his temper. His associates had to restrain him, and had they not done so, he would have physically attacked my friend.

So much for *"sinless perfection."*

SANCTIFICATION

The moment the sinner comes to Christ, at that moment he is *"Washed, Sanctified and Justified"* (I Cor. 6:11).

As we have previously explained, Sanctification is a Work of Grace which takes place immediately at Salvation. Actually, it is impossible for one to be Justified unless he is first made perfectly clean, which Sanctification does. It is a Free Gift from the Lord.

However, even though the believing sinner is made *"perfect"* in Christ, and because of his Faith in Christ, still, the *"sin nature"* remains, with the Sanctifying process continuing. Once again, as we have previously explained, the moment the sinner comes to Christ, he receives a *"Standing"* in the Lord at that time, which *never* changes. It is in Christ, so it cannot change. However, his *"State"* is something else altogether. It

NOTES

changes almost by the hour. This is what Scholars refer to, and rightly so, as *"Progressive Sanctification."* In other words, the Holy Spirit is working in the Believer's life, to bring his *"State"* up to his *"Standing."* Actually, it is a lifelong process, and will not conclude until the Believer is presented *"faultless before the Presence of His Glory with exceeding joy"* (Jude vs. 24).

One could say and be Scripturally correct, that *"one is Saved and is being Saved."* Or, *"One is Sanctified and is being Sanctified."*

There is also another teaching which is quite popular, which claims that the soul and the spirit are Saved while the body isn't. Consequently, they claim that when the Believer sins, that only the body sins, and not the soul and the spirit. (Others claim that it is the spirit only which does not sin, but the body and the soul.)

There is no truth to either of these claims. Whenever the Believer sins, he sins spirit, soul and body. That's the reason that Paul said, *"And the Very God of Peace Sanctify you wholly* (Progressive Sanctification)*; and I pray God your whole spirit and soul and body be preserved blameless unto the coming of our Lord Jesus Christ"* (I Thess. 5:23).

If the spirit was blameless, as some teach, then Paul's statement makes little sense.

There is another teaching which claims that sin is a consequence of the Law, which disappeared with the New Covenant. These individuals seem not to understand that sin existed before the Law of Moses, which Paul graphically describes in Romans Chapter 5.

In this thinking, they teach that any confession of sin by the Believer before God is error. Behavior is made right by *"confessing who one is in Christ Jesus,"* they say. Forgiveness of sin (I Jn. 1:9) then plays but little part in their present-day experience, at least in their thinking. Their whole conception is, that everything is made right by a proper confession, which does not include the confessing of any type of sin or failure. Of course, they deny the existence of a *"sin nature."*

DISCIPLINE!

Naturally, the Believer wants to know why the Lord allows the sin nature to remain in the Believer which seems to be the cause of so much trouble.

First of all, He does such for a purpose, to which we will momentarily address ourselves.

However, even though the *"sin nature"* is allowed to remain in the Believer, as we have already stated, it is now isolated, and if we properly follow Christ, it will cause no problem. Actually, it is not really the *"sin nature"* which causes the problem, but our own evil hearts (Mat. 15:18-19).

Someone has described the *"sin nature"* in the life of the unbeliever as a roaring conflagration, which it is. In other words, the unbeliever cannot help but sin because that's what he is — a sinner.

However, when the sinner comes to Christ, he is made a New Creature in Christ Jesus. At that time the *"sin nature"* is extinguished as far as its power is concerned. However, it is still present, somewhat like glowing embers, which cause no trouble unless fuel is applied to those embers.

Whenever the Christian sins, that is the fuel that's applied to the sin nature, which can cause great problems. If the situation is not understood correctly according to the Bible and handled according to the Bible, even as we are attempting to explain here the *"sin nature"* in the Believer can now roar into life, creating just as great a spectacle as it did even before Conversion. This is very confusing to many Believers, even as it was to Paul as outlined in Romans Chapter 7, which caused him to seek God for the answer to this dilemma, which was given in this 6th Chapter.

So, it is not really the sin nature that is the cause of our problems, and actually it should do us no harm or cause any problem whatsoever — that is, if we properly understand our Place and Position in Christ.

The Lord allows this thing to remain in our lives, for a disciplinary measure. The modern Christian has the same problems as the Jewish Believers of old. That problem is pride. It is so easy for the Believer to get lifted up in himself, with spiritual pride possibly being the worst pride of all.

After a little bit, at least if we are honest with ourselves, we begin to realize that to maintain the victory that Jesus Christ has won for us, and it is won totally and completely,

NOTES

one has to remain on one's face before God continually, seeking Him for Guidance, Leading and Strength. As stated, this is a disciplinary measure which every Believer needs, even one as close to God as the Apostle Paul (II Cor. 12:1-12).

So, the potential danger of the *"sin nature"* resident in all Believers, keeps the Believer on his face before God, leaning on the Lord, looking to Him for leading and guidance, trusting Him, and knowing that we *must* have His Strength and Power, if we are to be the overcomer expected of us. As well, as we learn the Leading and Guidance of the Holy Spirit, and His Working within our lives, little by little, we also learn how to give complete control to Him in all that we do. These things do not come easily, neither do they come quickly, and most of the time sad to say, they come about as a result of failure on our part, and then us seeking the Lord as to the reason why, etc. As stated, and which we will later study, this is the exact manner which Paul came to these Truths.

EMANCIPATION PROCLAMATION

In this great victory given to us by Christ, we have the Emancipation Proclamation issued by God in which the Christian has been released from slavery to the evil nature. But like many slaves after the Civil War, who were ignorant of Abraham Lincoln's Emancipation Proclamation, and who continued in the service of the slave-master, so Christians who are ignorant of Romans Chapter 6 continue to be slaves of the indwelling sinful nature to the extent that they are not gaining consistent victory over sin.

As we have already stated, Paul was in this very situation before he came to know the Truth of Chapter 6 which God gave to him, and he gave to us. He says, *"I am carnal, sold under sin.*

"For that which I do I allow not (I do not understand), *for what I would, that I do not; but what I hate, that I do"* (Rom. 7:14-15).

No! This is not an account of Paul before Conversion as many Preachers claim. It should be obvious that no unconverted person, irrespective of how religious he may be, would make such statements that we've just quoted from Paul. To be frank, sinners love sin. While they may hate the results of sin, they in no way hate the sin. That only comes about after the new nature of Christ has been placed in them.

Paul knew he was Saved, but he did not understand his Christian experience. The very thing he wished to do, namely, good, he did not do, and the very thing he did not want to do, namely, sin, he did do. The problem was, even as with many of us, he was struggling in his own strength to keep from sinning and to do what was right. However, he found that human endeavor was not equal to the task. Many Christians are in a like situation.

The Truth in Romans Chapter 6 enables the Believer to gain consistent victory over the indwelling sinful nature. The first fact that Paul brings out is that the sinful nature has had its power over the Believer broken. The Believer before Salvation was absolutely the slave of the evil nature. But since Grace has separated him from its power, he need not obey it.

CHRISTIANS ARE DEAD TO SIN

Just what does that mean?

Sin here, we have established, actually refers to the sin nature. So this means that we are dead to the sinful nature, even though it remains present within our lives — not sin, but the sin nature. Death means separation, but it does not mean extinction, and here lies the answer.

Physical death is the separation of a person from his body, while spiritual death, is the separation of the person from God. Consequently, we learn from this that the moment the sinner accepts Christ, a cleavage is consummated between the individual and his evil nature, even though it does remain. In other words, God uses His surgical knife to cut the believing sinner loose from his evil nature. This occurred potentially in the Mind and Purpose of God when the believing sinner, identified himself with the Lord Jesus Christ and His Death on the Cross of Calvary, which is the moment he placed his Faith in Jesus as Saviour.

Now, while God separated the believing sinner from the evil nature, He did not take it out of him, but left it in his inner being. John in his first letter (I Jn. 1:8) is most

careful to tell us that this evil nature remains in the Christian throughout his earthly life and is not eradicated until the Christian dies or is Glorified in the Coming Resurrection.

John is actually saying in the Greek; *"If we say that sin* (sin nature) *we are not constantly having, ourselves we are deceiving* (nobody else), *and the Truth is not in us."* John is not speaking here of a particular act of sin, but the nature of sin. The Greek brings this out:

First of all, John uses the word *"sin"* here a little different than Paul used it in Romans 5:20. While they both mean the same thing, Paul actually used the definite article of the Greek which in effect said, *"the sin,"* referring to the same thing of which John was speaking.

However, the manner in which John uses the word, does not require the definite article of *"the sin."* As with Paul, the Greek here, even though it does not have the definite article as it did with Paul, still emphasizes the nature of sin, because the word is used in the singular sense by John.

The word *"ourselves"* as John used it, is in the emphatic position, meaning that John was saying that any person who holds the theory that the sinful nature is eradicated at some point in the Christian's experience, is only deceiving himself. As well, he is also saying, that others are not deceived in beholding this individual, for they can see sin failure sticking out all over his life.

Consequently, let us, therefore, hold to this, that while there is a definite cleavage between the Believer and the sinful nature, yet that nature remains in him until he dies or is Glorified.

THE SEPARATION OF THE SIN NATURE FROM THE BELIEVER

When Paul said that we are dead to sin, he was referring to the cleavage or separation between the Believer and the sinful nature, which is a permanent one, a once for all disengagement of the person from the evil nature. In other words, this surgical operation spiritually speaking, is never repeated. So far as God is concerned, He has so thoroughly done His Work that the separation is permanent.

To use an illustration that will show the definite cleavage between the Christian and the evil nature, please allow me to use as an example a floor lamp connected to a wall outlet.

It derives its power to give light from the electric outlet in the wall. Just so, a sinner is connected to the evil nature, and derives his incentive and energy to sin, from the evil nature.

However, if one removes the connecting plug from the wall outlet, and the light ceases to function, this tells us its source of power has been cut off. Cut the connection between the sinner and the evil nature, and he ceases to function as a sinner. His source of sinful power has been cut off.

Upon no other basis can one explain the instantaneous and radical change in the outlook and actions of a sinner Saved by the Power of God. His outlook and actions instantly change from the life of gross sin he has once lived.

However, connect the floor lamp with the wall outlet again, and it will come to life again. Likewise, connect the Christian with the evil nature still in him, and he sins again. But the point is, he is under no compulsion to put himself back into the control of the evil nature again as he once was, nor can he do it habitually, nor frequently.

God has so adjusted things in the Believer's life, that, while he remains a free moral agent capable of choosing between obeying the Divine nature or the evil nature, yet, the preponderance of his choices are Godward, where they were once sinward (before Conversion). Thus, Paul declares the impossibility of a Christian habitually sustaining the same relationship to the evil nature which he sustained before he was Saved. In other words, there is no such thing as *"sinning a little bit everyday religion,"* or *"the Believer has to sin, he cannot help but sin,"* etc. Such thinking is not Scriptural, and probably shows that the person claiming such, has really never been Saved.

THE NEW NATURE

Even though the Christian at times will yield to the evil nature and sin, the fact is he doesn't have to do so, and if he truly understands his place and position in Christ, he will learn not to do so. No, that does not teach sinless perfection, for such cannot be reached this side of the Resurrection. But it does teach us victory over sin.

The point is, God has so constituted the Believer, that he need not fail. He has imparted the Divine Nature which gives the Christian a hatred of sin and a Love for Righteousness.

In addition to this, the Holy Spirit has been caused to take up His permanent residence in him and to aid him in this good fight of Faith, and in his effort to live the quality Christian Life which every Believer can have.

So Paul says, *"How is it possible for such as we who have died off once for all with respect to sin, any longer to live in it?"* Or to translate and interpret, *"How is it possible for such as we, Christians, to have been separated once for all from the sinful nature, any longer to live within its grip?"*

The Christian, to use another example, has the same power over the evil nature that he has over, for instance, his radio or TV set. When a program suddenly comes over the air unfit for Christian ears or eyes, he can shut the set off with a simple *"you cannot bring that smut into my life."*

Before Salvation, the evil nature had absolute dominion over the sinner. Since Salvation has wrought its beneficent work in our inner being, we now have absolute dominion over it. We must believe this, conducting ourselves as a Child of God, which we are, and then act upon it. The evil nature is a dethroned monarch.

Paul personifies this evil nature as a king reigning (Rom. 5:21). However, the Holy Spirit at the time of the sinner's Salvation, enthroned the Lord Jesus in the Throneroom of the Believer's heart. He stays on that Throne so long as the Believer keeps yielded to the Spirit and rejects the behests of the evil nature, actually letting Jesus live this life through him (Gal 2:20).

When the Believer sins, the dethroned king, the evil nature, mounts the throne, with the consequent dethronement of the Lord Jesus. These are cold, hard facts, yet, nevertheless true to the Word of God in its teaching on this subject.

However, such a procedure cannot go on indefinitely nor often, for God puts a curb upon such a thing by sending suffering and chastening, and the Christian is made most miserable by a guilty conscience and the indwelling Holy Spirit Who is grieved at such conduct.

(3) "KNOW YE NOT, THAT SO MANY OF US AS WERE BAPTIZED INTO JESUS CHRIST WERE BAPTIZED INTO HIS DEATH?"

The beginning of the question, *"Know ye not, that so many of us as were Baptized into Jesus Christ . . . ?"*, plainly says that this Baptism is into Christ and not Water (I Cor. 12:13; Gal. 3:27-29; Eph. 4:5; Col. 2:11-13).

"Baptism" in the Greek here is *"baptisma,"* which is slightly different than the normal word for Baptism, which is *"baptizo."*

The word is used in the classics of a Smith who dips a piece of hot iron into water, tempering it, also of Greek soldiers placing the points of their swords, and Barbarians, the points of their spears in a bowl of blood.

In Leviticus 4:6, it says, *"The Priest shall dip his finger in blood seven times and sprinkle of the blood seven times before the Lord."* Where *"dip"* is used, it relates to the word *"baptizo,"* and where *"sprinkle"* is used, it relates to the word *"rantizo,"* which refers to the action of placing the finger in the blood.

All of it refers to the placing of a person or thing into a new environment or into union with something else so as to alter its condition or its relationship to its previous environment or condition.

It refers to the Act of God introducing a believing sinner into vital union with Jesus Christ, in order that Believer might have the power of his sinful nature broken and the Divine nature implanted through his identification with Christ in His Death, Burial, and Resurrection, thus altering the condition and relationship of that sinner with regard to his previous state and environment, bringing him into a new environment, the Kingdom of God.

The conclusion of the question, *"Were Baptized into His Death?"*, refers to God placing us in Christ when He died so that we

might share His Death and thus come into the benefits of that identification with Him, namely, to be separated from the evil nature as part of the Salvation He gives us when we believe.

We were then placed in a new environment, Christ. The old one was the First Adam in whom as our Federal Head we were made sinners and came under condemnation. In our new environment in Christ we have Righteousness and Life. Our condition is changed from that of a sinner to that of a Saint, and instantly.

Whenever the sinner has *Faith* in what Christ did at Calvary, in effect, the Father places that sinner in Christ at the time of the Death of the Son of God, and in the Mind of God when Jesus paid the price, it was the same as the sinner paying the price, although in fact, it was no way for him to pay such except through Christ.

Nevertheless, what Jesus did is awarded to the believing sinner. The sin debt was completely paid by the Blood of Jesus poured out at Calvary, which meant that Satan has no more claim over the sinner, such claim being broken because the sin debt was once and for all and forever paid. As stated, and as we will continue to state, all of this comes by simple Faith in Christ (Jn. 3:16).

(4) "THEREFORE WE ARE BURIED WITH HIM BY BAPTISM INTO DEATH: THAT LIKE AS CHRIST WAS RAISED UP FROM THE DEAD BY THE GLORY OF THE FATHER, EVEN SO WE ALSO SHOULD WALK IN NEWNESS OF LIFE."

The phrase, *"Therefore we are buried with Him by Baptism into death,"* proclaims that Baptism is always by burial, regardless of what kind of Baptism it is (Acts 8:38), whether Water or into Christ. That's the reason that it is necessary for the one being Baptized, at least as it regards Water, to be completely immersed under the water, instead of sprinkling.

So, when Jesus died on Calvary and was placed in the Tomb (a form of burial), in effect, the believing sinner died with Him and was buried with Him. Actually, that was the entire purpose of Calvary. Jesus would take our place, die and be buried in our stead, with simple Faith in Him awarding the Believer what Jesus did. The Believer must always understand, that the Lord did all of this exclusively for sinners. In other words, nothing in Heaven needed such a thing, and above all, God certainly did not need such a thing. However, His Love was so great for fallen humanity, that He would become Man (Isa. 7:14), in effect being the Representative Man of the human race, and then do for us what we could not do for ourselves.

PERFECTION

Many people do not understand the perfection that God demands, and in effect, must demand. First of all, He demands a perfect birth. In other words, being born in original sin automatically doomed humanity, which is what Satan knew. However, it seems as if Satan never dreamed that God would do what He did, literally become Man, in order to Redeem man.

So, the Lord through the Power of the Holy Spirit would decree that Mary would become pregnant, which she did. Being a Virgin, consequently, having never known man, there was no taint of the Fall about Jesus' Birth. In fact, Mary only supplied a womb or house if you will, for some nine months, in order for that Holy Thing to be born. Consequently, Jesus as would be obvious, had no traits of Joseph whatsoever, but neither did He have any traits of Mary either. In other words, this biological Miracle did not use the sperm of Joseph (or any other man) nor Mary's egg. Mary simply provided the house for this particular period of time. Consequently, you and I receive the benefit of His Virgin Birth, which meant that God does not hold original sin against the Believer.

As well, Jesus had to be born of the Virgin Mary in the manner in which He did, in order to be the perfect Sacrifice at Calvary, for that alone was what God would accept.

For approximately 33 1/2 years He walked perfectly never failing even once. Consequently, the Believer is awarded His perfect Walk, which again fulfills the perfection demanded by God.

And then of course at Calvary, Jesus was the perfect Sin-Offering which paid for man's terrible sin debt, and which we are here discussing.

THE RESURRECTION

The phrase, *"That like as Christ was raised up from the dead by the Glory of the Father,"* presents the Resurrection which in effect, ratified what was done at Calvary. In other words, as should be obvious, if Jesus had not been raised from the dead, Calvary would have been in vain. So, Jesus not only had to be the perfect Sin-Offering, which He was, but God had to exhibit enough power to raise Him from the dead.

This is not to be taken merely at the weight of its face value. In fact, Jesus had raised several people from the dead, and God has the Power to raise any number of people from the dead, as should be obvious. However, what one must consider is this:

Satan did not mind Jesus dying at all. In fact, he would do all he could to hasten the process. Actually, he tried to kill Jesus in the Garden of Gethsemane hours before the Crucifixion (Lk. 22:39-45). I am sure that Satan knew what Calvary meant, hence, his efforts in the darkness of the Garden; however, if he could keep Jesus from rising from the dead, then Calvary would be of no consequence. As a result, he used all of his power respecting every single demon spirit in order to stop the Resurrection, but to no avail. *"Jesus was raised up from the dead by the Glory of the Father."*

The phrase, *"Even so we also should walk in Newness of Life,"* once again concerns the believing sinner as not only dying and being buried with Christ, but as well Resurrected with and in Him, and not that only, even as grand as that should be, but *"in Newness of Life."*

To say it another way, we were not only placed in Christ by God the Holy Spirit in order that we might share His Death and thus be separated from the evil nature, we were also placed in Him in order that we might share His Resurrection and thus have Divine Life imparted to us.

NEWNESS OF LIFE

The Newness of Life here does not refer to a new quality of experience or conduct but to a new quality of life imparted to the individual. Romans Chapter 6 does not actually deal with the Christian's experience or behavior. Paul treats that in Romans Chapters 12-16. In this 6th Chapter the key word is *"mechanics,"* one might say, of the Spirit-filled life. The Newness of Life, therefore, refers, not to a new kind of life the Believer is to live, but to a New Source of ethical and spiritual energy imparted to him by God by which he is enabled to live the life to which Paul exhorts in Romans Chapters 12-16.

THE WALK — OUR SANCTIFICATION

"Walk" in the Greek is *"peripateo,"* and means *"to order one's behavior, to conduct oneself."*

The word *"should"* as in *"even so we also should walk in Newness of Life,"* throws us off track somewhat. Even though the translation is correct, still, in our thinking respecting English as a language, the word *"should"* means that it is something that ought to be done, but not necessarily that it will be done. However, in Paul's Statement, it means for certain it shall be done. Consequently, to help us understand it better, it could be translated *"Even so we also will walk in Newness of Life,"* or better yet, *"Even so we also walk in Newness of Life."*

In other words, even as the sinner once walked in the oldness of death, brought on by Adam, the Believer now walks in Newness of Life, brought on by Jesus Christ.

Here we have the twofold result of the major surgical operation God performs in the inner being of the sinner when he places his trust in the Saviour. He is disengaged from the evil nature, separated from it, no longer compelled to obey it. He has imparted to him the Divine Nature (II Pet. 1:4) which becomes in him the new source of ethical, moral, and spiritual life, which causes him to hate sin and love Righteousness, and which gives him both the desire and the power to do God's Will. In other words, the Believer is a New Creature in Christ Jesus.

Paul, speaking of the same thing in Philippians 2:12-13, says, *"Carry to its ultimate conclusion your own Salvation, . . . for God is the One Who is constantly putting forth energy in you, giving you both the desire and the power to do His good pleasure."*

NOTES

THE CHRISTIAN'S WILL

The Christian's will has been made absolutely free. Before Salvation it was not free so far as choosing between good and evil was concerned. It was enslaved to the evil nature. But now, it stands poised between the evil nature and the Divine Nature, with the responsibility to reject the behests of the former and obey the exhortations of the latter. It is not so much as saying *"No"* to sin, but rather to saying *"Yes"* to Jesus, which becomes a habit, and then the victorious life has been reached.

Consequently, Paul has answered the question, *"Shall we as a habit of life continue to sustain the same relationship to the evil nature that we sustained before Salvation?"* By showing that this is a literal impossibility and for two reasons: A. The power of the sinful nature has been broken and, therefore, the Christian is not compelled to sin; and, B. The Divine Nature is imparted, and the Christian does not want to sin.

When a person does not have to do something which he does not want to do, he simply does not do it.

THE DIVINE NATURE IN THE BELIEVER

In addition to breaking the power of the evil nature (sin nature), God imparts His Own Divine Nature to us, even as we have stated. We have this Truth given us in Paul's Words in verse 4, *"Even so we also should order our behavior in the power of a new life imparted."*

This New Nature gives the Christian both the desire and the power to do God's Will, and the desire and the power to refuse to obey the evil nature.

Before Salvation, the sinner may have come to the place, which many do, that he hated the results of certain sins, and, therefore, attempted to say *"No"* to them, but found he was unable to do so. In fact, this is the hellish bondage of sin. It is of such power, fueled by Satan and death, that the human will is not able to overcome its dread demands. So, the Federal Government spending hundreds of millions of dollars in advertising displays, *"Say No To Drugs,"* despite the vast expense, simply will not work.

The addict is simply not able to say *"No,"* as no person is able to say *"No,"* to that which is stronger than he. In fact, man has no power that enables him within himself to overcome these impulses.

That's the reason that all the *"12-Step"* Programs in the world, cannot set the captive free. They may in fact, help a person to stop drinking, or taking drugs, or gambling, etc., but in doing so they have only dealt with the surface problem. The old nature remains and, therefore, the emptiness and loneliness. That's the reason that alcoholics in these programs, irrespective of how long they have stopped drinking, must forever say *"I am a recovering alcoholic."* They are telling the truth, in that they are still an alcoholic, even though they do not now drink.

However, when the Lord saves the sinner, He imparts into him the Divine Nature of God, which gives him power which he had not previously known. That power enables him to say *"Yes"* to the admonitions and commands of the Divine Nature. In fact, once he begins to say *"Yes"* to Christ and that Divine Nature, the easier it becomes to continue to say *"Yes,"* until it becomes a habit to do so.

Actually, one of the reasons that the unbeliever is not able to overcome the power of sin, is because he does not have Christ to Whom he can say *"Yes."* He can only say *"No"* to these terrible vices, which he has no power to uphold, which means that his *"No"* is useless.

TWO SUPERNATURAL CHANGES

To which we have already alluded, upon the acceptance of Christ, two supernatural changes take place in the inner being of the believing sinner at the moment he puts his Faith in the Lord Jesus.

The first is that Jesus breaks the power of indwelling sin.

The second is, that He imparts the Divine Nature to the believing sinner. This is all done by the believing sinner being Baptized into Jesus Christ, which is What and Who brings about this great Transformation.

The law of cause and effect requires that every effect must have an adequate cause. Since the breaking of the power of indwelling

sin and the impartation of the Divine Nature are operations which only God can perform, this Baptism must be, not Water Baptism, but a literal Baptism into Jesus Christ, which actually explains Salvation. In other words, Jesus Christ is Salvation.

THE HOLY SPIRIT BAPTISM

However, we would be remiss if we did not speak of the Holy Spirit Baptism, which Paul does not mention here, but addresses greatly in Romans Chapter 8. It is actually the Holy Spirit Who energizes this Divine Nature in the Believer, actually affording its power.

The word *"Baptize"* is the English spelling of the Greek word, not its translation. The Greek word itself means *"the introduction or placing of a person or thing into a new environment or into union with something else so as to alter its condition or its relationship to its previous environment or condition."* It refers here to the act of the Holy Spirit introducing or placing the believing sinner into vital union with Jesus Christ in order to alter that person's condition and environment.

While the Holy Spirit definitely comes into the believing sinner at Salvation, which speaks of the work of Regeneration, that within itself is not the Baptism with the Holy Spirit, as it took place on the Day of Pentecost.

As we have previously stated, if the believing sinner who definitely does have the Holy Spirit, however, stops there, and does not go on and be Baptized with the Holy Spirit according to Acts 2:4, the Holy Spirit is pretty well stopped regarding the things He can do in our hearts and lives.

In other words, even though the Believer is definitely *"born again,"* therefore, regenerated, which has been by the Holy Spirit, if he remains there and does not go on and be Baptized with the Holy Spirit, all of the attributes of Regeneration can little be brought about in the Believer's life. The Baptism with the Holy Spirit makes possible all the qualities and attributes of what Regeneration actually means, taking the Believer to ever higher heights and deeper depths in Christ Jesus. While being Baptized with the Holy Spirit definitely does not make one more Saved, that having been done by Faith in what Jesus did at Calvary, still, all that Salvation means, cannot be brought to bear in its resultant Fruit in the Believer's life, without that Baptism.

THE POTENTIAL OF THE HOLY SPIRIT

The Baptism with the Holy Spirit (Acts 2:4), is potential in nature.

By that I mean, that just because one has been Baptized with the Holy Spirit, such does not necessarily mean that all the wonderful things the Holy Spirit does within our hearts and lives are automatically done. In fact, very little is automatic, with the Holy Spirit awaiting the cooperation of the Believer. That's what I mean by being potential in nature.

In other words, the potential is there for all of the great things promised by God to be done, but they are not done without the proper consecration on the part of the Believer. Regrettably, it is only a few hearts and lives which really allow the Holy Spirit the latitude He desires, and actively cooperate with Him in bringing about the great qualities and attributes of Christlikeness in Believers. Most, sadly and regrettably, little advance beyond the speaking in Tongues stage. However, that is not the fault of the Holy Spirit, but of the Believer.

THE LAST ADAM, JESUS CHRIST

Before Salvation, the sinner stands in the First Adam as his Federal Head. In that position, he receives the position which the First Adam had as the result of the Fall, namely, guilty before God's Law, possessing a fallen nature, and unrighteous in his thoughts, words, and deeds. His physical body becomes subject to death. But all this is changed when the Holy Spirit takes him out of his first position, and places him in the Last Adam, Jesus Christ. The result is that this believing sinner stands now in his New Federal Head, absolutely Righteous before God's Law, the power of indwelling sin broken, and the Divine Nature imparted.

What a contrast this environment and condition is to the previous one he occupied. This introduction into Jesus Christ occurred potentially in the Mind and Purpose of God at the time the Lord Jesus hung on the Cross of Calvary, the results of which

NOTES

become operative in the life of the believing sinner when he places his Faith in Jesus as Saviour, and the Holy Spirit in answer to his Faith, places him in the Lord Jesus.

THE HATING OF SIN AND THE LOVING OF RIGHTEOUSNESS

In this new nature now possessed by the Believer, everything about him changes. He now loves Righteousness, where he once hated this great attribute of God, and now hates sin, which he once loved. As well, this new Divine Nature gives the Christian the impelling motive and the power to do God's Will. Thus, it is actually impossible for a Christian to live a life of habitual sin as he did before he was Saved.

CALVARY, THE ANSWER TO EVERYTHING

Some Believers have been erroneously taught that their Faith in what Jesus did at Calvary and the Resurrection was necessary in order to be Saved, but thereafter they are told, it has no bearing on the Believer's life and walk before God. Nothing could be further from the Truth.

Some of these Preachers then go on to say that Calvary is little more than *"past miseries."* They claim that we are people of the Resurrection, and as such, Calvary is of no more consequence. Many of them even go so far as to eliminate all songs about the Cross, the Blood of Jesus, or anything of this nature. As stated, they also deny the sin nature, claiming that a Believer's walk is determined by his confession alone. Consequently, all preaching against sin is banned, claiming that any preaching of this nature produces a sin consciousness. In other words, they claim that preaching against sin causes one to become conscious of sin, and then desire to sin. So, there is little or no preaching against sin in these particular Charismatic circles.

The Truth is, as I trust we have amply proved Scripturally, Faith in what Jesus did at Calvary and the Resurrection is definitely necessary for one to be Saved, but as well, continued Faith in that Atoning Work, is also necessary for one's victorious walk before God. In other words, Calvary is not only at the Core of our Salvation experience, but as well, of our daily walk before God. Failure to understand this, is simply to fail.

Faith in this Atoning Work regarding our victorious walk, is necessary each and every day of our lives, and is meant to be that way by the Holy Spirit.

Why does the Believer think that all of this teaching is given by Paul?

PAUL'S EXPERIENCE

As we will study in the 7th Chapter of Romans, which incidentally refers to Paul's after Conversion experience, and not his before Conversion experience, as many teach, we will learn some things.

Paul having come to Christ in the great Damascus Road experience, witnessed a radical change within his heart and life, even instantly as Jesus came in. As well, he was Baptized with the Holy Spirit some three days after his Conversion (Acts 9:8-9, 17).

Upon these twin great experiences of Salvation from sin and the Baptism with the Holy Spirit for power, Paul thought surely he could now live the victorious life over all the evil impulses of the flesh. To his chagrin, he found that even though Salvation was his, victory was alluding him, with him actually doing the things he did not want to do (Rom. 7:15).

At this stage, many Pentecostals make a mistake, thinking that the Baptism with the Holy Spirit provides all the power that one needs in order to overcome all things. Acts 1:8 is cited as an example.

While the Holy Spirit is definitely necessary in order for these great victories to be brought about in our lives, even as we have already spoken, still, the *"power"* spoken of by Jesus in Acts 1:8, more so speaks of *doing* what God wants rather than *being* what God wants. In fact, the sin question was not handled by the Holy Spirit, but by Jesus at Calvary and the Resurrection. While the Holy Spirit is the One, even as we have already explained, Who makes all of this real to our hearts and lives, still, it is that which Jesus did at Calvary which satisfied the claims of Heavenly Justice respecting sin, and, thereby, broke the grip of this monster from our hearts and lives. This is why Paul said,

NOTES

"I determined not to know any thing among you, save Jesus Christ, and Him Crucified" (I Cor. 2:2).

So, Paul went to the Lord, seeking His Face respecting the sin question, and the manner in which the Believer can walk in the Victory provided for him by Christ, and was given this great Truth of Romans Chapters 6-8. To be sure, if Calvary was a *once* situation, and no longer needed in the Believer's experience, then all of this teaching given by the Holy Spirit to Paul, makes no sense whatsoever.

No! Calvary is not a mere *"once"* situation, but figures prominently in our everyday walk before God, and will continue to do so until the Trump sounds.

(5) "FOR IF WE HAVE BEEN PLANTED TOGETHER IN THE LIKENESS OF HIS DEATH, WE SHALL BE ALSO IN THE LIKENESS OF HIS RESURRECTION:"

The phrase, *"For if we have been planted together in the likeness of His Death,"* proclaims that what Jesus did at Calvary, was totally and completely for the sinner. In effect, the believing sinner died in Him on the Cross, and was buried in Him as well.

This means that the price was totally and completely paid concerning the outstanding debt of sin and sins, with simple Faith all that is required on the part of the sinner, in order for this Standing in Christ to be freely given.

The phrase, *"We shall be also in the likeness of His Resurrection,"* means that it is impossible to have one (benefits of Calvary), without having the benefits of the other (Newness of Life).

To believe in Christ implies association with Him in His Death and Resurrection. His Death is called in verse 3 His Baptism. He was Baptized into Death, and all His members (sinners who have Faith in Him) were associated with Him in that Baptism; and His Death and Resurrection being inseparable in their purpose and efficacy, union with Him in the One carries with it participation in the Other.

Actually, this is what He was talking about in John 6, when He said, *"Except ye eat the Flesh of the Son of Man, and drink His Blood, ye have no life in you"* (Jn. 6:53).

Jesus was not speaking of literally eating His Flesh or drinking His Blood, but was using that as a metaphor respecting Faith in His Atoning Work (Jn. 3:16; 6:63).

TWO MAJOR FACTS

In verses 1-4, Paul has brought out two major facts:

1. When God saves a sinner, He separates him from the indwelling sinful nature, which cleavage is so effective, that the Believer is not compelled to sin anymore; he has been *permanently* delivered from its power; however, at the same time the Lord has also left the sin nature in the Believer *permanently*. As stated, this is done as a disciplinary measure.

2. Also, the Lord at the same time has imparted the Divine Nature, which gives the Believer both the desire and the power to do God's Will.

Now, in verses 5-10, Paul repeats these great Truths in the event that some of his readers may not have caught their full implications as presented in verses 2-4.

A FULFILLED CONDITION

Paul used the word *"if"* but it is the *"if"* of a fulfilled condition. In effect, he is saying, *"In view of the fact,"* or *"Since such and such a thing is so,"* etc.

"Have been planted together" in the Greek Text, speaks of a living, vital union of two individuals growing up together. Actually, the same word could be used of Siamese twins whose bodies were connected at one point, and whose bloodstream flowed through two physical bodies as it does normally through one. Actually, that is the best way to explain this union, and represents the close union between Christ and the Believer. God actually places the believing sinner into Christ at the Cross, to share His Death and Resurrection. As stated, this is done by Faith on the part of the Believer.

"Likeness" in the Greek Text is *"homioma,"* and means *"a likeness or resemblance which amounts almost to the same identity, as stated, even as close as Siamese twins."*

The idea is, that the believing sinner and

the Lord Jesus were united in a Death at Calvary, His Death, a vicarious one that had to do with the Salvation of the believing sinner from the guilt, penalty, and power of sin, actually, the sinner's death, one which he in justice should have died as a result of that sin, but which in the Grace of God was borne or carried as to its guilt and penalty by God's Son. Both deaths had to do with sin, but from different aspects — Jesus bearing the sin which the sinner has given Him.

SANCTIFICATION, NOT GLORIFICATION

The future aspect of the words *"We shall be"* is not that of a predictive future so far as time is concerned, but that of a logical future.

Paul says in his Greek, *"For, in view of the fact that we have become those permanently united with Him with respect to the likeness of His Death, certainly also* (as a logical result) *we shall become those who have become permanently united with Him with respect to the likeness of His Resurrection."*

Consequently, the physical aspect of the coming Resurrection of all of the Saints, which will at that time result in the Glorification of our bodies, is not in the Apostle's mind here, for he is writing in a context of Sanctification as it speaks of our walk before the Lord now, and not Glorification. To be sure, the Glorification will come, but Paul's subject does not pertain to that now, but rather the Believer's daily walk respecting overcoming victory.

So, the Saint in his new condition orders his behavior in the power of a new life imparted, namely, the Resurrection Life of our Lord. The little word *"also"* in verse 4 tells us all this. Our Lord's Resurrection Life is being lived in a new sphere, and so is that of the Believer.

Then Paul develops his thesis. As a result of the Believer having become united with Christ in His Death, the power of the sinful nature is broken, and this Paul treats in verses 6 and 7. In view of the fact that we have become united with Him in His Resurrection, the Divine Nature has been imparted. And this Paul speaks of in verses 8-10.

(6) "KNOWING THIS, THAT OUR OLD MAN IS CRUCIFIED WITH HIM, THAT

THE BODY OF SIN MIGHT BE DE-
STROYED, THAT HENCEFORTH WE
SHOULD NOT SERVE SIN."

The phrase, *"Knowing this, that our old man is crucified with Him,"* refers to that person the Believer was before he was Saved, totally depraved, unregenerate, lacking the Life of God.

There are two words in the Greek which mean *"man."* The first is *"anthropos,"* and is a generic, racial term, which is used for a male individual at times, but also has the idea in it of mankind in general, and, therefore, includes both men and women.

The other word is *"aner,"* and refers only to a male person.

The word *"anthropos"* is the word used by Paul, and refers, as stated, to an individual man or woman.

As well, there are two words in the Greek which mean *"old."* The first is *"archaios,"* and means *"old in point of time."*

The other word is *"palaios,"* and means *"old in point of use."* This is the word that Paul uses.

It describes something that is worn out, useless, fit to be put on the scrap pile, to be discarded. Consequently, that describes perfectly the *"old man"* which pertains to what we were before we were Saved, thereby brought to Christ.

(Some claim that the *"old man"* is Satan. However, as is obvious, there is nothing in the Greek Text that even remotely suggests such a thing. The idea altogether speaks of the person before Salvation.)

The phrase, *"That the body of sin might be destroyed,"* actually refers to the human body. *"Body"* in the Greek is *"soma,"* and means literally *"the human body."*

The word *"sin"* as it is used here, speaks of that monster possessing the human body, at least before Salvation. The idea is, that Satan uses the human body as the vehicle for temptation and, thereby, the carrying out of sinful desires.

The reference is, therefore, to the Believer's physical body before Salvation, possessed by, dominated and controlled by the sinful nature. The person the Believer was before he was Saved was crucified with Christ in order that his physical body which before Salvation

NOTES

was dominated by the evil nature, might be spiritually destroyed — that is, destroying the power of sin in the physical body.

"Destroyed" in the Greek is *"katargeo,"* and means *"to render idle, inactive, inoperative, to cause to cease."*

The phrase, *"That henceforth we should not serve sin,"* contains the following idea:

"Knowing this, that our old man, that person we were before we were Saved, was crucified with Him, in order that our physical body which at that time was dominated by the sinful nature, might be rendered inoperative in that respect, namely, that of being controlled by the sinful nature, in order that no longer are we rendering a slave's habitual obedience to the sinful nature."

As a result, the Believer no longer renders a slave's obedience to the evil nature habitually as he did before God Saved him. In other words, he has been set free from that bondage.

(7) "FOR HE THAT IS DEAD IS FREED FROM SIN."

The phrase, *"For he that is dead,"* is not speaking of physical death, but rather to the historic fact of a believing sinner being identified with Christ in His Death on the Cross.

The words *"is dead"* in the Greek Text have reference to a past action, which in effect is a once for all action. Thus, we have, *"The one who died off once for all,"* that is, off from the evil nature, this being a separation from that nature. It speaks of an action so complete and so final, that the Holy Spirit through the Apostle used the word *"dead."* If something is dead, that means it has no life in it, is not effective, carries no weight, can do nothing, with no danger from that source.

DEAD TO A CERTAIN THING

The Text as stated, is not meaning that the Believer is physically dead, or will be physically dead in the future, but is rather dead to a certain thing, in this case sin. As we will study in a moment, sin is not dead as is painfully obvious, but the Believer is dead to sin. The Believer in his past, which was an unbelieving state, was very much alive unto sin. All of this is now changed. However, due to the way it has been done, which pertains to being dead in Christ, the issue very quickly can become confusing.

IN CHRIST

Paul has laboriously defined this death, its type, and the manner in which it was done. It is all in Christ when He died on Calvary, and the believing sinner gains this status not by doing anything, but simply by having Faith in something that has already been done. However, here is the problem area:

If the Believer at any point in time steps outside of Christ, and I speak of the Believer's Faith in that Atoning Work at Calvary, in other words trusting in himself or others other than Christ exclusively, he will quickly find himself in serious consequences. This great position in Christ is so defined by the Holy Spirit, that one must remain constantly in Christ, and more particularly in that Finished Work, or one will quickly find that he is no longer dead to sin.

A CONTINUED FAITH

This means that the Faith which got us in, must continue to operate even on a daily basis, in order that we stay in. And this is where the trouble comes in. (We are not speaking here of Salvation, but rather of dominion over sin.)

The sinner under conviction by the Holy Spirit is quickly made to know how helpless he really is, and that he must be totally dependent upon Christ for Salvation. At that moment he throws himself on the Mercy and Grace of God, with his Faith in that Mercy and Grace instantly bringing Salvation. In fact, he knows very little about all the rudiments of that of which we speak, but exhibiting simple Faith guarantees him Salvation.

However, once this is done, the Believer begins to study the Bible, enjoying the Blessings of the Lord, even going on to be Baptized with the Holy Spirit (Acts 2:4). In respect to this, God begins to bless, as He always does. Now the danger flags begin to fly.

At this stage, and in fact all through the Christian experience, it is so easy for one to drift over into a position of spiritual elitism, in other words dependence on self. Inasmuch as self at times is so subtle, especially religious self, the transition is made without the Believer at times really realizing that

such is being done. Spiritual pride has that propensity.

The phrase, *"Is freed from sin,"* presents the Believer as being cut loose from the sin nature.

"Freed" in the Greek is *"dikaioo,"* and means *"to Justify, to declare Righteous, to render or make Righteous, acquit of a charge, to absolve."* It is a term having to do with the Law and the Courts of Law. Consequently, it deals with the Doctrine of Justification, which is a legal term. However, in this instance, Paul is not dealing with Justification, but rather with the Doctrine of Sanctification. Therefore, the idea of being *"set free"* growing out of the idea that a justified person is set free from the penalty of the Law, is used.

The one, Paul says, who died off once for all from the sinful nature, has been set free completely from it, with the present result that he is in a state of permanent freedom from it, permanent in the sense that God has set him free permanently from it, *and it is his responsibility to maintain that freedom from it moment by moment.*

GRACE

This which is taught by Paul and one might quickly add given to him by the Holy Spirit, is little accepted by the majority of Christianity. In fact, the vast majority of mankind accepts the human Doctrine of Salvation by merit; a very small minority believes the Divine Doctrine of Salvation by Grace. As the Lord Jesus Himself said, few tread that narrow way. The reason being, it is abhorrent to human pride.

As we have already stated, the Believer in Christ, trusting in what He did at Calvary and the Resurrection, is now dead to the monster of sin — in other words, dead to the sin nature. He is cut loose or freed from that monster. *However, that does not mean that sin or the sin nature is dead, with both continuing to be very much alive and just as much in existence as ever.* And yet, to the Believer sin or the sin nature need not be any problem whatsoever, providing he continues to have Faith moment by moment, and Faith in the right thing, namely in Christ.

MAINTAINING THE DISCONNECTION

The Christian is exhorted to maintain that relationship of disconnection which God has brought about between him and the indwelling sinful nature. However, God has not taken away the Christian's free will, and does not treat him as a machine. It is possible for the Christian by an act of his will to connect himself again with the evil nature, thus bringing sin back into his life.

However, he will not be able to do this habitually, and for various reasons. In the first place, it is not the Christian's nature to sin. He has been made a partaker of the Divine Nature which impels him to hate sin and to love Holiness.

In the second place, the minute a Christian sins, the Holy Spirit is grieved, and that makes the Believer decidedly uncomfortable, spiritually, and so much so that if Repentance is not enjoined quickly, the situation becomes intolerable.

At the same time, the Lord will also send suffering and chastening into the Believer's life as a curb to sin. All these things taken together, preclude any possibility of the Christian taking advantage of Divine Grace — in other words, the *"sinning a little bit everyday"* Doctrine, taught and practiced by some.

Thus, Paul has answered his hearer's question again, namely, that the believing sinner's death with Christ has disengaged that person from any connection with his indwelling sinful nature, resulting in that person's body being rendered inoperative so far as any control which the evil nature might exercise over it, is concerned.

(8) "NOW IF WE BE DEAD WITH CHRIST, WE BELIEVE THAT WE SHALL ALSO LIVE WITH HIM:"

The phrase, *"Now if we be dead with Christ,"* proclaims the result of this spiritual operation.

The word *"if"* would have probably been better translated *"since,"* thus reading, *"Now since we be* (are) *dead with Christ."* In other words, it is a settled, guaranteed disposition, which will accrue into very positive results.

The phrase, *"We believe that we shall also live with Him,"* presents the result of the surgical operation (spiritually speaking) of being freed from sin.

In other words, there was a purpose behind the Believer dying with Christ on Calvary and being buried with Him. Had it stopped there, the work would have only been half done. The purpose is not only to free one from sin, with the debt justly paid, even though that is an absolute necessity, but the end result of the *"New Life in Christ"* to which the Spirit is pointing.

Consequently, this shoots down the theory that the only difference in the Believer and the unbeliever, is the Blood of Christ. In other words, those who contend for that particular Doctrine are actually claiming that Believers sin just as much as unbelievers, but the difference is that one trusts Christ while the other doesn't. Nothing could be further from the Truth.

While the Blood of Jesus definitely is applied to the believing sinner, with all its wonderful, attendant results, still, there is a purpose in all of this, and it is to live the Resurrection Life free from sin's dominion.

WE BELIEVE

This latter phrase by the use of the words *"we believe"* proclaims the necessity of the continued use of Faith, respecting our continued victory over sin. This is absolutely imperative!

We are to simply believe that not only were our sins handled at Calvary, but as well, the Resurrection of Christ guaranteed our victorious walk over and above the dominion of sin. No, this does not mean sinless perfection. That will not come about until the First Resurrection of Life, when corruption will put on incorruption and mortality will put on immortality (I Cor. 15:51-57; I Thess. 4:13-18). It does mean though, that the Believer is *now* free from sin's dominion.

LIVE WITH HIM

"With Him" is a personal pronoun, and means that we live with respect to Him. That is, the Believer's New Life imparted to him at the moment of believing, is Life derived from Christ. We live by means of Him. The Believer derives his Spiritual Life from Christ in that sense.

Paul is not speaking here of the Believer's

fellowship with Christ here or in Eternity. He is speaking of what Christ did for us and our appropriation of that great victory within our hearts and lives.

How long does the Believer derive his Spiritual Life from the Lord Jesus? As long as Christ lives! Paul says He died once for all, and that death over Him will never again exercise lordship, thus, the Believer is sustained in his spiritual life for time and eternity, since Christ is in his life. In other words, as long as Christ lives, the Believer lives!

This great Divine Fact is to be believed, reckoned to be true, because it is true, and, as a consequence, the members of one's personal physical body are to be yielded to God as Weapons of Righteousness.

(9) "KNOWING THAT CHRIST BEING RAISED FROM THE DEAD DIETH NO MORE; DEATH HATH NO MORE DOMINION OVER HIM."

The phrase, *"Knowing that Christ being raised from the dead dieth no more,"* tells us several things:

1. All of this, His Death at Calvary and His Resurrection, actually the entirety of all that was done in the Incarnation, was done exclusively, totally, and absolutely for the human family, in other words, sinners. So, if He did all of this for us, and He did, then He surely wants us to have these great victories He has won.

2. In that He does not have to die anymore, tells us that His Work is a Finished Work, and in every capacity. In other words, nothing was left hanging. That's the reason it is so bad for anyone to add anything to the Finished Work of Christ.

3. *"Dieth no more"* has two meanings: A. He doesn't need to die again, as we said, because He paid it all the first time; and, B. All the powers of sin were broken, and that means broken in the heart and life of the Believer, for we are the ones for whom He died and rose from the dead.

The phrase, *"Death hath no more dominion over Him,"* presents *"dominion"* as the key word.

"Dominion" in the Greek Text is *"kurieuo,"* and means *"to rule, to be lord of, to exercise lordship over."*

"Death" in the Greek is *"thanatos,"* and

means *"deadly, or to be death."* In other words, it is a state of being or supremacy.

Death is here spoken of as it relates to sin, for the wages of sin is death. It speaks of the entirety of the hold over the human race, with all of its by-products of bondage, darkness, absence of life, and, in this case, an absence of spiritual life.

The idea is, that Jesus' Death, which speaks of His poured-out Life, relative to His poured-out Blood, satisfied the claims of Heavenly Justice. In that the sin debt was satisfied in this Act, Satan now has no more hold on the human family, at least those who believe in what Christ did. Therefore, the *"dominion"* of death with all of its attendant results is broken in the life of the Believer who accepts what Christ did. As death holds no more dominion over Jesus, it holds no more dominion over the Believer, and that refers to sin.

As we have repeatedly stated, the idea of all of this which Paul teaches is that sin no longer has dominion over the Believer. In fact, death and sin are both still a reality and very much in force, and will continue to be until the resolution of all things (I Cor. 15:24-28).

However, the force of both death and sin have no more hold in the Believer's life, with its dominion totally and completely broken. This is the Miracle and Wonder of the New Birth, and why Jesus is the only Answer for suffering, dying humanity. Every philosophy or religion pales into insignificance, actually into nothingness, in comparison to Jesus Christ and what He did at Calvary and the Resurrection.

(10) "FOR IN THAT HE DIED, HE DIED UNTO SIN ONCE: BUT IN THAT HE LIVETH, HE LIVETH UNTO GOD."

The phrase, *"For in that He died, He died unto sin once,"* actually means, *"He died unto sin once for all."*

The *"sin"* here of which Paul speaks, does not refer to particular acts of sin. That aspect of the death of our Lord, namely, that of paying the penalty for our sins, Paul took care of in 3:21-5:11.

Here he speaks of the relation of Christ's Death to the sinful nature of the individual. Our Lord's Death not only paid the penalty of human sin, but it was used of God to break the power of indwelling sin in the Believer's life. This is what the songwriter meant when he wrote concerning the Blood of Christ, *"Be of sin the double cure, save from wrath and make me pure."*

Even though this is very simple, it is something that many Believers have never heard, or else they have not thought of it in this sense. Considering how important that it really is, please allow us to say it again:

When Jesus died on Calvary, the terrible sin debt of man was then paid in full. And as we have said it so many times, Heavenly Justice was then satisfied.

That particular aspect of His Death did not really involve the sinner except in a distant way. In other words, all the sinner has to do is simply believe that, and Salvation is afforded.

However, Jesus also died not only that the great sin debt be paid, which it was, but also, that the believing sinner might be free from the dominion of sin and its effects thereafter. So as the song said, it was a *"double cure."*

Now this last aspect of His Death takes on a much more personal nature, even as Paul grandly explains in this 6th Chapter of Romans. Not only is the sin debt paid, but as well, its dominion is broken in the heart and life of the Believer.

It is brought about in relationship to the Believer literally dying with Him, and in effect, literally in Him, being buried in Him, and then Resurrected in Him. In this manner the dominion of sin was broken in the life of the Believer. But the Believer must continue to exercise Faith in this respect, and on a never-ending basis.

So, Christ's Death was twofold:

1. To pay the terrible sin debt.

2. To break the dominion of sin in the life of the Believer.

The phrase, *"But in that He liveth, He liveth unto God,"* concerns the very opposite of the first phrase.

The first phrase spoke of Jesus dying unto sin once, and that is all that would be necessary, and now it speaks of Him living, which is Life derived from God.

The phrase, *"He liveth unto God,"* tells us that all of this was instituted by God and

not by man.

As well, it speaks of Jesus doing all of this as the Representative Man, in effect, for us.

So, in essence, the gist of this statement as made by Paul, is that the only way this great victory can break down, is for God to die. Of course, we know that is impossible, and, therefore, it is impossible that the dominion of sin not be broken, respecting Believers who trust Christ.

One is not living according to one's own strength or ability or power, but rather that of God, i.e., *"unto God."*

The word *"liveth"* has a triple meaning:

1. It speaks of our daily walk and, consequently, daily victory over sin.

2. It speaks of more abundant life (Jn. 10:10).

3. It speaks of life sustained by God, and, consequently, infallible.

(11) "LIKEWISE RECKON YE ALSO YOURSELVES TO BE DEAD INDEED UNTO SIN, BUT ALIVE UNTO GOD THROUGH JESUS CHRIST OUR LORD."

The phrase, *"Likewise reckon ye also yourselves to be dead indeed unto sin,"* probably comes closer to a formula than anything else found in the Word of God.

We come now to Knowledge and Faith. In verses 1-10, Paul has presented two main facts: A. The Believer stands in the position of a permanent relationship of freedom to the sinful nature, and need not obey it; and, B. The Divine Nature is imparted by which he is given both the desire and the power to do God's Will.

This is the inner spiritual machinery God has installed whereby the Believer lives his Christian life. But, like an automobile engine, this machinery works best when it is serviced regularly.

There is always a change for the good in a new Convert's life. But if he does not understand this inner change and adjust himself properly to it, he lives a mediocre Christian life. This adjustment Paul speaks of in verses 11-13, namely, that which the Believer must do if he expects the best results from this inner change God has already wrought in him.

TWO THINGS THE BELIEVER MUST DO

A. The Believer is to reckon himself dead

to sin; and, B. Reckon himself alive to God.

The word *"reckon"* in the Greek is *"logizomai,"* and means *"to reckon, count, compute, to take into account."* Here Paul is exhorting the Saints that in their endeavor to live a life in accordance with the Word of God, they should take into account the fact that they are dead to sin, that they have been disengaged from the evil nature, that it has no power over them anymore, that they are scot free from it and can live a victorious Christian life. This is the *"knowledge"* of which we have spoken, which comes about through the teaching given by Paul in this 6th Chapter of Romans. The Believer is to also have Faith in this knowledge.

The Believer is also to take into account the fact that he is alive to God, that is, that the Divine Nature has been imparted with the result that this nature gives him both the desire and the power to regulate his life in accordance with the Word of God.

Now, reckoning oneself dead to sin and alive to God does not make one so. In other words, the mere fact of saying this, or even repeating it over and over, effects no positive results within itself.

One must have a working knowledge of what Jesus has done for us, understanding that a part of that great work was to give us dominion over sin in our everyday lives, having Faith in that, and a continuing everyday working Faith at that. That is what brings the victory. A reckoning in this manner becomes very profitable.

AN EXAMPLE

There is a game in which a blindfolded person is brought into a room, and made to stand on a table-board which rests on some books on the floor. Two young men lift the board about a foot, and warn the young man not to bump his head against the ceiling. Thinking that he is near the ceiling, he loses his balance and falls off. He lost his balance and fell because he reckoned himself to be where he was not.

Just so, a Christian who fails to count upon the fact that the power of the sinful nature is broken in his life, fails to get consistent victory over it, with the result that he lives a mediocre Christian life. He reckons himself

where he was not.

Another young man is blindfolded and stood on the board. He knows the game. When the board is lifted and he is warned not to bump his head against the ceiling, he remains perfectly straight and maintains his equilibrium, because he rightly reckoned himself where he was.

And so it is with the Christian who counts upon the fact that the power of the sinful nature is broken. He knows that he does not have to obey it, and that in fact, he has the power to ignore it in the sense of fear, etc., saying *"Yes"* to Jesus Christ, and saying *"Yes"* constantly, deliberately, totally, completely, and absolutely on a daily basis.

The phrase, *"But alive unto God through Jesus Christ our Lord,"* proclaims the Believer living this life in the strength of our Lord. The Christian who does not count upon the fact that the Divine Nature is implanted in his inner being, goes on living his Christian life as best he can, more or less in the energy of his own strength, with the result that he exhibits an up-and-down, even failing experience. But the Believer who counts upon the fact that he is a possessor of the Divine Nature, ceases from his own struggles at living a Christian life, and avails himself of the Life of God supplied in the Divine Nature. That is the secret of the victorious, overcoming Christian Life.

So the first adjustment the Christian should make is that of counting upon the fact that the power of the indwelling sinful nature is broken and the Divine Nature imparted, and order his life on that principle. So, several things are said here:

1. Upon the fact of what Jesus has done for us at Calvary and the Resurrection, and the Believer's knowledge of this glorious work, and Faith in that work, the Believer should *"reckon"* himself as in a certain victorious position. This is a concrete fact, with the Believer proclaiming its veracity in his own life.

2. He should reckon first of all that he is dead indeed unto sin. It has no more hold on him, with the sinful nature broken. As stated, sin no longer has dominion over him, with the Believer understanding that and proclaiming that.

3. He must reckon himself as well to be alive unto God, which pertains to all the things that God is. He must order his life accordingly. He has now been brought from darkness to light, and should act like it, talk like it, and in fact be what the Bible says he is.

4. All of this is *"through Jesus Christ our Lord,"* meaning, that He has done it all, with nothing left for us to do, except simply believe Him. Jesus is everything!

VICTORY AND OVERCOMING POWER

The Believer, consequently, is to never talk about trying to get victory over something, or trying to be an overcomer, etc. That is wrong terminology, and proclaims that the Believer does not fully understand what Jesus has done for him relative to dominion over sin. In fact and Truth, the Believer, even the weakest Believer, is already victorious in Christ and is already an overcomer as well. However, there are several problems with that — to be sure, not in the Finished Work of Christ, but in the Believer's position in Christ.

First of all, it is very difficult for the sinner to admit that there is nothing he can personally do to effect his Salvation. But that he must depend totally upon Christ. That is what keeps many if not most people from being Saved. They keep thinking they can effect their own Salvation in some way.

However, once the sinner comes to Jesus, that problem of self-sufficiency is still in the Believer, at least to a certain extent. All of it is a carry-over from the Fall in the Garden of Eden. As a result, the Believer begins to think that he can do something toward effecting his victory in Christ, or else he needs to do something, etc.

He then begins this round of self efforts, which negates the Grace of God, and only produces failure, as fail it must. To him, the Christian Life is a great struggle, which demands great effort on the part of the Believer. He finds himself fighting Satan, which is a battle he cannot win, and in fact does not need to win, considering that Jesus has already won that conflict.

So, it is very difficult for the Believer to fully rely on what Jesus has already done, or

else, he is blind to the fact of what the Atonement actually means in Christ. As we have already stated, he knows full well that Jesus has paid the penalty for sin, but he doesn't quite understand that He also broke sin's dominion. Of course, Satan always takes advantage of Biblical ignorance. In Jesus he already has the victory and is already an overcomer.

FIGHT THE GOOD FIGHT OF FAITH

There is only one fight that the Christian is to engage, and that is the *"good fight of Faith"* (I Tim. 6:12).

The Believer is not to fight the Devil, for Jesus has already fought him and won. The Believer is not to fight Demon Spirits, for they were fought and defeated at Calvary as well. He is to merely resist the Devil and Evil Spirits by using the Word of God and the Name of Jesus (Mk. 16:17; Eph. 6:13-17).

Every Believer must understand that the battle has already been fought and won and in every capacity, and by the Lord Jesus Christ. That is the reason Paul said, *"Through Jesus Christ our Lord."*

Whenever we try to fight these battles all over again, whether we realize it or not, we are in essence saying that what Jesus did was not enough, and our little part has to be added to His effort. But Paul also said, that Jesus *"died unto sin once,"* and as stated, it means *"once for all."* His victory was complete, and needs nothing added. In fact, whenever we begin to attempt to fight these battles all over again, which we do not need to fight, at the same time we stop the Grace of God from working on our behalf, which means we are doomed to failure. So, that effort is a losing operation all the way around.

While the Believer does fight the good fight of Faith, it is from a position of *maintaining* the Victory, and not trying to gain the Victory. As well, we do not try to become an Overcomer, in fact, we are already an Overcomer, in Christ.

Every Believer must know and understand, that if it was possible for us to overcome in our own strength and power, then Jesus wasted His time by coming down here and dying on Calvary. No! There was no way that we in ourselves could effect this great work, it had to be done for us, and was done by our Saviour.

THE REST THAT THE BELIEVER HAS IN CHRIST

Jesus said, *"Come unto Me, all ye that labour and are heavy laden, and I will give you rest"* (Mat. 11:28).

If one is to notice, He did not say that He would give us another conflict, or another battle, but rather *"rest."* That means *"rest"* from the struggle! *"Rest"* from self-efforts! *"Rest"* from the labor of trying to attain these things in Christ, which has already been done for us.

When Jesus came the first time, Israel was laboring under the heavy load of the Law, made even heavier by the added laws (hundreds of them) imposed by the Pharisees. Consequently, living for God had become a terrible chore, which was not the Plan of God. Hence, Jesus invited Israel, and the whole world for that matter and for all time, to come to Him, and that He would give us *"rest."*

With many Believers, living for Jesus is a battle of immense proportions, in fact, a battle they are always losing. The simple reason is, it is a battle that has already been fought and won. We do not need to take the land again, it has already been taken. We do not have to defeat the giants again, they have already been defeated. Actually, that is at least a part of what Calvary is all about.

OPPOSITION TO THE WORK OF GOD

Many Believers misunderstand or mistake one's Christian life in respect to one's Christian work. They are two different things altogether.

Respecting our life in Christ, it is to be one that is struggle free. As stated over and over again, the power of the sin nature has been broken once and for all. Sin no longer has dominion over the Believer. Consequently, living for God is supposed to be, and in fact is, the most delightful, glorious, wonderful, exciting, thrilling, heavenly, abundant life that anyone could ever think or contemplate, or comprehend. It is all in Jesus.

However, when it comes to our work for God, that is something else altogether. Satan

NOTES

opposes that work in every conceivable way possible, with Paul as an excellent example.

One would have to know and understand, that Paul had total victory in the realm of living for God. In other words, I think that he could certainly be an example, of course, with Christ as the Perfect Example. Nevertheless, Satan fought this Apostle, as he fought all the Apostles, and continues to do so unto this very hour, concerning Paul's work for God, and the work of all others as well.

Paul faced prison, beatings, stoning, in fact, about every negative thing that one could think, in his efforts to take the Gospel of Jesus Christ to a dying world. However, that is altogether different than one's life in Christ. So, the Believer must distinguish between the two, one's life and living *in* Christ, and one's work *for* Christ.

However, having said that, despite the hardships and difficulties which always come to one who is truly working for God, victory in that as well is ours, as we believe the Lord. Nevertheless, one must not think that this part of our Christian experience, our working for God, is uneventful, for it is not. Some have tried to claim it as such, but they found out to their dismay very shortly that what they were saying was not correct, or else they really were not working for the Lord to start with. The secret is this:

Even when Paul was in prison, his personal victory was complete. Even when they were stoning him, his victory and life in Christ were strong and powerful. In fact, these hardships and difficulties, could not take away from his personal victory, because he knew in *"Whom he had believed, and was persuaded that the Lord was able to keep that which he had committed unto Him against that day"* (II Cor. Chpt. 4; II Tim. 1:12).

THE HOLY SPIRIT

On top of this, and even as we have previously stated, but about which we could not say too much or too often, in all of this, our knowledge of what Christ has done for us, our Faith in that Finished Work, and our reckoning it as such, must be reinforced and strengthened constantly by the Holy Spirit. In fact, He Alone imparts this knowledge correctly to us, and He Alone energizes our

Faith. He is the One Who makes our *"reckoning"* a reality instead of a mere empty boast. That's the reason that Paul spoke of Him so strongly in the 8th Chapter of Romans.

I personally believe, that none of these great Truths, or the victories presented in these Truths, can be made a reality in the lives of Believers, without the Baptism with the Holy Spirit according to Acts 2:4. I realize that many would take exception to what I am saying, claiming that the Believer does receive the Holy Spirit at conversion, which within itself is correct.

But yet, even though the Spirit definitely does continue to perform a work in the Believer's heart and life even though they do not go on and be Baptized with the Holy Spirit, which incidentally does not come automatically at conversion, still, the full realization and reality of what He can do in the Believer's life can never be realized, without the Baptism with the Holy Spirit. That's the reason that Jesus commanded all Believers to be filled with the Spirit (Acts 1:4). That's the reason that the Twelve Apostles were changed men after the Day of Pentecost.

That is the reason the Baptism with the Holy Spirit is given such prominence in the Book of Acts (Chpts. 2, 8-10, 19). That's the reason that Paul gave such preeminence to the Spirit in the great 8th Chapter of this Book we are now studying.

All that Jesus did is made real only by the Holy Spirit. To exclude Him, to figure Him out, or even to misunderstand this great Work of Grace, greatly short-changes the Believer and cuts short all that Christ can be and do in one's life.

So, from now on, irrespective how one feels, one should always claim the victory, because in fact, in Jesus, one does always have the Victory, regardless of feelings. It was all done by Christ, and is just as valid today as when He did it some 2,000 years ago. Confess that! Shout that! Proclaim that! And believe it with all of your heart.

(12) "LET NOT SIN THEREFORE REIGN IN YOUR MORTAL BODY, THAT YE SHOULD OBEY IT IN THE LUSTS THEREOF."

The phrase, *"Let not sin therefore reign in your mortal body,"* presents sin or the

sin nature, as a principle of evil which dwells in the Christian's mortal body; however, it is not to reign there. This tells us several things.

First of all, this tells us that sin is not dead, nor is the Believer completely free from sin, even though he is free from its dominion.

"Reign" in the Greek is *"basileuo,"* and means *"to exercise kingly power."* In the Believer's heart and life, even though the sin nature is still there, it is a dethroned monarch. Consequently, the Believer has the responsibility of keeping it from mounting the throne of his heart, the place which the Lord Jesus Alone should occupy.

The Believer is well able to do this. His will is now free. Also, he has the Divine Nature and the Holy Spirit to urge him on, and give him the desire and the power to refuse this sinful nature and obey the Word. Paul says, *"Order your behavior in the sphere of, by means of, the Spirit, and you will positively not fulfill the desires of the flesh"* (Gal. 5:16).

The Apostle is also saying, *"Stop allowing the sinful nature to reign as king in your mortal body with a view to obeying it in the sphere of its passionate cravings."*

The phrase, *"That ye should obey it in the lusts thereof,"* tells us emphatically that the sin nature is still there, but that we do not have to obey it anymore.

Now to what does the word *"it"* refer, to the sinful Nation *or* the body?

Logic would lead us to relate this pronoun to the sinful nature; however, the Greek Text refers it back to our physical body. It is true that sinful desires originate with the evil nature, not with the physical body. But why does Paul in this instance relate them to the body?

The answer is found in the fact that the sinful nature is an intangible, invisible entity, and in fact, cannot be watched, as should be obvious. It is an unseen enemy whose tactics cannot be observed and, therefore, cannot be guarded against. However, the Saint *is* able to keep watch over the members of his physical body, what his eyes see, what his ears hear, what his mind thinks about, what his hands do, and where his feet carry him. Due to the Divine Nature in the

Believer, he now has the power to guide the actions of the physical body, which means exactly as Paul said, that he does not have to *"obey it in the lusts thereof."*

In fact, it is through the physical body that Satan hooks the individual. While sin definitely originates in the heart, it cannot be brought to full fruition, unless the physical body is engaged in some way. Therefore, the Believer finds that it is the physical body which is constantly giving him trouble respecting ungodly passions, etc. This is what Paul is talking about.

SINLESS PERFECTION?

I think it should be obvious from this 12th verse and related verses, that Sinless Perfection is not possible in the heart and the life of the Believer at present. In fact, and as stated, Paul is saying that the sin nature remains in the Believer. However, it does not *"reign"* or have dominion anymore over the Believer. That bondage is broken and forever. Nevertheless, the Believer, even the holiest among us, is continuing to *"come short of the Glory of God"* (Rom. 3:23).

The coming short of the Glory of God is not something that pertains only to the unbeliever as some think, but it pertains to the Believer as well, and speaks of something that is taking place constantly, and will continue to do so until the Resurrection. In fact, any person who is close to God to any degree, fully understands this. He realizes his shortcomings, flaws, and even occasional failures. It is not right, and the Believer is not forced to do such, but nevertheless it happens.

In fact, the degree of perfection demanded by God is so far beyond our understanding of such, that there is really no way to compare man's definition of perfection with that which God demands. In Truth, the Believer can only come up to that level in Christ; however, the Holy Spirit, nevertheless, is constantly working with us in these areas. Also, even though all are constantly coming short of the Glory of God, the Blood of Jesus at the same time, is constantly *"cleansing us from all sin,"* i.e., from coming short of His Glory.

No, this does not mean that the Lord automatically forgives sin when it is committed

by the Believer. When sin is purposefully committed, it must be purposely repented of before God (I Jn. 1:9). The coming short of the Glory, simply pertains to our everyday life and living, without any acts of sin, be they overt or covert, being purposefully committed. As stated, if one is close to the Lord at all, this reality will quickly become obvious in one's life. Actually, that is one of the things Jesus said in what we refer to as the Lord's Prayer, *"Forgive us our debts* (trespasses)*, as we forgive our debtors* (those who trespass against us)*"* (Mat. 6:12). While this pertains to known sins committed, it *also* pertains to things of which we are not at times fully aware.

As we have stated several times in the past, the sin nature is allowed to remain in the Believer as a disciplinary measure. To be sure it works well, helping the Believer to understand that within himself he is weak and unable to do what needs to be done, and must constantly depend on Christ.

(13) "NEITHER YIELD YE YOUR MEMBERS AS INSTRUMENTS OF UNRIGHTEOUSNESS UNTO SIN: BUT YIELD YOURSELVES UNTO GOD, AS THOSE THAT ARE ALIVE FROM THE DEAD, AND YOUR MEMBERS AS INSTRUMENTS OF RIGHTEOUSNESS UNTO GOD."

The phrase, *"Neither yield ye your members as instruments of unrighteousness unto sin,"* may seem somewhat like a contradiction, even as the previous verse, considering that the *"old man was crucified with Christ,"* and in effect *"the body of sin was destroyed"* (Rom. 6:6). However, it is *not* a contradiction.

It is explained in the presence of the sin nature remaining within our lives, and will remain until the Resurrection. The old man being crucified with Christ, and the body of sin being destroyed, has to do with Salvation and the power of the sin nature being broken in our lives, even though it does remain. The Believer is no longer under its dominion, even though its potential is still there.

Not only will the Saint who counts upon the fact that the power of the sinful nature is broken, stop allowing it to reign as king over him, he will also obey Paul's exhortation,

"Neither yield ye your members as instruments of unrighteousness unto sin." The Reader is to note, the Believer now has that power which he did not have before conversion, *he can yield or not yield*. In fact, there are three powerful words which figure prominently in this scenario of the Believer's Victory. Those words are: *"believe"* (vs. 8), *"reckon"* (vs. 11), and *"yield"* (vs. 13). These express the three energies of the Christian mind which secure and make real a life of Scriptural Sanctification.

In effect, Paul is saying *"Stop yielding,"* simply because the Believer now has the power to do that. We are to stop putting the members of our body at the disposal of, at the service of the sinful nature.

"Instruments" in the Greek is *"hopla,"* and refers to the weapons of a Greek soldier. Consequently, Paul thinks of the members (hands, eyes, ears, tongue, etc.,) of the Christian's body, as weapons to be used in the Christian warfare against evil. The Saint, counting upon the fact that he has been disengaged from the evil nature, does two things, he refuses to allow it to reign as king in his life, and he stops putting his members at its disposal to be used as weapons of unrighteousness.

The phrase, *"But yield yourselves unto God,"* refers to yielding one's will to God. As stated, the Believer now has the power to do this. In Christ, he can yield or not yield.

IS IT POSSIBLE FOR SATAN TO FORCE THE WILL OF A BELIEVER?

We will deal with this subject more broadly in the 7th Chapter, because it is there that Paul directly addresses this very important issue. However, simply because this question is of such great significance, I think it would be proper for us to look at the situation at least briefly.

Yes, Satan, contrary to the beliefs of most Christians, can override the will of a Christian, forcing the Christian to do something he does not want to do, and in fact is fighting with all his strength not to do, providing the Christian does not follow the path laid out by the Lord. As stated, that statement flies in the face of most teaching, but it happens to be true. And to be sure, it is a

NOTES

frightening prospect (Rom. 7:18).

Naturally, if this is so, and it is, then we certainly want to know the safeguards against such action, especially considering how so very important all of this is. In fact, this situation is far more common than most realize.

HOW CAN SATAN DO SUCH A THING?

First of all, and to which we have briefly alluded, if the Believer steps outside of the prescribed path laid down by the Lord, which in fact at times most do, then the Believer is left with nothing but his willpower to overcome Satan, which is woefully inadequate. In other words, irrespective of how strong the will of a Christian may be, within itself it is no match for Satan.

Paul said it very dogmatically in Romans 7:15, *"For that which I do I allow not: for what I would, that do I not; but what I hate, that do I."* No, this is not the account of Paul before his conversion, but rather after his conversion and even after being Baptized with the Holy Spirit. The Truth is, while the unsaved may hate the results of sin, they do not hate sin. In fact, they love sin, which is the reason many sinners do not want to give their hearts to Christ. They simply do not want to give up their sins. So, this statement, as well as others in Romans Chapter 7 proclaim the experience of the Apostle in trying with all his strength to do that which was right, and failing.

As well, in the 18th verse of that same Chapter he directly addressed the will of man and its inadequacy by saying, *"For to will is present with me; but how to perform that which is good I find not"* (Rom. 7:18).

So Paul here plainly says, that the will is not strong enough within itself to overcome Satan.

He also told us in his Epistle to the Galatians how to live the overcoming life. He then made the statement, *"I do not frustrate the Grace of God,"* simply meaning that it is possible to do such a thing (Gal. 2:20-21).

The idea is this: If we do not follow the Lord's prescribed path of victory, we will definitely frustrate the Grace of God, which means that God's Grace cannot function within us to bring about the holiness required, if we at the same time are attempting to do so within our own strength. Our own personal efforts in the wrong direction, cancel out the Grace of God, which invites Satan to ply his wares, making it impossible for us to obey. The Christian can only do what is right, by the enabling Grace of God, and if that is lacking he fails, irrespective of how hard he is trying to do otherwise.

WHAT IS THE PRESCRIBED PATH?

As I hope by now is obvious, this all-important answer is found in Romans Chapters 6 and 8 of this very Epistle. As well, Romans Chapter 7 is extremely significant as well, showing us as we shall see, the futility of the flesh.

The problem is self-will which translates into the flesh, in other words, attempting to solve the problem in our own strength. What makes this thing so subtle is that most of the time we think that our efforts in the flesh are really in the Spirit, when they aren't. Especially considering how religious our personal efforts are, we are easily fooled it seems.

The simple Truth is, if we follow God's glorious, prescribed methods, paid for by Jesus Christ and freely given unto any and all Believers, we cannot fail. If we follow other methods, irrespective of how well meaning and sincere we may be, we cannot help but fail. One must consider that if this problem is so severe (and severe it is) that Jesus had to die on Calvary in our place and be Resurrected from the dead, then we should realize that there is simply no other way for this great thing to be brought about, this continuous victory within our hearts and lives, except by that which He has done for us.

The trouble is, and which we have stated several times, Believers thinking they are walking after the Spirit, when in reality they aren't. To be frank, most Believers do not even know or realize, that Jesus won a twofold victory at Calvary. He paid the sin debt, which most Believers know and understand. However, He also broke the dominion of sin over us. Most Believers would claim knowledge of that, but the Truth is, most have little understanding of this great part of what Christ did at Calvary and the Resurrection.

NOTES

Consequently, they are prime targets for Satan, irrespective as to how dedicated to the Lord they may attempt to be.

The phrase, *"As those that are alive from the dead,"* refers to Believers who were dead to God before their conversion, and, consequently, had no power to yield the members of their physical body to that which was right, but rather were at the mercy of Satan. But now, after coming to Christ, with the power of the sin nature broken and with the Divine Nature imparted, the Believer, is now *"alive"* in the sense of being alive unto God, and has the power to do what he once could not do — *"yield unto God."*

POWER AVAILABLE NOW!

The phrase, *"And your members as instruments of Righteousness unto God,"* proclaims this power now available to the Believer, but only as he knows and understands what Jesus has done for him in breaking the dominion of sin in his life. Irrespective of Satan's power, and he does have power, the Believer can now yield himself as he should, and there is nothing that Satan can do.

As I trust we have properly explained, as Paul speaks of *"your members,"* he is speaking of our physical bodies, concerning our eyes, ears, tongue, feet, hands, in fact every member of our physical bodies. This is so important, and as previously stated, because it is in the physical body that Satan causes our problems. While sin definitely begins in the heart, it cannot actually come to fruition as stated, except through body members. This is where every evil impulse is carried out. However, the Believer now has the power to do the very opposite with the members of his physical body.

He does not have to use his eyes to look at filth over Television or anywhere else for that matter. He can yield his eyes to that only which is Holy and Righteous. The same goes for what he hears and for what he says. He does not have to hear gossip, neither does he have to peddle it with his tongue. He has the power now to yield his ears and tongue to that which is Righteous. As well, he now has the power to bring *"into captivity every thought to the obedience of Christ"* (II Cor. 10:5). Placing oneself in Christ at Calvary and the Resurrection, and understanding what it means, and understanding the Holy Spirit to help us in regard to energizing these great Truths to our hearts and lives, that which was formerly impossible now becomes not only possible, but easy. In other words, the struggle and the fight is gone, because Jesus has already fought and won that fight.

(14) "FOR SIN SHALL NOT HAVE DO-MINION OVER YOU: FOR YE ARE NOT UNDER THE LAW, BUT UNDER GRACE."

The phrase, *"For sin shall not have dominion over you,"* tells us several great and glorious things:

1. This Passage tells us that sin is still alive and as powerful as ever, but is not a danger to the Child of God who follows the prescribed pattern laid out by Christ.

2. The dominion of sin is broken respecting the Child of God. Actually, this happens at the very moment the person comes to Christ. But to *maintain* this victory, the Believer must understand what Christ has done for him in this respect, and have Faith that the Holy Spirit will energize this great Truth in his life.

3. The statement as given by the Holy Spirit through the Apostle, is dogmatic in that it is impossible for sin to have dominion over the Believer, as long as the Believer is abiding by the Word of God. The Saint should live his life everyday with the consciousness of that fact in his mind.

To say it again, and because it is so very important, when the Saint obeys the instructions laid down in these verses relative to his adjustment to the evil nature and the Divine Nature, Paul says, *"The sinful nature will not exercise lordship over you,"* and now he gives the reason:

The phrase, *"For ye are not under the Law, but under Grace,"* refers to the New Covenant, and the glorious provisions in that Covenant which guarantee the Believer the victory of Christ.

If Sanctification (and Sanctification is actually what we are talking about) were based upon the principle of Law-Obedience, i.e., upon works, it would be impossible to escape from the lawful dominion of sin, because a perfect obedience to Divine Law on the part of man is impossible. Consequently,

there is no victory in Law-keeping.

But being based upon the opposite principle of Grace, liberation from the power and dominion of sin, as a master, is secured and may be enjoyed every single day of our lives. Under Law, sin has a dominion, but it has no dominion under Grace. These are two totally independent realms.

To be under Law refers to a person who attempts to live in obedience to the Law of God in his own strength. To be under Grace is to be a person who has been the subject of a surgical operation, so to speak, in which the power of the sinful nature has been broken and the Divine Nature implanted.

The poet says, *"Do this and live, the Law commands, but gives me neither feet nor hands. A better word the Gospel brings. It bids me fly and gives me wings."* Wings in Scripture, speak of supernatural power.

WHY DID PAUL MENTION LAW HERE?

Paul is speaking of the Law of Moses and for the simple reason this Law is the Crown Prince of all Law, simply because it was given by God, and, was consequently perfect. However, it also refers to any type of Law which the Believer makes up, whatever it may be, or even Churches for that matter, with the intention of bringing about a righteous life.

The idea is this: whenever the Believer faces sin and fails, almost automatically, at least if he does not properly know the Word of God, he will institute a series of laws of his own making, or the making of someone else, thinking that by keeping these laws he will have victory. In other words, he will pray so much each day, or read so many Scriptures each day, or witness to so many people about Christ, etc. The list is almost endless.

While these things mentioned are very good within themselves and in fact, should be done and done constantly, but to use them to gain victory over sin, or victory in any capacity simply will not work. And there are two great reasons why they will not work:

1. Law cannot set anyone free, even as the Law of Moses never effected any type of Salvation or Victory for anyone. It was not designed by God for that purpose, nor intended to be used in that fashion. It was very valuable for that which it was intended,

but only for that which it was intended.

2. By doing these things, even as good as they may be, we are at the same time saying that what Jesus did at Calvary and the Resurrection is not enough. In other words, it needs our little contribution to make it effective. While we may not mean it in that fashion, such thinking is an insult to the Finished Work of Christ.

To be sure, Jesus paid the full price for sin, and as well, He paid the full price that sin may not have dominion over us.

WHY DO BELIEVERS RESORT TO LAW
OR SELF EFFORT SO OFTEN?

There are two main reasons why this error is committed:

1. There is something in man, even Godly Believers, that wants to do something to effect our Salvation or Victory. It is a bleed-over from the Fall. Sinner man thinks he is self-sufficient, and his biggest problem is a failure to humble himself before God. As stated, this carries over into the Believer. Somehow, it makes us feel good to think that we have contributed something toward whatever it is that we are seeking, even though in reality we have actually contributed nothing, and in fact are hindering what the Lord has already done.

But still, we continue to try to bring about these qualities and attributes in our hearts and lives by whatever methods are at our disposal, which makes us feel very religious and very worthy, when in reality, all we have done is hinder the Grace of God in our lives.

2. That many Believers attempt to do for themselves what in reality, Christ has already done, is simply because of an ignorance of the Scripture. They simply do not know what the Word of God says about the matter.

To be frank, I do not recall in all of my life ever hearing a Sermon preached respecting the subject we are presently engaging. Now I am certain that it has been preached many times in the past by some Preachers, but not often respecting the totality of the Church, etc.

The main reason it is not preached, which means that the people do not hear or know, at least for the most part, is simply because most Preachers, I think, do not know or

NOTES

realize, even as we have already said, that what Jesus did at Calvary and the Resurrection was in effect, a double cure.

He paid the sin debt, and He also broke the power of sin over the lives of Believers. This is a twofold work. Most readily understand the first part about Jesus paying the debt at Calvary, but they little understand the second part.

THAT WHICH JESUS DID

Once again as we have already stated, regarding the sin debt which Jesus paid, all one has to do is simply believe that He did it, and Salvation instantly comes to the believing sinner. However, if he stops there, even though Saved, he will have tremendous problems in his attempting to live the life of Holiness and Righteousness which he knows he must live. The latter part, which in reality is our Sanctification, can only come about as one knows and understands what Paul is teaching in Romans Chapters 6-8. These Chapters exclusively pertain to what Jesus did in the breaking of the dominion of sin in our lives, and how we may continue to walk in Victory according to the Divine Nature which is in us.

The gist of what Paul is saying in verse 14 is, that if we attempt to gain Victory under Law, sin definitely will have dominion over us. However, if we understand what Christ did, and that it was for us, and that in effect we were in Him when He did these great things, and accept all what He did by Faith, which guarantees us the Grace of God, the sin bondage will be forever broken. That is the Grace of God, which is opposed to the Law, which Law could never bring any type of victory.

(15) "WHAT THEN? SHALL WE SIN, BECAUSE WE ARE NOT UNDER THE LAW, BUT UNDER GRACE? GOD FORBID."

The question, *"What then?"*, presents Paul going back to the first question he asked in this Chapter. Due to the fact that the carnal mind, and especially the carnal religious mind, will *"read it wrong,"* Paul addresses the subject again, because it is so very important.

The question, *"Shall we sin, because we are not under the Law, but under Grace?",* proclaims some Believers once again thinking that if Grace is of such magnitude, we should not be concerned that much about sin.

In verses 2-14, Paul has answered the question regarding the proposed habitual yieldedness of the Believer to the evil nature, by showing that was a mechanical impossibility considering the way the Believer's inner spiritual set-up is arranged by God, the power of indwelling sin broken and the Divine Nature implanted.

Quite possibly another question could be asked in this fashion, *"Since Grace makes it impossible for the Believer to sin habitually like he did before he was Saved, cannot Christians live a life of planned, occasional sin, since they are not under the uncompromising rule of Law, but under the lenient scepter of Grace?"*

Actually, this is the question that is asked!

The answer is, that those who would ask such a question simply do not know Grace. While Law is uncompromising, Grace is never lenient. *Actually, it is far stricter than Law could ever be.* It is a far greater deterrent of evil than Law ever was. For instance, a half dozen motorcycle policemen with their motors tuned up, are a far greater deterrent to speeding, than any number of signboards along the road indicating the speed limit. The Holy Spirit, indwelling the Believer, takes notice of the slightest sin and convicts him of it, whereas the Law could act only generally and then only when the conscience of the individual cooperated with it. Consequently, Grace not only forgives, but teaches (Titus 3:11-14).

Just because the Believer is dead to the Law, does not mean that the Law itself is dead, or that the Believer can sin with impunity. Actually, it is the very opposite! There is a new propelling and compelling deterrent to sin, Divine Love, produced in the Believer's being which causes him to hate sin and obey the Word of God (Jn. 14:21-24; Gal. 5:13).

The two words, *"God forbid,"* is Paul's answer to such a preposterous question. It must be our answer as well.

Grace is never a license to sin, but rather the very opposite, actually, the liberty to live a Holy Life.

(16) "KNOW YE NOT, THAT TO WHOM

YE YIELD YOURSELVES SERVANTS TO OBEY, HIS SERVANTS YE ARE TO WHOM YE OBEY; WHETHER OF SIN UNTO DEATH, OR OF OBEDIENCE UNTO RIGHTEOUSNESS?"

The beginning of the question *"Know ye not, that to whom ye yield yourselves servants to obey, his servants ye are to whom ye obey?"*, presents Paul answering the question even to a greater degree by showing that the Believer has changed masters.

"Servants" in the Greek Text is *"doulos,"* and means *"the most abject, servile term for a slave in the Greek language."* So, instead of being translated *"servants"* it should have been translated *"slaves."*

The Believer was a slave of Satan before Salvation, but since he has been Saved, he is now a slave of the Lord Jesus. He has changed masters because he has a new nature, the Divine, and the evil nature which formerly compelled him to serve the Devil has had its power over him broken.

In the various meanings of this word *"doulos,"* we will trace Paul's argument to the effect that it is an impossibility for the Believer to live a life of planned occasional sin. While the Believer does occasionally sin, he does not provide in his life's plan for occasional acts of sin of any nature. He hates sin and endeavors to keep it out of his life, and in the event that he does commit an act of sin, he deals with it in confession to the Lord Jesus, putting it out of his life and receiving the cleansing the Blood of our Lord offers (I Jn. 1:9).

BORN INTO A CONDITION OF SLAVERY

The word *"doulos"* refers to one who is born into a condition of slavery. As we were born by natural generation, we inherited a totally depraved nature through our parents from Adam, a nature which made us love sin and compelled us to serve it habitually. Now, being born again by the act of Regeneration through the Agency of the Holy Spirit, we are given a new nature, the Divine, which gives us both the desire and the power to do God's Will. With our liberation from the compelling power of the evil nature and our acquisition of the Divine Nature, we have changed masters, from Satan to our Lord.

Paul argues that the Believer does not want to live even a life of occasional sin because, in the first place he does not have to, since the power of the evil nature over him is broken, and in the second place, he does not desire to do so, since his New Nature causes him to hate sin and love Righteousness, and when a person does not have to do what he does not want to do, he simply does not do it. As stated, the Believer has changed masters.

IN THE WILL OF GOD

Again, *"doulos"* means *"one whose will is swallowed up in the will of another."*

Paul argues that before Salvation, the person's will was swallowed up in the will of Satan, but since he has been Saved, his will is swallowed up in the sweet Will of God. And since that is so, he does not desire to live a life of occasional sin, in other words, he takes sin very seriously and never passes it off lightly.

BOUND TO ANOTHER

Again, *"doulos"* refers to one who is bound to another in bands so strong that only death can break them. The Believer's identification with the Lord Jesus in His Death, broke the bands which bound him to Satan. Now, he is bound to the Lord Jesus as His bondslave in bands so strong that only death can break them.

Since Christ is the Believer's life and He will never die again, the Believer is bound to Him forever. The only way he could live a life of planned occasional sin is to become again the slave of the evil nature and Satan. But his bands binding him to the Lord Jesus are unbreakable, at least as long as his desire is to serve God and, therefore, a return to Satan and his slavery is an impossibility under those circumstances.

IN DISREGARD OF HIS OWN INTERESTS

"Doulos" also means, *"one who serves another to the disregard of his own interests."* The sinner serves Satan to the disregard of his own best interest. He does so because he is compelled to do so. He gets sin and death,

sorrow and suffering.

The Believer, with his own will and accord, serves the Lord Jesus with an abandon that says; *"Nothing matters about me, just so long as the Lord Jesus is Glorified."*

Now, Paul argues, a person who does that, who disregards himself for the sake of the Lord Jesus, does not want to live a life of sin in any form.

The conclusion of the question, *"Whether of sin unto death, or of obedience unto Righteousness?"*, presents two masters here contrasted — sin and Righteousness. A man must be the servant of one or the other, for no man can serve two masters.

(17) "BUT GOD BE THANKED, THAT YE WERE THE SERVANTS OF SIN, BUT YE HAVE OBEYED FROM THE HEART THAT FORM OF DOCTRINE WHICH WAS DELIVERED YOU."

The phrase, *"But God be thanked, that ye were the servants of sin,"* speaks of a past tense. In other words, the Believer is no more a slave of sin, and because of the Power of God resident within Christ, and conveyed to the Believer by the Holy Spirit.

The phrase, *"But ye have obeyed from the heart that form of Doctrine which was delivered you,"* declares the Christian Faith to have been once for all delivered to the Church as fixed and complete, and, therefore, neither needing nor accepting additions. Into that form, as into a mould, the Roman Believers, and all others for that matter, were poured or *"delivered,"* and the two sides of that mould being *"Justification"* and *"Sanctification,"* it was manifest that anyone leading a sinful life had not been poured into the mould, or else are ignorant of the Word of God.

For as the subject of verse 1 to verse 11 is God *declaring* a sinner Righteous, i.e., Justification, so the theme of Romans 6:12 to Romans 8:39 is God *making* the Believer Righteous, i.e., Sanctification.

To better explain this statement by Paul, the word *"delivered"* in the Greek Text is somewhat different than normally used. Consequently, it would have been better translated, *"the form of Doctrine into which you were delivered."* While it is true that the Doctrines of Salvation were delivered to us, and we by the Grace of God believed them. However, that is not what Paul is saying here in the Greek. He is actually saying that the Believer was *delivered into "the form of Doctrine,"* that is, in Salvation, God constituted the Believer inwardly so that he would react to the Doctrines of Grace by nature (the Divine Nature) in such a way as to receive and obey them.

We were delivered into the teaching (Doctrine) in that we were constituted in Salvation so that we would obey it.

Paul thanks God that whereas before Salvation we were slaves of the evil nature, we were in Salvation delivered (handed over) to the teachings of Grace so that we become slaves of Righteousness (Wuest).

Consequently, the idea is, that the manner in which this thing is done respecting the life of the Believer, makes it impossible not to have Victory, that is, if the Believer knows and understands his place and position in Christ according to Romans Chapters 6-8.

To say it another way, the manner in which the Holy Spirit has described this Finished Work of Christ to the Believer, makes it impossible for the Believer to fail, that is if he obeys this Word. As stated, all it takes is knowing and understanding what has been done and having Faith in what has been done. Considering that the Holy Spirit will help us to do both, none of us have any excuse.

(18) "BEING THEN MADE FREE FROM SIN, YE BECAME THE SERVANTS OF RIGHTEOUSNESS."

The phrase, *"Being then made free from sin,"* actually means being free from the sin nature in that it has no more power over the Believer.

The phrase, *"Ye became the servants of Righteousness,"* actually says, that having been set free from the evil nature, and a slave to that nature, the Believer is now constituted a slave of Righteousness.

I realize that the word *"slave"* sounds very strong to the Believer, actually unappetizing. However, a slave of Jesus Christ is 180 degrees from being a slave of Satan. Jesus alluded to such when He said, *"Take My yoke* (slave yoke) *upon you, and learn of Me; for I am meek and lowly in heart: and ye shall*

find rest unto your souls.

"For My yoke (slave yoke) *is easy, and My burden* (demands) *is light"* (Mat. 11:29-30).

Being a slave of Christ is totally unlike the use of the word in any other capacity. While the meaning of the word is the same respecting Christ, the actual condition is altogether different — actually such a difference that it is impossible to even compare such.

To serve Christ is a pleasure. To give one's very life to and for Him is a privilege. He is so good to the Believer, so generous, so kind, so literally giving of Himself, that once one has served Him for any length of time, one delights in being His slave. To be frank, I would a thousand times rather be His slave, than to be Satan's king.

(19) "I SPEAK AFTER THE MANNER OF MEN BECAUSE OF THE INFIRMITY OF YOUR FLESH: FOR AS YE HAVE YIELDED YOUR MEMBERS SERVANTS TO UNCLEANNESS AND TO INIQUITY UNTO INIQUITY; EVEN SO NOW YIELD YOUR MEMBERS SERVANTS TO RIGHTEOUSNESS UNTO HOLINESS."

The phrase, *"I speak after the manner of men because of the infirmity of your flesh,"* actually has Paul apologizing for using the illustration drawn from human relations, that of a slave. But he says that he was forced to do so because of the frailties of the flesh.

The idea is, that these Romans to whom he was writing, plus all of the human family and for all time, had been slaves to the passions of sin before their conversion. The *"flesh"* being what it is, is very quickly enslaved to evil passions. I speak of alcohol, drugs, gambling, lust, hate, anger, greed, jealousy, etc.

The phrase, *"For as ye have yielded your members servants to uncleanness and to iniquity unto iniquity,"* details their lives, as well as all others, before coming to Christ. *"Uncleanness"* speaks of moral impurity, which plagues the human race. This is the very opposite of Righteousness, which speaks of moral perfection, and which only God has and can give.

The manner in which Paul uses the phrase, *"And to iniquity unto iniquity,"* speaks of the destructive power of sin. In other words, one iniquity leads to another, consequently, making it impossible for one to break out of such a bondage, at least within their own capabilities. It just cannot be! Only the Power of God can set the captive free.

A proper illustration would be that of quicksand. The more that one struggles in that mixture, it tends to have the very opposite effect than that desired. The person actually gets deeper into the quagmire, and thus, is sin. That is why David said, *"I waited patiently for the Lord; and He inclined unto me, and heard my cry.*

"He brought me up also out of an horrible pit, out of the miry clay, and set my feet upon a rock, and established my goings" (Ps. 40:1-2).

EVER UPWARD

The phrase, *"Even so now yield your members servants to Righteousness unto Holiness,"* presents the same principle as *"iniquity unto iniquity,"* but in the very opposite direction.

First of all, Paul is telling the Believer that since the power of the sin nature is broken, he no longer has to yield his physical members to unrighteousness, but can now yield them as slaves to Righteousness unto Holiness.

As well, as *"iniquity unto iniquity"* dragged the person down, even ever downward, and despite all he can do otherwise irrespective of what it might be, now the direction totally changes. Everything is ever upward. In other words, the Righteousness goes into Holiness, i.e., a holy life, and is a guarantee as the Believer follows the Divine Nature which is now within him and controlling him.

What we are now seeing, and what Paul is now explaining, is so beautiful as to defy description. It presents that which automatically comes with the born-again experience, providing the Believer understands his proper place in Christ, and what Christ did for him at Calvary and the Resurrection. The whole wicked process of the Fall is now reversed.

The tragedy about the Fall is, that the Falling never reaches a stopping place. In other words, despite all the centuries of education, technological advancement and higher learning, the Fall continues even unto

this hour, and will continue to continue. The actual Truth is that man is experiencing the very opposite of the erroneous teaching of evolution. He is not gradually getting better, but getting worse, and that despite all he can do otherwise.

As we have already stated, the 20th Century, which has been the century of the greatest education and advancement ever known to humanity, at the same time has seen the greatest bloodletting of any century in history. In stark reality, the ever-deepening horror of the Fall is made obvious to all who care to see, and I state again, that it is not possible for man to stop this downward slide within his own power or ability. That's the reason that man must be born again. Only God can stop this process, only God can reverse the direction, and He does it exclusively through His Son, The Lord Jesus Christ. Any other hope is a fool's hope and any other way is a fool's way.

(20) "FOR WHEN YE WERE THE SERVANTS OF SIN, YE WERE FREE FROM RIGHTEOUSNESS."

The phrase, *"For when ye were the servants of sin,"* should have been translated, even as we have stated, *"For when ye were the slaves of sin."* There could be no state worse than the state of one as a slave to sin. The pain and suffering which accompanies such bondage is actually beyond comprehension.

Beginning in the late Fall of 1991, we began to have two prayer meetings a day. One each morning and each night, minus Service times. I did this because the Lord instructed me to do so, and to be sure, it has been one of, if not the greatest thing, that has ever happened to my Christian experience. Each time occupies about an hour.

INTERCESSION AND TRAVAIL

During these times, the Lord has helped me to enter into Intercession, even into Travail for the lost, and in a way that I have never previously known. It is almost as if I can feel their pain and helplessness. They are locked in a prison in which the doors cannot be opened except by the Power of God.

To be frank, sinners love sin, but precious few of them if any, fully understand the implications of sin. It is a lark at the beginning, but swiftly goes into bondage. Most meet that bondage with denial, but the bondage is there just the same. And as Paul has stated, the situation does not get better, only worse.

After a while, the sinner wants out, but finds that he is trapped, and trapped so powerfully that he is unable to break the emotional and darkened spiritual chains which bind him.

In my spirit, even time and time again, I have seen these people, and as stated, I have felt their pain. To be sure, we have seen literal thousands instantly and gloriously set free by the Power of God, either through our Telecast, or in Crusades. But yet, the Spirit of God has moved upon me mightily, that I seek the Face of the Lord that He give us a greater enduement of Power from on High, that the Holy Spirit may work through us in order to bring conviction to these lost souls, and to help them to know and realize that the terrible bondages can be broken. The Lord is beginning to do that, even in a greater way than we've ever known before. It is being done for the *"slaves of sin,"* for it is for them for whom Jesus died!

The phrase, *"Ye were free from Righteousness,"* actually means that it was not possible in that state to have any Righteousness. Being a slave to sin, precludes all Righteousness. Of course, the type of *"Righteousness"* of which Paul speaks, is the Righteousness of God.

Man has forever attempted to bring about his own Righteousness. It is called self-righteousness. Man honors it and so does most of the Church, but not God. In fact, Isaiah referred to such by saying, *"But we are all as an unclean thing, and all our Righteousnesses are as filthy rags; and we all do fade as a leaf; and our iniquities, like the wind, have taken us away"* (Isa. 64:6).

Upon one's confession of Faith in the Lord Jesus Christ, Righteousness is freely and instantly imputed by God to the believing sinner. It comes only by Faith and Trust in Christ. It is given even to the worst of sinners, that is if they properly believe Christ (Eph. 2:7-8).

However, if man attempts in any way to offer to God that which is of his own efforts, it will be every time rejected. Only

the Righteousness of Christ is acceptable!

(21) "WHAT FRUIT HAD YE THEN IN THOSE THINGS WHEREOF YE ARE NOW ASHAMED? FOR THE END OF THOSE THINGS IS DEATH."

The question, *"What fruit had ye then in those things whereof ye are now ashamed?",* presents a very interesting spectacle.

The idea is, that there is absolutely nothing of any value which can come out of the sinful experience. There is *"fruit"* alright, but it is evil fruit! Irrespective of the efforts, irrespective of the amount of money spent, irrespective of the education, or anything else one might name, other than Christ there is no proper fruit. That means zero!

To be *"ashamed"* is the right description. To be frank, the shame of such activity is always awful. Without God, it is a world of immorality, lying, cheating, stealing, war, hurt, pain, loneliness, sickness, suffering, and every imaginable evil thing. Any satisfaction that one gets in that world, is fleeting and, consequently, soon gone. There is absolutely nothing that is positive or of any consequence in the world of sin, which is a world without Christ. It is only shame and disgrace.

The phrase, *"For the end of those things is death,"* proclaims again the ever-deepening of the destructive power of *"iniquity unto iniquity."* The end result is always death, that is if one could speak of this horror as having an end, which one really cannot. The final result is the Lake of Fire, which will never end.

(22) "BUT NOW BEING MADE FREE FROM SIN, AND BECOME SERVANTS TO GOD, YE HAVE YOUR FRUIT UNTO HOLINESS, AND THE END EVERLASTING LIFE."

The phrase, *"But now being made free from sin,"* tells us two things:

1. Paul is saying here that this great work has been carried out and finished in totality by Christ, and is now a fact respecting all Believers. It is somewhat like the price that Jesus has paid to satisfy the sin question respecting unbelievers.

When Jesus died on Calvary for the lost, He did so for every single human being who had ever lived, who was alive at the time, and who would live in the future. Of course, only those who had trusted Christ before

Calvary are included as should be obvious. Nevertheless, when Jesus died, He died for the entirety of the world. Consequently, in the Mind of God Salvation is available to all. They only have to come and partake of this Water of Life. In fact, the great invitation to all of humanity is *"Come"* (Isa. 55:1; Jn. 7:37; Rev. 22:17).

Likewise respecting every single Believer. As we have stated over and over, when Jesus died on Calvary, He not only satisfied the sin debt, but, as well, He broke the dominion of sin over the Believer. Consequently, every single Believer in the world can be free from all sin dominion, and in the Mind of God is in fact free — in other words, a present tense action. Regrettably, as most of the world does not take advantage of God's *Salvation Plan*, likewise, most Christians do not take advantage of God's *Victory Plan*.

2. The Believer can be free now, and without having to go through a long regimen of religious works, etc. In other words, the terrible struggle that many Believers are having with sin at this present time, can be ended instantly, once for all, exactly as Paul said, *"now!"* Jesus meant what He said, when He invited all to come to Him and *"rest"* (Mat. 11:28).

He was speaking of *"rest"* from this struggle against sin.

The phrase, *"And become servants to God,"* in essence means *"slaves to God, and not slaves to sin."*

Allow me to say it again, and because Paul did, it is a privilege and a pleasure to be a slave of the Lord. Perhaps the word *"slave"* is an unfortunate metaphor, for the simple reason that the term denotes a terrible state. However, where that is true with man, it is not true at all with God.

It is typified in the Old Testament by a slave who was given his freedom, but loved his master so much, and felt that he was treated so grandly and so kindly, that he actually did not want his freedom. In all Truth, he felt he had far more freedom serving his master, than he would have had otherwise. He was granted protection, security, given Love, blessed constantly, so why would he want to leave that!

When he made this decision, *"He shall*

bring him to the door, or unto the door post; and his master shall bore his ear through with an aul; and he shall serve him for ever" (Ex. 21:6; Deut. 15:17).

Spiritually speaking, I want both my ears pierced with an aul and for the simple reason, that it is a privilege and an honor to serve and worship the Lord of Glory — to be His servant, i.e., *"slave."*

The phrase, *"Ye have your fruit unto Holiness,"* i.e., a holy life, proclaims what God gives, versus the *"fruit"* of the world.

HOLINESS

Believers in every age have been called by God to be holy. There is no contradiction between the Old Testament and the New Testament concepts of Holiness, but there is a change in emphasis on what Holiness now involves.

HOLINESS IN THE OLD TESTAMENT

The root of the Hebrew words translated *"holy"* and *"holiness"* is *"qadas."* It means *"to be consecrated, to be dedicated, to be holy."* Anything that is *"holy"* is *"set apart."* It is removed from the realm of the common and moved to the sphere of the Sacred.

In the Old Testament the focus of the Sacred realm is God Himself, Israel's Holy One (II Ki. 19:22; Job 6:10; Ps. 16:10; 22:3; 71:22; 78:41; 89:18; Prov. 9:10; 30:3; Isa. 1:4; 5:19, 24; 10:17, 20; 12:6; 17:7; 29:23; Jer. 50:29; 51:5; Ezek. 39:7; etc.)

PLACES AND THINGS

"Holy" becomes a technical term used of persons, places, times, and things that were considered Sacred because they were associated with and consecrated to God.

For instance, the seventh day was holy, to be reserved for worship and rest (Gen. 2:3; Ex. 20:8-11; Deut. 5:12). Mt. Sinai was holy, for God appeared there in fire to give the Ten Commandments (Ex. 19:23).

The Priests of Israel were holy (Lev. 21:7), and everything associated with Worship and Sacrifice was to be considered holy. In a very significant sense Israel itself was considered holy, for this people was chosen by God to be His Own Special Possession (Deut. 7:6; 14:2, 21).

THE SACRED AND THE SECULAR

It is important to realize that great stress is placed in the Old Testament on maintaining the distinction between what is Sacred and what is secular. The holy must never be used in a common or profane way. That which was consecrated to God must be for His use alone — forever.

RITUAL HOLINESS

Israel's worship of God and service to God were both cultic (ritual) and moral. The cultic element established rituals and many aspects of the lifestyle of God's people.

A person was in a state of Holiness when he observed cultic restrictions. It was a responsibility of the Priests to *"distinguish between the holy and the common, between the unclean and the clean, and* (they were required to) *teach the Israelites all the Decrees the Lord* (had) *given them through Moses"* (Lev. 10:10-11).

As an example, essential nonmoral (that had nothing to do with morality) practices, such as not cooking a young goat and its mother's milk (Ex. 34:26), and religious ceremonies were aspects of ritual holiness. This is what is meant by the cultic or ritual.

MORAL HOLINESS

Two aspects of God's Nature are associated with Holiness in the Old Testament. One is His essential Power and Splendor. When two of Aaron's sons violated the ritual regulations governing worship, God, as quoted by Moses, announced: *"Among those who approach Me I will shew Myself Holy; in the sight of all the people I will be honoured"* (Lev. 10:3).

Fire flared from the Lord on that occasion and consumed the men who had treated Him with contempt by ignoring His Commands. God's Holiness was displayed in this exercise of awesome power.

Leviticus 19:2 displays a moral dimension to God's Holiness. *"Speak to the entire Assembly of Israel,"* the Lord told Moses, *"And say to them: 'Be Holy because I, the Lord your God, am Holy.'"*

The Commands that follow this statement are not ritual but are moral in character. They deal with idolatry, theft, lying, fraud,

slander, revenge, etc., and include the Command to Love one's neighbor. These Commands are punctuated regularly by the reminder, *"I am the Lord."*

HOLINESS AND GOD'S MORAL CHARACTER

In this Old Testament Passage and many others, God's Holiness is directly linked with His Own Moral Character. Holiness is displayed in His Moral Perfection and Faithful Commitment to Good and in His Judgment on those who desert the way of goodness for sin. As Isaiah says: *"The Lord Almighty will be exalted by His Justice, and the Holy God will show Himself Holy by His Righteousness"* (Isa. 5:16).

When Israel was set apart to God by God's Sovereign Choice, both the ritual and moral aspects of obedience to God were essential in their life of Holiness.

THE NEW TESTAMENT CONCEPT OF HOLINESS

Several words in Greek culture were associated with the idea of the Holy:

"Hieros" reflected the Old Testament emphasis on the ritually Holy. This word is rarely used in the New Testament (found only twice — I Cor. 9:13; II Tim. 3:15).

"Hagios" reflected the Law's expression of the Divine Will and human obligation to God. It had a strong moral overtone. It is this word that is the dominant one in the New Testament.

"Hosios" reflected piety or devoutness. It is used eight times in the New Testament — Acts 2:27; 13:34-35; I Tim. 2:8; Tit. 1:8; Heb. 7:26; Rev. 15:4; 16:5 — four of them in quotations from the Old Testament.

In addition, *"hosiotes"* is used twice in the New Testament (Lk. 1:75; Eph. 4:24), and *"osme"* is used once (I Thess. 2:10).

In the New Testament the most frequent use of *"Holy"* is in the designation of God's Spirit as the Holy Spirit. It is also used often in reference to Believers as God's *"Saints."* In the Gospels and Acts *"Holy"* may have either a ritual or a moral emphasis, just as *"qadas"* words do in the Old Testament.

It is in the New Testament, however, that we see a dramatic shift in the concept of the nature of practical Holiness.

THE HOLY LIFE

In the Old Testament, Holiness is expressed in strict separation. The clean were not permitted to come in contact with the unclean. Israel had to fiercely guard its differences from the surrounding Nations. Cultic commitments were, in part, designed to underline the uniqueness of Israel as a people set apart from all others to God.

The New Testament also has an emphasis on separation. But Christians do not live in a separate Nation. The Church is scattered as tiny Communities planted in every kind of human society. Paul wrote to Corinth: *"I have written you in my letter not to associate with sexually immoral people — however I am not speaking of the sinners of this world who are immoral, or the greedy and swindlers, or idolaters. In that case you would have to leave this world"* (I Cor. 5:9-10).

So, Paul is not preaching isolation, but rather separation. However, if we misunderstand separation and think that it speaks of a lack of contact between the clean and the unclean, the Sacred and the common, such thinking is incorrect. The New Testament presents a dynamic concept of Holiness as moral purity expressed in contact with the common and profane! Believers are to separate themselves from evil, but not from the people who remain uncommitted to the Divine Standards. In this way our Light is to shine.

THE CHRISTIAN EXPERIENCE

This is an extremely important reorientation. In Christian experience the Holy is not kept rigorously distinct from ordinary life. Instead, the essence of Holiness in the Believer, is a dynamic expression of the Divine within the normal processes of daily life. In other words, the Lord has not called us to isolate ourselves from the public, or in fact to separate ourselves from sinners, but to definitely separate ourselves from their sin.

We see this emphasis in nearly all of the Epistles. Peter expresses God's Call to Holiness in these words: *"Just as He Who called you is Holy, so be Holy in all you do; for it is written, 'Be Holy, because I am Holy'"* (I Pet. 1:15-16).

Peter goes on to explain this Holiness *"in all you do"* in the Second Chapter of the same Letter: *"You are a chosen people, a Royal Priesthood, a Holy Nation, a People belonging to God, that you may declare the Praises of Him Who called you out of darkness into His wonderful Light . . . Dear Friends, I urge you, as aliens and strangers in the world, to abstain from sinful desires, which war against your soul. Live such good lives among the Pagans that, though they accuse you of doing wrong, they may see your good deeds and glorify God on the day He visits us"* (I Pet. 2:9, 11-12).

It is as God's obedient Children, living by His Will as strangers within our cultures, that we fulfill the Call to Holiness.

JESUS AS THE CENTER OF OUR LIVES

This theme is developed in many of Paul's Epistles. Colossians is a good example. After presenting Jesus as the Center of our lives and our Christian experience, Paul looks at empty avenues to spiritual achievement. He dismisses ritualistic and ascetic religious practices as lacking any value (Col. 2:20-23).

Instead, he describes the Holy Life as one involving an inner separation from those passions that bubble up from our sinful natures (Col. 3:5-11). What marks Believers as *"God's Chosen People, Holy and dearly Loved"* (Col. 3:12) is their commitment to compassion, kindness, humility, gentleness, and patience. It is these things, with mutual forgiveness and deepening Love, that expresses the reality of Holiness (Col. 3:12-14).

In the New Testament, God's People are called *"Saints"* — His Holy Ones. This reflects our standing as those who have been set aside by God's Actions in Christ to be His Own Personal Possessions. But the term is also to reflect our experience.

We are daily to live out that moral Holiness and active Love that is revealed so beautifully in God's Own Character. The Call to Holiness in the New Testament is a Call to let our Father be seen and Glorified in our lives.

THE HOLY SPIRIT

Most New Testament uses of *"Holy,"* as we have stated, are in the title *"Holy Spirit."*

In the New Testament the Father and Son are sometimes also called *"Holy"* (Lk. 1:35; Jn. 17:11), but almost every mention of the Spirit includes the word *"Holy,"* thus, *"Holy Spirit."* This title is more than a reference to the Spirit's Deity; it is more specifically a reference to the nature of His Work.

Old Testament Cultic Holiness focused attention on Holy persons (Priests), places (the Temple, Jerusalem), and things (the Altar, the Temple Furniture, etc.). In the New Testament the Sacred is no longer seen in places or things. The focus of the Holy shifts dramatically to persons. *"Don't you know,"* Paul writes emotionally, *"that you yourselves are God's Temple and that God's Spirit dwells in you?"* (I Cor. 3:16).

In the New Testament, Holiness is linked with the Spirit's Working and with the product of His Work within human beings.

The Spirit is the Holy Spirit because He Himself is the Source of the Holy. Thus, New Testament Holiness is always rooted in a relationship with Jesus, Whom the Holy Spirit came to Glorify, and with the Spirit, Whom Jesus sends to be within every Believer.

CONSECRATION TO GOD

The idea of Holiness in Both Testaments is one of Consecration to God. In the Old Testament, and as we have stated, Holiness involves keeping both ritual and moral Commandments. Places and things and even persons were set aside as Sacred, to have no contact with the common or ordinary.

But the Old Testament consistently reminds us that the key to understanding Holiness is found in the Character of God. Holiness is expressed in His Power and His Own Moral Character. So True Holiness in His People will necessarily have a strong moral component.

HOLINESS IS AN EXPRESSION OF OUR INNER BEING

In the New Testament the ritual of the Old Testament is set aside. The emphasis in New Testament Teaching about Holiness is squarely on the moral. There is another shift in emphasis as well.

The Old Testament maintains strict separation between the Holy and the profane. In the New Testament, Holiness is true goodness woven through the lifestyle of the Believer and expressed in every daily activity and in every relationship.

In the Old Testament, God's People consecrated persons, places, and things solely for God's use. In the New Testament, God's Spirit Himself acts in Salvation to set us apart to God. In addition, the Holy Spirit continues to act in our lives to infuse us with Christ's Own Likeness and to enable us by His Power to express Christlikeness in our daily lives.

It is here that we find the True Holiness of the New Testament, all made possible by Jesus Christ, Who is the Example of True Holiness, and carried out by the Holy Spirit.

It is all a joyous commitment to God and to the truly good, expressed in everything we say and do.

(The thoughts on Holiness were provided by Dr. Lawrence Richards.)

The phrase, *"And the end Everlasting Life,"* presents the very opposite of sin which is death.

WHAT IS EVERLASTING LIFE?

Everlasting Life or Eternal Life is the opposite of eternal death. Eternal Life is eternal union with God by the cancellation of the eternal death penalty. It is God's Life infused in the Believer. It is never our life if we are not dwelling in God. It is ours only when we get into Christ and it is ours only as long as we abide in Him (I Jn. 2:24; 5:11-12). It is, therefore, something separate and apart from us and is imparted to us only when we are Saved and as long as we are Saved. Christ is our Life and we have it as long as we have Him (Jn. 15:1-7; Col. 2:6-7; 3:4).

THE CONDITIONS

The conditions which Jesus lays down for entering into this Life are Faith in Himself as the One Mediator of the Life, and the following of Him in a life of obedience. He Alone knows the Father and can reveal Him to others (Mat. 11:27). He Alone can give true rest and can teach men how to live, and give them the power to live that which He teaches (Mat. 11:28). The sure way to this Life is: *"Follow Me."*

His whole Ministry was virtually a prolonged effort to win confidence in Himself as Son and Mediator, to win obedience, and hence, bring men unto the spiritual relationships and activities which constitute the True Life.

In other words, Jesus is not only the Bearer of Everlasting Life, but as well, its Source.

LIFE

The fullest and richest teachings regarding Life are found in John's Gospel. Actually, the greatest word of this Gospel is *"Life."* John says he wrote the Gospel in order that *"Ye may have Life"* (Jn. 20:31).

Most of the teachings of Jesus recorded, circle around this great word *"Life."* This teaching is in no way distinctive and different from that of the other Gospels, but is supplementary, and completes the teaching of Jesus on the subject. The use of the word is not as varied, being concentrated on the one supreme subject.

John's Gospel represents Jesus the Logos as the Origin and Means of all Life to the world. As the Preincarnate Logos He was, and is, the Source of Life not only to mankind, but, as well, to the Universe (Jn. 1:4). As the Incarnate Logos He said His Life had been derived originally from the Father (Jn. 5:26; 6:57; 10:18). He then was and is the Means of Life to men (Jn. 3:15-16; 4:14; 5:21, 39-40); and this was the purpose for which He came into the world (Jn. 6:33-34, 51; 10:10).

The nearest approach to the definition of Eternal Life is found in John 17:3, and is in a prayer of Jesus, *"And this is Life Eternal, that they might know Thee the only True God, and Jesus Christ Whom Thou hast sent."*

(23) "FOR THE WAGES OF SIN IS DEATH; BUT THE GIFT OF GOD IS ETERNAL LIFE THROUGH JESUS CHRIST OUR LORD."

The phrase, *"For the wages of sin is death,"* speaks of spiritual death which is separation from God, and is the lot of those who follow this precarious path. On that broad way, there are no exceptions.

"Wages" in the Greek is *"opsoniom,"* and means *"whatever is bought or purchased to be eaten with bread, such as fish, etc."* It actually had reference to a Roman soldier,

and him being paid partially in money and partially in foodstuff. So, Paul is saying that sin does pay, but its wages is *"death."* It is not a very pleasant prospect!

The phrase, *"But the Gift of God is Eternal Life through Jesus Christ our Lord,"* portrays the totality of all things in this one verse. The former is *"death,"* while the latter is *"Life."*

However, the *"Life"* which is *"Eternal"* is found only *"through Jesus Christ our Lord."*

In all of this, Paul speaks of servants of iniquity who lead a life of uncleanness, up beside the servants of Righteousness, who lead a life of Sanctification. So long, therefore, as a man is the servant of the one he cannot obey the other. The one service is shameful and ends in death; the other is pure and ends in Life.

This Life is consciously Eternal and this Death is also consciously Eternal, the one being set over against the other. To be dead is horrible. To be consciously dead is more horrible. To be conscious that one is dead eternally, and to be eternally conscious of the fact, is most horrible.

The sinner earns his wages, but the Believer does not earn Eternal Life. It is a Free Gift, even as Paul says in this 23rd verse, and is from God. Its Channel is Christ and His Atoning Work.

God reckons the Believer in Christ to have died with Him. The Believer is to reckon this to be true. He is, therefore, dead to sin, to self, and to the world, and cannot, therefore, live in that to which he has died.

He is associated with Christ in His Death, and so freed from the dominion of sin, and he is associated with Christ in His Risen Life and consequently becomes the bondslave of Righteousness.

In the Death and Resurrection of Christ he is liberated from the one master, sin, in order to be handed over to the other Master, Righteousness. It is in that Risen Life that the Believer really knows Christ, and experimentally proves His Power to Sanctify him wholly (Williams).

"Oh let your soul now be filled with gladness, your heart redeemed, rejoice indeed!

"Oh may the thought banish all your sadness that in His Blood you have been freed."

"It is a good, every good transcending, that Christ has died for you and me!
"It is a gladness that has no ending there in God's wondrous love to see."

CHAPTER 7

(1) "KNOW YE NOT, BRETHREN, (FOR I SPEAK TO THEM THAT KNOW THE LAW,) HOW THAT THE LAW HATH DOMINION OVER A MAN AS LONG AS HE LIVETH?"

Romans Chapter 7 is at least one of the most important Chapters in the entirety of the Word of God, respecting the Christian walk and its Victory. And yet, most Believers pay scant attention to its contents, and for a variety of reasons.

Many simply don't understand it and, therefore, ignore it, or else just scan it when they come to its place in the order of Scripture.

I would pray that the Lord would help us, at least in some measure, to open up this Text, which is of such tremendous significance to any and all Believers.

Others give it little credence because they have been taught that it pertains to Paul's before-Conversion experience, of which they have little interest. However, that is error. I pray we will be able to properly expose that error and portray the Truth of this great Chapter.

That which makes the teaching in this Chapter so important to the Believer, is because Paul had some of the same problems that all of us have had. He thought surely after he was Saved and Baptized with the Holy Spirit, that he could live a victorious, overcoming Christian life, but to his dismay, found that he could not, at least with the Light he then had. That terrible situation caused him to exclaim, *"O wretched man that I am! Who shall deliver me from the body of this death?"* (vs. 24).

In that frame of mind Paul went to the Lord seeking an answer. The answer was

gloriously and wondrously provided, and given to us in these three Chapters, 6, 7, and 8 of Romans.

In this 7th Chapter, the Holy Spirit through the Apostle outlines the reason for the failure of the Believer. Sin is not to have dominion over us, but yet sin does have dominion in the lives of many Christians. Romans Chapter 7 tells us why, and if that is correct, and it is, then we are made to understand how vitally significant this Chapter really is.

The phrase, *"Know ye not, Brethren, (for I speak to them that know the Law,)"* presents Paul addressing himself to the Law of Moses.

Verses 1-6 reveal the Divine method of Sanctification, and sets out its impossibility under the bondage of Law and its certainty under the Freedom of Grace.

First of all, Paul is addressing his information to *"Brethren,"* meaning that he is speaking to Believers, as should be obvious. These were Believers who were having difficulties and problems with the sin question, and were seeking answers, exactly as Paul had sought such answers and which had been given unto him by the Holy Spirit.

As well, Paul is writing to Romans who are Gentiles, so why does he bring up the Law of Moses, when that in effect was strictly and more particularly a foundation of Judaism? The Law of Moses was totally fulfilled in Christ, and is not binding on Believers in the New Covenant, at least in a strict sense.

To portray the reason for the Believer's lack of Victory in his personal life, the Holy Spirit had Paul to address this Law, because in effect this figures into the dilemma that Believers find themselves, even though they are really not conscious of that fact.

Paul is now addressing his remarks to Gentiles who have gained some knowledge of the Law of Moses after coming to Christ. Inasmuch as this was a great controversy in the times of the Early Church, most Gentile Believers probably became at least somewhat acquainted with this Old Testament Foundation. So they knew what Paul was talking about.

Considering all the things that Paul says about the Law, and which some were apt to take wrongly, which he will address later, one is apt to think that the Law of Moses was evil, etc. However, nothing could be further from the Truth. In fact, the Law of Moses, which was really the Law of God, was Holy and Righteous, actually perfect in every respect. The giving of the Law by God to the Children of Israel, placed them in a position of a far greater advantage over all other Nations. While others had laws, they were all man-devised. But Israel's Law had come from God, and, consequently, gave these people a tremendous advantage in every respect.

SO, WHAT WAS THE PROBLEM WITH THE LAW?

First of all, the problem was not the Law, but rather Israel. Instead of accepting and using the Law of Moses as it was intended by God, they attempted to make Salvation out of its Commandments, which God never intended.

The Law of Moses, among many other things, was intended to point out and define sin. As well, it was to portray to man his total inadequacy and inability to keep the simple Commandments which God laid down (the Ten Commandments). He was then to throw himself on the Mercy and Grace of God for help and Redemption. While some few did exactly that, most did not.

Most of Israel became puffed up in their own self-righteousness, and despite the fact that they couldn't even keep the few Commandments that God had given, multiplied hundreds of others to go along with what was already there. Consequently, by the time that Jesus came, Who in effect was the Giver and Keeper of the Law, actually the only Man Who ever lived Who did such, they would not accept Him. Not only would they reject His Message, but in their evil they felt they had to destroy the Messenger, which they did by crucifying Him. Again we state, the Law of Moses was not the cause or fault of this, but rather the evil, wicked hearts of these people.

SO, HOW DOES THAT AFFECT GENTILES?

Whether it is the Law of Moses, or a Law of our own devising, man seeks to try to satisfy his spiritual needs by his own efforts.

He tries to do it with laws of one kind or the other, exactly as Israel did with the Mosaic Law. There is an innate spirit in man, even Believers, which is loathe to admit to himself or God that he cannot solve his own spiritual problems. All of this is a result of the Fall.

Among all the other reasons that the Holy Spirit had the Apostle to use the Law of Moses as an example, is that if man could not gain Righteousness by his attempts to keep the Law of Moses, considering it was from God and perfect in every respect, how in the world does he think he can bring about the same results through some pitiful laws of his own making? But yet, I think all of us have fallen into this trap in one way or the other.

Our trust is in our own laws, or efforts, etc., rather than in Christ. That in a nutshell, spells out our failure.

Man's self-sufficiency is his greatest enemy. In other words, we have met the enemy and he is us!

It is strange, Believers will look at the world and chide them for refusing to admit that they need Jesus, while we are at the same time doing the same thing. Too often we claim that we are leaning on Jesus, when in reality we are leaning on our own arm of flesh. All of it is so subtle and religious, and, consequently, deceives so many people.

SATAN AND LAW

The Evil One is quite content to allow us to struggle and strive in efforts of our own making, instead of trusting Christ. He knows that not only are we *not* going to get Victory in that manner, but that our situation is going to become progressively worse. For all attempts to bring about Victory in this way, can only lead to defeat, with each defeat becoming worse than the one preceding.

Satan is very content for man to be religious, even very religious, and for the simple reason that he knows that there is no Victory or Salvation in that sector. Actually, he even encourages these efforts. But the moment the Believer begins to depend totally on Christ, then the war begins as well. Strangely enough, most of the opposition will come from fellow Christians. That is sad, but true!

In this Chapter, Paul is going to open his soul as few Preachers ever have. He is going to portray his own failures, and the reason for those failures. While we are studying this, do not forget that the reason for his failures, is the reason for our failures as well! If the great Apostle could not bring about Victory by his own efforts, do any of us seriously think that we can succeed where he failed?

VICTORY AND THE LAW

The conclusion of the question, *"How that the Law hath dominion over a man as long as he liveth?"*, describes the person who is attempting to gain Victory by the Law, whether of Moses, or of his own making, which is more generally the case.

If a person attempts to gain Victory by using Law, in other words in his own strength and power, he will find that the Law has dominion over him. He will not obtain that of which he is seeking, Victory over the flesh, but rather the very opposite. So, Paul is now going to press home the point that the Believer is not under Law anymore, and that a Christian putting himself under Law and thus failing to avail himself of the resources of Grace is a defeated Christian, which was Paul's own experience after his Conversion, before he came into the knowledge given to him by Christ, and to which He gave us in Romans Chapter 6.

However, even though the Law will incite the Christian to more sin, which is the very opposite of what he wants, yet the Law is not responsible for that sin, but rather, the Sin Nature which is in the Believer, and which the Law excites, which it is actually intended to do.

The idea is, that as good as the Law of Moses was in itself and in the Divine intention, nevertheless, owing to the corruption of man's nature, which God knew all along, instead of the Law helping to make him good, actually did the very opposite. That sounds strange to the Bible Student.

One would quickly ask, if the Law of Moses stimulated sin in God's people, how could it be called good?

Once again, the problem was not in the Law, but in the corrupt nature of man. The Lord desired to show man just how corrupt he really was, and this was the best way to portray this fact.

It is somewhat like placing a certain type of medicine over a boil on the human body, which has a tendency to draw the corruption to the surface. The medicine has not caused the boil, nor is it the reason for the corruption. It just merely portrays the fact that the corruption is already there, by drawing it to the surface. So, if man attempts to gain Victory by attempting to keep the Law, he will have no more success than all who preceded him. The reason is simple.

Man has no power or ability to keep the Law.

IF GOD DEMANDED THAT IT BE KEPT, WHICH HE DID, WHY DID HE NOT GIVE MAN THE POWER TO DO SO?

To the natural mind it seems unfair, that God would give Law, demanding that man keep it, all the time knowing he could not. It becomes even more serious, when we realize that there is a severe penalty attached to not keeping the Law. Of course, for Law to truly be Law, there must be a penalty attached for disobedience.

While it is true that God did not give man any power to keep the Law, He did this for a purpose.

Man's problem has always been Pride, which was actually the cause of the Fall in the Garden of Eden. So, if God had given man the power to keep the Law, he would have only been lifted up further in his Pride, seeing less need of God than more, which was the intention to begin with. The Law, as stated, was intended to show man his inability, not to increase his problem with even more Pride.

DID NOT GOD KNOW THAT ISRAEL WOULD RESPOND TO THE LAW WRONGLY?

Of course He did! However, the Law did exactly what it was intended to do:

1. The Law gave man a correct pattern for living.

2. As stated, it pointed out sin and defined what it was.

3. It showed man his gross inadequacy to

keep or obey the simplest of Commandments.

4. It pointed to the ideal.

5. It addressed every single thing that pertained to man whether economically, physically, and socially. All of this along with the spiritual.

6. The Law portrayed man's obligations to his fellowman and his obligations to God.

So, even though the Law of Moses must be addressed in what seems to be a negative way, in fact, the Law was not negative at all, but the very opposite. As stated, the problem was on the part of man and not the Law.

In fact, some few Israelites down through the centuries treated the Law as God intended, and were blessed abundantly.

(2) "FOR THE WOMAN WHICH HATH AN HUSBAND IS BOUND BY THE LAW TO HER HUSBAND SO LONG AS HE LIVETH; BUT IF THE HUSBAND BE DEAD, SHE IS LOOSED FROM THE LAW OF HER HUSBAND."

The phrase, *"For the woman which hath an husband is bound by the Law to her husband as long as he liveth,"* presents the first statement of an analogy used by Paul to describe the Law and Believers under the New Covenant. First of all, the Bible Student must understand that Paul is not here teaching on the subject of divorce and remarriage, but rather using this as an analogy or comparison. Even though it seems somewhat confusing at first, it will become more clear as we go along, as to why the Holy Spirit chose this particular illustration.

The *"husband"* is here likened to the Law. The *"woman"* (wife) is likened to the Believer. As long as her husband (Law) is alive, she (the Believer) is bound to him (bound to the Law, which was the state of Israel before Christ).

The phrase, *"But if the husband be dead, she is loosed from the law of her husband,"* simply means that she is now free in the Eyes of God and man to marry again, if she so desires.

Continuing with that analogy, the Law is now dead, i.e., fulfilled by Christ. Consequently, the Believer is no longer bound to the Law, simply because it no longer exists. (In verse 4, Paul changes this analogy a little bit as we shall see, which tends to confuse

NOTES

the Reader, but which is done with purpose.)

The argument here is: that just as death is the only force that can liberate from the demands of sin (the Death of Jesus), so is it the only force that can liberate from the demands of the Law. This will be explained more fully as we go along.

(3) "SO THEN IF, WHILE HER HUSBAND LIVETH, SHE BE MARRIED TO ANOTHER MAN, SHE SHALL BE CALLED AN ADULTERESS: BUT IF HER HUSBAND BE DEAD, SHE IS FREE FROM THAT LAW; SO THAT SHE IS NO ADULTERESS, THOUGH SHE BE MARRIED TO ANOTHER MAN."

The phrase, *"So then if, while her husband liveth, she be married to another man, she shall be called an adulteress,"* presents the very opposite of the previous verse. Here, Paul uses the analogy of the husband not dying, but rather his wife divorcing him and marrying another man. Consequently, in the Eyes of God, and continuing to use this analogy, the woman now has two husbands. Those two husbands are the Law and Christ. Really, this is the gist of the entire analogy.

Paul is using this to portray the Believer attempting to serve two husbands, the Law and Christ, which is a literal impossibility. But yet, that is where many Believers, if not most, find themselves.

Paul is also saying, that irrespective as to what man may say of the woman (Believer), God calls her an *"Adulteress."*

That means that if the Believer attempts to serve Christ, but at the same time tries to hold on to some type of Law, in effect, that Believer is committing spiritual adultery. The Believer has pledged himself in totality to Christ, but as well is playing footsie with another effort or Law, attempting to attain the results which *only Christ* can give.

So, not only will the Believer not gain anything by this action, but will greatly hurt himself not only in the results, but in his relationship with Christ as well!

I realize that the Believer has some difficulty in understanding this. Perhaps we can be a little more clear:

ONLY CHRIST

What makes this scenario somewhat

confusing, is that the Believer most of the time is not deliberately trying to find Victory from other sources. He actually thinks he is depending solely upon Christ, while all the time depending on his own strength or even the strength of others. As well, his efforts are probably very spiritual, and he thinks even Scriptural. As stated, the effort is made mostly in ignorance.

Nevertheless, as should be obvious, irrespective of the good intentions, or Scriptural ignorance (most of the time that's what it is), the results are the same — wreckage. Having good motives and being sincere, as well as having good intentions, while good within themselves, never compensates for error. Wrong direction is wrong direction, irrespective as to the reasons why.

As we have repeatedly stated, most of the problem, at least as it pertains to the personal Victory of the Child of God over sin, is an ignorance of the teaching given in the 6th Chapter of this Book. We have all been taught greatly and grandly concerning the Price paid by Christ at Calvary regarding the terrible sin debt, making it possible for the sinner to be Saved; however, most of us have heard very little about the second benefit of Calvary, which is the Victory won by Christ in destroying the dominion of sin over the Believer.

Coming to Salvation is wonderful and great, but the Believer, even in the face of the Powers of Darkness, with all its attendant wickedness, must walk straight and clean before the Lord thereafter. Even though Jesus did pay the terrible sin debt and paid it in totality, sin, as a fact, was *not* eradicated or dissolved at that time. It is still very much real, and its bite causes just as much problem as it always did. What Jesus did in respect to breaking its dominion, was to literally build a spiritual shield between the Sin Nature and the Believer, effectively isolating that monster. However, even though that was done at Calvary and the Resurrection, and done in totality, most Believers little understand it, and even less know how to appropriate this great benefit.

CONTINUING FAITH

The second difficulty is that there must

NOTES

be a continuing Faith, which should not present a problem, but sometimes does.

Christians love to make everything final; however, while there is certainly a finality to what Jesus did respecting the destruction of the dominion of sin over the Believer, in another sense of the word it is not final. By that I mean that the Believer must continue to exercise Faith even on a moment-by-moment basis. To be sure, this is all done for our benefit, but at times it seems like anything but a benefit.

Once again, we come back to the foundation of the Word of God which demands that man go God's Way, and that nothing must be taken from that Way, or added to that Way. And this is man's great problem, even Believers. We either do not know the Way, or else we try to change the Way. Perhaps we do it in ignorance, even as I have already stated, but also as stated, the end results are the same — failure.

The phrase, *"But if her husband be dead, she is free from that Law,"* presents Paul proclaiming the situation as it ought to be.

The husband being dead, represents the Law being dead, in effect fulfilled by Christ. As a result, the Believer is no longer obligated to the law. He is free from its demands, simply because Christ has fulfilled those demands on his behalf.

The phrase, *"So that she is no adulteress, though she be married to another man,"* presents the Believer as now married to Christ, and no longer under obligation to the Law, because the Power of the Law is dead, at least as Paul draws the analogy. Israel was obligated under the Law, because Christ had not yet come. However, when Christ came, He took the place of the Law, and is to be the *only* husband. With Christ as the only Husband, the Believer is not looked at by God as committing spiritual adultery, as He did when the Believer was attempting to exert loyalty to both.

MARRIED TO CHRIST

In further pursuing the matter of the Christian's relation to Law as a method of Divine Dealing, Paul recurs to the substance of his statement in Romans 6:14, *"You are not under Law, but under Grace,"* i.e., *"married to Christ."*

To be under Law in a sense, is to be in the state of an unsaved person obligated to obey God's Law. However, the Law gives neither the desire nor the power to obey its precepts. Instead, it brings out sin all the more, because that's what it was designed to do. Its very presence incites rebellion in the totally depraved nature of the individual (Rom. 5:20).

Conversely, to be under Grace is to be a Christian, who has had the power of the evil nature broken in his life so that he does not need to obey it anymore, and has been given the Divine Nature which gives him both the desire and the power to do God's Will.

Consequently, we can now see how deadly it is to resort to any other method of Victory other than Christ. He is not only our Saviour from sin (the sin debt), but He is also our Saviour respecting the dominion of sin. It no longer rules us, and in fact cannot rule us, that is, as long as we depend on Christ.

(4) "WHEREFORE, MY BRETHREN, YE ALSO ARE BECOME DEAD TO THE LAW BY THE BODY OF CHRIST; THAT YE SHOULD BE MARRIED TO ANOTHER, EVEN TO HIM WHO IS RAISED FROM THE DEAD, THAT WE SHOULD BRING FORTH FRUIT UNTO GOD."

The phrase, *"Wherefore, my Brethren, ye also are become dead to the Law by the Body of Christ,"* presents the Passage which causes some confusion respecting this analogy drawn by Paul, respecting the husband who had died, etc.

Continuing that analogy, Paul would have said that the Law died, inasmuch as the dead husband represented the Law; however, he does not say that, rather saying that the Believer has become dead to the Law, instead of the Law being dead to the Believer.

The real point that Paul is making in this symbolism is of the woman, who is a type of the Believer, who attempts to be married to two husbands — the Law and Christ. Of course, such cannot be, as would be obvious.

Also, when he used the statement, *"Are become dead to the Law,"* he is referring to fellowship with Christ in His Death.

As well, he is using another analogy,

which in a sense turns the entire scenario around, by saying that when the husband (Law) dies, the wife also dies as far as that particular marriage relationship is concerned, and she is free to marry another. So, when Jesus died on Calvary, the Believer (wife, and continuing the analogy), died with Him (Rom. 6:6); therefore, the Believer is now free to marry Christ.

The phrase, *"Are become dead,"* in the Greek is *"thanatoo,"* and means *"Ye were made dead, put to death,"* which speaks of great violence. Alford says, *"The more violent word is used instead of 'apethanete (you died),' to recall the violent Death of Christ, in which, and after the manner of, Believers have been put to death to the Law and sin. In other words, there is absolutely no doubt that the Believer is dead to the Law and sin."*

THE STRUCTURE OF THE LAW

Now why did Paul change the structure of the analogy, and make the Believer dead to the Law, instead of the Law dead to the Believer, as was originally typified by the dead husband?

As we have already stated, the original intent was to portray the impossibility of the Believer attempting to be married to two husbands — Law and Christ. However, the reason that Paul did not say that the Law is dead to the Believer, but rather that the Believer is dead to the Law, is because the Law is not dead. It is very much alive, even at the present time.

Let me explain:

The Law of Moses although one, was somewhat divided into two parts: A. The Ceremonial Law, which consisted of the Feast Days, Circumcision, Sabbath-keeping and Sacrifices, etc.; and, B. The Moral Law, which consisted of the Ten Commandments (minus the Fourth).

The Ceremonial or Ritualistic part of the Law, which all the time pointed to Christ, and was meant to symbolize Christ, was all fulfilled when Christ came. Consequently, there was no more need for the symbolism. In regards to the Moral Law, which as stated was the Ten Commandments, minus the Fourth, was brought over into the New Covenant. In other words, that part of the

Mosaic Law is still incumbent upon Believers today, because Moral Law cannot change.

(The Fourth Commandment, *"Remember the Sabbath to keep it holy,"* was not brought over into the New Covenant, because it was between Israel and God exclusively. As well, it was the only One of the Ten Commandments which was not moral but rather ceremonial. If one carefully looks at the New Testament, after the Four Gospels, one will find that the Fourth Commandment is nowhere in view. In other words, Christians did not keep the Jewish Saturday, which was the Sabbath, but rather Sunday, which was the Day of the Resurrection.)

THE MORAL LAW

However, even though the Moral Law is very much alive and incumbent upon all Believers, that Law was and is kept in Christ, meaning that He lives in us, keeping the Moral Law (Gal. 2:20).

As well, Jesus Personally and perfectly kept the Moral Law (Ten Commandments) in every respect in the some 33 1/2 years of His earthly Life, and our Faith in Him grants us in the Eyes of God, the status of Law-keepers, instead of Lawbreakers.

The *"Body of Christ"* speaks of Christ offering His Physical Body as a Sin-Offering on Calvary's Cross. In the vehicle of His Body, He died to the Law, which means that Faith in Him and what He did, means that we died to the Law also. His dying means He suffered its penalty and met its demands.

The Believer is to never forget, that all of this was done for us, and not at all for Himself, because He had never broken the Law or incurred its curse. Inasmuch as He has done this strictly for us, surely it would stand to reason that He would want us to have all that His Great Victory affords. Once again, we go back to the fact that all of this (payment for sin and Victory over sin) was done at Calvary, and that its immediate effectiveness is carried out within our lives on a day-to-day basis, by continued Faith in what He did and our place in Him. This must never be misunderstood in that the Believer died in Him, was buried with Him, and rose from the dead with Him, to Newness of Life (Rom. 6:4). This is what is meant in Romans 6:3, *"Know ye not, that*

so many of us as were Baptized into Jesus Christ were Baptized into His Death?"

The believing sinner in order to be Saved, simply has to believe that Jesus died on Calvary for him, paying his terrible sin debt. Accepting what He did, and accepting Him as Saviour, guarantees Salvation.

DOMINION OF SIN BROKEN

However, the Believer, who is now in Christ, meaning he is already Saved, must now take his Faith to a much greater degree than that of the believing sinner. He must also believe that he was in Christ when these great things were done, including the Resurrection, and that this great happening broke the dominion of sin, and continued Faith in this great event and his part in it guarantees that it stays broken, even to where the Sin Nature is so isolated that it no longer is a bother or trouble to the Believer.

The phrase, *"That ye should be married to another,"* refers to Christ. He Alone can provide all that is needed and in whatever capacity. Now that we are dead to the Law, meaning that it has no more hold on us and because Jesus met its every requirement, we are free to marry Christ, which we have done.

(The keeping of the Law of Moses was incumbent upon all; however, all failed until Christ. As the Representative Man, Christ kept the Law of Moses in every single respect, and Faith in Him grants to the Believer the satisfaction of the Law in every respect also. Consequently, the Believer is no longer obligated to the Law because its demands have been met, with the Believer now free and qualified to marry the one who met those demands, namely Christ.)

The phrase, *"Even to Him Who is raised from the dead,"* presents the believing sinner as identifying with Christ in His Death, Burial, and Resurrection. Consequently, the Law now has no more jurisdiction over him, and for the obvious reasons. The *"old man (sinner)"* (Rom. 6:6) died and was buried with Christ, meaning the Law now has no more dominion over that person, especially considering that he has passed out of the realm where the Law holds sway. He is resurrected with Christ, in effect in Christ, *"to walk in Newness of Life,"* a life incidentally, free of the Law, because as stated, its demands have been met in Christ.

Paul's purpose now is to press home the point that the Believer is not under Law anymore; consequently, a Christian putting himself under Law and thus failing to avail himself of the resource of Grace is a defeated Christian, actually Paul's own experience before he came into the knowledge of Romans Chapter 6. While the Law incites the Christian to more sin, even as it always does, yet the Law is not responsible for that sin, but the evil nature, which only can be conquered as the Believer cries *"Who shall deliver me?"*, and thus looks away from himself and self-dependence to the Lord Jesus.

The phrase, *"That we should bring forth fruit unto God,"* proclaims the only way that such fruit can be brought forth. The hindrance to our living such a life is dependence on the flesh instead of Christ.

(5) "FOR WHEN WE WERE IN THE FLESH, THE MOTIONS OF SINS, WHICH WERE BY THE LAW, DID WORK IN OUR MEMBERS TO BRING FORTH FRUIT UNTO DEATH."

The phrase, *"For when we were in the flesh,"* can refer to the unsaved state, or to the Believer who is attempting to overcome the powers of sin by his own efforts, i.e., *"the flesh."* The end result is going to be the same in either case — failure. Actually, the entirety of this Chapter deals with the Believer who is trying to overcome sin in the wrong way. Actually there are only two ways that one can make this attempt, by the flesh or by the Spirit of God. If the Believer does not take advantage of what Jesus did for him at Calvary, understanding that Christ not only paid the sin debt, but as well broke the dominion of sin, then his only other recourse is the flesh. In other words, his attempts at Victory will be no more successful than the Alcoholic attempting to quit drinking through *"Alcoholics Anonymous,"* or one of a hundred other efforts made by men. There is Victory only in Christ, and only in following His prescribed Path.

THE FIVE OFFERINGS OF THE OLD TESTAMENT

It took Five Offerings as outlined in the

Old Testament to properly exemplify the one Sacrifice of Christ at Calvary. Those Five were: Burnt Offering, Food Offering, Peace Offering, Sin Offering and Trespass Offering. All were Offerings of clean animals (a lamb, a bullock, or a goat), with the exception of the Food Offering (Meat Offering). This was an Offering made of Grain and baked into cakes (Lev. Chpts. 1-7).

THE PEACE OFFERING

Of these Offerings, the Peace Offering typified the teaching given by Paul in Romans Chapter 6. It typified the Believer partaking of Christ in His Death, Burial and Resurrection (Rom. 6:3-6). The Type was carried out by the Worshiper partaking of the slain animal in a Feast after it had been cooked and prepared in a special way. He was even permitted to call in his friends to enjoy this Feast with him.

This is one of the reasons that the Believer should know and understand the Old Testament as well as the New. It lays the foundation for all that was done by Christ in His Perfect Birth, Perfect Walk, and Perfect Sacrifice. Actually, it is not really possible for anyone to understand the New Testament, unless they have a working knowledge of the Old.

THE LAW OF THE PEACE OFFERING

This is found in Leviticus Chapter 7. Unleavened cakes were to be used, which symbolized the sinless humanity of Christ. Leavened bread was to be used, symbolizing the sinful humanity of the worshiper. The One had sin on Him but not in Him; the other, had sin in him but not on him.

The Peace Offering for Thanksgiving was eaten the same day that it was offered; the Peace Offering for a vow, the same day or the next day — because a vow, or a voluntary offering, necessarily affected the heart more than an ordinary Thanksgiving.

This Law taught the Offerer to closely associate the Death and Sufferings of the slain lamb with the blessing that he gave thanks for. This Thanksgiving Offering was to be for every Blessing, for all Blessings come from God, but more primarily for that which the Lord would do at Calvary for the Believer, as typified by the slain lamb. Of course, the Offerer in Old Testament times, would not have had the full understanding of the things we are now discussing, but they definitely knew that the Sacrificial Offering of the clean animal represented the Sacrifice of the Coming Redeemer. The glass they saw through then was of necessity more shaded than present. Due to what Christ has already done, we at the present time have greater spiritual vision. Nevertheless, even now *"We* (continue to) *see through a glass, darkly."* However, when He comes back, we will *"then see face to face"* (I Cor. 13:12).

The lesson then taught to the worshipers continues to teach the same today. To disassociate worship and thanksgiving from the anguish and bloodshedding of the Lord Jesus is to offer to God an abomination and to bring death into the soul and into the Church.

CEREMONIAL CLEANLINESS

Ceremonial Cleanliness was obligatory before eating the Peace Offering (Lev. 7:20-21). Disobedience in this matter entailed death. To profess Faith in the Person and Atonement of Christ, and claim fellowship with Him, and be secretly unclean, ensures the Wrath of God.

Then, and of necessity, the cleansing was only ceremonial. Today it is a literal fact in that Christ makes one clean and keeps one clean, which the Peace Offering was all about.

THE FAT OF THE PEACE OFFERING

The fat of the Peace Offering was to be wholly given to God, because it symbolized the excellent affections and prosperity of God's dearly-beloved Son. In other words, God gave Heaven's very best when He gave Jesus. The *"fat"* which was to be burned upon the Altar, and the only part of this particular Offering which was so treated, was a sign of the Prosperity of God in every capacity. It pictured the Grace, Glory, Prosperity, Beauty, Health, and every other positive aspect of God's Gift to man, His Son, Jesus Christ.

Actually, the fat of any animal that died, or was accidentally killed, might be used for other purposes, but never eaten. Similarly was the Blood Precious.

THE WAVE BREAST AND HEAVE SHOULDER

Some parts of the slain and roasted animal were to be eaten by the Offerer, after it was cooked and suitably prepared. As stated, he could feel free to invite as many friends as he so desired to partake of this Feast. As the Offerer partook of this Feast, literally eating the flesh with the prepared cakes and bread, such symbolized the actual partaking of Christ in His Atoning Work at Calvary, and more perfectly, in His breaking the dominion of sin in the life of the Believer. Among other things, this is actually what it represented.

This tells us that the Believer is not only to accept the Vicarious Sacrifice of Jesus at Calvary concerning the terrible sin debt, but that also he is to liken himself as having died, been buried, and Resurrected with Christ. All of that was symbolized in the *"Peace Offering."*

Any type of sin in the life of the Believer destroys that Peace. It is only reinstated after proper Repentance, etc. However, to sin and repent, sin and repent, sin and repent, etc., is not God's Way, as should be obvious. And yet, that is where many Believers are, and the very reason that the Holy Spirit gave Paul this great solution in Romans Chapters, 6, 7, and 8. As the Offerer of old partook of the Peace Offering, the Believer is to partake of what Christ did at Calvary and the Resurrection, likening himself in the very acts which were carried out by the Son of God. This is what the Peace Offering represented, and which we are to enjoy today.

As is obvious, this was to be a Feast, which typified Joy, Peace, Prosperity, and Godliness. None of these things can be had by a sinning Salvation, or a constant Repentance, even though Repentance occasionally is always needed. The Lord intends for us to have total and complete Victory, which in effect we already have, and should maintain, and can do so in Christ, but only in Christ.

THE ONE WAS HEAVED . . .

This means that the shoulder of the animal after being prepared was lifted up before God as expressive of its preciousness and acceptability to Him. Christ's Shoulder upholds.

This also means, as is obvious, that the Believer's trust in Him respecting His breaking the dominion of sin in our lives, says that His *"Shoulder,"* typifying His Strength, has done for us what we could not do for ourselves. Paul said, *"For when we were yet without strength, in due time Christ died for the ungodly"* (Rom. 5:6). As obvious, this speaks of the person before Salvation. However, the Believer is also without strength when it comes to the dominion of sin, at least within himself. Our *"strength"* is in Christ, typified by the *"Heave Offering."*

THE ONE WAS WAVED . . .

The prepared Breast of the slain animal was lifted up and *"waved"* before the Lord, in effect presenting him to the four quarters of the Earth, as setting forth the sufficiency of this Offering to give life to the world.

Further, Christ's Shoulder upholds and His Breast consoles, all those who trust in Him; and they nourish those who serve Him in any form of Christian Ministry to others.

The reverence due to the Person and to the Work of the Messiah was enjoined by the two Laws respecting the *"fat"* and the *"Blood."* They expressed excellency and efficiency. *"This is My Beloved Son"* declared the One; and *"Peace through the Blood of His Cross"* proclaimed the other (Col. 1:20) (Williams).

All of the Peace Offering was a form of Thanksgiving, typifying the present Believer who should thank the Lord daily that Jesus not only paid the price for our Redemption, but as well, broke the dominion of sin within our lives, that it no longer rule over us. We actually should thank Him constantly, and which the Thanksgiving will always build Faith, never forgetting this which Christ did, which is an ever-present, effective work within our daily walk.

MOTIONS OF SINS

The phrase, *"The motions of sins,"* denotes being under the power of sin, and refers to the *"passions"* of sins. This speaks of the Sin Nature operating full blast, bringing about one sin after the other, which will always happen when the Believer relies on the

flesh instead of the Spirit. In other words, and as we have repeatedly said, he is attempting to obey some type of law which he has made up himself, or was made up by others, thinking that the obedience to such will bring about Victory, etc. Even though the intention may be good and the motive right, the results will be the same as it was before the Believer was Saved. While sin is *"motionless"* in the life of one who trusts Christ, it begins very much to stir into activity, when reliance shifts to something else.

That's one of the reasons that the Catholic Church has their Confessionals and why it is in operation constantly. Catholicism is a religion of works, as such, there is no Power of Christ represented. Therefore, the people are constantly sinning and constantly confessing. However, the Catholic has a threefold problem:

1. Very precious few Catholics are actually Saved.

2. They are depending on works to do with and for them whatever is needed, which can never be done.

3. Even their confessing has no effect, because they are confessing to a man expecting him to absolve their sin, which no man can do.

The phrase, *"Which were by the Law,"* seems to be negative on the surface as it regards the Law.

The effect of the Law, reveals sin, which it is actually designed to do, and because it does that, many think it is evil. However, the answer is that, on the contrary, *"the Law is holy"* (vs. 12).

Others say, granting that the Law is good in itself, yet it becomes evil to men because of its effects on them (vs. 13).

The reply to this is that its moral effect in them is beneficent, for its action reveals to them how evil they are, which is its intention all along.

An illustration may make this plain.

A piece of ground is barren. The Sun rises and shines upon it. Very quickly it is covered with weeds. Using the same analogy toward the Sun as many do toward the Law, they think, therefore, that the Sun must be to blame.

However, good Science rejects this, replying

that the Sun is good in itself.

Some may object to that saying that the Sun which might be good in itself becomes evil to the ground, and because the weeds were made manifest. To this Science replies that the Sun does not become evil to the piece of ground, but that the effect of its action is to reveal the evil that is in the ground and not in the Sun.

GOD'S LAW IS GOOD

God's Moral Law is holy and just and good. Man's fallen nature is evil. The effect of Law acting on that nature manifests not only the fact of the disease of sin, but the exceeding malignity of the disease.

Sin, i.e., the principle of evil lodged in fallen man, is manifested as exceedingly sinful, which the Law of God brings about, and is made evident to man's own consciousness (Williams).

The phrase, *"Did work in our members to bring forth fruit unto death,"* means that God's Moral Law does two things:

1. The Law of God, which of course is a Moral Law, does not cause the sin in the person's life, or have anything to do with its origination. *It only reveals what is already there.*

In other words, man was and is so deceived that he simply would not believe that his condition was as bad as it actually is. So, the Law of God showed him just how bad it was.

2. Not only did the Law of God show man how bad he was, in other words, revealing what was already there, but as well, showed man how weak he really is, respecting his efforts to address this terrible problem.

The Moral Laws of God as they were originally given in what is referred to as the *"Law of Moses,"* are ensconced in the Ten Commandments, minus the Fourth. To be frank, all Civil Law in the world has as its foundation the Moral Law of God, at least in one way or the other.

While the first Two of these Commandments, which deal with man's obligations to God, are basically ignored, the remaining Eight (minus the Fourth), form the groundwork and foundation of all Civil Law. These Moral Laws speak of taking God's Name in

vain, the honoring of one's Father and Mother, murder, adultery, stealing, lying, and covetousness.

MAN'S INABILITY

"Thou shalt not bear false witness," or *"Thou shalt not steal,"* etc., sound very simple, but man soon finds that he is unable to keep these Laws irrespective of how hard he may try. The problem is his depraved nature, which resulted in the Fall, and which has no power at all to do that which is right.

So, not only cannot he obey these Commandments, he as well, has no way within himself, and in any capacity, to remedy the situation. Man's every activity can only bring forth death, because man has no life within himself whatsoever.

However, man refuses to believe his situation is as bad as it actually is, and as a result, that he has no solution within himself. As we have stated in past Commentary, deception is a terrible thing. Such is man's problem, and is acute beyond belief. That's what Jesus was speaking of when He said, *"The Spirit of the Lord is upon Me, because He hath Anointed Me to . . . recover sight to the blind"* (Lk. 4:18).

He wasn't speaking of physical blindness, but spiritual blindness. In fact, man is so spiritually blind, that he cannot be reached intellectually. It takes a Revelation from God for this darkness to be penetrated, which can only be done by the Word of God and the Moving and Operation of the Holy Spirit upon that Word (Jn. 16:7-15).

As is now known, the word *"members"* as Paul uses it here, speaks of the physical members of our bodies, i.e., eyes, ears, tongue, feet, hands, etc. Acts of sin are carried out through these *"members."* Irrespective of what man may do regarding education, intellectualism, various philosophies, money, religion, etc., it can only *"bring forth fruit unto death."*

What does Paul mean by *"death?"*

He is speaking of the wages of sin which is death, which is produced by unregenerate man, and without fail! And as we have repeatedly stated, there is no way that man can ameliorate or change this direction, at least within himself. Man's problem is sin, which actually is a spiritual problem, and cannot be addressed from the economical, social, philosophical, religious, intellectual, psychological, etc. The only answer is Jesus!

The *"death"* mentioned here, is *"spiritual death,"* which means separation from God, Who Alone is the Life Source.

(6) "BUT NOW WE ARE DELIVERED FROM THE LAW, THAT BEING DEAD WHEREIN WE WERE HELD; THAT WE SHOULD SERVE IN NEWNESS OF SPIRIT, AND NOT IN THE OLDNESS OF THE LETTER."

The phrase, *"But now we are delivered from the Law,"* means that its demands were met in Christ. Inasmuch as we were in Christ (Baptism into Christ) when He died on Calvary and was raised from the dead, our Faith in Him, means that the demands of the Law were met in us as well.

In other words, the Law of God (Law of Moses) demanded and demands that all of it be obeyed by all, as should be obvious. Law is not law unless it demands obedience, and all Law has a penalty attached for failure. The problem was and is, man within himself could not and cannot keep the Law; consequently, it hung over his head as the sword of Damocles. And as well, there was no way out. The Law made its demands and man could not meet them, but yet must do so.

However, when Jesus came, He kept the Moral Law in every single respect, and then He satisfied the Curse of the Law by offering up Himself as a Sin-Offering at Calvary. So, in reality, man was delivered in a twofold way:

DELIVERED FROM THE CURSE

1. The terrible Curse (penalty) of the Law was satisfied by Jesus, when He offered up His Sinless, Perfect Body as a Sin-Offering, which satisfied the claims of Heavenly Justice and wiped the slate clean. He took the penalty Himself, which God accepted, and by simple Faith in Him, the charge and penalty of sin is instantly removed. So, at Calvary man was delivered from the penalty of the Law.

2. When Jesus came to this Earth, He perfectly kept in His daily Walk the Moral Law of God, never failing in even one point.

Consequently, as the Representative Man, Faith in Him also grants the Believer His Victory respecting the perfect keeping of the Law. Therefore, God grants to the Believer the Perfect Walk of Christ, in effect, as we have previously stated, making the Believer a Law-keeper, where he was once a Lawbreaker.

The phrase, *"That being dead wherein we were held,"* would have probably been better translated, *"Having died to that in which we were constantly being held down."*

Held by what?

That in which the Believer was constantly held before he was Saved is the *evil nature.* In the Greek, the manner in which Paul uses the term, portrays that the Sin Nature had absolute control over the unsaved person.

Some claim that Paul is speaking of the Law here being dead, but that is not so, due to the fact that he says the very opposite in the 4th verse. The Law does not die as he said, but the Believer dies to the Law. The Believer has now been delivered from the power of the Sin Nature, and in effect, it has no more control over him.

When Israel was under the Law, or if anyone puts himself under any type of Law at present, such will tend to bring out of the Believer infractions, and, consequently failure, even as Law is designed to do. But now that we are serving Christ, and at least have a rudimentary knowledge of what that service means, the power of the Law is broken within our lives, and, consequently, the Sin Nature is left without power as well.

THE HOLY SPIRIT

The phrase, *"That we should serve in newness of Spirit,"* refers to the Holy Spirit and not man's spirit. While the spirit of the Believer is certainly renewed at Regeneration, still, even the renewed spirit does not have the power to effect the work which is here noted and needed. That takes the Holy Spirit, which Paul graphically outlines in the next Chapter.

The distinction here is made between the Holy Spirit as the new method of Divine Dealing and the Law, which was God's old method. Paul's thought here is not that the Believer serves only in a new spirit, that is, in a new attitude and with new motives, which definitely does happen, but that he serves now in the Power of the Holy Spirit, under a new energy and control, rather than in an attempt to obey an objective Law. Once again we will quote the poet:

"Do this and live, the Law demands,
"But gives me neither feet nor hands.
"A better word the Gospel brings,
"It bids me fly and gives me wings."

The phrase, *"And not in the oldness of the letter,"* refers to the Law of Moses. The word *"letter"* in the Greek is *"gramma,"* and means *"a bond, a document, a letter one writes."* Here it refers to the Written Law of God as found in the Old Testament.

In the previous phrase, the word *"newness"* in the Greek is *"kainos,"* and means *"that which is new as to quality, as set over against that which has seen service, the outworn, that which is marred through age."* The Gospel as looked at here as *"new,"* as in respect it replaces the Law, which is old and worn out.

The word *"oldness"* in the Greek is *"palaios,"* and means, *"that which is old in point of use, worn out, useless."*

The Law of Moses fulfilled by Christ, which was abrogated at the Cross, is looked upon as outworn, useless, so that it has been set aside. Now, Spirit (Holy Spirit) and Law are contrasted.

Service in the *"letter"* means seeking Salvation by works, i.e., in union with the first husband (vss. 1-3). Service in the Spirit means enjoyment of Salvation in union with the second husband (vs. 4).

Thus, the Believer learns that association with Christ in His Death liberates him from Death as a King (Rom. Chpt. 5); from Sin as a Master (Rom. Chpt. 6); and from the Law as a Husband (Rom. Chpt. 7).

Romans Chapter 5: Sin on a person, i.e., condemnation. Romans Chapter 6: Sin over a person, i.e., domination. Romans Chapter 7: Sin in a person, i.e., desperation.

The only power that can deliver from these is not Law, but Grace; and the mode of liberation is death, i.e., the judicial death of the Believer at Calvary (Rom. 6:3-4).

In a sense, Death, Sin, and Law triumphed over Christ at Calvary, but only momentarily,

NOTES

and because He allowed it. But their dominion over Him ended directly when He was dead, which is what God planned, and which paid the sin debt and broke the grip of sin upon humanity.

In His Death the Believer died; and, consequently, their authority (Death, Sin, and Law) ended there for Him also, so that He is no longer in their dominion.

Risen with Christ — united to Him the New Husband — a life of Liberty and Sanctification is enjoyed in the life and energy of the Holy Spirit (Williams).

In these Passages, as well as scores of others, the Believer should easily see how that the Law pointed to Jesus. When He came, He fulfilled all its demands, with it no longer being held over the heads of God's people.

To which we have alluded, in all of this it may seem as if Paul is degrading the Law, but as he will show in the next verse, he is not doing so at all, only pointing out its true purpose, which it carried out very well. However, in that it very well fulfilled its task, even as designed by the Lord, and is now replaced by the Lord Jesus Christ, surely the Believer would not want to go back under the *"oldness of the letter."* But sadly, that is what we actually do so many times, and as well, we always reap bitter results — actually, the very opposite of what we intend.

(7) "WHAT SHALL WE SAY THEN? IS THE LAW SIN? GOD FORBID. NAY, I HAD NOT KNOWN SIN, BUT BY THE LAW: FOR I HAD NOT KNOWN LUST, EXCEPT THE LAW HAD SAID, THOU SHALT NOT COVET."

The question, *"What shall we say then?",* now addresses the question of Law (the Law of Moses), as to its purpose and effect.

In verses 1 through 6 of this Chapter, Paul has shown that the Believer is no longer under Law. In the remainder of the Chapter he shows that a Believer putting himself under Law, thus failing to avail himself of the resources of Grace, is a defeated Christian. He teaches that while the Law incites the Christian to more sin, that is, if the Christian tries to put himself under Law, which is actually what the Law was designed to do, yet the Law is not responsible for that sin, but rather the Believer himself, actually, the evil nature in the Believer's heart and life.

PAUL'S EXPERIENCE

As well, in the remainder of this Chapter, Paul gives his own experience as a Christian before he came into the knowledge of Romans Chapter 6. Consequently, he opens himself up that all may see.

In other words, and to which we have already alluded, once Paul was Saved while on the road to Damascus, and shortly thereafter Baptized with the Holy Spirit, noting the tremendous change within his life, he thought surely he could live the type of life he wanted to live and in fact, must live. However, to his dismay, and as we shall see, he found himself failing and failing repeatedly. In other words, his willpower was being overridden by the Powers of Darkness, which left him confused as to what was really happening. That is when he cried, *"O wretched man that I am! Who shall deliver me from the body of this death?"* (vs. 24).

It was then that the Lord gave him the great Truth of the *"Double Cure"* which he gave us in Chapter 6.

He learned that Jesus not only paid the sin debt at Calvary, but as well, broke the dominion of sin in the Believer's life. In fact, he learned many things.

He learned that even though the Believer was a New Creature in Christ Jesus, still the Sin Nature remained alive in that Believer, which could spring to life very quickly, which Paul had ingloriously experienced. In answer to that, he learned that the Believer actually died in Christ, was buried in Christ, and Resurrected in Christ. When the Believer understands this, and has Faith in that which Jesus has done, realizing that it was done for the sinner, he then learns that the power of the Sin Nature is broken, with him now able to walk in Victory as an Overcomer.

In other words, before he learned this, he was constantly trying to gain the Victory and trying to be an Overcomer, actually attempting to fight battles all over again which Jesus had already fought and won. He was frustrating the Grace of God.

VICTORY NOW!

Paul learned that the Believer, even the

moment that he accepts Christ as his Saviour, is Victorious, and is an Overcomer. It is not something he strives to do or strives to be, but in fact already is, but through what Jesus Christ did. However, if he does not know and understand that, there will be no Victory, and neither will he be an Overcomer.

Before these great Truths were shown to him by the Holy Spirit (which Truths he gave to us), Paul found himself attempting to keep the Law (the Moral Law) within his own power and strength, which he was unable to do. This is what frustrated him so very much. Surely, he thinks, inasmuch as I am Saved and Baptized with the Holy Spirit, I can do these things, which he knows must be done. But yet he found he could not keep these Moral Laws even though a Believer, and neither can anyone else — at least in their own strength. But then he found out as the Holy Spirit portrayed to him, how in fact, they can be kept and actually kept very easily! Consequently, what the Holy Spirit related to him, he relates to us.

As I dictate these words on November 10, 1997, I have to wonder in my spirit, considering today's modern Church, just how much it would accept Paul's words if being written presently? Self-righteousness is so rampant at the present time, and I say that with a grieving heart, that I'm not sure that Paul would have been given any credence at all. After all, Paul is openly admitting that he had failure in his Christian experience before he learned and understood these great Truths. So, I suspect that many, that is if Paul were writing these words presently, would hardly think that he would be entrusted by the Holy Spirit to write almost half the New Testament, and in fact, be given the New Covenant of Grace. But he was!

In Truth, I'm not so sure that his words were not met in his day and time with skepticism and even sarcasm. In fact, the questions he asked bear that out I think. Nevertheless, that which he was given was of God, and in fact, some of the greatest Truths found in the entirety of the Word of God.

That's the reason that the Believer must judge everything according to the Word of God, and never according to so-called popular opinion, and above all, they must not allow others to do their thinking for them. The Bible must be the criteria at all times, and, in fact, the only criteria. The tragedy is, most in Christendom blindly follow their Denominational Heads, irrespective as to what they say or do. This is a tragedy, and has led untold millions to die eternally lost.

THE BIBLE

When all of us stand before God, we will be judged according to that which is written in the Book called the Bible, and not according to what our Denomination said, taught or believed. Whatever policy they had or have, is one thing. What the Bible says, is something else altogether.

Regrettably, far too many Believers take the position, that these are things for Church Leaders to work out, and really does not involve them. Right and wrong involve everyone! Consequently, the moment that Denominational policy, or the policy of anyone for that matter, strays from the Word of God, the Believer had better follow the Bible, irrespective of what it means otherwise.

The question, *"Is the Law sin?"*, is asked because of the manner in which Paul has repeatedly addressed the Law.

In effect he is posing the question, *"What shall we say then to the fact that the desires or impulses in the evil nature in me were stirred into activity by the Law? Is the Law sinful or evil which does that?"*

The two words, *"God forbid,"* present his answer. These two words in the Greek are *"me genoito,"* and mean *"may it not become,"* that is, *"let not such a thing be thought of,"* or *"away with the thought."* This condition of man is not caused by the Law of God, but rather exposed. In other words, the Law brought out what was already in man's heart, exposed it to the light of day, showing what man really was.

WHAT THE LAW DOES

The phrase, *"Nay, I had not known sin, but by the Law,"* means that the Law defined what sin actually is. The Law did not originate sin or institute sin. In fact, it had nothing to do with the fact of sin, except to expose it. This it was designed to do, and this it did and very well.

NOTES

I heard a Jewish Journalist being interviewed, asked the question, *"Why is there such an animosity against the Jews?"*

The man's answer was somewhat revealing.

"God gave to the Jews the Ten Commandments, which informs as to what is right and wrong," he said, *"and the world has never forgiven us for that fact."*

Many erroneously believe that the Law of Moses was meant only for the Jews. It was meant for the entirety of the world.

Even though the Ritualistic and Ceremonial parts of the Law were definitely for the Jews, and for a particular purpose, however, the Moral Law was for all, because Moral Law cannot change. What was morally wrong for Jews was and is morally wrong for all.

Please forgive our repetition, but due to the complexity of some of these issues (and the Law is definitely one of those issues), some things have to be repeated more than once, and some things several times.

Even though there was only one Law of Moses, it was divided into two parts, the Ceremonial and the Moral. The Ceremonial consisted of the Sacrifices, Sabbaths, Feast Days, Circumcision, etc. This would have also included all of the Sacred Vessels of Furniture in the Tabernacle or Temple. Actually, all of these items and things pointed to Jesus. In other words, all were symbolic of Jesus.

The Moral part of the Law consisted of the Ten Commandments minus the Fourth. That Commandment alone was not Moral, but Ceremonial.

When Jesus came, He fulfilled all the Ceremonial parts of the Law, with it consequently no longer needed. He also kept completely and met the demands of the Moral Law. But due to these Commandments being Moral, they are still incumbent upon humanity as would be obvious. Nevertheless, man is no more capable of obeying these Commandments now than before. However, they *are* obeyed by the Believer totally in Jesus, with His obedience becoming our obedience.

Giving us the Power and the Strength, along with our understanding of what He has done for us, and our part in what He did at least according to Identification, we now keep these Moral Laws as well. But it is only *through, by, of,* and *with* the Lord Jesus Christ.

So, the Law of Moses very clearly and plainly portrayed the reality of sin which was already present, and as well, succinctly defined it.

The phrase, *"For I had not known lust, except the Law had said, Thou shalt not covet,"* tells us that the desire for what is forbidden is the first conscious form of sin. Paul is saying that the consciousness of sin awoke in him in the shape of a conflict with a prohibitive Law. In other words, the Law defined the covetous passion in Paul's heart. He wanted or lusted for something which belonged to someone else, or something which was not right, with the Law telling him and all others for that matter, what type of sin that he (or they) was now committing. The Law portrayed the presence of sin and its definition. *"Thou shalt not covet"* is the Tenth Commandment (Ex. 20:17).

(8) "BUT SIN, TAKING OCCASION BY THE COMMANDMENT, WROUGHT IN ME ALL MANNER OF CONCUPISCENCE. FOR WITHOUT THE LAW SIN WAS DEAD."

The phrase, *"But sin, taking occasion by the Commandment, wrought in me all manner of concupiscence,"* speaks to the fact that the moral effect of the Commandment manifested the depth of covetousness hidden in man's nature, and not only covetousness, but insensibility, for in the absence of Law sin is dead — not dead in relation to God, but dead to the sensibility of corrupt man (Williams).

"Sin" as here used by Paul, is once again *"The Sin,"* referring to the *"Sin Nature."* *"Occasion"* in the Greek is *"aphormen,"* and means *"to make a start from a place."* It is, therefore, *"a starting place, a base of operations, the means with which one begins."*

"Wrought" in the Greek is *"katergazomai,"* and means *"to accomplish, achieve an end, carry something to a conclusion."*

"Concupiscence" is *"epithumia,"* and means *"evil desire."*

The phrase, *"For without the Law sin was dead,"* means that the Law of Moses fully exposed what already was in man's heart. It not only exposed it, but as well, defined it. Consequently, the state of man thereafter was even worse, as would be obvious. That's the

reason our Jewish friend said that the world has never forgiven the Jews for God giving them the Moral Law. He meant that man now knowing the way, has no cloak for his sin. In other words, he can no longer plead ignorance.

THE LAW DID TWO THINGS:

1. It revealed sin, in other words what was already in man's heart. Law, and irrespective of what kind, excites men in one of two ways: it makes him either desire to break the Law, or to keep the Law. In other words, it has sort of compulsion to its nature. Respecting the Law of God, a desire to keep it of course is the right thing; however, man is shot down in either case.

First of all, if he sets himself to break these Laws, even as most do, he incurs the Wrath of God, which must come upon all sin. Such is the very Nature of God, and cannot be abrogated.

If he sets out to try to keep the Law, which some few attempt to do, he finds that he is woefully unable to do so. He simply does not have the moral capacity to obey. That's why he desperately needs Jesus!

2. According to the Law, he now knows what type of sin he is committing. As well, the Tenth Commandment puts a cap on the entirety of the Law, by actually saying in a sense that it's not only not good enough for man to not physically disobey these Commandments, but he must not even desire to do so. That is what covetousness means, desire, and in this case, *"evil desire."*

So, the Law portrayed to man what he actually was, depraved, without spiritual life, without ability to even obey the most simplest of moral commands. Consequently, he was then to throw himself on the Mercy and Grace of God for His Help, which He Alone could give. A few did, most didn't!

(9) "FOR I WAS ALIVE WITHOUT THE LAW ONCE: BUT WHEN THE COMMANDMENT CAME, SIN REVIVED, AND I DIED."

The phrase, *"For I was alive without the Law once,"* actually points to a double meaning:

1. Paul is speaking of himself and of the time of his Conversion. The Law had absolutely nothing to do with his Conversion,

played no part, at least directly, in that which Jesus did for him in the matter of Redemption, and with all for that matter.

At that moment, because of his acceptance of Jesus Christ he became spiritually alive unto God. It is the same with all, Law plays absolutely no positive part whatsoever in man's Redemption. While it is true that Jesus on our behalf, suffered the penalty of the broken Law, still, that does not affect the Believer at least as far as direct involvement is concerned.

2. The Fall of Adam illustrates verse 11, but also pertains to verse 9.

After Adam's creation and before the Commandment was given concerning his not eating of the Tree of the Knowledge of Good and Evil (Eve as well), there was no Law of any kind whatsoever.

During that time, ever how long it was, Adam and Eve were alive unto God, which enjoyed a state of bliss, of which now is little comprehension.

The phrase, *"But when the Commandment came, sin revived, and I died,"* once again points to two meanings:

1. Going back to Paul, after his Conversion and Baptism with the Holy Spirit, he enjoyed an abundant life which he had never known before. However, at the same time Satan brought about temptation regarding the Moral Law. At that time, Paul fell back on his own efforts attempting to throw aside the Temptation, and failed as fail he must. In fact, the harder he tried, the more he failed. Not understanding the great Truth which he was eventually given by the Lord, and attempting to keep the Commandment of Moral Law, he woefully found that he was unable to do so. Sin revived, and revived mightily. This means that he now found himself failing God just as much as he had before he had come to Christ. That's what he meant by the words *"And I died."* He was not meaning that he physically died, but that he died to the Commandment, in other words he failed to obey as hard as he tried.

In fact, the failure became worse and worse, with him ultimately crying the words of verse 24, *"O wretched man that I am! Who shall deliver me from the body of this death?"*

Of course, the answer to that is the great

Truths of Chapters 6, 7, and 8 of the Book of Romans.

THE SIN NATURE COMING ALIVE

The word *"revived"* in the Greek is *"anazao,"* and means *"to live again."* It speaks of the Sin Nature coming alive once again, giving him the same trouble he had before Conversion. Tragically, many modern Believers are in that very situation right now, and do not really know the reason for their problem, especially considering that they are trying with all their strength. They have little knowledge, if any at all, that even their trying is working to their detriment and not their good. Considering this is very little preached at the present time, puts these people in a dilemma, even as it did Paul so long ago. Observing the climate of the modern Church, most of them dare not say anything, for if they do, especially Preachers, they are consigned to spiritual oblivion, drummed out. So, such climate basically breeds hypocrisy. To be sure, it is not intentional hypocrisy, but nevertheless, that's what it amounts to.

2. Only one Commandment was given to Adam, he was not to eat of the Tree of the Knowledge of Good and Evil (Gen. 2:15-17). However, sin profited by that one Commandment, and used it as a point of attack, i.e., took occasion by it, deceived Adam and so slew him; for in that hour he died morally.

(10) "AND THE COMMANDMENT, WHICH WAS ORDAINED TO LIFE, I FOUND TO BE UNTO DEATH."

The phrase, *"And the Commandment, which was ordained to Life,"* refers to the Ten Commandments, or any one or more thereof.

In other words, these Commandments as given by God were right, and, therefore, pertained to Life. The idea is, that it is not the Commandment which is at fault. And yet this is where the great bone of contention is respecting much of modern Psychology and the Gospel.

Unconverted man carries with him guilt, which has a direct bearing on verse 10.

GUILT

In ordinary speech today, *"guilt"* most often indicates a feeling. However, in Scripture, *"guilt"* is a fact, not a feeling. For Believers, God forgives the sin that makes people guilty.

GUILT AND MODERN PSYCHOLOGY

Unconverted man carries guilt, but does not quite know how to define it, nor does he know or understand its cause.

Modern psychological counseling attempts to rid the person of that uncomfortable feeling by the use of therapy. Of course, such is impossible, simply because it in no way addresses the real problem, which is sin. So it attempts to address the situation in another way.

Modern Psychology basically claims that the Bible, i.e., The Commandment, is a throwback to superstition, and, accordingly, should be ignored. In other words, they are blaming *"The Commandment"* for the guilt, and if one does away with the Commandment, one then does away with the guilt.

They do not understand that the Commandment only exposes the real problem of sin, which causes the guilt. So, Psychology holds no answer whatsoever for man's guilt, because the problem cannot be treated externally, which is the only means available to Psychology, and anything that man may have to offer for that matter.

GUILT IN THE OLD TESTAMENT

While Hebrew words that mean *"iniquity"* and *"wickedness"* are sometimes translated *"guilt"* in particular versions of the Bible, the Hebrew term that means *"to be guilty"* is *"asam."*

This word and its many derivatives focus our attention on the full impact of guilt, which always involves three distinct aspects: A. There is an act that brings guilt; B. There is the condition of guilt that results from the act; and, C. There is the punishment that is appropriate to the act.

The stress in a particular verse may lie on the act itself, on the human condition, or on the punishment. But the Biblical concept of guilt always includes these elements.

Because all sin is an offense against God, guilt can be understood only by relating it to God. The issue in guilt is not how a person may feel about his or her actions; rather, the focus is on the fact that each human

being is responsible and will bear the consequences of his or her actions. In order to avoid those consequences, each person must let God deal with the sin and guilt.

GUILT IN THE NEW TESTAMENT

In the New Testament, *"guilt"* is a judicial concept, affirming criminal responsibility. This is true whether the court is human or Divine.

"Guilty" in Romans 3:19 in the Greek is *"hypodikos,"* and means *"to be guilty,"* or *"to be held accountable,"* in the sense of being forced to answer to the Divine Jurisdiction.

So, the New Testament reaches a little further than the Old, by counting the whole world as *"guilty before God."* Consequently, the world is not guilty merely because of a particular act which brings guilt, but rather because of original sin.

However, the difference is not noticeable simply because, unconverted man cannot help but commit acts of sin which automatically bring guilt.

THE DIVINE REMEDY FOR GUILT

The Bible's Message that human beings are accountable and must bear the consequences of wrong moral choices is taught in many ways.

However, the Divine emphasis is not on our failure. Instead, God comes to us with His unique Message of Hope. Even though you and I are guilty before God, we can be acquitted in the Divine Court!

The Lord shares with us in Scripture, especially in the teaching and actions of Jesus, His willingness to forgive.

Guilt is a reality. But so is forgiveness. In Jesus we find the perfect remedy for those tragic choices that have made us liable to judgment. In Jesus we have the Promise that no one can bring any charge against those whom God has Saved by their Faith in, and their acceptance of, His son, The Lord Jesus Christ.

The phrase, *"I found to be unto death,"* means that the Law revealed the sin, which wages are death.

The words, *"I found,"* literally in the Greek says, *"Was found."* That is, Paul expected his Christian Life under Law to issue in the production of a Testimony and Experience that would be a living one, alive with the Life of God. This was to be brought about and accomplished through his attempt at Law-Obedience. One must remember, all of this transpired after his Conversion.

But he found that mere effort at obeying an outside Law resulted in defeat. The Law, using the evil nature as a fulcrum, brought out sin all the more, and this condition he calls *"death."*

(11) "FOR SIN, TAKING OCCASION BY THE COMMANDMENT, DECEIVED ME, AND BY IT SLEW ME."

The phrase, *"For sin, taking occasion by the Commandment,"* in no way blames the Commandment, but that the Commandment actually did agitate the sin (the Sin Nature) and brought it to the fore, which it was designed to do. (The Commandment actually speaks of any of the Laws of God, but more particularly, the Moral Laws ensconced in the Ten Commandments.)

The phrase, *"Deceived me, and by it slew me,"* means that something happened which Paul did not in any way expect. He thought his great efforts to keep the Law (the Moral Law) would be met with success, especially considering that he now has Jesus in his heart, and is Baptized with the Holy Spirit. However, he was deceived respecting these thoughts, but the deception was on his part and not on God's.

How was he deceived?

Due to his new status in Christ, he thought surely that he now had enough strength to keep the Law. He was to find that God never intended for us to keep the Law by our own strength. That was never His Plan at all. The Law instead, is to be kept by Jesus living in us and by the Power of the Holy Spirit carrying out this which is demanded (Gal. 2:20).

Sadly, Paul was not the only one deceived, for literally millions of others have fallen into the same trap, and in fact, continue to do so. Now that they have the Lord, they think surely their strength is sufficient. They do not seem to realize that it is not strength which God is requiring, but rather Faith and Obedience.

He wants us to understand what Jesus did

for us at Calvary and the Resurrection, have Faith in that, in which the Power of God will then effect the situation, with sin being completely defeated within our lives. In fact, it is not a process, but rather an *"Act,"* i.e., the Act being that which Jesus did.

SIN AND THE LAW

Sin as an evil principle in man's nature makes use of Law to provoke men to the practice of sins that the Law forbids, and so plunges the soul into a conflict that, apart from Law, could not take place. But Law originates this conflict, which it is designed to do, and by making the sinner responsible, deposits the sentence of death in his conscience. The result is death in the conscience without any deliverance for the heart from the power of the disobedience.

THE COMMANDMENT AS THE INSTRUMENT OF DEATH

Law as a barrier to the will excites it; and the consciousness of sin thereby awakened, produces in the Presence of God a conscience under sentence of death. Thus, the Commandment ordained unto life becomes, in fact, the instrument of death. *"This do, and thou shalt live"* (Lk. 10:28), which is the Commandment, becomes death to man because his sinful nature refuses to obey; and in so refusing his own conscience condemns him to death.

Thus, the Law was holy and each of its Commandments just and good, but it condemned to death, even as Law must do, all who fail to render to it a perfect obedience, which none did except Jesus.

THE EFFECT OF DIVINE LAW

Such is the effect of Divine Law upon man's carnal nature; and the rest of this Chapter illustrates the Doctrine by showing how fruitless is the effort of the *"old man"* to live as the *"new man."* This emphasizes the absolute necessity of Regeneration; for it is impossible for an unconverted man, however moral and highly cultured he may think he is, to live the Christian Life. He is carnal, sold under sin, and all his Righteousness are as filthy rags in the sight of God.

(12) "WHEREFORE THE LAW IS HOLY,

AND THE COMMANDMENT HOLY, AND JUST, AND GOOD."

The phrase, *"Wherefore the Law is holy,"* points to this fact, because it is God's Revelation of Himself. As we have repeatedly stated, the Law was designed by God for a particular and specific purpose, which it accomplished greatly so.

The reason that Paul is having to do all of this explaining is because of two problems:

1. Israel perverted the Law, actually adding over 600 more Laws of their own making. They tried to make Salvation out of the Law, which basically reduced Judaism to a mere ethical form, which in effect made it little better than the religions of the world, etc. So, due to the manner in which the Law had been perverted by Israel, Paul's explanation is necessary.

2. The problem with Israel is the problem with us all, in that there is something in man, which came about as a result of the Fall, that makes him believe that he can actually live up to God's Holy Standards. In fact, most of the population of the world now, and in fact for all time, actually believe that they live up to God's Requirements. The Truth is, they have made up their own Moral Code, and in fact, don't even live up to it. Nevertheless, they are deceived, even as Paul said, making themselves believe that they are correct.

As we have already stated, this problem bleeds over into the hearts of Christians. We still like to think that we have contributed something toward whatever it is we are looking for respecting the Lord. The Truth is, we have contributed nothing at any time, before we were Saved or after we were Saved. The answer is simply Faith in what Jesus has already done.

The phrase, *"And the Commandment holy, and just, and good,"* addresses the demands of God as given in the Law:

1. These demands are *"holy"* and because their parent, the Law, is holy.

2. As well, they are *"just,"* meaning *"Righteous or right"* in their demands.

3. And last of all, they are *"good"* because they are *"right."*

The Holy Spirit through the Apostle goes into all of this explanation for the simple reason that man wants to blame God for his

dilemma. In the Garden, Adam blamed Eve, with Eve blaming the Serpent (Gen. 3:12-13). If we knew the full story, the poor Serpent probably blamed the Devil, which we all do in one way or the other, unless we are blaming God. The idea is, that man does not want to take responsibility for himself, which in one sense, the Law was actually designed to force him to do.

The idea is, *"Lord, You made me this way, so I am not responsible."*

No, God did not make anyone the way they are respecting sin, disobedience, and failure. They are that way as a result of their own actions.

However, it is not so much that which man has done, but rather that which man refuses to do. In other words, man really cannot help what Adam did, even though he suffers the consequences. What he can help, and that for which God holds him accountable, is his refusal to accept God's Atonement for the terrible dilemma in which he now finds himself. That Atonement is Jesus and what He did at Calvary and the Resurrection.

(13) "WAS THEN THAT WHICH IS GOOD MADE DEATH UNTO ME? GOD FORBID. BUT SIN, THAT IT MIGHT APPEAR SIN, WORKING DEATH IN ME BY THAT WHICH IS GOOD; THAT SIN BY THE COMMANDMENT MIGHT BECOME EXCEEDING SINFUL."

The question, *"Was then that which is good made death unto me?"*, is answered readily by the Apostle. Once again, it is not the Law that is at fault, but rather the sin in man which is opposed to the Law.

The two words, *"God forbid,"* places the Apostle in the position of responding emotionally, and rightly so! He will not tolerate the idea of God or His Word claimed as being the cause of all of these problems. He strongly denounces such a thought which some have suggested.

Man must always take the position that it is never God Who is at fault, and irrespective of what the situation may be. Admittedly, the fault may be with others or it may be with us, but it is never with God. Instead, *"His* (Thy) *Word is a Lamp unto my feet, and a Light unto my path"* (Ps. 119:105).

The phrase, *"But sin, that it might appear sin,"* proclaims the Divine intention of the Law, namely that sin might show its true colors.

This was necessary, because man before the Law would little admit that he was a sinner, but even if he did, he believed that he could effect his own Salvation. So, he has to be shown exactly what he is (without spiritual life, and, consequently, morally depraved), and that in no way can he live up to God's Standards, at least within himself.

A perfect example of this is found in the answer of Cain, after he had killed his brother Abel.

"And the Lord said unto Cain, Where is Abel thy brother? And he said, I know not: Am I my brother's keeper?" (Gen. 4:9).

He would not admit to sin, would not confess the sin, and complained at the restriction. So, Law was necessary in order to force mankind into the realization of what he is.

The phrase, *"Working death in me by that which is good,"* refers to Sin turning God's intended Blessing into a Curse. Nothing like the Law could more clearly show what sin is, or excite a stronger desire for deliverance from it. The excesses of sin reveal its real nature. Only then do some people get their eyes opened.

The phrase, *"That sin by the Commandment might become exceeding sinful,"* proclaims that as exactly what happened.

The Law demanded obedience, as all Law does, but which man could not carry out, irrespective as to how hard he tried. Actually, the more he tried, the worse the situation became, making an already out of control fire into a conflagration.

(14) "FOR WE KNOW THAT THE LAW IS SPIRITUAL: BUT I AM CARNAL, SOLD UNDER SIN."

The phrase, *"For we know that the Law is Spiritual,"* refers to the fact that the Law is totally of God, from God, and by God.

"Spiritual" in the Greek is *"pneumatikos,"* and means *"non-carnal, not of man,"* in other words, of the Holy Spirit.

The phrase, *"But I am carnal, sold under sin,"* refers to the fact that man within himself, has no spirituality whatsoever. In other words, he is completely void of a

NOTES

Spiritual or Divine Nature.

Here, Paul describes himself as carnal, in other words, as a Christian living, however unwillingly, more or less under the control of the evil nature from which he had been liberated; however he is back under its control, because he is living under Law instead of Grace. To be sure, it was done in ignorance, but the results were the same.

As such, he is sold as a slave under sin. *"Sold"* in the Greek is *"piprasko,"* and means *"sin has foreclosed the mortgage and owns its slave."*

Many may read this and claim that such is impossible respecting a Believer. However, not only is it possible, but in fact, the problem is pandemic throughout the Christian world.

I think the description as given to us here by Paul tells us, that unless the Believer knows and understands what Christ has actually done for him, and how that he figures into the entirety of that great Act at Calvary and the Resurrection, that it is inevitable that it conclude exactly as Paul describes here. There is no other alternative!

Having preached all over the world and for many years, while some few Believers do know and understand these great Truths, I know that most not only do not know them, but in fact, have never heard of such. So, if that is true, and it is, then one can readily see how serious this problem actually is.

Jesus said, *"And ye shall know the Truth, and the Truth shall make you free"* (Jn. 8:32). However, I might quickly add, it is only the Truth that one knows, which will make one free. Truth which is not known, which is the case with most Christians, has no effect whatsoever.

While it is true that the Holy Spirit *"guides . . . into all Truth,"* still, this is not by any means automatic but rather potential actually dependent on many things, such as obedience, consecration, dedication, and a sense or desire for all Godly things. Regrettably, many Christians do not fall entirely into these categories (Jn. 16:13).

Paul is the most perfect example of all. As sincere as he was, he only came by these great Truths, when in the position of acute desperation (vs. 24). Regrettably, it takes the same for most other Believers as well!

(15) "FOR THAT WHICH I DO I ALLOW NOT: FOR WHAT I WOULD, THAT DO I NOT; BUT WHAT I HATE, THAT DO I."

The phrase, *"For that which I do I allow not,"* presents not the words of an unsaved man, but rather a Believer who is trying and failing.

FRUSTRATION

"Allow" in the Greek is *"ginosko,"* and means *"to know by experience, to understand."* In effect he is saying, *"For that which I do, I do not understand."* He does not understand his experience as a Christian.

As stated, it is clear that Paul is recounting his experience as a Saved man, and not before his Conversion as many Preachers contend. He desires to do good and hates sin. To be frank, no unsaved man does that. The failure to achieve his purpose is found in the fact that he is attempting in his own strength that which can *only* be accomplished in the supernatural power of the Holy Spirit.

The phrase, *"For what I would, that do I not,"* refers to the obedience he wants to render to Christ, but rather failing.

The phrase, *"But what I hate, that do I,"* refers to sin in his life which he doesn't want to do and in fact hates, but finds himself unable to stop.

To be frank, this is the plight of untold numbers of Christians.

Why?

As we have stated, Paul's problem as all others in the same predicament, is that of attempting to carry out by one's own strength, which only the Holy Spirit can do. So, how do we come to the place, that we are depending on the Spirit and not on ourselves? To be frank, untold numbers of Spirit-filled Believers are in this same category, which leaves them exactly as Paul, meaning that they do not understand their predicament. They are Baptized with the Holy Spirit, just as Paul at this time was, so should not that take care of the problem?

Within itself, no!

OPERATING IN ONE'S OWN STRENGTH

I think I exaggerate not, when I say that the greatest problem with the Child of God, especially the one who seeks to do the Will

of God, is the problem of operating in our own ability, rather than in the Power and Ability of the Holy Spirit. It is so easy to do that whenever we load up our efforts with Scriptures, good intentions, even the doing of good things such as prayer or fasting, etc.

While all of these things are extremely commendable and helpful and even necessary in their own way, neither those things, nor any other attributes of the Word of God will bring about the Victory which one seeks, simply because the Holy Spirit will only function and operate in that which is Truth as it relates to the subject at hand.

Our problem too often is, if it is Biblical such as prayer, etc., then it is right.

While that is certainly true as far as it goes, however, we must ask ourselves, right in what capacity?

And then again, and as we have already stated, there is something in man, even Believing man, which wants to contribute at least something, as small as it may be, toward one's Victory, etc. We like to feel that we have contributed toward accomplishing the task, which makes us in our own eyes, big or greater than others. All of this, of course, is nothing more than pride. It is also an insult to Christ, because the very thought, in essence, says that what He did at Calvary and the Resurrection was not enough, and needs our little effort added to make it complete. Such is nothing short of crass, and as stated, an insult.

Other than the True Plan which the Lord laid out for the Apostle Paul, which is given in Chapters 6, 7 and 8, one can carry out any type of program they like respecting the overcoming of sin, and it is doomed to failure.

THE WORK OF THE HOLY SPIRIT

The Holy Spirit guides only into Truth (Jn. 16:13-15). That means Truth respecting the need at hand. While prayer, or fasting, or studying the Word of God, or witnessing to the lost, are all true things within themselves, and will benefit one greatly, still, one cannot set oneself to pray so much time each day thinking that such will overcome sin. It will certainly help in other ways, but it will not give one the Victory that one desires as Paul addresses here. The same goes for any other Biblical attribute or quality. These things definitely help the Believer in their own way, but once again, if we attempt to promote these things other than what Jesus has done as an answer to this problem, we have turned those great qualities into *"works,"* which God cannot recognize or bless.

I am not by any means saying that the Believer should not pray or fast, or any of these things we have named, but rather do them even in a greater way, but for the right purpose.

The Holy Spirit will only bring His Power to bear, whenever we are operating in Truth. He will not bless efforts of the flesh, irrespective as to how noble or right they may be within themselves.

Whenever we step into God's Plan, trusting and having Faith in what He has done for us, the Holy Spirit then brings His Power to bear, which assures all and sundry, is able to do whatever is needed. But it is only the Truth which He blesses and promotes.

WHAT IS THE TRUTH RESPECTING VICTORY OVER SIN?

Of course, we have given it in Commentary any number of times respecting Chapters 6 and 7, but due to the tremendous significance of that which we are discussing, and which the Holy Spirit thought so important that He would devote to the subject all this space, we will give it again.

THE DOUBLE CURE

1. The Believer must understand according to the Word of God, that Jesus not only satisfied the terrible sin debt which hung over the human race, but as well, broke the dominion of sin in the heart and life of the Believer. It is the *"Double Cure."*

IN CHRIST

2. As it deals with the breaking of sin's dominion, the Believer must understand that he was literally in Christ when Christ died on Calvary. Paul used the term, *"Baptized into His Death"* (Rom. 6:3). So, it is proper to say that we were literally in Him, at least by Faith, when He did this great thing.

Being in Him at His Death, we were also

"... buried with Him by Baptism into Death" (Rom. 6:4).

We must also know and understand that it was *"... our old man which was crucified with Him"* (Rom. 6:16), which speaks of the time we were dominated by the Sin Nature, in other words, a slave to sin and ungodly passions. We must know that all of that was buried with Him.

As well, we must understand that when He was Resurrected, we were Resurrected with Him, and in fact, in Him. However, it was not the *"old man"* that was Resurrected, but rather the *"new man"* walking in *"Newness of Life"* (Rom. 6:4). So, we *now* have a new life.

ENTIRELY FOR US

3. We must understand, that all of this was done for us. It is not that He merely allowed us to accompany Him in this great transformation, but that it was done exclusively for humanity in totality. Understanding that, we should also understand that He wants us to have the great Victory which He has paid for at such price.

FAITH

4. Knowing that we were not really there when Jesus died on Calvary and was Resurrected from the dead, we are to have Faith in this which Jesus did, and a continuing Faith at that. However, it is impossible to have Faith in something which is unknown. In other words, if the Believer does not know and understand this second part of what Jesus did at Calvary and the Resurrection regarding the breaking of sin's dominion, it is quite impossible for him to have Faith in such a thing. The Holy Spirit through Hosea said, *"My people are destroyed for lack of knowledge"* (Hos. 4:6).

So, to have Faith *in* what Jesus did, one must at least know something about *what* He did.

CONFESSION

5. Along with one's Faith one must reckon himself, or account himself as being *"... dead indeed unto sin, but alive unto God through Jesus Christ our Lord"* (Rom. 6:11). Such is the proper confession.

THE HOLY SPIRIT

6. Inasmuch as the Holy Spirit always responds to Truth and Faith, His Power is then brought to bear regarding the Sin Nature, with the reality of deliverance then instantly effected in the heart and life of the Believer. In other words, the Sin Nature was broken the moment Jesus died on Calvary. Consequently, its dominion was wrecked and destroyed regarding its hold on the Believer. However, inasmuch as the Believer did not know this, it again gained ascendancy. Now that the Believer knows and understands what Jesus has done for him, and he has Faith in that, the Holy Spirit will begin to apply His great Power to the problem, with it falling away easily and quickly. In other words, what was literally impossible for us, is not only entirely possible for Him, but in fact, very easy.

Satan does not dare attempt to usurp authority over the Holy Spirit, but to be sure, he will usurp authority over our error all day long and cause us tremendous problems, even as he did Paul.

ALL SIN

7. As well, the Believer must understand, that what Jesus did in the breaking of sin's dominion, includes every single type of sin that one could ever begin to think. In other words, nothing is left out with all included.

VICTORY

8. Consequently, and as we have stated, the moment the Believer accepts Christ, he has Victory and is an Overcomer. While there is a struggle, which we will address next, it is not from a position of trying to gain Victory, but rather from the position of *maintaining* the Victory.

The idea is, that the Believer is thinking wrong when he thinks of himself as having to try to gain something, especially considering that the Lord has already won that battle and His Victory is our Victory. We must understand that and act upon that.

Sadly, Satan is very successful at getting all of us to fight battles that we do not need to fight. In other words, the Lord has already fought these particular battles and won them at great price. Also, the very reason He fought them, is simply because we could not hope to win in any case. Our Victory is only in His Victory, as stated, and in fact, can only be in His Victory. There is no other recourse, as there need not be any other recourse.

DISCIPLINE

9. Whenever the Believer comes to Christ, even though the Sin Nature has its power broken and is isolated, still, it remains in the heart and life of the Believer. The Lord does that for a purpose. It is for our discipline, which teaches us trust, obedience, confidence in the Lord and dependence on Him. As we have stated, man's greatest problem, even with Believers, is self-dependence. That is probably the hardest thing for the Believer to break. God wants the Believer to depend totally and exclusively upon Him for everything. The reasons are obvious:

First of all, this situation is of far greater magnitude than any of us realize, and none of us are capable of coping with the Powers of Darkness on our own. We must look to the Lord and for all things.

THE FLESH AND THE SPIRIT

10. As well, even though we do not like to admit such, irrespective of the Believer knowing every single thing that Paul has taught in these Chapters, still, there will be occasional times of failure. To some that would seem like a bad confession. However, it is the Truth. This is what constitutes the tension between the flesh and the spirit (the regenerated spirit of man as well as the Holy Spirit in opposition to self-will, etc.).

However, the dominion of sin has been broken in the heart and life of the Believer, and properly understanding the Word of God totally brings to a halt the habitual sinning, i.e., habitual failures. The Believer can live a life of total and complete Victory as an Overcomer, but only as he understands his place and position in Christ, and properly walks after the Spirit (Rom. 8:1).

It is not the Will of God as should be obvious, for the Believer to live a life of failure, in other words, constantly sinning and repenting. While God will always forgive (I Jn. 1:9), it is the Will of God that we walk in Victory. The Work of Christ at Calvary and the Resurrection is a Finished Work. In other words, He did all that He set out to do, and did it totally and completely. He left nothing undone. His Victory is complete; therefore, our Victory is complete. He is a complete Overcomer and we are a complete Overcomer (Jn. 16:33).

(16) "IF THEN I DO THAT WHICH I WOULD NOT, I CONSENT UNTO THE LAW THAT IT IS GOOD."

The phrase, *"If then I do that which I would not,"* presents Paul as doing something which is against his will. In other words he doesn't want to do it, and is trying not to do it, but finds himself doing it anyway.

In reading what I have just said, many would conclude if Paul, or anyone for that matter, was doing something against his will, in other words, trying not to do the thing, then surely God would not hold him responsible for such action?

Yes, God did hold Paul responsible for these failures, and He holds all other Believers responsible as well.

It is the same principle with the sinner. He cannot help his condition because of original sin, and in Truth, God does not actually condemn him for that. No, that does not mean that such a condition or situation constitutes Salvation, for it does not. While God may not condemn the individual as such, the individual stands condemned already due to the very fact of original sin.

The idea is, that the accountability comes in by man refusing to accept God's Plan of Salvation which He has provided in the Atonement. In other words, God has the antidote for man's problem of sin, but most men refuse to accept it. That is where the condemnation comes in.

ACCOUNTABLE?

It works identically with the Believer. The fact of him having a Sin Nature is not his fault, being born into the world with this condition. However, the Lord has provided a remedy for the situation in what Christ did at Calvary. The Believer not taking advantage of that, whether through ignorance or self-will, is the problem. In other words, the solution is there if the Believer wants the solution. As with Paul it may not be

NOTES

easy in coming, and there might be quite a few failures before the Truth is reached. Nevertheless, the remedy is available. If he earnestly seeks God even as Paul did, which should serve as an example for us, the Holy Spirit will see to it that the remedy is found. In fact, we are giving here the remedy which is available to all.

So, no matter how hard one tries in the flesh, or how sincere one may be, or well-motivated, if one's efforts are misplaced, one will not find the victory which only Truth brings. So, the Believer is accountable in any case.

The phrase, *"I consent unto the Law that it is good,"* simply means that the Law of God is working as it is supposed to work. In other words, My wanting to do the opposite of what I do proves My acceptance of God's Law as good.

The idea is, that the Law has pointed out the sin in the Believer's life, also showing its terrible wrong. However, the Law gives no power to obey the Commandment, because it was never meant to give such power.

"Consent" in the Greek is *"sumphemi,"* and means *"to speak together with, concur with."*

Paul is saying, *"I don't want to do this thing which is wrong, and the Law does not want me to do this thing which is wrong."* Consequently, this whole scenario proves that the Law of God is performing its intended purpose.

Paul is also saying that it is not the Law's fault that he is failing, but rather his own fault. However, men have a tendency to want to blame the Law of God instead of their own evil and wickedness. No, the Commandment is not wrong, in fact, it is good. It is the sin in us and our approach to that sin, which is wrong.

(17) "NOW THEN IT IS NO MORE I THAT DO IT, BUT SIN THAT DWELLETH IN ME."

The phrase, *"Now then it is no more I that do it,"* has been grossly misunderstood by many, which they think is a license to sin.

Twisting and perverting Paul's words, many claim that they are not responsible for their sins. However, they *are* responsible for their sins, and Paul will now explain what he is saying.

The phrase, *"But sin that dwelleth in me,"* does not really refer to particular acts of sin, but rather the *"Sin Nature"* which dwells in every Believer.

In other words, and as Paul has already said, he does not want to do these things which are wrong, and neither does any True Believer. As we have stated, these are not the words or thoughts of an unsaved man. This is a Person who wants to do right and is actually trying to do right, but failing, and not really understanding the reason why. As we have stated, his Christianity is a mystery to him, at least before the great Truths of Victory in Christ were given to him.

Paul is activating the Sin Nature within himself, which is causing all kind of problems, and he really doesn't know how it is happening. He fights it very hard even as the next verse portrays, but instead of the situation growing better, it is actually growing worse.

Paul is not speaking here of the right or wrong of the situation, but rather the cause of what is taking place, which is the Sin Nature.

To be frank, when this problem was taking place in Paul's life, which was immediately after his Conversion, he did not really know or understand any of the things he is now explaining. Looking back, and considering that the Holy Spirit has led him into Truth, with its resultant Victory, he can now explain as to what was taking place at that time, and what brought on the failure.

(18) "FOR I KNOW THAT IN ME (THAT IS, IN MY FLESH,) DWELLETH NO GOOD THING: FOR TO WILL IS PRESENT WITH ME; BUT HOW TO PERFORM THAT WHICH IS GOOD I FIND NOT."

The phrase, *"For I know that in me* (that is, in my flesh,) *dwelleth no good thing,"* speaks of man's own ability, or rather the lack thereof, at least when it comes to spiritual things, in comparison to the Holy Spirit.

The idea is, that Paul found out that all of his struggles by his own self-efforts, even as dedicated or as sincere as they may be, brought about no Victory whatsoever. As the sinner has no solution to his spiritual dilemma within himself, likewise, the Believer has no solution within himself regarding these

problems. The answer in all cases is Jesus.

The Truth is, *"flesh"* in the Believer is just as ugly as *"flesh"* in the unbeliever. Actually, it is more ugly in the Mind of God, because so very unnecessary.

THE FLESH

As we have explained several times, the *"flesh"* speaks of man's frailty, inability, and the absolute futility of depending on such to bring about a spiritual change in one's life. Salvation is *all* of the Lord, and that means *"all."* Man does not need to add anything to this great Plan, and in fact, if he attempts to do so, which all of us have done, and Paul is here describing his own experience, all we do is *"frustrate the Grace of God,"* which means our efforts hinder Him from doing what He Alone can do (Gal. 2:21).

Likewise, many misunderstand this very verse also. They conclude that Paul is saying that the flesh is weak and, therefore, it is going to sin, and there is nothing the Believer can do about it. That is *not* what Paul is saying.

He is referring not to a sinning Salvation, but rather at the futility of trying to overcome sin in the flesh, i.e., by one's own efforts. Actually, the entirety of this scenario is a portrayal of what causes failure and how to have Victory over failure.

THE WILL

The phrase, *"For to will is present with me,"* in effect is saying that the *"will"* is not strong enough to overcome sin, at least within itself. That also means and as we have said, that Satan can override a Believer's will, that is if the Power of God does not accompany the will.

While it is true that the Believer has to will that which God wants, which is absolutely necessary, still, the will of man ideally, is only the trigger. It is not the actual power itself, exactly as the trigger on a gun is not the power of the gun, but rather the explosive charge. Likewise, it is the Holy Spirit Who is the Power, but is triggered by the will of the Believer.

However, that within itself is not enough. While the trigger for the gun is necessary, it must be pointing in the right direction to be effective. The Truth is, that the explosive power of the Holy Spirit will not work on our behalf unless we are pointed in the right direction, i.e., in the way of Truth. This pertains to the Believer knowing and understanding the Truth about what Jesus has done for us at Calvary, and how that in effect, we were in Him when this was done.

So, while the *"will"* of man is very important, it within itself cannot effect what needs to be done, as should be obvious.

GOD'S WILL

The idea is, that the Believer's will coincide with God's Will, which can only be done if the Believer satisfactorily knows God's Will. Merely saying it will not suffice. We must know God's Will, and we can only know that Will according to His Word.

"To will" in the Greek is *"thelo,"* and means *"being constantly desirous."* That is, Paul was constantly desirous of doing God's Will, but it still was not being done.

"Present" in the Greek is *"parakeimai,"* and means *"to lie beside."* This came from his Divine Nature (II Pet. 1:4), which meant that the Nature of God was in Paul which made him desire God's Will.

The phrase, *"But how to perform that which is good I find not,"* presents the problem. The will was there, but not the ability to do so.

The two words *"how"* and *"find"* are not in the Greek Text concerning this phrase. The word *"find"* was added by the translators to complete the thought. The word *"find"* one could probably say is a bad translation.

The literal Greek reads, *"But to perform the good, not."* Paul is saying that while the desire to do God's Will was always with him, the ability or power to perform it was not. Ignorant of the Truth of Romans Chapter 6, 7, and 8, he was depending upon his own efforts to do God's Will, which is never sufficient.

The Reader may wonder as to why the Lord has so constructed the situation in this manner? To one's thinking, the leaving of the Sin Nature in the Believer after Conversion, seems to be unnecessary, especially considering that in a sense it is the cause of so many problems. As well, I might quickly

add that one denying the presence of the Sin Nature really does not change anything. To be sure, one's friends and loved ones know it's there, because it is very obvious. In other words, if one thinks one has reached the stage of sinless perfection, let one know and understand at the same time that one's friends know better.

SPIRITUAL PRIDE

Man is so constituted, even Believers, that if we experience too much blessing even to the slightest degree, we quickly respond with spiritual pride. In other words, we become puffed up very quickly and very easily.

Allowing the Sin Nature to remain in the Believer, although isolated, has a tendency to constantly warn the Believer of his obvious frailty, whether he thinks so or not. We are quickly made to know and realize just how vulnerable we are, and, consequently, how much we must depend on the Lord, and depend upon Him constantly. In other words, the very moment we cease to look to Him, is the moment we veer off track, with the Sin Nature then springing to life, and quickly letting us know that the situation is going wrong. As a result, at least if we want to walk close to God, we find that we must constantly seek His Face, depend totally upon Him, ever learning more about Trust and Faith in Him. So, as stated, it was done for purpose and reason.

While Paul actually did find a way to perform that which was good, he did not find it within himself, which is what the Text actually means.

(19) "FOR THE GOOD THAT I WOULD I DO NOT: BUT THE EVIL WHICH I WOULD NOT, THAT I DO."

The phrase, *"For the good that I would I do not,"* means simply that no matter how hard he tried, and despite all the effort put forth, he simply could not live up to the Moral Law of God.

SELF-RIGHTEOUSNESS

I realize that many who have been touched somewhat by the plague of self-righteousness, contend that while some very weak Believers may fall into this category, that surely such does not touch them, especially considering that they are Faith giants.

However I remind such people, that if they believe such a thing, that means they are referring to the Apostle Paul as *"weak."* I also remind that person that Paul wrote almost half the New Testament and in fact, was given the New Covenant. Consequently, I would hardly think that the term *"weak"* could be rightly applied to him.

The Truth is, that all Believers and irrespective as to whom they may be, are *"weak"* within themselves. If we do not rightly understand that, then our fall will be even harder.

As well, if one truly understands that, one will never look askance at others who seem to be having difficulties in this area. In fact, they will have had the same difficulties themselves, and will realize that what they now have is not because of their own power or strength, but rather that of the Lord. Consequently, there is no room to boast.

The phrase, *"But the evil which I would not, that I do,"* completely lays to rest the idea that Paul is speaking here about minor things that are of little consequence. Paul is speaking of *"evil"* which means *"sin."*

I realize it is very difficult for us to grasp the fact that the mighty Apostle Paul actually failed God after his Conversion. However, the Text is very plain here that in fact he did, and repeatedly. I think the Reader would have to understand that Paul was a man of great personal courage, of strong determination, and of great resolution. However, these things within themselves were not, and are not, enough. No one, even the strongest among us, can overcome sin within his own strength. No matter how much he hates the thing, even as Paul did, the very evil which he does not want to do, that he will do.

IS SIN A MATTER OF CHOICE?

In the strict sense of the word, yes! However, it needs some explanation.

Anyone reading this Text will have to understand that Paul's choice was to do good. As well, his choice was *not* to do evil. So the *"choice"* which in effect is the *"will"* is not strong enough within itself. So, sin in that capacity is not merely a choice. If it was, Paul would not have had these great problems.

As well, there are many Christians even at this very moment who have made the choice not to do certain things which are wrong, but they have had that choice overrode time and time again. So, what is the answer?

WHAT TYPE OF CHOICE?

As we have already stated, and which the Text plainly bears out, if we try to make a choice respecting sin on the wrong basis, we will fail. In other words, it is not a matter of simply saying *"no"* to sin, etc. Were that true, then Jesus wasted His time in coming down here and paying the terrible price which He paid at Calvary.

I realize that the unconverted world does not say *"no"* to sin, and in fact, does not desire to say *"no."* In fact, they say *"yes"* to sin, and gladly so!

However, with the Believer the situation is altogether different. The moment the person comes to Christ, at that moment the power of the Sin Nature is broken, with the Divine Nature implanted within his heart and life. The Believer is now a New Creature in Christ Jesus (II Cor. 5:17).

But then the Believer finds that old sin impulses begin to come back. If he knows who he is in Christ Jesus and more particularly, what and why he is, he merely says *"yes"* to Christ, and the impulse dies as it is attempting to be born. Consequently, his Sin Nature remains dormant and doesn't come into play. The Believer is walking in Victory, even as intended.

HOWEVER!

Most of the time and regrettably so, it doesn't happen that way. The Believer attempts to overcome the evil impulse with his willpower and fails. In other words, he does what the sin impulse demands, which is evil, and which is sin. He feels terrible about the thing, instantly repents, and God instantly forgives, as He always will do (I Jn. 1:9).

However, the Sin Nature has now become active again, and because of the failure brings back the sinful impulse which rears its ugly head again, and again, and again, etc. The failures continue, even as Paul here explains, and the Sin Nature which has been dormant, with that dominion of sin broken, is now once again roaring into a conflagration, in other words out of control. The Believer, even though loving Jesus with all of his heart, and even though he will probably not even admit it to himself, is once again being controlled by the Sin Nature, exactly as he was before Conversion. This is the frustration which Paul felt, and which millions of others have felt after him.

To combat this thing, the Believer almost in panic, sets about to do whatever he can do which he thinks or hopes will bring Victory.

For instance, he asks for prayer in Church, with hands laid on him. Many times, the Power of God is very effective, with the Believer being touched mightily. He thinks surely that his problem is now solved, but finds that almost as quickly as he walks outside the Church Door, that the sinful impulse returns, and once again he is off to the races — a race incidentally, which he always loses. He is now more frustrated than ever. Doesn't the Power of God work? Isn't prayer effective?

He then resolves to try harder, which does not help the situation, but rather exacerbates it. Actually, and as we have stated, it tends only to frustrate the Grace of God (Gal. 2:21).

HOW LONG WILL GOD FORGIVE?

Despite what some Preachers say, God places no limitations on how many times He will forgive. As long and as often as the person is sincere in his heart, and truly seeking forgiveness, forgiveness will always be granted (Mat. 6:14-15; 7:1-5; I Jn. 1:9).

However, even though forgiveness is greatly needed and greatly appreciated, as would be obvious, that is really not the answer. Sinning and repenting, sinning and repenting, which regrettably is the case with many if not most, certainly should be obvious that such is *not* the Will of God. Jesus Christ did not die on Calvary, paying the terrible price which He paid, in order for the Believer to live a defeated life. While forgiveness is always afforded, at least if it is sought, that is only a temporary respite, and not the answer.

IS DELIVERANCE THE ANSWER?

Yes, but not in the sense in which most

people think. While deliverance plays a much greater role in all that God does for us than most anyone would be able to comprehend, still, deliverance in the sense of which most think, is not the answer. The reason is very simple:

If the person is delivered, without understanding what the Word of God says about this subject, they will be right back in the same position of defeat almost before the last Hallelujah dies down.

WHAT ABOUT DEMON SPIRITS?

While demon spirits definitely do play a part in anything which is not of God, still, it is not demon possession that is the problem, even though it certainly can go into demon oppression, which is a different thing altogether.

Nevertheless, as Biblical as is Anointing with Oil, and as Biblical as is Laying on of Hands, and as Biblical as is Deliverance, these things are not the answer for this of which Paul addresses.

And yet deliverance does play a role, but in a different way than most people realize.

When Jesus addressed His hometown of Nazareth, He made a bold and beautiful announcement. He said, *"The Spirit of the Lord is upon Me, because He hath Anointed Me to preach the Gospel to the poor; He hath sent me to heal the brokenhearted, to preach deliverance to the captives . . ."* (Lk. 4:18).

If one is to notice, He said *"to preach deliverance,"* rather than laying hands on the person and delivering them, which is a valid Scriptural Doctrine in certain situations.

What did He mean, *"preach deliverance?"*

He meant the same thing that I am saying in this Commentary, whether it is written, witnessed, or preached behind the pulpit.

The deliverance comes by the Truth being pointed out to Believers, exactly as the Holy Spirit pointed it out to Paul, with them seeing that Truth, acting on that Truth, and then deliverance coming by that Truth. I speak of Romans Chapters 6, 7, and 8. That is what He means by *"preach deliverance."* In fact, it is the only *"deliverance"* which will work in this type of situation, which incidentally, is available to all. Jesus said, *"Ye shall know the Truth, and the Truth shall make you free* (deliver you)" (Jn. 8:32).

CAN PSYCHOLOGICAL COUNSELING HELP IN THESE TYPE OF SITUATIONS?

For anyone to ask such a question, shows they have scant knowledge of the Word of God, or else they simply do not believe the Word of God.

The breaking of the dominion of sin by Christ in the lives of Believers, which was accomplished at Calvary and the Resurrection, presents a monumental Victory, as should be obvious. That tells us that the problem was and is of such magnitude, that man could not even begin to hope to deal with this monster. If he could, Jesus underwent this horror unnecessarily.

It is understandable as to how the world would resort to such choices. They do not know God and, consequently, do not believe God. So they resort to whatever they can. However, for Preachers who claim to believe God and claim to know the Bible, to even remotely suggest such a thing is an insult of the greatest magnitude to Christ and His Finished Work at Golgotha.

The problem is sin, not a quirk of nature, not a simple aberration, not a slight mendacity, nor even a personality problem. As stated, it is sin.

And if it is sin, and it is, even as Paul plainly states over and over again, then how does man think he can address himself to this situation with psychological counseling and expect favorable results? Don't Preachers know that this is the very reason that Jesus came to this world? Don't they know that He came to deliver men from sin? And paid a terrible price in order that this deliverance may be ours? In fact, deliverance from sin is the very foundation of the Gospel. It is what Redemption is all about. It is what Jesus did at Calvary and the Resurrection. That is the very reason He came.

So, how can the poor, pitiful, foolish, arcane prattle of man, which passes for wisdom, and in fact, is earthly wisdom, which is sensual and devilish — how can such help anything? (James 3:15-16).

The only answer to sin is Jesus. And this is that to which Paul is addressing himself.

To be frank, rather than gross unbelief on the part of Preachers, which is a sin of tremendous proportions, I would rather think that most Preachers have resorted to Psychology (psychological counseling) simply because they do not know the Truths presented here by Paul of Romans Chapters 6, 7, and 8. Not knowing what to do, and realizing that the laying on of hands although helping, has not really solved the problem, they had no answers; consequently, they turned to other sources.

However, even though that reason may be more noble, if in fact that is the reason with some, the end results will be the same, no help at all!

BELIEVERS LOVE TO PLACE THE BLAME ELSEWHERE

We have already addressed this, concerning the propensity of Adam after the Fall, blaming Eve. However, the world of Psychology offers another excuse for the Believer.

Of course, Psychology does not really believe there is such a thing as sin. They claim that man's problems, rather from originating inward, actually originate outward. The Bible claims the opposite, which is what this 7th Chapter of Romans is all about. They claim that all men are basically good and if they aren't, it is because of outward influences, which if corrected, the goodness will return. Of course, they claim they can correct the problem.

The Bible teaches the very opposite, in fact that man is inherently bad, and as such there is no good in him (Rom. 3:10-18). The Bible claims that this is the reason for all of man's problems. As well, it claims that the only solution is a miraculous change on the inside of man, called the *"born-again"* experience (Jn. 3:3, 16). The Bible claims that Jesus Alone can effect this miraculous New Birth experience, and that it comes only by one having Faith in Him (Acts 4:12; Eph. 2:8-9).

The Bible places the responsibility squarely on the person, while Psychology, as stated, blames outside forces, such as environment, lack of education or wrong education, abuse as a child, etc. Consequently, many Believers enjoy resorting to psychology, because this makes them think, at least for a short time anyway, that this problem of sin is not their fault or responsibility, but that of some-one else, or something else. Consequently, it is eagerly embraced by many, because many enjoy shifting responsibility.

The matter with the Lord is very simple. He only asks that the Believer admit that the situation or problem is sin, whatever type of symptom it may have. As well, he must ask the Lord to forgive him, and then to show him the Truth of the great Deliverance and Victory paid for by Jesus at Calvary and the Resurrection. The Lord will do exactly that, exactly as He did with Paul, and Victory can be instantly obtained.

Once the Believer knows what Jesus did, and his part in Jesus, and has Faith in that, the Holy Spirit will instantly take control, with Victory assured. Satan doesn't mind too very much what we do in the realm of personal opposition against him, but he cannot stand at all against Christ and the Spirit of God.

THE STRUGGLE!

If the Believer is fighting and winning, after a while he will fight and lose. That is a guaranteed conclusion.

The Believer is commissioned to fight only one fight, and that is the *"good fight of Faith"* (I Tim. 6:12). Other than that fight, we are not to fight at all, and because there is no need to fight.

That is why Jesus said, *"Come unto Me, all ye that labour and are heavy laden, and I will give you rest"* (Mat. 11:28).

Christianity is to be a *"rest"* in Jesus, not a continuous struggle against sin. While it is true that the flesh and the Spirit are con-stantly opposed to each other, still, if we follow after the Spirit, the *"rest"* will al-ways be ours.

(20) "NOW IF I DO THAT I WOULD NOT, IT IS NO MORE I THAT DO IT, BUT SIN THAT DWELLETH IN ME."

The phrase, *"Now if I do that I would not,"* is very similar to verse 17, but with one distinct difference.

In verse 17, Paul is establishing the fact of the Sin Nature in the life of the Believer.

In verse 20, he begins his teaching by de-claring in essence, that the Sin Nature is pow-erful because a particular Law enforces its activity. As we will see, this *"law"* mentioned

NOTES

by Paul, is not the Law of God, but rather *"the law of sin and death"* (Rom. 8:2).

The phrase, *"It is no more I that do it, but sin that dwelleth in me,"* emphatically states that the Believer has a Sin Nature. The idea is not getting rid of the Sin Nature, which actually cannot be done, but rather controlling it, which the Apostle has told us how to do in Romans Chapters 6 and 8.

"Dwelleth" in the Greek is *"oikeo,"* and means *"to occupy a house, reside, remain, to cohabit."* In other words, the Sin Na-ture will remain in the Believer, until the Trump sounds, and the Believer is then Glorified. Then and then alone, will ". . . *this corruptible* (must) *put on incorruption, and this mortal* (must) *put on immortal-ity"* (I Cor. 15:53).

However, even though it does remain in the Believer, even with a powerful law at-tached to it which makes it very effective, ideally it is to be isolated from the Believer, causing him no problem, and in fact is, as long as the Believer is fully trusting Christ (Gal. 2:20).

As should be obvious, the 20th verse shoots down the idea held by many Preachers, that there is no such thing as a Sin Nature.

(21) "I FIND THEN A LAW, THAT, WHEN I WOULD DO GOOD, EVIL IS PRESENT WITH ME."

The phrase, *"I find then a law,"* does not refer in this case to the Law of Moses as stated, but rather to ". . . *the law of sin and death"* (Rom. 8:2).

"Law" in the Greek is preceded by the ar-ticle, in other words, *"the law."*

The phrase, *"That, when I would do good, evil is present with me,"* carries the follow-ing idea:

As sure as ". . . *the Law of the Spirit of Life in Christ Jesus . . ."* guarantees Victory for the Believer, providing the Word is fol-lowed, as sure is the defeat if ". . . *the law of sin and death"* is allowed to have its way, with the Word being ignored (Rom. 8:2).

"Present" in the Greek Text is *"parakeimai,"* and means *"to lie near, be at hand."* The idea is, that this evil nature (Sin Nature) is always going to be with the Believer. There is no hint in the Greek, considering the words *"dwelleth"* and

"present" that their stay is temporary.

Paul brings out the same Truth in Galatians 5:17 where he says, *"The flesh (evil nature) has a passionate desire to suppress the Spirit, and the Spirit has a passionate desire to suppress the flesh. And these are set in opposition to each other so that you may not do the things which you desire to do."*

(22) "FOR I DELIGHT IN THE LAW OF GOD AFTER THE INWARD MAN:"

The phrase, *"For I delight in the Law of God,"* refers in this case to the Law of Moses, and more particularly to the Moral part of that Law. Due to now having the Divine Nature in him, Paul now loves the things of God, which he once hated, despite this war that is going on in his soul.

"Delight" in the Greek is *"sunadomai,"* and means *"to rejoice."* Once again, we know from this that Paul is not speaking of a pre-conversion experience, as many claim, for the simple reason that no unsaved person delights in the Law of God. It is simply not possible for him to do so, inasmuch as he has no Divine Nature in him whatsoever.

Despite the failure he loves God, wants to please God, loves the things of God, and all because he is a New Creature in Christ Jesus.

The phrase, *"After the inward man,"* refers to the new creation which has been brought about by and through the Lord Jesus Christ, in effect, creating a *"new man."* Before conversion, *"the inward man"* was corrupt, vile, ungodly, totally controlled by the sin nature. Now, *"the inward man"* is to be controlled by the Divine Nature (II Pet. 1:4). However, it refers as well to the following:

To which we have previously referred, man's real problem is from deep within himself. It is the law of sin and death which once bound him, but from which he is now free. Whenever Jesus saves the sinner, He does so by Regeneration, which is actually a Restoration (Titus 3:5). This takes place in the *"inward man,"* referring to the soul and the spirit. The Salvation process then works from inside outward, versus man's efforts which attempt to work from the outside inward, which are impossible. The latter is like attempting to assuage a poisoned well by building around it a garden. The garden

may be nice and beautiful, and even smell wonderful, but it doesn't change the poisoned water. For that to be changed, one has to go to the source, stopping that which is poisoning the spring. Only then will the water be pure and fresh. Thus, is the born-again experience.

(23) "BUT I SEE ANOTHER LAW IN MY MEMBERS, WARRING AGAINST THE LAW OF MY MIND, AND BRINGING ME INTO CAPTIVITY TO THE LAW OF SIN WHICH IS IN MY MEMBERS."

The phrase, *"But I see another law in my members,"* refers to *"the law of sin and death"* of Romans 8:2.

This has to do with the Sin Nature, and is that which provides its power. This *"law"* is not in the soul and the spirit, but rather in the physical members of the physical body, such as the eyes, ears, tongue, etc.

That does not mean that the soul and the spirit are unaffected by whatever happens regarding this law, but it does mean that the members of the physical body of the Believer is that which carries out the wishes of the Sin Nature, that is if the Believer yields to the evil impulse.

The phrase, *"Warring against the law of my mind,"* presents another *"Law."* This is the law of desire and willpower; however, let the Reader understand that this law is not more powerful than the law of sin and death.

So, we have three *"laws"* mentioned in verses 21-23. They are:

1. The law of sin and death (Rom. 8:2).
2. The Law of God (Rom. 8:2).
3. The law of the mind, which is the law of desire and willpower.

Of these three, the Law of God is far and away the most powerful, actually, All-powerful. But as stated, the law of sin and death is stronger than the law of the mind. Paul wanted to do right, as millions have, but the law of sin and death overrode the law of the mind, which it always will. So, Paul must find how to bring the Law of God to bear, which he does.

The phrase, *"And bringing me into captivity to the law of sin which is in my members,"* plainly tells us, as stated, that the law of sin is stronger and more powerful than the law of the mind.

The idea is, that the law of sin and death is warring against the mind, attempting to bring the Believer once again into bondage, actually a slave to the Sin Nature, even as was the case before coming to Christ.

I think one could say without exaggeration, that he succeeds most often, even as he succeeded for a period of time with the Apostle Paul.

Some people erroneously think that when this happens that the person is lost. That is ridiculous! And for the simple reason that there will be no *"war"* if the person is lost. The war is raging because the person belongs to God, loves God, and as in the case of Paul, may be in the process of being mightily used of God. In fact, this is the case oftentimes.

Some may wonder as to how a Believer could be used in this state, especially considering that he doesn't have Victory in this area, and at this point that he has once again become a slave to sin.

As to how long that Paul remained in this situation, we do not know. The Scripture is silent. However, it was long enough for him to learn these valuable lessons, which probably could not have happened over a period of only several days. Ever how long it was, however, the evidence surely is clear that the Lord was continuing to use Paul even during this time. The answer is not so complicated.

First of all, Paul loved the Lord very much, and was doing everything within his power to overcome this problem, whatever it was. As well, the Lord knew what the outcome would be, in that Victory would be obtained.

While the Holy Spirit definitely could not use Paul to the extent that He desired during this time, He still was continuing to work and to work mightily within his life.

It is the same with many modern Believers, and in fact always has been this way. There are many who are being presently used of God in a great way, but with problems of this nature in their lives, over which they are struggling and actually *"warring."* There is failure involved, even as Paul exclaims here, but as bad as that may be (and it is bad), that doesn't mean that Paul was lost, nor any other Believer who has fought this same battle. Were that the case, there would be few Saved, because all have fought this battle

NOTES

in one way or the other, I think I can say without fear of exaggeration.

Once again in this last phrase, Paul brings out the Truth that this *"law of sin"* carries out its evil desires through the physical members of the physical body. While sin begins in the heart, it has its conclusion in the members of the physical body. In other words, the eyes look at things at which they should not look, and the tongue says things it should not say, with the hands doing things they should not do, etc. This is why the physical body is the battleground!

(24) "O WRETCHED MAN THAT I AM! WHO SHALL DELIVER ME FROM THE BODY OF THIS DEATH?"

The exclamation, *"O wretched man that I am!"*, presents Paul now being brought to the place to where he can receive help. He has exhausted all of his own efforts, which worked not at all. His condition forces him to cry out to God for help.

It is unfortunate that most of us have to come to this place before help can be received. The battle and struggle is not necessary in the strict sense of the word, but it does seem to be necessary for most of us, even as it was for the Apostle Paul. Man, even Believers, must come to an end of themselves. In other words, the hope of the flesh must die in every respect. With no more hope left from that sector, we then cry out to God.

To be sure, the word *"wretched"* adequately describes the situation. It is a Christian who does not have Victory, but yet wants Victory with all of his heart. It might even possibly be an individual who is being mightily used of God while all of this is going on, even as Paul. However, Paul had one great disadvantage that none of us have, at least in a sense.

Even though this great Plan of Redemption which provided for Salvation from sin and Victory over sin, had been gloriously and wondrously consummated by Jesus Christ, and was now available to all, still, I am probably not exaggerating, when I say that not one single person in the world had this segment of Truth respecting this of what Jesus had done. Most likely it was Paul who was the first one to face this monster and also seek God until the answer came, which is given to us here.

And yet, I am not so certain if that was a disadvantage at all!

Most of the time other Believers can be of little help, and much of the time, even harm. Blessed is the Believer who does have the privilege of having someone join with him in seeking God and maybe, hopefully, one who knows the great Truths of these Chapters. Sadly, those are few and far between!

In fact, if Paul had been a member of some modern Pentecostal Denominations, the chances are great that he would have been unceremoniously drummed out of that particular organization. They could hardly afford to have had someone in their ranks, irrespective as to the Call of God on his life, or how much God was using him, who had obvious failure. Thank God, that albatross did not then exist.

The question, *"Who shall deliver me from the body of this death?"*, presents a wail of anguish and a cry for help. This was Paul's cry during the spiritual experience he describes of himself in this Chapter, Paul the Saint, ignorant of the Delivering Power of the Holy Spirit, concerning Whom he has so much to say in the next Chapter.

The minute he cries *"Who"* he finds the path to Victory, for he calls upon a person for help. Actually, the Greek Text is masculine, indicating a person. That Person is Jesus.

The words *"this death"* refer to the miserable condition of the Christian who is yet dominated more or less by the evil (sin) nature over which all the while he is desiring to gain Victory. It is the death Paul speaks of in verse 9.

The body here is the physical body, in which the sinful nature dwells and through which, when it is in control, it operates.

Paul is not crying out for egress from his body but for deliverance from the condition of defeat which his residence in his physical body makes a possibility, and his lack of spiritual knowledge up to that moment, resulted in (Wuest).

(25) "I THANK GOD THROUGH JESUS CHRIST OUR LORD. SO THEN WITH THE MIND I MYSELF SERVE THE LAW OF GOD; BUT WITH THE FLESH THE LAW OF SIN."

The phrase, *"I thank God through Jesus Christ our Lord,"* presents Paul giving the

NOTES

answer to his own question. Deliverance comes through Jesus Christ, and more particularly what Jesus did at Calvary and the Resurrection. Paul gives thanks to God for that fact.

In the words *"I thank God,"* one can see and feel the Victory which has now come to the Apostle, and for which he is so grateful. No longer does sin dominate him, and no longer does this battle rage within his soul. He has found *"rest"* in Jesus Christ.

While it is true that Satan will continue to oppose him greatly in respect to his work for God, which resulted in stonings, shipwrecks, imprisonments, etc., never again would Satan ever be able to rob him of this great Victory of Sanctification, which he now has in Jesus Christ.

THE WORD OF GOD

One can almost hear Paul crying to God in respect to this problem which threatened his very soul, for that was Satan's intentions. However, the answer came, and it came in detail, and it was meant to be given to all of us, hence it being written down in the Word of God, for it was and is, The Word of God.

No doubt, his thanks to God never ceased respecting this which the Lord had done, revealing the tremendous Truths imparted to him which meant not only his Victory, but the Victory of untold millions of others. Please allow me to say the following:

It is regrettable but true, that most great Victories are won and great Truths presented, even in that which seems to be terrible defeat, even as it was with Paul. Unfortunately, due to the Fall, man is so constituted that he is very reluctant to throw himself at the foot of the Cross, crying in desperation for help. And to be sure, even though these Victories always come through Jesus Christ, they all came through what He did at the Cross of Calvary.

God took that evil instrument of torture (the Cross) which Satan thought surely was the defeat of Jesus Christ, and turned it into the greatest Victory that man has ever known.

JESUS CHRIST

There is One, and One Deliverer only — The Lord Jesus Christ; for in response to the anguished cry, *"Who shall deliver me?"*, the answer is: that God can, and that the vehicle of the deliverance is through the Work and Person of Jesus Christ the Lord.

Thus, the three mighty Princes: death, sin, and law, lose their authority over all who by Faith become associated with Christ in His Death and Resurrection. With Him the Believer enters a new realm of Life and Righteousness; and, energized by the Holy Spirit, lives a life of True Sanctification.

If the Believer makes *"death"* his refuge, the Death of Christ, he is safe from the domination of sin. For what can Satan do with a dead man? (Williams).

The phrase, *"So then with the mind I myself serve the Law of God,"* presents the will of Paul, and all other Believers for that matter.

As stated, the will is the trigger, but it within itself can do nothing unless the gun is loaded with explosive power. That Power is the Cross, and more particularly, Jesus on that Cross. There He made it possible for Believers to *"serve the Law of God."* He actually does it through us (Gal. 2:20).

The phrase, *"But with the flesh the law of sin,"* is merely saying that if the Believer resorts to the *"flesh,"* i.e., self-will, self-effort, religious effort, he will *not* serve the Law of God, but rather *"the law of sin."* In other words, irrespective of his sincerity, motivation, consecration, or desire to do right, the end result of self-effort will always be *"the law of sin."*

The Holy Spirit emphasized through the Apostle, the term *"law"* over and over, and in respect to different situations. In effect He is saying, that these laws are immutable — not capable of or susceptible to change.

Even though the Apostle has spoken more of these negative laws in this Chapter, the positive *"Law of the Spirit of Life in Christ Jesus"* will be explained fully in the next Chapter. To be sure, this great and wonderful Law is magnified and proven to be so much greater than the laws of Satan, etc. Consequently, I think that tremendous blessing awaits us in the Commentary on the coming 8th Chapter of Romans.

*"My spirit, soul, and body, Jesus, I give
to Thee,*

"A consecrated offering, Thine evermore to be.
"My all is on the Altar; Lord, I am all Thine Own;
"Oh, may my Faith never falter! Lord, keep me Thine Alone."

"Oh Jesus mighty Saviour, I trust in Thy Great Name;
"I look for Thy Salvation, Thy Promise now I claim.
"Now, Lord, I yield my members, from sin's dominion free,
"For warfare and for triumph, as weapons unto Thee."

"Oh, blissful self-surrender, to live, my Lord, by Thee!
"Now, Son of God, my Saviour, live out Thy Life in me.
"I am Thine, Oh Blessed Jesus, washed in Thy Precious Blood,
"Sealed by Thy Holy Spirit, A Sacrifice to God."

CHAPTER 8

(1) "THERE IS THEREFORE NOW NO CONDEMNATION TO THEM WHICH ARE IN CHRIST JESUS, WHO WALK NOT AFTER THE FLESH, BUT AFTER THE SPIRIT."

The phrase, *"There is therefore now no condemnation to them which are in Christ Jesus,"* opens this great Chapter, which some have called the *"dynamics of the Holy Spirit."*

As the subject of Romans Chapter 3 is God declaring the sinner Righteous, so the theme of this 8th Chapter of Romans is God making the Believer holy. The former Chapter deals with Christ's Work *for* the sinner, i.e., Justification; the latter Chapter, Christ's Work *in* the Believer, i.e., Sanctification.

This Chapter opens with *"no condemnation,"* and closes with *"No separation."*

The subject of Romans 5:12-21, is *"condemnation"* for all who are in Adam; the theme of this 8th Chapter of Romans is *"no condemnation"* for all who are in Christ.

The special Greek word used for *"condemnation"* occurs only in Romans 5:16,

18, and Romans 8:1. It, therefore, links these two Passages.

This first verse, completes the teaching of Romans 7:24 and the first half of verse 25 (Williams).

The divided state of the Believer is glaringly obvious in Romans Chapter 7, which speaks of a terrible struggle due to the Believer not knowing or understanding what Christ has actually done for him at Calvary and the Resurrection, and his standing in that Finished Work. However, this divided state ends in the glorious triumph of the Spirit over the flesh — that is, if the Believer tenaciously clings to Christ.

"Condemnation" in the Greek is *"katakrima,"* and means *"an adverse sentence, the verdict."*

WHAT ADVERSE SENTENCE OR VERDICT IS PAUL TALKING ABOUT?

He is dealing with the struggle between the flesh and the Holy Spirit in the life of the Believer. Unless the admonition of Romans Chapter 8 is followed regarding the Work of the Holy Spirit, the flesh will triumph, which always brings condemnation. In other words, the Believer fails, despite the fact that he does not want to do so, and is trying not to do so with all his strength. That is the flavor of the struggle in Chapter 7 of Romans, which tells us in no uncertain terms that the Believer's efforts to overcome sin within his own strength are pointless and futile. Even though a New Creature in Christ Jesus, he is simply no match, at least within himself, against this monster of sin.

However, the Believer who knows the Truth, acts upon that Truth, which allows the Holy Spirit to perform His Office Work, which He can only do relative to Truth, is guaranteed Victory, and irrespective as to how bad the sin or bondage may be. As the Believer within himself is no match for sin; sin, Satan, and death are no match for the Holy Spirit. So, there is *"no condemnation"* because in following the Holy Spirit there is no failure. As well, the word *"now"* tells us that this condemnation free state is available this moment.

WHY DID PAUL USE THE WORD *"NOW?"*

Due to repeated failure, many have come

to believe that total Victory is not possible in this life, such awaiting the coming Resurrection when we shall be changed. However, the Holy Spirit through the Apostle is loudly debunking that erroneous thought by declaring, that Victory is possible now! To follow the prescribed methods of the Holy Spirit is to guarantee Victory. To ignore those methods, is to invite disaster.

The word *"now"* emphasizes the struggle-free Christian experience offered by Christ, when He said, *"Come unto Me, all ye that labour and are heavy laden, and I will give you rest"* (Mat. 11:28).

IN CHRIST JESUS THE SIN DEBT IS PAID

If one is to notice Paul uses the word *"in"* relative to the Believer and his relationship to Christ Jesus. He didn't say *"with"* but rather *"in,"* and for purpose and reason.

He is referring to the fact that one must understand and believe that when Jesus died on Calvary, the sinner upon his Faith is literally *"Baptized into Jesus Christ,"* actually *"Baptized into His Death"* (Rom. 6:3). In other words, Jesus did this for the sinner, and the sinner is actually in Christ as Christ dies on Calvary.

In that Death, which refers to the poured-out Perfect Life of Jesus represented in His Precious Shed Blood, the terrible sin debt of humanity was satisfied (paid), which means that the believing sinner no longer has a debt of sin against him. Consequently, Satan has no more hold or claim; therefore, the terrible wages of sin, which are death (spiritual death — separation from God), is no longer applicable to the believing sinner. He is now united with God, which means the enmity has been removed, which is called the *"born-again"* experience (Jn. 3:3). However, as great and wonderful as that is, it is only the first part.

DOMINION OF SIN IS BROKEN

The second part relates to Jesus breaking the dominion of sin, which also occurred in this great Sacrifice. This is primarily what is meant by Paul referring to the Believer being *"in Christ."*

Regarding Salvation, Jesus died *for* the

sinner. Regarding dominion over sin, the Believer died in Christ. The Believer must know and understand that, which regrettably, most don't I think! As Jesus dying for the sinner guaranteed Salvation, the sinner dying in Jesus guarantees sin's dominion as broken, thereby, Victory over sin. So, as we have repeatedly stated, the Work of Christ at Calvary, was in effect a *"Double Work,"* or a *"Double Cure."*

The first part of Jesus dying for the sinner on Calvary is known by all True Believers; however, the second Finished Work, which actually took place the same time as the first Finished Work, is not so readily known or understood by most Believers. Consequently, the terrible struggle of Romans Chapter 7 ensues.

The phrase, *"Who walk not after the flesh, but after the Spirit,"* plainly tells us that those who know and understand this second great Finished Work, meaning that they were *"in Christ"* when He died, and depend on this great Truth, will always have the help of the Holy Spirit, and, therefore, no failure.

AFTER THE FLESH

To *"Walk after the flesh"* is to depend on one's personal strength and ability, or else great religious efforts in order to overcome sin, which guarantees failure, no matter how sincere or motivated or consecrated the person may be. One would surely have to say that the Apostle Paul was all of these things and more. And yet, until this great Truth of *"In Christ"* was revealed to him, that part of his Christian experience was a total failure, even as Romans Chapter 7 portrays. Paul went into detail concerning his own personal experience, that you and I may not have to follow and walk the same path. Regrettably, however, most of us seem to have to learn this lesson the hard way, even as did Paul.

The word *"walk"* in the Greek is *"peripateo,"* and means *"to live, to deport oneself, to follow."* It speaks of our everyday walk, life, and living before God, which pertains to the totality of our Christian experience. As we have stated, this 8th Chapter concerns the Sanctification of the Believer.

(2) "FOR THE LAW OF THE SPIRIT OF LIFE IN CHRIST JESUS HATH MADE

ME FREE FROM THE LAW OF SIN AND DEATH."

The phrase, *"For the Law of the Spirit of Life in Christ Jesus,"* presents the Law which should govern the Christian, and in fact, will govern the Christian, but only with the Christian's cooperation.

If one is to notice, Paul has brought into this mix certain particular Laws in a stronger way than ever, beginning with the 21st verse of Romans Chapter 7, and continuing through verse 4 of this 8th Chapter of Romans. Even though the greatest concentration is here, some 8 Laws are referred to in the Book of Romans. They are as follows:

1. Law of Moses (2:12; 3:19; 7:12).
2. Law of Nature (2:14-15).
3. Law of Faith (3:27; 4:3-5, 11-24).
4. Law of the Mind (7:16, 21, 23).
5. Law of Sin (7:23, 25; 8:2).
6. Law of Righteousness (9:31).
7. Law of God (7:22, 25).
8. Law of the Spirit of Life in Christ Jesus: This is the most powerful Law in the universe, which alone can give victory over the law of sin and death (8:2).

AS PAUL USES THE WORD *"LAW,"* WHAT DOES IT MEAN?

Most of the time when Paul refers to *"Law,"* he is speaking of the Law of Moses (Rom. 2:12-15, 17, 20, 23, 27; 3:19-21; 4:13, 16; 5:20; 7:5-8, etc.). However, he does mention other Laws which we have enumerated.

The Holy Spirit through the Apostle uses the word *"Law"* in a specific sense, meaning that it is an operating and governing principle. In this sense Paul speaks of the *"Law of Faith"* (Rom. 3:27), which is contrasted with the Law of works. The contrast is that between the principle of Faith and that of works. It is the same idea that offers the best interpretation of the word *"Law"* in Romans 7:21, 23, 25; 8:2.

LAW AS AN OPERATING AND GOVERNING PRINCIPLE

Every Law mentioned in the Bible falls into this category, even the great Law of Moses. It means that the specific *"Law"* is designed by God to operate in a particular manner, which will bring forth particular results. In other words, those results are unvarying. That's the reason it is called *"Law."*

However, one cannot make these *"Laws"* work against God, in other words against His Nature, or against His Will. Inasmuch as these *"Laws"* are made and instituted by God, they are designed to operate in a particular framework.

In other words, there is a *"Law of Faith"* (Rom. 3:27). This means that if a Believer has Faith in God, which of course must be anchored in the Word of God, certain results without fail will be produced by this *"Law of Faith."* One can count on it, because it is a Law, and will always happen.

However, that does not mean that one can take this *"Law of Faith"* and use it against God, i.e., against His Will. These Laws have not been designed to do that, and cannot be used in that fashion, even though many have attempted to do so. In other words, the *"Law of Faith"* must give way at some point to the Will of God, which is the *"Law of God"* (Rom. 7:25). As well, *"The Law of Sin and Death"* has to give way to *"The Law of the Spirit of Life in Christ Jesus."*

It is the same way in Science. For instance, the *"Law of Gravity"* has to give way to *"The Law of Greater Power."* This speaks of any power that is strong enough to overcome the Law of Gravity, such as engines on an airplane, etc.

TO BE UNDER LAW

When the term *"To be under Law"* is used in the Bible, it is speaking of the Law of Moses, and not the other Laws mentioned. In other words, to be under this Law regarding New Testament Believers, excludes a person from the enjoyment of the Grace which the Gospel imparts; to be *"under Law"* is the opposite of being *"under Grace"* and means that the person is the bondslave of the condemnation and power of sin, which Paul has greatly discussed in Romans Chapter 7.

However, this has nothing to do with the various other Laws mentioned by Paul. To be frank, the Believer strongly desires to be under *"The Law of the Spirit of Life in Christ Jesus,"* and in fact, must be under this Law. As well, the Believer would strongly desire to be under the *"Law of Faith,"* and the

"Law of Righteousness," and the *"Law of God."* In fact, all of these Laws mentioned by Paul impact the Believer in one way or the other, constantly.

The *"Law of the Spirit of Life in Christ Jesus"* which makes real to the Believer the great Victory of Jesus Christ, cannot function in the life of the Believer as intended, if the Believer is frustrating that Law by obeying at the same time the *"Law of Sin."* It is like pouring water into a tank made for gasoline, and expecting the engine to continue to run. It won't!

What makes it so confusing is that the Believer's efforts to overcome sin by his own strength and abilities, i.e., *"the flesh,"* is actually bringing upon himself the *"Law of Sin."* While the efforts may be of the right motivation, and not necessarily sin within themselves, still, they will not work because they are of the flesh, which gives latitude to the *"Law of Sin."* Then the *"Law of Sin"* becomes predominant in the Believer's life, which means that the Sin Nature is now operating at full capacity, which causes all types of problems for the Believer.

WHAT ONLY GOD CAN DO

As well, the *"Law of the Spirit of Life in Christ Jesus"* is so designed by God, that it will not function or work, when the Believer attempts to do for himself, what only the Spirit of God can do. In other words, the Holy Spirit will *not* override the Believer's will, forcing him to let the Spirit take control instead of his own efforts.

The phrase, *"Hath made me free from the Law of Sin and Death,"* presents *"The Law of the Spirit of Life in Christ Jesus"* as the only Law, to which the *"Law of Sin and Death"* will yield. This is what makes modern Psychology so silly, and especially so-called Preachers of the Gospel running after this shamanism.

Every single person in the world is born under the dominion of *"The Law of Sin and Death."* It is called *"original sin."* This is the Law which Paul said works in the members of the physical body of the person (Rom. 7:23). It places one in bondage, making the person a slave to the Sin Nature.

Even though *"The Law of Sin and Death"*

is powerful, and has swept billions into its maw of sin and death, still, *"The Law of the Spirit of Life in Christ Jesus"* is more powerful, in fact, All-powerful. It is so powerful in fact, that there has never been a single person in history who has come to Christ, irrespective of their past and how sordid and bad it was, but that Jesus Christ took them and changed them, and made them *"free"* from this terrible *"Law."*

The Laws of God, at least as Paul mentions them here, are not so much written Laws, but rather a regulative principle which exercises a control over the life of the Believer. However, this control must be given by the Believer, it will not be forcibly taken.

Upon being freely given, this regulative control is exercised by the Holy Spirit in the form of energy given to the Believer both to desire and to do God's Will, this spiritual energy coming from the Life that God is. It is given to the Believer by reason of his position in Christ Jesus, but cannot be properly realized unless he *knows* his position in Christ Jesus.

THE LAW OF SIN AND DEATH

An Egyptian punishment at a particular time in their history was to fasten a criminal to a corpse, with the attachment continuing until death. It was a terrible bond as would be obvious, and the more so because the man bound knew that the bond would result in death. This was possibly before the Apostle's mind when writing verse 24 of the previous Chapter.

Such a helpless and hopeless prisoner, held in a bond so loathsome and fatal, would cry out with anguish: *"Who can deliver me from this dead body?"*

This is the moral condition of all who are in Adam.

THE GLAD TIDINGS OF THE GOSPEL

Christ took this very position at Calvary, even though He had never sinned, but in effect paying the sin debt of all humanity. To do this He had to die. But being God He rose from among the dead and ascended above the highest heavens, having by His Death destroyed death (Heb. 2:14), abolished sin (Heb. 9:26), and exhausted the

Curse of the Law (Gal. 3:13).

The Glad Tidings of the Gospel consist in the declaration that all who by Faith are in Christ died and rose with Him, and, consequently, there is no person, and no thing, that can condemn them. For Christ there is now no condemnation. He suffered its full intensity at Calvary. But He suffered that condemnation there on behalf of, and for the benefit of, all who believe upon Him. Hence, there is no condemnation for them.

They are in a new position entirely beyond and above the reach of everything to which condemnation attaches. Where Christ and His members now stand there can be no question of sin or of wrath or of condemnation or of imputation. All such questions were settled before He ascended thither; and He is on the Throne of God, His Person and Work accepted, because these questions were settled.

And the glorious Truth that liberates the Believer's heart is that he is there in that Glory with Christ where nothing that condemns can reach him (Eph. 2:6).

A LIFE OF POWER, HOLINESS, AND VICTORY

This is not only a new position in the Second Adam as contrasted with the old position in the First Adam, it is also a New Life — a Life of Power, Holiness, and Victory. The Christian Faith is not a scheme of Salvation intellectually accepted, but a Life of Power and Holiness experimentally enjoyed.

Immanuel's destruction of sin at Calvary may become to Faith a moral reality *now*, as it will become in the New Heavens and in the New Earth a physical fact; for in them Righteousness alone will dwell (Williams).

(3) "FOR WHAT THE LAW COULD NOT DO, IN THAT IT WAS WEAK THROUGH THE FLESH, GOD SENDING HIS OWN SON IN THE LIKENESS OF SINFUL FLESH, AND FOR SIN, CONDEMNED SIN IN THE FLESH:"

The phrase, *"For what the Law could not do,"* speaks of the Law of Moses. In other words, the Law of Moses could not condemn sin (destroy sin), but could only condemn the sinner, and this it did grandly.

The phrase, *"What the Law could not do,"*

could be rendered literally from the Greek, *"The impossible of the Law."* This was an impossible thing on the part of the Law, that it could condemn sin by giving power to sinners, in order to overcome this monster. This it could not do! In other words the Law of Moses demanded obedience, even as does all Law, but furnished man no power to obey its injunctions.

And yet, this is exactly what Israel tried to force it to do. Except for a small Remnant, the entirety of generation after generation was lost in this capacity, until finally it grew so bad that they murdered their Messiah, with the resultant loss of the entirety of nationhood. As a result, they wandered as vagabonds for about 1900 years, until finally becoming a Nation again in 1948.

Regrettably, as Israel tried to force the Law of Moses into a posture it was never intended, many of their modern Disciples attempt to force Faith into the same mold. God's Word must never be used against Himself, in other words, attempting to force it into that which it was never intended. In fact, this is the reason for all unscriptural Doctrines such as *"Unconditional Eternal Security," "The Ultimate Reconciliation of all Things," "The Modern Prosperity Gospel," "Works Righteousness," "The Hundredfold Return," "The Jesus Died Spiritually Doctrine," "Kingdom Now Philosophy,"* etc.

WEAK THROUGH THE FLESH

The phrase *"In that it was weak through the flesh,"* means that the only power the person had in order to keep the Law as given by God, was his own willpower, which was woefully insufficient. The *"flesh"* refers to the human frailties of each and all people. Man is so weak in fact, that he is not able, at least within his own power, to even keep the simple Laws of God laid down by the Creator, much less save himself.

"Weak" in the Greek is *"astheneo,"* and means *"impotent, without strength."*

The Law of Moses was like a mirror that showed man what he was, but gave man no power to change what he was. Consequently, there was no victory over sin in the Law (Rom. 7:7-12).

The phrase, *"God sending His Own Son,"*

refers to man's helpless condition, unable to save himself, unable to keep even a simple Law, and, therefore, in dire need of a Saviour.

God sending His Only Son, tells us two things: A. The tremendous Love of God for lost humanity; and, B. The terrible power of the bondage of sin, which could not be broken any other way, than by and through Jesus Christ. God had to deliver man, that is, if man was to be delivered, which He did through the Cross, and through the Cross Alone (Rom. 6:3-5).

The phrase, *"In the likeness of sinful flesh,"* says literally, *"Of the flesh of sin."* The choice of words is especially noteworthy:

Paul does not say simply, *"He* (Jesus) *came in flesh"* (I Tim. 3:16; I Jn. 4:2), for this would have expressed a bond between Christ's Manhood and sin.

Not *"in the flesh of sin,"* which would have represented Him as partaking of sin, which He did not.

Not in *"the likeness of flesh,"* since He was really and intensely human; but, *"in the likeness of the flesh of sin."*

This means that He was really human, conformed in appearance to the flesh which characteristic is sin, yet sinless.

Dickson said, *"Christ appeared in a Body which was like that of other men insofar as it consisted of flesh, and was unlike insofar as the flesh was not 'flesh of sin'."*

The phrase, *"And for sin,"* means *"to atone for sin, to destroy its power, and to save and sanctify its victims."* In other words, that was His Purpose for coming, and to be sure He carried out His Purpose in totality.

The phrase, *"Condemned sin in the flesh,"* means that as a Man, in fact, the Second Adam, He faced all the power of sin, Satan and death, everything which man faces and more, and never failed one time. As well, He not only did not fail, but He also destroyed the power of sin, dethroned death and defeated Satan. In other words, He condemned sin and all its power, breaking its hold over the human race.

Also, He did this not as a Deity, for such would not have sufficed, but as a Man, The Man Christ Jesus. The only help He had was the Holy Spirit, Who is available to all Believers as well.

In fact, at least as far as man was concerned, the only way that God could defeat sin and its result, which is death, is by God becoming Man. Inasmuch as dominion was vested in the First Adam (Gen. 1:28; Ps. 8), and then lost through forfeiture, which in effect gave Satan dominion, it had to be purchased back by another Adam, in effect, *"The Second Adam."* All was lost in this manner, and only could it be purchased back in this manner.

(4) "THAT THE RIGHTEOUSNESS OF THE LAW MIGHT BE FULFILLED IN US, WHO WALK NOT AFTER THE FLESH, BUT AFTER THE SPIRIT."

The phrase, *"That the Righteousness of the Law might be fulfilled in us,"* tells us that the Law of Moses contained Righteousness, as would be obvious, considering that it was given by God. However, for its Righteousness to be obtained by man, perfect obedience had to be rendered, which was impossible, because of the *"weakness of the flesh."*

The clause, *"Might be fulfilled in us,"* could be translated, *"Find its full accomplishment in us,"* not merely *"be performed by us."* The Apostle had a much deeper meaning, namely, that the aim of God in giving the Law might be accomplished in us, in our Sanctification, which is the ultimate end of our Redemption (Eph. 2:10; Col. 1:22).

THE SIGNIFICANCE OF THE LAW

I think we surely should understand from this verse as to just how significant the Law of Moses actually was. Even though it was given exclusively to the Jews, and for a particular purpose and reason, still, it was meant for the entirety of the world. These were God's Laws and they applied to all, and I speak primarily of the Moral Law, i.e., *"Ten Commandments."* As well, this Moral Law could not pass out of existence, because it is Truth, and Truth never changes. For instance, it was wrong to steal 4,000 years ago, and it is wrong to steal presently, and in fact, will always be wrong to steal, etc. So, God's Law was Righteous, and, as well, it had a Righteousness which could be obtained by obedience, but not by man in his fallen condition.

NOTES

However, Jesus as the Second Adam, totally kept the Moral Law in every respect, even throughout 33 1/2 years of public life, and being contested by Satan at every turn, and as well, took the penalty of the broken Law on the Cross of Calvary. He did this as the Representative Man, and Faith in Him (Jn. 3:16), grants the Believer a satisfied Judgment and the position of perfect Law-Keeper. His Victory upon Faith in Him becomes our Victory, which was intended.

RIGHTEOUSNESS

Upon simple Faith in Him, the most vile of human beings can become, and in fact, do become, instantly Righteous. Of course, the world can little accept this, thinking they can somehow earn this place and position. However, their efforts are doomed to failure, for such is impossible!

Some time ago Frances and I were taking a few days vacation. During this time of rest I was studying this very Passage of which we are now addressing, and as I read the Words, *"That the Righteousness of the Law might be fulfilled in us,"* the Presence of God came all over me. I sat there for a few moments weeping as I sensed the Lord impressing me as to the significance of this statement. It is something that only Christ can do and something which He gloriously did do. As a result, that for which He paid at such price, can now be ours by the simple act of Faith.

The phrase, *"Who walk not after the flesh, but after the Spirit,"* emphatically portrays to us that the *"Righteousness of the Law"* cannot be had by anyone who attempts to attain such by his own efforts.

The word *"walk"* as we have previously stated, refers to *"the order of one's behavior or conduct."*

"Flesh" can mean the frailty of human endeavors, but in this case it refers to the *"indwelling evil nature."* Of course, the *"Spirit"* refers to the *"Holy Spirit."*

"After" in the Greek is *"kata,"* and has as its root meaning *"down,"* which suggests domination.

In other words, a Christian is one who orders his behavior in such a way that it is not dominated by the evil nature (Sin Nature), but by the Holy Spirit (Wuest).

THE BELIEVER AND THE TWO NATURES

As a great portion of this Chapter constantly warns the Believer as to the possibility and danger of walking after the flesh, etc., such presents the great moral fact of the existence of these two natures in the Believer, and is actually the theme of this Chapter.

In a sense, the Believer is dead, for he was crucified with Christ. He, therefore, as a partner with Christ, enjoys all the advantages of the partnership acquired by Christ before he was brought into it. This is not necessarily an experience, it is rather a Divine operation apprehended and enjoyed by Faith.

However, the Believer is always very conscious that his carnal nature is not dead, but that between it and the new Spiritual Nature he received at Conversion (Eph. 1:13), there is a deadly warfare, that really never stops.

If the carnal nature were actually dead it would not be necessary to urge Christian people not to make provision to gratify its appetites (Rom. 13:14).

THE TEACHING OF THE NEW NATURE

This New Nature, which is energized by the Holy Spirit, hence our walking after Him, teaches that the Christian may enjoy such Victory, actually, a moral experience so liberating that the fact of indwelling sin may become to him only a matter of knowledge — because the Word of God asserts its existence — but not a painful fact of consciousness.

In other words, while it is true that this contest between the flesh and the Spirit is unending, if we follow after Christ exactly as we should, we are made to enjoy a *"rest"* that is actually beyond comprehension. While we do fight, it is only *"The good fight of Faith."*

Regrettably, most Christians have the opposite and, therefore, sad experience. They are painfully conscious of this principle of evil lodged in their nature, while the existence of the New Nature within them is a matter of belief because declared in the Scriptures, but not fully enjoyed at all!

Thus, verse 2 of this Chapter forms its keynote. It asserts the existence of these two natures in the Believer; but declares that the

New Spiritual Nature liberates from the old carnal nature.

So the subject of the Chapter is not the forgiveness of sins or Justification from them, but rather, liberation from the power of sin in order to live a life of Sanctification.

THE SPIRIT OF LIFE

To the Believer, *"the Spirit of Life"* is imparted, which is the New Spiritual Nature. That Nature operates with the regularity of a Law just as the principle of sin operates as a Law in its sphere. The one Spirit issues in Life; the other, death.

The Law of Moses could not make a man holy, not because of its impotency, but because of the impotency of man on whom it acted. As an example, if an old-fashioned railway engine were built of paper, steam would be powerless to move it, not because of any weakness in the power of steam, but because of the weakness of the material of which the engine was built.

But God does what the Law could not do, i.e., pardon the transgressor and give him a new nature, for He first in the sinless Flesh of His Beloved Son destroyed sin, condemning it to death, and then by the impartation of the Divine Nature to the Believer causes him by faultless conduct to satisfy all the Righteous requirements of the Law.

These Righteous requirements cannot be satisfied by anyone who walks *"after the flesh,"* who is controlled by the principle of sin in the flesh, but only by him who is controlled by the Holy Spirit (Williams).

THE HOLY SPIRIT

One cannot help but notice the emphasis that Paul places on the Holy Spirit in this 8th Chapter. As we have stated, it is called by some *"The Dynamics of the Holy Spirit."* And yet I am concerned that many do not know or understand properly what Paul is saying and what he means respecting the involvement of the Holy Spirit.

For instance, many in the modern Church do not subscribe to the Baptism with the Holy Spirit with the evidence of speaking with other Tongues (Acts 2:4). They claim that one receives the Holy Spirit at Conversion, and there is no more to receive.

They are wrong!

While the Holy Spirit is definitely involved in the Salvation process, even as He is involved in every single thing done by God on Earth, His participation in the New Birth other than conviction, is in the realm of Regeneration. However, if the Believer then does not go on and be Baptized with the Holy Spirit, which will always be accompanied by the speaking with other Tongues, the Holy Spirit is left pretty much dormant in the Believer's life, unable really to do much more (Acts 1:8; 2:4).

I think this is emphasized by the insistence in the Book of Acts of Believers being Baptized with the Holy Spirit. In fact, this is of such necessity that Jesus in effect told His followers not to go do anything for Him concerning His Work, until they first received *"the Promise of the Father."* He was speaking of the Holy Spirit, actually saying, *"For John truly Baptized with Water; but ye shall be Baptized with the Holy Spirit not many days hence"* (Acts 1:4-5). Of course, Acts Chapter 2 portrays that momentous occasion when they were filled.

Chapter 8 of the Book of Acts portrays this necessity to such an extent, that Peter and John were sent to Samaria immediately to pray for those who had been recently Saved under the Ministry of Philip, that they might be Baptized with the Holy Spirit, which they were.

In Acts Chapter 9, the Lord sent Ananias to the newly-converted Paul (Saul), that among other things, he might *"be filled with the Holy Spirit"* (Acts 9:17).

In Acts Chapter 10, Cornelius and his household were all filled immediately they were born again.

Acts Chapter 19 portrays Paul sensing the absence of Holy Spirit activity in some Ephesians, immediately asking them, *"Have you received the Holy Spirit since you believed?"* (Acts 19:2).

Paul prayed for them, and all Twelve were instantly filled.

Even though the Baptism with the Holy Spirit is definitely intended for power (Acts 1:8), Power to continue the Works of Christ, much more is involved here as well. Without the Baptism with the Holy Spirit, I feel

that the Scripture is replete with the fact that all He can do, and desires to do, in the hearts and lives of Believers, can little be done at all, unless the Believer is Baptized with the Holy Spirit with the evidence of speaking with other Tongues. Paul says as much with the statement, *"In Whom* (Jesus) *ye also are builded together for an habitation of God through the Spirit"* (Eph. 2:22).

So, I little think that all of this work mentioned by Paul, which only the Holy Spirit can carry out, can actually be done, without the Holy Spirit Baptism. The insistence by Jesus and the Spirit Himself in the Book of Acts, I think is replete.

SPIRIT-FILLED BELIEVERS

And now we come to Spirit-filled Believers. Just because a person has been Baptized with the Holy Spirit, does that mean they automatically have the benefit of these great Truths spoken of by Paul? The answer to that should be obvious, no they don't!

First of all, Paul was Saved and Baptized with the Holy Spirit, and he did not at the beginning have this great Victory within his life of which he portrays to us in these particular Chapters. So what was, or what is the trouble in this area!

First of all, being Baptized with the Holy Spirit actually guarantees little, but really only portrays the potential of what can be, that is if the Believer will cooperate with the Spirit of God. We have dealt with this previously, so I will be brief.

Were you to ask Spirit-filled Believers if they understood what Paul was saying in the 8th Chapter of Romans, most would probably nod in the affirmative. They have been Baptized with the Holy Spirit, so they automatically think that such within itself is all that is needed. They could not be more wrong.

The Truth is, that most spirit-filled Believers little know or understand that of which Paul speaks. There are many who are truly Baptized with the Holy Spirit, even with Gifts of the Spirit working through them, in other words, they are being used by the Lord, but at the same time are living lives of failure. They are frustrated! They do not know why! But nevertheless, the failure is ever present, and the situation does not seem to get better but rather worse.

In fact, that is true! It probably is getting worse. They know they are Saved and they know they are Spirit-filled, and so they cannot understand the failure, especially considering that they are trying so hard.

HOLY SPIRIT INVOLVEMENT

The manner in which the Holy Spirit works in this situation, is to energize the great Truths of Calvary in the heart and life of the Believer, bringing them to their full potential, realizing this great Victory purchased by Christ. However, if the Believer does not know this *"Truth,"* there is very little the Holy Spirit can do (Jn. 8:32).

To make the matter worse, and which further ties His Hands so to speak, the Believer at times, is working furiously within his own strength attempting to bring about Victory and constantly failing. This frustrates the Grace of God, and keeps the Holy Spirit from doing what He Alone can do.

It is somewhat like a swimmer who is drowning. He is flailing his arms and head with all of his strength, attempting to keep his head above water. Whenever someone comes to rescue him, sometimes they find it very difficult because of him fighting so severely. In other words, the drowning swimmer actually hinders his rescue by the person who has come to save him.

If he would just relax and quit fighting, the rescue would be much easier, where otherwise it is almost impossible. In fact, some drowning swimmers have actually had to be knocked out physically before they could be rescued.

The Christian who is fighting in the flesh, even though very sincere, is not really helping the situation, but as the drowning swimmer, is actually hurting his cause and severely.

Once the Believer knows the Truth of what Christ has done, and has Faith in that Great and Wondrous Work, the Holy Spirit can then take over and do all that needs to be done, making this Christian Life a tremendously pleasurable experience. Otherwise, it can be Hell on Earth! And that is not an exaggeration!

What do you think it was for Paul before

NOTES

he learned this great Truth, when he said, *"O wretched man that I am! Who shall deliver me from the body of this death?"* (Rom. 7:24).

(5) "FOR THEY THAT ARE AFTER THE FLESH DO MIND THE THINGS OF THE FLESH; BUT THEY THAT ARE AFTER THE SPIRIT THE THINGS OF THE SPIRIT."

The phrase, *"For they that are after the flesh do mind the things of the flesh,"* certainly can refer to the unsaved, but also to Christians. Actually, the thrust of the entirety of Paul's dissertation is to the Believer, which portrays the struggle between the flesh and the Spirit and how that the Believer is either in one or the other, or somewhere in between.

The Greek has it, *"For those who are habitually dominated by the flesh put their mind on the things of the flesh."* The *"flesh"* as it is here used, pertains to the Sin Nature. In other words, the Christian is dominated by the Sin Nature.

"Dominated" in the Greek is *"kata,"* and means *"down."* The manner in which it is used, refers to the state being continuous. This speaks of a person who is habitually dominated by the indwelling sinful nature.

This does not at all mean that the Christian desires this, but that it is happening (the domination) because of trusting in the flesh, i.e., self-efforts, for deliverance. It must ever be remembered, that the flesh cannot deliver from the flesh.

"Mind" in the Greek is *"phroneo,"* and means *"to exercise the mind, or have a sentiment or opinion."* Consequently, it means that the Believer who is dominated by the Sin Nature (flesh) has an improper understanding of the Word of God concerning this tremendous problem, and is, therefore, attempting to gain Victory in the wrong way. They are not necessarily doing it purposely or intentionally; nevertheless, the end result is the same, domination by the Sin Nature.

The phrase, *"But they that are after the Spirit the Things of the Spirit,"* presents the very opposite of the previous phrase.

AFTER THE SPIRIT

That which is *"after the Spirit,"* is that which is according to the Word of God. He cannot, nor will He function except according to the blueprint, which is the Word. While he will definitely help the seeking Believer find the Truth, He will not force such upon the disinterested.

What are the *"Things of the Spirit?"*

"Things" in the Greek is *"logos,"* and means *"something said, including the thought, by implication a topic* (subject of discourse), *also reasoning* (the mental faculty) *or motive, and above all the Divine Expression, i.e., Christ."*

So, Who Jesus is, what Jesus said, and what Jesus did, is the Eternal Logos, i.e., the Things of the Spirit. Even though it pertains to all things relative to Christ, more particular it refers to the great Truth of Him breaking the dominion of sin, at least in this case.

If the Believer sets his *"mind"* upon this of what Jesus has done, and believes it with all his heart, he will receive the *"Things of the Spirit"* which are total Victory, and in this case, over sin.

While the word *"Things"* has the same connotation or meaning concerning the *"flesh,"* it is there inverted. It presents the Believer who should be speaking the Words of Christ or the Spirit, rather speaking words of the *"flesh,"* which pertain to error, and most likely *"religious error."* It is difficult to explain, but in its most simplistic form, means that the Believer speaks the Words of Christ, versus the Believer who does not. However, the manner in which Paul made the statement needs more explanation.

MENTAL AFFIRMATION

It is possible for a Believer to know this Truth as laid out in Romans Chapters 6, 7, and 8, but actually know it only in his intellect. Consequently, he gives a mental assent or affirmation to this Truth, but really does not know it experimentally. In other words, it is not in his heart, and will consequently, bring forth few results.

To be frank, there are many who mistake mental affirmation for Faith, and are confused when it does not bring forth positive results. True knowledge of the things of God, pertains not only to a knowledge of the intellect, but as well that which gets down into one's spirit. That is how true

Faith springs forth.

So, the favorite statement of many people, *"I've tried that and it doesn't work,"* is the tip-off that true Faith is lacking, with the individual only giving mental assent to the subject at hand. Many people attempt to learn the Things of God, and above all the Word of God, even as they would learn Arithmetic, etc. It is not to be learned or understood in that fashion.

Jesus as the Eternal Logos must become a part of one's very spirit and being. In fact, when one truly has True Faith in God, it is quite possible they can exhibit Faith, but little explain what they are exhibiting. On the other hand, oftentimes those who have a mere mental assent, can in fact, properly explain what they believe, but obtain few results.

"After the Spirit" is a way of life. That's the reason Paul used the term *"After the Spirit."* The word *"after"* should have been translated *"dominated,"* for that is the actual Greek word used here.

Consequently it could be translated, *"For they that are dominated by the flesh do mind the things of the flesh; but they that are dominated by the Spirit the Things of the Spirit."* However, there is a difference in the way the word *"dominated"* is used.

The domination of the flesh sooner or later goes into compulsion. In other words, the individual is compelled by this domination to do those things which are wrong, which Paul outlines in Romans 7:15.

However, the word *"dominated"* as it is used concerning the Holy Spirit is the exact opposite. While the Holy Spirit will definitely dominate the Believer, it is only when the Believer freely gives control to the Spirit. In essence, the Spirit will never force a Believer to give Him control.

As well, the Holy Spirit dominates the Believer only in the sense of that which is good for the Believer, which is the very opposite of the flesh. He has our good at heart, and constantly pushes forth toward the realization of such good.

How wonderful it is to be led by the Spirit, guided by the Spirit, empowered by the Spirit, taught by the Spirit, and in fact to be *"after the Spirit."*

(6) "FOR TO BE CARNALLY MINDED

IS DEATH; BUT TO BE SPIRITUALLY MINDED IS LIFE AND PEACE."

The phrase, *"For to be carnally minded is death,"* springs back to the *"flesh"* of verse 5.

"Carnally minded" in the Greek is *"tophronema tes sarkos,"* and means literally, *"the mind of the flesh."* Again, *"flesh"* refers to the evil or Sin Nature. It means that the mind is possessed by, thus controlled or dominated by the evil nature, the description of an unsaved person or a Believer who is not dominated by the Spirit of God.

The word *"death"* speaks of spiritual death, i.e., separated from God. So, the question must be asked, *"Can the Believer continue indefinitely following after the flesh?"*

Of course the answer to that is *"No!"* But yet, there is no line drawn in the sand respecting that far and no further. Anytime anyone asks the Lord to forgive them and irrespective as to how bad the sin may be, or how many times they have been forgiven for that same sin, if they are truly sincere, God will always forgive (I Jn. 1:9). He puts no limitations on Forgiveness, Mercy, Grace, or His Love. Nevertheless, sinning and repenting, even though God's Provision, is definitely not His Will, which should be overly obvious.

THE FLESH AND DEATH

Irrespective of the things just said, the Believer must always understand that the *"flesh"* always leads to *"death."* That's why it is called *"The Law of Sin and Death"* (vs. 2). That means that while the Believer is under the domination of the Sin Nature, that he is plagued by misery, heartache, disappointment, frustration, pain, suffering, hurt, hopelessness, plus shame and humiliation. So, even though God will always forgive as long as the penitent is sincere, still, the price is incredibly high. Consequently, the Believer, and irrespective of the struggle, who is caught in this snare, must never give up, must never respond to hopelessness. It is my belief, and I think borne out by the experience of the Apostle Paul, that the Seeking Soul will always find the answer to that for which he seeks. The Lord has promised that (Lk. 11:9-13).

I write these words primarily to those of

you who would attempt to help Believers who are caught in this snare. That thing which dominates them, they do not want, and are trying with all their strength to overcome, but so oftentimes in the wrong way. I am cautioning you, the Reader, to be patient with them, loving, kind, compassionate, and considerate. Point out the great Truths given in these three Chapters, but never condemn. Who knows, you may be speaking to another Apostle Paul!

If you are reading these words and find yourself dominated by the terrible Sin Nature, prayerfully the Lord has helped us to properly explain these great Truths to such an extent, that the victory which you have long sought will now be yours. That is why Jesus came down here to die on Calvary. He paid such a price and He did it for you and me. He wants you to be free. He is not dangling a carrot in front of you, and then pulling it away at the last moment. Actually, He has brought you to this very place as you hold this Book in your hands. He has had me to write these very words to you and for you.

VICTORY IS YOURS IN CHRIST JESUS

The Victory you have so long sought is now yours. You know and understand what Jesus has done for you, and that by Faith you were actually in Him when it was carried out, even Baptized into His Death. As such, sin shall not have dominion over you. Once you know this Truth, and it is something you now know, Satan dare not usurp authority over the Holy Spirit, Who will now operate in power in your heart and life, because you now know the Truth. Actually, the next phrase will be yours, that for which you have sought and longed. Without money, without price, but yet purchased at such price, it is yours!

The phrase, *"But to be spiritually minded is Life and Peace,"* presents the most glorious, wonderful, fulfilling Life that one could ever know. This is what living is really all about. This is that which only God can give, and He reserves it for those who love Him and believe in His Great and Glorious Name. While it is for anyone, still, the requirements of Faith must be met.

The words *"spiritually minded"* in the Greek are *"to phronema tou pneumatos,"* and means literally, *"the mind possessed by the Spirit,"* thus, a mind controlled or dominated by the Holy Spirit.

Such a person possesses the Life that God is, Life and Peace.

The word *"Peace"* as it is here used, means *"to bind together that which has been separated."* Thus, the believing sinner, bound together with God and His Life after having been separated by sin (Wuest).

The *"Life and Peace"* here spoken, cannot be purchased by money, attained by education, discovered by Scientific theory, or earned by religious works. It is a Free Gift from God. As stated, it comes beautifully and simply by the vehicle of Faith, which means to simply believe what God has said and done.

However, and even though we have said it several times, please allow us to say it again.

One cannot have Faith in something of which one has no knowledge. While God doesn't require much, He does require some things. He requires that you know and understand that Jesus Christ not only paid the sin debt, but that He also broke the dominion of sin, and He did it for you. This is given to us in Romans 6:3-7. Actually, the entirety of the 6th Chapter portrays this great Truth, plus Chapters 7 and 8.

TWO WILLS

There are Two Wills contrasted in verses 5-8 — the will of the carnal nature and the Will of God. The carnal will being independent of God's Will is, consequently, hostile to it, and cannot be otherwise.

Therefore, all who are governed by the carnal will cannot, so long as they are thus governed, please God, be they ever so religious, moral, cultivated or noble. It is not that God takes no pleasure in noble actions performed by unconverted men, but that He cannot take pleasure in and accept religious worship and meritorious actions designed to purchase His favor which are prompted by the carnal mind. Hence, He rejected Cain's worship and offerings.

All who are controlled by the carnal will set their affections upon gratifying it. The

NOTES

opposite is true in the case of those controlled by the Divine Will. The one control ends in death, the other in Life.

(7) "BECAUSE THE CARNAL MIND IS ENMITY AGAINST GOD: FOR IT IS NOT SUBJECT TO THE LAW OF GOD, NEITHER INDEED CAN BE."

The phrase, *"Because the carnal mind is enmity against God,"* means that anything that is not of God and used in the manner in which God has intended, in effect creates a hostility toward God. As we have stated, the *"carnal mind"* is *"the mind of the flesh."* Again, it refers to the Sin Nature. In putting this in its proper focus, hopefully as the Spirit of God intended through Paul, please allow me to say it in this manner.

In effect, Paul is here explaining two things:

WORLDLINESS

1. He is warning all Believers of the danger of all things which are not totally of the Lord. To be sure, this covers a wide area. It speaks of the Believer's consecration and dedication. It speaks of their sincerity before God. It speaks of one's relationship with Christ, in other words, every facet of one's being in the Lord.

As well, it speaks of worldliness. By that I mean the things of this world, in which if engaged, will put one in the frame of a carnal mind, and ultimately will lead to spiritual death. Unfortunately, our Churches are full of people of this nature. They know far more about sporting events, or Hollywood, or Wall Street, or a hundred other things, which may not actually be sin within themselves, than they know about God. Such shows a *"carnal mind"* or at least, a mind that is leaning in that direction.

The interest of such a person, even though claiming Christ, is not really on the Lord, but on worldly things. Such is in the carnal direction, and will ultimately lead to a carnal mind, if not already!

THE WORD OF GOD

2. Paul is also speaking to the Believer who does not know the Truth of these three great Chapters and is overtaken by the Sin Nature, therefore, dominated by sin. His situation is miserable to say the least, irrespective

of how hard he may be trying to overcome this thing. However, the harder he tries, the worse the situation becomes.

The weapons being used are his willpower, or even spiritual things, which are good within themselves, but will not perform the intended task of freedom.

Even though the Believer does not think as such, attempting to use his willpower to overcome sin, constitutes a *"carnal mind."* It would actually be the same, were he using quite legitimate principles such as *"confession,"* or the *"laying on of hands,"* etc. One could name several other great Biblical principles as well.

We are certainly not saying that these things are wrong, when in reality they are right, and even very much right. However, to use such attributes in the capacity of that of which we speak, even as valuable as they are, is the same as a carpenter attempting to use a handsaw instead of a hammer, to drive nails. It simply won't work because it was not made for that purpose.

Satan tricks us by these things, simply because they are very good and actually bless us greatly. But we sadly and regrettably find, that they do not bring us the Victory which we seek and, in fact, must have.

But yet the Reader may ask, *"How could these things which are so right within themselves, even though used wrongly, be declared as 'enmity against God?'"*

"Enmity" in the Greek is *"echthra,"* and means *"hostility,"* and in this case, *"against God."*

The Reader who is caught in this trap, might quickly exclaim that he has no hostility against God, but rather the very opposite. That is correct but at the same time incorrect. The answer is found in the next phrase.

The phrase, *"For it is not subject to the Law of God, neither indeed can be,"* in its most simplest form means that what is being done, whatever it may be, is not in God's prescribed order, and, therefore, presents the person not going God's Way, which generates hostility, whether intended or not. In other words, every single thing that is not exactly as God intends for it to be, is in effect, at war with Him, whether the Believer understands that or not.

NOTES

THE DIVINE ORDER

"Subject" in the Greek is *"hupotasso,"* and is actually a military term meaning *"to arrange in order under."* In other words, God has a Divine Order, and all Believers are to come under that *"Order."* Such speaks of humility and, therefore, deals with the *"mind."* For instance, *"Let this mind be in you, which was also in Christ Jesus:*

"Who, . . . made Himself of no reputation, and took upon Him the form of a servant, and was made in the likeness of men: . . . He humbled Himself, and became obedient unto death, even the death of the Cross" (Phil. 2:5-8).

So the *"carnal mind"* is not a *"spiritual mind,"* and the reason being, is that it is not a *"humble mind."*

So, we find here, that one of the reasons for the *"carnal mind"* is a lack of humility and brokenness before God. I greatly suspect that this problem is so acute, that the best among us, whomever that may be, has far more spiritual pride, which is the worst type of all, than we realize (Isa. 66:2).

What is the Law of God?

It is the Word of God! It must be carefully and faithfully followed. That's the reason that it is so absolutely imperative that Believers know the Bible. As well, one must always understand, that it is virtually impossible to exhaust its treasures and resources. Considering that it is the Living Word of God, its meanings continue to enlarge and grow.

So, if the Believer takes the position that he already knows the Word, and, therefore, further study is little needed, he is greatly shortchanging himself. So much so, in fact, that it beggars description. Ever how much one may know, there is much more to know.

(8) "SO THEN THEY THAT ARE IN THE FLESH CANNOT PLEASE GOD."

Hebrews 11:6 says, *"But without Faith it is impossible to please Him."* So, we are told that *"Faith"* pleases God, while the *"flesh"* displeases God.

FAITH AND THAT WHICH IS OF GOD

Everything that God has, does, and uses in regards to the human family, originates totally, absolutely, completely, and altogether with Him. In other words, Salvation is all of God and not of man. That would include all of the nuances of Salvation as well, which pertains to Divine Healing, Sanctification, Righteousness, Leading, and Guidance by the Holy Spirit, etc.

That also means, that every single Word in the Bible, although penned by men and, therefore, used as instruments, is in fact, and in totality, Authored by the Holy Spirit (Mat. 4:4; II Pet. 1:21).

Inasmuch as everything originates with God, and is of a worth far beyond our capacity to grasp or understand, there is no way that sinful man can earn anything which is of God. Consequently, the only way anything can be obtained from the Lord is through the vehicle of Faith. In other words, man believes what God has said, taking it at face value. As well, True Faith in God also consecrates itself to do the Will of God in every respect that is humanly possible. That sounds very complicated, but actually, about all that man can do respecting the absolute Will of God, is to furnish a willing mind and obedient heart (II Cor. 8:12).

God does not look for ability, talent, resources, or self-will in man as a requirement, but rather the very opposite, which is a brokenness before Him, which in effect says that man knows that within himself he deserves nothing good from God (Isa. 66:2; Lk. 18:14). Actually, True Bible Faith does not really function very well outside the sphere of Biblical Humility.

THE FLESH AND DISPLEASING GOD

The *"flesh"* basically speaks of man's frailty, inability, and weakness, even impossibility, regarding spiritual things. Inasmuch as humanity is fallen, that means that within the *"flesh"* man has nothing good, can do nothing good, and cannot come up with anything which pleases God, as should be obvious. And yet, we seem to keep trying.

The whole idea is that if man tries anything within himself, whether Believer or otherwise, God simply cannot accept such. This is at least one of the reasons that God hates self-righteousness to such an extent, because it originates with the flesh, i.e., man's self-efforts, self-will. Consequently, it

is coming from a poisoned source, which can never be accepted by God.

As well, if self-righteousness becomes the attitude of a Believer, the *"flesh"* from such a source is just as hateful to God as it is in an unbeliever, actually far worse!

In the first place, the Believer should know that everything he has which is any good has come from God, and originated totally with God. This means that God does not need any help, and in fact, if man, even converted man, attempts to help God in these areas, which all of us have tried to do at one time or the other, it only tends to frustrate the Grace of God and, therefore, sully that which the Holy Spirit is attempting to do within our hearts and lives.

As the *"flesh"* keeps much of the human family from coming to God, likewise, the *"flesh"* is the greatest hindrance to the Believer. The temptation is always very heavy to add something to what Jesus has already done, or to take away from what He has already done, or to substitute something else altogether in its place. However, no matter how consecrated such an effort may be, it does not please God, and, in fact, cannot please God, and for the obvious reasons.

THE PERSONAL EXPERIENCE OF PAUL

When Paul wrote these words, he was writing something of which he knew firsthand. For a particular time in his Christian life, he attempted to overcome sin with the efforts of the *"flesh,"* his own willpower, ability, etc. It did not work, even as it cannot work. So, he knew firsthand of the terrible dangers and the futility of such an effort, and as well, how it displeases God for His Children to attempt such.

I look back in my own life and I tend to grieve when I realize how I have personally fallen into this trap so many times, and how it caused me so much heartache, troubles, and difficulty.

Paul learned that every effort by the flesh, no matter how well motivated, how well intentioned, how loaded down with Scriptures and religious effort, only tended to make the situation worse, with sin even more pronounced. In other words, instead of climbing out of the hole, he only tended to sink deeper (Rom. 7:15).

There are many reasons for this: First of all, and as we have stated, when one tends to make this effort, one is attempting to solve the problems of the flesh with the flesh, which are impossible. He is attempting to assuage a poisoned situation with water so to speak, from a poisoned spring. And irrespective of that, even if it was not poisoned and polluted, man simply does not have the strength to overcome sin within himself. It just cannot be done. The problem is of far greater magnitude than any human being could ever begin to realize, so bad in fact, that God had to become man, literally becoming a human Sacrifice, i.e., a Sin-Offering, in order for the terrible sin debt to be paid and its dominion broken.

As well, what Jesus did at Calvary completed the task of Victory and Deliverance over sin in totality. Nothing can be added, as nothing need be added. In fact, when we try to add something, we are insulting God.

AN EXAMPLE

To use a crude analogy, let's say that a man owed a Billion dollars at the Bank, and had absolutely no way to pay this terrible debt, actually being flat broke. A wealthy benefactor then steps in and pays the entirety of the debt, but as well, deposits a Billion dollars in cash in the same Bank, and tells the Bank Administrators, that this man who had formerly owed this terrible debt, is now free to write checks on this new account to his heart's content.

Of course the man is now very elated that this terrible debt has been paid, with him no longer owing anything. He is as well told of the tremendous amount of money that's in the Bank, on which account he is free to write checks for whatever he needs.

The man then has to purchase a piece of land which costs a million dollars. To purchase this land, he goes to the Bank and opens a new account depositing ten dollars, which is separate from the huge account that's already available to him in the Bank. He then writes the million dollar check on his new account to pay for the land, when in reality he only has $10 in the Bank, at least

NOTES

in his separate account which he has just recently opened.

The Banker says to him, *"Why are you doing this? Your $10 in the Bank will not cover a million dollar check, and you don't need to do this anyway considering that we have a Billion dollars in this Bank on which you can write as many checks as you like. I have also been told by your Benefactor, that if you exhaust this Billion dollars, they will instantly replenish it with as much as is needed."*

Considering what the Benefactor has done for this man, I should think that it would be obvious that he would not be too very much pleased at the foolish personal actions of this individual regarding finances. It is the same with the Lord.

Even though our illustration is very crude, this is exactly what we Believers have done many times. We have tried to take our two cents and purchase what only a Billion dollars could obtain, and which has already been provided, at least if we are allowed to use such an illustration.

Everything we need has already been done by Christ. So why do we insult Him by attempting to do it all over again ourselves, which is impossible anyway?

(9) "BUT YE ARE NOT IN THE FLESH, BUT IN THE SPIRIT, IF SO BE THAT THE SPIRIT OF GOD DWELL IN YOU. NOW IF ANY MAN HAVE NOT THE SPIRIT OF CHRIST, HE IS NONE OF HIS."

The phrase, *"But ye are not in the flesh,"* in one sense of the word is asking the question, *"Since you are now a Believer and no longer depending on the flesh, why are you resorting to the flesh?"*

The phrase, *"But in the Spirit,"* in effect is saying, *"You now have the Holy Spirit to help you."*

It is the Holy Spirit Who makes these great Truths real to the heart of the Believer, but as we have repeatedly stated, He cannot make anything real which Truth the Believer does not know, nor can He work on our behalf, when we are attempting to do the thing ourselves. This is what Paul is talking about.

The phrase, *"If so be that the Spirit of God dwell in you,"* in essence says, *"provided that,"* or *"assuming that."* That is, assuming that the Spirit of God dwells in you, that is an indication that you are not in the sphere of the evil nature.

"Dwell" in the Greek is "oikeo," and means "to live or dwell in a certain place as your home." The Spirit is not only resident in the Believer in the sense of position in him, but He is actively at home in him, living in him as His home.

A MINISTRY TO PERFORM

It further means that He is not there just to be there, but rather has a Ministry to perform in the Believer, namely, to give the Believer Victory over sin and produce His Own fruit. He gives the Believer Victory over sin by making real to him and energizing within him, the great Truth and Fact of what Christ did at Calvary and the Resurrection for him.

This, together with the presence of the imparted Divine Nature in the Believer, and the fact that God has broken the power of the evil nature, puts the Believer out of the sphere of the evil nature and within the sphere of the Holy Spirit. Consequently, the Believer is, therefore, not in the grip of the evil nature, but under the control of the Holy Spirit as he yields himself to Him.

However, these things of which we have said, are the ideal, meaning what is supposed to be. Too often the Believer does not know the full Truth of what Christ has done for him at Calvary and the Resurrection, giving the Holy Spirit little to work on and work with. As well, most Believers do not yield to the Holy Spirit too very well either, taking control out of His Hands. So, the Truth is, that the Holy Spirit in most Believers can only do and be to a limited degree, in comparison to what really can be done. In other words, most of us live so far beneath what we can truly be in Christ. We tie the hands of the Holy Spirit, grieving Him, wounding Him, actually allowing Him very little latitude within our lives. That's the reason that we have said that His Work is potential — only what we will allow Him to do, which too often, is not too very much.

The phrase, "Now if any man have not the Spirit of Christ, he is none of His," actually refers to the Holy Spirit. In other words, it is not possible for a person to be truly Saved

NOTES

without the Holy Spirit dwelling in them.

Some have thought that the "Spirit of Christ" referred to Christ's Personal Spirit; however, that is incorrect.

Paul is merely saying, that the Holy Spirit coming in to dwell within the heart and life of the Believer, is made possible only by what Christ did at Calvary and the Resurrection. There, Jesus satisfied the terrible sin debt, which meant that Satan no longer held a claim on anyone who evidenced Faith in Christ. Consequently, the Spirit of God since the Day of Pentecost, does not merely come to be with Believers, but rather in Believers (Jn. 14:17).

So, Paul is saying to failing Believers, that if they claim the Holy Spirit is not within their lives helping them, that means they are not even Saved. Because if they are Saved, the Holy Spirit is there, and is *ready* to do what He is there to do.

THE BAPTISM WITH THE HOLY SPIRIT

As we have said several times, and which I believe the Book of Acts and the Epistles bear out, if the Believer does not go on after Conversion, and be Baptized with the Holy Spirit, with the evidence of speaking with other Tongues, without this Baptism, the Holy Spirit is held somewhat dormant in the heart and life of the Believer, even though present. I realize that virtually all in the non-Pentecostal sector of the Church would strongly deny this, but I feel the Scripture bears it out and graphically so.

THE EXAMPLE OF THE WORD OF GOD

One must understand that the Word of God must stand as the criteria for all Faith and Belief. Agreeing upon that, our next task is to rightly divide the Word of Truth.

I believe the example of the Book of Acts and the Epistles as well, are replete with the fact that Believers in the Early Church had as the Foundation of their Faith, Salvation by Faith, the Baptism with the Holy Spirit, with the evidence of speaking with other Tongues, the mighty Power of God evidenced in the Healing of the sick and the working of Miracles, and the great Truth that Jesus Christ is coming again to set up a Kingdom on this Earth. If in fact that is the flavor of the Early Church, and it is, then our Churches should at least be similar at present. If not, then it's not truly Church, at least as God calls such.

It is the Holy Spirit Who makes real to the Believer all that Christ has done for the Believer. Therefore, if we ignore Him, disbelieve Him, or fail to give Him the latitude which He wants and seeks, He simply cannot do what needs to be done in our hearts and lives. It is absolutely imperative that the Holy Spirit have His Way. Regrettably and sadly, most Pentecostals and Charismatics who in fact are Baptized with the Holy Spirit, give Him very little latitude, and as a result, have but little of what He can really do.

(10) "AND IF CHRIST BE IN YOU, THE BODY IS DEAD BECAUSE OF SIN; BUT THE SPIRIT IS LIFE BECAUSE OF RIGHTEOUSNESS."

The phrase, *"And if Christ be in you,"* refers to a person having accepted Jesus as their own personal Saviour. Consequently, the Divine Nature, which is the Nature of God, is instantly deposited in the Believer. As well, and as we have just studied, the Holy Spirit has also taken up residence within the Child of God.

The phrase, *"The body is dead because of sin,"* speaks of the human body. Paul says it this way, in order that the Believer know and understand, that he must not try to gain Victory over sin by the means of his own physical body, i.e., self-will, personal efforts, one's own strength, etc.

The Believer's human body is dead in the sense that it has death in it because of sin, which speaks of Adam's sin which brought both spiritual and physical death to each member of the race. In view of that, and as Paul has already adequately explained, one's willpower alone, which has to do with the human body, simply cannot bring about the needed results, but actually can only hinder what the Spirit of God Alone can do.

So, Paul is saying that one is foolish to resort to these pitiful measures, when he already has tremendous firepower within his heart and life, in the form of Christ and the Holy Spirit to bring about what is needed.

The phrase, *"But the Spirit is Life because*

NOTES

of Righteousness," tells us several things:

THE SPIRIT

1. Paul is speaking of the Holy Spirit which is obvious. He is God, and as a result, can do anything. In other words, He is Almighty. So, one is not to think that his situation is so bad that the Holy Spirit is insufficient.

I remind the Believer, that this is the same Spirit of God Who *"moved upon the face of the waters"* in Genesis 1:2. The Earth at that time *"was without form, and void,"* and in six days time He brought it back to a habitable state, as well as creating all animals, fowls, fish, and human beings.

Understanding that, I think that the Holy Spirit has the Power to do whatever is necessary.

THE SPIRIT OF LIFE

2. He has *"Life"* and is actually the Source of Life.

Man has no Spiritual Life within himself due to his spiritual death. Even the Life which the Believer has, is that which is imparted by the Holy Spirit. So, to attempt to bring Life out of death (the physical body of the human being), is a futile effort. All Life is in the Spirit, and all Life emanates from the Spirit. It is obtained by Faith in Christ, and what He did for humanity at Calvary and the Resurrection.

RIGHTEOUSNESS

3. The *"Righteousness"* addressed here, is the Righteousness of God, which is given to any sinner upon Faith in Christ, and given instantly.

Within himself, man has no Righteousness, despite the fact that he attempts constantly to manufacture such, which the Bible calls *"self-righteousness"* (Lk. 18:9-14).

God's Righteousness is defined as *"moral perfection."* It is *"right"* because it is God's Way, and, consequently, absolutely devoid of any type of wrongdoing. As well, it is the Standard set by God, and not by man. It is the only Righteousness He recognizes, and as such, is instantly angry at man's efforts at self-righteousness, which God calls *"wicked"* (Ps. 7:11; Rom. 1:18).

(11) "BUT IF THE SPIRIT OF HIM THAT RAISED UP JESUS FROM THE DEAD DWELL IN YOU, HE THAT RAISED UP CHRIST FROM THE DEAD SHALL ALSO QUICKEN YOUR MORTAL BODIES BY HIS SPIRIT THAT DWELLETH IN YOU."

The phrase, *"But if the Spirit of Him that raised up Jesus from the dead dwell in you,"* tells us two things:

1. The same Power of the Holy Spirit which raised Jesus from the dead, dwells in Believers, and is available for our use. This is what Paul is saying.

The idea is, that there is no temptation of sin so black, so binding, or destructive, but that the Spirit of God can handle it, that is if we know the Truth respecting the Finished Work of Calvary. That same Resurrecting Power is available to all Believers.

2. That's the same Power that is dwelling in the Believer, and we are assured that He will use whatever part of it is necessary, in order that we might have the Victory for which we seek.

What a Promise!

The phrase, *"He that raised up Christ from the dead shall also quicken your mortal bodies by His Spirit that dwelleth in you,"* continues to express these two points:

1. Many claim that Paul is speaking here exclusively of the Coming Resurrection. While he is definitely speaking of that coming great event, still, by the use of the word *"mortal"* he is also speaking of our present experience in Christ.

In other words, the Holy Spirit will impart whatever power is needed to our present physical bodies (mortal), in order that we may have Victory in any and every capacity of life.

"Quicken" in the Greek is *"zooporeo,"* and means *"to cause to live, make alive, give life."* So, He will infuse Spiritual Life into these physical bodies, which always takes precedent over the *"death"* that is already there due to Adam's Fall.

Paul is dealing here not only with the fact of sin which we face everyday in our physical bodies, but also in the fact of original sin, which is the cause of the problem in the first place.

He imparts enough Life into these physical

bodies, which overcomes the death, and gives us strength to say *"Yes"* to Christ in whatever capacity that He requires.

2. Even though this of which we have stated is the thrust of Paul's Statement, nevertheless, he also in a secondary sense, is speaking of the Coming Resurrection of Life, when the Holy Spirit will also at that time give every Believer a new body (I Cor. 15:38, 51-57).

(12) "THEREFORE, BRETHREN, WE ARE DEBTORS, NOT TO THE FLESH, TO LIVE AFTER THE FLESH."

The two words, *"Therefore, Brethren,"* portray the fact that Paul is addressing his statements to Believers and not unbelievers.

Some Expositors claim that the *"carnally minded"* and those who are *"in the flesh,"* pertain to the unsaved.

While it certainly does pertain to the unsaved, the whole idea of what Paul is saying, that these things can come back into the hearts and lives of Believers as well, are those to whom this warning is directed. So, Paul is not speaking of the unsaved, but rather Christians who do not properly know their place in Christ, or else they are purposely drifting over into the ways of the world, etc. Either way, great problems will be the result.

The phrase, *"We are debtors,"* refers to that which we owe Jesus Christ.

"Debtors" in the Greek is *"opheiletes,"* and means *"one held by an obligation,"* in this case, as stated, to Christ.

The phrase, *"Not to the flesh,"* means that the Believer does not owe anything in that direction, and in fact, has done nothing but suffer from that means.

To be sure, Paul's Statement, although directed to the subject at hand, still, covers far more territory than meets the eye.

It has to do not only, with this struggle between the flesh and the Spirit, but as well, spreads out to include religious men who would attempt to force the Believer to abide by their man-devised religious laws. All of that is of the flesh, just as much as anything else one could name.

The idea is, that I as a Believer do not owe anything to another Christian, even as Paul will later say, except to Love him (Rom. 13:8). There Paul said, *"Owe no man any thing,"* or in other words, *"I am not a debtor to any man to obey him in anything as far as Believers are concerned, except to Love him in Christ."* Consequently, this shoots down all religious man-devised hierarchies.

THE BELIEVER OWES THE FLESH NOTHING

The phrase, *"To live after the flesh,"* refers to its dictates, and in this case the Sin Nature.

As a Child of God, I must order my life after the Holy Spirit, Who will always guide me according to Truth, i.e., the Word of God. As a Believer I owe the flesh nothing, and must not allow it to intrude in any part of my daily living.

Sin is no longer to control me in any capacity because its dominion is broken. I am not to be guided by fleshly lusts, or ungodly passionate desires. My hope alone is in Christ, and in Him I find all I need, and, actually, far more than I could ever need.

As a result, I do not guide my life after the conventional wisdom of the world, nor do I flow with its current. Its interests are not my interests. Its goals are not my goals. I am not moved by what moves it, nor do I respond to its appeal. There is a reason for all of that, which Paul beautifully gives us in the next verse.

(13) "FOR IF YE LIVE AFTER THE FLESH, YE SHALL DIE: BUT IF YE THROUGH THE SPIRIT DO MORTIFY THE DEEDS OF THE BODY, YE SHALL LIVE."

The phrase, *"For if ye live after the flesh, ye shall die,"* once again, has a far greater meaning than meets the eye.

The thrust of the subject is, as it is given by Paul, that a person who lives habitually under the dominion of the evil nature, and referring to Believers, that person will ultimately lose their soul. Consequently, this shatters the unscriptural Doctrine of Unconditional Eternal Security.

As we have stated, and as is obvious, Paul is speaking to Believers. He did *not* say that if this thing continues, the Sin Nature dominating the Believer, that one would lose fellowship with the Lord, but that ultimately, they would not only lose fellowship with the Lord, but would die spiritually, i.e., will lose their soul.

Whenever the word *"die"* is used in this

fashion, it actually refers to the final death in the Lake of Fire (Rev. 20:11-15). Consequently, the warning is double-barreled:

THE DOMINION OF SIN

1. This speaks primarily to the Believer, as is obvious, who does not avail himself of what Christ did at Calvary, therefore, continuing to live habitually under the dominion of sin. While God will always be patient, loving, longsuffering, and compassionate, and will forgive anytime and every time, irrespective of the sin, if the person is truly sincere (I Jn. 1:9), still, danger is, that the individual will begin to make allowances for his sin, quit seeking forgiveness, and lose his way totally.

No one can live with habitual sin, without reaping its bitter results, irrespective of the Forgiving Grace of God. Sin always takes a deadly toll. The only answer to sin, is what Jesus did at Calvary, and taking full advantage of that great Act of Saving and Delivering Grace.

THE WORLD SYSTEM

2. It also speaks of Believers playing loose with the world, actually becoming a part of the world, i.e., *"living after the flesh."*

Even though Paul is not here and now addressing this particular subject, the analogy, nevertheless, holds true. The world system is antagonistic to the Child of God. In other words, it is hostile to the Believer's Faith. That's the reason Paul did say, *"Wherefore come out from among them, and be ye separate, saith the Lord, and touch not the unclean thing; and I will receive you"* (II Cor. 6:14-18; 7:1).

If there is not a separation from that system, as well, the Believer who is constantly associating himself accordingly, will ultimately *"die,"* i.e., *"lose his soul."*

The phrase, *"But if ye through the Spirit do mortify the deeds of the body, ye shall live,"* tells us several things as well:

1. It is obvious that Paul is speaking here to Believers, because he is placing a choice before the Believer. First of all, how in the world can an unsaved person expect anything of the Spirit of God, when he doesn't even know the Spirit of God, and above all, does

not have the Spirit of God? No, Paul is speaking to Believers, and warning Believers!

2. We are told that it is only through the Spirit of God that we can overcome the Sin Nature. However, I remind the Reader, that this is done on the basis of the Believer knowing and understanding what Jesus has done for him at Calvary and the Resurrection, and his part in that great Act of Eternity. Again we say it, even at the risk of being overly repetitive, that the Presence of the Holy Spirit in the heart of the Believer is potential in nature. His Presence does not guarantee anything, without the full cooperation of the Believer. He has been sent to us to *"help,"* not to treat us as a slave (Jn. 16:7).

3. We are not to come to terms with the *"deeds of the body,"* i.e., the Sin Nature, but rather *"mortify them."*

"Mortify" in the Greek is *"thanatoo,"* and means *"to kill, put to death."* We are not to kill the body, but rather the deeds of the *"Sin Nature"* which have their expression in the body, i.e., *"physical body."*

4. This of which Paul says is not a suggestion or a request, but rather an ultimatum. We destroy by the Spirit the effectiveness of the Sin Nature, or it destroys us. Considering the results of not doing so, which is the loss of one's soul for all eternity, I think that we should take these statements very seriously.

5. If the Holy Spirit is given latitude, He will do these great things within our lives. Not only will He destroy the *"evil deeds of the body,"* as well, He will also give the Believer Life, i.e., *"ye shall live."* It functions in this capacity:

If the Believer insists upon *"living after the flesh,"* i.e., allowing the Sin Nature free course, more and more sin will be added, with the situation quickly becoming desperate. However, if the Believer allows the Holy Spirit His complete latitude, more and more Life will be the result, which in fact, will never end. Death never stops while Life never stops.

We must always remember, that we are speaking here of eternal things, and as such, should realize the seriousness of this which Paul is telling us.

If the Believer does not kill sin, sin will kill him. In effect, the Believer cannot kill

NOTES

sin, but he has received a power that can make dead all the passions of sin in the body, and that is the Power of the Holy Spirit.

(14) "FOR AS MANY AS ARE LED BY THE SPIRIT OF GOD, THEY ARE THE SONS OF GOD."

The phrase, *"For as many as are led by the Spirit of God,"* proclaims that which the Spirit wants to do. He wants to lead us according to the Will of God. As such, He will lead us out of this domination by the Sin Nature, and lead us into total Victory in Christ. That is where He has been instructed to lead us, and that is where He is leading us, providing we cooperate with Him.

The phrase, *"They are the Sons of God,"* pertains to what *"Sons of God"* do. They are led by the Spirit of God.

Paul in addressing the Corinthians said, *"Ye know that ye were Gentiles, carried away unto these dumb idols, even as you were led"* (I Cor. 12:2). As is obvious, he was speaking of the Corinthians before they gave their hearts to God. They were actually led by demon spirits, but now they are led by the Spirit of God. Of course, the same is apropos for all Believers, and for all time.

There are so many privileges attached to being a follower of Christ, that it is very difficult to properly enumerate them. However, being led by the Spirit of God has to be one of the greatest Attributes and Blessings afforded the Believer.

WHAT DOES IT MEAN TO BE LED BY THE SPIRIT OF GOD?

First of all, if one truly has Christ, i.e., *"born again,"* one at the same time has the Holy Spirit. It is impossible otherwise!

One cannot be united with Christ except through the Spirit (I Cor. 6:17), one cannot share Christ's Sonship without sharing His Spirit (Rom. 8:14-17; Gal. 4:6), one cannot be a member of the Body of Christ except by being Baptized into that Body (I Cor. 12:13).

This is not a Baptism into the Spirit as the Scripture seems to indicate on the surface, but into the Body of Christ. The Body here is the element one is Baptized into. The Spirit is the Agent Who does the Baptizing into the Body. The Believer is the candidate.

If it were the Spirit Baptism (Acts 2:4), Christ would be the Agent (Mat. 3:11) and the Holy Spirit would be the Element Baptized into. As such, the Spirit from above is the Power effecting the New Birth (Jn. 3:3-8; I Jn. 3:9), for the Spirit is the Life-Giver (Jn. 6:63), like a River of Living Water flowing from Christ bringing Life to him who comes and believes (Jn. 7:37-39).

THE SPIRIT OF GOD AND DIVINE POWER

It is important to realize that for the first Christians the Spirit was thought of in terms of Divine Power clearly manifest by its effects on the life of the recipient; the impact of the Spirit did not leave individual or onlooker in much doubt that a significant change had taken place in him by Divine Agency. Paul refers his readers back to their initial experience of the Spirit again and again. For some it had been an overwhelming experience of God's Love (Rom. 5:5); for others of Joy (I Thess. 1:6); for others of Illumination (II Cor. 3:14-17), or of Liberation (Rom. 8:2; II Cor. 3:17), or of Moral Transformation (I Cor. 6:9-11), or of various Spiritual Gifts (I Cor. 1:4-7; Gal. 3:5).

Actually, in Acts the most regularly mentioned Manifestation of the Spirit is the speaking with other Tongues, also with Prophecy and Praise, and bold utterance of the Word of God (Acts 2:4; 4:8, 31; 10:46; 13:9-11; 19:6). Over all, speaking with other Tongues is the initial physical evidence that one has been Baptized with the Holy Spirit (Acts 2:4).

All of these things put together tell us why the possession of the Spirit as such can be singled out as the defining characteristic of the Christian (Rom. 8:9; I Jn. 3:24; 4:13), and why the question of Acts 19:2 could expect a straightforward answer (Gal. 3:2). The Spirit as such might be invisible, but His Presence was readily detectable (Jn. 3:8).

THE GIFT OF THE HOLY SPIRIT

The Gift of the Spirit was thus not simply a corollary or deduction drawn from Baptism or laying on of hands but a vivid event for the first Christians, and continues to be such unto this hour. It is most probably to the impact of this experience to which Paul refers directly in Passages like (I Cor. 6:11; 12:13; II Cor. 1:22; Eph. 1:13).

According to the Book of Acts the first Christians adapted their way of doing, their way of being, and their way of worship, in accordance with the Spirit rather than vice versa (Acts 8:12-17; 10:44-48; 11:15-18; 18:25-19:6).

THE SPIRIT AS THE POWER OF THE NEW LIFE

According to Paul the Gift of the Spirit is also a beginning that looks to final fulfillment (Gal. 3:3; Phil. 1:6), the beginning and first installment of a life-long process of transformation into the Image of Christ which only achieves its end in the Resurrection of the Body which is yet to come (II Cor. 1:22; 3:18; 4:16-5:5; Eph. 1:13; II Thess. 2:13; I Pet. 1:2). The Spirit is the *"Firstfruits"* of the Harvest of Resurrection, whereby God begins to exercise His Claim over the whole man (Rom. 8:11, 23; I Cor. 3:16; 6:19; 15:45-48; Gal. 5:16-23).

LIFE FOR THE BELIEVER

Life for the Believer is, therefore, qualitatively different from what it was prior to Faith. His daily living becomes his means of responding to the Spirit's Claim, enabled by the Spirit's Power, which is what it means to be led by the Spirit (Rom. 8:4-6, 14; Gal. 5:16, 18, 25; 6:8). In other words, the Holy Spirit becomes the Guide into all Truth, the Leader of everything which is always toward Christ, and the final Word concerning every decision in the Life of the Christian, which is always according to the Word of God.

Actually, this was the decisive difference between a Bible Christianity and Rabbinic Judaism for Paul. The Jew lived by Law, the deposit of the Spirit's revelatory work in past generations, an attitude which led inevitably to inflexibility and a direct block to anything that God was now doing, since revelation from the past is not always immediately appropriate to the needs of the present. Regrettably, this applies also to every single modern religious Denomination which discounts the Baptism with the Holy Spirit, claiming that all is received at Conversion.

However, the Spirit of God brings an immediate, personal relationship with God, which actually fulfills all the great hopes of the past, and which makes worship and obedience something much more free, vital and spontaneous than mere ritual (Rom. 2:28; 7:6; 8:2-4; 12:2; II Cor. 3:3, 6-8, 14-18; Eph. 2:18; Phil. 3:3).

A FINAL FULFILLMENT?

At the same time, because the Spirit is only a beginning of final Salvation in this life, there can be no final fulfillment of His Work in the Believer as long as this life lasts. The man of the Spirit is no longer dependent on this world and its standards for his meaning and satisfaction, but he is still a man of human appetites and frailty and part of human society. Consequently to have the Holy Spirit is to experience tension and conflict between the old life and the New, between the flesh and Spirit, exactly as we are studying here (Rom. 7:14-25; 8:10, 12; Gal. 5:16; Heb. 10:29).

Strangely enough, to those who saw the characteristic Life of the Spirit in terms of Visions, Revelations, and the like, Paul replied that Grace comes to its full expression only in and through weakness (Rom. 8:26; II Cor. 12:1-10).

However, in all things in which the Spirit leads us, and in all things which the Spirit does for us, we must never forget, that the Holy Spirit is that Person and Power Who bears witness to Christ, always to Christ (Jn. 15:26; Acts 1:8; 5:32; Heb. 2:4; I Pet. 1:12; I Jn. 5:6-8; Rev. 19:10).

HIS OPERATION IN EVERY BELIEVER

A distinguishing feature of the Holy Spirit is that He is experienced by all and works through all, not just a select few (Acts 2:17; Rom. 8:9; I Cor. 12:7, 11; Heb. 6:4; I Jn. 2:20). Of course, I am speaking of those who have been Baptized with the Holy Spirit (Acts 1:4; 2:4). As we have already taught, the Believer who does not go on and be Baptized with the Holy Spirit, which will always include the speaking with other Tongues, although definitely Saved, will simply not have the Working of the Holy Spirit in his life accordingly. In Paul's

teaching it is only this common participation in the One Spirit that makes a group of diverse individuals one Body (I Cor. 12:13; II Cor. 13:14; Eph. 4:3; Phil. 2:1).

And it is only as each lets the Spirit come to expression in Word and Deed as a member of the Body, that the Body grows toward the maturity of Christ, and I speak of His Church (I Cor. 12:12-26; Eph. 4:3-16). This is one of the reasons why Paul both encourages a full range and free expression of the Spirit's Gifts (Rom. 12:3-8; I Cor. 12:4-11, 27-31; Eph. 4:30; 5:18; I Thess. 5:19), and insists that the Church test every word and deed which claims the Authority of the Spirit by the Measure of Christ and the Love He embodied (I Cor. 2:12-16; Chpt. 13; 14:29; I Thess. 5:19-22; I Jn. 4:1-3).

WORSHIP AND LEADING

The same twin emphasis on a Worship which is determined by immediate dependence on the Spirit (rather than in terms of a Sacred Place or Sanctuary) and in accordance with the Truth of Christ, is present in John 21:24.

Similarly John emphasizes that the Believer may expect an immediacy of teaching by the Spirit as the Counsellor, which is being led by the Spirit (Jn. 14:26; 16:12; I Jn. 2:27); but also that the New Revelation will be in continuity with the Old, in other words not contradicting the Old, a re-proclaiming if you will, even a reinterpretation of the Truth of Christ (Jn. 14:26; 16:13-15; I Jn. 2:24).

THE SPIRIT OF CHRIST

It is this tie-in with Christ which finally distinguishes the Christian's understanding of the Spirit from the earlier, less well-defined conception. The Spirit even as He now glorifies Christ in the heart and life of the Believer, is now definitively the Spirit of Christ (Jn. 7:38; 19:30; 20:22; Acts 2:33; 16:7; Rom. 8:9; Gal. 4:6; Phil. 1:19; Heb. 9:14; I Pet. 1:11; Rev. 3:1; 5:6).

Actually, the Other Counsellor Who has taken over Jesus' role on Earth (Jn. 14:16; I Jn. 2:1), means that Jesus is now present to the Believer only in and through the Spirit (Jn. 14:16-28; 16:7; Rom. 1:4; 8:9; I Cor. 6:17; 15:45; Eph. 3:1; I Tim. 3:16; I Pet. 3:18;

Rev. Chpts. 2-3), and that the Mark of the Spirit is both the recognition of Jesus' present status (I Cor. 12:3; I Jn. 5:6-12) and the reproduction of the character of His Sonship and Resurrection Life in the Believer (Rom. 8:11, 14-16, 23; I Cor. 15:45-49; II Cor. 3:18; Gal. 4:6; I Jn. 3:2).

(Bibliography: H. Berkhof, *"The Doctrine of the Holy Spirit"*; Bruner, *"A Theology of the Holy Spirit"*; Dunn, *"Baptism with the Holy Spirit."*)

The phrase, *"They are the Sons of God,"* speaks of present tense. In other words one is Saved *now*.

What Paul is speaking of relative to the Believer being a Son of God, is explained more fully in the next verse.

(15) "FOR YE HAVE NOT RECEIVED THE SPIRIT OF BONDAGE AGAIN TO FEAR; BUT YE HAVE RECEIVED THE SPIRIT OF ADOPTION, WHEREBY WE CRY, ABBA, FATHER."

The phrase, *"For ye have not received the spirit of bondage again to fear,"* speaks of several things:

LAW KEEPING

1. The *"spirit of bondage"* as Paul here uses the phrase, refers to the Old Mosaic Law. The Law demanded obedience, as all law demands obedience, and the person was a virtual slave to that process.

That does not mean that the Law was bad even as Paul has already addressed. Actually, he plainly said, *"The Law is Holy, and the Commandment Holy, and Just, and Good"* (Rom. 7:12).

However, the Law while good, still, made its demands, but gave no power to meet those demands. So, the Jew, at least those who tried to keep the Law, even as they certainly should, found themselves in bondage to that Law, because it was something they simply could not do (the keeping of it) as hard as they tried. And yet they knew they must!

Any Believer presently, who embarks upon an effort of Law-keeping, as possibly all of us have done in one way or the other, will find ourselves in that same bondage. I do not speak of the Law of Moses presently quite so much as the laws, rules, and regulations made up by many Churches. Nevertheless, it is Law,

NOTES

with some of it probably very good, etc.

Such efforts tend to fool people for the simple reason that many of these rules and regulations are good, just as the Law of Moses was good. Nevertheless, to reinstate Law in any fashion, and no matter how sincere we may be, such will not have the intended results of Holiness, but rather the very opposite.

FEAR

2. Efforts at Law-keeping always bring fear, for the simple reason, that the person is led to believe that their Salvation consists of keeping these Laws, i.e., rules and regulations of their Church, etc. So, their Christianity now becomes a bondage instead of a freedom — all of this, in attempting to be Holy and Righteous, which in fact only Jesus can give, which Law-keeping could never give, for the simple reason that the Law was always broken.

The very moment that the Believer attempts to keep Law of some making, the Holy Spirit withdraws His Help, with the Believer always failing sooner or later. The idea is not in the Believer keeping some type of Law, but rather in placing our trust in Christ Who has already kept the Law in every respect. In other words, it is a task already done, instead of being left up to us to do, which no one ever did but Christ.

Some people have the mistaken idea when they read that of which we have just said, that this means that Believers have a license to sin, etc. Quite the contrary!

In fact, the Believer is definitely to keep every Moral Law of God. That's one of the great facets of Christianity, that our lives are changed from the evil and the ungodly to the Righteous and the Holy. However, this process cannot be brought about by Law-keeping on our part, but only by trusting in Him. As a result of our trust, Jesus keeps the Moral Law through us, which is in accordance with our imputed Righteousness and Holiness (Gal. 2:20). He does this through the Power, Agency, Person, and Ministry of the Holy Spirit within our lives.

Now there is no *"fear."* The responsibility is not on my shoulders, but on Christ. As well, it is not that He will do these things, but in fact has already done these things.

A true relationship with Christ is always spelled out with one word *"done!"* The bondage of religion is always spelled out in one word *"do!"*

THE SPIRIT OF ADOPTION

3. If the Believer has in fact, received the *"spirit of bondage,"* it was not given to him by the Holy Spirit, but rather by his Church, or that of his own making and doing. So, the Believer needs to look at his situation, as to whether it matches up with this of which Paul brings to us, or rather something else.

The phrase, *"But ye have received the Spirit of Adoption,"* proclaims the manner in which all Believers are *"Sons of God."*

"Sons" in the Greek is *"huios,"* and means *"a mature Child of God in a legal standing with God."*

The Believer is not to confuse the statement *"Sons of God"* of verse 14 reflecting his status, with that of Jesus Who is *"The Son of God."* We are such by *"Adoption,"* while He is such as the Only Begotten Son of God (Jn. 3:16). John actually refers to Him in essence as the *"Only Begotten God"* (Jn. 1:18).

The Word *"Only Begotten"* does not only mean that our Lord was the Only Son of God in this manner, but that He as God the Son is Alone of His Kind, Unique, Begotten of God through eternal generations. He is the Image of God in the sense that He is a derived Representation of God the Father, co-existent eternally with Him, possessing the same Essence, Deity Himself. Being the only unique Representative, He is also, therefore, the Manifestation of God. He said to Philip, *"He that hath seen Me hath seen the Father"* (Jn. 14:9).

SONS OF GOD

He is also the One Who made Peace through the Blood of His Cross, meaning that He took away the enmity that was between God and man, because of man's Fall. That is, through His Substitutionary Death He satisfied completely all the claims which the Law of God had against us. We as lost sinners violated that Law. The Justice of God demanded that the penalty, death, be paid.

NOTES

But God in His Love desired to save those who would come to Him in Faith to appropriate Salvation.

So, He in the Person of His Son, Jesus of Nazareth, stepped down from His Judgment Throne to take upon Himself at Calvary your sin and mine, your penalty and mine. God's Law being satisfied, He is now free to Righteously bestow Mercy. Consequently, it is now possible for any sinner to be *"born again,"* and as such, to be brought into the Family of God by Adoption, thereby, becoming a *"Son of God."*

However, we should understand even as Paul tells us here, that adopted sons share the same rights and privileges as one born in the family.

Even though this Great Work was done by Jesus at Calvary, even as stated, still, it is the Holy Spirit who acts as the Legal Counsel, to bring the believing sinner into the Family of God.

When He does this, He is not bringing us into the position of slaves, which caused those under the Law to shrink from God in fear, because they had broken the Law, but rather into the great Family of God which gives freedom, purchased by Jesus Christ. As stated, this place and position is not one of fear, slavery and bondage, but rather the very opposite. Jesus has kept the Law in every respect, and upon Faith in Him, every Believer is given the status of Law-keeper, in other words, the same status that Jesus now has.

ROMAN LAW

The Holy Spirit is the One Who places Children of God as adult sons in a legal standing before God and in relation to Him.

Actually, what Paul is stating here, is a principle of Roman Law which was prevalent in his day, and served as an excellent example, contrary to Jewish Law which was somewhat different.

In Roman Law, the process of legal adoption by which the chosen heir became entitled not only to the rights of the property but to the Civil Status, to the burdens as well as the rights of the adopter — the adopted being made, as it were, the other self of the adopter, one with him.

As stated, this Roman Principle of Adoption

was peculiar to the Romans, unknown to the Greeks, unknown to all appearance, to the Jews, as it certainly is not found in the legislation of Moses, nor mentioned anywhere as a usage among the Children of the Covenant.

In essence, this tells us that the Adopted Son of God becomes, in a peculiar and intimate sense, One with the Heavenly Father. What an honor! What a privilege!

The phrase, *"Whereby we cry, Abba, Father,"* presents the status of the Adopted Believer. Slaves were never allowed to say *"Abba"* to a Master or *"Imma"* to a Mistress. *"Abba"* is a Syrian term which Paul translates in Greek *"The Father."* Jesus used the term *"Abba"* in His Gethsemane Prayer (Mk. 14:36) which Mark also translates into Greek.

However, Greek Scholars say, that the Greek word is not meant to be a mere translation of the Syriac, but that the Name *"Father"* is repeated. Robertson says it is a child's privilege to repeat the name, in other words, *"Abba, Father."* The Holy Spirit enables the Child of God to call God, Father, which is done so because of Jesus Christ.

In all of this Paul is telling us that the Believer has received the Power (his knowledge of what Christ has done and the Power of the Holy Spirit to make real that knowledge within his life) that can make dead all the passions of sin in the body. As stated, this is a Work of the Holy Spirit, and tells us that we are Sons of God. This Glorious Work does not put the Believer under the bondage of Law where he would be perpetually oppressed with doubts and fears as to whether he was Righteous before God, but it brings him into the High and Glorious Position of a child who, possessing his Father's nature, spontaneously cries out *"Abba, Father"* (Williams).

"Cry" in the Greek is *"krazo,"* and means *"a loud cry expressing deep emotion."* In other words, it speaks of much more than mere title, but rather *"relationship."*

(16) "THE SPIRIT ITSELF BEARETH WITNESS WITH OUR SPIRIT, THAT WE ARE THE CHILDREN OF GOD:"

The phrase, *"The Spirit Itself,"* should have been translated, *"The Spirit Himself."* The Holy Spirit is a Person, and, accordingly, should never be addressed as *"It."*

The phrase, *"Beareth witness with our spirit,"* means that He is constantly speaking and witnessing to us a certain thing. It is more, much more, than a witness when we first were Saved, but rather a continuing witness, something which never stops.

"Beareth witness with," in the Greek is *"summartureo,"* and means *"to bear joint witness with"* some other person, *"to bear joint-testimony with"* some other person. *"Our spirit"* refers to the Saint's human spirit energized by the Holy Spirit (Wuest). In other words, our own spirit tells us we are God's Children, but the voice with which it speaks is, as we know, prompted and inspired by the Divine Spirit Himself.

The phrase, *"That we are the Children of God,"* speaks of present tense, meaning *"right now."*

WHAT EXACTLY IS THIS WITNESS OF THE SPIRIT?

To be sure, it is something far higher than the mere knowledge of a philosophy, or even a personal experience we may have had. While personal experiences in the Lord are of extreme importance and never to be demeaned, still, the *"witness of the Spirit"* of which we speak, transcends all feelings, and means that it is stamped in the legal standing of the Word of God. It is a certitude (for certain) of the Spirit's Presence and Work continually within us, which takes us not only from experience to experience, but from Faith to Faith. It is manifested in His comforting us, His stirring us up to prayer, His reproof of our sins, His drawing us to works of Love, to bear testimony before the world, etc. On this direct testimony of the Holy Spirit rests, ultimately, all the regenerate man's conviction respecting Christ and His Work (Olshausen).

It is amazing that many in this modern climate claim that God no longer speaks to people presently. They should read Romans 8:16, where the infallible Word of God proclaims that the Spirit of God not only speaks to Believers, but as well speaks constantly. Perhaps these doubters do not know of this Truth, simply because He is not in their lives, i.e., they are not Born Again.

(17) "AND IF CHILDREN, THEN HEIRS;

HEIRS OF GOD, AND JOINT-HEIRS WITH CHRIST; IF SO BE THAT WE SUFFER WITH HIM, THAT WE MAY BE ALSO GLORIFIED TOGETHER."

The phrase, *"And if children, then heirs,"* speaks of a present position. *"If"* in the Greek is *"ei,"* and means *"a fulfilled condition."* In other words, the Spirit right now, is constantly bearing testimony right now, in company with our spirit right now, that we are Children of God right now.

The phrase, *"Heirs of God"* speaks of this *"Adoption"* as being the highest of all, not merely a secondary position, even as glorious as *that* would be. This is illustrated in the story given by Jesus of the Prodigal Son.

THE PRODIGAL

The Prodigal so sick of his lost condition with all of its attendant misery, was planning on going back to the Father and requesting of Him, *"Make me as one of thy hired servants"* (Lk. 15:19).

The *"hired servant"* did not even have the status of a regular servant who had full security and employment, but rather one who stood at the gate every morning, and took whatever work was available, irrespective as to its servility or shortness of duration.

However, when he came back to the Father, he found that the Father did not treat him as a servant, much less a *"hired servant,"* but brought him back to full status as a *"Son"* even with all of its full inheritance, even though the previous inheritance had been squandered. This is what Paul is talking about *"Heirs of God."*

Adam squandered the inheritance given to him by the Lord, and now guilty, his sons come back to the Father, and are received not as servants, but as *"Sons"* with all the privileges which the Father can give. In other words, total status and position are restored, with all rights reinstated.

If one is to notice, there was no condemnation whatsoever on the part of the Father as regarding the Prodigal Son, but rather the very opposite. Hence, Paul would say, *"There is therefore now no condemnation to them which are in Christ Jesus, who walk not after the flesh, but after the Spirit"* (Rom. 8:1).

THE LAST ADAM

The phrase, *"And joint-heirs with Christ,"* means, however, that we could never have this relationship with the Father, were it not for the Second and, therefore, Last Adam, The Lord Jesus Christ. He as our Representative Man, has done for us what we could not do for ourselves, and at tremendous price one might quickly add. So, this privilege and position of being a *"joint-heir"* with Him, is strictly because of His Mercy, Grace, Love, and Compassion, and not at all through anything that we have done. Simple Faith in Him, grants me all the privileges which He has with the Father, which makes me an *"Heir of God."*

Roman Law made all children including adopted ones, equal inheritors, which Paul no doubt had in mind.

By contrast, Jewish Law gave a double portion to the eldest son. However, Paul is saying that Jewish Law (the Law of Moses) does not apply here, because Grace lifts one to a higher status, and, therefore, gives us equal rights with Christ.

As one reads these Words, one is humbled, especially considering, the price that was paid, and how much none of us deserve any of this of which the Lord so freely gives.

Jesus is the Eldest Son, but He has purposely forfeited His place and position of the double portion, rather making all Believers equal with Himself regarding inheritance.

One can only shout *"Hallelujah!"*

The phrase, *"If so be that we suffer with Him,"* does not pertain to mere suffering, for such does not fulfill the condition. It is suffering *with* Christ.

SUFFERING

The idea is that the Holy Spirit also binds the heart of the Believer in sympathy with the suffering Creation and with all its pain and misery. Christ felt that sympathy; and anyone who believes himself to be a Christian but does not so suffer with Christ deceives himself, for only those who suffer thus in sympathy with the suffering Creation, and in this sense with Christ will be Glorified with Him (Williams). Verses 19-22 bear this out.

Any person who truly knows God, and, consequently, walks close to Him, cannot help but see the terrible conditions in the world such as starvation, war, sickness, pain, suffering, heartache, etc., which are brought about by the Fall. This will not, and in fact, cannot be changed until the return of the Lord. The unbeliever gropes in this darkness having no understanding of the future and little or nothing of the past and present. As Paul has already said, they are not led by the Spirit and, therefore, have little true understanding of anything. Those without God have a sordid past, a hurting present, and an unknown future.

THE CHURCH

As well, and certainly not secondary, the True Believer in Christ, who attempts to follow Him in all things, will find great opposition not only from the world, but, as well, from the Apostate Church. By the Apostate Church I mean the following:

There was a time, even as late as the 1960's that the line was pretty well drawn respecting Fundamentalism and Modernism. (Fundamentalists are those who claim to believe all the Bible.) However, that line has become so blurred presently as to be indistinguishable.

At the present time, and a situation I might quickly add which is going to continue to deteriorate, strong religious Denominations who once held for the Truth of the Gospel, have become so shot through with unbelief, that they no longer even remotely resemble what they once were. While there are some in these Organizations who still cling to the straight gate and the narrow way, for the most part its Leadership is not in that category.

One could easily speak of modern Psychology which is wholly unbiblical and in fact, anti-Biblical, with virtually all of Christendom having plunged into this pit, but in Truth, Psychology, which is the religion of Humanism, is but a symptom of the real problem. The real problem is a failure to follow the Word of God, either because of self-will or unbelief. Such mirrors perfectly the spiritual condition of the Israel of Jesus' day.

Israel had never been more religious than

NOTES

at the time of the First Advent of Christ. However, that was their problem! It was mere religion, with no relationship at all with God. Consequently, they murdered their Messiah, and in spirit, such continues to be done even unto this very hour.

For a long while I grieved concerning the Leaders of the Pentecostal Denomination with which I was formerly associated, thinking that if they would just come to our meetings, they would see the Moving and Operation of the Holy Spirit, and, consequently, would not be so antagonistic and even hostile. However, I finally came to see and understand, that it was the Moving and Operation of the Holy Spirit which they so greatly opposed. That was the very reason, the Anointing of the Holy Spirit in my life, for their intense dislike. The other things which they presented to the public were merely excuses and not true reasons. The reason is that of which I have spoken. Regrettably, as I dictate these words, the situation has not improved, but rather worsened.

CAIN AS AN EXAMPLE

And yet, the problem is not new, having even begun with Cain murdering his brother Abel at the very dawn of time. God approved of Abel's Sacrifice, while disapproving that of Cain. Consequently, Cain murdered his brother, which spirit has continued unto this very hour. That's what I mean by the Apostate Church (Gen. 4:3-9).

Joseph's suffering, even as Abel, was from his Brethren. David's great enemy was Saul and certain elements in Israel. It was Israel who killed their own Prophets, and not the heathen. It was the Church of Jesus' Day which crucified Him, and not actually heathenistic Rome. It was Apostasy which gradually weakened the Early Church, until finally the world was plunged into the Dark Ages. Regrettably, it continues unto the present, and due to the deception of these last days, will only grow worse, even ushering in the Antichrist.

The phrase, *"That we may be also Glorified together,"* pertains to the Coming Resurrection of Life, when every True Saint will be Glorified exactly as Christ now is.

The idea is, that if one is a True Believer,

and please understand that this number is not nearly as large as one would think, they are going to be opposed by the false way, which is actually one of the great signs of the True Way of the Word of God. Jesus suffered the opposition of the Apostate Church of His Day, and all others suffer accordingly, that is, if they truly know the Lord.

WHAT DOES IT MEAN TO BE GLORIFIED?

As stated, this pertains to the Coming Resurrection.

We can probably best answer the question by addressing ourselves to three questions:

1. What do we know of Resurrection as Transformation?

2. What do we know about the Resurrection State?

3. What is Resurrection Power?

THE RESURRECTION AS TRANS- FORMATION (TO BE GLORIFIED)

John wrote that God has made us His Own Children (I Jn. 3:1) and then added (I Jn. 3:2), *"What we will be has not yet been made known.*

"But we do know that when Jesus appears, we shall be like Him."

Paul in I Thessalonians 4:14 provides the broad outline of Resurrection when Jesus returns. He is speaking of the Rapture or the Resurrection, both words referring to the same event.

He spoke of those who had died in the Faith, in other words their soul and spirit going to be with Jesus, and then coming back with Him in the Resurrection. This has to do with that large group receiving a Glorified Body, which will be united with their soul and spirit. Those who are alive at that time will be instantly Glorified, meeting the Lord in the air (I Thess. 4:13-18).

There are more details in I Corinthians Chapter 15. To the questions *"How are the dead raised?"*, and *"With what kind of body will they come?"* (I Cor. 15:35), Paul simply notes that the Resurrection Body will correspond to our present Body, but in contrast it will be imperishable, glorious, infused with power — spiritual rather than natural. It will be in the likeness of Jesus,

through a transformation that will happen *". . . in the twinkling of an eye, at the last Trump."* Then the *". . . dead will be raised incorruptible, and we shall all be changed"* (I Cor. 15:35-52).

THE RESURRECTION STATE

What do we know about the Resurrection State? Very little, according to the Apostles Paul and John.

But many have found it fascinating to observe the capabilities of the Resurrected Jesus and speculate what being *"like Him"* might mean.

For instance, the Resurrected Jesus had *"flesh and bones"* (Lk. 24:39). Why not flesh and blood? It is because *"the life of the flesh is in the blood?"* (Lev. 17:11) and a Resurrected person is infused with a different kind of life!

The Truth is, that whereas the *"blood"* was that which formerly contained the life of the human body, now it will be the Holy Spirit.

Others have noted Jesus' sudden appearance among His Disciples in a locked room (Jn. 20:26). Is this teleportation? Or can a Resurrected person move between the atoms of the physical universe?

While all the questions are not now answered, this we do know. The limitations of our physical nature will then be gone, and whereas we are now perishable, we will then be imperishable. Power will replace weakness, and to such an extent as to be beyond present comprehension. As well, immortality (Eternal Life) will end mortality (death).

WHAT IS RESURRECTION POWER?

This is one of the most exciting of New Testament themes. Paul writes that, *"If the Spirit of Him Who raised Jesus from the dead is living in you, He Who raised Christ from the dead will also give life to your mortal bodies through His Spirit, Who lives in you"* (Rom. 8:11).

The point Paul makes is that the Holy Spirit, the Agent of Jesus' Resurrection, lives within the Believer. This means that Resurrection Power is available to us even in our mortal bodies. Through the Holy Spirit we are raised beyond our human limitations and enabled to live a Righteous Life, and as well, to do the Works of Christ (Jn. 14:12).

Actually, this Doctrine is sometimes overlooked, and certain Biblical Passages are, therefore, misinterpreted.

For instance, in Philippians Chapter 3, Paul is *not* expressing uncertainty about his own Resurrection when he yearns *"somehow, to attain to the Resurrection from the dead"* (Phil. 3:11). The entire sentence reads, *"I want to know Christ and the Power of His Resurrection and the fellowship of sharing in His Sufferings, becoming like Him in His Death, and so, somehow, to attain to the Resurrection from the dead"* (Phil. 3:10-11).

Actually, Paul's thought is focused on the present — living a Resurrection kind of life now — not on Eternity. He is expressing the desire, and even that which he definitely experienced, the Power of Jesus' Resurrection, at work in our lives presently. In other words, the same Power which raised Jesus from the dead, that it work in us now, and which it will, if we *"suffer with Him."*

THE DOCTRINE OF RESURRECTION AND CHANGE

The Greeks thought the soul had permanent existence and thought that it even possibly had renewed life through transmigration (to pass at death from one body or being to another, a form of reincarnation). However, they did not believe that the *"soul"* was the individual's conscious personality. Neither did they believe that this new state was a Resurrection. Resurrection was in fact so foreign to Greek thought as to be considered ridiculous. The idea was, *"Why would anyone want to go through all of this all over again?"* Of course, they had no knowledge of what True Resurrection actually meant.

THE JEWS

In the Jewish world of the First Century, opinion was divided. The Orthodox Pharisees were confident of a Resurrection, but the Sadducees denied the Doctrine. This division was possibly brought about by the lack of clear teaching in the Old Testament concerning this great Doctrine. However, while the teaching was not extensive, it was very clear in what little it did say (Job 14:14; Ps. 17:15; 49:7-20;

NOTES

73:23-26; Isa. 25:8; 26:19; Dan. 12:2).

THE RESURRECTION OF JESUS

It is the New Testament that makes God's Plan for individual human beings clear. There is an eternal destiny, a life beyond this life. Resurrection lies ahead. Jesus' Own Appeals to the Old Testament show evidence sometimes overlooked. But it is the Resurrection of Jesus that is the final proof.

Jesus' Resurrection not only declared Him to be what He claimed to be, the Son of God, but also provided a guarantee for us who believe. Because Jesus lives, we too will live. And we will share His Destiny, which is actually what we are studying in this 17th verse of Romans Chapter 8.

Again, as John said, *"When He appears, we shall be like Him, for we shall see Him as He is"* (I Jn. 3:2) (Richards).

(18) "FOR I RECKON THAT THE SUFFERINGS OF THIS PRESENT TIME ARE NOT WORTHY TO BE COMPARED WITH THE GLORY WHICH SHALL BE REVEALED IN US."

The phrase, *"For I reckon that the sufferings of this present time,"* speaks as we have stated, of the misery and ruin into which man and the Creation are fallen because of man's sin — whether in the world or the Church.

"Reckon" in the Greek is *"logizomai,"* and means *"to compute, to calculate."* The word implies reasoning. *"I judge after calculation made"* (Godet). The word refers to a process of reasoning which results in the arriving at a conclusion (Wuest).

When Paul used the words *"present time,"* he was speaking not only of his particular day, but of a condition which has existed ever since the Fall, and will exist until the Second Coming of the Lord. The Salvation of this world is the Second Coming of the Lord. To be sure, it is not one of several answers, but actually the *only* answer.

The phrase, *"Are not worthy to be compared with the Glory which shall be revealed in us,"* proclaims a comparison.

The future time for which man and the Creation hope, is the promised day of the Coming Resurrection when the Redeemed and the Creation will be delivered from the bondage of mortality and brought into the freedom of immortality. The glory of that future time will bear no relation to the misery of this present time (Williams).

The words *"Shall be revealed in us,"* in the Greek Text carries the idea of *"toward us and upon us."* In other words, it will be a reflected glory, reflected from our Lord in His Glory, that will make the Saints radiant when they return to the Earth with the Lord Jesus at the Second Advent.

THE PILLARS OF SOLOMON'S TEMPLE

An excellent example of this is found in Solomon's Temple of old. The two giant Pillars which stood in front of the Temple were actually there as ornamentation, not really holding up anything as Pillars normally do. As well, they were made of brass (I Ki. 7:13-22).

As is known, brass (copper) tarnishes easily, but when properly polished, presents a high gloss.

Inasmuch as the Temple faced the East, the Sun upon arising over Mt. Olivet would first strike the burnished brass of the two Pillars, creating a dazzling display of light. It is even said, that Traders coming into the City would purposely delay their arrival so they could stand on Olivet and watch the rising Sun as its rays struck the Pillars. It is stated that its beauty at this time was a wonder to behold. Perhaps this is what Jesus was speaking about when He said, *"Him that overcometh will I make a Pillar in the Temple of My God . . ."* (Rev. 3:12).

As the beauty of those Pillars was a reflection of the shining rays of the Sun, likewise, the Glory of the Believer is and shall be, the reflection of the rays of the *Son.*

(19) "FOR THE EARNEST EXPECTATION OF THE CREATURE WAITETH FOR THE MANIFESTATION OF THE SONS OF GOD."

The phrase, *"For the earnest expectation of the creature,"* would have been better translated, *"For the earnest expectation of the Creation."*

"Earnest expectation" in the Greek is *"apokaradokia,"* and means *"a watching with the head erect and outstretched."* Creation speaks of everything, both animate and

NOTES

inanimate (animate refers to that which has conscious life such as human beings and animals, etc., versus inanimate, which speaks of that which does not have conscious life, such as plants, etc.).

The phrase, *"Waiteth for the manifestation of the Sons of God,"* pertains to the Coming Resurrection of Life.

The idea is, that due to the Fall, everything is cursed (Gen. 3:17). Inasmuch, according to Psalm 8 that God had put the entirety of His Creation under the dominion of Adam (man), it seems like the entirety of the Creation, including outer space, etc., also suffered the result of the Fall. Consequently, nothing works as it should work and because of this Curse.

As well, in some mysterious way, even as the Holy Spirit through the Apostle here proclaims, the whole of Creation, both animate and inanimate, waits in suspense for the Coming Resurrection. In other words, it is not functioning as it was originally created, and cannot do so until the Creator returns and makes everything right.

"Waiteth" in the Greek is *"apodechomai,"* and means *"assiduously and patiently to wait for."*

MANIFESTATION

In essence, this tells us that all of Creation is involved in some way in the fortunes of humanity. But this, if Creation be personified, naturally leads to the idea of a mysterious sympathy between the world and man, and this is what the Apostle expresses. He is saying that Creation is not inert, utterly unspiritual, alien to our life and its hopes, but rather, the natural ally of our souls, because of being created by God.

"Manifestation" in the Greek is *"apokalupsis,"* and means *"an uncovering, a laying bare."* That is, the non-rational Creation, subject to the Curse put upon it because of man's sin, is expectantly waiting for the Glorification of the Saints, that it also may be delivered from the Curse under which it now exists. Inasmuch as man was given dominion over all of God's Creation (Ps. 8), then everything was subject to the Curse.

The *"Sons of God"* speaks of all Believers, even as Paul said in Romans 8:14, and are such because of what was done by the Second Adam at Calvary and the Resurrection. The First Adam brought on the Curse, with the Second Adam paying the price for deliverance from the Curse. Soon, the Curse in its totality will be lifted when Jesus returns.

However, this *"Manifestation"* will come in two parts. At the moment of the Resurrection (I Thess. 4:16-17), all Saints who have ever lived will be Glorified at that time. However, inasmuch as Jesus will not return to this Earth at that particular time, total Manifestation will not be brought about. That awaits some 7 years later, which will be after the Great Tribulation which will bring Israel back to God, which will occur at the Second Coming (Zech. Chpts. 13-14; Rev. Chpt. 19). For the *"Manifestation"* to be complete, the Jews must also return to the Lord.

Then the Curse will be lifted totally and completely from all things, with Christ reigning supremely on this Earth and in Person (Isa. 2:1-5; 4:2-6; 9:6-10; 14:1-8; 25:6-12; 26:1-4; 32:1-15; 33:6; 63:1-19).

FALSE!

There is a false teaching concerning the *"Manifestation of the Sons of God,"* which has been around for quite some time. It teaches that this *"Manifestation"* is already taking place, and has actually been enlarged on by the modern error of that which is referred to as *"Kingdom Now."*

Its proponents claim there will be no Rapture, which seems to indicate that they do not quite understand that the Rapture and the Resurrection are one and the same. As well, the idea is in this teaching, that this *"Manifestation"* will be ushered in by political means, with Christians being elected to public office, etc. In fact, a great part of the energy of the Church in the 1990's has gone toward this purpose, and not the real purpose of the Church, which should be World Evangelism — the Preaching of the Gospel to the lost in order to bring them to Christ.

No, this *"Manifestation"* of which Paul speaks, will be carried out at the Resurrection of the Just, and then the Second Coming of the Lord (Dan. 2:34-35).

(20) "FOR THE CREATURE WAS MADE

SUBJECT TO VANITY, NOT WILLINGLY, BUT BY REASON OF HIM WHO HATH SUBJECTED THE SAME IN HOPE,"

The phrase, *"For the creature was made subject to vanity,"* pertains to the fact, and as stated, that inasmuch as God gave Adam dominion over all His Creation, Adam's Fall signaled its Fall. As the Creation *"was made subject"* to Adam, it was also subject to his sin which resulted in a Curse on all things.

"Vanity" in the Greek is *"mataios,"* and means *"idle, resultless, futile, aimless, in other words, empty nothings."* It describes something that does not measure up to that for which it is intended.

Here, the Creation is viewed as originally created, a perfect Creation to Glorify God. When the Curse was put upon it, that purpose was interfered with in that a perishing and decaying Creation cannot perfectly Glorify Him. It was rendered relatively futile in that respect.

As we have stated, in some mysterious way, it senses that it is not fulfilling its intended purpose.

The words *"not willingly"* mean that Creation did not sin, even as such cannot sin, and, therefore, had no part in the reason for the Fall. However, inasmuch as Adam had dominion over all, all fell with him, including the whole of the human family.

In fact, due to the Fall, which has terribly adversely affected all of the Creation, man has absolutely no idea as to what it originally was before the Fall. Considering how beautiful that Creation is presently, which speaks of the animals and plant life, etc., as well as the Heavens, etc., one cannot help but wonder as to exactly how beautiful and glorious it was before the Curse of Sin perverted its true purpose!

However, what the First Adam lost, the Second Adam, The Lord Jesus Christ has Redeemed, with all, at least Believers and the Creation, eagerly awaiting His Return. As the song says:

"Our Lord is coming back to Earth again!"

The phrase, *"But by reason of Him Who hath subjected the same in Hope,"* speaks of God as the One Who passed sentence.

The Expositors say that Paul did not use the grammatical form which would express the direct agency of God, but rather that it was done *"by Him Who hath subjected."* In other words, it was done on account of Him, the idea being, that God had stated that if Adam disobeyed, Judgment would come, which is exactly what happened. It could probably be said to be *"the Law of Sowing and Reaping"* (Gal. 6:7). It was not so much that God directly did the thing (effected the destruction), but rather that He said that it would happen, and in essence, because of certain Laws which He had originally instituted. Consequently, it was Adam's sin and not God's Will directly which was the direct and special cause of the subjection to vanity. The supreme Will of God is thus removed *"to a wider distance from corruption and vanity"* (Alford).

It was on account of Him (God) — His Righteousness might be shown in the punishment of sin — that the sentence fell upon man, carrying consequences which extended to the whole realm intended originally for his dominion.

The words *"in Hope"* state that the sentence of man, however, was not hopeless, and Creation shares in his Hope as in his doom. When the Curse is completely removed from man, as it will be when the Sons of God are revealed, it will pass from Creation also, which will take place in the coming Kingdom Age, and for this, Creation sighs.

Creation was made subject to vanity on the footing of this Hope; the Hope is latent, so to speak, in the constitution of nature as it only can be, and comes out, in its sighing in some manner, to a sympathetic ear, which is actually that of the Lord (Denney).

(21) "BECAUSE THE CREATURE IT-SELF ALSO SHALL BE DELIVERED FROM THE BONDAGE OF CORRUPTION INTO THE GLORIOUS LIBERTY OF THE CHILDREN OF GOD."

The phrase, *"Because the creature itself also shall be delivered,"* presents the direction of this *"Hope."* The Hope is that of the subjected (Creation) not the Subjector (God). Nature possesses in the feeling of her unmerited suffering, a sort of presentment of her future deliverance (Godet).

However, the words *"shall be delivered"* in this phrase, tells us what type of *"Hope"* is here being addressed.

The word *"Hope"* as is normally used presently contains no certitude; however, that of which the Holy Spirit uses through the Apostle, speaks of a guaranteed positive conclusion, but not exactly known when. If one is to notice, Paul did not say *"the creature itself hopes to be delivered,"* but rather, *"shall be delivered,"* which speaks of that which is certain.

The phrase, *"From the bondage of corruption,"* speaks of mortality, i.e., *"death."* *"Corruption"* in the Greek is *"phthora,"* and means *"moral corruption, decay, ruin, depravity, wickedness."* It also speaks of that which is *"perishing and being destroyed,"* which is the application for *"Creation,"* in this case, mostly *"inanimate,"* but can include the *"animate,"* i.e., *"animals, fowls, fish, etc."*

The idea is not that animals will live forever in that coming time, but that they will function as God originally intended, which speaks of their nature being changed to that of docility (Isa. 11:6-9).

The phrase, *"Into the Glorious Liberty of the Children of God,"* expresses the mysterious sympathy which we have mentioned, between the creation and man. When man fell, Creation fell! When man shall be delivered, Creation will be delivered as well, and is expressed in the word *"also."*

"Glorious Liberty" can be translated *"the Liberty of the Glory."* It refers to the Glory of verse 18.

Then Redeemed man will be as he was before the Fall, but with one great difference. Redeemed man will be *"Glorified,"* which is far greater than what Adam previously had. That's the reason it is called *"Glorious."* The idea is, *"When sin abounded, Grace did much more abound"* (Rom. 5:20).

(22) "FOR WE KNOW THAT THE WHOLE CREATION GROANETH AND TRAVAILETH IN PAIN TOGETHER UNTIL NOW."

The phrase, *"For we know that the whole Creation,"* means exactly what it says, every single thing created by God, and all things created were created by Him (Jn. 1:3).

The phrase, *"Groaneth and travaileth in pain together until now,"* refers to the *common longing* of all the elements of the

Creation, not to its longing in common with God's Children (Vincent).

"*Groaneth*" in the Greek is "*sustenazo*," and means "*to experience a common calamity,*" which in this case refers to the Fall.

"*Travaileth*" in the Greek is "*sunodino*," and means "*pangs in company with or simultaneously.*" However, "*travaileth*" is different than "*groaneth,*" in that the "*travail*" carries with it an expectation of relief from suffering.

Even though this does speak of the entirety of the Creation, and is readily understandable concerning the inanimate Creation, and as well of Believers who truly know the Lord and are cognizant of the reason for man's present difficulties; however, it does not explain the unsaved of humanity who make up the far, far greater majority. One might argue that the word "*together*" does not include them; however, it does!

The unsaved "*groaneth,*" but for an entirely different reason. The Believer "*groans*" because he knows the cause of so much suffering (sin) and as well, the only deliverance, which is the Coming of the Lord. The unbeliever "*groans*" under the weight of rebellion against God, and the misery it brings, but never quite knowing the reason why.

The Believer "*travails*" but with the expectation of Deliverance, while the unbeliever does the same — but Deliverance from the wrong source, which in reality, is no Deliverance at all.

(23) "AND NOT ONLY THEY, BUT OURSELVES ALSO, WHICH HAVE THE FIRSTFRUITS OF THE SPIRIT, EVEN WE OURSELVES GROAN WITHIN OURSELVES, WAITING FOR THE ADOPTION, TO WIT, THE REDEMPTION OF OUR BODY."

The phrase, "*And not only they, but ourselves also,*" picks up on Believers, with Paul giving a greater explanation, and for the simple reason that it is Believers only, as we have stated, who know the true state of affairs. Believers know that Jesus is coming, that is if they truly know the Bible, and they know that He is the Answer to all things, hence, all True Believers say with John the Beloved, "*Even so, come, Lord Jesus*" (Rev. 22:20).

The phrase, "*Which have the Firstfruits of the Spirit,*" tells us, that even though

NOTES

Believers have the Holy Spirit, still, all that He can do, and all that He will do, will only be brought about at the Coming Resurrection.

UNIVERSAL SUFFERING

The phrase, "*Even we ourselves groan within ourselves,*" tells us in essence, that all that Jesus paid for and accomplished in the Atonement at Calvary's Cross, has not yet been realized, and will not be fully realized until the Resurrection. Believers, while in the body, are not yet exempt from our share in the universal groaning. In effect, Believers presently have "*the earnest of the Spirit*" (II Cor. 1:22), which means a down payment of all that He will yet do. As well, we now only have "*the earnest of our inheritance*" (Eph. 1:14), which speaks only of a part payment, with the full payment yet to come.

This answers many questions, or at least it should, concerning the reason for much Christian suffering. Unfortunately, some modern Bible Teachers have attempted to consider all present suffering and difficulties, as a lack of Faith. While a lack of Faith definitely does play a part in many things concerning Believers, still, no amount of Faith can bring the Blessing of the Coming Resurrection into the present.

The phrase, "*Waiting for the adoption,*" in essence could be translated, "*Waiting for the fulfillment of the process which adoption into the Family of God guarantees.*"

The phrase, "*To wit, the Redemption of our body,*" proclaims that (the Body) which has not yet been Redeemed.

The link which unites the Believer with the suffering Creation is his body. Because of sin it is subjected to pain, decay, and death. This connection with the Creation brings into conscious suffering the heart that is indwelt by the Love of Christ. It is the suffering of sympathy. The sense of the pain and evil that encompass the Creation oppresses him; and the more conscious he is of the indwelling warmth and liberty and power of the Divine Nature, which is Love, the more is he sensible of the weight of the misery introduced into the Creation by sin.

Thus, the Believer is united to the Creation by his physical body and to Heaven by the Spirit; and the sympathy which he feels for the suffering Creation is a Divine sympathy.

God, because of man's sin, subjected the Creation to death, even as verse 20 proclaims, but He did so in Hope. He looks forward to its recovery when man shall be fully Redeemed (Williams).

IS HEALING IN THE ATONEMENT?

This question has been heatedly argued I suppose almost from the time that Jesus died on Calvary.

The word *"Atonement"* means *"a making at one"* and points to a process of bringing those who are estranged into a unity. Its use in theology is to denote the Work of Christ in dealing with the problem posed by the sin of man, and in bringing sinners into right relation with God, which was done at Calvary's Cross.

In this, Jesus dealt with the sin question and all its effects. That means that the terrible sin debt was paid, with it no longer held against man, at least those who believe in Christ (Jn. 3:16).

In dealing with the sin question, which Jesus did in totality by offering up His pure, spotless, sinless Body as a Sin-Offering at Calvary, He settled the sin question and its effects once and for all (Isa. Chpt. 53). The effects speak of sickness, poverty, ignorance, and slavery. So, that means that Healing is definitely in the Atonement as well as prosperity, etc.

That means, that it is the Will of God, and *always* the Will of God to save from all sin, heal from all sickness, redeem from all poverty, deliver from all bondage and spiritually educate from all ignorance.

And yet we know, that despite this great thing which Jesus did at Calvary, Christians at times still sin, the sick are not always healed, prosperity is not the offing for all, and at times some spiritual bondages are not broken, at least not quickly, etc.

Why?

The answer is obvious. Even as Paul has so plainly said, Believers presently only have the *"Firstfruits of the Spirit,"* which means that all that Jesus did at Calvary has not yet come to the Believer, and in fact, will not come in totality until the Coming Resurrection. However, that doesn't mean that

Believers should live in a type of spiritual apathy of *"whatever will be, will be."* Many things can now be changed, and are in fact changed constantly, by Believers believing God, having Faith in Who He is and What He can do. So the Believer is to believe God for whatever is needed, irrespective that we now only have the *"Firstfruits."* But yet at the same time, Preachers should not claim that the failure or lack of one hundred percent of all of these things can be explained by a lack of Faith. That, as should be painfully obvious, is unscriptural!

THE MODERN FAITH MESSAGE

The following material has been previously printed in our Commentary on Daniel but due to the manner in which Commentaries are normally studied, and the significance of this subject, I have felt it proper to reprint this article at this time. As well, there is some repetition in the material, but which we think is necessary in order to properly develop the correct emphasis.

I feel like there are many elements in the modern Faith Teaching which are positive. Much of it is wholesome, edifying, and needful. Emphasizing Faith certainly does tend to elevate victorious Christian living, and this is definitely essential within the Body of Christ. If the *"Faith Teaching"* stopped there, it would be of untold value to the Work of God — but regrettably, much of it does not stop there. Sad to say, because of error, many individuals participating in this teaching have not been led to Victory but defeat, and complete defeat at that!

To the unlearned — those unfamiliar with the Word of God — it sounds logical, Scriptural, and inviting. This, of course, is why it ensnares so many people. Much error rides into the Church on the back of Truth.

The following lists some of the errors which I believe permeate the modern Faith Teaching. They are:

BIBLIOLATRY

Words of Scripture seem to be deified — apart from the Living God — and collected into various *"Laws"* which activate the forces of good and evil. Anyone who questions the specific interpretations is immediately branded as *"denying the Word of God and its Power."*

One could say that the sin of *"Bibliolatry"* is committed. This occurs when one makes an idol of the Bible or has excessive reverence for the letter of the Bible, in this case, claiming that certain Passages bring certain forces into play, etc.

As such, the Bible itself, apart from Christ, is looked at as the Source. This is idolatry just as surely as is the bowing down to heathenistic idols. However, it is very subtle and, therefore, far more dangerous because of its religious context.

KNOWLEDGE

Knowledge is said to be the way to achieve a Divine place in Creation. Attainment of *"a new-creature status for the Believer"* makes them part of a superior, elite, or master race, they teach.

This fits right in with the *"political message"* in the Christianizing of the culture and ultimately leading the world into the Millennium.

Just as with the ancient error of old, called *"Gnosticism,"* a superior knowledge is claimed! Consequently, whether the advocates realize it or not, *"knowledge"* becomes the way to Salvation instead of Christ.

CONFESSION

The Confession Principle is strictly adhered to, which teaches that the use of Scriptural formulas to *"confess"* results releases the forces of good on one's behalf.

And again, whether they realize it or not, the advocates of the Confession Principle are taking control out of the Hands of the Lord and placing it into their own hands.

In other words, they automatically conclude that they know the Will of God in any and all circumstances, which of course is untrue. The conclusion of that is to ultimately attempt to use the Word of God against God, which of course, the Lord will never allow to be done.

For instance, when the three Hebrew Children were facing the fiery furnace, they exclaimed that the Lord was able to deliver them. However, they went on to say, *"But if not, be it known unto thee, O King, that we*

NOTES

will not serve thy gods, nor worship the Golden Image which thou hast set up" (Dan. 3:17-18).

"But if not," would have been considered a bad confession by the so-called Faith people, but God did not call it such.

LAW

They teach that sin is a consequence of the Law, which disappeared with the New Covenant, and that confession of sin becomes a false perception because behavior is made right (they say) by confessing *"who one is in Christ Jesus."* Repentance then plays no part in our present-day experience, in their thinking, because it relates to sin — which ended with the Law.

As a result of this teaching, any Preaching that convicts of sin is called condemnation and is rejected out of hand. Actually, they little believe in Holy Spirit conviction, claiming that it represents a throwback to condemnation which ended with the abolishment of the Law (Law of Moses).

Any confession of sin is pretty much denied because it is a *"wrong confession"* of who one is in Christ. As a result, one of the great Office Works of the Holy Spirit — His convicting of *"sin, and of Righteousness, and of Judgment"* — is denied or erroneously interpreted (Jn. 16:8-11).

For instance, they claim that this pertains only to the *"world"* and not to the Believer. However, the word *"world"* simply means that it applies not only to the Jews, but also to Gentiles, in other words, to all people. John also said, *"And He is the Propitiation for our sins: and not for ours only, but also for the sins of the whole world"* (I Jn. 2:2).

Basically, this teaching claims that sin, conviction of the Holy Spirit, Repentance, etc., belong to the Old Covenant (Law) and have no validity under the New Covenant. Therefore, they have an erroneous conception of what sin is and its cure, which is Christ.

SIN NATURE

They basically deny human nature, claiming that the Christian is either Divine or Satanic, which is dualism. In other words, they deny *"the Sin Nature"* which goes along with their erroneous understanding of

"New Creationism."

Consequently, the struggle between the *"flesh"* and the *"Spirit,"* which characterizes the life of every Christian, is pretty much denied as well! *"How can there be a struggle if one is a 'New Creation?',"* they claim.

In answer to that theory, John the Beloved wrote, *"If we say that we have no sin* (Sin Nature), *we deceive ourselves, and the Truth is not in us"* (I Jn. 1:8).

SCIENTISM

Much modern Faith Teaching espouses a form of Scientism, teaching that *"Law"* and *"Formulas"* can control circumstances around us.

This harks back to point one, *"the deification of Scripture,"* and points to, *"the superior knowledge."*

SUFFERING

They deny, pretty much, Christian suffering in the bearing of the Cross of Christ, claiming that the Cross is in the position of *"past miseries."*

The Cross of Christ is little looked at as a Source of Victory, being replaced by *"proper confession."* In their idea, the Cross, even though necessary in its place, plays no part in our modern Victory. The Victory, they claim, is attained by the Resurrection.

Consequently, any and all songs about the Blood of Christ or the Cross are labeled as *"elementary"* and have little place in *"New Creationism."*

They show a lack of knowledge of the Atonement of Christ and what was accomplished both at Calvary as the Source and Key to all present Victory. In effect, this is the most dangerous part of their teaching because anything that demeans Calvary in any way or relegates it to a secondary position, is tantamount to spiritual suicide.

While it is certainly true that Calvary would have been of no effect without the Resurrection, it was not the Resurrection that Redeemed man from sin and all its consequences, but Calvary. This is the reason that Paul said, *"For I determined not to know any thing among you, save Jesus Christ, and Him Crucified"* (I Cor. 2:2).

Paul, who was no doubt the greatest

NOTES

Bible Scholar of his day, made this statement for purpose and reason: A. That which Paul said about Calvary was what the Holy Spirit demanded; and, B. By experience, Paul knew that Jesus satisfied the Sin Debt at Calvary, and as well, there broke the power of the dominion of sin in the heart and life of the Believer.

As one Godly Preacher has said, *"When the Church goes beyond Calvary, it has backslidden."* He meant that everything comes through Calvary: Salvation, the Baptism with the Holy Spirit, Divine Healing, Miracles, Overcoming Victory, Answered Prayer, Eternal Life, etc.

As stated, whether the present-day Faith Teachers realize it or not, their interpretation of the Atonement is not consistent with the tenor of teaching throughout the Word of God. This lies at the very heart of this teaching, and it strikes at the very core of Christian belief.

SCRIPTURE

One of the basic teachings of this element is that all Scripture is not the same. In other words, some Scriptures pertain particularly to those who are still in the realm of the *"senses* (flesh)"* — those who are sadly unenlightened.

Some of them even go so far as to say that the Apostle Paul demonstrated great lack of enlightenment in many of his experiences. I Corinthians Chapter 4 is considered an example of this. Actually, they say the same thing concerning all the Apostles in the days of the Early Church.

In other words, these Teachers say that if the Apostles of old had the knowledge that we posses today, they would not have been required to suffer many of the difficulties which they experienced.

In practice, only certain Scriptures are used by the Faith Teachers to support their contentions. Their basic difficulty with the Word of God is that they separate the Word from the Person of the Lord Jesus Christ. In short, they have replaced God with their chosen Scriptures, rationalizing that this will justify their actions. Consequently, certain Words of Scripture are deified — apart from the Living God — and exalted into various

"Laws" which bring the forces of good and evil as stated, into action.

They call themselves for the most part *"Word"* people, constantly quoting particular Scriptures, thereby, convincing the public that they are very Scriptural and very Spiritual — thus making their contentions trustworthy.

In Truth, they actually deny parts of the Bible as Revelation not illuminated with a higher knowledge.

THE OLD TESTAMENT

Even though they call themselves *"Word"* people, they rely on only a few selected Scriptural Texts, actually taking them out of Scriptural context. Consequently, they have very little respect for the Old Testament, seemingly suggesting that since Old Testament Personalities did not have the Written Word (or at least very much of it), they did not know very much. As a result, *"Word"* people basically only use isolated Texts from the Old Testament in their teaching. They seem to completely ignore the fact that the entire framework of New Testament context (thought) is derived from Old Testament Revelation.

Actually, one cannot arrive at a proper understanding of the New Testament unless he has a proper understanding of the Old Testament.

Years ago, I heard a Preacher make the statement that some individuals today worship the Bible apart from God Who inspired it. At first his statement puzzled me, but after some thought, I feel like I understand what he was saying.

Basically, he was suggesting, to which we have already alluded, that certain Scriptures, such as Mark 11:24 or John 15:7, etc., are taken out of context, used in some manner as a type of magic talisman (good luck piece).

In other words, he was saying that particular Scriptures are taken completely out of context and used to deal with situations, even though they have almost nothing to do with the present difficulty at hand. These Scriptures are quoted over and over again, with the individual using them as a sort of club to force God or circumstances to line up with the person's reasoning.

Also, many of them insist that Scriptures that do not line up with their way of teaching are just simply not relevant today. Again, we emphasize that they contend that if individuals such as the Apostle Paul had had their Scriptural knowledge, he would not have had to suffer persecution and trials.

They go on to tout their experience in the Word, meaning that they are more *"developed"* than the Apostles of old.

In Truth, most of these Teachers know very little about correct exegesis (interpretation) of Scripture — all the while proclaiming themselves to be *"Word"* people.

SUPERIORITY

As well, there is an air of superiority about these Teachers, their teaching, and their followers. They are the *"New Creation people."* They have *"the knowledge."*

Of course, even with a superficial investigation, this is absolutely opposed to the teachings of the Lord Jesus Christ. Humility was the Master's great hallmark. One of His last acts on Earth was the washing of the Disciples' feet. Superiority and lack of humility are always of Satan; these never come from God. They reveal the worldling, the ego of man, Believers in the so-called *"master race."*

They teach that one will continue to be a part of the *"master race"* unless one slips into using information from the *"sense world"* around them.

As a member of this superior mold (or master race), one is made to feel that he is entitled to all types of riches and rewards; hence, the Hundredfold Return Gospel. These Teachers do not seem to realize that to demand a hundredfold return from God on our investment is to again turn the Temple of God into a den of thieves, which is pretty well what it has become, at least in many circles.

THE PROSPERITY MESSAGE

Basically, the so-called Hundredfold Return Gospel intertwined with a master-race theory has little or nothing to do with the Love of God. It has little or nothing to do with the desire to promote God's Cause or to give to Him simply because we Love Him.

At best it is an investment or a gamble. At worse, it is a deception perpetrated by Satan. At its core, it is little better than the Las Vegas practice of enticing people into gambling casinos with the selfish lure of *"something for nothing."*

This is the *"Prosperity Message"* so prevalent today.

These Teachers hold the thought before their followers that their Faith (or knowledge) will deliver anything they desire. Consequently, they must drive the largest cars, live in the finest houses, wear the best clothes, the best jewelry, and so forth. This is an image they must maintain. It is somehow supposed to demonstrate their Faith. They are, in effect, role models for their followers.

As a result of this practice, the followers tend to look to the make of car, style of clothes, etc., as the mark of an individual's (or Teacher's) Faith.

Some time ago I heard one of their Preachers preach on the subject of *"K-Mart Faith."* His contention was, that any Christian who shopped at such a place evidently had little Faith.

To be frank, I did not hear the entire Message, because such drivel is so insulting to even elementary Scriptural intelligence, that one can only stand so much.

CO-DIVINITY

This teaching claims that man is basically victorious through his knowledge rather than through Christ. It elevates him beyond his basic position as merely mortal. He, in essence, becomes co-divinity with his Creator, or, in other words, a little Jesus.

This satisfies two perverted needs in fallen mankind:

1. The need to be one's own god, in control of all life.

2. The need to glorify oneself beyond one's proper place in Creation, which is what caused the Fall in the Garden of Eden to begin with.

These Teachers frequently use words like *"dummies"* or *"idiots"* to characterize those who do not believe in their particular way. This, of course, is a demonstration of one of man's basic problems today — ego. Man wants to *"play God."* In actuality, he wants

NOTES

to *"be God."* This is (and always was) Satan's problem too, and he has inoculated mankind with his desire for God/man equality.

Satan tempted Christ to misuse the Knowledge and Power of God when he suggested that Jesus create bread out of stones. The Lord gave Satan the correct reply, but this same desire — to misuse knowledge — is prevalent today.

They suggest, as stated, that there was a basic lack of knowledge of the laws of Healing and Salvation until Paul's time. Consequently, Old Testament Saints (according to these Teachers) underwent many unnecessary difficulties because of this lack of knowledge. Of course, this is absurd, but it is their excuse for any Scripture which conflicts with their misguided teaching.

Actually, there is a tendency to emphasize knowledge rather than Salvation. It is as though one becomes Saved, then becomes more Saved as his knowledge increases. It comes very close to ignoring the Blood Atonement of the Lord Jesus Christ, and actually does in some cases.

THE WILL OF GOD AND THE WORD OF GOD

In their deification of superior knowledge, they seem to have lost the realization that True Christian Belief is that the Will of the Father and the Words of the Bible are in perfect conformity; they give life to us as we move in the Knowledge of God according to the leading of the Holy Spirit, not in the bondage of a written formula that is separated and apart from our Living Saviour.

When God's Written Word is apart from His Person, a Scriptural Code of Law is developed. As with any Code of Law, legalism must develop — and with it the resultant condemnation whenever the Believer fails to keep one or several of the Laws.

If one would notice, Faith Teachers are often heard to say, *"It was your Faith that failed. God can never fail."* Consequently, the Believer becomes the one following the formula of Faith to its maximum and taking the blame for any ensuing failure. According to them, the *"Faith Law"* or *"formula"* always works! The only possibility of failure, therefore, lies in our Faith as revealed in our confession of the words or formulas.

In view of this, they say we should lean on our knowledge which will then control all circumstances around us. These Laws, or formulas, by their actions, are impersonal and divorced from any relationship except that of their mechanical performance.

By and large, as stated, this knowledge removes the control from God and His Will to an exercise of our will, using the formula (or Law). The line between God and man blurs, and man suddenly seems to become a Law unto himself. Of course, this totally ignores the fact that Jesus, although He was the Very Son of God, totally submitted Himself to the Will of the Father. It would seem prudent for us to do likewise!

KNOWLEDGE SALVATION

This *"Knowledge Salvation"* imposes a great burden on the Believer. He mustn't under any circumstances *"lose his confession."* If he does, all the results of the forces put into motion with the confession will be lost. One of their Teachers said, *"Action on the Written Word of God brings God onto the scene."*

It would seem from this teaching that God is automatically stirred into action by repetition of certain Words of Scripture. Consequently, the Believer acts solely upon the substance of his own Faith world — guided by specific Laws, confessions, and formulas.

THE LAW OF CONFESSION

Following hard on the heels of *"knowledge"* is *"confession."* Confession constitutes a major element in this so-called Faith Ministry.

Scriptural formulas confessing results into existence, thereby, releasing benevolent forces on our behalf, constitute a major force in this gospel. Their *"Law of Confession"* is a routine quoting of certain Scriptures. The Word of God is seen as a self-energizing entity — a deity within itself.

Specific Scriptures are utilized out of context most of the time, completely ignoring all related Scriptures addressing the same principles, which of course, is a violation of proper Scriptural interpretation.

By using these isolated Scriptures, God is

supposedly obligated to perform certain actions. The verbalized confession becomes the total force.

Of course, within this system the burden on the individual becomes almost too great to bear. Above all, he must not lose his confession; he must not weaken his confession; he must not err in his confession. No matter what happens, he is compelled to ignore reality and to maintain his confession.

As a result, sick people are prayed for and automatically declared healed.

Why?

Once the confession has been made, and because certain specific Passages of Scripture have been applied to their sickness, it is impossible for them not to be healed! In their thinking, the Word of God (which again has become a deity within itself) has been imprisoned within their Laws and the individual has to be healed.

In these matters, the Will of God, as well as all related circumstances, are totally ignored. The unfortunate individuals who find themselves under these Teachers are at times instructed not to see a doctor since this would counteract their positive confession, with the consequent loss of their healing. The sad fact is that some have actually died by observing this dangerous and hurtful teaching.

JESUS AND THE WORD

As stated, the Word of God is basically removed from the Person of the Lord Jesus Christ. Individuals are told they can do anything Jesus did — if they have the right type of knowledge, believe correctly, and have the right confession; they can have anything they confess. They are told that the Believer, infused with a new kind of nature (the new knowledge), can speak (even as God spoke) worlds into existence. This type of teaching is often termed *"the God-kind of Faith."*

Too often, this teaching basically denies the effect of sickness, death, trials, and problems in their lives when these problems are present. They seem to feel that they have the power to release *"forces of good"* as a consequence of their knowledge and confession. As such, they have little compassion for those who are sick or who suffer from trials or difficulties. They simply state with a cold, scientific logic, *"You are suffering because you have refused to know your place in Christ* (superior knowledge)."

They also say that if you pray according to God's Written Word and follow His Instructions, you will always get results. If you miss it (they say), it is your Faith that failed, not God.

They imply somewhat that prayer, in the sense of need, is the enemy of confession. They say that such prayer asks for help without denying that the circumstances exist; in other words, it is the opposite of confession. They suggest that rather than praying, we confess the answer, because in confessing the answer, we repeat the magic formula causing the negative factors to disappear.

PRAYER

They further imply that prayer (asking God for help) is a sign of weakness and dependence, so we should religiously avoid this type of praying. Instead, they say we should confess our position in Christ because confession has the ready answer, and all we really have to do is begin confessing.

In view of this, we are instructed not to pray as one normally would, since prayer, as indulged by most Christians, is really an enemy of Faith, they say. Prayer is talked about, but in reality there is very little praying in these circles, with what they refer to as prayer little more than words twisted to conform to the principle of confession.

Once again, the veil of condemnation falls heavily on the shoulders of the Believer. He is told that he can govern the circumstances around himself, using only the Written Word of God. He can use this as a club to force God into a particular position or at least as a magic talisman (good luck charm) that will banish all problems.

Trusting Believers are further told that results probably will not happen overnight just because we *"confess"* certain things once or twice. In other words, we must keep saying them over and over again and keep believing them.

Once again, the responsibility of the results falls entirely on the individual. Consequently, the individual is the one who is glorified if and when results occur. The Name

of God and His Word are spoken of constantly and are *"used"* continuously. But, in actuality, it is the individual who is glorified, and God receives very little of the praise. They even tell us that these are the same principles *"used"* by Jesus.

The Believer, as stated, is discouraged from the usual manner of praying since this would require him to repeat the problem allowed for all to hear. (This amounts to an acknowledgment of the problem which is a bad confession, they say!) Some insist that praying for help implies that God has left something undone, that Redemption is incomplete. Within this teaching nothing is considered incomplete.

REPENTANCE AND FORGIVENESS

We are even told, at least by some of these Teachers, that the prayer of Repentance and Forgiveness is not for the modern-day Saint and that no Christian should ever confess sin as one generally does. Some teach that a confession of sin should be replaced by a confession of who the Believer is — a New Creation in Christ. This is somehow supposed to erase the slip into sin consciousness.

If one would notice, these Preachers or Teachers seldom preach against any kind of sin. There is little said about it because (they say) it will cause people to have a *"sin consciousness."* As stated, and because it is so very important, we repeat it, they really do not believe in Holy Spirit Conviction either. They suggest that conviction is really condemnation, which completely ignores John 16:7-11.

Consequently, they pay lip service to getting people Saved, but to that effort devote little energy. Their brief, mechanical Altar Calls, if any at all, are little more than passing efforts. Their entire Movement depends on someone else winning souls to God. Only then do they come on the scene to elevate these to new levels of knowledge. As such, their teaching must be viewed as parasitical. In other words, if there were not true Preachers of the Gospel bringing people to Christ, the so-called modern Faith Teaching, would ultimately, simply disappear, simply because they bring precious few to Christ themselves.

As a result, they have very little regard for

World Evangelism, at least as we think of such, except in limited settings. This is not surprising in that their teaching of *"higher knowledge"* does not appeal too readily to many people in many parts of the world.

They do, however, mention *"thousands Saved."* This fits in with their confession concept. Even though there are few, if any, outward results, they tend to confess great results.

They also imply that the Believer no longer really needs God's Grace, but is himself invested with the ability to do what is necessary in life. Hence, one hears a great deal about the ability of God in the Believer. In other words, the Believer becomes something of a free agent or a franchisee, doing all sorts of great things.

PRESUMPTION

When this is carried to its final conclusion, it completely ignores the Will of God, falling into the err of presumption and leaving the Believer out of God's Will, exercising, instead, his own judgment and will which is the ultimate sin. He will then commit Satan's sin of using God's Word against His (God's) Purposes. Individuals are told to confess anything into existence — from Cadillacs to Resurrection — completely ignoring the Will of God in the matter. This is their *"right"* in their *"new knowledge in Christ Jesus,"* they say!

As we have previously stated, they basically deny the *"Sin Nature,"* teaching that one cannot have a human nature and a Godly Nature at the same time. One is either totally Divine or totally Satanic, never just human.

We are told that man is either operating totally in the *"flesh"* realm (the world of the senses) or in the spiritual realm. Therefore, they would convince us that sickness is purely spiritual in origin and must be healed on that level alone, instead of the physical level as well!

Consequently, they sometimes say that sickness is aligned with the sinful state of the ill person. It is always a spiritual problem (they say).

In view of all this, those adhering to this philosophy (and it is a philosophy; it is not the Gospel), do not feel that Christians truly

undergo trials and/or testings. If an individual appears to undergo such, then that person is operating, they say, in the realm of the senses, or the flesh realm — the world of carnality or of Satan.

I don't know in what state they would have placed the Apostle Paul, unless they claim, as some actually have, that if Paul had had their type of Faith, he would not have had so many problems and difficulties.

They equate any individual living completely free from all difficulties or problems as operating in the world of the Divine, which is God. It is always one or the other.

The individual is never just *"human"*; consequently, they would seldom say that they are *"tired"* or *"discouraged,"* etc. Converts are told never to confess any type of sickness. If they have a cold, they are to say (by Faith) that they do not have a cold because confessing something of this nature would indicate humanity. They, as they tell it, do not operate in the realm of the senses; they operate on a higher plane.

Anyone who prays, admitting total dependency on God, is filled with flaws and inconsistencies. To pray for God's Help would be considered foolish by these people. They simply do not have flaws or inconsistencies. They have already arrived at a state of co-Divinity with God.

PRIDE

These Teachers seem blind to man's basic human nature and thereby appeal to man's pride. They do not seem to realize, or will not admit, that we are actually poor, undeserving creatures desperately in need of God's Help, and, due to the Fall, we were born spiritually incomplete and inadequate, needing a Redeemer.

They do not seem to know or realize that only Jesus Christ is acceptable to God as our Saviour and Redeemer and that our relationship to God is according to our relationship with Christ, not some type of *"superior knowledge."*

They also tend to forget that when we are Saved (Born Again), our humanity does not cease. They ignore the fact that we still possess the flaws and inconsistencies of humans and, thereby, continue to fall short of the

Glory of God, and only God's Grace and Mercy — through Jesus Christ — allow us to enter into the Presence of God. They lose sight of the fact that within ourselves we are unworthy and, therefore, totally dependent upon the Lord for His Mercy and His Grace.

AN IMPROPER KNOWLEDGE OF THE CROSS OF CHRIST

This teaching, as stated, has an incomplete or faulty knowledge of the Cross of Jesus Christ. They basically teach that Jesus Christ became a partaker of the Satanic nature on the Cross. In other words, they suggest that He became identified with Satan. They claim He could not have died physically without first dying spiritually.

They seem to say, concerning the mortality of the Body of Christ, that His Death on the Cross was proof that He had ceased being the Son of God. They have a complete misconception of the Incarnation of Christ as the Perfect Sacrifice (a Sin-Offering).

Whether they realize it or not, they are teaching that Jesus was both Divine and Satanic, but not at the same time. In their view, He was Divine while in His Earthly Ministry but became sinful while on the Cross as He took our sins upon Himself.

The logical extension of their philosophy is that when Jesus took our sins upon Himself on the Cross, He became Personally in need of Redemption because of those sins. In short, because of this, they say, He died spiritually, went to Hell (the burning side), and as a result had to be Born Again exactly as we have to be Born Again presently.

They flaunt the Scripture which says He was the Firstborn of many creatures, and they distort this to suggest that He was Born Again (in the sense of a spiritual birth). They seem to ignore the fact that this refers to a physical birth, not a spiritual birth (Rom. 8:29).

GNOSTICISM

Irenaeus, the ancient Teacher who so strongly refuted Gnosticism (superior knowledge) which is so similar in many respects to the modern Faith Teaching, said, *"No creed is so blasphemous as theirs . . . , cutting off and dividing Jesus from Christ, Christ from*

Saviour, Saviour from Word, and Word from Only Begotten."

These Teachers claim that Jesus took on our Satanic flesh on the Cross and then died. They use the Scriptural reference of II Corinthians 5:21, completely pulling it out of context. They imply that the Cross is the place of the spiritual death of Jesus in addition to His physical death.

In Truth, this borders on blasphemy. It would seem that the Power and Forgiveness provided in the Atonement of the Lord Jesus Christ is lost to them, rejecting as they do their need for anything beyond knowledge.

One has the feeling that they come close to repudiating Calvary, consequently, making light of such songs as *"The Old Rugged Cross,"* etc. This type of song is looked at by them with disdain. They protest that they do not want to identify with the Death of the Lord Jesus Christ, only His Resurrection. One cannot help but conclude that they do not feel they have to go through Repentance and the Cross. As stated, it is ignored and treated as *"past miseries."*

Whether they realize it or not, such teaching also denies their Salvation.

The Truth is, as the Apostle Paul said in Galatians 6:14, *"But God forbid that I should glory, save in the Cross of our Lord Jesus Christ, by Whom the world is crucified unto Me, and I unto the world."*

Perhaps this error is merely Scriptural ignorance. However, the fact that one is not aware of error does not make the error any less destructive.

A GREAT LURE

Tragically, this teaching, because of its promise of worldly riches, holds out an exciting lure and attracts many followers. It attracts many because most Christians, sad to say, do not have the firm foundation they should have in the Word of God. Consequently, they are easy prey for this type of teaching. As stated, it has a powerful attraction!

The promise of instant riches appeals to the selfishness and greed in most people's hearts — even Christians. However, the only one getting rich is the Preacher or Teacher!

Because this teaching is covered with Scripture, although twisted and taken out of context, it has the apparent blessing of the Word of God. With these twin appeals, money and self-gratification, it exerts great allure. Individuals are promised instant health and wealth — and this is a heady gospel.

"Miracles" and *"Healings"* are spoken of constantly when, in reality, there are few Miracles, if any, and precious few Healings. Trusting followers are led to believe that God is continually speaking to these teachers. While it is certainly true that God definitely does speak to His people, still, the regularity and instant communication claimed by these individuals places the Teacher or Preacher in some type of spiritual atmosphere far above the lowly crowd.

FAITH?

As such, stupendous statements and claims are made — statements and claims having no documentation in fact. By *"Faith,"* great numbers are announced as being Saved. Miracles are tossed about as common occurrences, but with little basic substance or fact backing them up. Carelessness with facts becomes rampant — all under the guise of *"Faith."* The followers, often knowing little of the Word of God, are lulled into deception by eagerly accepting what really does not exist.

It sounds so Scriptural to the unknowing ear and eye! It sounds so plausible! It appears to be the dream of man, the answer to the cry of those desiring Victory within their lives. And there is some Truth, as we stated earlier, in what they teach.

This, of course, is what makes the error so much more difficult to recognize. Error surrounded by Truth finds it easy to entrap the unwary in its reaches.

Jesus told us we must judge a tree by the fruit it bears (Mat. 12:33; Lk. 6:43). For a moment, let us look at the *"fruit"* of the *"Faith Ministry"*:

1. Very little priority is placed on winning souls to Christ. Principle emphasis is placed on Money, Healings, Miracles, Faith, Knowledge, etc. Very little concern is demonstrated for the very core of True Christian Faith — the Salvation of the lost.

2. The taking of the Gospel of Jesus Christ to a lost world is little heeded. Consequently,

NOTES

areas of the world that cannot give a monetary return are, for the most part, ignored! This, within itself, is a complete denial of the Great Commission and actually denies the Last Words left by Christ before His Ascension (Mk. 16:15-20).

3. This teaching will not lead to Victory in the hearts and lives of any individuals because it is not Scriptural. In all cases, if followed to its conclusion, it will lead instead to future difficulties. People are promised all sorts of physical and material rewards, but very few of these promises ever materialize.

Consequently, the Believer is led to expect many things that God has never promised. Then when the expectant results fail to materialize, the individual ends up disappointed, at the least, and embittered, at the worst.

IT JUST DOESN'T WORK

When real tragedy befalls, as it does in many lives, this teaching of *"laws"* and *"formulas"* is applied, but to the Believer's dismay, they just don't work. The Believers have been promised that these are God's Laws, while in actuality they are nothing more than man's Laws.

It is in this way that many, due to this teaching, have abandoned their walk with God and become embittered. They end up denying God, His Work, His Church, and all that real Salvation comprises — all because they believed with all their hearts a premise built on a foundation of sand. The spiritual shores are littered with the wrecks of these hapless individuals. They placed their all in a false doctrine, but instead of gaining all, they lost all.

Sadly, these victims are ignored. There is no compassion for *"Faith drop-outs."* They are dismissed with a flippant *"they missed it"* and brushed aside like so much debris because there is always a fresh crop of gullible Believers to take their place.

In closing, I must echo the Words of Christ:

"... Except a corn of wheat fall into the ground and die, it abideth alone: but if it die, it bringeth forth much fruit.

"He that loveth his life shall lose it; and he that hateth his life in this world shall keep

it unto life eternal.

"If any man serve Me, let him follow Me; and where I am, there shall also My servant be: if any man serve Me, him will My Father honor" (Jn. 12:24-26).

(24) "FOR WE ARE SAVED BY HOPE: BUT HOPE THAT IS SEEN IS NOT HOPE: FOR WHAT A MAN SEETH, WHY DOTH HE YET HOPE FOR?"

The phrase, *"For we are Saved by Hope,"* refers to three things:

1. We have been Saved, we are being Saved, and we shall be Saved. This statement has to do with several things but primarily the fact that we must continue to trust and believe. Paul's statement completely refutes the unscriptural doctrine of Unconditional Eternal Security, which teaches that once a person is truly Saved, they cannot lose their Salvation irrespective of what they may do or not do. In other words, the Grace of God is taken to the extreme.

2. As we have stated, *"Hope"* is a guarantee of something which is coming to pass in the future, but not known exactly as to when.

3. The word *"Hope"* as used here, tells us that the greater part of our Salvation is yet future. We have now been Sanctified and we have been Justified; however, we have not yet been Glorified. That great event will take place at the Coming Resurrection, when we will then realize the totality of what Jesus did in the Atonement at Calvary's Cross (I Cor. 6:11).

The phrase, *"But Hope that is seen is not Hope,"* proclaims in another way the great Truth that all Salvation affords is not yet given unto the Believer. In fact, as far as the natural is concerned, we have not seen and neither can we see, at least at the present, that which is yet to come, except by Faith. This statement completely refutes the erroneous doctrine which claims that Christianity is going to gradually take over the world by political means, and has already made great strides in this direction, with some even claiming that we are now living in the Millennium.

False doctrines arise because of three things: A. Ignorance of the Word of God; B. Knowledge of the Word, but unbelief regarding what it says; and, C. Misinterpreting the

NOTES

Word because of pride.

Anyone who would read these Scriptures and draw such a political conclusion, obviously cannot understand simple language. The Truth is, that the Believer has not even remotely seen all of that which is yet to come (I Cor. 2:9).

The question, *"For what a man seeth, why doth he yet Hope for?"*, in effect tells us bluntly that what is coming is so far beyond that which is here at the present, as to be no comparison. Hope is the absolute conviction and assured expectation. Such Hope saves from depression and animates the heart. It is the Hope of verses 19 and 23 (Williams).

(25) "BUT IF WE HOPE FOR THAT WE SEE NOT, THEN DO WE WITH PATIENCE WAIT FOR IT."

The phrase, *"But if we Hope for that we see not,"* plainly tells us again that all that Salvation affords is not yet here. This speaks of the Believer and the great change that is coming respecting the physical body. It also speaks of the entirety of Creation, how it will be changed back to that which it originally was when first created by God before the Fall. In other words, a Restoration of all things is soon to come.

The phrase, *"Then do we with Patience wait for it,"* proclaims the certitude of its coming, because the Holy Spirit has promised that it would.

We do not see all that the Gospel holds out to us, but it is the object of our Christian Hope nevertheless; it is as true and sure as the Love of God which in Christ Jesus reconciled us to Himself and gave us the Spirit of Adoption, and, therefore, we wait for it in patience (Denney).

The idea of Paul's statement is, that just as sure as what we presently have, just as sure is that which is to come. Therefore, this *"Patience"* produces a joy in the heart of the Believer, which is the opposite of that of the world.

In other words, we presently enjoy so much what we now have in Christ Jesus, that it gives us a double joy in the anticipation of that which is yet to come.

(26) "LIKEWISE THE SPIRIT ALSO HELPETH OUR INFIRMITIES: FOR WE KNOW NOT WHAT WE SHOULD PRAY FOR

AS WE OUGHT: BUT THE SPIRIT IT-
SELF MAKETH INTERCESSION FOR US
WITH GROANINGS WHICH CANNOT BE
UTTERED."

The phrase, *"Likewise the Spirit also
helpeth our infirmities,"* tells us several
wonderful things:

THE HOLY SPIRIT IN THE BELIEVER

1. First of all, the Holy Spirit Who is
God, lives within our hearts and lives, which
was made possible by what Jesus did at Calvary and the Resurrection and the Exaltation and our acceptance of His Great Work.
This is at least one of the things that makes
the New Covenant of such greater magnitude than the Old Covenant. For one to
realize that God is with him and actually in
him (Jn. 14:17), is in a sense beyond comprehension. The idea is, that as far as the
person is concerned, God is directing all His
attention and help to that one person. Of
course we know that God is Omnipresent,
therefore, everywhere, but still, His help for
the Believer is of such a personal nature,
even as we are told here, that it is as if all of
God's Power and Wisdom are reserved for
the one Believer.

That is in no way meant to promote selfishness in the heart of the Believer, but
rather the extent of personal direction given
by the Lord.

HE HELPS US

2. *"Helpeth"* in the Greek is *"sunantilam-
bano,"* and means *"the action of a person
coming to another's aid by taking hold over
against that person, of the load he is carrying."* The one coming to help does not take
the entire load, but helps the other person
in his endeavor.

It speaks of the Holy Spirit indwelling the
Saint, coming to the aid of the Saint in the
Saint's spiritual problems and difficulties, not
by taking over the responsibility for him and
giving him an automatic deliverance without any effort on his part, but by lending a
helping hand, allowing him to work out his
problems and overcome his difficulties, with
the help of the Spirit.

It is done in this manner, to teach the
Believer responsibility, trust and dependence

on the Lord, and to bring us to a state of
maturity. If the Holy Spirit did everything
for us, without us having to do anything
ourselves, as should be obvious, this would
not be good for the Saint.

In other words, the Holy Spirit will not
promote the laziness of the Believer by having food brought to him, but He will help
him to go out and find a job. Even in that,
He will seldom bring the job to the person,
but will take the person to the job, at least if
they get out and try.

A perfect example is that of Ruth the
Moabitess. She had accepted the God of Israel and had come into His Covenant. However, needing food for she and Naomi, she
went out to glean in the fields, which was
the custom in Israel of that day concerning
people who had fallen for whatever reason,
on hard times.

The Scripture says, *". . . And her hap was
to light on a part of the field belonging unto
Boaz . . ."* (Ruth 2:3).

In other words, she went out looking for
a place to glean, not really knowing where
to go, but the Holy Spirit drew her to a certain place, even though she thought it just
happened by chance. However, nothing is
by chance concerning the Child of God.

PRAYER

3. *"Infirmities"* in the Greek is *"astheneia,"*
and means *"want of strength, weakness."*

The weakness spoken of here is defined by
the context which speaks of prayer, one of
the things in the spiritual realm in which
our weakness needs His Power. Although,
the word *"infirmities"* could speak of physical needs, it is basically, at least here, speaking of that which is spiritual.

The Holy Spirit here through the Apostle
is telling us how He wants to help us and how
that it is done. We find it in the next phrase.

The phrase, *"For we know not what we
should pray for as we ought,"* proclaims
prayer as the vehicle through which these
things are carried out.

The weakness addressed here concerns the
inability of the Saint to know what to pray
for. We do know what the general objects of
prayer are. But we do not know what the
specific, detailed objects of prayer in any given

emergency or situation are.

In the Greek the definite article is used before the word *"what."* Consequently, Paul actually said we do not know *"the what"* we should pray for, in other words, the particular what.

"As we ought" in the Greek is *"katho dei,"* and means *"What is necessary in the nature of the case for that we are to pray."*

According as the need is at the moment, we know the end, which is common to all who pray, but not what is necessary at each crisis of need in order to enable us to attain this end (Wuest).

The subject of prayer is of such importance that it needs greater treatment than just a few lines. We will address ourselves to that at the conclusion of the Commentary on this particular verse.

THE SPIRIT AND INTERCESSION

The phrase, *"But the Spirit itself maketh Intercession for us,"* should have been translated, *"The Spirit Himself . . . ,"* and for the reasons previously given.

"Intercession" in the Greek as used here is *"huperentunchano,"* and means *"to make a petition or intercede on behalf of another, or on behalf of."*

There are two major directions concerning the word *"Intercession"* as it is used here:

1. This is Intercession in respect to prayer, and not Intercession on behalf of one who has sinned, which can only be carried out by Christ, which He does constantly, with the Scripture saying, *"Seeing He ever liveth to make Intercession for them"* (Heb. 7:25). The Holy Spirit does not make this type of Intercession, only Christ. We will address ourselves to the Intercession of Christ when we get to verse 34.

2. The type of Intercession made by the Holy Spirit on our behalf in the realm of prayer is varied, even as we have already studied. However, this Intercession includes the manner and way for approaching a King, in other words, protocol. The Greek word is *"enteuxis,"* and is normally the noun used for *"prayer."* However, inasmuch as Paul uses verbs relative to Intercession, it does not show up in verses 26 or 27.

Nevertheless, the Holy Spirit not only

directs our attention to what we should pray for, but as well makes certain that what is said before the Father (His Translation), that it is terminology befitting a King, and in this case, The Lord of Glory.

As an example, I have had the occasion to meet a President of the United States two or three times, plus other World Leaders. Due to their office, one observes certain protocol, as would be obvious. In other words, one does not just barge in as in some cases with a friend. When meeting one of such high office there is certain things that one does and certain things that one does not do.

Using that as an example, it would hold even more true for the Creator of all the ages. Consequently, the Holy Spirit makes certain that we are approaching God as we should, even though within ourselves we do not have such knowledge.

What a Mighty God we serve!

GROANINGS

The phrase, *"For us with groanings which cannot be uttered,"* speaks of a burden of prayer which comes straight from the heart, and cannot really be put into words, at least successfully. This tells us that it is the state of the heart which the Lord looks at, and which approaches the Throne of God. In other words, the Holy Spirit is little interested in pious platitudes or beautiful phraseology in prayer. He is looking for a soul searching which cries to God to such an extent, that such a burden cannot really be put into words. Consequently, it can only be expressed in *"groanings."*

"Groanings" in the Greek is *"stenagmos,"* and means literally *"a cry."*

Many times in prayer the Holy Spirit will move through me in exactly this manner. The tears will begin to come as the Lord takes me into the very Throne Room of God. There is no way that one can properly express these times except with tears. At the same time, while the weeping or crying comes from my heart, it is the Holy Spirit Who is actually moving upon me, that this type of prayer would go forth. I personally feel it is the highest type of prayer.

This I do know, in times of prayer such as this, when the Holy Spirit does move in this fashion, in my own spirit I feel like I have gotten through to the Throne of God as at no other times. To fully describe what has happened, one is unable. And yet at the same time, there is a peace that fills one's heart at these times, because beyond the shadow of a doubt that which the Holy Spirit wanted has been done.

THAT WHICH THE LORD TOLD ME TO DO RESPECTING PRAYER

I have always had a strong prayer life, nurtured by my Grandmother when I was but a child. I was brought up with this, and when Frances and I married, it had become a daily staple in my life. Actually, that was my Bible School, my Seminary, the seeking God at my Grandmother's knee, so to speak. In that atmosphere she taught me to believe the Word of God and to have Faith in that Word. She taught me that there was nothing that God could not do.

I can hear her and even see her yet in my mind, as she would look at me but yet with a far-away look in her eyes, saying, *"Jimmy, God is a big God, so ask big!"* I have never forgotten that lesson, it has helped me to touch this world for Christ.

In the late Fall of 1991, with this Ministry in chaos and with Satan making every attempt to apply the death blow, all I knew to do was cry to God, imploring Him as to what I should do. Very clearly and plainly, He told me to have two prayer meetings a day, morning and night. We have done that from then until now and have no plans to stop. To be frank, I think that it is the greatest thing that has ever happened to me in my Christian experience. It has been a time of drawing nearer to the Lord, and Him dealing with my heart concerning many things which were desperately needed.

To be frank, I do not even feel comfortable addressing myself to this which the Lord has instructed me to do. But hopefully, it will be a blessing to others what little I have said and do say, respecting the tremendous privilege of prayer.

ASKING AND RECEIVING FROM GOD

Considering how many Promises we have in the Bible respecting prayer, and

NOTES

considering how Paul has brought it out extensively as to how the Holy Spirit helps us in this effort, and especially considering that this type of Intercession, which is the only type the Holy Spirit gives, is brought about only through prayer, by all means we should take advantage of this tremendous privilege.

The very idea that a mere mortal has the opportunity and privilege of going before the God of all the Ages, even encouraged to do so, knowing that He can do all things, presents a privilege of unparalleled proportions. And yet, most Christians take little advantage of this which is so very, very important.

Even though we have titled the beginning of this dissertation *"Asking and receiving from God,"* still, this only makes up a small part of prayer. Prayer is for consecration, for dedication, for the Will of God to be realized in one's life, for introspection by the Holy Spirit, in other words, there are really only three ways that one can properly communicate with the Lord. Those three ways are: A. The Word of God; B. Prayer; and, C. Worship. If the Believer lets down on any one of these three, sad will be the results.

A PERSONAL EXPERIENCE

A few paragraphs back, I briefly mentioned the Fall of 1991; however, I want to take the Reader to the Spring of 1988, actually, the month of March.

The largest Ministry in the world was in shambles. I did not know what to do, and the consternation was to a far greater degree than the problem at hand. I simply did not understand, considering that I was trying so very, very hard, as to how Satan could get the best of me, especially considering that the Lord was using me to touch much of the world for Christ, with untold thousands being brought to a saving knowledge of the Lord Jesus Christ.

I had always had a strong prayer life. My Grandmother, as stated, had taught me that as a child. As well, I was faithful with that prayer life, even to the extent that I was not only seeking the Lord an hour or more each day, but I had begun getting up at night and praying another hour. In fact, I was losing so much sleep that I could barely function during the day. Actually, I was fighting for my life and I did not know what else to do.

At that time, I did not understand the Cross as it regards Sanctification. I understood it as it regarded Salvation, and I preached it strongly. But when it came to Sanctification, living a victorious, overcoming Christian life, I had no idea the part the Cross played in that all-important endeavor. And when I failed, virtually the entirety of the Church offered no help at all, only criticism. In fact, when I mentioned my strong prayer life, they accused me of lying. In their thinking, because they did not understand the Cross either, they thought that if a person prayed as much as I said I did, then surely that person would have no problems whatsoever. So, in their minds, I must be lying. But I wasn't lying!

These disciplines, as important as they are, as valuable as they are, as helpful as they are, will never give one power over the powers of darkness. Sin cannot be overcome in this manner. Our Saviour said:

"You shall know the truth, and the truth shall make you free" (Jn. 8:32). And the truth, as it regards Sanctification, which pertains to the Cross, I simply did not know. Also, looking back, I didn't know a single person at that time who did.

A GREAT DAY

On this day in question, when I was suffering almost to the point of death, I had stayed home from the office with the intent of spending the entirety of the day in prayer, which I often did. While it was one of the saddest days of my life, at the same time, it would prove to be one of the greatest days of my life.

Frances had gone to the office, along with Donnie, and I was left alone. In those days, I generally walked while I prayed, and did so on the 25 acres that surround our home and Donnie's. I was at the back of the property, endeavoring to seek the Lord, with my heart broken in ten thousand pieces. As stated, I did not know what to do. More than all, I was more concerned about my own personal situation. How could I have failed? How was it possible? I was doing everything I knew

to do, but nothing seemed to help.

That morning as I began to pray, after just a few moments, the powers of darkness came against me, at least as great as I have ever experienced. I don't think I had ever experienced anything of this degree, as it regards oppression. It was so bad that I remember standing beside a fence that separated our property from our neighbor's, telling the Lord, *"No human being can stand this! Please, help me!"*

The Evil One was pushing about as hard as he could push, telling me, *"Get what money you have in the bank* (which was about $800), *get in your car, and leave. Just disappear! You have brought shame on your family, on your Church, and, above all, on the Work of God. You would do the Work of God a service, if you simply disappeared."* Those were the words of the Evil One.

And then, all of a sudden, it happened! It was like the Spirit of the Lord said, *"It is enough!"* The powers of darkness instantly dissipated, with the Power of God coming all over me. One moment I was as destitute as a human could be, in total despair. But the next moment, it was like I didn't have a single care in the world, as the Power of God enveloped me.

As I began to walk with my hands uplifted, worshipping and praising the Lord, all of a sudden, the Spirit of the Lord spoke to my heart. He said to me:

"I'm going to show you some things about the Holy Spirit you do not presently know!"

That was all He said. He did not mention the problem, my consternation, or the terrible situation in which I now found myself. Simply: *"I will show you things about the Holy Spirit you do not now know!"*

THE HOLY SPIRIT!

What did He mean? Of course, the Holy Spirit is God; consequently, there are untold numbers of things about Him I do not know. But yet, I knew that the Lord was speaking of my predicament. He only told me that He would show me this thing, but He did not say when. At any rate, I had a Promise! But, it was actually nine years before the Lord brought to fruition that great Promise. The answer would come in the Revelation of the

Cross; however, I had no knowledge whatsoever of that in 1988.

As I mentioned some paragraphs back, the Holy Spirit directed me to have two prayer meetings a day, which began in October of 1991. I faithfully followed that regimen all of those years. A little group of us would meet every morning at 10 a.m., and then again at night at 6:30 p.m. This occurred five days a week, including Saturday night.

All during this time, the Lord graciously moved upon my heart, and did so countless times. He gave me tremendous Promises, which strengthened me – Promises which are just now beginning to come to fruition. However, even though I remembered graphically what the Lord had told me regarding the Holy Spirit, still, as to exactly what that was, I didn't know.

THE REVELATION OF THE CROSS

During the six years of those prayer meetings, day and night, a regimen, incidentally, which I personally continue unto this hour, I really did not know that for which I was actually seeking the Lord. In other words, I wasn't praying for any specific thing, because I actually did not know what I really needed. The Lord had, in fact, spoken to me at the outset, saying, *"Do not seek Me so much for what I can do, but rather for Who I am."* And that's exactly what I did!

Little by little, the Lord began to reveal Himself to me, and in a more personal way than I had ever previously known. And then it happened!

It was some time in the Spring of 1997. I had gone to the office early, which I always did, to get ready for our morning program over SonLife Radio. I was studying the Book of Romans, actually preparing to write the Commentary on that great Epistle of Paul the Apostle. While I was studying, all of a sudden it happened. The Spirit of the Lord began to open up to me the meaning of the Sixth Chapter of Romans.

This is the great Chapter where Paul tells the Believer how to live for God. He first of all takes the Believer straight to the Cross (6:3-5). In a few words, he tells us how the Believer is baptized into the death of Christ, buried with Him by baptism into death, and

then raised with Him in newness of life. In other words, that is the foundation of our Christian experience, and of our Sanctification.

He then showed me, and did so through the writings of Kenneth Wuest, the Greek Scholar, as to the meaning of the word *"sin,"* as it is used in Paul's writings, especially in the Sixth Chapter of Romans. He explained from the original Greek Text, in effect, the way it was originally written, in that it referred to the *"sin nature."*

I will not go into any detail, but the moment I began to read those words, the Holy Spirit began to quicken my heart and mind, in order that I might properly understand this all-important aspect of Christian living. Tragically, most Christians don't have the foggiest idea as to what the sin nature actually is.

THE SIN NATURE

The sin nature is a result of the Fall, which took place in the Garden of Eden. Man fell from his position of total God-consciousness down to the far lower level of total self-consciousness. Sin, which is disobedience of the Word of God, characterizes the person's life. In other words, their very nature is toward sin. In fact, before the person comes to Christ, they are totally dominated by the sin nature, twenty-four hours a day, seven days a week. They know nothing else, simply because they cannot know anything else. Everything they do, in some way, is toward sin — hence, the sin nature.

Instantly, as this great Truth began to dawn on me, I knew this was the answer to my great question of *"Why?"* If the Believer doesn't properly understand the sin nature and how it works, and, above all, how to have victory over the sin nature, then, in some way, the sin nature is going to rule and reign in the heart of life of the Believer. It doesn't matter how zealous that person is for the Lord or how consecrated they are to the Lord. If they do not understand the sin nature, then, in some way, the sin nature is going to rule them, and they will be left extremely perplexed. That's why the great Apostle Paul said:

"For that which I do I allow (understand) *not: for what I would, that do I not; but*

what I hate, that do I" (Rom. 7:15). Please notice: I placed the word *"understand"* in parentheses, which is the way the Verse should have been translated, i.e., *"For that which I do I understand not."* This was before the Lord gave to the great Apostle the understanding of the Cross. But, to be sure, when Paul wrote this Seventh Chapter of Romans, he very well understood the Cross. He is telling us that if we do not understand and follow the teaching given in Chapter 6, we are bound to repeat Chapter 7, which refers to the sin nature ruling and reigning in one's life.

Paul was trying with all of his zeal and strength to overcome, but he simply could not do so. That's why he said, *"I don't understand what is happening,"* etc. How many Christians at this moment are failing miserably, despite all they try to do otherwise (and I speak of those who truly love the Lord and who are struggling with all of their strength and might to be what they ought to be in the Lord)?

THE TRUTH

I found out later from my study of the Word that as the Lord first of all gave me the understanding of the sin nature, likewise, this is the way it was with Paul. Actually, the sin nature is approached basically in one of several ways. They are:

1. Ignorance: Regrettably, even though this is one of the most important aspects of the Believer's life, most Christians don't have the faintest idea as to what the sin nature is. They are ignorant of what the Bible teaches in this respect.

2. License: Some few have some knowledge of the sin nature, but come to the conclusion that because the sin nature is running rampant in their lives, sin is excused. In other words, they think, *"Even though I am a Christian, I cannot help but sin every day."* The Apostle Paul answered this by saying, *"Shall we sin that Grace may abound?"* His answer was concise and to the point, *"God forbid!"* (6:1-2).

3. Denial: Believe it or not, despite all the teaching in the Word of God, there are many who claim that once the person comes to Christ, the sin nature is gone. In other

NOTES

words, they have no sin nature. Now, that's strange, when we consider that Paul mentions the sin nature some 17 times in Romans, Chapter 6. Actually, there is one time that it does not really refer to the sin nature, but to acts of sin, which is in the 15th Verse.

In the original Greek language, which is the language of the New Testament, the word *"sin,"* at least some 15 times in the Sixth Chapter of Romans, has what is referred to as the *"definite article"* in front it. In other words, in the original language, it actually reads: *"the sin."* This means it is not actually speaking of acts of sin, but rather the *"evil nature"* or the *"sin nature,"* both meaning the same thing.

That's the trouble with the Church presently. It mostly treats the symptoms of sin instead of what is causing the sin.

So, to deny that the Believer has a sin nature, especially in the face of a mountain of evidence otherwise, is foolishness indeed!

4. Struggle: There are many good Christians, and I speak of those who are truly consecrated to the Lord, who struggle daily with the sin nature, simply because they do not know or understand how it is to be addressed. In other words, they don't understand the Cross. So, their Christian experience is one gigantic struggle, which, to be frank, is a far cry from the *"more abundant life"* spoken of by Christ (Jn. 10:10).

5. Grace: This is the only way that the sin nature can be properly addressed. When the person comes to Christ, the sin nature is made dormant. In other words, it should not cause anyone any problem, whatsoever. However, if we attempt to live for God in the wrong way, which denies the Grace of God, then we will find ourselves once again being ruled by the sin nature. If we keep our Faith in Christ and the Cross, understanding that it's the Cross that makes available the Power of the Holy Spirit, then the Grace of God can flow uninterruptedly in our hearts and lives, thereby giving us perpetual victory, which means that the sin nature causes no problem.

But regrettably, most Christians are frustrating the Grace of God, which means they are trying to live for God without the help of the Holy Spirit. Paul said: *"I do not frustrate the Grace of God, for if righteous-ness come by the Law, then Christ is dead in vain"* (Gal. 2:21).

THE CROSS OF CHRIST

Even though the Lord had shown me that the problem was the sin nature, or rather an improper understanding of the sin nature, He still didn't tell me what the solution was. A few days after this first revelation had been given to me, in one of the morning prayer meetings, the Spirit of the Lord came upon me, and the Lord gently said to my heart, *"The solution for which you seek is found in the Cross, and is found only in the Cross!"* In fact, I was praying about this very thing. What was the answer to the sin nature? And then the Lord gave me the answer.

I was now beginning to understand the Scriptural rudiments of Sanctification. As wave after wave of the Spirit of God swept over my soul that morning in 1997, I knew that what the Lord was giving me was greater than I could even begin to comprehend. I remember requesting of Him that this door never close. Knowing that I could not ex-haust the potential of the Cross, i.e., *"the Finished Work of Christ,"* I asked the Lord if He would continue to open that door to me, in other words, to continue to give me more and more understanding of the Atonement.

To be sure, that He has! There is very seldom a day that I do not learn a little more about the Finished Work of Christ. It is a Perfect Work. It is so Perfect that it will never have to be amended. This is the rea-son Paul called it *"The Everlasting Covenant"* (Heb. 13:20).

From the information given by the Holy Spirit to me, as it regards the Cross, I knew that the Cross must be the object of my Faith. To be sure, that is so very, very important! The major problem with most Christians is an improper object of faith. In other words, they are placing their faith in something which may be good in its own right, but which is the wrong place for their faith. <u>Our Faith must be exclusively in Christ as the Source of all things and the Cross as the Means of all things.</u>

After the Lord gave me this Truth regard-ing the Cross, which was not new, but which

had been given to the Apostle Paul long ago, the thoughts entered my mind as to how the Holy Spirit figured into all of this. I knew that He did, but I didn't understand how.

For several weeks I cried to the Lord about this thing, asking Him to show me. And then it happened:

THE HOLY SPIRIT

It happened one morning, a few weeks after the Lord had given me the Revelation of the Cross. Actually, we were in the midst of our Radio Program, *"A Study in the Word,"* which airs seven days a week. Loren Larson was on the Program with me. I can-not recall who else was present, if anyone. Without premeditation, I made the state-ment, *"The Holy Spirit works entirely within the framework of the Finished Work of Christ."* I went on to say: *"He will not work outside of that framework, which demands that we have Faith exclusively in Christ and what Christ did for us at the Cross."*

It somewhat shocked me when these words came out of my mouth, because, as stated, they were not premeditated. There were a few moments of silence after these words were spoken, and Loren spoke up, ask-ing, *"Can you give me Scripture for that?"*

I sat there for a moment, and then the Holy Spirit brought to my mind Romans 8:2, *"For the Law of the Spirit of Life in Christ Jesus has made me free from the law of sin and death."* When I said it, the Spirit of the Lord entered the room. All of a sud-den I heard that still, small voice. *"This is what I told you back in 1988 that I would tell you about the Holy Spirit!"* It had taken nine years. I cannot even begin to tell you how I felt.

Of course, that which the Lord told me that day, He has enlarged upon from then until now. In effect, He told me how the Holy Spirit works. As stated, He works en-tirely within the framework of the Cross of Christ. In other words, what Jesus did on the Cross gave the Holy Spirit the legal right to do what He does in our hearts and lives (Jn. 14:17). For Him to work as He so de-sires, He only requires that our Faith ever be in Christ and the Cross. Then He will do great things within our lives, bringing about

Righteousness and Holiness (Rom. 6:3-5, 11, 14; 8:1-2, 11).

(27) "AND HE THAT SEARCHETH THE HEARTS KNOWETH WHAT IS THE MIND OF THE SPIRIT, BECAUSE HE MAKETH INTERCESSION FOR THE SAINTS ACCORDING TO THE WILL OF GOD."

The phrase, *"And He that searcheth the hearts,"* speaks of God the Father. Actually, all Three Persons of the Trinity search hearts: God the Father (I Chron. 28:9; Jer. 17:10); the Son (Rev. 2:23); and the Spirit (I Cor. 2:10).

However, there is a progression of order here which is not to be ignored. Even though the Holy Spirit is God, and, consequently, knows all things, still, His Purpose and Agenda is to carry out the Will of God in our lives, even as the last phrase in this verse proclaims. One could say that the Father *orchestrates*, the Son *institutes*, and the Spirit *executes*.

The phrase, *"Knoweth what is the Mind of the Spirit,"* refers to the special means of communication which can refer to praying in Tongues, but not necessarily so.

The idea is, that God the Father Who searches the hearts of His Saints, understands the intent or bent of our unutterable prayers, unutterable because we do not know the particular things for which we should pray in connection with a certain circumstance. He knows the Mind of the Holy Spirit praying for us and in our stead, according to the Plan of God for our lives (Wuest).

The phrase, *"Because He maketh Intercession for the Saints according to the Will of God,"* refers to the fact that the Holy Spirit is ensconced within our hearts and lives to carry out God's Will and not our will. He is not there to do our bidding, but the bidding of the Father, simply because the Father knows what we need.

The idea of all of this is twofold:

THE WILL OF GOD

1. For the Will of God to be carried out in the life of the Believer, there must be a strong prayer life involved. In this prayer life the Holy Spirit will at times move mightily upon the Believer, taking the Believer directly to the Throne of Grace, praying

through him that which is needed. Sometimes the Believer has knowledge of what is being carried out respecting the spirit world, and sometimes personal knowledge may be very slim. At times and as stated, the Intercession will be reduced to little more than *"groans"* or *"sighs,"* although uttered by the Believer, they are inspired by the Spirit.

A PLAN

2. God has a Plan for the entirety of the world and as well, a plan for each Believer. This Plan is ever the priority of the Holy Spirit respecting our hearts and lives. He has the overall Plan in Mind, and as well, our personal involvement in that Plan. He is there for the one purpose of realizing this which God desires.

For the Believer to work at odds with that which the Lord desires only creates conflict. To be sure, this is the reason for most disturbance in the hearts and lives of Christians. While they may think that the disturbance is caused by other things, the reality is that their struggle is with God. The struggle pertains to the pure and perfect Will of God for their lives.

The Patriarch Jacob is a perfect example. When his life was changed, it was the result of a wrestling match with God, which in effect was caused by self-will (Gen. Chpt. 32). In fact, self-will is the major problem in the lives of Believers. Someone has said and rightly so, that when Jesus died on Calvary, He died there to save us not only from *"sin,"* but as well from *"self."*

THE MINISTRY OF INTERCESSION

Even though verses 26 and 27 speak primarily of Intercession made by the Holy Spirit on our behalf, still, incorporated in the Text, is the Intercession which the Holy Spirit promotes in the hearts of praying Believers as they intercede for others. Actually, it is in this manner alone which various Moves of God take place all over the world. This is the reason for Revival in certain areas, for Movings and Operations of the Holy Spirit in certain parts of the world, even to conviction respecting individuals. None of that just happens, it is carried out through the Ministry of Intercession on the part of

Believers. Of course, and as stated, the Holy Spirit is the One Who executes all of this.

This is one of the ways that the so-called modern Faith Ministry has been such a detriment. It little teaches or believes in the Ministry of Intercession, at least as we are now portraying, but rather that such things be confessed into existence, which Doctrine has no Scriptural foundation.

To be a little clearer, the point I am attempting to make is, that every single person in this world who is Saved, and every Move of God which takes place somewhere (anywhere), that this has been brought about by Intercession on the part of Believers in some way. The Believers doing the Interceding, may have been very much acquainted with the people or situation, or not acquainted with them at all. But the Holy Spirit would begin to move upon the Believer's heart respecting Intercession for certain people, certain areas, certain parts of the world, many times areas to where the Intercessor has never been. As well, the Holy Spirit at the same time is probably moving on a number of Intercessors all over the world respecting this particular area or place, with none of these people acquainted with each other, but yet the Holy Spirit acquainted with all.

THE AUTHORITY OF THE BELIEVER

Even though the Lord needs nothing, He has allowed Believers a very prominent part in the carrying out of His Great Plan on this Earth. Actually, the involvement of Believers in that Plan is of such magnitude, that if we fall down at our task, the Work of God is very greatly hindered. Even though God's Plan is ultimately realized, although sometimes delayed, still, what the Believer does affects that Plan greatly, whether in a positive or negative sense.

The Believer's great part in this is characterized as the *"Great Commission"* (Mat. 28:18-20; Mk. 16:15-20; Lk. 24:49; Acts 1:8).

INTERCESSION

"Intercession" in the Hebrew is *"pagha,"* and means *"to make Intercession, to strike upon, or against, to assail anyone with petitions, to urge, and when on behalf of another, to Intercede"* (Gen. 23:8; Ruth 1:16;

Job 21:15; Isa. 53:12; Jer. 7:16; 27:18; 36:25).

In the New Testament, a similar word is used in the Greek, *"enteuxis,"* among several other Greek words, meaning *"to come between, to interpose on behalf of, to Intercede"* (Rom. 8:26-34; I Tim. 2:1; 4:5). Actually, the Greek word *"entugchano"* is found in Romans Chapter 8.

MAN'S INTERCESSION FOR HIS FELLOWMAN

Many such prayers are recorded in Scripture. The Sacrificial act of Noah may have been partly of this nature, for it is followed by a Promise of God on behalf of the race and the Earth at large (Gen. 8:20-22). Such also is Abraham's prayer for Ishmael (Gen. 17:18); Abraham's prayer for Sodom (Gen. 18:23-33); Abraham for Abimelech (Gen. 20:17). Jacob's blessing of Joseph's sons is of the nature of Intercession (Gen. 48:8-22).

His dying blessing of his sons is hardly to be regarded as Intercessory; it is, rather, declarative, although in the case of Joseph it does approach Intercession.

The absence of distinct Intercessory Prayer from Abraham to Moses is to be observed, and shows at least in part, the spiritual apathy of the time. In Moses, however, the social element finds a further development, and is interesting as taking up the Spirit of the Father of the Faithful.

The Intercessory Ministry of Moses is revealed in his prayer for the removal of the plagues regarding Egypt (Ex. 15:25); for water at Rephidim (Ex. 17:4); for victory over Amalek (Ex. 17:8-16); prayer for the people after the Golden Calf (Ex. 32:11-14, 21-34; 33:12). There are many other instances as well.

None of these prayers of Moses' are perfunctory. They are the vivid and passionate utterances of a man full of Divine enthusiasm and love for his people. It is Intercession wrung from a great and devout soul on occasions of deep and critical importance.

(In the history of Joshua we find only the prayer for the people after the sin of Achan, Josh. 7:6-9, although the communications from God to Joshua are numerous. A faint Intercessory note may be heard in Deborah's song as well, Judg. 5:13. Gideon's prayer seemed to reecho something of the words of Moses, Judg. 6:13. Manoah's prayers may be noted also, Judg. Chpt. 13. However, for the most part, from Moses to Samuel, even as it had been from Abraham to Moses, there seemed to have been very little Intercession. Again this shows the spiritual climate of that period.)

THE KINGS AND THE PROPHETS

Samuel is the real successor of Moses, and in connection with his life, Intercession again appears more distinct and effective. Hannah's song (Samuel's Mother) though chiefly of thankfulness, is not without the Intercessory spirit (I Sam. 2:1-11). Also Samuel's prayer at Mizpeh (I Sam. 7:5), and the recognition by the people of Samuel's place (I Sam. 7:8).

Going to others, one must note David's prayer for deliverance of the people from pestilence (II Sam. 24:17); Solomon's prayer for wisdom to govern the people (I Ki. 3:5-15); Solomon's prayer at the dedication of the Temple (I Ki. 8:12-61); Elijah's prayer for the widow's son (I Ki. 17:20); Elijah's prayer for rain (I Ki. 18:42); Elisha's prayer for the widow's son (II Ki. 4:33); Hezekiah's prayer (II Ki. 19:14-19).

Of course, there are many more of which we do not have space to enumerate.

Also, the Poetic Books furnish a few examples of Intercessory Prayer: Job's Intercession for his children (Job 1:5); the Lord's Command that Job should pray for his friends (Job 42:8).

In the Prophetical Books the note of Intercession also appears. The Prophet, though primarily a Messenger from God to man, has also something of the character of the Intercessor (Isa. Chpt. 6). In Jeremiah 42:4, the Prophet consents to the request of Johanan to seek the Lord on behalf of the people. The Book of Lamentations is naturally conceived in a more constantly recurring spirit of Intercession. In the Prophecies Jeremiah has been the Messenger of God to the people. But, after the catastrophe, in his sorrow he appeals to God for mercy upon them (Lam. 2:20; 5:1-19).

Ezekiel in the same way is rather the Seer of Visions and the Prophetic Representative

NOTES

of God. Yet at times he appeals to God for the people (Ezek. 9:8; 11:13).

INTERCESSION IN THE NEW TESTAMENT

In the New Testament, all prayer necessarily takes a new form from its relation to our Lord, and in these supplications before God, Intercessory Prayer plays its part.

At the outset, Jesus teaches prayer on behalf of those *"which despitefully use you"* (Mat. 5:44). How completely does this change the entire spirit of prayer! We breathe a new atmosphere of the high revelation of Love as characterized by Christ. As well, the Lord's Prayer (Mat. 6:9-13) is of this character. In fact, Christ's High-Priestly Prayer is the most sublime height of prayer to God and is Intercessory throughout (Jn. Chpt. 17).

THE ENTRANCE OF THE HOLY SPIRIT

Although the Holy Spirit has always been involved in man's prayer and petition to the Lord and as well, as stated, in Intercession, His filling the hearts of Believers after the Day of Pentecost, due to what Jesus did at Calvary, the Resurrection, and Exaltation, puts a brand-new perspective on this tremendous Ministry. It is even as we are now studying in Romans 8:26-27.

While it seems as if the entirety of the Text is devoted to the Spirit Himself Interceding on behalf of Believers, still, the word *"helpeth"* and the phrase, *"For we know not what we should pray for as we ought"* (vs. 26), lets us know that He is actually the One Who energizes the Believer respecting Intercession on behalf of others. Actually, the Divine Spirit is said to be a Spirit of Supplication (Zech. 12:10).

Actually, we see this Intercession at work throughout the entirety of the Book of Acts. Hence, the prayers of the Early Church Believers become Intercession at times, involving the wider outlook on others and on the world at large which Christianity has bestowed on men. Actually, they literally breathe the Spirit (Acts 2:24-30; 6:6; 7:60; 8:24; 9:40; 12:5-12; 13:3; 14:23; 15:40; 20:36).

THE INTERCESSION OF CHRIST

Even though this Ministry of Christ is on

a far higher plane than that of Believers, still, the example is very prominent before all.

The general conception of our Lord's Mediatorial Office is especially summed up in His Intercession in which He appears in His High-Priestly Office, and also as Interceding with the Father on behalf of that humanity whose cause He has espoused.

The function of Priesthood as developed under Judaism involved the position of mediation between man and God. The Priest represented man, and on man's behalf approached God; thus, he offered Sacrifice, Interceded, and gave to the offerer whom he represented the benediction and expression of the Divine acceptance.

THE WORK OF CHRIST

As in Sacrifice, so in the Work of Christ, we find the proprietary rights of the offerer in the Sacrifice. For man, Christ as One with man, and yet in His Own Personal Right, offers Himself (Rom. Chpt. 5; Gal. 4:5; Heb. 2:11).

There was also the transfer of guilt and its conditions, typically by laying hands on the head of the animal called the scapegoat, which then bore the sins of the offerer and was presented to God by the Priest. The acknowledgment of sin and the surrender to God is completely fulfilled in Christ's Offering of Himself, at His Death (Lev. 3:2, 8-13; 16:21; Isa. 53:6; II Cor. 5:21).

Our Lord's Intercessory quality in the Sacrifice of Himself is not only indicated by the imputation of guilt to Him as representing the sinner, but also in the Victory of His Life over Death, which is then given to man in God's acceptance of His Representative and Substitute.

ITS INTERCESSORY CHARACTER

In the Epistle to the Hebrews, the Intercessory character of our Lord's High-Priestly Office is transferred to the Heavenly Condition and Work of Christ, where the relation of Christ's Work to man's condition is regarded as being still continued in the Heavenly Place (Heb. 9:11-28). This entrance into Heaven is once for all, and in the person of the High Priest the way is open to the Very Presence of God.

NOTES

From one point of view (Heb. 10:12) the Priestly Service of the Lord was concluded and gathered up into His Kingly Office (Heb. 10:13-18). But from another point of view, we ourselves are bidden to enter into the Holiest Place; as if in union with Christ we too become a Kingly Priesthood (Heb. 10:19-22; I Pet. 2:9).

THE RIGHT OF ENTRANCE

It must not be forgotten, however, that this Right of Entrance into the Most Holy Place is one that depends entirely upon our vital union with Christ. He appears in Heaven for us and we with Him, and in this sense He fulfills the second duty of His High-Priestly Office as Intercessor, with the added conception drawn from the legal advocacy of the Roman Court.

The term *"Advocate"* in I John 2:1 is in the Greek *"parakletos,"* which in John 14:16 is translated *"Comforter."* The word has a familiar use in Greek for the legal Advocate in Roman Law who appeared on behalf of his client. Thus, in the double sense of Priestly and Legal Representative, our Lord is our Intercessor in Heaven. In other words, He guarantees our Salvation and Redemption. His Legal Representation is guaranteed by the *"Seal of Promise"* given by the Holy Spirit (Eph. 1:13; 4:30).

THE MANNER OF HIS REPRESENTATION

Of the modes in which Christ carries out His Intercessory Office, we can have little knowledge except so far as we may fairly deduce them from the phraseology and suggested ideas of Scripture. As High Priest, it may surely be right for us to aid our weak Faith by assuring ourselves that our Lord pleads for us, while at the same time we must be careful not to deprave our thought concerning the Glorified Lord by the metaphors and analogies of earthly relationship.

To be sure, it is done, but on a much higher plane and level, than we can too very well comprehend.

The Intercessory Work of Christ consequently, may be thus represented: He represents man before God in His Perfect Nature, His Exalted Office and His Completed Work.

The Scripture Word for this is *"To appear before the Face of God for us"* (Heb. 9:24). This plainly proclaims an active Intercession. This is the Office of our Lord as *"Advocate"* or *"Parakletos."* That this conveys some relation to the aid which one who has broken the Law receives from an Advocate cannot be overlooked, and we find Christ's Intercession in this aspect brought into connection with the Text which referred to Justification and its allied ideas (Rom. 8:34; I Jn. 2:1).

THE MANNER OF INTERCESSION AND REPRESENTATION

Whatever else it may include, the following must be a part of that which the Lord does for us as our Personal Representative in Heaven:

1. His appearing before God on our behalf, as the Sacrifice for our sins, as our High Priest, on the ground of Whose Work we receive the Remission of our sins, the Gift of the Holy Spirit, and all needed good.

2. Defense against the sentence of the Law and the charges of Satan, who is the great accuser.

3. His offering Himself as our surety, not only that the demands of justice shall be shown to be satisfied, but that His people shall be obedient and faithful.

4. The oblation of the persons of the Redeemed, Sanctifying their prayers, and all their services, rendering them acceptable to God, through the savor of His Own Merits.

Even this expression of the elements which constitute the Intercession of the Lord on our behalf, cautious and spiritual as it is in its application to Christian thought and worship, must be carefully guarded from a too complete and materialistic use.

Without this care, worship and devout thought may be degraded and fall into the mechanical forms by which our Lord's position of Intercessor has been reduced to very little more than an imaginative and spectacular process which goes on in some Heavenly Place.

It must not be forgotten that the metaphorical and symbolic origin of the ideas which constitute Christ's Intercession (for instance, the duties of the High Priests of old) is always in danger of dominating and materializing the spiritual reality of His Intercessional Office. (D. Bevan).

Nevertheless, even though of necessity our understanding is limited, still, the example portrayed by Christ in His Intercessory role on our behalf, at least should produce in us a Love for the lost and especially our fellow Believers.

(28) "AND WE KNOW THAT ALL THINGS WORK TOGETHER FOR GOOD TO THEM THAT LOVE GOD, TO THEM WHO ARE THE CALLED ACCORDING TO HIS PURPOSE."

There are two key words in this verse. They are *"Love"* and *"Purpose."*

The phrase, *"And we know that all things work together for good,"* presents the beginning of one of the most often quoted Scriptures in the Bible.

In view of the broad brush of this Text, and especially considering its vast consequences, one would not do violence to Scripture by asking the question, *"Do in fact, all things work together for good concerning Believers?"*

The answer is *"yes"* and *"no!"* *"Yes"* if the conditions are met, and *"no"* if they aren't met.

Paul begins this great Promise by saying *"We know,"* which means that not only does he know this, but as well, it is meant for every other Believer to know.

Also, *"all things,"* cover the entirety of the spectrum respecting Life and Godliness. It refers to every effort made by Satan against the Child of God, every scurrilous plan devised by him for our destruction, and even pertains to evil men working with him (whether they realize it or not) to further the designs of darkness concerning our own personal lives.

LOVE

The phrase, *"To them that love God,"* proclaims the first qualification. However, in the Greek Text, the Apostle designates the Believers as not merely loving God, but being beloved by God. The Divine side of our security from harm is brought out, as combining with and ensuring the other. We are sure that all things work for our good, not only because we Love Him Who worketh all things, but *also* because He Who worketh all things has loved and chosen us, and carried us through the successive steps of our spiritual life.

So, we learn from this Passage not only the requirements on our part, but as well, as to what the Lord is doing for the Believer.

The question could be asked if the phrase insinuates that there are some Believers who do not Love God?

No, that's not the idea. The idea of the Text is, that all Believers in fact do Love God. Actually, it would be impossible for a Believer not to do so (providing he is a True Believer), and for the reason that Believers at the moment of Conversion have the Divine Nature imparted unto them. To the degree of that Love, however, is something else again!

HIS PURPOSE

The phrase, *"To them who are the called according to His Purpose,"* proclaims the second qualification. Our lives must be for His Purpose, and not our purpose, and here is where the great conflict begins.

The working of the Holy Spirit in our lives, sent to us to carry out the Will of God, pertains here to the Calling of which the Apostle speaks. It is twofold:

1. First of all it is the Calling as it pertains to the everlasting Purpose of God, which was ordained before the foundations of the world were laid.

2. This Calling concerns, as we have previously stated, a personal objective, even as it is a part of the whole.

That spoken is the effort being carried out by the Holy Spirit and it is our business, to see to it that His Purpose is our purpose as well. Unfortunately, the terrible struggle of self-will enters in here, which greatly hinders the Holy Spirit and presents a conflict to the Believer not easily overcome. The *"flesh"* is so subtle, that most of the time it masquerades under great spiritual claims. It takes total consecration on the part of the Believer, in order for the Holy Spirit to point out these areas of spiritual weakness, sometimes which we think in our delusion are great spiritual strengths. In fact, it is a lifelong struggle. However, the Lord does not

NOTES

require perfection in this area, simply because were that the case, none would qualify. He does require Love for Himself, and that portrays the direction of our hearts.

In that view the Text literally reads, *"And we know with an absolute knowledge that all things are constantly working together, resulting in good for those who are loving God, for those who are Called ones according to His Purpose"* (Wuest).

Having these qualities of Love for God, and our Calling being according to His Purpose and not our own, all things then must work together for our good.

(29) "FOR WHOM HE DID FOREKNOW, HE ALSO DID PREDESTINATE TO BE CONFORMED TO THE IMAGE OF HIS SON, THAT HE MIGHT BE THE FIRSTBORN AMONG MANY BRETHREN."

The phrase, *"For whom He did foreknow,"* speaks of God's foreknowledge.

WHAT IS FOREKNOWLEDGE?

God is Omniscient, meaning that He knows everything, past, present, and future.

Consequently, *"foreknowledge"* is His Ability to look down through time in whatever capacity, or to whatever degree, and, therefore, to see and know what will take place at that particular time, and with whomever it involves.

It is true that the Scripture makes use of anthropomorphic (related in human terms) forms of expression regarding the way in which God obtains knowledge (Gen. 3:8), and sometimes even represents Him as if He did not know certain things (Gen. 11:5; 18:21); nevertheless the constant representation of the Scripture is that God knows everything. This perfect Knowledge of God, moreover, is not merely a knowledge which is practically unlimited for all spiritual purposes, but covers every aspect of all things in the strictest sense of the term.

In the Historical Books of the Old Testament the Omniscience of God is a constant underlying presupposition when it is said that God watches men's actions, knows their acts and words, and discloses to them the future; while in the Psalms, Prophets and Wisdom Books, this Divine Attribute becomes an object of reflection, and finds doctrinal expression.

ALWAYS HAS BEEN

It cannot, however, be said that this Attribute of God, the knowing of all things, appears only late in the history of Special Revelation; it is a characteristic of the Biblical idea of God from the very first, and it is only its expression which comes out with special clearness in the later Books. God's Knowledge, then, is represented as perfect. Since He is free from all limits of space, His Omniscience is frequently connected with His Omnipresence (He is everywhere).

GOD IS NOT BOUND BY TIME RESTRAINTS

God is also, according to the Old Testament, free from all limitations of time, so that His Consciousness is not in the midst of the stream of the succeeding moments of time, as is the case with the human consciousness.

God is not only without beginning or end of days, but with Him a thousand years are as one day or vice versa. Hence, God knows in one eternal intuition that which for the human consciousness is past, present, and future. In a strict sense, therefore, regarding the foreknowledge of God, and the distinction in God's Knowledge which we derive from His Word, such is actually the only way in which we can conceive of Divine Omniscience in its relation to time, and our understanding of such.

GOD'S KNOWLEDGE OF EVENTS

It is God's Knowledge of events which from the human point of view are future that constitute His Foreknowledge in the sense of that which we understand, or attempt to understand. God is represented as having a knowledge of the entire course of events before they take place. Such knowledge belongs to the Supernatural Power of God from the very outset of Special Revelation.

He knows beforehand what Abraham will do, and what will happen to him; He knows beforehand that Pharaoh's heart will be hardened, and that Moses will deliver Israel (Gen. 15:13; Ex. 3:19; 7:4; 11:1). Actually, the entire history of this period of Revelation exhibits plainly the Foreknowledge of God in this sense.

PROPHECY

Prophecy, which makes up about one-third of the Bible, is actually the Foreknowledge of God. This means that nothing future is hidden from Jehovah (Isa. 41:22; 42:9; 43:9-13; 44:6-8; 46:10; Dan. 2:22; Amos 3:7), and this Foreknowledge embraces the entire course of man's life, whoever that man may be (Ps. 31:15; 39:5; 139:4-6, 16; Job 14:5).

Passages from Isaiah show that it is from the occurrence of events in accordance with Jehovah's predictions that the Prophet will prove His Foreknowledge; and that in contrast with the worshipers of idols which are taken by surprise (in other words they don't know what is coming), Israel is warned of the future by the Omniscient Jehovah.

THE NEW TESTAMENT

In the New Testament likewise, God's Omniscience is explicitly affirmed. Jesus taught that God knows the hidden secrets of man's heart (Lk. 16:15); and this is also the teaching of the Apostles (Acts 1:24; 15:8; I Cor. 2:10; 3:20; I Thess. 2:4; Rev. 2:23).

In a word, according to the author of the Epistle to the Hebrews, everything is open to God, so that He is literally Omniscient, i.e., *"All-Knowing"* (Heb. 4:13).

Actually, Jesus asserts a Foreknowledge by God of that which is hidden from the Son, at least was hidden at that time (Mk. 13:32), and James asserts that all God's Works are foreknown by Him (Acts 15:18).

DOES GOD'S FOREKNOWLEDGE IMPACT FREE WILL?

Denials of the Divine Foreknowledge, have been occasioned by the supposed conflict of this Truth with human freedom, in other words, free will and choice on the part of man. It was supposed that in order to be free, an event must be uncertain and contingent as regards the fact of its future happening, and in the most absolute sense, that is, from the Divine as well as the human point of view. Hence, there have been many in the past who have denied the Foreknowledge of God.

It was supposed either that God voluntarily determines not to foresee the free volitions of man, or else that since God's Omniscience is simply the knowledge of all that is knowable, it does not embrace the free acts of man which are by their very nature uncertain and, consequently, unknowable, at least they say. And upon this view of freedom, this denial of God's Foreknowledge was logically necessary.

Of course, to take that view, one has to come to the conclusion, erroneously I might quickly add, that God has created all things, and merely sits by as an onlooker regarding the course of all events be they present or future, and which are necessarily entirely independent of His Purpose and Control. However, if anyone reads the Bible at all, we know this thinking has no place in Scripture, considering that God is involved in everything.

If God foreknows future events as certain, then they must be certain, and if so, then the certainty of their actually occurring must depend either upon God's Decree and Providential Control, or else upon a fate independent of God, which we know is not the case.

TO WHAT EXTENT?

It has been the thinking of some, that God has a knowledge of events as conditionally future, that is, events neither merely possible nor certainly future, but suspended upon conditions undetermined by God. However, this is not true. Besides being contrary to the Scripture in its idea that many events lie outside the decree of God, and that God must wait upon man in His Government of the world, there is really no such class of events as this theory asserts. As we have already stated, God is involved in everything.

If God foreknows that the conditions on which they are suspended will be fulfilled, then these events belong to the class of events which are certainly future; whereas if God does not know whether or not the conditions will be fulfilled by man, then His Foreknowledge is denied, and these events in question belong to the class of the happenchance. Nor do the Scripture Passages to which appeal is made to try to buttress such a Doctrine, such as Genesis 11:6; Exodus 3:19; Deuteronomy 7:3-4; I Samuel 23:10-13; II Samuel 12:8, etc., afford a basis

NOTES

for this Doctrine.

The Scripture recognizes that God has put all things in particular categories, and speaks of what can or cannot happen under such and such conditions; but none of these Passages assert or imply that the events are suspended upon conditions which are either unknown or undetermined, or not controlled by God.

GOD'S PLAN

God's Foreknowledge, according to the Scripture, is based upon His Plan or Eternal Purpose, which embraces everything that comes to pass. God is never represented as a mere onlooker seeing the future course of events, but having no part in them. That God has such a Plan is the teaching of the entire scope of Scripture. It is implied in the Old Testament conception of God as an Omnipotent (All-Powerful) Person governing all things in accordance with His Divine Plan.

This idea is involved in the Names of God revealed to the Patriarchs, *"El," "Elohim," "El Shaddai,"* and in the Prophetic Name *"Jehovah of Hosts."* This latter Name teaches not only God's Infinite Power and Glory, but also makes Him known as interposing in accordance with His Sovereign Will and Purpose in the affairs of this world, and as having also the spiritual powers of the Heavenly World at His disposal for the execution of His Eternal Purpose. Hence, the idea of God comes to signify the Omnipotent Ruler of the Universe (Ps. 24:10; Isa. 6:3; 51:5; 54:5; Jer. 10:16; Amos 9:5).

HUMAN HISTORY

Not only in this conception of God as Omnipotent and Sovereign Ruler is the thought of His Eternal Plan evolved, it is explicitly asserted throughout the whole Old Testament. The Purpose of God as determining human history in the Book of Genesis lies clearly upon the surface of the Narrative, as, for example, in the history of Abraham and of Joseph.

And where there is no abstract statement of this Truth, it is evident that the Writer regards every event as but the unfolding of the Purposes and Plan of God. In the Psalms, Prophets, and Wisdom Books, this Truth finds explicit and reiterated assertion. Jehovah has an Eternal Purpose (Ps. 33:11), and this Purpose will certainly come to pass (Isa. 14:27; 43:13).

As well, this Purpose includes all events and renders certain their occurrence (Isa. 14:24; 40:10; 46:9-10; Zech. 1:6).

Also, the Providential control wherewith Jehovah executes this plan includes the heart of man (Prov. 21:1).

Likewise, and stated, the New Testament regards all history as but the unfolding of God's Eternal Purpose (Acts 4:28), which includes man's Salvation (Eph. 1:4-5; II Tim. 1:9), the provision of Christ as Saviour (I Pet. 1:20), and the character and nature of the Christian (Eph. 2:10).

SO HOW DO WE ANSWER ALL THE QUESTIONS WHICH GOD'S FOREKNOWLEDGE PROPOSES?

Knowing and understanding that God is involved in every single event of human history, even to a far greater degree than our human minds can grasp, how are certain things reconciled? If one is to consider that the Lord notes every sparrow's fall, and numbers the hairs on each and every head of every person in the world (Mat. 10:29-30), then one has at least some idea as to the degree of involvement. As stated, it is beyond comprehension.

So how can God have this much involvement, thereby foreknowing all things, and not at the same time impact the free will of man? This we do know concerning man's free will:

While God speaks to men, deals with men, moves upon men, convicts and even pressures men, there is no record in the Word of God that He violates the free moral agency (free will) of any person. Actually, the entirety of the tone and tint of Scripture is *"Whosoever will"* (Rev. 22:17).

The only answer that one can give in respect to this question is that God, Who has and Who is Divine Power, Divine Knowledge and Divine Presence, can involve Himself in anything desired and to any degree desired, and at the same time, not affect man's free moral agency, at least to go beyond the normal appeal. Still, in every sense of the word,

NOTES

once a certain level is reached, God is beyond the comprehension of man.

The phrase, *"He also did predestinate,"* proclaims here the basic Bible Teaching of Predestination, which deals with God's Plan. However, Predestination does *not* pertain to individual conformity of free wills to that Plan. God has called all men and all are free to accept or reject the Call (Jn. 3:16; I Tim. 2:4; II Pet. 3:9; Rev. 22:17).

All who do accept, He has foreknown and predestinated to be conformed to the Image of His Son that His Son might be the firstborn among many Brethren.

Those who reject the Plan, He has foreknown and predestinated to be consigned to Eternal Hell as an everlasting monument of His Wrath on rebels (Isa. 66:22-24; Rev. 14:9-11; Mat. 25:41, 46).

PREDESTINATION AS A DOCTRINE

As is known, there are several views on this subject, with the view I have just given being that of this Writer.

Many in the Church world subscribe to the Calvinistic view of Predestination, that it is the aspect of foreordination whereby the Salvation of the Believer is taken to be effected in accordance with the Will of God, Who has called and elected him, in Christ, unto Life Eternal. In other words, the individual has nothing to do with his or her eternal destination, that having been decided by God from Eternity past.

However, this same teaching concludes that while God has elected some for Salvation, that there is nothing taught in Scripture which points to personal reprobation — in other words, that God has predestined some to be eternally lost, i.e., consigned to the Lake of Fire forever. However, to believe one is to believe the other. It is impossible to have it both ways.

If God has elected certain persons for Salvation, then simply by not being elected, automatically consigns them to eternal darkness.

Calvin's view of Predestination, which we believe to be rank error, had a strange way of addressing this problem. He said, *"Man therefore falls, God's Providence so ordaining, but he falls by his own fault."*

That statement is a contradiction in terms. How could he fall by his own fault, if God had so ordained it?

The argument may well be made, which it seems that Calvin tried to make, that God ordained the Fall only to the extent that through foreknowledge He knew it would happen.

However, once again the problem of contradiction arises. If God ordains the Fall, then man has no choice in the matter.

It is true that God has ordained, even as this 29th verse proclaims, that if man falls through his own free will, he will be eternally lost. (Fall is here used in the sense of dying lost.)

AUGUSTINE

Augustine lived about 400 years after Christ and was called by some *"The Father of Theology."*

In his teaching on the absolute Will of God, he made Divine Grace the only ground of man's Salvation; it was to him the irresistible power working Faith within the heart, and bringing freedom as its result.

He was partly right! Divine Grace is the only ground of man's Salvation (Eph. 2:8-9). However, Grace cannot be an irresistible power, for in so doing, it would cease to be Grace. As Grace is a free Gift of God, it must be freely offered, and the entire scope of Scripture maintains, that if it is Grace, it must be freely received.

Evidently, Augustine was attempting to reconcile the plain teaching of the Word of God respecting Grace with an erroneous view of Predestination.

Calvin's teaching on Predestination simply carried the Augustinian theory to its logical and necessary conclusion, and he was the first to adopt the Doctrine as the cardinal point of a theological system.

Calvin's mode of defining Predestination is that such is the Eternal Decree of God, by which He has decided with Himself what is to become of each and every individual. For all, he maintained, are not created in like condition; but Eternal Life is foreordained for some, eternal condemnation for others.

However, even Calvin confessed that his view of Predestination was a *"horrible decree."* But

NOTES

yet he somehow maintained that it was Love — *"the Fatherly Love of God,"* as he terms it — the efficiency of Saving Love — which fueled these decisions. (Calvin lived in the 16th Century.)

THE DOCTRINE OF UNCONDITIONAL ETERNAL SECURITY

From the teachings of Augustine and Calvin came the unscriptural Doctrine of Unconditional Eternal Security. In brief, this teaching claims that once a Believer is Saved, he cannot be lost irrespective of what he may do or how much he may habitually live in sin. However, most advocates of this Doctrine differ from Augustine and Calvin, in that man is Saved not because he is predestined to be so, but because of his own free will.

This Doctrine, as far as I am concerned is dishonest, in that it embraces part of Calvinism, while rejecting the rest.

Both Doctrines have caused untold millions to die eternally lost. If it is already predestined, then one should not even be concerned about one's soul, knowing that what will be, will be. As well, all Evangelism stops respecting Predestination. What's the point? Those who are going to be Saved, will be Saved, and those who are not going to be Saved, won't be Saved, irrespective in either case as to what anyone does. Some have attempted to address this glaring conclusion, by claiming that while it already has been decided, still, those who are Saved must work very hard to bring in the others. However, that is only a salve attempting to address the gross error.

Once again, if it is already predestined, what difference does it make as to how hard one works to bring others to Christ, it's all a moot point!

Likewise with Unconditional Eternal Security. Untold millions have been taught they could live any way they wanted to live after supposedly getting Saved, with no fear of the loss of their souls. Consequently, that's exactly what many who believe this Doctrine have done and are doing.

ARMINIUS

Jacob Arminius lived in the late 16th

Century. He strongly opposed Calvin's teaching on Predestination. It is his interpretation of the Scriptures respecting this subject, to which we basically subscribe.

Arminianism gives Grace a supreme place, and makes it, when welcome, pass into Saving Grace.

The idea of that statement is simply that it is by Grace that one is Saved (Eph. 2:8-9). However, it is only when Grace is welcomed and accepted, that it then becomes Saving Grace. In other words, the Grace of God is abundant to all, but can only be extended to those *"whosoever will"* so that it be extended to them (Rev. 22:17).

He made election depend on Faith, which is the condition of Universal Grace.

This statement means that God has elected people to be Saved who exhibit Faith in His Son, The Lord Jesus Christ, and the Sacrifice He gave of Himself at Calvary. While Grace is universal, meaning free to all, as it must be if it is to be Grace, the condition for receiving Grace is, as stated, *"Faith."*

Arminianism rejects the so-called Elect Grace of the Predestination Theory. This teaches that Grace is extended only to those who are predestined to be Saved. Of course, the Bible teaches no such thing.

Arminianism holds the awakened human will to cooperate with Divine Grace, in such wise that it rests with the human will whether the Divine Grace is really accepted or rejected.

Arminianism looks to Faith and Repentance as conditions of Personal Salvation (Acts 20:21). The Arminian standpoint admits the Foreknowledge of God, but denies foreordination (some ordained to be Saved and some ordained to be lost).

The Reader may think these Doctrines to be of little significance; however, to be blunt, there are untold millions at this moment in Hell simply because they had an erroneous view of these subjects as it concerned their soul's Salvation. No, these Doctrines are not of small consequence, but rather the very opposite. The Believer should know what he believes and why he believes it.

THE IMAGE OF HIS SON

The phrase, *"To be conformed to the Image of His Son,"* is the Predestination addressed

here, and the *only* Predestination addressed.

Those who of their own free will who accept Christ, are predestined to be conformed by the Holy Spirit, which we have been addressing here throughout the entirety of this Chapter, into the Christlike Image.

Let us observe the way in which Paul introduces this subject, so as to better understand his drift.

He has been speaking of the trials and imperfections of the present life, and urging his readers not to be discouraged by them, on the ground that if they continued to *"live after the Spirit,"* these things will by no means hinder, but rather further, the final issue. To strengthen this position he introduces the thought of God's Eternal Purpose.

The idea is that the Believer being in the State of Grace in which he now finds himself, is due to God's Eternal Purpose to call us to this State, and our having accepted. Consequently, it is impossible that the circumstances in which He has placed us, or any power thereafter, should thwart His Purpose, providing we continue to believe Him (Barmby).

"Conformed" in the Greek is *"summorphos,"* and means *"to be made like unto."* So, the idea is that the Believer become Christlike in every way. Hence, He said, *"Learn of Me"* (Mat. 11:29).

"Image" in the Greek is *"eikon,"* and means *"a copy, representation, resemblance."*

THE FIRSTBORN

The phrase, *"That He might be the Firstborn among many Brethren,"* has to do with Jesus being the prototype, which means the original model on which other things are patterned, in this case Believers.

Jesus as the *"Firstborn"* is the Only Begotten Son, meaning the first of all creatures (Incarnation) to be begotten of God, the Only One of all beings begotten of God, the first and Only One of the family of adopted and *"created"* Brethren begotten of God (Eph. 4:24; Col. 3:10).

The Church is the Called-out people of the One Who is the Firstborn (Heb. 12:23). Adam and Angels were by creation, not by begetting (Gen. 6:1-4; Job 1:6; 38:4-7; Lk. 3:38).

All Creation came into existence by creative acts, not by a begetting as in the case of Jesus. Even those many Brethren are not begotten in the sense Jesus was by the Holy Spirit. They (we) were begotten by men, not by God, and were thus brought into the human family, not the family of God. The only way one gets into God's Family is by adoption (Rom. 8:14-16; Gal. 4:5-6; Eph. 1:5). Jesus was not adopted, but Begotten, hence, the *"Firstborn."*

In the New Testament the word *"Firstborn* (prototokos)" appears only nine times. Twice it refers to Jesus in a literal way — that is, as the first child in the family of Joseph and Mary (Mat. 1:25; Lk. 2:7). This word occurs one time in the plural, to identify Believers as the *"Church of the Firstborn"* (Heb. 12:23).

This phrase suggests a position of special intimacy with God. One other use of *"prototokos"* is historical, a reference to the events of the Redemption of Israel from Egypt (Heb. 11:28).

BY AND LARGE ONLY TO JESUS

In most cases, however, *"prototokos"* serves as a technical theological term, applied only to Jesus (Rom. 8:29; Col. 1:15, 18; Heb. 1:6; Rev. 1:5).

This use is not literal but is intended to suggest Jesus' supreme rank and the uniqueness of His special relationship with the Father. In connecting the title of *"Firstborn"* with the Resurrection (Col. 1:18; Rev. 1:5), Scripture also offers us hope. Jesus has entered the realm of Glory. We too, though junior members of the family, will also share in the Glory Jesus now enjoys.

ERRONEOUS DOCTRINE

Some have contended from this verse, that Jesus was Born Again as any believing sinner is, therefore, the *"Firstborn."* Furthermore, they claim that this was done in Hell, in other words, that when He died on Calvary, He died as a sinner, went to Hell, and was Born Again in Hell.

Of course, there is nothing in Scripture to even remotely suggest such a thing. Jesus was not a sinner, and did not die as a sinner.

Jesus was the most Pure, Righteous,

Perfect Human Being Who ever lived. In fact, He had to be this way in order to be a Perfect Sacrifice, in order to be the Sin-Offering, which in effect was His Perfect Body. Any sin would have marred this Sacrifice, and made it unacceptable unto God (Ex. 12:5).

On the Cross Jesus was made to be a Sin-Offering, which paid the terrible penalty of man's sin, consequently, satisfying the Sin Debt. To satisfy that Debt, He had to die, but His Death had to be perfect, i.e., *"a Perfect Offering."*

While He did go to Paradise which was in the heart of the Earth and separated from the burning side of Hell only by a great gulf, there is no record in the Word of God that He went into the burning pit with all the lost souls, which are claimed by some (Lk. 16:23-31).

If one is to notice, the Scripture says *"The Firstborn among many Brethren,"* not *"The Firstborn among many lost."*

(30) "MOREOVER WHOM HE DID PRE-DESTINATE, THEM HE ALSO CALLED: AND WHOM HE CALLED, THEM HE ALSO JUSTIFIED: AND WHOM HE JUSTIFIED, THEM HE ALSO GLORIFIED."

The phrase, *"Moreover whom He did predestinate,"* refers <u>not</u> to some predestinated to be lost and others to be Saved, but rather refers back to the previous verse, in that <u>*those*</u> who accept Him of their own free will, He has *"predestinated* (them) *to be conformed to the Image of His Son."*

"WHOSOEVER WILL"

The premise of *"Whosoever will"* runs like a deep river all the way from the Book of Genesis through the Book of Revelation. Actually, the first invitation was given in the Garden of Eden immediately after the Fall, when *"The Lord God called unto Adam and said unto him, Where art thou?"* (Gen. 3:9). It closes out in the Book of Revelation with such an appeal that no one need misunderstand what is being said. As well, understanding that these were among the last words given by the Holy Spirit as He closed out the Canon of Scripture, there need not be any misunderstanding as to His intentions. Actually, it is the only time in the Bible that the Holy

Spirit refers to Himself as speaking, and says, *"And the Spirit and the Bride say, Come. And let him that heareth say, Come. And let him that is athirst come. And <u>whosoever will</u>, let him take the Water of Life freely"* (Rev. 22:17).

As well, in between those great beginning and ending Books of the Bible, the Words of Jesus echo to the whole of humanity, when He said, *"If <u>any man</u> thirst, let him come unto Me, and drink"* (Jn. 7:37). If one is to notice, He said *"any man,"* and He meant exactly what He said, which means the invitation is not extended to only a few who are predestinated. In fact, and as we have said, if men are already predestinated for Heaven, what's the point of the invitation anyway?

THE CALLED

The phrase, *"Them He also called,"* has a twofold meaning:

1. First of all, God has called, even as I think we have adequately illustrated, the whole of humanity, and for all time. If Salvation is available to one, then it must be available to all. As stated, that's the warp and woof of the entirety of the Bible. That means there is no such thing as a limited Atonement or a limited Salvation, or a limited Call for that matter (Jn. 3:16; 7:37).

Actually, God has to Call in order for anyone to be Saved. Man is so spiritually dead, that on his own he does not, and in fact, cannot Call upon God. With no spiritual life in him whatsoever, he is dead to all things which pertain to God. Therefore, no human being in his sinful, unconverted, unregenerate state, has ever called on God, without the Holy Spirit first of all in some manner awakening him to his need. As stated, that Call is going out to the whole of humanity, and has for all time.

This is done despite the fact, that God through foreknowledge knows who is going to accept and who is going to reject. Nevertheless, in respect to those who reject, when they stand at the Great White Throne Judgment (Rev. 20:11-15), they will not be able to say that they had no opportunity. Paul makes that abundantly clear in Romans 1:20.

About a thousand years before Christ, the Holy Spirit through Solomon said, *"Turn*

you at my reproof (repent)*: behold* (if you will do this), *I will pour out My Spirit unto you, I will make known My Words unto you.*

"Because I have Called, and ye refused; I have stretched out My Hand, and no man regarded;

"But ye have set at nought all My Counsel, and would none of My Reproof:

"I also will laugh at your calamity; I will mock when your fear cometh" (Prov. 1:23-26).

Predestination, erroneously thought, claims that all who are *"Called"* accept; however, the Word of God is clear and plain that all who are called do not accept.

2. As this *"Call"* is given *to* something, rather someone, it is also given *for* something, *"to be conformed to the Image of His Son."* The sinner is called from something, to something, in this case from darkness to light, from sin to Salvation, from lost to found, from Hell to Heaven, from spiritual death to Spiritual Life, from Satan to Jesus, etc.

JUSTIFICATION

The phrase, *"And whom He called, them He also Justified,"* means that God takes away the guilt and penalty for sins, and bestows upon the believing sinner a Positive Righteousness, even Jesus Christ Himself, in Whom the Believer now stands forever, innocent, uncondemned, and Righteous in every point of Law. This speaks of the Moral Law of Moses, which in reality is the Law of God, and is incumbent upon every human being who has ever lived. It cannot change, because it is Moral Law, therefore, it stands forever. I speak of the Ten Commandments, minus the Fourth, which was not carried over into the New Covenant, because it of all the Ten, was not moral but rather ceremonial.

GLORIFIED

The phrase, *"And whom He Justified, them He also Glorified,"* refers to the Act of God, yet to come, which will transform the Believer's body at the Rapture (Resurrection) into a body like the Resurrection Body of our Lord Jesus. As stated, this is a future event.

Yet the Apostle puts it in the past tense. How can he do this?

The Holy Spirit through Paul said these

Words in this way, because in the Mind of God, it is a guaranteed event although future. Actually, only God can guarantee future events. The idea is, that just as surely as the Believer has been Justified, just as surely will the Believer be Glorified.

The whole argument of Chapters 6-8 has been that Justification and the new life of Holiness in the Spirit are inseparable experiences. Hence, Paul can take one step to the end, and write, *"But whom He Justified, these also He Glorified."* Yet the tense in the last word is amazing.

It has been said, that this particular phrase is the most daring anticipation of Faith found in the entirety of the New Testament. As well, the life is not to be taken out of it by the philosophical consideration that with God there is neither before or after. The Glorification is stated as already consummated, though still future in the fullest sense.

The idea is this: the step implied in *"He Glorified"* is both complete and certain in the Divine Councils.

The Holy Spirit is explaining here the totality of Salvation. As such, He does it as only it can be done by proclaiming its totality. Consequently, even though the last step of Glorification the Saint does not yet have, its certitude is as sure as God. He has already decreed it; therefore, the Resurrection is certain (the Resurrection will be the time of Glorification).

In fact, Jesus is the Resurrection. When Martha said unto Him, *"If Thou hadst been here, my Brother had not died . . . Jesus saith unto her, Thy Brother shall rise again."*

Martha understood that to refer to the coming Resurrection of all Saints and answered accordingly. However, *"Jesus said unto her, I am the Resurrection, and the Life."*

In other words, He said to her, *"Martha look at Me, you are looking at the Resurrection, I am the Resurrection and the Life"* (Jn. 11:20-26).

(31) "WHAT SHALL WE THEN SAY TO THESE THINGS? IF GOD BE FOR US, WHO CAN BE AGAINST US?"

The question, *"What shall we then say to these things?"*, is meant to take the Believer far above the difficulties of this present time, in other words, looking to that Coming Day,

NOTES

the Resurrection, when all things will then be made right.

The two words *"these things"* refer to the suffering presently endured (vss. 17-18) in comparison with *"the Glory which shall be revealed in us."* The Apostle has disparaged the suffering in comparison with the Glory. He has interpreted it as in a manner prophetic of the Glory (vss. 19-27) (Denney).

The question, *"If God be for us, who can be against us?"*, puts everything in its proper perspective.

"If" in the Greek is *"ei,"* and means *"a fulfilled condition."* Consequently, it should have been translated, *"Since God is for us . . . ."*

As well, the words *"be"* and *"can be"* are in italics in your Bible, which means that they are not in the original Greek Text, but were supplied by the translators in an effort to fill out the thought.

The thought of Paul is not in the form of a hypothetical condition, as if it were a question whether God is for us or not. His thought is, *"In view of the fact that God is for us, who is or could be against us, so as to do us harm? That is, since God is for the Saints, on their side, who can harm them?"* (Wuest).

A PERSONAL EXPERIENCE

This particular question, actually asked in the form of statement, *"If God be for us, who can be against us?"*, is very dear to me personally, as it is, of course, to all who Love the Lord. What I'm about to relate is minor and of little consequence relative to the suffering for Christ which many have endured through the ages. However, it will, I think, make the point.

In our last Crusade in Houston, Texas, which was conducted in one of the Auditoriums in the City, the Lord moved mightily with many being Saved and Baptized with the Holy Spirit. Actually, the Saturday Night Service experienced a powerful Moving of the Holy Spirit. God Anointed me mightily to preach, with conviction touching the congregation in a strong way, with many responding to the Altar Call.

Having experienced this Move of God, and wishing that the entirety of the Church in Houston could have experienced that particular Service, and especially the Pentecostal Denomination with whom I had formerly been associated, I was heavy hearted because that had not been the case.

In fact, that particular Denomination had opposed us greatly, even to the point of threatening their people if they came to the meetings. As stated, I was heavy hearted over that and actually grieving in my spirit.

When Frances and I walked into the Hotel that Saturday night after the evening Service, and my mind heavily upon these things, the Spirit of the Lord came all over me in a powerful way, so strong in fact, that I began to weep.

I was thinking in my heart, *"Why do they oppose me so much, do they not know that the Spirit of God is moving greatly and why would they oppose that?"* As well, the thoughts were crowding my mind, as to how we could reach the people with that type of opposition, especially considering that it was almost total in its application?

To those thoughts the Lord spoke to my heart that night these very words, *"If God be for us, who can be against us?"*

It greatly comforted me, even tremendously so, even though the hurt and the grieving remained.

THE OPPOSITION

In fact, there are many who are *"against"* the Child of God, with much of the opposition sadly and regrettably, coming from the Church itself, even as it has always done. But at the same time, God is bigger than all of that, actually bigger than anything that may attempt to hinder. As someone has well said, *"God and one Believer, is a majority in any situation."*

Since 1988, I have watched and experienced the entirety of the News Media of this Nation, along with political efforts, to attempt to shut down this Ministry. Even above that, I have observed virtually all of the Church World who have done the same identical thing. The only thing that has not been done, at least to my knowledge, is that no one has been hired to attempt to kill us. Consequently, it has taken the Miracle-Working Power of God, even on a daily basis, to keep this Ministry alive. There has just been

simply no other way that it could survive.

In late 1991, even as I have mentioned, the Lord told me to have two prayer meetings a day which we have done, with the exception of Service times and Saturday morning. We have literally cried to God during these times, imploring Him for Leading, Guidance, and Direction, knowing that if He did not provide such that we would not be able to survive. The only way that David could survive Saul, was by the Miracle-Working Power of God.

Please be certain, that Saul did not die with that Monarch those many years ago. He is alive and well and still attempting to kill those who are of God, and are called of God, even as he tried to kill David.

But God did perform Miracle after Miracle, which He continues to do unto this very hour.

Having said that, thank the Lord that there is a segment of the Body of Christ around the world, with some few Spiritual Leaders who truly Love God, and are led by the Holy Spirit, who have been a great blessing to this Evangelist, to whom I will ever be grateful. There haven't been many, but those few have been very special, very precious, and have meant more to this Preacher, than words could ever begin to describe.

In all of this there is one thing that really matters and one thing alone, and that is that *"God be for us."* If the whole world is for us and God isn't, then nothing is going to work. Conversely, if the whole world is against us, and God is for us, it will turn out alright.

(32) "HE THAT SPARED NOT HIS OWN SON, BUT DELIVERED HIM UP FOR US ALL, HOW SHALL HE NOT WITH HIM ALSO FREELY GIVE US ALL THINGS?"

The phrase, *"He that spared not His Own Son,"* concerns the Great Gift of God, The Lord Jesus Christ.

"Spared" in the Greek is *"pheidomai,"* and means *"to treat leniently, to spare."* The idea is, that God did not treat His Son leniently or spare Him. He gave Heaven's best.

The idea is, that there was never any question that Love would do this thing, because Love must Redeem, at least if it is possible, but that the tremendous Cost and Price was ever before God, in this which He did.

The phrase, *"But delivered Him up for us*

all," concerns the whole of mankind, and not just a select, predestined few.

Delivered Him up to what?

JESUS

He delivered Him up to become a Man, which Form incidentally He will retain forever. That within itself, is altogether beyond anything that we could even begin to think. What He was, the Creator of the ages, *"Dwelling in the Light which no man can approach unto; Whom no man hath seen, nor can see,"* is beyond our comprehension (I Tim. 6:16).

For 33 1/2 years He lived as a Peasant, and during His 3 1/2 years of Public Ministry, was reviled, scorned, rejected, and then Crucified.

All of that was one thing, but the bearing of the sin penalty for all of mankind, was an act that was so absolutely unselfish, with that word being totally inadequate, but at the same time so awful, that even God could not look upon the scene, portrays that to which no other human being has ever experienced.

Even though He now resides in a Glorified Body, and will do so forever, still, that is a far cry from that which He once had, but will never have again, due to what He did for humanity.

The question, *"How shall He not with Him also freely give us all things?"*, lays bare before Believers the tremendous price paid for our Redemption. The idea is, that if God has done this, the giving up of His Only Son in order that we might be Saved, how can we think that He is going to allow us to be overcome by the Evil One, and I speak of those who truly want to live for God.

NO NEED FOR CONCERN

This does not mean that God will keep one against their will, but it does mean that irrespective of what comes or goes, those who want to live for God, irrespective of the opposition, need not fear. If the Lord did what He did respecting our Salvation, then one can be certain that He will do whatever it takes to keep that for which so much has been paid.

These things being so, if God be for us who can be against us so as to injure us? As well, Believers need not be anxious, for God

NOTES

being for us, fills the heart with a Rest and a Peace that shuts out all anxiety as to anything that could trouble it; for how could the Heart and the Hand that gave what was most precious to them fail in bounty, liberality and protection to those whom He has Saved? (Williams).

He Who has done so much, is certain to do much more.

In the first phrase of the Scripture, *"His Own"* in the Greek is *"idios,"* and means *"one's own peculiar, private possession."* Our Lord is the Father's Very Own, Private Possession, infinitely dear to Him (Wuest).

"Freely" in the Greek is *"dorean,"* and means *"without a cause, freely, gratuitously."* God freely gives us that which is most precious to Him, His Son.

In other words, God *"gives us all things,"* not because we deserve them, when in reality we deserve the very opposite. He does it because of His Love and His Grace. In other words, it is done not because of merit, nor is it expecting anything in return. It is a *"Gift."*

The phrase, *"He not with Him,"* speaks of both God the Father and God the Son, working in conjunction to bring about this great Redemption, and also working to give us Divine Protection, and as well, a guarantee that everything which goes with Salvation such as Glorification, will ultimately come.

(33) "WHO SHALL LAY ANY THING TO THE CHARGE OF GOD'S ELECT? IT IS GOD THAT JUSTIFIETH."

The question, *"Who shall lay any thing to the charge of God's Elect?"*, in effect means, *"Who shall pronounce those guilty whom God pronounces Righteous?"*

This means that every single sin by the trusting Believer which has ever been committed, has been washed away by the Precious Shed Blood of Jesus Christ, and because of one's Faith in that Shed Blood. As someone has well said, *"The Christian has no past, and Satan has no future!"*

This means that it is terribly improper, and actually an insult to God, for a Believer to bring up the sins of another which have long since been washed clean by the Blood of Jesus. As well, it is insulting to the Lord for the Believer to drag out his own sins again, which the Lord has already forgiven.

It does such a terrible injustice to the Mercy and Grace of God, considering that God does much more than merely forgive, but actually erases the sin from the account of the Believer, consequently, treating him as if the infraction was never committed. Actually, that is what Justification means. The sin is not only forgiven, but it is stricken from the record, and as far as God is concerned, it was never committed.

The phrase, *"It is God that Justifieth,"* means that no one, not even Satan or his evil angels, dare question or deny, God's great Plan of Justification.

Even God cannot do both, accuse and justify at the same time. And since our Justification resides in a Person, the Lord Jesus our Righteousness, in Whom we stand as uncondemned and unchargeable even as the Son Himself, it is impossible, after having been Justified, that we be again accused — and brought under condemnation (Wuest).

The word *"Elect"* in the Greek is *"eklektos,"* and means *"chosen out ones."* Paul's argument is, *"Who shall prefer any charge or accusation against the chosen-out ones of God?"*

WHAT DOES *"ELECT"* MEAN?

God's purpose is to save all who conform to His Plan — and this is His Choice or Election in the matter. By Grace, men who conform will become the Elect and be Saved, while those who do not will be damned (Mk. 16:15-16; Lk. 13:1-5; Jn. 3:16-18; I Tim. 2:4-5; II Pet. 3:9; Rev. 22:17).

The choice was first on God's part; but it must be accepted by men for them to receive the benefits and become a part of the Elect or Chosen Ones of God (Jn. 15:16; Eph. 1:4; 2:10; II Thess. 2:13); men must make their Calling and Election sure as stated in II Peter 1:10.

It is Scripturally erroneous to think that God has elected some people to be lost and some people to be saved, as some teach. Furthermore, according to this erroneous teaching, there is absolutely nothing they can do about their place or status. They are either doomed to die eternally lost, and they cannot stop it, or they are destined to go to Heaven, which will happen no matter what

they do. Such false doctrine, and false doctrine it is, is not taught in the Word of God.

The truth is: As the Gospel is preached, anyone, irrespective as to who they might be, if they will accept the Lord, they immediately become *"God's elect"* (Jn. 15:16; Rom. 8:33; Titus 1:1). Satan has caused many to be lost because they have believed the lie that they are elected to be lost.

Let us say it again: There could be nothing further from the truth. The Scripture still says, *"Whosoever will . . ."* (Rev. 22:17).

ELECTION FOR A SPECIAL PURPOSE

Election in this capacity, and which happens constantly, is the act of choice whereby God picks an individual or group out of a larger company for a purpose or destiny of His Own Appointment. The main Old Testament Word in the Hebrew for this is the verb *"beahar,"* which expresses the idea of deliberately selecting someone or something after carefully considering the alternatives. The word implies a decided preference.

The reason that God does this is known only to Him. Having perfect knowledge, He looks at a Believer and chooses that Believer on the basis of what He knows that Believer can and will be in Him. That means that every single Preacher of the Gospel, has in a sense been elected by God for this particular task, with God of course, knowing all they would be and do at the time of their Calling. So, He called David anyway, knowing that David would fail miserably in the case of Bathsheba and her husband Uriah. In fact, He chose Israel, knowing they would fail and even crucify His Own Beloved Son. This did not come as a surprise to Him.

WHY WOULD GOD ELECT SOMEONE KNOWING THAT THE END RESULT WOULD NOT BE GOOD?

First of all, if we judge anything accordingly by its present appearance, we are judging wrong. Anything and everything that God has elected, will ultimately come out to the good. In other words, Israel will one day be totally and completely restored. However, it will be at the time of their own volition, and as they make a choice to accept Jesus Christ as their Messiah and Saviour.

Admittedly, all of those who lived through the many centuries of rebellion and rejection will be and are eternally lost. Nevertheless, Israel will ultimately come back, even as God knew all along that they shall.

Despite the fact of the Apostate Church and lukewarmness, there is a Remnant, as there has always been a Remnant, who loves God and serves Him. They do it of their own choice, freely, willingly, loving Him out of their heart, which has to be of free will or it simply cannot be Love. In that case, it is *"A Glorious Church"* (Eph. 5:27).

(34) "WHO IS HE THAT CONDEMNETH? IT IS CHRIST THAT DIED, YEA RATHER, THAT IS RISEN AGAIN, WHO IS EVEN AT THE RIGHT HAND OF GOD, WHO ALSO MAKETH INTERCESSION FOR US."

The question, *"Who is he that condemneth?"*, is very similar to the question of the previous verse, but with one difference.

The climax of this Chapter is now reached and the Apostle triumphantly challenges anyone to lay anything to the charge of God's Elect. This glorious word *"Elect"* first occurs here in the Epistle.

The expiatory character of Christ's Death is affirmed in verse 34, and the meaning of Justification in verse 33. The challenge, *"Who shall bring a charge against God's Elect?"*, i.e., who shall pronounce those guilty whom God pronounces Righteous, makes clear its significance.

The only one who dares to condemn the Child of God, especially considering what Jesus Christ has done for him, and the price in which He paid, is Satan and his followers. The Scripture labels him as the *"Accuser of the Brethren"* (Rev. 12:10).

Consequently, when a Believer stoops to the low, low level of accusing or condemning another Believer, they have then joined the league of Satan, and have actually entered into a form of witchcraft.

WHAT DOES PAUL MEAN BY THE WORD *"CONDEMN?"*

Condemnation is an important concept. It is important both theologically and spiritually, for there are many persons whose sense of guilt leads them to fear condemnation. It is important even for those who need

not fear condemnation, for too often Christians are tempted to take God's place and judge (condemn) others!

THE OLD TESTAMENT CONCEPT

The Hebrew word usually translated *"condemn"* is *"rasa."* It means *"to be wicked"* or *"to act wickedly."*

Another word, *"asam,"* which means *"to offend"* or *"to be guilty,"* is also infrequently translated *"to condemn"* or *"to be condemned."* The thought is that the person who chooses a wicked rather than Godly lifestyle has brought himself or herself under condemnation.

It is important to remember that the wicked can turn from their ways (Ezek. Chpt. 18) and that Repentance and Confession can restore a right relationship with God.

THE GREEK WORDS

There is a large family of Greek words which can be translated *"condemn."* However, the basic word is *"krino,"* which means, *"to judge"* or *"to decide."*

There are a number of related words. The noun *"krima,"* is usually rendered *"condemnation"* and means *"to give judgment against,"* and thus, *"to condemn."*

Another Greek word *"kataginosko"* means *"to make a negative moral assessment,"* and thus, *"to blame."*

Another Greek word is *"katadikazo,"* and means *"to pass judgment on."*

Originally *"krino"* and its associate words indicated simply *"an assessment."* A person examined a matter and then came to a conclusion about it.

By New Testament times these words had become a part of the legal terminology used to speak of bringing charges, of judging, and of passing judgment. When used of God, *"krima* (judgment)*"* is understood as *"condemnation,"* for one judged by God is already condemned.

DIVINE CONDEMNATION IN THE NEW TESTAMENT

The New Testament reminds us that Jesus did not enter our world to condemn us. He came because humanity was already condemned (Jn. 3:17-18; Rom. 5:15-16). Those who fail to respond to God's Word are in a state of condemnation already (Jn. 3:36; 12:48).

Jesus came to save the world. His success has reflected in assertions such as this: *"There is now no condemnation for those who are in Christ Jesus"* (Rom. 8:1).

Because of Jesus, God's attitude toward Believers is not one of condemnation. What God still condemns is the sin in sinners (Rom. 8:3). We who respond to the Gospel Message in Faith have the assurance that no one can successfully charge us. Jesus, *"at the Right Hand of God,"* is *"also interceding for us"* (Rom. 8:34).

CONDEMNING OURSELVES AND OTHERS

Those who remain outside the circle of God's Grace by their refusal to respond to the Gospel (Jn. 3:18; 5:24) stand condemned; they are under Judgment for their sinful actions (Mat. 12:41-42; Jn. 5:29; 12:48). But we who have trusted Christ have passed beyond condemnation (Rom. 8:1).

God views us as being in His Son, and no charge can be lodged against us. Yet two important Truths are taught in the Scriptures about Believers and condemnation. First, we are to be careful to do what is right so that our consciences will not condemn us for actions we believe are wrong (Rom. 14:22; I Jn. 3:20-21).

And second, we are not to condemn fellow Believers (Rom. 14:3).

Theologically, condemnation can be avoided only by trusting in Jesus, Who bears our sin and thus removes us from the position of prisoners before the Bar of Divine Justice. Spiritually, we are to recognize the freedom from condemnation that Jesus brings us and learn to live as forgiven men and women.

Released from this burden ourselves, we are to bring the Gospel to others so that they may be freed as well (Richards).

The phrase *"It is Christ that died,"* refers to the price, great price, overwhelming price, a price absolutely paid which guarantees our Salvation. In other words, when one condemns a fellow Believer, one is condemning Christ, the Price He paid and the Victory He won. In effect, one is saying that the Price

is not enough, insufficient, inadequate, for to condemn the Believer is to condemn the Price.

PENANCE AND PUNISHMENT

Who would be so foolish as to dare do such a thing?

Of course, Satan would do such a thing, even as we already have said. However, for Believers to do such a thing, proclaims to all that they have left Grace and entered into Law. In other words, they are saying that the Believer simply having Faith in Christ and what He did at Calvary is not enough for their sins, but other penalties must be added as well. Whether such people say so or not, they are actually advocating the Catholic Doctrine of *"Penance."*

To do *"Penance"* is to carry out some task, whatever it may be, which is then supposed to pay for the sin, etc. In fact, the Major Pentecostal Denominations engage in this foolishness, at least with their Preachers. If something is done that is wrong, these Preachers are forced to get out of the Ministry for two years or some such period of time, and at times they are forced to move to another City, etc.

While they may personally deny that such is *"Penance,"* but rather *"Punishment,"* still, it all amounts to the same. In the first place, no Believer has the right, irrespective of who they may be, to condemn or to punish another Believer. The Lord has plainly said that *"Vengeance* (punishment) *is Mine; I will repay, saith the Lord"* (Rom. 12:19).

James asks, *"Who art thou that judgest another?"* In other words he is saying, *"Who do you think you are, thinking you are qualified to judge someone else?"* (James 4:12).

He then went on to say that the Lord was the only One Who was qualified to judge.

The phrase, *"Yea rather, that is risen again,"* refers to the ratification of that which He purchased for sinners in His Death. The Resurrection ratified the fact that Jesus was the Perfect Sacrifice, and that God accepted it as such. So, what is being said is this:

IS IT NOT ENOUGH?

If God has accepted the Sacrifice of His Only Son, and proven it by raising Him from the dead, which He did, then who are we, or anyone else for that matter, to question such by condemning those who have placed their Trust and Faith in Him!

These are bold statements, and every Believer should readily and soberly understand what is being said and adhere to it very cautiously.

The phrase, *"Who is even at the Right Hand of God,"* refers to the Exaltation of Christ.

When He ascended, He was then given His rightful place at the Throne of God. It is at His Father's Right Hand. This speaks of Power and Authority. Actually, Jesus said after His Resurrection, *"All Power is given unto Me in Heaven and in Earth"* (Mat. 28:18).

Our Faith should rest on Christ's Death, but to that must be joined His Resurrection and Dominion, for without such, His Death was to no avail. He as the Second Adam purchased back for us what the First Adam lost.

As well, we must ever understand, that at this very moment He is Exalted at the Right Hand of God, and there for a Divine Purpose.

The phrase, *"Who also maketh Intercession for us,"* tells us what that purpose is.

The *"Intercession"* He makes, is different, even as we have already said, than the Intercession made by the Holy Spirit for us. The latter is that of help, while the former is that of guaranteeing our Redemption and the Forgiveness, Cleansing, and Washing of all sin from our lives. His Intercession guarantees not only what He has already done respecting our Salvation, but guarantees any future sin to be Washed and Cleansed as well, at least upon Repentance and Confession (I Jn. 1:9).

UNDERSTANDING THE INTERCESSION OF JESUS ON OUR BEHALF

Most Believers think their understanding of the Intercession provided for us by Christ is correct, that is if they have thought of it at all. With some that certainly may be true, but with the majority, I fear their understanding is inadequate.

To properly understand His Intercession on our behalf, we have to understand it in

the same context as that of His Death and Resurrection. Actually, even as Paul here now makes the case, it is placed in that category, consequently, linked together.

THE PSALMS

Most would hardly understand the Psalms as being the explanation of this extremely important subject; however, it is!

In some Bibles, as the Psalm is listed, in the instructions before some of them, the words *"Messianic Psalm"* are applied. That means that this particular Psalm refers to Jesus in some way, whether to His Life or Mission. By these identification characteristics it is being said that only these Psalms apply to Jesus, with the others to other things, etc. However, the Truth is, all 150 Psalms refer to Jesus Christ in some way.

WHAT THE PSALMS TELL US

The Book of Psalms is a Volume of Prophecy; its principle predictions concern the Perfection, the Sufferings, and the Succeeding Glories of the Messiah.

God having been dishonored by human unbelief and disobedience, it was necessary that a Man should be born Who would perfectly Love, Trust, and Serve Him; and Who would be the True Adam, Noah, Abraham, Israel, Moses, David, etc.

God's moral Glory demanded that sin should be judged; that sinners should repent, confess, and forsake sin and worship and obey Him; and being God His Nature required perfection in these emotions of the heart and will.

Such perfection was impossible to fallen man, and it was equally out of his power to provide a Sacrifice that would remove his guilt and restore his relationship with God.

The Psalms reveal Christ as satisfying in these relationships all the Divine Requirements. He, though Himself sinless, declares Himself in these Psalms to be the Sinner; and He expresses to God the abhorrence of sin accompanied by the Repentance and Sorrow which man ought to feel and express but will not and cannot.

Similarly the Faith, Love, Obedience, and Worship which man fails to give He perfectly renders.

AS THE HIGH PRIEST OF HIS PEOPLE

Thus, as the High Priest of His people He, the True Advocate, charges Himself with the guilt of our sins; declares them to be His Own; confesses them, repents of them, declaring at the same time His Own sinlessness; and atones for them.

Thus, those Psalms in which the Speaker declares His sinfulness and His sinlessness become quite clear of comprehension when it is recognized Who the Speaker is.

This is the manner of His Intercession.

WHAT MOST THINK!

As stated, if most Believers think about it at all, they visualize Jesus as turning to the Father and asking Him to forgive us of our sins, etc. The Father hears Him, and does what He requests. However, that is not the way it happens.

When Jesus took our place at Calvary, He literally became the sinner, even though He never sinned. As a result, punishment was loaded on Him, with sin's demands met which was death, and the Curse of the Law satisfied. Upon Faith the Believer is literally in Him when He died (Rom. 6:3-4; 8:1). The same holds for His Burial and Resurrection.

If one is to notice, it continues in the Exaltation, even as Paul speaks here concerning Jesus at the Right Hand of God. Paul said, *"And hath raised us up together, and made us sit together in heavenly places in Christ Jesus"* (Eph. 2:6). So, as Christ is seated at the Right Hand of the Father, we are in effect seated with Him and in Him.

However, it does not stop there, but continues in the same manner respecting the failures and sins of Believers. Jesus takes these failures and sins, makes them His Own, seeks for forgiveness, even though He never failed. Because He has never failed, forgiveness is always automatic, which extends to the Believer, and because we are in Him.

So, His Intercession for us is of far grander magnitude than at first thought. It is not merely a request for others, even as important and wonderful as that would be, but in reality, the taking of our place, even as He has always taken our place.

THE WONDER OF IT ALL

When one thinks of this, it is beyond comprehension. It amazes us, even as it should amaze us. What a Mighty God we serve, and what a Wonderful Christ Who has Saved us.

God's Requirements must be satisfied, in order that His Righteousness not be abrogated. That is not a matter of stubbornness, but rather of necessity. God wants to approach us, and for us to approach Him, but in a sinful condition on our part, such could not be done. Therefore, He made it possible, by becoming Man, The Man Christ Jesus, and in so doing, served as the Representative Man, and for all who will believe, the Saviour of all the Ages.

When one thinks of what Paul is saying here, as already stated, it humbles one. Why He would Love us in this fashion, I think we will never know. But yet we know He does. Even at this very moment, 11-22-97, as I dictate these words, He is making Intercession for us, and the moment you read them, whatever time or day that is, He will be faithful in continuing this all-important task, until one day we stand before Him, even precious in His Sight.

There are many examples in the Psalms of His Personal Intercession. As He does this, even declaring Himself a Sinner, and I might quickly add, on our behalf, for He has never sinned, because of a lack of understanding of True Intercession on the part of many, they do not recognize these Psalms as being of Christ even as all the others. For instance, of all the many that could be chosen, Psalm 51 is perhaps the greatest example. It is the plea of David, but yet, of the Greater Son of David.

(35) "WHO SHALL SEPARATE US FROM THE LOVE OF CHRIST? SHALL TRIBULATION, OR DISTRESS, OR PERSECUTION, OR FAMINE, OR NAKEDNESS, OR PERIL, OR SWORD?"

The question, *"Who shall separate us from the Love of Christ?"*, if one is to notice, speaks of the Love of Christ for the Believer, instead of the Believer's love for Christ.

In verses 35-39, some have attempted to promote the unscriptural Doctrine of Unconditional Eternal Security, which teaches that after one is truly Saved, they cannot be lost irrespective of what they may do, or how deep they may go out into sin and remain there, etc. Of course, this Doctrine is not Scriptural and for many and varied reasons. However, the main reason is that it abrogates all personal responsibility, as well as violating the free moral agency of man. In effect, and as we have already stated, it is another form of the erroneous Doctrine of Predestination, which teaches that all are either predestined to be Saved or lost, and there is nothing anyone can do to change that situation.

GOD WILL NOT PROTECT US FROM OURSELVES

While it is true that God protects the Believer as is recorded here from all outside adversity, there is nothing in these Passages which says that God protects the Believer from Himself. In other words, the Believer still retains the power of choice, and it is that choice that decides his eternal destiny. No! It is not that man's choice is greater than God. Such thinking is silly. But God has given man the privilege of choice, and in effect, the love spoken here, has to be by choice, or it simply cannot be love, whether it is on the part of God or man.

In other words, the very nature of one's living for God has to be on the principle of choice. It is the same as a husband and wife. One cannot force the other to love. That must be one's own prerogative. It is the same with God. We must freely love Him, or else it is not love.

In fact, this is the manner in which God made man in the very beginning. Had He wanted some type of human computer, He would have easily made man without a *"will."* However, to obtain that which He desired, which is that man would love Him, man *had* to be given the Power of Choice.

The question, *"Shall tribulation, or distress, or persecution, or famine, or nakedness, or peril, or sword?"*, presents the foe's armory as containing seven weapons — the whole of his resources.

But however these weapons may disfigure, deform, degrade, or denigrate the Believer, Christ will still Love and Prize him.

NOTES

For instance, Joseph was just as dear to that love when lying in the dungeon as when seated on the Throne. It is possible to separate from human love, but not from Christ's Love.

For instance, a man may love his betrothed very deeply, but if by the power of an enemy her beauty and her character be destroyed, it is possible his love for her can die. But not that of God toward those who are His.

That of which the Text speaks, and that of which we have spoken, pertains to the love of Christ for the Believer. However, on the other side of the coin, these things are allowed by God, as detrimental as they may seem on the surface, to rather deepen our love for God, rather than the opposite. And so it does!

Satan uses these weapons to try to separate us from the Love of Christ, not so much regarding the Lord loving us, for the enemy knows that is impossible. However, he does have the mistaken idea that these foes will weaken our love for God. There is a reason for that.

JOB

Satan claimed that Job loved God not because of Who God is, but for what God had done for Job (Job Chpt. 1). Actually, that is the entire contention of Satan against God.

He claimed then that men loved God because of the wonderful things the Lord did for them, and he continues to do the same presently. He refuses to admit that men love God simply because of Who He is. In other words, we will love Him, irrespective of what He does for us in the material and physical sense. Whether it is poverty or riches, we will love Him. Whether it is health or sickness, we will love Him. That and that alone is True Christianity.

Satan refuses to acknowledge that, which actually is the bedrock of serving God. In other words, we serve Him for Who He is, rather than for the things He gives us.

ONE REASON THAT THE MODERN PROSPERITY GOSPEL IS SO EVIL

This so-called Gospel, which in reality is *"another Gospel,"* makes money the priority. In other words, and irrespective as to how much it is denied, money and money alone is that Gospel. Jesus Christ and what He did at Calvary, plus the entirety of the Plan of Salvation to Redeem humanity from sin's terrible bondage, is cheapened to mere *"things."* Hence, Jesus said, *"Take heed, and beware of covetousness: for a man's life consisteth not in the abundance of the things which he possesseth"* (Lk. 12:15).

While God definitely does bless people, and financially as well, still, this is not the main thrust of the Gospel, and in fact, never has been. It plays right into Satan's hands with his age-old contention that no one truly loves God. Any supposed Love, he says, is merely a ploy to get things, etc. So, the Preachers who claim this as their Message, are not preaching the Gospel, are not winning people to Christ, and are actually playing into the hands of the Evil One.

If we forget the True Purpose for which Jesus came, which is to Redeem man from sin, then we have totally abrogated all that He did at Calvary, the Resurrection, and the Exaltation. Then as stated, we are preaching *"another Gospel"* (II Cor. 11:3-4).

THE ENTIRETY OF THE SO-CALLED CONFESSION MESSAGE

This false message which is prominent today, and has been prominent for several decades, claims that if the Believer has enough Faith, and his confession is proper, he can void all these tribulations, distresses, etc. This fits right in with the Prosperity Message, and in fact, is the Prosperity Message.

However, the entirety of the tenor of the Bible presents the very opposite of that preached. The Believer is not exempt from these things, but actually the very opposite. The people in the world who are giving Satan great problems, are the True Believers in Christ. Consequently, he will use every means at his disposal, to attempt to stop the Child of God, as should be obvious. In fact, the Believer is at war, and will be at war with the Evil One, at least regarding his Faith, until the Trump of God sounds.

However, if one will study Church History, one will find that great opposition and persecution by the Powers of Darkness, and in whatever manner these came, even to the giving up of one's life, have never weakened

or hurt the True Church of the Living God. For all who were snatched from its ranks, several others took their place, even knowing that it could mean their lives, as well. So, persecution has really never hurt the Church, actually only strengthened the Church, i.e., the individual Believer. To be frank, this is one of the very reasons it is allowed by the Lord.

That which weakens, hinders, stunts the spiritual growth, and turns aside the Believer, is the opposite message, with which we have been regaled for the last several decades — the false Prosperity Message.

LEAVEN

I realize that the Reader may think I am overly hard upon this particular subject. However, if that be the case, it is not Preachers per se proper to whom I address these remarks, but rather the message itself. It is the lie to which I am opposed, and not the people themselves. And yet, I realize that it is very difficult to separate the man and his message, perhaps impossible. Consequently, it is incumbent upon the Preacher of the Gospel not to allow his heart to be adversely affected by the propagators of this false message, but to stay focused on the true task at hand, the Evil One who is behind all of this, Satan himself.

Let not the Believer think that Satan doesn't know what he is doing. In fact, his greatest weapon is to make his message sound as near to the True Message as possible, so near in fact, that it takes one truly close to God to actually see the difference. In fact, he loads up his lie with Truth, which makes it very plausible. However, it is the *"leaven"* in the Truth which must be exposed, and which causes so much danger respecting the Believer (I Cor. 5:6). Irrespective as to how small the amount of *"leaven"* may be at the beginning, if it is not removed, it will ultimately take over the whole, until there is nothing left but leaven. That is Satan's purpose, and he is very good at what he does — mixing error with Truth.

(36) "AS IT IS WRITTEN, FOR THY SAKE WE ARE KILLED ALL THE DAY LONG; WE ARE ACCOUNTED AS SHEEP FOR THE SLAUGHTER."

The phrase, *"As it is written, For Thy sake we are killed all the day long,"* is taken from Psalm 44:22.

If one carefully reads that particular Psalm, it speaks of God Who had done great things for His people, but then seemingly withdraws His Hand of help and protection, allowing His people to seemingly be overcome. However, verses 20 and 21 tell us why.

Israel had strayed, and *"God (would) search this out, for He knoweth the secrets of the heart."*

The Lord allows tribulation for two purposes: A. To expose the *"leaven"* in our lives; and, B. To draw us nearer to God. It is sad that Believers need such chastisement, but often we do.

The phrase, *"We are accounted as sheep for the slaughter,"* proclaims a Great Truth that we should learn.

THE LIFE OF THE BELIEVER

When the sinner comes to Christ, his life ceases to be his own, it then becoming the property and possession of our Lord. Consequently, at that moment, we give up our lives, which is exactly what Jesus told us to do. He said, *"For whosoever will save his life shall lose it: and whosoever will lose his life for My sake shall find it"* (Mat. 16:25).

One of the great problems of the modern Believer is that he is attempting, erroneously I might add, to build a Paradise out of this present life, which makes him not too desirous of the one to come. If one is to notice the attitude of the Early Church, their hearts were on things above. I am afraid that presently, too many of us have our hearts on things below. Once again, and even though I am overly repetitive, the modern Prosperity Gospel fits perfectly into this scheme.

While the Believer has a great work at this present time to do, and while that work is of extreme importance, still, the Believer must ever know and realize that the Sons of God have not yet been manifested. That will happen only when Jesus comes. Please allow me to ask this question:

How many Believers and for whatever reason, truly want Jesus to come at this present time?

Some few do, while most know nothing

about His Coming, or else they have been erroneously taught, thinking that His Coming depends on them. Nothing could be more crass, even the height of prideful absurdity. Such is the modern Kingdom Message.

(37) "NAY, IN ALL THESE THINGS WE ARE MORE THAN CONQUERORS THROUGH HIM THAT LOVED US."

The phrase, *"Nay, in all these things we are more than conquerors,"* means that such has never stopped the True Church of God, and such will never be successful in that effort.

The phrase, *"More than conquerors,"* in the Greek is *"hupernikao,"* and means *"to conquer, to carry off the Victory, come off Victorious."* However, the Greek word *"huper"* attached to *"nikao,"* means *"above,"* thus, *"to come off more than Victorious, to gain a surprising Victory."* It is a holy arrogance of Victory in the Might of Christ (Meyer).

Perhaps it is a mistake to define in what the *"more"* consists; but if we do, the answer must be sought on the line indicated in the note on *"For thy sake we are killed all the day long"*; these trials not only do *not* cut us off from Christ's Love, they actually give us more intimate and thrilling experience of it (Denney).

The phrase, *"Through Him that loved us,"* means that He allowed these things to come to pass, not to destroy us, but rather the very opposite. It is because of His Love, which some have called *"Tough Love,"* that He allows adversities.

Such not only draws the Believer closer to God, and for the simple reason that we know our only hope is in Christ, but as well, these great Victories won by the Child of God despite the worst of adversities, portray to all of Heaven, as well as the darkened host of Satan, that God's people do not serve Him for *"things,"* but rather because they love Him. In other words, they are willing to lay down their lives for His Sake.

The *"conquering"* carries the idea, not so much of deliverance from these things, but rather that we did not allow these adversities to sully our Testimony, but rather to sharpen our Testimony.

In other words, these who have gone through such trials, and many have, did not do so because of a lack of Faith, but rather because of their Great Faith. Actually, it was meant to strengthen their Faith, which it did.

(38-39) "FOR I AM PERSUADED, THAT NEITHER DEATH, NOR LIFE, NOR ANGELS, NOR PRINCIPALITIES, NOR POWERS, NOR THINGS PRESENT, NOR THINGS TO COME,

"NOR HEIGHT, NOR DEPTH, NOR ANY OTHER CREATURE, SHALL BE ABLE TO SEPARATE US FROM THE LOVE OF GOD, WHICH IS IN CHRIST JESUS OUR LORD."

The phrase, *"For I am persuaded,"* comes from the heart of the Apostle, meaning that he has faced the things of which he now speaks.

There are probably few people in history, if any, who have suffered as Paul suffered in order to take the Gospel of Jesus Christ to a hurting world. While the Victory of his heart, even according to this 8th Chapter, was overflowing with strength and power, with Satan making no headway there, still, the Evil One fought the Apostle on every hand, with beatings, stonings, shipwreck, and about everything that one could possibly think. So, when he says, *"I am persuaded,"* it refers to something, or rather someone who has stood the test, namely himself.

The phrase, *"That neither death,"* means that Jesus has pulled the teeth of that monster. The True Believer no longer fears death, with untold numbers down through history, who have willingly laid down their lives for the Cause of Christ. In fact, not long after the writing of the Book of Acts, Rome turned ugly toward the Church, with the floors of its Arenas turning red with the spilled blood of those who died for Jesus.

The world of that day other than Christendom, was plagued with a myriad of gods. In other words, there were all types of gods worshiped by all types of people. Consequently, the Roman Senate voted that their Caesar, whoever he would be, would be declared as *"deity"* or *"god."* Most of the Caesars realizing their humanity and, consequent frailty, refused to have such a title attached to their name. However, Nero demanded to be called *"god."* Consequently, untold thousands died at the mercy of wild animals and Roman spears, simply because they would

NOTES

not say *"Caesar is Lord."* Their cry even unto death was, *"Jesus is Lord!"*

What a Testimony!

APOSTASY OF THE CHURCH

As well, down through the Dark Ages, the Church itself turned ugly, forsaking Christ, gradually evolving into what became known as the Catholic Church, attempting to bring about the Kingdom of God by force. As a result, untold thousands, with some even claiming millions, died for the Cause of Christ simply because they refused allegiance to the Catholic Church and the Pope. It was called the *"Dark Ages"* for a reason.

So, the great freedoms we presently have, did not come cheaply. They were paid for with blood, and not only on the field of battle, but even more so in the spirit world.

The phrase, *"Nor life,"* refers to the vicissitudes or difficulties of life which come to the Believer, even as Paul has here enumerated. Someone has said, and perhaps rightly so, that at times it is harder to live for God, than it is to die for Him.

FALLEN ANGELS

The phrase, *"Nor Angels,"* refers to Fallen Angels, who threw in their lot with Lucifer, himself an Angel, when he rebelled against God in the ages of the past (Isa. Chpt. 14; Ezek. Chpt. 28).

These Fallen Angels are powerful beings, helping Satan orchestrate and manage his Kingdom of Darkness. Consequently, they are very much involved in the opposition against the Child of God, helping to carry out these evil schemes. We are here assured, however, that if we will cling to Jesus, that their power is foiled irrespective as to what they may attempt.

The phrase, *"Nor Principalities,"* refers to the Satanic powers of Ephesians 2:2; 6:12.

These are Fallen Angels who are of greater power than normal, who are in fact, in charge of certain areas of the world. They are Chief Rulers of the highest rank and order in Satan's Kingdom (Col. 2:10).

The phrase, *"Nor Powers,"* again refers to Fallen Angels, who derive their power from and execute the will of the Chief Rulers, i.e., Chief Angels.

If one is to notice, this speaks of the world being divided into areas, with powerful Fallen Angels in charge of certain sections, with other Angels under them carrying out instructions, all under the Chief Fallen Angel, Satan himself. This is evident in Daniel Chapter 10. The powerful Fallen Angels which were being fought by Gabriel and Michael, themselves the most powerful Angels in God's Kingdom, concerned spiritual authority in the world. (Please see our Commentary on Daniel, Vol. 5, which covers both Ezekiel and Daniel.)

The phrase, *"Nor things present,"* refers to present trials engineered by these *"Principalities and Powers."*

The phrase, *"Nor things to come,"* refers to the plans being made at this very moment against the Kingdom of God by these fallen beings, which will materialize in the future. However, we need not fear, knowing that Jesus has defeated all of these Powers of Darkness.

The phrase, *"Nor height, nor depth,"* refers to Satan as the *"Prince of the Powers of the air,"* and to the horrors of Hell itself (Eph. 2:2).

"Height, nor depth," also refers to the severity of Satan's planned attack against the Child of God. It will fail, as fail it must!

The phrase, *"Nor any other creature,"* is not meant to insinuate that there are other spheres of operation which can oppose the Child of God, other than Satan, his Fallen Angels and Demon Spirits, but is meant to cover any and all things, that may conceivably oppose the Believer. In other words, the Holy Spirit through the Apostle is saying that there is absolutely nothing which Satan can originate or institute against the Believer that will be successful, that is, if the Believer will cling tenaciously to Christ.

The phrase, *"Shall be able to separate us from the Love of God,"* guarantees the conclusion.

The phrase, *"Which is in Christ Jesus our Lord,"* refers to everything we have, everything we have been given, every privilege and blessing which has come our way, our Salvation, our Baptism with the Holy Spirit, our Eternal Life, our Redemption in totality, all, and He means all, being in, through, of, and

NOTES

by the Lord Jesus Christ. He is the Manifestation of the Father, and in Him are all things. He is Life, Salvation, Grace, Mercy, Compassion, and Resurrection. He is our Saviour today, and will be our Judge tomorrow.

JESUS AND HIS PEOPLE

His people love Him and believe in the fidelity of His Love to them; for trials do but assure the heart which knows His Love that nothing can separate from it; and they know well that being Called, Justified, and Glorified no link is wanting in the golden chain that binds them to His Heart.

That chain begins in the immeasurable past and reaches into the immeasurable future. It stretches from one Eternity to the other. Love and purpose planned that they should have the one and same portion with Himself.

This Faith makes them more than conquerors over *"all these things,"* i.e., these trials. Joseph, Daniel, etc., are examples.

THE ENEMY OF OUR SOULS

Let the enemy search death and life and the present and the future; let him mount to the greatest heights or descend to the lowest depths; let him turn to all created things, and to men, Angels, and Demons, and he will fail to find any power that can separate the Redeemed from the Love of God which is in Christ Jesus the Lord.

A PERSONAL NOTE

The Lord Saved me when I was eight years of age and Baptized me with the Holy Spirit a few weeks later. When I was nine years old I knew that I would be an Evangelist, and I knew that this Ministry would be worldwide.

When I was about ten years old, I had an experience which was but a portend of that which was to come. Strangely enough it was not in a Prayer Meeting or a Church Service, but rather while I was alone, with me at this time not actually remembering the setting.

How it happened and what brought it on, I also fail to remember. But this I vividly remember.

For the first time in my life I sensed the Powers of Darkness. At that time, and at that very early age, Satan or else one of his demon spirits began to speak to me, telling me, *"I will stop you, you will not succeed in doing what God has called you to do."*

At that time, I seemed to see a globe of the Earth and it spinning slowly, showing the continents of the world. This thing was so strong, that I became extremely fearful, not really knowing or understanding what was happening. In later years I would know, and to be sure.

Satan meant what he said, and set out almost from that moment to carry out his threats. For me to enumerate all of these efforts by the Evil One, would be pointless at this particular time. All Believers suffer opposition from the Powers of Darkness. However, I share the sentiments of the great Preacher E. M. Bounds, who said, *"Those who are a great threat to Satan, feel the power of his opposition keenly."*

I may not have his exact words, but that is close to his statement, and ever so true.

THE ATTITUDE OF THE BELIEVER

No, I am not blaming wrongdoing or failure on Satan, for the simple reason that all wrongdoing is the fault of the individual irrespective of the circumstances. However, for anyone to think that the matter is simple, that person is either hypocritical or else he has never faced the Powers of Darkness.

Some time ago I read a Message by a Preacher who lived and ministered in the 1700's. In his Message he made a statement which I think is well worth repeating, even though I have quoted it elsewhere in these Volumes. It is as follows:

1. When one hears something negative about a fellow Believer one should treat it as gossip, which means to ignore it, and above all to never repeat such slander, because slander is what it is.

2. Even if one feels one has firsthand knowledge of the circumstances, still, are you sure that you know and understand the degree of spiritual warfare involved?

3. If you had been placed in the same circumstances, would you have done any better or even as well?

A long time ago, the songwriter said:

"I have seen the lightning flashing, I have heard the thunder roll,

"I have felt sin's breakers dashing, trying to conquer my soul.
"But I hear the Voice of Jesus, telling me Fight On.'
"He has told me I'll never leave you, I'll never leave you alone."

"No never alone, no never alone,
"He promised never to leave me, never to leave me alone.
"No never alone, no never alone,
"He promised never to leave me, never to leave me alone."

However, as I close the Commentary on this Chapter, I want to go back to its 2nd verse and say with the Apostle Paul, and do so with great Joy and Thanksgiving, *"For the Law of the Spirit of Life in Christ Jesus hath made me free from the Law of Sin and Death."*

I wish the whole world could say the same thing. As well, every single Believer who has ever lived and who stands victorious in Christ Jesus, must say the same thing, because elsewhere no Victory is possible! It is ever *"In Christ Jesus,"* and Christ Jesus Alone!

As someone has well said: Satan says things about me. People say things about me. God says things about me.

It is only what God says that matters.

CHAPTER 9

(1) "I SAY THE TRUTH IN CHRIST, I LIE NOT, MY CONSCIENCE ALSO BEARING ME WITNESS IN THE HOLY SPIRIT,"

Chapters 9, 10, and 11, deal with the Jewish question, and in every capacity. As well, the erroneous manner in which the Doctrine of Predestination is often presented will be refuted, as Paul explains Israel's present state of unbelief, and that despite being originally elected by God. And yet Paul will wondrously and grandly portray in Chapter 11 their coming Restoration.

PROMISES TO ISRAEL

Paul is now dealing with Israel according to the fullness and freeness of the Gospel, as the Power of God unto Salvation to everyone that believeth. Consequently, a question naturally arises, not unaccompanied with painful difficulty, respecting the exclusion of that people, as a people called Israel, to whom God's Promises were made. With this national rejection of Israel the Apostle now deals.

The Abrahamic Covenant, promised Israel the possession of the land from the modern Suez Canal on the Southwest to the Euphrates on the Northeast and East, actually, from the Mediterranean Sea on the West to the Euphrates on the East. The extreme Northern Boundary would have taken in all of modern-day Syria, actually coming close to modern Turkey. As well, it would have included ancient Phoenicia, which is modern Lebanon.

The boundaries include the modern Sinai Peninsula, which Israel actually did possess in modern times until it was given back to Egypt in 1983, I believe it was. Also, the boundaries include the Arabian Peninsula which incorporates most of the Arab countries, even including a good part of Iraq. Consequently, the totality of the Abrahamic Covenant includes an area approximately one-third the size of the United States. Even though much of that area is now desert, in the coming Millennium when Israel will claim the entirety of this Promise, the Scripture plainly says that such will *"blossom as the rose,"* i.e., become tremendously fertile (Isa. 35:1).

As well, the Davidic Covenant promised Israel an Eternal Dynasty of Kings of Whom the last One would be an Eternal Person, actually, the Lord Jesus Christ. Of course, up to the time of the writing of this Book of Romans, these Promises had not been fulfilled, and in fact, still have not been fulfilled. Paul will explain the reason why.

From the Prophecies of old he explains how that Israel will be brought back in Sovereign Grace, Saved, and Restored to its land under its Covenanted King, the Lord Jesus, but as well according to their own will. In other words, they will seek the Lord, even as the Prophets of old predicted, and He will be found of them.

THE WORD OF THE HOLY SPIRIT TO ISRAEL

The phrase, *"I say the Truth in Christ, I*

lie not," is proclaimed by Paul in this manner, in order to refute the accusation that in preaching to the Gentiles he is now animated by hostility to the Jews.

The two words *"In Christ,"* mean that he speaks in fellowship with Christ, so that falsehood is impossible (Alford).

The phrase, *"My conscience also bearing me witness in the Holy Spirit,"* proclaims what he is about to say as being given to him by the Holy Spirit. As well, his phraseology proclaims that he in his own spirit is exactly in tune with the Holy Spirit.

(The two words *"Ghost"* and *"Spirit"* come from the same Greek word *"Pneuma."* The word *"Ghost"* is obsolete English, and it should be translated *"Spirit."* Why the King James Translators used the word *"Ghost"* has never been satisfactorily explained, as far as I know. It should have been translated *"Spirit"* because that's what the Word actually is.)

"Conscience" in the Greek is *"suneidesis,"* and means *"co-perception, i.e., moral consciousness."*

"Witness" is *"summartureo,"* and means *"to testify jointly, i.e., to corroborate by concurrent evidence."*

The idea is, that Paul was perfectly satisfied in his own spirit, that what he had been given was definitely from the Lord, of that he had no doubt. The strong manner in which he addressed the subject in this first verse tells us that he went to whatever lengths he thought necessary in order to verify and ascertain that he had definitely heard from the Lord. It was not the idea of not wanting to do the Will of the Lord, but of ascertaining for certain that it was the Lord, and that such thought or Doctrine was not coming out of his own mind.

Actually, this is a problem that every True Preacher of the Gospel faces. Satan is constantly inserting things in one's mind, which seem to be very plausible and very right, at least on the surface, which make some think that it is from the Lord, when actually it is the opposite. That is the reason the Preacher of the Gospel or anyone for that matter, must be in tune with the Lord constantly, walking close to Him, in order that they not mistake another voice for His. *"God told me,"* consequently, carries little weight, for the very reason of which I am addressing. People think it is God, when many times it is not.

(2) "THAT I HAVE GREAT HEAVINESS AND CONTINUAL SORROW IN MY HEART."

The phrase, *"That I have great heaviness,"* speaks of Paul's grieving over the plight of the Israel of his day.

"Heaviness" in the Greek is *"lupe,"* and means *"sorrow, pain, grief,"* used of mourning.

The phrase, *"And continual sorrow in my heart,"* is in the same vein.

"Sorrow" is *"odune,"* and means *"consuming grief,"* which means *"to cause intense pain, to be in anguish, to be tormented."*

"Continual" is *"adialeiptos,"* and means *"unintermitted, unceasing, without leaving off."*

PAUL AND ISRAEL

I think it is safe to say without fear of contradiction that no one in the world of Paul's day knew Israel and her plight exactly as did the Apostle. Having been a champion of the Law at his Conversion, and probably knowing the Law of Moses as no other man alive of that time, he above all others saw the terrible direction in which these people were heading. They had crucified their Messiah, in effect, murdering Him, and since that time of approximately 25 or 30 years before, there had been no Repentance, but rather a deepening of rebellion against God.

In fact, Israel would be totally destroyed as a Nation about ten years from this present time (A.D. 70), which as well he no doubt felt heavily in his spirit this impending doom, that was soon to come.

This section of Romans begins with Paul's sorrow as to Israel's failure (Rom. 9:1-5), and it closes with Paul's joy as to Israel's future (Rom. 11:33-36), despite what is happening presently.

In between this opening and this close is set out God's purpose respecting *"some"* (a Remnant — Rom. 9:6-29), and His purpose respecting *"all"* (Rom. 11:1-32), while between these purposes he records Israel's rejection of the Messiah despite the Prophets (Rom. 9:29-33), despite the Law (Rom. 10:1-13), and despite the Gospel (Rom. 10:14-21).

MODERN DENOMINATIONS?

Leaving Paul's day and coming to the present, and knowing that this is the age of Apostasy, even as predicted by Paul (II Tim. 4:3-4), one cannot help but experience deep sorrow at the spiritual plight of modern Religious Denominations, and especially those of the Pentecostal variety which have been given so much by the Lord. It is very obvious from all accounts in the Word of God, that the Antichrist will be heralded by the Apostate Church, which should take place immediately following the Rapture of the True Church (II Thess. 2:3-12).

As Israel rejected Jesus, they did not at all diminish in their religious capacity, if anything, increasing in intensity. Such mirrors modern Denominations, and especially the Pentecostal variety. That which has had so much, at least in a spiritual sense, is fastly coming down to so very little. To be sure, I say that with great sorrow, at times even grieving at what I know the future will be, unless there is Revival. As True Biblical Repentance was the only answer for Israel of old, and which opportunity was grandly presented under the Ministry of John the Baptist, but rejected, likewise, it is the same for the modern Church. However, it is very difficult to bring people to Repentance, who do not at all see their need for such. Self-righteousness is a dreadful thing, and was actually the plight of Israel. It is also the present plight.

In these last days, I feel that the Scripture teaches that there is going to be a tremendous *"falling away from the Gospel"* (II Thess. 2:3), but at the same time, a great *"outpouring of the Holy Spirit"* (Acts 2:17-21). It will be, and in fact already is, similar to two streams running side by side, but in opposite directions.

In the final alternative, there were actually only a few Jews in the time of the Early Church who were truly Saved, at least in comparison to the whole. Is it going to be the same way with the modern Church?

I am concerned that it cannot be any other way.

(3) "FOR I COULD WISH THAT MYSELF WERE ACCURSED FROM CHRIST FOR MY

BRETHREN, MY KINSMEN ACCORDING TO THE FLESH:"

The phrase, *"For I could wish that myself were accursed from Christ for my Brethren,"* presents a moot point, for such is impossible.

Paul giving his soul away to eternal perdition, would have absolutely no bearing whatsoever regarding the Salvation of Israel, or anyone else for that matter. Actually, such would have the opposite effect, if anything.

It is a moot point as Paul will ultimately exclaim, for the simple reason that Salvation, or the very opposite, a lost condition, cannot be transferred from one person to another. Every person must answer himself for his own soul (Jn. 3:16; Rev. 22:17).

Considering that such is impossible, why did the Holy Spirit permit Paul to include such a thought?

I think the answer is found in this phrase, *"My kinsmen according to the flesh."*

Some have said that there is a passion in Paul's statement even more profound than that of Moses' prayer in Exodus 32:32. Moses identifies himself with his people, and if they cannot be Saved, would perish with them; Paul could find it in his heart, were it possible, to perish for Israel, if in fact, it would mean their Salvation.

Such being impossible, the Holy Spirit proclaims the love the Apostle had for his people, which as well carried over into loving all people everywhere, which is portrayed in his efforts to take the Gospel to the lost everywhere.

The words *"I could wish,"* in the Greek Text mean that such being impossible, it was not entertained at all.

"Accursed" in the Greek is *"anathema,"* and means *"a curse, a man accursed, devoted to the direst woes."* In this case, it means *"doomed and separated from Christ."* It never denotes simply exclusion or excommunication, but always perdition, i.e., *"hellfire"* (Alford).

Did Paul really mean what he said? Did he mean that he would burn in Hell forever if such would guarantee the Salvation of Israel?

The question is purely academic, therefore, moot, because such is not possible. But it does show as stated, the great love the

Apostle had for his people, as he put it, *"My kinsmen according to the flesh,"* which rebutted the accusations of his detractors.

Paul sacrificing himself would not help Israel, or even bring one soul to Christ, for there is only One Sacrifice appropriate for that, and that is the Sacrifice already offered by Jesus Christ, which alone God would and did accept, and which Paul preached so grandly. But yet the burden and love shown by the Apostle, characterizes the same type of burden and love shown by the Lord. Jesus did give Himself, and we are to do the same, at least as far as is possible respecting our energies, time, self-will, and personal wants and desires. In other words, our self-will is to be totally swallowed up in Christ.

(4) "WHO ARE ISRAELITES; TO WHOM PERTAINETH THE ADOPTION, AND THE GLORY, AND THE COVENANTS, AND THE GIVING OF THE LAW, AND THE SERVICE OF GOD, AND THE PROMISES;"

The phrase, *"Who are Israelites,"* is actually the answer to Paul's phrase in the last verse regarding his *"Kinsmen."* But yet for clarification I will now pose it as a question:

WHO ARE ISRAELITES?

Actually, verses 4 and 5 proclaim who and what Israel as a people actually are. In brief, their significance is given not only for the past, which should be obvious, but as well for the future. To have an improper understanding of Israel as a people, and especially regarding the Promises of God relative to them, is to have an improper understanding of the Plan of God in general. Regrettably, many, if not most, modern Believers have insufficient understanding concerning the history and especially the future of Israel. Actually, many modern Believers have the erroneous idea that Israel has no future, at least as far as God is concerned. They base their conclusion on Israel's rejection of her Messiah and the world's Saviour, the Lord Jesus Christ. However, even as Paul will graphically outline in Chapter 11, and even as the Prophets of old foretold in illuminating terms, Israel will be restored. Actually, her Restoration is absolutely necessary for the Plan of God to be fully realized, and because of *"the Promises."*

IN A SENSE ISRAEL ACTUALLY BEGAN IN THE GARDEN OF EDEN

Immediately after the Fall of Adam and Eve, which in effect doomed the entirety of the race, the Lord said to the serpent, *"And I will put enmity* (hatred) *between thee* (Satan) *and the woman, and between thy seed* (unredeemed men) *and her Seed* (Jesus)*; it* (He) *shall bruise* (the Cross) *thy head* (Satan's head)*, and thou shalt bruise* (Calvary) *His* (Jesus') *Heel"* (Gen. 3:15).

This statement must have confused Satan tremendously so. In the first place, the female gender has no seed, that belonging exclusively to the male gender. But yet Satan knew from this statement that the Lord had already taken measures.

WHY DID THE *"SEED"* NOT COME IMMEDIATELY?

What other information the Lord gave to Adam and Eve we are not told; however, it is obvious that they were given a great deal of information respecting the Sacrifices, in a sense as a means to approach God, and as an Atonement for their fallen spiritual condition. Even though the majority of the Adamic Covenant is negative, still the very last part was positive (Gen. 3:14-21). In the *"Coats of skins,"* which the Lord made for Adam and Eve to cover their nakedness, animals gave their lives to provide this covering, which served as a Sacrifice in looking forward to the Promised Redeemer (Heb. 9:22).

In fact, when Cain was born, Eve said, *"I have gotten a man from the Lord,"* with the appellative *"Lord"* referring to *"Covenant God."* In other words, Eve thought that Cain was the Promised Redeemer, when in fact he would be a murderer (Gen. 4:1-8).

By the time *"Seth"* was born, Eve had lost confidence in the Covenant, for she no longer referred to Jehovah as *"Lord,"* but rather *"God"* (Gen. 4:25).

In fact, *"Seth"* was in the Promised Lineage of the Coming Redeemer (Lk. 3:38).

The Lord could not send the Redeemer immediately after the Fall, because He was not wanted or desired. Actually, the Scripture says concerning this period before the flood of approximately 1600 years, *"And God saw that the wickedness of man was great in the Earth, and that every imagination of the thoughts of his heart was only evil continually"* (Gen. 6:5).

It was actually so bad, that God had to perform major surgery on the Earth in order that mankind could be Saved. It then came down to only Noah and his family (Gen. 6:6-13).

ABRAHAM

For the Lord to bring the Second Adam into the world, which would have to be done in order to redeem humanity, certain things would have to be done. Due to the terrible spiritual degeneration of these times, there were no people on the face of the Earth, at least as far as a Race or Tribe was concerned, which would serve this purpose. Evil, wickedness, and ungodliness were so pronounced, that the Messiah simply could not be given to any people that then existed.

Approximately 400 years after the flood, the Lord chose a man by the name of Abraham, even though at the time he was an idolater (Josh. 24:2). Abraham responded favorably to that Call, even though it meant leaving all that he held dear, even going to a place called Canaan of which he was not familiar (Gen. 12:1-3). From this man, the Lord would bring a people into the world who in effect, would serve as the Womb of the Messiah. Consequently, the Lord was referred to as the *"God of Abraham, of Isaac and of Jacob."* This was strictly on the basis of Faith. In other words, these men believed what God said about the Coming Promised Messiah, and how they were to be instrumental in this greatest of all happenings in the world.

Actually, from Jacob, Abraham's Grandson, came the sons who would be the titular heads of the Thirteen Tribes of Israel. In fact, Jacob's name was changed to *"Israel,"* meaning *". . . As a Prince hast thou power with God and with men, and hast prevailed"* (Gen. 32:28). Hence, those who would follow him, being born in his lineage, would be called *"The Children of Israel."* These were the only people on the face of the Earth at that time, at least that is recorded, who were serving God. Actually, some of the sons of Jacob little lived for God at the outset, even though they bore the names of those whom God would use.

JOSEPH

As Bible Students know, Joseph was sold into Egypt by his ungodly Brethren (they would later change), to which it seems that God used for a blessing instead of the curse in which it was originally intended. Ultimately, Joseph became the Viceroy of Egypt, then the most powerful Nation on Earth. In fact, under Pharaoh, he was the most powerful man at that time in the world.

Ultimately, he revealed himself to his brothers, with his Father Jacob and the entirety of the clan, moving to Egypt, which was sanctioned by the Lord.

Even though they came in only 70 souls (Gen. 46:27), as the years passed, they grew into a mighty Nation of millions of people. Regrettably, succeeding Pharaohs enslaved these Children of Israel, putting them through terrible hardships.

Quite possibly it was necessary that this be done, or else it is doubtful that the Children of Israel would have desired to leave Egypt. The oppression became so severe, however, that they cried to God for deliverance, and deliverance came.

MOSES

Under Moses these people who would serve as the Womb of the Messiah, were delivered from slavery in Egypt. They were led by God to Canaan, the Land promised to their forefathers by the Lord.

There the family took on another dimension, becoming a Nation as well as a people. The Mosaic Law was the national code as well as the religious code for Israel. At times in the Old Testament, *"Israel"* stands for the Nation (Judg. 19:1; II Sam. 1:12; I Ki. 9:5). In the same sense, it stands for the Land occupied or claimed by the Nation.

DAVID

Along with the Second Adam redeeming humanity, Who would come through these people, with them prepared especially for this very purpose, dominion as King

NOTES

would also have to be established. Adam forfeited everything by his Fall in the Garden of Eden, with dominion of the Earth being lost to Satan in every respect. Now, Satan ruled and in effect, ruled over the entirety of the Earth. As stated, the only people who were not ruled and controlled by the Evil One, were the select few down through history who served God.

For the first 1600 years (until the flood), only two men were recorded as living for God, those two being *"Abel"* who was murdered by his brother Cain, and *"Enoch"* who walked with God, and was consequently, translated (Gen. 5:21-24).

After Noah died, we have little information given to us concerning his three sons *"Shem, and Ham, and Japheth,"* except that given to us in Genesis 9:22-27.

There is some small evidence that Shem may have lived for God, with some thinking that he was the one who possibly witnessed to Abraham. However, there is no Biblical proof for that suggestion. Nevertheless, Abraham definitely was in the lineage of Shem (Gen. 11:10-26). (It has been suggested that Melchizedek, King of Salem — Jerusalem — may have actually been Shem, but again with no concrete proof.)

Of the Tribes of Israel, Judah was chosen as the Kingly Tribe, for it would be through this Tribe that the Messiah would come. Jacob prophesied this before his death (Gen. 49:8-12).

Consequently, David would be of the Tribe of Judah, and through whom the Messiah would come, not only as Redeemer but as King (II Sam. Chpt. 7).

For Redemption the Sacrifice of the Messiah would be offered up, and for Dominion, He will one day be established as King, even though rejected originally by Israel.

So the die is now cast in the fulfillment of the Promise given in Genesis 3:15. A special people were prepared, for the coming of the Redeemer, and actually for all things to be regained which Adam and Eve had lost.

A DIVIDED KINGDOM

After the death of Solomon, David's son, the Nation was divided geographically. The territory occupied by the Ten Northern Tribes became the separate Kingdom of Israel.

The area occupied by the two Southern Tribes became the separate Kingdom of Judah. (Simeon probably went with Judah, inasmuch as her territory was actually in the confines of Judah, giving the Northern Kingdom actually only Nine Tribes.)

During this era, the history of which is given from I Kings Chapter 11 through II Kings Chapter 25, *"Israel"* is sometimes used to designate this Northern Kingdom, and sometimes it is used in other senses.

The Northern Kingdom was destroyed in 722 B.C., and in 586 B.C. the people of the Southern Kingdom were deported as well to Babylon. After a time of exile, a group of the Jewish people returned to the Promised Land. However, due to their rebellion against God, they were not allowed by Jehovah to set up an independent Nation again, but rather remained a Province in a larger Empire, which at that particular time was the Medo-Persian Empire. However, they would remain under the domain of other Empires until they were finally destroyed by the Romans in A.D. 70.

THE BIRTH OF JESUS

In the Books of Ezra and Nehemiah and in the Gospels, *"Israel"* is used in most of the Old Testament senses to indicate the religious community, the land, and the ethnic entity that looked forward to a restored national identity.

Consequently, when Jesus was born, and even during His dramatic Ministry, He was not recognized at all, even though this was the very purpose of their identity. Their eyes, as stated, were looking forward to a restored national identity. If He fit into that scheme, they would possibly have some use for Him, but otherwise not so.

So, the very purpose for which they came, and the very reason for their identity, were missed completely when after all the many centuries of preparation, Jesus was not even recognized for Who He really was, Israel's Messiah, and the world's Redeemer.

Noting the spiritual declension of Israel, and that it was so bad that they actually murdered the Lord of Glory, one is made to realize how bad it really was before this time,

which prevented the coming of the Second Adam until the appointed time.

For His Coming, a special people would have to be prepared, which they were from the loins of Abraham, and even though they little lived up to the demand, they were supposed to be a holy people, all for the very purpose of getting the world ready for the Coming Redeemer. However, when He did come, and according to the appointed time, sadly and regrettably, the very people who were raised up specifically for this very purpose, did not even know Him (Jn. 1:11).

THE PROPHECIES

Despite Israel's terrible problems, there was always a Remnant in the Nation who truly lived for God. Not many, but always some. To be sure, it was these who made up the True Israel. As such, the Old Testament portrays a bright destiny for the descendants of Jacob, despite their sordid history. This destiny involves a Spiritual Conversion, reestablishment of a national identity, reoccupation of the Promised Land (which has already begun), and many associated Blessings. Often in the Old Testament the Prophets speak of *"Israel"* in ways that incorporate all these meanings (Isa. 44:21-23; 45:17; Jer. 31:21-37; Amos 9:7-15).

Despite being a special people, actually raised up by the Lord and for a specific purpose, many of the physical descendants of Israel had no vital personal relationship with the Lord. Paul argues in Romans Chapter 9 which we are now addressing, *". . . Not all who are descended from Israel are Israel . . . It is not the natural children who are God's Children, but it is the Children of the Promise who are regarded* (truly) *as Abraham's offspring"* (Rom. 9:6-8).

PAUL

Paul also presents the stunning fact that through the Gospel, Gentiles are brought into the Covenant and thus into the community of the Redeemed (Eph. 3:6; Heb. Chpt. 8). In this limited spiritual sense, all Believers are *"Israel"* and Abraham's spiritual descendants.

Even though the Prophets in the Old Testament graphically described Israel's coming

Restoration, not too much is said in the New Testament about this coming day. While the New Testament does not go into detail about the future, Jesus' Own Prophetic Statements are in harmony with the Old Testament picture. When the question, *". . . Are You at this time going to restore the Kingdom to Israel?"*, was asked by His Disciples (Acts 1:6), Jesus replied that only the Father knows the times and dates (Acts 1:7).

Dealing with the question in depth, Paul devotes Chapters 9 through 11 of Romans to examine the situation of Israel. He portrays the opening of the door of Faith to the Gentiles as the grafting of a wild olive tree into a cultivated olive tree and promises that this purposeful setting aside of Israel is not permanent.

Looking back to the Old Testament, Paul praises God, for *"God's Gifts and His Call are irrevocable"* (Rom. 11:29). Thus, the Old Testament picture of Israel's future still awaits realization at the return of Christ, which most definitely will happen.

Israel rejected her Messiah and, consequently, the Kingdom when it was first offered. They will not reject it the second time. They will then accept the King and the Kingdom, humbling themselves before the very Lord of Glory Who they crucified. They will even ask Him, *". . . What are these wounds in Thine Hands?" Then He shall answer, "Those with which I was wounded in the house of My friends"* (Zech. 13:6).

Israel will then be completely restored, with all the Promises of God finally realized in them, *"And the Lord shall be King over all the Earth: in that day shall there be one Lord, and His Name One"* (Zech. 14:9).

GOD'S PECULIAR PEOPLE

The phrase, *"To whom pertaineth the adoption,"* refers to the selection of Israel to be God's peculiar people (Ex. 19:5). The Lord also said, *". . . Israel is My Son, even My Firstborn"* (Ex. 4:22), and *"Ye are the Children of the Lord your God . . ."* (Deut. 14:1). As well, *"When Israel was a child, then I loved him, and called My son out of Egypt"* (Hos. 11:1).

The phrase, *"And the Glory,"* refers to the Presence of God, which Israel alone was

privileged to have (Ex. 16:7, 10; 40:34-35; Deut. 5:24; I Sam. 4:21-22).

The intensity of Paul's distress, and of his longing for the Salvation of his countrymen are partly explained in this verse. It is the greatness of his people, their unique place of privilege in God's Providence, the splendor of the inheritance and of the hopes which they forfeit by unbelief, that make their unbelief at once so painful, and so perplexing.

Actually, the pronoun *"Who,"* as it refers to these people, emphasizes character and quality, namely, *"Who are of such a character or quality as to be"* Israelites.

The name *"Jew"* speaks of him in his national distinction from a Gentile. The term *"Israelite"* refers to him as a member of the theocracy, and a partaker of the theocratic privileges and glorious vocation of the Nation Israel and an heir of the Promises.

The term *"theocracy"* in the Greek means literally *"the Power of God."* It speaks of Israel as the Nation which enjoys the privilege of having a unique relationship to God as its Sovereign, a privilege which is not accorded the Gentile Nations. Israel in its apostate condition, repudiated this honor (Denney).

So, Israel truly partook of the *"Glory of God,"* and in fact, were the only people on Earth who were so privileged.

The phrase, *"And the Covenants,"* referred to the various Covenants God made with Israel such as the Abrahamic, first of all promising Salvation by Faith (Gen. 15:6), and as well promising to make of Abraham a great Nation and giving him possession of the Land from the Suez to the Euphrates (Gen. 15:18), and then the Davidic, promising to that Nation an Eternal Dynasty of Kings stemming from David (II Sam. 7:11-16).

In fact, God never made any Covenants with the Gentiles. He made these Covenants with Israel because that Nation was to be used as a channel to bring Salvation to the entirety of the human race, which would of course, include the Gentiles. However, as far as Evangelism was concerned, Israel failed miserably, becoming sectarian in their self-righteousness, which destroyed them.

The phrase, *"And the giving of the Law,"* refers of course to the Mosaic Law which was given exclusively to Israel, and never pertained to the Gentiles (Wuest).

Actually, this means that Israel in having the Mosaic Law, was the most privileged people on the face of the Earth. No other Nation in the world could boast of such legislation, especially concerning its fairness, integrity, justice, and absolute equality. As well, the Moral Law (Ten Commandments) was and is the Standard and Basis of all Law in the world and changes not, because Moral Truth does not need to change, and in fact, cannot change. So, these were a privileged people indeed!

The phrase, *"And the Service of God,"* pertained to the Tabernacle, Offerings, and Priesthood as found in Exodus and Leviticus.

The phrase, *"And the Promises,"* referred to the Messianic Promises, which in fact, were the greatest Promises ever given to man at any time, at any place.

(5) "WHOSE ARE THE FATHERS, AND OF WHOM AS CONCERNING THE FLESH CHRIST CAME, WHO IS OVER ALL, GOD BLESSED FOR EVER. AMEN."

The phrase, *"Whose are the Fathers,"* refers basically to Abraham, Isaac, and Jacob.

As we have previously stated, these men are noted for their Faith in God. They believed in what He told them, thereby giving up everything in order that their lives would be used for God's Glory, and most of all that through them, the Messiah and Redeemer of all mankind, would ultimately come into the world.

The greatness of its ancestry ennobled Israel, and made its position in Paul's time harder to understand and to endure. Who could think without the keenest pain of the sons of such Fathers forfeiting everything for which the Fathers had been called? (Denney).

This tells us that each generation must have its Revival, or that which preceded it will be lost. The Faith of the Patriarchs would not suffice for the spiritual guides of the people during the time of Christ. Their experience with God was woefully lacking, and, consequently, they lost all understanding of their true mission and purpose.

This does not mean that the Faith of the Patriarchs, or the true sons of Israel who followed was in vain. In fact, that which they

believed came to pass exactly as they believed it, but was not shared or enjoyed by the generation of the culminating time, which spoke of their destruction.

In fact, Faith can never die. Even though others may forfeit and fall down, the one who believed, even though long gone even as the Patriarchs, will ultimately see the Promise realized, even as Faith claimed its Blessing. Hence Jesus said, *"Your Father Abraham rejoiced to see My Day: and he saw it, and was glad"* (Jn. 8:56).

The phrase, *"And of whom as concerning the flesh Christ came, Who is over all,"* proclaims the supreme distinction of Israel, even though they were not aware of this glorious time.

The word *"Christ"* is the English spelling of the Greek word *"Christos,"* which in turn is the translation of the Hebrew word for Messiah, both words meaning *"The Anointed."* The Messiah, so far as His Humanity is concerned, came out of Israel. But so far as His Deity is concerned, Paul says, *"God blessed for ever. Amen."*

Paul's Greek here is *"out from whom as a source* (Israel) *the Christ came according to the flesh* (the Incarnation — His Humanity), *the One Who is above all things* (Deity), *God eulogized forever"* (Wuest).

The word *"Amen,"* simply means that this will never change.

(The phrase *"Who is over all,"* and as it speaks of Christ, concerns the Incarnation, and refers to being over all of humanity.)

(6) "NOT AS THOUGH THE WORD OF GOD HATH TAKEN NONE EFFECT. FOR THEY ARE NOT ALL ISRAEL, WHICH ARE OF ISRAEL:"

The phrase, *"Not as though the Word of God hath taken none effect,"* means that the Word of God did not fall to the ground, and by no means has come to nought (Thayer).

In other words, because Israel ultimately failed, in no way means that the Word of God failed. In fact, it cannot fail, but will always carry out its intended purpose.

THE BIBLE

Holy Scripture is not simply a collection of religious books: still less does it consist of mere fragments of Jewish and Christian thought and literature. It belongs to the conception of Scripture, that, though originating by divers portions and *"in divers manners"* (Heb. 1:1), it should yet, in its completeness, constitute a unity, evincing, in the spirit and purpose that bind its parts together, the Divine Source from which its Revelation comes.

The Bible is the record of God's Revelations of Himself to men in successive ages and dispensations (Eph. 1:8-10; 3:5-9; Col. 1:25-26), till the Revelation culminates in the Advent and Work of the Son, and the Mission of the Spirit. It is this aspect of the Bible which constitutes its grand distinction from all collections of Sacred Writings — the so-called *"Bibles"* of heathen religions — in the world.

These, as the slightest inspection of them shows, have no unity. They are accumulations of particular materials, presenting, in their collocation, no order, progress, or plan. The reason is, that they embody no historical Revelation working out a purpose in consecutive stages from germinal beginnings to perfect close.

The Bible, by contrast, is a single Book because it embodies a single Revelation, and exhibits a single Purpose. The unity of the Book, made up of so many parts, is the attestation of the reality of the Revelation it contains.

ITS SPIRITUAL PURPOSE

This feature of Spiritual Purpose in the Bible is one of the most obvious things about it. It gives to the Bible what is sometimes termed as its *"organic unity."* The Bible has a beginning, middle, and end. The opening Chapters of Genesis have their counterpart in the *"New Heaven and New Earth"* and Paradise restored in the closing Chapters of Revelation, 21-22.

Man's sin is made the starting-point for disclosures of God's Grace. The Patriarchal history, with its Covenants and Promises, is continued in the story of the Exodus and the events that follow, in fulfillment of these Promises.

Deuteronomy recapitulates the Lawgiving at Sinai, as Joshua sees the people put in possession of the Promised Land. Backsliding,

rebellion, failure, do not defeat God's purpose, but are overruled to carry it on to a sure completion. The Monarchy is made the occasion of new Promises to the House of David (II Sam. Chpt. 7).

The Prophets root themselves in the past, but, at the very hour when the Nation seems sinking in ruin, hold out bright hopes of a brighter future in the extension of God's Kingdom to the Gentiles, under Messiah's rule.

FULFILLMENT IN CHRIST

In Truth, even though the efforts of the history given in the Old Testament proclaimed that which was imperfect, transitional, even temporary, still, all was brought to a realization and completion in the Redemption and Spiritual Kingdom of Christ, upon His Advent into the world. Christ is the Prophet, Priest, and King of the New Covenant, and actually the sole Person to Whom the Old Testament (Old Covenant) points.

His Perfect Sacrifice, *"once for all,"* supersedes and abolishes the typical Sacrifices of the Old Economy (Heb. Chpts. 9-10).

His Gift of the Spirit realizes what the Prophets had foretold of God's Law being written in men's hearts (Jer. 31:31-34; 32:39-40; Ezek. 11:19-20).

His Kingdom is established on moveless foundations, and can have no end (Phil. 2:9-11; Heb. 12:28; Rev. 5:13). In tracing the lines of this Redeeming Purpose of God, brought to Light in Christ, and Christ Alone, we gain the key which unlocks the inmost meaning of the whole Bible. It is the Revelation of the *"Gospel,"* i.e., *"The Lord Jesus Christ."*

BIBLICAL INSPIRATION

Inspiration is the guarantee of God that the Bible is a True Record of a Progressive Revelation. It guarantees its contents of the discovery of the Will of God for man's Salvation, of the Prophetic and Apostolic Standing of its writers, of the unity of spirit and purpose that pervades it.

It is difficult for any honest person, if not impossible, to deny that a quite peculiar Presence, Operation, and Guidance of the Spirit of God are manifest in its production. The belief in Inspiration, it has been seen, is implied in the formation of these Books into a Sacred Canon.

Here it need only be said that the claim for Inspiration in the Bible is one made in fullest measure by the Bible itself. It is not denied by any that Jesus and His Apostles regarded the Old Testament Scriptures as in the fullest sense inspired. The appeal of Jesus was *always* to the Scriptures, and the Word of Scripture was final with Him, *"Have you not read?"* (Mat. 19:4).

"Ye do err, not knowing the Scriptures, nor the Power of God" (Mat. 22:29). This because *"God"* speaks in them (Mat. 19:4).

Paul esteemed the Scriptures *"The Oracles of God"* (Rom. 3:2). They are *"God-inspired"* (II Tim. 3:16).

As well, that New Testament Prophets and Apostles were not placed on any lower level than those of the Old Testament is manifest from Paul's explicit words regarding himself and his fellow-Apostles. Paul never faltered in his claim to be *"An Apostle of Jesus Christ by* (through) *the Will of God"* (Eph. 1:1) — *"... Separated unto the Gospel of God ..."* (Rom. 1:1) — who had received his Message not from man, but by *"Revelation"* from Heaven (Gal. 1:11-12).

The *"Mystery of Christ"* had *"now been revealed unto His Holy Apostles and Prophets in the Spirit,"* in consequence of which the Church is declared to be *"built upon the foundation of the Apostles and Prophets, Jesus Christ Himself being the Chief Cornerstone"* (Eph. 2:20; 3:5).

THE DENOUNCING OF NATIONAL SALVATION

The phrase, *"For they are not all Israel, which are of Israel,"* is meant to denounce national Salvation, in other words, that one is Saved just because he is an Israelite.

In essence, Paul is saying that physical circumcision has nothing to do with Salvation. It actually meant nothing, at least in the spiritual sense, that a Jew practiced circumcision. Circumcision of the heart is what really mattered, which could only come about as a result of the Born-Again experience.

It is not rituals or ceremonies which save people. It is Faith in Christ and what Christ did for us at the Cross.

NOTES

Israel had reached the place as many modern Churches, that simply being a Jew, with some few exceptions such as Publicans, etc., guaranteed Salvation, or so they thought. Likewise, many Churches claim the same.

For instance, the Catholic Church teaches that a person is right with God if they are faithful to the Catholic Church, irrespective of their spiritual condition, etc. The same can be said for some Protestant Denominations. Millions are deceived into believing that they are Saved simply because they belong to a certain Church, have been Baptized in Water, take the Lord's Supper, etc. Israel substituted nationality for Jesus, and their modern counterparts substitute Religious Denominations for Jesus. The end result is the same in both cases, eternally lost.

(7) "NEITHER, BECAUSE THEY ARE THE SEED OF ABRAHAM, ARE THEY ALL CHILDREN: BUT, IN ISAAC SHALL THY SEED BE CALLED."

The phrase, *"Neither, because they are the seed of Abraham, are they all children,"* further debunks the nationalistic Salvation theory.

The idea is, that the Promises to the Patriarchs (Abraham, Isaac, and Jacob) never, from the first, implied the spiritual inheritance of them by all the physical descendants of those Patriarchs; even in Israel there is a recognized distinction between being of the people of Israel and being the True Israel of God, which Paul addresses next.

The phrase, *"But, in Isaac shall thy seed be called,"* is meant to exclude Ishmael, although a son of Abraham.

In the original Promise to Abraham the descendants of Ishmael (though equally with those of Isaac, his physical seed) were excluded.

So, Paul uses this as an example to further his contention, that all works of the flesh (which Ishmael was), are excluded from the Promise. As it held true for Ishmael, it continues to hold true unto the present. The next verse throws more light on the subject.

(8) "THAT IS, THEY WHICH ARE THE CHILDREN OF THE FLESH, THESE ARE NOT THE CHILDREN OF GOD: BUT THE CHILDREN OF THE PROMISE ARE

COUNTED FOR THE SEED."

The phrase, *"That is, they which are the children of the flesh, these are not the children of God,"* is meant to address itself to Israel, which again debunks their national Salvation theory (Saved simply because they are a Jew), but as well it holds true in all facets of the Work of God.

WHAT DOES PAUL MEAN BY THE PHRASE *"CHILDREN OF THE FLESH"*?

Inasmuch as Paul is using Abraham and Isaac as examples, we will continue in that vein.

To bring about a special family of people, who in effect would be the Womb of the Messiah, God chose Abraham and Sarah. Through them He would bring a *"Seed,"* in this case Isaac, and ultimately through this lineage, the Messiah, the Redeemer of mankind, would be born (Gen. 12:1-3).

Even though God had given a Promise to Abraham and Sarah, the years rolled by without Sarah conceiving. In fact, she was barren, unable to conceive (Gen. 11:30).

Abraham knowing and understanding the seriousness of this situation, and that the entirety of humanity depended upon the coming of the Redeemer, and the part he was to play in this, proceeded to attempt to *"help"* God, respecting Sarah's difficulty. Consequently, Sarah conceived of a plan to which Abraham agreed, that they would substitute Hagar, her Egyptian maid, in order to bear this child (Gen. 16:1-12).

In fact, this was an accepted custom in those days, providing the wife could not bear children. However, it was that which God would not accept, simply because it was brought about as a result of the *"flesh,"* i.e., the efforts and ingenuity of man instead of God. Consequently, that *"work of the flesh"* (the Arabs), has brought Israel untold trouble from that day until the present.

The child that would be born of Abraham and Sarah, must be strictly of those two, and due to the barrenness of Sarah, could only be brought about by the Power of God. Consequently, it would take a Miracle of Healing on both Abraham and Sarah for the child to be conceived, which is exactly what happened. When all hope of the flesh was gone,

in other words Abraham and Sarah could not do anything within themselves to bring about this Promise, then God brought everything to fruition (Gen. 17:15-19; 21:1-8). So, the birth of Isaac was all of God and none of man, at least respecting capability.

SALVATION IS ALL OF THE SPIRIT AND NONE OF THE FLESH

That simply means that nothing man does in his own ability or efforts, can bring about Salvation of any nature. Redemption is a *"Gift of God"* (Eph. 2:8-9), and is obtained by Faith alone. So, when man attempts to save himself, by joining Churches, good deeds, the giving of money, religious efforts, or in any other manner of that nature, such are likened to *"children of the flesh"* and are, therefore, unacceptable. Emphatically Paul states, *"These are not the children of God."*

This situation is very simple but very subtle at the same time. Because men load their efforts with religious works, they are easily fooled into believing that they are Saved. For instance, untold thousands each and every Sunday Morning walk down aisles in Churches, shake a Preacher's hand, and by that act are thought to have Salvation. If they are in doubt at the moment, all their fears are dispelled surely when they join the Church sometime later.

While some few of these people may truly have accepted Christ as their Saviour, the Truth is that most have not. They have engaged in a *"work of the flesh,"* and because it was religious, it deceived them into thinking that they were now Redeemed.

IN A SETTING OF THIS NATURE, HOW COULD SOME FEW BE SAVED, WHILE MOST ARE NOT?

Continuing to use this particular analogy, which actually could apply to many types of efforts, Salvation is a matter of the heart. In other words, from the heart a person believes and accepts Christ, and at that time is definitely Saved (Jn. 3:16). So, in that type of setting, some definitely do accept Christ, and are definitely Saved.

However, many only mentally affirm that which they are hearing, and think within their hearts that the act they are performing, such as shaking the Preacher's hand, or joining the Church, effects Salvation, which it does not. In fact, it cannot effect Salvation, simply because those things contain no Salvation. Jesus Alone is Salvation. And He is not received by proxy, in other words by performing religious acts.

A person is Saved by simply believing in his heart that Jesus Christ is the Son of God, and the Redeemer of mankind, and that He paid the price for man's Redemption at Calvary's Cross. If the sinner believes that, accepting what the Lord did, desiring to follow Him all of one's life, at that moment, one is Saved (Rom. 10:9-10, 13). It does not matter whether the sinner is in a Church, on a street corner, watching a Christian Television Program, or where he may be. The place does not Save him, neither some particular religious act performed as stated, but rather a simple Faith in Christ.

THE PROMISE

The phrase, *"But the children of the Promise are counted for the Seed,"* once again goes back to Abraham, and the Promise God gave him respecting this coming *"Seed."*

Even though the birth of Isaac would be a natural birth, still, the Genesis of the matter was wrapped up in Abraham's Faith. In other words, Abraham *believed* that God would do what He said He would do, and *"God accounted it to him for Righteousness"* (Gen. 15:6).

So, the argument is that this Promise did not contemplate the children born of Abraham's body (Ishmael and others), but those born of Abraham's Faith — *"The children of the Promise,"* i.e., all who should exercise the same Faith as Abraham did in God Who brings life out of death and Who is the God of Resurrection. So, the Promise concerned some and not all.

Even though the *"Promise"* in this instance pertained to Isaac, it actually pertained to Jesus Christ, Who was the ultimate Purpose and the actual *"Seed."* It was all about Jesus being brought into the world, Who would serve as the Second Adam, thereby redeeming humanity, at least all who will believe. For man to be Saved, it

NOTES

was an absolute necessity that God become Man, hence, the great significance of what happened to Abraham.

Consequently, the question must be asked, *"Are you a 'child of the flesh' or a 'Child of the Promise'?"*

If you are a *"Child of the Promise,"* it is not because you are a member of the Baptist Church, or Assemblies of God, or the Methodist, or the Catholic, etc. As well, it is not because you have been Baptized in Water, or take the Lord's Supper, as important as those things may be. As well, it is not because you speak in Tongues, or anything else of that nature, but rather, because you have exhibited simple Faith in the Lord Jesus Christ, trusting Him implicitly, and have given Him your heart and life. Nothing else will suffice.

(9) "FOR THIS IS THE WORD OF PROMISE, AT THIS TIME WILL I COME, AND SARAH SHALL HAVE A SON."

The phrase, *"For this is the Word of Promise,"* pertains to the next phrase, and speaks of that which God had promised, namely the birth of Isaac.

It is not that Isaac as a person had anything to do with one's Salvation, for he does not. He just happened to be the one who was promised by God, who would figure into the coming of Christ. The emphasis is on the *"Promise of God,"* not on Isaac, or even Abraham for that matter.

That is the problem. Man tends to get his eyes on the peripheral things, instead of the Promise, Who is Christ, always Christ!

The phrase, *"At this time will I come, and Sarah shall have a son,"* refers to Genesis 18:10. Once again, Abraham is not the principle figure, neither is Sarah, or Isaac for that matter. Only the *"Promise"* which would ultimately figure into Christ.

(10) "AND NOT ONLY THIS; BUT WHEN REBECCA ALSO HAD CONCEIVED BY ONE, EVEN BY OUR FATHER ISAAC;"

The phrase, *"And not only this,"* pertains to what he has just said, but will now give another example.

The idea is, that God did not choose Ishmael nor any of the sons of Keturah which would yet be born, but only Isaac; and if the Jews urged that these offspring, were not the sons of Sarah, but they (the Jews) were, implying that the analogy did not fit, Paul replies by now pointing to Jacob.

Knowing that the Jews were smug in their confidence as the heirs of both Abraham and Sarah, he will now counter with an even more compelling argument. He is striking hard at this idea of one being Saved simply because they are of a certain nationality, have certain forefathers, have done certain good things, or belong to certain Churches, etc. However, despite what the Holy Spirit gave through the Apostle, this problem is just as persistent presently in the modern Church, as it was in Israel of old. Man loves to believe that he is Saved simply because he has done something, rather than believe he is Saved because Christ has done something.

The phrase, *"But when Rebecca also had conceived by one, even by our father Isaac,"* makes the argument even more ironclad. Whereas the Jews could claim that Paul's analogy of Abraham did not apply to them, simply because they were definitely of the seed of Isaac and not Ishmael, etc., Paul now introduces Rebecca as the mother of two sons, Esau and Jacob, with only one (Jacob) accepted by God. So, if the first analogy of Abraham weakened the contention of the Jews, this one blows it all to pieces. He will now show them that having Abraham and Sarah as Father and Mother, does not of itself mean anything, with the same holding for Isaac and Rebecca.

Once again, he is hitting hard this idea that one is Saved simply because they are in the lineage of Abraham and Sarah, i.e., a member of a certain Church, etc.

This is exactly what John the Baptist was talking about when he said, *"Bring forth therefore fruits meet for Repentance:*

"And think not to say within yourselves, We have Abraham to our Father: for I say unto you, that God is able of these stones to raise up children unto Abraham" (Mat. 3:8-9).

He then said, and speaking of the idea of the Jews regarding parental or national Salvation, *"And now also the axe is laid unto the root of the trees* (that which one believes)*: therefore every tree which bringeth not forth good fruit* (True Salvation) *is hewn down*

(God rejects everything other than Christ), *and cast into the fire"* (Mat. 3:10).

(11) "(FOR THE CHILDREN BEING NOT YET BORN, NEITHER HAVING DONE ANY GOOD OR EVIL, THAT THE PURPOSE OF GOD ACCORDING TO ELECTION MIGHT STAND, NOT OF WORKS, BUT OF HIM THAT CALLETH;)"

The phrase, *"For the children being not yet born, neither having done any good or evil,"* refers to Esau and Jacob, who were twins.

Paul's argument is along this track: a Jewish opponent might say, *"Ishmael was an illegitimate child, who naturally had no rights as against Isaac; we are the legitimate descendants of the Patriarch Abraham, and our right to the inheritance is indefeasible* (not capable of being annulled, voided, or undone).*"*

To this the Apostle replies in verses 10-13. Not only did God make the distinction already referred to, but in the case of Isaac's children, where there seemed no ground for making any distinction whatever (neither had done any good or evil at this point), He in fact did distinguish again, and said, *"The elder shall serve the younger."*

Jacob and Esau had one father, one mother, and were twin sons; the only ground on which either could have been preferred was that of priority of birth, and this was disregarded by God; Esau, the elder, was rejected, and Jacob, the younger, was made heir of the Promises. However, there was a reason that the Lord did this.

The phrase, *"That the Purpose of God according to Election might stand,"* speaks of God's foreknowledge.

God is always true to His Nature and His Word; therefore, God does not elect anyone to be Saved or to be lost, irrespective of their choice. It is always *"Whosoever will"* (Rev. 22:17).

Inasmuch as God is Omniscient (All-knowing), which means He can see all things into the future, it is perfectly understandable as to Him looking ahead and seeing what the response of particular individuals will be, incidentally of their own choice, and then making a decision based upon that fact, although future, but yet certain. That is the sum total of *"Election."*

The phrase, *"Not of works, but of Him that calleth,"* pronounces the entire basis of God's dealings with men and His manner of operation.

"Works" in the Greek is *"ergon,"* and means *"the act of doing labor or work."* In this case, it refers to one attempting to earn his Salvation or place with God, by *"works,"* i.e., something the person does which makes him think that he has now earned Salvation, etc. In effect, the Jews thought they had merited Salvation because of being in the lineage of Abraham, and having done some good things whether real or imagined. With God, *"works"* count for nothing. It is only Faith in Christ which God honors.

"Calleth" in the Greek is *"kaleo,"* and means *"to call, to bid, to urge, or to hail."*

In this capacity, it is not used in the sense of forcing one to do something, but rather that they have the opportunity, whether accepted or not. In other words, the individual's power of choice is not abrogated.

(12) "IT WAS SAID UNTO HER, THE ELDER SHALL SERVE THE YOUNGER."

The phrase, *"It was said unto her,"* refers to the Lord speaking to Rebecca and is found in Genesis 25:23. Exactly how the Lord spoke to her we are not told. At any rate, the prediction as given by the Lord, forecasts exactly who and what Esau and Jacob would be.

The phrase, *"The elder shall serve the younger,"* contains a much wider application than merely referring to Esau and Jacob, even though it did begin with them (Gen. 25:29-33). Regarding these two, the Birthright should have gone to Esau, inasmuch as he was the firstborn; however, he sold it to Jacob.

From Esau came the people known as the *"Edomites,"* and from Jacob, those known as the *"Israelites."*

Even though the phrase, *"The elder shall serve the younger,"* actually pertained to the ultimate ascendancy of Jacob over Esau, which happened centuries later, still it has even a greater spiritual meaning.

The word *"elder"* actually refers to the sin nature, with which every individual, as a result of the Fall, is born. The *"younger"* refers, spiritually speaking, to the *"Divine Nature,"* which enters into the heart and life of the person at conversion (II Pet. 1:4). To be sure, the struggle may be intense, as it regards the sin nature and the Divine Nature, which in fact it is; however, if the Believer will place his Faith in Christ and the Cross, the Holy Spirit will work mightily in the heart and life of such a person, and it will come out exactly as was stated so long ago, *"The elder shall serve the younger."* In other words, the sin nature will serve the Divine Nature, instead of the other way around.

But tragically, that's not the way it is in the lives of most Christians. In most lives, even those who truly love the Lord, the sin nature is ruling supreme, which makes for a miserable existence. But it doesn't have to be that way. God's Prescribed Order of Victory is constant Faith in Christ and what Christ has done for us at the Cross, which then gives the Holy Spirit latitude to work in our lives. This means that the Believer must understand that every single thing he has from the Lord comes to him solely through the means of the Cross (Rom. 6:3-5, 11, 14; 8:1-2, 11; Gal. 6:14).

(13) "AS IT IS WRITTEN, JACOB HAVE I LOVED, BUT ESAU HAVE I HATED."

The phrase, *"As it is written,"* is taken from Malachi 1:1-3.

The phrase, *"Jacob have I loved,"* presents such being predicated on one thing, and gives us great information respecting God's dealings with the human race.

First of all, God loved Jacob because Jacob loved Him. It does not speak of the moral perfection of Jacob, because such was not evident. Actually, it was the very opposite. In fact, Jacob was anything but lovable, at least for about the first hundred years of his life. But yet, there was something in Jacob's heart despite his problems, which reached out after God, and was ultimately rewarded (Gen. 32:24-30).

In fact, there is surely nothing in the life of any unbeliever which would speak favorably to God, nor in any Believer for that matter, with the exception of that which the Lord infuses into him (the Divine Nature). So, the Lord does not love us because of our attributes, qualities, talents, abilities, etc.

These things count none at all to Him, and in fact, there is absolutely nothing that anyone can do to personally endear themselves to God, with the exception of one thing:

When the Lord appeals to the heart of the sinner, and that sinner responds favorably with Faith, it pleases God, and it is that of which I speak (Heb. 11:5-6).

The phrase, *"But Esau have I hated,"* once again was done simply because Esau hated God. He did not want the Things of God, did not desire the Ways of God, and despised the Birthright, which spoke of all things of God (Gen. 25:34).

The idea is, that God did not indiscriminately love Jacob, nor did He indiscriminately hate Esau.

In these Statements, the idea of God loving all of humanity, even *"while we were yet sinners,"* is not in question (Rom. 5:8). In fact, the greatest picture of God's Love is Jesus dying for the ungodly and actually the unlovable. There is no greater Love than such, nor can there be any greater Love.

The idea of the entirety of this scenario directs attention to the lifestyles of these two men and their attitudes toward God and His Work, which Paul will address in the next verse.

(14) "WHAT SHALL WE SAY THEN? IS THERE UNRIGHTEOUSNESS WITH GOD? GOD FORBID."

The question, *"What shall we say then?"*, is meant to counter the claim that God was unfair in this disposition toward Jacob and Esau.

The question, *"Is there unrighteousness with God?"*, Paul meets head on.

The phrase, *"God forbid,"* is the answer of the Holy Spirit through the Apostle.

NO UNRIGHTEOUSNESS WITH GOD

It must be settled in the heart and mind of every Believer that everything that God does is right. It's not right simply because He does it, but it's right because it is right. In other words, there is no unrighteousness with God whatsoever.

The Lord doesn't function the same way as humans do. He has no evil passions. So when words like *"jealous"* or *"hatred"* are used in respect to God, they don't mean the same as when they are used respecting men. The passions of the Lord are without guile and without favoritism. He loves all alike; however, His Righteousness will never allow Him to condone sin in any fashion. In dealing with Israel, no one can say that God did not show great Mercy, Kindness, Patience, and Longsuffering. Actually, He has shown the same to all of us. To be sure, He never takes opposite measures, until there is absolutely no choice. In other words, the Lord really never leaves anyone. It is the person who leaves the Lord.

Israel left God, even murdering her Messiah, which left God with no choice.

CERTAIN DOCTRINES WOULD BE UNRIGHTEOUS IF IN FACT THEY WERE TRUE, WHICH THEY ARE NOT

First of all I speak of the Doctrine of Predestination as it is taught by many. If God arbitrarily predestined some to Heaven and some to Hell, or if God arbitrarily loved Jacob and arbitrarily hated Esau, such would be unrighteous, which should be obvious. And yet, that is what many people teach and believe.

However, that particular Doctrine is patently untrue. God does not predestine anyone to Heaven or Hell. In fact, He opens the door of Salvation to all (Jn. 3:16).

While it is true that some have more opportunities than others, still, the fault is not with God, as it never is with God, but lies elsewhere. Yes, God is all-powerful, consequently, able to do anything; however, He has purposely limited Himself in some ways respecting man's free moral agency. In other words, it would be very easy for God to force a person to live for Him, but that He will not do, and for all the obvious reasons. If He did so, He would not really have children, but rather slaves.

If God rewarded unrighteousness, or cursed Righteousness, or at least the attempts by man to be so, that would be grossly unrighteous on the part of God. However, God is totally fair and equitable with all. The Scripture plainly says that He *"is no respecter of persons"* (II Sam. 14:14; Acts 10:34; Col. 3:25; I Pet. 1:17). Anyone who meets God's conditions, will be treated accordingly, and those who refuse to do so,

NOTES

will suffer the consequences.

(15) "FOR HE SAITH TO MOSES, I WILL HAVE MERCY ON WHOM I WILL HAVE MERCY, AND I WILL HAVE COMPASSION ON WHOM I WILL HAVE COMPASSION."

The phrase, *"For He saith to Moses,"* has Paul once again going back to the Old Testament which he was constantly doing. Even though we have said it several times, due to its significance please allow me the latitude of warning the Bible Student once again of the danger of ignoring the Old Testament. I say this because of the untold numbers of Charismatics who have been erroneously taught that the Old Testament is of little consequence. Nothing could be further from the Truth.

At least one of the reasons that some come up with weird Doctrines, is because they do not have a proper Foundation, and by Foundation I speak of the Old Testament. In fact, one simply cannot understand the New unless one understands the Old. The Bible is a story and runs like an unbroken line from the Book of Genesis through the Book of Revelation. To ignore any part of its content, is to do so at one's peril. Paul referred to the Old Testament over and over because it was the Word of God. Although much of it has been fulfilled in Christ, it is still the Word of God. In fact, to properly understand Jesus, one must have a working knowledge of the Types, Symbols, Shadows, and Metaphors of the Old Testament, with all picturing Jesus whether in His Redeeming Work or Personal Life.

The phrase, *". . . I will have Mercy on whom I will have Mercy, and I will have Compassion on whom I will have Compassion,"* is taken from Exodus 33:19.

THE TERMS OF MERCY AND COMPASSION

Moses had besought the Lord to show him His Glory as a token that he and the people had found Grace in His Sight. The Lord, in answer to his prayer, makes *"all His Goodness pass before him,"* in token that such Grace had been found; but declares, in the words quoted, that all such Grace accorded was not due to any claim on the part of man,

NOTES

but to God's Own Good Pleasure (Barmby).

Paul shows us here that God is Sovereign over His Mercy; however, this doesn't mean that He indiscriminately shows Mercy to some and withholds it from others. God is always perfectly fair and just in His dealings with man. He has laid down certain conditions. If those conditions are met, irrespective as to who it might be, Mercy will be shown.

The idea is that God is laid under no obligation by a human will or a human work. In other words, one cannot merit the Mercy or Compassion of the Lord. Such is literally not possible!

However, at the same time, the *"will"* of an individual is definitely involved, even as the Scripture says, *"Whosoever will"* (Rev. 22:17). However, the *"will"* alone is not enough. There are untold millions who *"will"* the Mercy and Compassion of the Lord, while all the time continuing to rebel against Him. In fact, much of the world and for all time, falls into that category. However, such is not to be, because such cannot be.

As well, there is no *"work"* that can endear one to God, thereby earning or meriting God's Mercy or Compassion. But at the same time, one must be willing that a *"Work of God"* (not a work of man) be carried out in one's life, for Mercy and Compassion to be shown. God does not expect man to do anything to earn Salvation, for such cannot be done. But He does expect man to be willing to conform to the Ways of God as the Lord gives him power and strength to do so. The trouble with man is, too oftentimes he wants sin and Salvation at the same time. He wants his own way and God's Way concurrently. He wants rebellion and then continued Mercy and Compassion. Such is not to be, as such cannot be!

The idea is, God sets the rules, not man. To be frank, that is the entire upshot of it all. Man wants to change the rules, but God plainly says to Moses, and to Paul, and to everyone else for that matter, that such is not to be.

WHAT IS MERCY AND COMPASSION?

In the New Testament the Greek word *"oiktirmos"* is translated either *"mercy"*

(Rom. 12:1) or *"compassion"* (II Cor. 1:3). So as would be obvious, they are both very closely related.

The Bible makes many statements about God. One of the most comforting teaches us that *"Our God is full of Compassion"* (Ps. 116:5). Consequently, it is to this Attribute of God that we wish to address ourselves.

COMPASSION AS A RESPONSE TO NEED

In the Old Testament, the Hebrew word *"Hamal"* is translated *"to have pity,"* *"to spare,"* or *"to have compassion."*

The word indicates *"that emotional response which results* (or may result) *in action to remove its object . . . from impending difficulty."* The word describes human as well as Divine emotion.

Pharaoh's daughter, for example, was moved by *"Hamal"* (compassion) when she saw the baby Moses in the rush basket and took him into her home to raise as her son (Ex. 2:6).

However, almost half of the occurrences of this word are in the negative: they speak of *not* having compassion. For instance, the Babylonian captivity had a good and purifying purpose, but to the Exiles it felt as though God simply did not care (Lam. 2:2; 3:43). But God does care, deeply, even for those undergoing discipline. So Malachi looks ahead and records God's Promise of Restoration: *"They will be Mine, says the Lord Almighty, in the day when I make up My treasured possession. I will spare them, just as in compassion a man spares his son who serves him"* (Mal. 3:17).

COMPASSION AS AN EXPRESSION OF LOVE

The Hebrew word *"raham,"* means *"to love deeply"* and thus, *"to be compassionate,"* or *"to have mercy."* This word with its derivatives is found 133 times in the Old Testament. Of the 47 uses of the verb, 35 speak of God's Love for human beings (Ex. 33:19; Deut. 13:17; 30:3; II Ki. 13:23; Ps. 102:13; 103:13; 116:5; Isa. 9:17; 13:18; 27:11; 30:18; 49:10, 13; 54:8, 10; 60:10; Jer. 12:15; 13:14; 31:20; 33:26; Lam. 3:32; Ezek. 39:25; Hos. 1:6-7; 2:23; 14:3; Micah 7:19; Zech. 1:12; 10:6).

NOTES

The word clearly indicates the depth of the relationship God has with His Children (Ps. 103:13; Micah 7:19). But as we are here studying (Rom. 9:15), it also reflects God's conditions under which Mercy and Compassion are tendered.

One fascinating Old Testament theme links Compassion with Prophecy. The future that God has announced will not only bring Him Glory but will also show His deep Love and Compassion for His people (Isa. 14:1; 49:13; 54:7; Jer. 12:15; 33:26; Ezek. 34:25; Micah 7:19; Zech. 1:16).

MERCY AND COMPASSION AS PORTRAYED IN THE NEW TESTAMENT

Three Greek words communicate a sense of Mercy, Pity, or Compassion. *"Eleos"* is *"Mercy."* *"Oiktirmos"* is a pitying exclamation torn from the heart of the sight of another's suffering. *"Oiktirmos"* is translated either *"Mercy"* (Rom. 12:1) or *"Compassion"* (II Cor. 1:3), as stated. God compassionately and truly cares about what happens to us (Rom. 12:1; II Cor. 1:3). We are to imitate our Heavenly Father (Lk. 6:36) and let His kind of caring bind Believers to each other in unity (Phil. 2:1; Col. 3:12).

The third Greek word is *"splanchnizomai"* and is not used frequently in the New Testament. But its occurrences seem especially important. The noun is found in Luke 1:78; Acts 1:18; II Corinthians 6:12; 7:15; Philippians 1:8; 2:1; Colossians 3:12, plus several other places.

The word originally indicated the inner parts of the body and came to suggest the seat of the emotions — particularly emotions of Pity, Compassion, and Love. This is the word used in the Gospels to speak of Jesus having Compassion on someone in need.

THE COMPASSION OF CHRIST

When Jesus' response is such that He is described as being moved by Compassion, the occasion is often the turning point in someone's life.

For instance, a leper came to Jesus and begged for healing. Jesus, *"filled with Compassion,"* reached out to touch and heal (Mk. 1:40-42). Traveling in the towns and villages of Judea, Jesus saw the confused crowds and *"had Compassion on them"* because they were like sheep without a Shepherd (Mat. 9:33-38).

Thereupon Jesus immediately gave His Disciples authority to heal and drive out Evil Spirits. He sent His Disciples to travel through the land (Mat. Chpt. 10). Compassion moved Jesus to take action that affected the lives of those whose needs moved Him.

ANOTHER EXAMPLE

We see this same active aspect of Compassion in two Parables Jesus told. In Matthew Chapter 18 there is the story of a servant who owed an unpayable debt. He begged the King to whom he owed the money to give him time to pay it. But the King knowing the man could not pay, was so moved by Compassion that he canceled the debt. Luke Chapter 15 tells the story of the Prodigal Son. The wayward youth returned home to confess his sins and beg for a job as a hired man. But the Father was *"filled with Compassion for him"* and welcomed him back as a son. The loving Compassion of one person literally changed the life of another, for the person who cared was moved to act and so set the needy person on a new course in life.

God calls you and me to have compassion on others. That Call is more than an appeal for us to feel with and for the needy. It is a Call to care enough to become involved and to help by taking some action that will set others' lives on a fresh, new course.

The idea is, as God has shown great Compassion on us, we should reciprocate and show the same to others. To not do so, is a sin of unimagined proportions.

(Most of the material on Compassion was derived from Lawrence O. Richards.)

(16) "SO THEN IT IS NOT OF HIM THAT WILLETH, NOR OF HIM THAT RUNNETH, BUT OF GOD THAT SHEWETH MERCY."

The phrase, *"So then it is not of him that willeth, nor of him that runneth,"* once again proclaims the great Truth that Mercy and Compassion cannot be earned or merited by the sinner, irrespective of what he may do. Consequently, this completely rules out a *"works"* Salvation.

The phrase, *"But of God that sheweth*

Mercy," proclaims all conditions on the part of God. In other words, the Lord lays down the rules Himself as to how and to whom Mercy is shown. As we have stated, man keeps trying to change those rules, but they are not to be changed.

Israel had it in her mind that due to some 2000 years of history, and especially considering that the Law had been given to them, as well as the entirety of the Word of God, that this merited them some type of favor with God. Paul's entire thrust is to debunk this idea respecting them, as well as all others. Despite the 2000 years of history, Israel merited nothing. In fact, even on their own grounds they were woefully lacking. They had not contributed anything to God, with Him rather having contributed everything to them. They had it in their minds that they were something special because God had given them the Law and the Prophets, etc.

The facts were, that God did not choose them because of their personal righteousness, nor did He give them the Law and the Prophets because of any personal goodness. Actually, He gave them these things despite what they actually were, not because of what they were. Paul in Romans Chapters 2-3, graphically outlines what they were, and it definitely was not what they thought they were. So, the very thing they are demanding, that God reward them because of the some 2000 years of history, is actually the very thing they do not want. On that basis they are shot down before they start, considering that the entirety of this 2000 years is sprinkled with rebellion against God in one form or the other.

Such was not only so with Israel, but continues to be so with all others as well. The last thing any man wants to do is to demand justice from God. We want Mercy and Compassion, but we must understand that we are not due any Mercy or Compassion, and the very moment we think we are, that is the moment we nullify these Attributes. One receives such from God by admitting that he does not deserve such, but rather the very opposite. He does not present to God any of his so-called accomplishments or qualities. As well, he desires that his life be changed, realizing that only God can do such. On this basis alone, will God show *"Mercy and Compassion"* (Isa. 66:2; Lk. 18:14).

In fact, the Lord plainly lays down the conditions for receiving Mercy and Compassion when He said, *". . . For every one that exalteth himself shall be abased; and he that humbleth himself shall be exalted"* (Lk. 18:14).

I don't know how much clearer it could be. Such statements completely nullify the idea that God arbitrarily chooses certain individuals upon whom He will lavish Mercy and Compassion, while refusing to do so with others, irrespective of circumstances. As we have repeatedly stated, God lays down the conditions, and if we meet those conditions, we will obtain the Promise.

(17) "FOR THE SCRIPTURE SAITH UNTO PHARAOH, EVEN FOR THIS SAME PURPOSE HAVE I RAISED THEE UP, THAT I MIGHT SHEW MY POWER IN THEE, AND THAT MY NAME MIGHT BE DECLARED THROUGHOUT ALL THE EARTH."

The phrase, *"For the Scripture saith unto Pharaoh,"* is taken from Exodus 9:16.

The phrase, *"Even for this same purpose have I raised thee up,"* presents the Lord using what is there, but not forcing the issue. In other words, God did not predestine Pharaoh to take a position of rebellion, with him having no choice but to do so, in order that God may show His Power, etc. Such *would* be unrighteous.

However, through foreknowledge, God saw and knew what Pharaoh would do and how he would react, using that, exactly as He uses such all over the world constantly.

Pharaoh didn't have to do what he did as it regards God's dealings with him. He could have yielded to Jehovah, and Egypt would have been spared. But this he would not do! Therefore, God was left with no choice but to act as He did.

The phrase, *"That I might shew My Power in thee, and that My Name might be declared throughout all the Earth,"* portrays that which God did and that which He does constantly, even at this very moment.

The Scripture says, *"Surely the wrath of man shall praise Thee"* (Ps. 76:10). What does that mean?

Pharaoh is a perfect example. It would have been greater praise to God for Pharaoh to have humbled himself before the Lord and thereby, have received Mercy and Grace. Nevertheless, God would be honored and praised even in this man's rebellion, in that the mighty Power of God was manifested in the destruction of Pharaoh, which struck fear to the whole world of that day. It is not that God wants or desires the wrath of man, for in reality, He desires the very opposite. Nevertheless, whichever direction that man takes, God will ultimately be praised even as with Pharaoh.

(18) "THEREFORE HATH HE MERCY ON WHOM HE WILL HAVE MERCY, AND WHOM HE WILL HE HARDENETH."

The phrase, *"Therefore has He mercy on whom He will have mercy,"* concerns God's conditions, which will not change. Many claim that God is unfair in His dealings with man, considering that the human race had absolutely nothing to do with the actions of Adam and Eve. In other words, they are claiming that it is unfair for God to hold mankind responsible for something they did not do — something in which, in fact, they had no part whatsoever. How could an act carried out by two people who lived at the dawn of time, namely Adam and Eve, affect the entirety of the human race, and in a very detrimental way? Therefore, men argue with God, concluding that He is unfair.

The truth is: if God left the situation as it is, men may have an argument. Two factors are involved:

1. The argument that because something happened long, long ago, over which they had no control, it should, therefore, not affect them, simply won't hold water. All of us are affected, even on a daily basis, by things which happen many miles away or happened many years ago, over which we had no control. Those are the facts of life, and is something the human race lives with constantly. So that complaint is invalid.

2. If God allowed the situation of man's lost condition to remain that way without doing something about it, man might have an argument; however, the Lord did not, to say the least, take that course. God became

Man, came down to this world, and died on a Cross, in order that man may be salvaged from this terrible dilemma of spiritual lostness. In effect, a price was paid that is so staggering, it beggars description. So, if man says that God is unjust and unfair, it is an argument that has no validity (Jn. 3:16).

The phrase, *"And whom He will He hardeneth,"* in the Greek *"hardeneth"* is *"skleruno,"* and means *"to make hard, to harden, to render obstinate, stubborn."*

Three words are used in the Hebrew to describe the hardening of Pharaoh's heart. The one which occurs most frequently, properly means *"to be strong,"* and, therefore, represents the hardness as foolhardiness, infatuated insensibility to danger (Ex., Chpt. 14).

The word as used in its positive sense, hardens, not merely permits to become hard. In Exodus the hardening is represented as self-produced (Ex. 8:15, 32; 9:34), and as produced by God (Ex. 4:21; 7:3, 9:12; 10:20, 27; 11:10). Paul here chooses the latter representation.

We are *not* to understand in the latter instance that God arbitrarily and directly forced upon Pharaoh an obstinate and stubborn resistance to Himself. Evil cannot be laid at the door of God. God not only does not solicit a sinner to do evil (James 1:13), but He also does not cause man to do evil. When man does wrong, that wrong comes from his own totally depraved nature (James 1:14).

PHARAOH AND HIS OWN STUBBORN WILL

When Pharaoh acted in stubborn rebellion against God, all of that rebellion came as a result of his own depravity, not any directly from God. When God is said to harden Pharaoh's heart, it is that He demanded the release of Israel, which confronted the Monarch with an issue which he did not wish to meet. It is like the case of a naughty boy whose violent temper is incited to greater effort by the demand of his mother that he behave himself.

WHOM HE WILL HE HARDENETH

"Will" in the Greek is *"thelo,"* and means *"to be resolved, to be determined, to purpose."*

NOTES

As this word is used of God, it is used in the sense of a Decree. God's resolve to use Pharaoh as an example of His Sovereignty was issued in a Decree that he be so used. Pharaoh was incorrigible, and God simply used him as He found him to demonstrate His Power to the human race, in the last analysis, an act of mercy to the larger number, while also an act of perfect justice toward Pharaoh, for what God was demanding was right and just.

Because of Pharaoh's own choice he was in this position, which God would use, and did use. Because of Pharaoh's stubbornness and resistance to God, which was his own will and choice, God's Power was shown in the Miracles by which Pharaoh and Egypt were visited, and God's Name is proclaimed to this day wherever the story of the Exodus is told (Wuest and Denney).

(19) "THOU WILT SAY THEN UNTO ME, WHY DOTH HE YET FIND FAULT? FOR WHO HATH RESISTED HIS WILL?"

The phrase, *"Thou wilt say then unto me,"* purposes Paul answering the questions of the Jews. Paul knew the Jewish mind to a far greater degree than anyone else, not merely because he was Jewish himself, but rather because he had once championed this very cause for Israel. Israel could not even remotely conceive that God would deal with them as He dealt with the Gentiles. Consequently, the idea that all must come on the same basis, the basis of Faith, left them cold. Paul knew and understood this thinking, because it had once been his thinking and his lot in life — that is, until he met Jesus on the road to Damascus.

As well, if one is to notice, Paul addressed himself to these subjects pretty much as a lawyer would do presently. In fact, Paul definitely would have met the criteria respecting that particular position of that day, especially considering, that he probably knew the Law of Moses better than any man on Earth.

In fact, his knowledge of that Law was very much skewed before his Conversion, and for the obvious reasons. Now that he knows Christ, he sees the Law as God intended for it to be seen and for it to actually be. Unfortunately, the Israel addressed by Paul, was unconverted and, therefore, blind to the true things of God. So, they could not see what he could see. However, their blindness was a judicial blindness, in other words visited upon them by God, and because it was a willful blindness on their part. In fact, the experience of Pharaoh was very similar in one respect to that of Israel, in that it was a willful blindness on the part of both.

In the sight of so many Miracles, Pharaoh had all the evidence he needed as to Who God was, and that He Alone should be worshiped and obeyed. But Pharaoh ignored this obvious evidence, continuing to rebel and resist. Israel did the same identical thing, with Jesus performing Miracle after Miracle, which left them without excuse. Both Pharaoh and Israel resisted, and both Pharaoh and Israel were destroyed!

The question, *"Why doth he yet find fault?"*, pertains to man finding fault with God.

Considering that God is perfectly fair in His dealings with all of humanity, and that He is no respecter of persons, why do men continue to find fault with Him?

Can he find fault with God's Love for humanity? Considering the price He paid in the giving of His Only Son to save humanity, no fault can be found there.

Can man find fault in God's Plan of Redemption? Considering that God offers Salvation to all alike, and on the same terms, meaning that all one has to do to receive this great Salvation is to simply have Faith, no fault can be found there as well.

Can the Mercy and Grace of God be found to have fault? Considering that this is the very subject of this discourse, and that God has laid down the conditions respecting the receiving of His Mercy and Grace, and that those conditions are applicable and can easily be met by all, one can find no fault in that either.

There is fault alright, but the fault is on the part of man and not God. That is what Paul is driving at, and the conclusion which must be reached by all, that is if we are to have the favor of God.

It is man who has sinned against God, and not God Who has sinned against man. It is man who is lost, and not God. Therefore, the fault is in man and man alone.

NOTES

The question, *"For who hath resisted His Will?"*, simply means that God has laid out His Plan concerning Redemption for humanity, and despite men resisting that Plan, it continues to stand and will never change, simply because God cannot change.

Irrespective of the amount of false doctrine which has been perpetrated through the ages, concerning the Word of God, the True Word still stands, and changes not. Despite the great number of Pharaohs who have lifted themselves up against God, in effect *"resisting His Will,"* His Will is the same today as it was then, and ever shall be. Once again, it changes not.

In fact, entire Nations such as Israel have attempted to resist God, but as someone has said, *"The hammers break, the anvil remains."*

In fact, most of humanity, and for all time, and fueled by the Powers of Darkness, have attempted to resist the Will of God, but they have never been successful, and they never will be successful. The idea is not to resist that Will in order to attempt to change it, which is impossible, but rather to conform to God's Will, thereby getting in line with God's Word, which will then garner His Blessings.

(20) "NAY BUT, O MAN, WHO ART THOU THAT REPLIEST AGAINST GOD? SHALL THE THING FORMED SAY TO HIM THAT FORMED IT, WHY HAST THOU MADE ME THUS?"

The question, *"Nay but, O man, who art thou that repliest against God?"*, can be answered in the experiences of Isaac and Joseph.

Isaac, though he knew the Will of God, willfully determined to bless Esau, and he *"trembled exceedingly"* when defeated. He *"loved"* Esau which was the opposite of God, and *"hated"* Jacob, which was as well the opposite of God (Gen. 25:28; 27:1-4, 33).

Likewise, when Joseph saw his aged father placing his right hand of Blessing upon the head of Ephraim, his younger son, moved by the energy of the flesh, he attempted to prevent the action. He also was defeated (Gen. 48:17-22).

So, no one who resists God, or who repliest against God, even His Chosen such as Isaac and Joseph, are successful, for such cannot be successful. Therefore, if these two could not circumvent the Plan of God, how is it possible for others with not nearly the standing of these two to do so?

The question, *"Shall the thing formed say to Him that formed it, Why hast Thou made me thus?"*, presents that which is foolish.

It is foolish and irreverent for the creature to judge the Creator. If the creature were sinless he might, perhaps, claim liberty of criticism, but being sinful he can make no such claim.

WHY HAS GOD MADE MAN THUS?

Both questions of this verse imply a spirit of contention. The idea is, that man is blaming God for his predicament, whatever that predicament of disturbance may be.

From the time of the Fall, man has not yet desired to take responsibility for his actions. Adam blamed Eve for the Fall, as Eve blamed the Serpent. None took responsibility for themselves (Gen. 3:9-13).

So, on this premise let's look at this question.

THE MANNER IN WHICH MAN IS MADE

Human nature can be understood only when it is seen in its relationship with God. Any philosophical or psychological school that attempts to treat human nature apart from God must reach inadequate or wrong conclusions.

Our understanding of the human race in Biblical perspective must begin with the Genesis account of Creation. Here we discover a number of ways in which humanity is carefully distinguished from the rest of Creation:

1. Man alone was created in the Image and Likeness of God (Gen. 1:26-27). Even after the Fall, this Image persists, continuing to set humanity apart and to make each individual life precious (Gen. 9:6).

2. Man alone was created with distinct elements, the body having been shaped from the Earth and given the breath of life (Gen. 2:7).

3. Man alone is described as directly and personally shaped by the Creator, rather than being simply called into existence by the Creator's spoken Word (Gen. 2:7).

4. Man alone was given the right to subdue the material creation and to rule all

living beings as God's Representative (Gen. 1:26, 28-30; Ps. 8).

5. Man alone has a nature that requires relationships with his fellows on multiple levels of personality (Gen. 2:18-25).

6. Man alone was made morally responsible to obey God's Commands and to care for the Garden of Eden (Gen. 2:15-17).

HUMAN DESTINY ESTABLISHED IN REDEMPTION AND RESURRECTION

As stated Human nature can be understood only when it is seen in its relationship with God. Any attempts to understand man outside of the Bible, will always result in error. This is the reason that modernistic psychoanalysis is woefully inadequate.

In the Old Testament, the focus of Revelation rests on Creation, with mankind viewed as created in the Image of God.

In the New Testament, the focus of Revelation is on man's alienation from God and on God's remedy in Christ — Redemption and Resurrection.

Rather than look at mankind in the abstract, the Bible always reminds us that man is a creature. Once more, man is a fallen creature. Human potential and personality have been warped by sin. Rather than live in fellowship with God, human beings rebel and look at the Lord with enmity (Rom. 1:18-32). Humanity is not and cannot be subject to God's Law, at least on its own (Rom. 8:14-25).

"The sinful mind is hostile to God. It does not submit to God's Law, nor can it do so" (Rom. 8:7). As persons who are fully responsible for their acts, human beings are under the Wrath of God, for He, as Righteous Judge, must punish sin.

AS MAN IS!

The vision of man as sinner is within itself inadequate. Even those explorations of the impact of sin on personality and relationships, while they give insight into the current state of the race, do not adequately explain mankind.

The Bible tells us that human beings remain the objects of God's Love. In virtue of the uniqueness of humanity, which flows from a creation endowment, each individual has an eternal destiny. No individual is simply snuffed out of existence at death.

THAT WHICH GOD HAS DONE ABOUT THE SITUATION

God's concern for us as unique beings is shown in the decision of the Triune God to effect our Salvation. The Father planned and predestined; the Son entered the human family to die; and the Spirit breeds Life into all who believe, bonding each Believer to the Body of Christ.

To effect this Plan, the Son Himself actually took on humanity (Heb. 2:14-18) and then died as a human being to effect our Redemption. In His Resurrection we have not only a guarantee of forgiveness but also a vision of our own final destiny.

So the Scripture draws our attention to Christ and to the Redemption He provides and the Resurrection He Promises. Through Jesus, there is the possibility of an inner transformation, through which sin's impact will be canceled and our lives will bring forth beauty. Through Jesus, there is the prospect of full restoration to God's ideal for mankind — when the Resurrection occurs.

It is clear, then, according to Scripture that mankind could never be understood simply by looking at man's present experience in this world. To grasp who and what human beings are, we must look back to Creation, look to the continuing impact of Redemption, and look ahead to the ultimate transformation that will be effected by Resurrection.

When each human being is understood as an ever-living person — unique, and precious to God — then and only then will we begin to understand the nature of mankind.

THE OLD MAN AND THE NEW MAN

The Bible is realistic about man's natural capability. Human nature is presently in the grip of sin, twisted beyond hope. The New Testament term *"old man"* indicates all that is misshapen within the personality of the Believer (Rom. 6:6).

But the term *"new man"* represents God's dynamic New Creation. That *"new self"* is *"being renewed in knowledge in the Image of its Creator"* (Col. 3:10). It recaptures in

NOTES

time what was lost in the Fall, and it gives a taste of the feast that awaits Believers (Richards).

ABILITY TO *"WILL," "REASON,"* AND TO *"CHOOSE"*

This Attribute of God as given to man in his creation, which is at least a part of the *"Image of God,"* sets man apart from all Creation. While animals do have a will and a limited power of choice, it is very abbreviated and functions more so in the realm of instinct. As well some animals such as dogs, may have a tiny bit of reasoning ability, but miniscule.

While man has instinct as well, his ability to reason and to choose, is of far greater magnitude than any of God's other Creation. It is of such magnitude that it can actually create, which again is the Image of God, and which it seems even Angels cannot do.

In this ability to reason, to will, and to choose, tremendous vistas are opened to man, actually in almost an unlimited manner. But yet, with the vast wonder of this ability, there is an inherent danger.

The Philosopher Bertrand Russell once asked the question as to why God, if there is a God as he put it, did not make man with a will so strong that it would be impossible to fail? Of course, such a question is an oxymoron. Such a will in fact, would not be a will.

For such to be, privilege and choice must be available.

So, God made man with the ability of reason, choice, and a will. As such, man chose wrongly, which is why he is as he is. In other words, God did not form man as a sinner, lost, without direction, unable to do the right thing, and, therefore, suffering the consequences, but rather the opposite.

MAN'S CONTENTION

Now we come down to the meat of the entire contention, *"Why hast Thou made me thus?"*

Man argues that it is not his fault regarding his present condition, inasmuch as it was brought about by Adam, a situation over which all descendants had no control, etc.

While that is true, at least as far as it goes,

the basic problem that God has with man, is not his fallen condition, as terrible as that is, but rather his refusal to accept God's Remedy for that condition, which is His Son The Lord Jesus Christ.

While it is true that man had no choice over his situation as he was born, he does have a choice as to whether he will remain degenerate or become regenerate.

Man's original Creation was of such magnitude that God gave him dominion over all of His Creation (Ps. 8). For us to imagine or comprehend such a thing, is absolutely impossible, at least at present. Adam originally before the Fall, had to be of such magnitude in the intellectual sense as to defy all description. As well, considering that his physical body would never have died, and that he, due to his constant association with God, would have continued to grow even more intelligent, all of this due to his spirituality, i.e., Godly association, it is difficult to even begin to guess as to his original spiritual and intellectual posture.

The Fall destroyed all of that, actually positioning him in the very opposite posture, and growing regressively worse.

The entirety of the remedy centers up in Jesus Christ. He and He Alone is the Answer to the dilemma. As we have previously stated, considering what God has done to redeem humanity, no fault can ever be laid at His Feet.

The fault in the beginning was that of man, and the fault now is that of man.

(21) "HATH NOT THE POTTER POWER OVER THE CLAY, OF THE SAME LUMP TO MAKE ONE VESSEL UNTO HONOUR, AND ANOTHER UNTO DISHONOUR?"

The beginning of the question, *"Hath not the Potter power over the clay . . . ?"*, presents God as the Creator, and as such perfectly capable of creating what He desires.

Considering God's creative abilities, one must not lower God down to the level of the inane thoughts of man. In other words, the ways of the Creator are past finding out by the Creation.

However, man is not only a creature, he is a fallen creature, which makes it doubly worse. In other words, man does not have the ability to comprehend God in the fashion

as He really is. Consequently, he has warped ideas about God.

Man is looked at here as *"clay,"* which he actually is, and which is of the Earth, earthy. By contrast, *"God is a Spirit"* (Jn. 4:24). Consequently, the difference in Deity and Dust is considerable, as should be obvious.

In essence, Paul is telling man that he does not have the right or the intellectual ability in any capacity to say the least, to tell God how He should make and form the clay. Concerning His Creation, the Scripture says, *"And God saw every thing that He had made, and, behold, it was very good"* (Gen. 1:31).

Incidentally, the formula *"The Scripture saith,"* as given in verse 17, asserts the Inspiration of the Bible. What God says, the Scripture says, and what the Scripture says, God says.

The conclusion of the question, *"Of the same lump to make one vessel unto honour, and another unto dishonour?"*, proclaims what Paul has been saying all the time.

"Make" in the Greek is *"poieo,"* and means *"to make or do in a very wide application, more or less direct. It refers to a single act."*

The idea is, that in the making of man, God knew that man would Fall. He also knew that He would provide a Redeemer, with some accepting, which would bring man *"honor."* He also knew that many would not accept, which would cause them to go further into *"dishonor."*

Once again, we come back to the question, as to why God made man as He did, knowing that most would remain in *"dishonor"* (Mat. 7:13).

For God to obtain what He desired in His Creation, man had to be made in the manner in which he was made. For man to Love God, which is what God intended in man, he must do so willingly, of his own free choice, and with reason. Otherwise it is not Love, and man is no more than a machine such as a computer, etc.

It is not that God predestined some to *"honor"* and some to *"dishonor,"* but that He did predestine that man would have a choice, and that the choice would fall out to either *"honor"* or *"dishonor."*

Such is God, and such is Creation!

(22) "WHAT IF GOD, WILLING TO

SHEW HIS WRATH, AND TO MAKE HIS POWER KNOWN, ENDURED WITH MUCH LONGSUFFERING THE VESSELS OF WRATH FITTED TO DESTRUCTION:"

The phrase, *"What if God, willing to shew His Wrath, and to make His Power known,"* is in effect saying, inasmuch as there are vessels of dishonor, there is a Divine necessity, that God should demonstrate the Power of His Wrath as well as the Riches of His Mercy.

The phrase, *"Endured with much longsuffering the vessels of wrath fitted to destruction"* proclaims the very opposite of predestination as it is commonly taught. If these *"vessels of wrath"* which if they stayed in that condition were *"fitted for destruction,"* were predestined to this darkness, what point would the *"longsuffering"* of God be?

No! The *"longsuffering"* is actually the Mercy of God extended to rebels for an inordinate period of time, with the hope that they may repent. Of course God in His Omniscience knows who will and who will not repent. Nevertheless, He is *"longsuffering"* to all irrespective of their final decision, in order that there be no accusation against God at the Great White Throne Judgment (Rev. 20:11-15).

(23) "AND THAT HE MIGHT MAKE KNOWN THE RICHES OF HIS GLORY ON THE VESSELS OF MERCY, WHICH HE HAD AFORE PREPARED UNTO GLORY,"

The phrase, *"And that He might make known the riches of His Glory on the vessels of mercy,"* pertains to those whether Jews or Gentiles who accept the *"riches of His Glory"* unto Salvation.

If one is to notice, Paul used two terms *"vessels of wrath"* and *"vessels of mercy."* The first speaks of the *"Wrath of God"* against those who continue to rebel against His Grace and Mercy, while the second speaks of the *"Mercy of God"* extended to those who willingly and graciously accept such Mercy.

The phrase, *"Which He had afore prepared unto Glory,"* does not mean that God predestined these for Salvation, but does mean that He predestined that those who accepted His Mercy and Grace would be *"prepared unto Glory."* This was decided *"afore,"* i.e., in eternity past.

Who would receive this predestined

"Glory," is up to *"whosoever will"* (Jn. 3:16; Rev. 22:17).

Looking at the other side of the analogy that Paul has drawn respecting the *"potter"* and the *"clay,"* the Believer must yield to the Potter's hand in allowing the proper molding and construction of the *"vessel."* Too oftentimes the will of the *"vessel"* is at cross purposes with the Will of God, which actually finds ourselves resisting His Will. He has a perfect Plan for our lives, but for that Plan to be realized, there must be cooperation on our part.

As well, and as is obvious from the very analogy drawn, the Believer does not begin as a finished *"vessel,"* but rather as a lump of unmolded clay. To be sure, the Potter (the Holy Spirit) knows exactly what type of vessel that He is to prepare. As well, it is the work of a lifetime, which means as should be obvious, that it is not easy nor quick.

OBVIOUS FLAWS

When I first went on Radio and Television back in the late 1960's and early 1970's, there was a deep Moving and Operation of the Holy Spirit within my life to prepare me for this particular work. It was not something I purposely engaged, for I really did not have the spiritual depth to contemplate such. However, the Holy Spirit knew what was needed and began to develop the process.

I have always had a very strong prayer life, which was actually encouraged by my Grandmother when I was but a child. Thankfully, I never strayed from her inspiration and direction in this capacity. But at this particular time, it seemed as if the Holy Spirit moved upon me exceedingly so to seek the Face of God, to spend time with Him, to allow the searchlight of the Spirit to penetrate every fiber and core of my being. During this time there were many mighty Movings of the Holy Spirit, some grander than any I had ever known before. It was during this period that the Lord began to launch us out into World Evangelism, especially in the field of Television. It was then that He gave me greater insight respecting the Holy Spirit, and how that thousands would be filled in our meetings, which they were.

During this particular time, and believing

that I was closer to God than ever before, which I believe actually was the case, still, I felt more undone than I ever had in my life, at least in a spiritual sense.

THE LIGHT

The purpose of this following illustration either was given to me in a dream, or while I was in prayer. I really cannot remember which. Nevertheless, ever how it came to me, I related to the Lord that even though I felt I was closer to Him than ever before, still, ugly flaws of which I had not previously been aware, now had become obvious to me. It was what seemed to be a dichotomy.

THAT WHICH THE LORD
SPOKE TO ME

The Lord spoke to my heart relating to me the reason for this. As I said, it was either in a dream or during a time of prayer.

"The closer you get to the Light, the more the flaws begin to be apparent," was His Answer to me.

So many times, we are too far from Him, to properly see ourselves as we really are. However, the closer that one gets to Him, the brighter the Light shines upon one, and then one begins to see what is really there. I think I can say without fear of exaggeration, that irrespective as to who we are, or how close to God we may think we are, we will find during these times that the flaws in our character are of far greater dimension than we had ever begun to realize.

At the present I realize I have yet a long way to go, and say as Paul, *"Not as though I had already attained, either were already perfect: but I follow after, if that I may apprehend that for which also I am apprehended of Christ Jesus"* (Phil. 3:12).

As I look back, I see so much which I thought was the Spirit of God, but actually was the flesh. To be sure, and among other things, this is the position into which the Holy Spirit is attempting to mold every Vessel, that everything in our lives be of the Spirit, and none of the flesh. I am convinced that this is the grand purpose. If that can be realized, then whatever the Plan of God is for the Believer, can be brought about.

The following is a Chapter taken from the Book *"God's Eagles"* written by George Watson. I feel it has a strong bearing on the working of the Holy Spirit in the hearts and lives of Saints, as He makes us into that which He desires.

GOD'S EAGLES

There are many places in the Bible where God mentions Eagles, and in such a way as to indicate that the term applies to a class of the Servants of God, who have in them those qualities that correspond with Eagles in the rank of nature. God has put a language into all things of His Creation. There is a spoken language for Angels and men, and then there is an unwritten language in all the Works of God, just as distinctly and clearly as the spoken language.

God puts a language into trees and rocks, leaves and birds, beasts, fishes, the sea and the sky, a language known to Himself, and doubtless a language in due time to be perfectly interpreted to the Saints of God.

Using symbols, God calls His people by the names of Cattle, Sheep, Doves, and Eagles. Just as there are Sheep among human Saints which are not four-legged animals, so there are Eagles in human character, which are distinct from rapacious Birds. God compares Himself to a Great Eagle, and compares His True Saints to Eagles. The Lord says in the Book of Exodus, *"I bare you on Eagles' wings and brought you to Myself."*

In David's lament over the death of Saul and Jonathan, he said, *"They were swifter than Eagles, and stronger than Lions."*

The Psalmist says that those who wait upon the Lord shall renew their strength and mount up with wings as Eagles.

We are told in the Book of Revelation of the Four Living Creatures, one of those beings having the form of *"a flying Eagle."*

SAINTS OF GOD

In everyone of these Scripture references, the Eagle is used in a good sense to signify the Saints of God, who are taking rank in the Kingdom of God, corresponding to the rank of Eagles in the realm of nature.

The most striking Passage bearing on this subject is found in Deuteronomy 32:11-12, *"As an Eagle that stirreth up her nest, fluttereth over her young, spreadeth abroad her wings, taketh them, beareth them on her wings;*

"*So the Lord* (Jehovah) *Alone did lead him, and there was no strange God with them.*" These words give us a beautiful insight into God's method of dealing with His people, as to how He draws them to Himself, and as to how He makes Eagle Saints and what Attributes they are possessed with.

There are various ranks among the Servants of God, corresponding to the different ranks among birds, or among trees, or among the stars, and Paul tells us that as one star differs from another star in Glory, so will it be in the Resurrection of the Saints.

GOD'S PLAN

In the first place, let us notice how God makes His Eagles. God makes all things by a Plan in His Own Mind, as He told Moses to make the Tabernacle according to the pattern shown him on the Mount. When God makes a tree, or a world, or a race of beings, He works according to a Plan, and hence, when He makes a class of Saints which ranks as Eagles, He works by a method which is set forth in the Text.

The first step in the process of making an Eagle Saint is to stir up the nest. The Eagle builds its nest on a lofty mountain crag, or in the highest tree it can find, and forms it of sticks and branches of trees and then lines it with softer things like wool, or paper, or rags, or the skins of animals, making it soft for its young. When the young Eagles have become large enough to fly, the Mother Bird forces them out of the soft nest by tearing away the soft lining and throwing everything out of the nest that would make it comfortable, and letting the young birds down on the sharp sticks and thorns, so that they become dissatisfied with their home and are willing to move somewhere else.

This is the way God deals with those of His Servants that He calls into close and heroic union with Himself. He begins by stirring up their nests, and making them unhappy, that they become willing to move out into a new place of experience, and thought, and life.

This is the way He stirred the nests of the Israelites in the land of Egypt.

When the Hebrews first went into Egypt, God built a fine nest for them under the administration of Joseph, for they had the fat of the land, and for many years they had prosperity and an excellent living. But when the time came for God to take them out of Egypt, He knew they would not be willing to leave unless their nest was stirred, and the soft lining was all removed. Hence, God allowed the Egyptians to treat them awfully, with hard bondage and poverty, and distress, and this bondage waxed worse and worse, until in their desperate sorrow, they cried as the voice of one man to the God of Abraham for deliverance. This is the way God stirs the nest of those of His Servants that He wants to lift into the altitudes of Faith and Service.

It may be He breaks up the home life, or the Church life, or takes away property, or removes loved ones, or by a series of strange providences takes away the soft lining of our lives, our earthly, or social, or religious comforts, and lets us down upon the sharp thorns, and the hard sticks of trouble and suffering, until like the Hebrews in Egypt, we cry out to the Living God for deliverance.

THE APOSTLES

All the Apostles had their nests stirred, all the Reformers and great Evangelists and great Religious Leaders had their nests stirred, until they were willing to immigrate into new quarters, or go to the ends of the Earth, or change their locality, or change their relationships, or change a traditional theology, or move out into a new realm of thought, or prayer, or work, or experience. We can never move into a new locality without breaking our relationship with the present locality. We can never go into a better climate without disrupting from the climate we are now in. We can never move toward God without leaving something of Adam. We can never migrate toward the West without leaving the East. We can never step toward Holiness without breaking with unholiness.

God takes away the soft things on which we lean, the dear old props of nature, of friends, of old forms, and old ceremonies, and old comforts. He undermines our natural foundations, and lets us down on the bare rock. If God did not thus stir our nest, we would be unwilling to move out into His Realm.

Abraham is a pattern, and he was God's immigrant, and all True Saints are immigrants from the old nest of natural things into the upper air of the things of God.

THE REVELATION OF GOD TO THE BELIEVER

The second step in the making of an Eagle is, the Mother Bird flutters over them. The young birds hear the sound of wings to draw their attention from the thorns and sticks to her. The Mother Eagle will watch her young, and when they begin to whine and complain, and move uneasily, and hunt for some easy place, and cannot find it, then the Mother Bird rises over the nest and flutters her feathers, and shakes out her wings right over their heads, with a most peculiar sound, to draw the attention of their eyes from the painful thorns and sticks in the bottom of their nest.

Oh, what a language there is in the sound of wings, a language perfectly intelligible to the young Eagles. When they hear that peculiar sound, the young birds look up to the parent. This is just what God does in the making of His Saints.

When God allows trouble, sorrow, sickness, poverty, bereavement and desolation to come to us, and we weep and cry and murmur, and find fault, and get sad, and blue, and look around as to find something to lean upon, and hunt for comfort in the creature, in that which is of the Earth, and find nothing but sharp briars and piercing trials, then God flutters over us, and we hear the sound of His Wings.

God does it to draw our attention to Himself, and for us to look away to Him, to look away above us, from the coffin, from the grave, from the old house, from the deserted farm, from departed friends, from earthly property, from a good reputation, from human comfort.

We look up to catch the sound of those mysterious wings that flutter in the ears of our souls. God draws us to look up to Him with sounds we have not heard before, and like the Prophet Ezekiel, God causes us to

hear the noise of wings.

THE SPREADING OF THE WINGS

The next step in the process of making Eagle Saints is, he spreadeth abroad his wings. No bird in all the world has wings like the Eagle, and the Mother Eagle is always larger than the male bird, and her wings are the largest. Many an Eagle measures 14 feet from tip to tip when its wings are spread out.

When you see the wings folded, you would not think they were over two feet long, but when those wings are stretched out it is amazing how long they seem. If the young Eagles could talk they might say to their Mother, *"I never saw you look so big before, for when you were here with us in the nest, you looked rather small, but since those wings are spread out at their full length, we are amazed at the magnitude of your protection and strength."*

The spreading abroad of the Eagle's wings is a revelation to her young of her strength. This is the way God deals with us. He not only flutters over us to draw our attention to Himself, but *"He spreadeth abroad His wings."* When we get our attention on God He unfolds His magnitude to our Faith. He spreads abroad the great wings of His Attributes, His Majesty, His Power, His Glory.

There have been times in some of our lives in which we lost apparently everything on the Earth, when property and friends, and health, and prospects were swept away as in a storm, and at those times we heard the flutter of the Divine Wings, and looked up and saw God spread abroad His Wings, and unfold to our earnest Faith the marvelous strength of His Perfection.

It is an epoch in our lives when God unfolds Himself to us, when He gives us a Vision of His infinite providence, the vastness of His resources, the Revelation of His inward feelings, the largeness of His arrangements, the delicacy and minuteness of His care over us, the far sweep of His Eternal Purposes.

HIS MIGHTY POWER

What a thrill of inspiration goes through our souls when we see the great wings of the Jehovah Eagle spread abroad above our heads, those wings that stretch from horizon to horizon, that spread out without beginning and without ending, from the eternal past into the eternal future, those wings that can support worlds on worlds as easily as carrying an insect, and those wings whose feathers are the Attributes of Almighty God, are stretched out for our safety, our Salvation, our security.

We never see the infinite merit of Jesus until revealed to us by the Holy Spirit in the outspreading wings of the Atonement of the Precious Blood. Just as the spreading abroad of the Eagle's wings is the great Revelation that the young Eagles have of the parent bird, so the spreading abroad of God's Eagle Wings constitutes that Revelation of Himself to us of His unlimited perfection. It is then that the wings of the Mother Bird become larger and softer than all the comforts found in the nest. It is when God spreads abroad His Wings over us, and around us, that we see He is infinitely greater than everything in nature, or than everything in our dreams, or our air castles, that He has sufficiency in Himself, infinitely beyond all our wants and all our imaginations.

Are you an orphan? Is your husband dead, or your wife dead? Are your parents dead? Are you poor, or hated, or cast out? Are you criticized, or ostracized, or minimized, or undersized? Are you perplexed? Are you barefooted, hungry, homeless, etc.? If you are in such a condition, and you could see God spread abroad His Wings, and unfurl the blue sky of His Attributes above you, and around you, you would cease to feel sorrow, you would be lifted above your circumstances, you would have an inspiration from above that would be more than a match for all the ills of this world. The sight of God's infinite Wings spread abroad would make us forget the tearing up of any earthly nest.

GOD BEARS US UP

The next step in the process of making Eagles, the Mother Bird taketh them, and beareth them on her wings. She stands on the edge of the nest, and lays her wings down so the young Eagles can climb up on her wings and fasten their young claws into her feathers, preparatory for a great flight up in the air.

NOTES

See how God stirred the nest of the early Christian Church in Jerusalem by the beheading of James, and the persecution, and how the infant Church was apparently torn to pieces, and how they were scattered everywhere, preaching the Word. But for the stirring of their Jerusalem nest, they would not likely have gone 50 miles away, but by stirring the nest up they were scattered to the four corners of the Earth.

The Mother Bird spreads out her long wings flat down on the nest, and the young Eagles are glad to step from the briars and thorns, and sharp sticks, upon their Mother's soft great wings. When the young birds have fastened their claws on the Mother's wings, then she prepares for a great flight.

Taking the young birds one at a time on her wing, the Mother Bird will soar from 4,000 to 5,000 feet up in the blue sky, and then give a certain sudden lurch, and throw off the young Eagle. The young bird tumbles and rolls over, and puts out its wings, and beats the air while it is falling, but the Mother Bird watches her young, and when the helpless little thing is halfway down to the Earth, she shoots downward with the accuracy and the speed of a bullet, and catches the young bird again on her wing, and again soars aloft in the sky, and repeats this process until the young Eagle has learned how to fly.

This illustrates in the spiritual life the way God teaches the Believer to live by Faith, and to exercise the Spirit's Gifts and Graces, and to form habits of perfect trust against what seems to be utter ruin and absolute failure.

When the Eagle has formed habits of flying, it will stem terrific storms, and beat its way up against the channel of the wind, and surmount the elements against all ordinary calculations. It is thus that God takes the Eagle Saints on His Wings, and carries them aloft in glorious flights of rich and rare experience, and then suddenly seems to drop them and leave them to themselves, that they may learn the Divine art of perfect trust against all odds and difficulties and all failures.

THE BELIEVER LEARNS TO TRUST GOD

The trust which is developed by this process, brings us to a much higher level of experience than we have known previously.

In other words, the Believer learns to trust in God Alone, without leaning on past experiences, or any feeling, or religious emotion, without leaning on other Saints, or on the Church, or on circumstances, but to run the tremendous risk of falling helpless into hands of infinite Love.

It is then that God turns loose His Eagles in a thunderstorm, at midnight, or a cold, winter's day, with the wind blowing a gale, or to face a blizzard of circumstances, and to practice that venturesome and seemingly reckless reliance on God's Word, and on His Character. This is the way that God makes those Eagle Saints which are to take rank in His Coming Kingdom.

THE QUALITIES OF EAGLES

We now come to consider what are the qualities of Eagles. There are certain moral and spiritual qualities that constitute a fitness for rank in the Kingdom of God, and as there are various ranks in the Kingdom of Heaven, and each of these ranks is marked by certain qualities peculiar to its own, so there are certain qualities in the Eagle which are typical of Front Rank Saints.

In the first place, the Eagle is the King of the air, just as the Lion is the King among beasts. Jesus appropriates the name of Lion to Himself in referring to His conquest of the Earth, and we see in the writings of Moses that Jehovah appropriates the name of Eagle to Himself, in referring to His supernatural power, in working the great Miracles in Egypt, and lifting His people out of bondage to bear them on His Wings into the land of Canaan (Ex. 19:4).

The Lion is not the largest of animals, but it is the King among all animals just the same. There are some birds which are larger than the Eagle, but the Eagle is emphatically the King of the air, and over all other birds. There is a royalty and majesty in the Eagle which belongs to no other bird or fowl. This is true of Eagle Saints, for they constitute a race of rulers who are to reign in the Coming Kingdom.

The man that governs the air governs the world. At first, men fought with clubs and stones; later on, they fought with arrows and spears; still later on, they fought

with gunpowder and bullets; then came the era of warfare in battleships, and the conquest of Navies on the Sea, but in these times they are carrying on the art of war up in the air and down under the Sea, which is a clear sign of the winding up of this age and the concluding of the drama of man's rule in the Earth and the preparation for the final scene of this world's history in its present fallen condition.

THE GREAT EYES OF EAGLES

The Eagles are great watches. There is not an eye in all the world like the Eagle's eye. The Eagle has an eye both telescopic to discern things afar off and microscopic to see the smallest. The eye of the Eagle can penetrate a great distance and discover things that no other eye on Earth could find at such a long range. It is said by the best authority that it is impossible to deceive an Eagle.

They may be captured when young, or shot, or conquered in battle, but they cannot be deceived in a matter of vision.

Audubon knew more about birds than any man in the world, and he gives it out that he never could succeed in deceiving the Eagle. He once climbed a mountain crag, near an Eagle's nest and hid himself, as he thought, perfectly private to the habits of the Mother Bird. When the Mother Eagle would return, she soared aloft, round and round about her nest, piercing every nook and corner of the mountain, until she spied Audubon in his hiding place, and then dropping the prey that she was bringing to her young, gave a loud scream to her mate which was miles away, notifying him that their nest had been discovered.

This quality of Eagle vision is referred to by our Saviour concerning those Saints which He pronounces to be the *"Elect."* Remember that the word *"Elect"* in the Bible does not refer to Salvation, but it refers to a rank which people take after they are Justified, and mostly the term refers to Sanctification, and to being in the company of the bridehood Saints.

DECEPTION

Not one of God's Eagles will ever be deluded by Mormonism, or Christian Science so-called, or Spiritualism, or Russellism, or any other *"Ism,"* because they are Divinely illuminated with that Apostolic Light which Jesus and the Prophets and the Apostles had.

The Apostle Peter refers to some Christians who are nearsighted, and cannot see afar off, but he distinctly affirms that such Christians are nearsighted, because they have not escaped the corruption or the depravity which is in the world, and because they have not added to their Faith, Virtue, Knowledge, Temperance, Patience, Godliness, and Brotherly Kindness.

He is describing a soul that is Sanctified, and filled with the Holy Spirit, and then says, he that lacks these things is nearsighted, and cannot see afar off; in other words, he may be a Christian, a weak Christian; he may get to Heaven, but he is not one of God's Eagles, and does not possess that keen penetrating vision which can see things afar off, and distinguish between Truth and error.

THE VISION

It is amazing how multitudes of good people can be hoodwinked and fooled in so many ways, and by so many people. It is said that the Patriarchs had such vision that they saw the Promises of God afar off. They had an Eagle vision to see things thousands of years ahead of them, not only as to the First Coming of Christ, but also to His Second Coming, and to that City which had foundations, and whose Builder and Maker is God.

The reason they could see these things, is because of their great spiritual height. Eagles prefer great heights. They build their nests on high mountain peaks and in the highest trees they can find. They love to soar miles and miles above the Earth, and the vast upper blue sky, far above the flight of all other birds. Their instincts are lofty, they spurn low spots for their resting places. This is a trait of Eagle Saints. Their song is:

"You need not look for me down in Egypt's sand,
"For I have pitched my tent far up in Beulah Land.
"Lord, lift me up and let me stand,
"By Faith on Heaven's table land."

SANCTIFICATION

An Eagle Saint is one who has been delivered from the old Adam, and filled with Divine Love — the Love that came down from the Godhead, and the Love that instinctively arises to dwell with God in the heavenly places.

The first man had two names. His first name was Adam, which signifies *"Red Earth,"* and indicates the Earth nature of fallen man.

His second name was *"Ish,"* translated by the word *"Man,"* but this name *"Ish"* indicates the higher spiritual part of a man's life (the man Adam).

The Greek word which we translate *"Sanctification,"* signifies *"to take the Earth out."* The word is *"hage,"* a combination of two words. The word *"Ge,"* always in the Greek Testament means *"Earth,"* and the prefix *"ha"* is the strongest negative, and means *"no Earth."*

Now that is the word that the Holy Spirit has selected for Holiness, or Sanctification. Thus, you see the word *"Adam"* means *"Red Earth,"* and the word *"Hage"* or *"Holiness"* means *"No Earth."* Thus, when a Believer is truly Sanctified, and the Earth, or the old Adam, is taken out of him, and he is filled with the Holy Spirit, he is lifted into the heavenly places, and his Faith and Prayer and Spiritual Life ascends to those spiritual regions which correspond with the lofty flight of the Eagle.

HIGH MOTIVES AND LOFTY PRAYERS

Eagle Saints have high motives, and lofty prayers, and heavenly aspirations. In giving their money, and in their spiritual work, they are wider than sectarian bonds, and higher than sectarian walls, and far above selfish motives.

There is a word in the Song of Solomon which says, *"Let us look from the top."* This is the lofty Eagle vision of those who have, in the truest and best sense, entered the higher life. Such Believers soar in their Faith and Prayer and Love above narrow boundaries, above national lines and see the great world, with its teaming millions, from God's standpoint, and see the affairs of this world in the light of Heaven and Eternity.

In the language of Isaiah, they dwell on high, and their defense is the munitions of rocks. They mount up with wings as Eagles, and grasp things that are above the world.

STRENGTH

Last of all, the Eagles are strong of wing. An Eagle can knock a man down with his wing.

The power of the Ostrich is in his foot, and they have been known to kill horses with a kick.

The power of the Lion is in his mouth, by which he can tear flesh. But the power of an Eagle is mainly in his wing.

A man in the Alps stood on a mountain and watched an Eagle fighting two Rams, and saw how the Eagle would strike the great Sheep with his wings and hurl him over on the ground. The strength of the Eagle wing is seen in his flight, in the great speed, and in their great length.

The power of the Eagle's wing sets forth the supernatural strength of Eagle Saints in Prayer, and Faith, and Endurance, and Long-suffering. There is a strange Divine Power in Saintly Souls which outmatches all physical strength, or all intellectual sharpness, or all subtlety of philosophy, or all the ordinary strength of human beings.

There are little women, and sickly men, and poor people, who have reached a place in God where in spiritual things they are giants, and are like Lions and Eagles in the natural world. There are those who seem to be full of weakness, and yet by the power of Prayer and the loftiness of Faith they are carrying burdens, bearing troubles, enduring sorrows and accomplishing things through the Holy Spirit beyond all the natural strength of man, and beyond all the intellectual greatness of Scholars and Orators and this world's great ones so-called.

They have that strength of the Eagle's wing by which in union with Jesus Christ which through the Holy Spirit they bear all things, and endure all things, and hope all things.

This is a Divine Strength just beyond all fanaticism, or fleshy demonstrations; it is above all boasting, or all self-conceit; it is higher than air castles, stronger than a mere notion, but firm with a rock bottom, and a

sky-blue clearness which is attained only through the indwelling of the Holy Spirit.

These qualities of God's Eagles are obtained by that perfect attitude of abandonment, and Obedience, and Faith that waits on the Lord, until the strength is renewed, and in that strength the soul mounts up with wings as Eagles and runs and is not weary, and walks and is not faint.

(24) "EVEN US, WHOM HE HATH CALLED, NOT OF THE JEWS ONLY, BUT ALSO OF THE GENTILES?"

The phrase, *"Even us, whom He hath called,"* refers to several things:

1. First of all it is God Who initiates the Call. Unbelieving man is totally bereft of all spiritual life. Consequently, there is nothing in him toward God. As a result, God must initiate the approach in every respect, which He does through the preaching of His Word, and by the Moving and Operation of the Holy Spirit.

In other words, we did not find the Lord, the Lord found us.

2. This Call is to all, and is proclaimed as such by the words *"Whosoever will"* (Jn. 3:16; Rev. 22:17).

It is not a limited Call to a select few from among humanity, but to the whole world. We know this because the Scripture plainly says that *"God so loved the world, that He gave His Only Begotten Son, that whosoever believeth in Him, should not perish, but have Everlasting Life."*

Jesus Loved the entirety of the world, and He died for the entirety of the world. Consequently, all are called, even though only a few favorably respond (Mat. 7:14).

3. Of all the appeals to man, this is by far the greatest Call he will ever receive. For God to call, there could be nothing higher or greater. As well, that He would condescend to call such as we, is beyond comprehension. However, it is the Love of God which fuels His Call, consequently, it is the Call of Love.

The question, *"Not of the Jews only, but also of the Gentiles?"*, is meant to be enlarged upon, which Paul will do in the coming verses. He will plainly tell us that God has always intended that the Gentiles be included as well, which corresponds of course with John 3:16.

(25) "AS HE SAITH ALSO IN OSEE (HOSEA), I WILL CALL THEM MY PEOPLE, WHICH WERE NOT MY PEOPLE; AND HER BELOVED, WHICH WAS NOT BELOVED."

The phrase, *"As He saith also in Osee (Hosea),"* is taken from Hosea 2:23.

The phrase, *"I will call them My people, which were not My people; and her beloved, which was not beloved,"* is used by Paul in the context of the Gentiles, even though it was originally meant for the Jews. That he does so, is manifest from the words themselves and from the transition to the Jews in verse 27.

A great lesson is learned here, in that the Word of God can always be broadened to include as much as is needed, even all, providing the spirit of the Text is not interrupted.

It is obvious that Hosea is addressing his remarks to the Jews, which the Holy Spirit intended, and is actually referring to the coming Kingdom Age when Israel will finally accept Jesus as her Messiah and Saviour. However, the Holy Spirit allows Paul latitude to include the Gentiles even though that was not the original intention. So, if the Promise is to one, the Promise is to all, at least in a general sense.

(26) "AND IT SHALL COME TO PASS, THAT IN THE PLACE WHERE IT WAS SAID UNTO THEM, YE ARE NOT MY PEOPLE; THERE SHALL THEY BE CALLED THE CHILDREN OF THE LIVING GOD."

The phrase, *"And it shall come to pass,"* is taken from Hosea 1:9-10.

The phrase, *"That in the place where it was said unto them, Ye are not my people; there shall they be called the Children of the Living God,"* proclaims Paul once again, taking a Passage that was given exclusively to Israel, and broadening it in order that it cover the Gentiles.

The idea seems to be that Paul brings the Gentiles forward to show that it is in keeping with what we know of God's dealings, *"To receive as His people those who were formerly not His people."* In effect, the spirit of that which applied to Israel, now fits perfectly with the Gentiles as well, as an investigation of the Text proves.

One could say, that Israel in this as in so many other things was the Prophetic mirror in which God foreshowed on a small scale, His future dealings with mankind (Alford).

In this as well, we see the Loving Heart of God Who wants grandly so to bring lost sinners to Himself.

(27) "ESAIAS (ISAIAH) ALSO CRIETH CONCERNING ISRAEL, THOUGH THE NUMBER OF THE CHILDREN OF ISRAEL BE AS THE SAND OF THE SEA, A REMNANT SHALL BE SAVED:"

The phrase, *"Esaias (Isaiah) also crieth concerning Israel,"* proclaims the Apostle drawing attention from the Gentiles back to Israel.

"Crieth" in the Greek is *"krazo,"* and means *"an impassioned utterance, mostly an inarticulate cry."*

The Prophet in an awful earnestness, and as with a scream of anguish, cries over Israel (Morrison).

The phrase, *"Though the number of the Children of Israel be as the sand of the Sea, a Remnant shall be Saved,"* proclaims that all of Israel, despite being children of both Abraham and Sarah, and a recipient of the Promises, still, most did not truly know the Lord. Even from the very beginning only a small *"Remnant"* in Israel were actually Saved, as is obvious when one begins to study the history of these people. How large that *"Remnant"* was, only the Lord knows, but to be sure, it was probably far smaller than most realize. As well this phrase deals with the coming Great Tribulation, which only a *"Remnant"* of Israel will survive, which we will later address.

It is the same presently with the Church. For instance, in America alone, over 100 million people claim to be Born Again. That means these people are religious after a fashion, with at least the far greater majority associated with some particular Church. But yet, only a small *"Remnant"* of all those who profess, are actually and truly Born Again. Once again, I greatly suspect that this particular number is overwhelmingly small.

HOW MANY ARE ACTUALLY SAVED?

In fact, there are approximately two billion people at present who claim Christianity in some fashion. The number is about evenly divided with approximately a billion Catholics and approximately a billion Protestants. All in some way claim Salvation.

Even though what I say may seem to be harsh; however, it is not meant that way, but only to be Truthful.

If we take the Bible as our guide, which of course *is* in fact the criteria, the situation begins to narrow down dramatically.

Catholic Doctrine is not Biblical in any sense of the word. Consequently, the percentage of Catholics who truly are Saved would be minuscule to say the least. However, among the approximately one billion Protestants, the situation is little better. Most of the Old-Line Denominations have almost totally repudiated the Word of God, mostly preaching a social Gospel, if any Gospel at all, which means that precious few in those ranks are truly Born Again.

In the so-called Fundamentalist ranks, Legalism is of such magnitude, with such an opposition to the Holy Spirit, that once again the number, although greater than the previous, would still be very small concerning those who are truly Saved. Sadly and regrettably, the same must presently be said for the Pentecostal Denominations as well. The spiritual declension in these Organizations has been so widespread, and at such a fast pace, to be almost unbelievable. So the numbers there which alone God knows, I'm afraid are little better than the Fundamentalists, if any at all.

Concerning the Independent and Charismatic Churches, the situation might be a tiny bit better, but not much. The Truth is, that despite all the claims, and all the religiosity, and all the millions who go to Church on Sunday, precious few are truly Born Again. Jesus said so (Mat. 7:14).

Regarding other countries, I suspect from my years of experience in preaching in many of these countries, that the number of professing Believers who are truly Born Again, would probably be somewhat higher than in the States and Canada. Once again, only the Lord truly knows that number, but from experience, it is my belief that my thought is correct. Irrespective, I am concerned that despite all the claims of nearly two billion adherents to Christianity,

NOTES

the number is shockingly small for those who truly know Jesus Christ as their Lord and Saviour. The use of the word *"Remnant"* by Paul is appropriate.

"Remnant" in the Greek is *"kataleimma,"* and means *"a few."*

Going back to verses 25 and 26 where Paul pulled the Gentiles into these verses originally meant for the Jews, and the Commentary I gave regarding the spirit of the Text, please note the following:

As we have stated, every part of the Word of God applies to you the individual, providing it does not violate the spirit of its intent. Let me give an example:

BARTIMAEUS, ABRAHAM, AND SARAH

Jesus called blind Bartimaeus to Him, and said unto him, *"What wilt thou that I should do unto thee?"* (Mk. 10:51).

Even though this question was directed personally to Bartimaeus, it can as well apply to anyone, and so doing does not violate the spirit of the Text. In essence, Jesus is asking the entirety of the world that very question, at least those who will come to Him.

As another example in the opposite direction, the Lord promised Abraham and Sarah a son even though Abraham was a hundred years old and Sarah was ninety (Gen. 17:17; 21:1-8).

However, even though the Lord did this for the Patriarch and his wife, He has not promised that He would give a child to others of the same age. Therefore, it is not Scriptural for one to take this Promise given to Abraham and Sarah in this regard, and try to force it into an application regarding themselves, even as some have attempted to do. Such is a violation of the spirit of the Text.

As another example, of which the Bible is replete with many, the Lord told Moses that He would give the Children of Israel the land of Canaan as their inheritance. However, He has not given unto me, or anyone else for that matter, that same Promise. Consequently, it would be improper for me to attempt to obtain such.

FAITH IN THE WORD OF GOD

My purpose for making these statements is twofold:

1. Most of the so-called Christian world, denies the Promises of the Word of God. They either try to claim that these Promises were for yesterday or possibly will be for tomorrow, but according to these people they are never for the present. To be frank, almost all of the old-line Church world falls into this category. Consequently, they belittle anyone who believes God for anything, which basically makes the Bible a dead letter, at least as far as they are concerned.

They preach that God no longer heals today, no longer answers prayer, no longer speaks to people, no longer reveals Himself to anyone, and that whatever is in the Bible was meant only for those particular individuals, and does not include anyone presently. I think it should be obvious as to how wrong that is.

On the Day of Pentecost, Peter said, *"This is that which was spoken by the Prophet Joel"* (Acts 2:16). Had he the spirit of many modern Preachers, he would have claimed that such applied only to Joel and those of his day, and had no bearing on the present. The same goes for what Paul said, and a host of others.

Yes, the Promises of God are given to us presently, and are meant to be used by us presently. In fact, God is not a yesterday God or a tomorrow God, but always a *"now God."* The Scripture says, *"God is our Refuge and Strength, a very <u>present</u> help in trouble"* (Ps. 46:1).

2. As many deny everything that God has promised, others attempt to claim that which has not been promised to them, which in effect is *"presumption."* Most of the time, self-will is the cause of this presumption, which always leads to disappointment. When we seek the Will of God, and truly have the Will of God, we will not ask for silly things, attempting to force the issue by claiming that which has not been promised to us. As denial brings reproach to the Lord, presumption does likewise.

(28) "FOR HE WILL FINISH THE WORK, AND CUT IT SHORT IN RIGHTEOUSNESS: BECAUSE A SHORT WORK WILL THE LORD MAKE UPON THE EARTH."

The phrase, *"For He will finish the Work, and cut it short in Righteousness,"* actually

NOTES

has to do with the coming Tribulation, when Israel through much suffering will finally come back to God. So, the word *"Remnant"* actually has two meanings, first of all the small number down through history regarding Israel and all for that matter, who are truly Saved, and as well, it pertains to the small number left after the Great Tribulation, who according to the Prophet Zechariah will finally accept the Lord (Zech. 13:1).

Paul is probably taking this statement from the Words of Jesus when He said, *"And except those days should be shortened, there should no flesh be Saved: for the Elect's sake* (Israel) *those days shall be shortened"* (Mat. 24:22).

Jesus is speaking of the great number who will die in the Great Tribulation, as well as the Battle of Armageddon, which will close out that horrible time in history.

The phrase, *"Because a short work will the Lord make upon the Earth,"* refers to the Second Coming, which will be in the midst of the Battle of Armageddon (Rev. Chpt. 19), which will cut it short.

The word *"work"* in the Greek Text is *"logos"* and should have been translated *"Word"* in both cases. It actually has to do with a prophetic utterance, and could have been translated, *"For He will finish the Prophetic Word and cut it short in Righteousness: because a short Prophetic Word will the Lord make upon the Earth."*

The idea is, that of all the great Prophecies which are yet to be fulfilled respecting the coming rise of the Antichrist, the Great Tribulation, the Battle of Armageddon and the Second Coming of the Lord, once it begins such will be fulfilled speedily, i.e., *"a short work."* The idea is, that *"Righteousness"* is going to Prevail and Reign and not the Antichrist. Jesus is Righteousness.

(29) "AND AS ESAIAS (ISAIAH) SAID BEFORE, EXCEPT THE LORD OF SABAOTH HAD LEFT US A SEED, WE HAD BEEN AS SODOMA, AND BEEN MADE LIKE UNTO GOMORRHA."

The phrase, *"And as Esaias* (Isaiah) *said before,"* is taken from Isaiah 1:9.

One should ever be reminded as to how much Paul referred back to the Old Testament, as so did Jesus. In other words, the

Word of God was the Foundation for all that was said and done, and it must be the same presently, or it is simply not of God.

The phrase, *"Except the Lord of Sabaoth had left us a Seed,"* actually means *"The Lord of Hosts,"* referring to the Lord of a great army.

It actually refers to the Second Coming, with the Lord bringing a great Heavenly Host (army) with Him, which will quickly defeat the Antichrist (Ezek. Chpt. 39). The *"Seed"* is the *"Remnant"* which will be left after the Battle of Armageddon (Zech. 13:8-9).

The phrase, *"We had been as Sodoma, and been made like unto Gomorrha,"* refers to the destruction of Sodom and Gomorrah (Gen. Chpt. 19), with not one single person left.

Paul is pursuing this line of thought because it refers to the manner in which Israel will be brought back to God. In a state of denial and rebellion, it is going to take judgment of unprecedented proportions to bring them to their spiritual senses, which will happen in the coming Great Tribulation.

In likening the situation to Sodom and Gomorrah, the idea is projected that Israel was just as bad as those people of old, and even worse. Jesus said of the situation, *"But I say unto you, that it shall be more tolerable for the land of Sodom in the day of judgment than for thee"* (Mat. 11:24).

(30) "WHAT SHALL WE SAY THEN? THAT THE GENTILES, WHICH FOLLOWED NOT AFTER RIGHTEOUSNESS, HAVE ATTAINED TO RIGHTEOUSNESS, EVEN THE RIGHTEOUSNESS WHICH IS OF FAITH."

The question, *"What shall we say then?"*, finds Paul desiring to say something good about the spiritual condition of the Jews, but forced to face the Truth that there is nothing good to say.

ISRAEL AND THE GENTILES

The Apostle now discusses the problem raised by the relation of the Jews to the Gospel. He has shown in verses 6-29 that they have no claim as of a right to Salvation. Their whole history, as recorded and interpreted in the Scriptures, portrays them to be a people of Rebellion. Paul now proceeds

to show more definitely that it was owing to their own guilt that they were rejected.

They followed, and persisted in following, a path on which Salvation was not to be found; and they were inexcusable in doing so, inasmuch as God had made His Way of Salvation plain and accessible to all.

The phrase, *"That the Gentiles, which followed not after Righteousness,"* has reference to the fact that these Pagans did not pursue after God or Righteousness, of which their history is replete. They were idol worshipers. They did not believe in the God of Israel, nor did they pursue Him, at least for the most part. How to be right with God was not their main interest, or any interest at all for that matter.

By contrast, Israel was the very people raised up by God to exhibit Righteousness to the world. They were given the Law, the Prophets, and actually were the only people on Earth who knew anything about Jehovah. In effect, they were the bearer of the Light for the entirety of the world which lay in darkness.

The phrase, *"Have attained to Righteousness,"* refers to the Gentiles who did obtain this great Attribute of God, even though it had not been sought by them, or even understood by them, whereas Israel who should have been the recipients, received Righteousness not at all.

In fact, this is what angered the Religious Leadership of Israel so greatly against Paul. The very idea, that he would claim that they had been set aside, and these Pagan Gentiles, who had been idol worshipers all of their existence, were in fact given Righteousness, was that which the Jews could not accept. In fact, they met this claim with outright hostility, desiring to kill Paul, and would have done so, if the opportunity had presented itself.

THE PRESENTATION OF THE GOSPEL

I suspect if Paul were alive now, that the majority of the Church world would descend upon him heavily, and attempt to force him to moderate his Message. The idea that he cut no slack at all, which in fact infuriated the Jews, and even some Christians, seemed to slow him not at all. He had but one purpose and that was to preach the Truth. And this must always be understood in reference to Truth:

Truth not only projects the right way, but it also lays bare that which is the wrong way. In fact, it is impossible for it to do otherwise.

So, Preachers who claim to preach the Truth, but never offend anyone at all, I think is obvious they are actually not preaching the Truth.

Am I mean or hostile simply because I plainly state that Catholic Doctrine is not according to the Word of God; therefore, adherents to that Doctrine are not Saved?

On a cold, stormy night, if a man learns that the bridge ahead is out, is he mean or hostile if he waves a lantern in the road to stop traffic, in order to save their lives? I think the answer to that is obvious.

Popularity is not the business of the Preacher of the Gospel. Preserving unity is not his business either. Hearing from Heaven, and then delivering to men what God has given him to deliver, is his business, and his only business. How that men react to his Message is something else altogether. Actually, that is not his affair. His affair is to hear the Word, and deliver the Word.

No! I think if Paul were ministering presently instead of nearly 2,000 years ago, he would have been caricatured, lambasted, lampooned, and rejected. As well, I doubt very seriously he would have been able to have associated with many, if any, of the modern Religious Denominations. He was simply too controversial, and if there is anything that modern Denominations do not want, it is that which is controversial.

However, there is a problem with that. The True Gospel of Jesus Christ is controversial, and extremely so I might quickly add!

The phrase, *"Even the Righteousness which is of Faith,"* in fact is the only Righteousness which God will accept.

With reference to the Gentiles appropriating a Righteousness which comes by Faith, it is not surprising that a Righteousness of this sort should be found even by those who are not in quest of it: its nature is that it is brought and offered to men, and Faith is simply the act of appropriating it, with it

being made available to all (Denney).

This was Israel's objection. In their thinking, how in the world could these Pagans be given Righteousness, when they did not previously know God, had no history with God, were actually opposed to God, that is if they believed in Him at all, and as well, had not been given any of the Attributes of God, such as the Law, the Prophets, etc.?

Paul coming along, and telling the Gentiles that all they had to do to know God, and to receive of the Lord, was to simply have Faith in Him, and all would be immediately given unto them, i.e., Righteousness, caused the Jews to treat such with absolute disdain. However, on this simple act of Faith, many Gentiles responded eagerly.

In fact, God had offered unbelieving Israel, Life and Righteousness, under the Prophets, under the Law, and under the Gospel, but they rejected all three offers.

WHAT IS RIGHTEOUSNESS?

Righteousness is simply that which is *"right,"* but yet the Standard which God has set and not man. It is moral perfection, but again moral perfection according to God's Standards.

In an absolute sense, *"Righteousness"* is wrapped up in the Ten Commandments, minus the Fourth, which was not brought over into the New Covenant. Remember the Sabbath to keep it holy, was between God and Israel exclusively, and was the only Commandment which was not of moral content.

The Righteousness which God demands of necessity must be, and is, a Perfect Righteousness. Of course, man cannot come up to that Standard, which is portrayed miserably so in Israel, with that Nation and those people ultimately destroying themselves attempting to attain to a Righteousness which comes by obedience and performance, which man cannot do.

The Gift of God's Righteousness involves entry into the new realm of Divine Salvation, furnished entirely by Jesus Christ, which is the Gift of Eternal Life under the Reign and Rule of God (Rom. 6:12-23; II Cor. 6:7, 14; Eph. 4:24; Phil. 1:11).

Hence, the extrinsic Righteousness imputed through the Cross finds inevitable expression in the intrinsic Righteousness of a life which in a new way conforms to the Will of God, even through the ultimate realization of this conformity must await the consummation of the Kingdom (I Cor. 13:12; Phil. 3:12-14; II Pet. 3:11-13; I Jn. 3:2).

THE DIVINE WILL

The New Testament uses Righteousness in the sense of conformity to the demands and obligations of the Will of God, the so-called *"Righteousness of the Law,"* of which we will discuss to a greater extent at a later time (Gal. 3:21; Phil. 3:6, 9; Tit. 3:5).

Human attainment of Righteousness is at points relatively, positively viewed (Mat. 5:20; Lk. 1:6; 2:25), but in the end this attainment in all men falls far short of a true conformity to the Divine Will (Lk. 18:9-14; Jn. 8:7; Rom. 3:9-20).

In contrast to this human unrighteousness stands the Righteousness of God (Rom. 1:17) which in consistency with Old Testament understanding conveys the thought of God's active Salvation of man in the Miracle of His Grace.

JESUS CHRIST

This Righteousness is proclaimed by Jesus as a Gift to those who are granted the Kingdom of God (Mat. 5:6). By Faith in Jesus Christ and His Work of Atonement man, unrighteous sinner though he is, receives God's Righteousness, i.e., he is given a true relationship with God which involves the forgiveness of all sin and a new moral standing with God in union with Christ *"The Righteous One"* (Rom. 3:21-31; Chpt. 4; 10:3; I Cor. 1:30; II Cor. 5:21; Phil. 3:9).

By dealing with all the consequences of man's sin and unrighteousness (both Godward and manward) in the Cross, God at once maintains the moral order in which alone He can have fellowship with man and in Grace deliver the needy (Rom. 3:26).

RIGHTEOUSNESS IN EVERYDAY LIVING

In all our thought of Righteousness it must be borne in mind that there is nothing in New Testament Revelation which tells us what Righteousness calls for in every particular circumstance. The differences between earlier

NOTES

and later practical standards of conduct and the differences between differing standards in different circumstances have led to much confusion in the realm of Christian thinking.

We can keep our bearing, however, by remembering the double element in Righteousness which should always be before us. It is, first of all *"the will to do right,"* and second, *"the determining in any given circumstance by the help of the Lord just what the right is."* The larger Christian conceptions always have an element of expansiveness, in other words to be somewhat fluid.

For example, it is clearly a Christian obligation to treat all men with a spirit of goodwill and with a spirit of Christian Love. But what does Love call for in each particular case?

We can only answer the question by saying that Love seeks for whatever is best, for him who receives and for him who gives. This may lead to one course of conduct in one situation and to quite a different course in another.

We must, however, keep before us always the aim of the largest life for all persons whom we can reach. Christian Righteousness today is even more insistent upon material things, than even was the Law of Moses. Consequently, the obligation to use the latest knowledge for the welfare of all is just as binding now as then, but *"the latest knowledge"* in any given circumstance, is a changing term. Material progress, technological advancement, education, spiritual instruction, are all influences which really make for full life.

The only way these everyday occurrences can be addressed, and which arise constantly in the lives of Believers, is that we allow Jesus to live full and complete within our lives, even as Paul said (Gal. 2:20). Christlikeness guarantees the Righteousness of Christ, which is actually what this Christian life is all about. However, the True Righteousness of Christ can only be evident in the ongoing, everyday living of the Believer, facing all circumstances and in every situation, by a close relationship with Him. In fact, if Righteousness does not carry over into everyday living, then the Holy Spirit is not being allowed to have His Way within our lives, which way will always Glorify Christ.

THE POWER OF RIGHTEOUSNESS

Not only is present-day Righteousness social and growing; it is also concerned, to a large degree, with the thought of the world which now is. As stated, if it doesn't translate into everyday living, then the Holy Spirit is not being allowed to have His Way respecting our Sanctification.

Righteousness has too often been conceived of merely as the means of preparing for the life of the future Kingdom of Heaven. Present-day emphasis has not ceased to think of the life beyond this, but the life beyond this can best be met and faced by those who have been in the full sense Righteous in the life that now is. There is no break here in True Christian continuity. In fact, those who have understood Christianity best have always insisted that to the fullest degree the present world must be able to *view* the Righteousness which is ensconced in the heart and life of the Believer, which actually makes Christianity different than anything else on Earth.

However, we always must understand that all earthly Righteousness takes its start from Heavenly Righteousness, or, rather, that the Righteousness of man is to be based upon his conception of the Righteousness of God, and in reality, man's Righteousness must be that of God, or it is not Righteousness which God will recognize.

Righteousness in its truest sense must always be a manifestation of God's Holy Love as is evidenced toward others from our hearts and lives. The chief channel, and in fact, the only real channel which is living and moving, through which Holy Love is to manifest itself, is the conscience and Love of the Christian Believer.

We are to never allow the Love of God within us, which True Righteousness always expresses, to get out of touch with everyday life. There is an experience of Love which exhausts itself in well-wishing, which in reality exhibits nothing. Such is found in the Parable of the Good Samaritan.

Some passed the man by never stopping to help at all, which is a perfect example of that of which I speak. Their so-called Righteousness, was an untouchable Righteousness,

NOTES

which of course was self-righteousness. The man who stopped, who was a Samaritan incidentally, portrayed the Love of God to a wounded brother, which in effect, is Righteousness in action (Lk. 10:30-37).

The phrase, *"Even the Righteousness which is of Faith,"* presents God's Righteousness which is found only in Christ, and is obtained only by Faith.

WHAT DO WE MEAN WHEN WE SAY *"OF FAITH,"* OR *"BY FAITH?"*

Few words are more central to the Christian Message or more often used to describe Christian experience than *"Belief"* or *"Faith."* Yet these words are often corrupted by a misunderstanding of their Biblical meaning.

People today may use *"Faith"* to indicate what is possible but uncertain. However, the Bible uses *"Faith"* in ways that link it with what is assuredly and certainly true. Christians may sometimes speak of *"believing,"* as if it were merely a subjective effort (according to one's own experience and interpretation), as if our act of Faith or strength of Faith were the issue. But the Bible shifts our attention from our own personal experiences and centers it upon the object of our Faith, or what should be the object of our Faith — God Himself. In reality all Faith must have as its object, The Lord Jesus Christ, Who Alone is the Door and Way to God. *"Looking unto Jesus the Author and Finisher of our Faith"* (Heb. 12:2).

It is exciting to look into the Scriptures and there rediscover the full meaning of Faith and Belief. There we grasp the great Promise that Faith holds out to all mankind: transformation through a personal relationship with God in Jesus Christ.

THE OLD TESTAMENT CONCEPT OF FAITH

When we read *"Belief"* and *"Faith"* in the Old Testament, the Hebrew word most used is *"Aman."* This word indicates firmness and certainty; it actually means *"to be certain," "to believe in,"* or *"to be assured."*

Other forms of the word denote Faithfulness, Fidelity, Steadiness, Faith, Certainty, Firmness, and Truth. This powerful Old Testament term, which captures the Biblical meaning of Faith, affirms certainty, never doubt. It expresses firm conviction — conviction based on the reliability of what is believed.

It can be found in the following verses, to name a few (Gen. 15:6; 45:26; Ex. 4:1, 5, 8-9, 31; 14:31; 19:9; Num. 14:11; 20:12; Deut. 1:32; 9:23; Jud. 11:20; I Sam. 27:12; Ps. 27:13; 78:22, 32; 106:12, 24; 116:10; 119:66; Isa. 7:9; 28:16; 43:12; Jer. 12:6; Micah 7:5; Hab. 1:5).

Another Hebrew word *"Batah"* used for Faith or Believing, turns our attention to the Believer and expresses the inner result of having someone or something in which to place confidence. That outcome is a feeling of well-being and security. However, the word *"Aman"* captures the fullest meaning of spiritual Faith: it portrays an informed decision to commit oneself to God. *"Batah"* captures the release that comes with our surrender.

PREVALENT DANGERS IN FAITH

But just as *"Aman"* can be false if the object of Faith is something other than the True God, so *"Batah"* is false if what we have trusted ourselves to is unable to guarantee our safety.

The Old Testament speaks of several false sources of security. It holds each of them up and examines them in contrast to the security that is ours in the Lord. We are foolish if we turn from reliance on God to seek security in man (Ps. 118:8; 146:3; Jer. 17:5), in violence (Ps. 55:23; 62:10), in riches (Ps. 49:6; 52:7), in military power (Deut. 28:52; Ps. 44:6; Jer. 5:17), or in our own goodness (Ezek. 33:13; Hos. 10:13).

There is another Hebrew word related to Faith or Trust, which is *"Mahseh,"* and means *"to seek refuge."* It suggests that a person is helpless and in danger and is rushing to find a secure hiding place. The Psalmists speak words of hope to the insecure and fearful, reminding them that God, our Rock and Strength, is Himself the Refuge of His people (Ps. 14:6; 46:1; 62:8; 71:7; 91:9).

GOD IS FAITHFUL

The Old Testament concept of Faith as certainty and safety is deeply rooted in the Old Testament view of God. Faith fastens on God as One Who by His Nature is the sole certain and sure reality. God is faithful and unchanging, established in eternity; and because He is Who He is, we can commit ourselves to Him.

Because God also commits Himself to us in Covenant relationship, placing our confidence in Him brings us true well-being and safety.

The Old Testament views human response to God as vital in the matter of True Faith. But the Old Testament emphasis (as expressed in the words chosen to express Faith) is on this fact: our response to God has validity because God Himself is utterly faithful and trustworthy.

ABRAHAM'S FAITH

When we look into the Old Testament to see how *"Faith"* words are used, we are drawn at once to the experience of Abraham. Not that *"Faith"* is used often to describe Abraham's relationship with God. In fact, it is so used only in Genesis 15:6. But we turn to Abraham because of the pivotal nature of that verse and because the New Testament again and again points us to Abraham as Faith's primary example.

ABRAHAM'S EXPERIENCE

Genesis Chapter 15 describes Abraham, then a very old man, in dialogue with God. Abraham complained that God had given him no children of his own, despite an earlier Promise (Gen. 12:2).

God responded by amplifying the Promise. Abraham looked to the sky, filled with its numberless stars, and heard God say, *"So shall your offspring be"* (Gen. 15:5). The next verse tells us, *"Abram believed the Lord, and He credited it to him as Righteousness"* (Gen. 15:6).

The Apostle Paul says of this incident: *"Against all hope, Abraham in hope believed . . . . He faced the fact that his body was as good as dead — since he was about a hundred years old — and that Sarah's womb was also dead. Yet he did not waver through unbelief regarding the Promise of God, but was strengthened in his Faith and gave Glory to God, being fully persuaded that God had power to do what He promised"* (Rom. 4:18-21). Abraham examined the circumstances and, despite everything, decided that God was to be trusted. He chose to put his trust in God, and this act of Saving Faith was accepted by the Lord in place of a Righteousness that Abraham did not actually possess.

THE BIBLICAL ILLUSTRATION

Abraham was not perfect, by any standard. But his life, as reported in the Old Testament, shows again and again that he trusted God and acted on God's Promises, certain the Lord could be counted on (Heb. 11:8-12).

The example of Abraham stands as the Biblical illustration of Faith as believing response to God. God spoke in Promise and Command. Abraham trusted himself to God. And Abraham's Faith was demonstrated as he subsequently acted on what God had said (Gen. Chpts. 12-22).

GOD'S WORD

Faith is not some response to evidence, as important as that may be, even when that evidence is clearly miraculous. Rather than believing the Miracle, Abraham believed God. His Faith was a response to God Himself, not to something that God did or would do.

That word from God is far more compelling for Faith than any Miracles performed in the material universe.

All of us have a tendency to get our eyes on the gift, instead of the Giver. God was to tell Abraham, *"I am thy Shield, and thy exceeding great reward"* (Gen. 15:1). In other words, God was Abraham's reward, and not the things that God could do.

That is extremely important in the sense, that True Faith always enlarges God in our eyes, instead of things He accomplishes. All of us have a tendency to get our eyes off of Him and onto the things he does, which always causes one to be weakened.

This is why that some of the modern Faith Teaching has been negative. It has tended to reduce God to a supplier of things, instead of learning Who God is regarding His Person. As stated, the object of Faith must ever be Jesus, and not what Jesus can do, even as important as those things may be.

THE TOTAL PERSON

Faith in God also engages the total person. It is expressed in perception and action. Abraham was well aware of his and Sarah's advanced age. But Abraham also considered God's Power and Faithfulness.

This fact of God so transformed Abraham's perspective that he easily accepted God's Promise, although fathering a son was humanly impossible for him.

By contrast, Israel, poised on the borders of Canaan, with God ready for them to go in, and all of Heaven standing ready to help them in whatever capacity that was needed, instead, refused to go in, seeing only the military strength of that land's inhabitants. In other words, they treated God *"with contempt"* (Num. 14:11; 16:30) by refusing to consider His Power and Reality. They refused to believe Him, and an entire generation was lost.

When one places his Faith in God, the total person is to be involved. In other words, one is to look to God in any and all circumstances, for any and all things, respecting any and all direction.

While it is true, that we are in the world, and as such, must avail ourselves of daily communion with our fellowman, and as well must seek to exhibit the Love of God to all who are around us, still, it is God to Whom we look for all we need, and not man, even religious man.

This danger is far more acute than one realizes, with many Believers looking to their Church, their Religious Denomination, or other people for leading and guidance, which always tends to weaken one's Faith.

Lest there be misunderstanding, in no way do we demean or belittle the help of others, which all of us need. However, all of that which man can do, advise and counsel, must always be subject to the Word of God. For in that alone, the Word of God, our Faith must abide (Rom. 10:17).

DEMONSTRATION OF FAITH

The outcome of Faith is always demonstrated in some way. When a person responds to God's Self-disclosure, Faith-generated obedience leads to blessing.

Abraham believed God and knew God's protection during his lifetime. When he was told to go to Canaan, he packed up and went (Gen. Chpt. 12). By contrast, when the Exodus generation was told to conquer the land, they refused even to try. They were betrayed by their *"unbelieving heart."* In other words, they did not trust God. Consequently, whereas Abraham went on to spiritually take the land, the unbelieving generation who had been delivered from Egyptian bondage, wandered back into the wilderness, to die in its desolate wastes.

FAITH IN THE NEW TESTAMENT

Actually, Faith does not change from the Old Covenant to the New. It simply refers to believing God.

The major Greek word for Faith is *"Pistis"* which means *"Faith and Belief."* There are other related words also which deal with relationships established by trust and maintained by trustworthiness.

However, whatever word is used in the New Testament for Faith, it stresses faithfulness to the agreement made or trustworthiness in keeping Promises. In fact, the Message of Faith is shaped and molded by the dynamic Message of the Gospel, which is based strictly on Faith in Christ.

For instance, respecting the New Testament, *"to believe"* is used in the sense *"to be convinced of"* or *"to entrust."* It is often used with the word *"that"* which indicates something of which the individual is convinced. It means *"to give credence to"* or *"entrust oneself to."*

Without going into all the Greek nuances, Faith in a sense, means *"to believe through,"* which indicates the way by which a person comes to Faith (Jn. 1:7; I Pet. 1:21). *"Faith in"* indicates the realm in which Faith operates (Eph. 1:15; Col. 1:4; II Tim. 3:15).

FAITH IN THE EARLY CHURCH

This most important construction (Faith in) is unique to the New Testament, at least as it is expressed, and is actually an invention of the Early Church which expresses the inmost secret of our Faith. That construction links Faith with the Greek preposition *"eis,"* which means *"to"* or *"into."* This is

NOTES

never done in secular Greek, because there is simply no call for such in secular life.

However, in the Gospel this type of Faith portrays a person committing himself or herself totally to the Person of Jesus Christ, for our Faith is actually *"into Jesus."* The reason is clearly expressed by Jesus Himself. He said, *"I am the Way and the Truth and the Life. No one comes to the Father except through Me"* (Jn. 14:6). In other words, God the Father has revealed Himself in the Son. Consequently, the Father has set Jesus before us as the One to Whom we must entrust ourselves for Salvation. It is Jesus Who is the Focus of Christian Faith.

In the context of our Faith and in our relationship with Jesus, *"Believing"* has come to mean: A. The happy trust that a person places in the Person of Jesus Christ; and, B. The allegiance to Him that grows out of that very personal commitment.

This is actually the type of Faith to which Paul points, which obtains the Righteousness of God. It is total Faith in Jesus Christ, Who He is, and What He has done.

(31) "BUT ISRAEL, WHICH FOLLOWED AFTER THE LAW OF RIGHTEOUSNESS, HATH NOT ATTAINED TO THE LAW OF RIGHTEOUSNESS."

The phrase, *"But Israel, which followed after the Law of Righteousness,"* presents this which Israel did, but in the wrong way, by works.

"Followed" in the Greek is *"dioko,"* and means *"to run swiftly in order to catch some person or thing, to run after, pursue."* It means *"to seek after eagerly, earnestly endeavoring to acquire."*

The phrase, *"Hath not attained to the Law of Righteousness,"* presents that which is blunt or emphatic. In other words, works did not bring Salvation, as works *cannot* bring Salvation.

"Attained" in the Greek is *"katalambano,"* and means *"to lay hold of so as to make one's own, to appropriate, take possession of."*

The repetition of the word *"Righteousness"* is striking: it is the one fundamental conception on which Paul's Gospel rests; the questions at issue between him and the Jews were questions as to what it was, and how it was to be attained.

WHAT IS THE LAW OF RIGHTEOUSNESS?

Speaking of Israel in pursuit of the Law of Righteousness, the idea is not that Israel was in quest of this Law, which pertains to the means by which Righteousness can be attained, for in fact, every Israelite believed himself to be, and already was, in possession of such a Law.

It must rather be that Israel aimed incessantly at bringing its conduct up to the standard of this Law in which Righteousness was certainly held out, but in fact, was never able to achieve its purpose. The Law of Righteousness, the unattained goal of Israel's efforts, is of course the Mosaic Law. However, whereas the Law of Moses did exhibit Righteousness, it did not bestow Righteousness. Nevertheless, Israel kept trying to attain to, to arrive at, the Righteousness of that Law, but it remained out of their reach, even as it always does, that is within the sphere of one's own efforts. In other words, legal religion proved a failure then, and legal religion is a failure now.

A PERFECT PERFORMANCE

While the Law of Moses definitely did contain Righteousness, that is if it was perfectly obeyed, the trouble was, fallen man, even God's Chosen People the Israelites, could not obey its Commands. They could not and neither can anyone else. The reason is simple.

Due to the Fall, man has no capability within himself of keeping the Ten Commandments, irrespective as to how hard he may try. While he may boast within himself, thinking he has kept some of the Commandments, when he gets to the Tenth, *"Thou shalt not covet,"* he then realizes that the true concept of these Commandments is not in the mere fact of not breaking them in the actual sense, but not even desiring to do so. No human being can say that his heart has not desired unlawful things, even though the actual carrying out of such an act may not have been consummated (Rom. 7:7).

That is why the Pharisees, who incidentally claimed obedience to the Law, hated Jesus so much. He took them past the mere legalism, to the very heart of the matter, by telling them that the mere fact of not committing adultery was not enough. They must not desire such in their hearts. He said, *"But I say unto you, That whosoever looketh on a woman to lust after her hath committed adultery with her already in his heart"* (Mat. 5:28).

So, I think one can see from that, if one is going to attempt to attain Righteousness by one's performance, one is shot down before he even begins. Consequently, the only Performance which can be looked at and presented, is the Performance of the Lord Jesus Christ. One's Faith in Him grants one in the Sight of God, the perfect Performance of Christ. On that basis alone, will God recognize the believing sinner, and impute to him freely *"Righteousness."*

Again we state, the Law of Moses had Righteousness, but it was unattainable by Israel, as it was unattainable by all. And yet, it can be reached and obtained, by one's Faith and Trust in Christ, which is actually the only way.

(32) "WHEREFORE? BECAUSE THEY SOUGHT IT NOT BY FAITH, BUT AS IT WERE BY THE WORKS OF THE LAW. FOR THEY STUMBLED AT THAT STUMBLINGSTONE;"

The question *"Wherefore?"*, in effect asks as to why Israel did not, and in fact, could not attain to the Law of Righteousness?

The phrase, *"Because they sought it not by Faith,"* is obvious as to its meaning.

The end of all Faith and for everyone, is Jesus Christ. In fact, Israel did have Faith, but it was in themselves, their abilities, their good works, etc., even as most of the world. The object of their Faith was wrong, which has been the lot of so many. In fact, the problem of Israel is the problem of most.

Israel wanted to believe that all of her association with God through the Law and the Prophets, etc., earned her something with God, even as millions of people presently think that their association with the Church, which they equate with God, surely must earn them something as well. It does not!

Association with the things of God, does not bring Salvation. The reason is simple, there is no Salvation in the Church, or its so-called Sacraments.

Last night I heard a Catholic Priest say over Television as to how certain people had now become faithful to the Church. He said this because he actually believes as a Priest in the Catholic Church, that faithfulness to the Church equates with Salvation. Once again, it does not! In fact, if one thinks that faithfulness to such equates with Salvation, they are automatically lost. That means they are trusting something other than Christ.

We must never equate religious things with Christ. We must never equate good works as a substitute for Christ. Actually, this is one of Satan's biggest traps. Even as Israel of old, modern man attempts to make religious things into Salvation. It fools men, simply because it is religious.

One must have a personal relationship with Christ, with the emphasis on the word *"personal."* While the Church, at least the True Church, belongs to Christ, it within itself is not Christ. While the Sacraments or Ordinances belong to Christ, still, they are not Christ. They may be symbolic of Him, but they are not in fact, actually Him. Consequently, one cannot reach Him through these means. One can only reach Christ by personally exhibiting Faith in Him, and never by proxy, i.e., substituting things to take His place.

Men are not Saved because they belong to a certain Church, but because of their simple Faith in Christ Alone. Israel could never see that, and neither can most modern Church members.

The phrase, *"But as it were by the works of the Law,"* refers to Israel attempting to attain Righteousness by the method of *"works of Righteousness,"* in other words by attempting within their own strength to keep the Law of Moses.

DID NOT GOD INTEND FOR THEM TO KEEP THE LAW?

Most definitely He did! Even though the Old Testament is full of these admonitions to keep the Law, at least beginning with the giving of the Law as recorded in the Book of Exodus, most probably it is summed up in Deuteronomy 28:15-68, as to leave absolutely no doubt. So the admonition was clear and

plain, and Israel was definitely to make every attempt to obey the Lord, and God blessed abundantly all those who attempted to do so (Deut. 28:1-14).

However, there was no Salvation in the Law, meaning that the fact of the Law, Israel having the Law, and even attempting to keep the Law, did not save anyone. The Remnant in Israel who truly attempted to live for God, ever what that number may have been down through the centuries, were Saved (right with God) not because of the Law of Moses, but because of the Covenant of Abraham (Gen. Chpt. 15).

As such, their Salvation depended on their Faith in that Covenant, and was portrayed in the offering up of Sacrifices as prescribed by the Lord, which was a Type of *"The Sacrifice"* which was to come, The Lord Jesus Christ. Pure and simple that was their Salvation.

In fact, as should be obvious, it was no different then than now. All before Christ were Saved by Faith, as all after Christ are Saved by Faith. Actually, this is what Paul is discussing.

SO HOW DID ISRAEL GO WRONG?

While the majority in Israel continued to believe in the Covenant of Faith given to Abraham, instead of attaching the Covenant of Law to that of Faith, they inverted these Laws, attempting to attach Faith to Law. In other words, they made the Law of Moses preeminent, which it was never intended to be.

In essence, they then made a religion or a god out of the Law of Moses, glorying in the fact of the Law, and especially that they were the only people in the world who had such legislation. In fact, this decline into a Salvation by Law-keeping, did not really come about until after the Dispersion. During the approximate 500 years from that time unto the Birth of Christ, this problem became more and more acute, coming to a head during the time of Christ.

From the time of the Prophet Malachi to that of John the Baptist, a period of about 400 years, Israel for the first time in her history, had no Prophet. Down through the centuries, these great men of God whether heeded or not, with thundering tones, if not whipping Israel into line, at least laid down the Standard as to what was right and wrong. However, during this 400 year period of Prophetic silence, religion abounded, even as religion always does when the voice of the Prophet is silent. Consequently, the Pharisees, who probably had a righteous beginning, gradually succumbed to a works Salvation, so by the time of Christ, they had added over 600 oral laws to the original Law of Moses. In other words, if some is good, a lot more is much better, or so they thought.

By the time of Christ, the Nation was fully ensconced in the religion of Judaism, which had degenerated to a mere system of ethics, which meant it was almost altogether now man-devised and man-instituted. Consequently, it was not of God by any shape, form, or fashion.

THE END RESULTS OF
SUCH AN EFFORT

Trying to earn one's Salvation by *"works of the Law,"* whether the Law of Moses, or some other devised law, always without exception, breeds self-righteousness. As well, the characteristics of self-righteousness always exclude all others who do not conform to its particular regimen. Inasmuch as Christ adhered strictly to the True Law of Moses, ignoring all of the hundreds of added laws by the Pharisees, a clash soon developed between Christ and these adversaries, with the hostility on the part of the Pharisees becoming more pronounced by the day. It finally ended with the Sadducees and the Pharisees joining together, the two major Religious Parties in Israel who normally hated each other, and crucifying Christ. Sadly and tragically, they killed the Lord in the Name of the Lord.

To be sure, their modern counterparts, barred by the Law of the Land from carrying out actual murder, still continue to oppose the True Work of God in every way they can. They *"kill"* and *"crucify"* in various different ways. What Jesus said about the Pharisees in Matthew Chapter 23, holds true presently, and in fact always has, for those who follow in the same spirit.

NOTES

WHAT IS THE IDEA OF SALVATION BY *"WORKS OF THE LAW"*?

Whether in Jesus' day, or the time of Paul, or now for that matter, the idea is that one is Saved because they do certain things. In Israel's case, they were extremely religious (at least the so-called spiritual guides of the people), which means they involved themselves in all types of religious activity, but almost altogether in the laws, rules, and regulations they had self-devised. That is what Jesus was talking about when He said, *"Woe unto you, Scribes and Pharisees, hypocrites! For ye . . . have omitted the weightier matters of the Law, Judgment, Mercy, and Faith: . . . .*
"Ye blind guides, which strain at a gnat, and swallow a camel" (Mat. 23:23-24).

These people had no Faith in God, only in their own *"religious doing."* It is the same presently with millions, and in fact, always has been. Millions subscribe to a particular religious regimen, whether it's the activities of a Church, or whatever, thinking somehow this brings them Salvation.

In fact, major Religious Denominations, even those who began in the right way, oftentimes degenerate into a *"works righteousness,"* which in the Eyes of God, is no righteousness at all.

The telltale signs begin to appear in these Denominations, as they leave the Word of God, more and more relying on their self-made rules and regulations, until finally the Bible has little place at all. In other words, they do not use the Bible as their Standard and Guide, but rather their own Constitution and Bylaws, which they feel free to change constantly, etc.

I was discussing Bible Doctrine with a Catholic Priest once, when he said to me that the Catholic Church had changed its rules in some things. As a result of that change, what had formerly been sin was now no longer sin, etc.

I asked him how it was possible to change the Word of God, because he had been insisting that Catholic Theology was Biblical? I went on to say, *"My Brother, one cannot change the Word of God, don't you realize that?"*

He sat there stunned for a few moments saying nothing at all, realizing the incongruity of his position. I then kindly said to him that his position (that of the Catholic Church) was completely unscriptural.

He finally mumbled something about both the Bible and the Church being right, but if there was a difference, the Church took precedence.

Well of course, if one believes the Bible at all, that position is untenable. And that is the problem not only with the Catholic Church, but many others as well! They leave the Word of God, with it ceasing to be the Standard for Righteousness, instead, substituting their own standards, etc.

The phrase, *"For they stumbled at that stumblingstone,"* presents the necessity of Faith in The Lord Jesus Christ, the One Who all the Sacrifices had symbolized.

In their foolish course Israel thought that they were advancing on a clear path, and lo! All at once there was found in this way an obstacle on which they were broken; and this obstacle was the very Messiah Whom they had so long invoked in all their prayers (Godet).

Faith in the Messiah was also a rock of offence. The offence of the Cross, at which they stumbled, is not simply the fact that it *is* a Cross, whereas they expected a Messianic Throne; the Cross offended them because, as interpreted by Paul, it summoned them to begin their spiritual life, from the very beginning, at the foot of the Crucified, and with the sense upon their hearts of an infinite debt to Him which no *"works"* could ever repay (Denney).

(33) "AS IT IS WRITTEN, BEHOLD, I LAY IN SION A STUMBLINGSTONE AND ROCK OF OFFENCE: AND WHOSOEVER BELIEVETH ON HIM SHALL NOT BE ASHAMED."

The phrase, *"As it is written,"* is taken from Isaiah 8:14. Once again, Paul refers to the Old Testament as the Foundation for all he is teaching.

The phrase, *"Behold, I lay in Sion* (Israel) *a Stumblingstone and Rock of Offence,"* refers to Jesus Christ.

WHY WAS JESUS A STUMBLINGSTONE AND ROCK OF OFFENCE TO ISRAEL?

As He was to Israel so is He as well to most of the world.

But first Israel.

In fact, and according to the Prophecies of Daniel (Dan. 9:24-26), Israel was expecting the Messiah at approximately the time that Jesus was born. In fact, the Prophecies down through the ages had been abundant, respecting His Coming, even beginning in the Garden of Eden with the Lord's threat to Satan and Promise to the world (Gen. 3:15). So, the fact of His Coming and the time of His Coming, were an expected event. However, Who He would be, and how He would be, due to their straying from the Scriptures, were as we would presently say, off the wall.

Without going into detail, they thought He would be a mighty conqueror, leading them once again to their place of glory, even as they had been under David and Solomon, a thousand years before.

In other words, they had no interest whatsoever in a Saviour, for the simple reason that they already imagined themselves to be righteous and holy. They wanted a conqueror, and more perfectly, one who would do their bidding.

WHO JESUS WAS!

Despite their straying from the Word of God, they knew this Coming One would be in the lineage of David, and would once again occupy David's Throne. They believed this, because it fit in with their thoughts of a Conquering Messiah. But of course with Jesus, there the similarity ended.

In fact, His lineage was perfect back to David. He went back to David through Solomon, which was actually the Kingly Line through His foster-father Joseph. He also went back to that point through Nathan, another son of David, through Mary His Mother. Of course, He was of the Tribe of Judah, even as Jacob had long ago prophesied (Gen. 49:8-12).

However, Jesus did not come to this world as a mighty King, but rather as the very opposite. He was a Man of humility, actually a Man of sorrows. Such a One, Israel would not accept, even though this manner had been clearly prophesied by Isaiah (Isa., Chpt. 53).

Inasmuch as He was a Peasant, made no attempts to use His Power to overthrow Rome, but rather preached the Kingdom of

God, rather than the Kingdom of Israel, He was rejected — and that despite the fact that He fulfilled all the Prophecies, even down to the most minute detail.

In their self-righteousness, they were so blinded to what they really were, and Who He really was, that both He and the Cross were a terrible *"Stumblingstone and Rock of Offence."* To trust such a One for Salvation, was unthinkable! Especially considering the manner in which He died, which was by Crucifixion, and which they knew spelled the Curse of God (Deut. 21:22-23), how could such a One at least in their thinking, be the Messiah?

THE CURSE OF THE BROKEN LAW

While it was indeed true, that Jesus suffered the curse of the broken Law which was Death (Rom. 6:23), still, they understood not at all, that He suffered this not because of personal sin, but in order to bear the sin penalty of the world.

However, there was absolutely no excuse for them not understanding this, considering that the offering of every single Sacrifice spelled out the terrible Judgment of God which would fall upon this coming Sin-Offering, instead of sinners, who rightly deserved its wrath. In glaring, obvious, stark reality, this was carried out with the offering of every Lamb, with its shed blood representing His poured-out Blood, and the fire consuming the carcass on the Altar, that representing the Judgment of God and Calvary's Cross. As no other people on Earth they knew this, and as no other people on Earth, they should have understood.

But they didn't! As well, untold millions of others follow in their footsteps. Many do not believe in Jesus at all, with others believing in Him as merely a good Man, but deceived! Of course, the question must be asked, as to how a person could be a good man and at the same time a deceiver?

No! Jesus was the Son of God Who gave Himself for the sin of man, thereby making it possible for any and all to be Saved, that is, if they will only believe (Jn. 3:16; Rom. 10:9-10, 13; Rev. 22:17).

The phrase, *"And whosoever believeth on Him shall not be ashamed,"* once again,

portrays that Salvation is open to all, and not to a select predestined few, as many teach.

Either the Holy Spirit meant what He said, when He had the Apostle to use the word *"whosoever,"* or He didn't. I happen to believe, that He meant exactly what He said. *"Whosoever"* means the entirety of mankind. In other words, the door is open to all!

As well, all who have put their trust in Him, for there is no other, have His Promise, which I believe with all of my heart, that we *"shall not be ashamed,"* i.e., *"disgraced."*

"Ashamed" in the Greek is *"kataischuno,"* and means *"to shame down, to disgrace, put to the blush, confounded, dishonored."*

Instead of *"shame,"* in fact, all who trust Him, will reap His Glory, which is beyond parallel. The Truth is, all who do *not* trust Him, will stand ashamed at the last day, and greatly so, and especially those of Israel, His Chosen, who down through the many centuries rejected Him. The shame then will be awful!

"I am happy today and the Sun shines bright,
"The clouds have been rolled away;
"For the Saviour said whosoever will,
"May come with Him to stay."

"All my hopes have been raised, Oh His Name be praised,
"His Glory has filled my soul;
"I've been lifted up and from sin set free,
"His Blood hath made me whole."

"Oh what wonderful Love, Oh what Grace Divine,
"That Jesus should die for me;
"I was lost in sin, for the world I pined,
"But now I am set free."

"Whosoever, surely meaneth me, surely meaneth me, Oh surely meaneth me;
"Whosoever, surely meaneth me, whosoever, meaneth me."

CHAPTER 10

(1) "BRETHREN, MY HEART'S DESIRE AND PRAYER TO GOD FOR ISRAEL IS, THAT THEY MIGHT BE SAVED."

The one word *"Brethren,"* refers to the Saints in the local Church at Rome, actually to whom he was writing. They were Gentiles, with the exception of probably a few Jews in the area who had accepted Christ, and were a part of the Church.

It is somewhat ironic, the Jewish Synagogues had a few Gentiles generally who attended, and now the Churches have a few Jews.

The bond ties of Christianity, evidenced by the word *"Brethren"* which makes this the greatest family in the world, provides a *"oneness"* through Jesus Christ, which sets it apart from every other union. In fact, the closeness and union of the Saints in Christ, even surpasses that of our own blood kin who do not know Jesus.

The phrase, *"My heart's desire,"* has it in the Greek, *"the desire of my heart."*

"Desire" in the Greek is *"eudokia,"* and means *"will, choice, delight, pleasure, satisfaction."*

Of all people, Paul, no doubt greater than anyone else, knew of Israel's plight. He had once been a part of this unbelief and hostility toward Christ. Consequently, he knew their thinking and above all, the lie they were now living. I have an idea as well, that he sensed their impending doom, which would come just a few years from this particular time (A.D. 70). So, for him, the pain and grief over Israel's rejection, were doubly hard.

The phrase, *"And prayer to God for Israel,"* concerns as is obvious, his supplication on their behalf.

I personally think that in his seeking God for them, he had given up hope respecting the Salvation of the Nation, and was rather believing for individual Jews to come to Christ, which some did.

The phrase, *"That they might be Saved,"* proclaims the main attraction of his concern. They were lost! Despite all their religion and history, they were lost!

Several things are brought into focus here:

1. We have here the necessity and the power of prayer. *"Prayer"* in the Greek as used here, is *"deesis,"* and means *"request, supplication, petition."* In other words, Paul was interceding on behalf of Israel, and more direct, Jews in particular.

2. Considering the authority placed in

the hands of Believers (Mk. 16:15-18; Jn. 14:13-14; 15:7; 16:23), everything done on Earth for the Lord must in some sense, go through the Body of Christ. This speaks of Intercessory Prayer most of all, as well as the Work of God respecting Evangelism, etc.

In essence, this means that every single person in the world who comes to Christ, in some sense, somewhere, Saints of God have interceded for that person, even though the far greater majority of the time the person is unknown to the Intercessor. The Holy Spirit moves upon the Believer concerning a certain part of the world, and the Believer intercedes respecting that which the Spirit desires, with things then beginning to happen. In fact, this may go on for quite some time, even years, before great results are seen. But from the moment, the Spirit of God begins to move on the heart of the Believer to intercede for certain areas, at that moment things are set in motion in the spirit world in order that a Move of God may be brought about. That comes under the Authority of the Believer.

3. Regrettably, because of much false teaching, very little Prayerful Intercession is presently being offered. Consequently, until at least some part of the Body of Christ sees this ancient Truth, and, thereby, follows after the Holy Spirit in this capacity, there may be some things break out which people think are from the Lord, but no true Move of God will be forthcoming.

(2) "FOR I BEAR THEM RECORD THAT THEY HAVE A ZEAL OF GOD, BUT NOT ACCORDING TO KNOWLEDGE."

The phrase, *"For I bear them record that they have a zeal of God,"* should read, *"for God."*

Using such a strong term *"For I bear them record,"* proclaims Paul alluding to his conduct of former days, in essence saying, *"I know something of it, of that zeal."* The phrase *"Zeal for God"* is the genitive of description, defining just what kind of zeal it is. It is a zeal which has to do with God as its object (Godet).

When Paul spoke about their rejection from the inheritance of the Promises, he appropriately dwelt on their ancient privileges; here, where he has in view their own failure to respond to God's purpose for them, he as appropriately refers to their undoubted zeal, which he regrets should be misdirected (Barmby).

The phrase, *"But not according to knowledge,"* pertains to the right kind of knowledge.

"Knowledge" in the Greek is *"epignosis,"* and means *"full, correct, vital, experiential knowledge."* That is, the Jews' zeal for God was not conditioned nor characterized by a complete, but rather a partial, insufficient knowledge, which because insufficient, led them astray as to the method whereby they could appropriate Salvation (Wuest).

WHY DID ISRAEL NOT HAVE THE CORRECT KNOWLEDGE?

Of all the people in the world, these are the very ones who should have known all things about God, at least that which He had revealed. They were the people of the Covenants, the Law, and the Prophets.

I think the great Annals of God will show that the blindness of Israel which caused them to not even recognize their Messiah when He came, and then worse still, to murder Him, is by far the most awful happening of all. Everything else pales up beside the plight of Israel.

The tragedy is, the *"knowledge"* was before them all the time in the form of the Word of God.

So I guess the question would be as to why they forsook the Knowledge of God, substituting in its place their own knowledge? The answer is in the following verse.

(3) "FOR THEY BEING IGNORANT OF GOD'S RIGHTEOUSNESS, AND GOING ABOUT TO ESTABLISH THEIR OWN RIGHTEOUSNESS, HAVE NOT SUBMITTED THEMSELVES UNTO THE RIGHTEOUSNESS OF GOD."

The phrase, *"For they being ignorant of God's Righteousness,"* spells the story not only of ancient Israel, but almost the entirety of the world, and for all time.

IGNORANT?

"Ignorance" in the Greek is *"agnoeo,"* and means *"not to know through lack of information or intelligence, or by implication to ignore through disinclination,"* of which the

NOTES

latter was Israel's problem. They had the Word of God, but they simply ignored it.

The ignorance of the world is different than the ignorance of the Church. While neither is excusable, that of the Church is far less excusable.

Those who are unsaved by which we constitute the world, cannot understand the Word of God even if they have it in their possession (I Cor. 2:14). However, the world is very strongly inclined to substitute their own Righteousness for that of God's. Such stems from Adam's Fall, and the reason for that Fall, which was the placing of self ahead of God. As a result, man has been loathe ever since to admit his dependence on the Creator, claiming self-sufficiency in all things. Consequently, he thinks he can save himself by his good works, or some type of self-achievement. However, with the Church, the situation is far more acute.

The Church, as Israel of old, professes to know the Way of God. So, their ignorance is a contrived ignorance, which results in a judicial blindness. Even though the Church has the Word of God, and purports to know the Word of God, still, it chooses to ignore what God has said about these matters, thereby substituting self-righteousness for *"God's Righteousness."*

Consequently, many in the modern Church have great difficulty understanding how one can be unrighteous one minute and perfectly righteous the next, simply by believing the Lord Jesus Christ. While for the most part, it claims to believe Him, much of the time it insists upon *"penance"* of some sort.

Whenever Family Worship Center was established, in the setting of the criteria for association with the Church, I was somewhat surprised at the demands made by some of the Preachers. They demanded a long list of do's and don'ts.

I asked as to why simple Faith in Christ was not enough? My thoughts were, if it's good enough for the Lord, it should be good enough for us.

After all had their say, I went ahead and instituted that which I felt was Biblical, which was simple Faith in Christ. Once again, adding Law to Grace has never helped the situation, with hypocrisy almost always being the result of such an amalgamation.

WHAT IS GOD'S RIGHTEOUSNESS?

As Paul will say in the next verse, Christ is the Righteousness of God. In other words, God's Righteousness is not a philosophy, a theory, a Church, or a Law. It is a Person, The Lord Jesus Christ.

The Righteousness of Christ is the only Righteousness that God will accept. As well, He makes the Righteousness of Christ available to all who have simple Faith in Him, admitting that they have no Righteousness of their own, and are totally dependent on God for everything. Believing in what Jesus did at Calvary and the Resurrection, affords one instant Righteousness, which is referred to as *"Imputed Righteousness"* (Eph. 2:8-9).

In other words, God imputes to the believing sinner that which he does not have, and which in no way he can have, at least within himself. It is a Free Gift, and must be freely received.

The phrase, *"And going about to establish their own Righteousness,"* presents Israel's problem, and, actually, the problem of most of humanity.

HOW DID THEY ATTEMPT TO ESTABLISH THEIR OWN RIGHTEOUSNESS?

"Establish" in the Greek Text is *"histemi,"* and means *"to set up,"* which indicates their pride in their endeavor. In effect, they would erect a Righteousness of their own as a monument to their own glory, not to God's.

"Going about" in the Greek is *"zeteo,"* and means *"to seek,"* in other words, to seek something which was not necessary to seek, and because it had already been provided.

"Their own" in the Greek is *"idios,"* and means *"one's own private, personal possession, in a class by itself, peculiarly one's own."*

The Righteousness the Jews desired was a Righteousness that was in character their own, one tinged with their own endeavors, the product of their own efforts, one that would glorify themselves, not one characterized by what God is in His Glorious Person, not one handed to them as a gift for which they would feel obligated to thank Him (Wuest).

Their manner of doing this lay in their efforts to obtain Righteousness by keeping the Law of Moses.

First of all, it was proper that they make every effort to keep the Law, and in fact were commanded by God to do so (Deut. 28:15-68). So that within itself was not wrong, but rather right.

A TWOFOLD PROBLEM

Their problem was twofold: A. They claimed they were keeping the Law when they were not; and, B. They made a religion out of the effort. Consequently, if Ten Commandments were good, many, many Commandments would be even better. So, as stated, they added about 600 oral laws to the original Ten, even claiming that these man-devised laws were of greater import than the original Ten. As a result, by the time of Christ the entirety of the Nation was literally swimming in religious laws of every nature.

As an example, one of those 600 odd laws was that a person could not drag a chair across the floor on the Sabbath, because some dust may be moved by the chair, which could be construed as plowing, which was forbidden on the Sabbath in the original Law of Moses. As well, a woman could not comb her hair on the Sabbath, because a speck of dust might be moved, and she would be guilty of plowing, etc. When one begins to realize that there were approximately 600 laws like this, all man-devised, then one begins to get the general idea of them attempting to establish their own Righteousness.

There is something about all this religious effort that makes a man feel he is doing something to contribute toward his Salvation. Consequently, the more he becomes involved in religious effort, the more righteous he becomes, at least in his own eyes. In a sense religion is a narcotic.

This is at least one of the reasons they hated Jesus to such an extent. He ignored all of their man-devised laws, and even above that proclaimed the clarion call to all, *"Come unto Me, all ye that labour and are heavy laden, and I will give you rest"* (Mat. 11:28).

Rest from what?

Rest from all this weary legalism, which

never brought peace of mind, or instituted Righteousness whatsoever, at least that which God would accept.

SUBMISSION

The phrase, *"Have not submitted themselves unto the Righteousness of God,"* proclaims what must be done in order for one to be Saved.

"Submitted" in the Greek is *"hupotasso,"* and is a military word which means, *"to arrange under, to subordinate, as soldiers in a battalion under a Commanding Officer, to put oneself under orders, to obey."*

This means that the appropriation by Faith of God's Righteousness found only in Jesus Christ, involves not only the discarding of all dependence upon self and self-effort for Salvation, but also the heart's submission or capitulation to Jesus as Saviour and Lord. This the Jews would not do, and this most of the world will not do!

Submitting oneself to the *"Righteousness of God"* involves only one thing, but actually in two parts:

1. To which we have already alluded, the sinner must submit himself to Jesus Christ, Who in effect, is the Righteousness of God, and to that which He did to redeem humanity. There is no other Saviour except Christ. In fact, regarding all the major religions of the world, such as Islam, Buddhism, Hinduism, etc., not one of the founders of these philosophies ever claimed to be God. However, Jesus Christ did claim to be God, and proved He was God in many ways, by the performing of an untold number of Miracles, as well His Resurrection from the Dead certainly not being the least of such proof. So, it is Jesus with Whom man must deal.

If men attempt to circumvent the Plan of God in any way regarding Jesus Christ, they automatically forfeit their Salvation. Because in the words of Simon Peter *"Neither is there Salvation in any other: for there is none other name under Heaven given among men, whereby we must be Saved"* (Acts 4:12). So, as blunt as it seems, submission must be to Christ, or there is no Salvation.

IT IS NOT CHRIST PLUS!

Also, submission must be to Christ Alone,

NOTES

without tacking anything onto the condition of Faith. For example, when Catholics tack the Church or Mary onto Jesus regarding Salvation, that automatically forfeits this grand privilege. Whenever the Church of Christ tacks Water Baptism onto Jesus, the results are the same, *"forfeiture."* When Seventh Day Adventists tack on Saturday to Jesus, they have followed the same path. When certain Pentecostals tack on Tongues, the results are the same.

Anytime, anyone adds anything to Jesus Christ, such constitutes *"works,"* and nullifies Faith in Christ. God does not demand scholarship, morality, good works, money, education, or anything else for that matter, in order for a person to be Saved, only trust exclusively and totally in Jesus Christ and what He did at Calvary. The Lord does not even demand that the sinner understand very much about this great work, which in fact he doesn't. The Lord only demands Faith, which simply says *"I believe in Jesus Christ, and what He did at Calvary and the Resurrection and I give my life to Him."* If they mean it with all of their heart, irrespective as to whom they are, or where they are, at that moment that person is Saved (Jn. 3:16; Rom. 10:9-10, 13). Then the Righteousness of God is instantly and freely imputed to the believing sinner.

THE RIGHTEOUSNESS OF GOD

2. The Word of God proclaims to all what the *"Righteousness of God"* actually is. Actually, that subject is the foundational study of the entirety of the Bible.

Man forfeited his Righteousness in the Garden of Eden, and God set about immediately to restore that which was lost. That He did this thing in Jesus Christ, is the story of the Bible. God's dealings with man is the portrayal of the *"Righteousness of God."*

Man has no Righteousness within himself, cannot obtain Righteousness within himself, cannot earn Righteousness irrespective as to what he might do, but yet Righteousness is demanded by God. Consequently, the Lord made it possible through His Son Jesus Christ that Righteousness could be afforded to humanity, and that it be given upon simple Faith. Nothing could be more fair, more honest, more equitable, or more forthright. The condition is the same for all, whether rich or poor, whether great or small, whether old or young, whether red, yellow, brown, black, or white. The condition is Faith in Christ.

This means that the worst sinner in the world, whoever he or she might be, can throw himself or herself at the Feet of the world's Redeemer, as soiled and polluted as is possible to be, and in a few moments' time arise totally Justified, and completely Righteous. Of course, Israel of old had problems with that, and so does most of the world. They keep trying to earn this which in fact cannot be earned, and can be obtained only as a Free Gift from God.

In the Fall of 1997 a Catholic Nun referred to as Mother Teresa passed away. Noted for so-called *"good works,"* she was heralded all around the world as Righteous and Holy. However, such were claimed on the basis of *"good works,"* and not Faith in Jesus Christ. If that continued to be her claim when she died, she then died unsaved, despite all the good works, which within themselves are very commendable. However, such does not bring Salvation, even as Paul is here graphically discussing.

Some may object to me using this dear woman's name. However, there are untold millions in Hell at this very moment, and will be there forever and forever, wishing that a Preacher somewhere would have told them the Truth, and I mean the plain, unvarnished Truth, whereas no one would have any difficulty understanding what was being said. This we have attempted to do!

(4) "FOR CHRIST IS THE END OF THE LAW FOR RIGHTEOUSNESS TO EVERY ONE THAT BELIEVETH."

The phrase, *"For Christ is the end of the Law,"* speaks of the Law of Moses.

"End" in the Greek is *"telos,"* and means *"the termination or limit at which a thing ceases to be"* (Wuest).

The idea of this statement is, that the entirety of the Law of Moses as it was given by God, whether in the Ceremonial or the Moral, was fulfilled totally and completely in Christ. In fact, the Law pointed to Christ in every respect.

Regarding the Ceremonial, which included the Sacrifices, Feast Days, Sabbath Keeping, Circumcision, etc., every single one of these things, were symbolic of Christ.

The Sacrifices were a Type of what He would do at Calvary, in taking the Judgment of God upon Himself, on our behalf, in fact, that which we rightly deserved. When He came and died on Calvary and rose from the dead, the Sacrifices which were only meant to point to Him anyway, were no longer needed, as should be obvious.

Sabbath keeping was meant to point to the coming *"Rest"* which one would have in Christ as one's Redeemer. That is to what Jesus refers in Matthew 11:28-30. Consequently, inasmuch as Jesus our *"Rest"* has come, Sabbath keeping is no longer necessary.

Likewise, all the Feast Days such as the Passover, etc., typified Christ in a part of His Redemptive Role, and upon these things being done, the Feast Days are no longer necessary to be observed. Circumcision is the same, which symbolizes separation unto God, with one's allegiance to Christ now fulfilling that role.

THE MORAL LAW

Regarding the Moral Law, i.e., the Ten Commandments, Jesus is the end of that as well. However, the Moral Law unlike the Ceremonial Law did not pass away, with the exception of the Fourth Commandment. It is still incumbent upon all. However, Jesus kept the Moral Law in every single respect, that which man within himself could not do. Consequently, our Faith in Him, guarantees the believing sinner the Obedience and Moral Perfection of Christ. The believing sinner is no longer a Lawbreaker, but due to Christ, now a Law keeper.

The phrase, *"For Righteousness to every one that believeth,"* has reference to the fact that even though the Law did in fact have Righteousness, man could not obtain it, simply because he could not render that which was required, a perfect obedience. But Faith in Christ (every one that believeth) guarantees the Righteousness which the Law had, but could not give.

So, this tells us that the way to Righteousness is not the observance of statutes, no matter that they have been promulgated by God Himself; it is Faith, the abandonment of the soul to the Redeeming Judgment and Mercy of God in His Son (Denney).

As well, to simply believe in the Lord and what He has done to Redeem mankind, is not difficult. While I will admit that some Preachers have made it difficult, the Truth is, that all one has to do is just simply believe what God has said. To do that, one does not have to be a Scholar, or rich, or an intellectual, etc., just simply have the capacity to say *"Lord I believe."* At the moment that is done, and if one is truly sincere, desiring to make Jesus Christ the Lord of one's life, Salvation (Righteousness) is instantly imputed to the believing sinner (Eph. 2:8-9).

As well, it includes *"everyone"* exactly as it says here in the Scripture, not merely some select few. When God says *"everyone,"* He means everyone!

(5) "FOR MOSES DESCRIBETH THE RIGHTEOUSNESS WHICH IS OF THE LAW, THAT THE MAN WHICH DOETH THOSE THINGS SHALL LIVE BY THEM."

The phrase, *"For Moses describeth the Righteousness which is of the Law,"* tells us plainly that the Law did contain a Righteousness of God. In other words, if an Israelite, or anyone for that matter, could keep all of the Moral Law, not only in fact but also in heart, not failing even one time, even as Jesus did and Jesus Alone, then such a person could claim the Righteousness of God. However, Righteousness on the principle of Law Obedience was impossible of attainment owing to man's incapacity to give such an obedience.

The phrase *"That the man which doeth those things shall live by them,"* is taken from Leviticus 18:5. However, Paul uses it in a little different manner than it was originally given.

Paul is simply saying that no matter how hard a person tried to render perfect obedience, he would not be able to do so. Consequently, to bring about Salvation on that basis was and is literally an impossibility. All that men could succeed in doing by looking to the Law was not Salvation, but rather failure, for it really contained no Salvation, but actually only a curse. The Law condemned

NOTES

and cursed, even as it was designed to do (Deut. 27:26; Rom. 3:19-20; Gal. 3:10-13). This shows the impossibility of being Saved by the Law.

In fact, there was Salvation in Old Testament times, but it was not in the Law, but rather in the Sacrifices, and more perfectly, Faith in that, or rather to Whom the Sacrifices pointed, The Lord Jesus Christ.

However, Israel tried to force Salvation into an ethical cult where obedience to the Old Testament Decalogue would bring Salvation. Such was impossible. Paul is combating this. Israel sought a Righteous Standing by Law Obedience. Paul says it can be appropriated only by Faith. He presents such in the next three verses.

(6) "BUT THE RIGHTEOUSNESS WHICH IS OF FAITH SPEAKETH ON THIS WISE, SAY NOT IN THINE HEART, WHO SHALL ASCEND INTO HEAVEN? (THAT IS, TO BRING CHRIST DOWN FROM ABOVE:)"

The phrase, *"But the Righteousness which is of Faith speaketh on this wise,"* is now about to proclaim the wonderful and beautiful simplicity found only in Christ.

The only type of Righteousness which God will accept is the Righteousness that is afforded by Christ, which, upon simple Faith in what Jesus did at the Cross, is given to man upon simple faith. It is freely imputed, meaning that it cannot be earned, purchased, bought, or sold. It is free, afforded by Christ, and, in a sense, is ours for the asking (I Cor. 6:11; II Cor. 5:17-18).

The phrase, *"Say not in thine heart, Who shall ascend into Heaven? (that is, to bring Christ down from above:),"* presents Paul proclaiming the beautiful simplicity of Gospel Salvation. The idea is this:

For one to be Saved, one does not have to perform some Herculean task, such as bring Christ down in Person from Heaven. In other words, and as we shall see, God's Word is enough.

(7) "OR, WHO SHALL DESCEND INTO THE DEEP? (THAT IS, TO BRING UP CHRIST AGAIN FROM THE DEAD.)"

As no one has to go up to Heaven and bring Christ down Personally in order to secure Salvation, neither does one have to go into the grave or the nether world to bring Christ up from the dead. In the first place, the Incarnation, Resurrection, and Ascension are a fact, which speaks of a Finished Salvation.

In essence, Paul is saying, let not the man who sighs for deliverance from his own sinfulness suppose that the accomplishment of some impossible task is required of him in order to enjoy the Blessings of the Gospel. Let him not think that the Personal Presence of the Messiah is necessary to insure his Salvation.

Christ needs not to be brought down from Heaven, or up from the abyss, to impart to the sinner forgiveness and holiness. No! Our Christian Message contains no impossibilities. We do not mock the sinner by offering him happiness on conditions which we know that he is powerless to fulfill. We tell him that Christ's Word is near to him: so near, that he may speak of it with his mouth, and meditate on it with his heart . . . .

Is there anything above human power in such a confession, and in such a belief? Surely not! It is graciously adapted to the necessity of the very weakest and most sinful of God's creatures (Wuest).

(8) "BUT WHAT SAITH IT? THE WORD IS NIGH THEE, EVEN IN THY MOUTH, AND IN THY HEART: THAT IS, THE WORD OF FAITH, WHICH WE PREACH;"

The question, *"But what saith it?"*, now proclaims God's beautiful Plan of Salvation, which all can receive, and easily so, if they so desire. It is not some difficult thing such as attempting to keep the Law of Moses, but rather by simple Faith, which Paul will now explain.

So, the question *"What saith it?"*, as it pertains to Salvation, is without a doubt, the single most important question ever asked by anyone. Paul will now explain it step-by-step.

The phrase, *"The Word is nigh thee,"* presents a simple Word, which is simply said, that Jesus died for sinners and rose from the dead. It is not hard, not complicated, does not have many parts to have to grasp, only the simple admonition given.

As well, that *"Word"* is near everyone. It is probably the most proliferated Word on

NOTES

the face of the earth. So, there is no excuse for anyone.

The phrase, *"Even in thy mouth,"* speaks of the confession which must come from the mouth, even as Paul will say in the next verse, in order for one to be Saved.

That does not mean that merely speaking words, even the right words, saves someone, for it does not. It just simply means, that sooner or later one must confess Christ before others.

The phrase, *"And in thy heart,"* proclaims the part of man in which Faith begins, otherwise, it is mere mental affirmation, and will effect no Salvation at all. Jesus said, *"For out of the abundance of the heart the mouth speaketh"* (Mat. 12:34).

"Heart" in the Greek is *"kardia,"* and means *"the thoughts or feelings."* So Salvation must begin in the heart.

The phrase, *"That is, the Word of Faith, which we preach,"* presents the declaration by Paul that Justification is on the Faith-Principle as opposed to the Works-Principle.

"Word" is *here* translated *"Rhema,"* with it normally being translated *"Logos."*

"Logos" refers to the total expression of some idea or person. *"Rhema"* is used of a *part* of speech in a sentence. In other words, to be Saved, one does not have to know all about what Jesus has done for him, but actually only a part of what was done, namely that He died for sinners and then rose from the dead (Jn. 3:16).

So from this, we can see how easy the Holy Spirit has made the Plan of Salvation, in order that anyone may be able to accept. It is the Message of Salvation in which Faith is the appropriating method of obtaining Redemption. The sinner simply has to believe that Jesus did this thing for him, and if he believes it out of his heart, he is Saved (Jn. 3:16).

As Paul preached this, likewise, we must preach it as well!

(9) "THAT IF THOU SHALT CONFESS WITH THY MOUTH THE LORD JESUS, AND SHALT BELIEVE IN THINE HEART THAT GOD HATH RAISED HIM FROM THE DEAD, THOU SHALT BE SAVED."

The phrase, *"That if thou shalt confess with thy mouth the Lord Jesus,"* means to be in agreement with all that Scripture says about Him, which includes all that these two names imply. *"Jesus"* is the Greek transliteration of the Hebrew name *"Jehoshua."* It means *"Saviour"* or *"Jehovah saves."*

"Lord" in the Greek is *"Kurios,"* which has the same meaning as the Old Testament version of *"Jehovah."* It implies *"Deity."*

Thus, to confess Jesus as Lord includes a heart belief in His Deity (Jesus is God), Incarnation (God becoming Man), vicarious Atonement (what He did at Calvary), and Bodily Resurrection (He rose from the dead).

The phrase, *"And shalt believe in thine heart that God hath raised Him from the dead,"* pertains as is obvious, to the Bodily Resurrection of Christ.

The phrase, *"Thou shalt be Saved,"* consequently, points to two requirements:

1. One must believe that Jesus Christ is God, and that as a Man He died for lost sinners, and, therefore, is the Saviour.

2. One must believe as well, that God raised Jesus from the dead, i.e., *"The Resurrection."*

In the late 1970's when we began to conduct citywide Crusades with thousands of people in attendance, and all over the world for that matter, the Lord began to deal with me about people who were coming forward to accept Christ. He told me that I should not take it for granted that they know how to pray or to accept the Lord. In other words, I must lead them into this, and that I was to use this very Scripture (vs. 9) in what I refer to as the *"Sinner's Prayer."*

Through the years in giant Crusades all over the world, I have had untold thousands to pray this Prayer with me. I cannot honestly say that all who prayed thusly were Saved, but untold numbers were and continue to be.

Countless times, when I would come to the part where I would have the believing sinner to repeat after me, *"With my mouth, I confess the Lord Jesus, and with my heart I believe that God has raised Jesus from the dead,"* I would greatly sense the Presence of God, with such evident on the countenance of the seekers as well. Also, I have had untold numbers to pray accordingly with me by Television, in other words, giving their hearts and lives to the Lord Jesus

NOTES

Christ even in the privacy of their own home, or in a hotel room, etc.

That which the Lord told me to do those many years ago, I continue to do unto this very hour, when praying with the lost to be Saved. When the believing sinner is led step-by-step into Salvation, even to the prayer he or she is praying, it makes it much easier for them, just as the Lord told me those many years ago, resulting in many more people actually finding Christ.

(10) "FOR WITH THE HEART MAN BELIEVETH UNTO RIGHTEOUSNESS; AND WITH THE MOUTH CONFESSION IS MADE UNTO SALVATION."

The phrase, *"For with the heart man believeth unto Righteousness,"* portrays the word *"believing"* in a mode of *"thinking,"* not of feeling.

The phrase, *"And with the mouth confession is made unto Salvation,"* presents Heart-Faith, which must confess itself.

To separate the two phrases in this verse, looking for an independent meaning in each, is a mistake: a heart believing unto Righteousness and a mouth making confession unto Salvation, are not really two things, but two sides of the same thing.

The idea is, when Faith comes forth from its silence to announce itself, and to proclaim the Glory and the Grace of the Lord, its voice is *"confession"* (Morrison).

WHAT IS SALVATION

Actually, the words *"Salvation"* or *"Saved"* denotes simply *"deliverance,"* and this in almost any sense.

First of all it means to be delivered from the penalty of sin, and then from sin itself.

This is all because of Faith — specifically, Faith in Christ. God does not visit the penalties of sins on Believers, but treats them as if they were Righteous (Rom. 5:1).

But this is not because of a quality in the Believer or in the Faith for that matter, but because of an act that preceded any act of Christian Faith, namely, the Death of Christ on the Cross. Through this Death God's Mercy could be extended safely, while before this the exercise of that Mercy had proved disastrous (Rom. 3:25-26). As well, the Death of Jesus was a Sacrifice, in essence, a

Sin-Offering (Rom. 3:25).

Paul presents a double line of thought in the remission of penalties through the Atoning Death of Christ and the destruction of the power of sin through strength flowing from Christ, the human element in both cases being Faith.

SALVATION IN THE PRESENT AND IN THE FUTURE

Salvation is both a present and a future matter for Believers. The full realization of all that God has in store will not be ours until the end of human history, but the enjoyment of these Blessings depends on conditions fulfilled in us and by us now. But a foretaste of the Blessings of Forgiveness of sins and growth in Holiness is given on this Earth. The pardon depends on the fact of God's Mercy through the Death of Christ, and evident Faith on the part of the believing sinner.

But strength comes from God through the Glorified Christ (made possible by the Holy Spirit), this vital union with God being a Christian fundamental.

That human effort is an essential in Salvation is not to be denied in the face of all the New Testament evidence. However, by effort we mean *"a willing mind and an obedient heart."* To be frank, no one with the faintest conception of what Salvation means would think of coming before God to claim merit. Salvation is first and foremost a *"Gift"* (Eph. 2:8-9).

(11) "FOR THE SCRIPTURE SAITH, WHOSOEVER BELIEVETH ON HIM SHALL NOT BE ASHAMED."

The phrase, *"For the Scripture saith,"* is derived by combining parts of Isaiah 28:16, with Isaiah 49:23.

The phrase, *"Whosoever believeth on Him,"* proclaims the fact that Salvation is reachable by all. The Lord has so devised a Plan that reaches any and all strata of society. It is a Plan so grand and glorious, that it could not have been devised by man, in fact it is devised to be accepted only by man.

Once again, the emphasis on the pronoun *"Him"* proclaims Jesus as the Sole Figure in the realm of Salvation. The reasoning is simple. It is Jesus Who satisfied sin's penalties at

NOTES

Calvary's Cross, and it is Jesus Who rose from the dead, ratifying that which was done on the Cross. So, Jesus must without fail be the Object of one's Faith (Heb. 12:2).

The phrase, *"Shall not be ashamed,"* in essence says, *"Shall not be put to shame."*

The idea of this phrase is not that of being ashamed of the Lord Jesus, for such is not in the Apostle's mind. Rather, he says that the sinner who places his Faith in the Lord Jesus will not be defeated, disappointed, or suffer a repulse in his life.

(12) "FOR THERE IS NO DIFFERENCE BETWEEN THE JEW AND THE GREEK: FOR THE SAME LORD OVER ALL IS RICH UNTO ALL THAT CALL UPON HIM."

The phrase, *"For there is no difference between the Jew and the Greek,"* actually should read, *"between the Jew and the Gentile."*

Respecting the availability to all, this sums up Paul's statement respecting who can be Saved. It refers to all, irrespective as to whom they may be.

This is what angered the Jews so much. The very idea, that Paul would put Jews with Gentiles was unthinkable. As well, and worse still, he placed no difference between the Jews and the Gentiles.

"Difference" in the Greek is *"diastole,"* and means *"to draw asunder, divide, distinguish, or distinction."* In other words, Paul placed no distinction between the two, making all one outside of Christ (sinners needing Redemption) and one in Christ (those Redeemed).

The phrase, *"For the same Lord over all is rich unto all that call upon Him,"* tells us several things:

1. There is One Saviour and Redeemer for the entirety of the world, Who is, *"The Lord Jesus Christ."* Furthermore, emphasized by the title *"Lord,"* Jesus is God!

2. The Lord is *"over all,"* in the sense that He is the Creator of all. Consequently, all answer to Him, and that is to be taken literally.

Men will answer to Him now as Lord and Saviour, or else they will answer to Him at the Great White Throne Judgment, when He will then be their Judge (Rev. 20:11-15).

3. Anyone is free to *"Call upon Him"* anytime they desire, and are actually encouraged

to do so. In fact, He is the only One Who can meet any need, answer any prayer, do anything which needs to be done, and defeat any power of darkness. In essence, Satan and every Fallen Angel and Demon Spirit, have already been defeated.

Actually in all of history, there has never been even one who has called upon Him respecting Salvation, but that He did not answer, and always answered favorably. As should be obvious, that is quite a record.

4. Not only will the Lord hear all who call upon Him, at the same time, he will be *"rich"* unto them, and irrespective as to who they are, or what they have done. *"Rich"* in the Greek is *"plouteo,"* and means *"to be wealthy or increased with goods."*

It means that whatever is needed, the Lord has an abundant supply, and dispenses it freely and liberally.

(13) "FOR WHOSOEVER SHALL CALL UPON THE NAME OF THE LORD SHALL BE SAVED."

The words, *"For whosoever,"* taken from Joel 2:32, made it evident to the Hebrew people that Life and Righteousness were offered to Faith and not to merit or to privilege, for it was manifest that the word *"whosoever"* embraced the entire world without distinction.

The phrase, *"Shall call upon the Name of the Lord shall be Saved,"* speaks of the sinner coming to Christ, but can refer to any Believer and with whatever need.

When a person evidences Faith in Christ, that is the same as believing in Him. Faith is very easy to understand. It is simply believing God and His Word.

Whereas the *"Name of the Lord"* referred to many things in the Old Testament, in the New Testament it refers to *"The Lord Jesus Christ."*

Much of the world claims a belief in God, but much of the world disagrees as to how to reach Him. Jesus said, *"I am the Way, the Truth, and the Life: no man cometh unto the Father, but by Me"* (Jn. 14:6).

That's the reason that one must call upon the *"Name of the Lord,"* that Name being Jesus. As stated, He is the One Who has paid the price for man's Redemption, and, consequently, it is His Name which

opens the Door (Jn. 10:1-10).

(14) "HOW THEN SHALL THEY CALL ON HIM IN WHOM THEY HAVE NOT BELIEVED? AND HOW SHALL THEY BELIEVE IN HIM OF WHOM THEY HAVE NOT HEARD? AND HOW SHALL THEY HEAR WITHOUT A PREACHER?"

The question, *"How then shall they call on Him in Whom they have not believed?"*, is meant to direct attention by Paul to several areas:

1. He directs the question to Israel, in effect saying, that they will not call upon the Lord for Salvation, for the simple reason that they do not believe they need Salvation, and furthermore they do not believe in God's Salvation Plan, which is Faith in Christ.

2. Paul is also addressing this question to the Gentile world, referring to the fact that they have not believed in Jehovah in the past, rather believing in their own heathen gods, etc. However, he is now going to state how this problem can be remedied, in fact, with the remedy already having begun.

Much of the world presently lies in unbelief. Actually, Jesus said of the Holy Spirit, *"And when He is come, He will reprove* (convict) *the world of sin, and of Righteousness, and of Judgment:*

"Of sin, because they believe not on Me" (Jn. 16:8-9).

However, Paul will go on to say that a great cause of unbelief is in the fact that the Gospel is not properly preached. Actually, I think we can say from these Texts that this *is* the greatest cause of unbelief in the world.

The question, *"And how shall they believe in Him of Whom they have not heard?"*, tells us several things.

Paul himself wrote in Romans Chapter 1 that man is without excuse referring to the fact of the existence of God. Creation demands a Creator (Rom. 1:20). However, the mere knowledge of God has nothing to do with Salvation. In other words, people are not Saved simply because they know and believe there is a God. Something else is needed, and that something else is the Gospel of Jesus Christ preached unto them. In other words, they must hear!

This Passage plainly tells us that ignorance is not Salvation. We know from the Word of

God, that a person must believe in the Lord Jesus Christ in order to be Saved (Jn. 3:16; Rom. 10:9-10). However, they cannot believe if they have not heard that in which they are to believe. Consequently, that's the reason that the last Message of Jesus Christ was what is commonly referred to as *"The Great Commission"* (Mk. 16:15-20).

THE PRIMARY EFFORT

For every person in the world who does not have an opportunity to hear the True Gospel of Jesus Christ, as far as that person is concerned, all that God did to Redeem humanity in the sending of His Only Son, The Lord Jesus Christ, was in vain.

When one thinks of the Gospel Story, considering the large number of Missionaries in the world, and the ways and means that the Gospel is being proclaimed, one might have a tendency to think that this task is adequately being carried out. However, that is not the case, as it has never been the case.

To be frank, out of all the Missionaries in the world today, there are only a few of them who are really preaching the Gospel of Jesus Christ. Actually, that number is even smaller than most would even dare realize. Having preached all over the world, and having a Call of God on my life to take the Gospel to the world, I would think that I have a little more knowledge in this field than most.

MISSIONARIES?

When one realizes, that many Missionaries to the foreign field, are mainly there in a social position, the number of the truly God-called is narrowed down dramatically. In other words, these people, whomever they may be, function as little more than a religious peace corps. They are not there to preach the Gospel, for the simple reason they don't even really believe in the Gospel. They call themselves Missionaries, and they are sent out by their respective Churches, but their work among the natives wherever they may be, is mostly in the realm of social activity. Whatever they are doing may be of some small help to the people, but it does not address the subject of lost souls; spiritually speaking, these people are of no consequence.

Coming down to Missionaries who are

NOTES

under the Pentecostal banner, while some few of them definitely do preach the Gospel, and are gloriously and wondrously used of God, sadly and regrettably, the majority do not fall into that category. Many, and I know what I am talking about, are little more than religious Psychologists. In other words, they place very little credence in the True Gospel of Jesus Christ. These people are of no worth or value to the Kingdom of God.

Even many in the Charismatic realm, even those of note, little preach a Salvation Message, if at all. In other words, very little attempt, if any, is made to get people to Christ. The Truth is this:

Even though there are some few men and women of God on the field around the world who are grandly proclaiming this Great and Glorious Gospel of Jesus Christ, to be factual, that number is precious few. To be frank, most of the money given for that which calls itself *"Foreign Missions,"* is by and large wasted.

TELEVISION

In the mid 1970's the Lord began to speak to my heart about World Evangelism. He told me that the manner in which it was presently carried out, was woefully insufficient. In other words, the population of the world is so great, that even though one-on-one Evangelism is of immense significance, and will never lose its place as should be obvious, still, if it is limited to that, most will never have the opportunity to hear. Consequently, He told me to place our Telecast in every Nation in the world that would open the door to the Gospel. From that moment forward, this we have attempted to do, and with astounding results I might quickly add.

Please do not misunderstand. Television cannot take the place of Churches in these areas or consecrated Missionaries, or any other type of worker for the Lord for that matter. Actually, that is not the idea. The idea is Mass Evangelism.

With a program over Television, we can reach more people in one week with the Gospel of Jesus Christ, than most Churches can in the entirety of their existence. However, in no way does that mean we don't need

Churches. In fact, we need *more* Churches, far more.

The Lord has helped us to see literally hundreds of thousands of people brought to a Saving knowledge of Jesus Christ through our Television Program aired all over the world, even translated into various languages. To be sure, after these people come to Christ, they need, and in fact must have, a good Church to attend. So, in no way are we demeaning the Church, actually, we are making it stronger.

However, just anyone on Television will not see those kind of results. There must be a Call of God for this specific purpose, at least to see the results of which I speak. I am not on Television simply because I have seen a need and am responding accordingly. I am on Television with the Gospel, because the Lord has called me to do so. In other words, woe unto me if I do not preach the Gospel over Television.

THE ANOINTING OF THE MESSAGE

As well, the Lord has Anointed me to preach His Word, and that is the second reason for the results we see. That is the reason I lay on my face crying to God, that He will help me, will give me His Word which He wants me to deliver, and then Anoint me to deliver that Word. The same Anointing that Jesus had, as a Minister of the Gospel, I as well must have that Anointing. This is so important, please allow me to say it in another way.

If Jesus had to have the Anointing of the Holy Spirit to do what He did, even more, is that Anointing incumbent upon me as a poor mortal (Lk. 4:18-19).

The question, *"And how shall they hear without a Preacher?"*, proclaims God's method of proclaiming His Message.

GOD'S PROGRAM MUST NOT BE CHANGED

God has chosen the manner of Preaching to proclaim His Word. Of course, that can be done in several ways, such as Gospel Literature or even Gospel Music, etc., but however it is proclaimed, it must be the True Word of God.

There is absolutely nothing in the world more powerful than a Holy Spirit-Anointed

Preacher of the Gospel. I speak of a man or woman who has been truly called of God, and who walks close to God, and is Anointed by the Holy Spirit. They have something to say, and they say it in a powerful way.

When I say these things, I am not speaking of oratorical capabilities, or even educational or intellectual knowledge. I am speaking of one who has heard from Heaven, has been given a Message by the Lord, and the Anointing of the Holy Spirit to deliver that Message. There is nothing in the world more powerful than that.

It is that means chosen by the Lord to take His Word to a hurting world.

When men attempt to substitute political means and ways in place of the Preaching of the Gospel, such is not the Will of God. As well, whenever a Church ceases to be strong in its Preaching, that Church has begun to die. As strong as is the Pulpit, as strong as is the Pew.

Nothing will ever take the place of Preaching and Teaching the Word, as nothing can take the place of Preaching and Teaching the Word.

If one were to look back in history, one would find that events turned not so much on military conflict or even revolution, but rather on the Preaching of the Gospel.

As an example, England was heading the same way as France regarding revolution, which would have totally destroyed the Nation, had it not been for the preaching of John Wesley. His Messages Anointed by God stirred the Nation, and pulled it to the place that it should be in a political sense, as well as other ways. While many other things may be given the credit, if the Truth be known, it was the preaching of John and Charles Wesley which turned the tide.

Had it not been for the Preaching and Ministry of Charles Finney, there may not even be a United States as it is presently. In thundering tones, he whipped New England toward God, which greatly decided the course of this Nation.

As well, it must be quickly added, that if one will carefully study the Messages of Wesley and Finney, and hundreds of others like them, one will find they did not preach a political Message, but rather the pure and plain Gospel of Jesus Christ. Man's problem is not political, or economical, or social, but rather spiritual. In other words, a black, evil, wicked heart is man's problem. The only solution to that is the Gospel of Jesus Christ, which alone can change men's hearts. That is your answer, and your only answer.

For the Church to spend all its energies trying to elect particular individuals to public office, thinking somehow to change the course and the direction by that means, is futile indeed. Even though those things certainly hold some significance, still, that is not God's Way, respecting the Church. The business of the Church is to preach the Gospel of Jesus Christ, and that alone.

(15) "AND HOW SHALL THEY PREACH, EXCEPT THEY BE SENT? AS IT IS WRITTEN, HOW BEAUTIFUL ARE THE FEET OF THEM THAT PREACH THE GOSPEL OF PEACE, AND BRING GLAD TIDINGS OF GOOD THINGS!"

The question, *"And how shall they preach, except they be sent?"*, tells us in no uncertain terms, that the ones who send the Preacher, are just as important as the Preacher.

THE SENDER AND THE SENT

Of course, we know that it is God Who sends His Preachers. But at the same time, He uses a multitude of people to support the one He has sent. That is His Way.

As an example, the Lord has called me to preach the Gospel by Television. He has given me the Message, and as stated, has Anointed me to deliver that Message.

Irrespective, I have to have an army of people to help me do this. The production costs and air time for Television are considerable, as should be obvious. Television reaches a tremendous number of people, and in fact, the cost per person of taking the Gospel to them is actually the least expensive of any presentation. In other words, due to the tremendous number of people reached by Television, the cost per person is lower than any other form of Evangelism. In fact, much lower! However, due to the tremendous number reached, the sum needed for this presentation, is more than any one person can handle.

So, when the Lord calls someone such as

NOTES

myself for a particular Ministry, He also calls others to support that Ministry. In other words, their Call in the Sight of God, is just as important as the Call on the part of the Preacher. Without the sender the Preacher cannot be sent.

DOES THE SENDER REALLY KNOW JUST HOW IMPORTANT HE IS TO THE WORK OF GOD?

I am sure that some few do know. But the Truth is, most, I think, do not really know or understand how important their place actually is respecting the greatest of all works — the taking of the Gospel to the world. I want to say it again, I believe that God actually calls people for this purpose, even associating them with a particular Ministry, for the greatest of all tasks, World Evangelism, to be carried out. As a result, their place and position is of tremendous significance.

At the same time, Satan will do everything within his power to divert that person from their called task. He will try to make them lose confidence in the person they are supporting. He will bring about events to where they will stop their support, and use any and every tactic to do so.

To be frank, Satan's greatest method to hinder, is to use other Christians. That is sad but true! If he can get Religious Leaders to oppose one who God has truly called, and that's not too very difficult to do, he knows that many people will then stop their support.

In fact, he will use any tactic at his disposal, telling any lie, use any method, doing anything, irrespective as to what it is to gain his purpose. He wants the Gospel of Jesus Christ to stop.

He knows who God has called, and he makes that Preacher his target. Of course, that does not condone wrongdoing on their part in any capacity, but it does make the task much more difficult. As well, irrespective as to how much God has Called a Preacher, or Anointed that Preacher, if Satan can be successful in stopping the ones who *"send"* that Preacher, then he has accomplished his task.

He tries to stop the Preacher who is Called of God. If he cannot do that, he will attempt to stop those who send that Preacher, and he is a master at these tactics. Actually, he does not care how he accomplishes the task, just so he stops the Gospel.

A MUCH BELIEVED ERROR

Many Believers think that God has many Isaiahs, or Jeremiahs, or Pauls, or Simon Peters, etc., but He does not. There was only one of these individuals.

By that I mean, that much of the Church believes that if the Lord doesn't use one person to take the Gospel to others, He will use somebody else. In other words, it is not something to be excited about, because in their thinking, God has many to take the Gospel all over the world.

That is simply untrue!

While the Lord at times certainly does have more than one, still, there aren't the great number available as is popularly believed. In other words, in some situations, there is in fact only one person to accomplish the task. Let me give an example:

Years ago I heard H. B. Garlock speak of his years of service in West Africa. God used him mightily in this area to see untold numbers of souls brought to Christ. In fact, he was one of the first to open up West Africa to the Pentecostal Message.

His time there reads like the Book of Acts. The things that the Lord did, are absolutely miraculous to say the least.

He went on to mention that villages as far as several hundreds of miles away, would send runners to his Church, pleading with him to come to their village with the Gospel, or at least to send someone. Many times, there was no one to send.

For those villages where no one could be sent, did they ultimately hear the Gospel?

Probably not! So I'm saying, that God does not have great numbers of people to send all over the world. There aren't that many who are truly called of God.

To use a Biblical example, Ezekiel was given a Message to deliver by the Lord. He was told to tell the people what God told him to say, and if the people would not hear, then he (Ezekiel) had done all he could, he had delivered his soul.

But the Lord also told him, that if he refused to take them the Message, *"The*

same wicked man shall die in his iniquity; but his blood will I require at thine hand" (Ezek. 3:17-19).

At least in this situation, Ezekiel was the only one to take the Message. I am persuaded that the situation is the same oftentimes.

A COP-OUT!

Most of the time, it is a cop-out when people take the attitude that they need not be too concerned about the situation, because God has many people to send to the lost, etc. The Truth is this:

Every *single* Believer has a responsibility to do what he or she can do to help take the Gospel of Jesus Christ to the world. Although only a few are called directly to Preach the Gospel, in fact, *all* Believers are called in some capacity respecting World Evangelism.

First of all, every single Believer can pray, and should pray constantly respecting the Salvation of the lost all around the world. The Believer should ask the Lord to burden their hearts respecting particular places, and which the Holy Spirit most definitely will do.

As well, every Believer can give, and I speak of our financial abilities. In fact, every single Believer should delegate a certain part of their giving to go to World Evangelism. Also, the Believer should seek the Lord earnestly as to where this money ought to go.

However, this area of one's consecration, which is probably the single most important part of a Believer's life, in fact, is treated most of the time with less responsibility than anything else.

Most Believers just simply give to their Church, and then have no idea what happens to the money or where it goes. In some cases it is used legitimately and performs a Work for God. In many cases, and actually in most cases, it does *not* perform a Work for God. So, the Believer should earnestly seek the Lord regarding where his or her money should go respecting the taking of the Gospel to the world. One must look beneath the surface, past all the glitter and the claims, because to be sure, every Preacher in the world claims he is doing exactly what God wants him to do, etc. The Truth is, that only a very special few are actually in that category.

WHAT SHOULD THE CRITERIA BE?

In fact, it is not really that difficult to ascertain what is right and what is wrong respecting these things of which we speak. As stated, all types of claims are made, so if one is going to go exclusively by that, one will be led astray.

First of all, a Ministry must be totally *Biblical*. By that I mean, people must be Saved under that Ministry, Baptized with the Holy Spirit under that Ministry, delivered under that Ministry, and healed under that Ministry.

Satan is very good at camouflaging that which isn't, making people think it is. For instance, there are many Ministries which claim all types of Miracles and Healings, when in reality very few people are being Saved, or Baptized with the Holy Spirit, and if the Truth be known, very few people are being healed as well. The point I wish to make is this:

In those types of situations, the priorities are wrong. While Healings and Miracles are definitely a part of a Biblical Ministry, if one is to use the Bible as a Standard, those things are not to be the Foundation but only a part. *People being Saved and Baptized with the Holy Spirit must be the Foundation*, with all these other things being a part of the major thrust of the Gospel, which always must be the Salvation of souls. That is the Book of Acts criteria, and, consequently, what is laid down by the Holy Spirit, and if it is not followed, it means that one's Ministry is unbiblical in some fashion, and as a result, will not truly accomplish for the Lord what should be done.

STEWARDSHIP

To be sure, when every Believer stands at the Judgment Seat of Christ, we are going to have to give an account for every single thing we've done. If we have been unwise in our stewardship, we will have to answer for that. To be frank, there are going to be many which will lose some of their reward, and some that will lose all of their reward, even though their souls will be Saved (I Cor. 3:15).

NOTES

As a result, every Believer must live his or her life, doing every single thing, as if it was being tried before the Judgment Seat of Christ presently. In other words, we should do everything in the Light of that Judgment.

The phrase, *"As it is written, How beautiful are the feet of them that preach the Gospel of Peace, and bring glad tidings of good things,"* is taken from Isaiah 52:7. One is struck by Paul's constant reference to Old Testament Scripture. Such must be an example for all others, exactly as the Holy Spirit intends.

"Beautiful" in the Greek is *"horaioi,"* and means *"the time of full bloom or development, as well as blooming maturity and vigor."*

The word *"feet"* carries the idea of swift, vigorous feet. Feet, emphasizing the rapid approach of the Messenger.

The *"Gospel of Peace,"* presents the Message which if accepted, will make things right between the sinner and God. There is an enmity now between God and unbelieving man. Man has sinned against God, in essence, rebelling against Him. To express the degree of the terribleness of this sin is virtually impossible. About as close as one can come referring to such an explanation, is a child murdering its parents. More perfectly, to imagine the parents as Good, Righteous, and Holy, makes the situation even worse. Even though that explanation is woefully inadequate, it gives one somewhat of an idea as to what man has done against God, his Creator.

PEACE!

It was not Satan who gave man Life, but rather God. In fact, Satan has done nothing but steal from man, using him, and then discarding him on the garbage dumps of refuse. To be sure, that is done everyday by the millions.

Man does not feel this enmity nearly as much as God, simply because it is God Who has been wronged, and not man.

So, when the Preacher of the Gospel proclaims the Good News and it is accepted, it brings *"Peace"* between God and man, because the enmity is removed. The sinner has admitted culpability, thrown himself or herself on the Lord for Mercy, which is always instantly granted, with the record cleansed.

As well, whenever the sinner accepts Christ, not only is *"Peace"* brought about as a result of the enmity being removed, but as well there are all types of other *"glad tidings of good things."*

GOOD THINGS?

What are those good things?

In just about any and every way that one could think, things begin to change for the better. When the heart of the sinner is changed, that person has a totally different outlook on everything. In fact, they are a New Creature in Christ Jesus. In other words, the old person doesn't live there anymore.

The very nature and character of the person changes, with them having a totally different outlook on all things. In other words, *"Old things are passed away; behold, all things are become new"* (II Cor. 5:17).

Along with all these other Blessings, at the moment of Conversion, the New Believer enters into the Economy of God. As such, his economic situation instantly begins to improve. He is no longer at the whim of Wall Street, or Washington, or what other people do, but now, the Lord is his Protector, Benefactor and Guide (Mat. 6:25-34).

For those who do not know God, life is a gamble, and in worldly parlance, the luck of the draw, a roll of the dice. However, with the Child of God there is purpose and direction now in his life. He is led not by whim or chance, but by the Holy Spirit (Rom. 8:1-2). The Holy Spirit through the Apostle explained it perfectly. Truly, *"good things"* says it all!

PEACE WITH GOD

As we have stated, for sinful man there must first be Peace with God, the removal of sin's enmity through the Sacrifice of Christ (Rom. 5:1; Col. 1:20). Then inward Peace can follow (Phil. 4:7), unhindered by the world's strife (Jn. 14:27; 16:33). Peace between man and man is also part of the purpose for which Christ died (Eph. Chpt. 2) and of the Spirit's Work (Gal. 5:22); but man must also be active to promote it (Eph. 4:3; Heb. 12:14), not merely as the elimination of discord, but as the harmony and

true functioning of the Body of Christ (Rom. 14:19; I Cor. 14:33).

PEACE IN A TROUBLED WORLD

Peace seems impossible to achieve in our troubled world and, for those struggling with anxiety or disappointment, in individual lives.

Peace, admittedly, is a complex concept. In the Old Testament particularly, Peace is a powerful theological term, with the nature of Peace deeply rooted in Scripture's view of relationships and of humanity's deepest needs.

The New Testament provides clear guidance as to how we can experience Peace — a Peace that our world neither understands, nor gives, nor can take away.

THE OLD TESTAMENT CONCEPT OF PEACE

The Hebrew word for *"Peace"* is *"Shalom."* It is derived from a root that conveys the image of wholeness, unity, and harmony — something that is complete and sound. Although *"Peace"* is essentially a relational concept in the Old Testament, it also conveys the idea of prosperity, health, and fulfillment.

The word *"Shalom"* occurs over 200 times in the Old Testament. In 50 or 60 of these occurrences, the emphasis lies in the absence of strife. Thus, the tension and antagonism that had developed between Isaac's servants and the people of Abimelech, a Philistine King, were resolved with a Feast and a Treaty, after which the people of Abimelech *"left him in Peace"* (Gen. 26:31).

The same use of *"Peace"* affirms a lack of international strife, as well as the beneficial effect of such Peace on a Nation's citizens.

"During Solomon's lifetime Judah and Israel, from Dan to Beersheba, lived in safety, each man under his own Vine and Fig Tree" (I Ki. 4:25). This is the Blessing that came from having *"Peace on all sides"* (I Ki. 4:24).

THE WELFARE OF A PERSON OR NATION

While most of the uses of *"Shalom"* in the Narrative Books of the Old Testament focus on interpersonal or international harmony, the concept does expand to refer to an individual's or a Nation's welfare. For example, when the Prophet Elisha saw a close friend hurrying to him, he sent his servant to greet her with a series of questions, *"Are you all right (Shalom)? Is your husband all right (Shalom)? Is your child all right (Shalom)?"* (II Ki. 4:26).

Thus, health, personal fulfillment, and prosperity are all included in the concept of Peace. And, in the 25 or so times when *"Shalom"* is used as a greeting or farewell, it is the extension of a Blessing — a wish for the recipient's welfare.

Peace takes on its deepest significance as we move into the Psalms and the Prophets. Through the Old Testament, some two-thirds of the uses of this word express the fulfillment that comes to human beings when they experience God's Presence.

THE PRESENCE OF GOD AND PEACE

The Sovereign God of Israel will bless *"His people with Peace"* (Ps. 29:11). But more than national blessing is involved in the Peace that God gives. David, fleeing from Absalom during that son's rebellion, felt intense pressure (Ps. 4:1-2). But David fixed his thoughts on God and remembered the joy that came with trust in Him. Comforted and at rest despite overwhelming danger, David concluded, *"I will lie down and sleep in Peace, for You Alone, O Lord, make me dwell in safety"* (Ps. 4:8).

For us as for David, Peace in difficult circumstances is a result of our relationship with the Lord. *"Great Peace,"* David says, *"have they who love Your Law"* (Ps. 119:165). The one whose life is in harmony with God's Revealed Will experiences inner harmony as well. It is not surprising, then, to find Psalm 37 contrast the *"wicked and ruthless"* with *"the man of Peace"* (Ps. 37:35-37).

The man of Peace lives in a right relationship with God, for God Alone is the Source of human rest and fulfillment. For those who have missed the Way of Faith and are struggling to find fulfillment apart from God, there is no such Blessing. As Isaiah warns, *"The wicked are like the tossing sea, which cannot rest, whose waves cast up mire and mud.*

"'There is no Peace,' says my God, 'for the wicked'" (Isa. 57:20-21).

THE PEACE OF GOD

Actually, the type of Peace of which we have spoken respecting David, etc., is really *"Sanctifying Peace"* or what one might refer to as *"The Peace of God."* Such is different than *"Peace with God"* which comes at Salvation. Every single Believer has *"Peace with God,"* but all Believers, regrettably, are not as David of old, able to sleep in the midst of obvious danger. Such is the *"Peace of God,"* or *"Sanctifying Peace,"* that comes with absolute trust in the Lord regarding all things. In other words, the Believer knows, as David of old, that whatever the situation, the Lord is in control. David had nothing in his heart against God, and had fully repented of all wrongdoing, so could expect that God would protect him. Consequently, he could sleep in *"Peace."*

The modern Believer should do the same. At least, this is the place to which the Holy Spirit is endeavoring to bring us, the place of total dependence on the Lord. Such is the *"Peace of God,"* and is the answer, to worry, anxiety, fear, stress, nervous disorders, and everyday vicissitudes of life. Such is a Blessing of unparalleled proportions.

THE PRINCE OF PEACE

The Prophets added yet another dimension to the theological shape of *"Peace."* God not only brings an inner harmony and Peace to those who live in a right relationship with Him, but He also intends to bring Peace to the Nations.

This Peace too will come only with God's Presence. The Prophets promised the coming of a *"Prince of Peace"* (Isa. 9:6) and looked forward to the day when *"of the increase of His Government and Peace there will be no end"* (Isa. 9:7).

God says that when the Messiah comes to establish His Kingdom and pour out His Spirit, *"The Fruit of Righteousness will be Peace; the effect of Righteousness will be quietness and confidence forever.*

"My people will live in peaceful dwelling places, in secure homes, in undisturbed places of rest" (Isa. 32:17-18).

One Old Testament Prophecy (Ezek. 34:20-31) declares that God will be Personally

Present and *"will be their God"* (Ezek. 34:24) and that David's descendant (The Lord Jesus Christ) will rule, confirming God's *"Covenant of Peace"* with His People (Ezek. 34:25).

Of course, Isaiah and Ezekiel are speaking of the coming Kingdom Age, which will commence immediately upon the Second Coming of The Lord Jesus Christ, and will usher in the greatest time of Peace the world has ever known. The reason is simple, the *"Prince of Peace"* is now present, and there can now be Peace.

The following is a beautiful thought but unknown by the world, that from the time that Jesus was born, until His Ascension approximately 33 1/2 years later, there was Peace in the world. It is said, that the great war gates of *"Janus"* in Rome were closed for the first time in their history, signifying that Roman Armies were at Peace all over the Roman Empire.

Little did Rome, or anyone else for that matter, know and understand, that the reason for this Peace was the Birth of a Child in a tiny place called Bethlehem. As well, almost no one knew that at the moment of His Birth the Angels sang, *"Glory to God in the highest, and on Earth Peace, good will toward men"* (Lk. 2:14).

Almost immediately upon the Ascension of Christ, war broke out again, and has continued ever since. Actually, Jesus said, *"And ye shall hear of wars and rumours of wars . . .*

"For Nation shall rise against Nation, and Kingdom against Kingdom . . ." (Mat. 24:6-7). The idea is, Israel rejected the *"Prince of Peace"*; consequently, the world was subjected to continued war and bloodshed, which has lasted now for approximately 2,000 years since Christ. As stated, only when He returns, will there be *"Peace"* for the Nations.

THE PRICE THAT JESUS PAID FOR OUR PEACE

Peace in the Old Testament, then, speaks of the blessing of inner and outer harmony that comes to a person or people who live in a close relationship with God. Believers can, like David, experience Peace despite dangerous circumstances by being conscious of God's Presence, or at least of His Sure Promises. Ultimately the world will know

international and interpersonal Peace as well, as the very Presence of God in the Person of Jesus halts strife and war.

But Peace is not purchased cheaply. Alienation from God and antagonism toward others flows from twisted human nature. Isaiah gives us a hint of the price of Peace in his description of the suffering servant:

"He was pierced for our transgressions, He was crushed for our iniquities; the punishment that brought us Peace was upon Him, and by His Wounds we are Healed" (Isa. 53:5).

THE PEACE OFFERING

One of the Old Testament Offerings was called the *"Peace Offering"* (Selem). It is mentioned over 80 times in the Old Testament. This Offering, which came after the Sin-Offering, was partially burned and partially eaten by the worshipers. Thus, it symbolized the *"Shalom,"* the overflowing joy and fulfillment, that forgiveness brings us, causing us to be at Peace with the Lord.

PEACE IN THE NEW TESTAMENT

The Greek word *"Eirene,"* originally referred to that orderly, prosperous life that is possible when there is no war. Only much later did Philosophers begin to apply the concept to an inner personal Peace.

But the New Testament use of *"eirene"* (90 occurrences) does not reflect the culture of the Greeks. Instead, *"Peace"* in the New Testament is defined and enriched by the Old Testament's *"Shalom."*

In every theologically significant use, *"Peace"* is something rooted in one's relationship with God and testifies to the restoration of human beings to inner harmony and to harmonious relationships with others. Our once-shattered lives are again made whole, and we become in Christ what God originally intended us to be. The vital health and wholeness of a restored humanity are available only in Jesus.

THE PEACE THAT JESUS BRINGS

Multiplied greetings and farewells in the Epistles are wishes that the believing readers will receive Grace, Mercy, and *"Peace."* This Peace is *"from God our Father, and from*

The Lord Jesus Christ" (Rom. 1:7; I Cor. 1:3; II Cor. 1:2; Gal. 1:3; Eph. 1:2; Phil. 1:2; Col. 1:2; II Thess. 1:2; I Tim. 1:2; II Tim. 1:2; Titus 1:4; Phile. vs. 3; II Jn. vs. 3). As in the Old Testament, the New Testament affirms that the Lord is *"The God of Peace"* — the Source and Bringer of Peace (Rom. 15:33; 16:20; I Cor. 14:33; Phil. 4:9; I Thess. 5:23; Heb. 13:20).

PEACE WITH GOD

First and foremost, the Peace human beings need, as stated, is Peace with God. This is ours only in Jesus; *"Since we have been Justified through Faith, we have Peace with God through our Lord Jesus Christ"* (Rom. 5:1). Ephesians 2:14 adds that Jesus *"Himself is our Peace."*

God's Peace may be an inner experience, but the wholeness that is suggested by *"Shalom"/"Eirene"* is also visibly expressed in the believing community. Among God's people, Peace means that hostility has been replaced by unity (Eph. 2:14-17; 4:3). It means order and harmony (I Cor. 14:33). It means a commitment to harmony that is as much the Christian's calling as is Holiness (II Tim. 2:22; Heb. 12:14).

Paul beautifully portrays Peace as it is experienced by the believing community living in fellowship with the Lord: *"As God's Chosen People, Holy and dearly loved, clothe yourselves with compassion, kindness, humility, gentleness and patience. Bear with each other and forgive whatever grievances you may have against one another. Forgive as the Lord forgave you. And over all these virtues put on Love, which binds them all together in perfect unity.*

"Let the Peace of Christ rule in your hearts, since as members of one Body you were called to Peace. And be thankful" (Col. 3:12-15).

PEACE DESPITE SUFFERING

Jesus warns His Disciples not to imagine that His Presence means they will be freed from external pressures and strife (Mat. 10:34; Lk. 12:51). Instead, Jesus focuses on Peace despite suffering.

John most clearly develops this theme. He reports Jesus' Words of Peace: *"Peace I leave*

NOTES

with you; My Peace I give you. I do not give to you as the world gives. Do not let your hearts be troubled and do not be afraid" (Jn. 14:27).

And then He said, *"I have told you these things, so that in Me you may have Peace. In this world you will have trouble. But take heart! I have overcome the world"* (Jn. 16:33). Jesus provides an inner Peace that lets the Believer face danger and suffering without fear or a trembling heart. Through Jesus, an inner Peace is possible, no matter how turbulent the external situation may be. This is, as stated, the *"Peace of God."*

In fact, the entirety of the New Testament links Peace directly to Jesus, even as the Old Testament points in that direction. God, the God of Peace, Who Alone brings Peace, has acted in Jesus to bring the Blessings of Peace to man. Peace with God should overflow in the experience of those who follow Christ — both in the quality of relationships among Believers as a community of Faith and in the inner life of each Believer.

(Most of the thoughts on Peace were supplied by Dr. Lawrence O. Richards.)

(16) "BUT THEY HAVE NOT ALL OBEYED THE GOSPEL. FOR ESAIAS (ISAIAH) SAITH, LORD, WHO HATH BELIEVED OUR REPORT?"

The phrase, *"But they have not all obeyed the Gospel,"* means that all who hear the Gospel, will not heed the Gospel, in other words will not *"obey."*

However, there is a slant in the Text, including verses 14 through 18, which insists, as should be obvious, upon every person in the world *hearing* the Gospel, therefore, having an opportunity to accept, whether they do or not. There seems to be an unction by the Holy Spirit in this regard. As stated, such should be obvious, due to the fact that Jesus died for all of humanity. However, for those who do not know, as previously stated, His Death is in vain. Nothing could be more tragic than that.

In this phrase, the Holy Spirit is warning the Preacher that not all will obey, and in fact, only a few will actually hear and believe (Mat. 7:14).

The question, *"For Esaias* (Isaiah) *saith, Lord, who hath believed our report?"*, comes from Isaiah 53:1.

Paul's statements are at least in part in response to the Jews, who evidently were claiming that if the Gospel of Jesus Christ was genuine, that all would receive its Message. He counters with the words of Isaiah, with the insinuation that very few would actually believe the *"report."*

That of which Isaiah was speaking, and Paul is reiterating, pertains to The Lord Jesus Christ. Despite Him truly being the Messiah, only a few actually believed in Him. In fact, almost none of the ruling Hierarchy of Israel believed in Him. In Truth, the way the Holy Spirit phrases the question through Isaiah, very few in Israel actually believed the *"report,"* i.e., Jesus Christ.

It is the same presently with the world. However, irrespective as to the small number who actually believe by comparison to those who hear, we are not to be discouraged, continuing to proclaim the Greatest Story every told.

(17) "SO THEN FAITH COMETH BY HEARING, AND HEARING BY THE WORD OF GOD."

The phrase, *"So then Faith cometh by hearing,"* means that Faith is out of the source of that which is heard. It is the publication of the Gospel which produces Faith in it (Alford).

The phrase, *"And hearing by the Word of God,"* concerns that which is heard. In other words, Faith does not come simply hearing just anything, but rather by *hearing God's Word.*

The idea is this: The sinner hears the Word of God as it is preached by the Power of the Holy Spirit, and accordingly, the sinner then either believes or disbelieves. If he tends to accept the Gospel, Faith begins to come, which means that the sinner begins to have confidence in what he is hearing. He believes, accepts, and is Saved.

However, such does not stop with Salvation. As the New Believer grows in Christ, his Faith continues to grow according to his knowledge of the Word of God. It is impossible otherwise!

That is the reason the Believer should make the Bible a lifelong study. If he is to have Faith, and if his Faith is to grow, it is

absolutely imperative that the Word of God be imbibed, studied, digested, and practiced daily. As well, it is absolutely impossible to exhaust the Word of God; consequently, it is impossible to exhaust the amount of Faith that one can have.

As the Believer *"keeps hearing"* what the Spirit is saying through the Word, Faith likewise, *"keeps coming."*

One of the major problems with Believers is, they are constantly reading books about the Bible, instead of the Bible. While some of the books may be very good, the Truth is, that most are not. To be frank, most books presently in Christian Bookstores, are little more than pop psychology. Consequently, even though the Word of God may be casually mentioned, it is only in passing.

For the Believer, there is nothing greater than his everyday study of the Word of God, or Commentaries on the Word, such as this very book. Anything that helps one understand the Scripture better, is of inestimable value.

(18) "BUT I SAY, HAVE THEY NOT HEARD? YES, VERILY, THEIR SOUND WENT INTO ALL THE EARTH, AND THEIR WORDS UNTO THE ENDS OF THE WORLD."

The question, *"But I say, Have they not heard?"*, proclaims Paul bringing the subject matter back to the Jews, with the previous verses dealing with them as well, but in a partial manner.

In fact, even though Paul is by and large speaking to the Church in verses 14 through 17, regarding World Evangelism, still, it cannot be fulfilled in totality until the coming Kingdom Age, which will definitely include the Jews.

When Isaiah originally uttered the words of verse 15, he closed it by saying, *"That saith unto Zion, Thy God reigneth"* (Isa. 52:7).

Only the Jews will be able to utter those words, and they will do so not long after the Second Coming, when Jesus rules and reigns, and they have accepted Him as Lord and Messiah. Then as Isaiah also said, *"The Earth shall be full of the knowledge of the Lord, as the waters cover the Sea"* (Isa. 11:9).

Respecting the Jews, and concerning the Gospel, there is a note of sarcasm in his question, *"Have they not heard?"*

The phrase, *"Yes, verily, their sound went*

into all the Earth, and their words unto the ends of the world," plainly proclaims the fact that Israel knew about Jesus Christ. Paul is actually quoting from Psalm 19:4. Even though this Passage speaks of the Revelation of God in nature, which actually has nothing to do with Salvation, still, Paul uses this verse respecting Israel's opportunity to hear and know the Gospel. The fact is, they knew the Gospel very well, but simply refused to believe. They would not believe, and in fact, could not believe, simply because they refused Jesus Christ.

One must remember, that Paul knew as no other person the extent to which the Gospel had been proclaimed in his day. It was as widely spread as the diaspora (the Jews scattered throughout the Roman Empire).

Actually, the word *"world"* is used not of the entirety of the planet concerning Paul's day, but to the extent of the Roman Empire.

Israel's rejection of God's Gift of Righteousness in Christ is predicted and declared in verses 14-21. They heard the Gospel, for Preachers Divinely sent announced it to them (vss. 14 and 15), but they did not obey it (vs. 16). It was a Message from God; and if they had listened to it and believed it (vs. 17) they would have become partakers of the Peace and the good things it proffered.

They all heard it for it was proclaimed throughout the whole world (vs. 18). This throws an interesting light upon the diffusion of the Scriptures throughout the whole known world, prior to, and at the time of, the First Advent (Williams).

(19) "BUT I SAY, DID NOT ISRAEL KNOW? FIRST MOSES SAITH, I WILL PROVOKE YOU TO JEALOUSY BY THEM THAT ARE NO PEOPLE, AND BY A FOOLISH NATION I WILL ANGER YOU."

The question, *"But I say, Did not Israel know?"*, pertains to the Gospel being given to the Gentiles, which it was after the Day of Pentecost. Israel also knew, as Paul will now recall, that it had been prophesied that Israel would reject the Gospel. Paul now calls these Prophecies into account.

The phrase, *"First Moses saith, I will provoke you to jealousy by them that are no people, and by a foolish Nation I will anger you,"* is derived from Deuteronomy

32:21. As far back as some 1600 years before Paul's day, Moses prophesied the acceptance of the Gospel by the Gentiles.

Did not Israel know these Texts? More so did they understand these Texts?

There was no reason they did not know, nor was there any reason for them not to understand. The problem was this:

Israel like so many modern Christians, promoted only the parts of the Word of God which fit their self-will. They imagined themselves as God's Chosen People, claiming great Righteousness while at the same time demeaning the Gentiles, when in reality, even though they spoke of the Lord with their lips, their hearts were far from Him (Mat. 15:7-9).

As well, they added awfully so to the Word of God, actually over 600 more Laws to the original Law of Moses. Many of them even claimed that these oral Laws were even more important than the original Laws given by God.

It happened exactly as the Holy Spirit said it would through Moses, Israel became *"jealous"* of the Gentiles who accepted the Lord, and they were *"angered"* by this wonderful and notable thing.

Whenever a Church or even the entirety of a Religious Denomination, begins to turn its back on God, these two things characterize their attitude, *"jealousy and anger."*

They become very jealous of the Moving and Operation of the Holy Spirit in the life or lives of others, and as well, they become *"angry."* In their self-righteousness, they reason that this should not be, finding themselves, at least in their own eyes, greatly superior to the ones being used by the Lord, whomever those individuals may be.

As Israel of old, instead of meeting such with Repentance and thanking God for what He is doing, they attempt to claim that it is not God, or else, whatever it is, it does not meet with their approval. And as Israel attempted to destroy Paul, as well, the modern variety has the same spirit. What they cannot control, they attempt to kill. However, I emphasize again, that these two works of the flesh *"jealousy and anger,"* are characteristics of a backslidden condition.

(20) "BUT ESAIAS IS VERY BOLD, AND SAITH, I WAS FOUND OF THEM

THAT SOUGHT ME NOT; I WAS MADE MANIFEST UNTO THEM THAT ASKED NOT AFTER ME."

The phrase, *"But Esaias* (Isaiah) *is very bold, and saith,"* is taken from Isaiah 65:1-2.

The phrase, *"I was found of them that sought Me not; I was made manifest unto them that asked not after Me,"* proclaims basically the same Message as that given by Moses. He predicts that the Gentiles will hear and receive the Gospel.

As we have previously stated, this Passage pretty well says the same thing as Romans 9:30.

The Gentile world, as stated, did not seek after God, because they did not believe in Jehovah. They worshiped and served their own gods, having no inclination toward Israel's God. The idea that He was the Creator of all things, was foreign to them. They simply did not believe it.

Up unto Alexander the Great, which was about 300 years before Christ, most Nations and Tribes credited their god, whatever they called him, with their military victories, etc. As well, they normally worshiped several gods, which played a major part in every facet of their lives, even with their clothing or the furniture in their homes modeled after their particular deity, whatever it was. These gods were called by various names, Baal, Bel, Chemosh, Asherah, Hadad, etc.

When one Nation or Kingdom was conquered by another, it was thought that the god of the conquering Nation was stronger than the god of the conquered, or perhaps, the ones vanquished were being punished by their god for whatever reason. However, most of the time the Nation defeated, was looked at as having an inferior god. That's the reason that Sennacherib the Assyrian Monarch ridiculed Jehovah when demanding the surrender of Jerusalem. He had recently defeated the Northern Kingdom of Israel, and believing that Jehovah was their God as well, he felt confident that his god (Ashur) could defeat Judah without any problem.

He did not realize that the Northern Kingdom of Israel had long since departed from Jehovah, and was now worshiping golden calves. Now when he truly comes up against Jehovah of Judah, Who Alone is God, with his god no more than an invention of man,

NOTES

he was to find out Who Jehovah actually was. It would be an expensive lesson (II Chron. 32:17-21).

So, the Gentiles of Paul's day, were not seeking the Lord, nor were they asking about Him. However, when the Gospel was presented to them, the Holy Spirit began to convict their hearts, and they began to accept Christ as their Saviour, and thus became the Church. Whereas the Church had begun exclusively Jewish, and in Jerusalem at that, it soon became almost exclusively Gentile.

(21) "BUT TO ISRAEL HE SAITH, ALL DAY LONG I HAVE STRETCHED FORTH MY HANDS UNTO A DISOBEDIENT AND GAINSAYING PEOPLE."

The phrase, *"But to Israel he saith,"* continues the Prophecy of Isaiah 65:1-2.

The phrase, *"All day long I have stretched forth My Hands unto a disobedient and gainsaying people,"* predicts not only that the Gentiles would hear and receive the Gospel, but as well, that Israel would reject it. Irrespective, even after they murdered their Messiah, the Holy Spirit would keep appealing to them through the Ministry of the Apostles, and strongly so through the Apostle Paul, but to no avail.

The idea is of God stretching both Hands toward them, pleading that they would come to Him. He promises to accept them even though they have been *"a disobedient and gainsaying people."*

As well, in the fulfillment of the Prophecy of Isaiah, which pertained to Paul's day, the appeal would be heavy, for the simple reason, that in a few short years Israel would be totally destroyed as a Nation. This would happen in A.D. 70. A continued rejection of the Lord by Israel, guaranteed a coming Judgment. There was no alternative!

By their rejection, the majority of Israel by their self-will and unbelief fashioned themselves into vessels of wrath, for they rejected Christ as announced by the Prophets, by the Law, and by the Gospel.

THE DECLARATION OF THE GOSPEL

In this Chapter, as in the prior one, the entire argument of Paul and its dogmatic statements, are based upon the Divine and conclusive foundation of the Inspired

Scriptures, which should be overly obvious (Williams).

The Gospel is thus set out in this Chapter:

Its provisions: Life (vs. 13) and Righteousness (vs. 4).

Its simplicity: within reach (hand), well-known (mouth), easily understood (heart) (vs. 8).

Its conditions: Faith and submission (vs. 9).

Its freeness: *"Whosoever"* (vs. 11).

As I dictate these notes on Saturday morning, December 13, 1997, I have just returned from preaching a funeral.

I did not know the deceased, having only seen him a few hours in the Hospital before his demise. Actually, even though Donnie and I prayed for him, he was unconscious and really did not know we were there.

His wife insinuated, that he really had not known the Lord as his Saviour. At least, that is the way I understood her statements.

She related to me how that he had begun watching our Telecast several months before his death. She mentioned as to how he would not miss a single Program, and irrespective as to who was there, or what other type of programs were on other Channels, he demanded that our Program be watched. His wife who is a Believer, had been praying for him for many years. The Holy Spirit knowing that this man was soon going to die, began to deal with his heart and used our Program to do so. To be sure, it was not me, but the Gospel I preach.

At any rate, about four days before he died, one of our Associate Pastors had gone to visit him in the Hospital. On this particular day, he was lucid, therefore, able to understand what was being said. Dave prayed the Sinner's Prayer with him, and due to the months of the Gospel being preached to him by Television, he made Jesus his Saviour just hours before he died.

When I stood there that day to preach the funeral, even though I had no knowledge of this man's history except recent days, still there was a joy that filled my heart as I began to minister to his family. I knew he was Saved and at that moment with The Lord Jesus Christ.

Much of the world cannot accept or understand how that one can be Saved that

NOTES

quickly. Even many in the Church desire to add something to the Great Finished Work of Christ. But Salvation is not of works, lest any man should boast, it is the Gift of God. As Paul said, *"For by Grace are ye Saved through Faith"* (Eph. 2:8-9).

This man was Saved in his last hours by simply believing in his heart that Jesus had died for him, and then accepting Him as his Saviour. It was that simple, because it is meant to be that simple.

As I have briefly given this man's Testimony, I could give the Testimonies of untold numbers of others who have been convicted by the Holy Spirit as we have preached the Gospel by Television or in Crusades, and have given their hearts and lives to The Lord Jesus Christ. I speak not only of the United States and Canada, but many of the Nations in the world, with the Program translated into various different languages. There is nothing more important than the Gospel of Jesus Christ. There is nothing more important than the Salvation of souls. We only understand its vast significance, when we begin to understand the terrible price paid by the Lord for the Redemption of mankind. Then and only then, do we get a true picture of an eternal soul.

"Cross of Jesus, Cross of sorrow,
"Where the Blood of Christ was shed,
"Perfect Man on thee did suffer, Perfect God on thee has bled!

"Hear the King of all the ages,
"Throned in light ere worlds could be,
"Robed in mortal flesh is dying, crucified by sin for me.

"Oh mysterious condescending!
"Oh abandonment sublime!
"Very God Himself is bearing all the sufferings of time!

"Evermore for human failure,
"By His passion we can plead;
"God has born all mortal anguish; surely He will know our need."

CHAPTER 11

(1) "I SAY THEN, HATH GOD CAST

AWAY HIS PEOPLE? GOD FORBID. FOR I ALSO AM AN ISRAELITE, OF THE SEED OF ABRAHAM, OF THE TRIBE OF BENJAMIN."

The question, *"I say then, Hath God cast away His people?"*, is so phrased in the Greek Text that it requires a negative answer. Actually, Paul is not raising a question. He is driving home the fact that God did not, and has not, cast Israel away.

This 11th Chapter of Romans is to be added to the myriad of Prophecies in the Old Testament concerning the Restoration of these ancient people (Isa. 11:11; 14:1-2; 27:12-13; 43:5-6; 66:20; Jer. 3:17-18; 23:3-8; 24:5-7; 30:3; 31:40; 33:6-26; 46:27-28; 50:19-20; Ezek. 11:17-20; 16:60-63; 20:33-44; 28:25-26; 36:6-38; Hos. 1:10-11; 3:4-5; Joel Chpt. 3; Amos 9:9-15; Obad. vss. 7-21; Micah 2:12-13; 4:1-8; 5:3-15; Zeph. 2:7; 3:20; Zech. 2:8-13; 8:1-8; Chpts. 12-14; Mal. 3:2-5; 4:1-6, etc.).

Actually we have given only a few of the references in the Old Testament which predict the coming Restoration of Israel, which other than the predictions of the Coming Lord Himself, is the most solid, pronounced prediction in the entirety of the Old Testament, and the New for that matter. Consequently, how any Preacher could read any of these predictions by the Prophets of old, and especially this 11th Chapter of Romans, and continue to come to a conclusion that Israel is no more, is beyond my comprehension.

Paul will discuss in this Chapter how that Israel has been set aside respecting the great Plan of God for these people, because of their terrible rebellion. He will now discuss how the Church has stepped in to take their place, at least at this time, respecting the great Work of God on Earth. However, he plainly proclaims, even as the Prophets of old, that Israel will be restored, although in this Chapter he only alludes to the fact and does not go into any detail. However, we know from Ezekiel, Chapters 37-48 and Zechariah Chapters 12-14, that this will take place at the Second Coming. Of course, there are many other references to this particular time as well.

To throw Israel out, as many in the modern Church are attempting to do, is to deny one of the Cardinal Truths of the Word of God concerning their Restoration. To be sure, it is not that the people of Israel are of such special consideration, but rather the Plan of God. Concerning Bible Prophecy, if Preachers, or anyone for that matter, do not have at least a working knowledge of future events as taught in the Word of God, that might be a clue that they do not know too very much about present events either. In other words, the entirety of their Gospel presentation just might be skewed.

NOTES

THREE REASONS

Paul is going into great detail respecting this subject and for particular reasons. They are as follows:

1. The Holy Spirit desired that he do so.

As we have said over and over, inasmuch as Israel figures so prominently in the Plan of God, the Church must not lose sight of that fact. To do so is to misunderstand the entirety of God's Plan, which in essence will confuse all issues. At the same time, when one considers that the great Prophecies of old respecting these people, are already beginning to be fulfilled, the entirety of the present Body of Christ should be immensely interested in these things.

2. Israel had recently murdered her Messiah, and was continuing to oppose the Gospel, ever continuing to grow harder, which was pointing toward sure judgment. Consequently, many during Paul's time were no doubt wondering as to exactly where these people stood in the Plan of God at present. Were they cast off entirely? Considering what they had done, had they forfeited all rights and even abrogated the Prophecies of old? These questions were no doubt in the minds of many at that time, and especially considering the many Prophecies, Paul is led by the Holy Spirit to address this very important subject.

3. In Chapter 2 of Romans, Paul had addressed the Jewish question of exclusive Salvation very strongly. In other words, he had completely shot to pieces the Jewish claim that they were the only bearers of the Light, and that all Gentiles were excluded, unless they became Jewish proselytes, etc. In the great Gospel Plan of Salvation, which Christ afforded by His Death, Resurrection,

JIMMY SWAGGART BIBLE COMMENTARY

and Ascension, and to which the Old Testament constantly pointed, Paul places all, Jews and Gentiles alike, on the same ground, and, therefore, having to come in the same identical way. In other words, all were lost and all could be Saved. However, all must be Saved, and in fact could be Saved only by accepting Christ. Of course, this infuriated the Jewish Leadership of Israel at that time. To be frank, it did not set too well even with the Jews who were followers of Christ. As the record shows in the Book of Acts, they were still attempting to cling to the old Mosaic Law, while at the same time trusting Christ. Actually, this is the very thing that Paul hit so hard in his Epistles.

ISRAEL AND SALVATION

Having addressed himself in this manner to the question of Salvation, which the Book of Romans is all about, some may have gotten the opinion that he was writing off the Jews as a people and as they related to the great Promises of God. Consequently, he addresses this issue, projecting the very opposite.

It should be understood, however, in Paul's question, *"Hath God cast away His people?"*, that by him using the term *"His people,"* referring to God's people, Israel, he is referring only to their place in the Plan of God, and not to personal Salvation.

Actually, this is his very contention, that Israel does not have Salvation simply because they were chosen of God. However, they came to believe that all the rights and privileges granted them, translated into Salvation, which it did not. Even as we have previously stated, there were always only a Remnant in Israel who truly knew the Lord, with all others, sadly and regrettably, being lost. In fact, every single Jew who has ever been Saved, even from the very beginning, has had to be Saved in the same manner even as Gentiles, i.e., by accepting Christ. There has never been but one way of Salvation, and that is Jesus.

It was to Jesus, ever Jesus, to Whom the Sacrifices ever pointed, even from the Garden of Eden. It is to Calvary now, that great, supreme Sacrifice, to which all of history points, be it past, present, or future.

(Of course when one mentions Calvary it

automatically assumes the Resurrection.)

ISRAEL'S FUTURE

The following is an abbreviated account of Israel at present, and what the Bible predicts concerning their future:

1. According to the Prophecies, Israel must be restored to her homeland as a Nation. In fact, this was done in 1948. All the many Scriptures given at the beginning of this Chapter concerning her Restoration demand this.

Isaiah prophesied that Israel would be *"outcasts"* all over the world, and would be gathered together from many Nations. He even said, *". . . The four corners of the Earth"* (Isa. 11:11-12). This is exactly what happened in 1948, and has continued even unto this very hour, with the several hundreds of thousands coming from Russia being only the latest gathering.

In fact, this is the reason that Adolph Hitler instigated the Holocaust, murdering some 6 million of these people. Of course, he did not know the reason why, but Satan through him, was attempting to slaughter so many that they would not be able to establish a Nation. In fact, the Holocaust was the most horrifying event in human history. Its magnitude only tends to signify the significance of the great prophetic events which are about to be fulfilled in the world. In other words, we are living in the last of the last days.

2. Israel will accept the Antichrist as the Messiah:

Actually, the Antichrist will not be revealed until after the Rapture (Resurrection) of the Church (I Thess. 4:13-18; II Thess. 2:3-12). So, considering that this is soon to come, this should tell the Church how close we are to the Resurrection.

Jesus pointedly spoke of this time when He said, *"I am come in My Father's Name, and you received me not: if another* (the Antichrist) *shall come in his own name, him you will receive"* (Jn. 5:43). As well, Daniel spoke graphically of this coming time (Dan. 8:23-25; 9:27; 11:35-45; 12:1).

In 1996 (I believe it was) Israel signed the Palestinian Accords, thinking it would help bring peace to the region. However, it has not brought peace, even as it cannot bring peace. Consequently, the problems of Israel and the Middle East will continue to increase, until the Advent of the man of sin, i.e., the Antichrist.

When this man makes his appearance on the scene, he will come at first in the capacity of peace (Dan. 9:27; Rev. 6:1-2). He will be inspired by Satan as no other human being in history. In fact, and to use modern vernacular, this will be Satan's trump card.

Israel will accept him as the Messiah, which means he will be a Jew. In fact, the entirety of the world will praise him and for many and varied reasons. At the outset, he will satisfy the Israeli/Palestinian problem, i.e., Moslem problem, etc. Bringing peace to this troubled region, will greatly increase his stature throughout the world. Israel will announce to the world at that time, even as Jesus predicted, that their Messiah has finally come, and the world at that time will rejoice with her.

In fact, the Antichrist will sign a seven-year treaty with Israel and many other Nations, which will bring about all of these great happenings of peace, etc. (Dan. 9:27).

3. The Antichrist will break his agreement with Israel:

As Israel will be lulled even deeper into her spiritual sleep, thinking that this evil one is her Messiah, he will show his true colors, breaking his agreement with Israel at the midpoint of this seven-year treaty, actually attacking her and defeating her for the first time since she became a Nation in 1948 (Dan. 8:9-14, 23-26; 9:27).

In fact, the Antichrist, at least for a short period of time, will change his headquarters to Jerusalem, actually taking over the Temple.

4. Israel's terrible time:

This period is that referred to by the Prophet Jeremiah as *"... The Time of Jacob's Trouble..."* (Jer. 30:7). As well, John prophesied on the Isle of Patmos, that at this time they would flee *". . . Into the wilderness, where she hath a place prepared of God ..."* (Rev. 12:6). Actually, at this time, the Antichrist would completely destroy Israel but for the protection of the Lord, also prophesied by John (Rev. 12:13-16). As well, the Antichrist at this time according to Daniel,

NOTES

will be distracted by other events, and will go North and East to fight great battles, which will give Israel a time of respite (Dan. 11:44).

5. The Battle of Armageddon:

After the Antichrist defeats other enemies, which will take the better part of three years, consolidating his forces, he will then come down upon Israel, who will then have filtered back into Jerusalem, in what is known as the Battle of Armageddon (Rev. 16:16). Ezekiel gives the full account in Chapters 38 and 39 of his Book.

Why is the Antichrist so determined to destroy Israel considering that she is of little consequence as a Nation, and at this time friendless in the world?

Empowered by Satan, the Antichrist will know of the predictions of the Prophets in the Word of God concerning the Restoration of these people. If he can destroy them, then the Word of God falls to the ground, and in effect, Satan has won. Consequently, he will reserve his greatest effort against Israel.

6. The Second Coming of the Lord:

Zechariah prophesies that the Antichrist will come very close to succeeding in his efforts, even with two-thirds of the Jews being killed at this time, even with half of Jerusalem falling to the man of sin (Zech. 13:8; 14:1-2).

Facing total extinction, Israel will then begin to call on God for her Messiah as she has not heretofore done. In Truth, this is the major reason for the coming Great Tribulation, the humbling of Israel, and bringing her back to God. To be sure, she will be heard by the Lord, with the Scripture saying, *"Then shall the Lord go forth, and fight against those Nations, as when He fought in the Day of Battle"* (Zech. 14:3).

This is the Second Coming, and that which will rescue Israel, defeating the Antichrist, with Jesus Personally leading this great charge, even accompanied by every Saint of God who has ever lived (Zech. 14:3; Rev. 19:11-21).

7. The Restoration:

Then Israel will repent, accepting Jesus as her Messiah and Saviour, restored to her rightful place as the leading Nation of the world (Zech. 13:1-6; 14:8-21).

As well, the Prophet Ezekiel proclaims as to how Israel will function as the leading Nation in the coming Kingdom Age under Christ (Ezek. Chpts. 40-48).

The phrase, *"God forbid,"* proclaims Paul's answer to the question, *"Hath God cast away His people?"*

The phrase, *"For I also am an Israelite, of the seed of Abraham, of the Tribe of Benjamin,"* presents an interesting statement concerning the people of Israel.

An Israelite was seen as a member of the theocracy and thus, an heir of the Promises God gave to that Nation. Actually, *"Israelite"* is the most august title of the three names, *"Israelite, Hebrew, and Jew."*

The title *"Hebrew,"* at least in Paul's day, spoke of a Hebrew-speaking Jew against a Greek-speaking Jew. The name or title *"Jew"* referred to national distinction relative to a Gentile.

The phrase, *"The seed of Abraham,"* refers to the true lineage of Isaac and not Ishmael. (The Moslems claim Ishmael as the true seed, while the Jews, as well as the Church, claims Isaac, Gen. 17:19-21.)

Paul was proud of his tribal affiliation of Benjamin, in that this Tribe remained with Judah when the Nation broke apart after the death of Solomon (I Ki. Chpt. 12).

(2) "GOD HATH NOT CAST AWAY HIS PEOPLE WHICH HE FOREKNEW. WOT YE NOT WHAT THE SCRIPTURE SAITH OF ELIAS? HOW HE MAKETH INTERCESSION TO GOD AGAINST ISRAEL, SAYING,"

The phrase, *"God hath not cast away His people which He foreknew,"* refers to Israel as a Nation, and the many Promises made respecting the future of these ancient people. Thus, the Covenant of God with Israel, having been national, shall ultimately be fulfilled to them as a Nation: not by the gathering in merely of individual Jews, or of all the Jews individually, into the Christian Church — but by the National Restoration of the Jews, not in unbelief, but as a Christian believing Nation, to all that can, under the Gospel, represent their ancient preeminence, and to the fullness of those Promises which have never yet in their plain sense been accomplished in them (De Wette).

"Foreknew" in the Greek is *"proginosko,"*

and means *"the appointing of a person or people to a certain destiny."*

GOD'S SELECTION

The idea is, that God in His Own Eternal Decree before the world was ever created, selected as the chosen Nation, these people, to be His Own. They would be the depository of His Law, the vehicle of the theocracy, from its first Revelation to its completion in Christ's future Kingdom. Consequently, this makes their rejection incredible or rather impossible.

In essence, Paul is saying that God knew what Israel was before He chose her as a Nation. He knew from the first what it would be. Israel stood before God's Eyes from Eternity as His People, and in the immutableness of the Sovereign Love with which He made these people His, lies the impossibility of her rejection.

In other words, Israel was predestined as a people by God for certain things, and to be sure, God's Plan for these people will be fulfilled in totality, with not one single Promise falling to the ground in any capacity.

WHAT DOES THAT MEAN EXACTLY?

Predestination or *"foreknowledge"* as Paul here uses the word, does not refer to every single Jew being Saved, even as the following Scriptures prove. In fact, most Jews were not Saved, and, consequently, died eternally lost.

However, there was always a Remnant who truly served the Lord, and it is through this Remnant that the Lord worked in Old Testament times.

All down through the many centuries since their rejection of Christ, the Lord has watched over them as a people, even though they have suffered terribly. In fact, only a precious few during this long period of time have actually been Saved. However, as a particular people, even in all their wanderings, God has guided them from afar. He has kept them from destruction, even despite Satan's greatest efforts in that capacity, in order that His future Plan for them will be fulfilled, which it shall in the coming Kingdom Age. As well, it seems that then, the entirety of the Nation of Israel will truly follow the Lord, which is something that was never done in the past (Zech. 13:1-6).

The question, *"Wot ye not what the Scripture saith of Elias* (Elijah)*?"*, is taken from I Kings 19:10, 14.

The phrase, *"How he maketh Intercession to God against Israel, saying,"* presents an interesting statement.

The answer to Elijah by the Lord, even as we shall see, portrays the thought, I think, that the Prophet should have pleaded *for* Israel and not against Israel.

The petition to the Lord by any Believer, and especially one of the status of Elijah, carries tremendous weight. In fact, and as we have addressed in the past, this refers to the *"Authority of the Believer"* (Jn. 14:12-14; 15:7; 16:23).

Due to the power of the Believer's petition, this is at least one of the reasons that Jesus told us to, *". . . Love your enemies, bless them that curse you, do good to them that hate you, and pray for them which despitefully use you, and persecute you"* (Mat. 5:44).

Paul might have said something similar of his own time, for his circumstances were not totally unlike those of Elijah. The Apostle, like the Prophet, was lonely and persecuted, and Israel as a whole seemed to have abandoned God or been abandoned by Him. But, due to the great Covenant of Grace, Paul understands God's Way and His Faithfulness better than that Prophet of old. Consequently, he pleads *for* them.

(3) "LORD, THEY HAVE KILLED THY PROPHETS, AND DIGGED DOWN THINE ALTARS; AND I AM LEFT ALONE, AND THEY SEEK MY LIFE."

The phrase, *"Lord, they have killed Thy Prophets,"* at this particular time, referred to the Northern Kingdom of Israel, to whom Elijah had been sent. The account of his Ministry is given in I Kings Chapters 17-22, and II Kings Chapters 1-2.

Bible history records that the Northern Kingdom of Israel had not one righteous king, and in fact rebelled totally against God, worshiping golden calves, etc. They survived as a Nation for about 250 years. Even though the Scripture does not give the account, it is obvious from the statement of Elijah, that some Prophets were killed during this time

NOTES

under the rulership of some of these wicked kings (I Ki. 18:4).

The phrase, *"And digged down thine Altars,"* means to destroy, or to demolish. In other words, the true worship of God at that time, was forsaken, and in its place idols were substituted (I Ki. 12:28-33).

The phrase, *"And I am left alone, and they seek my life,"* presents that spoken by the Prophet which was only partially correct. It was true that they did seek his life, but it was not correct that he was the only one in the Northern Kingdom of Israel who truly served the Lord, even as the Lord will now answer him.

(4) "BUT WHAT SAITH THE ANSWER OF GOD UNTO HIM? I HAVE RESERVED TO MYSELF SEVEN THOUSAND MEN, WHO HAVE NOT BOWED THE KNEE TO THE IMAGE OF BAAL."

The question, *"But what saith the answer of God unto him?"*, proclaims to us detail which is very important, not only regarding that which happened so long ago with Israel, but as well with every modern Believer.

The phrase, *"I have reserved to myself seven thousand men, who have not bowed the knee to the image of Baal,"* presents Paul adding the words *"to Myself,"* to the statement given by God to Elijah in I Kings 19:18. Consequently, several things are said here:

1. First of all we are told in this Passage, that God is very jealous over each one of His Children. The Text proclaims the fact that the spiritual condition of each one is known minutely to the Lord, and Jealously guarded.

2. In the exact number being given, we learn just how important these people are and in fact, continue to be.

3. Paul being led by the Holy Spirit to add the two words *"to Myself"* suggests that God has a purpose of His Own which is identified with these people. God has reserved the seven thousand; He has reserved them for Himself. In fact, this is proof that He had not cast them off, and in fact, there has always been a certain number of Jews who have eagerly served Christ. Of course, the Lord numbers each believing Gentile in the same manner.

4. The proof of the Faith of these Israelites of old, was that they *"had not bowed the*

knee to the image of Baal." This tells us that True Faith always has the attachment of spiritual action. In other words, it will always fall out to the upholding of God's Standard, in this case the refusal of the image of the idol. To be sure, as was no doubt true, those who were placed in this category, endangered their lives, with some even possibly forfeiting their lives for their Biblical stand. No less is demanded presently!

(5) "EVEN SO THEN AT THIS PRESENT TIME ALSO THERE IS A REMNANT ACCORDING TO THE ELECTION OF GRACE."

The phrase, *"Even so then at this present time also there is a Remnant,"* brings the situation from the time of Elijah, up to Paul's day. The *"time"* to which Paul had reference was strategic, one marked by the inclusion of the Gentiles together with the Jews in the one Body of Christ, a time at which, while the Gentiles gladly received the Word, Israel was apostate, a time at which despite Israel's apostasy, there was a *"Remnant"* in Israel Saved who had not followed their Leaders into rebellion (Wuest).

In fact, even at that particular time, there were possibly some 50,000 Jewish Saints in Jerusalem alone, with others in most every Church planted by the Apostle Paul over the Roman Empire, which no doubt included those planted by the Apostles and others as well.

THE REMNANT

"Remnant" in the Greek is *"lima,"* and means *"to leave."* Thus, a Remnant is that which is left, in other words, a select group.

As we have previously stated, not only was it true of Israel that throughout the entirety of their existence, only a *"Remnant"* had truly served the Lord, the same holds true in the Church. Untold numbers profess, but there is only a *"Remnant"* with God Alone knowing the exact number, even as He did with Israel of old, who are truly Born Again.

The phrase, *"According to the Election of Grace,"* definitely speaks of Predestination, but not as many think.

It is the *"Remnant"* that is elected or predestined, and not who will be in the Remnant. The number in the *"Remnant"* is pulled strictly from *"Whosoever will,"* and is

guaranteed by the word *"Grace."*

"Election" in the Greek is *"eclogue,"* and means *"to pick out, to choose out from a number."* However, the word *"Grace"* describes how that number is chosen out. The ground or motivating factor in this choice of certain in Israel, or presently in the Church for that matter, who were and are objects of the choice of God for Salvation, was and is Grace, the spontaneous overflowing Love of God bestowing the Gift of Salvation upon anyone who will meet God's conditions.

For *"Grace"* to be Grace, that which is offered, in this case Salvation, must be freely given, and freely received. In other words, if God predestined certain ones to be Saved as is commonly taught respecting *"Predestination"* or *"Election"* then it is impossible of Grace.

In effect, all of Israel and all the world for that matter, are called to become God's Elect or chosen ones, and can be if they will choose God. In other words, the matter is not left up to the Lord, for He has already made His Will known regarding the Salvation of all mankind (II Pet. 3:9), but to the personal choice of the individual himself (Mat. 11:28-30; 20:16; Jn. 1:12; 3:16-20; 6:37; Eph. 1:4; II Thess. 2:13; I Tim. 2:4; James 2:5; Rev. 17:14; 22:17).

(6) "AND IF BY GRACE, THEN IS IT NO MORE OF WORKS: OTHERWISE GRACE IS NO MORE GRACE. BUT IF IT BE OF WORKS, THEN IS IT NO MORE GRACE: OTHERWISE WORK IS NO MORE WORK."

The phrase, *"And if by Grace, then is it no more of works,"* proclaims the manner of Salvation. Several things are said:

1. Salvation is one hundred percent by Grace. That means that no one, not even the Jews of old could point to their religious works as grounds for Salvation, and neither can anyone else for that matter.

2. The moment that *"works"* are added in any capacity, at that moment *"Grace"* is nullified.

3. Salvation by Grace in its most simple form, means that the sinner does not deserve such, and in fact can do nothing within himself to deserve such, and that God freely gives, simply out of the purity, love, and

goodness of His Heart. The only thing required on the part of the sinner, is Faith. In other words, the sinner believes that Jesus is the Son of God, and died on Calvary for the sinner, and rose from the dead on the third day. If he truly believes that, accepting Christ as his Saviour, he is at that moment truly Saved (Jn. 3:16; Rom. 10:9-10, 13; Rev. 22:17).

The phrase, *"Otherwise Grace is no more Grace,"* proclaims as stated, that the addition of any works, nullifies this great Gift of God. In fact, this is one of the single most important verses in the entirety of the Word of God.

The greatest problem in the Church is, and always has been, the Church attempting to add something to the Finished Work of Christ. Of course, if it is finished, it needs nothing added.

For instance, most Catholics believe that one has to be a member of the Catholic Church, and faithful to its Sacraments so-called, in order to be Saved. That is *"works"* pure and simple, which nullifies the Grace of God, and means that very few Catholics actually are Saved, which should be overly obvious.

However, even as we have previously stated, this problem is not limited to Catholicism, but is rife in Protestant Churches as well. For instance, many Baptists believe that unless one is associated with their particular Church, that one is not Saved. That as well, is *"works."* A certain segment of Pentecostals believe that one has to be Baptized in Water using a certain formula, and speak in Tongues in order to be Saved. That as well, nullifies the Grace of God. Many Seventh Day Adventists believe that one has to keep the old Jewish Sabbath, with many in the Church of Christ believing that one has to be Baptized in Water, etc. In fact, the list is almost endless.

Paul's words scream out at us, and due to their simplicity, must not be taken lightly. The moment that one inserts anything into the Finished Work of Christ other than Faith, at that moment, the Grace of God is nullified, and that means the individual is not Saved.

The phrase, *"But if it be of works, then is it no more Grace,"* is a repetition of the previous phrase, but said in a little different way. The Holy Spirit desires to make certain that no one misunderstand.

The phrase, *"Otherwise work is no more work,"* is very important as well!

The Holy Spirit through the Apostle is not meaning to denigrate *"works,"* only their wrong disposition, i.e., attempting to bring about Salvation by works, which cannot be done. In fact, *"works" are* very important, but must be kept in their rightful place.

Water Baptism is important, as well as the Lord's Supper, etc. In fact, any good thing done for the Lord is important.

Of course, the Law of Moses given to Israel, was very important, respecting its Feast Days, Circumcision, Sabbath-keeping, etc. The Moral Law was of utmost importance. So, the idea is not to demean all of these things, but rather that they not be wrongly used.

The idea is, that if any of these great and true things given by God and extremely helpful in their place, are wrongly used, their veracity is then impugned.

In other words, Water Baptism looked at and acted upon wrongly, nullifies its true meaning, which holds true as well for all other great Ordinances of the Lord. That is why Paul said, *"Otherwise work is no more work."*

(7) "WHAT THEN? ISRAEL HATH NOT OBTAINED THAT WHICH HE SEEKETH FOR; BUT THE ELECTION HATH OBTAINED IT, AND THE REST WERE BLINDED."

The question, *"What then?"*, was asked by Paul regarding Israel, but can also apply to the Church as well! The answer as we shall see is blunt, and should be taken very seriously, especially considering that Paul is discussing the Salvation of the soul.

The phrase, *"Israel hath not obtained that which he seeketh for,"* emphatically states that Salvation cannot be obtained in any manner or way other than God's Way. If God would not allow Israel to come in by her works, how in the world do Gentiles think they can follow the same course and be successful? Actually, this is the very crux of the argument.

Israel demanded that her 2,000 years of history had earned them something. Especially considering that they were God's Chosen, the people of the Law, the people of the Book, the people of the Prophets, surely they thought, this earned them something!

In fact, it earned them much, but not Salvation. As we shall see, Paul will warn the Gentiles that if Israel could not qualify on the basis of works, most assuredly the Gentiles cannot.

The phrase, *"But the election hath obtained it,"* refers to the Jews who did not attempt to claim Salvation by merit, but rather by Grace (the Election of Grace).

In fact, God elected that the entirety of Israel would be Saved, but it was only those who elected to go God's Way, which was and is the Way of Grace, who in fact, obtained Salvation. So, *"Election"* actually works two ways, and in fact, must do so, in order that the prize be obtained.

The phrase, *"And the rest were blinded,"* refers to a judicial blindness. In other words, if men demand their own way, instead of God's Way, *"blindness"* will always be the result.

"Blinded" in the Greek is *"poroo,"* and means *"to cover with a thick skin, to harden by covering with a callous,"* metaphorically, *"to make the heart dull"* (Jn. 12:40) (Wuest).

(8) "(ACCORDING AS IT IS WRITTEN, GOD HATH GIVEN THEM THE SPIRIT OF SLUMBER, EYES THAT THEY SHOULD NOT SEE, AND EARS THAT THEY SHOULD NOT HEAR;) UNTO THIS DAY."

The phrase, *"According as it is written,"* is taken from Isaiah 6:10; 29:10.

The phrase, *"God hath given them the spirit of slumber,"* pertains to the judicial blindness.

"Slumber" in the Greek is *"katanuxis,"* and means *"severe sorrow, extreme grief, insensibility or torpor of mind, a spirit of stupor."*

Once again, the Lord did not arbitrarily do this thing, but such is the result of *"sowing and reaping."* If men do certain things, such as resist God's Way, God has ordained that certain things will naturally follow in its course. In this case, judicial blindness. God cannot be blamed for the situation, but rather the stubbornness of the individuals involved.

LIGHT REFUSED

In effect, this proclaims to us, and even as

NOTES

I have said many times in past Commentary, if Light is given and refused, not only is the Light lost which is offered, but even what little Light the person has previously had is lost as well. That is the reason Jesus said, and concerning this very thing, *". . . And the last state of that man is worse than the first . . ."* (Mat. 12:45).

The phrase, *"Eyes that they should not see, and ears that they should not hear,"* refers to not being able to *"see"* even though the evidence is plainly visible, or to *"hear"* even though the words are plainly said. Paul is addressing something here that is extremely serious, which should be obvious.

This has to do with unbelief, and as is all unbelief, it pertains to evidence rejected, even though obvious and plain. Such is the Gospel Program.

The Plan of God for the Salvation of man is so absolutely clear, plain, and simple, that there is no reason for anyone not to understand. Of course, I speak of those who have had the privilege to hear the Gospel, but have rejected the Gospel. When that happens, this willful rejection, the individual is left more calloused and hardened, making it even more difficult to accept or believe once the Gospel is presented again. In fact, with each rejection, the situation becomes more and more serious, with the person becoming more and more hardened. Such can easily affect Believers as well!

BELIEVERS

If a Believer refuses added Light, the same *"spiritual blindness"* and *"spiritual deafness"* sets in upon him as well. God's Revelation has always been progressive. If progression is denied, ultimately what Light the Believer presently has, is also withdrawn.

Even though the situation involves many directions, I will use the Baptism with the Holy Spirit as an example.

When the Light of this Biblical experience began to be given at approximately the turn of the century, which fulfilled Joel's Prophecies concerning the Latter Rain outpouring (Joel 2:23), as should be obvious, it was available to all. In fact, many old-line Denominational people did receive. However, as a whole, it was rejected by the Leadership of these respective Denominations.

God in His patience continued to deal with these people, but with each rejection, their spiritual sensibilities were more and more hardened. As a result, and for all practical purposes, these particular Denominations have pretty much been set aside, as far as the Work of God is concerned. They rejected the Light that was given; consequently, they not only lost that Light, but what little Light they did have.

Regrettably, major Pentecostal Denominations are following in the same train. If anything, their situation is worse, because they are rejecting Light which they had once enjoyed. For Light to be rejected when it is offered is bad enough, but to be rejected after it has been received, is worse than all.

The phrase, *"Unto this day,"* refers to a condition that will not correct itself, but actually grows worse.

Despite the greatest array of Miracles the world had ever known referring to the Ministry of Christ, Israel stubbornly refused to see or hear irrespective of the evidence. To sin in ignorance is one thing, but to sin against Light, and above all, the greatest *"Light"* the world had ever known, is something else altogether. In fact, the words *"Unto this day,"* apply to Israel at this moment, just as it did in Paul's day. However, this past nearly 2,000 years have not been uneventful to say the least. Actually, it has been a time of untold spiritual sorrow and extreme grief, exactly as the word *"slumber"* proclaims.

(9) "AND DAVID SAITH, LET THEIR TABLE BE MADE A SNARE, AND A TRAP, AND A STUMBLINGBLOCK, AND A RECOMPENCE UNTO THEM:"

The phrase, *"And David saith,"* is taken from Psalm 69:22-23.

The phrase, *"Let their table be made a snare,"* refers to their prosperity.

In the giving of the Law to Israel, prosperity in every facet accompanied the Word of God, even as it always does.

When their Leadership was even halfway following the Lord, they were blessed in every way imaginable. This speaks of financial prosperity, physical healing and more importantly, even Divine health, and

in every other way that one might think. Actually, a list of these Blessings is outlined in Deuteronomy 28:1-14.

The manner in which it became *"a snare,"* is that they equated these Blessings of God with the approval of God.

This is the reason that modern Believers must not altogether take the Blessings of God as the approval of God. Those very things which are in fact, great Blessings, can in fact, become *"a snare."* In Truth, it has happened to millions.

The phrase, *"And a trap,"* pertains to the end result of the *"snare."* In other words, the *"snare"* leads the victim into the *"trap."*

The phrase, *"And a stumblingblock,"* refers to the fact that Israel stumbled over the very Blessings which were intended for her betterment.

The idea is, that they got their eyes on the gifts instead of the Giver. This is when Blessings become *"a snare."*

I wish to make it clear, even as we have already stated, that this problem was not indicative to Israel only, but is just as much a present danger as then. In fact, Blessings often turn out to be the opposite of what God intends. That's the reason it is very difficult for Him to bless some people.

Of course, all of us think that we will conduct ourselves exactly as we should if such is forthcoming. However, the Truth is, that such seldom is the case. The far greater majority of the time, these things prove to be a *"stumblingblock."*

The phrase, *"And a recompence unto them,"* actually refers to a negative end result.

"Recompence" in the Greek is *"anatapodoma,"* and means *"a just retribution."* They brought the problems on themselves!

(10) "LET THEIR EYES BE DARKENED THAT THEY MAY NOT SEE, AND BOW DOWN THEIR BACK ALWAY."

The phrase, *"Let their eyes be darkened that they may not see,"* pertains to that which is sure to happen in such cases, and in fact did happen. By the time of Christ, Israel, at least as far as its Leadership was concerned, was so far gone, that their situation was hopeless.

The phrase, *"And bow down their back alway,"* refers to them coming under the burden of captives, which is exactly what happened.

Israel from then until now, has *"bowed down their back"* without respite, i.e., *"back alway."*

THE MOST DISASTROUS THING THAT COULD EVER HAPPEN!

Paul says all in Israel not included in the Remnant were hardened. He explains this hardening in that God gave them a spirit of slumber, an insensibility of heart that made them insensible to the Gospel, sightless spiritual eyes, and deaf ears. How are we to understand this?

Moses records the fact that God hardened Pharaoh's heart, but not until Pharaoh had first hardened his own heart. The original hardening came from his totally depraved nature.

Then God hardened Pharaoh's heart by forcing him to an issue which he did not want to meet. The more God demanded that he let Israel go, the more Pharaoh rebelled. The more he rebelled, the harder his heart became. So with Israel.

LIGHT REJECTED!

Israel rejected God and His Word, and the more it did so the harder its heart became. Light rejected, blinds. In addition to this natural hardening of the heart, there was God's judicial action of hardening as a just judgment upon the sin of rejection.

Paul does not say how they were hardened or by whom: there is the same indefiniteness here as in *"vessels fitted to destruction"* in Romans 9:22. It may be quite possible to give a true sense to the assertion that they were hardened by God, although the hardening in this case is always regarded as a punishment for sin, that is, a confirming in an obduracy which originally was not of God, but their own: as if the idea were, first they would not, and then, in God's reaction against their sin, they could not (Wuest and Denney).

THE CONSTANT DANGER

This is the most dangerous thing that could happen to anyone, and for the simple reason that we are speaking of the soul of man. That's the reason that the heart must stay pliable before God, in order that He

may correct us and that we may constantly yield to Him.

This condition is always accompanied by spiritual stiffness and pride, in other words, the very opposite of humility. Consequently, brokenness before God is ever imperative. To a broken heart God can speak. With an humbled man, God can deal. That's the reason that David said, *"The Sacrifices of God are a broken spirit: a broken and a contrite heart, O God, Thou wilt not despise"* (Ps. 51:17).

That of which David said was the opposite of Israel, and regrettably, is the opposite of most of the modern Church as well!

(11) "I SAY THEN, HAVE THEY STUMBLED THAT THEY SHOULD FALL? GOD FORBID: BUT RATHER THROUGH THEIR FALL SALVATION IS COME UNTO THE GENTILES, FOR TO PROVOKE THEM TO JEALOUSY."

The question, *"I say then, Have they stumbled that they should fall?"*, refers to falling in the sense that they will never be restored. As Paul will graphically state, the answer to that is *"No!"*

As we have stated over and over again, how anyone can read these Passages and continue to come to the conclusion, that Israel is no more, at least as far as the Promises of God to the Nation are concerned, is beyond me. It is my opinion that Preachers who claim such, really do not know the Bible. Or else they do know the Bible, but in a twisted way. In other words, they try to make the Scriptures fit their Doctrine, or whatever it is they want their Doctrine to be, rather than allowing their Doctrine to be molded by the Scriptures.

The phrase, *"God forbid,"* is Paul's answer to his own question, and a term he is fond of using.

It is meant to make a very forceful expression, leaving absolutely no room for doubt concerning the correct answer.

The phrase, *"But rather through their fall Salvation is come unto the Gentiles,"* is another manner of expressing the formation or building of the Church.

WAS THE CHURCH ALWAYS THE PLAN OF GOD?

In a word, *"No!"* However, it was always God's intention, that the Gospel be given to the entirety of the world, even as the Promise was given to Abraham (Gen. 12:3).

To take this thought to its final conclusion, however, one would have to ascertain that neither was it God's perfect will regarding the bringing of Israel into existence.

Knowing that sin is never the Will of God, one must come to the conclusion, as should be overly obvious, that it was certainly not God's Will for Adam and Eve to fall in the Garden of Eden. However, through foreknowledge, God knew that such would happen, and provided a contingency. That contingency was Israel.

In this fallback plan, that is if one would be allowed to refer to it as such, it was God's intention that Israel would accept the Kingdom on the First Advent of the Messiah, which would have made the formation of the Church, at least as we know such, unnecessary. That's the reason both John the Baptist and Jesus came preaching, ". . . *Repent: for the Kingdom of Heaven is at hand*" (Mat. 4:17). Actually, the term *"Kingdom of Heaven,"* is a dispensational term and refers to Messiah's Kingdom on Earth. It was rejected so was postponed until the Second Coming, when Israel will then accept Christ as Saviour, Lord, and Messiah (Mat. 11:12, 20-24; 27:22-25; Lk. 19:11-27; Acts 1:6-7; 3:19-26).

Israel rejecting the Kingdom, subjected the world to another period of wars, insurrections, sickness, suffering, and plagues, which have continued for nearly 2,000 additional years.

WHY IS ISRAEL SO SPECIAL RESPECTING THE USHERING IN OF THE KINGDOM?

In fact, and as we have previously stated, before the Kingdom can commence, Israel must in fact accept Jesus as Messiah and Saviour. Only then can everything be brought into proper balance, with the Nations of the world being blessed as God originally intended. However, for this to be, Israel must serve in the capacity of Leadership. This is because of the Promises made to Abraham and to David.

The Divine Monarchy is in the lineage of David, and, consequently, Jesus as the *"Son of David"* must ultimately sit upon that Throne, which He shall in the coming

Kingdom Age. As we have stated, these people were brought about for the very purpose of giving the world the Word of God, serving as the womb for the Messiah, and regaining the dominion lost by Adam through the Throne of David (Gen. 12:1-3; Chpt. 15; 17:19; II Sam. Chpt. 7).

Inasmuch as Israel lost the position of Leadership to Nebuchadnezzar about 600 years before Christ, and missed the opportunity to regain it at the time of Christ, this period which has now lasted for about 2600 years, is referred to by Jesus as *"The Times of the Gentiles"* (Lk. 21:24).

This ". . . *Times of the Gentiles . . ."* will not end until the Second Coming (Rev. 19).

THE CHURCH!

Knowing that Israel would reject Him, but offering the Kingdom anyway, Jesus also foretold, ". . . *And upon this Rock I will build My Church . . .,"* which is the first mention of the New Testament Church (Mat. 16:18).

The Church is the Body of Christ made up of all Born-Again Believers, irrespective as to whom they may be, whether Jew or Gentile (Acts 15:13-18; I Cor. 12:13; Eph. 2:20-22; 4:13).

If one is to notice, the Church is not mentioned anywhere in the Old Testament, with the exception of it being referred to in shadow by the use of the word *"Gentiles."* Actually, Isaiah alone spoke of the Gentiles in this capacity, with the exception of Malachi (Isa. 11:10; 42:1, 6; 49:6, 22; 60:3; 62:2; 66:19; Mal. 1:11).

If the Church had been intended by God, at least as we now know such and which has existed since the Day of Pentecost, the Old Testament would have had far greater reference to this extremely important economy of God.

The idea of the phrase as given by Paul, *"But rather through their fall Salvation is come unto the Gentiles,"* is rather intended to say that the Fall of Israel did not stop the Gospel from coming to the Gentiles. In fact, it was God's Plan all along, that Israel would be the bearer of Glad Tidings to the Gentiles. However, as they more and more rebelled against God, they more and

NOTES

more withdrew into their own self-righteous shell, actually referring to Gentiles as *"dogs."* Nevertheless, the Lord would still use a Jew, namely the Apostle Paul, to bring this grand and glorious Message to the Gentile world. In fact, he called himself an Apostle to the Gentiles (II Tim. 1:11).

The phrase, *"For to provoke them to jealousy,"* harks back to the Prophecy of Noah after the flood, when he said, *"Blessed be the Lord God of Shem* (who spawned Israel and the Messiah), . . . *God shall enlarge Japheth, and he shall dwell in the tents of Shem . . ."* (Japheth will receive the Blessings intended for Shem) (Gen. 9:26-27).

All the Tribes of the Earth are direct descendants of the sons of Noah, *". . . Shem, Ham, and Japheth . . ."* (Gen. 10:1).

Israel, the descendants of Shem, was to receive the Blessings of the Messiah, and in fact did bring the Messiah into the world, but rejected Him. However, the descendants of Japheth, who make up the white Caucasian Race, did accept The Lord Jesus Christ as the Messiah and Lord and Saviour. As a result, and as is plainly obvious all over the world, and has been for these nearly 2,000 years, the Blessing has gone to Japheth, i.e., *"Japheth has dwelt in the Tents of Blessing originally promised to Shem."*

This to be sure has provoked Israel to jealousy, knowing that this Blessing of Leadership in the world rightly belonged to them. However, they have only themselves to thank for the terrible unfortunate turn of events.

(12) "NOW IF THE FALL OF THEM BE THE RICHES OF THE WORLD, AND THE DIMINISHING OF THEM THE RICHES OF THE GENTILES, HOW MUCH MORE THEIR FULNESS?"

The phrase, *"Now if the Fall of them be the riches of the world,"* tells us several things:

1. The manner of the translation makes it seem as if the world has been greatly enriched by the Fall of Israel. However, that is not the case!

God intended all along, even as we have stated, that the entirety of the world would be enriched with the Gospel of Jesus Christ. The idea is, and as stated, that their Fall did not stop the Gospel from coming to the world.

2. The word *"riches"* is used, telling us that every advancement in the world has been as a direct result of the Gospel of Jesus Christ. This means that all freedom, prosperity, blessing, education, equality, etc., have come about, solely because of the Gospel of Christ. And this, one might quickly add, despite the fact that even so-called Christian Nations, such as America, etc., give Christ little credit, if any at all. Most of the time, these Blessings are placed in the category of man's own ingenuity and abilities instead of God.

The Moslems are fond of pointing toward America as the greatest Christian Nation in the world, and then loudly trumpeting the great amount of vice and crime rampant in this Nation. Of course, they link these negatives to Christianity.

The Truth is, that the vice and crime exist because of America's rejection of Bible Christianity. In fact, there is only a small Remnant in America who are truly Born Again, but this small Remnant carries a weight and authority all out of proportion to its size. In other words, great Blessings have come to this Nation and the world, because of this *"Salt"* and *"Light"* (Mat. 5:13-14). In fact, if this *"Salt"* and *"Light"* were suddenly taken out of the world, even as it will be at the First Resurrection (I Thess. 4:13-18), the entirety of the world will then be plunged into Great Tribulation as it has never known before (Mat. 24:21).

The phrase, *"And the diminishing of them the riches of the Gentiles,"* once again states that even though their Fall and Diminishing, have greatly delayed the Plan of God, still, the Gospel being offered to the Gentiles, and in fact accepted, has not been delayed.

As we have previously stated, in all the annals of human history, the Fall of Israel is without a doubt, the greatest catastrophe that humanity has ever known. There is actually no way that words can properly describe the awfulness of this horror. It is inconceivable to think of people in a state of preparation for some 2,000 years to bring the Messiah into the world, actually raised up for this very purpose, and then when He finally did come, not even recognize Him. One wants to ask, and even as we have stated, *"How could this happen?"*

But it did happen! And Paul will very

succinctly warn the Gentile world as well, i.e., the Church, that we are not immune from such a possibility ourselves, and must never forget that fact.

The question, *"How much more their fulness?"*, carries with it a meaning and worth all out of proportion to the brevity of its thrust.

In this one question, Paul implies Israel's rightful place in the Kingdom of God, which will then bring everything into line, with her being the great Blessing that God always intended.

ISRAEL'S PLACE AND POSITION

When I speak of Israel, I am not speaking of Israelites as individuals, but rather Israel as a Nation. Actually, this is what Paul is addressing as well.

As a Nation, God has outlined a particular program for these people which has not yet been realized, and actually was delayed critically by her rejection of Christ, her Messiah. In essence, the entirety of the Rule of God, at least concerning the *"Kingdom of Heaven"* on Earth, is wrapped up in the Nation of Israel. So, for certain things to be brought about, Israel must regain this place of ascendancy, but must do so in the Will of God and not according to her own will.

This was the major problem with Israel during the time of Christ. She understood her place in the Kingdom, and greatly chaffed under Roman Rule, but refused to admit that she was in this condition because of her spiritual failure. Consequently, she was looking for a Messiah Who would restore her place and position in the order of Nations as God originally intended. However, such was impossible at the time because of her spiritual condition. In fact, had Israel been made the conqueror instead of the conquered, she would have been a far worse tyrant than Rome ever dared to be. The reason is simple, there is no tyranny like religious tyranny.

In fact, Jesus did offer the Kingdom to Israel at that time, but on His terms and not theirs, which they would not accept (Mat. 4:17).

WHY WAS ISRAEL CHOSEN?

Whenever God created Adam and Eve, He gave Adam dominion over all the work of

NOTES

His Hands (Gen. 1:28; Ps. 8).

At the Fall, Adam lost this dominion, with it in essence, at least to a certain degree, being taken over by Satan (II Cor. 4:4; Eph. 2:2). For rulership and dominion to be taken back, God could not simply speak it into existence, as He had done all other things (Gen. Chpt. 1). When He gave the dominion to Adam, it was not a pseudo dominion, but in fact, total and complete. So, for such to be brought back into its rightful place, man would have to do so of his own volition. In other words, God could not force man's will, because this would be against creation and the way that He had purposely designed and created man.

God must always abide by His Nature and Character. Even though He is Sovereign, His Sovereignty will never violate those things which He has laid down actually as Laws of the Universe.

So the dominion given to man was real and not imagined, and, it now must be won back.

To do that, God would have to send a Second Adam into the world, who we now know as The Lord Jesus Christ. However, this could not be done immediately for the simple reason that the world was not ready for the Redeemer and would have to be prepared. In fact, the situation was so critical, that God could not use a single Nation, Tribe, or Family to bring about this task. He would actually have to formulate or devise a special people for the coming of the world's Redeemer.

For this task, God chose a man by the name of Abraham, and from him He would build or make a family of people who would be holy, and in fact, would serve as the womb for the Messiah, or Redeemer (Gen. 12:1-3). Consequently, Israel began with Abraham.

THE PREPARATION OF ISRAEL

In fact, the very reason that the appellative *"The God of Abraham, and of Isaac, and of Jacob"* is so special, is simply because these men had Faith in God. In other words, they believed what He said to them about a coming Redeemer, and strongly desired to be used in this which God would do. To be factual, these men were not perfect, but they did believe God, and this is what made them so very special. In fact, at least as far as we know, there were no other men at that time on the face of the Earth who had any Faith in God whatsoever, or even believed in Him at all. As we have stated, the world was in such a condition, that it was not ready at this time for the Redeemer.

From Jacob's loins came the sons who would make up the heads of the 13 Tribes, which would then make up the Family of God in the world of that day. So, God prepared them for this special purpose of bringing the Redeemer into the world, a preparation we might quickly add, which took nearly 2,000 years (4,000 years from the time of Adam).

PROMISES MADE BY GOD

During this time, the Lord told Israel that she would be the head Nation in the world (Deut. 28:13). Actually, the Lord said of them, ". . . *The people* (Israel) *shall dwell alone, and shall not be reckoned among the Nations*" (Num. 23:9).

This simply means they were a special people, and had a special purpose.

The prophetic future of Israel has been fulfilled from that time until now. They have never lost their identity as a people; and have never intermarried with Gentiles, except for a very few. They have maintained their own customs, traditions, and religion, segregated from the people among whom they have dwelt, and will continue to do so (Gen. 12:1-3; 17:6-8; Isa. 11:10-12; Ezek. Chpt. 48).

Their not being *"reckoned among the Nations"* literally means that they would remain a distinct people from all others, and that God would not deal with them on the basis of being one with the Gentiles. In effect, they will always be a separate class of people and a distinct Nation, because of the reasons stated (I Cor. 10:32).

DOMINION

As well, this rulership or dominion includes the Kingship of the Earth. In other words, for the dominion to be regained, the Second Adam would have to regain the rulership of the Earth lost by the First Adam. The Promise was given to David, that it would be through his family that this rulership

would be regained. Hence, Israel knew that the *"King"* would be the *"Son of David,"* who was actually The Lord Jesus Christ.

Regrettably, sadly, and tragically, Israel rejected her King, choosing Caesar instead (Jn. 19:15). So, when they rejected the King, they also rejected the Kingdom, for it is impossible to have the Kingdom without having the King. And that King is The Lord Jesus Christ, and no other!

So, for the Kingdom to commence, Israel must accept the Messiah, Who must be and is, The Lord Jesus Christ, which will take place at the Second Coming (Rev. Chpt. 19).

At that time, and according to the Prophets, Jews will be brought to Israel from all over the world, with virtually all of them accepting Christ as Messiah and Saviour, which will then commence the Kingdom, with Israel in her rightful place.

Ezekiel graphically portrays what type of Nation these people will be, in Chapters 40 through 48 of his Book. They will then be what God originally intended for them to be, a holy people (Lev. 11:44-45; 20:7; 21:6; Num. 15:40; Deut. 7:6; 14:2, 21; 26:19; 28:9).

THEIR FULLNESS

So, Japheth has dwelt in the tents of Shem, exactly as Noah prophesied about 4400 years ago. However, Shem (Israel) will ultimately regain the Blessing, even as all the Prophets foretold. The Nations of the world will then be grandly blessed, with Israel in her rightful place and position. The Times of the Gentiles will then be over (Lk. 21:24).

The great question asked by the Disciples of Jesus, ". . . *Lord, wilt Thou at this time restore again the Kingdom to Israel?"*, will finally be answered (Acts 1:6).

That *"Kingdom"* will be restored, and then the *"fullness"* will come in, even as the Lord told Abraham so long ago (Gen. 12:3).

The answer to the entirety of the scenario is *"Jesus!"*

Think of it – the Lord Jesus, Personally reigning on the Throne of David in Jerusalem, the Nation of Israel Saved, Satan bound, and Universal Righteousness, Peace, and Prosperity for 1,000 years, *"That the residue of men might seek after the Lord, and all the Gentiles . . ."* (Acts 15:17) (Robinson).

(13) "FOR I SPEAK TO YOU GENTILES, INASMUCH AS I AM THE APOSTLE OF THE GENTILES, I MAGNIFY MINE OFFICE:"

The phrase, *"For I speak to you Gentiles,"* carries a far weightier meaning than at first meets the eye.

Paul is now going to relate as to how the Lord has grafted in the Gentile Church, because even though the Church is for all people, in fact containing some Jews even as was Paul, still, the greater majority have been and are Gentiles.

The way that Paul uses the word *"Gentiles"* is done so by the Holy Spirit in order that they (we) might know, that we are grafted in, not because of any merit of our own, for in fact we had none, but purely because of the Grace of God. When Jesus died on Calvary, He died for the entirety of the world; consequently, the manner in which God will reach the Gentile world, which of course makes up all of mankind, with the exception of the Jews, is now unfolded.

THE GENTILE WORLD

The Greek word *"ethnos"* signifies Gentile, Pagan, or, in the plural, a Nation or Nations as distinct from Israel.

The root of the concept is found in the Old Testament, in the words *"goy"* and *"goyim."* These Hebrew words, usually translated *"Nation"* or *"Nations,"* originally indicated any people who could be distinguished as a group by their political, territorial, or ethnic identity. In the early Books of the Old Testament these terms are applied to Israel as well as to other Nations. But increasingly as sacred history moves on, God's Old Testament people develop a sense of their unique identity as a Covenant people.

THE DIFFERENCE

Israel was bonded to the Lord and was significantly different from the Pagan peoples surrounding the Jewish homeland, to which we have briefly alluded. Increasingly history shows that the Pagan peoples around Israel seduced them from Faith in the Lord and were the antagonists and persecutors of Israel.

After the captivity, Gentile world powers were dominant over the Holy Land, a fact that galled the Jews of Jesus' time. The Prophets portrayed the Gentiles as enemies, the objects of Divine Judgment. And yet the Prophets testified of a day when even the Gentiles would know God's Salvation.

WITHOUT GOD'S WRITTEN REVELATION

The New Testament portrays the Gentiles as people who were without God's Written Revelation (Rom. 2:14), who were led astray by futile thoughts (Acts 14:16; Eph. 4:17), and who were captive to idolatry (I Cor. 12:2). The Bible's moral description of the Gentiles is found in Romans 1:18-32, and their spiritual condition is portrayed in Ephesians 2:11-22.

Gentiles were *"separate from Christ,"* excluded from citizenship in Israel and foreigners to the Covenants of the Promise, without hope and without God in the world.

Yet the Message of Christ is announced to the Gentiles, so that those *"Who were once far away"* may be *"brought near,"* to be united with believing Jews in the One Body of Christ.

THE GOSPEL

The Message of the Gospel breaks down the wall of hostility and antagonism that has divided humanity, and it unites people from every culture and society in the single spiritual organism created by the Death and Resurrection of Jesus.

THE RELATIONSHIP

The Gentiles were far less sharply differentiated from the Israelites in Old Testament times than in New Testament times. Under Old Testament regulations Gentiles were simply non-Israelites, not from the stock of Abraham, but they were not hated or despised for that reason, and were to be treated almost on a plane of equality, except certain Tribes in Canaan with regard to whom there were special regulations of nonintercourse.

Actually, the Gentile stranger enjoyed the hospitality of the Israelite who was commanded to love him (Deut. 10:19), to sympathize with him, *". . . For ye know the heart of the stranger, seeing ye were strangers in the land of Egypt"* (Ex. 23:9).

The Gentiles had the right of asylum in the cities of refuge in Israel, the same as the Israelites (Num. 35:15). They could even inherit land in Israel even as late as the Exile (Ezek. 47:22-23). They were also allowed to offer Sacrifices at the Temple in Jerusalem, as is distinctly affirmed by Joshua, and is implied in the Levitical Law (Lev. 22:25).

However, as we approach the time of Christ, the attitude of the Jews toward the Gentiles changes, until we find, in New Testament times, the most extreme aversion, scorn, and hatred.

They were regarded as unclean, with whom it was unlawful to have any friendly intercourse. They were the enemies of God and His people (at least as Israel then treated them), to whom the knowledge of God was denied unless they became proselytes, and even then they could not, as in ancient times, be admitted to full fellowship.

Jews were forbidden to counsel them, and if they asked about Divine things they were to be cursed. All children born of mixed marriages were Bastards. That is what caused the Jews to be so hated by Greeks and Romans, even as we have abundant evidence in the writings of Cicero, Seneca, and Tacitus.

THE REASON?

If we inquire what the reason of this change was we shall find it in the conditions of the Exiled Jews, who suffered the bitterest treatment at the hands of their Gentile captors and who, after their return and establishment in Judaea, were in constant conflict with neighboring Gentile Tribes, etc.

Some of the Gentile Rulers not long before the time of Christ, attempted to blot out their religion and to hellenize them, which brought about a desperate struggle for independence, creating in them a burning patriotism and zeal for their Faith which culminated in the rigid exclusiveness of New Testament times.

However, the basic reason for their problem went deeper than their maltreatment at the hands of Gentiles, even though that was a factor. It pertained to their changing the Word of God according to the desires of their self-will, actually making a religion out of the Law of Moses, even adding over 600 Laws

of their own devising. Consequently, Judaism had basically sunk to the level of a mere ethic, which brought on acute self-righteousness, which such always does.

They now placed themselves on a high spiritual pedestal, looking down on all others. Hence, when their own Messiah came, they did not know Him, and despite incontrovertible evidence as to Who He really was, the Messiah of Israel and the Saviour of the world, they murdered Him. So, their attitude toward Gentiles, was in a sense, their attitude toward God.

PAUL THE APOSTLE

The phrase, *"Inasmuch as I am the Apostle of the Gentiles,"* speaks of Paul's special Calling by the Lord. These were the words that the Lord gave Ananias to give to this newly-converted Jew, *". . . For he is a chosen vessel unto Me, to bear My Name before the Gentiles . . ."* (Acts 9:15). So, the Lord would take the greatest Christ-hater of them all, and make of him the greatest voice for Christ of his day, and maybe for all time.

Paul alone, to a far greater degree than all others, felt the burden of taking the Gospel to the Gentiles, and carried out that burden by taking the Gospel to almost all the world of his day, the Roman Empire. Paul as no other man, helped fulfill that which was given to Abraham by the Lord, *". . . In thee shall all families of the Earth be blessed"* (Gen. 12:3).

The phrase, *"I magnify mine office,"* has a twofold meaning:

1. Paul took his Apostleship respecting the Gentiles very seriously. He gave it all diligence, feeling the burden keenly, and doing all within his power to carry out the task of getting the Gospel to the Pagans of the world.

2. In doing so, as the next verse portrays, it was his strong desire that Israel would note the Blessings of the Lord upon the Gentiles, thereby provoking them to jealousy, which hopefully would stimulate a desire for their share of the Gospel.

(14) "IF BY ANY MEANS I MAY PROVOKE TO EMULATION THEM WHICH ARE MY FLESH, AND MIGHT SAVE SOME OF THEM."

The phrase, *"If by any means I may provoke to emulation them which are my flesh,"* presents somewhat of an irony.

God's Plan in the beginning had been that the Gentiles would see the Blessings of God upon Israel, and be provoked to jealousy, desiring what they had. They would then inquire after Israel's God. In fact, that's exactly what happened during the times of David and especially that of Solomon (II Chron. 9:23). So now Paul will use the same process, praying it will have some success with the Jews. However, there was a vast difference in the situation as it is presented.

The Gentile Nations were not eaten up with self-righteousness and, had little compunction about seeking guidance from Israel, at least in a spiritual sense. However, for Israel, the situation was far different. She was eaten up with spiritual pride, and would do almost anything before she would seek that which was possessed by the Gentiles.

"Emulation" in the Greek is *"parazeloo,"* and is the same word which is translated *"provoke to jealousy"* in verse 11.

The phrase, *"And might save some of them,"* tells us several things:

1. Despite all their religion, Israel was not Saved. I speak of the Nation which as a whole had rejected Christ. To be frank, most in modern Christendom although very religious, are not truly Saved.

2. This was Paul's only concern regarding his people. He knew they were lost, and as such would die without God. Consequently, the thing that was constantly on his mind was not a theological argument, but rather the Salvation of their souls.

In that same manner, God has given me a special burden for the Catholics. Many misunderstand, thinking, that I am opposed to Catholics as people. Nothing could be further from the Truth!

The Truth is, I know that virtually all of them are lost without God, and my heart's cry is that they may be Saved, which I know cannot be brought about by devotion to the Church or Mary worship.

3. False Doctrine damns souls and damns them eternally. There was no way that the Jews could reject Christ, and be Saved. There is no way that anyone can reject Christ, or

even relegate Him to a secondary position and be Saved.

The Law of Moses could not save Israel, and neither can the Church save the Gentiles. Jesus in both cases was and is the Saviour, and the only Saviour!

It is not enough that people be sincere in what they believe. Paul plainly said, and on which we have already commented, that Israel had *". . . a zeal of God, but not according to knowledge"* (Rom. 10:2). Such describes, regrettably so, much of the modern Church.

4. Paul's statement, *"And might save some of them,"* completely refutes the erroneous Doctrine of Predestination. If the Doctrine of Predestination as it is taught in many circles, is correct, then the word *"might"* referring to *"hopefully,"* or *"maybe,"* would not here apply. However, it does apply, simply because the Gospel is presented to the entirety of the world, and it's to *"whosoever will"* respecting those who are actually Saved (Rev. 22:17).

(15) "FOR IF THE CASTING AWAY OF THEM BE THE RECONCILING OF THE WORLD, WHAT SHALL THE RECEIVING OF THEM BE, BUT LIFE FROM THE DEAD?"

The beginning of the question, *"For if the casting away of them be the reconciling of the world . . . ?"*, proclaims here a great Truth.

As we have stated several times, it was always God's Plan that the Gospel be given to the whole world. In fact, it was His Plan that Israel would be that vehicle or instrument to perform this task.

However, inasmuch as Israel would not obey the Lord in this matter, but rejected His Plan, despite the fact that they were His Chosen People, He purposely set them aside, in order that the Gospel may go to the entirety of the world. From this, we should learn just how important it is that this great Message of Redemption be given to all mankind.

The word *"if"* which Paul uses throughout his argument here, is not the *"if"* of a hypothetical condition, but the *"if"* of a fulfilled condition. In other words, Paul is not arguing upon the basis of a hypothesis, but on the basis of facts. Actually, the translation should read *"since"* or *"in view of the fact."*

The casting away of Israel the Nation, refers to the Act of God setting Israel aside *temporarily* as a channel through which to bring the Good News of Salvation to the world, and in their place the substitution of the Church, this with a view to bringing Israel back into fellowship with Himself and service in the coming Millennium (Wuest).

"Reconciling" in the Greek is *"katallage,"* and means *"adjustment, restoration, atonement."*

Through the acceptance of the Gospel Message, the unsaved are reconciled to God in the sense that their attitude of unbelief and hatred is turned to one of Trust and Love, and all because of Jesus Christ.

Due to the Fall, man is at cross purposes with God, and can only be reconciled to Him by the acceptance of Jesus Christ as Lord and Saviour. Jesus paid the price, removing the sin debt in order that this may be done. The only requirement is *"Faith"* (Jn. 3:16; Rom. 10:9-10, 13; Eph. 2:8-9).

The conclusion of the question, *"What shall the receiving of them be, but life from the dead?"*, refers to that wonderful time when Jesus returns to this world (Zech. Chpt. 14), when all Israel shall be Saved (Rom. 11:26). This will be *"life from among the dead,"* in that the Nation that then is, will be Saved by the Grace of God out from a spiritually dead state and from among those who remain spiritually dead.

Of course, this speaks only of those who are alive at that time, the time of the Second Coming (Rev. Chpt. 19).

(16) "FOR IF THE FIRSTFRUIT BE HOLY, THE LUMP IS ALSO HOLY: AND IF THE ROOT BE HOLY, SO ARE THE BRANCHES."

The phrase, *"For if the Firstfruit be Holy,"* refers to the Patriarchs of Israel, Abraham, Isaac, and Jacob.

The idea is, that the Foundation of Israel was spiritually solid, i.e., *"Holy."* However, the word *"Holy"* as it here applies, refers to that which God has done, and not to the personal attributes of the men in question. In fact, as is obvious, Abraham, Isaac, and Jacob were not perfect. They were constantly building Altars, for the simple reason that they were constantly failing. So, how could

God refer to them as *"Holy?"*

They were referred to as *"Holy"* because what was done in their lives was all of God and none of man. In other words, it was a Work of the Holy Spirit, and any Work of the Holy Spirit is *"Holy."* It is the same presently!

No Believer within himself can attain to the status of *"Holiness."* However, if the Work in us, is totally of the Lord, and none of man, despite our failures, each Believer, and irrespective as to whom they may be, is described by God as *"Holy."* Paul said, ". . . *But ye are washed, but ye are Sanctified* (made Holy), *but ye are Justified in the Name of the Lord Jesus, and by the Spirit of our God"* (I Cor. 6:11).

The phrase, *"The lump is also holy,"* refers to the Nation of Israel. However, once again their designation as *"Holy"* is not given because of their own personal attributes, and in this case, does not even refer to Salvation. It simply means, that Israel has been called of God, and set apart by God for a special task. As a result, that task will ultimately be performed.

The phrase, *"And if the Root be Holy,"* refers to the reason that the *"lump"* is Holy, which pertains to all of this being a Work of the Holy Spirit.

The phrase, *"So are the Branches,"* refers to the fact that if the Root is Holy, of necessity the *"Branches"* must be Holy.

As stated, the entirety of Paul's statement refers to Israel as being called of God for a special purpose. Also as stated, none of this has any reference whatsoever to the Salvation of the Nation, or the Salvation of individual Jews. It simply means that Israel has been set apart for God as a chosen Nation through which Salvation could be produced and channeled to the rest of the human race. This pertains to their work, their reason for being!

(17) "AND IF SOME OF THE BRANCHES BE BROKEN OFF, AND THOU, BEING A WILD OLIVE TREE, WERT GRAFFED (GRAFTED) IN AMONG THEM, AND WITH THEM PARTAKEST OF THE ROOT AND FATNESS OF THE OLIVE TREE;"

The phrase, *"And if some of the Branches be broken off,"* refers to Israel being *"cast away"* or set aside, despite their Calling, and because of unbelief. Irrespective that they were designated as *"Holy,"* as stated, this was their Call and not necessarily their Salvation, although it definitely could be and was actually meant to be. But the *"Branches"* of this tree were broken off because of unbelief, even as verse 20 states.

This statement actually refers to the rejection of the Apostate Nation, its dispersion in A.D. 70, and God's act of setting it aside temporarily as the channel through which He would work.

SOME OF THE BRANCHES

If one is to notice, Paul did not say that all the *"Branches"* were broken off, but only some of them. What did he mean by that?

If all the Branches had been broken off leaving none, this would mean that Israel has ceased to be respecting the Plan of God, and will never experience Restoration, but have doomed themselves in entirety. However, that is *not* what it means.

Even though Israel as a Nation is today out of the Will of God, still denying her Messiah The Lord Jesus Christ, nevertheless, the ultimate Plan of God for these people is still intact. The prophetic Branches of a coming Restoration remain on this Tree. In other words, even though Israel has greatly hurt herself, even to the extent of untold sorrow, still, there will be an ultimate Reconciliation and Restoration. Almost every Prophet of old predicted such, as the Holy Spirit moved through them. Consequently, those particular Branches remain.

GENTILES

The phrase, *"And thou, being a wild Olive Tree, wert graffed* (grafted) *in among them,"* pertains to the Gentiles being included.

It refers to the Act of God in breaking down the wall of separation between Jew and Gentile at the Cross by the abrogation of the Mosaic Economy, and the inclusion of the Gentile with the Jew in One Body, the Church (Eph. 3:6).

The phrase, *"And with them partakest of the Root and fatness of the Olive Tree,"* simply means that the Church derives its life from the common Root that was originally given to Israel of long ago. In effect, the

life-force and the Blessing are received by the Gentile through the Jew, and not the Jew through the Gentile. The spiritual plan moves from the Abrahamic Covenant downward, and from the Israelitish Nation outward (Dwight).

This is why Jesus said in speaking to the Samaritan woman, *"Ye worship ye know not what: we know what we worship: for Salvation is of the Jews"* (Jn. 4:22).

Paul's statement here is remarkable in the sense that the normal agricultural process of grafting is the insertion of *"the good into the inferior stock."* Paul reverses this process.

It has been suggested in explanation that Paul took the figure merely at the point of inserting one piece into another, meaning that he was ignorant of the agricultural process. In fact, in the Kingdom of Nature generally, certainly in the case of the olive, the process referred to by the Apostle never succeeds. If one grafts the good upon the wild, which is the natural process, and which is the opposite of which Paul states, it will conquer the wild, even as nature intends. However, it is virtually impossible to reverse the process with success, so why does Paul use this type of metaphor?

THE WONDER AND BEAUTY OF THIS ILLUSTRATION

The Holy Spirit had the Apostle to use this illustration in exactly this manner, even though it is contrary to the laws of nature. It is meant to suggest or to promote the great Gospel of Grace.

It is only in the Kingdom of Grace that a process thus contrary to nature can be successful; and it is this circumstance which the Apostle has seized upon to magnify the Mercy shown to the Gentiles by grafting them, a wild race, contrary to the nature of such operations, into the good Olive Tree of Israel, and causing them to flourish there and bring forth fruit unto Eternal Life.

The Apostle lived in the land of the olive, and was in no danger of falling into a blunder in founding his argument upon such a circumstance in its cultivation. Actually, Paul plainly says in verse 24 that what he is stating is *"contrary to nature."*

This is the reason that we previously stated

that the Church was not God's original intention. It became necessary when some of the Branches of Israel had to be cut off. However, the original Plan of God has not been disturbed, for the simple reason that the *"Root"* of the Tree, and actually the Tree itself, which denotes the original Plan of God, is still very healthy. The Church was graffed *"grafted"* into this Olive Tree, as Paul uses it as an illustration, which means as stated, that it was not the original Plan of God, but has been made a part of that Plan.

(18) "BOAST NOT AGAINST THE BRANCHES. BUT IF THOU BOAST, THOU BEAREST NOT THE ROOT, BUT THE ROOT THEE."

The phrase, *"Boast not against the Branches,"* refers to several things:

1. The Church has not replaced Israel in the Plan of God. While the Church definitely is now involved in that Plan, and is carrying forth the Work of God which Israel forfeited, nevertheless, Israel will yet fulfill her eternal destiny.

2. As we have already stated, the Church (Gentiles) was admitted strictly on the basis of Grace and never of any personal merit or worth. Consequently, we have no reason to boast.

3. As stated, the *"Root"* and the Tree itself are healthy, which refers to the original Plan of God. From this we must understand that men may fail but God never fails. His Plan is insured of success, and will always ultimately succeed.

The phrase, *"But if thou boast, thou bearest not the Root, but the Root thee,"* is meant to set the Church straight.

In essence, Paul is saying that the Church has nothing to boast about, and if it thinks that it is carrying forth the Plan of God, it should understand that the reverse of that thought is actually the Truth. The Plan of God, i.e., *"the Root"* is carrying the Church and not the opposite. God's original plans for Israel are still in force, and that is something for which we should ever be thankful.

The very means of His guaranteeing their ultimate Survival and Restoration also guaranteed that the Gospel would be brought to the Gentile world.

NOTES

It meant that my family who in effect were, *"aliens from the Commonwealth of Israel, and strangers from the Covenants of Promise, having no hope, and without God in the world,"* nevertheless, would have an opportunity to hear and accept this great and glorious Gospel of Jesus Christ, and thereby, to be Saved.

The wonder of it all is beyond the comprehension of mere mortals. But that He loved us enough that He would graft us in, even though it was contrary to nature, presents a Miracle of Grace which will be the song of the Redeemed forever and forever.

"Wonderful Love that rescued me, sunk deep in sin,
"Guilty and vile as I could be, no hope within, when every ray of light had fled,
"Oh glorious day! Raising my soul from out the dead, Love found a way."

"Love brought my Saviour here to die on Calvary,
"For such a sinful wretch as I, how can it be?
"Love bridged the gulf twixt me and Heaven, taught me to pray,
"I am redeemed, set free, forgiven — Love found a way."

"Love opened wide the gates of light, to Heaven's domain,
"Where in eternal power and might Jesus shall reign, Love lifted me from depths of woe.
"To endless day; there was no help in Earth below — Love found a way."

"Love found a way to redeem my soul,
"Love found a way that could make me whole,
"Love sent my Lord to the Cross of shame, Love found a way, Oh Praise His Holy Name!"

(19) "THOU WILT SAY THEN, THE BRANCHES WERE BROKEN OFF, THAT I MIGHT BE GRAFFED (GRAFTED) IN."

The phrase, *"Thou wilt say then,"* anticipates the possible boasting of those grafted in. The Believer must constantly suppress the idea that our place and position in Christ are due to our qualities or consecration, etc.

Naturally, one's consecration to God is very important; however, irrespective of our efforts in this capacity, within itself it merits nothing. All is strictly by the Grace of God.

The phrase, *"The Branches were broken off, that I might be graffed* (grafted) *in,"* presents that which is *not* the idea at all.

The Church must ever know and understand, that it was and is second choice. The Truth is, even as the next verse proclaims, the Branches were broken off not because of a need to make room for the Church. As stated, the Church was not really in the Plan of God, at least as we know it presently. It was God's original Plan that Israel would be the instrument of World Evangelism. She forfeited that, even as we are studying here. However, she will ultimately carry out this task in the coming Kingdom Age (Isa. 66:19).

(20) "WELL; BECAUSE OF UNBELIEF THEY WERE BROKEN OFF, AND THOU STANDEST BY FAITH. BE NOT HIGH-MINDED, BUT FEAR;"

"Well" in the Greek is *"kalos,"* and means *"a form of irony."* Paul does not think it worthwhile to dispute the assertion of verse 19 though as it stands it is by no means indisputable; he prefers to point out what it overlooks — the moral conditions of being broken off and of standing secure, in other words *"Why!"*

The phrase, *"Because of unbelief they were broken off,"* as is obvious, states the reason.

WHAT TYPE OF UNBELIEF?

The root type of unbelief addressed here, pertains to the Word of God, but saw its climax in the rejection of The Lord Jesus Christ.

If the Leadership in Israel had given due diligence to the Word of God, understanding what it said, and believing what it said, and not tried to insert their own gloss, they would have known Who Jesus was, and What Jesus was, i.e., The Son of God, The Messiah. Exactly Who and What He would be, was graphically portrayed and outlined by the Prophets. Consequently, there was no excuse for their ignorance, just as there is no excuse for ignorance presently.

Unbelief is expressed by two Greek words

in the New Testament, *"apistia"* and *"apeitheia."* Both words refer to disobedience, rebellion, and contumacy. It is a want of *"Faith and Trust."*

"Apistia" is a state of mind, and *"apeitheia"* an expression of it. Unbelief towards Himself was the prime sin of which Christ said that the Spirit would convict the world (Jn. 16:9). Consequently, unbelief in all its forms is a direct affront to the Divine veracity (I Jn. 5:10), which is why it is so heinous a sin.

The Children of Israel did not enter into God's *"Rest"* for two reasons. They lacked Faith (*"apistia,"* Heb. 3:19), and they disobeyed (*"apeitheia,"* Heb. 4:6). Unbelief finds its practical issue in disobedience (Heb. 3:12).

THAT WHICH GOD DEMANDS

When God has spoken, in Precept and yet more in Promise, distrust involves, at least potentially, an element of disobedience. His supreme claim is to be trusted to Command only what is right, and to Promise only what is true.

He is infinitely sympathetic in His insight, and infallibly knows where distrust comes only of the dim perceptions and weak misgivings of our moral nature, and where, on the other hand, a moral resistance lies at the back of the non-confidence. But the presence of that darker element (lack of confidence in God) is always to be suspected, at least, and searched for in serious self-examination.

UNBELIEVERS

"Unbeliever" is a general term that can be applied to anyone who has not yet put his trust in Christ. Such persons are characterized by unbelief, even as Christians are characterized by their believing attitude toward God.

We are taught to associate with unbelievers — even with the immoral at times, which pretty much characterizes all unbelievers (I Cor. 5:9-13). After all, God may open eyes blinded by Satan through our presentation of the Gospel (II Cor. 4:4). In other words, the Bible teaches separation, but it does not teach isolation.

However, we are to remain spiritually

sensitive, avoiding compromising situations (I Cor. 10:27-33). We are also to avoid entering into *"yoked"* relationships with unbelievers (II Cor. 6:14).

Whereas *"unbeliever"* is simply a term that characterizes one who is not yet a Christian, *"unbelief"* has strong negative overtones. The anxious father can struggle between belief and unbelief (Mk. 9:24). Paul can see the relationship between his early unbelief and Old Testament sins of ignorance (I Tim. 1:13).

But at heart, unbelief is staggering back from God's Revelation of Himself, refusing to respond as Abraham did, with Trust (Rom. 4:20). Thus, unbelief exhibits a sinful heart *". . . that turns away from the Living God"* (Heb. 3:12).

The phrase, *"And thou standest by Faith,"* proclaims that the Church was brought in because of Faith and not merit, and stands in its present position by Faith and not merit. In its simplest form, the Jews would not believe in Christ, while the Gentiles did! And as well, Israel will not, and in fact, cannot, be restored until she herself likewise *"comes to Faith."*

THE CRITERIA IS FAITH

We know that it is the Word of God which fuels Faith (Rom. 10:17).

We also know that without Faith it is impossible to please God (Heb. 11:6). However, there is a certain requirement on the part of the Believer which must be met, in order for Faith to be realized in the heart. I speak of humility.

I do not think the proud can come to Faith, even as Jesus outlined in Luke Chapter 18 concerning the Publican and the Pharisee.

Even though the Scripture does not plainly say, with the word *"Faith"* not even being used in this scenario; nevertheless, Jesus said, and concerning the Publican, *". . . This man went down to his house justified rather than the other; for every one that exalteth himself shall be abased; and he that humbleth himself shall be exalted"* (Lk. 18:14).

Even though Faith is not mentioned, we do know that it would have been impossible for this man to have received from God without Faith. However, to come to Faith, he

had to first come to self-abasement.

On the other hand, the Pharisee exhibited no humility, but rather pride, and entertained no Faith whatsoever, and, consequently, received nothing from God.

In fact, the very first Beatitude is, *"Blessed are the poor in spirit* (broken, humbled)*: for theirs is the Kingdom of Heaven"* (Mat. 5:3). As well, it seems that David in his prayer of repentance seemingly did not come to Faith until he said, *"The Sacrifices of God are a broken spirit: a broken and a contrite heart, O God, Thou wilt not despise"* (Ps. 51:17).

Faith tends to fill the broken and contrite spirit, even the broken heart, simply because the person has come to the end of himself. He realizes that God is the only Answer. As well, he also realizes that he deserves nothing good, but rather the opposite. He also knows that he can do nothing within himself to alleviate his situation. Consequently, he must trust the Lord, which in fact is Faith. God then moves, as only then He can move!

So, even though there is no Scripture which distinctly points to humility as a requirement of Faith, still, the inference is there in countless Passages and illustrations.

The phrase, *"Be not highminded, but fear,"* in effect, says exactly what I have attempted to portray.

"Highmindedness" is the very opposite of *". . . meek and lowly in heart . . ."* (Mat. 11:29). So, one cannot be *"highminded"* and at the same time have *"Faith."*

"Highminded" in the Greek is *"hupselophroneo,"* and means *"lofty in mind, i.e., arrogant."*

Paul said, *"Let this mind* (humility) *be in you, which was also in Christ Jesus . . .* (Who) *made Himself of no reputation, and took upon Him the form of a servant, and was made in the likeness of men . . . He humbled Himself, and became obedient unto death, even the death of the Cross"* (Phil. 2:5-8).

"Fear" in the Greek is *"phobeo,"* and means *"to be in awe, exceedingly reverent."* The reason why is given to us in the next verse.

(21) "FOR IF GOD SPARED NOT THE NATURAL BRANCHES, TAKE HEED LEST HE ALSO SPARE NOT THEE."

The phrase, *"For if God spared not the natural Branches,"* speaks as is obvious, of Israel.

This means that as far as comparisons can be made at all in such things, the Jews had been more securely invested in the Kingdom than the Gentiles. They were, in the language of the figure, not artificially grafted, but native Branches, on the Tree of God's people; yet even that did not prevent Him from cutting off those who did not believe (Wuest).

The phrase, *"Take heed lest he also spare not thee,"* refers again as is obvious, to the Church.

The idea is, if the Lord did not spare Israel, He will not spare Gentiles either, if in pride they fall from Faith. As well, one should take note that the Holy Spirit through the Apostle is not speaking of the Gentile world in general, but rather those who profess Salvation.

GOD DEMANDS SEPARATION REGARDING HIS PEOPLE

Regarding Israel's Fall the first time, which was approximately 600 years before Christ, they violated this Command respecting separation, in fact, becoming worshipers of idols as the surrounding Nations. Despite repeated warnings by the Prophets and the longsuffering of God, Israel would not hear, but instead went even deeper into sin. The writer of Chronicles said, *"But they mocked the Messengers of God, and despised His Words, and misused His Prophets, until the Wrath of the Lord arose against His people, till there was no remedy"* (II Chron. 36:16). Their problem was worldliness.

However, by the time of Christ they had gone in the exact opposite direction, turning worldliness into isolation. In other words, they became so lifted up in themselves, so self-righteous, that they held the Gentile world in disdain, isolating themselves, which was not the Will of God. In fact, the Church fights the exact same problem, except in reverse.

Not so long after the turn of the 20th Century, legalism was the great problem of the Church. Legalism as with Israel of old, always breeds self-righteousness, and brings

NOTES

about isolation, which is never the Will of God. If one is isolated, how can one's light shine?

However at present, even though some legalism still exists, the major problem of the modern Church is worldliness, which is a violation of God's Command of separation (II Cor. 6:14-18).

THE DISPENSATION OF GRACE

The modern Church foolishly and erroneously has the idea that Israel of old fell because they were under Law and, therefore, the Judgment of God. It presently reasons that we now live under the Dispensation of Grace; therefore, there is no worry or concern regarding Judgment. Nothing could be further from the Truth. In fact, God demands far more under Grace than He ever did under Law. Paul plainly said, *"And the times of this ignorance* (before Grace) *God winked at; but now* (under Grace) *commandeth all men every where to repent"* (Acts 17:30).

He also said, *"For the Wrath of God is revealed from Heaven against all ungodliness and unrighteousness of men, who hold the Truth in unrighteousness"* (Rom. 1:18).

I remind the Reader, that both times in which Paul spoke these words, he was speaking to Gentiles. In fact, the danger facing the modern Church is far more acute than Israel of old for two reasons:

1. This is the Age of Grace and God expects more out of the Church. In fact, Israel existed about 37 years (from the Day of Pentecost) under Grace, but was destroyed because of her refusal of the great Plan of God. So, the Church, even as Paul said, should look at Israel and *"fear."*

2. The Church, even though under Grace, doesn't have the status that Israel did, because she was the *"natural Branches,"* whereas the Church is *"a wild Olive Tree,"* i.e., *"Branches."*

GOD'S STANDARD

To which we have already alluded, God did not have one Standard for Israel and now another for the Church. The Standard has always and without exception, been Faith. It was Faith then, it is Faith now!

Considering all of this, the Church ought

to have a deep and abiding Love for Israel. And of course, True Christians do have that type of Love.

When I speak of Love, I am not speaking of the type of Love that all Believers should have for all men. I speak of the understanding and knowledge as to who and what exactly is Israel.

Even though Believers have sympathy for individual Arabs and should demand fair treatment for all, still, the Believer must ever understand that Israel's fight in the Middle East, is in a sense, the fight of the Church as well. To be blunt, the Moslem world is not of God, has never been of God, and never will be of God. So if it is not of God, then it is of Satan. In fact, Islam is the greatest threat to world peace on the horizon presently. It is Satan's great effort against Israel in these last days. The tragedy is, I think that most of the political leaders in America little understand the religion of Islam, as to its hatred, and especially its hatred for America. It sees America as the *"great Satan,"* and the only thing that stands in the way of world domination by the Moslem Religion, and above all, the destruction of Israel.

American politicians should know and understand, that if the Leaders of Islam had their way, there would not be a single American left alive anywhere in the world. The streets would run red with blood, with our Cities becoming graveyards. The only thing that stops them is not lack of will, but rather the might and power of the United States. Some may argue that I am overstating the case. I am not! If anything, my statements are understated instead of overstated.

The Koran promises Paradise to all who kill the infidels. And to be sure, all Christian Americans are looked at by the Moslem Leadership as infidels.

THE LAST DAYS

Getting back to the Church, and the statements as given by the Apostle Paul, in fact, most in the present Church are not going to be spared. They will come under the Judgment of God.

Paul also said, *"For the time will come when they will not endure sound Doctrine;*

but after their own lusts shall they heap to themselves teachers, having itching ears;

"And they shall turn away their ears from the Truth, and shall be turned unto fables" (II Tim. 4:3-4).

That time of which Paul spoke, is no longer in the future, in fact, it has already come. I know what I am talking about.

Of all the Christian Television Stations in America and Canada, we are able to air our Program on approximately ten percent of these Stations (none in Canada at all). Irrespective of the excuses given, as to why the approximate 90 percent won't air the Program, the real reason is, they simply do not believe in what we preach, or that for which we stand. It doesn't matter that the Spirit of God is in the Program in a great way, in fact, greater than ever. Neither does it matter that untold thousands of people have come to a Saving Knowledge of Jesus Christ through this Ministry, and continue to do so unto this hour. It doesn't matter that untold lives have been gloriously and marvelously changed by the Power of God relative to what we preach, in fact, those things count not at all.

If the Truth be known, the True Moving and Operation of the Holy Spirit is that to which they are opposed. Sadly and regrettably, the situation will not improve but rather get worse.

And then again money is the excuse for many of these Stations. They are afraid that some of their supporters may not want our Program aired and, therefore, might stop their giving. In other words, what God wants matters little.

Yes, there are some few Preachers on these Stations and Networks who are preaching the Gospel, at least as far as it goes. But again if the Truth be known, precious few people are actually being Saved, precious few lives are truly being changed, and precious few Believers are truly being Baptized with the Holy Spirit. In fact, almost none on all counts. But yet, there is great religious activity, with many people thinking that much is being done, when in reality, precious little is actually being done for the Cause of Christ.

DECEPTION

Deception is a very subtle thing and by its

very nature is designed to deceive. Satan little minds Preachers preaching the Truth respecting Salvation, if they deny or ignore the Holy Spirit. He knows that even though some Truth is being preached, very little is going to be done for the Cause of Christ, because it takes the Power of the Holy Spirit for these things to be done. As well, he doesn't mind at all if some Preachers extol some of the Gifts of the Spirit as preeminent, while ignoring the major thrust of the Gospel, which is the Salvation of souls, the Deliverance of men from sin, and Believers being Baptized with the Holy Spirit. He knows that such will arouse a tremendous amount of activity, but again, that very little will actually be done to hinder his kingdom of darkness.

So he does not oppose those Preachers, at least not too very much. They are doing him and his kingdom little harm, so there is little opposition in that direction.

He saves his efforts for that which is strictly according to the Word of God, and is accordingly empowered by the Holy Spirit. Then souls will be Saved, lives will be changed, bondages will be broken, sick bodies will truly be healed, and Believers will be Baptized with the Holy Spirit. That is what he opposes and strongly! Sadly and regrettably, his greatest sphere of operation, and that which he uses to the greatest extent of all to oppose the True Work of God, is not so much the world, but rather the Church itself. In other words, he uses those who profess and claim to be followers of the Lord.

So, the Church is facing the same dilemma as Israel of old. And as Israel of old, only a *"Remnant"* will be Saved.

(22) "BEHOLD THEREFORE THE GOODNESS AND SEVERITY OF GOD: ON THEM WHICH FELL, SEVERITY; BUT TOWARD THEE, GOODNESS, IF THOU CONTINUE IN HIS GOODNESS: OTHERWISE THOU ALSO SHALT BE CUT OFF."

The phrase, *"Behold therefore the goodness and severity of God,"* speaks of the positive and the negative regarding God.

God's Righteousness demands certain things. His Righteousness demands that if anyone humbles themselves before Him, seeking His Mercy and Grace, in effect, throwing themselves on His Mercy and Grace,

knowing that they deserve neither, He will always respond with *"goodness"* (Isa. 1:18; 66:2; Hos. 14:2-6; Mat. 11:28-30; Rom. 10:9-10, 13; Rev. 22:17).

However, for those who claim to be followers of the Lord (for it is those to whom the Holy Spirit speaks), and they rebel against God's Ways, repudiating His Word, holding themselves in pride and self-righteousness, those people, and without exception, will be met with *"severity,"* i.e., *"Judgment"* (Prov. 1:24-33; Isa. 1:2-6, 19-20; Lk. 19:41-44; Rom. 6:23; Rev. 21:8).

To be blunt, even as Paul exclaims here, one is a fool who discounts the Righteousness of God in any manner!

"Goodness" in the Greek is *"chrestotes,"* and means *"benignity and kindness."*

"Severity" in the Greek is *"apotomia,"* and means *"the nature of that which is cut off, abrupt, precipitous like a cliff, rough."*

And I remind the Reader, that the criteria with the Lord is not obedience to some Denomination which in fact is demanding that which is unscriptural, or to any man for that matter, but rather brokenness, contrition and humility before God. That is God's Way, and that which He demands (Ps. 51:17; Isa. 66:2; Lk. 18:9-14).

The phrase, *"On them which fell, severity,"* speaks of Israel.

THE WORD OF GOD

The Jews lost their standing because they had come to believe that they were indefectible, and independent of moral conditions. They did not believe the Word of God, in fact, the same problem which the modern Church is facing presently, and in every strata, from Presbyterians to Pentecostals.

Due to a lack of belief in the Word, they refused Christ when He came. However, as a prideful spirit always does, they were not content with merely refusing Him, they must murder Him as well! Regrettably, the modern Church, at least for the most part, carries the identical spirit. It is not content to merely oppose, it must as well, attempt to destroy.

The phrase, *"But toward thee, goodness, if thou continue in His Goodness,"* proclaims the condition.

First of all, this shoots down the unscriptural Doctrine of Unconditional Eternal Security.

God shows goodness to those who humble themselves before Him, even as we have already stated; however, one must *"continue in His Goodness,"* which means to continue in His Word. In fact, this has always been the condition of Eternal Life (Jn. 6:27).

The phrase, *"Otherwise thou also shalt be cut off,"* I think should be understood by the Reader, that God means exactly what He says. We must learn to take God at His Word. If He says that He is going to do something, then we must understand that's exactly what He will do (Rom. 2:11).

If the Gentile Church commits the same mistake that Israel did, it will incur the same doom, and in fact, this is exactly what is going to happen.

It is not to Israel only God may say, *"The Kingdom is taken from you, and given to a Nation bringing forth the Fruits thereof."* The visible organized Church on Earth today is for the most part modernistic, i.e., unbelieving, and at the Resurrection (Rapture) will be set aside in favor of Israel which will then be restored as the final channel through which God will work to bring the Good News of Salvation to the entirety of the human race. This will take place in the coming Kingdom Age.

In this sense, the Gentiles will be cut off as Israel was in A.D. 70, and for the same reason, failure to function as the means through which God works for the Salvation of sinners.

(23) "AND THEY ALSO, IF THEY ABIDE NOT STILL IN UNBELIEF, SHALL BE GRAFFED (GRAFTED) IN: FOR GOD IS ABLE TO GRAFF (GRAFT) THEM IN AGAIN."

The phrase, *"And they also, if they abide not still in unbelief, shall be graffed* (grafted) *in,"* lays down the condition which is Faith, and also completely refutes the unscriptural Doctrine of Predestination, which teaches that some are predestined to be lost and some to be Saved.

WHAT IS THE CURE FOR UNBELIEF?

Of course, there is nothing that can be

done, which will absolutely guarantee that an individual will without fail say *"yes"* to Jesus Christ. But yet, there are certainly some things which can be done which will guarantee that some will yield to the Lord.

The coming seven-year Great Tribulation, called *"... The Time of Jacob's Trouble ..."* (Jer. 30:7), among other things, will be brought about for that specific purpose — to bring Israel back to God. Israel today does not know God, and in fact has not known Him for over 2,000 years. Of course, there have been individual Jews who have been Saved, thereby serving Jesus Christ, but the Jews as a whole have remained adamant in their unbelief.

Tribulation (Dan. 9:27; Mat. 24:21), will bring Israel to the place that her only hope is God, in fact, the coming of the Messiah (Zech. 14:1-9). Great trouble, and this trouble will be the greatest that Israel has ever faced in all of her long history, has a tendency to cause people to look to God. Man has a tendency to depend upon himself; however, when he has exhausted his options, many will then cry to God, which Israel shall do at that day. Actually it will be during the Battle of Armageddon, when it looks like Israel will be totally destroyed. In fact, the Prophet Zechariah said that the situation will become so critical that half of Jerusalem will fall (Zech. 14:1-2).

THE COMING OF THE LORD

The Lord will hear their cry and deliver them, which will be carried out by His Second Coming, which will in fact, be the greatest moment in the history of all mankind. The Coming of the Lord will be accompanied by every Child of God who has ever lived, both Jews and Gentiles. These will be the great group who has had part in the First Resurrection (Rev. 20:5-6). Israel will then accept the Lord Jesus Christ as their Saviour and Messiah and be fully restored (Zech. 12:10-14; 13:1, 6).

The phrase, *"For God is able to graff* (graft) *them in again,"* refers to the Restoration of Israel.

When the Holy Spirit uses the word *"again,"* this simply means that it has been done before.

As well, irrespective of the problems of the past regarding Israel, if they will once again evidence Faith, which in this case means to trust and accept the Lord Jesus Christ as their Saviour and Messiah, the Lord, irrespective of the seeming impossibilities *"is able to graff* (graft) *them in again."*

One should never think that any situation is impossible, that is if a person will believe God. Whatever the past has been, whatever its difficulties and even impossibilities, if a person turns to Faith in God, God will never disappoint that person, but will always make Himself real unto them. As Paul said, *"God is able!"*

(24) "FOR IF THOU WERT CUT OUT OF THE OLIVE TREE WHICH IS WILD BY NATURE, AND WERT GRAFFED CONTRARY TO NATURE INTO A GOOD OLIVE TREE: HOW MUCH MORE SHALL THESE, WHICH BE THE NATURAL BRANCHES, BE GRAFFED INTO THEIR OWN OLIVE TREE?"

The phrase, *"For if thou wert cut out of the Olive Tree which is wild by nature,"* refers to the Gentile world, and in this case the Church.

The phrase, *"And wert graffed contrary to nature into a good Olive Tree,"* refers to the Church being grafted into this *"good Olive Tree,"* i.e., Israel, i.e., The Plan of God.

As we have previously stated, a fruitless Branch grafted to a good tree is contrary to custom and is simply not done. It is somewhat like putting a rotten apple into a barrel of good apples. The good apples never make the bad apple good, but the opposite always happens, with the bad apple corrupting the good apples.

However, by the Grace of God, the Lord allowed this wild Olive Branch to be grafted into the good Olive Tree, and by His Power, made it work, *"That He might present it to Himself a Glorious Church, not having spot, or wrinkle, or any such thing; but that it should be holy and without blemish"* (Eph. 5:27).

The question, *"How much more shall these, which be the natural Branches, be graffed into their own Olive Tree?"*, speaks of Israel.

The idea is: it is not natural at all to

NOTES

graft an inferior branch into a superior tree; however, it is perfectly natural to graft in good branches.

Some may complain that Israel did not turn out to be a *"Good Olive Tree;"* however, it is not so much Israel that is in question here, but rather the Plan of God. That and beyond the shadow of a doubt, is a *"Good Olive Tree."*

Israel happened to be a part of that Plan. Israel failed, but the Plan did not fail. That which God had ordained, the Salvation of sinners, has been done and is being done, irrespective of Israel's failure. However, Israel will be brought back, and will evangelize the world as originally planned, which will take place in the coming Kingdom Age (Isa. 66:19).

(25) "FOR I WOULD NOT, BRETHREN, THAT YE SHOULD BE IGNORANT OF THIS MYSTERY, LEST YE SHOULD BE WISE IN YOUR OWN CONCEITS; THAT BLINDNESS IN PART IS HAPPENED TO ISRAEL, UNTIL THE FULNESS OF THE GENTILES BE COME IN."

The phrase, *"For I would not, Brethren, that ye should be ignorant of this mystery,"* pertains to that of which Paul has been speaking, the setting aside of Israel with the inclusion of the Gentiles.

In fact, Paul uses the word *"mystery"* quite often. The Greek word is *"musterion,"* which means *"something previously hidden, which is now fully revealed."* Most of that which is labeled as a *"mystery"* comes from the Old Testament, although given to us in the New. Many things in the Old Testament were in shadow or type, meaning that they pointed to something that was to come, which would be the reality of the shadow, etc. Consequently, as the shadow or the type could not fully reveal what the Lord intended, it remained a mystery.

Paul used the word more than anyone else, because it was to Paul that the Meaning of the New Covenant was given. Consequently, he had a better grasp or understanding of the Scriptures, I think, than anyone else. As well, he knew the Law of Moses as no other person in the world of his day. In fact, before his conversion to Christ, he had been the fair-haired boy of the Pharisees, so to speak, groomed to take the place of the great Scholar, Gamaliel. So, these *"mysteries"* became quite clear to the Great Apostle. As a result, in his Epistles, he gave us the clear meaning of many of these mysteries, thereby clearing up the confusion.

Even though the word *"mystery"* is not found in the Old Testament, which means it is altogether in the New, still, as stated, the *"mystery"* began in Old Testament times. This is one of the reasons that presently we have a much Better Covenant, based on much Better Promises, than those of the Old Covenant. It is admitted that we presently still *"see through a glass darkly"*; still, the information we currently have, all due to the New Covenant, is far ahead of that which was given under the Old Covenant.

For instance, in Old Testament times, the Doctrine of the Resurrection, although known, was still dim. It was not until Christ came, Who is the Resurrection and the Life, that it was finally made clear. That information also was given to the Apostle Paul, as he gave to us in the great Fifteenth Chapter of I Corinthians.

The phrase, *"Lest ye should be wise in your own conceits,"* simply means that the Gentiles were not pulled in because of any merit or righteousness on their part, but strictly because of the Grace of God.

In effect, this which the Lord has done respecting Israel and the Gentiles, should create a wonder and awe at the Mercy and Grace of God, in allowing these wild Olive Branches to be grafted into the *"Good Olive Tree."* In other words, the thoughts of such, should humble one, instead of having the opposite effect.

And if the Lord did that, and He certainly did, He will surely be able to bring Israel back.

The phrase, *"That blindness in part is happened to Israel,"* is the *"mystery"* of which Paul speaks.

THE GRACE OF GOD

As I have attempted to write Commentary on this Chapter, I have sensed the Presence of God I think, in a greater way than any of our other efforts in this respect. The Holy Spirit speaking through the Apostle has made me realize more than ever, how wonderful is the Grace of God.

Even though this of which the Lord has done is far greater than the mind of man can even comprehend, perhaps one can only fully understand it, at least somewhat, by that which the Lord has done in one's own immediate family.

I was born into a home on March 15th, 1935, that did not know God. In fact, until my Dad was 25 years old, which was when I was five years of age, he had never even seen a Bible. He had never attended a single Church Service anywhere at anytime. He had never heard a Gospel Song in all of his life. My Mother was pretty much in the same category.

Consequently, but for the Grace of God, there was no way that my family could know the Lord. We were doomed to an eternal darkness, without God and without hope.

But yet the Grace of God, brought this great Gospel to our little hometown of Ferriday, Louisiana, with ultimately the entirety of my family coming to a Saving Knowledge of the Lord Jesus Christ.

"Oh happy day, Oh happy day,
"When Jesus washed my sins away."

ISRAEL

However, part of that which I feel so strongly concerning this Chapter, is as well a sorrow for Israel. As I have previously stated, beyond the shadow of a doubt, their Fall is the greatest catastrophe in the history of man. As well, let not anyone think that their Fall affected only themselves, but let all know and understand that it actually affected the entirety of the Earth.

While it is true that their Fall did not stop the great Plan of God from being fulfilled, in that the Lord grafted in the Gentiles, still, the loss was awful, not only for Israel, but as stated, for the entirety of the world.

In the first place, their rejecting Jesus Christ, which constituted their Fall, submitted this world to what is now another 2,000 years of war, famines, pestilences, earthquakes, and sorrows (Mat. 24:6-8).

The idea is, the world has been submitted to that, when it could have had Peace (Isa. 2:4), the very nature of all of Creation changed (Isa. 11:6-9), universal Healing (Isa. 35:3-6), an end to hunger (Isa. 35:1), honest government (Isa. 9:6-7), and eternal security (Isa. 65:18-23). As well, there will be Eternal Life for all who call upon His Name (Isa. 58:9).

So, even though we have only touched the surface, I think it should be obvious as to what the world has suffered by Israel's Fall. How so it will be blessed, when Israel returns.

The phrase, *"Until the fulness of the Gentiles be come in,"* speaks of the completion of the Mystical Body of Christ made up of both Jews and Gentiles, in what is commonly referred to as the *"Church."* It speaks of all Jews and Gentiles Saved from the Day of Pentecost to the Rapture of the Church (Resurrection).

THE TIMES OF THE GENTILES AND THE FULLNESS OF THE GENTILES

These are two different terms, and should not be confused.

The *". . . Times of the Gentiles . . ."* is that which Jesus spoke of in Luke 21:24.

It refers to that time from Nebuchadnezzar's deportation of the dynasty of David and will conclude with the defeat of the Antichrist at Armageddon. This time has lasted already for about 2600 years. It is during which the Gentiles have ruled over the Jews.

The *"Fullness of the Gentiles"* refers to the Church. It speaks of the completion of the Mystical Body of Christ made up of both Jew and Gentile as stated, who have been Saved from the Day of Pentecost to the coming Resurrection (Rapture of the Church) (Acts 15:14; Eph. 4:11-13; I Cor. 12:12-13).

The hardening of Israel extends to the time when the last sinner comes in to Salvation, completing this Age of Grace, completing the Body of Christ. The Rapture occurs, the Seventieth Week of Daniel comes sometime after this event, and at the Second Advent, Israel will then be Saved (Restored).

FOUR RAPTURES

Actually, the First Resurrection will continue on into the Great Tribulation. The Scripture actually speaks of Four Raptures. They are:

NOTES

1. That which is referred to as the main Rapture (I Thess. 4:16-17).

2. The 144,000 Jews, who will be saved in the first three and a half years of the Great Tribulation. They will be raptured at the midpoint (Rev. 7:1-8; 12:5; 14:1-5).

3. There will be many people who will come to Christ in the Great Tribulation, who will pay with their lives. They will be included in the First Resurrection (Rev. 6:9-11; 7:9-17; 15:2-4; 20:4-6).

4. The two witnesses, who will be Enoch and Elijah, will be raptured at the very conclusion of the Great Tribulation. This will end what is referred to as the *"First Resurrection"* (Rev. 11:7-11).

In fact, the words *"Rapture"* and *"Resurrection,"* at least as it refers to the First Resurrection, actually mean the same thing. The details of the Resurrection are given to us in the Fifteenth Chapter of I Corinthians.

(26) "AND SO ALL ISRAEL SHALL BE SAVED: AS IT IS WRITTEN, THERE SHALL COME OUT OF SION THE DELIVERER, AND SHALL TURN AWAY UNGODLINESS FROM JACOB:"

The phrase, *"And so all Israel shall be Saved,"* refers to the individual Salvation of each member of the Nation of Israel living at the time of the Second Advent. Zechariah 13:1 predicts this cleansing of Israel from its sins in the words, *"In that day there shall be a fountain opened to the House of David and to the inhabitants of Jerusalem for sin and uncleanness."*

This individual cleansing from sin will be followed by a National Restoration to the Messianic Kingdom with the Messiah reigning on the Throne of David in Jerusalem as King of kings and Lord of lords for 1,000 years and then forever.

Actually, every Jew on the face of the Earth at that time, will be brought to Israel. The indication is that all will then accept Christ as their Saviour and Messiah (Isa. 11:11-12; 14:1; 27:12; 41:9; 43:5; 60:9; 66:20; Jer. 30:10; 31:8; 32:37; 33:7; 46:27; 50:4; Ezek. 16:53; 20:33-40; 34:11; 36:24; Hos. 2:14; 3:5; Zech. 2:6; 10:6, 9).

The phrase, *"As it is written, There shall come out of Sion the Deliverer, and shall turn away ungodliness from Jacob,"* is quoted from a combination of Isaiah 27:9; 59:20-21.

Jesus Christ will be the Deliverer, Who will deliver Israel from the Antichrist, and more importantly, will deliver them from their sins. He Alone can *"turn away ungodliness from Jacob!"*

(27) "FOR THIS IS MY COVENANT UNTO THEM, WHEN I SHALL TAKE AWAY THEIR SINS."

One is struck by the constancy of Paul's reference to Old Testament Scriptures. As well, oftentimes he combines Passages even as here. This shows us two things:

1. Paul was, without a doubt, the greatest Old Testament Scholar of his day. His knowledge of the Law of Moses, and the Promises of God in general, proclaims a vast knowledge of God's Word to man.

2. As well, we are shown here the veracity of the Scriptures, whenever the Holy Spirit allows the Apostle to join particular Scriptures, taken from totally different parts of the Word of God, and at the same time maintain their integrity. Even though this does show Paul's knowledge of the Word, even more so it shows the absoluteness of the Scriptures as the Word of God, i.e., the Living Word of God which cannot fail. This shows us the immutability of the Scriptures. God keeps His *"Covenants,"* irrespective as to what those Covenants may be.

(28) "AS CONCERNING THE GOSPEL, THEY ARE ENEMIES FOR YOUR SAKES: BUT AS TOUCHING THE ELECTION, THEY ARE BELOVED FOR THE FATHERS' SAKES."

The phrase, *"As concerning the Gospel, they are enemies for your sakes,"* refers to the Gospel of Jesus Christ.

The attitude of God with regard to Israel is determined by or with reference to, the Gospel and its rejection. In view of that rejection, God counts Israel as an enemy.

"Enemies for your sakes," means by rejecting and opposing the Gospel, such has been the occasion of the Gentiles having been now called in. And yet, down through the nearly 2,000 years of Israel's blindness, there is no record, at least that of which I am aware, of Jews taking up arms against Christians. In fact, even now, despite their rejection of the Gospel, and despite their

NOTES

integrity of Zionism, there is an unspoken kindred spirit (and sometimes not so much unspoken), between Israel and the Nations of the world which by and large embrace Protestant Christianity.

But yet, for all of these centuries, Jews have had a misconceived idea respecting Christianity. Considering what she faced one can well comprehend the misunderstanding.

In about the Third Century the Church began to apostatize, gradually degenerating into what is now known as the *"Catholic Church."* In fact, the apostasy was just about complete by the beginning of the Seventh Century, if not before. Inasmuch as the greater majority of those who referred to themselves as followers of Christ were in Truth unregenerate, animosity toward Jews was quite strong. In fact, of those who truly followed the Lord, thereby being truly Born Again, such constituted only a small Remnant.

During the times of the Crusades, Jews were slaughtered by the Crusaders about as readily as were the Moslems. Consequently, as far as Jews were concerned, those who called themselves *"Christians"* were their biggest enemies, and rightly so. To be sure, the Catholic Church has never expressed any Love for the Jews. In fact, it did very little to stem the tide of the Holocaust, even when opportunities presented themselves. In fact, Adolph Hitler called himself a *"Christian,"* and in his warped, demented, demon-possessed mind, considered himself doing the world a favor by ridding it of Jews.

Irrespective that he was a demon-possessed maniac, Jews actually thought of him as a *"Christian,"* and with some justification.

RECENT TIMES

Only since World War II has True Christianity, at least for the most part, begun to make itself felt. In fact, this (True Christianity) is the very reason for America's stand respecting the protection of the State of Israel. It is difficult for Israel to understand this, but it is so. Not meaning to be negative, but at the same time desiring to be forthright, if America was basically Catholic as many countries, such protection would not be afforded. To be frank, even as with England where a false Christianity prevails in the nature of the Church of England, etc., the same animosity as with Catholicism rears its ugly head against the Jews. It is only the True Christians in this world who truly stand with Israel, and for the obvious reasons. They know the Word of God, and, consequently, know exactly what Paul is addressing in this 11th Chapter of Romans, plus the Old Testament Prophets.

Even though Israel is an enemy as it concerns the Gospel, still, the Covenant of God continues to hold true respecting these people, when He said, ". . . *I will bless them that bless thee, and curse him that curseth thee . . .*" (Gen. 12:3). God meant exactly what He said!

AMERICA

America's stand with Israel, is one of the things that insures the Blessings of God for this Country. It is at least one of the reasons that this Nation is the only super power left in the world. It is the reason that America is the Nation of choice for most of the world. It is also the reason, whether America likes it or not, that this Country is the policeman of the world. Among other things, God has appointed this Nation as the guardian of Israel during this very particular trying time. In fact, were it not for the United States, and more particularly, God using this Country, there would not be any Israel as a Nation.

The phrase, *"But as touching the Election, they are beloved for the Fathers' sakes,"* speaks of their Calling.

It does not mean that particular Jews are elected to be lost while others are elected to be Saved. It does mean, that Israel has been elected for a particular purpose, which in effect is the basic story of the Bible. That *"Election"* is very special in the Eyes of God, and should be very special in the eyes of every Believer.

As we have said innumerable times, Israel was raised up, i.e., elected: A. To give the world the Word of God; B. To bring the Messiah into the world; and, C. To evangelize the world with the Gospel. They failed on the last point, but will yet carry out even that Command in the coming Kingdom Age.

Knowing that everything we have in the

NOTES

realm of the Word of God has come into this world because of the Faith of Abraham, Isaac, and Jacob, with whom God made an Everlasting Covenant, the reason for the Love of the Believer for Israel should be overly obvious. In fact, the world owes a debt of gratitude to the Jew, of which it can never repay. Every iota of freedom, prosperity, and that which is sensible and right, have come into this world because of the Word of God and the Advent of the Lord Jesus Christ. As repeatedly stated, the vehicle for this action was Israel.

So, when one reads the stories of Abraham, Isaac, and Jacob in the Old Testament, one is not merely reading a biography or even a history, but rather the struggle of Redemption. In effect, the Salvation of humanity was hinged on their Faith. So, when Paul says, *"They are beloved for the Fathers' sakes,"* the weight of such a statement is of far greater magnitude than meets the eye.

(29) "FOR THE GIFTS AND CALLING OF GOD ARE WITHOUT REPENTANCE."

God is not a man that He should lie, neither the Son of man that He should repent. In other words, when the Lord calls someone, He will not change His mind about that Call; irrespective of the situation of the individual, the Call remains. In fact, some may fail the Lord, and thereby fail to carry out the Call on their lives. But the Call remains! It only awaits the individual getting right with God, and then the carrying out of the Call can proceed.

"Gifts" as here used in the Greek is *"Charisma,"* and means *"a favor which one receives without any merit of one's own."* These *"Gifts,"* according to Godet, are not the moral and intellectual qualifications with which Israel was endowed for its mission in the world, but the privileges of Grace spoken of in Romans 9:4.

"Calling" in the Greek is *"klesis,"* and means regarding Israel, *"God's authoritative invitation to be a part in the Messianic Kingdom."* From Israel these things can never be withdrawn.

The words *"Without repentance"* in the Greek are *"ametameletos,"* and mean, *"that the Gifts and Calling of God are not subject to a change of mind on God's part."* That is, He will not change His Mind regarding His Chosen People, the Jews, and their God-ordained mission and destiny, or anyone else for that matter whom He has called.

A VERY PERSONAL EXPERIENCE

Knowing the Call of God, and how Satan opposes that Call, I suppose that my empathy for Israel may be somewhat greater than normal.

Wanting the Reader to understand that failure is never permissible with God and never condoned in any way for that matter, still, it is only those who have never fought any battles who have all the answers. In fact, armchair Generals, and Monday morning quarterbacks are a dime a dozen. Unfortunately, those particular ranks in the Church are overly swollen, and seem to always remain in that capacity.

God called me when I was but a child, and without going into detail, considering the hundreds of thousands of people we have seen brought to a Saving Knowledge of Jesus Christ, I think the veracity of that Calling should be obvious, at least for those who desire the Truth.

At the same time, I know what it is to face the Powers of Darkness to such an extent that as Paul said, *". . . We were pressed out of measure, above strength, insomuch that we despaired even of life"* (II Cor. 1:8).

In October of 1991, not knowing what else to do, with this Ministry looking as if it was completely destroyed, all I knew to do was to cry to God from the position of a broken heart. Actually, Preachers galore were telling me in essence that we should quit, the Call of God was no longer there, or we had forfeited that Call, etc. In fact, the Denomination with which we had formerly been associated, and in whose Churches we had placed literally tens of thousands of converts all around the world, had grandly announced to the world in every way that was humanly possible, that our *"Gifts and Calling"* were no longer valid. Almost every other Denomination, and in fact every Denomination as far as I knew, followed suit.

WHAT DID THE LORD SAY?

As for our wilderness experience, it did

NOTES

not begin in October of 1991, but as far as I am concerned, the instruction by the Lord did begin at that critical juncture. I have learned to depend totally and completely on Him, because there was no other on whom I could depend. Man not only would not help me, but most were doing all within their power to destroy me. So, if God did not give direction, there was no direction forthcoming, at least that offered any hope whatsoever. If God did not meet the need, the need simply could not be met. Consequently, there was only one way that direction and provision could be sought, and that was in prayer and supplication before the Lord.

At that time, the Lord told me to begin two Prayer Meetings a day, one in the morning and then during the evening. This we did, having only missed two days during all of these years, with the exception of the times that Frances and I were out of town. Even then, the Prayer Meetings continued without me, with Donnie in charge, etc.

THE PRAYER MEETINGS

To be frank, I know I could not have made it without these constant times before the Lord. Time and time again, when it looked like there was no hope, and the Ministry would surely drown beneath every type of onslaught, the Lord would give me assurance in prayer and direction. Time and time again, when I would be so discouraged that it seemed impossible to continue, the Spirit of God would move mightily in one of the Prayer Meetings, and I would leave literally floating on air, as the Lord would lift us up. He has been, and is, and to be frank ever shall continue to be, our only Source. He has taught me to trust Him and Him completely. He has weaned me away from Denominational Religion, on which most Preachers rely, and which I once relied. He has taught me that He can set a table even in the wilderness. In fact, I have watched Him perform Miracle after Miracle in every sense.

In the financial sense, He has literally performed a Miracle for us every single day. To be sure, I exaggerate not. With almost every Preacher in the world vehemently denouncing us, or else strongly discouraging anyone from supporting us, only God could perform the impossible, which He does day after day. Of course, most of the Church world denies that it is God, but attributes such to manipulation or whatever. But I know that it is the Lord, and that's all that matters.

THE GOOD FIGHT OF FAITH

In this Good Fight of Faith, for that's what it is, Frances and Donnie, along with quite a number of the people in our Church, Family Worship Center, have stood with us in this vigil of Prayer and Supplication, daring to believe God for great and mighty things. We are not asking Him only for the survival of this Ministry, but that we may finish this Course laid out for us, which is to touch this world with the Gospel of Jesus Christ. As I dictate these words, He has already begun to move in a mighty way, which I believe will ultimately result in the greatest Move of God we have ever seen, and which I believe the world has ever seen as well. Of course, His Moving and Operation will be with many, but I definitely believe that we will have a part in that which He is doing and shall do.

THE EXACT WORDS . . .

At the darkest time in that month of October, that Thursday night in 1991, not knowing what to do, not knowing where to turn, and with almost all of the Church world demanding that we close the doors, I took the entirety of the situation to the Lord in prayer. There were eight or nine of us present that night. At a particular point, the Spirit of God began to move in that room, and in one of the greatest ways I have ever known.

In my petition to Him, all I wanted was His Will. What did He want us to do? What was His Will for my life and this Ministry?

At a particular point in time that night, even as the Spirit of God moved mightily in that room, a Message came forth in Prophecy. It was to the point and very direct. *"I am not a Man that I should lie, neither the Son of Man that I should repent. What I have blessed nothing can curse."* Those were His exact words!

When that Word was given, there was no doubt in the room that it was from God.

NOTES

The Spirit of God moved in such a way as I think I have never seen Him move. Every person in that room was powerfully touched, even some who were not too accustomed to this of which I speak. To be sure, the situation was so dark, that more than likely most there thought the same as much of the Church world. We should quit, which was probably uppermost in their minds.

It was instantly obvious as to what the Lord was saying. He had called us for a particular task. That task was and is World Evangelism. When He called us, He did not lie about the Calling. Neither has He repented or changed His Mind about the matter. Respecting that, we have His Blessings, and every effort of Hell, despite its severity, is doomed to failure.

There is no way that I can properly explain as to exactly how I felt that night. I knew God had spoken. I knew what I was to do. I realized that it would not be easy, not at all! I knew that Satan would not discontinue his efforts, even though God had made His Will plainly known. I knew that the Church so-called, would fight us severely and even to a greater extent. But the Lord had told me what to do, and this I must do.

To be sure, things have come very slowly. As with Abraham and Sarah, Isaac was not born quickly. And yet I see a greater Moving and Operation of the Holy Spirit within my own personal life today than I have ever previously known. As well, what I presently see, only makes me know and realize there is much more needed and I believe much more to come. So, this 29th verse as given by the Apostle Paul, is very dear to me because it is the Word of God. But on a personal basis, it is very special, because at a period of time in my life, it was a Passage to which I could hold. Thank God it was a Solid Rock!

(30) "FOR AS YE IN TIMES PAST HAVE NOT BELIEVED GOD, YET HAVE NOW OBTAINED MERCY THROUGH THEIR UNBELIEF:"

The phrase, *"For as ye in times past have not believed God,"* concerns the Gentile world which lived outside of the Promises of God for about 4,000 years. In fact, they not only lived outside the Promises, but actually did not even believe in God.

As Paul addressed the Athenian Philosophers in Acts Chapter 17, it is obvious despite all their learning, that they had no knowledge of God whatsoever. They had little progressed, if at all, beyond the worship of reptiles and animals, etc. In fact, the best they could do, was call down some devised gods who supposedly lived somewhere in the heavens, etc. The True God, Who Paul introduced to them, was exactly as they had said, *"Unknown!"* (Acts 17:23).

The phrase, *"Yet have now obtained Mercy through their unbelief,"* refers to the unbelief of Israel.

Israel being called of God to present the Gospel to the Gentiles, not only refused to fulfill that Calling, but refused to even believe the Gospel themselves. As a result, it seems as if God accelerated the process of World Evangelism, despite the attitude and unbelief of the Jews. Two things are here in view:

1. Israel's rejection did not stop the propagation of the Gospel.

2. As well, and as stated, the Text implies that God accelerated the situation. Mostly through one man, Paul, a great part of the Roman World would be evangelized. It is as if God said that Mercy would not be withheld from the Gentiles even in their lost condition, irrespective of Israel's unbelief. The Gospel would be presented to them, even as it was.

IS THIS ATTRIBUTE OF GOD POSSIBLE AS WELL IN THE CHURCH?

By that we are asking a question concerning the Mercy of God.

If certain segments of the Church function in unbelief, which is meant to stop the Work of God, even as Israel functioned in her unbelief, does that mean the Work of God is stopped? It does as far as that segment of the Church is concerned. However, I believe that the Holy Spirit through the Apostle, is telling us here that the Lord will rather accelerate Mercy through the segment of the Church which believes Him, even as small as that segment or Remnant may be.

Israel of New Testament times, was not willing to simply reject the Gospel, but rather felt she had to stop its propagation as well.

Even though she did everything within her power to carry out this wicked task, still, every evidence shows that she did not succeed, and that great Churches were built all over the Roman Empire, as the Mercy of God was shown, even accelerated and exaggerated to the Gentiles.

Many in the modern Church functioning in unbelief, have the same spirit. They not only reject what God is doing, but attempt to destroy that which He is doing. From these Texts and personal experience, I believe that God in fact, does increase Mercy in these circumstances, at least to those who believe Him. Men rule, but God overrules! As well, I believe that opposition tendered by those who claim His Name, but actually do not possess the proper ownership of that Name, only tend to accelerate the Mercy of God extended to those, as stated, who dare to believe Him.

(31) "EVEN SO HAVE THESE ALSO NOW NOT BELIEVED, THAT THROUGH YOUR MERCY THEY ALSO MAY OBTAIN MERCY."

The phrase, *"Even so have these also now not believed,"* pertains once again to Israel, and the fact that even though they are now in unbelief, this will ultimately change.

The phrase, *"That through your Mercy they also may obtain Mercy,"* can be explained in this way.

Upon Israel's failure, the Lord grafted in the Gentiles, i.e., The Church. The Church has done two things: A. Continued the Work of God in taking the great Message of Redemption to sinners; and, B. Has stood in Israel's place during this time, in effect keeping this place and position for her until she returns, which she shall.

In this manner, the Mercy which was extended to the Gentiles, will ultimately bring Israel back as well, with the entirety of the Plan of God now coming full circle.

(32) "FOR GOD HATH CONCLUDED THEM ALL IN UNBELIEF, THAT HE MIGHT HAVE MERCY UPON ALL."

The phrase, *"For God hath concluded them all in unbelief,"* contains the thought that God confined both Jew and Gentile within the scope of one kind of guilt, that of unbelief. The past unbelief of the Gentiles and the mercy they presently enjoy, the present unbelief of the Jews, and the mercy they are determined to enjoy in the future — these things not only correspond to each other, but they are interwoven with each other; they are parts of a system which God controls, and in which every element conditions and is conditioned by all the rest. The idea is this, at least as it pertains to this scenario.

When it is all concluded, Israel will not be able to say, even as she once did, that she is worthy of Salvation due to the fact of being God's Chosen People, etc. Due to her terrible night of unbelief, which she brought upon herself, she will know and beyond the shadow of a doubt, in that coming glad day when she is finally brought to a proper realization of the Lord Jesus Christ, that her Restoration is strictly through the Mercy and Grace of God and for no other reason.

As well, the Gentiles will likewise know and understand, that their being grafted in was not because of any merit on their part, but likewise, because of the Grace of God.

The phrase, *"That He might have Mercy upon all,"* proclaims God's condition of dealing with the entirety of the human family, both Jew and Gentile, as that of *"Mercy!"*

All were in unbelief, all were shown *"Mercy,"* and all who evidenced Faith, were Saved.

In fact, this is nothing new with God, in that this has been His Word all along. While the Gentiles knew that they had no merit with God, or at least surely should know, Mercy being their only Salvation, Israel refused to come on that basis. Surely, at least in her thinking, she would not be demanded to come the same way as Gentile dogs! Most certainly, at least in her thinking, the privileges afforded her, merited her at least something with God!

ALL BY FAITH

That all must come by Faith, having no merit whatsoever, throwing themselves on the Mercy of God, Israel could not accept; therefore, she has to be brought to the place, and will be brought to that place through her own volition, that she ultimately will cry for Mercy, realizing it is her only hope, and then will be Saved.

One is not to think that God has changed His Plan of Redemption, for He definitely

has not. Israel has to be made to conform to that Plan, which she shall!

Jew and Gentile alike must be made to feel the need of Grace by being shut up under disobedience. It is within Paul's thought to say that the sin of Jews and Gentiles to whom he preached the Gospel, did not lie outside the control, or outside the redeeming purpose of God; but it does not mean to say or to be within Paul's thoughts, that God ordained sin in general for the sake of, or with the view to, Redemption. While God subordinates sin to His Purpose, it is not a subordinate element in His Purpose. In other words, God never receives Glory from sin, but He does receive Glory from victory over sin.

To say it another way, God never forces a person to sin or leads one into sin, in order that they may learn a lesson; however, He definitely does allow Believers or those as Israel who claim Faith, but really do not possess such, to go their own way of disobedience, that they may ultimately learn a lesson. In fact, while God uses everything, be it Satan or sin, He is not the cause of such, that being the evil hearts of men. God is *never* the author, instigator, perpetrator or originator of disobedience, sin, unrighteousness, or wrongdoing of any nature. He *never* elects or ordains such. That in its entirety, as stated, comes from the wicked, unregenerate, evil hearts of unbelief in men. However, and as stated, He does use these things once they are perpetrated, in order to bring about His Perfect Will. Again, to say it another way, Satan will ultimately do the Will of God, although it will be for the ultimate Plan and Purpose of God, not for himself. Satan will ultimately be lost forever (Rev. 20:10).

(33) "O THE DEPTH OF THE RICHES BOTH OF THE WISDOM AND KNOWLEDGE OF GOD! HOW UNSEARCHABLE ARE HIS JUDGMENTS, AND HIS WAYS PAST FINDING OUT!"

The phrase, *"O the depth of the riches both of the Wisdom and Knowledge of God,"* presents that which is beyond the comprehension of man.

Paul, greatly disturbed by the spiritual condition of the Jews, fearing they are utterly lost because of their rejection of the Gospel, sought the Lord earnestly concerning the future of these people, his People. Are they out forever? Are they no more, at least as far as God is concerned?

In his seeking the Lord, Revelation was afforded and given unto him respecting that which the Lord will do with Israel in the future. This he gives us in this 11th Chapter.

In no way does this mean that all those in the meantime will ultimately be Saved, for they shall not. It only pertains to those who are alive at the time of the Second Coming, who will then be redeemed by the Grace of God, and will fulfill the Purpose of God concerning their destiny. All of this is by the Grace of God.

Paul well knows and understands what the Prophets of old have said concerning Israel's Restoration. Nevertheless, he no doubt wondered how this could be, especially considering that Israel had not only rejected her Messiah, she had in fact, murdered Him. Paul knew this very well, having himself once been the great opposer of the Gospel and, thereby, of Jesus Christ.

However, when the Lord gave to the Apostle the Revelation of not only the means of Grace by which Israel would be restored, but as well, the place and position of the Church in the entirety of the scheme of things, Paul could only exclaim at the *"depth of the riches both of the Wisdom and Knowledge of God!"*

It is something he had not known, despite his vast knowledge of the Scriptures, but now sees so clearly in Scripture, telling us, that the *"depth of these riches"* is all ensconced in the Word of God. In other words, there is no *"Wisdom or Knowledge"* on the part of God that is not given somewhere in His Word, that is if proper interpretation is accorded, which can only come by the illumination of the Holy Spirit (I Cor. 2:14).

The phrase, *"How unsearchable are His Judgments, and His Ways past finding out,"* pertains to man's own intellect or brain power. However, the Spirit of God, even as with Paul, can reveal these *"Judgments"* and *"Ways."*

"Past finding out" in the Greek is *"anexichniastos,"* and means *"that which cannot be traced out."* The word could be

NOTES

used of a blood-hound who found it impossible to follow the scent of a criminal, or of a guide who could not trace out or follow a path in the woods (Vincent).

Once again, this speaks of man's natural ability, even that of the Believer. These things are not *"past finding out"* to the Holy Spirit, and He will reveal the Word of God to those who will dare to believe Him, seeking His Wisdom, even as Paul here portrays.

(34) "FOR WHO HATH KNOWN THE MIND OF THE LORD? OR WHO HATH BEEN HIS COUNSELLOR?"

The question, *"For who hath known the Mind of the Lord?"*, as well as the next, was probably derived from Isaiah 40:13-14.

The only way for the *"Mind of the Lord"* to be known, even as we have already stated, is for it to be revealed by the Holy Spirit. However, Paul is dealing with the idea of Omniscience which means that God is All-Knowing, past, present, and future. Consequently, it is impossible for man to comprehend such!

The question, *"Or who hath been His counsellor?"*, would have to be answered *"no one."*

The idea is, that Lucifer whose name means *"morning star or light bearer,"* thinks he is wiser than God. In fact, the Scripture does say about him, *". . . Thou sealest up the sum, full of wisdom, and perfect in beauty"* (Ezek. 28:12).

He has deceived himself into believing that his wisdom is greater even than that of his Creator. And to be sure, he *is* far beyond the ability or intelligence of men. However, he is not Omniscient as God; consequently, God's abilities are far above this creature.

That is at least one of the reasons it is so foolish for Believers to trust in worldly wisdom, especially considering, that the wisdom of the ages is available to all who will simply seek its knowledge. It is found in the Word of God, and careful consecration will enlist the help of the Holy Spirit, which gives the Believer a decided advantage.

(35) "OR WHO HATH FIRST GIVEN TO HIM, AND IT SHALL BE RECOMPENSED UNTO HIM AGAIN?"

This Passage is derived from Job 41:11.

The original Hebrew says, *"Who hath first given unto Me, that I should repay him?"*

This Passage in Job actually speaks of

Satan. In essence, the Lord is saying that all the trouble and heartache that Satan has caused, are going to be brought back on his own head. In effect, the Lord has thrown out the gauntlet, in a sense daring Satan or any of his fallen angels to try to stop him. The King James Version from Job 41:11 says, *"Who hath prevented Me, that I should repay him? . . ."* From this and other Passages (Rev. 20:10), we know that Satan is doomed. Admittedly, it is a mystery, to which we have already alluded, as to why God has allowed him to continue this long. However, in the light of eternity, in other words in the manner in which God looks at things, this past 6,000 years have been a very short period of time. His destruction and all he represents, is soon to be brought about, even sooner than anyone thinks.

(36) "FOR OF HIM, AND THROUGH HIM, AND TO HIM, ARE ALL THINGS: TO WHOM BE GLORY FOR EVER. AMEN."

The phrase, *"For of him,"* refers to Creation. God is the Creator of all things, and all things which He has created are *"very good"* (Gen. 1:31). This refers to His Omnipotence, i.e., All-Powerful.

The phrase, *"And through Him,"* refers to His Omniscience, i.e., perfect knowledge, past, present, and future. So, this means that Satan must go *"through"* the Lord for everything he does, with the Lord allowing only certain latitude (Job Chapters 1-2).

The phrase, *"And to Him,"* refers to his Omnipresence, i.e., His Presence is everywhere. He Alone is the First Cause.

The phrase, *"Are all things,"* means exactly what it says.

Nothing is done in God's vast Creation, without His overshadowing Presence. As we have stated, Satan must ask His permission for whatever is done, and permission is given only in the context as to the Will of God, and not Satan (Job Chpt. 1). Anyone who has the power to note every sparrow's fall to the ground, and is able to number the very hairs of each head of each person in the world, and to do so constantly, points to a degree of intelligence and involvement which are beyond comprehension (Mat. 10:29-30). When He said *"all things,"* He meant *"all things!"*

NOTES

The phrase, *"To Whom be Glory for ever,"* refers to the fact that all of this portrays the Glory of God and will do so *"forever."*

So, even all of these thousands of years of sorrow and heartache brought about by the Evil One, will ultimately fall out to the Glory of God. That means that Satan never takes best, and in fact, can never take best. No matter how the situation may look at present, and irrespective as to how long it may take, all will ultimately fall out to the Glory of God.

Of course, God never receives Glory out of sin, failure or disobedience; however, He does receive Glory out of victory over these things, which is always the ultimate goal in one way or the other. God cannot be defeated and, consequently, will not be defeated!

The word *"Amen,"* simply means that this situation will not change respecting the Power and Glory of God. Who He is, and What He is, is a foregone conclusion.

James said, *"Every good gift and perfect gift is from above, and cometh down from the Father of Lights, with Whom is no variableness, neither shadow of turning"* (James 1:17).

"How firm a foundation, ye Saints of the Lord,
"Is laid for your Faith in His excellent Word!
"What more can He say than to you He hath said,
"To you who for refuge to Jesus have fled?"

"Fear not, I am with thee; Oh be not dismayed,
"For I am thy God, and will still give thee aid;
"I'll strengthen thee, help thee, and cause thee to stand,
"Upheld by My Righteous, Omnipotent Hand."

"When through fiery trials thy pathway shall lie,
"My Grace, all sufficient, shall be thy supply:
"The flame shall not hurt thee; I only design,
"Thy dross to consume, and thy gold to refine."

*"The soul that on Jesus hath leaned
    for repose,
"I will not, I will not desert to his foes;
"That soul, though all Hell should en-
    deavor to shake,
"I'll never, no, never, no, never for-
    sake!"*
Amen.

CHAPTER 12

(1) "I BESEECH YOU THEREFORE, BRETHREN, BY THE MERCIES OF GOD, THAT YE PRESENT YOUR BODIES A LIVING SACRIFICE, HOLY, ACCEPTABLE UNTO GOD, WHICH IS YOUR REASONABLE SERVICE."

Now that Paul has outlined to us in the 11th Chapter of Romans, how that the Lord in His Mercy and Grace has allowed the Gentile Church to be grafted into the *"Good Olive Tree,"* and that it is through no merit of our own that we are there; he now tells us in the concluding Chapters of this Great Epistle of Romans, how in fact, we should conduct ourselves as Believers.

Beautifully and amazingly enough, he starts out with instruction respecting our physical bodies offered as a Living Sacrifice. Why does the Holy Spirit through the Apostle present this first of all?

As Paul addressed in Romans Chapter 7, it is through the physical members of our bodies in which sin and disobedience are carried out. In the 8th Chapter of Romans he tells us how the Holy Spirit gives us victory over the flesh, according to what Jesus did for us at Calvary and the Resurrection, which are outlined in Romans Chapter 6. So now, he comes to the practicalities of our living for God.

It is said in Romans Chapters 1-8, that Paul explains the Doctrines of Condemnation, Justification, Sanctification, and Glorification. In Romans Chapters 9-11, he explains to Israel why the Abrahamic and Davidic Covenants have not been fulfilled. Now, in Romans Chapters 12-16, the Apostle exhorts to a life in conformity with

NOTES

the exalted position in which Romans Chapters 1-8 place the Believer, and in view also of the God-given ability which the Believer has to live such a life.

Romans Chapters 1-8 consist of Doctrine which must always precede exhortation since in Doctrine the Saint is shown his exalted position which makes the exhortation to a holy life a reasonable one, and in Doctrine, the Saint is informed as to the Resources of Grace he possesses with which to obey the exhortations (Wuest).

The phrase, *"I beseech you therefore, Brethren,"* begins Paul's exhortation.

"I beseech you" in the Greek is *"parakaleo,"* and means *"I beg of you, please."* The word *"therefore,"* reaches back to the contents of the previous Chapters.

If one is to notice, Paul under Grace does not command, as did Moses in the Law. He beseeches; he is but a fellow servant, with his Brethren, of Christ; he does not *"Lord it over God's heritage."*

A TREMENDOUSLY IMPORTANT THOUGHT RESPECTING CHURCH GOVERNMENT

The only thing any Brother or Sister in the Lord owes another Brother or Sister is *"to love them,"* which Paul will address in Romans 13:8. Of course, and to which we will address ourselves to a greater extent in the next Chapter, if one truly loves another with the God kind of Love, he would never do anything to hurt that person.

If anyone had the right, at least in the natural, to order and command people to do certain things, Paul certainly had that right. However, even as we shall see over and over, he never conducted himself in that manner, because it would not have been pleasing to the Lord. As we have stated, under Grace he beseeched, while under Law, Moses commanded. Unfortunately, we have many in the present Economy of God who are still trying to function under Law instead of Grace. So they *"Command!"*

ACCOUNTABILITY

I have had many Preachers mention to me in the last few years, that *"One must be accountable."* Of course that is correct, at least as far as it goes. However, one must ask the question, *"Accountable to whom?"*

The true accountability that every Believer should show, and in fact must show, is to the Word of God, and that refers to all things. In other words, whatever the Word says, that we must do. That is true accountability. Without going into detail, the Word of God must always set the criteria.

However, the type of so-called accountability, that most of these Preachers are speaking of, has nothing to do with the Word of God. In other words, they are saying, *"You are to be accountable to me, and do whatever I tell you to do."* My answer to that is simple:

I will do anything that one tells me to do, providing it is Scriptural. If it is obviously unscriptural, I'm not going to do it irrespective as to what is demanded. I, as every Believer, must answer first of all to God. That allegiance in totality must never be abrogated.

When anyone commands that I quit preaching, irrespective of whom they may be, that is a command that I cannot obey, simply because it violates the Scriptures. God is the One Who has called me to preach, and not man. If He tells me to quit, then I will quit. But of course, in all of history, He has never told any Preacher to stop preaching and in fact, never will. Paul said it very well, *"For the Gifts and Calling of God are without repentance,"* meaning that no man or woman can stop doing what God has called them to do (Rom. 11:29).

SUBMISSION

I love all Brothers and Sisters in the Lord, and will do anything and everything that is possible to get along with them, and to be Christlike toward them. However, when any man says to me, or acts toward me in a manner that says, *"I am your superior, and you are to do what I tell you to do,"* automatically I know that man is unscriptural and out of order. Such speaks of Religious Hierarchy which is not Scriptural, and is the opposite of that which is Christlike.

There is only one Superior respecting Ministry, and that is the Senior Pastor in a *Local* Church. Peter said, *"Likewise, ye younger* (younger Preachers), *submit yourselves unto the Elder* (Pastor) . . ." (I Pet. 5:5).

When one reads the first five verses of the 5th Chapter of I Peter, it is obvious that Peter is referring to a Local Church, and not some type of Religious Headquarters, etc. In fact, in the Book of Acts, which is the story of the Early Church, as given by the Holy Spirit, and in the Epistles, there is no Central Authority respecting the Government of Churches. Jerusalem was not that Authority, nor any other City or Church. Each Local Church was the highest authority respecting its own autonomy, and all matters were settled in the Local Church, with no outside influence. While some did seek the advice and counsel of the Apostle Paul, even as they should have so done, and for the simple reason that he planted most of these Churches; still, even in the gravest of matters, he beseeched them to do what should be done, with no hint of commands.

Unfortunately, most of the modern Church has drifted so far away from the Word of God, that anymore it little knows what it says about these matters. It has been so educated into following self-appointed shepherds, little by little made to believe that whatever these shepherds say is law and gospel, that most just blindly follow and regrettably, many will follow to perdition.

The criteria always must be the Word of God. What do the Scriptures say?

As we study these Epistles, over and over again, we see Paul referring to the Scriptures. Not one time does he refer to any of the other Apostles, at least in matters of Doctrine, even though he no doubt respected them highly. He always referred to the Word of God for his Foundation, his Criteria, and his Direction.

TO WHOM SHALL WE FOLLOW?

Jesus asked His Disciples once, ". . . *Will ye also go away?"* (Jn. 6:67), referring to the many who had already left His Side.

Peter answered Him and said, ". . . *To whom shall we go? Thou hast the Words of Eternal Life"* (Jn. 6:68).

Believers can follow the Lord, or they can follow man. They cannot follow both! And to be sure, this is one of Satan's greatest efforts in his work of darkness.

In his efforts to deceive, he always violates the Scripture. But he does it in such a way that many people cannot see it or understand. He covers it up with so much religious phraseology, and to be sure, he has many Believers who play into his hands, willing to do what he desires, because it fits in with their self-will.

For instance, most of the modern Church world follows self-appointed men, and not those who have been Called of God. They follow Denominational Leaders, when in fact, the office that most of these men occupy, is not Scriptural, which means they carry no spiritual authority whatsoever. However, because they have been elected on a popular ballot, most people think they are Religious Leaders, when in fact, at least in the Eyes of God, Whose Eyes Alone matter, most are not.

GOD'S ORDER

God has set in the Church *". . . Apostles; and some, Prophets; and some, Evangelists; and some, Pastors and Teachers."*

He then said, *"For the perfecting of the Saints, for the Work of the Ministry, for the edifying of the Body of Christ"* (Eph. 4:11-12).

It does not say that He has set in the Church, or has given, *"Superintendents, Presidents, Bishops, Moderators, Overseers,"* etc. Actually, it is not wrong or unscriptural for these administrative offices to exist. In fact, if they are conducted in a Scriptural manner, they can be a blessing to the Body of Christ. However, one must ever know and realize that Spiritual Authority is ensconced in *"Apostles, Prophets,"* etc., and not the other.

In fact some, if not almost all of those elected to these man-devised administrative offices, are no doubt in fact, Pastors or Teachers, etc., which mean they are Called of God; however, these man-devised offices do not in any way, at least according to the Bible, increase the Spiritual Authority of these individuals, whomever they may be.

I realize that to most laypersons, these things may not seem to be important. However, they are extremely important and for the following reason:

Every Believer in the world is going to follow some Preacher. And to be sure, this

NOTES

is not unscriptural. However, they must make certain that the one they follow is truly Called of God, and is functioning in the Leading and Guidance of the Holy Spirit, strictly according to the Word of God. Otherwise, they will suffer great spiritual declension or deception.

In fact, and to be blunt, untold millions are following particular Preachers and Priests into Eternal Darkness. They are being led astray, and simply because they are being led away from the Word of God.

That's the very reason that I am very particular about what Preachers I hear or what I read. I know the Bible too well to listen to that which is obviously unscriptural. As well, that which is dishonest regarding wild claims, also is intolerable. In view of the fact that we are speaking of the single most important thing in the world, our souls, consequently, we must not be ignorant of Satan's devices (II Cor. 2:11).

The phrase, *"By the Mercies of God,"* speaks of the Sanctification, Justification, and Glorification of the Believer. In other words, all of this is given to the Believer not because of merit on the Believer's part, but strictly because of the *"Mercy of God."*

A RIGHTEOUS LIFE

The exhortation to a Holy Life in conformity to the exalted position of the Saint *in Christ Jesus* is to be obeyed in view of these *"Mercies."* Thus, in view of the fact that we are Justified persons, Righteous in our standing before God, we are under obligation to live a Righteous Life.

In view of the fact that we are the objects of the Holy Spirit's Work of Sanctification, we are to live such lives in the spiritual energy He supplies. As well, considering that we are yet to be Glorified, we are to look forward to our Lord's Coming, and in so doing, purify our lives in anticipation of this coming grand time (Wuest).

The phrase, *"That ye present your bodies a Living Sacrifice,"* presents the fact that the first evidence of real Christian Life is consecration to God and transformation from the world. This is not merely an outside mechanical action, but rather an action on the outside which springs from an inward perpetual renewing of the mind which seeks for discerning, and doing the Will of God (Williams).

If this consecration is outward only, which it is with many, it is only legalism, which means the person's experience has degenerated into nothing more than religion. In other words, if I abide by a certain set of rules outwardly, that means I am holy, etc.

To be frank, such is the bane of True Bible Christianity. Everything that pertains to Christ must begin at the heart, and flow outward, which makes Christianity, at least Bible Christianity, totally different than any religion in the world, which is outward only.

"Present" in the Greek is *"paristemi,"* and means *"to place beside or near, to present, to offer, to put at one's disposal."* It is the technical term for presenting the Levitical victims and offerings.

In the Levitical Sacrifices of old, the offerer placed his offerings so as to face the Most Holy Place, thus bringing it *"before the Lord."*

To be sure, those Levitical Offerings of old, were to be the very best of the flock, actually *"without blemish"* (Ex. 12:5), because the Offering was to represent Christ, i.e., *"a Type of Christ as The Lamb of God"* (Jn. 1:29; I Pet. 1:19; Rev. 5:6-10). Of course the difference is, that we are now to present our bodies as a *"Living Sacrifice,"* contrary to the Offerings of old which were dead. However, the comparison in effect still holds, because we as Believers are *". . . to be dead indeed unto sin, but alive unto God through Jesus Christ our Lord"* (Rom. 6:11).

So, as the offerers of old were to offer a Sacrifice without blemish before God, likewise the Believer is to do the same respecting his physical body.

THE PHYSICAL BODY

Even as we have previously stated, the physical body of the Believer constitutes the vehicle through which either Righteousness or unrighteousness is carried out. Consequently, it is the target of Satan more than anything else, and includes the *"mind"* as well, as we shall see.

The bodies of Christians are *"Members of Christ, Temples of the Holy Spirit, consecrated*

to God, and to be devoted to His Service" (I Cor. 6:15); and not in heart only, but in actual life and conduct, of which the body is the agent, we are to offer ourselves after the example of Christ.

God demands that what we offer be *"Holy"* which in the Greek is *"hagios,"* and means *"that which is set apart for God."* It actually has the same meaning as Sanctification, and in effect, is Sanctification.

The idea is as follows:

SANCTIFICATION

Inasmuch as the Lord *"Sanctified"* us at Conversion, which means from that moment that we were set apart for God, and through the vehicle of Faith only, we are to continue to walk in this *"Standing"* provided for us by the Lord (I Cor. 6:11). So, the type of holy body which God demands, accrues to itself the idea of purity and freedom from sin in that the God of the Christian is both infinitely pure and is also free from sin.

Thus, the physical body of the Believer, put at the disposal of God, presented to Him, is holy, both in the sense of being set apart for His use, and holy in the sense of being used for pure and righteous purposes, and thus, free from sinful practices (Wuest).

The phrase, *"Acceptable unto God,"* actually means that a holy physical body is all that He will accept.

"Acceptable" in the Greek is *"euareston,"* and means *"acceptable, pleasing, approved, satisfactory, actually well approved, eminently satisfactory, or extraordinarily pleasing."*

Of course, it should go without saying, that a Perfect, Holy, and Righteous God, can accept nothing less than perfection.

The phrase, *"Which is your reasonable service,"* simply means that God is not asking something which is unreasonable.

"Reasonable" in the Greek is *"logikos,"* and means *"rational, agreeable to reason, following reason."*

Israel preached the Gospel through the use of object lessons, such as the Tabernacle, Priesthood, and Offerings, etc. In other words, these things represented something, and more particularly, they represented Christ.

Likewise, the Church preaches the same Gospel in abstract terms, meaning that these same object lessons are to be carried out in our everyday walk before God, i.e., our physical bodies.

"*Service*" in the Greek is "*latreia,*" and means "*the service or worship of God according to the requirements of the Levitical Law.*" It is used in Hebrews 9:6 of the Priests who performed the Sacred Service. Thus, it speaks of Priestly Service.

Doubtless, in the thinking of Paul, the word is used here to speak of the Believer in a sense serving as a Priest unto God, but yet not as the Levitical Priests, offering a Burnt Sacrifice which was apart from themselves, but rather, a Living Sacrifice which is not only a part of ourselves but also entails the giving of ourselves in connection with the giving of our bodies to the Service of God. The idea is, that a person cannot act independently of his physical body (Wuest).

DOES IT SEEM UNREASONABLE, THAT WHICH GOD DEMANDS?

Paul outlined this problem in Chapter 7 of this Epistle. No matter how hard he tried, and in fact, the harder he tried, the worse the situation became, with him failing God constantly, that which he did not want to do.

In this scenario, this attempt to live a Godly, Righteous life, he found that God's Demands were anything but reasonable, in fact, totally unreasonable! So much so, that Paul would cry, "*O wretched man that I am! Who shall deliver me from the body of this death?*" (Rom. 7:24). In fact, by the use of the term "*body of this death,*" Paul could very well have been thinking of one of the Egyptian manners of execution.

They would tie a dead corpse to the living body of the condemned. It would remain there until the condemned died the most horrible death that one could ever begin to imagine, as would be obvious. So, the Lord is demanding Holiness and Righteousness, and Paul in his own efforts, and despite how hard he tried, is producing the very opposite.

How many Saints have read these Words in Romans 12:1, and wondered in their hearts how that God could call such "*reasonable*"?

GOD'S DEMANDS *ARE* REASONABLE . . .

In fact, if God demanded such from our

NOTES

own power, strength, and ability, it would be not only unreasonable, but terribly unreasonable, in other words, impossible. However, God does not demand such from that basis.

As Paul outlined in Romans Chapter 6, the Lord showed him how that victory is sure through the Death and Resurrection of Christ. He showed him, and which we have already stated in previous Commentary, the "*double cure.*"

Jesus paid the sin debt owed by humanity, by the offering up of Himself as a Perfect Sin-Offering. It was perfect because He had never sinned; consequently, God could accept this Offering without reservation, which He did.

However, Christ also effected another Work in His Sacrificial Offering. He as well, broke the grip of sin from the Believer's life.

Consequently, the Believer is to understand that when Jesus died on Calvary, He in effect was "*Baptized into His Death.*" He as well, is to understand that he was ". . . *buried with Him by Baptism into Death.*" Also, he is to understand "*that like as Christ was raised up from the dead by the Glory of the Father, even so we also* (were raised up and) *should walk in newness of life . . .*" (Rom. 6:3-5).

Understanding this, and having *Faith* in this, we should understand ". . . *that the body of sin* (was) *destroyed, that henceforth we should not serve sin*" (Rom. 6:6).

THE HOLY SPIRIT

In the 8th Chapter of Romans, Paul outlines the Power and Ability of the Holy Spirit to make real these Great Truths within our life, that is if we follow after Him, and not after our own efforts (Rom. 8:1-13). However, if we attempt to do what is demanded of us by our own efforts, despite what Christ did at Calvary, we will find that the demands of God are not reasonable, with failure being the obvious outcome.

When we consider that Jesus has done all of this for us, and actually that this is the very reason for which He came, and that He has given us the Holy Spirit to Lead, Guide, and Empower, in effect doing it all for us, with our only contribution being Faith, then we must come to the understanding that what God demands, is, in fact, *"reasonable."*

This is, as stated, what makes Bible Christianity different than anything else in the world. While particular religions may subscribe to a code of ethics, in fact, things which are good, still, there is no power in those Religions to help the person achieve that code of ethics.

For example, Buddhism has a code of ethics, but according to their own admission, no one has ever reached that place called *"Nirvana."* The goal is there, but elusive, as indeed, it must be. The simple fact is man, in his fallen condition, cannot live up to what he knows is right, even as was perfectly symbolized in the giving of the Law of Moses, which no one kept, except Christ. Man did not keep this Law, because man could not keep this Law, at least within his own power and strength. Such is simply not sufficient, irrespective of the effort.

However, when Christ came and did all of these things for us, and then gave us the Holy Spirit to help us do that which He demands, considering that the Holy Spirit is God, and can do anything, that is if we will only acquiesce and submit to Him, He has the perfect right to demand of us what He desires, especially considering that in effect, He does it for us.

This Truth is glorious, but yet at times not so simple to apply, as all of us have found out at times, to our dismay.

The fact is, the physical body of the Believer presents a dichotomy. In it is the seed of victory and as well the seed of defeat. If we depend upon the physical resources of the physical body alone, we will fail in keeping the Moral Law every single time. However, if we depend not at all upon the flesh, but totally and completely on the Holy Spirit, knowing and understanding what Jesus has done for us at Calvary and the Resurrection, and having Faith in that, we will find that the Holy Spirit can do, what we with all of our efforts, even as Paul found out, could not do. What is impossible for us, victory over sin, is totally possible with Him, because He is God. In fact, He is sent to help us do this very thing within our lives, in other words, that our walk may be perfect

NOTES

before God. However, at times, and despite all this help that He has given us, we still find ourselves in a mode of failure, having to ask the Lord to forgive us for that which we have done which is wrong, which He always does (I Jn. 1:9). Still, we must know and understand, that the dominion of sin is broken within our lives, and this is what is so very important. While there may be occasional failure, there must not be habitual failure. If we look to Him, and to be sure, He will be very Longsuffering and Patient with us, we are assured of victory, which has been so elusive regarding our own efforts.

(2) "AND BE NOT CONFORMED TO THIS WORLD: BUT BE YE TRANSFORMED BY THE RENEWING OF YOUR MIND, THAT YE MAY PROVE WHAT IS THAT GOOD, AND ACCEPTABLE, AND PERFECT, WILL OF GOD."

The phrase, *"And be not conformed to this world,"* begins now to portray the results of one presenting one's physical body as a Living Sacrifice unto God. The purpose is to bring the Saint into conformity to the *"Perfect Will of God."*

"Conformed" in the Greek is *"sunschematizo,"* and means *"the assuming of an expression that is patterned after some definite thing."*

The Greek word *"schematizo"* which has the prefix *"sun"* removed, has the very opposite meaning, which *"speaks of an individual assuming an outward expression that does not come from within him, nor is it representative of his inner heart life."*

So, Paul exhorts the Saints, *"Stop assuming an outward expression which is patterned after the world, an expression which does not come, nor is it representative of what you are, in your inner being as a regenerated Child of God."* It could be translated, *"Stop masquerading in the habiliments of this world, its mannerisms, speech expressions, styles, habits"* (Wuest).

"World" in the Greek is *"aion,"* and means *"all that floating mass of thoughts, opinions, maxims, speculations, hopes, impulses, aims, aspirations, at any time current in the world, which may be impossible to seize and accurately define, but which constitute a most real and effective power, being the*

moral, or immoral atmosphere which at every moment of our lives we inhale, again inevitably to exhale" (Trench). The idea is, Believers in the world, but not of the world — at least they are not supposed to be. It is the spirit or world of men who are living alienated to and apart from God.

THE WORLD

The Greek word *"kosmos"* means *"the ordered world."* It is used in the New Testament, sometimes for what we should call the *"universe,"* the created world, described in the Old Testament as *"all things"* or *"Heaven and Earth"* (Acts 17:24).

The *"world"* as far as Creation is concerned, was made by the *"Word,"* i.e., *"The Lord Jesus Christ"* (Jn. 1:10); and it was this *"world"* of which Jesus was speaking when He said it would not profit a man anything if he gained the whole of it and lost his soul in the process (Mat. 16:26).

MANKIND

Due to the fact that mankind is the most important part of the universe, the word *"kosmos"* is more often used in the limited sense of human beings, i.e., *"the inhabited Earth."*

It is into this *"world"* that men are born, and in it they live till they die (Jn. 16:21). It was all the Kingdoms of this world that the Devil offered to give to Christ if He would worship him (Mat. 4:8-9). It was this world, the world of men and women of flesh and blood, that God loved (Jn. 3:16), and into which Jesus came when He was born of a human mother (Jn. 11:27).

REBELLION

It is, however, an axiom of the Bible that this world of human beings, the climax of the Divine Creation, the world that God made especially to reflect His Glory, is now in rebellion against Him. Through the transgression of one man, sin has entered into the world (Rom. 5:18) with universal consequences of tragedy. It has become, as a result, a disordered world in the grip of the Evil One (I Jn. 5:19). And so, very frequently in the New Testament, and particularly in the Gospel and Epistles written by John, the

NOTES

word *"kosmos"* has a sinister significance.

It is not the world as God intended it to be, but *"this world"* set over against God, following its own wisdom and living by the light of its own reason (I Cor. 1:21), not recognizing the Source of all true life and illumination (Jn. 1:10).

PRIDE AND COVETOUSNESS

The two dominant characteristics of this world are *"pride,"* born of man's failure to accept his creaturely estate and his dependence on the Creator, which leads him to act as though he were the Lord and Giver of Life; and *"covetousness,"* which causes him to desire and possess all that is attractive to his physical senses (I Jn. 2:16). And, as man tends in effect to worship what he covets, such covetousness is idolatry (Col. 3:5).

Accordingly, worldliness is the enthronement of something other than God as the supreme object of man's interests and affections. Pleasures and occupations, not necessarily wrong in themselves, become so when an all-absorbing attention is paid to them.

THE SPIRIT OF THIS WORLD

"This world" is pervaded by a spirit of its own, which has to be exorcised by the Spirit of God, if it is not to remain in control over human reason and understanding (I Cor. 2:12).

Man is in bondage to the elements which comprise the world (Col. 2:20) until he is emancipated from them by Christ. He cannot overcome them until he is himself *"born of God"* (I Jn. 5:4).

Legalism, Asceticism (self-denial), and Ritualism are this world's feeble and enfeebling substitutes for True Salvation (Gal. 4:9-10); and only a true knowledge of God, as revealed by Christ, can prevent men from relying upon them.

It was because the Jews relied upon these things (Legalism, Asceticism, and Ritualism) that they did not recognize either the Christ in the days of His Flesh (Jn. 1:11) or His followers (I Jn. 3:1). Similarly, false prophets who advocate such things, and who are antinomian in their teaching, will always be listened to by those who belong to this world (I Jn. 4:5).

(Antinomianism is the Doctrine which claims that under the Gospel dispensation of Grace the Moral Law is of no use or obligation because Faith alone is necessary to Salvation. There is some Truth in this false teaching, which makes it appealing.

In fact, Faith alone is necessary to Salvation; however, True Faith will always produce a Holy Life.)

THE LORD JESUS CHRIST

Christ, Whom the Father sent to be the Saviour of this world (I Jn. 4:14), and Whose very presence in it was a judgment upon it (Jn. 9:39), freed men from its sinister forces by Himself engaging in mortal combat with its *"Prince,"* the perpetual instigator of the evil within. The crisis of this world came when Jesus left the Upper Room (Last Supper) and went forth to meet this Prince (Jn. 14:30-31).

By voluntarily submitting to death, Jesus brought about the defeat of him who held men in the grip of death, but who had no claims upon Himself (Jesus) (Jn. 12:31-32; 14:30).

On the Cross, Judgment was passed on the Ruler *". . . Prince of this world . . ."* (Jn. 16:11); and Faith in Christ as the Son of God, Who offered the Sacrifice which alone can cleanse men from the guilt and power of sin (a cleansing symbolized by the flow of water and blood from His stricken Side, Jn. 19:34), enables the Believer to overcome the world (I Jn. 5:4-6), and to endure the tribulations which the world inevitably brings upon him (Jn. 16:33).

LOVE FOR GOD

The Love of a Christian for God, the Father of Jesus Christ his Redeemer, Who is the Propitiation for the sins of the whole world (I Jn. 2:2), acts with the explosive power of a new affection; it makes the spirit of the world abhorrent to him to set his affections any longer upon *"this world,"* which, because it is severed from the True Source of Life, is transitory and contains within itself the seeds of its own decay (I Jn. 2:15-17).

A man who has come to experience the higher Love for God, and for Christ and His Brethren, must abandon the lower love for it is contaminated by the spirit of the world:

NOTES

"friendship of the world is (of necessity) *enmity with God"* (James 4:4).

JESUS' PRAYER FOR BELIEVERS

Jesus, in His last prayer in the Upper Room, did not pray for the world, but for those whom His Father had given Him out of the world. By this *"Gift,"* these men whom Jesus described as *"His Own"* ceased to have the characteristics of the world; and Jesus prayed that they might be kept safe from its evil influences (Jn. 17:9).

He knew that after His Departure they would have to bear the brunt of the world's hatred which had hitherto been directed almost entirely against Himself. As the Risen and Ascended Christ He still limits His Intercessions to those who draw near to God through Him (Heb. 7:25); and He continues to manifest Himself not to the world but to His Own who are in the world (Jn. 14:22).

THE FIELD IS THE WORLD

It is very certain that Christ's Disciples cannot and must not attempt to retreat from this world. The Lord has called us to separation but never to isolation. It is into this world, all the world (Mk. 16:15), that He sends them.

They are to be its *"Light"* (Mat. 5:14); and the *"field"* in which the Church is to do its work of witnessing to the Truth as it is in Jesus, is no less comprehensive than the world itself (Mat. 13:38).

For this world is still God's world, even though at present it lies under the Evil One.

In the end, *"Earth's true loveliness will be restored"*; and, with all evil destroyed and the Sons of God manifested, the whole Creation will be *"set free from its bondage of corruption and* (will then) *obtain the glorious liberty of the Children of God"* (Rom. 8:21). Then God will be *"Everything to everyone"* (I Cor. 15:28); or, *"Present in a total manner in the universe."*

John on the Isle of Patmos sees the day when great voices in Heaven will proclaim: *". . . The Kingdoms of this world are become the Kingdoms of our Lord, and of His Christ, and He shall reign forever and ever"* (Rev. 11:15).

(The above outline on the world was

derived from the book by J. Hering, the *"Vocabulary of the Bible."*)

The phrase, *"But be ye transformed,"* presents that which only the Power of God can accomplish, but yet, in which the cooperation of the Believer is absolutely necessary.

TRANSFORMED

"Transformed" in the Greek is *"metamorphoomai,"* which speaks *"of the act of a person changing his outward expression from that which he has to a different one, an expression which comes from, and is, representative of his inner being."*

This same word is used in Matthew 17:2 where it is translated *"transfigured."*

Consequently, the translation concerning the transfiguration of Jesus could read, *"The manner of His outward expression was changed before them, and His Face shone as the Sun, and His clothing was white as the light."*

The usual manner of our Lord's outward expression during His humiliation was that of the Man Christ Jesus, a Man of sorrows and of grief, the itinerant Preacher and Teacher from Nazareth dressed in the homespun of a Galilean peasant. But here, our Lord allows the Glory of the essence of His Deity that came from His Inner Being as Deity and was representative of Him as such, to shine through His human Body.

This radiance caused His Face to shine and His Garments to appear white as the Sun.

Paul, therefore, says in effect to the Saints, *"Change your outward expression, your attitude, your demeanor, your conduct, your ways, your direction, your habits, your friends, your patterns, your ambitions, your direction from that which you had before Salvation, an expression which came from your totally depraved nature and was representative of it, to an expression which comes from your regenerated inner being and is representative of it."*

HOW IS THE SAINT TO DO THIS?

The phrase, *"By the renewing of your mind,"* tells us how.

"Renewing" is *"anakainosis,"* and means *"the gradual conforming of the man more and more to that new spiritual world into*

which he has been introduced, and in which he now lives and moves; the restoration of the Divine Image; and in all this so far from being passive, he must be a fellow-worker with God."

The idea is, that this change of outward expression, which refers to a total change, is dependent upon the renovation, which is the complete change for the better of the Believer's mental process. This is accomplished through the Ministry of the indwelling Holy Spirit, Who when definitely, and intelligently, and habitually yielded to, puts sin out of the Believer's life and produces His Own Fruit.

He does this by controlling the mental processes of the Believer, but it is control which the Believer must willingly give to the Holy Spirit, for the Spirit will never take such control by force.

In effect, the Believer can do little more than furnish a *"willing mind and obedient heart"* (I Chron. 28:9). Even in the *"obedient heart"* about all that the Believer can do, is to be willing that the heart be made obedient to the Lord.

When the believing sinner is Born Again, the Holy Spirit automatically comes in, imparting to the Believer the Divine Nature (Jn. 3:3; II Cor. 5:17). As well, the Spirit of God sets about to bring the Believer to conformity to the Image of Christ (Rom. 8:29). In this the Holy Spirit also brings great Power which is now available to the Believer (Acts 1:8; 8:12).

COOPERATION WITH THE SPIRIT

However, the full quantity and quality of what the Holy Spirit can do within our lives, is dependent, as stated, upon our cooperation. This has to do with the Believer's Sanctification, with the Holy Spirit unable to accomplish these tasks within our hearts and lives without the full consecration of our self-will into that of Christ. It is not a matter at all of the Believer becoming passive, but in reality the very opposite. It speaks of the will being submitted to Christ to the extent, that His Will becomes our will. It is somewhat like meekness. This attribute is not weakness but rather controlled strength. The Will of God carried out in the Believer's life, is never passivity, but rather controlled direction, i.e., controlled by Christ, but only with our compliance.

Actually, this is the prescription of the Apostle: *"Habitually be ordering your behavior within the sphere and by means of the Spirit, and you will positively not fulfill the desire of the flesh* (sin nature)*"* (Gal. 5:16).

As well, the *"renewed mind"* will always be in the realm of the *"Mind of Christ,"* which denotes humility (Phil. 2:5-8).

The phrase, *"That ye may prove what is that good, and acceptable, and perfect, Will of God,"* presents that which the Holy Spirit is attempting to bring about within our lives. His Purpose in our lives is not to do our will, but the Will of God, and more perfectly, the *"Perfect Will of God,"* which alone God accepts.

"Prove" in the Greek is *"dokimazo,"* and means *"to put to the test for the purpose of approving, and finding that the thing tested meets the specifications laid down,"* in other words to put one's approval upon it.

As a result of the Spirit's control of the mental processes of the Saint, the latter is enabled to put his life to the test for the purpose of approving it, the specifications being that it conform to the Word of God. Thus, experiencing what obedience is to the Word, and finding out what it feels like to have the Word saturate and control the life, the Believer now sees the road of victory in all things, and lays his claim to that direction.

The Lord was speaking of the same thing when He said, *"If any man will do His Will, he shall know of the Doctrine, whether it be of God, or whether I speak of Myself"* (Jn. 7:17). In other words, and according to the old adage, *"The proof of the pudding is in the eating."*

THE WILL OF GOD

Satan is very adept at making both unbelievers and Believers think that which is wrong concerning the Will of God.

To the unbeliever, he tells how many wonderful things he will have to give up to live for God. He also tells him how boring it will be to be a Christian. Of course, he is lying, but the unbeliever much of the time believes him.

NOTES

The unbeliever does not understand that once coming to Christ, his entire nature changes. In effect, Divine Nature is imparted into him, with everything about him changing. In other words, he doesn't really have to give up anything of the world, he just simply doesn't want it anymore, having that which is so much better.

As well, whereas going to Church and doing those types of things, once was an extreme weariness, due to the great change in his life, he now loves Church and the worship of God, such actually becomes the highlight of his life. However, he cannot see these things as an unbeliever.

In fact, the True Biblical Christian life, is the single most wonderful, fulfilling, expanding, all-encompassing experience that one could ever have. There is nothing in the world which can remotely compare with living for Jesus. As the Apostle said, *". . . (We) rejoice with Joy unspeakable and full of Glory"* (I Pet. 1:8).

Regarding Believers, Satan often lies to them, attempting to make them believe that the Perfect Will of God contains some awful thing and which they will not desire to do. Consequently, many Believers do not properly consecrate to the Lord for this very reason. Nothing could be further from the Truth.

First of all, the Lord never makes one's life less, but always more. In fact, it is *"more abundant life"* (Jn. 10:10).

As well, anything He desires that a person do, He first gives a Love for that thing in the Believer's heart. The Believer is not a slave of the Lord, but rather treated in a sense by God as an equal to Christ (Rom. 8:14-17).

A PERMISSIVE WILL OF GOD?

We have already dealt with this subject in other Commentary, so suffice to say that there is no such thing as a *"permissive Will of God,"* as taught by some. God has only one Will, and that is His *"Perfect Will of God."* That is the only thing that is *"acceptable"* unto Him. As well, it is *"good."*

"Perfect" in the Greek is *"peleios,"* and means *"brought to its end, finished, wanting nothing necessary to completeness"* (Wuest).

Every Believer must strive for the *"Perfect*

Will of God," making it the goal, and, in fact, the only goal in one's life. As the word *"perfect"* outlines, that is the end of all things, the totally, fulfilled Life. It is found only in Jesus and is always anchored in the Word of God (Mat. 11:28-30).

(3) "FOR I SAY, THROUGH THE GRACE GIVEN UNTO ME, TO EVERY MAN THAT IS AMONG YOU, NOT TO THINK OF HIMSELF MORE HIGHLY THAN HE OUGHT TO THINK; BUT TO THINK SOBERLY, ACCORDING AS GOD HATH DEALT TO EVERY MAN THE MEASURE OF FAITH."

The phrase, *"For I say, through the Grace given unto me,"* refers to Paul's Apostleship by the Grace of God (Eph. 3:8).

The idea in this statement is that *"humility is the immediate effect of self-surrender to God"* (Gifford). Paul illustrates in his own person, in giving this advice, the rule he is laying down for the Church. He speaks *"through the Grace given him,"* and, therefore, without presumption; but he does speak, and so puts Wisdom and Love at the service of the Church . . . everybody in the Church needs this word, the word of humility (Wuest).

HUMILITY

The phrase, *"To every man that is among you, not to think of himself more highly than he ought to think,"* is the Word the Church needs.

To himself, every man is in a sense the most important person in the world, and he always needs much Grace to see what other people are, and to keep a sense of moral proportion.

There are various degrees of self-estimation proper, for God gives one more and another less; but all are fundamentally regulated by humility, for no one has anything that he has not received from God in the first place.

Understanding how greatly significant this matter of humility is in the life of the Believer, still, I think that Paul was coming from the perspective of his experience as a Jew, as well as the common need in the Church.

Israel had fallen, and the reason at least in part was because of this very thing — a prideful, unscriptural evaluation of themselves. In

NOTES

other words, they definitely thought of themselves far more highly than they ought to have thought. Paul knew, having been a part of that system for many years. So, even though he does not mention Israel here, I think the experience of his own people, must at least have played a part in his thinking respecting this admonition.

The phrase, *"But to think soberly,"* means not to be high-minded above that which one ought to be minded, but to be so minded as to be sober-minded. All of which goes to say that a Christian should appraise the Gifts God has given him fairly, glorifying God for their bestowal, and their exercise through dependence upon the Holy Spirit, and not in mock humility make light of them (Wuest).

"To think" in the Greek is *"phronein."*

"To think more highly" in the Greek is *"huperphronein,"* and means *"to over-think, to think above, thus to proudly think."* The Believer is *"to think"* that is, appraise his Gifts rightly, but not become proud of them.

"To think soberly" in the Greek is *"sophronein,"* and means *"to be in one's right mind."* Actually, Paul is here treating conceit as a species of insanity (Robertson).

THE MEASURE OF FAITH

The phrase, *"According as God hath dealt to every man the measure of Faith,"* has somewhat of a double meaning.

First of all, it pertains to God giving a measure of Faith to the believing sinner.

The idea is, that the Holy Spirit convicts of sin in the heart of the sinner, with the Lord at the same time granting the sinner *"a measure of Faith."* Were it not for the Grace of God in this capacity, the sinner would not have any capacity to believe whatsoever, due to the fact, that there is nothing spiritual in the unregenerate heart. Regrettably, many refuse to believe, even though this measure of Faith is granted unto them.

As well, after the believing sinner has come to Christ, the Lord then bestows particular Gifts on that person respecting his work. At the same time He does this, He also gives to the person *"a measure of Faith"* to carry out these Gifts and to perform and accomplish their intention.

Consequently, as there is no excuse for

the sinner not to accept Christ after the measure of Faith is granted, there is no excuse for the Believer to not carry out the task assigned to him by the Lord concerning Gifts furnished.

The idea of the Text is that our estimate of our Gifts is to be governed by *"the measure of Faith"* God gives each of us.

Its meaning, therefore, must not be strictly limited to the conception of Justifying Faith in Christ, though that conception includes and is really the basis of every wider conception. Justifying Faith is that which is given to the sinner, even as we have just spoken.

As well, it is Faith as the condition of the powers and offices of Believers, Faith regarded as spiritual insight, which, according to its degree, qualifies a man to be a Prophet, a Teacher, a Minister, etc.

As Faith is the sphere and subjective condition of the powers and functions of Believers, so it furnishes a test or regulative standard of their respective enduements and functions.

With *"the measure of Faith"* a Believer receives power of discernment as to the actual limitations of his Gifts. Faith, in introducing him into God's Kingdom (Salvation), also introduces him to new standards of measurement, according to which he accurately determines the nature and extent of his powers, and so does not think of himself too highly. This *"measure"* is different in different individuals, but in every case Faith is the determining element of the measure.

COMMENSURATE WITH THE CALL

If God has called a person to do a certain thing, even if that thing is overly large such as Paul's Ministry for instance; still, irrespective of the Call, the Lord had to grant Paul *"the measure of Faith"* commensurate with the Call, or else it could not have been done. If one properly understands this, knowing that it is God Who has called, and God Who has granted *"the measure of Faith"* in order that the Call may be accomplished, there is no room for prideful thinking.

Even though some may be given a much higher, and, therefore, more responsible Call than others, still, the weight of such responsibility quickly humbles one, having a great

tendency to subdue pride, that is if that danger lurks as it generally does.

If one is to notice, Paul used the term *"the measure of Faith"* instead of *"a measure of Faith."* It specifies *"the measure"* for the particular task at hand, whether the sinner coming to Christ, or the Believer carrying out that which God has called him to do. It portrays a perfect organization on the part of God, which should be obvious.

As well, the idea is, that if God has truly given the Call, at the same time He will grant *"the measure of Faith"* for the Call to be exercised. No Faith, no Call!

(4) "FOR AS WE HAVE MANY MEMBERS IN ONE BODY, AND ALL MEMBERS HAVE NOT THE SAME OFFICE:"

The phrase, *"For as we have many members in one body,"* refers to every person who is in the Body of Christ, for Christ is the Object as the Head of the Church (Eph. 1:22).

The phrase, *"And all members have not the same Office,"* presents that which is obvious, but yet the reminder is needed.

"Office" in the Greek is *"praxis,"* and means *"a mode of acting or a function."* The insinuation of the Text is, that every single member in the Body of Christ, has been Called of God for a particular *"Office."* If the Believer does not already know what that *"Office"* is, he should seek the Lord accordingly, and to be sure, the Holy Spirit will without fail, make the designation known to the heart of the seeker.

I think it should be obvious to each Believer just how important this is, especially considering the attention given to these Offices by the Holy Spirit through the Apostle. And yet many, if not most Believers, do not have the slightest idea as to what their particular *"Office"* is, concerning the Work of God. Prayerfully, the following Commentary on the subsequent Scriptures will be of service respecting this very important subject.

(5) "SO WE, BEING MANY, ARE ONE BODY IN CHRIST, AND EVERY ONE MEMBERS ONE OF ANOTHER."

The phrase, *"So we, being many, are One Body in Christ,"* speaks to the entirety of the Church, and the unity which ought to be prevalent within the Body. Paul addresses this very graphically in I Corinthians 12:12-31.

NOTES

The phrase, *"And every one members one of another,"* in effect says that whatever is true according to one, is also true according to the other. This does not speak of *"Offices"* but rather of being a member of the Body.

All who are truly Saved, came in the same way, that is by Faith (Eph. 2:8-9). Consequently, all are kept by the Power of God, which speaks of continued Faith. As well, the Bible is to be the Standard and the Rule for all things. The commonality produces a bond between Believers, which is supposed to be expressed by Love one for another (Jn. 13:35; 15:12-13, 17; I Thess. 4:9; Heb. 13:1; I Jn. 3:14).

(6) "HAVING THEN GIFTS DIFFERING ACCORDING TO THE GRACE THAT IS GIVEN TO US, WHETHER PROPHECY, LET US PROPHESY ACCORDING TO THE PROPORTION OF FAITH;"

The phrase, *"Having then Gifts differing according to the Grace that is given to us,"* speaks of different *"Gifts"* or *"Offices."*

The word *"Grace"* is used in the sense, that none of us deserve these *"Gifts,"* but they are given to us strictly by the Grace of God, and not according to merit. Accordingly, the Believer, irrespective of the Gifts, or their number possessed, must never think of himself or herself as worthy of such, i.e., more highly than one ought to think. This is where humility must ever be prevalent.

The phrase, *"Whether Prophecy,"* refers to the Gift that speaks to men to *"edification, exhortation and comfort"* (I Cor. 14:3-6). Paul is using this as an example, even as he will use other things, as we shall see.

The phrase, *"Let us prophesy according to the proportion of Faith,"* has to do with *"the measure of Faith."*

I think it would be difficult to fully explain the full complement of what Paul is saying here respecting each individual; however, perhaps in generalized terms we can be of some service.

Continuing to deal with the Gift of *"Prophecy,"* I think I can say without fear of contradiction, that each person who has this Gift (or any Gift for that matter), if they will think and pray about the matter somewhat, they will be able to realize and understand approximately what is their measure of Faith.

First of all, and I think I can say without contradiction, most of us never live up to the full potential of our Faith. In other words, we are not nearly exhausting *"the measure of Faith"* given unto us respecting the Gift or Gifts in which we are now used. As well, I think if the Believer reaches the proportion of Faith allotted to him or her, a request placed with the Lord can no doubt enlarge the capacity of Faith. The Lord never discourages growth, but rather the opposite!

"Proportion" in the Greek, is *"analogia,"* and actually refers to *"a mathematical term."* Consequently, we are not to overstep the boundaries. Regarding this, there need not be any fear in the heart of the Believer, especially considering that we are led by the Holy Spirit, that is if we are truly following the Spirit (Rom. 8:14).

(7) "OR MINISTRY, LET US WAIT ON OUR MINISTERING: OR HE THAT TEACHETH, ON TEACHING;"

The phrase, *"Or Ministry,"* refers to either a Pastor or Deacon. *"Ministry"* in the Greek is *"diakonia,"* and is one of the Greek words for *"servant."* It represents the servant in his activity (Trench). The word, therefore, refers to one who serves.

The phrase, *"Let us wait on our Ministering,"* would have been better translated, *"Let us Minister according to the proportion of Faith."*

The phrase, *"Or he that teacheth, on Teaching,"* carries the same idea.

The idea of all of this is, that the one who is given a particular Gift, whether it be Ministry, or Teaching, etc., should remain within the exercise of that Gift. It is a wise man who stays within the sphere of service for which God the Holy Spirit has fitted him, and does not invade some other field of service for which he is not fitted (Wuest).

(8) "OR HE THAT EXHORTETH, ON EXHORTATION: HE THAT GIVETH, LET HIM DO IT WITH SIMPLICITY; HE THAT RULETH, WITH DILIGENCE; HE THAT SHEWETH MERCY, WITH CHEERFULNESS."

The phrase, *"Or he that exhorteth, on exhortation,"* once again comes under the same heading that such should be done according to *"the measure of Faith."*

"Exhorteth" in the Greek is *"parakaleo,"* and means *"to call aside, make an appeal to by way of exhortation, entreaty, comfort, or instruction."* This has to do with Preaching in any capacity.

The phrase, *"He that giveth, let him do it with simplicity,"* proclaims *"giving"* as a *"Gift"* or *"Office."*

"Giveth" in the Greek is *"metadidomi,"* and means *"to impart of one's earthly possessions."*

"Simplicity" in the Greek is *"haplotetes,"* and means *"singleness, simplicity, sincerity, mental honesty, the virtue of one who is free from pretense and hypocrisy, openness of heart manifesting itself by benefactions and liberality"* (Thayer).

This is the way that God gives, and it is the way we ought to give as well.

RELIGIOUS HIERARCHY

The phrase, *"He that ruleth, with diligence,"* refers to anyone placed in a position of authority, whatever that may be, i.e., Pastor, the head Deacon, Superintendent of a department in the Church, etc.

"Diligence" in the Greek, is *"spoude,"* and means *"to make haste, do one's best, take care,"* etc. The word speaks of intense effort and determination.

Some have attempted to expand the word *"ruleth"* into Religious Hierarchy, etc. However, as I think should be obvious, words or statements such as this in the Bible, must never be taken beyond Scriptural precedent. In other words, inasmuch as such (Ruling Hierarchy) is not mentioned in the Book of Acts or the Epistles, we violate the spirit of the Text to force the issue accordingly. *"Ruleth"* as given here, has to do with the Local Church, and the Work of God in that capacity. While it certainly can include an outside forum, it must never be taken beyond the true Scriptural meaning.

The phrase, *"He that sheweth Mercy, with cheerfulness,"* concerns ministering to the sick, the infirm, the helpless, or the discouraged.

"Cheerfulness" in the Greek, is *"hilarotes,"* and means *"cheerfulness, readiness of mind, joyfulness, the amiable Grace, the affability going the length of gaiety, which makes the person so gifted a literal sunbeam penetrating into any place there is such need."*

I think one would hardly think of *"showing Mercy"* as a *"Gift"* or *"Office."* Nevertheless, the Holy Spirit through the Apostle definitely portrays such as a very worthy effort for the Cause of Christ.

Looking at these *"Gifts"* or *"Offices,"* one is quickly made aware of the fact that the Holy Spirit addresses both Preachers and Laypersons.

"Ministry" or *"Teaching,"* or *"Exhortation,"* applies mostly to Preachers of the Gospel. *"Prophecy"* can apply to either, whether Preacher or Layperson.

"Giving" as well as *"Ruleth,"* and *"showing Mercy"* can apply to all also. However, that which stands out so graphically is, that all are included. As stated, every single Believer should know and understand as to the *"Gift"* or *"Office"* given to him by the Lord, and seek to function properly, according to *"the measure of Faith."*

As well, Paul only mentioned a few of the Gifts, with many, many more available, and in whatever capacity. For instance, there are nine Gifts of the Spirit respecting I Corinthians 12:8-10, while Paul only mentioned one of those Gifts, Prophecy.

As well, there are many other Gifts, all given and superintended by the Holy Spirit. To name a few, one thinks of prayer, music, singing, business ability, etc.

To go back to two Gifts which Paul named, *"Giving"* and *"Showing Mercy,"* all Believers should engage in these qualities; however, to those who have a special *"Gift"* in this capacity, one will find that this becomes a Ministry with them, which makes them more successful in this which they do, and because they stand in this particular *"Office."*

(9) "LET LOVE BE WITHOUT DISSIMULATION. ABHOR THAT WHICH IS EVIL; CLEAVE TO THAT WHICH IS GOOD."

The phrase, *"Let Love be without dissimulation,"* refers to the fact that it should be real and not feigned.

"Dissimulation" in the Greek, is *"anupokritos,"* and means *"don't play the hypocrite."*

The phrase, *"Abhor that which is evil,"* means that the Christian is to express his hatred of evil by a withdrawal from it and a loathing of it.

"Evil" in the Greek, is *"poneros,"* and

speaks of that which is *"inactive appositive to the good."*

The phrase, *"Cleave to that which is good,"* means to cement, to join, or fasten firmly together.

(10) "BE KINDLY AFFECTIONED ONE TO ANOTHER WITH BROTHERLY LOVE; IN HONOUR PREFERRING ONE ANOTHER;"

The phrase, *"Be kindly affectioned one to another with brotherly Love,"* speaks of the brotherhood of Believers.

"Kindly affectioned" in the Greek, is *"philostorgos,"* and means as it refers to Christians, *"bound by a family tie."*

"Brotherly Love" in the Greek, is *"philadelphia,"* and means *"to love the Brethren in the Faith as though they were Brethren in blood."* The word *"kindly"* is the key, and gives the real sense. *"Kind"* is originally *"kinned,"* and *"kindly affectioned is having the affection of kindred."*

The Family of God is the greatest family in the world. In fact, and as we have previously stated, Believers are closer to fellow Believers in the Lord, than they are even to their own blood kindred who do not know Jesus.

This should not be difficult seeing that the Love of God is shed abroad in the hearts and lives of all True Believers. Consequently, the fact of having and expressing that Love should be a simple thing, actually second nature.

BETWEEN CHRISTIANS

Within the Christian community, Love should respond to Love, and find its fulfillment, for there all men are, or should be, God's Sons actually, *"... because the Love of God hath been shed abroad in our hearts, through the Holy Spirit which was given unto us"* (Rom. 5:5). And this mutual Love within the Christian brotherhood is called, as stated, *"philadelphia"* (I Pet. 5:9).

However, Love is not really Love, until it is shown, and even under the most adverse circumstances. In other words, Love is the same at all times.

When one is down and cannot defend himself, and anyone can do any negative thing they like to such a person without any fear of censure, but will actually be applauded, one then finds who truly has the Love of God within his or her heart. Thankfully,

there are some few, but not many!

THE STOICS

This twofold ideal of social morality as universal benevolence and mutual affection in Paul's day, had been foreshadowed by the Stoics. Men as citizens of the world should adopt an attitude of Justice and Mercy toward all men, even slaves, they said. However, not knowing the Lord, even though the Greek schools saw at least a part of the light, they had no power to carry out such action or attitude. Only with the advent of Christianity was there success in organizing and realizing in intense and practical fellowship, the ideal that remained vague and abstract in the Greek schools.

"See how these Christians Love one another." It was their Master's example followed, and His Commandment and Promise fulfilled: *"... Love one another; as I have Loved you ...; By this shall all men know that ye are My Disciples ..."* (Jn. 13:14, 34-35).

Paul in his earliest Epistle bears witness that the Thessalonians practiced Love *"... toward all the Brethren that are in all Macedonia,"* even as they had been taught of God, but urges them to *"abound more and more"* (I Thess. 4:9-10).

THE CHRISTIAN ADVANCE ON HEATHEN THOUGHT

For the healing of differences, and to build up the Church in order and unity, Paul urges the Romans, even as we are now studying, *"in love of the Brethren* (to) *be tenderly affectioned one to another..."* (Rom. 12:10). Christians must even *"... forbear one another in Love"* (Eph. 4:2) and *"walk in Love, even as Christ also loved you ..."* (Eph. 5:2; Phil. 2:1-2).

True Love expressed, involves some suffering and sacrifice. The author of the Epistle to the Hebrews recognizes the presence of *"Love of the Brethren,"* and urges that it may continue (Heb. 13:1). It is the direct result of Regeneration, of purity and obedience to the Truth (I Pet. 1:22-23).

It proceeds from Godliness and issues in Love (II Pet. 1:7). *"Love of the Brethren"* (Agape) is the one practical topic of John's Epistles. It is the Message heard from the beginning, ". . . *that we should Love one another"* (I Jn. 3:11, 23).

It is the test of light and darkness (I Jn. 2:10); life and death (I Jn. 3:14); Children of God or children of the Devil (I Jn. 3:10; 4:7-12).

Without it there can be no knowledge or Love of God (I Jn. 4:20), but when men Love God and Obey Him, they necessarily Love His Children (I Jn. 5:2). No man can be of God's Family, unless his Love extends to all its members (Rees).

The phrase, *"In honour preferring one another,"* proclaims by the Holy Spirit the manner in which this *"Brotherly Love"* is shown.

"Honour" in the Greek, is *"time,"* and means *"a valuing by which the price is fixed, deference, reverence, veneration, honor."* Hence, the word means *"that respect shown another which is measured by one's evaluation of another"* (Wuest).

"Preferring" in the Greek is *"proegeomai,"* and means *"to go before and lead, to go before as leader, one going before another as an example of deference."* In simple terminology, it means the honoring of another in allowing them to take the lead. It means to recognize and honor God's Gifts in a brother.

(11) "NOT SLOTHFUL IN BUSINESS; FERVENT IN SPIRIT; SERVING THE LORD;"

The phrase, *"Not slothful in business,"* pertains to anything that the Believer sets out to do. It is to be done with fervency, diligence, attention to detail, and with responsibility.

In other words, the Christian can be trusted, his word is his bond, and he gives an honest day's work, etc.

"Slothful" in the Greek is *"okneros,"* and means *"to delay, to feel loath, to be slow, to hesitate, to be lazy."*

How many Christians are just plain lazy?

"Business" in the Greek, is *"spoude,"* and is the same word translated *"diligence"* in Romans 12:8. It denotes the moral earnestness with which one should give himself to his vocation (Luther).

The phrase, *"Fervent in Spirit"* actually should have been translated *"Fervent in the Holy Spirit."*

"Fervent" in the Greek, is *"zeo,"* and means *"to boil with heat, be hot, in this case for that which is good."*

"Spirit" in the Greek is *"pneuma,"* and

due to the fact that it carries with it the definite article, which actually says *"The Spirit,"* as stated, it should have been translated *"Holy Spirit."* Consequently, Paul is exhorting fervency in the Christian life which is engendered by the Spirit, not produced by the flesh (self-effort).

The idea is, that many people will seem to be fervent in certain activities, but in reality are only doing such to impress others. In other words, it is all for *"show."*

By contrast, the Believer is to attend his duties with diligence and responsibility, whether anyone sees him or not, but knowing that God sees all things. This is to be done, because the Holy Spirit says it is to be done.

That means if a Christian is the President of a country, he is to be diligent in his efforts, doing everything he does as unto the Lord, and giving it the very best he has. As well, if the Christian is digging ditches for a living, he should do his very best to dig the very finest ditch that is possible to dig. If he or she is working at McDonald's, in other words, any and all menial tasks, he or she should be the very finest preparer of hamburgers in the place, or whatever they may be doing, even if it is mopping the floor.

PRACTICAL CHRISTIANITY

We must understand, even as Paul relates here, that this is what the Holy Spirit demands of the followers of the Lord.

Frances and I, along with others, were in Russia in 1985. Of course, this was before the demise of Communism.

In speaking with one of the Russians on the trip, he remarked as to how the State had severely persecuted Christians at the outset of Communism in 1917 and following. However, he went on to relate, how that the State began to notice, even as the years passed on, that those who called themselves Christians, were the most diligent workers in the entirety of the country. They noticed that Christians did not come on the job drinking, neither did they steal, nor would they lie. Consequently, it was a perfect example of practical Christian living, which makes an impression, which it is intended to do.

The phrase, *"Serving the Lord,"* refers to the fact, which is very important, that every single thing done by the Believer, even his secular work as we have mentioned, is looked at by the Holy Spirit as *"serving the Lord."*

The idea is, that the face of the Christian is to not only be Christlike in Church, but in every single thing he or she does. This makes for better employees, better associations, better business deals, in fact, better in everything that is done, because, as stated, it is *"serving the Lord,"* whether spiritual, secular, domestic, or whatever!

(12) "REJOICING IN HOPE; PATIENT IN TRIBULATION; CONTINUING INSTANT IN PRAYER;"

The phrase, *"Rejoicing in hope,"* actually means, *"rejoicing in the sphere of hope."* That is, when earthly prospects are dim, the Christian's rejoicing should be in the sphere of hope that the Lord will send deliverance, and in the meantime take care of His afflicted Child (Wuest).

The phrase, *"Patient in Tribulation,"* presents that which comes at times to all Believers, irrespective of the degree of their Faith.

"Patient" in the Greek, is *"hupomeno,"* and means *"to remain under,"* that is, to remain under the test in a God-honoring manner, not seeking to escape it but eager to learn the lessons it was sent to teach (Wuest).

"Tribulation" in the Greek, is *"thlipisis,"* and means *"a pressing together, pressure, oppression, affliction, tribulation, distress, straits."*

TRIBULATION

In no place does the Word of God make the claim that if a Believer has a certain degree of Faith, that all Tribulation, i.e., affliction, can be avoided. While some problems definitely come to Believers because of a lack of Faith, such would not include all.

At times, Believers suffer tribulation because of attacks by Satan, circumstances over which they have no control, or because of lessons which need to be learned and can be learned no other way.

Irrespective, the Believer is to always understand, that any and all things which happen to him, irrespective as to what they may

NOTES

be, are either caused or allowed by the Lord. The Believer belongs to Christ, and as such, is not subject to whim or fancy, or to those things which unbelievers face. Believers are under, and in, the Economy of God, and as such, are protected, guided, led, superintended, and instructed by the Holy Spirit.

In this process, if the Lord allows *"Tribulation,"* He does so for a purpose, and it is up to us to know what that purpose is, thereby learning the lesson which is being taught.

The phrase, *"Continuing instant in prayer,"* proclaims the privilege of the Child of God of being able to speak on a constant basis to the Creator of all things.

"Continuing instant" in the Greek is *"proskartereo,"* and means *"to persevere, to give constant attention to a thing, to be devoted or constant to one, to be steadfastly attentive to, to give unremitting care to, to wait on continually, to be in constant readiness for one."* The word is used of the soldier who waited on Cornelius continually (Acts 10:7), and of the Twelve who said, *"We will give ourselves continually to prayer . . ."* (Acts 6:4) (Wuest).

The idea is, that we pray about everything continually, and be quick to do so.

It also means to not let go easily respecting that which we believe the Lord has promised to us. To be sure, Satan will fight the prayer life of the Believer as he fights nothing else. The reason is obvious, prayer is the strength of the Believer in the sense that this is where we receive our Leading, Guidance and Direction by the Holy Spirit. As well, in prayer, the Believer is addressing someone Who can do anything, irrespective of the need, for with God all things are possible.

PRAYER AND THE HOLY SPIRIT

It was in a praying atmosphere that the Church was born (Acts 1:14; 2:1); and throughout its early history prayer continued to be its vital breath and native air (Acts 2:42; 3:1; 6:4-6).

The Epistles abound in references to prayer. Those of Paul in particular contain frequent allusions to his own personal practice in the matter (Rom. 1:9; Eph. 1:16; Phil. 1:9; I Thess. 1:2, etc.), and many exhortations to his readers to cultivate the praying habit (Rom. 12:12; Eph. 6:18; Phil. 4:6; I Thess. 5:17, etc.).

But the new and characteristic thing about Christian prayer as it meets us now is its connection with the Holy Spirit. It has literally become a Spiritual Gift (I Cor. 14:14-16); this is the reason the Baptism with the Holy Spirit is so very important. Part of the Believer's prayer life should be that we *"pray in the Spirit"* whenever we come to the Throne of Grace (Eph. 6:18; Jude vs. 20).

The Holy Spirit, as promised by Christ (Jn. 14:16), has raised prayer to its highest power by securing for it a Divine cooperation (Rom. 8:15-26; Gal. 4:6).

Thus, Christian prayer in its full New Testament thought is prayer addressed to God as Father, in the Name of Christ as Mediator, and through the enabling Grace of the indwelling Spirit (Lambert).

(13) "DISTRIBUTING TO THE NECESSITY OF SAINTS; GIVEN TO HOSPITALITY."

The phrase, *"Distributing to the necessity of Saints,"* pertains to concern and generosity.

"Distributing" in the Greek, is *"koinoneo,"* and means *"to enter into fellowship, make oneself a sharer or partner."* The exhortation is to make oneself as sharer or partner in the needs of our fellow-Saints in the sense that we act as if those needs were our own. We would satisfy our own needs, and the contention is where possible, to satisfy those of our Christian brother as well (Wuest).

However, in no way is Paul meaning that laziness should be rewarded, especially considering that he has just said *"not slothful (lazy) in business."* In fact, he also said, ". . . *If any would not work, neither should he eat"* (II Thess. 3:10). In fact, the Christian work ethic has no place for laziness or slothfulness. Industry and in whatever capacity, should always be the hallmark of the Child of God.

The phrase, *"Given to hospitality"* pertains to a lifestyle.

"Given" in the Greek, is *"dioko,"* and means *"to pursue, to seek after eagerly, earnestly endeavor to acquire."*

"Hospitality" in the Greek, is *"philoxenia,"* and means *"fondness or affection for strangers, hospitality."*

This was a necessary injunction when so

many Christians during Paul's time were banished and persecuted. The indication of the word is, that not only is hospitality to be furnished when sought, but that Christians are to seek opportunities of exercising this Grace.

The hospitality referred to here is the giving of food, clothing, and shelter to persecuted Christians who have lost these, due to their Testimony of the Lord Jesus (Vincent).

Once again, and as should be obvious, in no way is this an injunction to reward laziness, etc.

(14) "BLESS THEM WHICH PERSECUTE YOU: BLESS, AND CURSE NOT."

The phrase, *"Bless them which persecute you,"* as well as the entirety of this Scripture, is probably derived by Paul from the Words of Jesus in Matthew 5:44. It is believed that the Book of Matthew may have been written as long as 15 to 20 years before Paul wrote Romans.

"Bless" in the Greek, is *"eulogeo,"* and means *"to speak well of a person, to eulogize him."* It also means *"to bless one, to praise, celebrate with praises"* (Thayer).

"Persecute" in the Greek, is *"dioko,"* and means *"to follow after, to press forward, with the idea of overtaking someone and hurting them."*

The exhortation is to bless our persecutors in the sense of returning kindness and love to those who mistreat us because of our Testimony of the Lord Jesus. It is *"to speak them good."*

The phrase, *"Bless, and curse not,"* concerns that which is emphatic. In other words, the Christian is to only bless, and not pronounce judgment on others, even our most strident enemies.

"Curse" in the Greek is *"kataraomai,"* and means *"to curse, doom, imprecate evil on."* From this we understand that the word *"curse"* as used here, does not have the usual present-day meaning of profanity, but rather of calling down Divine curses upon a person. This the Believer is not to do!

THE CURSE

What does it mean that God cursed the ground? And why was there an immediate reaction, as reported in Deuteronomy, when a young man of mixed parentage cursed his parents? And what about the curses that stand in contrast to the Blessings listed in Mosaic Law? (Deut. Chpt. 28).

The English concept of *"curse"* is complicated. The Old Testament concept is even more complex. But we can understand the various meanings of *"curse"* by considering Hebrew and Greek words and the context of the Biblical world.

THE SOLEMN WARNING

The Hebrew word *"alah"* means *"to swear a solemn oath."* It is used of promises that people make and of testimony they give in court. It is also found in Passages that speak of the Covenant that exists between God and His People (Deut. 29:12).

Although an oath statement may make a promise as well as define a penalty, *"alah"* is most often used in warnings. A curse made God's People aware ahead of time of the Judgments that would follow should they break their Covenant obligations (Deut. 29:14-21; Isa. 24:6; Jer. 23:10; Dan. 9:11).

THE BINDING ACT

The Hebrew verb *"arar"* is found 63 times in the Old Testament, and a derivative noun, *"m'erahm,"* is found fives times (Deut. 28:20; Prov. 3:33; 28:27; Mal. 2:2; 3:9).

Twelve times *"arar"* stands in opposition to *"barak,"* which means *"to bless."*

In such Passages it functions much like *"alah"* as a statement of consequences imbedded within the framework of God's Law (Deut. 27:15-16; 28:16-18). Such warnings are bold and clear: *"The Lord will send on you curses, confusion and rebuke in everything to which you put your hand to, until you are destroyed and come to sudden ruin because of the evil you have done in forsaking Him"* (Deut. 28:20).

But this word goes beyond the definition of the consequences of disobedience. It also serves to announce punishments that God has imposed.

The root idea expressed in *"arar"* is to bind so as to reduce ability or to render powerless. When God announced that because of sin His curse was upon the Earth, He declared that Earth's original spontaneous

fertility had been stunted.

The land was no longer able to produce to its earlier capacity. Human beings were no longer able to enjoy Earth's produce without labor.

CAIN AND BALAAM

Two other examples deserve mention:

1. One is the curse on Cain the farmer (Gen. 4:2-3, 11-12), which included driving him from the ground (banning him from enjoying the land's productivity).

2. The second is that of Balaam; he was hired by Balak to curse Israel, because Balak wanted the Seer to neutralize Israel's military power (Num. 22:4-6).

A person or thing that is cursed, then, is in some significant way bound: that person or thing is unable to do what he, she, or it was once able to do.

MAGIC?

People of the ancient world (and some in the present) considered that curses were magic tools to be used to gain power over enemies. In Scripture the curse is notably a consequence of violating one's relationship with God. Thus, *"curse"* is a moral rather than a magical term.

The association of the curse with magic is sometimes reflected in the term *"qabab."* All of its eight Old Testament uses are associated with the story of Balaam. Certainly Balak wanted the Seer to utter magical words that would immobilize his enemy; however, he was to find that Balaam was not able to utter any type of *"curse"* on God's People, Israel. In fact, the Lord spoke through the wayward Prophet concerning this very thing, saying, *"Surely there is no enchantment against Jacob, neither is there any divination against Israel: according to this time it shall be said of Jacob and of Israel, What hath God wrought!"* (Num. 23:23).

Let the Believer understand, that this holds true not only for Israel of old, but for all who Name the Name of Jesus. No curse is effective against the Believer.

To be sure, if Satan had his way, he would have wreaked death and destruction upon all followers of the Lord from the very beginning.

He hasn't done so, simply because he cannot do so. Believers do not belong to him, but rather, belong to God.

Peter said, *"But ye are a Chosen Generation, a Royal Priesthood, an Holy Nation, a Peculiar People; that you should shew forth the Praises of Him Who hath called you out of darkness into His Marvelous Light"* (I Pet. 2:9).

The word *"peculiar"* actually means *"possession,"* and in fact, *"God's Own Possession."*

It is somewhat like the Lord drawing a circle, placing the Believer inside the circle, and then saying to Satan, *"Everything on the inside of this circle is Mine, and to what is inside this circle you have no access, unless I permit such."* So, Satan's curses do not work on the Child of God.

A PERSONAL EXPERIENCE

I have used the word *"personal,"* even though I was not directly involved, but yet an indirect part of that which happened.

Our Ministry built about 35 Schools in the little Island Nation of Haiti. These were very elementary affairs, costing approximately $50,000 per School, and only went through the 6th grade. However, these Schools were such a blessing to the people, inasmuch as they were for the very poor. Actually, we provided a hot meal at noon each day for each child, in many cases, the only hot meal the child would get.

With many of these Schools, we also built a Church nearby, sometimes even physically connected with the School.

In one particular part of *"Port'au'Prince"* the Lord began to bless one of the Churches to such an extent, that it fastly outgrew its quarters. Many people were coming to Christ, with many lives being changed. It was pastored by a Native Haitian.

There are probably more Witch Doctors in Haiti commensurate to its size than any other Nation in the world. Except for the Light of the Gospel, this little Island Nation has been given over to Satan, who has wreaked his destructive force upon its people. These Witch Doctors specialize in putting *"curses"* upon people, hiring out their services, etc.

So many people had come to Christ, that

the lead Witch Doctor in this area had grown incensed at the Pastor and at me personally, because I had built the Church. All the people coming to Christ, was cutting down on his revenue, etc., and probably as important, his control over them.

A CURSE THAT BACKFIRED

There was a chance meeting on a certain day of the Pastor in question and this particular Witch Doctor. Angry at the Pastor, he began to revile and to place a *"curse"* upon him. Actually, he said, *"In 30 days you and Jimmy Swaggart will be dead,"* which was his most powerful curse.

The Pastor said to him in return, *"No, your curse be back upon your own head, in 30 days you will die."*

In 30 days the Witch Doctor was dead, causes unknown!

Inasmuch as Paul by the Holy Spirit had forbidden such activity on the part of the Believer, quite possibly the Pastor was not right in that which he did. However, at the same time, I doubt very seriously if he was that much aware of what the Word of God said respecting Paul's admonition. Irrespective, it is very obvious as to the residue of power in the heart and life of the Pastor and not the follower of Satan. John said, *". . . Because Greater is He that is in you, than he that is in the world"* (I Jn. 4:4).

As stated, a curse issued by Satan or his followers has no affect upon the Child of God; however, that said by the Believer has great affect, and that is the reason we are admonished to only *"bless"* and not *"curse."*

The Hebrew word *"qalal"* means *"to be slight."* The one cursed experiences reduced circumstances. Often this curse of reduced position, power, wealth, or honor is occasioned by the breaking of God's Covenant.

The noun *"q'lalah"* emphasizes the loss or absence of the state of blessing, a state that God yearns for His People to enjoy.

The verb may be used in the sense of pronouncing a curse or to indicate that someone is in the state of being cursed. Again, the Pagans felt that by uttering magical words they could attack and diminish an enemy. This may be reflected in the phrase in the Abrahamic Covenant, *"He who curses (qalal) you."* It is also likely that the case reported in Leviticus 24:11, in which the *"Son of an Israelite woman blasphemed the Name of the Lord with a curse,"* reveals an attempt to use God's Name in a magical incantation against someone the young man viewed as an enemy.

But God says, *"He who curses you, I will curse"* (Gen. 12:3). The use of *"magic"* against Believers is done before Almighty God, Who Himself puts persons and competing powers in a state of powerlessness or reduced ability.

When we understand the background of the ancient Near East, the Command *"If anyone curses his father or mother, he must be put to death . . ."* (Lev. 20:9) takes on a different meaning. The individual is not uttering careless oaths in anger. He is turning to magic in a conscious effort to harm his parents, whom God has commanded him to honor (Lev. 20:6-8).

THE NEW TESTAMENT

Two different Greek roots are reflected in the use of this word *"curse."*

One concept is expressed in words linked with *"anathema,"* which means *"accursed."* The root indicates dedication to destruction: an anathematized object or person is delivered up to the Judgment of God.

Paul, touchingly eager for the Salvation of his Jewish Brethren, wished that, if such a thing were possible, he might be accursed that they might be Saved (Rom. 9:1-3). But the wish could not be granted — for him or for anyone else who has been Saved through the Blood of Jesus.

Words compounded with *"anathema"* are generally translated *"accursed."* Two other Greek words are *"katara"* or *"kataraomai."* These words correspond closely to *"qalal"* and suggest the opposite of Blessing.

THE CURSE OF THE LAW

In Paul's argument in Galatians 3:10-14, he looks back into history at the Blessings and curses of the Law. Paul says that Law requires us to *"continue to do everything"* written in it if we are to be Blessed.

Regrettably, all fall short of doing everything. Thus, all who rely on the Law must

NOTES

in fact fall under the curse rather than the Blessing!

Thus, Law itself, when taken as a means to Life, becomes a curse, from which we can be released only by Faith in Jesus.

THOSE WHO WOULD CURSE US

According to the instructions in the New Testament about those who curse us, actually that which we are now studying, we are to do nothing that might diminish their situation nor wish them ill. The reason should be obvious.

First of all, when we as Believers were once loaded with sin and, therefore, under its curse, which is death, upon Faith in Christ, the Lord lifted the curse from us, giving us the Blessing of Redemption and Eternal Life. Inasmuch as the Lord has done that for us, we are to show kindness to others in the same capacity, even though they may be bitter enemies.

As well, irrespective as to what others may try to do to us in a harmful sense, if we trust the Lord, they cannot succeed. So, we should reward them by Blessing them instead of cursing them. This shows the Divine nature of the Child of God.

Also, if the Believer does curse someone (pronounce judgment upon them), such words coming from a Believer have a powerful effect, and can actually come to pass. In view of this fact, no Believer should ever desire to bring judgment on the head of anyone. This is God's prerogative Alone (Rom. 12:17-21).

The business of the Believer is to bring Life instead of death. This is the reason that Jesus told Israel that He did not come to condemn, but rather to bring Life (Jn. 10:10).

To be sure, it takes the Grace of God to speak well of, to eulogize, to praise the very one who is attempting to hurt us. However, that is the business of the Grace of God, to enable the Believer to do what within himself is impossible.

BELIEVERS GOING BACK UNDER THE CURSE

The writer of Hebrews mentioned Believers who were in danger of being cursed (Heb. 6:8). They were in danger of slipping out of the realm of Blessing into the opposite experience, for they were considering turning back to the Old Testament ways of worship, away from Jesus.

To go back under the Old Testament Law, thereby denying the Finished Work of Christ, to Whom the Law actually pointed as its completion, is to bring back upon oneself the *"Curse of the Law,"* which means eternal damnation. To do such is unthinkable, but yet many have!

Jesus Himself provides all the Blessings the Old Testament holds out — and much, much more! Actually, every iota of the Mosaic Law pointed to Jesus. The Sacrifices, Feast Days, Circumcision, even the very Temple itself, were all Types of Christ. All pointed to Him, as the only One who could deliver from the Curse of sin and death. Consequently, if one repudiates Him, even attempting to go back to the Old Law, the results will only be a *"curse"* and not the opposite. Jesus is the only One Who could deliver and can deliver from that *"curse."*

FAITH IN CHRIST

When we read *"curse"* in the Bible, the reference is not to swearing. Usually it does not even refer to that magical kind of curse that is pronounced by witches and warlocks.

The people of the Biblical world thought of curses as magical incantations that harnessed the supernatural in order to harm enemies. At times the Old Testament uses the word *"curse"* in this Pagan sense, as in the prohibition against cursing one's parents. But the True Biblical meaning of *"curse"* is quite distinct.

A curse is essentially a Divine Judgment. A curse may be uttered as a solemn oath, warning of what God will do if His Covenant is violated.

A curse may also be the Judgment itself, spoken of after it has been imposed. Such a curse binds and limits its object. It brings about diminished circumstances that stand in contrast to the Blessing God yearns to provide.

In the Old Testament, Blessing and Cursing are intimately associated with the Mosaic Law. That Law defines the way of Life that those in relationship with a Holy God must follow.

NOTES

Those who obey are to be blessed; those who will not obey are to experience the curse. But, as the New Testament points out, with these conditions the Law itself proved to be a curse, for no one could keep it perfectly.

It is wonderful that in His Death, Jesus won release for us from the Curse of the Law. Through Faith in Christ, we have been given Blessings that we could never have earned.

And it is significant that though the Old Testament speaks often of curses that God's sinning people must endure, there is no hint in the New Testament of a curse for those who continue to follow Jesus.

(15) "REJOICE WITH THEM THAT DO REJOICE, AND WEEP WITH THEM THAT WEEP."

The phrase, *"Rejoice with them that do rejoice,"* speaks of the Believer being sincerely glad for the Blessings of others.

The phrase, *"And weep with them that weep,"* expresses the Believer being sincerely sorry for and with those who experience tribulation and sorrow.

Over and over again, as we have seen and as we shall see, the Holy Spirit through the Apostle directs the attention of the Believer to others. In the Spirit of Christ we are to bless them, whomever they may be, even enemies, sincerely rejoicing at their Blessing and sincerely feeling the sorrow of their hurt. To be sure, only in Christ can this be done.

(16) "BE OF THE SAME MIND ONE TOWARD ANOTHER. MIND NOT HIGH THINGS, BUT CONDESCEND TO MEN OF LOW ESTATE. BE NOT WISE IN YOUR OWN CONCEITS."

The phrase, *"Be of the same mind one toward another,"* in respect refers to having the Mind of Christ (Phil. 2:5-11).

If one is to recall, the example of Christ in His dealings with people from all walks of life is to be the criteria. He did not at all grovel before the high and mighty nor seek their pleasure in any way. He was kind to them as He was to all, and that's the point. He treated all just alike. Actually, the Scripture says, *". . . And the common people heard Him gladly"* (Mk. 12:37).

The idea of Paul's statement is, that if all are truly followers of the Lord, and are truly seeking to do His Will, all will have the Mind of Christ. The idea, is to enter into the feelings and desires of the other as to be of one mind with Him (Gifford). It is not uniformity but unanimity of which Paul is speaking here.

The phrase, *"Mind not high things,"* clues us in even more so to the previous phrase.

DISCRIMINATION

If the Believer does not have and practice the Mind of Christ, he will begin to discriminate, which is the spirit of the world. To understand this even more, it is somewhat necessary to understand the culture and social climate of Paul's day.

The entirety of the world of that day was very class conscious, actually with much of the human race being slaves. Even among Romans there were three classes: A. Those of the ruling class who were of certain financial status, and to show this they wore a certain type of garment with a wide band conspicuously displayed, which portrayed their place; B. Those who were of somewhat lesser status and of finances as well, but still men of substance, wore a band on their tunic or garment which was about half the width of the highest rank; and, C. Last of all, the common people who were not allowed to wear any type of recognition at all, at least as the other two groups, even though Roman citizens. So, as stated, class consciousness was rife in the world of Paul's day.

However, Christianity began to change this class distinction, with all being treated equal. In other words, when people came together to worship the Lord, and in whatever capacity, at times wealthy landowners sat side by side with slaves. All were supposed to be treated alike, whether they were rich, poor, great, small, male or female, Roman or otherwise. All are one in Christ (Col. 3:10-11). In fact, Christianity alone ultimately banished the horrible scourge of slavery from the face of the Earth, at least where Christianity holds sway. While it is true that it did not come quickly, and actually little by little, still it was done. Men do not give up their sins easily!

CHRISTIAN TREATMENT

The Believer is to look at all other human

beings as made in the Image of God, whatever their present status, and as a result, of great worth and value (Mat. 12:12).

The phrase, *"But condescend to men of low estate,"* continues this thought in the same vein.

Please allow me to say it in this fashion:

The manner in which you the Believer treats a person who occupies the lowest station of life, whatever that might be, and when no one else is seeing or hearing, is what you are. In other words, if you treat them unkindly in any manner, that shows what you really are. Conversely, if you treat them with dignity and respect, that as well, shows Christlikeness, again what you are.

I personally feel that this is the greatest test of all as to what a person really is, irrespective of their claims.

"Condescend" in the Greek, is *"sunapago,"* and means *"to lead away or together."* In a sense, it speaks of making friends with people who have no status or position in the world, as well as making friends with those who do, at least if it is possible.

The word *"low"* or *"lowly"* in the Greek is *"tapeinos,"* and means *"not rising far from the ground, of low degree."*

The Greek word *"tapeinophrosune,"* taken from the word *"tapeinos,"* means *"having a humble opinion of oneself; a deep sense of one's* (moral) *littleness, modesty, humility, lowliness of mind."*

"Tapeinosis" means *"spiritual abasement leading one to perceive and lament his* (moral) *littleness and guilt."* In other words, lowly things or lowly men would be those of no great consequence so far as the spirit of this age is concerned. They would be those who in self-abasement and humility walk this Earth with a deep sense of their moral littleness.

PRIDE

Pride is probably the worst sin there is, at least as it blinds people to their true spiritual condition. Of the seven sins which the Scriptures state as an abomination unto God, *"pride"* leads the list (Prov. 6:16-19). It is this *"prideful look"* by Israel which rejected Christ, and ultimately crucified Him. As well, it has caused most of the world to be lost, and is the ruin of entire Church Denominations. It translates into self-righteousness, plus a host of other sins and abominations. While it certainly would not include all, still, men of high estate, even in the Church, often fall into the category of pride.

The phrase, *"Be not wise in your own conceits,"* proclaims the antipathy felt by the Apostle to every sort of spiritual aristocracy, to every caste-distinction within the Church, which breaks out again in the word *"conceits"* (Wuest).

Denney says, *"Be not men of mind in your own conceit. It is difficult to put our judgment into a common stock, and estimate another's as impartially as our own; but love requires it, and without it there is no such thing as 'being of the same mind one toward another.'"*

The idea of this phrase contains the thought that if our knowledge or wisdom is based on self-worth, while we put others down, it is not wisdom at all, but rather *"conceits."* It goes back to the 3rd verse where Paul said that a man should *"not think of himself more highly than he ought to think,"* and I might quickly add, for all the obvious reasons.

(17) "RECOMPENSE TO NO MAN EVIL FOR EVIL. PROVIDE THINGS HONEST IN THE SIGHT OF ALL MEN."

The phrase, *"Recompense to no man evil for evil,"* plainly and clearly says what is to be done. Even though individuals may seek to harm us, and in fact, may harm us, we are not to repay in like kind, even if such is within our power, but rather with the very opposite.

"Recompense" in the Greek, is *"apodidomi,"* and means *"to give back, to requite."*

How many Christians can honestly say that they have adhered to this Command as given by the Holy Spirit?

A better question yet, how far removed from Biblical Christianity as outlined here by Paul, is the modern Church?

The phrase, *"Provide things honest in the sight of all men,"* does not really speak of the handling of money as many think, but of course could include that.

"Provide" in the Greek, is *"pronoeo,"* and means *"to perceive beforehand, foresee, to*

think beforehand."

"Things honest" in the Greek, is *"kala."* The word is one of the two words which the Greeks have of describing that which is good, *"agathos"* referring to intrinsic goodness, and *"kalos,"* which is our word here which speaks to exterior goodness, or goodness that is seen on the exterior of a person, the outward expression of an inward goodness.

When this outward expression conforms to the inward goodness, then that expression which a Christian gives of himself is an honest one, one conforming to the inner facts. But if the Christian assumes an outward expression which is patterned after this age, that expression not representing what he is, a Child of God, but giving the beholder the impression that he is a person of the world, that expression is a dishonest one.

The Christian is exhorted to take careful forethought that his manner of life, his outward expression conforms to, is honestly represented of what he is as a Child of God (Wuest).

As stated, the idea as Paul expresses this statement, is of far greater magnitude than monetary or material honesty, but rather referring to what we really are in Christ Jesus. In other words, if we are truly Saved, we should act like it.

(18) "IF IT BE POSSIBLE, AS MUCH AS LIETH IN YOU, LIVE PEACEABLY WITH ALL MEN."

Sometimes it is impossible owing to the conduct of others.

"If it be possible" is objective only — not *"if you can"* but *"if it be possible"* — if others will allow it.

"As much as lieth in you live peaceably with all men," means that all your part is to be peace: whether you actually live peaceably or not, will depend solely on how others behave towards you. The Believer has no control over the conduct of another, but the idea is, that the initiative in disturbing the peace is never to lie with the Christian.

(19) "DEARLY BELOVED, AVENGE NOT YOURSELVES, BUT RATHER GIVE PLACE UNTO WRATH: FOR IT IS WRITTEN, VENGEANCE IS MINE; I WILL REPAY, SAITH THE LORD."

The phrase, *"Dearly beloved, avenge not*

yourselves," proclaims action respecting fellow human beings.

"Avenge" in the Greek, is *"ekdikeo,"* and means *"to vindicate one's right, do one justice, to avenge oneself."*

The idea is, that even when the Christian has been wronged, he is not to take the Law into his own hands, and right or vindicate himself (Denney).

The phrase, *"But rather give place unto wrath,"* simply means that one should not try to avenge oneself. We are to leave it up to the Lord, allowing Him to do what only He can do. If the other person is wrong, the Lord plainly and clearly says, *"I will repay."*

"Wrath" in the Greek is preceded by the article, actually saying *"the Wrath"* which points to a special Wrath, God's Wrath.

To give place to God's Wrath means to leave room for it, not to take God's proper work out of His Hands (Wuest).

The phrase, *"For it is written, Vengeance is Mine; I will repay, saith the Lord,"* refers to the Lord as the Maintainer of moral order in the world, and that the righting of wrong is to be committed to Him.

"Vengeance" in the Greek, is *"ekdikesis,"* and means *"a revenging punishment."*

The idea is not that instead of executing vengeance ourselves we are to abandon the offender to the more powerful vengeance of God, but that God as the Righteous Judge will do right.

In fact, God cannot be said to have vengeance in the sense that a person has vengeance, namely a retaliatory feeling which prompts a vindictive requital. The Lord judges from Perfect Knowledge and Perfect Righteousness. As such, His Judgment, unlike ours, is not only right, but always right.

"Repay" in the Greek, is *"antapodidomi,"* and means *"to give back or requite."*

The idea comes from Matthew 7:1-2, where Jesus said, *"Judge not, that ye be not judged.*

"For with what judgment ye judge, ye shall be judged: and with what measure ye mete, it shall be measured to you again."

Paul's statement, prefixed by the words, *"For it is written,"* was probably derived from Deuteronomy 32:35.

(20) "THEREFORE IF THINE ENEMY HUNGER, FEED HIM; IF HE THIRST, GIVE HIM DRINK: FOR IN SO DOING THOU SHALL HEAP COALS OF FIRE ON HIS HEAD."

The phrase, *"Therefore if your enemy hunger, feed him; if he thirst, give him drink,"* refers to the opposite tact of the world. The attitude of the world is: *"Get even"*! The Believer is to do the very opposite.

The phrase, *"For in so doing thou shall heap Coals of Fire on his head,"* has been debated by expositors since it was written.

Of the many explanations I have read or heard, the two following I think, come closer to the meaning:

1. The Greek Scholar, Kenneth Wuest gives the following:

In Bible times an Oriental needed to keep his hearth fire going all the time in order to insure fire for cooking and warmth. If the fire went out in his house, he had to go to a neighbor for some live Coals of Fire. These he would carry on his head in a container, oriental fashion, back to his home.

The person who would give him live coals would be meeting his desperate need and showing him an outstanding kindness.

If he would heap the container with coals, the man would be sure of getting some home still burning.

Bringing the illustration to bear with Paul's admonition, the one injured would be returning kindness for injury, the only thing a Christian is allowed to give back to the one who has injured him. This act of kindness God could use to soften the heart of the person and lead him on to Repentance and the Offering of a Recompense for the injury sustained. In this way the Christian would overcome evil with good.

2. Another interpretation which I have read or heard (I don't remember which), concerns the Coals of Fire which were taken from the Brazen Altar, and placed on the Altar of Incense, in the Holy Place in the Temple.

This was done at least twice a day, with incense poured over these coals, which in effect has to do with one's Worship and Prayerful Intercession before the Lord. The Altar of Incense sat immediately in front of the Holy of Holies, which contained the Ark of the Covenant and the Mercy Seat. So, there was a Sweet Savour which came up before God constantly, and which, as stated, represents Prayerful Worship.

Whenever the Believer extends a kindness to one who has wronged him, he is in effect, making it possible for this person to repent, because spiritually speaking, the Coals of Fire have been taken from the Brazen Altar to the Altar of Incense, i.e., the Head, The Lord Jesus Christ.

The Coals of Fire from the Brazen Altar represent the Judgment of God, which would be poured out upon God's Son, instead of on the sinner. So, in effect, the Believer performing a kindness to an enemy, diverts the Judgment that should come upon this enemy instead to The Lord Jesus Christ, that is, if the offender will only repent.

It is my thinking, that this last explanation is probably what Paul meant.

There is a tremendous power in that which the Holy Spirit demands respecting situations of this nature. When the Believer treats ill will and hurt with kindness, the power of evil is broken. Another course is now charted, and the way is now open for the offender to make things right, with the way in fact, now being much easier.

As well, this speaks of forgiveness on the part of the offended one, even though the offender has not asked for forgiveness. Having the power to do that, which every Believer has, and then the using of that power in this fashion, presents a powerful force. The initiative now changes from evil to good.

(21) "BE NOT OVERCOME OF EVIL, BUT OVERCOME EVIL WITH GOOD."

The phrase, *"Be not overcome of evil,"* has reference to the fact that we should not meet evil with evil. If we attempt to do that, every time we will be *"overcome of evil,"* i.e., make the situation nothing but worse.

The phrase, *"But overcome evil with good,"* presents that which we have just stated, which changes the initiative from evil to good, and is actually the only way that situations of this nature can be changed.

HOW FAR SHOULD ONE GO IN MAKING THESE ATTEMPTS?

Paul answered that question by saying, *"If it be possible, as much as lieth in you,"*

NOTES

which means *"If it be possible"* — *"if others will allow it."*

I think one of the greatest examples of what Paul is saying here, is found in the story of Joseph (Gen. Chpts. 37-50).

JOSEPH THE EXAMPLE

The story of Joseph, the son of Jacob, the Grandson of Isaac and the Great-Grandson of Abraham, is striking indeed! In fact, Joseph is a Type of Christ, which makes the example even more wonderful. For instance, of all the Bible Characters, Joseph is the only one of whom no wrongdoing whatsoever is recorded.

This does not mean that he was perfect, for the Scripture says different, *"All have sinned, and come short of the Glory of God"* (Rom. 3:23). But being a Type of Christ, especially in view of his character, he was a very Godly man.

HIS BROTHERS

Regrettably, the other sons of Jacob, the brothers of Joseph, with the exception of Benjamin, did not fall into the same category as Joseph. In fact, they were men of murderous hearts, who hated Joseph so severely, that they would have killed him had it not been for the Intercession of Reuben (Gen. 37:18-22). Judah as well, would play a part in his life being spared, but did suggest that they sell him as a slave to the *"Ishmeelites,"* which they did (Gen. 37:23-28).

(It seems as if Reuben left the company of his brothers for some time, and was intending all along to rescue Joseph and return him to his Father Jacob. However, they had already sold Joseph when Reuben returned, with him now, it seems, becoming a part of the conspiracy to hide the fact from Jacob, of what had been done.

THE ASCENDANCY OF JOSEPH

Years passed, with Joseph ultimately becoming the Viceroy of Egypt, second only to Pharaoh, which meant he was the second most powerful man in the world.

Famine gripped the Middle East, which necessitated Joseph's brothers coming to Egypt in order to purchase food, etc. Of course they had no idea that Joseph was now the Viceroy of Egypt, and neither did they recognize him when they were ushered into his presence. As far as they were concerned, he was an Egyptian (Gen. Chpt. 42).

THE CONDUCT OF JOSEPH

It is very interesting, that Joseph did not reveal himself at all to his brothers when they first came to Egypt. In fact, he instituted a series of tests to ascertain the present condition of their hearts.

In fact, he demanded on their next trip that Benjamin be brought with them, who it seems did not accompany them on this first trip. Simeon was kept in Egypt to insure that Benjamin be brought. How many times, if any, that Joseph visited him during this period is not known.

On their second trip, this time with Benjamin, Joseph again instituted further tests to insure the condition of their hearts. The idea is, that he would not reveal himself to them, at least in a friendly fashion, if they were still the same men who had sold him into Egypt. Beautifully so, their actions portrayed that they were, indeed, changed men. Then and then only, did he reveal himself to them and then loaded them with kindnesses, etc.

THE MORAL OF THIS ILLUSTRATION

While it is possible to be kind to our enemies, even as Paul states here, and which the Holy Spirit demands; still, until True Repentance is enjoined, there can be no fellowship, even as the experience with Joseph illustrates.

As well, I think it is incumbent upon the Believer, even as Joseph, to ascertain the validity of one's spiritual claims. If one has truly repented, there will be telltale signs and obvious to all, even as with the brothers of Joseph. If one has not repented, those signs will be there as well!

To be kind and gracious to an enemy is not only possible but demanded; however, for true fellowship to be restored, there must be Repentance on the part of the offender.

HOW BROAD SHOULD REPENTANCE BE?

Repentance should be as broad as the offense.

If the situation is contained between two parties, the Repentance need only include that one party, with of course Repentance toward God mandatory in all circumstances. If the offense is broader, it should include all who have been offended.

If the offense has been public, the Repentance should be public as well.

The situation with Joseph and his brothers, included only the family. Consequently, there is no record that Joseph ever revealed to Pharaoh, or anyone else for that matter, this situation which had existed between him and his brothers. It was in the family, so it remained in the family, even as it should have.

"I think of my Saviour, His Love and His Favor,
"And all of His Mercy Divine;
"A new heart He gave me, and thus He did save me, this wonderful Saviour of mine."

"The moment so precious, so holy and gracious,
"I think of it joyfully still,
"When Jesus renewed me, with power endued me, and humbled my heart to His Will."

"How close is the union, and rich the communion,
"Between the Dear Lord and my soul;
"'Tis joy full of sweetness, my heart in completeness, I yield to His Holy Control."

"In glad exultation o'er conscious Salvation,
"I praise His Adorable Name;
"A new heart He gave me, and thus did He save me, and I will His Goodness proclaim."

CHAPTER 13

(1) "LET EVERY SOUL BE SUBJECT UNTO THE HIGHER POWERS. FOR THERE IS NO POWER BUT OF GOD: THE POWERS THAT BE ARE ORDAINED OF GOD."

After dealing with the formation of the

Church in Chapter 11, Paul deals with the subject of mutual responsibilities and duties of Christians in the Body of Christ in Chapter 12.

The Apostle now passes to the duty of Christians toward Civil Government and the Laws of the country in which they lived. There is a reason why Paul abruptly changes the subject.

The Roman Empire of Paul's day looked at Judaism and the Church as pretty much the same, even though Jews who were not Christians (and most were not), despised those who were. Besides that, all the Apostles were Jewish, and Paul, the greatest Evangelist in the world of that day, was Jewish as well; consequently, in the Roman mind there was little difference in Judaism and Christianity.

CITIZENS!

The Jews of the Roman Empire were notoriously bad citizens. Many held on the ground of Deuteronomy 17:15 that to acknowledge a Gentile Ruler as such, was sinful. Actually, this was the spirit back of the question of the Pharisees who asked Jesus, *"Is it lawful to give tribute to Caesar, or not?"*

Also, there were some Jews who were Christians. To be sure, even though their thinking would not have been rabid as the non-Christian Jews, still, their attitude toward Gentiles left something to be desired. Gentiles, in contact with such Jewish Christians, and especially Jews who were non-Christians, could well imbibe the spirit of anarchy which such an attitude would foment. Thus, Paul, as led by the Holy Spirit, writes in this Chapter certain instructions, to make certain that Christians understand their relations and obligations to Civil Government.

His statement could be summed up in the following words: *"Law and its representatives are of God, and as such are entitled to all honor and obedience from Christians"* (Denney).

It was, therefore, peculiarly needful that the Christian Community should be cautioned to disprove the attitude and disposition of most Jewish Communities, by showing themselves in all respects good law-abiding subjects.

GOVERNMENT

To be sure, this was not necessarily easy, especially considering that Nero was now Caesar, a man demented, demon possessed, consequently, carrying out very little of good Government. Nevertheless, Christians are commanded to obey, that is if Scripturally possible. Peter and John, and rightly so, had at first defied the authority even of the Sanhedrin in matters touching conscience (Acts 4:19).

However, wherever it is possible to obey Civil Government, that is when it does not violate the conscience or Biblical Authority, Paul, therefore, lays down the rule that Civil Government, and in whomsoever hands it might be, is, no less than the Church, a Divine Institution for the maintenance of order in the world, to be submitted to and obeyed by Christians within the whole sphere of its legitimate authority. In his admonitions, at least here in Romans Chapter 13, he does not refer to cases in which it might become necessary to obey God rather than man: his purpose here does not call on him to do so; nor were the circumstances so far such as to bring such cases into prominence; for he, as stated, was writing in the earlier part of Nero's reign, before any general persecution of Christians had begun.

Nor does he touch on the question whether it may be right in some cases for subjects to resist usurped power or tyranny, or to take part in political revolutions, and even fight for freedom. Such a question was apart from his subject, which is the general duty of obedience to the Law and Government under which we are placed by Providence.

This is the only Passage in which he treats the subject at length and definitely.

In a doctrinal and practical treatise like this Epistle, addressed as a statement of the Holy Spirit to the metropolis of the world and the Seat of Government (Rome), it was fitting that he should express clearly the attitude of the Body of Christ with regard to Civil Order.

As well, his teaching in other Epistles is in accordance with this; as where (I Cor. 7:21) he bids slaves acquiesce in the existing Law of slavery, and (I Tim. 2:1, etc.) he desires especially prayers to be made on behalf of

Kings and Rulers (Barmby).

ORDAINED OF GOD

The phrase, *"Let every soul be subject unto the higher powers,"* refers to Human Government which is ordained as a principle by God. It does *not* mean that all the people involved in Human Government are ordained by God, but that God does ordain Government. However, every single Government functionary, and in whatever capacity, irrespective of his lowliest position or his highest, will one day answer to God for his service in this capacity. While this service has absolutely nothing to do with Salvation, it does have something to do with God's Order, and as such, all will ultimately give account.

"Every soul" in the Hebrew actually refers to *"every person."*

"Be subject" in the Greek is *"hupotasso,"* and refers to *"a military work speaking of soldiers arranged in order under a General."* In other words, they are subject to his orders. The translation reads, *"Let every soul place himself habitually in subjection to the higher powers."*

"Higher powers" is literally *"authorities which have themselves over,"* that is, authorities who are over the citizen (Wuest). (*"Higher Powers"* does not refer to Deity.)

The phrase, *"For there is no power but of God,"* refers to the fact that God has ordained Government. In fact, Human Government is a Divine Institution, instituted by God when Noah came out of the Ark, the basic Law of which is Capital Punishment for the murderer duly convicted of his crime (Gen. 9:5-6).

Lacking Government, anarchy reigns, which is the worst thing that can ever happen to any people, insuring their destruction. Anarchy is *"a state of lawlessness or political disorder due to the absence of Governmental Authority."* In such a case, with no restraints, lawlessness reigns, which refers to the criminal element of whatever variety, doing whatever they desire to the helpless.

OF GOD!

"Of God" in the Greek is *"hupo theou,"* and literally means *"by means of God,"* that is, constituted such by God.

The phrase, *"The powers that be are ordained of God,"* refers to Human Government being a permanent institution brought into being by God for the regulation of human affairs.

Consequently, the powers or authorities here are seen, not in their individual personalities, but as Officers of the Law, whose positions are ordained by God. That is, the various Offices of Civil Authority are appointed by God. The structure of Government and the Laws connected with it are appointed by God as a means of promoting Law and Order on Earth. The incumbents of those Offices, as should be obvious, are not always ordained of God. In fact, we know that demon spirits have a great deal to do with various Governments, at times literally taking over particular Governments of the Earth, which constitute untold suffering for the citizens of that particular land. Yet, the Christian is obligated to honor and obey the Magistrates under whose jurisdiction he lives, that is if the laws formulated by such Governments do not violate his conscience or Scripture.

In fact, as we have stated, we may observe that the Apostle here pays no regard to the question of the duty of Christians in revolutionary movements, etc. His precepts regard an *"established power,"* be it what it may. It, and all matters lawful (lawful to Scripture), we as Christians, are bound to obey. However, and as stated, if the Civil power commands us to violate the Law of God, we must obey God before man. If it commands us to disobey the common laws of humanity, or the Sacred Institutions of our country, our obedience is due to the higher and more general Law, rather than the lower and unscriptural Law.

These distinctions must be drawn by the wisdom granted Christians in the varying circumstances of human affairs. All powers among men must be in accord with the Higher Power of God, and always refer to the moral sense.

But even where Law is hard and unreasonable, not disobedience, but legitimate protest, is the duty of the Christian (Wuest).

IN PAUL'S DAY

In fact, very shortly after Paul penned

these words, the Roman Government under Nero began to demand of Christians that which was unscriptural, and, consequently, which they could not do. Therefore, untold thousands died in the Roman arenas, horrible deaths I might quickly add, simply because they would not acquiesce to Nero's demands which violated their conscience and the Word of God.

NERO

The first five years of Nero's reign were characterized by good Government at home and in the provinces, and popularity with both the Senate and the people. Many reforms during this time were initiated, financial, social, and legislative.

During this time, Nero was anything but Righteous and Just, actually giving himself over to the greatest excesses and with the most profligate companions. However, the Government was basically operated by Seneca and Burrus, two powerful Roman Sages. However, the evil bent of Nero was soon to manifest itself.

THE SECOND PERIOD

Nero surrounded himself with the most dissolute companions conspicuous among whom were Salvius Otho and Claudius Senecio.

The former had a wife as ambitious as she was unprincipled, and endowed, according to Tacitus, with every gift of nature except an *"honorable mind."* Already divorced before marrying Otho, she was minded to employ Otho merely as a tool to enable her to become Nero's consort. This opens the second period of Nero's reign. She proved his evil star.

Under her influence he shook off all restraints, turned a deaf ear to his best advisors, and plunged deeper into immorality and crime, even to the awfulness of murdering his own Mother, who this evil woman considered a rival.

In A.D. 62 Burrus died, which weakened the restraint on this despot. As well, Seneca, the other guiding light of the tyrant, was made to retire from the court.

Oddly enough, Poppaea Sabina, for that was her name, died during pregnancy, of a cruel kick inflicted by Nero in a fit of rage.

This was in A.D. 65.

BANKRUPTCY OF THE GOVERNMENT

Along with the immorality and crime of Nero, he had also exhausted the well-filled treasury which Claudius, the former Emperor, had left him. Huge amounts of money were squandered on foolish extravagances, etc. He was now driven to fill his coffers by confiscations of the estates of rich nobles against whom one of his lackeys would trump up charges, etc. However, even this did not prevent a financial crisis — the beginning of the bankruptcy of the later Roman Empire.

The Provinces which at first enjoyed good Government under his reign were now plundered; new and heavy taxes were imposed. Worst of all, the gold and silver coinage was depreciated, and the Senate was deprived of the right of alleviating the situation.

THE GREAT FIRE

This difficulty was much increased by the great fire which was not only destructive to both private and state property, but also necessitated providing thousands of homeless with shelter, and lowering the price of corn. On July 18, 64, this great conflagration broke out in Circus Maximus. A high wind caused it to spread rapidly over a large portion of the city, sweeping before it ill-built streets of wooden houses.

At the end of six days it seemed to be exhausted for lack of material, when another conflagration started in a different quarter of the City. Various exaggerations of the destruction are found in Roman Historians' accounts: of the 14 City regions, seven were to have been totally destroyed and four partially.

Nero was at Antium at the time. He hastened back to the City and apparently took every means of arresting the spread of the flames. He superintended in person the work of the fire brigades, often exposing himself to danger. After the fire he threw open his own gardens to the homeless.

The catastrophe caused great consternation, as would be obvious, and, for whatever reasons, suspicion seemed to fix upon Nero.

Rumor has it, that he had often deplored the ugliness of the City and wished an opportunity to rebuild it. It is said that he actually did not start the fire, but suspicion did continue to cling to him.

THE PERSECUTION OF CHRISTIANS

Now begins the persecution of Christians by the State, which ultimately was to cost Paul his life.

Such calamities as the great fire of Rome, were generally attributed, in those days to the wrath of the gods. In the present case everything was done to appease the offended deity(s). Yet, despite all this, suspicion, as stated, still clung to Nero. Wherefore in order to allay the rumor, he began to cast aspersions on Christians in Rome, claiming they were the cause of the calamity.

He reasoned that this *"Christus"* (Christ), from whom the name Christians was derived, was punished by the procurator Pontius Pilate in the reign of Tiberius; therefore, this noxious form of religion, which had broken out again in Judaea, its original home, and also throughout the City of Rome and throughout the Roman Empire, must be stopped. Therefore, all who confessed to being a Christian were arrested on trumped-up charges. They were implicated, not so much on the charge of starting the great fire, but as for hatred of the human race, of all things.

They died by methods of mockery; some were covered with the skins of wild beasts and then torn by dogs, some were crucified, some were burned as torches to give light at night, with such extreme cruelty spreading throughout the entirety of the Roman Empire. Such is the earliest account of the first heathen persecution. Tacitus, the Roman Historian, clearly implies that the Christians were innocent, and that Nero employed them simply as scapegoats.

WHY CHRISTIANS?

The question has been asked as to why the Christians were selected as scapegoats rather than the Jews, who were both numerous and had already offended the Roman Government and had been banished in great numbers? Or why not the many followers of other types of religions in Rome, which had proved more than once to be obnoxious?

Strangely enough, Poppaea, the evil wife

of Nero, was favorable to Judaism and had certainly enough influence over Nero to protect the Jews. Actually, she was regarded by them as a proselyte and is termed such by Josephus the Jewish Historian.

When the populace and Nero were seeking victims for revenge regarding the fire, the Jews, it is thought, may have been glad of the opportunity of putting forward the Christians and may have been encouraged in this by Poppaea. (The great fire in Rome took place about a year before Poppaea was murdered by Nero.)

Farrar in his book *"The Early Days of Christianity,"* sees in the proselytism of Poppaea, guided by Jewish malice, the only adequate explanation of the first Christian persecution.

Closely connected with this was doubtless the observation by the Roman Government that Christianity was an independent Faith from Judaism, which was against Roman Law. This may have been brought home to the authorities by the trial of Paul before Nero as suggested by Ramsay.

Judaism was a recognized and tolerated religion, and Christianity when divorced from Judaism became illegal, and, therefore, punishable by the State. Christianity first rose *"under the shadow of licensed Judaism."*

As Christianity formed a society apart from Roman society, all kinds of crimes were attributed to its followers, actually, the most preposterous of things.

As well, the enthusiasm and evangelism of Christians which were so different from the despair of heathen religions, no doubt added to the charges and suspicion.

Incidentally, Nero died a suicide, with his last words being *"Too late — this is fidelity."*

THE FIRST PERSECUTION

The first persecution to which Christianity was subjected came from the Jews. At the beginning this was centered up in Jerusalem as the Religious Leadership of Israel began to persecute the followers of Christ, who were then virtually all Jews. Actually, Paul was one of the ringleaders in this opposition. After Paul's Conversion, Jews strongly opposed him in every City in which he went spreading the Good News of the Gospel. Actually they tried a number of times to kill him, and would have done so, had it been in their power (Acts Chpt. 9).

THE FIRST HEATHEN PERSECUTION

The first heathen persecution took place under Nero, to which we have already alluded. Actually, the name *"Nero"* does not occur in the New Testament, but he was the Caesar to whom Paul appealed (Acts 25:11) and at whose tribunal Paul was tried after his first imprisonment.

It is quite likely that Nero heard Paul's case in person, for the emperor showed much interest in provincial cases. It was during the earlier years of Nero's reign that Paul addressed his Epistle to the Christians at Rome, and was probably in the last year of Nero's reign (A.D. 68) when Paul was executed in Rome.

ROME AND CHRISTIANITY

Through the first five years of Nero's reign, the Roman Government had been on friendly terms with Christianity, as Christianity was not prominent enough to cause any disturbance of society, or was concluded by the Romans to be the same as Judaism.

But soon, whether because of the trial of Paul, a Roman citizen, which took place in Rome about A.D. 63, or the growing hostility of the Jews, or the increasing numbers and alarming progress of Christianity, the distinction between Christianity and Judaism became apparent to the Roman authorities. If it had not been prescribed as an unlicensed religion, neither had it been admitted as approved.

Christianity was not in itself as yet a crime in the eyes of Rome. Its adherents were not liable to persecution *"for the Name."* However, the situation with Nero and the great fire of Rome changed all of that.

The idea seems to be, that even though the Neronian persecution was in the beginning, an isolated thing, to satisfy the revenge of the mob, etc., still, little by little, and using all types of excuses, Christians came to be established in Roman eyes as enemies of society. Christianity thus became a crime and was banned by the authorities. Consequently, in the coming years thousands died,

NOTES

or possibly even tens of thousands, simply because among other things, they would not say *"Caesar is Lord."*

(2) "WHOSOEVER THEREFORE RESISTETH THE POWER, RESISTETH THE ORDINANCE OF GOD: AND THEY THAT RESIST SHALL RECEIVE TO THEMSELVES DAMNATION."

The phrase, *"Whosoever therefore resisteth the power, resisteth the Ordinance of God,"* presents Government in the Earth as of Divine Ordination. The Magistrate is a Minister of God, at least in the sense in carrying out this Ordination of God. It has nothing to do with Salvation, as should be obvious.

The sword in his hand is a Divine instrument for the punishment of evildoers. He is responsible to use it; and, consequently, all Christians are responsible to aid him in the discharge of this duty, at least where the demands do not violate the Word of God. It is, therefore, lawful for a Believer to be a policeman or a soldier; and, further, it is his duty to be such if the Magistrate so commands.

But if the Magistrate, as stated, uses the sword not against evildoers, but against the innocent, then the servants of God are not bound to obey him. The question whether the persons to be punished are innocent or guilty is always one of difficulty. The Believer has to make a value judgment in such cases. However, the basic responsibility lies with the Government rather than the private soldier or police officer, etc.

If it is to be noticed, no form of Government is attacked or recommended here, only the principle of Government itself. Authority in these matters is recognized as from God, and should be treated accordingly.

"Resisteth" in the Greek is *"antitasso,"* and means *"to arrange in battle against, to oppose oneself, resist."* The idea is, that one who sets himself against the authorities, withstands what has been instituted by God.

This means that all militia groups which have become prominent on the American scene presently, which for the most part are opposed to Government, or what they conclude to be less than satisfactory Government, etc., are actually in rebellion against God.

While there is no such thing as a perfect Government in the world, and for the simple reason that it is carried out by humans, and will not be perfect until Jesus comes to reign Personally (Isa. 9:6-7), still, for all of its problems, there is absolutely no reason that Government in America should be resisted in this fashion. In fact, there are very few Governments presently in the world, if any, which are any more fair or equitable than Government in this country. While there is much room for improvement, and for which Christians should seek to bring about, still, people who set themselves against Government by unlawful means, even as we have lately seen (Waco, Oklahoma City, etc.), sin greatly against God, and which the State of necessity must take stringent measures, to bring such to a halt.

The phrase, *"And they that resist shall receive to themselves damnation,"* does not necessarily refer to damnation from God, although it definitely does in an indirect sense. The nerve of the whole Passage is that most Commentators seem to regard it as coming through the human authority resisted.

ARE CHRISTIANS EVER ALLOWED TO RESIST HUMAN GOVERNMENT?

To which we have already spoken, yes, but only as the demands of Government violate the Word of God. As stated, tens of thousands of Christians during the time of the Early Church gave up their lives, rather than obey a Government demand that they give allegiance to Caesar by stating *"Caesar is Lord."*

In fact, many years before, the Roman Senate had voted that Caesar, whoever he would be, would be looked at as Divinity or Deity. With the heathen world worshiping all types of gods, they reasoned that the one who headed up the mighty Roman Empire surely, should be looked at as Deity.

Most Caesars realizing their all too obvious humanity, treated this Law as a joke, demanding not at all its enforcement. However, upon the advent of Nero, and some who followed him, such allegiance was demanded, which of course, Christians could not obey, or Jews either, for that matter. Consequently, they had to decide between *"Jesus as Lord"* or *"Caesar as Lord."*

However, the manner in which they resisted

this ungodly Law, was merely by refusing to obey the Law.

In such a situation, I would not go so far as to say that it never would be permissible for a Believer to take up arms respecting insurrection against an evil, oppressive Government; however, in almost all cases, I would think that the Bible teaches a peaceful and prayerful resistance.

(3) "FOR RULERS ARE NOT A TERROR TO GOOD WORKS, BUT TO THE EVIL. WILT THOU THEN NOT BE AFRAID OF THE POWER? DO THAT WHICH IS GOOD, AND THOU SHALT HAVE PRAISE OF THE SAME:"

The phrase, *"For Rulers are not a terror to good works, but to the evil,"* concerns the Divine right of Government to oppose crime and to protect its citizens. It is as if Paul says: *"Recognize the Divine right of the State, for its representatives are not a terror — an object of dread — to the good work, but to the bad."* Such is taken for granted that the State will not act in violation of its own purpose, and identify itself with the bad. Regrettably, there are Governments in the world, which are in fact criminal. However, even that type of Government, is better than no Government at all.

BIBLICAL FACTS ABOUT HUMAN GOVERNMENT

Government in the Greek is *"exousia,"* and means *"delegated authority."* This simply means that government is ordained by God. Were it not for government, anarchy would prevail. There could be nothing worse than anarchy, which refers to everyone taking the law into their own hands. This doesn't mean, however, that God condones bad government. Still, bad government is better than no government at all. That's the reason that Christians should pray for their governmental leaders, and do so constantly (I Tim. 2:2).

INSTITUTED BY GOD

We find Government identified in the Bible almost throughout its entirety (Gen. 9:1-7; Rom. 13:1-6; I Pet. 2:13-17).

Without Government, anarchy is the result, which was the mode and method of man before the Flood, a period of about 1600 years. Consequently, this period ended in such evil as defies all description, necessitating the Lord overthrowing the entirety of man and all he had done, leaving only Noah and his family. After Noah, Human Government was instituted as a Divine Institution, necessary for the betterment of humanity.

Without Government evil men will soon control the State, with all such attendant evil results. Consequently, Government is to oppose crime and must be given any legal power to do so, even up to and including the death penalty, which is Biblical (Gen. 9:6). In connection with this is the responsibility of Government to protect its law-abiding citizens (Gen. 9:6; Isa. 11:4-9; 65:20; Dan. 2:21; 4:17-25; 5:21; Rom. 13:1-6; I Pet. 2:13-17).

THE TEN COMMANDMENTS

The basis for all Civil Law should be the Ten Commandments, minus the Fourth, which was not brought over into the New Covenant. Actually, the Fourth Commandment, *"Remember the Sabbath to keep it holy,"* was the only Commandment which did not have a moral content, but was ceremonial only. It was a Commandment strictly between Israel and God for particular reasons. When Jesus came, He fulfilled the *"Type"* which is actually what it was, with it no longer being necessary. If one is to notice, the Book of Acts and the Epistles do not project or countenance the keeping of this particular Commandment at all, and for all the obvious reasons.

If the legislative bodies of Government stray outside of the remaining Nine Commandments (Ex. Chpt. 20), unfairness and iniquity, are the result, even with a continued deterioration. The legalization of Abortion and Gambling in this country are but two examples, of which we will momentarily deal with the latter.

THE DUTY OF CHRISTIANS

It is the duty of Christians, as stated, to pray for those in authority, and to do our very best to support good government, all which is in the Will of God, and which will always play out for the betterment of humanity (Rom. 13:1; I Pet. 2:13-17).

While Christians are to do all within their

NOTES

power to aid and abet good Government, even to the point of Christians seeking political office, however, that should be confined to the Laity and almost never regarding Preachers of the Gospel, and for the obvious reasons. However, such involvement must always be with the understanding that Christians can only make the situation a little better by their involvement, with the greatest thrust always remaining in the realm of the spiritual.

In other words, Believers are little going to change society by electing particular people to political office, so should labor in this arena with that understanding. The greatest help afforded by Believers, is in the realm of prayer and opposing the Powers of Darkness in the spirit world, which are really the cause of most political, economic, and spiritual disturbance. As stated, Preachers are called to Preach the Gospel, and not run for political office, etc.

TO USE FORCE IF NECESSARY

The question is often asked, *"Is it wrong for a Christian to fight and even kill during times of war?"* Some Christians think that the Sixth Commandment, which states, *"Thou shalt not kill"* (Ex. 20:13), means that it is wrong for a Believer to serve in the Armed Forces; but, if for some reason he must serve, he should not engage himself in battle; and, if that happens, he should not kill, etc. I do not think this is valid reasoning, and I will give the reasons why.

ETHICAL CONSIDERATIONS

First of all, God ordained human government to help Him enforce moral laws. Even though governments are appointed by God, this can in no way mean He is responsible or accountable for their actions. Of course, if they get out of line, God will judge them as He will anyone or anything else.

Second, to murder is always to kill, but to kill is not always to murder. There are scores of times in the Bible when God ordered particular nations, peoples, or individuals to be destroyed (killed). Why would God do this? He did it because of their great wickedness (Deut. 7:2).

Numbers 35:9-34 speak of killing a man

unawares, that is, by error, or unwittingly. Even in our governmental system in modern-day United States, we recognize degrees of guilt. For example, people can be tried and/or convicted for first-degree, second-degree, or third-degree murder, manslaughter, etc. An individual could even kill intentionally and yet it would not be murder. We are told that if a thief, breaking into a house, be smitten so that he die, there shall no blood be shed for him (Ex. 22:2-3). In other words, the man defending his home or property would not be punished for that killing. It would not be murder. The Bible recognizes an individual's right to defend his person, his property, his dear ones, and his country.

WAR

If a Christian in the United States enlists or is drafted into the army during a time of war — or war breaks out while he is serving — and that Christian is placed on the front lines of battle (or any place of this nature), he should defend himself and his country to whatever extent is necessary. If this means having to take the life of the enemy, he should do this.

No one, and this would also include those serving our country, should conduct himself in an attitude of desiring to kill. But where there is no choice or alternative in the matter, a soldier (or policeman, or other law enforcement authority) can certainly discharge such duties with a clean conscience. God would not hold them accountable for murder or for any lesser crime of that nature. In other words, they would not (if their actions and motives are right) be guilty of breaking any kind of law, anywhere, either moral or Scriptural.

WORLD WAR II

Let us look at World War II. Germany and Japan, I think most people would agree, were the aggressors in that conflict. Germany, under the leadership of Adolf Hitler, murdered some six million Jews in the horrible Holocaust, plus untold millions of other people, as well. This madman would have enslaved the world except for the intervention of the United States of America. Admittedly, other nations also contributed

greatly to his defeat, but it was the might and the power of this country that ultimately brought him to his knees and to destruction.

What kind of world would we have now if Hitler had been allowed to follow his course to completion? I think the answer is fairly obvious. So, moral government is required by God to put down bandit nations that would endeavor to exert their dictatorial authority and enslave millions of people. This Scripture plainly says:

"Because sentence against an evil work is not executed speedily, therefore the heart of the sons of men is fully set in them to do evil" (Eccl. 8:11).

LEGALIZED GAMBLING AS A CASE IN POINT

Even though it is not possible to legislate morality at least as far as the heart of man is concerned, still, it is the duty and business of good Government to protect its citizens from that which is harmful, such as Gambling. Regrettably, America has entered into a wind of legalized Gambling, which will, and without fail, reap a whirlwind.

In many States of the Union, Gambling is now legal in many forms, whether in State Lotteries or Casinos, etc. As stated, this is an ill wind which will blow no good.

IS GAMBLING A SIN?

Yes, unequivocally, Gambling is a sin.

The final Commandment of the Ten is *"Thou shalt not Covet . . ."* (Ex. 20:17). Gambling is *"covetousness"* in its most impure form.

As well, one must understand that the Ten Commandments, minus the Fourth, are the groundwork and foundation for all morality in the Earth. They were not meant for Old Testament times only, but are just as incumbent upon modern society. These Commandments are the Righteousness of God in written form, and, therefore, Truth. As such, they are, ideally, to undergird all Moral Law in the Earth.

To be sure, Gambling is not the only form of covetousness, with the potential for this sin obvious in the form of all activities of life; however, as stated, Gambling is definitely one of its most impure forms.

THE JUST SHALL LIVE BY FAITH

As well, the Scripture tells Believers that *"The Just shall live by Faith"* (Hab. 2:4; Rom. 1:17).

This means that Believers are not to *"carry on the duties of life"* by so-called whims of chance, the luck of the draw, or the variances of fate. Believers are to believe God for His daily care, which He has promised to give (Mat. 6:25-34).

To the world (unbelievers) life in fact, is a gamble. However, to Christians, it is the very opposite.

"Luck" which is the so-called mainstay of Gambling, has its roots in *"witchcraft, signs, omens, magic,"* etc., and is forbidden by God. Paul said to the Corinthians, *"Ye know that ye were Gentiles, carried away unto these dumb idols, even as ye were led"* (I Cor. 12:2).

In other words, and as is blatantly clear, those who engage in Gambling are being led by demon spirits, which is of course, anathema to a Believer, who is led by the Holy Spirit (Rom. 8:14-15).

GAMBLING AND ADDICTION

We are told that approximately five percent of the people who gamble become addicted, which poses all types of problems. If the Truth be known, the number is probably far higher.

Addiction is bondage, which means that the victim has lost control, and, furthermore, will do most anything to feed the addiction. I speak of stealing, robbery, embezzlement, fraud, lying, cheating, etc., even to the point of murder in some cases. Consequently, as should be obvious, the individual's life is now destroyed, and will in the process, destroy others, even loved ones, and especially loved ones.

The idea as held by some that Gambling is not a sin, is shot down immediately by the threat of addiction. There is nothing that God has or is, or to which He submits His Children, which ever leads to addiction of any type. Such is always reserved for the Powers of Darkness. In fact, the very purpose of the Gospel, is to set people free from the addiction of sin, of which Gambling is but a part.

While many claim they will never become addicted, still, the fact is, that every single one who is addicted, began this journey thinking it could not happen to him or her as well. The Truth is, that every single Gambler in the world began his addiction by placing his first bet. As well, every Alcoholic began by taking their first drink. The list goes on.

So, the idea *"you can beat Satan at his game,"* is foolish and facetious indeed! As stated, anyone who sows to that wind, will always reap the whirlwind.

IF ONE DOES NOT BECOME ADDICTED, IS IT SIN?

Actually, the addiction has little to do with the principle of sin, only being the result. Whether addicted or not, Gambling is a sin and a grievous sin at that. The reason is this:

Even if one does not become addicted, and they look at it only as a form of entertainment, or their losses are minimal, it is still wrong.

First of all, the Gambler who does not become addicted to this vice, serves as bait for those who do. As such, they do a terrible disservice to their fellowman, which is a violation of the Word of God, that *". . . Thou shalt Love thy neighbour as thyself"* (Mat. 19:19).

As well, the greed manifested in the hearts of Gamblers to win, presents another sin against their fellowman.

Anyone who wins at Gambling, ultimately wins from those who can ill afford the loss. In other words, the winnings of any Gambler, do not actually come from the *"House,"* or the *"State,"* but rather from the losers, who have in some cases, lost their homes, their self-respect, their marriages, and everything, all because of their addiction. The whole apparatus of Gambling, whether it is operated by the State or whether it is operated by businessmen, is based on the losses of the losers. Without that, Gambling cannot exist.

As well, no True Believer could take the position that these nameless, faceless people are incidental, in other words, *". . . Am I my Brother's keeper?"*, which is the same question asked by Cain the murderer (Gen. 4:9). Surely, no Believer could be so cold-hearted, as to take the position that those who are addicted, which supply a great percentage of the winnings, are of no consequence. The idea being that if they are that weak they should not participate. Such is cruelty of the greatest magnitude.

THE RESPONSIBILITY OF THE STATE

To which we have already alluded, the business of Government is to protect the weak and helpless, even at times, and to be sure much of the time, from themselves. The Lottery is an excellent case in point.

Most, if not all of this form of Gambling, is controlled by the State. As well, many if not most of the participants in the Lottery, are those who can ill afford to lose any sums of money. In other words, those who are on welfare, old-age pensions, or work at minimum wage jobs. These are the very ones whom the State is supposed to protect, but regarding the Lottery and Gambling, are doing the very opposite.

In fact, the Lottery is the most expensive form of taxation there is, for the simple reason that it takes from those who can ill afford to lose anything. At this moment, how many hundreds of thousands of the poorest of the poor in America are addicted to the Lottery, actually the very people whom Government is supposed to protect? In fact, nothing could be more cruel, and as stated, America is going to reap the whirlwind of this terrible sin, and, in fact, has already begun to do so.

While State controlled Lotteries certainly cannot be put in the class of despotic Governments, still, it is a sad beginning on the road downward, which had already begun with legalized Abortion, i.e., *"murder!"*

Government has said in America that they cannot, and in fact will not, protect the unborn, and now they are saying they will not protect the weak and helpless.

It is ironic that the News Media holds up to ridicule any elderly people or the poor, who give to the Work of God, or any Preacher who asks for such support, but never says a word about the millions of elderly and very poor, who purchase Lottery Tickets, at times going hungry to do so. As well, they are all too pleased to spotlight the Lottery Winner which in reality is nothing more than sucker bait, while they never mention any precious soul who has given to the Work of God and been greatly blessed by doing so.

Of course, the reasons are obvious.

DOESN'T GAMBLING PROVIDE EXCELLENT EMPLOYMENT FOR THE COMMUNITY IN WHICH IT OPERATES?

In a word, *"No!"*

Of course there is employment provided, but at what expense?

The type of employment provided, is for the most part, that which is not desired. I speak of extra policemen, extra social workers, larger prisons, the greater need for more security guards, the need for more Judges in Courts concerning increased crime and bankruptcies, etc.

It is a proven fact that no Community has ever benefitted strictly from Gambling. It has always suffered a net loss. Consequently, the fabrication (and that's what it is) that the State will be able to fund education, etc., with its Gambling Profits, is one of the biggest lies of all. The amount actually received by Education or any particular public need, is minimal to say the least, and is terribly offset by the losses on the other side of the coin.

The reasons ought to be obvious. Gambling does not produce anything as far as goods, services, or products are concerned. Consequently, none are bettered with the exception of the Casino owners. And, as stated, they are bettered at the expense of great loss on the part of many. Even the State is not bettered, as we have already explained, actually experiencing a great loss. In fact, it is the taxpayer who has to ultimately foot the bill, at least as far as money is concerned.

In our City of Baton Rouge, there was a large sign on the side of the Interstate near downtown, which promised a 98 percent return on slot machines at a certain River Boat. I wondered as to how that could be any type of attraction, considering that they are plainly saying that ultimately the Gambler playing the slots is guaranteed to lose two percent.

Perhaps they are advertising the fact that the losses at their River Boat, at least as it concerns the slots, will be less than in others.

How stupid!

BUT ISN'T GAMBLING THE SAME AS PLAYING THE STOCK MARKET, ETC.?

No!

There is a vast difference in investment and Gambling. While there is a risk involved in any investment, the risk is predicated on goods or product of some sort. If the goods or product turn out to be what the Investor hopes, everyone benefits, those who provide the capital to make the effort possible, those who labor to bring it forth, and those who purchase the product, whatever it is, because it is a benefit or help in meeting a need.

If the goods or product prove to be less than expected, money is often lost. That is the risk; however, it is not a gamble respecting the roll of the dice, etc. It is a risk which entails ability, effort, ingenuity, and hard work. If it succeeds everyone profits. If it doesn't, there is always a reason or factor involved, which common sense demands as an accounting at the outset.

In fact, God has always blessed the Entrepreneur and Investor, providing it is done according to that which is right and honest. Jesus said, *"For which of you, intending to build a tower, sitteth not down first, and counteth the cost, whether he has sufficient to finish it?"* (Lk. 14:28).

However, while the Lord does encourage business activity I think, He does warn us against covetousness, saying, *"Lay not up for yourselves treasures upon Earth, where moth and rust doth corrupt, and where thieves break through and steal:*

"But lay up for yourselves treasures in Heaven, where neither moth nor rust doth corrupt, and where thieves do not break through nor steal;" (Mat. 6:19-20).

He then said, *"For where your treasure is, there will your heart be also"* (Mat. 6:21).

The question, *"Wilt thou then not be afraid of the power?"* simply means that Civil Government should be respected, and fear of breaking the Law should be the feelings of all.

The phrase, *"Do that which is good, and thou shalt have praise of the same,"* refers to obeying the Law, as all Christians ought to do. As well, it assumes that the Laws are right and just.

(4) "FOR HE IS THE MINISTER OF GOD TO THEE FOR GOOD. BUT IF THOU DO THAT WHICH IS EVIL, BE AFRAID; FOR HE BEARETH NOT THE SWORD IN VAIN: FOR HE IS THE MINISTER OF GOD, A REVENGER TO EXECUTE WRATH UPON HIM THAT DOETH EVIL."

The phrase, *"For he is the Minister of God to thee for good,"* proclaims Government as a Divine Institution.

"Minister" in the Greek is *"diakonos,"* and means *"a servant as seen in his activity."* It means that the Civil Magistrate, Saved or unsaved, is a servant of God in the sense that since God has instituted Human Government as a means of regulating the affairs of the human race, a Magistrate who carries out the Law, acts as a servant of God.

(The word *"Minister"* as used here, has nothing to do with Preaching the Gospel, or Salvation in any spiritual sense.)

The phrase, *"But if thou do that which is evil, be afraid; for he beareth not the sword in vain,"* refers to two things:

1. There is a penalty for breaking Civil Law, and the State has the right to execute that penalty.

2. The sword is the symbol of the Magistrate's right to inflict Capital Punishment. The reference of it here is among the many Testimonies borne by Scripture against the attempt to abolish the infliction of the penalty of death for capital crimes (Gen. 9:6).

While the death penalty should be used very sparingly, only in the case of cold-blooded murder, still, it should be used.

WHY IS CAPITAL PUNISHMENT SCRIPTURAL?

In the English language there are many words that portray the killing of human beings; they include *"destroy," "kill," "massacre," "murder," "slaughter,"* and *"slay."* There is a similar range of terms in Hebrew and Greek. In fact, the very variety of terms and settings that have to do with the taking of life complicates the debates over the morality of killing.

This debate has extended throughout the Christian Era. Some people just a few generations removed from the Apostolic period refused to give evidence in capital cases, lest they be responsible for an execution. Some soldiers in the Roman Army who had accepted Christ, refused to fight and were thereupon executed by their officers.

The moral issues are many and complicated. What about killing in war? Capital punishment for capital crimes? Killing in defense of one's life or property?

While convictions may differ, still, the testimony of the Words of Scripture always must set the Standard, thereby providing the guideline. Personal convictions must be based upon the Word of God, or else one is guilty of establishing his own morality, which in reality is the problem with the world presently, and in fact, always has been.

THE BIBLICAL IDEAL

The Old Testament tells of God's Personal and Unique Creation of human beings (Gen. Chpts. 1-2). Only man shares the Image and Likeness of God.

Humanity is granted dominion over Creation, but the first two Chapters of Genesis record no provision for the rule of man over man.

Genesis Chapters 1-2 establishes the ideal. But Chapters Genesis 3-4 shows why the ideal has never been approached in history. Adam and Eve sinned, and death struck the race.

One expression of death was demonstrated when a jealous and angry Cain killed his younger brother, Abel (Gen. Chpt. 4). Cain was unable to master the sinful passions that gripped him (Gen. 4:7). He did the unthinkable: he took the life of a being who, like himself, was shaped in the Divine Image.

OLD TESTAMENT WORDS

The Old Testament is filled with Words that portray killing and death, because history is filled with events duplicating the first killing, as indeed it must be, because of the Fall.

We read in the Bible of *"Nakah,"* which means *"to smite," "attack," "kill,"* and of *"Sahat,"* which means *"slaughter."*

We read of those who caused the death (*"mut"*) of others, who killed (*"harag"*) and who murdered (*"rasah"*). The multiplicity

NOTES

of such words testifies to the awful impact of sin, which shattered our every hope of realizing God's ideal, even as Cain's blow shattered the body of his brother, spilling his blood on God's new, but now stained Earth.

JUSTIFICATION?

There is no way to justify murder. Any act of murder falls short of God's ideal and crushes a being shaped in God's Image.

But man does not live in an ideal world. Each of us lives in a world in which killing does take place. The problem we face thus is clear, even though it is complex. How do we affirm the ideal and honor the Image of God that is stamped on every human being, while at the same time responding to the reality of the killing that does take place?

To explore this question, we need to look at two of the key Hebrew words for *"killing"* and *"murder,"* and explore the question of war along with Capital Punishment, which we will do momentarily.

KILLING AS A SAD FACT OF LIFE

The Hebrew word *"harag,"* though one of several used for *"to kill,"* is significant in that it is usually used of the violent killing of people by other people. It is used of Cain's killing of Abel (Gen. 4:25), of Moses' killing of an Egyptian slave master (Ex. 2:14), of Saul's murder of a family of Priests (I Sam. 22:21), of the killing of the False Prophets of Baal at Elijah's behest (I Ki. 19:1), and of the Jews' killing of their enemies in Esther's day (Esther 9:6, 10, 12).

It is used of Jezebel's killing of Jehovah's Prophets (I Ki. 18:13), and of God's killing of the firstborn of Egypt in the culminating judgment on that people who held Israel in slavery (Ex. 13:15).

This brief survey shows that the word is used of unjustified murder and of what might be considered justified killings, and it is even used of Divine Judgments. In this present world, warped as it is by sin, killing is a fact of life which we must deal with. Are there any theologically crucial Passages that may guide us?

WHAT THE WORD SAYS

Genesis 4:8-16: Cain killed (harag) Abel.

Confronted by God and driven from his abode, Cain complained of his fate: *". . . I will be a restless wanderer on the Earth, and whoever finds me will kill* (harag) *me"* (Gen. 4:14).

But God placed a mark on Cain *". . . so that no one who found him would kill* (harag) *him"* (Gen. 4:15).

Genesis 9:5-6: God announced after the Flood, *". . . From each man, too, I will demand an accounting for the life of his fellowman.*

"Whoever sheds the blood of man, by man shall his blood be shed; for in the Image of God has God made man."

Although it uses none of the Hebrew words for killing, this Passage introduces the principle of social responsibility. Human beings are now charged by God as participants in the Divine Call for an accounting. Actually, even as we have previously stated, this is the foundation of the Divine Institution of Government.

Respecting Government, this Passage is foundational relative to Capital Punishment, which affirms the Image of God in man by placing the only possible equivalent value on it — that of another life:

1. Capital Punishment for capital crimes is established here by God as a necessary part of Moral Government. Contrary to what many people think, Capital Punishment was not instituted by God as a deterrent to crime, but because man was originally created in the Image of God and the value of such must not be lost in the mind of man.

Nations of the world which subscribe to the Biblical definition of human life, that man is created in the Image of God, spirit, soul, and body, and as such will live forever, whether with the Lord or in Eternal Hell, place a high value on the worth of man. Otherwise, life is cheap!

2. God has Himself set the penalty that society is to require.

3. The failure of society to accept this responsibility implies social consent to murder and a lowering of the value placed on human life.

In this view, David's execution (harag) of the murderers of Ishbosheth (II Sam. 4:11-12) is not only a case of justified execution, but also a case in which execution was a moral necessity.

Deuteronomy 13:6-11: This Passage in the Mosaic Law shows how Israel is to protect itself from Pagan influences. If anyone, no matter how close the relationship, suggests the worship of other gods, that person is to be put to death. *". . . Show him no pity,"* the Passage reads. *"Do not spare him or shield him. You must certainly put him to death* (harag). *"Your hand must be the first in putting him to death* (harag), *and then the hands of all the people . . . ."*

Again the concept of social responsibility is implicit. In a world marred by sin, there are actions that call for the taking of a life, as distasteful as it might be. Unfortunately, we do not live in an ideal world, but must face reality as it is according to Biblical concepts.

Individuals in the community of Israel itself are called by God to accept responsibility for its own purification, and God Himself passes sentence for His People, defining acts that call for the death sentence.

MANSLAUGHTER AND MURDER

In the Old Testament, *"rasah"* is the only uniquely Hebrew term for killing. The word carries a range of what we may call *"personal"* killings, from manslaughter to premeditated murder. Also, the word may be used of assassination (II Ki. 6:32) and revenge killings (Num. 35:27-30), but it is not used of killing in war or of judicial executions.

Two contexts in which it is employed are critical on this point. First, the Ten Commandments.

Here we read, *"You shall not kill"* (rasah) (Ex. 20:13; Deut. 5:17). What it means is, *"You shall not murder"* (or *"You shall not kill a person"*) — which means more than simply killing, but rather, as stated, murder.

ISRAEL AS A NATION

In Numbers Chapter 35 we are given the Judicial Regulations by God as to how Israel was to deal with murder when the Nation was established.

This Chapter establishes *"Cities of refuge"* to which a person who killed another might flee. This protected the killer from the vengeance of a member of the family of

NOTES

the person killed, until a trial could take place.

This account carefully establishes and defines the personal killing that merits a death penalty. There is motivation (hostility, intent), method (shoving, throwing, hitting, etc.), means (iron, wooden, or stone objects, or fist), and results (death). In such cases the murderer is to be put to death by society.

As well, this Chapter goes on to deal with killing without hostility, in other words accidental. It speaks of someone suddenly shoving another or throwing something at him unintentionally, or without seeing him, drops a stone that hits him, and he dies.

Since he was not his enemy and he did not intend to harm him, the assembly must judge between him and the avenger of blood (a family member who desired revenge) according to these regulations. The assembly must protect the one accused of murder (Num. 35:22-25).

So, accidental homicide, while still killing, is not murder, and the killer in such cases, deserves the protection of society.

THE SERIOUSNESS OF THE MATTER

Also in Numbers Chapter 35, it is specified that the facts of a capital case must be established *". . . only on the testimony of witnesses. But no one is to be put to death on the testimony of only one witness"* (Num. 35:30).

The idea is, that human life is of such value, that even though Capital Punishment is mandated for cold-blooded murder, still, the evidence must be absolutely irrefutable for this sentence to be carried out.

In fact, and as stated, such was so stringent, that even one eyewitness account of the murderer would not be sufficient for a death penalty. There must be two or more witnesses. So, one could well imagine that there were not many executions, even in the case of cold-blooded murder.

One other regulation is also worth nothing: *"Do not accept a ransom for the life of a murderer, who deserves to die. He must surely be put to death"* (Num. 35:31).

CONCLUSIONS DRAWN FROM THE OLD TESTAMENT

Even though we shall presently see what

the New Testament says about this extremely important question, still we should note the following facts established in the Old Testament, which we will find are carried over into the New:

1. Human beings, shaped in God's Image, are precious to Him.

2. The unwarranted taking of another's life is prohibited.

3. The Old Testament recognizes the reality of war and does not expressly forbid killing in war.

4. The Old Testament recognizes offenses for which the death penalty is prescribed.

5. The Old Testament held the Society of Israel responsible for carrying out the death penalty where it is ordained by God.

6. Personal killing is forbidden in the Ten Commandments.

7. The death penalty is prescribed when personal killing is premeditated or an expression of murderous hostility.

8. Witnesses must give uncontrovertible evidence before the death penalty can be carried out.

9. Accidental killing of persons does not merit the death penalty, nor does manslaughter, and the person who kills accidentally is to be protected by society from vengeful family members.

THE NEW TESTAMENT

Three Greek words are translated *"kill"* or *"murder"* in English Versions. In 21 of its 23 occurrences in the New Testament, one of those words *"anaireo"* is used in the sense of *"to kill"* (all in Matthew, Luke, and Acts) — the two exceptions being in Acts 7:21 and Hebrews 10:9. It is used, for example, of Herod's killing of the children after Jesus' Birth (Mat. 2:16), of the killing of Jesus (Lk. 22:2; Acts 2:23), and of the plot to assassinate Paul (Acts 9:23).

"Apokteino" is another Greek word, actually the most common term for *"kill"* in the New Testament; it includes any way of depriving another of life. Earlier generations of Jews killed the Prophets (Mat. 23:37), just as Jesus' Own generation killed Him (Mat. 26:4; Lk. 18:33; Jn. 5:18; Acts 3:15; I Thess. 2:15). This word is also used figuratively, to indicate depriving something of its vitality, force or

power (Rom. 7:11; II Cor. 3:6; Eph. 2:16).

MURDER

The distinctive word translated *"murder"* from the Greek is *"phoneuo."* It is used 12 times in the New Testament, including each occurrence of the Commandment *"Do not murder"* (Mat. 5:21; 19:18; Mk. 10:19; Lk. 18:20; Rom. 13:9; James 2:11).

The Greek noun for *"murder," "phonos"* (also used 12 times in the New Testament), is found in every list where killing as murder is identified as a sin flowing from man's corrupt and evil nature (Mat. 15:19; Mk. 7:21; Rom. 1:29; Gal. 5:21).

The related noun for *"murderer"* is *"phoneus"* (used seven times in the New Testament), two of its uses being in connection with Jesus' death — once in Jesus' parabolic prediction of His Own death (Mat. 22:7) and once by Stephen in his accusation of the Jewish Leaders responsible for Jesus' Crucifixion (Acts 7:52).

THE EVIL OF THE HUMAN HEART

The New Testament uses none of the three Greek words in a positive or approving way. In each case, killing is seen to involve the guilty persons violating the rights of the innocent. Whether the slaughter of the innocents, the persecution of the Prophets, or the plot against Jesus, the killings the New Testament deals with are criminal as well as sinful acts, whatever pseudo — legal justification such acts may have claimed.

Yet it is significant that *"phoneuo," "to murder"* is used distinctively and is set apart in two ways from the more general words for *"kill"*:

1. It alone is in each case where the New Testament restates the Old Testament Commandment against murderer, i.e., *"rasah."*

2. It alone is used when the root of murder in the evil heart of humanity is examined. Jesus states clearly that murder is not a matter of circumstances caused by social or economic deprivation: murder is like adultery, evil thoughts, immorality, theft, false testimony, and slander. It comes *"out of the heart"* (Mat. 15:19). It is a work of the flesh (Gal. 5:21).

Consequently, this shoots down the psychological theory that economic deprivation is the cause of such acts, and that if the Government would alleviate this cause, most if not all capital crimes would cease.

The Bible teaches that the only way to deal with such evil is to deal directly with the human heart. In other words, man's environment or lack of education, or lack of economic opportunity is not the problem. In fact, it is only by the New Birth that one's heart can be renewed, and it is only by the Fruit of the Spirit that Love can replace the hostility and hatred that stimulate murder and other such crimes.

THE ROLE OF GOVERNMENT

One of the striking differences between the Old Testament and the New Testament is that the New Testament does not go into nearly the detail concerning this all-important question as the Old Testament.

In fact, that which Paul tells the Roman Believers, and all others for that matter, that Human Governments, as agencies instituted by God for the control of sin in society, do *". . . not bear the sword for nothing . . ."* (Rom. 13:4), sums it all up. More significantly, the same verse adds that Government is *". . . God's servant, an agent of wrath to bring punishment on the wrongdoer."*

In fact, this Passage carries forth the injunctions of the Old Testament of the right of Government and its responsibility for carrying out God's established principles of justice, which includes the carrying out of the punishment the Old Testament indicates is appropriate for cold-blooded murder.

THE DIFFERENCE

Another reason that the New Testament does not go into detail concerning this very important question as the Old Testament, pertains to the fact that Israel was a Nation, and as such, needed the regulations of Moral Government. In fact, they were to be the leading Nation, serving as an example to all others, actually, the only Nation in the world which had the Government of God.

By contrast, the Church is a community that has no existence as a Nation or State. Instead, the Church exists across the ages as communities of God's People within many different States and subject to the Laws of their respective States.

The Christian Church does not control society, nor are the Church's standards necessarily the standards a State will adopt.

Nevertheless, and as Paul graphically illustrates, Believers are to be subject to Civil Government, and the closer the State is to the Bible regarding its Government, the more fair and equitable it will be to its subjects.

THE OLD TESTAMENT AND THE NEW TESTAMENT ARE THE SAME REGARDING THIS ISSUE

Does this mean that Old Testament social principles provide sufficient guidance and are still in force?

Does the Spirit of the New Testament, which emphasizes forgiveness now but judgment to come, demand new social attitudes and a new approach to the reality of murder?

Those who answer *"yes"* to the latter question must do so only after careful consideration, for God's Old Testament Commands concerning putting a murderer to death are stated in the strongest possible way. As well, and as we have stated, Paul brings the Old Testament injunction regarding murder and Capital Punishment over into the New.

At the same time, and as we have also stated, those who answer *"no,"* even as we have done, must likewise do so only after careful consideration, for the Law that guided society in Old Testament times was very careful to protect the innocent by setting up evidential safeguards. In fact, I seriously doubt if we are as careful today to condemn only murderers whose convictions are based on absolutely incontrovertible evidence.

We must never forget that God's Standards of Morality are far higher than those of man's. Everything He does is right, not because He does it, but because in fact, it is right. So, to second guess God, is always in some way, to fall out ultimately to a violation of human rights.

WHAT ABOUT KILLING IN WAR?

Accounts of war and tragedy abound in the Old Testament. The Bible focuses on the role of God in war and on the attitude of

the Believer toward war.

It is true that the Bible makes a clear distinction between murder and killing in war. But surely war is an evil, causing untold suffering. How are we as Christians to view war today? How does God view war?

THE BIBLE VISION OF A WORLD WITHOUT WAR

Perhaps the most famous of Scripture's Words of Peace are found in Isaiah 2:3-4: *"Many peoples will come and say, 'Come, let us go up to the mountain of the Lord, to the house of the God of Jacob. He will teach us His Ways, so that we may walk in His Paths.' The Law will go out from Zion, the Word of the Lord from Jerusalem.*

"He will judge between the Nations and will settle disputes for many peoples. They will beat their swords into plowshares and their spears into pruning hooks. Nation will not take up sword against Nation, nor will they train for war any more."

These Words do not stand alone in portraying God's Promise of International Peace (Micah 4:1-5; Zech. Chpt. 14). But such words offer little support for those who suppose that Peace can come to our war-weary world by one Nation unilaterally abandoning weapons. For these words, and others like them, appear in a particular context.

CONDITIONAL!

That context is first of all conditional.

These words of Peace are associated with the time of history's end. Peace will be possible then because the Lord will be established in the hearts of redeemed humanity and will be Personally Present to *"judge between many people"* and to *"settle disputes for strong Nations"* (Micah 4:4).

It is on the day that, as Zechariah said, *". . . The Lord my God will come and all the holy ones with Him"* (Zech. 14:5) that Peace will be imposed then upon the world.

OF WARFARE!

The context is also, surprisingly, one of warfare.

Peace will not come by abandoning conflict, as some think. Peace in the Old Testament is associated with war waged by God

Himself against an arrogant, rebellious humanity. It is outlined in the New Testament, in fact, in Revelation Chapter 19.

Peace will come when it is imposed by the *". . . dread of the Lord and the splendor of His Majesty, when He rises to shake the Earth"* (Isa. 2:21). In other words, God is going to force the issue, even as the Prophets of old and Jesus predicted (Mat. Chpt. 24).

In reality, one of the most striking aspects of Scripture's vision of a final Peace is that it is achieved only through the ultimate warfare (Isa. 13:4; 24:21-23; 29:5-8). Even in Micah's exalted description, God's Promised Peace (Mic. 4:1-5) will come after many Nations will have gathered against Israel, and God will cry to her, *"Rise and thresh, O Daughter of Zion, for I will give you horns of iron; I will give you hoofs of bronze and you will break to pieces* (the Peace of) *many Nations"* (Mic. 4:13).

GOD'S INVOLVEMENT IN ISRAEL'S WARS

The Hebrew language has two major words that mean *"war," "battle,"* or *"fighting"*: *"laham"* and *"saba."* *"Laham"* is *"to fight or wage war."* It occurs 171 times in the Old Testament; and its derivative, *"milhamah,"* is found 319 times.

The word *"sbaot"* (*"armies"*), a derivative of *"saba,"* is associated with God's Name some 285 times in the Old Testament, as He is called *"God of Hosts"* or *"God of armies."*

This phrase means *"Almighty,"* stressing the fact that God is the Ultimate Ruler of the Universe, but it also reflects something basic in the Old Testament's view of God and His relationship to Israel's wars.

We see that view in multiplied Passages, such as Psalm 44:

"With Your hand you drove out the Nations and planted our Fathers; You crushed the peoples and made our Fathers flourish.

"It was not by their sword that they won the land, nor did their arm bring them victory; it was Your Right Hand, Your Arm, and the Light of Your Face, for You loved them.

"You are my King and my God, Who decrees victories for Jacob.

"Through You we push back our enemies; through Your Name we trample our foes.

"I do not trust in my bow, my sword does not bring me victory;

"but You give us victory over our enemies, You put our adversaries to shame.

"In God we make our boast all day long, and we will praise Your Name forever" (Ps. 44:2-8).

This view is firmly rooted in the Pentateuch and Israel's history. God promised to do battle for Israel when she went to war (Ex. 14:14; Deut. 1:30; 3:22; Neh. 4:20; Ps. 118:10-14; 124:1-3; Jer. 21:5).

The forces of Israel were the Armies of Jehovah. David even identified the Lord as the Source of his skill in warfare: *"Praise be to the Lord my Rock, Who trains my hands for war, my fingers for battle"* (Ps. 144:1).

CHALLENGED!

This bold identification of God with Israel in warfare has been challenged by Commentators on the basis of a supposed inconsistency with the Character of God as displayed in Jesus. However, those who think such, do not understand the character of the Old Testament or the New for that matter. First of all, we must see war in the Old Testament in that Covenant's own frame of reference. Two common Old Testament themes are important in understanding the nature and significance of war as it was engaged at that time:

ISRAEL AS GOD'S PEOPLE

1. Israel existed in Covenant relationship with Jehovah. In fact, they were the only people on Earth who were serving Him, actually, people who He had raised from the loins of Abraham for the express purpose of sanctifying His Name in the world. As such, Israel was surrounded by Nations which did not know God, and because of a fallen nature, were very hostile at times toward the People of God, with these scenarios of course, devised by Satan. In fact, Satan tried repeatedly to destroy these people called Jews, and for the obvious reasons. If they could be destroyed, God's Witness in the world would be destroyed, plus all of His Plans to bring a Redeemer through these people in order to save man.

As a result of His Covenant Relationship

with Israel, it was His Obligation to come to their aid, which He did time and time again.

2. God is the Moral Judge of the Universe. The Old Testament affirms that many of Israel's wars were determined by God, Who used His People in a Judicial way to punish evildoers (Deut. 7:1-2, 16; 20:16-17). This is particularly significant in the wars of *"devotion,"* in which the enemy was to be totally destroyed (Deut. Chpt. 20).

The concept is introduced in the time of battle for the Promised Land: *"When the Lord your God brings you into the Land . . . and . . . has delivered them over to you and you have defeated them, then you must destroy them totally. Make no treaty with them, and show them no mercy"* (Deut. 7:1-2; Josh. 6:17-19, 21; 11:11-12, 14, 20-21).

WHY WOULD GOD DO THIS?

The destruction of the people of Canaan was ordered in part because the moral and religious practices of these people would surely have drawn Israel's hearts away from God (Deut. 7:3-6). But Genesis 15:16 gives us another clue.

There God told Abraham about the 400 years that his descendants had to be in Egypt before they would take possession of Canaan. He explained, *". . . For the sin of the Amorites has not yet reached its full measure."*

The idea is, that God did not act to destroy the people of Canaan until such action was demanded by the overflowing flood of sin and debauchery in their society. In fact, one Archaeologist stated, *"The God of the Old Testament Who gave instructions that certain Tribes were to be destroyed in totality, did future generations, and in fact the entirety of the world an untold service."*

Why would he make such a statement?

He was speaking of the very thing of which the Lord had spoken to Abraham concerning the Amorites. These particular Tribes which inhabited Canaan at that time, had grown so wicked and evil, in the form of Homosexuality, Bestiality, Pedophilia, Pederasty, and Human Sacrifice, that they had to be excised even as a cancer is excised from a human body. Exactly as the Archaeologist said, *"Such executions* (genocide) *did future generations and the world in general an untold service."*

God, then, identified Himself with Israel in her wars because of the Covenant and because He also used Israel as an instrument of His Judgment on sin.

It is also noteworthy that God used other Nations to wage wars of Judgment on Israel when His Own People sinned against Him and refused to repent (Isa. 63:10; Amos 3:14-15).

BABYLON, A CASE HISTORY

The Old Testament view of God as Judge extends His responsibility for the Moral Governancy of the Universe beyond His responsibility for Israel, as should be obvious. God is responsible for all the Nations of the world. Old Testament wars are often viewed in the framework of Judgment. It is sin that moves a people to overstep their boundaries and crush their neighbors. That sin itself leads to further wars, which come as Divine Judgments.

A few extended Passages relate war and world politics to God's overarching control (Isa. Chpts. 13-23; Jer. Chpts. 46-51; Ezek. Chpts. 25-32; Amos Chpts. 1-2).

Babylon, which emerged as a world power some 600 years before Christ, provides us with a fascinating case history. Habakkuk cried to the Lord because of the injustices he saw in Israel (Hab. 1:1-4).

God responded by saying that He would raise up the Babylonians to wage war against multiplied Nations and that He would punish Israel for their sin (Hab. 1:5-11).

Habakkuk realized that the Lord had *". . . appointed them to execute Judgment . . ."* (Hab. 1:12). But clearly the Babylonians were less righteous than the Nations they destroyed, and their victories led them to view force itself as their god, and thus, they failed to acknowledge the Universal Lord.

The Prophet wondered how God could permit that (Hab. 1:13-17). God answered by displaying some of the principles of Judgment that operate in history (Hab. Chpt. 2):

". . . Woe to him who piles up stolen goods and makes himself wealthy by extortion! How long must this go on?

"Will not your debtors suddenly arise? Will they not wake up and make you tremble? Then you will become their victim.

"Because you have plundered many

Nations, the peoples who are left will plunder you. For you have shed man's blood; you have destroyed lands and cities and everyone in them" (Hab. 2:6-8).

JUDGMENT

War establishes a hatred that generates its own judgment. The oppressors themselves are destroyed as the hatred that war generates is turned against them. Just as God used Babylon to execute His Judgments on Assyria (Isa. 10:5-19) and on Israel (Hab. Chpt. 1), so the Lord would use another Nation, the Medes, to crush Babylon (Isa. 13:17).

The course of history, then, as illustrated in Babylon, is one of successive wars. Each war was an expression of evil and sin (Isa. 13:11), and each succeeding war was an expression of the Divine Judgment that must come when any Nation plunders another and sheds human blood. In other words, their time will come, as it always has.

In September of 1939, Germany attacked Poland, in effect, beginning World War II. For about a year Hitlerite Germany ran roughshod over Europe, enslaving hundreds of millions and wreaking terrible pain and suffering. The Jews were a special case in point, with some six million being slaughtered by the monsters of the Third Reich.

However, Germany unleashed a tidal wave of hatred which engulfed them, leaving her cities in total ruin, with nearly 20 million dead. The Judgment was of the Lord. Consequently, the soldiers who fought on the side of the Allies were in effect serving God. This is the case in all wars of this nature. However, this does not make excuses or allowances for cruelty or murder.

(Soldiers fighting in legitimate battles are not guilty of murder; however, in all war, irrespective of the supposed Righteousness of one side, killing for the sake of killing is not allowed. Righteousness on the side of America or any of the Allies, in no way tendered excuse for brutality, cruelty, or as stated, murder.)

WAR IN THE NEW TESTAMENT

The New Testament is nearly silent on the subject of war. The words of warfare appear, but they are almost always used in a figurative sense. Irrelevant Greek terms are *"strateuo"* (*"to serve as a soldier"*), *"polemeo"* (*"to make war, or fight"*), *"polemos"* (*"battle"* or *"war"*), and *"mache"* (*"battle," "fighting,"* often in the sense of quarrels and disputes).

Because the Church is a Faith entity, not a national one, there are no guidelines given for waging war, and no prohibitions against war are stated. Yet many in the earliest centuries of the Church refused to serve in the military. Many were even executed for their convictions.

But there is no direct Biblical prohibition against military service. When John the Baptist was asked by soldiers what they should do to demonstrate Repentance, he did not tell them to resign from the army. Instead he simply said, *". . . Don't extort money and don't accuse people falsely — be content with your pay"* (Lk. 3:14).

Many references in Revelation point to the final battle at history's end, even as we have already stated, of which the Prophets prophesied. In the Gospels, Jesus warned that until then, history will be filled with wars and rumors of war (Mat. 24:6; Mk. 13:7; Lk. 21:9).

FIGHTS AND QUARRELS AMONG CHRISTIANS

James wrote of *". . . fights and quarrels . . ."* among Christians (James 4:1). This Passage does not speak directly of war, but it may be relevant as an analysis of the causes of interpersonal and international conflicts:

". . . They come from your desires that battle within you . . . You want something but don't get it. You kill and covet, but you cannot have what you want. You quarrel and fight . . ." (James 4:2). The origin of those quarrels that lead to fighting is rooted in man's sinful nature, in covetousness.

Paul's argument that *"we do not wage war as the world does"* is not an anti-war statement, nor does it imply a rejection of war. It is simply an affirmation that Christians are engaged in spiritual warfare and that it is not appropriate for them to approach that warfare (spiritual warfare) in a worldly way.

In fact, the New Testament is almost silent on the question of war, with the exception of the first seven verses of Chapter 13, which only address the subject in an off-hand way. However, the New Testament does recognize war as a reality that must be confronted.

SCRIPTURAL GUIDANCE

It is my opinion that Scripture is clear respecting the overall principle of our discussion regarding the taking of human life and the times when it is necessary. However, as should be obvious, the Holy Spirit does not go into detail concerning every single question one may have.

War is unquestionably an evil, and the shedding of man's blood must never be done except under certain circumstances.

However, as awful as war is, living as we do in a world warped by sin and marred by war, we are never told that Nations are not to defend themselves.

In the Old Testament we have a model in Israel of a Faith Community that is also a Nation. God's People were actually expected to go to war, and often God identified Himself with their cause. God fought for His Covenant People and used them as instruments to punish evildoers.

The Old Testament also gives case histories of Pagan Nations. Some developed into Empires by the use of war. Each of them was ultimately destroyed by war. Those who engage in war suffer war's destruction as an appropriate retribution. Here war is a means used by God as Moral Judge to maintain moral balance in international relations.

For the Believer to desire the protection of the State, even as Paul outlines in this Chapter, and then not be willing to aid the State respecting just causes, even such as war, presents a double standard, and I think, unscriptural.

Had it not been for America in World War II, Hitler would have overrun the world, which would have plunged it into unimaginable cruelty. As such, America along with other Nations, were morally obligated to oppose such tyranny and to do so by force. Consequently, the men who fought on the front lines, who dropped the bombs from the airplanes, and who waged war, were not sinning, nor violating Scripture in any manner. However, and as stated, a just cause never

NOTES

gives license for brutality, cruelty, or wanton killing. In fact, killing should be avoided if at all possible, but as is understood, war is all about killing.

Continuing to use this Nation as an example, I feel the war in Korea was just. The same could be said for the conflict in the Gulf, etc.; however, Vietnam was another story, and America is still paying for that debacle. Nevertheless, that does not implicate the men who fought in that conflict, but actually only the Leaders who should have known better.

Whether America likes it or not, she is at the present time elected by the Lord to serve as the Policeman of the world. Such may be an appellative not enjoyed at all, or even denied; nevertheless, due to the strong Christian principle of this Nation, right and wrong according to the Word of God is understood more perfectly here than anywhere else, one could say. And yet, that knowledge is flawed and weakening fast, and will continue to deteriorate without a Holy Spirit Revival. However, it is the responsibility of this Nation to keep peace in the world, to put down bandit Nations, and to use whatever force is necessary to do so. To not favorably respond to such responsibility, is to submit great parts of the world to increased tyranny and unwarranted slaughter. That's the reason that Believers should pray for those in authority that they may have the Mind of God in these decisions, whether they personally realize or understand such or not (I Tim. 2:1-3).

ONE DAY WAR WILL BE FOREVER OVER

The Prince of Peace, The Lord Jesus Christ was rejected the first time which subjected the world to continued war and rumors of war. However, He is coming back, and even though His very Coming will be in the midst of war, He at that time will institute Peace such as the world has never known before. The Prince of Peace will be here, and, therefore, Peace will reign.

Until He returns, man's efforts at Peace, although commendable, are futile. Such can only be brought about by the One Who is Peace (Isa. 11:3-9; Rev. Chpt. 19).

About 2,000 years ago, actually at the

Birth of the Prince of Peace, the Angels praised God, saying, *"Glory to God in the highest, and on Earth Peace, good will toward men"* (Lk. 2:13-14).

One day soon, this accolade of praise will be realized in totality.

(Most of the material on Capital Punishment and War was derived from that developed by Dr. Lawrence O. Richards.)

The phrase, *"For he is the minister of God, a revenger to execute wrath upon him that doeth evil,"* proclaims the principle of the right of the State as ordained by God, to use whatever force is necessary to stop *"evil,"* i.e., crime. As we have stated, to deny Government that right, is to take away its power of enforcement, which then makes Government inconsequential.

(5) "WHEREFORE YE MUST NEEDS BE SUBJECT, NOT ONLY FOR WRATH, BUT ALSO FOR CONSCIENCE SAKE."

The phrase, *"Wherefore ye must needs be subject,"* plainly tells us that Christians are subject to the Law of the Land, that is if it does not violate the Word of God. Of course, if an unscriptural Law is forced upon Believers, they must be prepared to pay the price for a lack of obedience, which could mean a jail term or even the loss of one's life. In fact, and as we have stated, untold thousands of Early Christians died in the Roman Arenas, simply because among other things, they would not say *"Caesar is Lord."*

The phrase, *"Not only for wrath, but also for conscience sake,"* refers to a higher principle than that of the unbeliever.

Most people obey Laws simply because they fear the consequences of not doing so, i.e., *"wrath."* However, on the part of the Child of God, obedience of the Law should be because of *"conscience sake,"* i.e., because it is the right thing to do.

The Believer should always have the good of all in mind. In other words, the ideal demands that Believers think in the same capacity as the Lord.

(6) "FOR FOR THIS CAUSE PAY YE TRIBUTE ALSO: FOR THEY ARE GOD'S MINISTERS, ATTENDING CONTINUALLY UPON THIS VERY THING."

The phrase, *"For for this cause pay ye tribute also,"* refers to the paying of taxes.

NOTES

"Pay" in the Greek is *"teleo,"* and means *"to fulfill, to complete, carrying the sense of the fulfillment of an obligation."* In other words, it is money that is owed.

"Tribute" in the Greek is *"phoros,"* and means *"that which is brought,"* taxes. Tertullian said, *"That which the Romans lost by the Christians refusing to bestow gifts on their heathen Temples, they gain by their conscientious payment of taxes."*

TAXES IN BIBLE TIMES — THE OLD TESTAMENT

The Old Testament refers to two types of *"taxes"*:

1. The first is a Temple tax that was imposed on all males as *"a ransom"* when the first Exodus census was taken (Ex. 30:11-16).

That money was used to support services at the Tabernacle and later the Temple (Mat. 17:24). At one time a special tax was levied for the repair of the Temple (II Chron. 24:5-12).

2. The Old Testament also speaks of taxes collected by the Pagan Kings who ruled Judea as a Province (Ezra 4:13, 20; 7:24; Neh. 5:4).

It is in the New Testament, however, that we learn about taxes in a more modern form.

TAXES AND TAX COLLECTING IN NEW TESTAMENT TIMES

The practice in New Testament times was for the Government (Rome) to fix an amount due from a Province or area and sell the right to collect the tax. The successful bidder then hired Tax Collectors (Publicans, *"telones"*) from the local population.

The original contractor, his agents, and the local collectors all made their profit by collecting more than was due the Government. The abuse of this system and the proverbial greed of the Tax Collectors generated the Jews' hatred of their fellow citizens who collected these taxes, a hatred we see reflected in the Gospels.

The burden of this system was multiplied when we realize that in addition to the basic tax, custom stations were established everywhere to collect more tolls and taxes when a person crossed bridges, used roads, came to market to sell, etc. It is no wonder that Jesus' willingness to associate with *"Tax Collectors and sinners"* was a cause for intense criticism (Mat. 9:9-11; 11:19; Mk. 2:15-16; Lk. 5:30; 7:34).

Yet these outcasts of society were often more ready to respond to Jesus than were the *"Righteous"* (Mat. 10:3; Lk. 15:1; 18:10-14).

TAXES TO CAESAR

Many in Judea in Jesus' day resented the fact that they had to pay taxes to their Roman oppressors. Rome brought stability to the ancient world, but the tax burden on its Provinces was staggering. Contemporary records indicate a tax rebellion was the root of the revolt of Judea that led to the destruction of Jerusalem in A.D. 70. So the issue was politically explosive when Jesus was asked if it was *"right"* to pay taxes to Caesar (Mat. 22:17; Mk. 12:14; Lk. 20:22; 23:2).

The particular term used in Matthew and Mark, indicates the Poll Tax. Jesus called for a coin, and, pointing out that Caesar's picture was on it, said to render to Caesar what is Caesar's and to God what is God's. This silenced those who had hoped to trap Him.

SET THE TONE

Jesus' response also sets the tone for the New Testament's teaching on taxes. It is appropriate for a Nation's citizens to support their Government, which God has ordained for His Own good purposes, with the taxes that are due it (Rom. 13:6-7). However, there is also a word for the tax collector.

John the Baptist told tax collectors who heard his Call to Repentance and asked what to do, *"Don't collect any more than you are required to . . ."* (Lk. 3:13).

There was no need to resign from the despised profession, according to both John and Jesus, but there was a need for followers of the Lord who were employed in this occupation to be honest and fair, as would be obvious.

JESUS AND THE TEMPLE TAX

According to Matthew 17:24-27, tax collectors asked Peter if Jesus paid the annual Temple Tax. Peter blurted out, *"Yes, He does . . . ."*

Then he went into the house where Jesus was, and Jesus asked him, *". . . From whom*

NOTES

do the kings of the earth collect duty and taxes — from their own sons or from others?"

Peter answered correctly: *"From others . . . ."* Jesus nodded and observed, *". . . Then the sons are exempt . . . ."*

Often we focus on the fish Peter caught, which had a coin in its mouth worth enough to pay Jesus' and Peter's tax. But the real focus is on Jesus' question and his conclusion.

As Son of God, Jesus was exempt from the Temple Tax. But the very fact that God called for such a tax in Old Testament times may have been intended to show that the Israelites, despite their Covenant relationship with the Lord, were not yet sons.

Throughout the centuries, the existence of the Temple Tax on all Israelite males could be taken as an indication that each individual must go beyond the rights obtained by birth to find a personal relationship with God through a Faith like that of Abraham (Richards).

The phrase, *"For they are God's ministers, attending continually upon this very thing,"* refers to public servants.

"Minister" in the Greek, at least as it is used here, is *"leitourgos,"* and means *"a public minister, a servant of the State."* The word brings out more fully here the fact that the ruler (Government official or officer in whatever capacity) like the Priests, discharges a Divinely-ordained service. Government is thus elevated into that of a Divine principle or ordinance.

(7) "RENDER THEREFORE TO ALL THEIR DUES: TRIBUTE TO WHOM TRIBUTE IS DUE; CUSTOM TO WHOM CUSTOM; FEAR TO WHOM FEAR; HONOUR TO WHOM HONOUR."

The phrase, *"Render therefore to all their dues,"* means that it is proper and right for all people to pay taxes, and Christians as well.

"Render" in the Greek is *"apodidomi,"* and means *"to give over."*

"Dues" in the Greek is *"opheile,"* and means *"that which is owed, a debt."* The word has in it the idea of a moral obligation (Wuest).

This also means, as is obvious, that it is permissible for Believers to legally avoid paying taxes, that is, to take advantage of whatever allowances allowed by the Government.

However, it is never right in a Scriptural sense to evade taxes.

The phrase, *"Tribute to whom tribute is due,"* refers to that which is owed, and which should be paid.

The phrase, *"Custom to whom custom,"* addresses hidden taxes, etc.

"Custom" in the Greek is *"telos,"* and means *"an indirect tax on goods."*

So we are told here, that as good citizens and good Christians, we are not only morally obligated to pay income tax, but, as well, hidden tax, which is normally levied on everything purchased.

The phrase, *"Fear to whom fear,"* refers to the fact that Government as an institution is to be respected.

The phrase, *"Honour to whom honour,"* refers to such respect extending to all Civil servants from the lowest to the highest.

(8) "OWE NO MAN ANY THING, BUT TO LOVE ONE ANOTHER: FOR HE THAT LOVETH ANOTHER HATH FULFILLED THE LAW."

The phrase, *"Owe no man any thing,"* in one sense of the word seems like a contradiction, especially considering that Paul has repeatedly stated in the first seven verses of this Chapter, that Believers definitely do *"owe"* to the Government, taxes, fear, honor, and respect.

The idea is, that Christians do not *"owe"* their Brethren in the Lord the same obedience as is owed Civil Rulers.

As well, this phrase has nothing to do with owing just debts of money and other material things. However, we are obligated as Believers, as should be obvious, to pay all just debts.

CIVIL GOVERNMENT AND CHURCH GOVERNMENT

Some Church Leaders have attempted to pull the admonitions of Paul from verses 1-7 concerning Civil Government and Christian obligation, over into Church Government. In fact, this is the greatest problem presently, and always has been, the adoption into the Church of Civil forms of Government. The two are not the same, and are not intended by the Lord at all to be the same.

As a Believer, I owe Civil Government fear

NOTES

and taxes. I do not owe either to so-called Church Leaders. I only owe them Love.

CIVIL HIERARCHY AND RELIGIOUS HIERARCHY

Civil Government has a Civil Hierarchy which is obvious, and which is necessary. Were such not the case, Civil Government could not survive, and for a lack of authority. However, regarding the Book of Acts and the Epistles, there is no such thing as a Religious Hierarchy. Such did not exist then, and if the Holy Spirit had in fact wanted this, that certainly would have been the time for such to have been instituted.

OLD TESTAMENT TIMES

Israel of old was governed by a Theocracy. This is Government of a State (for Israel was a Nation) by immediate Divine guidance or by officials who are regarded as Divinely guided. In that sense, Israel could be said to have been governed by a Religious Hierarchy.

Almost immediately after Israel was delivered from Egyptian bondage, the Lord leading them toward a land which would be theirs, would now give the Law to them, which was to be their form of Government. We find this in three of the Books of the Pentateuch (Exodus, Leviticus, and Deuteronomy). In fact, the Law did much more than merely state the Ten Commandments, it actually structured all of society. It provided wide-ranging Laws that dealt with situations involving servants (Ex. 21:2-11), personal injury cases (Ex. 21:12-36), property rights (Ex. 22:1-15), destructive social relationships (Ex. 22:16-31), conducting law suits (Ex. 23:1-9), and religious duties (Ex. 23:10-19).

As well, other extended Passages touched on other aspects of national and community life. By following the social order laid down in the Law, Israel was to create a just, moral community, in which even poverty would be eliminated.

ISRAEL WAS NOT GIVEN LEGISLATIVE POWERS

Under the Theocracy, the burden of making Laws and establishing the social order was that of God Himself. The people of Israel were not given legislative powers. But the other function of Government, that of enforcing the Laws on the community, was delegated in accordance with the principle laid down in Genesis Chapter 9. The individual is to be held responsible for his actions by others. Society is accountable for punishing wrongdoers, actually, exactly as it is presently.

The unique feature of Israel's Theocracy in regard to administration of Law, is that no central controlled structures were originally established to administer justice. The responsibility to hold members of the community accountable to God's Laws were distributed to the community as a whole, in other words divided up all over the Nation.

A PARTICIPATION BY MANY

This meant that individuals who had some personal knowledge of a situation were to be called as witnesses and were to tell the truth if an individual was brought to suit or trial. Suits were conducted within the community, with the Elders of the local community serving as Judges and Jury. The community leaders were responsible for settling the cases, based on principles expressed in the Law's codes.

In the case of sins like idolatry, which threatened the well-being of Israel itself because it provoked God's anger (Josh. Chpt. 7), it was the responsibility of individuals to bring charges and thus, to discharge the community of responsibility.

When a case was too difficult for local Elders to settle, it was possible for the Elders to take it to the Priests, who served God at Israel's single place of Worship. There were also provisions by which a case that could not be settled in any other way might be brought directly to God, Who would serve as final Judge.

RESPONSIBILITY OF EACH

The most significant element in the system was the principle of distribution of responsibility to every member of the community. In ancient Israel no one could stand by when a crime was being committed and then give the excuse that he did not want to become involved or that it was police business.

In Israel each person was to hold himself

NOTES

responsible for the holiness of society. Each was to accept personal responsibility for seeing that all the people carried out God's Just and Holy Laws.

NEVER FULLY IMPLEMENTED

This Theocratic system, despite its wise structure and beauty, was never implemented in Israel. With the exception of a single generation (Deut. 4:4; Josh. 24:31), Israel failed to follow the Lord.

The social order that depended on the presence of a majority of righteous persons was warped and twisted by sin, and God's Good Laws could not be administered as He intended (Hab. 1:4).

The fault was not in the system, for it was given by God. The fault was in the weakness of sinful flesh (Rom. 8:3). No system of Government that attempts to rely on innate human goodness for its operation can ever succeed in maintaining the social order as it should.

So, one could say that Israel did have a loose Hierarchy of sorts, and because of the combination of Civil and Religious Authority. As well, Israel was a Nation, and, therefore, in a sense, somewhat political. Consequently, a Hierarchy of sorts was necessary.

NEW TESTAMENT TIMES

The Epistles in the New Testament proclaim to the Body of Christ instructions respecting the great Covenant of Grace. The Book of Acts, presents these instructions or directions being carried out in everyday life and in the Work of God. Consequently, Acts and the Epistles are the guideline for all things relative to the Church, and as well, as it regards Church Government.

Some have claimed that very little instruction is given in Acts and the Epistles regarding Church Government; however, that is totally incorrect. Not only do we learn from what it said, but we also learn from what is *not* said. Actually the whole of Acts and the Epistles is Government — the Government of God. Let's look at that for a moment:

BIBLICAL DIRECTION

The Local Church in New Testament times was the highest Spiritual Authority. In other words, even though advice and counsel could come from outside the Local Church, nothing must take precedent over that Local Body. This meant there was no such thing as a Religious Hierarchy. So, if such was not the case then, it should not be the case now.

In fact, if the Holy Spirit had desired such, that would have been the opportune time. Jerusalem would have been the place, and the Twelve Apostles would have been the people. However, even though Jerusalem was very important, and for obvious reasons, still, we find that the center of activity respecting the Work of God, gradually shifted from Jerusalem to Antioch (Acts Chpt. 13).

As well, while the original Twelve were greatly used of God, we find Paul being chosen as the instrument for the major thrust. So, there was no Hierarchy.

(A Religious Hierarchy is a ruling body of clergy organized into orders or ranks each subordinate to the one above it.)

When Jesus addressed Himself to the seven Churches of Asia, He did so to each respective Church, and more particularly, to each Pastor of these Churches (Rev. Chpts. 2-3). Had there been a Hierarchy, He would have addressed these letters to its ruling member or members, for them to filter the message out to those beneath them. However, He did not do this, because such did not exist. To have done so, would have abrogated His place and position as the Head of the Church.

As well, when the Holy Spirit gave the Epistles to Paul, He did not address those Epistles to Jerusalem or to the Twelve Apostles, but rather, directly, to the Churches themselves, or to individuals in particular. Once again, this was done, because the Local Church was the highest Spiritual Authority. This is obvious by the action of the Holy Spirit in the dissemination of directive information.

RELIGIOUS DENOMINATIONS?

A Religious Denomination is basically a name designation, a general name for a category, a religious organization uniting in a single legal and administrative body a number of local or national or even international congregations.

As well, such did not exist in New Testament times, the Churches being more so a fellowship than anything. They were to be of like Doctrine and like purpose, and in fact, would be that way as the Holy Spirit was allowed preeminence.

Each Local Church was to settle its own problems and make its own determination under the Lord, without interference from an outside governing body, etc.

However, in the strict sense of the word, there is nothing unscriptural concerning the formation, having or joining a Religious Denomination, providing it remains in its proper administrative capacity. Likewise, there is nothing unscriptural about a Central Headquarters, as far as organization is concerned. In fact, if it's conducted correctly, it can be a great blessing to the Work of God all over the world.

The wrong is brought about, when control is taken away from the Local Church, forcing the issue, whatever it may be, according to outside desires. It then becomes unscriptural.

SPIRITUAL AUTHORITY?

In the Local Church and throughout the Body of Christ, the Lord has established Spiritual Authority:

1. It is headed up in Himself as the *"Head"* of the Church (Eph. 1:20-23).

Satan attacks the Headship of Christ more than anything else. He does so through religious men forming and making offices which are not Scriptural, and little by little taking the Authority which belongs only to Christ. Christ is a very active Head of His Church, and not passive, as some think. As well, the Church belongs to Him, and not others.

Satan does these things by instituting a form of Government into the Church which is not Scriptural, and consequentially has no Scriptural precedent. I think I can say without exaggeration, that he has used this tactic to weaken, hinder, and even destroy the Work of God more so than anything else.

2. The Lord as the Head of the Church delegates Spiritual Authority to *"Apostles, Prophets, Evangelists, Pastors and Teachers."*

The Scripture plainly says, *"He* (Jesus)

gave," meaning that this is His prerogative Alone, and is never given to anyone else (Eph. 4:11). He is the One through the Holy Spirit, Who calls and appoints.

All of this is *"for the perfecting of the Saints, for the Work of the Ministry, for the edifying of the Body of Christ"* (Eph. 4:12). (If one is to notice, it is for the *"perfecting of the Saints,"* and *not* for the *"covering of the Saints."* Our *"Covering"* is Christ Alone and not men.)

He does not use Church Denominations to do this, elected Religious Officials, etc. It is done by His Callings and Designations, or it is not done. So the authority as given by Christ, rests in these particular Callings, and in nothing else.

Now, it is quite certain that some or all Preachers who are elected by popular ballot to particular administrative offices in a Denomination are already one or more of these designations. However, being elected to one of these man-devised offices, in no way enhances or increases the Spiritual Authority they already have under Christ. However, this is where many in the modern Church go wrong. They think that these man-devised offices constitute some type of Spiritual Authority which must be obeyed, when in reality and according to the Scriptures, it does nothing of the sort. But Satan has successfully used this to insert his own pseudo-authority, which means, that anything which is not totally of the Lord, which means it has its foundation in Scripture, is actually of Satan.

The modern Church today, is little guided by Christ or those of His designations, but rather by those in man-instituted offices, elected on popular ballots, claiming this gives them some type of added Spiritual Authority. However, if God's Rule of Government is violated, the Holy Spirit withdraws to a great degree, and sometimes in totality. The Lord will not in any fashion share control. And yet, this is where the battleground is, in the sphere of *"control."*

IMPROPER DESIGNATIONS

Religious Denominations are not the only ones guilty of adding to that which the Lord has already given respecting

Church Government. Many who are not associated with Denominations fall into the same trap. As the Lord warned His Disciples, men love to lord it over others, and religious men love to do so most of all (Mat. 20:24-28).

For instance, the names or titles of *"Pastor, Shepherd, Presbyter, Bishop, or Elder"* all mean the same thing, *"Pastor."* These titles were used interchangeably by Paul and others, but they all referred to the same thing, the Pastor or Pastors of a Local Church. Unfortunately, some have attempted to make the title *"Bishop"* mean something else altogether. I speak of some type of special calling, or else a spiritual leader over a designated area, which includes a number of Churches, etc.

None of this is Scripturally proper. As stated, *"Bishop"* means no more than the Pastor of a Local Church, and never refers to some type of higher spiritual order.

Neither do the names, *"Superintendent, Presbyter* (as Presbyter is often used), *President, Moderator, Overseer,"* etc. These are all man-derived designations, or else used improperly.

It is not unscriptural or improper for any of these names or designations to be used, providing they are used properly. In other words, the title *"Superintendent,"* or *"Moderator,"* does not signify any added Spiritual Authority. Neither does the title *"Bishop,"* other than its designation as *"Pastor."*

Men are always attempting to make more than God intends, or less!

DISCIPLINE

There is nowhere in the Book of Acts or the Epistles, that authority is given for any man or even a Church, or even a Church Denomination, to punish another person, be they Preacher or otherwise.

First of all, the responsibility of whatever action is taken is to be left with the Local Church with which the individual is associated, even as Paul wrote to the Church at Corinth (I Cor. Chpt. 5). If sin is involved, Repentance is demanded. If proper Repentance is enjoined, the matter stops there (II Cor. Chpt. 2). As well, the Lord has the same Standard for both Laity and Preachers, which as stated, is Repentance. Nothing is to be added to that or taken from that (I Jn. 1:9).

To do so, insults Christ, and all that He did at Calvary.

As well, it is not difficult at all to see if an individual has truly repented. It will soon become obvious if he has and obvious if he hasn't. The idea that even if one does repent, they still must be punished, holds no precedent at all in Scripture, and actually is the very opposite of the Word of God, and glaringly so. And yet, this is the criteria of most Denominations. The Scripture says the very opposite, *"restore"* (Gal. 6:1).

If an individual, Preacher or otherwise, refuses to repent, or else it becomes obvious that there has not been True Repentance, the individual is then to be disfellowshiped (I Cor. Chpt. 5). That means they are told to go elsewhere to Church, or wherever they desire, other than the Local Church of their present position (Mat. 18:15-17).

THE NATURE OF AUTHORITY WITHIN THE BODY OF CHRIST

The Scriptures teach and assume that in a world warped by sin, governing authorities are a necessity. But a vital question for Christians has to do with the nature of authority within the Body of Christ.

In its philosophical and theological sense as freedom of action to control or limit the freedom of action of others, do Christian Leaders really have authority within the Church? And if they do, to what extent is that authority?

The issue is an important one and deserves much study and debate, even as we are attempting to do here. But a number of observations should be made to help us think about this issue more clearly. And above all to be certain that all actions coincide with the Word of God.

THE BIBLE DOES NOT TEACH CONTROL BY CHRISTIANS, OR EVEN CHURCH LEADERS OVER OTHERS

For instance, Jesus delegated authority to His Disciples (Mk. 3:15; 6:7; Lk. 9:1; 10:19), but this was authority over demons and diseases. No Passage suggests freedom to exercise control over other human beings. In fact, the freedom of choice of those to whom these Disciples came is clearly protected (Mk. 6:11; Lk. 10:8-12).

NOTES

One incident reported in the Synoptics is especially significant. Matthew Chapter 20, Mark Chapter 10, and Luke Chapter 22 all tell of a heated debate among the Disciples over which of them would be greatest. Jesus took that opportunity to instruct them on leadership and its character within the Church. Each Passage reports that Jesus said, *". . . You know that the rulers of the Gentiles lord it over them, and their high officials exercise authority over them"* (Mat. 20:25).

In each Passage Jesus bluntly rules out this kind of leadership authority for them: *". . . Not so with you!"* (Mat. 20:26).

SERVANT LEADERSHIP

The alternative that Jesus spells out is Servant Leadership. And a Servant is a far cry from a Ruler!

It is fascinating to compare these three Passages in Matthew, Mark, and Luke, and to note that one of them uses the Greek word *"exousia"* to indicate the authority exercised by secular officials.

The other two (Mat. 20:25; Mk. 10:42) use the Greek word *"katexousiazo,"* and is found only in these two places in the New Testament.

The latter word means *"authority over"* but it also implies a tendency toward whatever compulsion is required to gain compliance.

These Passages suggest strongly that whatever authority Christian Leaders may have, their freedom of action does not include the right to control the actions and choices of their brothers and sisters in the Lord.

USING PAUL AS AN EXAMPLE

The Apostle Paul is deeply aware of the fact that as an Apostle he does have authority. He speaks of it in II Corinthians Chapters 10 and 13.

He told the Corinthians that the Lord gave him authority with a specific purpose: *". . . For building you up, not tearing you down"* (II Cor. 10:8; 13:10). In II Corinthians Chapter 13 Paul speaks of his concern not to be *"harsh in the use of* (his) *authority"* (II Cor. 13:10).

The context shows that the Christians in Corinth refused to admit that Christ was speaking through this servant leader. Paul did not respond by threatening. He did not try to manipulate or to coerce. He simply reminded them, *". . . He (Christ) is not weak in dealing with you, but is powerful among you"* (II Cor. 13:3).

JESUS AS THE HEAD OF THE CHURCH

Paul had no need to resort to manipulation or to coercion, because Jesus was alive and acting as Head of His Church.

Jesus remained powerful among His People and was free to exercise His Authority in disciplining ways. Paul relied on Jesus to bring about a response to the words that He, Jesus, had given to Paul to speak to the Corinthians.

These Passages, and studies of Paul's style of leadership, suggest strongly that in the Church God limits the authority given to leaders. The leaders' authority is not an authority of control, but an authority to help the Believer to use his or her freedom to respond willingly to Jesus.

JESUS AND LEADERSHIP

Those living in the First Century had secular models of leadership on which to draw. These models viewed authority as vested in a person. The Roman system was a highly developed bureaucratic model. Although there were checks and balances, an official in the system spoke as a representative of the supreme authority himself, Caesar.

A leader thus had the power to tell a person, *"Do this"* and he or she had to do it.

There was another model implicit in the pattern originally provided in the Old Testament, even to which we have already alluded. In this model, God was the Living King, and local Elders acted to guide the community to live by His Laws. But for this model to be effective, total dedication to the Lord was demanded. Inasmuch as that was not forthcoming, it was replaced in Israel by Charismatic Judges and later by hereditary kings.

We need to have some insight into the view of leadership prevalent in the New Testament world to sense the impact of some of the statements of Jesus.

WHAT JESUS SAID . . .

In a world where leaders spoke as representatives of a person with supreme power

— with total authority to command the behavior of ordinary folk, and that which His followers understood — Jesus told His Disciples, to which we have alluded:

". . . You know that the rulers of the Gentiles lord it over them, and their high officials exercise authority over them.

"Not so with you. Instead, whoever wants to become great among you must be your (a) *servant, and whoever wants to be first must be your* (a) *slave — just as the Son of Man did not come to be served, but to serve, and to give His Life as a ransom for many"* (Mat. 20:25-28).

Jesus' proclamation of leadership is also reflected in His Judgment on the Religious Leaders of Israel — *"The Teachers of the Law and the Pharisees . . ."* (Mat. 23:2) — who claimed that they had authority to command the faithful. Jesus, in light of their leadership, told His Disciples: *"But you are not to be called 'Rabbi,' for you have only one Master and you are all brothers. And do not call anyone on earth 'Father,' for you have one Father, and He is in Heaven. Nor are you to be called 'Teacher,' for you have one Teacher, the Christ. The greatest among you will be your servant. For whoever exalts himself will be humbled, and whoever humbles himself will be exalted"* (Mat. 23:8-12).

These and other statements of Jesus stand in stark contrast to the cultural concept of Church leadership as it is presently viewed, and especially the bringing of secular Government into the Church.

CHRIST, THE LIVING HEAD OF HIS BODY

Leadership in the Church is viewed against a new reality. The Church is an organism, with Christ the Sole and Living Head. There is no need for intermediaries to represent Him, whether they be Catholic or Protestant Popes, for *". . . Christ died and returned to life so that He might be the Lord of both the dead and the living"* (Rom. 14:9).

As we see in Matthew Chapter 20, Jesus decisively rejected the image of the secular ruler. Instead, He pointed to the servant and to His Own Servanthood as the Will of God.

In the words of Lawrence O. Richards,

"Human leaders in the Church must not adopt the patterns and methods of their society if they are to provide effective Church Leadership."

The phrase, *"But to Love one another,"* proclaims the only requirement between Believers. And yet, this requirement is quite enough.

One cannot really expect Love between unbelievers; therefore, there has to be authoritative Government, etc. With Believers, and where Love should reign supreme, if such is practiced, one would not do anything to dispute or harm in any way, at least knowingly, a fellow Believer. If we truly Love one another, we will respect their rights, respect their place and position, value their friendship, and seek to show every act of kindness.

So, the real *"Government"* among Believers should be that of *"Love,"* and we speak of the *"God kind of Love."*

The phrase, *"For he that loveth another hath fulfilled the Law,"* pertains to what the Law of Moses intended, but never brought about, simply because no power was afforded helpless man in order that the Commandments be kept. However, under the New Covenant, power is afforded the Child of God through the Person and Agency of the Holy Spirit, Who, if given satisfactory control, will help the Believer to do that which should be done (Rom. 8:1-2).

THE MANNER OF LOVE

Love transforms character. The Christian is a person who is in the process of transformation toward Christlikeness. Many Passages in the New Testament provide a description of the kind of person the Believer is becoming, or is supposed to be (I Cor. 13:1-7; Col. 3:12-17).

It is the fact of our transformation toward Christlikeness that explains the relationship that the New Testament postulates between Love and Law.

The Law expressed Righteousness in the form of external Commandments. Love moves the Believer to actually be righteous in his every relationship. Therefore, *"Love is the fulfilling of the Law"* (Rom. 13:10; Gal. 5:23).

(9) "FOR THIS, THOU SHALT NOT

COMMIT ADULTERY, THOU SHALT NOT KILL, THOU SHALT NOT STEAL, THOU SHALT NOT BEAR FALSE WITNESS, THOU SHALT NOT COVET; AND IF THERE BE ANY OTHER COMMANDMENT, IT IS BRIEFLY COMPREHENDED IN THIS SAYING, NAMELY, THOU SHALT LOVE THY NEIGHBOUR AS THYSELF."

The phrase, *"For this, Thou shalt not commit adultery,"* is Commandment number Seven of the Ten (Ex. Chpt. 20).

This Commandment prohibits all unlawful sexual relationship and upholds the Sacredness and Divine appointments of marriage for the propagation and multiplication of the human race.

That which is unlawful pertains to sex in any form outside of marriage (Gen. 2:23-24).

The phrase, *"Thou shalt not kill,"* is the Sixth Commandment.

To which we have already discussed, this Law does not prohibit killing as punishment for crimes, or killing in a just war, which God Himself commanded Israel at times to do; however, it does prohibit killing for malice, and premeditative and wilful destruction of man who was made in the Image of God.

(The word *"kill"* should have actually been translated here *"murder."*)

The phrase, *"Thou shalt not steal,"* presents the Eighth Commandment.

This Commandment prohibits the taking of the property of another, or even the injury of such property, even to the point of carelessness.

The phrase, *"Thou shalt not bear false witness,"* presents the Ninth Commandment.

This prohibits false testimony in Courts of Justice, and lying about the acts, words, and property of a neighbor.

The phrase, *"Thou shalt not covet,"* presents the Tenth and final Commandment of the Decalogue.

This last Commandment prohibits the inward desire of the heart from longing for, scheming, and putting forth any effort to acquire anything that belongs to another (Prov. 6:25; Mk. 7:19-21; James 1:13-15). If one is to notice, Paul deals with the Commandments which have to do with our fellowman, which means if we truly *"Love"* we won't do these things to them.

The phrase, *"And if there be any other Commandment, it is briefly comprehended in this saying, namely, Thou shalt Love thy neighbour as thyself,"* proclaims the Words of Jesus (Lk. 10:27). The word *"Love"* as it is used here and in verse 8, is *"Agapao,"* and means *"Divine Love produced by the Holy Spirit, self-sacrificial in its nature"* (Wuest).

WHO IS MY NEIGHBOR?

This question was posed by a so-called expert in the Scriptures, when Jesus told him to Love his neighbor (Lk. 10:29). It led to an explanation from Jesus that is particularly important for us today.

Two Hebrew words are most often found where English Versions read *"neighbor"* in the Old Testament.

1. The first is *"saken,"* and simply indicates inhabitants of neighboring areas, whether they are friendly or unfriendly.

2. The second and most used word is *"rea."* The basic idea is that of having something to do with one another. That is, neighbors refer to persons who in some way contact me and affect my experience. *"Rea"* is found some 187 times in the Old Testament, and has a very broad application, which is obvious.

It is used both of a close friend and, as well, of a chance acquaintance. While at times it seems to indicate relationships between members of the Covenant People (Lev. 19:18-32), in early times it was used not only to indicate a fellow Israelite (Ex. 2:13) but also the Egyptian oppressors (Ex. 11:2).

NOT SO KNOWLEDGEABLE IN THE WORD

This man who approached Jesus, who was called a *"lawyer,"* was supposed to be an expert in the Law of Moses. Consequently, the broad use of *"rea"* as it is used in the Old Testament concerning the word *"neighbor,"* actually made the question Jesus was asked unnecessary. *". . . Love your neighbor as yourself . . ."* (Lev. 19:18) should have been given the broadest possible interpretation, which this man professed to know, which would have, and in fact, explained what Jesus said readily.

But out of the desire for self-justification,

the *"expert"* in the Law asked the question *"Who is my neighbor?"*, in an attempt to narrow the responsibility that the term implied.

WHAT JESUS SAID

The answer Jesus gave used the most common Greek word for neighbor — *"plesion."* This word is used in each of the nine New Testament Passages in which the Old Testament injunction to Love one's neighbor is repeated (Mat. 5:43; 19:19; 22:39; Mk. 12:31, 33; Lk. 10:27; Rom. 13:9; Gal. 5:14; James 2:8).

In answering this man, even though his question was sarcastic, Jesus told of the Good Samaritan (Lk. 10:25-37), who, upon passing a Jewish stranger who had been stripped and beaten by robbers, took pity on him. The Samaritan stopped, helped him to the nearest Inn, and took responsibility to pay for his care.

After establishing the fact that the neighbor was one who had mercy on the needy stranger, Jesus told his questioner, *". . . Go and do likewise"* (Lk. 10:37).

JESUS' MESSAGE WAS CLEAR

The story extends rather than narrows the concept of *"neighbor."*

In the story, the injured man was a Jew, someone traditionally hostile to Samaritans. There was no bond of personal relationship between the two. They were simply two human beings, one in need and the other able to meet the need.

Jesus' Message was clear for those who heard Him then, and it is clear for us today.

Our *"neighbor"* is any person we may come in contact with who has a need. And to Love one's neighbor means to be moved by compassion to reach out and to seek to meet that need (Richards).

(10) "LOVE WORKETH NO ILL TO HIS NEIGHBOUR: THEREFORE LOVE IS THE FULFILLING OF THE LAW."

The phrase, *"Love worketh no ill to his neighbour,"* in effect, speaks of the Commandments just listed, and proclaims that followers of Christ, that is if they are fully obeying Christ, will *"work no ill"* in any form toward their *"neighbor."*

The phrase, *"Therefore Love is the fulfilling*

of the Law," proclaims the fact, that this is all that is formerly required by the Law. Therefore, Love is Law's fulfillment. Of course, Love is an inspiration rather than a restraint, and transcends Law as embodied in merely negative Commandments. As well, as should be obvious, this is the Mosaic Law of which Paul speaks, and not Law in general. It is from it the prohibitions are derived on the grounds of which the Apostle argues, and to it, therefore, we must apply his conclusion (Wuest).

The Law of Moses was God's Standard of Righteousness and Morality. It is on this foundation that all just, fair, and equitable Laws are based. To ignore or violate these Moral Laws as laid down by God, is to bring hurt and harm to one's fellowman in some manner. If Legislative bodies ignore these Laws, such form of Government always proves to be unfair, unjust, and harmful to the populace as a whole. I speak primarily of the Ten Commandments, minus the Fourth, plus the Words of Jesus in Luke 10:27.

(11) "AND THAT, KNOWING THE TIME, THAT NOW IT IS HIGH TIME TO AWAKE OUT OF SLEEP: FOR NOW IS OUR SALVATION NEARER THAN WHEN WE BELIEVED."

The phrase, *"And that, knowing the time,"* is meant to bring into proper perspective the significance of the Christian experience. *"Time"* in the Greek, as it is used here, is *"kairos,"* and means *"season, a special, critical, strategic period of time."* Paul is urging the significance of the foregoing exhortations in view of the immanency of the Rapture and the Judgment Seat of Christ. It is *"time"* regarded as having a character of its own, full of significance for the Believer (Wuest).

The phrase, *"That now it is high time to awake out of sleep,"* refers to the apathy and lethargy of many Believers, and how spiritual deadness must be shaken off.

"Sleep" in the Greek is *"hypnos,"* and *"indicates a deep sleep and is used metaphorically of insensitivity to the significance of one's present life in Christ."*

The phrase, *"For now is our Salvation nearer than when we believed,"* actually speaks of the coming Resurrection and the Believer at that time being Glorified.

NOTES

"Salvation" as used here in the Greek is *"soteria,"* and means *"rescue or safety."* It carries the idea of being rescued or saved by a *"Deliverer,"* i.e., God or Christ: — Saviour (Soter).

Salvation is actually in three tenses:

1. Past, which refers to Justification, the removal of the guilt and penalty of sin from the believing sinner and the bestowal of Righteousness, which is Christ Jesus Himself, this occurring at the moment of believing.

2. It pertains as well to the present, which speaks of Sanctification, the continuous process by which the Holy Spirit puts sin out of our lives, produces His Own Fruit, gradually conforming us to the Image of our Lord.

3. Salvation also points to the future, which speaks of Glorification, the transformation of our bodies at the Rapture (Resurrection) into perfect bodies of a new nature. As stated, it is of this third phase of Salvation which Paul is speaking.

The idea is, that the completion of our Salvation is nearer to us than the day we first placed our Faith in the Lord Jesus (Wuest). Properly understanding what Paul is saying, makes one realize just how close *now* we are to this coming miraculous, wondrous event.

(12) "THE NIGHT IS FAR SPENT, THE DAY IS AT HAND: LET US THEREFORE CAST OFF THE WORKS OF DARKNESS, AND LET US PUT ON THE ARMOUR OF LIGHT."

The phrase, *"The night is far spent, the day is at hand,"* refers to everything up unto the coming Resurrection, as *"night."* The coming Resurrection and after, is referred to as *"day,"* with both night and day used as symbols.

Knowing that the Holy Spirit inspired these words to Paul, we are made to realize, at least as far as we can presently comprehend, just how different this coming day is going to be. Actually, I think it is not possible for even the most ardent Believer to properly comprehend what is coming, relative to this grand time.

The idea is also present in this phrase, that we are to live constantly and constantly live, as if this *"day"* will come at any moment.

The phrase, *"Let us therefore cast off the*

works of darkness," could be translated, *"Let us therefore cast off the clothes of darkness."*

Former habits of life are here, as elsewhere, regarded as clothing once worn — a man's habitual investment, though not part of his real self — which is to be put off.

Due to Jesus at Calvary not only having paid the sin debt, but, also, having broken the grip of sin, the Believer is no longer under bondage to the works of darkness. Through the Person and Ministry of the Holy Spirit, he now can simply *"cast off"* this old clothing, so to speak, which is filthy. Therefore, we are without excuse regarding the continuing in these darkened works.

The phrase, *"And let us put on the armour of Light,"* could as well be translated, *"And let us put on the clothes of Light."*

As we *"cast off"* the other, we now *"put on"* the new investment, the Graces and Virtues, supplied to us from the region of Light, which constitute the Christian Character (II Cor. 6:7; Eph. 6:11; I Thess. 5:8).

In all these Passages the new clothing to be put on is designated as armour, the idea being carried out in detail in Ephesians 6:11; and thus, the further conception is introduced of Christians being as soldiers on the watch during the watches of the night, awaiting daybreak, equipped with arms of heavenly proof, careful not to sleep on their posts, or to allow themselves in revelry or any deeds of shame, such as are done in the night under the cover of darkness (Barmby).

(13) "LET US WALK HONESTLY, AS IN THE DAY; NOT IN RIOTING AND DRUNKENNESS, NOT IN CHAMBERING AND WANTONNESS, NOT IN STRIFE AND ENVYING."

The phrase, *"Let us walk honestly, as in the day,"* refers to what we are in Christ, at least what we are supposed to be.

"Walk" in the Greek is *"peripateo,"* and means *"to conduct oneself, order one's behavior."*

"Honestly" in the Greek is *"euschemonos,"* and means *"in a seemly manner, decently."* The idea is, of the Saints giving an honest impression of themselves to the world. They should conduct themselves in a manner befitting their high station in life, as Saints of the Most High God (Wuest).

We should act like Christians, talk like Christians, walk like Christians, think like Christians, and be like Christians, because we are Christians. The idea is, there are no closet Christians.

The phrase, *"Not in rioting and drunkenness,"* speaks of the drunken revelry which characterizes so many in the modern world. According to some modern news reports, such is the scene in many modern sporting events. The situation has become so critical in some places, that there is even some talk of banning alcohol, i.e., beer, etc. However, inasmuch as such is the stay of the modern world, and perhaps ever has been, it is extremely doubtful that they would ever go to such righteous lengths, regardless of the danger of the present situation. Of course that is but one example of which there are many.

The phrase, *"Not in chambering and wantonness,"* speaks of sexual immorality of every nature, unbridled lust, excess, licentiousness, shamelessness, insolence, etc.

The phrase, *"Not in strife and envying,"* pertains to the constant manipulation and exploitation to best others regarding business, place, or position. In other words, the *"rat-race."*

(14) "BUT PUT YE ON THE LORD JESUS CHRIST, AND MAKE NOT PROVISION FOR THE FLESH, TO FULFIL THE LUSTS THEREOF."

The phrase, *"But put ye on the Lord Jesus Christ,"* refers to clothing the soul in the moral disposition and habits of Christ. In effect, the clothing seen here, for that is the reference, is the Lord Jesus Christ so fully covering the Christian that Christ Alone is seen.

This is actually what Paul was speaking of when he said, *"I am crucified with Christ: nevertheless I live; yet not I, but Christ liveth in me: and the life which I now live in the flesh I live by the Faith of the Son of God, Who loved me, and gave Himself for me"* (Gal. 2:20).

The Believer is to take full advantage of all that Christ offers, which in reality is inexhaustible. Jesus is all in all. He is the One Who has paid the price for man's Redemption, and the One Who also broke the grip of sin by His Atoning Work at Calvary and the Resurrection. By the Power of the Holy Spirit, He and all that He is, can be made real to the Believer, and in any and every capacity. In other words, Jesus is all that one needs, but to avail oneself of this which He has done and fully intends for us to have, one must at least have some knowledge of His Great Atoning Work.

(For further Commentary on this extremely important subject, please carefully study Romans Chapters 6, 7, and 8.)

The phrase, *"And make not provision for the flesh, to fulfill the lusts thereof,"* presents the very opposite of Christ.

The *"flesh"* as Paul here uses the word, has to do with the sin nature which still resides in the Believer, although the Believer is Born Again.

This injunction proves the fact of sin in the Christian, for he could not make provision for gratifying the appetites of that which does not exist. Mark 7:21-23 says that these appetites have their roots in the heart (Williams).

The slightest interest in the sin nature will bring sin into the life. Paul means that in the case of the evil nature, we are to take the attitude that such has no part in our lives, and thus, we will not provide for it under any circumstances.

"Provision" in the Greek is *"pronoia,"* and means *"provident care or supply."* It is *not* the idea of not allowing sin in the life to not gain an upper hand, but rather that we do not allow it at all. Even though the sin nature does remain in the Believer, if we wear Christ, it will lie dormant causing no problem. However, unless we avail ourselves of all that Christ has done and is to us, and that speaks of a present help, to be sure, the sin nature will cause us great problems.

The sin nature, i.e., *"the flesh,"* contains *"lusts."* That word in the Greek is *"epithumia,"* and means *"a craving, passionate desire, good or bad, depending upon the context, here an evil one."*

Exactly what are those lusts?

Paul outlines them in Romans 1:21-32; I Corinthians 6:9-11; Galatians 5:19-21; Colossians 3:5-10. They are referred to as *"works of the flesh."*

"All that I am or hope to be, Oh Son of God, I owe to Thee,

"For Thou has bought me; I am Thine, and by Thy Mercy Thou art mine."

"Thy blessed Cross has sealed my peace, Thy sorrows make my own to cease;
"Thy power has cleansed me from all sin, Thy Presence keeps my conscience clean."

"Thy cruel wounds my own have healed; Thy broken heart my pardon sealed;
"Thy death, Oh Christ, means life for me, a life for all eternity."

CHAPTER 14

(1) "HIM THAT IS WEAK IN THE FAITH RECEIVE YE, BUT NOT TO DOUBTFUL DISPUTATIONS."

The phrase, *"Him that is weak in the Faith receive ye,"* has to do with Christians, whether Jews or Gentiles, who were still holding to certain particular Laws or Rulings regarding the eating or not eating of certain types of food, or the keeping of certain days, etc.

Regarding the Jewish Christians, some were still attempting to hold on to parts of the old Law of Moses respecting the not eating of certain foods such as pork, etc., and especially the keeping of the Sabbath.

Regarding the Gentiles who had come to Christ, they remembered that certain types of foods had been consecrated to their heathen gods, with the eating of these foods giving them favor with these gods, etc. Now that they had come to Christ, some felt they could not partake of these foods any longer, considering what it had once represented.

The phrase, *"Weak in the Faith,"* pertains to one who does not fully appreciate what his Christianity means; in particular, he does not see that the soul which has committed itself to Christ for Salvation is emancipated from all ritual and ceremonial Law, irrespective of it being Jewish or Gentile. Of course, it was still incumbent upon Believers to keep the Moral Law.

As well, there were, no doubt, some Christians who were practicing an overscrupulous asceticism, which practices strict self-denial of most anything which is pleasurable, and is austere in appearance, manner, and attitude.

THESE PROBLEMS IN THE CHURCH

Many from the beginning, even as we see here, have attempted to attach certain types of man-made rules and regulations to their Salvation. In other words, they felt or feel (bringing it up to modern times) that the doing or not doing of these particular things, whatever they may be, has something to do with their Holiness, Sanctification, or even Salvation as stated.

For instance, I have heard of Christians who would not read a newspaper on Sunday, because they thought it was a violation of the Sabbath, not realizing it seems, that first of all Sunday is not the Sabbath, and that the old Jewish Sabbath is not incumbent upon Christians. Others feel that a lady not wearing any type of makeup, constitutes Holiness, etc. Others have stated that no woman should wear any type of jewelry, etc. Others have claimed that long sleeves should be worn, irrespective of the climate, and by both men and women.

Many years ago, some Churches would not have a piano to accompany their singing, because such instruments were also used in places of ill fame.

The list goes on, probably including almost anything of which one could think, which somebody thinks that they should or should not do, and we speak of certain rituals or ceremonies, which they think the doing or the not doing adds something, or takes away something from their Salvation respecting Holiness or Sanctification, etc.

HOLINESS

Doing certain things or not doing certain things does not make one holy. And yet, that is the manner in which most of modern Christendom attempts to come by the great attribute of Holiness. The truth is: there is absolutely nothing that the human being can do, irrespective as to how consecrated he may be, how dedicated he may be, or even how much he might love the Lord, that will make him holy. And yet, we are commanded to be holy! (II Pet. 3:11)

NOTES

Some time back, I was reading after one particular Preacher, who has long since gone on to be with the Lord. He made a statement which, to me, said it all. He was discussing, in his book, the attire of the High Priest of the Law of Moses. He then wrote:

"Turn your eyes away from your ten thousand failures and look at the golden plate on the Mitre of the High Priest, which says 'Holiness unto the Lord.'" The meaning is clear:

Our Holiness resides totally and completely in Christ, of which the High Priest of old was a Type. We attain to that Holiness simply by exhibiting Faith in Christ and what Christ has done for us at the Cross. Carrying that out on a constant basis, the Holy Spirit then perfects Holiness within our lives, which is the only way it can be done. (Gal. 2:20).

WHAT SHOULD THE MORAL STANDARD BE FOR THE CHILD OF GOD?

The word *"moral"* is the key. If it is not immoral, then it is not wrong.

If one is to notice, all of the Ten Commandments with the exception of the Fourth, *"Remember the Sabbath to keep it holy,"* are moral. As well, if one is to notice, this Fourth Commandment was not brought over into the New Covenant, while all the others were. The reason is obvious! All the others are moral, while Sabbath-keeping was ritualistic and ceremonial only. In other words, the doing or not doing of it had nothing to do with one's morals.

Of course one could argue that if God commanded something to be done, even as He did with Sabbath-keeping in the Old Testament, that it would be immoral to disobey Him. That certainly is true. However, that was the only moral attachment to this particular Commandment, as the Commandment within itself contained nothing moral; consequently, this Commandment was not brought over into the New Covenant, and for the obvious reasons. It only served as a Type of the spiritual rest one would receive by accepting the Atoning Work of the coming Messiah respecting Salvation. When He came, the *"Type"* or *"Symbol"* was no longer needed, once again as should be obvious.

A man or a woman wearing certain types of jewelry carries no moral connotations, so there is nothing wrong with that practice, if one so desires such. As well, a lady wearing makeup has nothing to do with morals one way or the other. Neither does clothing, providing it is decent. The same can be said for all types of things which men conjure up in their minds respecting Holiness or Sanctification.

People are not holy because they wear a ring or do not wear a ring. Neither are they holy, because they will not read a newspaper on Sunday, etc. These things are silly, and common sense should tell one that the doing or not doing of such has no bearing on one in a spiritual sense.

IMMORALITY

On the other hand, there are many things which are immoral, and with which Christians should not associate.

Due to the sorrow and heartache it causes, I think that any type of alcoholic beverage is immoral. Even though it is certainly true that many Believers could drink a glass of wine each day without becoming addicted, or causing anyone else problems; still, due to the fact that every Alcoholic began by taking his or her first drink, and considering all the sorrow and heartache that alcohol brings to the world, I personally feel that the Believer for the sake of morality and to set a Standard, should not imbibe at all.

Also, there are some things that a Christian should not read, and for the simple reason that it is immoral. The same should go for things watched over Television, Movies, etc. The Believer must discriminate because of morals, and to be sure, the Holy Spirit will help the Believer in this regard (Jn. 16:7-15).

There are many places as a Christian that I will not go, many things I will not read, and many things that I will not watch over Television, or listen to over the Radio. It is either immoral or not edifying.

However, if other Believers do not see eye to eye with me on all of these things, unless it is blatantly wrong respecting what is being done, I will not comment on their convictions in these areas or the lack thereof. I

will leave that between them and the Lord.

As well, there are many things immoral, which many Christians do not think of as such. For instance, slander and gossip are immoral, probably far more immoral than nicotine or gambling, as bad as those things are. Spiritual pride is immoral. Jealousy and envy are immoral. Pharisaism is grossly immoral and so is Denominationalism. Racism, prejudice, bias, and discrimination, are immoral, and grossly so!

To be frank, these latter things named, are of far greater immorality than many vices which we label as sin, and which in fact are sin. The Truth is, most people know those things (vices) are sin, while they seek to overlook these things which are at times, of far greater magnitude. For instance, Jesus said, *"Woe unto you, Scribes and Pharisees, hypocrites! For ye pay tithe of mint and anise and cummin, and have omitted the weightier matters of the Law, Judgment, Mercy, and Faith: these ought ye to have done, not to leave the other undone"* (Mat. 23:23).

I think that says it about as well as it can be said.

THE PRACTICE OF HOLINESS

One of the most powerful Chapters in the entirety of the Word of God is the Twelfth Chapter of Exodus. In fact, it is one of the pivot Chapters of the Bible. It is that which delivered Israel out of Egyptian bondage. The pattern laid down in that Chapter for their deliverance has not changed, at least as far as principle is concerned. All the great miracles performed in Egypt, as valuable as they were, did not deliver the Children of Israel. But the slaying of the lamb, which typified Christ dying on the Cross, with the blood being applied to the doorposts of all the houses, occasioned their deliverance.

The Wrath of God was about to be poured out on Egypt, which would claim the firstborn of every home, and even the firstborn of all animals. The Lord would strike a blow at the very heart of the religious system of Egypt, which was centered up in their firstborn. Death would come to every home in Egypt which did not have the blood applied to the doorposts.

All of this was a Type of what Christ would

do and the Redemption of humanity as it regards the Cross. It must ever be understood that, from the beginning of the Bible until it closes with Revelation 22:21, the theme is *"Jesus Christ and Him Crucified"* (I Cor. 1:23).

WHEN I SEE THE BLOOD

As it regards Holiness, the following truth must be paramount in our thinking, that is, if we are to properly understand Holiness. When the blood was applied to the doorposts, the Lord plainly said, *"When I see the blood, I will pass over you, and the plague shall not be upon you to destroy you"* (Ex. 12:13).

Now please notice what the Lord said:

He didn't say, *"When I see Abraham and Sarah, or Zechariah, in the house,"* or *"When I see the Baptist Church or the Methodist Church, etc.,"* but rather, *"When I see the blood, I will pass over you."* Faith in that atoning blood put each Israelite inside the house. Faith presently in the atoning blood puts us in Christ (Gal. 2:20). In fact, this is the theme, the core, the very power of Christianity (I Cor. 1:18).

We must ever understand that we aren't holy because we don't do certain things or because we do certain things. In fact, there is absolutely nothing that we, within ourselves, can do, as stated, which can make us holy or keep us holy. But, at the same time, there are plenty of things we can do that will make us unholy, and fast!

The way we maintain holiness is by keeping our Faith in Christ and what Christ did for us at the Cross. It always comes back to the statement, *"When I see the blood, I will pass over you."* When the Lord looks at us, He looks at us through Christ and what Christ has done for us at the Cross.

PERFECTION

It should not come as a surprise that God can accept nothing but perfection. No, the Bible doesn't teach sinless perfection, as it regards the Saints. Anyone who thinks they are sinlessly perfect, to use some street vernacular, is smoking something. However, the One Whom we serve is Perfect, and His Name is Jesus. Not only is Christ Perfect, but His Sacrifice on the Cross of Calvary was

a Perfect Sacrifice — so perfect, in fact, that God accepted it in payment for all sin, past, present, and future, at least for those who will believe (Heb. 10:12). So, when God looks at us, He actually sees His Son, our Saviour, the Lord Jesus Christ. Consequently, we maintain Holiness by continuing to look to Christ and His Substitutionary Work, all on our behalf, just as the Father looks at Christ.

Let us say it again: Jesus Christ is the Source of all things, including Holiness, and the Cross is the Means by which everything is given to us, which is made real to us and effective by the Power of the Holy Spirit, Who lives within our hearts and lives (I Cor. 3:16).

OF WHAT KIND OF FAITH IS PAUL SPEAKING HERE?

He is speaking of Justifying Faith.

Justifying Faith pertains to that which Christ did for all at Calvary and the Resurrection. There He paid the sin debt of man, and as well broke the grip of that evil monster on the human race, at least those who will believe. As well, His Work is a Finished Work, meaning that it was done in totality, and nothing need be added.

Consequently, everything is wrapped up in what Jesus did at Calvary — our Salvation, our Holiness, and our Sanctification. Simple Faith in Him, guarantees all that He did in totality, for the Believer. Nothing must be taken from His Finished Work, and nothing must be added to His Finished Work.

Consequently, anyone attempting to add to what He did, which is normally the case, such as the keeping of certain days, or doing or not doing certain things which have no moral bearing, thinking this adds to one's Holiness or Sanctification, and even Salvation as some believe, shows that person to be *"weak in the Faith."* In other words, they do not fully understand what Jesus did at Calvary and the Resurrection, or else they do not fully believe what He did.

PURELY BY FAITH IN CHRIST

A person's Salvation, which also means their Holiness and Sanctification, is purely by Faith in Christ, and not by works of any nature (Eph. 2:8-9). The moment the sinner believes, at that moment he is Saved (Jn. 3:16), and Sanctified (made Holy), and Justified (declared Holy) (I Cor. 6:11). Upon Faith, these things are given freely by the Grace of God. All the rituals or ceremonies that one may engage or do, does not add one iota to that which is given freely by Christ. For one to attempt to earn such by works is literally impossible. It simply cannot be done. The *only* way these wonderful and glorious Graces can be received, is simply as a Gift, and the Gift is received by Faith, which means we believe it and He gives it to us. It is just that simple! (Jn. 3:16; Rev. 22:17).

The phrase, *"But not to doubtful disputations,"* is directed toward strong Believers and not those *"weak in the Faith."* It means that the strong, who welcome those of weak Faith into the fellowship of the Church, are to do so unreservedly, not with the purpose of judging and attempting to rule their minds, etc.

The word *"receive"* in the Greek is *"proslambano,"* and refers in this instance to *"God's gracious acceptance of men."* In other words, as God has been gracious to accept us, we should be gracious to accept those of weak Faith, and not demand that they change their particular scruples, etc. Let the Holy Spirit tend to that, as the strong in Faith extend fellowship, love, and warmth to these individuals, without making them feel inferior, or without condemning them.

However, if those of *"weak Faith"* would attempt to impose their rituals or thinking on others, the Pastor of the Church would have to take a loving, kind, but firm stand. If something is not plainly condemned in Scripture, even as we have already stated, while we are certainly free to have our personal convictions about such things, we are not to attempt to impose those convictions on others.

(2) "FOR ONE BELIEVETH THAT HE MAY EAT ALL THINGS: ANOTHER, WHO IS WEAK, EATETH HERBS."

The phrase, *"For one believeth that he may eat all things,"* pertains to the strength of one's Faith, based on a proper understanding of what Jesus did for us at Calvary and the Resurrection.

The phrase, *"Another, who is weak, eateth*

herbs," points to those who are *"weak in the Faith."* They do *not* understand the Finished Work of Calvary as they should and, therefore, think by not eating certain things, that such is aiding their Salvation, Sanctification, and Holiness.

Paul is using the word *"herbs"* as a metaphor, which actually means these people were vegetarians, but, could apply to anything.

(3) "LET NOT HIM THAT EATETH DESPISE HIM THAT EATETH NOT; AND LET NOT HIM WHICH EATETH NOT JUDGE HIM THAT EATETH: FOR GOD HATH RECEIVED HIM."

The phrase, *"Let not him that eateth despise him that eateth not,"* speaks of the spirit of spiritual superiority.

Even though the one *"strong in the Faith"* knows that the weak Brother's convictions are of no Biblical consequence, he is to respect his Brother in the Lord, and never do or say anything that would wound the weak Brother respecting these convictions.

The phrase, *"And let not him which eateth not judge him that eateth,"* is the same thing in reverse.

The spirit of spiritual superiority or spiritual pride, is no respecter of persons. It can fasten itself to either group, and with equal tenacity. To be frank, it is probably more bold in those who *"eat not,"* than in those who *"eat."* Considering, that they think their Sanctification or Holiness is wrapped up some way in this particular conviction, many in this vein are very quick to condemn others who do not see eye to eye with them, claiming they are not Holy, etc. If such happens, which it often does, spiritual elitism is the result. However, it should be noted, that those in this segment who conduct themselves accordingly, are not looked at by the Holy Spirit as *"elite,"* but rather *"weak."*

And yet at the same time, many have attempted to take their Christian liberty into license, claiming that Grace covers all, and that basically, nothing is wrong. This element is very widespread in the Church as well. Paul's answer to that is, *"God forbid!"* (Rom. 6:1-2). As we have attempted to convey, both extremes are allied to spiritual pride.

The phrase, *"For God hath received him,"*

speaks of the individuals in either case.

GOD HATH RECEIVED HIM

In other words, when the individual, irrespective as to whom he or she may be, believed on Christ, at that moment they were Saved. They were Saved irrespective of their observance of certain days or the lack thereof. They were Saved at that moment, and it had absolutely nothing to do with what type of food they ate or did not eat. Once again, Paul is pointing to the requirement of Salvation, which is Faith and Faith alone, and which has nothing to do with anything else.

So, the Apostle is in essence saying, that all of these other things are extracurricular, and as such, should be treated accordingly. Whenever the sinner *"believed"* God, the Lord instantly received that sinner, thereby, and in a moment's time, making him or her a new creature in Christ Jesus (II Cor. 5:17-19).

The Apostle is saying, that if God has received the person, who are we not to receive him?

And yet, there are millions of Christians who will not receive certain people, simply because their particular Denomination to which they belong, does not receive them.

Why will they not receive them?

Even as Paul speaks here, the lack of receiving has nothing to do with the basic fundamentals of the Faith, but rather that the person will not do some ritual or ceremony which is man-devised. In other words, such a Denomination or these people, have based Salvation or acceptance solely on other than the Biblical account. This is far more widespread than many think.

For instance, Catholics do not accept non-Catholics as Saved, because they are not associated with the Catholic Church. In fact, many Baptists are the same way. Some Pentecostals fall into the same category.

Others will not accept fellow Believers unless they are Baptized in Water according to a certain formula. Others, unless they speak in Tongues.

Men love to make rules and demand that other men keep those rules. If some refuse to keep them, they are quick to be branded as unacceptable, irrespective of the fact that these rules, whatever they may be, have no

NOTES

bearing in Scripture whatsoever.

Any man or woman, boy or girl, who accepts Christ as their Lord and personal Saviour, is my Brother and Sister in the Lord. I must accept them as such, simply because God has received them, exactly as He said He would (Jn. 3:16, 27; 6:37). It also means, that if any Brother or Sister has sinned, but truly repents of that sin, turning away from it, I must receive that Brother or Sister, forgetting what has happened in the past, in effect, receiving them exactly as the Lord does. If I do not do such, I am seriously jeopardizing myself, because every single Believer at one time or the other, and in fact many times, has had to ask the Lord for forgiveness. The sin may have been in secret or it may be known, but the results are the same. All have had to go before the Lord many times asking for Mercy and Grace, as should be obvious. Consequently, we should treat others as we desire to be treated ourselves (Mat. 6:14-15; 7:1-5; Gal. 6:1-3).

The Believer places himself in serious jeopardy, when he will not receive what God has received. In placing himself in this position, he is in effect setting up his own Salvation, which will ultimately have the effect of shutting him out, unless he repents. These five words, *"For God hath received him,"* are serious indeed, and should be treated accordingly.

AN ILLUSTRATION!

Many years ago, a young lady and young man fell in love with each other, and announced that they were to be married. They both were associated with the same Church, and in fact, were both very close to the Lord, serving Him diligently.

However, even though the young lady had not been previously married (neither the young man), she did have a sordid past. In fact, she had been Saved out of a life of prostitution.

Many in the Church knowing this, began to raise objections to this proposed union, claiming that the boy should not marry this girl, etc.

The situation grew quite heated, with finally the entirety of the matter being brought before the Body of the Church. One can quite well imagine how embarrassing it was for this young couple, and especially the young lady, with many people standing to their feet voicing their disapproval, which by its very spirit cast aspersions on her.

Finally one elderly lady stood to her feet and asked permission to speak. Granted permission, she asked one simple question:

"Does the Precious Shed Blood of Jesus Christ cleanse from all sin, or does it not cleanse from all sin?"

It is said that a hush settled over the congregation.

Someone finally stood and almost in a whisper said, *"The Blood of Jesus Christ cleanses from all sin, and if it does not, all of us are in trouble."*

The elderly Sister then spoke again, saying, *"Then the matter is settled, when this young lady gave her heart and life to Christ, which we all know is the case, and which her life proves, she is just as clean as is possible for one to be, and this young man will be very blessed to have her as his wife."*

It is said that the Power of God fell on that congregation at that moment, and because what the lady said was right. The Blood of Jesus does cleanse from *all* sin (I Jn. 1:7).

In fact, John made it crystal clear, that the basis of *"fellowship one with another,"* is not based upon Denominational rituals or man-devised regulations, but rather that *". . . The Blood of Jesus Christ His* (God's) *Son cleanseth us from all sin"* (I Jn. 1:7). If we use anything else as a basis for fellowship, we have *". . . trodden under foot the Son of God, and hath counted the Blood of the Covenant wherewith he was Sanctified, an unholy thing, and hath done despite unto the Spirit of Grace"* (Heb. 10:29).

(4) "WHO ART THOU THAT JUDGEST ANOTHER MAN'S SERVANT? TO HIS OWN MASTER HE STANDETH OR FALLETH. YEA, HE SHALL BE HOLDEN UP: FOR GOD IS ABLE TO MAKE HIM STAND."

The question, *"Who art thou that judgest another man's servant?"*, in effect presents an emphatic statement presented as a question.

In the Greek, the word *"thou"* is emphasized, actually saying, *"As for you, who are you to judge God's Servant?"* This is almost identical to what James, the Lord's Brother, had written about 12 or 13 years earlier (James 4:12).

NOTES

OF WHAT TYPE OF JUDGING DOES PAUL SPEAK HERE?

Inasmuch as this is a very serious topic, and especially considering that this sin is so easily committed, I think an evaluation of the subject would be proper.

The sad thing is, many Christians think nothing about glibly judging another, which is in direct violation of the Word of God, and shows an acute misunderstanding or lack of knowledge, as to the grievousness of this sin, or what God says about the matter. Consequently, we will look at the subject from the perspective of both the Old and New Testaments.

We are plainly told in the New Testament, even as we are studying here, that we are not to judge another. Yet we are also told to maintain Church discipline! Does the Bible solve such puzzles? Yes it does!

THE OLD TESTAMENT CONCEPT OF JUDGING

Two Hebrew synonyms are translated *"judge"* and *"judgment"* in the Old Testament. *"Din"* is one of those words, and occurs 43 times, usually in the Psalms and the Prophets.

The other word is *"sapat,"* and means *"to judge, to govern."* This particular word also has a Hebrew derivative *"mispat,"* which means *"judgment, or decision."*

Each of these words expresses the idea of governing and implies every function of Government. Each includes executive and legislative as well as judicial functions.

In our modern culture the various functions of Government are divided, and the separation of powers is fiercely guarded. In the Old Testament world such departmentalization did not exist. A Ruler decided disputes and acquitted or punished the accused.

But the Ruler also had legislative and executive responsibility, as he led his people.

So we are misled if we think of the Biblical *"Judge"* only in a modern judicial sense. Like the *"Judges"* who ruled Israel after Joshua, such persons were Governors in the fullest sense. Consequently, when we read the word *"Judge"* in the Old Testament, we need to keep the broad meaning of *"rule"* or *"ruler"* in view.

GOD, THE ULTIMATE JUDGE

The Old Testament makes it clear that the Ultimate Ruler of the universe is God. All human governing authority is derived from Him. Often where the Old Testament speaks of God as Judge, it is His ultimate Sovereignty as Governor of the universe, not simply His role as Moral Arbiter, that is in view. We see this interplay clearly in Psalm 96:10-13, where God is pictured as *"Judge"* in all the rich meaning of that word.

"Say among the Nations, 'The Lord reigns.' The world is firmly established, it cannot be moved; He will judge the people with equity.

"Let the heavens rejoice, let the earth be glad; let the sea resound, and all that is in it; let the fields be jubilant, and everything in them. Then all the trees of the forest will sing for joy; they will sing before the Lord, for He comes, He comes to judge the earth. He will judge the world in Righteousness and the people in His Truth."

God's judicial acts are but one aspect of His Rule. To affirm God as Judge is to assert that He is Governor of all, not only with every right to command but also with responsibility to vindicate and to condemn.

THE NEW TESTAMENT CONCEPT

A single family of Greek words is used to express the many shades of meaning in the New Testament references to judging.

"Krino" is one word, and means one or more of the following in a given usage: to judge, evaluate, decide, assess, distinguish between, pronounce judgment, select, or prefer.

The whole process of evaluation is thus expressed by this one word, with the context helping to determine if the focus is on process or product.

Another Greek word is *"anakrino,"* and means *"to investigate or examine."*

Another is *"katakrino,"* and means *"to condemn." "Krites,"* means *"to be a judge,"* and *"krisis,"* means *"to come to a decision,"* with *"krima,"* meaning *"to arrive at a verdict."*

By New Testament times these words were entrenched in the legal system and are often used in the New Testament in reference to

some aspect of the judicial process — of bringing to trial, condemning, and punishing.

THE WORD *"JUDGE"*

But *"judge"* is not used in the New Testament only in a legal or semilegal way. This family of words is used where the Bible speaks of evaluating, considering, making a decision, approving, and preferring.

Still, when a word like *"judge"* or *"judgment"* has a number of possible meanings, it is easy to become confused, as many Christians are about the Bible's teaching concerning judging others. The best way to develop our understanding of what the Bible teaches on this important subject is to examine key Passages in the New Testament.

GOD ALONE IS JUDGE

The New Testament, like the Old Testament, strongly affirms God as ultimately the only qualified Judge. Consequently, all Believers must understand that our judgment at best is faulty; therefore, even at times when a judgment is necessary, we should always understand and consider how limited we are in knowledge, and at the same time how unworthy all of us are to attempt to judge anything, even though at times such is required.

James emphasizes the Old Testament concept of a judge as a ruler when he writes, *"There is only One Lawgiver and Judge, the One Who is able to save and destroy. But you — who are you to judge your neighbour?"* (James 4:12).

In this dominant legal or judicial sense, only God has the right or knowledge to judge (Jn. 8:15-16). All will have to *". . . give an account to Him Who is ready to judge the living and the dead"* (II Tim. 4:1, 8; Heb. 10:30; 12:23; 13:4; I Pet. 4:5).

The fact that God Alone is competent to pronounce judgment on human beings is basic to our grasp of what the Bible says about judging, and should never be forgotten.

THE MANNER IN WHICH GOD JUDGES

Even though God is the Ultimate Judge, and does so with perfect Righteousness and Knowledge, yet He is not eager to judge. This is borne out in Scripture. John writes that Jesus was sent into the world, not to condemn (judge), but so that all who believe might be Saved (Jn. 3:17).

The verdict of condemnation is passed on the lost by their own condition and actions. Jesus, the Light, has come into the world; those who love darkness will reject Him and turn away (Jn. 3:19-21). The Father *". . . has entrusted all judgment to the Son"* (Jn. 5:22).

A person's response to Jesus has become the dividing line between life and death (Jn. 5:19-30). So Jesus announced to the crowds during the week of His Death: *"As for the person who hears My Words but does not keep them, I do not judge him. For I did not come to judge the world, but to save it. There is a Judge for the one who rejects Me and does not accept My Words; that very Word which I spoke will condemn him at the last day. For I did not speak of My Own accord, but the Father Who sent Me commanded Me what to say and how to say it"* (Jn. 12:47-49).

GOD'S KINDNESS

Romans picks up the theme and portrays God, moved by kindness, waiting patiently in order that people will respond and repent (Rom. 2:4). *"But for those who are self-seeking and who reject the Truth and follow evil, there will be wrath and anger"* (Rom. 2:8).

Those who reject the Divine Pardon must in the end stand before God as Judge. In that Judgment based on evaluation of each person's works (Rev. 20:12), *"God will give to each person according to what he has done"* (Rom. 2:6).

Those who know the Revealed Law of God will be judged by its Standard. But even those who do not know the Will of God as unveiled in the Written Word have *"the requirements of the Law . . . written on their hearts . . ."* (Rom. 2:15), so they are without excuse.

God has created human beings with a moral sense, which gives inner testimony to right and wrong. Tragically, human beings are so warped by sin that the inner witness accuses but does not lead to righteous living.

And so the day is coming when God will act as the Moral Governor of our universe.

NOTES

He will put aside His Patience to carry out the verdict that people pronounce against themselves by their actions and by their refusal to accept God's Pardon in Jesus, for Jesus is always the End of all things.

WHAT ARE WE NOT TO JUDGE?

In affirming God as Judge, the Scripture also limits those ways in which human beings are to judge others. A number of Passages help us understand the limitations:

Matthew 7:1-2; Luke 6:37-38: The verses in Matthew record Jesus' warning as follows: *"Do not judge, or you too will be judged. For in the same way you judge others, you will be judged, and with the measure you use, it will be measured to you."*

The thought is that we must not assume the right to condemn others. Luke adds, *". . . Forgive, and you will be forgiven."* The faults of others are to occasion forgiveness, not condemnation, or else we bring to a halt God's Mercy and Grace extended to us personally, which is a frightful thing.

Romans 2:1-3: Paul speaks passionately of passing judgment on others. He warns, *". . . At whatever point you judge the other, you are condemning yourself. . . ."*

MORAL SUPERIORITY?

To pass judgment implies the assumption of a moral superiority that we simply do not possess. We have all failed, and even continue to fail at times; no human being is able to judge others without becoming vulnerable to the same judgment.

Romans 14:1-18: Paul looks at convictions in the Christian community, even as we are now studying. Then, as today, Believers differed about what was right to eat or drink or do. While each person should develop his or her own convictions based on the Word of God, and live by them, no one has the right to look down on or condemn a Brother or Sister for his or her practices. If something is obviously unscriptural, it should be addressed; however, still, it must be done with Love, Patience, Mercy, and Concern.

Paul says we must see Jesus as sole Lord and each other as His servants. So each Believer is responsible to the Lord, not to the conscience of other Christians. Paul does appeal for unity. But Christian unity is based on: A. The freedom of each individual to be responsible to Jesus; B. A nonjudgmental approach to differences of conviction; and, C. A willingness to consider others when deciding whether or not to use one's freedom to follow one's own convictions.

I Corinthians 4:3-5: Paul himself was being judged by Believers in Corinth. He wrote, *"I care very little if I am judged by you or by any human court. . . ."* The Greek word here is *"anakrino,"* and refers to undertaking an investigative process that is intended to lead to a verdict.

Paul rejected the right of the Corinthians to convene such a court or call his faithfulness as Jesus' servant into question. Paul, though his conscience was clear, was not even competent to judge himself and his possibly hidden motives. What were Paul's conclusions?

". . . It is the Lord Who judges me," he said; *"therefore judge nothing before the appointed time; wait till the Lord comes. . . ."*

I Corinthians 5:12: Paul taught the Corinthians not to relate to non-Christians in a judgmental way. Their sins might be many, but it is not the business of Christians to *"judge those outside the Church."* The issue in the case of unbelievers is not their morality but their relationship with Christ. When Jesus enters their lives, their practices will change (I Cor. 6:9-11).

Colossians 2:16: Judging creates pressure that is designed to force conformity. Paul urges the Believers in Colosse to resist this kind of thing. It denies not only Christian freedom but also Jesus' Lordship.

"Therefore do not let anyone judge you by what you eat or drink, or with regard to a religious festival, a New Moon Celebration or a Sabbath Day."

James 4:11-12: James sees a critical approach to others as slander.

Talking against our Brothers is wrong because it implies becoming a judge of the Law rather than a doer. James' argument is that God gave us the Law, not to use against others, but that we might be responsive to it on a personal basis.

Only God, Who as Governor of the universe

gave the Law, has the right to judge human beings by the Law.

SCRIPTURE CONDEMNS SUCH ACTIONS

In each of these Passages we have just given as examples, *"judging"* carries quasi-legal meanings. The choices or the motives of others are called into question, and a condemning verdict is passed in each. Each part of this process is ruled out by the Scriptures we have given.

Human beings are not competent to call another's motives or practices into question. Even when actions are clearly wrong, forgiveness, not condemnation, is the appropriate response. A judgmental attitude and punitive attempts are both wrong. We are to draw back, remembering that God Alone is competent to judge, and to stop judging others.

WHAT ARE WE COMMANDED TO JUDGE?

Christians are not to judge others, as I hope by now is obvious. But this does not mean that we are not to use the capacity God has given us to evaluate and make judgments. It does not even mean that *"judging"* is wrong in every single circumstance!

Romans 13:1-7: God has established human Government. He has given to Governing Authorities responsibility for all functions of rule, including the judicial functions. Thus, the administration of Criminal and Civil Law by Judges is a right and a responsibility delegated to organized society. The Ruler is *". . . God's servant, an agent of wrath to bring punishment on the wrongdoer."*

I Corinthians 2:15: Paul says, that *"The spiritual man makes judgments about all things, but he himself is not subject to any man's judgment."*

The Greek word here is *"anakrino,"* and means *"to examine or discern."* Believers possess God's Holy Spirit, and they also have been given the very Mind of Christ. Believers can thus evaluate from the Divine perspective and can also sense God's individual guidance.

I Corinthians 5:12-13: Is the Church to stand in judgment on fellow Believers? The apparent contradiction is resolved when we understand the nature of Church discipline, which we will address momentarily.

I Corinthians 6:2-5: The fellowship of Believers in Corinth was being marred by some of the Believers taking their disputes into secular Law Courts. Paul urges Christians to ask other Believers to serve as a panel to resolve such *"trivial matters"* rather than go to Court before unbelievers.

I Corinthians 10:15; 11:13: Paul's exhortation *"Judge for yourselves . . ."* suggests here that the right answer is obvious. But not every matter Christians are called on to examine has an obvious answer. However, God expects us to examine the issues of our lives and develop convictions based on principles found in God's Word.

I Corinthians 11:31-32: Paul calls on us to judge ourselves. He points out that at times God disciplines us because we have not evaluated our own actions, recognized them as sin, and confessed the sin.

"If we judge ourselves," he writes, *"we would not come under judgment."*

CHURCH DISCIPLINE

Some of the following material on Church Discipline has been given in other of our Commentaries. But due to the significance of this subject, I feel it proper to repeat at least some of the information.

In I Corinthians Chapter 5, Paul expresses shock because the Corinthians were passively accepting sexual immorality, with the perpetrator not at all showing any sign of repentance.

Looking at this case, Paul wrote, *"I have already passed judgment on the one who did this, just as if I were present,"* and he goes on to command, *"When you are assembled in the Name of our Lord Jesus . . . hand this man over to Satan."* The Believers are *"not to associate with anyone who calls himself a Brother,"* and consistently practices sin; Paul says, *"With such a man do not even eat."*

Looking at this, we must square what Paul has said, and rightly so, with the many New Testament Passages that tell Christians not to judge one another.

GOD AS THE MORAL ARBITER

The answer is found in the affirmation of

Scripture that God is the Ruler of the universe and is the final moral Arbiter. He, the Judge, had already announced His verdict on the practices of which Paul was writing.

He had identified these practices as sin. As such, what the Church is called on to do is to agree with God in the Divine assessment of the actions of this one who *"calls himself a Brother."* As a community, the Church is to *". . . expel the wicked . . ."* from its fellowship, and of course this speaks of those who refuse to repent (I Cor. 5:13).

Condemning someone by calling into question that person's motives, actions, or personal convictions is vastly different from accepting God's verdict that certain actions are sins and that those who practice them, refusing to stop, must be ostracized.

A number of aspects of New Testament Church Discipline help us understand Paul's insistence that the immoral person be expelled. Please note the following:

THE CHOICE TO PRACTICE SIN

What necessitates discipline is an individual's choice to practice what the Bible identifies as sin, and who refuses to stop.

The Truth is, that all of us may fail often and have to come to the Lord in confession. For this there is no call for discipline. Discipline is applied only when a person refuses to acknowledge that his practices are sin and refuses to change his ways.

RESTORATION

Even when discipline must be entered into by the Church, the goal of such discipline must always be Restoration and certainly not destruction.

In the case mentioned by Paul, *"The punishment inflicted on him* (the offender) *by the majority . . . ,"* in withdrawing fellowship (II Cor. 2:6) was sufficient, and the guilty man repented.

Paul then called on the Corinthians to accept him back and *"to reaffirm their love for him"* (II Cor. 2:8).

(Some claim this is not the same man; however, irrespective, the principle is the same.)

SPIRITUAL REALITY

The rationale for Church Discipline is

found in spiritual reality.

Sin in fact alienates from God, cutting off the individual from fellowship (I Jn. 1:6). As stated, we are speaking of one who practices sin, and refuses to repent.

In Church Discipline, the Body of Christ acts out this spiritual reality in its relationship with the sinner. A person expelled from the local community (Church) senses the fact of lost fellowship, and hopefully will be induced to repent.

THE PRACTICE OF SIN

The occasion for Church Discipline, and the only occasion, is moral fault: the practice of sin. The Church is not permitted to discipline for other deviations.

Difference in convictions or even doctrinal differences do not call for Church Discipline. It is only the consistent practice of sin without acknowledgment of the fault that occasions discipline.

THE MANNER OF PROCEDURE

The responsibility for Church Discipline rests on the local Church, and not some far off headquarters, etc. The ones who are familiar with the situation and circumstances should be the ones to attend to the matter. Matthew 18:15-17 is generally understood to outline a process that Christians should follow.

An offended person should approach the sinner and explain the fault. One or two members of the congregation should go with the first member if the sinning Saint refuses to listen. The whole Church is to be informed if the individual still refuses to listen.

Then the person is to be ostracized (disfellowshiped). This joint responsibility is reflected also in Corinthians, where Paul writes of expelling the sinning person when the Church is ". . . *assembled in the Name of our Lord Jesus . . .*" (I Cor. 5:4).

DISCIPLINE AND JUDGING

Exercising Church Discipline is very different from adopting the judgmental and condemning attitude against which Scripture speaks. In Church Discipline we see the loving action (or at least it should be loving) of the Christian community, committed to obedience, in tending through the Discipline to

NOTES

help the Brother or Sister turn from sin and find renewed fellowship with the Lord.

Every Christian has a need for wisdom to make judgments about how to live from day-to-day. How wonderful to know that God through His Word has already equipped us to judge. By judging only those things that God calls on us to judge and by refusing to be trapped into judging others, we will be enabled to live productive and peaceful lives.

(The material on Judging was derived from Lawrence O. Richards.)

The phrase, *"To his own master he standeth or falleth,"* refers to the fact that the Lord is the *"Master"* of all His Children, and as such, is the One Who is the final Judge. Two things are said here:

1. It is only God Who has the power, and Who extends that power to His Children, which enables any of us to *"stand."*

2. It is God Who is the final Judge in all these matters, and it is what He says that counts, and *only* what He says that counts. As we have said several times, *"The stands may cheer or the stands may jeer, but it is the man in the striped suit who calls the game."*

Even though this is the case irrespective of what people say or do, still, the idea is that Believers should conduct themselves accordingly. If the Word of God does not back up what is said or done, then it has no Scriptural validity. But sadly, many Believers, and especially some so-called Church Leaders, all too often make up their own rules, which have no Scriptural validity. The tragedy is, that most of the Laity follows without question.

Many are very quick to allude to certain individuals as *"fallen,"* when there is no Scriptural validity for such. What those people should readily understand, is that whatever sentence we judgmentally pass, has absolutely no bearing whatsoever on that which is reality. Beside that, the ones who falsely accuse or falsely sentence, only hurt themselves and the Work of God. It is God Who says, *"He stands,"* or *"He is fallen!"* As well, it is clearly spelled out in God's Word as to who stands or falls. It is not nearly as elusive as one might think.

TRUSTING CHRIST

No one in the Bible is judged as *"fallen,"*

who continues to trust Christ. It is only the person who discontinues that privilege who is judged as *"fallen."*

For instance, Peter failed miserably in denying Christ just hours before the Crucifixion. However, he continued to trust Christ, consequently, was forgiven, and continued in the Lord.

By contrast, Judas ceased to trust Christ and, therefore, was *"fallen."* Actually, the Scripture says, *". . . From which Judas by transgression fell . . ."* (Acts 1:25).

No matter what the sin has been, if the Believer goes before the Lord in humble confession and contrition, Mercy and Grace are always extended, with the individual instantly restored (I Jn. 1:9).

In fact, were this not the case, every single Believer on the face of the earth who has ever lived, would be concluded as *"fallen,"* because all have failed at one time or the other (I Jn. 1:10).

FAILURE AND FALLEN

Many Believers get the two confused. As we have stated, every Christian sadly and regrettably has failed the Lord many times, consequently, having to go to Him, confessing the wrong, asking for Mercy and Grace. As we have also stated, He never fails respecting forgiveness, that is, if we are sincerely repentant (I Jn. 1:9).

To fail the Lord in any capacity is very grievous; however, that in no way means that one is fallen. So, no Believer should confuse the issue.

To address the subject on a personal note, it is somewhat confusing to me how that Believers, who on a personal basis have had to ask forgiveness from the Lord many times, are very quick to deny others the same privilege, rather referring to them as *"fallen."* Perhaps they are thinking of certain types of sin.

While some sins are definitely worse than others, still, if a person truly trusts the Lord, the Scripture does not limit forgiveness to any particular sins. The Scripture plainly tells us, *"The Blood of Jesus Christ His* (God's) *Son cleanseth us from all sin"* (I Jn. 1:7).

For instance, David failed the Lord and failed miserably, respecting two awful sins, adultery and murder. However, as grievous as

these sins were, and they were grievous to the very extent of utter failure, still, David in the Eyes of God was not *"fallen,"* simply because he continued to trust the Lord (Ps. 51).

This is not to say that there were no grievous ramifications to these sins, as there are to all sin. Even though God readily forgives, the idea that sin does not have severe penalties is foolish indeed! However, those penalties are never to be leveled by other Believers, but only by God.

Absalom thought he would take advantage of this particular situation and dethrone his Father. In fact, he had the majority of Israel on his side. David had failed and failed miserably; therefore, this was the opportunity of his ambitious son to take the Throne by force, even though God had not called him for such. Unfortunately, failure such as David's, also exposes what is in the hearts of others. Oftentimes, even as with Absalom and much of Israel, it was not good. It cost Absalom his life, as well as the lives of many Israelites. The Lord plainly says, *"Touch not Mine Anointed, and do My Prophets no harm"* (Ps. 105:15). Israel forgot that, and suffered greatly! Regrettably, Israel has not been the only one to fall into such a trap.

THE MEANING OF THE WORD *"FALLEN"*

There are a number of Greek words whether in the form of nouns or verbs which pertain to the words *"fall," "fallen," "falling," "fell."* We will look at these words as they apply to the subject at hand.

The first Greek word is *"ptosis,"* and is used metaphorically by Luke of the spiritual fall of those in Israel who would reject Christ (Lk. 2:34). The fall would be irretrievable, as should be obvious. If one refuses to trust Christ, there remains no other direction.

Another Greek word is *"paraptoma,"* and refers to this subject of the sin and downfall of Israel in their refusal to acknowledge God's claims in His Christ; by reason of this the offer of Salvation was made to Gentiles (Rom. 11:11-12).

"Apostasia," means *"a defection, revolt, or apostasy,"* and literally means *"a falling away from the Faith,"* which once again refers to a falling away from Christ (II Thess. 2:3).

"Ekpipto," refers to falling from Grace due to placing dependence in the Law, i.e., *"works"* (Gal. 5:4).

"Peripipto," is another Greek word which means *"a falling away from the realities and facts of the Faith"* (Heb. 6:6).

"Aphistemi," means *"to apostatize,"* which again, refers to falling away from the Faith (I Tim. 4:1; Heb. 3:12).

"Parabaino," means *"to fall away"* as Judas (Acts 1:25).

"Pipto," refers to Revelation 2:5, and speaks of one falling from his First Love, and refusing to repent.

In essence, all of these Greek words which refer to *"fall," "fallen," "falling,"* and *"fell,"* speak of departing from Christ, and in a more direct sense, ceasing to trust Him.

So, as stated, there is a vast difference in one who has *"failed,"* even as Peter did, and in fact, all Believers have at one time or the other, and one who has *"fallen,"* as Judas did. The one who fails continues to trust Christ, while the one who falls ceases to trust Christ, and is, therefore, lost.

The phrase, *"Yea, he shall be holden up: for God is able to make him stand,"* has reference to the fact that God is the only One Who can do this and not man. The idea is that God is powerful to sustain His Children, and to God Alone the Believer is accountable.

Having already addressed the principle of accountability, we will not do such again, at least here; however, this plainly tells us that it is to God Alone that man is truly accountable. The idea is, if man is faithful to God, he will also be faithful to his fellowman, in that he will always be careful to pay him the love *"owed"* (Rom. 13:8).

GOD IS ABLE

The three words *"God is able"* carry with them the all-encompassing power that God is able, irrespective of the problem, the difficulty, the opposition, or in other words whatever man or Satan can do. The only manner in which God can be limited, is that we limit Him by unbelief (Ps. 78:41). Faith in God, produces the Ableness or Power of God.

Consequently, the Believer must look to the Lord, and not other men, that is, if he is to receive the help which God Alone can give.

MODERN PSYCHOLOGY

Since the 1950's much of the modern Church has experienced a gradual slide (and sometimes not so gradual) toward Modern Psychology. I say *"modern"* simply because this idea (psychotherapy) was basically given birth by Sigmund Freud in the 1880's. Many so-called Church Leaders, losing Faith in Christ and His Word, have opted for this religion (Faith?) of humanism. (The Philosophy of Humanism asserts the dignity and worth of man and his capacity for self-realization through reason, which rejects God, His Word, and anything that is supernatural.) All of this is promoted while the Bible plainly says that *"God* (Alone) *is able to make him* (Believers) *stand."*

Many in the modern Church would claim that God uses Psychology, etc. My answer to that is in the form of a question:

What did the Lord use before the advent of this nefarious shamanism? As well, another question comes to mind. Does God need help from humanists? Another question may be asked: *"Is that which was done by Christ at Calvary and the Resurrection a Finished Work, or does it need something added?"*

TWELVE-STEP PROGRAMS

A short time back a secular Cartoonist portrayed his observation of the 12-step programs used in the world of Psychology.

He drew the 12 steps leading upward, even as steps normally do, but pictured the last step as a precipice down to the floor, where many devotees of this Philosophy conclude.

It is amazing that this secular Cartoonist could see this, while many so-called Church Leaders cannot.

In the January 5th, 1997 issue of the *"Pentecostal Evangel,"* the weekly Publication of the Assemblies of God, the advertisement on page seven recommends a Christ-centered, 12-step Program, as they put it, for those addicted to alcohol and drugs.

How can a program be Christ-centered, when its victims (and victims they are) are told that first of all they must put their trust and confidence in a *"higher power."* However, they are quick to explain that this

NOTES

"higher power," can be Mohammed, Jesus Christ, Buddha, the Virgin Mary, or a big tree if they so like.

The Truth is, there is no help in these programs. In fact, anything that deals with the human need respecting spirituality, answers can be found only in Christ. The price He paid at Calvary and the Resurrection was total and complete. Irrespective as to what the bondage, the sin, or the aberration may be, the only answer is Jesus, and He does not need other types of help, which in Truth are no help.

One cannot have it two ways. Jesus either paid it all at Calvary, thereby setting the captive free, at least for those who believe, or else He did not do so, and His Salvation needs help. I believe that He did pay the price, and that it was and is complete (Jer. 33:3; Mat. 11:28-30; Lk. 4:17-19; Jn. 3:16; 10:10; Rom. 14:4; II Pet. 1:3-4; etc.)

WHY CANNOT CHRISTIANITY AND PSYCHOLOGY BE MIXED?

The answer to that is very simple.

One is totally of God, and the other is totally of man.

Anyone who knows the Bible at all, and so-called Religious Leaders certainly should, know and understand, that Salvation is all of God. The moment that man tries to insert his own efforts into Salvation in any capacity, it not only does not help, but immediately nullifies the Work of God and the help which God Alone can give (Eph. 2:8-9). So, the idea that Secular Psychology can be mixed with Christian Faith in order to make one's Christianity more viable, and, consequently, more helpful, violates the very foundation of the Word of God, which should be readily understood by any serious Bible Student (II Pet. 1:3-4).

The Truth is this:

1. Most Preachers do not know the Bible.

2. What little they do know, they simply do not believe.

The Truth is, that it is Biblically impossible to mix the two. The attempt to do so, only leaves a watered-down Christianity, which in fact, is no Christianity at all.

IS PSYCHOLOGY A TRUE SCIENCE?

No!

NOTES

I think I can probably say without fear of contradiction, that most who claim that Psychology is a Science, are those who are trying to parade under the guise of Christendom, in other words, a wolf in sheep's clothing (Mat. 7:13-20).

The idea is, that if something is truly scientific, then it must be true. However, Psychology is exactly what Paul said, *"Science falsely so called"* (I Tim. 6:20).

All True Science is based on Mathematics. The reason is simple, and to use a trite adage, *"Liars may figure, but figures do not lie."* In other words, no matter what Atheists or anyone else of that ilk may attempt to do, two and two is still four. These are Laws laid down by God, and these Laws uphold His Creation, and cannot be changed.

If one has any knowledge of Psychology whatsoever, one knows that it is filled with theories which blatantly oppose each other.

"Psyche" as in Psychology, is derived from the Greek word *"psuche,"* which means *"soul"* (Ps. 107:9; Mat. 10:28; 22:37; Acts 2:27; Eph. 6:6; etc.) However, from 25 to 50 percent of Psychologists (according to what poll is correct) claim to be Atheists. Consequently, they little believe that man has a soul, at least in the realm of that which pertains to God. So, Psychology, ignoring the true meaning of the word, turns it into a study of the mind.

The way that Psychology attempts to add the word Science or Scientific to this Philosophy is as it regards *"symptoms."* In fact, Psychology is expert in its definition of symptoms. People with certain aberrations act a certain way, and because this is true in any case, or at least most, some people erroneously think that Psychology is truly scientific because it predicts these symptoms with a degree of accuracy. In fact, almost all of the claims in this realm pertain to predictions in this capacity. In other words, Pavlov's dog will respond the same way each time, if certain things are done.

THE CAUSE!

However, when it comes to the *cause* of man's aberrations and problems, the world of Psychology does not have a clue. The Bible teaches that the problem in any case, is inside of man, i.e., a wicked, evil heart (Jer. 17:9). In fact, Jesus plainly pointed to the cause of man's problems, when He said, *"For out of the <u>heart</u> proceed evil thoughts, murders, adulteries, fornications, thefts, false witness, blasphemies: these are the things which defile a man . . ."* (Mat. 15:19-20).

Psychology teaches the very opposite, that man's problems are all caused by external forces. In other words, the Bible teaches that all men are evil and must have a change of heart, which can only be brought about by the Lord Jesus Christ, while Psychology teaches that all men are basically good, and have been made evil, if in fact they are, by outside forces, etc. Consequently, the very premise of the teaching of this philosophy is totally antagonistic to the Word of God, which means in no way can the two be joined or melded.

Not only does Psychology not know the *cause*, neither does it have a *cure*. In fact, and as stated, it only knows and understands symptoms.

However, telling a person as to how he is going to act under certain circumstances, is not really helping him.

IN FACT, WHAT HELP DOES PSYCHOLOGY (PSYCHOTHERAPY) OFFER?

None!

It not only does not help and because it cannot help, but it actually harms the person, in leading them away from the only help there is, the Word of God and a reliance on Christ. I want to be bold with my statement, simply because it is true. I do not want the Reader to misunderstand what I say.

The world of Psychology is a lie. It is a lie because it is based on other than the Word of God. The father of it is a lie, and its practitioners are liars. Now you know and understand why I am not too well liked in most of the Religious Community. However, what I am trying to point out is this:

It is understandable that the world would reach for this false hope, for the simple reason that they have no other. But it is not understandable at all, how those who call themselves *"Christians,"* and above all, *"Spiritual Leaders,"* at the same time, could recommend this shamanism to fellow Believers.

Once again, if they truly believe the Bible, how could they do such a thing?

Does the Reader know and understand, that the world of Psychology has no medicine or antibiotics of any nature that they can prescribe? (Psychiatrists who are also Medical Doctors, can prescribe medicines, etc. However, their prescriptions, at least as it pertains to the mind, are at least one of the greatest causes of prescription drug addition. Actually, this problem is so acute in America, that there are twice as many prescription addicts than the street variety — 12 million and 6 million respectively.)

So, if the Psychologist cannot prescribe medicines, etc., what can he do?

Talk!

That's right, the only thing he has to offer is talk.

The Reader must consider and understand, that if the problem of mankind, which is an evil nature, can be talked away, then why did Jesus have to come down from Heaven and die on a cruel Cross?

In fact, this problem of sin is so awful, so terrible, that even God could not speak it out of existence, even though He had the Power to speak Creation into existence (Gen. Chpt. 1). That should tell us something.

So, in the realm of *"talk"* what can they say or do?

Some label themselves as *"Christian Psychologists,"* which incidentally, is a misnomer, for there is not such a thing. There may be Psychologists who are Christians, but there is no such thing as *"Christian Psychology."* Such simply does not exist.

These particular Psychologists practice the latest theory on their patients (victims), whatever that might be, until it is proven wrong, as it always is. What might these theories be?

Just about anything that one could begin to imagine.

Some time back, a Reporter for a major magazine in the United States told me that her next assignment was to write a story on the latest fad (latest then) which was all the rage in Psychological Therapy at that time.

I asked her what it was, and she smiled and said, *"All those who participate in this therapy, completely disrobe and sit around* in a circle. They close their eyes and then reach out and feel of each other."

I asked her as to how that could help anyone? She laughed, shaking her head in the negative, in essence saying, *"I don't know."*

The right word for that is *"stupid!"*

BUT WHAT ABOUT CHRISTIAN PSYCHOLOGISTS?

Many so-called Christian Psychologists attempt to paper their efforts with some type of Biblical or Spiritual jargon. I will give you an example.

Richard Dobbins, a practicing Psychologist and also an ordained Minister with the Assemblies of God, in his book *"Your Spiritual and Emotional Power"* wrote, respecting the type of counseling that he does, etc.

He said, *"Learn to create Bible scenes in your mind when you are anxious or afraid. The Word of God is filled with restful, relaxing scenes. Often, calm can be restored to an anxious person through effective use of mental imagery. That is how I was able to help Gail.*

"In getting acquainted with Gail, I discovered she was very imaginative. Most people who are anxious and fearful have active imaginations, but they are focused on the wrong kind of mental images. Wanting her to discover how her imagination could work for her rather than against her, I asked, 'Gail, what are your three favorite Bible scenes?' She listed them: 'The Twenty-Third Psalm, the Good Shepherd and the one lost sheep, and Jesus calming the storm on Lake Galilee.'

"'Good,' I said, 'Now I want these scenes to minister to you. First, I want you to take three deep breaths.'

"When she had finished her deep-breathing exercises, dropped her shoulders, and closed her eyes, I suggested, 'While your eyes are closed and you are enjoying such a good relaxed feeling, why don't you picture in your mind the one Bible scene you like most. When you have it in focus, tell me which one it is.'

"Gail's first choice was the Twenty-third Psalm. She worked with that scene until she could picture the green pastures, locate the stream, see the surrounding hills, hear

NOTES

the sound of the Shepherd's staff and the bleating of the sheep. I also helped her to develop the ability to fix her other favorite Bible scenes in her imagination.

"Gail was instructed to take a few moments before leaving the house to recreate one of these scenes in her mind. Then I reminded her that each of them emphasized the reality of Christ's Presence with her everywhere she went. By beginning to focus on an awareness of God's Presence and assuring herself that she could do all things through Christ (Phil. 4:13), she was able to drive to her sessions after the first five weeks. By that time, she was also able to shop more comfortably."

CAN THE READER HERE SEE WHAT IS BEING DONE?

To those who have little understanding of the Word of God, the above advice may seem to be practical and helpful. However, in reality, Dr. Dobbins is plain and simple portraying in the words of the Apostle Paul *"another Christ"* (II Cor. 11:4).

This is another form of mind-science called Mental Imagery. It is used by all the Cults and New Agers, and is in fact occultic. Using the Bible in this fashion, only deepens the error, and in no way makes it legitimate.

I do not know what was wrong with Gail, but I do know what Paul said, and what he said is the answer to her dilemma, as well as the dilemma of all others, *"For I am not ashamed of the Gospel of Christ: for it is the Power of God unto Salvation to every one that believeth . . ."* (Rom. 1:16).

The *"Power of God"* is the solution for hurting humanity, and not mental images. Paul here spoke of *"believing"* the Word of God, and that means believing what it says to us and about us. It does not say anything about Mental Imagery, at least in the way that it is advocated by this Psychologist.

An excellent place to start for those who are fearful or heavy laden as Gail, is found in the Words of Jesus. He said, *"Come unto Me, all ye that labour and are heavy laden, and I will give you rest. Take my yoke upon you, and learn of Me; for I am meek and lowly in heart: and ye shall find rest unto your souls"* (Mat. 11:28-29).

Believing on and learning of Him will supply the *"rest,"* not some type of mental exercise which has its roots in Eastern Religions, and is, therefore, of the Devil.

All of these things are solved by the Power of God, and Faith in the Power of God.

The True Gospel still works! There are literally hundreds of millions of people in the world at this present time, who have been delivered by the Power of God from every type of bondage. Untold millions have been set free, liberated by the Gospel of Jesus Christ. It was done without any Psychology, and in fact where Psychology is mixed with the Gospel, the Gospel is instantly nullified. As we began this statement on Psychology, we will close this statement on Psychology.

Either what Jesus Christ did at Calvary's Cross and the Resurrection is a Finished Work, which means total and complete, with nothing needed to be added, or else it is not a Finished Work, and needs the help of Freud, Maslow, and Rodgers, etc.

Thank you kindly, but I believe it is a Finished Work. You can have the prattle of those mentioned, but as for me and my house, we will take Matthew, Mark, Luke, and John, etc.

"God is able to make him stand."

(5) "ONE MAN ESTEEMETH ONE DAY ABOVE ANOTHER: ANOTHER ESTEEMETH EVERY DAY ALIKE. LET EVERY MAN BE FULLY PERSUADED IN HIS OWN MIND."

The phrase, *"One man esteemeth one day above another,"* is actually referring back to the Jewish Sabbaths. Actually, no particular Sabbath is commanded in the New Testament. In fact, *nothing* in the Christian Faith is of a legal or statutory nature, not even the observance of Sunday. That observance originated in Faith, and because it is the day on which Jesus arose, it cannot be what it should be except it be maintained by Faith.

In other words, Christianity is not in any manner an observance of rules or regulations, etc. It is purely and simply by Faith. What do we mean by that?

I am not Saved, and neither do I have Holiness nor Sanctification, nor Victory of any nature, because I keep certain rules, do certain things, or observe certain things, but rather because I have Faith in what Christ

has already done at Calvary's Cross. Paul plainly said if it is works, it is not of Faith and if it is of Faith, it cannot be of works (Rom. 3:27-28; 11:6).

The phrase, *"Another esteemeth every day alike,"* in effect says, *"Judge every day, that is, subject every day to moral scrutiny."* Actually this is the proper course.

The phrase, *"Let every man be fully persuaded in his own mind,"* means to be fully convinced or assured. The idea is this:

The Holy Spirit through the Apostle is not speaking of things which are morally wrong, and which the Word of God has already condemned. That being discussed pertains to particulars which have no bearing morally on anyone whether it is done or not. So, the Apostle is saying, if a person feels he should do a certain thing or not do a certain thing which pertains basically to a ritual only, he should do what he feels he ought to do. However, he should not try to impose his own particular conviction regarding these matters on others. In other words, let the Believer be content by being *"persuaded in his own mind,"* and not try to persuade others.

(6) "HE THAT REGARDETH THE DAY, REGARDETH IT UNTO THE LORD; AND HE THAT REGARDETH NOT THE DAY, TO THE LORD HE DOTH NOT REGARD IT. HE THAT EATETH, EATETH TO THE LORD, FOR HE GIVETH GOD THANKS; AND HE THAT EATETH NOT, TO THE LORD HE EATETH NOT, AND GIVETH GOD THANKS."

The phrase, *"He that regardeth the day, regardeth it unto the Lord,"* means that the Believer, whatever type of ritual he may be attempting to keep, is supposed to be doing it unto the Lord, and not for some personal satisfaction, etc.

The phrase, *"And he that regardeth not the day, to the Lord he doth not regard it,"* actually has the same meaning as the previous phrase. The interest of the Lord should be in view in either case.

For his own personal reasons, which he feels the Lord wants him to do, one regards a particular ritual as being pleasing to the Lord for him to keep. The other addresses the same ritual, whatever it may be, and feels that his Faith in Christ has nothing to do with that particular thing, consequently, ignoring it. As stated, both are to have the same end in view — namely, the interest of the Lord. However, again we emphasize, one must not attempt to impose one's convictions in these matters on others.

The phrase, *"He that eateth, eateth to the Lord, for he giveth God thanks,"* proclaims that what he is doing is unto the Lord; his Faith is sufficient and whatever the food might be, is of no consequence.

The phrase, *"And he that eateth not, to the Lord he eateth not, and giveth God thanks,"* once again, exactly as stated in the previous Scripture, has the same end in view, or at least it should — to please the Lord.

One may wonder why Paul would devote this much space to that which seems to be inconsequential?

The Truth is, even as Paul says, these things are inconsequential; however, the problem is, many Believers make much out of these situations, which causes all type of problems in the Church, and individually as well.

Problems of this nature are caused because of a lack of Faith, and a lack of Faith is caused by a lack of knowledge of the Word of God.

LET ME GIVE A PERSONAL EXAMPLE

When Frances and I first began in Evangelistic Work back in 1956, after a period of time the Lord made it possible for me to record our music and offer it to the people in the Churches. Actually, He told me to do so.

He had given me the talent to play the piano, and as well, to sing, and above all, to be led by the Spirit in doing so, which has been a blessing to people, for which we give the Lord all the Praise and Glory.

As well, what little profit there was from the sale of these items, actually made it possible to remain in Evangelistic Work, for the simple reason that the offerings in most Churches were very small. This in no way is meant to demean the Pastor or the people of these Churches, for in many cases, they were giving all they could give, for which we were very thankful. But the fact remained, that with that alone I am not sure if we could have remained on the field, simply not having enough funds to even sustain ourselves. So, the profit from the sale of the recordings

NOTES

was very helpful, and the recordings were a blessing to the people.

The recordings were set up in the lobby of the Church, and Frances would serve the people respecting which recordings they wanted, if any, etc. If I mentioned them at all during the Service it would only be to just simply tell the people they were there.

In one particular Church, the Pastor told me that I could not set the recordings up in the lobby or anywhere in the Church for that matter. Of course we were not there for the purpose of selling recordings, we were there to preach and to see a Move of God in the Church, which incidentally, the Lord helped us to see greatly so in this particular Church.

He finally gave his consent, but his reasons for his attitude is what I want to call to your attention.

A LACK OF KNOWING THE WORD OF GOD

When at first he told me that it would not be permissible to set up the recordings, which were actually very few in number and took up very little room, I asked him *"Why?"*

His answer was, *"This is the House of God, and nothing should be sold here."*

He was older than I and respecting his age, I answered him very carefully.

Very kindly I told him, *"Sir, a Church Building is not the House of God, it is merely a place to keep out the weather."* I then said, *"We (Believers) are the House of God, not a Building"* (I Cor. 3:16).

To be frank, he was not too very happy with this young upstart correcting him, irrespective that I did so very kindly. But to his credit, he did hear what I said, and I could tell that it registered.

After a few moments, he said, *"Well, you can put them here in the lobby, but they are to be covered up on Sunday and not offered."*

I asked, *"Why not on Sunday?"*

His reply was if I remember correctly, *"That is the Sabbath, and we must remember to keep it Holy,"* or words to that effect.

Again, very kindly I said to him, *"Sir, Saturday is the Sabbath, not Sunday, and Jesus fulfilled all of that at Calvary and the Resurrection, and such is not incumbent on Christians."*

He looked at me for a few moments, thinking it over, and I do not actually remember what he said, but whatever it was I do remember that we ultimately had permission to offer the recordings in the Church for the entirety of the time we were there.

I do not want to leave the impression that this man was lacking in love for God. Actually, I personally felt and do feel that he was a very Godly man and loved the Lord supremely. We had a tremendous Revival in his Church, with tremendous numbers of people being Saved and Baptized with the Holy Spirit.

He simply did not understand the Word of God about these matters as he should have, and, therefore, had some ideas in his mind which were not Scripturally correct.

There was nothing wrong with offering the recordings in the lobby of his Church, in fact, it was what the Lord had told us to do, and they were a great blessing to the people. As well, Sunday was no different than any other day of the week, as far as the Lord was concerned, which should be our concern also. And as stated, the Lord blessed abundantly.

MUCH TROUBLE!

Even though these things are small, as stated, they have been the cause of much trouble in Churches even from the very beginning. If people do not properly know and understand the Word of God, their Faith will be insufficient in some manner, and as a result, they will come up with some conclusions which can cause problems, especially if they try to foster them off on others.

On the other side of the coin, if the Brother in question of whom I have just spoken, had a conviction in his heart about him selling anything in the manner in which we have discussed, there is no problem with that whatsoever. He should heed that conviction as unto the Lord. But at the same time, he should not try to foster off that conviction upon me.

However, having said that, this was his Church. And as such, irrespective of what I thought about his rules and regulations, while there I must abide by what he says and for all the obvious reasons. Thankfully, he

NOTES

was kind enough to acquiesce to my requests. However, had he not done so, inasmuch as he was the Pastor of the Church, I must not attempt to force my convictions on him, and must yield to him as a matter of ethics, etc.

In fact these things are small, and have no bearing on anything, but as stated, they have been the cause of much contention in the Church, but need not be, if we will only follow the admonition as given here by the Holy Spirit through Paul.

(7) "FOR NONE OF US LIVETH TO HIMSELF, AND NO MAN DIETH TO HIMSELF."

The interpretation of this verse would seem to say that *"every man's conduct affects others for better or for worse,"* etc. However, the Greek Text does not bear that out, having a far higher view in mind.

It means, *"No Christian is his own end in life; what is always present to his mind, as a rule of his conduct, is the will and interest of his Lord"* (Wuest).

Even though what we do definitely does affect others, still, that is not the import of this verse, it is speaking to a higher order. Every Believer should have in mind one thing, and that is to please God in all things.

What does the Lord want for my life? What is His direction? What work does He have for me to do?

As well, the idea is, and which should be very comforting to all Believers, is that the Lord sets the time for our death. We die when the Lord wills, as the Lord wills, and then by our death glorify Him.

He has a work for us to do, and if we truly follow Him, trusting Him, we will not die until that work is complete.

IS IT POSSIBLE FOR A BELIEVER TO CUT HIS LIFE SHORT?

Yes it is!

Of course, God still has the final say, but our action or reaction regarding certain things, can cause Him to shorten our days.

For instance, Paul in explaining the Lord's Supper (I Cor. 11:23-30), said, *"For he that eateth and drinketh unworthily, eateth and drinketh damnation* (judgment) *to himself, not discerning the Lord's Body. For this cause many are weak and sickly among you, and many sleep* (die prematurely)."

The word *"unworthily"* in the Greek is *"anakios,"* and means *"irreverently."* It actually has the same meaning as *"unworthy."*

The idea in Paul's warning is in two directions:

1. If a Believer takes the Lord's Supper with unconfessed, unrepentant sin in his or her life, he is eating and drinking damnation (judgment) to himself, and if the situation is not ultimately remedied, it could cut his life short (I Cor. 11:27-28).

2. The Believer must properly discern the Lord's Body regarding what He did at Calvary. We must understand that He died for us that not only would our sins be washed away, but as well, that we might be physically healed, for Healing is in the Atonement (Isa. 53:4-5; Mat. 8:17; I Pet. 2:24).

In other words, one could say that Healing is in the Cup, that is if we rightly discern what Christ has done for us. Of course, if one does not believe that Jesus Christ heals today, and that all passed away with the Apostles as many Preachers teach, the Believer's life could be cut short by sickness, simply because he does not properly appropriate for himself what Jesus bought and paid for at Calvary and the Resurrection.

PEOPLE WHO ARE UNSAVED

There are many Church Members who are really not Born Again, who take the Lord's Supper regularly, but seemingly suffer no ill effects. The reason is simple. These people do not belong to the Lord irrespective of being Church Members and habitually taking the Lord's Supper, for such does not save. Inasmuch as they do not belong to Him, under normal circumstances that which they do, at least that of which we are discussing, has no effect on them. For instance, the Lord chastises those He loves and for the obvious reasons (Heb. 12:5-8).

However, there are many people who call themselves Christians, who obviously are not living right, but never seem to suffer any chastisement whatsoever. The reason is obvious, these people really do not belong to the Lord, irrespective of their claims, and in reality are as the Scripture says *"bastards, and not sons"* (Heb. 12:8).

(8) "FOR WHETHER WE LIVE, WE LIVE UNTO THE LORD; AND WHETHER WE DIE, WE DIE UNTO THE LORD: WHETHER WE LIVE THEREFORE, OR DIE, WE ARE THE LORD'S."

The phrase, *"For whether we live, we live unto the Lord; and whether we die, we die unto the Lord,"* reinforces that which Paul said in the previous verse.

The Believer belongs to the Lord, and as such, is to do the Lord's bidding. This refers not only to Preachers of the Gospel, but to laypersons as well, actually to whom Paul is speaking. This means that every facet of one's life, secular employment, domestic involvement, whatever ministry one may have, all belong to the Lord.

It also means, that which we conclude to be ours, is also the Lord's. That speaks of our income, family, occupation, i.e., *"everything!"*

The phrase, *"Whether we live therefore, or die, we are the Lord's,"* reflects Him having total control over our lives and our deaths, which we must desire that He use to the fullest.

The prominence given to *"the Lord"* three times in this verse, shows that the one Truth present is the all-determining significance of our relation to Christ respecting our conduct. The crowning saga of the Believer is to understand the preeminence of the Lord in his life, and that everything done must be done with the view in mind that we belong to the Lord, and, consequently, we do only what He wants and desires, and in the way He wants and desires. That is the road to fulfillment of life, security, happiness, well-being — one completely lost in Christ, and in doing so, one truly finds oneself.

(9) "FOR TO THIS END CHRIST BOTH DIED, AND ROSE, AND REVIVED, THAT HE MIGHT BE LORD BOTH OF THE DEAD AND LIVING."

The phrase, *"For to this end,"* refers to the fact of Christ's absolute Ownership of the Believer, spirit and soul and body. Such is a most precious fact for the heart of the Christian (Williams).

This ideally determines everything, alike in life or death; and all that is determined by what is right.

The phrase, *"Christ both died, and rose, and revived,"* have to do as obvious, with His

Death and Resurrection. In other words, we are bought with a price, and in fact, a price of such magnitude, that it absolutely defies description. Had that price not been paid, we would have died eternally lost. Consequently, in view of the price paid, and Who paid it, it should go without saying that we belong entirely to Him, and rightly so!

However, His Ownership of us, is in no way for our hurt or detriment, but rather the very opposite. It is for our life, and above all, our Eternal Life. In fact, this is the only way, the acceptance of Christ and what He did at Calvary and the Resurrection, in which one can be Saved.

The phrase, *"That He might be Lord both of the dead and living,"* refers to the Lordship of Christ of all Saints, whether alive or having passed on. Jesus Christ is Lord, and it is to Him that men must answer. He is today the Saviour, tomorrow He will be the Judge, whether of the Judgment Seat of Christ which pertains to Believers only, or to the Great White Throne Judgment, which pertains to unbelievers only. This means that the entirety of mankind, and for all time, will ultimately answer to Him.

(10) "BUT WHY DOST THOU JUDGE THY BROTHER? OR WHY DOST THOU SET AT NOUGHT THY BROTHER? FOR WE SHALL ALL STAND BEFORE THE JUDGMENT SEAT OF CHRIST."

The question, *"But why dost thou judge thy Brother?"*, carries several connotations:

1. Is any Believer qualified to judge another Believer? The Bible resoundingly answers *"No!"*

2. Understanding our common responsibility to the Lord, how dare we judge each other.

3. Considering the love we are supposed to have for our Brother, love simply will not allow us to do such a thing.

4. The phrase, *"Your Brother"* is another reason for not judging: it is inconsistent with a recognition of the brotherhood of Believers (Wuest).

The question, *"Or why dost thou set at nought thy Brother?"*, in effect refers to Believers drawing up their own rules, which by their very nature are not of God and simply because they are not Scriptural, and freezing out all who do not comply with these rules.

How close does the modern Church comply with this laid down by the Holy Spirit through the Apostle?

There is only one Biblical reason for *"setting at nought"* (setting aside, refusing fellowship) any Believer. That reason is unconfessed, unrepentant, habitual sin in a person's life (I Cor. Chpt. 5). Even then, it is more so the wrongheaded spirit and rebellious attitude of the individual against God and His Word, rather than the sin itself, whatever it may be (I Cor. 5:6).

However, the fact is, many are *"set at nought"* simply because they refuse to obey some man-directed rule which has no basis in Scripture whatsoever, and actually is a violation of Scripture. The tragedy is, if so-called Spiritual Leaders, take such a stand, almost always, those in their Churches or entire Denominations for that matter, follow suit. It is said as a joke but nevertheless true, that one particular large Pentecostal Denomination, has so many man-made rules, that not a single one, or at least very few, of the Bible Greats, whether Old or New Testaments, could be an ordained Preacher in that particular Denomination. In other words, David or Peter or Paul, would not be welcome, because they are not *"good enough."* I have chosen these three as an example, but it would apply to any.

Why would these three not be accepted, or any of the Bible Greats for that matter?

WHY?

First of all the situation with David concerning Bathsheba and her husband Uriah, would have instantly disqualified him. No, his repentance before God would have mattered not at all respecting this particular Denomination, and probably a number of others as well.

Paul would have been disqualified because he was too controversial. Anyone who caused an uproar wherever he went, and even near riots in some places, and who spent years in prison, simply would not be acceptable. To be frank with you, Paul would be the least acceptable of all, due to the fact that he could not be controlled — man-controlled and not God-controlled. The fact is, Paul was controlled by Christ in totality, but he was not controlled by man.

Peter denied the Lord, and despite his repentance, he would have been forced to have stepped aside for several years, which means he would not have been present on the Day of Pentecost, would not have preached the Inaugural Message of the Church on that day, nor would he have had any part whatsoever, at least for a number of years.

THE WORD OF GOD MUST BE THE CRITERIA

I make these statements attempting to show to the Reader how far many Church Leaders have drifted away from the Word of God, in fact making up their own rules. I am attempting to emphasize the fact that the Word of God must be our criteria in all things, and I mean all things. The moment we insert our own man-devised rules, or whatever, into the plain, clear teaching of the Bible, then the effort ceases to be of God, and becomes that of man and man alone. God will be patient with all of us, as He always is; however, the business of the Holy Spirit is to lead all of us, including so-called Spiritual Leaders, to the Truth of the Word, and the Word exclusively (Jn. 16:12-15).

Some Believers have the mistaken idea that whatever a major Religious Denomination does, it is right. However, nothing could be further from the Truth. It does not matter what or who it is, whether an individual, or a Denomination, the Word of God is applicable to all, and if the Word is not followed, great harm always will be the result.

The phrase, *"For we shall all stand before the Judgment Seat of Christ,"* refers to the fact, that there is coming a time when every Believer will have to stand at this Judgment Seat, meaning that we will all stand at one Bar, with Jesus as the Universal Judge.

WHAT IS THE JUDGMENT SEAT OF CHRIST?

This Judgment will be for Believers only, and not unbelievers. Inasmuch as all sins of Believers were judged at Calvary, those sins can never again be brought up and held over the Believer. They are forever done away and are no longer against him (Ps. 103:12; Isa. 43:25; 44:22; Acts 3:19). So

this Judgment will not pertain to the Believer's sins, for he has none, but rather his *"works"* (I Cor. 3:8-15).

At this Judgment the souls of Believers cannot be lost, but reward for works definitely can be lost, and in fact in many cases, will be lost (I Cor. 3:15).

Paul is here warning the Church, that we must all understand, that one day we will stand at the Judgment Seat of Christ to give account. As well, we will all stand on the same basis, none better than the other, and be judged accordingly. There we will answer, and there we will give account. So, whatever we do now, regarding motives, actions, attitudes, decisions, direction, in fact, anything and everything, must be done with the understanding, that one day an account will be called, and we will answer. Consequently, we *must* do everything in the light of that coming Judgment.

THE BASIS OF THIS JUDGMENT

The basis will be, as stated, our works, both good and bad (Mat. 16:27; Rom. 2:6; Chpt. 14; I Cor. 3:11-15; II Cor. 5:10; Col. Chpt. 3; II Tim. 4:14).

Paul plainly said, *"And every man* (every Believer) *shall receive his own reward according to his own labour* (works)*"* (I Cor. 3:8).

When it comes to our *"works"* for the Lord, of course, motive must play a tremendous part in all that we do. Why do we do it? What is our purpose and reason? What do we hope to get out of these things which we do for the Lord? What is our purpose?

Perhaps I could explain it better by giving the following illustration.

THE APOSTLE PAUL

Some time ago, Frances and I, along with Donnie, Gabriel, and Matthew, plus others, were in the city of Rome, Italy. If I remember correctly, we had just come from seeing the Coliseum. We walked down a long street, where had once been the very heart and center of Rome, when it was at the height of its power. In fact, this is where all the governmental buildings stood, when Rome ruled the world. But it was what was at the other end of the this street which interested me.

At the end of the long street is the

Mammertine Prison. It is not at all large. Actually, the part that I wished to see was underground in Paul's day. I speak of the cell where he spent his last few months, from which he wrote I and II Timothy. It is said that they took him out of this cell and down the Ostian Way, where he was executed. Little did they realize that they were executing the man, the Jew from Tarsus, who had done more than any man alive to establish Christianity, on which the very foundation of Western Civilization is constructed. But Rome had no idea of all of this.

THE PRISON

During Paul's day, there was no outside entrance to this cell. In fact, Paul would have had to have been lowered down through the ceiling by a rope, for the only entrance was a trap door in the ceiling, with another cell above this cell. As stated, that's where he spent the last few months of his life. It was an underground cavern, possibly about 30 feet by 20 feet, if I remember correctly. It had been carved out of solid rock. In fact, it had been used as a granary years before; however, at the time of Paul, Rome used it as a prison.

Presently, it has steps that lead down into the cell. All of us walked down, some 20 or 25 of us, filling the room. Realizing the history that it held, I took out my New Testament and began to read aloud some of Paul's last words. He wrote them in this very place. He said:

"For I am now ready to be offered, and the time of my departure is at hand.

"I have fought a good fight, I have finished my course, I have kept the faith:

"Henceforth . . ."

When I reached that particular part, I could not continue. For a few moments, I saw the aged Apostle standing in the room. He had just finished writing II Timothy. He knew it would be his last Epistle. He also knew that he had only a few days left.

The moral of my illustration is: there is no one who had greater Faith, I think, than the Apostle Paul. As well, there was no one who worked any harder for Christ than did this Great Apostle. But the main thing was that his motives were correct. If a human

being can be any type of example, I know that Paul was. I think we would do well to emulate him as best we can, at least as far as his motives were concerned. Then, when we stand at the *"Judgment Seat of Christ,"* there will be no fear, only thankfulness.

WHAT WILL BE THE MANNER OF ASCERTAINING THE VALIDITY OF OUR WORKS?

Paul said, *"For the day shall declare it, because it shall be revealed by fire; and the fire shall try every man's work of what sort it is"* (I Cor. 3:13).

In all of this the Holy Spirit through the Apostle uses symbolisms to describe the substance or lack of such. For instance, that which is built on the solid Foundation of the Word of God, are likened to *"gold, silver, and precious stones"* (I Cor. 3:12). These are materials that fire will not burn.

That which is not built on the proper Foundation, *"which is Jesus Christ,"* such works are likened to *"wood, hay, and stubble."* Obviously, such material easily burns. The Word of God is the test, and Jesus Christ is the Foundation (I Cor. 3:11).

Paul deals with this in two ways: A. In Romans Chapter 14, which we are now studying, he directs attention to our attitude toward and treatment of people, and especially Brothers and Sisters in the Lord; and, B. In I Corinthians 3 he deals with our own personal motives respecting our Work for God, whatever that may be.

I think our motives will pretty well decide how we treat people. If we are building properly upon Christ, our treatment of others will be accordingly. Otherwise, that will be obvious as well!

(11) "FOR IT IS WRITTEN, AS I LIVE, SAITH THE LORD, EVERY KNEE SHALL BOW TO ME, AND EVERY TONGUE SHALL CONFESS TO GOD."

The phrase, *"For it is written,"* is derived from Isaiah 45:23.

The phrase, *"As I live, saith the Lord,"* in effect constitutes a vow or even an oath. Isaiah says it in this manner, *"I have sworn by Myself, the Word is gone out of My Mouth in Righteousness, and shall not return . . ."* (Isa. 45:23), meaning it cannot be altered.

What God says will happen, will happen!

The idea is, that if God can die, His Word can die. Of course, God cannot die, so His Word cannot die.

The phrase, *"Every knee shall bow to Me, and every tongue shall confess to God,"* states that which will be done.

"Confess" in the Greek is *"exomologeo,"* and means *"to acknowledge or profess from the heart."* Thus, in a context like this, it means *"to make a confession to one's honor, hence to praise"* (Vincent).

Paul also said, *"That at the Name of Jesus every knee should bow, of things in Heaven, and things in earth, and things under the earth;*

"And that every tongue should confess that Jesus Christ is Lord, to the Glory of God the Father" (Phil. 2:10-11).

This means every Angel in Heaven, every person who has ever lived on the earth, and every Demon and Fallen Angel in the infernal underworld (Ps. 16:10; Mat. 12:40; Eph. 4:8-10; I Pet. 3:19; II Pet. 2:4; Jude vss. 6-7).

Men can bow to Him in Worship and Praise because they love Him, as all certainly should, or else they can bow to Him in Worship and Praise because of being forced to do so. However, irrespective, all are going to bow and all are going to worship, whether voluntarily or involuntarily.

(12) "SO THEN EVERY ONE OF US SHALL GIVE ACCOUNT OF HIMSELF TO GOD."

"Give account" in the Greek is *"doseo logon,"* and refers *"to an account in a ledger which a bookkeeper enters"* (Robertson). The idea is this:

A record is kept in Heaven of all things done on earth by each and every person. If sins before the Lord have been properly confessed and repented of, that part of the record is cleansed, never to show against the Believer. However, all works and motives are diligently accounted, and to these, every single Believer must answer. In other words, no Believer will ever be able to deny what is written there, knowing that the account is infallible. He will answer to that account and to God.

As well, and as should be obvious from the Text, none will be excused, *"Every one shall give account of himself to God."*

(13) "LET US NOT THEREFORE JUDGE ONE ANOTHER ANY MORE: BUT JUDGE THIS RATHER, THAT NO MAN PUT A STUMBLINGBLOCK OR AN OCCASION TO FALL IN HIS BROTHER'S WAY."

The phrase, *"Let us not therefore judge one another any more,"* can be translated, *"Let us no longer have the habit of criticizing one another."*

This is perhaps, one of the most oft committed sins by Believers. As well, it is of far greater magnitude than most realize. The idea is this:

Whenever we criticize another Brother or Sister in the Lord, we are in effect judging that person, hence, Paul's prohibition. So, the admonition is clear and plain, *"Don't do such."*

Laying everything else aside, plus all the reasons, etc., the real reason we are not to judge or criticize another, is simply because they belong to the Lord. Consequently, when one criticizes that which belongs to Him, in effect, we criticize Him. As such, it is a finding of fault with the Work of the Holy Spirit in his or her life.

I do not think any Christian, that is if he is in his right mind, would purposely or knowingly criticize the Lord. However, when we criticize His property, we criticize Him.

The phrase, *"But judge this rather, that no man put a stumblingblock or an occasion to fall in his Brother's way,"* tells us in fact, what is permissible to judge.

As Believers, we are to judge every Brother and Sister and situation which surrounds them, irrespective as to what it might be, as to how we can *help* that Brother or Sister, instead of harming them.

To judge in the sense of criticizing, can cause the one who is being treated accordingly, to become so discouraged, that the thing becomes *"a stumblingblock,"* which can *"occasion the fall"* of the individual.

How many people have quit living for God, or have been seriously hindered in their spiritual walk, because of the criticism of fellow Believers? Of course, only the Lord knows the answer to that question; however, of this one can be assured, the number is large.

So, the question should be asked as to this situation, concerning the veracity of our action as Believers.

Are we finding ways to be of kind and gracious service to a fellow Believer in helping them along their way, or are we instead, doing that which falls out to a *"stumblingblock"* before them? The idea is this:

Even if the Believer has failed, that gives us no excuse to criticize them, for the simple reason that we have failed as well. Also, at the very time such persons are needing kindness the most, oftentimes, they receive the very opposite from fellow Believers. In this state, no one needs a diagnosis as to why certain things have happened, but rather encouragement respecting Faith in God that victory is going to be won. It is sad, when many if not most Christians spend their lives, serving as *"stumblingblocks,"* instead of *"supports."* Which are you, a stumblingblock or a support?

(14) "I KNOW, AND AM PERSUADED BY THE LORD JESUS, THAT THERE IS NOTHING UNCLEAN OF ITSELF: BUT TO HIM THAT ESTEEMETH ANY THING TO BE UNCLEAN, TO HIM IT IS UNCLEAN."

The phrase, *"I know, and am persuaded by the Lord Jesus,"* means that this declaration is in the Lord, and not merely in his own reasoning power. One would have to understand Paul, in order to fully comprehend this statement.

First of all, being a *"Hebrew of the Hebrews,"* Paul would have once (before his Conversion) been rabid concerning the eating or not eating of particular foods, or the keeping or not keeping of certain days, etc. Consequently, the evidence is, that Christ had performed such a work in this man's life, that his belief system was brand new, carrying with it no clinging vines of the past. In other words, he knew what Salvation in the Lord Jesus Christ meant, and it had nothing to do with rituals and ceremonies.

The phrase, *"I know and am persuaded,"* in the words of Bengel, presents *"a rare conjunction of words, but fitted here to confirm against ignorance and doubt."*

"Know" in the Greek is *"oida,"* and means *"absolute, positive knowledge."*

"Am persuaded" is *"peitho,"* and is given in the perfect tense. It means that Paul's position had come to this point due to a Revelation

NOTES

from Jesus Christ, with the result that he now stands in a place and position regarding these things, which are permanent. He stands persuaded. Wuest said, *"He could not be budged from his conviction, so sure was he of the Truth of the matter."*

OF ITSELF!

The phrase, *"That there is nothing unclean of itself,"* means to be unfit on the grounds that it is unholy or impure in a ritualistic or ceremonial fashion. The word *"unclean"* at least in this case, speaks of ceremonial impurity, not of actual immorality. It had to do with religious scruples regarding animal flesh and a vegetarian diet, along with the keeping of one day as against another in a special observance (Wuest).

Does this mean that alcohol or drugs are placed in this category as well?

No! If one looks at the statement, it says *"Nothing unclean of itself."* That means in the manner in which it was originally created by the Lord, there is nothing unclean. However, that which the Lord originally created can be distorted, which it often is, and quickly made to be unclean.

For instance, *"corn"* is a grain, and is a very healthy staple as food; however, it can be made into strong drink, which is *"unclean,"* for the simple reason that it is immoral and for all the obvious reasons. The same could be said for many other types of ingredients.

There are many types of plants which produce certain types of chemicals which are very helpful. However, if the wrong chemicals are mixed together, they can be very harmful, such as certain types of drugs, etc.

"Of itself" means none of these things created by God have any connotation of evil or wrong, but only when distorted or changed in a detrimental way from their intended purpose. Trees are not evil or wrong, but if one is cut down in order to make an idol, it then becomes *"unclean,"* i.e., sin.

The phrase, *"But to him that esteemeth any thing to be unclean, to him it is unclean,"* is this way because of one thing, a lack of Faith.

LACK OF FAITH

What do we mean by that?

Paul will say at the conclusion of this Chapter, *". . . For whatsoever is not of Faith is sin"* (vs. 23).

The idea pertains to a lack of knowledge concerning the Finished Work of Christ. This means that the believing sinner can do nothing regarding any type of works respecting Salvation, except simply have Faith in what Jesus did at Calvary and the Resurrection. In other words, his Salvation stands in Faith alone. Consequently, it has nothing to do with whatever one eats or does not eat, wears or does not wear, what days one may or may not observe, etc. All of that, and a hundred and one other things, which at times become a part of religion, is in effect a tremendous insult to Christ, which by its very nature claims that He has not paid the price, and something else needs to be added. So, if a person imagines something of this nature to be unclean, claiming it is a sin if such be done, etc., in fact, to that person it *is* sin.

(15) "BUT IF THY BROTHER BE GRIEVED WITH THY MEAT, NOW WALKEST THOU NOT CHARITABLY. DESTROY NOT HIM WITH THY MEAT, FOR WHOM CHRIST DIED."

The phrase, *"But if thy Brother be grieved with thy meat, now walkest thou not charitably,"* proclaims direction given by the Holy Spirit, that even though such may be silly, and I speak of the eating or not eating of certain things, etc., the one strong in Faith must not wound this weak Brother or Sister.

The word *"charitably"* speaks of love. The idea concerns the love we all must have for one another, and that we must not do anything, at least if it is within our power, to cause grief for a Brother or Sister in the Lord.

The phrase, *"Destroy not him with thy meat, for whom Christ died,"* lends credence to the fact that Jesus paid a terrible price for this person's Redemption. Consequently, the small price we are asked to pay regarding concern for a weaker Brother or Sister, is not unreasonable to say the least.

As well, if Jesus paid such a price for man's Redemption, and we know that He did, should we not hold this person's Redemption as priceless, and do nothing to offend in any way, irrespective as to how inconsequential

NOTES

it may actually be!

THE MAIN IDEA

Paul was not laying down firm and fast rules, for to do such, would have of itself taken it out of the realm of Faith. The idea is simple, that we show love and concern for our fellow Christians. As stated, the Lord paid a terrible price for the Salvation of all. Consequently, the last thing we want to do as Believers is to be a stumblingblock for others.

To be frank, what we are seeing here respecting these admonitions, is exactly that which Paul did when he went into the Temple in Jerusalem, entering into a purification process which pertained to the Mosaic Law. It is recorded in Acts 21. Many of the Jerusalem Jews were weak in this area of Faith, thinking they had to continue parts of the Mosaic Law irrespective of the fact that Jesus had come, thereby fulfilling all of that Law. While they believed in Christ, they still held to parts of the Old Law.

So as not to wound their weak conscience, Paul bent over backwards, to accommodate their thinking, although knowing that Jesus had already fulfilled all of this; consequently, it was now of no import.

Even though Paul made himself well known respecting the Gospel and that such was no longer necessary (the Law), still, knowing that entering into the Temple regarding this process held nothing spiritual one way or the other, he would accommodate his Brethren by joining with them upon the request of James (Acts 21:18-24).

ARE THERE LIMITS TO THIS?

Of course there are limits. If anything done violates the Word of God, it cannot be entered into, irrespective as to what people may think. Whether one eats or does not eat a certain type of food does not involve the Word of God in any manner. The same is true for the keeping of certain days, and many other things one could name. Actually the purification process of which we have just discussed, once was a valid requirement before Jesus came. When He came, its Type was fulfilled, consequently, it being of no more spiritual value. So, the doing or not doing this thing now was no longer of any spiritual significance.

There are some Christians I think who have taken this too far, and violated the Word of God, claiming they did not desire to offend their Brethren, etc. As an example, I speak of American Christians drinking wine with their French Brethren, or beer with their German Brethren. I feel like they are violating the Word of God when they do such a thing.

Some may disagree, but I feel that alcoholic beverage is immoral. I feel like the record bears it out, and as we have already stated, Believers should set the example by not imbibing at all.

For those who disagree with me, I will make my views known, and will stand by my convictions; however, concerning those who are doing something I feel is Scripturally wrong, still, I will love them, and can fellowship with them without any animosity whatsoever, at least on my part. If they see things differently than I in this respect, I will not fall out with them over that. They are my Brother and Sister in the Lord, and as such, I love them dearly, and will stand by them and with them irrespective.

HOW FAR SHOULD SEPARATION GO?

The matter I have just discussed involves separation. But yet, it does not have to involve isolation. And this is the problem with the modern Church, separation is taken into isolation, which is never commanded in the Bible.

I purposely choose to separate myself from many and varied things constantly. But I do not choose to isolate myself. Many Believers have thought that isolation translates into some type of holiness, but it does not.

As an example, Believers associate with unbelievers constantly. In fact, this is the very means in which the Light of the Believer can shine, and in fact, the manner in which it is supposed to shine. If it is isolated, it cannot shine. However, even though I associate with these people in business activities, I do not join in with their revelry or wrongdoing. As stated, the Believer is to always be separated, but never isolated.

This is the reason that communities which

have featured Christians only, have never been a success. In the natural it would seem to be the thing to do. However, such is not pleasing to the Lord.

How can we be a witness, if we are isolated from everyone? The Truth is, we cannot!

(16) "LET NOT THEN YOUR GOOD BE EVIL SPOKEN OF:"

It is of vital import not to violate the conscience. To the conscience that esteems something to be unclean in the Levitical sense, which under the Gospel is really not so, to that conscience it becomes unclean. So the Believer's liberty of action is affected, and he must *not* by eating idol-offered meat grieve or wound the conscience of his Brother in the Lord; for to do so would not be walking in love toward him, but, on the contrary, could cause the person to have severe spiritual difficulties, a person incidentally, for whom Christ died to save.

"Your good" pertains to the liberty which is found in Christ, which is very good, but which because of the possible injury it could do to another, is pointed to by others as evil. So, this *"good"* must be exercised with a gracious spirit, always considering others.

(17) "FOR THE KINGDOM OF GOD IS NOT MEAT AND DRINK; BUT RIGHTEOUSNESS, AND PEACE, AND JOY IN THE HOLY SPIRIT."

The phrase, *"For the Kingdom of God is not meat and drink,"* actually refers to rules, regulations, ceremonies, or rituals of whatever stripe. This is extremely important for the simple reason, that in many Churches, the *"Kingdom of God"* is exactly what Paul says here it isn't. In other words, it is more Law than Grace, in reality not much Grace at all.

The phrase, *"But Righteousness, and Peace, and Joy in the Holy Spirit,"* tells us what the Kingdom of God actually is.

Righteousness here is not used in its judicial sense of Justifying Righteousness, that is the Righteousness which was imputed to us when we were Saved, but in its *"practical, ethical sense, as shown in moral rectitude toward men"* (Vincent).

"Peace" as it is used here, is not speaking primarily of Peace with God, which it usually means, but rather in this case, *"mutual*

concord among Christians."

In other words, the True Kingdom of God does not produce dissention and quarreling among Christians, but rather *"Peace."* It is only these man-devised rules and regulations which bring discord.

"Joy" is *"common joy, arising out of the prevalence of rectitude and concord in the Church."* The whole Chapter is concerned with the mutual relations of Christians, rather than their relations to God (Vincent).

The qualifying phrase *"In the Holy Spirit,"* refers to all three terms, *"Righteousness, Peace, and Joy."* It is this Divine Guest Who — by His Presence, produces them in the Church (Godet).

Denney says, *"One may serve Christ either eating or abstaining, but no one can serve Him whose conduct exhibits indifference to Righteousness, Peace, and Joy."*

(18) "FOR HE THAT IN THESE THINGS SERVETH CHRIST IS ACCEPTABLE TO GOD, AND APPROVED OF MEN."

The phrase, *"For he that in these things serveth Christ is acceptable to God,"* means that *"Righteousness, Peace, and Joy"* are acceptable to the Lord, but not contention, quarreling, and fighting in the Church, which should be obvious.

The Kingdom of God, at least in this instance, refers to Gospel fellowship. In such fellowship the Holy Spirit by His Energy and Government actuates Righteousness, Peace, and Joy, i.e., uprightness in conduct, concord in brotherhood, and joy in experience.

The Apostle says that these are the great matters in the Church, not eating food and drinking wine, etc.

Parts of Christianity which are corrupt, declare the contrary, for it says that the most important spiritual exercise of a Christian congregation is the eating of bread and drinking of wine in what is known as the Mass, or as the Lord's Supper in other particular Churches. The Apostle here plainly says that eating and drinking are not essential in Christian Fellowship, but Righteousness, Peace, and Joy which are absolutely fundamental (Williams).

The Christian heart should have but one thought, one direction, one desire, and that is to do things which are *"acceptable to God,"*

irrespective of whether it is acceptable to men or not. It is Him Alone Who matters!

The phrase, *"And approved of men,"* does not mean as it appears on the surface that all will agree with what is done, and may even go so far as to hate and persecute the true servant of Christ; nevertheless, much of the surface quarreling will stop.

"Approved" in the Greek is *"dokimos,"* and means *"to put to the test for the purpose of being approved, and having met specifications, have the stamp of approval."*

The idea is, that the only thing in the Church which will work, and, therefore, place one on the correct road of life, is *"Righteousness, Peace, and Joy in the Holy Spirit."* Anything else will have the opposite effect, and simply because it is not of the Spirit.

(19) "LET US THEREFORE FOLLOW AFTER THE THINGS WHICH MAKE FOR PEACE, AND THINGS WHEREWITH ONE MAY EDIFY ANOTHER."

The phrase, *"Let us therefore follow after the things which make for peace,"* refers to the things of God, which Paul here clearly outlines, and not things which are devised by men. Man is either following the Lord or that devised by other men, he cannot follow both.

The phrase, *"And things wherewith one may edify another,"* refers to that which is produced by the Holy Spirit, and not by man.

Churches have fights and squabbles, too often over very nonessential things. Men are always tempted to attempt the adding of particulars to the Finished Work of Christ. It was a problem then, and it is a problem now. The Word of God must be the criteria for all things.

When Family Worship Center was formed in Baton Rouge, Louisiana in the early 1980's, some of the Preachers then on our staff desired to form all types of rules and regulations to which one had to adhere in order to be a member of the Church. I heard them out, and then said, *"No, the only requirement we are going to have to join this Church, is the same requirement the Lord has for entrance into His Kingdom, which is to be 'Born Again'"* (Jn. 3:1-2; Rom. 10:9-10, 13; Eph. 2:8-9).

That is what we did; however, two or three

of the Preachers grew angry and left, and I am told that was the reason.

Why is it that what is good enough for the Lord, is not good enough for some people?

These individuals, whomever they may be, have an erroneous concept of what Church really is. The earthly organization which we refer to as *"Church,"* is just that earthly. It is man-devised, but hopefully for the purpose of spreading the Gospel of Jesus Christ. Associating with it or not associating with it, as such, carries no spiritual connotation one way or the other.

The real *"Church,"* the *"Called-out ones,"* called out of the world, has been referred to as the *"Mystical Body of Christ,"* which it rightly is. It has nothing to do with human organization, is strictly of God, and one enters into this *"Church,"* by being *"Born Again."* As mean joining the Kingdom of God. That comes about by being Born Again.

Please allow us to say it again, the Word of God must be the Foundation, Base, Criteria, and Pattern for all that is done. It must be obeyed, at least to the best of our ability. When we do otherwise, we do not help the Kingdom of God, but rather hurt the Kingdom of God.

(20) "FOR MEAT DESTROY NOT THE WORK OF GOD. ALL THINGS INDEED ARE PURE; BUT IT IS EVIL FOR THAT MAN WHO EATETH WITH OFFENCE."

The phrase, *"For meat destroy not the Work of God,"* presents a command which regrettably, has not all the time been obeyed.

"Destroy" in the Greek is *"kataluo,"* and means *"to tear down,"* as one would tear down a building.

Normally the Greek word for *"destroy,"* is *"apollumi,"* which means *"to destroy or ruin."* But here it refers to a building being torn down brick by brick or plank by plank. Consequently, we should ask ourselves, if what we are doing, is building up the *"Work of God,"* or tearing down the *"Work of God."*

In essence, the *"Work of God"* is people. So if we tear down people over nonessential things, we are tearing down the *"Work of God."* The phrase, *"All things indeed are pure,"* refers to that which are created by God.

This of which Paul speaks is the principle of the strong in Faith. The difficulty is to get

the enlightened to understand that an abstract principle can never be the rule of Christian conduct. The Christian, of course, admits this principle, but he must act from love.

To know that all things are clean, does not (as is often assumed) settle what the Christian has to do in any given case. It does not define his duty, but only makes clear his responsibility.

Acknowledging that principle, and looking with love at other Christians, and the effect of any given line of conduct on them, the Christian has to define his duty for himself. All meat is clean, but not all eating (Denney).

The phrase, *"But it is evil for that man who eateth with offence,"* refers to the man who is *"weak in Faith."* However, the tone of Paul's direction is also to the strong as well as the weak. The idea is, that whatever we do, even though in our heart we may know there is no wrong attached, still, weaker Brethren must be considered, and everyone for that matter. The whole idea is consideration for others.

"Pure" in the Greek as used here, is *"kathara,"* and means *"ceremonial purity."* It is nonmoral in its implications. In other words, Paul is not addressing himself to things which are immoral and, therefore, impure, but rather only things which are ritualistic or ceremonial and contain no moral aspect. Unfortunately, many have attempted to take the word *"pure"* as it is here used, and make it apply to all things, seeking to justify that which is immoral.

(21) "IT IS GOOD NEITHER TO EAT FLESH, NOR TO DRINK WINE, NOR ANY THING WHEREBY THY BROTHER STUMBLETH, OR IS OFFENDED, OR IS MADE WEAK."

Throughout this Chapter, Paul in essence is saying that *"it is good"* to be strong in the Faith, knowing and understanding liberties afforded us by Christ. However, he now says in this verse, that *"it is good"* if we not avail ourselves at times of all of these liberties, for the simple reason that to do so might cause one to be offended or to stumble.

"Stumbleth" in the Greek is *"proskopto,"* which means *"to strike the foot against; to err from the truth."* So, what we are discussing

here is that which could cause someone to lose his soul, which as obvious, is no trifling matter.

"Offended" in the Greek is "skandalizo," which means "to wound one's spirit or to offend." The Believer must ever take the attitude that we must help fellow Believers along the way instead of hindering them.

The phrase, "Or is made weak," has reference to the fact that whatever action is brought about, does not cause the individual to become stronger in the Lord, but rather weaker.

"Weak" in the Greek is "asthenos," which means "strengthless, without power to properly distinguish the difference between what is right and what is wrong."

When it comes to Salvation, people are to be handled delicately. If proper love, concern, and sensitivity, are not shown, some can become confused, and discouraged, thereby turning back to the old life of sin.

If these were not real dangers, and in fact a problem which often surfaces, the Holy Spirit would not have devoted this much explanation through the Apostle to the Body of Christ. It *is* a serious problem!

The idea is, that love is to be the ruling guide, and not our freedom of liberties.

(22) "HAST THOU FAITH? HAVE IT TO THYSELF BEFORE GOD. HAPPY IS HE THAT CONDEMNETH NOT HIMSELF IN THAT THING WHICH HE ALLOWETH."

The question, "Hast thou Faith?", is addressed to the strong.

The phrase, "Have it to thyself before God," has reference to the fact that the one strong in Faith should not run the risk of injuring a Brother's conscience, merely for the sake of exercising in a special way the spiritual freedom which he has the happiness to possess — whether he exercises it in that way or not (Denney).

Incidentally, even though Paul is not addressing the following directly, still, this Passage does cover that of which I will now say.

There are many things that we as Believers feel in our heart that God has told us. Our Faith is that He definitely has. However, in many cases, we should keep it to ourselves, in other words between us and the Lord. To proclaim it to others, whatever it might be, may at times, prove to be detrimental in the long run.

By that I mean, that there are times when we believe the Lord has spoken something to us, when in reality He has not. Consequently, if it does not come to pass, but rather the very opposite, if it has remained between the individual and the Lord, there is no embarrassment to the person or the Work of God.

In no way is this advice meant to cast aspersions on the Word of God, but rather the very opposite. The Word of God cannot fail. If God has truly told us a certain thing, it will happen exactly as He has said. However, we as Believers are not perfect. Even the best of us at times make mistakes. That is the reason if we have Faith for a certain thing, we should keep it between the Lord and ourselves, until we are absolutely certain on all counts of what we say.

The phrase, "Happy is he that condemneth not himself in that thing which he alloweth," refers to this being joy enough, without us taking our liberty further, that is if such is the case, thereby hindering a weaker Brother or Sister.

(23) "AND HE THAT DOUBTETH IS DAMNED IF HE EAT, BECAUSE HE EATETH NOT OF FAITH: FOR WHATSOEVER IS NOT OF FAITH IS SIN."

The phrase, "And he that doubteth is damned if he eat, because he eateth not of Faith," proclaims to us the absolute power which is indicative of True Faith in God.

To try to better understand this of which Paul is speaking, first of all we must grasp the fact that if the individual does not eat the particular meat, etc., in Faith, in the Eyes of God his conduct actually constitutes sin. Actually, it is not the eating of the meat (or whatever) that is the sin, but not having Faith. In one sense of the word it means even as Paul said about the Lord's Supper, "For he that eateth and drinketh unworthily (in this case, without Faith), eateth and drinketh damnation to himself, not properly discerning the Lord's Body" (I Cor. 11:29). As we said in Commentary at the beginning of this Chapter, such an individual does not fully know or understand what Jesus did for them at Calvary and the Resurrection. The Word also says, "... People are destroyed for lack of knowledge ..." (Hos. 4:6), i.e., a lack of knowledge of the Word of God.

The phrase, *"For whatsoever is not of Faith is sin,"* in few words embodies the great principle of Biblical Christianity.

The phrase means that whatsoever is not of Faith in Christ and the Cross constitutes sin. This means if we place our faith in anything, and I mean anything, other than Christ and the Cross — let us say it again — we sin.

Once again, this tells us that Bible Christianity is not a religion, but rather a relationship with a Person, The Lord Jesus Christ, which relationship is tendered by Faith. The Lord has done a great Work for all who will believe. Everyone who has *"Faith"* in what He did, is Saved. Hence, the entirety of the principle of Christianity rests upon *"Faith"* (Eph. 2:8-9).

RELIGION

Religion is a personal set or institutionalized system of religious attitudes, beliefs, and practices originated by man. It may be an effort made by man to reach God, or to bring about some ethical result. In any case, it is from man to God, or man to man, and not God to man.

As such, it is not of God, and can effect no positive result in the realm of spirituality.

By contrast, Christianity is not a religion in any sense of the word, but rather a relationship, even as we have said, with Christ. Jesus is the total Focus of Christianity, being the One Who is the Door to the Father, and the One Who has paid the price for all that we have relative to Salvation. Faith in Him is the great principle on which Christianity turns.

> *"Jesus, Master, Whose I am, purchased Thine Alone to be, by Thy Blood, Oh spotless Lamb,*
> *"Shed so willingly for me, let my heart be all Thine Own, let me live to Thee Alone."*

> *"Other lords have long held sway; now Thy Name Alone to bear, Thy dear Voice alone obey,*
> *"Is my daily, hourly prayer; Whom have I in Heaven but Thee? Nothing else my joy can be."*

NOTES

> *"Jesus, Master, I am Thine; keep me faithful, keep me near; let Thy Presence in me shine,*
> *"All my homeward way to cheer. Jesus at Thy Feet I fall; Oh, be Thou my All in All."*

CHAPTER 15

(1) "WE THEN THAT ARE STRONG OUGHT TO BEAR THE INFIRMITIES OF THE WEAK, AND NOT TO PLEASE OURSELVES."

It is unfortunate that the King James Translators placed the Chapter division here. The 14th Chapter of Romans would have probably been better ended immediately following Verse 7, with the 15th Chapter of Romans beginning with Verse 8.

The phrase, *"We then that are strong ought to bear the infirmities of the weak,"* has the end result in mind of these weaker Brethren also becoming strong in Faith and Knowledge of the Lord.

"Strong" in the Greek is *"dunatos,"* and means *"powerful, or able to do whatever is necessary."* In this instance it means to be *"strong"* in the Word, understanding primarily what Jesus has done for us at Calvary and the Resurrection. It takes its cue from Verse 9 of Romans Chapter 14.

If one does not properly understand all that was done for sinners by Christ in His vicarious, Atoning Death at Calvary and the Resurrection, even as explained by Paul in Chapter 6 of Romans, one will have an improper view or knowledge of all else which pertains to Christianity. One could say that an improper knowledge of what Christ did there, brings about an improper knowledge of everything else. This is the basic reason for much if not all false Doctrine. We will momentarily address this to a greater extent.

"Ought" in the Greek is *"opheilo,"* and means *"to be a debtor, to be under obligation, bound by duty."* It means that this admonition to help the weak is not a suggestion, but rather a moral obligation.

"Bear" in the Greek is *"bastazo,"* and means *"to bear what is burdensome."* In

this case it means the strong Believer will go the extra mile to help the one weaker in Faith, but again with the end in view of making the weaker Believer strong.

"Infirmities" in the Greek is *"asthenema,"* and means *"physical or mental weakness."*

"Weak" in the Greek is *"adunatus,"* and means *"unable, impotent."*

The phrase, *"And not to please ourselves,"* strikes at the very heart of True Christianity.

In the Image and Likeness of Christ, the Believer is to always have others in mind. As stated, this is the very heart of True Christianity. Williams said, *"Pleasing self ruins Christian fellowship."*

Denney said, *"It is very easy for self-pleasing and mere wilfulness to shelter themselves under the disguise of Christian Principle. But there is only one Christian Principle which has no qualification — Love."*

WHAT DID JESUS DO FOR THE HUMAN RACE AT CALVARY AND THE RESURRECTION?

There is almost no end to what one could say on this subject of all subjects. Nevertheless, for the sake of brevity, we will attempt to touch the basic Principles:

1. Jesus effected the double cure which addressed the double curse:

A. The double curse was the sin debt of man and the sin grip on man. In other words, the debt was so horrible that man could not pay, and the grip so tight that he could not break.

B. When Jesus died on Calvary He paid all of the sin debt of man, leaving nothing owing. To receive its benefits, all one has to do is to believe (Jn. 3:16).

Once the person comes to Christ, he is then to believe that he was literally in Christ when Jesus died, was buried and rose from the dead (Rom. 6:3-11). In the Believer's understanding of this, sin's grip is broken.

So, at Calvary the wages of sin which are death are set aside, and the grip of sin which is bondage is broken, thereby, effecting the double cure.

Consequently, the Believer is to look to Calvary not only as the place and time of his Conversion, but also of his continued victory. All that we have in Christ is tied to His

NOTES

Death, Resurrection, and Exaltation, and not to rules, regulations, works, ordinances, or self efforts of any nature. Faith is the only requirement, and more particularly, Faith in what Jesus did at that time and at that place.

2. The Atonement, for that is what we are actually speaking about, includes not only the sin question being handled, but as well, healing for the sick, knowledge for ignorance, and prosperity for poverty (Isa. Chpt. 53; Mat. 21:22; Mk. 11:24; Jn. 14:14; 15:7; I Pet. 2:24).

In effect, the Atonement addressed everything man lost in the Fall. Consequently, healing includes not only the physical body, but as well, the mind and spirit (Lk. 4:18).

However, it must be understood that even though the Atonement addressed everything, all of its results are not yet possible for the Believer. The Believer is now Sanctified and Justified. However, his Salvation, at least as far as the totality of the Atonement is concerned, will not be completed, until he is Glorified. That will take place at the coming Resurrection (I Cor. Chpt. 15).

So, even though the Atonement addressed all sin, and removed its curse and bondage, still, Believers can still sin, and, regrettably, sometimes do (I Jn. 1:9).

As well, due to the fact that we still live in a mortal body, even though Jesus heals, this mortal body still grows old, and as a result suffers the effects which include sickness, etc.

Also, due to the fact that Believers continue to live in a system which in effect is governed by Satan, even though Christ meets the needs of every Believer in a material, financial sense, still, Believers, due to living in this system, at times, suffer material disadvantages.

All of this, although addressed at Calvary and the Resurrection, will not be totally brought to its positive conclusion, until the Resurrection. Then the results of the Believer's present Salvation will be complete.

3. What Jesus did at Calvary and the Resurrection by removing the sin debt, now makes it possible for Believers to be Baptized with the Holy Spirit, which opens up the entirety of the vista of personal Christlikeness (Jn. 16:7-15; Acts 2:4; Rom. Chpt. 8).

The Spirit-led and Spirit-directed life,

opens up the entirety of the Plan of God to the Believer. This speaks of the Revelation of the Word to the Believer, and the Place and Position of the Believer in Christ. In other words, everything the Lord does on this earth, He does through the Ministry, Power, Agency, and Office of the Holy Spirit. As stated, all of this was made possible by the price paid by Christ at Calvary.

Even though we have only touched the high points of this all-encompassing subject, still, what little we have given proclaims to the Believer the absolute necessity of a proper understanding of the Atonement.

(2) "LET EVERY ONE OF US PLEASE HIS NEIGHBOUR FOR HIS GOOD TO EDIFICATION."

The pleasing one's neighbour in this context refers to the act of the Believer foregoing a legitimate act because a weaker Christian thinks it to be wrong. It pleases the weaker Believer because it removes a source of temptation to him to do that thing, and makes easier his attempt to live a life pleasing to God. However, and even as we have stated, the stronger Christian is to do this only in the instance where the weaker Christian would be edified or built up in the Christian life. Paul then enforces his exhortation by citing the example of our Lord Jesus Who pleased not Himself, as we shall see (Wuest).

"Edification" in the Greek is "oiko-dome," and means "the act of building," in this case, the promotion of spiritual growth. In other words, spiritual growth should always be in mind.

This does not refer to the entire Church, or a single Believer for that matter, giving over to someone who has a contentious spirit. There are some people who consider themselves to be super spiritual, attempting to force the entirety of the Church to adhere to their silly notions. These Passages as given by Paul, have absolutely nothing to do with that type of person. In fact, if the Church heeds that type of ruling, contentious spirit, as should be obvious, it will destroy the local congregation. These people are the architects of their own brand of Holiness apart from the Bible.

AN EXAMPLE!

We have Prayer Meeting each night with

the exception of Service nights, in one of the major assembly rooms of the College Dorms, which are immediately across the street from Family Worship Center.

It was December of 1996. I had just arrived for Prayer Meeting, having just gotten out of the car. Before going inside, a man who had been in our Church for several years, who considered himself to be super spiritual, and had caused problems, confronted me about the Christmas Tree which some of the Students had set up in this large room. He was demanding that it be removed, and if not he would take his family and go elsewhere. To his surprise, at least that is what registered on his face, I reached out my hand and shook his, telling him that I hoped he would be happy wherever it was that he went. We would not take down the Tree.

Actually, as far as I knew, that was the only place on the Ministry Compound where someone had decorated a Christmas Tree. We do not erect one in the Church, although there would be nothing wrong with it if we did. As stated, there is nothing moral or immoral about a Christmas Tree, unless someone falls down and worships the thing, which I have really never heard of anyone doing.

This man was not a new convert, as were most if not all those of whom Paul spoke, but rather considered himself as spiritually elite. These people, as I trust we have explained, have to be dealt with somewhat differently.

(3) "FOR EVEN CHRIST PLEASED NOT HIMSELF; BUT, AS IT IS WRITTEN, THE REPROACHES OF THEM THAT REPROACHED THEE FELL ON ME."

The phrase, "For even Christ pleased not Himself," actually means that had He done so He might have avoided the hatred of man's heart to God. That He was so hated is a testimony to His Deity, for only God could be thus hated by man (Williams).

The entirety of the Life and Ministry of Christ was to do the Will of the Father (Ps. 40:8; Heb. 10:7).

The phrase, "But, as it is written, the reproaches of them that reproached Thee fell on Me," is taken from Psalm 69:9.

The idea is, that all the hatred of God by fallen man, and hatred it was, was taken out on Christ. Evil men could not reach God, but they could reach Christ when He came. Their treatment of Him makes it obvious, as to their hatred of God.

More particularly, this was the hatred of religious men who claimed to be of God, rather than those who were of the world. As we have said many times, there is no hatred like religious hatred.

Why did Paul use this example of Christ respecting hatred for Him?

The idea is, if Jesus could undergo the extreme persecution which He did, even unto death, seeking not at all to please Himself, but rather His Heavenly Father, how much more should we be willing to forego some small things in order to strengthen a weak Brother! Comparison is not really the idea, but rather example. As the Life and Ministry of Christ, as stated, were always for others, likewise, should be our lives.

(4) "FOR WHATSOEVER THINGS WERE WRITTEN AFORETIME WERE WRITTEN FOR OUR LEARNING, THAT WE THROUGH PATIENCE AND COMFORT OF THE SCRIPTURES MIGHT HAVE HOPE."

The phrase, *"For whatsoever things were written aforetime were written for our learning,"* refers to the whole of Old Testament Scriptures (Lk. 24:44; Jn. 5:39; I Cor. 10:1-11; II Tim. 2:15; 3:15-16; etc.).

If the Holy Spirit through the Apostle grandly proclaims the validity and necessity of our *"learning"* the Old Testament, then by all means, He should be taken seriously. I say this because many Charismatics claim that the Old Testament has little validity now, considering that we presently have the New Covenant. However, the idea is, that one cannot fully understand the New Covenant, unless one has a proper working knowledge of the Old Covenant. In fact, the Old Testament is the Foundation for the New Testament. Consequently, to lack understanding in that capacity means that one lacks a proper Foundation.

In fact, a lack of understanding of the Old Covenant, is at least one of, if not the major reason, for false Doctrine.

The phrase, *"That we through patience and comfort of the Scriptures might have hope,"* as given by the Holy Spirit, takes the Apostle to a much greater depth concerning

NOTES

this issue.

"That" in the Greek is *"hina,"* and means *"in order that."* This introduces God's Purpose, which is wider than the immediate purpose of the Apostle. Paul meant to speak only of bearing the infirmities of the weak, but with the quotation of Psalm 69:9 there came the idea of the Christian's sufferings generally, and it is amid *them* that God's Purpose is to be fulfilled (Denney).

The idea is, that there are sufferings and reproaches attached to the Christian Life which cannot be avoided, and that the Word of God provides *"Patience"* and *"Comfort"* that the Believer might maintain a brave and cheerful spirit.

"Patience" in the Greek is *"hupomone,"* and means *"cheer, hopeful, endurance and continuance."*

"Comfort" in the Greek is *"paraklesis,"* and means *"a calling near, a summons, supplication, encouragement, consolation and solace."*

In respect to these two attributes, the Scriptures give us examples which give direction, and encouragement. Faith is the end result, which brings forth the *"Patience and Comfort."*

"Hope" in the Greek is *"elpis,"* and means *"to anticipate with expectation, which brings pleasure, and which generates Faith."*

To be frank, the *"Scriptures,"* whether of the New Testament or the Old, Alone bring the help which is needed. Only the Lord knows the answer to life's problems, and His directions are found in the Scripture. It is sad, when much of the modern Church recommends instead, the wisdom of the world, found in modern Psychology, etc. As well, even as these Passages proclaim, there is no way that the Believer can confess away all of the problems and vicissitudes of life. While a proper confession is certainly important, and very beneficial, still, a certain degree of difficulties are going to come the way of the Christian irrespective of the degree of one's Faith. Spiritually speaking, Believers live in an alien and foreign society. As such, the Believer spiritually, swims against the tide instead of with the tide.

(5) "NOW THE GOD OF PATIENCE AND CONSOLATION GRANT YOU TO BE LIKEMINDED ONE TOWARD ANOTHER

ACCORDING TO CHRIST JESUS:"

The phrase, *"Now the God of Patience and Consolation grant you to be likeminded one toward another,"* presents God as the Author of the Patience and Consolation lodged in the Scriptures, which nourish the Hope of Believers (Williams). In other words, the Word of God is given to the Believer for this very purpose, among other things.

The phrase, *"According to Christ Jesus,"* proclaims by Paul, that the moral judgment and temper of all Believers may be determined by Jesus Christ. In this case there will be the harmony which the disputes of Chapter 14 of Romans disturbed (Denney).

Believers are to imitate Christ by receiving one another to the Glory of God as Christ received us to that same Glory (Williams).

(6) "THAT YE MAY WITH ONE MIND AND ONE MOUTH GLORIFY GOD, EVEN THE FATHER OF OUR LORD JESUS CHRIST."

The phrase, *"That ye may with one mind and one mouth Glorify God,"* proclaims the Christlikeness of the previous Verse, as the only manner in which these differences can be correctly settled.

All the Saints are to have *"one mind,"* which is to be the *"Mind of Christ"* (Phil. 2:5-8). The *"Mind of Christ"* is the *"Servant Mind,"* which is to be the same in the Believer (Phil. 2:7).

If we speak as *"one mouth,"* it means we will speak the Word of God. Only then can God be properly Glorified.

The phrase, *"Even the Father of our Lord Jesus Christ,"* contains the rendering of Christ pleasing the Father, Who we must desire to please accordingly. When the Church glorifies God with one heart and one mouth, it will have transcended all the troubles of Chapter 14 of Romans (Denney).

(7) "WHEREFORE RECEIVE YE ONE ANOTHER, AS CHRIST ALSO RECEIVED US TO THE GLORY OF GOD."

The phrase, *"Wherefore receive ye one another,"* speaks of Christian acceptance and fellowship.

"Receive" is *"proslambano,"* and means *"to take to oneself, to grant one access to one's heart, to take into friendship and fellowship."*

The phrase, *"As Christ also received us to the Glory of God,"* refers to the sinner being

NOTES

Born Again, and that such a one being brought from darkness to Light brings *"Glory to God."*

"Us" covers all parties in the Church, however they may be distinguished. If Christ received both, they are bound to receive each other (Denney).

A STRONG APPEAL

The idea is, as should be obvious, that if one is Born Again, one is to be received as a Brother or Sister in the Lord. The emphasis is on the Salvation experience, whatever peripheral differences there may be. This is a strong appeal for unity, but as well, strongly based, even in a concrete fashion, on Biblical Salvation.

The strength of this appeal at the same time, shuts out those who do not have or believe in, the Born-Again experience (Jn. 3:3). In essence, if one is not Saved by truly expressing Faith in Christ and what He did at Calvary, one cannot be considered a Brother or Sister in the Lord.

PREDICATED ON BIBLICAL SALVATION, HOW FAR SHOULD ACCEPTANCE REACH?

If one is truly Born Again, peripheral beliefs, according to the Holy Spirit through the Apostle Paul, should not, and in fact must not, stand in the way of acceptance. The idea is, if Christ has received us from darkness unto Light, who are we not to receive one whom Christ has received!

When one looks at the modern Church, one finds that these Passages are not adhered to very readily. In other words, they are little obeyed.

For instance, in the non-Pentecostal Church world, very few Preachers who believe in being Baptized with the Holy Spirit, with the evidence of speaking with other Tongues (Acts 2:4), are welcome to minister in any of those respective Churches. Consequently, at least in those circles, Biblical Salvation is not the basis for fellowship, but rather one's belief respecting the Baptism with the Holy Spirit.

Likewise, in many Pentecostal Denominations, thousands of Preachers are shut out simply because they will not adhere to a man-devised rule, etc. Once again, Salvation which should be the only issue, is not the issue, but rather something else.

When the Church strays from the Word of God, division and hurt are always the results. In that climate, God receives little Glory.

(8) "NOW I SAY THAT JESUS CHRIST WAS A MINISTER OF THE CIRCUMCISION FOR THE TRUTH OF GOD, TO CONFIRM THE PROMISES MADE UNTO THE FATHERS:"

The phrase, *"Now I say that Jesus Christ was a Minister of the circumcision for the Truth of God,"* proclaims the fact that Jesus was obligated first of all to the Jews, and for particular reasons.

He explains this Himself in His Answer to the Disciples who misunderstood His Answer to the woman, *". . . I am not sent but unto the lost sheep of the House of Israel"* (Mat. 15:24).

The phrase, *"To confirm the Promises made unto the Fathers,"* proclaims the fulfillment of the Messianic Promises to Israel. Actually, the Jews were raised up for the very purpose of giving the world the Word of God, and serving as the womb of the Messiah. Consequently, the obligation was to them first.

However, this was but a means to an end, even as the next Verse proclaims, that the Gentiles might be reached through Israel and thus Glorify God for His Mercy (Wuest).

The argument of Verses 7-13 supports the command, *". . . Receive ye . . ."* of Romans 14:1.

The argument is: that just as Christ as a Minister (one who serves) in the Hebrew Church, received the Gentiles into that Fellowship, even as Paul described in Chapter 11 of Romans, so weak Believers should be received into Christian Fellowship. It is quite an argument as is obvious.

And, further, that the right to Fellowship was not agreement on petty points of observance, but on the fact of reception by Christ, and of recognition of Him as the Head and the Center of the Fellowship (Williams).

This is most important, and this argument of the Apostle shows how essential to right Christian conduct, both in the Church and in the world, is intelligence in Dispensational Doctrine, i.e., the activities of the Divine Purpose in the various periods of human history,

as revealed in the Scriptures.

In other words, one must know and understand from the Word of God, how that God issued His Plan into the world by raising up a special people (Jews) from the loins of Abraham, and how He included the Gentiles in that Plan.

The *"Truth of God"* as presented in this Verse, is the Fidelity of God to His Promises made to Israel. Consequently, the Jewish claim was based on the Fidelity of God as promised; the Gentile hope is somewhat different, in fact, based on the *"Mercy of God,"* even as the next Verse proclaims.

(9) "AND THAT THE GENTILES MIGHT GLORIFY GOD FOR HIS MERCY; AS IT IS WRITTEN, FOR THIS CAUSE I WILL CONFESS TO THEE AMONG THE GENTILES, AND SING UNTO THY NAME."

The phrase, *"And that the Gentiles might Glorify God for His Mercy,"* has reference to the fact that Gentiles are grafted in not because of any merit on their part, but strictly because of *"Mercy"* on His Part.

The idea is, in Verse 8, Jesus is seen as the Center of the Believing Fellowship of Israel, and in Verse 9, as the Center of Believing Pagans, while in Verses 10-11 He is presented as the Center of a vast Fellowship formed of all people, both Jews and Gentiles, now united in Christ.

The phrase, *"As it is written,"* once again harks back to the Word of God as the Foundation for all things.

The phrase, *"For this cause I will confess to Thee among the Gentiles, and sing unto Thy Name,"* is taken from Psalm 18:49.

Christ is assumed here to be the Speaker, even as He is in all the Psalms, and He gives thanks to God among the Gentiles when the Gentiles give thanks to God through Him (Heb. 2:12) (Denney).

Understanding that the Psalms constituted earth's first Songbook, and that it was meant for the Glory of God, means that those of Israel who were in Faith, were a singing people. Such is the same for the Gentile Church. Lord we *"Sing unto Thy Name."*

(10) "AND AGAIN HE SAITH, REJOICE, YE GENTILES, WITH HIS PEOPLE."

This Passage is derived from Deuteronomy 32:43.

By joining *"Gentiles"* with Israel, *"His People,"* Moses predicts the grafting of the *". . . Wild Olive Tree . . .",* into the *". . . Good Olive Tree . . .",* as Paul exclaims in Romans 11:17-24. So, one sees how these Revelations of Paul were already ensconced in the Old Testament Scriptures. To be sure, the Lord fleshed it out greatly to Paul, giving him understanding, but the Foundation of the New Covenant was already in the Word of God.

(11) "AND AGAIN, PRAISE THE LORD, ALL YE GENTILES; AND LAUD HIM, ALL YE PEOPLE."

This is taken from Psalm 117:1.

It predicted the day that the Gentiles would Praise the Lord, and would *"Laud Him,"* meaning to extol His Grace and Virtue.

The true beginning of this actually took place on the Day of Pentecost, at least that which made it possible. Even though only Jews that day were Baptized with the Holy Spirit, still, the stage was set for the Gospel to go to the entirety of the world. In fact, the last Words of Jesus before His Ascension were in effect, *". . . Go ye into all the world, and preach the Gospel to every creature"* (Mk. 16:15).

So, the Gospel going to the Gentiles should not have been a shock to Israel, as it had been predicted by the Prophets of old, even as Paul here reiterates, and even as Jesus proclaimed must be done.

Incidentally, the rendering in Psalms is *"O Praise the Lord, all ye nations: Praise Him, all ye people."* *"Nations"* as it is used in the Old Testament, always refers to the Gentiles, unless Israel is specifically mentioned. In fact, this is about the closest that the Old Testament comes respecting predictions concerning the coming *"Church,"* which actually came into being on the Day of Pentecost.

(12) "AND AGAIN, ESAIAS (ISAIAH) SAITH, THERE SHALL BE A ROOT OF JESSE, AND HE THAT SHALL RISE TO REIGN OVER THE GENTILES; IN HIM SHALL THE GENTILES TRUST."

The phrase, *"And again, Esaias* (Isaiah) *saith,"* is found in Isaiah 11:10.

The phrase, *"There shall be a root of Jesse,"* refers to David the son of Jesse, but

more particularly, to the Incarnation respecting Jesus, Who would be, and in fact was, *"The Greater Son of David."*

The phrase, *"And He that shall rise to reign over the Gentiles,"* proves several things:

1. This by Isaiah predicted the coming of the Messiah, Who would be Jesus Christ, and because He was in the lineage of David, i.e., *"Root of Jesse."*

2. He being Jewish will bring together both Jew and Gentile, which is here predicted, and which shall happen in the coming Kingdom Age.

3. This predicts that the Gentiles would look to Him, trusting Him for Salvation.

4. It predicts that Jesus will ultimately *"reign"* as King over the entirety of the world.

The phrase, *"In Him shall the Gentiles trust,"* came to pass exactly as predicted. Today the Church is almost entirely made up of Gentiles, and in fact, was that way almost from the beginning. In fact, Paul was the Great Apostle to the Gentiles.

(13) "NOW THE GOD OF HOPE FILL YOU WITH ALL JOY AND PEACE IN BELIEVING, THAT YE MAY ABOUND IN HOPE, THROUGH THE POWER OF THE HOLY SPIRIT."

As someone said, *"Hope springs eternal."* However, for hope to be proper it must ever be in Christ and the Cross.

The phrase, *"Fill you with all Joy and Peace in believing,"* means that this which the Lord imparts to Believers, rests on Faith (in believing).

"In believing," in the Greek is *"en toi pisteuein,"* and means *"in the believing,"* which is interpreted, *"in the sphere of the act of habitually believing, which means continuing to believe."*

"Joy" in the Greek is *"chara,"* and means *"cheerfulness, calm, delight, exceeding fulsomeness."* As stated, the source of this *"Joy"* is Faith, with God Himself as the Ground and Object, God Who we know and have in Christ.

"Peace" is *"eirene,"* and means *"prosperity, quietness, rest, to set at one again."*

What we are seeing here is the true meaning of Life. It is the fulfillment, the finding, the goal of the human soul and spirit. As stated, it can only be found in Christ, and the vehicle is Faith in Him. These things money cannot buy, the world cannot give, and man cannot bring about at all on his own.

The phrase, *"That ye may abound in hope,"* speaks of the *"more abundant Life"* promised by Christ (Jn. 10:10).

"Abound" is *"perisseuo,"* and means *"to exceed a fixed number or measure, to be over, to exist in abundance, to be in affluence."* The noun *"perissos,"* means *"more than is necessary, superadded."* These words speak of a superabundance.

"Hope" in the Greek is *"elpis,"* and means *"to anticipate with pleasure, to have expectative confidence."* It is actually tied to *"Faith."*

The idea is, that the *"Joy"* and *"Peace"* which we now have in Christ, will not only *not* be lost, but will continue to grow, actually super-abounding. Wonderfully enough, this has nothing to do with circumstances, whatever problems there may be, but continues right on irrespective of these things.

Whatever happiness or peace the world may have, is totally dependent upon outward circumstances, and is, therefore, here today and gone tomorrow. However, that which is given of the Lord is not affected at all, by the variances of particular happenings, whatever they may be. In other words, what saddens the world does not sadden us, and what gladdens the world, does not gladden us, and for the simple reason that our Power Source is within us, even as the next phrase proclaims.

The phrase, *"Through the Power of the Holy Spirit,"* tells us several things:

1. First of all, the Holy Spirit resides in the heart and life of the Believer, and does so continually and perpetually.

2. Being God, He has the *"Power"* to do whatever is necessary, and in whatever capacity.

3. He is there to use His Power on behalf of the Child of God, but only according to the directions given by the Father *". . . according to the Will of God"* (Rom. 8:27).

4. The *"Joy"* and *"Peace"* here addressed, plus all else from the Lord, cannot possibly be brought about in the heart and life of the Believer, without the *"Power"* of the Holy Spirit.

5. This should unequivocally state to all Believers, that the modern humanistic manner of Psychology (Psychotherapy) has no place in the thinking of the Child of God.

NOTES

In fact, such as given here in the Word of God, is totally foreign, and, therefore, anathema to Humanistic Psychology. The sadness is, that most in the modern Church, even many of its so-called Spiritual Leaders, do not anymore believe in the *"Power of the Holy Spirit,"* that is if they ever did.

Incidentally, the word *"Ghost"* in the Greek is *"Pneuma,"* and means *"Spirit,"* and should have been translated accordingly.

(14) "AND I MYSELF ALSO AM PERSUADED OF YOU, MY BRETHREN, THAT YE ALSO ARE FULL OF GOODNESS, FILLED WITH ALL KNOWLEDGE, ABLE ALSO TO ADMONISH ONE ANOTHER."

The phrase, *"And I myself also am persuaded of you, my Brethren,"* means to suggest that what he wrote in Chapter 14 was not meant to insinuate them defective either in intelligence, or love, or both. Paul disclaims any such inference by this phrase (Denney). Vincent says that with this verse the Epilogue of the Epistle begins.

The phrase, *"That ye also are full of goodness,"* means that they had such because of Christ, and not because of what he had ministered to them, for in fact, he had not ministered to them at all before this Epistle, except for those in the Church who he had previously known elsewhere.

The context defines this goodness, not as goodness in general, but the Christian Love which bears the infirmities of the weaker Brother (Wuest).

The phrase, *"Filled with all knowledge,"* refers to Christian knowledge in its entirety, and not in an absolute sense, which should be obvious.

The phrase, *"Able also to admonish one another,"* means that there was sufficient knowledge of the Word of God among the Saints in Rome, that they could correct each other if the need be. Actually, this is the ideal under the Lord for all Churches.

As should be known, there were not many Spiritual Leaders in those days of the Early Church. Mostly, Leaders were raised up among their own. This of course had its drawbacks; however, it also had its attributes.

Too often at the present time, many congregations little seek to learn the Word of God themselves, but rather rely on their Pastor for almost all instruction. In other words, if they like the man, whatever he says they go along with his line of thought. Such is extremely dangerous, at least in a spiritual sense.

While the Pastor should be loved, respected, and trusted, still, the Believer must know the Word of God as well, in order that the veracity of any Bible Subject is known and understood irrespective as to who stands behind the pulpit.

(15) "NEVERTHELESS, BRETHREN, I HAVE WRITTEN THE MORE BOLDLY UNTO YOU IN SOME SORT, AS PUTTING YOU IN MIND, BECAUSE OF THE GRACE THAT IS GIVEN TO ME OF GOD."

The phrase, *"Nevertheless, Brethren, I have written the more boldly unto you in some sort,"* has to do with the *"goodness"* mentioned in the previous Verse. He believed they would receive what he had to say.

"The more boldly" in the Greek is *"tolmeroteros,"* and means, *"with greater confidence than otherwise."*

In fact, Paul was always bold in his presentation of the Gospel. He had to be, for it needed boldness to declare man's hopeless depravity; to teach Justification and Sanctification in Christ apart from works; and to prove that the Gentiles were branches in the Good Olive Tree of Divine privilege, and consequently members of the Body of Christ. To be sure, these Doctrines pretty well rubbed everyone the wrong way.

Most of humanity does not think of itself as without God, and, consequently, utterly depraved. It is very fond of pointing to its alleged good works, of whatever sort.

Likewise, the idea that *"works"* of all sort were out, especially considering Justification and Sanctification, was not exactly easy for most to swallow. Once again, man likes to think he can contribute something toward his spiritual welfare.

And then of course, the idea that God had included Gentiles did not set well with many Jews, especially considering, that all now had to come on the same basis — that of Faith in Christ. So, it took a holy boldness, which the Holy Spirit readily gave to the Apostle, and which he used constantly.

The phrase, *"As putting you in mind, because of the Grace that is given to me of*

God," proclaims the fact that even though the Church at Rome was not one of his own foundation, nor did he have a desire, there or elsewhere, to *"build upon* (on) *another man's foundation"* (vs. 20), yet his peculiar mission as Apostle to the Gentiles gave him a right to admonish them.

The reason thus given is, it will be observed, a confirmation of the view, otherwise apparent, that the Roman Church consisted principally of Gentile Believers (Barmby).

(16) "THAT I SHOULD BE THE MINISTER OF JESUS CHRIST TO THE GENTILES, MINISTERING THE GOSPEL OF GOD, THAT THE OFFERING UP OF THE GENTILES MIGHT BE ACCEPTABLE, BEING SANCTIFIED BY THE HOLY SPIRIT."

The phrase, *"That I should be the Minister of Jesus Christ to the Gentiles,"* presents by Paul, his Calling as an Apostle to the Gentile Church.

"Minister" is not here the usual word translated *"Minister,"* namely, *"diagonos"* (a servant), but *"leitourgos,"* used here by Paul as referring to Sacred Things of the Priests of the Jerusalem Temple (Heb. 8:2).

Paul uses this word to speak of his Ministry of preaching the Gospel as a Priestly Ministry, and of equal value and Sacredness to the Ministry of the Priesthood of the Old Testament.

The phrase, *"Ministering the Gospel of God,"* is used in the sense of the Priests and Levites of old, who were busied with the Sacred Rites in the Tabernacle and Temple. The word *"Ministering"* is again another of those words speaking of a Ministry that is sacred, in the Greek *"leitourgeo"* (Wuest).

The phrase, *"That the Offering up of the Gentiles might be acceptable,"* presents Paul conceiving himself as presenting to God the Gentile Church as an *"Offering."* The Priestly function in the exercise of which this Offering is made is the Preaching of the Gospel (Denney).

As should be obvious, Paul gloried in his appointment as a Preacher to the Gentiles. With him, and as it should be with all, Preaching was the highest service of all, even greater than the working of Miracles, etc. In fact, he alludes to this in Verse 18.

The phrase, *"Being Sanctified by the Holy*

Spirit," presents the manner in which this is done.

The Holy Spirit here symbolically pictures the Apostle as a Priest of the Old Testament Economy (Num. 8:11). He is pictured as offering up the Gentiles as a pure Sacrifice acceptable to God because they were washed in the Blood, and Sanctified by the Holy Spirit. The Jews had always regarded the Gentiles as *"unclean,"* which in fact they were. However, Calvary corrected that, with the Holy Spirit making it possible for the purpose of the Finished Work of Christ to be made applicable to believing sinners, which was and is done by Faith. In Truth the Jews were unclean as well, but were loathe to admit such. In any case, the Shed Blood of Jesus Christ was absolutely needed as the cleansing agent for sinners, which applies to all men (Rom. 3:23).

(17) "I HAVE THEREFORE WHEREOF I MAY GLORY THROUGH JESUS CHRIST IN THOSE THINGS WHICH PERTAIN TO GOD."

The phrase, *"I have therefore whereof I may glory through Jesus Christ,"* despite the apologetic tone of Verse 14, proclaims Paul as not without confidence in writing to the Romans (Denney). However, there is no personal assumption in this, for he has this authority only in Christ Jesus, and as Vincent translates, *"I have my glorying in Christ Jesus."*

The phrase, *"In those things which pertain to God,"* is in Jewish liturgical language a denoting of functions of worship (Heb. 2:17; 5:1).

The idea is, that all of his Ministry and in whatever capacity, is ordered and directed by the Holy Spirit, signifying the Divine Order. Everything is of God, according to the directions of the Lord, instituted by God, all in Christ Jesus, and Anointed and carried out by the Holy Spirit through the Apostle.

(18) "FOR I WILL NOT DARE TO SPEAK OF ANY OF THOSE THINGS WHICH CHRIST HATH NOT WROUGHT BY ME, TO MAKE THE GENTILES OBEDIENT, BY WORD AND DEED,"

The phrase, *"For I will not dare to speak of any of those things which Christ hath not wrought by me,"* carries the idea, that all

that Paul has done and has written, has been totally of the Lord. Denney says, *"All other boasting he declines . . . in effect this means, I will not presume to speak of anything except what Christ wrought through me. This is the explanation of 'I therefore have my glorying in Christ.'"*

The phrase, *"To make the Gentiles obedient by word and deed,"* proclaims the vindication (if such is needed) of Paul's action in writing to the Church in Rome. It is not on his own impulse, but in Christ that he does it; and the Romans as Gentiles lie within the sphere in which Christ works through him (Wuest).

Paul's purpose in relating these things in these verses is to allege proof of his being a True Apostle with the right to speak with authority to the Gentiles.

It does not follow from his statements, although it is possible, that in his asserting his claim respecting his Apostleship, that he had in mind the Judaizers who denied that claim. Still, he may have suspected that some might possibly have been busy there, as they were in other places; and, however that might be, writing as he was to a Church not founded by, and as yet unvisited by, himself, he might think distinct assertions of his claim to be desirable.

PAUL THE APOSTLE

Studying the New Testament, of which Paul wrote almost half, it is presently unthinkable that anyone would question his Apostleship. But to be sure, Paul was not granted the accord then as one might think. He was very controversial, but not in the sense of his own nature, but rather because of the Mission appointed him by the Holy Spirit.

The Great Gospel of Grace which was given him, in effect the New Covenant, and in effect made him the Moses of the New Testament, greatly impacted the Jews. The New Covenant of Grace basically states that the Old Covenant was fulfilled in Jesus, which means it was to be set aside having run its course. There was no more need for Types when the Antitype had now come. There was no more need for Symbols when the Reality, namely Christ had now come, fulfilling all the Symbols. The Old Covenant had done its work well, pointing to the One Who was to come, which was basically its purpose. It now must be set aside in favor of the New.

Jesus had alluded to this when He said, *"No man putteth a piece of new cloth unto an old garment, for that which is put in to fill it up taketh from the garment, and the rent is made worse"* (Mat. 9:16).

He then said, further reinforcing His previous statement, *"Neither do men put new wine into old bottles* (old wineskins)*: else the bottles* (skins) *break, and the wine runneth out, and the bottles* (containers made of skins) *perish: but they put new wine into new bottles* (new skins), *and both are preserved"* (Mat. 9:17).

Even many of the Jews in the Early Church who were followers of Christ, did not readily accept this new wineskin of the Gospel of Grace as readily as they should. Many of them kept attempting to combine the two, which as is blatantly obvious, was directly contradictory to what Jesus had said. Men do not easily give up that which they have known all their lives, even though it is inferior to the New, at least as it refers to the Great Gospel of Grace.

THE LORD'S CHOICE OF PAUL

Many in the Early Church attempting to discredit the Message, made their greatest thrust in this effort in an attempt to discredit the Messenger. Most of the Book of II Corinthians was written in respect to the situation. To counter these efforts by the Judaizers (those who attempted to combine the Law with Grace), Paul constantly reinforced his Calling as an Apostle. In fact, the salutation of most of his Epistles begins with the words, *"Paul, an Apostle,"* or words to that effect.

As well, even though he ministered to the Jews in a major way, still, his major thrust was always toward the Gentiles, because that was the thrust of the Holy Spirit. Even as Paul has said in this very Chapter, this was always the intention of the Lord, as was given in the Scriptures concerning the Prophets of old.

(19) "THROUGH MIGHTY SIGNS AND WONDERS, BY THE POWER OF THE

SPIRIT OF GOD; SO THAT FROM JERUSALEM, AND ROUND ABOUT UNTO ILLYRICUM, I HAVE FULLY PREACHED THE GOSPEL OF CHRIST."

The phrase, *"Through mighty signs and wonders,"* proclaims the Mighty Power of God in operation.

"Signs" in the Greek is *"semeion,"* and means *"indication,"* in other words, an indication that the Power of God is working, which indicates that the Holy Spirit is present.

"Wonders" are *"teras,"* and mean *"something extraordinary or inexplicable, a marvelous, unusual accomplishment or deed."*

These things no doubt included Healings and Miracles, even extraordinary things such as the opening of blinded eyes, or one being delivered from demon spirits, etc. Of course, anything that God does is extraordinary, irrespective as to what it may be; however, the *"Signs"* and *"Wonders"* mentioned here, speak of that which is totally out of the ordinary, that is if anything the Lord does could be labeled as *"ordinary."*

The idea is, that these extraordinary events and happenings, could not have happened of themselves, and could be explained only as a display of the Power of God.

WERE THESE THINGS MEANT TO CONTINUE AFTER THE EARLY CHURCH?

Most definitely!

Jesus said, *". . . These signs shall follow them that believe . . ."* (Mk. 16:17). He then gave a list of what those *"signs"* included:

The casting out of demons, speaking with other Tongues, putting away demon spirits from areas and localities, power to overcome threats on one's life, Prayer for the sick and seeing them Healed (Mk. 16:17-18). Jesus put no time limit or termination date on these things, with the Greek Text actually portraying otherwise, continuing as long as the Church is in the world. So that means, that whatever happened then, should happen now as well, and in fact does.

PERSONAL EXAMPLES

As a child of about 11 or 12 years old, I was wondrously Healed in answer to Prayer. Before my healing, despite the efforts of the

Medical Profession, my situation steadily grew worse, until the School Authorities told my Parents that if the situation did not improve, I would have to be taken out of School. Their words were, *"We don't want him to die on our hands."* However, to make the story short, the Lord Wondrously and Gloriously Healed me and I have not been sick since.

In fact, untold numbers of people have been Healed by the Power of God down through the ages, whether in Old Testament times, New Testament times, or at the present. The Lord does not change. Preachers who claim these things are done away, mostly fall into the camp of those who deny the Baptism with the Holy Spirit with the evidence of speaking with other Tongues (Acts 2:4; Chpts. 10; 19).

At the same time, there have been many wild claims made regarding Healings and Miracles, which have no validity in fact. God does not want, nor will He accept false glory. However, despite the unbelief and false claims, the Lord has always, and continues, to do great and mighty things among those who will dare to believe Him.

The phrase, *"By the Power of the Spirit of God,"* proclaims the manner in which these things were done. It is always by the *"Spirit of God."*

WHAT DOES THIS MEAN?

There is one God, but manifested in Three Persons, *"God the Father," "God the Son,"* and *"God the Holy Spirit."* To help us understand it better, even at the risk of gross oversimplification, one can think of *"God the Father"* as the Architect of all things, with *"God the Son"* as the Builder, and *"God the Holy Spirit"* as the One Who does the actual construction (Gen. 1:2; Jn. 1:1-5; I Cor. 15:28). In other words, every single thing done on this earth which emanates from the Godhead, is actually carried out through and by the Person, Ministry, Office, and Work of the Holy Spirit.

When the Godhead determined to bring this world back to a fruitful, habitable condition, even though God the Father spoke such into existence, still, it was the Holy Spirit Who performed the actual work (Gen. 1:1-2).

As well, it was the Holy Spirit Who actually

dwelt between the Mercy Seat and the Cherubim in the Tabernacle and Temple of old. We know this from the fact that it is the Holy Spirit Who now indwells Believers, with Believers now serving as His Temple (I Cor. 3:16).

Likewise, it was the Holy Spirit Who came upon and within Christ, enabling Him to do the mighty works which He did (Lk. 4:18-19; Jn. 1:33). In fact, the Holy Spirit is so prominent in the Book of Acts, which is meant to serve as our Pattern, that His Name in one way or the other, is used over 50 times.

WHAT CAN THE BELIEVER DO WITHOUT THE HOLY SPIRIT?

Of course, many in the Church World would argue that all have the Holy Spirit at Conversion. They are right and at the same time they are wrong.

As we have already stated, every single thing done on this earth by the Godhead, is done by and through the Person and Ministry of the Holy Spirit. It is the Holy Spirit Who gives the Word to the Preacher or witness of any nature. It is also the Holy Spirit Who Anoints the person to deliver that Word. As well, it is the Holy Spirit Who convicts the sinner of sin upon hearing the Word (Jn. 16:7-15).

When the Work of Redemption is carried out in the heart and life of the believing sinner, it is the Holy Spirit Who effects the Work of Regeneration. So, in that sense, every Believer most definitely receives the Holy Spirit, which is a given, that is if one is truly Born Again.

However, being *"Born of the Spirit"* is totally different than being *"Baptized with the Spirit"* (Acts 2:4). It is the Work of the Spirit, referred to as the *"Baptism with the Holy Spirit"* of which we now speak.

This experience comes after Salvation, and in fact, must come after Salvation. The Holy Spirit can only dwell in a Temple which has been cleansed by the Precious Shed Blood of Jesus Christ (I Jn. 1:7). In fact, Jesus said that the world could not receive the Holy Spirit, and for all the obvious reasons, that being reserved for the Saint who has been cleansed by the Blood of the Lamb (Jn. 14:17).

Once the sinner is Saved, thereby, now a Believer, he is a candidate for the Baptism with the Holy Spirit, which will *always* be accompanied by speaking with other Tongues (Acts 1:4; 2:4; 10:46; 19:1-6).

Whenever the Believer is Baptized with the Holy Spirit, which is an experience different and set apart from Salvation, and is received as stated, after Salvation, *"Power"* is infused into the Believer's heart and life (Acts 1:8). It is this *"Power"* which helped Paul to perform these Miracles, as well as help given to every other Spirit-filled Believer. Of course, the Baptism with the Holy Spirit is not solely for Power, but that is one of the greatest attributes of His Indwelling.

In fact, it is the Holy Spirit who makes real and understandable all that Jesus has done for the Believer at Calvary and the Resurrection, in other words, one's place and position in Christ, as Paul carefully outlined in Romans Chapter 8. So, the quantity and quality of His Help, are beyond definition.

POTENTIAL!

However, the Baptism with the Holy Spirit does not guarantee anyone anything, His Presence actually being in the realm of potential. That means He has the potential to do all of these things, whether He is allowed to or not.

Being used by the Holy Spirit is another thing altogether, and requires much consecration and dedication to the Lord. As someone has stated, the more of Jesus that one has in one's life, the more the Holy Spirit can operate and work. One can turn it around and also say, that the more of the Holy Spirit one allows to work and operate in one's life, the more that Jesus will be Glorified.

There are untold numbers who are Baptized with the Holy Spirit with the evidence of speaking with other Tongues, who do little or nothing for the Lord. The potential is there, but it has never been realized in their lives, and because of many and varied factors, such as lack of consecration, lack of a prayer life, etc.

The Lord Jesus is the Greatest Example, being yielded to the Holy Spirit as no other human being who has ever lived. This total yielding and moral perfection on the part of

NOTES

Christ, gave the Holy Spirit such unlimited access to Christ, that great and mighty things could be done, which in fact, were done.

However, I maintain from the Word of God, of which I believe Acts is the perfect example and pattern, that without the Baptism with the Holy Spirit, with the evidence of speaking with other Tongues, which we believe the Bible solidly expresses, very little, if anything, is going to be done for God. The reason is simple, it is the Holy Spirit Who does these things, using the Spirit-filled Believer as an instrument, and if He is not allowed such access, nothing can be done. That's the reason that most of what is done in the Church World is man-instituted, man-directed, and man-operated, which means it is not of God, and will bring forth nothing for the Lord (Acts 1:4, 8).

MODERN PENTECOSTAL DENOMINATIONS

The fundamental difference that I personally have, even with many of the Pentecostal Denominations, centers up in the Moving and Operation of the Holy Spirit. Actually, the very thing that made these Denominations great, and helped them touch the world for Jesus Christ, which is the activity of the Holy Spirit, I personally feel is being pushed aside in favor of other particulars. I do not say this from personal pique or animosity, but from having been associated with one of these organizations for over 50 years.

To be frank, there are still Preachers and Laity in all of these Denominations who really love God and are doing all they can to further the Cause of Christ, and to be sure, they are certainly led by the Holy Spirit. However, that number is fastly diminishing. What I have just said can also apply, and in fact does apply, to some of the Leadership, and especially in some foreign countries. But as a whole, the Leadership is going, I believe, in the opposite direction.

THE CAUSE

Paul mentioned that Israel had attempted to establish their own righteousness, and as a result, did not submit themselves unto the *". . . Righteousness of God"* (Rom. 10:3).

I do not really feel that is the problem

with the modern Pentecostal Denominations. I personally feel that the situation is, again as Paul wrote (that is if he wrote Hebrews), *"Take heed, Brethren, lest there be in any of you an evil heart of unbelief, in departing from the Living God"* (Heb. 3:12).

I think pure and simple, it is *"unbelief."*

I do not see how that anyone who claims to know the Bible, could at the same time embrace the humanistic philosophy of Psychology (Psychotherapy). The two, the Gospel of Jesus Christ, and the Psychological Way are antagonistic by their very nature. Without going into a long dissertation, it is my belief that those who embrace this philosophy, and especially those who claim to be Spirit-filled, must do so only after having rejected the Spirit of God. In other words, they simply do not believe that Jesus Christ delivers mankind, and, consequently, is the Answer to the ills of humanity. The idea that He would need the help of Humanistic Psychology, which is totally antagonistic to the Word of God, as I have already stated, either shows a lack of knowledge of what Psychology really is, or the Bible, or both. I do not think it is a lack of knowledge, but rather *"unbelief."*

It all goes back to the Power of the Holy Spirit, His Leading, Guidance, and Anointing. We either believe what the Bible says about the Working and Moving of the Holy Spirit, eagerly allowing Him to have His Way, or else we do not believe the Word of God in this respect, and look to other avenues or sources. I maintain that most of the modern Pentecostal Denominations are looking elsewhere.

Many people believe that the events of 1988 are the cause of the rupture between me and the particular Denomination with which I was associated. It was not, it was only an excuse.

Do not misunderstand, I take full responsibility for my actions and as it pertains to me, lay the blame totally at my own feet; however, I am not to blame for their unscriptural actions. The real reason for this rupture is that of which we are presently addressing, the preeminence of the Holy Spirit or the lack thereof. To be sure, that difference is fundamental and cannot be bridged, unless there is a fundamental change in direction.

NOTES

IS IT SCRIPTURAL?

I believe the Bible must be the guide in all matters. The first question always ought to be, *"Is it Scriptural?"* Unfortunately, most Denominational Leadership little considers the Word of God, but rather makes decisions from a political viewpoint. Of course that is common, when Jesus is no longer the Head of the Church, but rather that it is now headed up by man. There is a Bible Way for everything. The Holy Spirit addressed Himself to every particular regarding living and life, and meant for us to abide by what He has given (II Pet. 1:3-4).

If wrong is committed, and in whatever capacity, there is only one solution, and that is to do what the Bible says do, which is to repent of the situation, whatever it might be, and get back on track with the Word of God. When one tries to address any problem in any manner other than that which is Scriptural, no matter how good it may seem to people on the surface, it will lead to no good. We must not add to the Word of God, and we must not take away from the Word of God (I Jn. 1:9).

As a Christian I respect my Brothers and Sisters in the Lord. I submit to them exactly as the Word of God demands, which submission is always to be reciprocal (Eph. 5:21). However, I will not do anything demanded of me which is unscriptural, irrespective as to who makes the demand. My first allegiance and always my allegiance, must be to the Word of God.

THE RESULTS

Attempting to define the information which I have, it is my estimation that only about a third of the people in modern Pentecostal Denominations actually claim to be Baptized with the Holy Spirit. If that is in fact true, that means these Denominations cannot honestly refer to themselves anymore as Pentecostal. In Truth, and with some exceptions, they are not. To be sure, the Pentecostal Way is far more than merely speaking with other Tongues, as important as that might be. It incorporates a total lifestyle, as well as a particular view of the Word of God. In brief, it means that the

Book of Acts should be duplicated in our present-day Churches.

The Assemblies of God with which I was once associated, I still hold in high regard. Some may deny that, considering the things I have just written; however, I say these things not out of bitterness or animosity, but rather because I am grieved at the present situation. This Organization began as a Fellowship. That is Scriptural. Its Government, I think then was right, at least in spirit; however, the Assemblies of God of today, is not the Assemblies of God of 50 years ago. Having over a half century of experience in this capacity, I know what I am talking about. What this Organization was nearly a half century ago, is what I am now and continue to be. In that mode, depending on the Holy Spirit, and for the simple reason it had nothing else on which to depend, it touched the world. Today, at least in a spiritual sense, it touches much of nothing.

Back in 1989 and 1990, the grief over the prevailing situation almost killed me. I would remonstrate to myself and to others, that if their Leaders would just come to the Meetings, or one of our Campmeetings, they would surely see and sense the Spirit of God at work, and would change their minds. However, I gradually came to understand that it was the Spirit of God that they did not want or desire.

I do not say those words in any particular sense toward individuals, because I have no one in mind. In fact and as stated, I am not now acquainted with very many of its present Leadership. Nevertheless, the drift, sadly and regrettably, continues in the same direction.

WHY AM I SAYING THESE THINGS?

First of all I believe the Lord has directed me to do so. As well, He still governs His Church through *"Apostles, Prophets, Evangelists, Pastors and Teachers"* (Eph. 4:11), and not through Denominational Structures. That (Denominational Structures) may be the way man governs, but not God. As Paul said, I will speak only of those things *". . . which Christ hath wrought by me . . ."* (Rom. 15:18).

By the Grace of God, I have seen hundreds of thousands brought to a Saving Knowledge

NOTES

of Jesus Christ, for which we give God all the Praise and all the Glory. As well, I have seen literally tens of thousands Baptized with the Holy Spirit. Untold numbers have had their lives wondrously and gloriously changed, sometimes from the worst bondages imaginable, by the Gospel we preach. Such continues unto this hour, and is the proof of what I say. I am not a novice, and the *"Fruit"* of this Ministry is obvious all over the world. *That* is the Biblical criteria and sanction (Mat. 7:20), and not the praise of men.

The phrase, *"So that from Jerusalem, and round about unto Illyricum, I have fully preached the Gospel of Christ,"* refers to Jerusalem as the starting point, with his Ministry reaching to what is present-day Yugoslavia. As well, he would minister in Rome, but had not done so when this Epistle was written. As well, and as we shall see in Verse 24, he planned to go to Spain, but there is no record in Scripture or history that this journey was ever undertaken.

The words *"fully preached"* are from the Greek verb *"pleroo,"* and means *"to fulfill, to perfect, to consummate, to make complete in every particular."*

The idea is, that he preached all of the Gospel, Salvation by Faith, the Baptism with the Holy Spirit with the evidence of speaking with other Tongues, and Divine Healing by the Power of God, over all the areas mentioned.

There is nothing in the world more important than the Gospel of Jesus Christ. Everything else pales by comparison. Whatever Jesus did at Calvary and the Resurrection is all in vain, for those who do not know. It is incumbent upon every Believer to do everything within his or her power, in order that the entirety of mankind know of Jesus and His Power to save. As well, it must be the same Gospel as preached by Paul, a Gospel of Power, which sets captives free, and not a watered-down, compromised version, which denies the Power of God. Paul plainly said of that, *". . . From such turn away"* (II Tim. 3:5).

(20) "YEA, SO HAVE I STRIVED TO PREACH THE GOSPEL, NOT WHERE CHRIST WAS NAMED, LEST I SHOULD BUILD UPON ANOTHER MAN'S FOUNDATION:"

The phrase, *"Yea, so have I strived to preach the Gospel,"* speaks of his earnest zeal.

"Strive" in the Greek is *"philotimeomai,"* and means *"from a love of honor to strive to bring something to pass, to be ambitious."*

Vincent says, *"The correct sense is 'to prosecute as a point of honor.'"* However, the word *"prosecute"* here does not mean to attempt to convict as in the action of a prosecuting attorney, but rather, *"of prosecuting a project, a proposed piece of work, carrying it on to a successful termination."*

The phrase, *"Not where Christ was named,"* means that Paul never sought to evangelize where Christianity was already established. From the word *"strive"* as it refers to *"honor,"* it was a point of honor with him, but not of rivalry.

This phrase does not mean that Paul never preached where Christ had already been proclaimed, but that his Missions endeavors, as directed by the Holy Spirit, always led him to uncharted territory, at least where the Gospel was concerned. The main thought presented here, even though other ideas are involved, is that the Gospel be taken to those who have not had the privilege of heretofore hearing this Message of Life. As that was the thrust of the Apostle then, it must ever continue to be the thrust of all involved in this grand Gospel of Christ Jesus.

The phrase, *"Lest I should build upon another man's foundation,"* indicates several things:

1. As stated, the major thrust should always be to take the Gospel to those who have not had the privilege to know and hear, or else have had very little opportunity.

2. Jesus as the Head of the Church gives direction through and by the Holy Spirit to particular workers. In other words, it was the Holy Spirit Who directed Paul, and also directed others. At this time, every evidence is that the original Twelve were also taking the Gospel to various places. This would have also included others not of that group, or even named in the Bible, but yet greatly used by God. Again, there was so much space to cover, that duplication was not exactly desired.

3. If one is truly God-Called, that Call will include not only the place but the Message as well. As such, other voices, especially if they

are not totally sensitive to the Holy Spirit, could bring dissention. To be frank, these problems were rife in the Churches built by Paul, with Judaizers coming in attempting to subvert what Paul had preached, and even attempting to turn the people against him, which they nearly succeeded doing in some places.

These individuals could not bring people to the Lord themselves, and especially considering that what they were preaching was a false message, they attempted to parasite the Foundation as laid by the Apostle.

To be sure, this problem did not die with the Early Church. It is alive and well presently, and is actually one of Satan's greatest efforts to subvert the Work of God.

AN EXAMPLE

To use a case in point, there are some Godly Preachers and Teachers in what is presently referred to as the *"Faith Ministry;"* however, for the most part, this particular Gospel is in fact *"another Gospel,"* and basically survives and even thrives on the Foundation of others. Very few people are Saved and very few people are Baptized with the Holy Spirit in these circles. So, they have to depend on someone else bringing people to the Lord, or else they have little if any Ministry. Such a Ministry does not coincide with the Book of Acts and, therefore, for the most part is not Scriptural.

(21) "BUT AS IT IS WRITTEN, TO WHOM HE WAS NOT SPOKEN OF, THEY SHALL SEE: AND THEY THAT HAVE NOT HEARD SHALL UNDERSTAND."

The phrase, *"But as it is written,"* refers to Isa. 52:15. Once again, Paul refers to Scripture on which his entire effort is based.

The phrase, *"To whom He was not spoken of, they shall see,"* refers as is obvious to the Message of Redemption going to the Gentiles. The pronoun *"He"* refers to Jesus. Paul was the very one who helped the Gentiles to *"see."*

The phrase, *"And they that have not heard shall understand,"* presents that which previously had not been the case.

Until the First Advent of Jesus, the Gentiles had almost no understanding at all of the Lord, in fact, what little they did have, which only pertained to a minute few, they had learned in the Jewish Synagogues. Other than that, there was no knowledge of God. They worshipped idols and paid homage to many gods, which in fact were fabrications of man.

In fact, if the Holy Spirit had not desired the Gospel to go to the Gentiles, which is of course unthinkable, there is no way without His help that they could have understood the Word of the Lord whatsoever. These things are spiritually discerned, and concerning spiritual things, to those the Gentiles were dead (I Cor. 2:14).

This prophecy by Isaiah was that the time would come, which it now had, that the Gentiles would hear and understand the Word of God, thereby accepting Christ as Saviour. It is ironical, they who had been pagans since the dawn of time, now had understanding, but the Jews who were the very people who gave the world the Word of God, did not understand. That had been predicted as well (Isa. 6:9). Jesus referred to this account Himself (Mat. 13:14, 15; Mk. 4:12; Lk. 8:10; Jn. 12:39-40).

(22) "FOR WHICH CAUSE ALSO I HAVE BEEN MUCH HINDERED FROM COMING TO YOU."

The phrase, *"For which cause,"* refers to Paul preaching these number of years in areas that did not have the Gospel. Consequently, even though he wanted to go to Rome, there simply had not been the time.

WHY ROME?

The same question might be asked concerning this Epistle. Why did he address it to the Romans, considering that he had never ministered in the Capital City of the Roman Empire?

As is obvious in this Epistle, he chose this time to systematically put in writing the great Fundamentals of the Faith and their meanings. As we have already stated, Romans is the ABC's of the Gospel. Not only are the great Fundamentals addressed, but, as well, the great benefits of Calvary and the Resurrection are given here as in no other Epistle.

Rome as the Capital City of the Empire carried great weight respecting the entirety of the world of that day as would be obvious, but as well pointed to the future. Everything

Paul did was meant not only to firmly establish the Church, but as well, to evangelize the world. Rome would figure into this, which was a necessity considering its prominence. If Christianity was to girdle the globe, which it must do, and which was of absolute necessity, it was helpful that it be established at this time in Rome, hence Paul's interest.

As well, if Paul wrote the Book of Hebrews, which I think he did, then we have two powerful Epistles, Romans directed toward the Gentiles and Hebrews toward the Jews. Consequently, the statement is made.

The phrase, *"Also I have been much hindered from coming to you,"* tells us several things:

1. Implies a succession of hindrances.

2. We can tell from this statement plus others, that Paul felt he must go to Rome, and which is borne out by the appearance of Christ to him in Jerusalem (Acts 23:11).

3. As an Apostle, and most likely the leading Apostle of his day, everything he did was of great significance. So, his desire to Minister in Rome was not born out of personal ambition, but was directed by the Holy Spirit concerning his Apostleship.

Even though we will study the word *"Apostle"* to a greater extent when we come to the Epistle to the Ephesians, it is my belief that this high calling of the Holy Spirit, always effects the entirety of the Church, even around the world, in one way or the other. In fact, the individual so called of the Lord may not even be known by many in the world, or may not even be respected, etc. However, if the person is truly a God-called Apostle, whatever it is that the Lord gives him to do, whatever the Mission, it will in some way have some effect on the entirety of the Body of Christ, and one could probably say for all time.

(23) BUT NOW HAVING NO MORE PLACE IN THESE PARTS, AND HAVING A GREAT DESIRE THESE MANY YEARS TO COME UNTO YOU;"

The phrase, *"But now having no more place in these parts,"* means he had now planted the Gospel in all the principle centers, leaving Disciples and converts, and probably an ordained Ministry, to carry on the work and extend it even unto the regions beyond (Barmby).

The phrase, *"And having a great desire these many years to come unto you,"* proclaims that which had been strong within his heart. This would materialize, his going to Rome, and because it was the Will of God, but at this stage, Paul did not dream that it would come about in the manner in which it actually did — him being taken a prisoner to that city.

The manner and ways in which the Lord sometimes works, are at times totally different than we had at first imagined, and even at times, ways in which we do not understand. God being God and, therefore, all-powerful and infallible, can do anything He so desires. But yet, many times He does not make it easy for His Children, and at times for reasons known only to Himself.

(24) "WHENSOEVER I TAKE MY JOURNEY INTO SPAIN, I WILL COME TO YOU: FOR I TRUST TO SEE YOU IN MY JOURNEY, AND TO BE BROUGHT ON MY WAY THITHERWARD BY YOU, IF FIRST I BE SOMEWHAT FILLED WITH YOUR COMPANY."

The phrase, *"Whensoever I take my journey into Spain, I will come to you,"* now brings another country into the mix, but with no record that Paul ever went to Spain. He may have, but history is silent, whether Biblical or otherwise.

The phrase, *"For I trust to see you in my journey, and to be brought on my way thitherward by you,"* implies that he hoped to take a select number into Spain with him from the Church in Rome. The word *"brought"* in the Greek bares this out.

The phrase, *"If first I be somewhat filled with your company,"* refers to his proposed stop in the Imperial City on his way to Spain. He no doubt planned to stay as long as he could, and desired to minister unto them.

Where the Church or Churches were now located in Rome we are not told. Actually, they were probably in people's houses; however, when persecution arose a few years later, the Church for the most part, if not altogether, moved into the underground catacombs, where the dead were buried.

I have personally been in these catacombs. And there are markings on the walls, which

NOTES

are reputed from those particular times.

As stated, Paul would go to Rome, but he would not be able to Minister in any of the Churches, being a prisoner of the Roman Empire. However, every indication is, that the Church did come to him in his own hired house, even though he was chained to a Roman soldier.

(25) "BUT NOW I GO UNTO JERUSALEM TO MINISTER UNTO THE SAINTS."

The phrase, *"But now I go unto Jerusalem,"* is recorded regarding these happenings in Acts Chapters 20-21. Actually, the Epistle to the Romans was written from Corinth.

The phrase, *"To minister unto the Saints,"* speaks particularly of taking the contributions of the Gentile Saints to the poor Jewish Saints in Jerusalem which would not only supply their needs, but also, hopefully, bring about a better understanding between Gentiles and the Jews in the Church at large. The account of Paul receiving these offerings is recorded in II Corinthians Chapters 8-9.

(26) "FOR IT HATH PLEASED THEM OF MACEDONIA AND ACHAIA TO MAKE A CERTAIN CONTRIBUTION FOR THE POOR SAINTS WHICH ARE AT JERUSALEM."

The phrase, *"For it hath pleased them of Macedonia and Achaia,"* speaks of modern day Greece. Corinth and Athens were in the area of Achaia, with Thessalonica and Philippi in Macedonia. In fact, Macedonia was in a state of poverty itself, due to political problems, but yet, the Churches there although impoverished themselves, insisted upon giving to the poor Saints in Jerusalem, and actually gave even more than Paul had thought they could give. It was so much in fact, that he actually did not want to accept it, considering their personal privation, with them pressuring him to do so (II Cor. 8:1-5).

The phrase, *"To make a certain contribution,"* shows by the word *"certain"* that there was no assessment to raise a prescribed amount. The giving was more or less according to the willingness of the individual and the circumstances he was in (Denney).

The phrase, *"For the poor saints which are at Jerusalem,"* had to do with the persecution levelled at the Church there by the Jewish Sanhedrin.

Following the Day of Pentecost, many thousands of Jews accepted Christ as their Saviour. In turn, they were immediately excommunicated from the Synagogue, which meant that they were cut off from everything. Synagogues in Israel served as the meeting house for all things, such as Schools for the children, a clearing house for employment, with many legal matters attended there, all as well as a place of worship.

Consequently, when one was excommunicated from the Synagogue, it meant their Children could no longer attend School, most of the time they were deprived of employment, and often they were evicted from their rented flats or houses, etc. Consequently, thousands were destitute, hence these contributions or offerings and their significance.

(27) "IT HATH PLEASED THEM VERILY; AND THEIR DEBTORS THEY ARE. FOR IF THE GENTILES HAVE BEEN MADE PARTAKERS OF THEIR SPIRITUAL THINGS, THEIR DUTY IS ALSO TO MINISTER UNTO THEM IN CARNAL THINGS."

The phrase, *"It hath pleased them verily,"* refers to the reaction of the Churches in Achaia and Macedonia, when Paul related to them the need. Of course, all the Saints in Jerusalem were not poor, but these were stretched to the limit, as stated because of the great influx of people, and the many being excommunicated from the Synagogues. So, it pleased these Churches in Greece to be of help. In other words, they took great delight in doing so, even though some of them, even as we have already stated, were in dire straits themselves.

The phrase, *"And their debtors they are,"* refers to the Jews being the bearers of Salvation, even though the greater majority rejected Christ. As a nation raised up for this very purpose, the Holy Spirit through them, had given the world the Word of God, and the Messiah. So, in a sense, even as Paul here explains, the Gentiles owe a debt of gratitude to the Jews.

THE JEWS

In fact, the entirety of the world even *now*, owes a debt of gratitude to the Jews. Every iota of freedom and prosperity in the world

today, has as its base and foundation the great principle of Bible Christianity, which has its roots in Judaism. However, the world has little understood this *"debt,"* and in fact, has conducted itself in the very opposite manner, oftentimes making the Jews the scapegoats of the world.

One day the world will realize its error, but that will not be until the Second Coming of the Lord. Then the Jews will be given their rightful place in the world, and will be given the honor due them, but only after they accept their Messiah, The Lord Jesus Christ.

The phrase, *"For if the Gentiles have been made partakers of their spiritual things, their duty is also to minister unto them in carnal things,"* portrays God's plan relative to the establishment of His Church. It is as follows:

1. The carnal things which the Gentiles ministered to the Jews were the necessities of life, food, clothing, shelter, in short, money.

2. The word *"contribution"* is *"koinonia"* in the Greek text, the verb form of which means *"to participate jointly with some other person, to have fellowship."* Here it speaks of the Gentile Saints participating jointly or having fellowship in the sending of money to the Jewish Saints in Jerusalem and of having fellowship with them in their necessities by making these necessities their own.

The same word is translated *"communicate"* in Hebrews 13:16 and means there, *"share what you have with others"* (Wuest).

3. This passage also proclaims the necessity of Churches taking care of the material needs of their Pastors, as the Pastors attend to the spiritual needs of the congregation.

4. It also pertains to people who are blessed, instructed, and helped through and by the Word of God, through a Television Ministry, Radio Ministry, Literature Ministry, etc. If you as a Believer receive some of your spiritual instruction and nourishment from such a Ministry, even as millions do, it is in turn your duty to minister unto that particular effort in *"carnal things,"* i.e., money.

5. Inasmuch as the Holy Spirit is laying this out so graphically, there is no excuse for any Believer not having proper knowledge in this area.

Having been on Television since 1975, in

effect using this media to minister over much of the world, I would perhaps have more knowledge than most in this particular area. Only the Lord knows the number of letters we have received through the years from people who have watched the program faithfully, and in their communication have told us that almost all they know about the Bible, they learned through the Telecast, or else the program ministered to them even to the extent of bringing them the Gospel which effected their Salvation. And yet many of these will say, even after being blessed and helped for years, *"Brother Swaggart, I have never written you before . . ."* In essence, they are saying that they have never supported whatsoever.

I think it should be easily discerned from the statement given here by Paul, that such does a gross injustice to the Work of God, and shows a lack of gratitude to the Lord for seeing to it that such a Ministry be brought into the lives of those who are in serious need of the Gospel.

(28) "WHEN THEREFORE I HAVE PERFORMED THIS, AND HAVE SEALED TO THEM THIS FRUIT, I WILL COME BY YOU INTO SPAIN."

The phrase, *"When therefore I have performed this,"* has to do with Paul first of all going to Jerusalem to deliver the contributions there so desperately needed.

The phrase, *"And have sealed to them this fruit,"* concerns the Offerings as given by the Saints in Macedonia and Achaia. Everything the Believer does for the Lord, or even the spiritual growth in one's life, is looked at by the Holy Spirit as *"fruit."*

The fruit bearing process was outlined graphically by Jesus in John Chapter 15, and ought to be studied minutely.

The phrase, *"I will come by you into Spain,"* refers to Rome being a stopover on the way to that distant land. However, how different were the circumstances of Paul's first visit to Rome which we know from Acts, than that which he had previously thought. Man proposes, but God disposes, and all for final good (Phil. 1:12).

That Paul carried out his intention of visiting Spain, and to which we have already alluded, cannot be alleged with certainty;

however, there is a tradition that he did so, but with no proof.

(29) "AND I AM SURE THAT, WHEN I COME UNTO YOU, I SHALL COME IN THE FULNESS OF THE BLESSING OF THE GOSPEL OF CHRIST."

The phrase, *"And I am sure that, when I come unto you,"* proclaims a certitude in Paul's heart concerning his visit to Rome, which was no doubt placed there by the Holy Spirit. At this time, the Lord had not Personally addressed him about this situation as He later would in Jerusalem (Acts 23:11). However, the Holy Spirit had already begun to deal with Paul's heart concerning this matter.

The phrase, *"I shall come in the Fulness of the Blessing of the Gospel of Christ,"* proclaims the fact of great Truths held by Paul, actually given to him by Christ (Gal. 1:11-12), which he wished to give to the Roman Church. Paul, being the recipient of the great Covenant of Grace, of necessity had more knowledge in this area than actually anyone in the world of that day. Also, all the Churches desperately needed the *"Fulness"* of this Message. Actually, that's the very reason for this Epistle, plus all his Epistles. As well, he would visit Churches as often as he could, in order that he may personally proclaim to the congregations this Glorious Covenant of Grace.

Also, that this great *"Gospel of Christ"* was a great *"Blessing"* is without question. It was freedom personified. It was the culmination of the Law, and actually all to which the Law of Moses had pointed. The man was full of his Message, and to be sure, the Message, i.e. *"Christ"* had transformed the man. In fact, Christ is the Message!

(30) "NOW I BESEECH YOU, BRETHREN, FOR THE LORD JESUS CHRIST'S SAKE, AND FOR THE LOVE OF THE SPIRIT, THAT YE STRIVE TOGETHER WITH ME IN YOUR PRAYERS TO GOD FOR ME;"

The phrase, *"Now I beseech you, Brethren,"* presents one of Paul's most oft used phrases.

"Beseech" in the Greek is *"parakaleo,"* and means *"I beg of you, please."*

The phrase, *"For the Lord Jesus Christ's sake,"* refers to the Work of God. Even though the Lord has paid the price for man's Redemption, it is men such as the Apostle Paul, who take that Message to the world. As such, they are a prime target of Satan, which should be understood. And yet I'm afraid that in many cases, many Believers think of people such as Paul as not needing prayer. In other words, that their Faith is of such magnitude, that they do not have ordinary needs such as other men.

Such as should be obvious, is simply not the case. In fact, if anything, greater Supplication and Intercession are needed, and because these are the very ones who Satan is attempting to hinder the most. This should be obvious, but I'm afraid it isn't in many Christian circles.

The phrase, *"And for the Love of the Spirit,"* concerns the Will of God. In other words, the Apostle is asking the Saints to pray for him, that he will not miss the Will of God, but will be successfully led by the Holy Spirit.

The *"Love of the Spirit"* is the Divine Love which the Holy Spirit produces in the hearts of the Saints (Rom. 5:5; Gal. 5:22). Alford says, *"A Love which teaches us to look not only on our own things but on the things of others."*

The phrase, *"That ye strive together with me, in your prayers to God for me,"* proclaims the humility of this man, and the power of Prayer.

"Strive together" in the Greek is *"sunagonizomai,"* and means *"to contend along with, to share in a contest."* Paul asks the Roman Saints to contend with him in prayer against the opposition of the hosts of wickedness, contending with him as athletes would do with one another, with intensity of purpose and in perfect cooperation (Wuest).

If one is to notice throughout his Epistles, Paul is constantly requesting prayer (I Thess. 5:25; II Thess. 3:1; Heb. 13:18).

As well, this is almost the opposite of what presently is the case. Very seldom do we hear notable preachers request prayer. Too often, they are constantly telling people to send them their prayer requests, etc. While this is certainly right, and in fact should be done, still, I as an Evangelist desperately need for you to pray for me, even on a daily basis.

Therefore, as Paul, I beseech you to do so, knowing the significance of prayer and having faith and confidence in your touch with God as well. Yes, I have prayed for untold thousands, and continue to this very hour, even seeing tremendous answers to these prayers, but still, I need your prayers also, and so does every other man and woman of God.

(31) "THAT I MAY BE DELIVERED FROM THEM THAT DO NOT BELIEVE IN JUDAEA; AND THAT MY SERVICE WHICH I HAVE FOR JERUSALEM MAY BE ACCEPTED OF THE SAINTS;"

The phrase, *"That I may be delivered from them that do not believe in Judaea,"* proclaims the idea that Paul was already having warnings in his spirit concerning that which was to come, and which would increase greatly so as he went toward Jerusalem.

As one Scholar said, it was not the unbelieving Jews only who hated or disliked Paul. To them he was an apostate who had disappointed all their hopes; but even Christian Jews in many cases regarded him as false to the nation's prerogatives, and especially to the Law of Moses.

In fact, the prayers of these Romans and others were answered, in that Paul was ultimately delivered from the unbelieving Jews in Jerusalem; however, it did not come quickly or easily. In fact, they would have killed him, even as Acts, Chapters 21-23 proclaim, had he not been rescued by the Roman Captain. Even then he would languish for some two years in prison in Caesarea. So, his appeal to these Saints for prayer on his behalf was not without foundation.

The phrase, *"And that my service which I have for Jerusalem may be accepted of the Saints,"* concerns the Offering for the poor Saints in Jerusalem who were in desperate need.

This statement by Paul sounds somewhat strange, unless one knows his reason for saying such a thing.

There *was* a real danger that the contribution he brought from the Gentile Churches might not be graciously accepted, even accepted at all; it might be regarded by them as a bribe, in return for which Paul's opposition to the Law, at least as they saw such, would be condoned, and the equal standing of his upstart Churches in the Kingdom of God acknowledged.

It was by no means certain that it would be taken as to what it actually was — a pledge of Brotherly Love; and God Alone could dispose *"the Saints"* to take it as simply as it was offered.

THE LAW/GRACE ISSUE

It did not set well during Paul's time with many Christian Jews, that the Law, being fulfilled in Christ, was now no longer applicable. Of course, we are speaking of the Ceremonial and Ritualistic part of the Law of Moses. That Faith alone in Christ was all that was necessary for Salvation, and especially considering that Gentiles could come the same way, was not to the liking of many Christian Jews.

GENTILES?

I think in the entirety of the mix, the pride factor loomed large. The Law of Moses was the distinguishing characteristic of Israel. It set them apart from the entirety of the world, and in a positive way. And now Paul comes along, in effect stating that the Law is out, or at least that it had been fulfilled in Jesus, and now all, even Gentiles can come in the same manner, and in fact must come in the same manner, which is by Faith and Faith alone, in a sense strips the Jews of their peculiar and prideful characteristic. That which made them Jews is no more. Paul being the one who championed this new direction, was not too well liked, even though the Old Testament Scriptures had foretold all that now is.

PAUL'S ATTITUDE AND SPIRIT

To be rejected by one's own nation is bad enough, even as was Paul. To be sure, he was probably the most hated man as far as the nation of Israel was concerned.

I'm sure that grieved him, but more than all it must have grieved him greatly, that many Christian Jews did not as well, hold him in very high regard. He was the target! He was the one accused of taking away their identity.

So I guess I'm saying, that not many men could have stood the pressure that he stood,

NOTES

taken the abuse he took, and still maintained spiritual and mental equilibrium. His relationship with Christ alone enabled him to *"fight this good fight and stay the course."*

(32) "THAT I MAY COME UNTO YOU WITH JOY BY THE WILL OF GOD, AND MAY WITH YOU BE REFRESHED."

The phrase, *"That I may come unto you with joy by the Will of God,"* refers to the fact that it definitely was the Will of God for Paul to go to Rome, but I'm not so sure if the *"joy"* prevailed as he would have desired, considering the manner in which he arrived in the Imperial City. And yet, the *"joy"* of the Apostle depended not upon circumstances or surroundings, but rather from an inner peace which was altogether of Christ. In that context, the *"joy"* was abundant.

The phrase, *"And may with you be refreshed,"* pertains, even as the last Chapter reveals, that Paul had many friends in Rome, hence the warmness of his statements. It is obvious that he is writing to people, at least some of them with whom he is acquainted. He longs to see them, and as well, the Church in Rome is something special, especially considering that this was the Capital City of the world. He takes great joy in knowing that Christianity has spread this far and with this much strength. As well, some of these people, even as we shall see, are his converts from other times and other places. So, it will be *"refreshing"* to see them, be with them, and discuss the great Work of God together.

(33) "NOW THE GOD OF PEACE BE WITH YOU ALL. AMEN."

In effect, this Scripture is the first of what seems to be benedictions (Rom. 15:33; 16:20, 24, 27).

"No blood, no altar now, the Sacrifice is o'er!
"No flame, no smoke ascends on high, the Lamb is slain no more.
"But richer blood has flowed from nobler veins,
"To purge the soul from guilt, and cleanse the vilest stains."

"We thank thee for the Blood, the Blood of Christ, Thy Son:
"The Blood by which our peace is made,

our victory is won:
"Great victory o'er hell, and sin and
woe
"That needs no second fight, and leaves
no second foe."

"We thank Thee for the Grace, descend-
ing from above,
"That over-flows our widest guilt eter-
nal Father's love.
"Love of the Father's everlasting Son,
"Love of the Holy Spirit, Jehovah, Three
in One."

"We thank Thee for the Hope, so glad,
and sure, and clear;
"It holds the drooping spirit up till the
long dawn appears;
"Fair hope! With what a sunshine does
it cheer
"Our roughest path on earth, our drea-
riest desert here."

"We thank Thee for the Crown of Glory
and of Life;
"'Tis no poor withering wreath of earth,
man's prize in mortal strife;
"'Tis incorruptible as is the Throne,
"The Kingdom of our God and His In-
carnate Son."

CHAPTER 16

(1) "I COMMEND UNTO YOU PHEBE OUR SISTER, WHICH IS A SERVANT OF THE CHURCH WHICH IS AT CENCHREA:"

The phrase, *"I commend unto you Phebe our sister,"* presents the first name of the 28 mentioned in Verses 1-16, 20 men and 8 women. It is interesting that the first name is that of a woman and that she was a deaconess of the Church at Cenchrea, and some even say its Pastor. Ministry in the primitive Church was not confined to men.

Cenchrea was the Port of Corinth, and about nine miles from that city.

PETER

In this Chapter, Paul will greet any number of people, but not one time does he mention Simon Peter. Now, if Peter was at Rome, and our Catholic friends say he was at this

particular time, then surely the Apostle Paul would have said something about the Prince of the Apostles.

Paul, however, said nothing, which leads us to conclude that Peter simply wasn't in Rome. In fact, there is no solid historical reference that Peter was ever in Rome. So this completely destroys the idea that Peter was the first Pope. Actually, the time frame of a man being referred to as *"Pope"* was not until the early 600's. In other words, that which we know today as the Catholic Church came into being over a protracted period of time, as the Early Church gradually apostatized.

"Commend" in the Greek is *"sunistemi,"* and means *"to recommend, vouch for."* So Paul commends this gracious lady.

It is assumed that Phoebe was a widow, on the ground that she could not, according to Greek manners, have been mentioned as acting in the independent manner described, either if her husband had been living or if she had been unmarried.

The phrase, *"Which is a servant of the Church which is at Cenchrea,"* presents this woman as very active in that particular Church. It was probably an extension of the Church at Corinth.

"Servant" in the Greek is *"diakonos,"* a word that could be used in either the masculine or feminine genders. Our words *"deacon"* and *"deaconess"* are derived from it, showing that its Scriptural for a woman to serve in this capacity as well as a man. The word means *"a servant as seen in his activity,"* and can refer, as stated, to a Minister of the Gospel as well.

Paul is commending this dear lady to the Church at Rome for several reasons. The foremost being that this Epistle was carried by her over the long and dangerous journey to Rome. Renan says: *"Phoebe carried under the folds of her robe the whole future of Christian Theology."* The Roman Letter was written at and sent from Corinth. God's watchful care was over both the bearer and the Letter.

Paul calls Phoebe *"our sister,"* that is *"Christian Sister."*

It appears that Phoebe may have had business at Rome, perhaps of a legal kind.

Paul took advantage of her going, to send the Letter by her, desiring also to list the aid of fellow Christians at Rome and furtherance of her business, whatever it might be.

Her having business at Rome, and her having been *"a succourer of many,"* suggests the idea of her being a lady of means (Barmby).

(2) "THAT YE RECEIVE HER IN THE LORD, AS BECOMETH SAINTS, AND THAT YE ASSIST HER IN WHATSOEVER BUSINESS SHE HATH NEED OF YOU: FOR SHE HATH BEEN A SUCCOURER OF MANY, AND OF MYSELF ALSO."

The phrase, *"That ye receive her in the Lord, as becometh Saints,"* refers to receiving into companionship and fellowship.

The idea was more than a mere reception, but rather that she was to be received in every capacity, and not be barred from any type of spiritual intimacy. In other words, this was a woman who could be trusted and who loved the Lord extensively. What a privilege to be recommended thusly by the Apostle Paul.

The phrase, *"And that ye assist her in whatsoever business she hath need of you,"* suggests, as we have stated, that she may have had business in Rome of a legal nature. They were to assist her any way they could in whatever endeavors she sought.

The phrase, *"For she hath been a succourer of many, and of myself also,"* lends credence to the idea that her house was always open to Ministers of the Gospel, a place where Paul had evidently frequented when in the vicinity.

One can tell from Paul's statements, that the times the weary Apostle was able to avail himself of her hospitality, were refreshing indeed!

(3) "GREET PRISCILLA AND AQUILA MY HELPERS IN CHRIST JESUS:"

Priscilla and Aquila are mentioned first in Acts 18:2. Aquila was born in Pontus which is on the Black Sea, but of Priscilla no information is given concerning her birth.

Paul first met them at Corinth. They were refugees from the cruel and unjust edict of Claudius which expelled all Jews from Rome in A.D. 52.

Paul stayed with this couple in Corinth,

working with Aquila at tentmaking, which was the craft of both. When Paul left Corinth, it seems they left with him, accompanying him as far as Ephesus (Acts 18:18-28). They are always mentioned together as man and wife, with Priscilla usually mentioned first, some suggesting that she was the stronger of the two respecting the Christian Faith (Acts 18:2, 18, 26; Rom. 16:3; I Cor. 16:19; II Tim. 4:19).

After Ephesus it seems, perhaps taking advantage of relaxations towards Jews after Claudius' death, it seems they went back to Rome, at least for a period of time. Hence, Paul greets them.

As stated, it seems as we shall see, that he had previously known quite a few people who were now in Rome, which had in some way drifted toward the Capital.

(4) "WHO HAVE FOR MY LIFE LAID DOWN THEIR OWN NECKS: UNTO WHOM NOT ONLY I GIVE THANKS, BUT ALSO ALL THE CHURCHES OF THE GENTILES."

The phrase, *"Who have for my life laid down their own necks,"* refers to Priscilla and Aquila. Exactly how they risked their lives for Paul is not exactly known. It may have been at Corinth at the time of the Jewish insurrection against Paul (Acts 18:12), or at Ephesus at the time of the tumult raised by Demetrius the Silversmith (Acts 19:23), when Paul had been in imminent danger, which is probably the case.

The phrase, *"Unto whom not only I give thanks, but also all the Churches of the Gentiles,"* presents the idea that the Lord used this couple to save the life of the Apostle, and in doing so greatly endangered themselves. Of course if Paul had been killed at Ephesus or wherever the situation occurred of this particular Text, it would have been a tremendous blow to the Kingdom of God, i.e., *"all the Churches of the Gentiles."*

Some believe the situation at Ephesus occurred at about A.D. 58. As well, it is believed that Paul was executed in about A.D. 68. If these dates are correct, he was given about ten more years to plant Churches and to anchor those already planted.

(5) "LIKEWISE GREET THE CHURCH THAT IS IN THEIR HOUSE. SALUTE MY WELLBELOVED EPAENETUS, WHO IS

THE FIRSTFRUITS OF ACHAIA UNTO CHRIST."

The phrase, *"Likewise greet the Church that is in their house,"* speaks of the house of Priscilla and Aquila. I Corinthians 16:19 also records that they had used their house as a Church while in Corinth. It is also mentioned that there was a Church in the house of Nymphas (Col. 4:15), and that of Philemon (Phile. vs. 2). A similar gathering may be implied in Romans 16:14-15 as well.

Bishop Lightfoot says there is no clear example of a separate building set apart for Christian worship within the limits of the Roman Empire before the Third Century. The Christian congregations, due to the times, were, therefore, dependent upon the hospitality of prominent Church members who furnished their homes for this purpose. As stated, upon the coming persecution which took place a little later, Christians in Rome ultimately had to transfer their meeting places from houses to the underground Catacombs.

The phrase, *"Salute my wellbeloved Epaenetus, who is the firstfruits of Achaia unto Christ,"* speaks of Corinth. There is no concrete proof, but it is believed that this man possibly was of the house of Stephanas (I Cor. 16:15).

The word *"firstfruits"* means that he was among the first ones in Corinth who gave their hearts to Christ.

(There are some who claim the Text should have read *"Asia"* instead of *"Achaia"*; however, there is no real proof of that.)

(6) "GREET MARY, WHO BESTOWED MUCH LABOUR ON US."

Other than this statement, no other information is given concerning this dear lady. Where Paul knew her is not said, or what she did is not related. However, from this example we learn several things:

1. A record is kept in Heaven of all that is done, of which all of us should be well aware.

2. Paul did not take these kindnesses for granted, and neither should we. They are to be forever remembered.

3. When this dear lady helped Paul and whatever it was she did, she little realized that untold millions would read these words about her, and be thankful for what she did

NOTES

to help the Apostle.

4. Any and everything done for Satan is lost except to infamy. All that is done for the Lord lives forever.

(7) "SALUTE ANDRONICUS AND JUNIA, MY KINSMEN, AND MY FELLOW PRISONERS, WHO ARE OF NOTE AMONG THE APOSTLES, WHO ALSO WERE IN CHRIST BEFORE ME."

The phrase, *"Salute Andronicus and Junia, my kinsmen,"* probably refers to fellow Jews, and not blood relatives.

"Kinsmen" in the Greek is *"suggenes,"* and means, at least in this case, *"of the same race, a fellow-countryman."*

The phrase, *"And my fellowprisoners,"* implies that these two had been, like himself, at some time imprisoned for the Faith, but it does not follow that he and they had been imprisoned together (Barmby).

The phrase, *"Who are of note among the Apostles,"* does not mean they were Apostles themselves, but that they were well-known to the original Twelve. And yet, some claim that the Greek Text lends some weight to the fact that these two were Apostles as well, which certainly is possible.

The phrase, *"Who also were in Christ before me,"* simply means that their conversion predated his.

(8) "GREET AMPLIAS MY BELOVED IN THE LORD."

This man is mentioned only here, but evidently was known of Paul at an earlier time in another field of Paul's endeavors. And yet, due to his friendship with the Apostle, he is mentioned forever in the Eternal Word of God.

(9) "SALUTE URBANE, OUR HELPER IN CHRIST, AND STACHYS MY BELOVED."

As well, these two men are mentioned only here, and refers to the fact that they had been helpers of Paul in earlier times.

(10) "SALUTE APELLES APPROVED IN CHRIST. SALUTE THEM WHICH ARE OF ARISTOBULUS' HOUSEHOLD."

The phrase, *"Salute Apelles approved in Christ,"* could possibly mean that there had formerly been some question about this Brother's Salvation, but that his Faith in Christ had laid that to rest. Or else it could mean that Paul was just simply saying something kind about him, referring to the fact that he had once been of help in some endeavor in the planting of a Church, etc.

Incidentally, the word *"salute"* simply means to *"greet."*

The phrase, *"Salute them which are of Aristobulus' household,"* probably refers to slaves who had once belonged to this man.

In those days when slaves were purchased by another master, they continued to bear the name of their former proprietor. Lightfoot the Historian says that some of the slaves of the household of Aristobulus had become Christians.

Some think that Aristobulus might be a grandson of Herod the Great, as mentioned by Josephus. Evidently, and in whatever case, Paul had become acquainted with these slaves, and now greets them.

(11) "SALUTE HERODION MY KINS-MAN. GREET THEM THAT BE OF THE HOUSEHOLD OF NARCISSUS, WHICH ARE IN THE LORD."

The phrase, *"Salute Herodion my kins-man,"* refers evidently to another Jew.

The phrase, *"Greet them that be of the household of Narcissus, which are in the Lord,"* once again does not refer to Narcissus personally, but to slaves of his household, at least those who were followers of the Lord.

It is thought that this Narcissus was the powerful freedman of Claudius, mentioned by Tacitus, and by Suetonius. He appears to have been put to death on the accession of Nero in A.D. 54, with his property passing to the possession of Nero, which would have included his slaves. That being the case, they would have become a part of Caesar's house-hold, and as stated, would have continued to be called by their late master's name.

It is observable that, at a later period, the Apostle, writing from Rome to the Philippi-ans, sends special greetings from them *"that are of Caesar's household,"* which may well have been these very slaves mentioned (Phile. vss. 23-24) (Barmby).

(12) "SALUTE TRYPHENA AND TRYPHOSA, WHO LABOUR IN THE LORD. SALUTE THE BELOVED PERSIS, WHICH LABOURED MUCH IN THE LORD."

The phrase, *"Salute Tryphena and Tryphosa, who labour in the Lord,"* presents

two more slaves, for theirs are slave names. These two as well had been used by the Lord in some manner to help the Apostle, and their names are forever recorded.

The phrase, *"Salute the beloved Persis, which laboured much in the Lord,"* refers to a woman.

From the manner in which the Apostle describes this lady, she must have been known by him personally, and had done work of which he was cognizant. As well, it is to be observed how, in calling her *"the beloved,"* he avoids, with delicate propriety, adding *"my"* as he does in speaking of his male friends (Barmby).

(13) "SALUTE RUFUS CHOSEN IN THE LORD, AND HIS MOTHER AND MINE."

The phrase, *"Salute Rufus chosen in the Lord,"* is probably the one mentioned in Mark 15:21. He was probably the son of Simon of Cyrene who helped Jesus bear the Cross.

The phrase, *"And his mother and mine,"* evidently means that this dear lady, the wife of Simon had been of gracious kindness to Paul. So much is said in these few words.

That notable day when Simon of Cyrene happened to be in Jerusalem and happened to be near the route which Jesus would be taking on His way to Calvary, as horrible as it was for the Saviour, would prove to be the greatest day of this man's life. But in es-sence, and in totality, this is why Jesus came.

(14) "SALUTE ASYNCRITUS, PHLEGON, HERMAS, PATROBAS, HERMES, AND THE BRETHREN WHICH ARE WITH THEM."

What a privilege for one to have his name listed, especially in a positive way, in the Word of God.

(15) "SALUTE PHILOLOGUS, AND JULIA, NEREUS, AND HIS SISTER, AND OLYMPAS, AND ALL THE SAINTS WHICH ARE WITH THEM."

To what degree Paul had previously known these people we are not told. However, for him to take the time to list these individu-ally, insinuates at least, that they were more than passing acquaintances. In some way, and in some place where Churches were planted elsewhere in the Roman Empire, they had been of help and strength to Paul. Conse-quently, their names would be forever en-shrined on the greatest record that humanity has ever known, the Word of God.

Incidentally, all Born-Again Believers are referred to as *"Saints"* (Acts 9:13, 32, 41; 26:10; Rom. 1:7; 8:27; 12:13; 15:25-26, 31; 16:2, 15; I Cor. 1:2; 6:1-2; 14:33; 16:1, 15; Eph. 1:1, 15, 18; 2:19; Heb. 6:10, etc.). Consequently, the Catholic claim of *"Saints"* has no Scriptural validity whatsoever. The idea that good works or even the performing of Miracles makes Saints is completely foreign to the Word of God. Believing sinners are instantly made Saints because of their Faith in Christ, and what He has done for them. In other words, the word *"Saint"* is attached to the Believer not because of what the Believer has done, other than to have Faith, but because of what Christ did at Calvary, the Resurrection, and the Exaltation.

(16) "SALUTE ONE ANOTHER WITH AN HOLY KISS. THE CHURCHES OF CHRIST SALUTE YOU."

The phrase, *"Salute* (Greet) *one another with an holy kiss,"* presents that which was the custom of all Oriental people at that time, not only Christians. Shaking of hands is our custom of greeting presently, and pretty well the custom of much of the world.

People who seek to continue this ancient custom are simply carrying on an ancient Oriental practice, which actually has no spiritual bearing. In no way is Paul issuing a command or even a suggestion that such a custom be continued.

The idea was that the kiss (on the cheek, incidentally), was not to be hypocritical as it was with so many who were not followers of Christ, but that it be sincere. Incidentally, men kissed men and women kissed women.

The phrase, *"The Churches of Christ salute you,"* refers to the Churches planted by Paul, and who in turn were greeting the Church in Rome.

In this one short statement we have at least the possibility that quite a few others knew that Paul was writing this Epistle to the Romans. It is suggestive that there were many questions concerning the great Doctrines of the Faith, and that Paul had reiterated to others that these questions would be addressed in this particular Epistle. Whether copies were made of the original which was sent to Rome we are not told; however, I

NOTES

would think that it was almost imperative that Paul had several copies of all his Epistles.

Inasmuch as he knew that what he was writing was the Word of the Lord, and that these Epistles were intended not only for the destination in question, but rather all Churches, it stands to reason that copies would have been made (Eph. 3:4; Col. 4:16; I Thess. 5:27).

THE CHURCH

"Church" in the Greek is *"ekklesia,"* which means *"called out."* In this case, it refers to a body of people called out of the world system into the system or government of the Lord, and done so by and through the Born-Again experience. The *"Church"* of the Lord Jesus Christ is made up of people of all walks of life, who, as stated, have been Born-Again (Jn. 3:3). In actuality, *"Church,"* as it is given in the Word of God, has absolutely nothing to do with institutionalized religion.

This doesn't mean that it is wrong to form Denominations, to have Denominations, or to be associated with Denominations, as such! In fact, a Denomination, in the strict sense of the word, is simply a tool, which supposedly can help spread the Gospel of Jesus Christ around the world. The problem, however, with Denominations is *"Denominationalism."*

"Denominationalism" is pretty much the same as *"racism."* I speak of the idea that belonging to a certain Denomination affords one a certain spirituality. It doesn't! Belonging or not belonging to particular Denominations has absolutely nothing to do with one's walk with the Lord, etc. However, what is preached behind the pulpit, and I speak of the Message, can be, ideally, of great benefit to Believers; on the other hand, it can be a great detriment, that is, if it is false doctrine. But simply belonging to a Denomination, as many believe, carries no spiritual connotation and no spiritual enrichment or improvement. A Denomination is simply something that is man-devised and, therefore, man-made.

JESUS CHRIST, THE HEAD OF THE CHURCH

We must never forget that Christ is the

NOTES

"Head" of the Church (Col. 1:16-20). To be sure, He is a very active Head and never a passive Head. One might say that He functions through the Holy Spirit, Who functions through Believers. We must never forget that it is His Church, and we speak of those who have been called out of darkness into light.

One of the great problems in the modern Church, however, is the abrogation of the Headship of Christ. In fact, that has always been the problem and the cause of untold difficulties. When men devise something, they tend, after a fashion, to desire to force other individuals to belong to their group or else destroy them — literally kill them, as was done in the Middle Ages. But now, due to the law of the land, they limit the destruction to the person's character, etc. Whenever this sectarian spirit prevails, i.e., "Belong to us or else!" one can be certain that such a Denomination or group is no longer being led by the Lord, but rather by men — and more particularly, by Satan.

(17) "NOW I BESEECH YOU, BRETHREN, MARK THEM WHICH CAUSE DIVISIONS AND OFFENCES CONTRARY TO THE DOCTRINE WHICH YE HAVE LEARNED; AND AVOID THEM."

The phrase, "Now I beseech you, Brethren," presents Paul once again using a favorite phrase. As stated, it means "I beg of you, please."

The phrase, "Mark them which cause divisions and offences contrary to the Doctrine which ye have learned," refers to false teachers.

"Mark them" in the Greek is "skopeo," and means "to look at, observe, contemplate, to fix one's eyes upon, direct one's attention to, scrutinize."

This means that all Believers should carefully analyze that which is being taught respecting the Gospel. Does it line up with the Word of God? Does it draw attention to the Preacher or to Christ? Is what is being taught pulled out of context with the balance of the Word of God?

This means that all Believers must know and understand the Word for themselves, and not depend upon someone else to lead them. While the Lord has surely put into the

Church, "Apostles, Prophets, Evangelists, Pastors and Teachers," for the "perfecting of the Saints, for the Work of the Ministry, for the edifying of the Body of Christ," still, Believers must know the Word, in order that they may know if what is being taught is Biblical and, therefore, right. Not everyone who preaches and teaches is truly Called of God, and then again, some have been truly Called of God, but have turned away from the Truth, and now present ". . . another Gospel . . ." (II Cor. 11:4).

"Division" in the Greek is "dichostasia," and means "disunion, in the sense of pulling one away from Christ."

"Offenses" in the Greek is "skandalon," and means "an impediment placed in the way and causing one to stumble or fall."

"Doctrine" in the Greek is "didache," and means "instruction or teaching regarding the act or matter under discussion." In this case it refers to the New Covenant, which of course has its roots in the Old Covenant, and does not at all contradict that Covenant.

FALSE TEACHERS

As now, so then, false teachers were everywhere, who Paul will describe in the next verse. Even though he has not preached in Rome, consequently not founding that Church, still, due to the fact that he mentions all of these friends he has known in other places, but are now in Rome, and who are well acquainted with his Gospel, in essence he is saying, "Mark them which cause divisions and offenses contrary to the Doctrine which you have learned of me." Of these people he had named, he knew they were loyal to the Word of God as it had been given to him, and that the others in the Roman Church believed accordingly, or else these friends of Paul would not have been welcome there.

The phrase, "And avoid them," means "turn away from, keep aloof from, and shun these."

These people are not the same as those who Paul identifies in Chapter 14 of Romans. Those people believed the Fundamentals of the Faith, but due to their spiritual weakness, had some peculiar ideas. These of which Paul warns against here, attack the very Fundamentals of the Faith, which are the Grace of God. There can be no fellowship with these people.

WHAT ARE THE FUNDAMENTALS OF THE FAITH?

First of all the word *"fundamental"* means *"that which relates to a supporting existence or determining essential structure or function. It is that without which a thing or a system would not be what it is."* In this case, we are addressing ourselves to the fundamental structure of Salvation and not peripheral events as important as they may be. In other words, we are addressing ourselves to that which one must believe in order to be Saved (Jn. 3:3, 16).

JESUS IS GOD

In order to be Saved, the sinner must believe that Jesus Christ is God (Isa. 7:14; Jn. 1:1-5; 5:26; 6:35; 7:29; Eph. 1:2-3).

To believe in Jesus as merely a good Man, or a Prophet, or even a Miracle-Worker, is not enough. One must know and understand that Jesus is God.

JESUS IS THE ONLY SAVIOUR

One must understand that Jesus Alone can save.

Peter said, *"Neither is there Salvation in any other: for there is none other Name under Heaven given among men, whereby we must be Saved"* (Acts 4:12).

Peter is speaking of *". . . Jesus Christ . . ."* (Acts 4:10).

Jesus is not One among several saviours, but rather the *"Only Saviour."*

JESUS DIED ON CALVARY TO PAY THE PRICE FOR MAN'S REDEMPTION

Whether the unbelieving sinner understands it or not, he has a debt of sin on him which is against God (Rom. 3:9-18, 23).

There is no way that man could or can pay that debt; consequently, God literally became Man, Who we know as Jesus Christ, in order that He might pay the debt for us. He did so by dying on Calvary, in essence taking our place, providing a Sacrifice which God would accept. In other words, Jesus died for sinners, which all men are (Rom. 5:8).

NOTES

In order to be Saved, the sinner must believe that Jesus died for him, in effect taking his place (Jn. 3:16).

MAN MUST KNOW AND UNDERSTAND THAT HE IS A SINNER

If he does not believe, know, and understand, that he is a sinner, lost without God, there is no way that he can be Saved. In effect, the fact of man being a sinner, is the cause of his guilt (Rom. 3:23).

One of the basic problems of humanity is, that man does not want to admit that he is a sinner, and, consequently, in dire need of a Saviour, Who Alone is The Lord Jesus Christ. In fact, this is why the Preaching of the Gospel is so necessary! The Gospel preached under the Anointing of the Holy Spirit brings conviction to the sinner, awakening him to his spiritual need (Jn. 16:7-11).

GOD GIVES SALVATION AS A FREE GIFT, WHICH IS BY GRACE

The word *"Grace"* means *"unmerited favor."* In other words, man cannot earn, merit, or do anything that makes himself worthy of this Gift of God. Even though it came at such price, God freely gives Salvation to believing sinners. Paul said, *"For by Grace are ye Saved through Faith; and that not of yourselves: it is the Gift of God:*

"Not of works, lest any man should boast" (Eph. 2:8-9).

So the believing sinner must understand that there is nothing he can do to merit Salvation, but that it is freely given to him by God, which refers to the Grace of God. This is an absolute Fundamental of the Faith.

BELIEVING SINNERS MUST RECEIVE SALVATION STRICTLY BY FAITH

This simply means that the sinner believes what Jesus did for him at Calvary and the Resurrection, a Faith incidentally which must come from the heart, and if he sincerely believes, he is instantly Saved (Jn. 3:16).

The Truth is, that the believing sinner may not understand very much about what the Lord has done for him at Calvary, and in fact, at the beginning cannot have much understanding concerning this tremendous thing which has been done in order to save men. It is not a matter of having great understanding, but rather believing what little that one does know, which simply means *"I believe that Jesus died for me."*

That's the reason that Paul said, *"That if thou shalt confess with thy mouth the Lord Jesus, and shalt believe in thine heart that God hath raised Him from the dead, thou shalt be Saved"* (Rom. 10:9).

And then he said, *"For with the heart man believeth unto Righteousness; and with the mouth confession is made unto Salvation"* (Rom. 10:10).

And last of all he said, *". . . For whosoever shall call upon the Name of the Lord shall be Saved"* (Rom. 10:11-13).

That above in brief addresses the great Fundamentals of the Faith, which speak of that which one must believe in order to be Saved. Of course, there are many peripheral Doctrines, such as the Baptism with the Holy Spirit with the evidence of speaking with other Tongues, Divine Healing, much teaching concerning Prophecy, etc.; however, whether one believes absolutely correctly concerning these particular peripheral Doctrines, while it may impact their Sanctification, it cannot impact their Justification, i.e., Salvation, that is, as long as they continue to trust Christ for Salvation, and not their own good works, etc.

(18) "FOR THEY THAT ARE SUCH SERVE NOT OUR LORD JESUS CHRIST, BUT THEIR OWN BELLY; AND BY GOOD WORDS AND FAIR SPEECHES DECEIVE THE HEARTS OF THE SIMPLE."

The phrase, *"For they that are such serve not our Lord Jesus Christ, but their own belly,"* here gives the motive.

"Belly" in the Greek is *"koilia,"* and means *"the whole belly, the entire cavity, in this case, the satisfaction of the creature needs."*

The idea is, that it is not the Lord Whom they serve, but on the contrary, their own base interests. It is a bitter contemptuous way of describing a self-seeking spirit, rather than an allusion to any particular cast of Doctrine (Denney).

To the utmost, this describes the modern Prosperity Doctrine, plus any other so-called Gospel, which in effect is serving its

own purpose instead of the Lord's.

In fact, I think one can say that any gospel which does not lead men to Calvary, is in Truth not the Gospel. In other words, if it leads men to money, to self-service, to place and position, or to anything else rather than Jesus and Him Crucified, it may be a gospel, but it is not the Gospel of Jesus Christ (I Cor. 2:2).

This of which Paul states actually refers to both the false teachers and those who are unfortunate enough to listen to them. False teachers have motives other than Christ, i.e., self is placed first, consequently, they appeal to base or selfish interests in their followers.

Many presently are attempting to use Christ to get rich. While the Lord definitely does bless people in a financial sense, that is not the end motive of the Gospel.

WHAT PAUL SAID

The Apostle addressed himself to this very thing by saying, *"Perverse disputings of men of corrupt minds, and destitute of the Truth, supposing that gain is Godliness: from such withdraw thyself . . ."* (I Tim. 6:5-8).

He then said, *"But they that will be rich fall into temptation and a snare, and into many foolish and hurtful lusts, which drown men in destruction and perdition.*

"For the love of money is the root of all evil: which while some coveted after, they have erred from the Faith, and pierced themselves through with many sorrows" (I Tim. 6:9-10).

He then said, *"But thou, O man of God, flee these things; and follow after Righteousness, Godliness, Faith, Love, Patience, Meekness"* (I Tim. 6:11).

The phrase, *"And by good words and fair speeches deceive the hearts of the simple,"* refers to those who have little true understanding of the Word of God.

"Good words" in the Greek is *"chrestologia,"* and means *"fair speaking, a smooth and plausible address."*

"Fair speeches" is *"eulogia,"* and means *"praise, laudation, polished language."*

The first refers to an insinuating tone, and the second refers to the fine style of many false teachers.

The word *"deceive"* although proper,

would probably have been better translated *"beguile."* The idea is, that the hearers of this false message, are lulled or even somewhat hypnotized by what they hear.

ERROR

The Gospel of Jesus Christ has the Power of the Holy Spirit behind its thrust. Error as it pertains to the Gospel, at least that which is blatantly opposed to Scripture, is initiated by demon spirits (I Tim. 4:1; I Jn. 4:1-6). Consequently, the error is not easy to break and because of the attending Powers of Darkness.

The *"simple"* refers to those, as stated, who are not knowledgeable in the Word, or as knowledgeable as they ought to be, thereby providing prey for false teachers.

By the use of the word *"hearts"* we know that this is a matter far deeper than the mere intellect. It has to do with one's very spirit, which speaks of who and what the person actually is. While the intellect is involved, it is more so the spirit of the person which is far deeper. While a person definitely believes with his mind, which is the seat of the intellect, more than all his will is brought to bear which comes from his spirit.

(19) "FOR YOUR OBEDIENCE IS COME ABROAD UNTO ALL MEN. I AM GLAD THEREFORE ON YOUR BEHALF: BUT YET I WOULD HAVE YOU WISE UNTO THAT WHICH IS GOOD, AND SIMPLE CONCERNING EVIL."

The phrase, *"For your obedience is come abroad unto all men,"* refers to Paul not linking the Saints in the Church in Rome with these false teachers, whomever they may be.

In the Greek the pronoun *"your"* is in the emphatic position, meaning that he has confidence in their being grounded in the Word, but yet he conveys a feeling of anxiety which should be read carefully by all Believers, for none are immune to the wiles of Satan.

The phrase, *"I am glad therefore on your behalf,"* expresses his joy at their maturity in the Lord, which quite possibly had been related to him by one or more of his acquaintances there, actually those mentioned here in this Chapter.

The phrase, *"But yet I would have you*

NOTES

wise unto that which is good, and simple concerning evil," expresses several things:

1. He wanted them to be so grounded in the Word, that they would instantly know false doctrine when it came their way.

2. It was not possible that they should be immune from the efforts of Satan in this manner, as it is not possible for any Believer to be immune. Actually it is something that Believers have to constantly face.

3. The phrase, *"And simple concerning evil,"* is a beautiful way of saying that they could easily discern the difference between the true and the false. Not only did it not coincide with the Word, but, as well, it did not agree with their rejuvenated spirit.

The entirety of this phrase, *"But yet I would have you wise unto that which is good, and simple concerning evil,"* goes back to *"... the Tree of the Knowledge of Good and Evil ..."* in the Garden of Eden (Gen. 2:17).

Adam and Eve disobeyed God by partaking of the fruit of this Tree, thereby suffering a cataclysmic Fall, which affected not only themselves, but all of future humanity. Believers are told here by Paul, not to make the same mistake as made by Adam and Eve. Evil should hold no curiosity, and, therefore, must be rejected out of hand.

(20) "AND THE GOD OF PEACE SHALL BRUISE SATAN UNDER YOUR FEET SHORTLY. THE GRACE OF OUR LORD JESUS CHRIST BE WITH YOU. AMEN."

The phrase, *"And the God of Peace,"* is used by Paul with special reference to the Divisions referred to in Verse 17 (Denney). Divisions in the Church are Satan's work, which destroy the Peace of the Church, and of individuals as well. The suppression of these *"Divisions"* by the *"God of Peace"* is a victory over Satan.

The Greek word for *"Peace"* is *"eiro,"* at least as it is used here, and means *"to bind together that which was separated."* When that happens, the result is Peace.

The phrase, *"Shall bruise Satan under your feet shortly,"* has one meaning, but with two fulfillments:

1. For all who are anchored in the Word and are led by the Spirit, even though Satan may attack, the end result for the individual will always be victory, with Satan defeated,

i.e., *"under your feet."*

2. Satan's defeat will be twofold: At the Second Coming and then at the end of the Millennium (Rev. 20:1-10).

"Bruise" in the Greek is *"suntribo,"* and means *"to crush, trample under foot."* It is not to be a partial, but rather a total victory. It is hinged on what Jesus did to Satan at Calvary, the Resurrection, and the Exaltation.

"Shortly" in the Greek is *"en tachei,"* and refers to *"quickness, speed, speedily, soon."* The idea is, that whatever attack by Satan may be enjoined, his defeat is certain, and the good fight of Faith will not be one of long duration.

The phrase, *"The Grace of our Lord Jesus Christ be with you. Amen,"* presents the standard Benediction of Paul, which he uses in one form or the other in all his Epistles, even Hebrews.

Paul was the Apostle of Grace, the great Covenant of Grace having been given to him. In effect the words of John the Baptist as recorded by John the Apostle sum up this great Covenant. John said, *"For the Law was given by Moses, but Grace and Truth came by Jesus Christ"* (Jn. 1:17).

The closing word *"Amen,"* proclaims the veracity of the statement, and that it will never change.

(21) "TIMOTHEUS MY WORK FEL-LOW, AND LUCIUS, AND JASON, AND SOSIPATER, MY KINSMEN, SALUTE YOU."

The phrase, *"Timotheus my workfellow,"* refers to Timothy, Paul's young understudy and fellow worker. Timothy was probably converted in the meetings conducted by Paul and Barnabas in Lystra and Derbe, cities of Lycaonia, and recorded in Acts 14:6-7. This was where the townspeople concluded the Apostles to be two gods, at least after the crippled man was healed. However, they soon changed their minds, stoning Paul, almost killing him (Acts 14:8-20). Timothy is mentioned in Acts 16:1, with inference back to this meeting. He traveled with Paul quite extensively.

Quite possibly, the one referred to here as *"Lucius"* could be *"Luke,"* who wrote the Gospel which bears his name and also the Book of Acts. There is, however, no proof of that, only speculation.

The phrase, *"And Jason,"* could refer to the one mentioned in Acts 17:5, 7, otherwise unknown.

The phrase, *"And Sosipater,"* may be the same one mentioned in Acts 20:4.

The phrase, *"My kinsmen, salute you,"* refers to the greetings sent to the Christians in Rome by these so named. Once again, the word *"kinsmen"* probably refers to fellow Jews, and not blood relatives.

(22) "I TERTIUS, WHO WROTE THIS EPISTLE, SALUTE YOU IN THE LORD."

The phrase, *"I Tertius, who wrote this Epistle,"* simply means that he was Paul's Secretary or Scribe to whom Paul dictated the Letter to the Romans. It seems that Paul was in the habit of dictating his letters to such a one (Gal. 4:13-15).

The phrase, *"Salute you in the Lord,"* indicates that it is as a Christian, not in virtue of any other relation he has to the Romans, that Tertius salutes them (Denney).

This shows Paul's courtesy in leaving Tertius to salute or greet in his own name. To dictate to him his own salutation, would be to treat him as a machine (Godet).

(23) "GAIUS MINE HOST, AND OF THE WHOLE CHURCH, SALUTETH YOU. ERASTUS THE CHAMBERLAIN OF THE CITY SALUTETH YOU, AND QUARTUS A BROTHER."

The phrase, *"Gaius mine host,"* probably means that Paul was staying in this man's home. Inasmuch as the Epistle to the Romans was written from Corinth, this hospitable Christian is probably the same who is mentioned in I Corinthians 1:14 (Denney).

The phrase, *"And of the whole Church, saluteth you,"* could mean that the Church was meeting in the home of Gaius.

The phrase, *"Erastus the Chamberlain of the city saluteth you,"* is probably the one mentioned in II Timothy 4:20 and Acts 19:22. Denney defines Erastus' position as City Treasurer. Vincent says that he probably was the Administrator of City Lands. Irrespective, he seemed, at least for a time, to have held some position in City Government at Corinth.

The phrase, *"And Quartus a brother,"* is mentioned only here.

(24) "THE GRACE OF OUR LORD JESUS

CHRIST BE WITH YOU ALL. AMEN."

In a sense, this is the third Benediction; however, the following may explain this peculiarity.

The close of the 15th Chapter of Romans actually closes the Epistle, at least as far as instruction is concerned, with the exception of Verses 17-20, in Chapter 16 of Romans. And yet, the 33rd Verse of the 15th Chapter of Romans, does not close with Paul's usual Benediction, even though he does add the word *"Amen,"* signifying the finish or close.

The idea seems to be that even though the instruction closed with the 15th Chapter of Romans, he knew he would add the following pertaining to greetings. In the midst of these greetings, he saw fit to add an admonition to unity and sound Doctrine, which closed this part with the 20th Verse, and his usual Benediction. Once again, *"Amen"* is added.

Then beginning with the 21st Verse down through the 24th, it seems as if Tertius may have reminded him of others which needed to be included, and with Paul telling him to add his own greeting, which he did (vs. 22). Once again, the 24th Verse concludes with the usual Benediction of *"The Grace of our Lord Jesus Christ. . . ."*

The last three Verses, 25-27 some think may have been added by Paul's own hand a short time later, when Tertius was not present. This could very well have happened, and in fact, probably did, with the Holy Spirit desiring this last long sentence.

(Of course, when Paul wrote this Epistle there were no Chapters or Verses, that being later added by the Translators. However, in describing the possibility of the manner of these Benedictions, for clarity I have used the words *"Chapters"* and *"Verses,"* even though, those things were not in Paul's mind when the Epistle was written.)

(25) "NOW TO HIM THAT IS OF POWER TO STABLISH YOU ACCORDING TO MY GOSPEL, AND THE PREACHING OF JESUS CHRIST, ACCORDING TO THE REVELATION OF THE MYSTERY, WHICH WAS KEPT SECRET SINCE THE WORLD BEGAN."

The phrase, *"Now to him that is of Power to stablish you according to my Gospel,"*

NOTES

refers to The Lord Jesus Christ, Who is given *". . . all Power in Heaven and in Earth"* (Mat. 28:18). The song says:

"I've anchored in Jesus, the storms of life I'll brave,
"I've anchored in Jesus, I'll fear no wind or wave,
"I've anchored in Jesus for He hath Power to Save,
"I've anchored to the Rock of Ages."

This establishing is to take place *"according to my Gospel."*

The expression *"My Gospel"* used by Paul, implies not only that Paul's Gospel was his own, in the sense that he was not touted by any man (Gal. 1:11), but also that it had something characteristic of himself about it.

The characteristic feature, to judge by this Epistle, was his sense of the absolute freeness of Salvation (Justification by Faith, apart from works of Law), and of its absolute universality *"for every one that believeth"* (Denney).

As we have stated, Paul was given by Jesus Christ the Great Gospel of Grace (Gal. 1:12). He wasn't being egotistical in his statement, not at all! Even as he had already warned the Romans (Rom. 16:17-20), and all others for that matter, many would attempt to subvert this *"Gospel."* Consequently, he is saying that the only true establishment is that in which he preaches, and that all others must preach the same or else it is error, and because it was given to him by Jesus Christ.

The phrase, *"And the preaching of Jesus Christ,"* has to do with the manner in which Jesus Christ is preached. It was the proclamation of Jesus Christ in Paul's Gospel to which the Apostle has reference. If He is preached in any other way other than *"according to my Gospel,"* it is then *". . . another Jesus . . ."* being preached (II Cor. 11:4).

The phrase, *"According to the Revelation of the Mystery,"* proclaims that which is now revealed in his Gospel.

"Mystery" in the Greek is *"musterion,"* and means *"something hidden and unknown but later revealed and then understood."*

This Mystery is God's world-embracing Purpose of Redemption, as it is set out conspicuously in this Epistle. The Gospel as

Paul understood it was a Mystery, because it could never have been known except through Divine Revelation (Denney).

The phrase, *"Which was kept secret since the world began,"* presents the second part of this *"Mystery"* which in effect, was double:

1. The first part of the Mystery is that the Gospel was given in the Old Testament, but not understood due to the fact that no one had the key, which could be given only by Revelation.

2. The second part has to do with the fact, that this was kept secret for so long.

"Kept secret" in the Greek is *"sigao,"* and means *"to keep silence, to hold one's peace."*

"Since the world began," in the Greek is *"chronos aionios,"* and means *"through times eternal, or the eternal ages before creation."* However, since it can only refer to humanity *"since the world began,"* this is the time that is applicable.

(26) "BUT NOW IS MADE MANIFEST, AND BY THE SCRIPTURES OF THE PROPHETS, ACCORDING TO THE COMMANDMENT OF THE EVERLASTING GOD, MADE KNOWN TO ALL NATIONS FOR THE OBEDIENCE OF FAITH:"

The phrase, *"But now is made manifest,"* concerns the *"Mystery"* of Verse 25.

"Made manifest" in the Greek is *"phaneroo,"* and means *"to make visible, to make known what has been hidden or unknown."* The actual Greek reads, *"But now has been made known through Prophetic writings"* (Wuest).

The phrase, *"And by the Scriptures of the Prophets,"* refers to the Old Testament which Paul constantly used in preaching his Gospel, and in whatever capacity.

For him the Old Testament was essentially a Christian Book. His Gospel was witnessed to by the Law and the Prophets, and in that sense the Mystery was made known through them. However, their significance only came out for one who had the Christian key — the Knowledge of Christ which Revelation had given to Paul (Denney).

THE MANNER IN WHICH THE REVELATION OF THE NEW COVENANT WAS GIVEN TO PAUL

As we have already stated, the New Covenant

was given to Paul not by man or even through his own ingenuity, but rather *". . . by the Revelation of Jesus Christ"* (Gal. 1:11-12). However, the question is, *"What manner did Jesus choose to make known this Revelation to the Apostle?"*

Before his Conversion Paul was a Bible Scholar; however, he actually only knew the Letter of the Old Testament, for that was the Bible of his day, and not the spirit of the Old Testament. In fact, no unsaved person can truly know the Word of God, even as Paul would write, and no doubt from his own experience, *"But the natural man receiveth not the things of the Spirit of God: for they are foolishness unto him: neither can he know them, because they are spiritually discerned"* (I Cor. 2:14). So, he only really began to know and understand the Scriptures after his Conversion.

THE EVIDENCE IS CLEAR

After the Damascus Road experience, the Word of God took on a completely new complexion for Paul. From his writings, it seems he began to literally devour the Scriptures. As he did this, even as he now says in this 26th Verse, the Holy Spirit begins to open up the great Prophecies to him concerning the Plan of God for the human race.

For instance, he sees Salvation by Faith in Genesis Chapter 15, even as he beautifully outlines in Romans Chapter 4. Likewise, he sees Jesus as the Suffering Messiah in Isaiah Chapter 53, which was the exact opposite of what the Jews were contending. They were looking for a conquering Messiah, Who in fact will ultimately come, but not at the First Advent. It is Jesus on both counts. Paul had, no doubt, read Isaiah Chapter 53 any number of times before his Conversion, but actually did not really understand what he read. But now the Holy Spirit opens up the entirety of the Plan of God to him, making clear what is going to be done. Over and over again, Paul refers to the Gospel going to the Gentiles, even as it was predicted by the Prophets (Rom. Chpt. 15).

When Paul accepted Christ, Jesus came into his heart, which made everything possible. This is the Revelation of which he speaks, which gave the Holy Spirit access to his life, Who carried out the Revelation of the New Covenant.

The phrase, *"According to the Commandment of the Everlasting God,"* actually means according to the appointment of God, that the *"Mystery"* should thus be now at last made known.

The idea is that only an express Command of the Eternal God could justify the promulgation of the secret He had kept so long (Denney).

The phrase, *"Made known to all Nations,"* refers actually to the Great Commission (Mk. 16:15).

The Truth is, that for every person who does not truly know what Jesus has done at Calvary and the Resurrection, this Great and Glorious Gospel is still a *"Mystery"* to him. It is absolutely incumbent upon the Church that every person hear, even as is evidenced in the life and Ministry of Paul, and especially his Epistles.

The phrase, *"For the obedience of Faith,"* proclaims the Way of Salvation. This speaks of the Christian Faith as a system of Truth.

When men believe God, i.e., *"believe His Word,"* they are then being *"obedient,"* i.e., having Faith.

The entirety of the idea is that Jesus Christ is to be preached. In Him and Him Alone, is Salvation for all Nations on the principle of Faith-Obedience (as opposed to works) and this is Commanded by the Everlasting, Eternal God.

(27) "TO GOD ONLY WISE, BE GLORY THROUGH JESUS CHRIST FOR EVER. AMEN."

The phrase, *"To God only wise,"* refers to the fact that God not only has wisdom, He is Wisdom. In fact, there is no True Wisdom outside of Him.

The phrase, *"Be Glory through Jesus Christ for ever. Amen,"* means that which Jesus did for the Salvation of the human race, the Great Price He paid, the Great Sacrifice made, will forever bring Glory to God, in the fact that it has brought about the Salvation of untold numbers of souls. As well, what He did forever defeated the Evil One and, thereby, forever freed man from the unbreakable grasp of darkness — unbreakable to all except Jesus Christ.

NOTES

It is Tuesday, 12:07 p.m., January 27th, 1998, as I dictate these last words respecting the Commentary on Romans. To try to distinguish the greater parts of this Epistle is simply an impossible task. Each word being the Word of God, one is loathe to even attempt to differentiate.

And yet, if it is possible for any Chapter to stand out above the others, I think the 11th Chapter fits that description. As Paul began to explain how the Lord allowed admission by the Gentiles, and all because of His Grace and Mercy, at that moment it all began to come home. That Grace included my family, as well as untold numbers of others. The songwriter said:

"Oh Lord, haste, Thy Mission high fulfilling,
"To tell to all the world that God is Light;
"That He Who made all Nations is not willing one soul should perish,
"Lost in shades of night."

"Behold how many thousands still are lying,
"Bound in the darksome prison house of sin,
"With none to tell them of the Saviour's dying,
"Or of the life He died for them to win."

"Proclaim to every people, tongue, and Nation,
"That God, in Whom they live and move, is Love:
"Tell how He stooped to save His lost creation,
"And died on Earth that man might live above."

"Give of thy sons to bear the Message Glorious;
"Give of thy wealth to speed them on their way;
"Pour out thy soul for them in prayer victorious;
"And all thou spendest Jesus will repay."

"He comes again: Oh Zion, ere thou meet Him,
"Make known to every heart His Saving Grace;

*"Let none whom He hath ransom fail
    to greet Him,
"Through thy neglect, unfit to see His
    Face."*

NOTES

INDEX

The index is listed according to subjects. The treatment may include a complete dissertation or no more than a paragraph. But hopefully it will provide some help.

As well, even though extended treatment of a subject may not be carried in this Commentary, one of the other Commentaries may well include the desired material.

For all information concerning the
Jimmy Swaggart Bible Commentary,
please request a Gift Catalog.

You may inquire by using Books of the Bible.

- Genesis (639 pages) (11-201)
- Exodus (639 pages) (11-202)
- Leviticus (435 pages) (11-203)
- Numbers
  Deuteronomy (493 pages) (11-204)
- Joshua
  Judges
  Ruth (329 pages) (11-205)
- I Samuel
  II Samuel (528 pages) (11-206)
- I Kings
  II Kings (560 pages) (11-207)
- I Chronicles
  II Chronicles (528 pages) (11-226)
- Ezra
  Nehemiah
  Esther (288 pages) (11-208)
- Job (320 pages) (11-225)
- Psalms (688 pages) (11-216)
- Proverbs (320 pages) (11-227)
- Ecclesiastes
  Song Of Solomon (11-228)
- Isaiah (688 pages) (11-220)
- Jeremiah
  Lamentations (688 pages) (11-070)
- Ezekiel (508 pages) (11-223)
- Daniel (403 pages) (11-224)
- Hosea
  Joel
  Amos (496 pages) (11-229)
- Obadiah
  Jonah
  Micah
  Nahum
  Habakkuk
  Zephaniah *(will be ready Spring 2014)* (11-230)

- Matthew (880 pages) (11-073)
- Mark (606 pages) (11-074)
- Luke (626 pages) (11-075)
- John (532 pages) (11-076)
- Acts (697 pages) (11-077)
- Romans (536 pages) (11-078)
- I Corinthians (632 pages) (11-079)
- II Corinthians (589 pages) (11-080)
- Galatians (478 pages) (11-081)
- Ephesians (550 pages) (11-082)
- Philippians (476 pages) (11-083)
- Colossians (374 pages) (11-084)
- I Thessalonians
  II Thessalonians (498 pages) (11-085)
- I Timothy
  II Timothy
  Titus
  Philemon (687 pages) (11-086)
- Hebrews (831 pages) (11-087)
- James
  I Peter
  II Peter (730 pages) (11-088)
- I John
  II John
  III John
  Jude (377 pages) (11-089)
- Revelation (602 pages) (11-090)

For telephone orders you may call 1-800-288-8350 with bankcard information. All Baton Rouge residents please use (225) 768-7000. For mail orders send to:

Jimmy Swaggart Ministries
P.O. Box 262550
Baton Rouge, LA 70826-2550

Visit our website: www.jsm.org

NOTES

NOTES

NOTES

NOTES

NOTES

NOTES

NOTES

NOTES

NOTES

NOTES

NOTES